The World's Major Languages

The World's Major Languages

Second Edition

Edited by
Bernard Comrie

Routledge
Taylor & Francis Group

LONDON AND NEW YORK

KH

First edition published in 1987 by Croom Helm
Reprinted with revisions and additions in 1989 by Routledge

Second edition published in 2009 by Routledge
2 Park Square, Milton Park, Abingdon, Oxon OX14 4RN
www.routledge.co.uk

Simultaneously published in the USA and Canada
by Routledge
270 Madison Avenue, New York NY 10016
www.routledge.com

Routledge is an imprint of the Taylor and Francis Group, an informa business

© 2009 Bernard Comrie

Typeset in Times New Roman by
Taylor & Francis Books
Printed and bound in Great Britain by
TJ International Ltd, Padstow, Cornwall

British Library Cataloguing in Publication Data
A catalogue record for this book is available from the British Library

Library of Congress Cataloguing-in-Publication Data
A catalog record for this book has been requested

ISBN 978-0-415-35339-7 (hbk)
ISBN 978-0-203-30152-4 (ebk)

9/3/09

Contents

Contributors

Daniel Abondolo
University of London

Robert Austerlitz
Columbia University,
deceased

Philip Baldi
Pennsylvania State University

Michael Branch
University of London

Wayles Browne
Cornell University

George Cardona
University of Pennsylvania

Ross Clark
University of Auckland

R.G.G. Coleman
University of Cambridge, deceased

Bernard Comrie
Max Planck Institute for Evolutionary
Anthropology and University of
California Santa Barbara

Greville Corbett
University of Surrey

Scott DeLancey
University of Oregon

Edward Finegan
University of Southern California

John N. Green
University of Bradford

Einar Haugen
Harvard University, deceased

John A. Hawkins
University of California Davis;
University of Cambridge

Robert Hetzron
University of California Santa Barbara,
deceased

Thomas John Hudak
Arizona State University

Grover Hudson
Michigan State University

Brian D. Joseph
Ohio State University

Yamuna Kachru
University of Illinois at
Urbana-Champaign

Alan S. Kaye
California State University Fullerton,
deceased

M.H. Klaiman
Independent scholar

Jan G. Kooij
University of Amsterdam

Jaklin Kornfilt
Syracuse University

Charles N. Li
University of California Santa Barbara

Silvia Luraghi
University of Pavia

D.N. MacKenzie
University of Göttingen, deceased

Behrooz Mahmoodi-Bakhtiari
University of Tehran

Graham Mallinson
Independent scholar

Monique Monville-Burston
University of Cyprus

Nam-Kil Kim
University of Southern California

Đinh-Hoà Nguyễn
Southern Illinois University at Carbondale,
deceased

Paul Newman
University of Michigan

Michael P. Oakes
University of Sunderland

Ọlanikẹ Ọla Orie
Tulane University

Stephen Parkinson
University of Oxford

J.R. Payne
University of Manchester

Douglas Pulleyblank
University of British Columbia

Lawrence A. Reid
University of Hawaii

Paul Schachter
University of California Los Angeles

Masayoshi Shibatani
Rice University

David Short
University of London

Sanford B. Steever
Independent scholar

David Strecker
Independent scholar

Gerald Stone
University of Oxford

Uri Tadmor
Max Planck Institute for Evolutionary
Anthropology

Sandra A. Thompson
University of California Los Angeles

Nigel Vincent
University of Manchester

Benji Wald
Independent scholar

Linda R. Waugh
University of Arizona

Julian K. Wheatley
Massachusetts Institute of Technology

Gernot L. Windfuhr
University of Michigan

Preface

In the preface to the first edition of this work, published in 1987, I noted that it represented the fruits of the collaboration of 44 scholars with international reputations ranging across a broad spectrum of the world's languages. This new edition adds two new languages (Javanese and Amharic) and increases the number of such scholars to 52: the authors of the two new chapters plus eight scholars who have either substantially revised or completely rewritten existing chapters. The second edition contains 52 chapters, each dealing with a single language, group of languages or language family, in addition to my Introduction. The chapters that are not completely new have been revised, at times substantially, from their original version published in 1987, although in 19 chapters this has been restricted primarily to my updating the bibliography.

Perhaps the most controversial problem that I, as editor, have continued to face in the second edition has been the choice of languages to be included. My main criterion has, admittedly, been a very subjective one: what languages do I think the volume's readership would expect to find included? In answering this question I have, of course, been guided by more objective criteria, such as the number of speakers of individual languages, whether they are official languages of independent states, whether they are widely used in more than one country, whether they are the bearers of long-standing literary traditions. These criteria often conflict – thus Latin, though long since deprived of native speakers, is included because of its immense cultural importance – and I bear full responsibility, as editor, for the final choice. I acknowledge that the criterion of readership expectation has led me to bias the choice of languages in favour of European languages, although over half of the volume is devoted to languages spoken outside Europe.

The notion of 'major language' is obviously primarily a social characterisation, and the fact that a language is not included in this volume implies no denigration of its importance as a language in its own right: every human language is a manifestation of our species' linguistic faculty and any human language may provide an important contribution to our understanding of Language as a general phenomenon. In the recent development of general linguistics, important contributions have come from the Australian Aboriginal languages Warlpiri and Dyirbal. My own research work has concentrated largely on languages that do not figure in this volume, such as Chukchi of eastern Siberia, Huichol of Mexico, Maltese of the Mediterranean, Haruai of the New Guinea Highlands and Tsez and Bezhta of the North Caucasus. Other editors might well have come up with different selections of languages, or have used somewhat different criteria. When linguists learned of the death in 1989 of the last speaker of Kamassian, a Uralic language originally spoken in Siberia, who had kept her language alive for decades in her prayers – God being the only other speaker of her language – they may well have wondered whether, for Klavdija Plotnikova, *the* world's major language was not Kamassian.

Contributors were presented with early versions of my own chapters on Slavonic languages and Russian as models for their contributions, but I felt it inappropriate to lay down strict guidelines as to how each individual chapter should be written, although I did ask authors to include at least some material on both the structure of their language and its social background. The main criterion that I asked contributors to follow was: tell the reader what you consider to be the most interesting facts about your language. This has necessarily meant that different chapters highlight different phenomena, e.g. the chapter on English, the role of English as a world language; the chapter on Arabic, the writing system; the chapter on Turkish, the grammatical system. But I believe that this variety has lent strength to the volume, since within the space limitations of what has already grown to be quite a sizeable book it would have been impossible to do justice in a more comprehensive and homogeneous way to each of over 50 languages and language families.

The original impetus for the first edition, published by Croom Helm (since merged into Routledge/Taylor & Francis), came from a meeting with Jonathan Price, at that time the publisher's Linguistics Editor, who also worked with me editorially on the first edition and earned my eternal gratitude. This role was taken on for the second edition by Kate Aker, Director of Development at Routledge Reference, whom I thank not only for her editorial work but also for her patience during delays that were wished upon her. I would also like to thank Ulrike Swientek for her sterling efforts during the production phase of the volume. Finally, I am grateful to Routledge/Taylor & Francis for assuming the editorial costs involved in preparing the second edition.

Some of the authors who contributed to the first edition have since passed on: Robert Austerlitz, R.G.G. Coleman, Einar Haugen, Robert Hetzron, Alan S. Kaye (who completed his revisions shortly before his untimely death), D.N. MacKenzie, Dinh-Hoa Nguyen and D.J. Prentice. I dedicate this second edition to their memory.

Bernard Comrie
Leipzig/Santa Barbara, July 2008

Abbreviations

* The asterisk is used in discussion of historical reconstructions to indicate a reconstructed (non-attested) form. In synchronic discussions, it is used to indicate an ungrammatical item; (* X) means that inclusion of X makes the item ungrammatical; * (X) means that omission of X makes the item ungrammatical.

In the chapters on Tamil and Vietnamese, a subscript numeral n after a word in the English translation indicates that that word glosses the nth word in the Tamil or Vietnamese example.

In the chapters on the Romance languages, capitals are used to represent Latin or reconstructed Proto-Romance forms.

1	first person	asp.	aspirated
2	second person	aspc.	aspect
3	third person	athem.	athematic
abilit.	abilitative	aux.	auxiliary
abl.	ablative	Av.	Avestan
abs.	absolutive	ben.	beneficiary
abstr.	abstract	BH	Biblical Hebrew
acc.	accusative	BN	B-Norwegian
acr.	actor	Boh.	Bohemian
act.	active	BP	Brazilian Portuguese
act.n.	action nominal	Br.	British
adj.	adjective	c.	common
adv.	adverb	Cast.	Castilian
Alb.	Albanian	Cat.	Catalan
Am.	American	caus.	causative
anim.	animate	cc	class concord
aor.	aorist	Cent.	Central
Ar.	Arabic	circ.	second element of circumfix
Arm.	Armenian		
art.	article	cl.	class(ifier)
Ashk.	Ashkenazi(c)	clit.	clitic

cmpr.	comparative	gr.	grade
comp.	complementiser	GR	Gallo-Romance
conj.	conjunction	gutt.	guttural
conjug.	conjugation	H	High
conjv.	conjunctive	Hier. Hitt.	Hieroglyphic Hittite
cont.	contemplated	Hitt.	Hittite
conv.	converb	hon.	honorific
cop.	copula	IE	Indo-European
cp	class prefix	imper.	imperative
crs.	currently relevant state	imperf.	imperfect(ive)
Cz.	Czech	inanim.	inanimate
Da.	Danish	incl.	inclusive
dat.	dative	indef.	indefinite
dbl.	double	indic.	indicative
decl.	declension	indir.	indirect
def.	definite	infin.	infinitive
dem. prox.	proximal demonstrative	inst.	instrumental
dem. dist.	distal demonstrative	inter.	interrogative
dent.	dental	intr.	intransitive
deriv. morph.	derivational morpheme	inv.	inversion particle
det.	determiner	irr.	irrational
de-v.	deverbal	It.	Italian
dir.	direct	i.v.	intransitive verb
disj.	disjunctive	L	Low
Dor.	Doric	lab.	labial
drc.	directional	Lat.	Latin
du.	dual	Latv.	Latvian
dur.	durative	LG	Low German
d.v.	dynamic verb	lig.	ligature
E.	Eastern	lingu.	lingual
Eng.	English	lit.	literally
ENHG	Early New High German	Lith.	Lithuanian
EP	European Portuguese	loc.	locative
erg.	ergative	m.	masculine
ex.	existential-possessive	MBs.	Modern Burmese
f.	feminine	ME	Middle English
fact.	factive	med.	medio-passive
fact. n.	factive nominal	MH	Middle Hebrew
foc.	focus	MHG	Middle High German
Fr.	French	mid.	middle
fut.	future tense	MidFr.	Middle French
g.	gender	ModE	Modern English
gen.	genitive	ModFr.	Modern French
ger.	gerund(ive)	MoH	Modern Hebrew
Gk.	Greek	Mor.	Moravian
gl.	glottalised	MP	Middle Persian
Gmc.	Germanic	n.	noun
Go.	Gothic	necess.	necessitative

neg.	negative	Po.	Polish
NHG	New High German	pol.	polite
nm.	nominal	pos.	position
NMLZ	noun-forming affix	poss.	possessive
NN	N-Norwegian	pred.	predicate
nom.	nominative	prep.	preposition
noms.	nominalisation	prepl.	prepositional
NP	New Persian	pres.	present tense
nt.	neuter	pret.	preterit
numb.	number	prim.	primary
Nw.	Norwegian	prog.	progressive
O.	Oscan	proh.	prohibitive
OArm.	Old Armenian	pron.	pronoun
obj.	object	Ptg.	Portuguese
obl.	oblique	Q	question
OBs.	Old Burmese	rat.	rational
Oc.	Occitan	recip.	reciprocal
OCS	Old Church Slavonic	red.	reduplication
OE	Old English	refl.	reflexive
OFr.	Old French	rel.	relative
OFri.	Old Frisian	rep.	reported
OHG	Old High German	res.	result
OIc.	Old Icelandic	Ru.	Runic
OIr.	Old Irish	Rum.	Rumanian
OIran.	Old Iranian	Rus.	Russian
OLat.	Old Latin	Sard.	Sardinian
OLith.	Old Lithuanian	SCr.	Serbo-Croat
ON	Old Norse	sec.	secondary
OP	Old Persian	Seph.	Sephardi(c)
opt.	optative	sg.	singular
OPtg.	Old Portuguese	S-J	Sino-Japanese
orig.	original(ly)	Skt.	Sanskrit
OS	Old Saxon	Slk.	Slovak
OV	object–verb	s.o.	someone
p.	person	SOV	subject–object–verb
pal.	palatal	Sp.	Spanish
part.	participle	spcf.	specifying form
pass.	passive	spec.	species
past.	past tense	s.t.	something
pat.	patient	st.	standard
PDr.	Proto-Dravidian	su.	subject
perf.	perfect(ive)	subj.	subjunctive
pers.	person	sup.	superlative
PGmc.	Proto-Germanic	s.v.	stative verb
PIE	Proto-Indo-European	SVO	subject–verb–object
PIt.	Proto-Italic	Sw.	Swedish
Pkt.	Prakrit	tap.	tense/aspect pronoun
pl.	plural	temp.	temporal

them.	thematic	v.	verb
Tk.	Turkish	vd.	voiced
tns.	tense	Ved.	Vedic
Toch.	Tocharian	VL	Vulgar Latin
top.	topic	vls.	voiceless
tr.	transitive	v.n.	verbal noun
transg.	transgressive	VO	verb–object
t.v.	transitive verb	voc.	vocative
U.	Umbrian	VSO	verb–subject–object
unint.	unintentional	YNQ	yes/no question marker

Introduction

Bernard Comrie

1 Preliminary Notions

How many languages are there in the world? What language(s) do they speak in India? What languages have the most speakers? What languages were spoken in Australia, or in Mexico before European immigration? When did Latin stop being spoken, and when did French start being spoken? How did English become such an important world language? These and other similar questions are often asked by the interested layman. One aim of this volume – taking the Introduction and the individual chapters together – is to provide answers to these and related questions, or in certain cases to show why the questions cannot be answered as they stand. The chapters concentrate on an individual language or group of languages, and in this Introduction I want rather to present a linking essay which will provide a background against which the individual chapters can be appreciated.

After discussing some preliminary notions in Section 1, Section 2 of the Introduction provides a rapid survey of the languages spoken in the world today, concentrating on those not treated in the subsequent chapters, so that the reader can gain an overall impression of the extent of linguistic diversity that characterises the world in which we live. Since the notion of 'major language' is primarily a social notion – languages become major (such as English) or stop being major (such as Sumerian) not because of their grammatical structure, but because of social factors – Section 3 discusses some important sociolinguistic notions, in particular concerning the social interaction of languages.

1.1 How Many Languages?

Linguists are typically very hesitant to answer the first question posed above, namely: how many languages are spoken in the world today? Probably the best that one can say, with some hope of not being contradicted, is that at a very conservative estimate some 6,000 languages are spoken today. Laymen are often surprised that the figure should be so high, but I would emphasise that this is a conservative estimate. But why is it that linguists are not able to give a more accurate figure? There are several different reasons conspiring to prevent them from doing so, and these will be outlined below.

Even a couple of decades ago one could reasonably have observed that some parts of the world were simply insufficiently studied from a linguistic viewpoint, so that we did not know precisely what languages are spoken there. There are very few parts of the world where this still holds, since our knowledge of the linguistic situation in remote parts of the world has improved dramatically in recent years – New Guinea, for instance, has changed from being almost a blank linguistic map in the first half of the twentieth century to the stage where nearly all languages can be pinpointed with accuracy: since perhaps as many as one-fifth of the world's languages are spoken in New Guinea, this has radically changed any estimate of the total number of languages. Although new languages are still being discovered, this is no longer the major factor it would have been in the past.

A second and more important problem is that it is difficult or impossible in many cases to decide whether two related speech varieties should be considered different languages or merely different dialects of the same language. Native speakers of English are often surprised that there should be problems in delimiting languages from dialects, since present-day dialects of English are in general mutually intelligible (at least with some familiarisation), and even the language most closely related genetically to English, Frisian, is mutually unintelligible with English. With the languages of Europe more generally, there are in general established traditions of whether two speech varieties should be considered different languages or merely dialect variants, but these decisions have often been made more on political and social rather than on strictly linguistic grounds.

One criterion that is often advanced as a purely linguistic criterion is mutual intelligibility: if two speech varieties are mutually intelligible, they are different dialects of the same language, but if they are mutually unintelligible, they are different languages. But if applied to the languages of Europe, this criterion would radically alter our assessment of what the different languages of Europe are: the most northern dialects and the most southern dialects (in the traditional sense) of German are mutually unintelligible, while dialects of German spoken close to the Dutch border are mutually intelligible with dialects of Dutch spoken just across the border. In fact, our criterion for whether a dialect is Dutch or German relates in large measure to social factors – is the dialect spoken in an area where Dutch is the standard language or where German is the standard language? By the same criterion, the three nuclear Scandinavian languages (in the traditional sense), Danish, Norwegian and Swedish, would turn out to be dialects of one language, given their mutual intelligibility. While this criterion is often applied to non-European languages (so that nowadays linguists talk of the Chinese languages rather than the Chinese dialects, given the mutual unintelligibility of, for instance, Mandarin and Cantonese), it seems unfair that it should not be applied consistently to European languages as well.

In some cases, the intelligibility criterion actually leads to contradictory results, namely when we have a dialect chain, i.e. a string of dialects such that adjacent dialects are readily mutually intelligible, but dialects from the far ends of the chain are not mutually intelligible. A good illustration of this is the Dutch–German dialect complex. One could start from the far south of the German-speaking area and move to the far west of the Dutch-speaking area without encountering any sharp boundary across which mutual intelligibility is broken; but the two end points of this chain are speech varieties so different from one another that there is no mutual intelligibility possible. If one takes a simplified dialect chain A – B – C, where A and B are mutually intelligible, as are B and C, but A and C are mutually unintelligible, then one arrives at the contradictory result that A and B are dialects of the same language, B and C are dialects of the same language, but A and C are different languages. There is in fact no way of resolving this contradiction if we maintain the traditional strict difference between language and dialects, and what such examples show is that this is not an all-or-nothing distinction, but rather a continuum. In this sense, it is not just difficult, but in principle impossible to answer the question how many languages are spoken in the world.

A further problem with the mutual intelligibility criterion is that mutual intelligibility itself is a matter of degree rather than a clear-cut opposition between intelligibility and unintelligibility. If mutual intelligibility were to mean 100 per cent mutual intelligibility of all utterances, then perhaps no two speech varieties would be classified as mere dialect variants; for instance, although speakers of British and American English can understand most of one another's speech, there are areas where intelligibility is likely to be minimum unless one speaker happens to have learned the linguistic forms used by the other, as with car (or auto) terms like British *boot, bonnet, mudguard* and their American equivalents *trunk, hood, fender.* Conversely, although speakers of different Slavonic languages are often unable to make full sense of a text in another Slavonic language, they can usually make good sense of parts of the text, because of the high percentage of shared vocabulary and forms.

Two further factors enter into the degree of mutual intelligibility between two speech varieties. One is that intelligibility can rise rapidly with increased familiarisation: when American films were first introduced into Britain they were initially considered difficult to understand, but increased exposure to American English has virtually removed this problem. Speakers of different dialects of Arabic often experience difficulty in understanding each other at first meeting, but soon adjust to the major differences between their respective dialects, and Egyptian Arabic, as the most widely diffused modern Arabic dialect, has rapidly gained in intelligibility throughout the Arab world. This can lead to 'one-way intelligibility', as when speakers of, say, Tunisian Arabic are more likely to understand Egyptian Arabic than vice versa, because Tunisian Arabic speakers are more often exposed to Egyptian Arabic than vice versa. The second factor is that intelligibility is to a certain extent a social and psychological phenomenon: it is easier to understand when you want to understand. A good example of this is the conflicting assessments different speakers of the same Slavonic language will often give about the intelligibility of some other Slavonic language, correlating in large measure with whether or not they feel well disposed to speakers of the other language.

The same problems as exist in delimiting dialects from languages arise, incidentally, on the historical plane too, where the question arises: at what point has a language changed sufficiently to be considered a different language? Again, traditional answers are often contradictory: Latin is considered a dead language, although its descendants, the Romance languages, live on, so at some time Latin must have changed sufficiently to be deemed no longer the same language, but a qualitatively different one. On the other hand, Greek is referred to as 'Greek' throughout its attested history (which is longer than that of Latin and the Romance languages combined), with merely the addition of different adjectives to identify different stages of its development (e.g. Ancient Greek, Byzantine Greek, Modern Greek). In the case of the history of the English language, there is even conflicting terminology: the oldest attested stages of English can be referred to either as Old English (which suggests an earlier stage of Modern English) or as Anglo-Saxon (which suggests a different language that is the ancestor of English, perhaps justifiably so given the mutual unintelligibility of Old and Modern English).

A further reason why it is difficult to assess the number of languages spoken in the world today is that many languages are on the verge of extinction. While it has been the case throughout human history that languages have died out, recent social changes have considerably accelerated this process, as the languages of smaller speech communities are endangered by those with more speakers and more prestige. Economic factors often make it difficult for modern services (health, education, etc.) to be provided in the languages of smaller speech communities, and members of smaller speech communities interested in integrating into wider social networks often feel impelled to abandon their own language in favour of a language of wider currency or at least to encourage their children to do so. This is not just the ever increasing use of English as a result of globalisation. At a more local level, smaller languages are endangered in particular situations by French, Spanish, Indonesian, Swahili – even Tsamai (the last-mentioned a language of Ethiopia with around 10,000 speakers, to which the few remaining speakers of Birale are assimilating). Documentation and, where possible, preservation of endangered languages is one of the major tasks facing linguists in the twenty-first century.

1.2 Language Families and Genetic Classification

One of the basic organisational principles of this volume, both in Section 2 of the Introduction and in the arrangement of the individual chapters, is the classification of languages into language families. It is therefore important that some insight should be provided into what it means to say that two languages belong to the same language family (or equivalently: are genetically related).

It is probably intuitively clear to anyone who knows a few languages that some languages are closer to one another than are others. For instance, English and German are closer to one another than either is to Russian, while Russian and Polish are closer to one another than either is to English. This notion of similarity can be made more precise, as is done for instance in the chapter on the Indo-European languages, but for the moment the relatively informal notion will suffice. Starting in the late eighteenth century, a specific hypothesis was proposed to account for such similarities, a hypothesis which still forms the foundation of research into the history and relatedness of languages. This hypothesis is that where languages share some set of features in common, these features are to be attributed to their common ancestor. Let us take some examples from English and German.

In English and German we find a number of basic vocabulary items that have the same or almost the same form, e.g. English *man* and German *Mann*. Likewise, we find a number of bound morphemes (prefixes and suffixes) that have the same or almost the same form, such as the genitive suffix, as in English *man's* and German *Mann(e)s*. Although English and German are now clearly different languages, we may hypothesise that at an earlier period in history they had a common ancestor, in which the word for 'man' was something like *man* and the genitive suffix was something like *-s*. Thus English and German belong to the same language family, which is the same as saying that they share a common ancestor. We can readily add other languages to this family, since a word like *man* and a genitive suffix like *-s* are also found in Dutch, Frisian and the Scandinavian languages. The family to which these languages belong has been given that the proto-language is not an attested language – although if written records had gone back far enough, we might well have had attestations of this language – but its postulation is the most plausible hypothesis explaining the remarkable similarities among the various Germanic languages.

Although not so obvious, similarities can be found among the Germanic languages and a number of other languages spoken in Europe and spreading across northern India as far as Bangladesh. These other languages share fewer similarities with the Germanic languages than individual Germanic languages do with one another, so that they are more remotely related. The overall language family to which all these languages belong is the Indo-European family, with its reconstructed ancestor language Proto-Indo-European. As is discussed in more detail in the chapter on Indo-European languages, the Indo-European family contains a number of branches (i.e. smaller language families, or subfamilies), such as Slavonic (including Russian and Polish), Iranian (including Persian and Pashto), and Celtic (including Irish and Welsh). The overall structure is therefore hierarchical: The most distant ancestor is Proto-Indo-European. At an intermediate point in the family tree, and therefore at a later period of history, we have such languages as Proto-Germanic and Proto-Celtic, which are descendants of Proto-Indo-European but ancestors of languages spoken today. Still later in history, we find the individual languages as they are spoken today or attested in recent history, such as English and German as descendants of Proto-Germanic and Irish and Welsh as descendants of Proto-Celtic. One typical property of language change that is represented accurately by this family-tree model is that, as time goes by, languages descending from a common ancestor tend to become less and less similar. For instance, Old English and Old High German (the ancestor of Modern German) were much closer to one another than are the modern languages – they may even have been mutually intelligible, at least to a large extent.

Although the family-tree model of language relatedness is an important foundation of all current work in historical and comparative linguistics, it is not without its problems, both in practice and in principle. Some of these will now be discussed.

We noted above that with the passage of time, genetically related languages will grow less and less similar. This follows from the fact that, once two languages have split off as separate languages from a common ancestor, each will innovate its own changes, different from changes that take place in the other language, so that the cumulative effect will be increasing divergence. With the passage of enough time, the divergence may come to be so great that it is no longer possible to tell, other than by directly examining the history, that the two languages do in fact come from a common ancestor. The best-established language families, such as Indo-European or Sino-Tibetan, are those where the passage of time has not been long enough to erase the obvious traces of genetic relatedness. (For language families that have a long written tradition, one can of course make use of earlier stages of the language, which provide more evidence of genetic relatedness.) In addition, there are many hypothesised language families for which the evidence is not sufficient to convince all, or even the majority, of scholars. For instance, the Turkic language family is a well-established language family, as is each of the Mongolic and Tungusic families. What is controversial, however, is whether or not these individual families are related as members of an even larger family. The possibility of an Altaic family, comprising Turkic, Mongolic, and Tungusic, is rather widely accepted, and some scholars would advocate increasing the size of this family by adding Korean and perhaps Japanese.

The attitudes of different linguists to problems of this kind have been characterised as an opposition between 'splitters' (who require the firmest evidence before they are prepared to acknowledge genetic relatedness) and 'clumpers' (who are ready to assign languages to the same family on the basis of quite restricted similarities). I should, incidentally, declare my own splitter bias, lest any of my own views that creep in be interpreted as generally accepted dogma. The most extreme clumper position would, of course, be to maintain that all languages of the world are genetically related, although there are less radical positions that would posit such 'macro-families' as Eurasiatic or Nostratic (including, inter alia, Indo-European, Uralic and Altaic), Dene-Caucasian (including, inter alia, Na-Dene, Sino-Tibetan, East Caucasian and West Caucasian), and Austric (including at least Austronesian and Austro-Asiatic). In the survey of the distribution of languages of the world in Section 2, I have basically retained my own splitter position, although for areas of great linguistic diversity and great controversy surrounding genetic relations (such as New Guinea and the Americas) I have simply refrained from detailed discussion.

While no linguist would doubt that some similarities among languages are due to genetic relatedness, there are several other possibilities for the explanation of any particular similarity, and before assuming genetic relatedness one must be able to exclude, at least with some degree of plausibility, these other possibilities. Unfortunately, in a great many cases it is not possible to reach a firm and convincing decision. Let us now examine some of the explanations other than genetic relatedness.

First, two languages may happen purely by chance to share some feature in common. For instance, the word for *dog* in Mbabaram, an Australian Aboriginal language, happens to be *dog*. This Mbabaram word is not, incidentally, a borrowing from English, but is the regular development in Mbabaram of an ancestral form something like **gudaga*, which is found in forms similar to this reconstruction in other related languages (it is usual to prefix reconstructed forms with an asterisk). If anyone were tempted to assume on this basis, however, that English and Mbabaram are genetically related, examination of the rest of Mbabaram vocabulary and grammar would soon quash the genetic relatedness hypothesis, since there is otherwise minimal similarity between the two languages. In comparing English and German, by contrast, there are many similarities at all levels of linguistic analysis. Even sticking to vocabulary, the correspondence *man*: *Mann* can be matched by *wife*: *Weib*, *father*: *Vater*, *mother*: *Mutter*, *son*: *Sohn*, *daughter*: *Tochter*, etc. Given that other languages have radically different words for these concepts (e.g. Japanese *titi* 'father', *haha* 'mother', *musuko* 'son', *musume* 'daughter'), it can clearly not be merely the result of chance that English and German have so many similar items. But if the number of similar items in two languages is small, it may be difficult or impossible to distinguish between chance similarity and distant genetic relatedness.

Certain features shared by two languages might turn out to be manifestations of language universals, i.e. of features that are common to all languages or are inherently likely to occur in any language. Most discussions of language universals require a fair amount of theoretical linguistic background, but for present purposes I will take a simple, if not particular profound, example. In many languages across the world, the syllable *ma* or its reduplicated form *mama* or some other similar form is the word for 'mother'. The initial syllable *ma* enters into the Proto-Indo-European word for 'mother' that has given English *mother*, Spanish *madre*, Russian *mat'*, Sanskrit *mātā*. In Mandarin Chinese, the equivalent word is *mā*. Once again, examination of other features of Indo-European languages and Chinese would soon dispel any possibility of assigning Chinese to the Indo-European language family. Presumably the frequency across languages of the syllable *ma* in the word for 'mother' simply reflects the fact that this is typically one of the first syllables that babies articulate clearly, and is therefore interpreted by adults as the word for mother. (In the South Caucasian language Georgian, incidentally, *mama* means 'father' – and 'mother' is *deda* – so that there are other ways of interpreting baby's first utterance.)

Somewhat similar to universals are patterns whereby certain linguistic features frequently co-occur in the same language, i.e. where the presence of one feature seems to require or at least to foster the presence of some other feature. For instance, the study of word universals by Greenberg (1966) showed that if a language has verb-final word order (i.e. if 'the man saw the woman' is expressed literally as 'the man the woman saw'), then it is highly probable that it will also have postpositions rather than prepositions (i.e. 'in the house' will be expressed as 'the house in') and that it will have genitives before the noun (i.e. the pattern 'cat's house' rather than 'house of cat'). Thus, if we find two languages that happen to share the features: verb-final word order, postpositions, prenominal genitives, then the co-occurrence of these features is not evidence for genetic relatedness. Many earlier attempts at establishing wide-ranging genetic relationships suffer precisely from failure to take this property of typological patterns into account. Thus the fact that Turkic languages, Mongolic languages, Tungusic languages, Korean and Japanese share all of these features is not evidence for their genetic relatedness (although there may, of course, be other similarities, not connected with recurrent typological patterns, that do establish genetic relatedness). If one were to accept just these features as evidence for an Altaic language family, then the family would have to be extended to include a variety of other languages with the same word order properties, such as the Dravidian languages of southern India and Quechua, spoken in South America.

Finally, two languages might share some feature in common because one of them has borrowed it from the other (or because they have both borrowed it from some third language). English, for instance, borrowed a huge number of words from French during the Middle Ages, to such an extent that an uncritical examination of English vocabulary might well lead to the conclusion that English is a Romance language, rather than a Germanic language. The term 'borrow', as used here, is the accepted linguistic term, although the terminology is rather strange, since 'borrow' suggests a relatively superficial acquisition, one which is moreover temporary. Linguistic borrowings may run quite deep, and there is of course no implication that they will ever be repaid. Among English loans from French, for instance, there are many basic vocabulary items, such as *very* (replacing the native Germanic *sore*, as in the biblical *sore afraid*). Examples from other languages show even more deep-seated loans: the Semitic language Amharic, for instance, has lost the typical Semitic word order patterns, in which the verb precedes its object and adjectives and genitives follow their noun, in favour of the order where the verb follows its object and adjectives and genitives precede their noun; Amharic is in close contact with Cushitic languages, and Cushitic languages typically have the order object–verb, adjective/genitive–noun, so that Amharic has in fact borrowed these word orders from neighbouring Cushitic languages.

It seems that whenever two languages come into close contact, they will borrow features from one another. In some cases the contact can be so intense among the languages in a given area that they come to share a significant number of common features, setting this area off from adjacent languages, even languages that may happen to be more closely related genetically to languages within the area. The languages in an area of this kind are often said to belong to a sprachbund (German for 'language league'), and perhaps the most famous example of a sprachbund is the Balkan sprachbund, whose members (Modern Greek, Albanian, Bulgarian, Macedonian, Rumanian) share a number of striking features not shared by closely related languages like Ancient Greek, other Slavonic languages (Bulgarian is Slavonic), or other Romance languages (Rumanian is Romance). The most striking of these features is loss of the infinitive, so that instead of 'give me to drink' one says 'give me that I-drink' (Modern Greek *ðos mu na pjo*, Albanian *a-më të pi*, Bulgarian *daj mi da pija*, Rumanian *dǎ-mi sǎ beau*; in all four languages the subject of the subordinate clause is encoded in the ending of the verb).

Since we happen to know a lot about the history of the Balkan languages, linguists were not deceived by these similarities into assigning a closer genetic relatedness to the Balkan languages than in fact holds (all are ultimately members of the Indo-European family, though from different branches). In other parts of the world, however, there is the danger of mistaking areal phenomena for evidence of genetic relatedness. In South-East Asia, for instance, many languages share very similar phonological and morphological patterns: in Chinese, Thai and Vietnamese words are typically monosyllabic, there is effectively no morphology (i.e. words do not change after the manner of English *dog*, *dogs* or *love*, *loves*, *loved*), syllable structure is very simple (only a few single consonants are permitted word-finally, while syllable-initially consonant clusters are either disallowed or highly restricted), and there is phonemic tone (thus Mandarin Chinese *mā*, with a high level tone, means 'mother', while *mǎ* with a falling–rising tone, means 'horse'), and moreover there are a number of shared lexical items. For these reasons, it was for a long time believed that Thai and Vietnamese were related genetically to Chinese. More recently, however, it has been established that these similarities are not the result of common ancestry, and Thai and Vietnamese are now generally acknowledged not to be genetically related to Chinese. The similarities are the results of areal contact. The shared vocabulary items are primarily the result of intensive Chinese cultural influence, especially on Vietnamese. The tones and simple syllable structures can often be shown to be the result of relatively recent developments, and indeed in one language that is genetically related to Chinese, namely Classical Tibetan, one finds complex consonant clusters but no phonemic tone, i.e. the similarities noted above are neither necessary nor sufficient conditions for genetic relatedness.

In practice, the most difficult task in establishing genetic relatedness is to distinguish between genuine cognates (i.e. forms going back to a common ancestor) and those that are the result of borrowing. It would therefore be helpful if one could distinguish between those features of a language that are borrowable and those that are not. Unfortunately, it seems that there is no feature that can absolutely be excluded from borrowing. Basic vocabulary can be borrowed, so that for instance Japanese has borrowed the whole set of numerals from Chinese, and even English borrowed its current set of third person plural pronouns (*they*, *them*, *their*) from Scandinavian. Bound morphemes can be borrowed: a good example is the agent suffix *-er* in English, with close cognates in the other Germanic languages; this is ultimately a loan from the Latin agentive suffix *-arius*, which has however become so entrenched in English that it is a productive morphological device applicable in principle to any verb to derive a corresponding agentive noun.

At one period in the recent history of comparative linguistics, it was believed that a certain basic vocabulary list could be isolated, constant across languages and cultures, such that the words on this list would be replaced at a constant rate. Thus, if one assumes that the retention rate is around 86 per cent per millennium, this means that if a single language splits into two descendant languages, then after 1,000 years each language would retain about 86 per cent of the words in the list from the ancestor language, i.e. the two descendants would then share just over 70 per cent of the words in the list with each other. In some parts of the world, groupings based on this 'glottochronological' method still form the basis of the only available detailed and comprehensive attempt at establishing genetic relations. It must be emphasised that the number of clear counter-examples to the glottochronological method, i.e. instances where independent evidence contradicts the predictions of this approach, is so great that no reliance can be placed on its results.

It is, however, true that there are significant differences in the ease with which different features of a language can be borrowed. The thing that seems most easily borrowable is cultural vocabulary, and indeed it is quite normal for a community borrowing some concept (or artefact) from another community to borrow the foreign name along with the object. Another set of features that seem rather easily borrowable are general typological features, such as word order: in addition to the Amharic example cited above, one might note the fact that many Austronesian languages spoken in New Guinea have adopted the word order where the object is placed before the verb, whereas almost all other Austronesian languages place the object after the verb; this happened under the influence of Papuan languages, almost all of which are verb-final. Basic vocabulary and bound morphology are hardest to borrow. But even though it is difficult to borrow bound morphology, it is not impossible, so in arguments over genetic relatedness one cannot exclude a priori the possibility that even affixes may have been borrowed.

2 Distribution of the World's Languages

In this section, I wish to give a general survey of the distribution of the languages of the world, in terms of their genetic affiliation. I will therefore be talking primarily about the distribution of language families, although reference will be made to individual languages where appropriate. The discussion will concentrate on languages and language families not covered in individual chapters, and at appropriate places I have digressed to give a brief discussion of some interesting structural or sociological point in the language being treated.

2.1 Europe

Europe, taken here in the traditional cultural sense rather than in the current geographical sense of 'the land mass west of the Urals', is the almost exclusive preserve of the Indo-European family. This family covers not only almost the whole of Europe, but also extends through Armenia (in the Caucasus), Iran and Afghanistan into Central Asia (Tajikistan), with the easternmost outpost of this strand the Iranian language Sarikoli, spoken just inside China. Another strand spreads from Afghanistan across Pakistan, northern India and southern Nepal, to end with Bengali in eastern India and Bangladesh; an off-shoot from northern India, Sinhalese, is spoken in Sri Lanka, and the language of the Maldives is the closely related Maldivian.

In addition, the great population shifts that resulted from the voyages of exploration starting at the end of the fifteenth century have carried Indo-European languages to

9

many distant lands. The dominant languages of the Americas are now Indo-European (English, Spanish, Portuguese, French), as is the dominant language of Australia and New Zealand (English). While in some countries these languages are spoken by populations descended primarily from European settlers, there are also instances where a variety of the European language is spoken by a population of a different origin, perhaps the best-known example being the creolised forms of European languages (especially English, French and Portuguese) spoken by the descendants of African slaves in the Caribbean. It should be noted that these population shifts have not led exclusively to the spread of European languages, since many languages of India, both Indo-European and Dravidian, have also extended as a by-product, being spoken now by communities in the Caribbean area, in East Africa, and in the South Pacific (especially Fiji).

Of the few European languages not belonging to the Indo-European family, mention may first be made of Basque, a language isolate, with no established genetic relations to any other language. It is spoken in the Pyrenees near the French–Spanish border. Basque is perhaps most noted for its ergative construction, whereby instead of having a single case (nominative) for both subjects of intransitive verbs and subjects (agents) of transitive verbs, with a different case (accusative) for objects (patients) of transitive verbs, Basque uses one case (absolutive) for both intransitive subjects and objects of transitive verbs, and a different case (ergative) for subjects of transitive verbs, as in the following sentences:

Jon etorri da.   'John came.'
Neska-k gizona ikusi du.   'The girl saw the man.'

In the first sentence, *Jon* is intransitive subject, and stands in the absolutive (no inflection); in the second sentence, *neska-k* 'girl' is transitive subject, and therefore stands in the ergative (suffix *-k*), while *gizona* 'man' is transitive object, and therefore stands in the absolutive, with no inflection.

Some other languages of Europe belong to the Uralic family. These include Hungarian, Finnish, Estonian, and Saami (formerly also called Lappish – properly a group of mutually unintelligible languages rather than a single language), to which can be added a number of smaller languages closely related to Finnish and Estonian. Other members of the Uralic family are spoken on the Volga and in northern Eurasia on both sides of the Urals, stretching as far as southern Siberia.

Turkish as spoken in the Balkans represents the Turkic family in Europe, but this is primarily an Asian family, and will be treated in the next section. The same is true of Afroasiatic, represented in Europe by Maltese.

2.2 Asia

Having just mentioned Turkish, we may now turn to the Turkic family, which is spoken in Turkey, parts of the Caucasus, some areas on the Volga, most of Central Asia (and stretching down into north-western Iran), and large parts of southern Siberia, with one off-shoot, Yakut, in north-eastern Siberia. Turkic is perhaps to be joined in a single language family (Altaic) with the Mongolic and Tungusic families. The Mongolic languages are spoken predominantly in Mongolia and northern China, though there are also isolated Mongolic languages in Afghanistan (Moghol) and just to the north of the Caucasus mountains (Kalmyk); the main member of the family is the language Mongolian (sometimes called Khalkha, after its principal dialect), which is the official language of Mongolia. The Tungusic languages are spoken by numerically small population groups in Siberia, spreading over into Mongolia and especially north-eastern China. The Tungusic language best known to history is Manchu, the native language of the Qing dynasty that ruled China from 1644 to 1911; the Manchu language is, however, now almost extinct, having been replaced by Chinese. Whether Korean or Japanese can be assigned to the Altaic family is a question of current debate.

This is a convenient point at which to discuss a number of other languages spoken in northern Asia. All are the languages of small communities (a few hundred or a few thousand). They are sometimes referred to collectively as Paleosiberian (or Paleoasiatic), although this is not a genetic grouping. Three of them are language isolates: Ket, spoken on the Yenisey river, and the sole survivor of the small Yeniseic family; Yukaghir, spoken on the Kolyma river; and Nivkh (Gilyak), spoken at the mouth of the Amur river and on Sakhalin island. The small Chukotko-Kamchatkan family comprises the indigenous languages of the Chukotka and Kamchatka peninsulas: Chukchi, Koryak, Kamchadal (Itelmen); it has been suggested that they may be related to Eskimo-Aleut, which we treat in Section 2.5 on the Americas. Finally, we may mention here the recently extinct Ainu, apparently a language isolate, whose last native speakers lived in Hokkaido, the most northerly Japanese island.

One of the geographic links between Europe and Asia, the Caucasus, has since antiquity been noted for the large number of clearly distinct languages spoken there; indeed it was referred to by the Arabs as the 'mountain of tongues'. Some of the languages spoken in the Caucasus belong to other families (e.g. Armenian and Ossetian to Indo-European, Azerbaijani to Turkic), but there are in addition a number of languages with no known affiliations to languages outside the Caucasus: these are the Caucasian languages. Even the internal genetic relations of the Caucasian languages are the subject of debate. Few scholars now accept the genetic relatedness of all Caucasian languages, but there is ongoing debate over whether West Caucasian and East Caucasian together form a single North Caucasian family. The Kartvelian or South Caucasian family includes Georgian, the Caucasian language with the largest number of speakers (over four million) and the only Caucasian language to have a long-standing literary tradition (dating back to the fifth century). The West (North-West) Caucasian languages are on and close to the Black Sea coast, though also in Turkey as a result of emigration since the mid-nineteenth century; one Caucasian language, Ubykh, which died out in Turkey towards the end of the twentieth century, is noteworthy for the large number of its consonant phonemes – at one time it was considered the world record-holder. The East (North-East) Caucasian (or Nakh-Daghestanian) languages are spoken mainly in Daghestan, Chechnya and Ingushetia in the Russian Federation; the best-known language is Chechen with about a million speakers, though the family also includes languages like Hinuq, spoken by about 500 people in a single village.

Turning now to south-western Asia, we may consider the Afroasiatic family, which, as its name suggests, is spoken in both Asia and Africa. In Asia its main focus is the Arab countries of the Middle East, although Hebrew and Aramaic are also Afroasiatic languages of Asia, belonging to the Semitic branch of Afroasiatic. In addition Arabic is, of course, the dominant language of North Africa, where Afroasiatic is represented not only by a number of other Semitic languages (those of Ethiopia, the major one being Amharic), but also by Berber, the Cushitic languages of the Horn of Africa (including Somali, the official language of Somalia), and the Chadic languages of

11

northern Nigeria and adjacent areas (including Hausa). One branch of Afroasiatic formerly spoken in Africa, Egyptian (by which is meant the language of ancient Egypt, not the dialect of Arabic currently spoken in Egypt), is now extinct.

In South Asia (the traditional 'Indian subcontinent'), four language families meet. Indo-European languages, more specifically languages of the Indo-Aryan branch of Indo-European, dominate in the north, while the south is the domain of the Dravidian languages (although some Dravidian languages are spoken further north, in particular Brahui, spoken in Pakistan). The northern fringe of the subcontinent is occupied by Sino-Tibetan languages, to which we return below. The fourth family is Austro-Asiatic. The languages in this family with most speakers are actually spoken in South-East Asia: Vietnamese in Vietnam and Khmer (Cambodian) in Cambodia, and they are the only languages of the family to have the status of national languages. Languages of the family are scattered from central India eastwards into Vietnam, Western Malaysia and the Nicobar Islands. In India itself, the Austro-Asiatic language with most speakers is Santali. It is only relatively recently that the assignment of Vietnamese to this family has gained widespread acceptance. In addition, there is one language isolate, Burushaski, spoken in northern Pakistan, while the genetic affiliations of the languages of the Andaman islands remain unclear.

We have already introduced a number of South-East Asian languages, and may now turn to the other two families represented in this area: Tai-Kadai (also called Kadai and Kam-Tai) and Sino-Tibetan. While the Tai-Kadai group of languages, which includes Thai (Siamese) and Lao, was earlier often considered a branch of Sino-Tibetan, this view has now been abandoned; Tai-Kadai languages are spoken in Thailand, Laos, southern China, and also in parts of Burma (Myanmar) and Vietnam. Sino-Tibetan contains the language with the largest number of native speakers in the world today, Chinese (and this remains true even if one divides Chinese into several different languages, in which case Mandarin occupies first position). The other Sino-Tibetan languages traditionally form the Tibeto-Burman branch, which includes Tibetan and Burmese, in addition to a vast number of languages spoken predominantly in southern China, Burma (Myanmar), northern India and Nepal. Finally, the languages of the Hmong-Mien (Miao-Yao) family are spoken in southern China and adjacent areas.

In East Asia we find Korean and Japanese (the latter together with the closely related Ryukyuan varieties), whose genetic affiliations to each other or to other languages (such as Altaic) remain the subject of at times heated debate.

The Austronesian family, though including some languages spoken on the Asian mainland, such as Malay of Western Malaysia and Cham spoken in Cambodia and Vietnam, is predominantly a language of the islands stretching eastwards from the South-East Asian mainland: even Malay–Indonesian has more speakers in insular South-East Asia than on the Malay peninsula. Austronesian languages are dominant on most of the islands from Sumatra in the west to Easter Island in the east, including the Philippines, but excluding New Guinea (where Austronesian languages are, however, spoken in many coastal areas); Malagasy, the language of Madagascar, is a western outlier of the family; Austronesian languages are also indigenous to Taiwan, though now very much in the minority relative to Chinese.

2.3 New Guinea and Australia

The island of New Guinea, which can be taken linguistically together with some of the smaller surrounding islands, is the most differentiated area linguistically in the whole world. Papua New Guinea, which occupies the eastern half of the island, contains some 800 languages for a total population of about five and a half million, meaning that the average language has just under 7,000 speakers. In many of the coastal areas of New Guinea, Austronesian languages are spoken, but the other languages are radically different from these Austronesian languages. These other languages are referred to collectively as either 'non-Austronesian languages of New Guinea' or as 'Papuan languages', though it should be realised that this is a negatively characterised term, rather than a claim about genetic relatedness. Though much work remains to be done, there has been considerable recent progress in classifying the Papuan languages genetically; in particular, there is growing evidence for a Trans-New Guinea family containing a large number of languages running east–west across the middle of the main island and on to some of the smaller islands to the west.

One syntactic property that is widespread among the Highland Papuan languages is worthy of note, namely switch reference. In a language with a canonical switch reference system, a sentence may (and typically does) consist of several clauses, of which only one is an independent clause (i.e. could occur on its own as a free-standing sentence), all the others being dependent; each dependent clause is marked according to whether or not its subject is the same as or different from the subject of the clause on which it is dependent. The examples below are from Usan:

Ye nam su-ab, isomei.   'I cut the tree and went down.'
Ye nam su-ine, isorei.   'I cut the tree and it fell down.'

The independent verbs, *isomei* and *isorei*, are respectively first person singular and third person singular. The dependent verbs, *su-ab* and *su-ine*, have respectively the suffix for same subject and the suffix for different subject. In the first example, therefore, the subjects of the two clauses are the same (i.e. I cut the tree and I went/fell down), while in the second sentence they are different (i.e. I cut the tree and some other entity – from the context only the tree is available – went/fell down). The words *ye* and *nam* mean respectively 'I' and 'tree'. One effect of switch reference is that the speaker of a language with switch reference must plan a discourse ahead to a much greater extent than is required by languages lacking switch reference, since in switch reference languages it is nearly always the case that the dependent clause precedes the independent clause, i.e. in clause *n* one has to mark the co-reference relation that holds between the subject of clause *n* and the subject of clause *n* + 1. This should, incidentally, serve to dispel any lingering notions concerning the primitiveness or lack of grammar in the languages of other societies. Although switch reference is found in many other parts of the world (e.g. in many indigenous languages of the Americas), it is particularly characteristic of the languages of the New Guinea Highlands.

Although the genetic classification of the indigenous languages of Australia, which numbered over 250 at the time of contact with Europeans, is the subject of at times acrimonious debate, there is a general consensus that a large Pama-Nyungan family can be identified, comprising most languages spoken in the south and centre and some in the north, while the other languages of the north form a number of small families and language isolates.

The Australian languages overall are characterised by an unusual consonant system, from the viewpoint of the kinds of consonant systems that are found most frequently across the languages of the world. Most Australian languages have no fricatives, and no voice opposition among their stops. However, they distinguish a large number of places of articulation, especially in terms of lingual articulations: thus most languages have, in addition to labial and velar stops, all of palatal, alveolar, and retroflex stops, while many languages add a further series of phonemically distinct dentals. The same number of distinctions is usually found with the nasals, and some languages extend this number of contrasts in the lingual stops to the laterals as well. One result of this is that Europeans usually fail to perceive (or produce, should they try to do so) phonemic oppositions that are crucial in Aboriginal languages, while conversely speakers of Australian languages fail to perceive or produce phonemic oppositions that are crucial in English (such as the distinction among *pit*, *bit*, *bid*).

One Australian language, Dyirbal, spoken in the Cairns rainforest in northern Queensland, has played an important role in recent discussions of general linguistic typology, and it will be useful to make a short digression to look at the relevant unique, or at least unusual, features of Dyirbal – though it should be emphasised that these features are not particularly typical of Australian languages overall.

In English, one of the pieces of evidence for saying that intransitive and transitive subjects are just subtypes of the overall notion 'subject' is that they behave alike with respect to a number of different syntactic processes. For instance, a rule of English syntax allows one to omit the subject of the second conjunct of a coordinate sentence if it is co-referential with the subject of the first conjunct, i.e. one can abbreviate the first sentence below to the second one:

I hit you and I came here.
I hit you and came here.

It is not possible to carry out a similar abbreviation of the next sentence below, since its subjects are not co-referential, even though the object of the first conjunct is co-referential with the subject of the second conjunct:

I hit you and you came here.

In the above examples, the first clause is transitive and the second clause intransitive, but the notion of subject applies equally to both clauses. If we think not so much of grammatical labels like subject and object, but rather of semantic labels like agent and patient, then we can say that in English it is the agent of a transitive clause that behaves as subject. In the corresponding Dyirbal sentences, however, it is the patient that behaves as subject, as can be seen in the following sentences:

Ngaja nginuna balgan, ngaja baninyu.	'I hit you and I came here.'
Ngaja nginuna balgan, nginda baninyu.	'I hit you and you came here.'
Ngaja nginuna balgan, baninyu.	'I hit you and you came here.'

In these sentences, *ngaja* is the nominative form for 'I', while *nginuna* is the accusative form for 'you'; the verbs are *balgan* 'hit' (transitive) and *baninyu* 'come here' (intransitive). In the third sentence, where the intransitive subject is omitted, it must be interpreted as co-referential with the patient, not the agent, of the first clause. In Section 2.1 we mentioned ergativity in connection with Basque case marking. These Dyirbal examples show that Dyirbal has ergativity in its syntactic system: patients of transitive verbs, rather than agents of transitive verbs, are treated as subjects, i.e. are treated in the same way as intransitive subjects. Note that in this sense Dyirbal grammar is certainly different from English grammar, but it is no less well defined.

Another unusual feature of Dyirbal is sociolinguistic. In many, if not all languages there are different choices of lexical item depending on differences in social situation, such as the difference between English *father* and *dad(dy)*. What is unusual about Dyirbal is that a difference of this kind exists for every single lexical item in the language. Under certain circumstances, in particular in the presence of a taboo relative (e.g. a parent-in-law), every lexical item of ordinary language (Guwal) must be replaced by the corresponding lexical item from avoidance style (Jalnguy). No doubt in part for functional reasons, to ease the memory load, it is usual for several semantically related words of Guwal to correspond to a single Jalnguy word, as when the various Guwal names for different species of lizard are all subsumed by the one Jalnguy word *jijan*.

The surviving textual materials in the Tasmanian languages, extinct since the end of the nineteenth century, are insufficient in scope or reliability to allow any accurate assessment of the genetic affiliations of these languages – certainly none is immediately apparent.

2.4 Africa

Africa north of the Sahara is the preserve of Afroasiatic languages, which have already been treated in Section 2.2. This section will therefore concentrate on the sub-Saharan languages, though excluding languages introduced into Africa by external colonisation (though one such language, Afrikaans, a descendant of colonial Dutch, is a language of Africa by virtue of its geographic distribution), and also Malagasy, the Austronesian language of Madagascar. It is useful to take as a starting point the classification of the sub-Saharan African languages into three groups as proposed by J.H. Greenberg in the mid-1960s – Niger-Congo, Nilo-Saharan and Khoisan – while keeping in mind that some of these groupings remain controversial, either in general or in particular details.

The Niger-Congo (Niger-Kordofanian) family covers most of sub-Saharan Africa, and includes not only major languages of West Africa such as Yoruba but also, as a low-level node on the family tree, the Bantu languages, dominant in most of East, Central and southern Africa. The assignment of some groups of languages to Niger-Congo, such as the Kordofanian languages spoken in the Kordofan mountains of Sudan and the Mande languages of western West Africa, remains controversial.

More controversial is the proposed Nilo-Saharan family, which would include languages spoken in a number of geographically discontinuous areas of northern sub-Saharan Africa including parts of southern Sudan running through northern Uganda and western Kenya to northern Tanzania, northern Chad and neighbouring areas and the bend of the Niger river in West Africa. While the languages of the first group form a well-defined language family, Nilotic, at the opposite extreme inclusion of Songhay on the bend of the Niger river is widely rejected.

Finally, the three main groups within Khoisan as proposed by Greenberg, namely Northern, Central (Khoe) and Southern, all spoken in southern, mainly south-western Africa, plus two geographically isolated languages of Tanzania, Hadza and Sandawe, are individually well-defined language families (or isolates). However, grouping them together as a single larger family is generally considered at least premature. Typologically, Khoisan languages are most noted for having click sounds as part of their regular phoneme inventory, a sound type that has also been borrowed into some neighbouring Bantu languages such as Zulu and Xhosa.

2.5 The Americas

The genetic classification of the indigenous languages of the Americas is overall the most contentious, with proposals ranging from a single family covering nearly all these languages, associated especially with the name of J.H. Greenberg, to around 200 distinct families and isolates. Even widely cited intermediate proposals, such as the Hokan and Penutian families, remain controversial. In what follows, I have concentrated on some of the more widespread established families and on some of the other languages with relatively large numbers of speakers.

Two population groups of North America are distinct ethnically from the remainder, namely the Eskimos (Inuit, although this latter term properly only refers to part of the Eskimos overall) and Aleuts. The Eskimo-Aleut family contains two branches, Aleut and Eskimo. Eskimo is properly a number of different languages rather than a single language, and is spoken from the eastern tip of Siberia through Alaska and northern Canada to Greenland; in Greenland it is, under the name Greenlandic, an official language.

Another language family centred in Alaska is the Athapaskan family (more properly: Athapaskan-Eyak, with inclusion of the Athapaskan or Athabaskan languages and the single language Eyak as the two branches of the family). Most of the Athapaskan languages are spoken in Alaska and north-western Canada, though the Athapaskan language with most speakers, Navajo, is spoken in Arizona and adjacent areas. Navajo is the indigenous language of North America (Canada and the USA) with the largest number of speakers, about 150,000. Athapaskan-Aleut is related to Tlingit, together forming a grouping often referred to as Na-Dene, although this term is also used to include Haida, which may well rather be a language isolate.

Among the other major families of North America are Iroquoian (around Lakes Ontario and Erie), Siouan (the Great Plains), and Algonquian (much of the north-eastern USA and eastern and central Canada, though also extending into the Great Plains with Arapaho and Cheyenne). One interesting feature of the Algonquian languages to which it is worth devoting a short digression is obviation. In Algonquian languages, a distinction is made between two kinds of third person, namely proximate and obviative, so that where English just has one set of third person pronouns (e.g. *he, she, it, they*) and morphology (e.g. the third person singular present tense ending *-s*), Algonquian languages distinguish two sets. In a given text span (which must be at least a clause, but may be longer), one of the third person noun phrases is selected as proximate (the one which is in some sense the most salient at that part of the text), all other third person participants are obviative. In the remainder of the text span, the proximate participant is always referred to by proximate morphology, while other participants are referred to by obviative morphology. In this way, the ambiguity of an English sentence like *John saw Bill as he was leaving* (was it John that was leaving, or Bill?) is avoided. The following examples are from Cree:

Nāpēw atim-wa wāpam-ē-w, ē-sipwēhtē-t.
'The man saw the dog as he (the man) left.'

Nāpēw atim-wa wāpam-ē-w, ē-sipwēhtē-ýit.
'The man saw the dog as it (the dog) was leaving.'

In both sentences, 'the man' is proximate (indicated by the absence of any affix on *nā pēw* 'man'), and 'the dog' is obviative (indicated by the suffix *-wa* on *atim-wa* 'dog'). The morphology of the verb *wāpam-ē-w* 'he sees him' indicates that the agent is proximate and the patient obviative (this is important, since the word order can be varied). The prefix *ē-* on the second verb indicates that it is subordinate ('conjunct', in Algonquianist terminology). In the first sentence, the suffix *-t* on this second verb indicates a proximate subject, i.e. the subject must be the proximate participant of the preceding clause, namely *the man*. In the second sentence, the suffix *-ẏit* indicates an obviative subject, i.e. the subject of this verb must be an obviative participant of the preceding clause, in this sentence the only candidate being *the dog*.

Another important family, Uto-Aztecan, includes languages spoken in both North America (the South-West) and Central America. Its Aztecan branch includes Nahuatl, whose varieties have in total over a million speakers. The ancestor of the modern dialects, Classical Nahuatl, was the language of the Aztec civilisation which flourished in Central Mexico before the arrival of the Spanish. Spoken to the south of Nahuatl entirely within Central America, the Mayan family has an equally glorious past, because of its association with the ancient Mayan civilisation. Mayan languages are spoken in southern Mexico and Guatemala, with some overspill into neighbouring Central American countries; the Mayan language with the largest number of speakers is Yucatec, with about 700,000, although several others have speaker numbers in the hundreds of thousands.

The major families of South America include Carib, Arawakan and Tupi. These language families do not occupy geographically continuous areas: Carib languages are spoken to the north of the Amazon, and predominate in the eastern part of this region; Arawakan languages, once also spoken in the West Indies, dominate further west and are also found well south of the Amazon; while Tupi languages are spoken over much of Brazil south of the Amazon and in Paraguay. One Tupi language, (Paraguayan) Guarani, with about five million speakers, is a co-official language of Paraguay and is unique among indigenous languages of the Americas in that most of its speakers are non-Indians. Hixkaryana, a Carib language spoken by about 600 people on the Nhamundá river, a tributary of the Amazon, has become famous in the linguistic literature as the first clear attestation of a language in which the word order is object–verb–subject, as in the following sentence:

Toto yahosɨye kamara.   'The jaguar grabbed the man.'

In Hixkaryana, *toto* means 'man', *kamara* means 'jaguar', while the verb *yahosɨye* has the lexical meaning 'grab' and specifies that both subject and object are third person singular. Since there is no case marking on the nouns, and since the verb morphology is compatible with either noun as subject or object, the word order is crucial to understanding of this Hixkaryana sentence (which cannot mean 'the man grabbed the jaguar'), just as the different subject–verb–object word order is crucial in English.

Quechua – properly a family of often mutually unintelligible languages rather than a single language – has about ten million speakers, primarily in Peru and Bolivia, though with offshoots north into Ecuador and Colombia and south into Chile and Argentina. It is of uncertain genetic affiliation, though often claimed to be related to the neighbouring Aymara language. Quechua was the language of the Inca civilisation, centred on Cuzco in what is now Peru.

3 The Social Interaction of Languages

As was indicated in the Preface, the notion of 'major language' is defined in social terms, so it is now time to look somewhat more consistently at some notions relating to the social side of language, in particular the social interaction of languages. Whether a language is a major language or not has nothing to do with its structure or with its genetic affiliation, and the fact that so many of the world's major languages are Indo-European is a mere accident of history.

First, we may look in more detail at the criteria that serve to define a language as being major. One of the most obvious criteria is the number of speakers, and certainly in making my choice of languages to be given individual chapters in this volume number of speakers was one of my main criteria. However, number of speakers is equally clearly not the sole criterion.

An interesting comparison to make here is between Chinese (or even more specifically, Mandarin) and English. Mandarin has far more native speakers than English, yet still English is generally considered a more useful language in the world at large than is Mandarin, as seen in the much larger number of people studying English as a second language than studying Mandarin as a second language. One of the reasons for this is that English is an international language, understood by a large number of people in many different parts of the world; Mandarin, by contrast, is by and large confined to China, and even taking all Chinese dialects (or languages) together, the extension of Chinese goes little beyond China and overseas Chinese communities. English is not only the native language of sizable populations in different parts of the world (especially the British Isles, North America and Australia and New Zealand) but is also spoken as a second language in even more countries, as is discussed in more detail in the chapter on English. English happens also to be the language of some of the technologically most advanced countries (in particular of the USA), so that English is the basic medium for access to current technological developments. Thus factors other than mere number of speakers are relevant in determining the social importance of a language.

Indeed, some of the languages given individual chapters in this volume have relatively few native speakers. Some of them are important not so much by virtue of the number of native speakers but rather because of the extent to which they are used as a lingua franca, as a second language among people who do not share a common first language. Good examples here are Swahili and Indonesian. Swahili is the native language of a relatively small population, perhaps a couple of million, primarily on the coast of East Africa, but its use as a lingua franca has spread through much of East Africa (especially Kenya and Tanzania) and beyond, so that the language is used by a total of perhaps around 50 million people. The Indonesian variety of Malay–Indonesian is the native language of perhaps 23 million, but is used as a second language by about 140,000,000 in Indonesia. In many instances, in my choice of languages I have been guided by this factor rather than by raw statistics. Among the Philippine languages, for instance, Tagalog does not have the largest number of native speakers, but I selected it because it is both the national language of the Philippines and used as a lingua franca across much of the country. A number of Indo-Aryan languages would surely have qualified for inclusion in terms of number of speakers, but they have not been assigned individual chapters because in social terms the major languages of the northern part of South Asia are clearly Hindi–Urdu and Bengali.

Another important criterion is the cultural importance of a language, in terms of the age and influence of its cultural heritage. An example in point is provided by the Dravidian languages. Tamil does not have the largest number of native speakers; it is, however, the oldest Dravidian literary language, and for this reason my choice rested with Tamil. I am aware that many of these decisions are in part subjective, and in part contentious. As I emphasise in the Preface, the thing furthest from my mind is to intend any slight to speakers of languages that are not considered major in the contents of this volume; much of our knowledge of Language as a general characteristic of the human species comes precisely from the study of smaller, often endangered languages.

Certain languages are major even despite the absence of native speakers, as with Latin and Sanskrit. Latin has provided a major contribution to all European languages, as can be seen most superficially in the extent to which words of Latin origin are used in European languages. But even those languages that have tried to avoid the appearance of Latinity by creating their own vocabulary have often fallen back on Latin models: German *Gewissen* 'conscience', for instance, contains the prefix *ge-*, meaning 'with', the stem *wiss-*, meaning 'know', and the suffix *-en* to form an abstract noun – an exact copy of the Latin *con-sci-entia*; borrowings that follow the structure rather than the form in this way are known as calques or loan translations. Sanskrit has played a similar role in relation to the languages of India, including Hindi. Hebrew is included not because of the number of its speakers – as noted in the chapter on Hebrew, this has never been large – but because of the contribution of Hebrew and its culture to European and Middle Eastern society.

A language can thus have influence beyond the areas where it is the native or second language. A good example to illustrate this is Arabic. Arabic loans form a large part of the vocabulary of many languages spoken by Islamic peoples, even of languages that are genetically only distantly related to Arabic (e.g. Hausa) or that are genetically totally unrelated (e.g. Turkish, Persian and Urdu). The influence of Arabic can also be seen in the adoption of the Arabic writing system by many Islamic peoples. Similarly, Chinese loan words form an important part of the vocabulary of some East Asian languages, in particular Vietnamese, Japanese and Korean; the use of written Chinese characters has also spread to Japan and Korea, and in earlier times also to Vietnam.

It is important to note also that the status of a language as a major language is far from immutable. Indeed, as we go back into history we find many significant changes. For instance, the possibility of characterising English as the major language of the world is an innovation of the twentieth century. One of the most important shifts in the distribution of major languages resulted from the expansion of European languages, especially English, Spanish, Portuguese, and to a lesser extent French as a result of the colonisation of the Americas: English, Spanish and Portuguese all now have far more native speakers in the New World than in Britain, Spain or Portugal. Indeed, in the Middle Ages one would hardly have imagined that English, confined to an island off the coast of Europe, would have become a major international language.

In medieval Europe, Latin was clearly the major language, since, despite the lack of native speakers, it was the lingua franca of those who needed to communicate across linguistic boundaries. Yet the rise of Latin to such pre-eminence – which includes the fact that Latin and its descendants have ousted virtually all other languages from south-western Europe – could hardly have been foreseen from its inauspicious beginnings confined to the area around Rome. Equally spectacular has been the spread of Arabic, in the wake of the spread of Islam, from being confined to the Arabian peninsula to being the dominant language of the Middle East and North Africa.

In addition to languages that have become major languages, there are equally languages that have lost this status. The earliest records from Mesopotamia, often considered the cradle of civilisation, are in two languages: Sumerian and Akkadian (the latter the language of the Assyrian and Babylonian empires); Akkadian belongs to the Semitic branch of Afroasiatic, while Sumerian is as far as we can tell unrelated to any other known language. Even at the time of attested Sumerian inscriptions, the language was probably already approaching extinction, and continued to be used in deference to tradition (as with Latin in medieval Europe). The dominant language of the area was to become Akkadian, but in the intervening period this too has died out, leaving no direct descendants. Gone too is Ancient Egyptian, the language of the Pharaohs and whose earliest texts are roughly contemporaneous with those of Sumerian. The linguistic picture of the Mediterranean and Near East in the year nought was very different from that which we observe today.

Social factors and social attitudes can even bring about apparent reversals in the family-tree model of language relatedness. At the time of the earliest texts from Germany, two distinct Germanic languages are recognised: Old Saxon and Old High German. Old Saxon is the ancestor of the modern Low German (Plattdeutsch) dialects, while Old High German is the ancestor of the modern High German dialects and of the standard language. Because of social changes – such as the decline of the Hanseatic League, the economic mainstay of northern Germany – High German gained social ascendancy over Low German. Since the standard language, based on High German, is now recognised as the standard in both northern and southern Germany, both Low and High German dialects are now considered dialects of a single German language, and the social relations between a given Low German dialect and standard German are in practice no different from those between a High German dialect and standard German.

One of the most interesting developments to have arisen from language contact is the development of pidgin and creole languages. A pidgin language arises from a very practical situation: speakers of different languages need to communicate with one another to carry out some practical task, but do not speak any language in common and moreover do not have the opportunity to learn each other's language properly. What arises in such a situation is, initially, an unstable pidgin, or jargon, with highly variable structure – considerably simplified relative to the native languages of the people involved in its creation – and just enough vocabulary to permit practical tasks to be carried out reasonably successfully. The clearest examples of the development of such pidgins arose from European colonisation, in particular from the Atlantic slave trade and from indenturing labourers in the South Pacific. These pidgins take most of their vocabulary from the colonising language, although their structure is often very different from those of the colonising language.

At a later stage, the jargon may expand, particularly when its usefulness as a lingua franca is recognised among the speakers of non-European origin, leading to a stabilised pidgin, such as Tok Pisin, the major lingua franca of Papua New Guinea. This expansion is on several planes: the range of functions is expanded, since the pidgin is no longer restricted to uses of language essential to practical tasks; the vocabulary is expanded as a function of this greater range of functions, new words often being created internally to the pidgin rather than borrowed from some other language (as with Tok Pisin *maus gras* 'moustache', literally 'mouth grass'); the structure becomes stabilised, i.e. the language has a well-defined grammar.

Probably at any stage in this development, from inception to post-stabilisation, the pidgin can 'acquire native speakers', i.e. become the native language of part or all of the community. For instance, if native speakers of different languages marry and have the pidgin as their only common language, then this will be the language of their household and will become the first language of their children. Once a pidgin has acquired native speakers, it is referred to as a creole. The native language of many inhabitants of the Caribbean islands is a creole, for instance the English-based creole of Jamaica, the French-based creole of Haiti, and the Spanish- and/or Portuguese-based creole Papiamento (Papiamentu) of the Netherlands Antilles and Aruba. At an even later stage, social improvements and education may bring the creole back into close contact with the European language that originally contributed much of its vocabulary. In this situation, the two languages may interact and the creole, or some of its varieties, may start approaching the standard language. This gives rise to the so-called post-creole continuum, in which one finds a continuous scale of varieties of speech from forms close to the original creole (basilect) through intermediate forms (mesolect) up to a slightly regionally coloured version of the standard language (acrolect). Jamaican English is a good example of a post-creole continuum.

Even with hindsight, as we saw above, it would have been difficult to predict the present-day distribution of major languages in the world. It is equally impossible to predict the future. In terms of number of native speakers, it is clear that a major shift is underway in favour of non-European languages: the rate of population increase is much higher outside Europe than in Europe, and while some European languages draw some benefit from this (such as Spanish and Portuguese in Latin America), the main beneficiaries are the indigenous languages of southern Asia and Africa. It might well be that a later version of this volume would include fewer of the European languages that are restricted to a single country, and devote more space to non-European languages. Another factor is the increase in the range of functions of many non-European languages: during the colonial period European languages (primarily English and French) were used for most official purposes and also for education in much of Asia and Africa, but the winning of independence has meant that many countries have turned more to their own languages, using these as official language and medium of education. The extent to which this will lead to increase in their status as major languages is difficult to predict – at present, access to the frontiers of scholarship and technology is still primarily through European languages, especially English; but one should not forget that the use of English, French and German as vehicles for science was gained only through a prolonged struggle against what then seemed the obvious language for such writing: Latin. (The process may go back indefinitely: Cicero was criticised for writing philosophical treatises in Latin by those who thought he should have used Greek.) But at least I hope to have shown the reader that the social interaction of languages is a dynamic process, one that is moreover exciting to follow.

Bibliography

The most comprehensive and up-to-date index of the world's languages, with genetic classification, is Gordon (2005); while some data are no doubt questionable, this is certainly the most reliable such index available. For a more splitter-oriented classification, see Dryer (2005); for a more clumper-oriented one, Ruhlen (1991). Two series dealing with particular language families are the Cambridge Language Surveys (http://www.cup.cam.ac.uk/series/sSeries.asp?code=CLS) and the Routledge Language Family Series (http://www.routledge.com/books/series/Routledge_Language_Family_Series); the former concentrates on general properties of the language group in question, while the latter, initially inspired by the first edition of the present work, provides sketches of individual languages. Though outside these series, Heine and Nurse (2000) provides a good overview of languages of Africa. Among several recent publications on endangered languages are Abley (2003) and Harrison (2007); see also http://www.ethnologue.com/nearly_extinct.asp for a list of 'nearly extinct' languages, i.e. for which 'only a few elderly speakers are still living'.

Readers wanting to delve deeper into problems of genetic classification should consult a good introduction to historical and comparative linguistics, such as Campbell (2004). For discussions of language universals and typology, reference may be made to Comrie (1989) or Croft (2002). A good introduction to language contact is Thomason (2001).

References

Abley, Mark. 2003. *Spoken Here: Travels among Threatened Languages* (Heinemann, London; Houghton Mifflin, Boston).

Campbell, L. 2004. *Historical Linguistics*, 2nd edn (Edinburgh University Press, Edinburgh).

Comrie, B. 1989. *Language Universals and Linguistic Typology*, 2nd edn (Basil Blackwell, Oxford; University of Chicago Press, Chicago).

Croft, W. 2002. *Typology and Universals*, 2nd edn (Cambridge University Press, Cambridge).

Dryer, M.S. 2005. 'Genealogical Language List', in M. Haspelmath, M.S. Dryer, D. Gil and B. Comrie (eds) *The World Atlas of Language Structures* (Oxford University Press, Oxford), pp. 584–644.

Gordon, R.G., Jr (ed.) 2005. *Ethnologue: Languages of the World*, 15th edn (SIL International, Dallas). Online version http://www.ethnologue.com/

Greenberg, J.H. 1966. 'Some Universals of Grammar with Particular Reference to the Order of Meaningful Elements', in J. H. Greenberg (ed.) *Universals of Language*, rev. edn (MIT Press, Cambridge, MA), pp. 73–112.

Harrison, K. David. 2007. *When Languages Die: The Extinction of the World's Languages and the Erosion of Human Knowledge* (Oxford University Press, Oxford).

Heine, B. and Nurse, D. (eds) 2000. *African Languages: An Introduction* (Cambridge University Press, Cambridge).

Ruhlen, M. 1991. *A Guide to the World's Languages, Vol. I: Classification*, rev. edn (Stanford University Press, Stanford).

Thomason, S.G. 2001. *Language Contact: An Introduction* (Edinburgh University Press: Edinburgh).

Sources

I owe the Mbabaram example to R.M.W. Dixon. The Basque examples are from R. Etxepare (2003), 'Valency and Argument Structure in the Basque Verb', p. 364, in J.I. Hualde and J. Ortiz de Urbina (eds) *A Grammar of Basque* (Mouton de Gruyter, Berlin), pp. 363–426; the system is somewhat more complex than indicated in my text. The Usan examples are to be found in Ger P. Reesink (1983), 'Switch Reference and Topicality Hierarchies', *Studies in Language*, vol. 7, pp. 215–46. The discussion of Dyirbal is based on R.M.W. Dixon (1972), *The Dyirbal Language of North Queensland* (Cambridge University Press, Cambridge), especially Section 5.2.2 and Chapter 8. The Cree examples are from H. C. Wolfart and J.F. Carroll (1981), *Meet Cree*, 2nd edn (University of Alberta Press, Edmonton), p. 26. The Hixkaryana example is taken from D.C. Derbyshire (1985), *Hixkaryana and Linguistic Typology* (Summer Institute of Linguistics, Dallas; University of Texas at Arlington, Arlington) p. 32.

1

Indo-European Languages

Philip Baldi

1 Introduction

By the term *Indo-European* we are referring to a family of languages which by about 1000 BCE were spoken over a large part of Europe and parts of southwestern and southern Asia. Indo-European is essentially a geographical term: it refers to the easternmost (India) and westernmost (Europe) pre-colonial expansion of the family at the time it was proven to be a linguistic group by scholars of the eighteenth and nineteenth centuries (the term was first used in 1813). Of course, modern developments which have spread Indo-European languages around the world now suggest another name for the family, but the term *Indo-European* (German *Indogermanisch*) is now well rooted in the scholarly tradition.

Establishing languages as members of linguistic families is a process which must be accomplished using proven methods and principles of scientific analysis. During the approximately two centuries in which the interrelationships within the Indo-European family have been systematically studied, techniques to confirm and quantify genetic affiliations among its members have been developed with great success. Chief among these is the comparative method, which takes shared features among languages as its data and provides procedures for establishing protoforms (reconstruction). The comparative method is supplemented by the method of internal reconstruction and the application of principles of typological inference, which can be utilised together with the comparative method to achieve reliable reconstructions. But since space is limited and the focus of this chapter is Indo-European and not methods of reconstruction, we will restrict ourselves here to a brief review of the comparative method as it applies under normal conditions, using only data from Indo-European languages, though it should be pointed out that the method is generally applicable to the world's languages, regardless of family affiliation.

When we claim that two or more languages are genetically related, we are also claiming that they share common ancestry. And if we make such a claim about common ancestry, then our methods should provide us with a means of recovering the ancestral system, attested or not. The initial demonstration of relatedness is only a first step;

establishing well-motivated intermediate and ancestral forms is somewhat more complex. Among the difficulties are: which features in which of the languages being compared are older? which are innovations? which are the result of contact? how many shared similarities are enough to prove relatedness conclusively, and how are they weighted for significance? what assumptions do we make about the relative importance of lexical, morphological, syntactic and phonological features, and about directions of language change?

With these questions in mind, we begin the reconstruction process with the following assumption: if two or more languages share a feature which is unlikely to have arisen by accident, borrowing or as the result of some typological tendency or language universal, then *under normal circumstances* (i.e. in contrast with the rare instances of language mixing), the feature is assumed to have arisen only once and to have been transmitted to the two or more languages from a common source. The more such features are discovered and securely identified, the firmer the relationship.

In determining genetic relationship and reconstructing proto-forms using the comparative method, we usually start with vocabulary. Table 1.1 contains a number of words from various Indo-European languages which demonstrate a common core of lexical items too large and too basic to be explained either by accident or borrowing. A list of possible cognates which is likely to produce a maximum number of common inheritance items, known as the basic vocabulary list, provides many of the words we might investigate, such as basic kinship terms, pronouns, major body parts, lower numerals and other lexical fields which have proven to be resistant to borrowing in this family. From these and other data we seek to establish sets of equations known as *correspondences*, which represent statements that in a given environment X phoneme of one language will correspond to Y phoneme of another language *consistently* and *systematically* if the two languages are descended from a common ancestor.

Table 1.1 Some Basic Indo-European Terms

A NUMERALS	*one*	*two*	*three*	*four*	*five*	*six*	*seven*	*eight*	*nine*
Skt.	éka-	dvā́, dváu	tráya-	catvāra-	páñca	ṣáṭ-	saptá-	aṣṭá(u)	náva
Gk.	oînos 'ace'	dú(w)ō	treîs	téttares, téssares	pénte, pémpe	héks	heptá	oktṓ	enné(w)a
Lat.	ūnus	duo	trēs	quattuor	quīnque	sex	septem	octō	novem
Hitt.		dā-	tēri-	Hier. Luv.	paⁿta		šipta-		
Toch. A			wu	tre	śtwar	päñ	ṣäk	ṣpät	okät	ñu
B			wi	trai	śtwer	piś	ṣkas	ṣuk(t)	okt	ñu
OIr.	ōen	dāu, do	trī	ceth(a)ir	cóic	sē	secht	ocht	noī
Go.	ains	twai	þreis	fidwōr	fimf	saíhs	sibun	ahtau	niun
OCS	(jed)inŭ	dŭva	trĭje	četyre	pętĭ	šestĭ	sedmĭ	osmĭ	devętĭ
Lith.	víenas	dù	trŷs	keturì	penkì	šešì	septynì	aštuonì	devynì
Arm.	mi	erku	erekʻ	čorkʻ	hing	vecʻ	evtʻn	utʻ	inn
Alb.	nji, një	dü	tre, tri	katër	pesë	gjashtë	shtatë	tetë	nëndë

Table continued on next page.

Table 1.1 (continued)

B	ANIMAL NAMES	mouse	wolf	cow	sheep	pig	dog	horse
Skt.		mū́ṣ-	vŕ̥ka-	gáv-	ávi-	sūkará-	śvá-	áśva-
Gk.		mûs	lúkos	boûs	ó(w)is	hûs	kúōn	híppos
Lat.		mūs	lupus	bōs	ovis	sūs	canis	cquus
Hitt.								
Toch. A				ko			ku	yuk
B			walkwe	keu	eye	suwo	ku	yakwe
OIr.			olc 'evil'	bō	oī		cū	ech
OHG		mūs	wulfs	OIc. kȳr OHG ouwi		swein	hunds OE eoh	
OCS		myšĭ	vlĭkŭ	gomŭno 'threshing floor'	ovĭnŭ	svinija	Russ. súka; 'bitch'	
Lith.			vil̃kas Latv. gùovs Lith.		avìs Latv.	suvęns	šuō (OLith.)	ešvà, ašvà, 'mare'
Arm.		mukn		kov	hoviw 'shepherd'		šun	ēš
Alb.		mī	ulk			thi		

C	BODY PARTS	foot	heart	eye	tongue
Skt.		pád-	śrád-dhā- 'put the heart in trust'	ákṣi-	jihvā́
Gk.		poús (gen. podós)	kardíā	óp-somai 'I will see'	
Lat.		pēs (gen. pedis)	cor (gen. cordis)	oculus	lingua
Hitt.		pāta-(Luw.)	kard-		
Toch. A		pe	kri 'will'	ak	kāntu
B		paiyye	kāryāñ (pl.)	ek	kantwo
OIr.		īs 'below'	cride	enech	teng
Go.		fõtus	haírtō	augō	tuggō
OCS		pĕšī 'on foot'	srŭdĭce	oko	językŭ
Lith.		pādas 'sole'	širdìs	akìs	liežùvis
Arm.		otn	sirt	akn	lezu
Alb.		(për)posh 'under'		sü	

D	KINSHIP TERMS	mother	father	sister	brother
Skt.		mātár-	pitár-	svásar-	bhrā́tar-
Gk. (Dor.)		mā́tēr	patḗr	eór (voc.) (Dor.)	phrā́tēr < 'member of a brotherhood'
Lat.		māter	pater	soror	frāter
Hitt.					
Toch. A		mācar	pācar		pracar
B		mācer	pācer		procer
OIr.		māthair	athair	siur	brāthair
OIc.		mōðir Go. fadar		swistar	Go. brōþar
OCS		mati		sestra	bratrŭ, bratŭ
Lith.		mótė 'woman'		sesuō	brólis
Arm.		mair	hair	k'oir	ełbair
Alb.		motrë			

Table continued on next page.

25

Table 1.1 (*continued*)

E	GENERAL TERMS	*full*	*race, kind*	*month*	*die, death*	*old*	*vomit*
	Skt.	pūrṇá-	jánas-	mā́s-	mṛtá-	sána-	vámiti
	Gk.	plḗrēs	génos	mḗn	ámbrotos 'immortal'	hénos 'last year's'	eméō
	Lat.	plēnus	genus	mēnsis	mortuus	senex	vomō
	Hitt.				mer-		
	Toch. A			mañ			
	B			meñe			
	OIr.	lān	gein 'birth'	mī	marb	sen	
	Go.	fulls	kuni	mēna, mēnōþs	maúrþr	sineigs OIc	vāma 'sickness'
	OCS	plŭnŭ		OBulg. měsęcǐ	mĭrǫ		vémti
	Lith.	pìlnas		mė́nuo	mir̃tis	sẽnas	
	Arm.	li	cin 'birth'	amis	mard 'mortal'	hin	
	Alb.	plot		muai			

In order to illustrate the comparative method we will briefly and selectively choose a few items from Tables 1.1 and 1.2, restricting our data to fairly clear cases.

	mouse		*mother*		*nine*
Skt.	mū́ṣ-		mātár̃		náva
Gk.	mū̂s	(Dor.)	mā́tēr		enné(w)a
Lat.	mūs		māter		novem
OHG	mūs	OIc.	mōðir	Go.	niun

	dead		*dog*		*race, kind*
Skt.	mṛtá-		śvá-		jánas-
Gk.	ámbrotos 'immortal'		kúōn		génos
Lat.	mortuus		canis		genus
Go.	maúrþr 'murder'		hunds		kuni

	I am		*vomit*		*old*
Skt.	ásmi		vámiti		sána-
Gk.	eimí		eméō		hénos 'last year's'
Lat.	sum		vomō		senex
Go.	im	OIc.	vāma 'sickness'	Go.	sineigs

We will first look only at the nasals *m* and *n*. Lined up for comparative analysis they look like this:

	mouse	*mother*	*nine*	*dead*	*dog*	*race, kind*	*I am*	*vomit*	*old*
Skt.	m-	m-	n-	m-	-∅-	-n-	-m-	-m-	-n-
Gk.	m-	m-	-nn-	-m(b)-	-n	-n-	-m-	-m-	-n-
Lat.	m-	m-	n-	m-	-n-	-n-	-m	-m-	-n-
Gmc.	m-	m-	n-	m-	-n-	-n-	-m	-m-	-n-

Before we begin reconstructing we must be sure that we are comparing the appropriate segments. It is clear that this is the case in 'mouse', 'mother', 'dog', 'race, kind', 'I am', 'vomit' and 'old', but less clear in 'nine', 'dead' and 'dog'. What of the double *n* in Gk. *enné(w)a*? Internal reconstruction reveals that *en-* is either a prefix or the

Table 1.2 Inflectional Regularities in Indo-European Languages

A Examples of Verb Inflection

		I am	*he, she is*
Skt.		ásmi	ásti
Gk.		eimí	estí
Lat.		sum	est
Hitt.		ēšmi	ēšzi
Toch.	A		
	B		ste
OIr.		am	is
Go.		im	ist
OCS		jesmĭ	jestĭ
OLith.		esmì	êsti
Arm.		em	ē
Alb.		jam	është

B Examples of Noun Inflection

tooth

		Skt.	*Gk.*	*Lat.*	*Go.*	*Lith.*
Sg.	nom.	dán	odṓn	dēns	*tunþus	dantìs
	gen.	datás	odóntos	dentis	*tunþáus	dantiẽs
	dat.	daté	odónti	dentī	tunþáu	dañčiui
	acc.	dántam	odónta	dentem	tunþu	dañtį
	abl.	datás		dente		
	loc.	datí				dantyjè
	inst.	datā́				dantimì
Pl.	nom.	dántas	odóntes	dentēs	*tunþjus	dañtys
	gen.	datā́m	odóntōn	dentium	tunþiwē	dantũ
	dat.	dadbhyás	odoūsi	dentibus	tunþum	dantìms
	acc.	datás	odóntas	dentēs	tunþuns	dantìs
	abl.	dadbhyás		dentibus		
	loc.	datsú				dantysè
	inst.	dadbhís				dantimìs

C Examples of Pronoun Inflection

I, me

	Skt.	*Gk.*	*Lat.*	*Hitt.*	*Go.*	*OCS*
nom.	ahám	egṓ	ego	uk	ik	azŭ
gen.	máma(me)	emoû(mou)	meī	ammēl	meina	mene
dat.	máhyam(me)	emoí(moi)	mihī	ammuk	mis	mĭnē(mi)
acc.	mā́m(mā)	emé(me)	mē(d)	ammuk	mik	mene(mę)
abl.	mát		mē(d)	ammēdaz		
loc.	máyi			ammuk		mĭnē
inst.	máyā					mŭnojǫ

you (sg.)

	Skt.	*Gk.*	*Lat.*	*Hitt.*	*Go.*	*OCS*
nom.	tvám	sú	tū	zik	þu	ty
gen.	táva(te)	soú(sou)	tuī, tīs	tuēl	þeina	tebe
dat.	túbhyam(te)	soí(soi)	tibī	tuk	þus	tebē(ti)
acc.	tvā́m(tvā)	sé(se)	tē(d)	tuk	þuk	tebe(tę)
abl.	tvát		tē(d)	tuēdaz		
loc.	tváyi			tuk		tebē
inst.	tváyā					tobojǫ

Note: Forms in parentheses are enclitic variants.

outcome of some pre-Greek phonological process; in either case, the first *n* is definitely outside the comparative equation. Likewise with Gk. *ámbrotos* 'immortal': the *a-* is a prefix meaning 'not' (= Lat. *in-*, Go. *un-*, etc.), and the *b* results from a rule of Greek in which the sequence *-mr-* (a-mrotos) results in *-mbr-*, with excrescent *b* (cf. Lat. *camera* > Fr. *chambre*). Similarly with Skt. *śvá-* 'dog', which has no *n* itself, but reveals an *n* in the stem of the genitive case form *śúnas*. So the nasals in these sets do indeed align, leaving us with consistent *m* and *n* correspondences in their respective sets:

$$m : m : m : m \qquad n : n : n : n$$

These alignments represent the horizontal or comparative dimension of the reconstruction process. Next we 'triangulate' the segments, adding the vertical, or historical dimension:

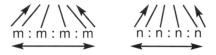

Finally, after checking all the relevant data and investigating their distributional patterns, we make a hypothesis concerning the proto-sound. In these two cases there is only one reasonable solution, namely **m* and **n*:

At this stage of the analysis we invert the equation, so that it reads '**m* > (develops into) *m* and **n* > *n*' in the specified daughter languages.

Neat correspondences such as these are more the exception than the rule in comparative analysis. It is far more common to find sets in which only a few of the members have identical segments. But the comparative method does not require that segments **match**, only that they **correspond** systematically. Consider the following data from Table 1.1, supplemented by some additional material:

	pig	*old*	*race, kind* (gen. case)	*be*
Skt.	sūkará-	sána-	jánasas	ástu 'let him be!'
Gk.	hûs	hénos 'last year's'	géneos (génous)	éō (ô) 'I might be'
Lat.	sūs	senex	generis	erō 'I will be'
Go.	swein	sineigs	(OCS slovese 'word')	ist 'he/she is'

We are concentrating here on the correspondences which include *s*, *h* and *r*. In 'pig' and 'old' we have the set *s* : *h* : *s* : *s* initially (cf. also 'six' and 'seven'). In final position we find ∅ : *s* : *s* : *s* in 'pig' and 'old' (cf. also 'one', 'three', 'mouse' and 'wolf', among others). And in medial position we have *s* : ∅ : *r* : *s* in 'race, kind' (gen.) and 'be'. What is (are) the proto-sound(s)?

A brief look at the languages in question takes us straight to *s for all three correspondences: *s > h in Greek initially (weakens), and disappears completely medially (éō), yielding a phonetically common pattern of s > h > ∅; Sanskrit final ∅ in 'old' is only the result of citing the Sanskrit words in their root forms; the full nominative form (as in the other languages) would contain s as well (ékas, etc.); and the medial Latin r is the result of rhotacism, whereby Latin consistently converts intervocalic s to r (cf. es- 'be', erō 'I will be'; (nom.) flōs 'flower' (gen.) flōris).

From these few, admittedly simplified examples we can get an idea of the comparative method which, when supplemented by adequate information about the internal structure of the languages in question and by a consideration of all the relevant data, can produce consistent reconstructions of ancestral forms. It is with such methods that Proto-Indo-European (PIE) has been reconstructed.

2 The Languages of the Indo-European Family

The Indo-European languages are classified into eleven major groups (ten if Baltic and Slavonic are considered together as Balto-Slavonic). Some of these groups have many members, while some others have only one. Of the eleven major groups, nine have modern spoken representatives while two, Anatolian and Tocharian, are extinct.

2.1 Indo-Iranian

The Indo-Iranian group has two main subdivisions, Indo-Aryan (Indic) and Iranian. The similarities between the two subdivisions are so consistent that there is no question about the status of Indo-Iranian intermediate between Proto-Indo-European and the Indic and Iranian subgroups. The Indo-Aryan migrations into the Indian area took place some time in the second millennium BCE.

2.1.1 Indo-Aryan (or Indic)

(See Chapter 20.)

2.1.2 Iranian

(See Chapter 24.)

2.2 Hellenic (Greek)

(See Chapter 19.)

2.3 Italic

(See Chapter 7.)

2.4 Anatolian

The Anatolian languages were unknown to modern scholars until archaeological excavations during the first part of the last century in Boğazköy, Turkey, yielded texts which were written primarily in Hittite, the principal language of the Anatolian group. The texts, which date from approximately the seventeenth to the thirteenth centuries BCE, were written in cuneiform script and contained not only Hittite, but Akkadian and Sumerian as well. Decipherment proceeded quickly and it was demonstrated by B. Hrozný in 1915 that the Hittite in the texts was an Indo-European language. It was later shown that Hittite contained a large number of archaic features not found in other Indo-European languages, which resulted in revised reconstructions of the proto-language. Now totally extinct, the Anatolian group contains, in addition to the amply attested Hittite, Luwian (Cuneiform and Hieroglyphic), Lycian, Palaic, Lydian, and possibly Carian.

2.5 Tocharian

Around the turn of the twentieth century a large amount of material written in an unknown language was discovered in the Chinese Turkestan (Tarim Basin) region of Central Asia. The language represented in these texts is now known as Tocharian; it was quickly recognised as Indo-European, despite its extreme eastern location. The Tocharian documents are chiefly of a religious nature, but also contain commercial documents, caravan passes and medical and magical texts. There are two dialects of Tocharian: Tocharian A, also known as East Tocharian or Turfan, and Tocharian B, also known as West Tocharian or Kuchean. The texts found in Chinese Turkestan are all from the period CE 500 to 1000, so this language has not played the same role as other twentieth-century discoveries like Hittite and Mycenaean Greek in the shaping of reconstructed Proto-Indo-European.

2.6 Celtic

The Celtic languages are largely unknown until the modern period, though it is clear from inscriptional information and place and river names that Celtic languages were once spread over a fairly wide section of Europe in the pre-Christian era. The Celtic languages are commonly classified into two groups: the Continental group, comprising the extinct Celtiberian (Hispano-Celtic), Gaulish and Galatian; and the Insular group, which contains two subdivisions, namely the Gaelic (Goidelic) group, made up of Irish, Scots Gaelic and the extinct Manx, and the Brythonic (Brittanic) group, made up of Welsh, Breton and the extinct Cornish. The oldest records of Celtic are some sepulchral inscriptions from the fourth century CE, and Old Irish manuscripts which date from the late seventh to early eighth century CE.

Many specialists believe that the Celtic and Italic languages have a remote relationship (Italo-Celtic) intermediate between the disintegration of Proto-Indo-European and the establishment of the separate Celtic and Italic groups.

2.7 Germanic

(See Chapter 2.)

2.8 Slavonic

(See Chapter 14.)

2.9 Baltic

This highly conservative group of Indo-European languages has played a significant role in Indo-European studies. Despite the fact that the oldest useful recorded material from Baltic dates from the mid-fourteenth century CE, Baltic has preserved many archaic features, especially in morphology, which scholars believe existed in Proto-Indo-European.

Only two Baltic languages are spoken today, Lithuanian and Latvian (or Lettish). Many others are now extinct, including Semigallian, Selonian, Curonian, Yotvingian and Old Prussian. Old Prussian is the most important of these; it became extinct in the early eighteenth century, but provides us with our oldest written documentation of the Baltic group.

The Baltic languages are considered by many specialists to be in a special relationship with the Slavonic languages. Those who follow such a scheme posit a stage intermediate between Proto-Indo-European and Baltic and Slavonic called Balto-Slavonic.

2.10 Armenian

Armenian was probably established as a language in its historic homeland in the southern Caucasus and western Turkey by the sixth century BCE. The first records of the language are from the fifth century CE, and it shows considerable influence from Greek, Arabic, Syriac and especially Persian. In fact, so extreme is the foreign influence on Armenian that it was at first thought to be a radical dialect of Persian rather than a language in its own right. Written in an alphabet developed in the fifth century, the language is quite conservative in many of its structural features, especially inflectional morphology and, by some accounts, consonantal phonology.

2.11 Albanian

The remote history of Albanian is unknown, and although there are references to Albanians by Greek historians in the first century CE, we have no record of the language until the fifteenth century. Much influenced by neighbouring languages, Albanian has proven to be of marginal value in the reconstruction of Proto-Indo-European. There are two principal dialects of Albanian: Gheg, spoken in the north and in parts of the former Yugoslavia, and Tosk, spoken in southern Albania and various communities in Greece and Italy.

2.12 Fragmentary Languages

In addition to the eleven major groups, there remain a number of 'minor' Indo-European languages which are known only in fragments, glosses, inscriptions and other unpredictable sources. Though there is some dispute about the Indo-European character of some of these languages, scholars generally agree on the following as Indo-European: Ligurian (Mediterranean region), Lepontic (possibly affiliated with Celtic), Sicel (possibly affiliated with Italic), Thraco-Phrygian (frequently connected with Armenian and Albanian), Illyrian (especially prevalent along the Dalmatian coast), Messapic (with uncertain Italic or Albanian connections), and Venetic (probably connected with Italic). None of these languages exists in sufficient material detail to be of systematic value in the reconstruction of Proto-Indo-European.

3 The Structure of Proto-Indo-European

There have been many attempts to reconstruct Proto-Indo-European from the evidence of the daughter languages. The discoveries of Hittite, Tocharian and Mycenaean Greek in the last century have modified the data base of Indo-European studies, so it is not surprising that there have been frequent changes in views on Proto-Indo-European. Also, there have been a refinement of technique and an expansion of knowledge about language structure and language change which have modified views of the protolanguage. In this section we will briefly review past and present thinking on Proto-Indo-European phonology, and we will then discuss commonly held positions on the morphological and syntactic structure of the proto-language.

3.1 Phonology

3.1.1 Segmental Phonology

The first systematic attempt to reconstruct the sound system of Proto-Indo-European was by A. Schleicher in the first edition of his *Compendium der vergleichenden Grammatik der indogermanischen Sprachen* in 1861. Using the sound correspondences worked out by his predecessors, Schleicher proposed the consonant system as in Table 1.3 (from the 1876 edition, p. 10).

Schleicher's three-vowel system of *a*, *i* and *u* was based primarily on the pattern found in Sanskrit whereby 'basic vowels' are modified by combinatory processes which the Indian grammarians called *guṇa* 'secondary quality' and *vṛddhi* 'growth, increment'. By these processes the basic three-vowel system is modified by the prefixation of *a* as follows (1876: 11):

Basic Vowel	First Increment	Second Increment
a	a + a → aa	a + aa → āa
i	a + i → ai (e)	a + ai → āi
u	a + u → au (o)	a + au → āu

The reconstructed PIE system is not identical to the Sanskrit system; it is, however, patterned on it.

Schleicher's model soon gave way to the one proposed by the Neogrammarians, a group of younger scholars centred at Leipzig who had quite different views about Proto-Indo-European, and about language change generally, from their predecessors.

Table 1.3 Schleicher's Reconstructed System

	unaspirated		aspirated	spirants		nasals	r
	vls.	vd.	vd.	vls.	vd.	vd.	vd.
Guttural	k	g	gh				
Palatal					j		
Lingual							r
Dental	t	d	dh	s		n	
Labial	p	b	bh		v	m	

The Neogrammarian system is embodied in the classic work of K. Brugmann (1903: 52), as in Table 1.4.

Brugmann's system is much more elaborate than Schleicher's in almost every respect: there are more occlusives (stops), more fricatives, diphthongs, etc. But probably the most significant difference is in the vowel system. Brugmann proposes a six short, five long vowel system which is much more like that of Greek or Latin than that of Sanskrit. This change was brought about by the discovery that a change had taken place whereby Sanskrit collapsed PIE *ĕ, *ŏ, *ă into ă (cf. Lat. *sequor*, Gk. *hépomai*, Skt. *sáce* 'I follow' (*e*); Lat. *ovis*, Gk. *ó(w)is*, Skt. *ávi-* 'sheep' (*o*); Lat. *ager*, Gk. *agrós*, Skt. *ájra-* 'field, plain' (*a*)). From this it could be seen that Sanskrit was not to be considered closest to the proto-language in all respects.

The Neogrammarian system, which in modified form still finds adherents today, was put to the test by the theories of Saussure (1879) and the findings of Kuryłowicz (1927) and others. Based on the irregular behaviour of certain sounds in the daughter languages, Saussure proposed that Proto-Indo-European had contained sounds of uncertain phonetic value which he called 'coefficients sonantiques'. According to Saussure, these sounds were lost in the daughter languages but not before they left traces of their former presence on the sounds which had surrounded them. For example, there is no regular explanation for the difference in vowel length between the two forms of Gk. *hístāmi* 'I stand' and *státos* 'stood'. Saussure theorised that originally the root had been *steA (A = a coefficient sonantique). The A had coloured the *e* to *a* and had lengthened it to *ā* in *histami* before disappearing. The major changes ascribed to the action of these sounds include changing *e* to *o*, *e* to *a* and lengthening preceding vowels.

This new theory, based on abstract principles, was put to use to explain a wide range of phonological and morphological phenomena in various Indo-European languages. It came to be called the 'laryngeal theory', since it is thought that these sounds may have had a laryngeal articulation. Proposals were made to explain facts of Indo-European

Table 1.4 Brugmann's Reconstructed System

Consonants

Occlusives:	p		ph	b	bh	(labial)			
	t		th	d	dh	(dental)			
	k̂		k̂h	ĝ	ĝh	(palatal)			
	q		qh	g	gh	(velar)			
	qu̯		qu̯h	gu̯	gu̯h	(labio-velar)			
Fricatives:	s		sh	z	zh	þ	þh	ð	ðh	(j)
Nasals:	m		n	ñ	ŋ				
Liquids:	r		l						
Semi-vowels:			i̯	u̯					

Vowels

A	Vowels:	e	o	a	i	u	ə
		ē	ō	ā	ī	ū	
B	Diphthongs:	ei̯	oi̯	ai̯	əi̯		eu̯	ou̯	au̯	əu̯
C	Syllabic Liquids and Nasals:	l̥	r̥	m̥	n̥	ñ̥	ŋ̥
		l̥̄	r̥̄	m̥̄	n̥̄	ñ̥̄	ŋ̥̄

Source: Brugmann 1903: 67, 89, 122–38.

root structure, ablaut relations (see Section 3.2.2) and other aspects of PIE phonology and morphology. Many proposals concerning the exact number of laryngeals, and their effects, were made. Some scholars worked with one, others with as many as ten or twelve. It remained an unverified theory until 1927, when Kuryłowicz demonstrated that Hittite preserved laryngeal-like sounds (written as ḫ or ḫḫ) precisely in those positions where Saussure had theorised they had existed in Proto-Indo-European. Some examples: Hitt. *ḫanti* 'front': Lat. *ante*; Hitt. *ḫarkiš-* 'white': Gk. *argés* Hitt. *palḫiš*; 'broad': Lat. *planus*; Hitt. *meḫur* 'time': Go. *mēl*; Hitt. *u̯aḫanzi* 'they turn': Skt. *vāya-* 'weaving'; Hitt. *newaḫḫ-* 'renew': Lat. *novāre*.

The empirical confirmation that Hittite provided for Saussure's theories led to a reworking of the Proto-Indo-European sound system. We may take the scheme proposed by W. Lehmann (1952: 99) as representative of these developments as in Table 1.5.

There are many differences between Lehmann's system and that of Brugmann. Note in particular the postulation of only one fricative, *s*, the lack of palatals, diphthongs, voiceless aspirates and schwa. These were all given alternative analyses, partly based on the four laryngeals which Lehmann assumed.

In a further refinement, O. Szemerényi (1999: 150) proposed the system in Table 1.6, which is a bit more robust than that of Lehmann, say, but not as elaborate as that of Brugmann. It is a system that many specialists feel best represents the facts of the IE languages. Note the absence of laryngeals in Szemerényi's account of this stage of PIE.

Table 1.5 Lehmann's Reconstructed System

Obstruents:	p	t	k	k^w		
	b	d	g	g^w		
	b^h	d^h	g^h	g^{wh}		
		s				
Resonants:	m	n				
	w	r	l	y		
Vowels:		e	a	o	e	
	i·	e·	a·	o·	u·	
Laryngeals:		x	γ	h		ʔ

Table 1.6 Szemerényi's Reconstructed System

Obstruents:	p	p^h	b	b^h		
	t	t^h	d	d^h		
	(k′	k'^h	g′	g'^h?)		
	k	k^h	g	g^h		
	k^w	k^{wh}	g^w	g^{wh}		
Nasals	n	m				
Semivowels	y	w				
Liquids	l	r				
Fricatives	s	h				
Syllabic Liquids and Nasals:			ṇ	m̥	ṇ̄	m̥̄
			l̥	r̥	l̥̄	r̥̄
Vowels:						
	i	u			ī	ū
	e ə o				ē	ō
	a				ā	

Criticisms of the traditional system centre on the typological naturalness of the overall system. While faithful to the comparative method, such a system seems to be in conflict with known patterns of phonological structure in attested languages. One problem lies in the presence of the voiced aspirated stops without a corresponding series of voiceless aspirates. A principle of typological inference stipulates that the presence of a marked member of a correlative pair implies the presence of the unmarked member of that pair: thus *bh* ⊃ *ph*. And as T. Gamkrelidze puts it (1981: 591): 'Reconstructed systems should be characterised by the same regularities which are found in any historical system.'

Pursuing the dicta of typological structure and dependency, some scholars have recently followed a different approach to Indo-European sound structure. The focus of the effort has been the obstruent system of the proto-language, which has long presented special challenges to Indo-European scholars. Chief among the problems are the following:

(a) The traditional system without voiceless aspirates is in violation of certain markedness principles. But the solution which calls for a voiceless aspirated series only begs the question, since only one language (Sanskrit) has the four-way distinction of voiced/voiceless, aspirated/unaspirated. Thus the elaborate Proto-Indo-European system seems to rely far too heavily on Sanskrit, and is unjustified for the other groups.

(b) There has always been a problem with *b. It is extremely rare, and those few examples which point to *b (e.g. Lith. *dubùs*, Go. *diups* 'deep') are by no means secure.

(c) There are complicated restrictions on the co-occurrence of obstruents in Proto-Indo-European roots (called 'morpheme' or 'root structure' conditions) which are only imperfectly handled with traditional reconstructions. They are that a root cannot begin and end with a plain voiced stop, and a root cannot begin with a plain voiceless stop and end with a voiced aspirate, or vice versa.

(d) Plain voiced stops as traditionally reconstructed almost never occur in reconstructed inflectional affixes, in which Proto-Indo-European was rich. This is a distributional irregularity which cannot be explained under the traditionally reconstructed system.

(e) It has long been a curiosity to Indo-European scholars that both Germanic and Armenian underwent similar obstruent shifts (the Germanic one came to be celebrated as 'Grimm's Law', and forms the backbone of much pre- and post-Neogrammarian thinking on sound change):

'Grimm's Law' and the Armenian Consonant Shift

PIE					*Gmc.*				*Arm.*			
*p	t	k	k^w	>	f	þ	h	h^w	h	tʻ	s	kʻ
*b	d	g	g^w	>	p	t	k	k^w/k	p	t	c	k
*bh	dh	gh	gh^w	>	b	d	g	g^w/g	b	d	j	g

In the revised reconstruction of the obstruent system (commonly known as the 'glottalic theory'), the pattern in the occlusives is based on a three-way distinction of voiceless stops/ voiced aspirates/glottalised stops (see Hopper 1981, Gamkrelidze 1981, Gamkrelidze and Ivanov 1995). The traditional plain voiced stops are now interpreted as glottalised stops (ejectives).

Reconstructed Obstruents in the 'Glottalic Theory'

	I Glottalised	II Voiced Aspirates/ Voiced Stops	III Voiceless Aspirates/ Voiceless Stops
Labial	(p')	b^h/b	p^h/p
Dental	t'	d^h/d	t^h/t
Velar	k'	g^h/g	k^h/k
Labio-velar	k'^{w}	g^{wh}/g^w	k^{wh}/k^w

The distribution of these segments has been a matter of some debate, and indeed each Indo-European language seems to have generalised one allophone or another, or split allophones, according to differing circumstances.

This new system seems to provide phonetically natural solutions to the five problems posed above:

(a) The system with the three-way distinction above violates no naturalness condition or typological universal. In fact, it is a system found in modern Armenian dialects. Under this view, Indo-Iranian is an innovator, not a relic.

(b) The near absence of *b now finds a simple solution. In systems employing glottalised stops, the labial member is the most marked. Thus this gap, unexplained by traditional views, is no longer anomalous.

(c) The complicated morpheme structure restrictions turn out to be fairly simple: two glottalised stops cannot occur in the same root; furthermore, non-glottalised root consonants must agree in voicing value.

(d) The absence of plain voiced stops in inflections turns out to be an absence of glottalics in the new reconstruction. Such a situation is typologically characteristic of highly marked phonemes such as glottalised sounds (Hopper 1981: 135).

(e) Under the new system the parallel Germanic and Armenian consonant 'shifts' turn out to reflect archaisms rather than innovations. All the other groups have undergone fairly regular phonological changes which can be efficiently derived from the system just outlined.

Proto-Indo-European generally, not just in phonology, is a 'rolling' concept. That is, this unwritten proto-language, which has been dated to anywhere between 2500 and 7000 BCE, certainly underwent many changes of its own during its evolution and eventual break-up into the attested descendant systems. What this means is that arriving at a uniform reconstruction that captures all the internal developments and external influences that must have affected the language over many millennia is a formidable task. In this context it is not surprising that differences exist among investigators on the structure of the phonology of PIE.

3.1.2 Ablaut

In the oldest stages of Proto-Indo-European, word roots were differentiated in their various grammatical functions by a modification of the root-vowel, a pattern which is recoverable throughout the attested languages. For example, in Latin there are three forms *tegō/toga/tēgula* 'I cover/toga (garment)/roof tile', which represent three different forms of the root *teg-* 'cover', each with a different vowel (*e/o/ē*). The same pattern can be seen in various representations of the 'father' word in Greek: *patéra/*

eupátora/pat'ér. This type of vowel modification or alternation is known as 'ablaut' or 'vowel gradation'.

Vowel gradation patterns were based on the interplay of both vowel quality such as *e/o* (qualitative ablaut) and vowel quantity or length such as *e/ē* (quantitative ablaut). The main alternations were between the basic root-vowel, usually *e*, called the 'normal grade', alternating with *o* ('*o*-grade'), zero (∅) ('zero-grade'), lengthened grade (*ē*) and lengthening plus change (lengthened *ō*-grade). In what follows the quantitative and qualitative ablaut types will be presented separately, though it should be emphasised that this is one system, not two. The two are separated here because the daughter languages typically generalised either the qualitative or quantitative system, or eliminated ablaut altogether.

	e-grade		*o-grade*		*∅-grade*	
Gk.	pét-omai	'I fly'	pot-é	'flight'	e-pt-ómēn	'I flew'
Gk.	ékh-ō	'I have'	ókh-os	'carriage'	é-skh-on	'I had'
Lat.	sed-eō	'I sit'	sol-ium	'throne'		
			(<*sodium)			
Lat.	reg-ō	'I rule'	rog-us(?)	'funeral-pyre'		
Lat.	teg-ō	'I cover'	tog-a	'a covering'		
Gk.	leíp-ō	'I leave'	lé-loip-a	'I left'	é-lip-on	'I left'
Lat.	fid-ō		foed-us	'agreement'	fid-ēs	'trust'
	(<feidō)	'I trust'				
Gk.	peíth-ō	'I persuade'	pé-poith-a	'I trust'	é-pith-on	'I persuaded'
Gk.	dérk-omai	'I see'	dé-dork-a	'I saw'	é-drak-on	'I saw'
Gk.	pénth-os	'grief'	pé-ponth-a	'I suffered'	é-path-on	'I suffered'

Qualitative Ablaut

The primary qualitative relations were based on the vowels *e ~ o ~ ∅ (ei ~ oi ~ i; er ~ or ~ r̥; en ~ on ~ n̥, etc.)*. Different forms of a morpheme were represented by different ablaut grades. This system is rather well preserved in Greek, but is recoverable in nearly every Indo-European language to one degree or another. (Note: *e ~ o ~ ∅* alternation is not the only series, nor does this account consider the many interactions between vowel length and quality.)

Quantitative Ablaut

Quantitative ablaut patterns are primarily based on the alternations of 'normal', 'lengthened', and 'reduced' varieties of a vowel, e.g. *o : ō : ∅; e : ē : ∅; a : ā : ∅*. While represented vestigially in a wide number of Indo-European languages, (cf. Lat. *pēs*, gen. *pedis* 'foot'; *vōx* 'voice', *vocō* 'I call'; Gk. *patér*, *patrós* (gen.), *patéra* (acc.) 'father'), the quantitative system is most systematically represented in Sanskrit. A few good examples are:

Normal grade	*Lengthened grade*	*Reduced grade*
pát-ati 'he/she flies'	**pāt**-áyati 'he/she causes to fall'	pa-**pt**-imá 'we flew'
kar-tr̥- 'doer'	**kār**-yá- 'business'	kr̥-tá- 'done'

Quantitative vowel alternation, in conjunction with the qualitative type, was an important means of morphological marking in Proto-Indo-European, providing a basis for distinguishing different grammatical representations of a morpheme.

3.1.3 Accent

Because of the widely different accentual patterns found in the daughter languages, reconstructing the accent of Proto-Indo-European has proven challenging. The most widely accepted accounts of Proto-Indo-European accent, which rely heavily on the evidence of Sanskrit, Greek, Baltic and Slavic, suggest that it was a dominantly pitch accent system. Every word (except clitics, which were unaccented) had one accented syllable which received high-pitch accent. The accent was 'free' in that it could fall on any syllable in a word, its specific position being conditioned by morphological considerations. Accent was one means of marking grammatical categories in Proto-Indo-European. (For a parallel, cf. Eng. *rébel* (n.): *rebél* (v.); *cónflict* (n.): *conflíct* (v.).)

For example, in certain nouns some cases are typically accented on the inflections, while others are accented on the root, as can be seen in some representatives of the word for 'foot'. The nominative and accusative cases, the so-called 'strong cases', have root accent, while the genitive and dative, locative (and instrumental) have inflectional accent, indicating that accent is interacting with case markers to indicate grammatical function.

Root/Inflectional Accent (Nouns)

	Gk.	*Skt.*
nom.	poús	pā́d
acc.	póda	pā́dam
gen.	podós	padás (gen./abl.)
dat.		padé
loc.	podí (actually dat.)	padí

Similarly, some verbal forms are accented on roots, some on inflections, as can be seen in the Sanskrit verb 'to turn': *vártāmi*, (pres.) *vavárta* (perf. sg.) *vavṛtimá* (perf. pl.) *vṛtanáḥ* (part.).

3.2 Morphology

The unevenness of historical records and huge chronological gaps among many of the languages (e.g. ca. 3,000 years between Hittite and Lithuanian) pose special problems for the reconstruction of PIE. These problems surely exist in the reconstruction of morphology, perhaps even more dramatically than in phonology because of the much larger inventory of morphological elements. Many of the older, well-documented languages, especially Latin, Greek, Baltic, Slavonic and Sanskrit, have very complex morphologies: they have well-developed case systems in nouns, adjectives and pronouns; they have finely marked gender and number categories with fixed concord relations. In the verb they have elaborate systems of tense, voice, mood and aspect, as well as number markers and even gender concord in some forms, all marked with complex morphological formatives.

Many Indo-European languages reflect this complex morphology to one degree or another: Celtic, Armenian and, in part, Tocharian, in addition to the groups just mentioned. But many of the other languages of which we have adequate records show much less morphological complexity, with fewer formal categories and distinctions; and it is not only the modern ones. Hittite, Germanic, Tocharian (in part) and Albanian do not agree with the other groups in morphological complexity.

How does the analyst approach these problems in applying the comparative method? The answer is: cautiously. We must not think of Proto-Indo-European as a single monolithic entity, uniform and dialect-free, which existed at a certain time in a single place before it began to disintegrate. Rather, we must recognise that this language was itself the product of millennia of development. As Ivanov puts it (1965: 51):

> Within the limits of the case systems of the Indo-European languages it is possible to distinguish chronological layers of various epochs beginning with the pre-inflectional in certain forms of the locative and in compound words ... right up to the historical period when the case systems were being formed ... Between these two extreme points one must assume a whole series of intermediate points.
>
> (Quoted from Schmalstieg 1980: 46)

We will now proceed to a discussion of the traditional ('classical') system as reconstructed in the nineteenth and early twentieth centuries, and refined in more recent literature. This system represents one, surely very late, stage of Proto-Indo-European from which some, but not all of the daughter languages descended. In this context it has validity as the most probable system based on the comparative method.

3.2.1 Nominal and Pronominal Morphology

Traditionally, Proto-Indo-European is considered to be a fusional (inflectional) language which uses case markers to indicate grammatical relations between nominal elements and other words in a sentence, and to indicate gender and number agreement between words in phrases.

Based primarily on the evidence of Latin, Greek, Sanskrit, Baltic and Slavonic languages and to an extent Armenian, PIE is reconstructed with eight cases: nominative (subject of sentence), genitive (adnominal case), dative (beneficiary), accusative (direct object), ablative (source), locative (place where), instrumental (means and agent) and vocative (direct address). In addition, nouns and adjectives were inflected in three genders (m., f., n.), and three numbers (sg., pl., du.).

The structure of the noun was based on the following scheme: a *root*, which carried the basic lexical meaning, plus a *stem*, which marked morphological class, plus an *ending*, which carried grammatical information based on syntactic function. Thus a word like Lat. *lupus* (OLat. *lupos*) 'wolf' would be *lup+o+s*. Generally we recognise consonantal and vocalic stem nouns. Some examples of consonantal stems are **ped-* 'foot' (Skt. *pád-*, Gk. (gen.) *podós*, Lat. (gen.) *pedis*); **edont-/*dont-/*dent-* 'tooth' (Skt. *dánt-*, Gk. (gen.) *odóntos*, Lat. (gen.) *dentis*); **ĝʰom-* 'man' (Lat. *homo*, Go. *guma*); **māter* 'mother' (Skt. *mātár-*, Gk. *mḗtēr*, Lat. *māter*); **ĝonos-/*ĝenos-* 'race' (Skt. (gen.) *jánasas*, Gk. (gen.) *géneos* (< **génesos*), Lat. (gen.) *generis* (< **genesis*)).

To illustrate some of the vocalic stems we may cite the *i*-stem form **egnis/*ognis* 'fire' (Skt. *agní-*, Lat. *ignis*) or **potis* 'master' (Skt. *páti-*, Gk. *pósis*, Lat. *potis*); an *-eu-* diphthongal stem like **dyeu-* 'sky, light' (Skt. nom. *dyáus*, Gk. *Zeús*, Lat. *diēs*, *-diūs*); and finally the *o*-stem **wl̥kʷos* 'wolf' (Skt. *vŕ̥ka-*, Gk. *lúkos*, Lat. *lupus*).

Through a comparison of the various languages we arrive at the following reconstruction of case endings (Szemerényi 1999: 160; the order of cases as in the original). These endings represent a composite set of possibilities for the Proto-Indo-European noun; no single stem class reflects them all.

Reconstructed Case Endings

	Sg.	Pl.	Du.
Nom.	-s,-∅	-es	
Voc.	-∅	-es	-e, -ī/-i
Acc.	-m/-m̥	-ns/-n̥s	
Gen.	-es/-os/-s	-om/-ōm	-ous? -ōs?
Abl.	-es/-os/-s;	-bh(y)os, -mos	-bhyō, -mō
	-ed/-od		
Dat.	-ei	-bh(y)os, -mos	-bhyō, -mō
Loc.	-i	-su	-ou
Inst.	-e/-o, -bhi/-mi	-bhis/-mis, -ōis	-bhyō, -mō

The Proto-Indo-European adjective followed the same declensional pattern as the noun. Adjectives were inflected for gender, number and case, in agreement with the nouns which they modified. Some adjectives are inflected in masculine, feminine and neuter according to masc. *-o* stem, fem. *-ā* stem and neut. *-om* patterns, as in **newos*, **newā*, **newom* 'new' (cf. Skt. *návas*, *návā*, *návam*, Gk. *né(w)os*, *né(w)ā*, *né(w)on*, Lat. *novus*, *nova*, *novum*). Other adjectival forms have identical masculine and feminine forms, but separate neuter (cf. Lat. *facilis*, *facile* 'easy'), and still others have all three identical in some cases (cf. Lat. *ferens* 'carrying' (< **ferentis*)).

Adjectives were compared in three degrees, as in English *tall*, *taller*, *tallest*. Comparative forms are typically derived from positive forms through the suffixation of **-yes*, **-yos* (cf. Lat. *senior* 'older' *(senex)*, Skt. *sánya-* 'older' *(sána-)* and with **-tero-* (cf. Gk. *ponērós* 'wicked', cmpr. *ponēróteros*). Superlatives are often found with the suffixes *-isto-* and *-samo-*, though there are others. Some examples: Gk. *béltistos*, Go. *batista* 'best', Skt. *návistha-* 'newest' *(náva-)*. For **-samo-*, cf. Lat. *proximus* 'nearest', *maximus* 'greatest', OIr. *nessam* 'next'. As with Gk. *béltistos*, Go. *batista*, adjectival comparison was occasionally carried out with suppletive forms, cf. Lat. *bonus*, *melior*, *optimus* 'good, better, best'.

Proto-Indo-European distinguished many different types of pronouns. A short sample of personal pronouns is given in Table 1.2. Pronouns followed the same general inflectional patterns as nouns, though they have their own set of endings for many of the case forms, except personal pronouns, which are almost entirely different from nouns and did not mark gender. In addition to the personal pronouns 'I/we', 'you/you' *(*eĝ(h)om, egō/*wei, *n̥smés; *tū, *tu/*yūs, *usmés)*, Proto-Indo-European also had demonstrative pronouns with the form (m.) **so*, (f.) **sā*, (n.) **tod* and **is*, **ī*, **id*. These also served the function of third person pronouns in many of the Indo-European languages. The first of these is represented in Skt. *sa*, *sā*, *tad*, Go. *sa*, *so*, *þata* and Gk. *ho*, *hē*, *tó*. The latter Proto-Indo-European demonstrative forms are represented in Lat. *is*, *ea*, *id* and in various forms in Sanskrit and Germanic such as Skt. nom. sg. n. *id-ám*, acc. sg. m. *im-ám*, f. *im-ám* and Go. acc. sg. *in-a*, nom. pl. m. *eis*, acc. pl. *ins*.

Interrogative and relative pronouns are also well represented, though it is not possible to reconstruct a single relative. From a PIE (anim.) **kʷis*, (inanim.) **kʷid*, which had either interrogative or indefinite meaning, we find Lat. *quis*, *quis*, *quid*, Gk. *tís*, *tís*, *tí*, Hitt. *kwis*, *kwit*, Skt. *kás*, *kā́*, *kím*, and a number of variants of this stem with interrogative or indefinite meaning. In Italic, Tocharian, Hittite, Celtic and Germanic the root **kʷis*, **kʷid* also functioned as a relative pronoun (as does Eng. *who*). In Indo-Iranian, Greek and Slavonic a different form **yos*, **yā*, **yod* served the relative function (cf. Skt. *yás*, *yā́*, *yád*, Gk. *hós*, *hḗ*, *hó*). There is also a recoverable reflexive form **sew-*, **sw* (OCS *sę*, Lat. *se*, Go. *si-k*).

40

3.2.2 Verb Morphology

The Proto-Indo-European verb presents the analyst with many of the same issues as the noun. The various daughter languages show wide variation in formal categories and inflectional complexity; some of the ancient classical languages, especially Greek, Latin and Sanskrit, have highly diversified formal structure characterised by intricate relations of tense, mood, voice and aspect. Others, like Hittite and Germanic, have fairly simple morphological systems with few formal distinctions. We can contrast formal complexity by the following simple chart.

Verbal Categories

	Voices	Moods	Tenses
Greek	3	4	7
Sanskrit	3	4	7
Hittite	2	2	2
Gothic	2	3	2

As with the noun, we may take several paths to a reconstructed system. We can propose a robust Proto-Indo-European system with losses and syncretisms in Hittite and Gothic, we may propose a simple Proto-Indo-European system with additions and splits in Greek and Sanskrit, or we may assume different periods of development and break-off from the parent language. Accepting this final alternative, realistic though it is, in effect prohibits us from reconstructing a single system which underlies the others. All we can do, then, is to present one version, surely quite late, of the Proto-Indo-European verbal system as traditionally reconstructed, recognising that many unanswered chronological questions remain which are outside the scope of this chapter.

The classical reconstruction of the Proto-Indo-European verbal system posits two voices, four moods and from three to six tenses. In addition, there were person and number suffixes and a large number of derivational formatives by which additional categories were fashioned. The verb categories are as follows:

Voice refers to the relationship of the subject to the activity defined by the verb, i.e. whether the subject is agent, patient or both. In Proto-Indo-European there were two voices, active and medio-passive. An active verb is one in which the subject is typically the agent, but is not directly affected by the action (e.g. *John called Bill*). Medio-passive is a mixed category which includes the function of middle (= reflexive) and passive. When the subject of the verb is both the agent and the patient, the verb is in the middle voice (e.g. Gk. *ho paîs loúetai* 'the boy washes himself', Skt. *yájate* 'he makes a sacrifice for himself'). When the subject of the verb is the patient, but there is a different agent, the verb is in the passive voice (e.g. Gk. *ho paîs loúetai hupò tês mētrós* 'the boy is washed by his mother'). In general, the various Indo-European languages generalised either the middle or the passive function from the Proto-Indo-European medio-passive. For example, in Sanskrit the middle function dominates, the passive being late and secondary. In Greek the middle and passive are morphologically identical in all but the future and aorist tenses, with the middle dominating. Italic and Celtic have mostly passive use, though there are ample relics of the middle in deponent verbs like Lat. *loquitur* 'he speaks', OIr. *-labrathar* 'who speaks', as well as Lat. *armor* 'I arm myself', Lat. *congregor* 'I gather myself', and others. Germanic has no traces of the middle, while Hittite shows a largely middle function.

Mood describes the manner in which a speaker makes the statement identified by the verb, i.e. whether he believes it is a fact, wishes it, doubts it or orders it. In Proto-Indo-European there were probably four moods: indicative, optative, subjunctive and imperative. With the indicative mood the speaker expresses statements of fact. Indicative is sometimes marked by a vowel suffix (thematic class) and sometimes not (athematic class), e.g. Skt. *rud-á-ti*, Lat. *rud-e-t* 'he cries' (thematic); Skt. *ás-ti*, Lat. *es-t* 'he is' (athematic). The optative mood is used when the speaker expresses a wish or desire, and is also marked by a vowel which depends on the vowel in the indicative, e.g. OLat. *siet*, Gk. *eíē*, Skt. *syā́t* 'let him be'. The subjunctive is used when the speaker is expressing doubt, exhortation or futurity. Its theme vowel depends on the vowel of the verb in the indicative, though it is common with *e/o* ablaut. Some examples are Lat. *erō* 'I will be', *agam*, *agēs* 'I, you will/might drive', Gk. *íomen* 'let us go'. The final mood is the imperative, which is used when the speaker is issuing a command. The imperative was formed from the bare verbal stem, without a mood-marking vowel as with the other three. Imperatives are most common in the second person, though they are found in the first and third as well. Examples are (second person) Gk. *phére*, Skt. *bhára*, Lat. *fer* 'carry' (sg.) and *phérete*, *bhárata*, *ferte* (pl.). There were other imperative suffixes as well which need not concern us here.

Tense refers to the time of the action identified by the verb. The original Proto-Indo-European verb was probably based on aspectual rather than temporal relations (aspect refers to the type of activity, e.g. momentary, continuous, iterative, etc.), though tense comes to dominate in most IE languages, Slavonic being a prominent exception. We usually identify three tense stems, the present, the aorist and the perfect. The present stem identifies repeated and continuing actions or actions going on in the present (= imperfective aspect): Lat. *sum*, Gk. *eimí*, Skt. *ásmi* 'I am', or Lat. *fert*, Gk. *phérei*, Skt. *bhárati* 'he carries'. The aorist stem (= perfective aspect) marks actions that did or will take place only once, e.g. Gk. *égnōn* 'I recognised', Skt. *ádāt* 'he gave', Gk. *édeikse* 'he showed', Skt. *ánaiṣam* 'I led'. The final stem is the perfect stem (= stative aspect), which describes some state pertaining to the subject of the verb. Examples are Skt. *véda*, Gk. *oĩda*, Go. *wáit* 'I know'.

The exact internal structure of the various tense systems is extremely complicated. A number of formal types exist, including stems characterised by ablaut, reduplication, prefixation (augment), infixation and a wide variety of derivational suffixes. An interesting fact is that though tense was not directly and explicitly marked in Proto-Indo-European, most of the daughter languages generalised tense as the defining characteristic of their respective verbal systems.

In addition to the tense, voice and mood categories, the Proto-Indo-European verb carried at the end of the verbal structure a set of endings which indexed first, second or third person and singular, plural or dual number, and also carried much of the information on voice and tense in the daughter languages. There were different sets of endings for different voices, tense stems and moods. Here we list only the principal 'primary' and 'secondary' endings; they are identical except for the final *-i*, an earlier particle which marks the primary endings. These endings were originally used with specific tenses and moods, but have been largely generalised in the daughter languages.

Verbal Endings

	Primary	*Secondary*
1st sg.	-mi (Skt. bhárāmi)	-m (Lat. sum)
2nd sg.	-si (Skt. bhárasi)	-s (OLat. ess)
3rd sg.	-ti (Skt. bhárati)	-t (Lat. est)
3rd pl.	-nti (Skt. bháranti)	-nt (Lat. sunt)

We can schematise the overall structure of the Proto-Indo-European verb as follows:

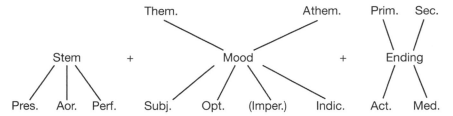

The Structure of the Indo-European Verb

A few examples:

Lat.	am	ā	s	'you love'	(Pres. indic. 2nd pers. sg. act.)
	am	ē	s	'you might love'	(Pres. subj. 2nd pers. sg. act.)
	am	ā	ris	'you are loved'	(Pres. indic. 2nd pers. sg. pass.)
	am	ē	ris	'you might be loved'	(Pres. subj. 2nd pers. sg. pass.)
Gk.	paideú	ei	s	'you teach'	(Pres. indic. 2nd pers. sg. act.)
	paideú	ē	s	'you might teach'	(Pres. subj. 2nd pers. sg. act.)
	paidcú	oi	s	'may you teach'	(Pres. opt. 2nd pers. sg. act.)
Skt.	bhár	a	ti	'he carries'	(Pres. indic. 3rd pers. sg. act.)
á	neṣ		vahi	'we two led ourselves'	(Aor. indic. 1st pers. du. mid.)
	sunu		yáma	'we might press'	(Pres. opt. 1st pers. pl. act.)

Besides the finite verb forms which we have been discussing, Proto-Indo-European also made use of a number of derivative forms which were nonfinite, i.e. they did not stand as independent tensed predications. We include here a number of infinitive forms, which were originally noun forms in various oblique cases (mostly accusative and dative) and became re-analysed as part of the verbal system: cf. Skt. *dātum* (acc.), *dātave* (dat.) 'to give'. There were also participial formations represented in most of the languages from Proto-Indo-European formations in *-nt-* (e.g. Go. *bairands*, Skt. *bháran-*, Lat. *ferens* 'carrying'), as well as others in *-wes-* (cf. Skt. *vidvás-* 'knowing'), *meno-* (cf. Gk. *hepómenos* 'following') and *-to-* (cf. Lat. *amātus* 'loved'). These secondary formations, as well as a number of others such as gerunds, gerundives, supines and other verbal nouns, are widely represented and used throughout the Indo-European family.

3.3 Syntax

The reconstruction of syntax has lagged behind the reconstruction of the phonological, morphological and lexical structures of Proto-Indo-European. This is initially surprising given the central role played by syntax and syntactic theory in modern linguistics. There are many reasons for this lag; among them are the following:

(a) The lack of native speakers. Modern linguistics draws its data from the speech and intuitions of native speakers, but of course a reconstructed language has no such data source.

(b) The abstractness of syntax. Phonological, morphological and lexical units are more concrete units than rules or patterns of syntax. Fewer theoretical notions are

43

required in order to isolate concrete units, whereas in syntax, nothing exists pre-theoretically. Syntax is a set of principles, requiring abstract theories before even data organisation can begin.

(c) The structure of the descendant languages. The Indo-European daughter languages are of a highly inflecting type, and carry out a great deal of their 'syntax' in morphological expressions. Consider the difference between (1) and (2) in English:

(1) The boy sees the girl.
(2) The girl sees the boy.

The Latin equivalents to these sentences can have the words arranged in any order without affecting the agent/patient relations:

(1′)	i	Puer	puellam	videt.
		Boy	girl	sees
	ii	Puellam	puer	videt.
		Girl	boy	sees
	iii	Videt	puer	puellam.
		Sees	boy	girl
			etc.	

(2′)	i	Puella	puerum	videt.
		Girl	boy	sees
	ii	Puerum	puella	videt.
		Boy	girl	sees
	iii	Videt	puella	puerum.
		Sees	girl	boy
			etc.	

From these few examples we can readily see that the morphology/syntax division in fusional languages is quite a different matter from the same division in a language like English.

(d) The data. The Indo-European languages on which the reconstruction of Proto-Indo-European is based are simply not uniform enough to allow a straightforward account of syntactic patterns. The problem is no greater, and no less, than that found in phonology and morphology.

We will move now to a brief and highly selective review of some major features of Proto-Indo-European syntax. Because the citation of examples is extremely complicated, data will be cited sparingly.

3.3.1 Word Order

Late Proto-Indo-European was most likely a subject–object–verb (SOV) language with attendant adjective–noun (*good boy*), genitive–noun (*John's hat*), standard–marker–adjective (*John than bigger*) order, postpositions (*the world over*) and the preposing of relative clauses (*the who I saw man*). The reconstruction of these structural patterns is based on principles of typological inference developed largely by W. Lehmann (e.g. 1974), who extended the concepts of word order harmony formulated by J. Greenberg

(1963) to historical syntax. According to these principles, there are major structural configurations in languages which are harmonious or compatible with each other. They take the form of statements like the following: if a language has some property P, then it will also have some property Q. For example, if a language is SOV in its basic sentence pattern, it will also have postpositions; if it is SVO, it will have prepositions.

Lehmann has put such 'implicational universals' to work in the reconstruction of Proto-Indo-European word order patterns. For example, Hittite, Vedic Sanskrit and Tocharian are SOV; Latin is predominantly SOV (Homeric Greek is apparently alternately SVO/SOV). Concentrating on Hittite, we find that it has postpositions and adjective–noun order, and dominant genitive–noun and relative clause–noun order. This seems to be ample evidence for an SOV Proto-Indo-European, a conclusion which is strengthened by the existence of SOV-harmonic forms in otherwise SVO languages. For example, we find relic postpositions in Slavonic and Baltic, as well as large numbers of postpositions in the Italic languages which, though they are mostly SOV, are moving towards SVO. The archaic-like nature of the frozen postpositions in Latin *mēcum* 'with me', *tēcum* 'with you' (not *cum mē*, *cum tē*, as expected; cf. *cum puellā* 'with the girl') can be taken as an indication of early SOV structure, even in languages like Latin which show a move towards SVO structures. Discovering such patterns and drawing inferences for reconstruction depends crucially on the assumption that such marked structures as the Latin postpositions are indeed archaisms and not innovations.

There has been much criticism of this approach to syntax. For one thing, it has been noted that inflected languages have much freer word order possibilities than do languages like English, which rely on word order for marking grammatical function. According to this view, the word order issue is a false one, since word order serves mainly secondary functions like marking topic or focus relations

Another problem with the approach is the fact that the pure types are very rare (in the Indo-European family only Celtic is consistent, and it is VSO!). But the method has a built-in escape: languages which are internally inconsistent, like English with its SVO but adjective noun structures, are said to be in transition from one type to another; the process is not yet complete. This begs the issue, because languages are always in such a transitional state. In other words, Greenberg's observations should be regarded as frequently occurring and interesting tendencies which should not be elevated to the status of explanatory devices. Furthermore, there is ample evidence that such implicational universals do not serve as reliable predictors of future syntactic change in a language.

Finally there are matters of method. Typological inferences often are based on data being used in a circular manner, viz. if a language is SOV, one expects postpositions. And if a language is SVO but a stray postposition is found, one assumes that it must have been SOV at one time. There is also the issue of 'marked' vs 'unmarked' structures. Determining that a language is SOV or SVO when both are present in the data requires a judgement that one of the structures is more natural, more basic, more regular than the other. The problem with ancient languages with no native speakers is that judgements about marked/unmarked structures often reduce to simple frequency counts, and this is not adequate.

3.3.2 Ergative vs Nominative/Accusative Structure

It is clear from the daughter languages that late (classical) Proto-Indo-European was of the nominative/accusative type. That is, the agent of the verb was inflected in the nominative case, and the patient or goal was inflected in the accusative: cf. Lat. *Marc-us amat puell-am* 'Marcus loves the girl'. But there is evidence that Proto-Indo-European was at one time of the ergative type, i.e. a language in which the subject of a transitive verb is in a different case from the subject of an intransitive verb. There are many instances throughout the early Indo-European languages of agents in the genitive case: cf. OArm. *ēr nora* (gen.) *hraman aireal* 'he (of him) had received a promise', Lat. *attonitus serpentis* 'astonished by (of) the serpent'. There are other cases where the real object of a verb of perception is in the accusative while the producer of the perceived act is in the genitive: cf. Skt. *vácam* (acc.) *śṛṇóti* 'he hears a voice' vs *devásya* (gen.) *śṛṇóti* 'he hears a god'. These agentive genitives may at one time have been the subjects of intransitive verbs with genitive agents, as would be found with ergative languages. As Proto-Indo-European developed its complex nominal and verbal morphology, these genitives were reinterpreted as objects of transitive verbs and are now considered simply irregular formations.

3.3.3 Some Further Syntactic Characteristics of Proto-Indo-European

Proto-Indo-European made use of a simple phrase structure principle by which the verb was the only obligatory constituent of a sentence. The subject of the verb was in the nominative, the object in the accusative and a number of other grammatical functions were served by the remaining cases. Verb structures could be expanded with case expressions of time, place-to, place-in, place-from, goal, possession and a number of other qualifiers. Conjunction of both noun phrases and other constituents was possible, including sentence conjunction. Simple sentences could be extended by the use of cases, adverbs and particles to indicate circumstance, purpose, result or manner. Particles were used to introduce different types of clauses (e.g. subordinate, interrogative, relative, co-ordinate). The modality of a sentence, as well as tense and aspect, were expressed inflectionally, though they may have been originally marked only by particles. Finally, there is evidence of a well-developed. noun-compounding system, represented chiefly by Sanskrit.

As a final note to the structure of Proto-Indo-European, it may be useful to take a brief look at a version of a reconstructed Proto-Indo-European sentence. This sentence is from Lehmann and Zgusta's (1979: 462) reinterpretation of Schleicher's famous Indo-European fairy tale, which was written in 1868.

			Owis	ekwōsk^{w}e		
			Sheep	horses-and		
G^{w}ərēi	owis,	k^{w}esyo	wḷhnā	ne	ēst
Hill-on	sheep,	of whom	wool	not	is
ekwōns	espek̂et	oinom	ghe	g^{w}ṛum	
horses	he-saw,	one	emph. prt.	heavy	
woĝhom	weĝhontṃ	oinomk^{w}e	meĝam		
load	pulling,	one-and	great		
bhorom	oinomk^{w}e	ĝhṃenṃ	ōk̂u	bherontṃ	
burden	one-and	man	swiftly	carrying.	

The sheep and the horses

On a hill, a sheep which had no wool saw horses, one pulling a heavy load, one carrying a great burden and one (carrying) swiftly a man.

4 Aspects of Proto-Indo-European Culture and Civilisation

When we reconstruct a proto-language, we are by implication also reconstructing (parts of) a proto-culture and civilisation. But linguistic evidence alone is not sufficient to provide a complete picture of a proto-culture; it must be supplemented by information from archaeology, history, folklore, institutions and other sources. The question 'Who were the Indo-Europeans?' has been studied ever since the Indo-European family was established. Where was their homeland, when (if ever) were they a unit, and what was the nature of their culture?

Many different areas of the world have been suggested for the Proto-Indo-European homeland. Central Asia was an early favourite because of the strong Biblical tradition that this was the home of mankind; the Baltic region, Scandinavia, the Finnic area, Western Europe, the Babylonian Empire, southern Russia, the Mediterranean region and a number of other places have been advanced as possibilities. The reason such a wide variety of views exists lies not only in the complexity and ambiguity of the issues, but also in the trends of the times and the prejudices of individual investigators, many of whom were motivated by racial or ethnic considerations rather than scientific investigation. For example, many of the early researchers, lacking the insights of modern anthropology, believed that the obviously strong and warlike Indo-European people could only have been blond, blue-eyed Aryans who must have originated in Northern Europe, and not Asia or the Mediterranean region, for example. Such a confusion of the matters of race, culture and language, fuelled by religious prejudice and scientific immaturity, produced much speculation on the homeland issue.

A famous argument about the homeland was made by Thieme (1953, summarised in 1958). Using the word for 'salmon' *laĥs (Eng. *lox* < Yiddish *laks*), Thieme argued that these fish fed only in the streams of northern Europe in the Germano-Baltic region during Indo-European times. Since *laĥs is recoverable with the meaning 'salmon' in Germanic and Baltic and 'fish' in Tocharian, this distribution suggests a northern homeland. In Indo-Iranian a form Skt. *lakṣá* 'one hundred thousand' is interpreted by Thieme as an extension of the uncountable nature of a school of salmon. Thieme concludes that the existence of this root in Indo-Iranian and Tocharian, spoken in areas where salmon are unknown, confirms the Germano-Baltic region as the original homeland.

Thieme uses similar argumentation with the reconstructed words for 'turtle' and 'beech tree'. There is a botanical line where the beech flourished about five thousand years ago, as well as an area which defines the limits of the turtle at the time. Finding these roots in a number of Indo-European languages where the physical objects are unknown suggests the north European region again.

Of course, the problem with such argumentation is that the botanical evidence for the beech line of five thousand years ago is not conclusive. Also, it is well known that speakers frequently transfer old names to new objects in a new environment, as American speakers of English have done with the word *robin*. Thus the root *bhāgo- may have been used to designate trees other than the beech in some dialects.

This brief review provides us with some background to consider current thinking on the Indo-European homeland. A widely held view is that of M. Gimbutas, who argued in a number of research articles (largely collected in Gimbutas 1997) that the Proto-Indo-European people were the bearers of the so-called Kurgan or Barrow culture found in the Pontic and Volga steppes of southern Russia, east of the Dnieper river, north of the Caucasus, and west of the Ural mountains. The Kurgan culture (from Russian *kurgan* 'burial mound') is typified by the tumuli, round barrows or 'kurgans', which are raised grave structures from the Calcolithic and Early Bronze Age periods. Evidence from the Kurgan archaeological excavations gives clear evidence of animal breeding, and even the physical organisation of houses accords with the reconstructed Proto-Indo-European material. For example, Go. *waddjus* 'wall' is cognate with Skt. *vāya-* 'weaving', which reflects the wattled construction of walls excavated from the Kurgan sites.

Kurgan culture is divided into three periods, beginning in the fifth millennium BCE. The Indo-Europeanisation of the Kurgan culture took place during the Kurgan II period, roughly 4000–3500 BCE. Kurgan sites from this period have been found in the north Pontic region, west of the Black Sea in the Ukraine, Rumania, the former Yugoslavia and Eastern Hungary. During the Kurgan III period (c. 3500–3000 BCE), Kurgan culture spread out across Central Europe, the entire Balkan area and into Transcaucasia, Anatolia and northern Iran. Eventually, it also spread into northern Europe and the upper Danube region. During the final period, Kurgan IV, waves of expansion carried the culture into Greece, West Anatolia and the eastern Mediterranean.

According to Gimbutas, the archaeological evidence attesting to the domesticated horse, the vehicle, habitation patterns, social structure and religion of the Kurgans is in accord with the reconstruction of Proto-Indo-European, which reflects a linguistic community from about 3000 BCE.

For additional discussion of this topic see Mallory and Adams (1997), Fortson (2004). For a proposal to locate the PIE homeland east, in Anatolia at a much earlier date (ca. 7000 BCE), see initially Renfrew (1987) and many subsequent publications.

Salient lexical items which give insight into Proto-Indo-European culture can be cited. In the remaining space we will note those items which are particularly useful in developing a view of Proto-Indo-European culture. Mallory and Adams (1997) provides an encyclopaedic account of PIE cultural vocabulary.

Physical Environment. One or more words for *day, night*, the *seasons, dawn, stars, sun, moon, earth, sky, snow* and *rain* are plainly recoverable. A number of arboreal units have been identified and successfully reconstructed. Words for *horse, mouse, bear, wolf, eagle, salmon, beaver, otter, dog, cattle, sheep, pig, goat, wasp, bee* and *louse* can also be reliably postulated. It is interesting that no single word for *river* or *ocean* can be established.

Family Organisation and Social Structure. The Proto-Indo-European family was probably patriarchal and patrilocal, living in small houses and adjacent huts. Villages were small, distant and presumably exogamous. There is good evidence for patriliny, and cross-cousin marriage was probably not permitted. Kinship terms are reconstructible for *father, mother, brother, sister, son, daughter, husband's in-laws* and *probably grandrelatives*. The word for husband means 'master' and the wife was probably 'a woman who learns through marriage'. Evidence for Proto-Indo-European patriarchal kinship comes not only from the lexicon, but also from epic songs, legal tracts and ethnological sources from the various ancient Indo-European languages.

There is widespread evidence of a word for *tribal king*, giving some indication that government was established.

Technology. The Indo-European languages confirm the technological advancements of the proto-culture. Evidence from farming and agricultural terms indicates small-scale farmers and husbandmen who raised pigs, knew barley, and had words for *grain, sowing, ploughing*, *grinding*, *settlement* and *field* or *pasture*. We can also safely reconstruct words for *arrow*, *axe*, *boat*, *gold*, *wagon*, *axle*, *hub* and *yoke*, showing a rather advanced people with knowledge of worked metals and agriculture.

Religion and Law. From lexical, legal and other sources we find clear indications of a religious system among the Proto-Indo-European people. There is a word for *god*, and a designation for a *priest*; words for *worship, prayer, praise* and *sacred* give clear indications of organised religion. There is lexical evidence and evidence from ancient institutions for legal concepts such as *religious law, pledge, justice* and *compensation*.

Bibliography

General overviews of the Proto-Indo-European and the Indo-European languages include Ramat and Ramat (1998) and Fortson (2004). Meillet (1937) remains a lucid exposition of the principles of Indo-European linguistics, while Szemerényi (1999) is currently the most authoritative handbook. For a general text on historical linguistics and its methods, see Campbell (2004).

Pokorny (1951–59) is the standard in Indo-European etymology and lexicography, while Buck (1951) is a resource of synonyms arranged by semantic class. More recent accounts are Mallory and Adams (1997), Watkins (2000), Rix (2001), and a number of on-line resources.

References

Brugmann, K. 1903. *Kurze vergleichende Grammatik der indogermanischen Sprachen* (Trübner, Strassburg)

Buck, C.D. 1951. *A Dictionary of Selected Synonyms of the Principal Indo-European Languages* (University of Chicago Press, Chicago)

Campbell, L. 2004. *Historical Linguistics: an Introduction*, 2nd edn (MIT Press, Cambridge)

Fortson, B.W., IV. 2004. *Indo-European Language and Culture: An Introduction* (Blackwell, Oxford)

Gamkrelidze, T.V. 1981. 'Language Typology and Language Universals and Their Implications for the Reconstruction of the Indo-European Stop System', in Y.L. Arbeitman and A.R. Bomhard (eds) *Bono Homini Donum: Essays in Historical Linguistics in Memory of J. Alexander Kerns* (John Benjamins, Amsterdam), pp. 571–609

Gamkrelidze, T.V. and Ivanov, V.V. 1995. *Indo-European and the Indo-Europeans.* (Part 1, The text; part 2, Bibliography, indices.), Trends in Linguistics: Studies and Monographs, 80 (Mouton de Gruyter, Berlin and New York). [English version by J. Nichols of *Indoevropejskij jazyk i indoevropejcy.* 1984 (Tbilisi University Press, Tbilisi)]

Gimbutas, M. 1997. *The Kurgan Culture and the Indo-Europeanization of Europe: Selected Papers from 1952 to 1993* (Institute for the Study of Man, Washington)

Hopper, P. 1981. '"Decem" and "Taihun" Languages: An Indo-European Isogloss', in Y.L. Arbeitman and A.R. Bomhard (eds) *Bono Homini Donum: Essays in Historical Linguistics in Memory of J. Alexander Kerns* (John Benjamins, Amsterdam), pp. 133–42

Ivanov, V.V. 1965. *Obăceidoevropejskaja praslavjanskaja i anatolijskaja jazykovye sistemy* (Nauka, Moscow)

Kuryłowicz, J. 1927. 'ə indo-européen et h hittite', in *Symbolae Grammaticae in Honorem Ioannis Rozwadowski* (Drukarnia Uniwersytetu Jagiellońskiego, Cracow), pp. 95–104

Lehmann, W.P. 1952. *Proto-Indo-European Phonology* (University of Texas Press, Austin)

Lehmann, W.P. and Zgusta, L. 1979. 'Schleicher's Tale After a Century', in Bela Brogyanyi (ed.), *Festschrift for Oswald Szemerényi on the Occasion of his 65th Birthday* (John Benjamins, Amsterdam), pp. 455–66

Mallory, J.P. and Adams, D. (eds) 1997. *The Encyclopedia of Indo-European Culture* (Fitzroy Dearborn, London)

Meillet, A. 1937. *Introduction à l'étude comparative des langues indo-européennes*, 8th edn (reprinted by University of Alabama Press, University, Alabama, 1964)

Pokorny, J. 1951–9. *Indogermanisches etymologisches Wörterbuch* (Francke, Bern and Munich)

Ramat, P. and Ramat, A. 1998. *The Indo-European Languages* (Routledge, London)

Renfrew, C. 1987. *Archaeology and Language: The Puzzle of Indo-European Origins* (Cape, London)

Rix, H. 2001. *Lexicon der indogermanischen Verben (LIV)* (Reichert, Wiesbaden)

Saussure, F. de. 1879. *Mémoire sur le système primitif des langues indo-européennes* (Teubner, Leipzig)

Schleicher, A. 1876. *Compendium der vergleichenden Grammatik der indogermanischen Sprachen* (Böhlau, Weimar)

Schmalstieg, W.R. 1980. *Indo-European Linguistics: A New Synthesis* (Pennsylvania State University Press, University Park)

Szemerényi, O. 1999. *Introduction to Indo-European Linguistics* (Oxford University Press, Oxford) [English translation based on 4th German edn, 1990]

Thieme, P. 1953. 'Die Heimat der indogermanischen Gemeinsprache', in *Abhandlungen der geistes- und sozialwissenschaftlichen Klasse* (Akademie der Wissenschaften und Literatur, Wiesbaden), pp. 535–610

—— 1958. 'The Indo-European Language', *Scientific American*, vol. 199, no. 4, pp. 63–74

Watkins, C. 2000. *The American Heritage Dictionary of Indo-European Roots*, 2nd edn (Houghton Mifflin, Boston)

2

Germanic Languages

John A. Hawkins

The Germanic languages currently spoken fall into two major groups: North Germanic (or Scandinavian) and West Germanic. The former group comprises: Danish, Norwegian (i.e. both the Dano-Norwegian Bokmål and Nynorsk), Swedish, Icelandic, and Faroese. The latter: English (in all its varieties), German (in all its varieties, including Yiddish and Pennsylvania German), Dutch (including Afrikaans and Flemish) and Frisian. The varieties of English are particularly extensive and include not just the dialectal and regional variants of the British Isles, North America, Australasia, India and Africa, but also numerous English-based pidgins and creoles of the Atlantic (e.g. Jamaican Creole and Pidgin Krio) and the Pacific (e.g. Hawaiian Pidgin and Tok Pisin). When one adds to this list the regions of the globe in which Scandinavian, German and Dutch are spoken, the geographical distribution of the Germanic languages is more extensive than that of any other group of languages. In every continent there are countries in which a modern Germanic language (primarily English) is extensively used or has some official status (as a national or regional language). Demographically there are at least 450 million speakers of Germanic languages in the world today, divided as follows: North Germanic, over 18 million (Danish over 5 million, Norwegian over 4 million, Swedish approximately 8.8 million, Icelandic 260,000 and Faroese 47,000); West Germanic apart from English, approximately 125 million (90 million for German in European countries in which it has official status, German worldwide perhaps 100 million, Dutch and Afrikaans 25 million, Frisian over 400,000); English worldwide, 320–80 million first language users, plus 300–500 million users in countries like India and Singapore in which English has official status (cf. Crystal 2003).

There is a third group of languages within the Germanic family that needs to be recognised: East Germanic, all of whose members are now extinct. These were the languages of the Goths, the Burgundians, the Vandals, the Gepids and other tribes originating in Scandinavia that migrated south occupying numerous regions in western and eastern Europe (and even North Africa) in the early centuries of the present era. The only extensive records we have are from a fourth-century Bible translation into Gothic. The Goths had migrated from southern Sweden around the year nought into the area around what is now Gdańsk (originally Gothiscandza). After AD 200 they moved south into what is now Bulgaria, and later split up into two groups, Visigoths and Ostrogoths. The Visigoths established new kingdoms in southern France and Spain (AD 419–711), and the Ostrogoths in Italy (up till AD 555). These tribes were subsequently to become absorbed in the local populations, but in addition to the Bible translation they have left behind numerous linguistic relics in the form of place names (e.g. *Catalonia*, originally 'Gothislandia'), personal names (e.g. *Rodrigo* and *Fernando*, compare Modern German *Roderich* and *Ferdinand*), numerous loanwords (e.g. Italian-Spanish *guerra* 'war'), and also more structural features (such as the Germanic stress system, see below). In addition, a form of Gothic was still spoken on the Crimean peninsula as late as the eighteenth century. Eighty-six words of Crimean Gothic were recorded by a Flemish diplomat in 1562, who recognised the correspondence between these words and his own West Germanic cognates.

The earliest records that we have for all three groups of Germanic languages are illustrated in Figure 2.1. These are runic inscriptions dating back to the third century AD and written (or rather carved in stone, bone or wood) in a special runic alphabet referred to as the Futhark. This stage of the language is sometimes called Late Common Germanic since it exhibits minimal dialect differentiation throughout the Germanic-speaking area. Further evidence of early Germanic comes from words cited by the classical writers such as Tacitus (e.g. *rūna* 'rune') and from some extremely early Germanic loanwords borrowed by the neighbouring Baltic languages and Finnish (e.g. Finnish *kuningas* 'king'). The runic inscriptions, these early citations and loans, the Gothic evidence and the method of comparative reconstruction applied to both Germanic and Indo-European as a whole provide us with such knowledge as we have of the Germanic parent language, Proto-Germanic.

There is much uncertainty surrounding the origin and nature of the speakers of Proto-Germanic, and even more uncertainty about the speakers of Proto-Indo-European. It seems to be agreed, however, that a Germanic-speaking people occupied an area comprising what is now southern Sweden, southern Norway, Denmark and the lower Elbe at some point prior to 1000 BC, and that an expansion then took place both to the north

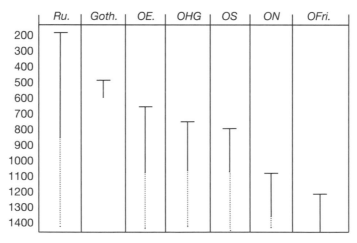

Figure 2.1 The Earliest Written Records in the Germanic Languages.
Source: Kufner 1972.

and to the south. Map 2.1 illustrates the southward expansion of the Germanic peoples in the period 1000 to 500 BC. A reconstruction of the events before 1000 BC is rather speculative and depends on one's theory of the 'Urheimat' (or original homeland) of the Indo-European speakers themselves (see pages 25–26). The pre-Germanic speakers must have migrated to their southern Scandinavian location sometime before 1000 BC and according to one theory (cf. Hutterer 1975) they encountered there a non-Indo-European-speaking people from whom linguistic features were borrowed that were to have a substantial impact on the development of Proto-Germanic from Proto-Indo-European. According to Hutterer as much as one-third of the vocabulary of the Germanic languages is not of Indo-European origin (see page 56).

The major changes that set off Proto-Germanic from Proto-Indo-European are generally considered to have been completed by at least 500 BC. In the phonology these were the following: the First (or Germanic) Sound Shift; several vowel shifts; changes in word-level stress patterns; and reductions and losses in unstressed syllables.

The First Sound Shift affected *all* the non-nasal stops of Proto-Indo-European and is illustrated in Figure 2.2.

The reconstructed Proto-Indo-European consonants of Figure 2.2 are those of Brugmann (1903) (see Baldi, this volume, page 11). According to this reconstruction Proto-Indo-European had a voiceless and a voiced series of consonants, each of which could be unaspirated or aspirated, and within each series there was a bilabial, a dental, a palatal, a velar and a labio-velar (labialised velar) stop, as shown. Proto-Germanic abandoned the palatal/velar distinction throughout, and collapsed the unaspirated and aspirated series of voiceless stops. Unaspirated voiced stops shifted to their voiceless counterparts (see, for example, Lat. *decem*, Eng. *ten*), voiceless stops shifted to voiceless fricatives (e.g. Lat. *tres*, Eng. *three*), and aspirated voiced stops shifted to voiced fricatives (most of which subsequently became voiced stops). The dotted lines in Figure 2.2 indicate the operation of what

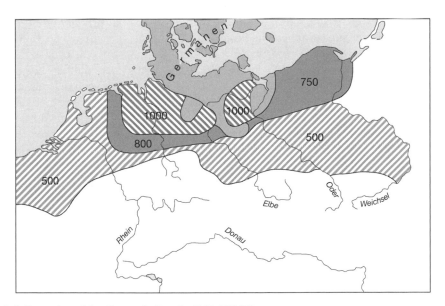

Map 2.1 Expansion of the Germanic People 1000–500 BC.
Source: Adapted from Hutterer 1975.

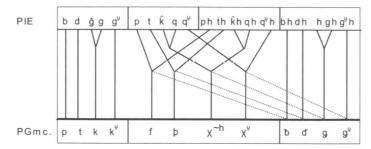

Figure 2.2 The First (Germanic) Sound Shift.
Source: Adapted from Krahe 1948.

is called 'Verner's Law'. Depending on the syllable that received primary word stress, the voiceless fricatives of Germanic would either remain voiceless or become voiced. For example, an immediately following stressed syllable would induce voicing, cf. Go. *fadar* 'father' pronounced with [ð] rather than [θ], from PIE *pətér*, cf. Skt. *pitár-*, Gk. *patér*.

According to the more recent Proto-Indo-European consonantal reconstruction of Gamkrelidze (1981) (see Baldi, this volume, page 14) the unaspirated voiced stops of Figure 2.2 were actually glottalised stops, which lost their glottalic feature in Proto-Germanic, resulting in the voiceless stops shown. For further details, and also a critique, of this reconstruction see Voyles (1992).

The vowel shifts are illustrated in Figure 2.3. Short *a*, *o* and *ə* in Proto-Indo-European were collapsed into Germanic *a* (compare Lat. *ager*, Go. *akrs* 'field, acre'; Lat. *octo* (PIE *oktō*), Go. *ahtau* 'eight'; PIE *pəter*, Go. *fadar* 'father'). The syllabic liquids and nasals of Proto-Indo-European became *u* plus a liquid or nasal consonant. Long *ā* and *ō* collapsed into *ō* (Lat. *fräter*, Go. *brōþ*ar* 'brother'; Lat. *flōs* (PIE *bhlōmen*), Go. *blōma*, 'flower, bloom'), and the number of diphthongs was reduced as shown.

The changes in word stress resulted in the many word-initial primary stress patterns of the Germanic languages where in Proto-Indo-European the stress had fallen on a variety of syllable types (the root, word- and stem-forming affixes, even inflectional endings). This shift (from a Proto-Indo-European accentual system that has been argued to be based on pitch originally, i.e. high versus low tones) is commonly assumed to have occurred after the First Sound Shift, since the operation of Verner's Law pre-supposes variable accentual patterns of the Indo-European type that were subsequently neutralised by the reassignment of primary stress. Thus, both PIE *bhrāter* 'brother' and *pətér* 'father' end up with primary stress on the initial syllable in Go. *brōþar* and *fádar*, and yet the alternation between voiceless [θ] in the former case and voiced [ð] in the latter bears testimony to earlier accentual patterns. Had the stress shifted first, both words should have changed *t* in the same way. A major and lasting consequence of initial stress was the corresponding reduction and loss of unstressed syllables. This process was well underway in predialectal Germanic and was to continue after the separation of the dialects. Indo-European final *-t* was regularly dropped (Lat. *velit*, Go. *wili* 'he will/wants'), and final *-m* was either dropped or reduced to *-n* (OLat. *quom*, Eng. *when*). Final short vowels were dropped (Gk. *oĭda* 'I see', Go. *wait* 'I know'), and final long vowels were reduced in length.

The extremely rich morphology of Proto-Indo-European was reduced in Proto-Germanic. The Proto-Indo-European noun distinguished three genders (masculine, feminine, neuter),

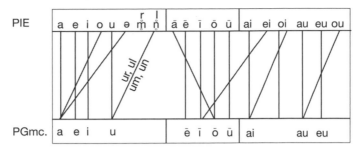

Figure 2.3 Germanic Vowel Shifts.
Source: Krahe and Meid 1969.

three numbers (singular, plural, dual) and eight cases (nominative, vocative, accusative, genitive, dative, ablative, instrumental and locative). The three genders were preserved in Germanic, but special dual inflections disappeared (though residual dual forms survive in the pronominal system of the early dialects). The eight cases were reduced to four: the original nominative, accusative, and genitive preserved their forms and functions; the vocative was collapsed with the nominative; the dative, instrumental and locative (and to some extent the ablative) were united in a single case, the Germanic dative, though occasional instrumental forms are attested; and some uses of the ablative were taken over by the genitive.

Proto-Indo-European nouns were also divided into numerous declensional classes depending on the final vowel or consonant of the stem syllable, each with partially different inflectional paradigms. These paradigms survive in Germanic, though some gained, and were to continue to gain, members at the expense of others (particularly the PIE *o*-class (Gmc. *a*-class) for masculine and neuter nouns, and the PIE *ā*-class (Gmc. *ō*-class) for feminine nouns). The inflectional paradigm for masculine *a*-stems in the earliest Germanic languages is illustrated in Table 2.1.

The syncretism of the case system was accompanied by an expansion in the use of prepositions in order to disambiguate semantic distinctions that had been carried more clearly by the morphology hitherto.

The pronouns of Germanic correspond by and large to those of Indo-European, except for the reduction in the number of dual forms.

As regards the adjective, Germanic innovated a functionally productive distinction between 'strong' and 'weak' inflections, which is still found in Modern German (cf. pages 97–98 for illustration). Proto-Indo-European adjectival morphology was fundamentally similar to that for nouns. The Germanic strong adjective inflections were formed from a fusion of pronominal inflections with the declensional paradigm for nouns and adjectives ending in a stem vowel, while the weak adjective inflections were those of nouns and adjectives with *n*-stems. Strong and weak adjectives in the early dialects carried a meaning difference similar to that of the indefinite versus definite articles of the modern Germanic languages, and it is no accident that adjectives within indefinite versus definite noun phrases are typically strong and weak respectively in German today.

Proto-Indo-European verbal morphology was considerably reduced in Germanic. The Proto-Indo-European medio-passive voice was lost (except for a few relics in Gothic and Old English), and only the active survives. Distinct subjunctive and optative forms were

Table 2.1 The Inflectional Paradigm for Germanic Masculine *a*-Stems

		Go.	*ON*	*OE*	*OS*	*OHG*
Sg.	Nom.	dags	dagr	dæg	dag	tag
	Gen.	dagis	dags	dæges	dages	tages
	Dat.	daga	dege	dæge	dage	tage
	Acc.	dag	dag	dæg	dag	tag
	Voc.	dag	(= Nom.)	(= Nom.)	(= Nom.)	(= Nom.)
	Inst.	—	—	dæge	dagu	tagu
Pl.	Nom.	dagōs	dagar	dagas	dagos	taga
	Gen.	dagē	daga	daga	dago	tago
	Dat.	dagam	dǫgom	dagum	dagum	tagum
	Acc.	dagans	daga	dagas	dagos	taga

Notes: Germanic *a*-stems exemplified by Gothic *dags* 'day' and cognates in the other Germanic dialects derive from Indo-European *o*-stems (cf. Latin *lupus*, earlier *lupos* 'wolf').

collapsed, and only two of several tense and aspect distinctions were maintained in the Germanic present versus past tenses. Separate verb agreement inflections for dual subjects survive only (partially) in Gothic and Old Norse. A special innovation of Germanic involved the development of a systematic distinction between strong and weak verbs. The former (exemplified by Eng. *sing/sang/sung*) exploit vowel alternations, or 'ablaut' (see pages 14–15), in distinguishing, for example, past from present tense forms, the latter use a suffix containing a dental element without any vowel alternation (e.g. Eng. *love/loved*). The verbal morphology of Proto-Germanic has been maintained in all the modern Germanic languages (though the number of strong verbs has been reduced in favour of weak ones), and in addition new periphrastic forms have evolved for the tenses (e.g. perfect and pluperfect) and voices (the passive) that were lost in the transmission from Proto-Indo-European to Proto-Germanic.

The Germanic lexicon, like the phonology and morphology, reveals clearly the Indo-European origin of Germanic. Yet, as pointed out earlier, Hutterer (1975) argues that as much as a third of Germanic lexical items cannot be derived from Proto-Indo-European. These items, far from being peripheral, belong to the core of the basic vocabulary of Common Germanic. They predominate in the following semantic fields: seafaring terms; terms for warfare and weaponry; animal names (particularly fish) and terms for hunting and farming; communal activities and social institutions and titles; and miscellaneous terms. Some examples (taken from English) are: *sea, keel, boat, rudder, mast, steer, sail*; *sword, bow*; *carp, eel, calf, lamb*; *thing* (originally a communal meeting), *king, knight*; and *leap, bone*. In the absence of independent evidence for the Germanic substrate language, arguments for lexical borrowing, or for other distinctive features of Germanic from the substrate must be considered speculative. More recent studies of early Germanic such as Voyles (1992) and Robinson (1992) do not refer to it. On the other hand, the Dutch dictionary of Marlies Philippa et al. (2003) gives systematic attention to the substrate idea, and unless Indo-European etymologies can be found for these basic vocabulary items in Germanic it must be considered a serious possibility worthy of further research.

Common Germanic also took numerous loanwords from neighbouring Indo-European peoples, especially from Latin, though also from Celtic. The Latin loans reveal the strong influence of Roman culture on the early Germanic peoples in areas such as agriculture (cf. Eng. *cherry*/Lat. *ceresia*, *plum/pluma*, *plant/planta*, *cheese/caseus*), building and con-struction (*street/strata*, *wall/vallum*, *chamber/camera*), trade (*pound/pondo*, *fishmonger/ mango* (= slave-trader), *mint/moneta*), warfare (*camp/campus*). Most of the days of the week are loan translations from the Latin (e.g. *Sunday/solis dies*, etc.).

There is much less certainty about the syntax of Proto-Germanic, though the word order of the earliest inscriptions (Late Common Germanic) has been quite extensively documented by Smith (1971). He establishes that the basic position of the verb was clause-final (62 per cent of the clauses he investigated were verb-final, with 19 per cent verb-second and 16 per cent verb-first). Within the noun phrase, however, the pre-dominant order of adjectival modifiers and of possessive and demonstrative determiners is after the noun, and not before it, as in many OV languages. In the earliest West Germanic dialects, by contrast, the verb is correspondingly less verb-final, and modifiers of the noun are predominantly preposed.

The precise manner in which the proto-language split up into the three groups (North, East and West) is a question of long-standing dispute. With the exception of the earliest runic inscriptions, the tripartite division is already very clearly established in the earliest records of Figure 2.1: each of the groups has undergone enough characteristic innovations to justify both the existence of the group itself and the assumption of a period of separate linguistic development for the languages involved following migra-tion from the homeland. But whether these innovations point to the existence of, for instance, a West Germanic parent language which split off from Proto-Germanic and from which all the later West Germanic dialects are descended, or whether the innova-tions are the result of contact and borrowing between geographically proximate tribes speaking increasingly distinct dialects whose common point of departure was the Germanic parent language, is almost impossible to tell. Some scholars argue against the assumption of a West Germanic parent language on the grounds that a threefold dialect grouping within West Germanic (into North Sea Germanic, Rhine-Weser Germanic, and Elbe Germanic – also called respectively Istveonic, Ingveonic and Erminonic) can be reconstructed back as early as the second century AD. The runic inscriptions of this early period do not lend credence to such an early dialect split, however.

Bibliography

For the Indo-European background, see Baldi (Chapter 1, this volume), Brugmann (1903), Krahe (1948), and Gamkrelidze (1981). Van Coetsem and Kufner (1972) contains many papers (in English) on the phonology, morphology and syntax of Proto-Germanic, on the position of Germanic within Indo-European as a whole and on the reconstruction of developments within Germanic prior to the first records. It includes Kufner's (1972) summary and synthesis of the different theories concerning subgroupings within Germanic.

For the phonology and morphology of early Germanic languages, see Krahe and Meid (1969), Voyles (1992) and Robinson (1992). Robinson also includes discussion of syntax. Hutterer (1975) is a general compendium of the grammars and histories of all the Germanic languages and of the cultures of their speakers. Smith (1971) gives a summary of word order in early Germanic.

The chapters in König and van der Auwera (1994) give grammatical summaries (in English) of all the modern Germanic languages, including Germanic creoles (Romaine 1994). This volume also includes an overview chapter on the Germanic languages (Henriksen and van der Auwera 1994), a chapter on Gothic and the reconstruction of Proto-Germanic (W.P. Lehmann 1994), plus chapters on the historical stages of North and West Germanic languages.

References

Baldi, P., this volume. 'Indo-European Languages'

Brugmann, K. 1903. *Kurze vergleichende Grammatik der indogermanischen Sprachen* (Trübner, Strassburg)

Crystal, D. 2003. *English as a Global Language*, 2nd edn (Cambridge University Press, Cambridge)

Gamkrelidze, T.V. 1981. 'Language Typology and Language Universals and Their Implications for the Reconstruction of the Indo-European Stop System', in Y.L. Arbeitman and A.R. Bomhard (eds), *Bono Homini Donum: Essays in Historical Linguistics in Memory of J. Alexander Kerns* (John Benjamins, Amsterdam), pp. 571–609

Henriksen, C. and van der Auwera, J. 1994. 'The Germanic Languages', in E. König and J. van der Auwera (eds) *The Germanic Languages* (Routledge, London), pp.1–18

Hutterer, C.J. 1975. *Die germanischen Sprachen: ihre Geschichte in Grundzügen* (Akadémiai Kiadó, Budapest)

König, E. and van der Auwera, J. (eds) 1994. *The Germanic Languages* (Routledge, London)

Krahe, H. 1948. *Indogermanische Sprachwissenschaft* (Walter de Gruyter, Berlin)

—— and Meid, W. 1969. *Germanische Sprachwissenschaft*, 2 vols (Walter de Gruyter, Berlin)

Kufner, H.L. 1972. 'The Grouping and Separation of the Germanic Languages', in F. Van Coetsem and H.L. Kufner (eds) *Toward a Grammar of Proto-Germanic* (Max Niemeyer, Tübingen)

Lehmann, W.P. 1994. 'Gothic and the Reconstruction of Proto-Germanic', in E. König and J. van der Auwera (eds) *The Germanic Languages* (Routledge, London), pp. 19–37

Philippa, M., Debrabandere, F. and Quak, A. (eds) 2003. *Etymologisch Woordenboek van het Nederlands*, Vol. 1 (Amsterdam University Press, Amsterdam)

Robinson, O.W. 1992. *Old English and its Closest Relatives: A Survey of the Earliest Germanic Languages* (Stanford University Press, Stanford)

Romaine, S. 1994. 'Germanic Creoles', in E. König and J. van der Auwera (eds) *The Germanic Languages* (Routledge, London), pp. 566–603

Smith, J.R. 1971. 'Word Order in the Older Germanic Dialects' (PhD dissertation, University of Illinois, available from University Microfilms, Ann Arbor, Mich.)

Van Coetsem, F. and Kufner, H.L. (eds) 1972. *Toward a Grammar of Proto-Germanic* (Max Niemeyer, Tübingen)

Voyles, J.B. 1992. *Early Germanic Grammar: Pre-, Proto-, and Post-Germanic Languages* (Academic Press, San Diego)

3

English

Edward Finegan

1 Introduction

Readers of *The World's Major Languages* may be assumed to have more than a nod-
ding acquaintance with the English language. English is, moreover, widely studied and
has received significant attention from distinguished grammarians since the nineteenth
century. It thus seems appropriate here to discuss English in terms not entirely parallel
to those in which other languages, perhaps less familiar, are described in this book. In
somewhat more detail than is possible at present for most other languages, this chapter
will describe the structural variation that characterises English functionally and socially,
as well as some salient historical and regional variation.

Section 2 describes the status of English throughout the world, along with its social
history and past contact with other languages. Section 3 offers a historical sketch of its
lexicon, phonology, morphology and syntax, followed by a brief account of orthographic
practices. Section 4 treats regional, social and functional variation in present-day English.

2 Status of English

2.1 Current Status of English

Although Chinese is spoken by a greater number of people, English is spoken around
the globe with a wider dispersion than any other language. From its earlier home in
Britain (now with 60 million speakers), it has spread to nearby Ireland (4 million),
across the Atlantic to North America (where some 215 million residents over the age of
five speak it in the United States and as many as 20 million in Canada) and across the
world to Australia and New Zealand (with more than 20 million speakers).

English is the sole official language in more than a score of other countries: Ghana,
Liberia, Nigeria, Uganda and Zimbabwe in Africa; Jamaica, the Bahamas, Dominica
and Barbados in the Caribbean; and the Solomon Islands in the Pacific, to name a
sample. Elsewhere it shares official status with one or more languages in a score of

nations, including Tonga, Tanzania, Cameroon, Kenya, Nigeria, South Africa, Singapore, the Philippines, Western Samoa, Kiribati, Pakistan and India (where it is an associate official language alongside Hindi). In still other nations, English holds no official status only because its widespread use in government (often alongside an indigenous tongue) and in trade is taken for granted. The United States, with no designated official language, is the most prominent of such cases. In still other nations, English is of such commercial and scientific advantage that consideration is repeatedly given to making it an official language.

Substantial portions of the populations of the United States and Canada speak English as a second language, many of them immigrants, but others born there and raised in families and neighbourhoods struggling to preserve the language and culture of ancestral lands. One well known example is that of French speakers in Canada, who constitute a majority only in Quebec province but whose influence is so strong nationally that Canada is officially a bilingual nation. Less well known is how many speakers of languages other than English reside in the United States. The United States Census reports that in 2003 more than 48 million residents over the age of five spoke a language other than English at home. This suggests that a good many residents of the United States speak English as a second language. Los Angeles is a sufficiently bilingual city that balloting materials for all elections are available in Spanish, Chinese, Japanese, Vietnamese, Korean and Tagalog, and similar multilingualism characterises voting materials in other American cities. Elsewhere, Nigeria, Ghana and Uganda have almost two million speakers of English as a second language each and the Philippines more than 11 million. Likewise, the millions who speak English in Pakistan and India have learned it, for the most part, not in their infancy but as a second language, a lingua franca for governmental and educational functions.

Beyond its uses as a first and second language in ordinary intercourse, English is the lingua franca of much scholarship, particularly of a scientific and technical nature. In addition, throughout the world are English-speaking universities in which instruction and textbooks use English as a principal medium. Reflective of its widespread dissemination and perhaps its adaptability is the fact that Nobel Prizes in literature have been awarded to more writers using English than any other language and, in particular, that these laureates have been citizens of Australia, Ireland, India, Trinidad, St. Lucia, Nigeria and South Africa, as well as the United States and Britain. At the United Nations, English is an official language, alongside Arabic, Chinese, French, Russian and Spanish. A quarter of the world's population is said to be competent in English—that would be 1.5 billion people (Crystal 2003).

2.2 Possible Reasons for Widespread Use of English

The widespread use of English around the globe is often attributed to social prestige and the need for English in technological advancement. Some also credit the simplicity of its inflections and the cosmopolitan character of its vocabulary. These latter features are influential only when coupled with social, historical and economic factors, for other languages and other peoples share them, though with different outcomes.

Among reasons sometimes suggested for the extension of English is the spread of technology, for the diffusion of American technologies during the twentieth and twenty-first centuries likewise spread English words for them, as with *television* and *HDTV* (high definition television). Likewise in other arenas, cultural artifacts have spread their English names in their travels, from concrete objects like *jeans* and *discos* (both of which are originally French) to the intangible and ubiquitous *OK*.

English words have not always been welcomed abroad. Troubling such watchdog institutions as the *Académie française*, Anglo-Americanisms like *weekend* and *drugstore* have been banned in France, while guardians of German balked at the introduction of words like *Telefon* for the native *Fernsprecher*. Elsewhere, people are more open to English loanwords. The Japanese, for example, have drafted the words *beesubooru* 'baseball', *booringu* 'bowling' and *futtobooru* 'football', along with the games they name, trading them for *judo, jujitsu* and *karate*, which have joined the English team.

Further contributing to the popularity of English may be its inflectional structure, for it exhibits notable inflectional simplicity compared to languages like German and Russian. Assuming, as many linguists would, that a language simple at one level will be compensatorily complex elsewhere in order to carry out equivalent communicative tasks, it is difficult to assess the impetus of grammatical simplicity on the spread of a language. To be sure, English inflections are few and relatively easy to learn compared to heavily inflected languages. English nouns, for example, generally have only two variants in speech, a marked variant for possessive singulars and all plurals, an unmarked one for all other functions. Aside from a few exceptions like *teeth* and *oxen*, plurals are formed by adding /-s/ or /-z/ or /-əz/ to the singular, according to straightforward conditions detailed below (Section 3.1.1). As for possessives, the rules are identical to those for the plural, but without exceptions. Further, English exhibits no variation in adjectives for number, gender, or case, there being but one form each in the positive degree (*tall, beautiful, old*) although comparative (*-er*) and superlative (*-est*) degrees are marked by inflection or, under specified circumstances, analytical forms with *more* and *most*. Verbs are only minimally inflected, with suffixes for third person singular concord, present participle (*-ing*), past tense (/-t/, /-d/, /-əd/) and past participle. In all, there are but eight productive inflectional suffixes in present-day English: two on nouns, four on verbs and two for adjectives. There are no inflectional prefixes or infixes.

Breadth of vocabulary is an oft-cited reason for the acceptance of English around the globe. *Webster's Third New International Dictionary* (1961) boasts that it contains some 450,000 words. A four-volume supplement to the *Oxford English Dictionary* was completed in 1986, updating the original with words and senses that had arisen or been recognised during the decades of publication between 1884 and 1928 and afterward, and the entries in these supplements are incorporated into the twenty-volume second edition; a third edition in progress can be engaged online. At the *Oxford English Dictionary* website, lists of new entries, subentries and senses appear regularly. A list posted in 2007 displays the nouns *wiki, technopreneur, tighty-whities, tweener, lightstick, irritainment, HDTV, edamame, bad girl* and *asswipe*; the verbs *cannonball, dog-pile* and *virtualize*; and the adjectives *caramelized, cardiothoracic, fricking* and *trepidatious*. Not all these words are new to English, but even this small selection illustrates the vitality of shortening, compounding, borrowing, affixation and functional shift as processes continuing to expand the word stock.

Still further evidence of the abundance of English words can be seen in the fact that the number of synonyms or near synonyms for many words is large, each reflecting some variation on a semantic core or use in different situations. A thesaurus can provide scores of synonyms for the adjective *inebriated* and more than a dozen for the noun *courtesy*, to offer only two examples from different parts of speech (and without intending to suggest the relative richness of these notions among English speakers).

English also boasts a distinctively cosmopolitan vocabulary, having borrowed extensively from its Germanic cousins and Latin and French, but absorbing tens of thousands of words from scores of languages over the centuries. From earliest times English has exerted a remarkable magnetism for loanwords, not only in foods and toponyms but also in virtually every other arena of human activity. Some indication of this cosmopolitan nature is suggested by words like *alcove*, *alcohol* and *harem* (from Arabic), *tycoon* and *ikebana* (Japanese), *taboo* (Tongan), some 10,000 words of French origin added during Middle English and an even larger influx from Latin during the Renaissance. Recent borrowings reveal an extraordinary range of donor languages, more than seventy-five in number. French provides most items, followed by Japanese, Spanish, Italian, Latin, Greek, German, Yiddish, Russian, Chinese, Arabic, more than two dozen African and three dozen other languages around the globe.

Maps of the English-speaking parts of the world are dotted with borrowings from many sources. Hundreds of streets in Los Angeles exhibit names of Spanish origin (from *La Cienega* to *Los Feliz*) as does the city itself. Elsewhere in the USA, place-names like *Mississippi* and *Minnesota* come from Amerindian languages, while *Kinderhook*, *Schuylerville* and *Watervliet*, all in New York State, come from Dutch. In England, common place name designations come from the Scandinavian languages (as discussed in Section 2.3) and after the Norman invasion from French.

Names for popular foods such as *taco*, *burrito*, *chili* and *guacamole* (from Mexican Spanish), *hamburger*, *frankfurter* and *wiener schnitzel* (German), *teriyaki* and *sukiyaki* (Japanese), *chow mein* and *foo yong* (Cantonese), *kimchi* (Korean), *pilaf* (Persian and Turkish), *falafel* (Arabic) and a thousand others indicate the catholic tastes of the English tongue both gustatorily and linguistically. Playing a special role, French culinary words have leavened the English lexicon in kitchens around the world: *hors d'œuvre*, *quiche*, *pâté*, *fondue*, *flambé*, *soufflé*, *sauté*, *carrot*, *mayonnaise*, *bouillon*, *flan*, *casserole*, a whole series with *crème* including *crème brûlée*, *crème caramel*, *crème de menthe* and *crème de cacao*, and now stretching beyond the dining room are such mainstays as *à la* 'in the manner of' (*à la mode* and *à la carte*) and *crème de la crème* 'the best (of anything)'. A wide stripe of languages is represented by other familiar culinary words: *semolina* (Italian), *chocolate* (Nahuatl, via Spanish and French), *coleslaw* (Dutch), *chutney* (Hindi), *moussaka* (Greek), *bamboo* (Malay), *gazpacho* (Spanish), *yoghurt* (Turkish), *kebab* (Arabic), *caviar* (Persian, via Turkish, Italian and French), *pepper* (Latin), *whiskey* (Irish), *maize* (Taino—an Arawakan language—via Spanish) and *blintz* and *knish* (both Ukrainian, via Yiddish).

Another suggested reason for the spread of English is the simplicity of its common words. In the 100-million-word British National Corpus all of the fifty most frequent words in both speech and writing are monosyllabic. Of the fifty next most frequent written words, none contains more than two syllables and only eleven are disyllabic (Leech et al. 2001). Similar information for a wide range of languages might make it clear that, in accordance with Zipf's law, languages generally abbreviate words of frequent use. English has had an additional historical impetus in that most disyllabic words ending in an unstressed syllable became monosyllabic in early Modern English, as described below (Section 3.2).

One final explanation offered by some scholars for the diffusion of English lies in the supposed nature of the relationships between grammatical structures and the processing mechanisms for comprehension. Though not universally accepted, this explanation relies on the claim that SVO languages like English are perceptually simpler than languages whose basic orders are SOV or VSO. Proponents of this view point out that, even granted their sociological and political statuses, it is noteworthy that Chinese, French, Russian and Spanish are SVO and of wide diffusion, as is the spoken form of Arabic that is spreading. The putative perceptual advantage of SVO languages over SOV or VSO languages is the ready identification of subjects and objects by virtue of their being separated by the verb. It might also be mentioned that English tends to have topics in sentence-initial position (though to a lesser degree than many other languages); given its preference for SVO word order, subject and topic often coincide, a coincidence that may enhance processability, especially when the subject is the semantic agent.

2.3 English and its Social History

English did not always hold so prominent a position among the world's languages as it holds today. Even in England it has faced competitors at times. Nor has it always been clear that the United States and Canada would be English-speaking countries, and encroachments by Spanish and French on the status of English in North America remain vigorous.

English derives from the West Germanic branch of the Indo-European family of languages. It is most closely related to the Low German dialects in northern Germany and to Dutch and Frisian, sharing with them the characteristic absence of the Second, or High, German Sound Shift, occurring around AD 600 and markedly differentiating the phonology of the West Germanic varieties of the highland south from those of the lowland north. Geographically separated from the Continent since the middle of the fifth century, English would not have been subject to this shift, but its origins in the northernmost part of the Germanic-speaking area would also have spared it.

It was in AD 449, according to Bede's *Ecclesiastical History of the English People*, that bands from the three Germanic tribes of Angles (after whom England and its language were named), Saxons and Jutes began leaving the area known today as northern Holland and Germany and southern Denmark. These Teutons sailed to Britain, which had been deserted by the Romans four decades earlier, to assist the Celtic leader Vortigern, who had called upon them to help repulse the invading Picts and Scots from the north of Britain. Preferring Britain to their continental homelands, the Teutons settled, driving the hapless Celts into remote corners, where their descendants remain to this day.

Surviving the Roman occupation of the British Isles there remain but few linguistic relics of Latin origin, including the second element of such place names as *Lancaster*, *Manchester* and *Rochester* (from Latin *castra* 'camp'). This influence of Latin through Celtic transmission was the slightest of several Latin influences on the English lexicon. As for direct Celtic influence on the early Germanic settlers, it is noticeable only in place-names like *Dover, Kent, York*, possibly *London*, and a few other toponymics like the river names *Avon, Thames* and *Trent*. In 563 St Columba established an Irish monastery on the island of Iona off the coast of Scotland, and his missionary activities introduced a few Celtic words like *cross* and perhaps *curse* into the English word stock.

It is not until the end of the seventh century that we have written records of a Germanic language spoken in England and not until the reign of King Alfred (871–99) that we have 'Englisc' recorded in quantity. In 597, St Augustine (not the bishop of Hippo known for his fifth-century *Confessions* and *City of God*) christianised the English people, giving them scores of Latin words like *abbot, altar, angel, cleric, priest* and *psalm* in the religious sphere and others like *grammatical, master, meter, school* and *verse* in learned arenas.

In the eighth and ninth centuries, a series of invasions by the Scandinavians brought a secondary Germanic influence into the Anglo-Saxon lexicon, though it does not vigorously manifest itself in the written record until after the eleventh century. Sporadic raids started in 787, with monasteries sacked and pillaged at Lindisfarne and Jarrow (Bede's monastery). In the year 850, as many as 350 ships carried Danish invaders up the Thames. At length King Alfred defeated these Vikings in 878 and signed the Treaty of Wedmore with Guthrum, who agreed to become Christian. There followed a period of integration during which bilingualism prevailed in the Danelaw, an area governed by Danish practices and including Northumbria, East Anglia and half of central England.

The intermingling of these groups brought an influx of more than 900 everyday words from the Scandinavian tongues, including such homely nouns as *gift*, *egg*, *skirt*, *skill*, *skin* and *sky* and the verbs *take*, *give* and *get*. In addition, about 1,400 Scandinavian place-names pepper English maps, besides some 600 ending in -*by* (as in *Derby*, *Rugby*), 600 in -*thorp* or -*thwaite* (*Kettlethorpe*) and another hundred or so in -*toft* (*Lowestoft*), all Scandinavian. Besides this toponymic evidence, the close relationship between the Scandinavians and the English is suggested by the possibility that both pronoun and verb in the phrase *they are* derive not from OE *hīe sindon* but from Scandinavian sources.

In the development of English, the most significant historical event is the invasion by the Normans in 1066. In that year William, Duke of Normandy, crossed the Channel and with his French-speaking retinues established an Anglo-Norman kingdom in England. During the following century and a half, one could not have confidently predicted the reemergence of English and its eventual triumph over French in all domains. Only a series of extraordinary social events contributed definitively to reestablishing a Germanic tongue emblematic of England.

After 1066 the Normans established themselves in the court, in the church and her monasteries, throughout the legal system and the military and in all other arenas of wealth and power. The upper class spoke only French, while English remained chiefly on peasant tongues. Naturally, between those social extremes a significant number of bilinguals eventually used English and French, but for generations England was ruled by French-speaking monarchs, unable to understand the language of many subjects and unable to be understood. Only when King John lost Normandy to King Philip of France in 1204 did the knot between England and the Anglo-Norman language start to come undone. Following other political and military antagonisms, the linguistic tide turned.

Finally, the Black Death struck England in 1348, wiping out perhaps 30 per cent of the population and increasing the value of every peasant life. Ironically, this plague lifted the English-speaking lower classes to positions of greater appreciation and enhanced the value of their work. Along with a rise in their stature came increased stature for their language. In 1362 Parliament passed the Statute of Pleading, which mandated that all court proceedings, conducted solely in French since the Norman conquest, should thenceforth use English. By about 1300 all the inhabitants of England knew English, and French began to fall into disuse. During the fourteenth century, English again became the language of England and her literature. (Details of this story are well told in Baugh and Cable (2002).)

Literature in English is known since Old English times. *Beowulf*, a 3,000-line heroic poem, is still studied even in secondary schools. The surviving manuscript dates probably from the late tenth century, but the poem was likely composed in the eighth. Other texts also survive: poetry (starting at the end of the seventh century), translations of the Bible, chronicles and religious writings particularly from the time of Alfred. Besides known translations, including Boethius's *Consolation of Philosophy*, Alfred is thought to have translated Bede's *History* from Latin and is credited with establishing the practice of maintaining the Anglo-Saxon Chronicles. Reigning from Wessex, his kingdom lay within the West Saxon dialect area, making West Saxon the basis for the study of Old English even though it is not the ancestor of the London dialect of Chaucer that is the basis of modern standard English.

Less was written between 1066 and the thirteenth century, but English language traditions remained vital enough for the fourteenth century to produce Chaucer (1340–1400) and his *Canterbury Tales*, an extraordinary work still enjoyed for its earthy, humorous narrative and poetic achievement. From quite early times English has been robust in its literary manifestation, except for the period of Anglo-Norman dominance from which it nevertheless emerged a great literary language, lexically enriched and inflectionally simplified.

3 English Structure and Its History

English is usually divided into three major periods: Old English, dating from either the arrival of the Germanic tribes in 449 or the earliest documents, about 700, to about 1100 (shortly after the Norman conquest); Middle English from about 1100 to 1500; and, from 1500, Modern English, including an early Modern English period between 1500 and 1700. These dates are somewhat arbitrary in that English did not develop at the same rate in all regions nor at all levels of the grammar. The dates are in fact more appropriate to a phonological than a grammatical history because Modern English morphology and syntax displayed essentially their current form by about 1400, the year of Chaucer's death.

Old English had four principal dialect areas: Northumbrian, Mercian, Kentish and, representing most extant texts, West Saxon. In Middle English, Mercian is divided into West Midland and East Midland dialects, and East Midland, which incorporated features of other dialects, gave rise to standard Modern English. In the discussion to follow, little detail is provided for Middle English because it represents a transitional period whose general nature can be inferred from knowledge of Old English and Modern English; because while spoken English remained vital, written documents are relatively scarce; and because Middle English is far more diverse in its regional dialects than is susceptible to a brief exposition. (Details about Middle English can be traced in Mossé (1968).)

3.1 Lexicon

Enriched by compounding of native elements and by borrowing from other languages, the English word stock has grown continuously although the chief mechanisms for enriching it have shifted in the course of time. The Old English lexicon shows traces of Latin and Celtic influence but is almost purely Germanic. To a great extent it shares etymons with the other Germanic languages and like them developed its word stock chiefly by compounding, as well as by prefixing and suffixing. Compounds were especially frequent and imaginative in Old English poetry, and the resulting kennings enhanced poetic resources as in these examples from *Beowulf*: *seglrād* 'sail road' and *hrōnrād* 'whale road' for sea and *bānhūs* 'bone house' for body. Old English nouns productively suffixed *-dōm*, *-hād*, *-ere* and *-scipe* (all with reflexes in Modern English), as in *wīsdōm* 'wisdom', *cildhād* 'childhood', *wrītere* 'writer' and *frēondscipe* 'friendship'.

Verbs commonly prefixed *ā-*, *be-*, *for-*, *fore-*, *ge-*, *mis-*, *of-*, *ofer-*, *on-*, *tō-*, *un-*, *under-* and *wiþ-*. From *settan* 'to set' Old English could create: *āsettan* 'place', *besettan* 'appoint', *forsettan* 'obstruct', *foresettan* 'place before', *gesettan* 'people, garrison', *ofsettan* 'afflict', *onsettan* 'oppress', *tōsettan* 'dispose', *unsettan* 'put down' and *wiþsettan* 'resist' (Baugh and Cable 2002). It prefixed *wiþ-* to 50 verbs, only one of which (*withstand*) survives in Modern English (*withdraw* and *withhold* originated in Middle English).

The Norman invasion gave new impetus to linguistic borrowing and when English reemerged in the thirteenth century it did so in a context in which anybody who was anybody spoke French and many of the elite spoke little or no English. From that period on, besides smithing with native elements, English has energetically imported words from the languages with which its speakers came into contact. Forty per cent of all French words in English were borrowed between 1250 and 1400 (according to Baugh and Cable (2002)), a period during which English came again to be used for official and learned purposes. From this flood of 10,000 French words inundating Middle English, 75 per cent remain in use. English had earlier borrowed from the Celtic tongues and Latin and, during the ninth and tenth centuries, from its Viking cousins, as we saw. Still, one effect of the invasion was to promote borrowing above the more characteristic English word-smithing practices of affixing and compounding, which formerly had been the most productive springs of new words and would become so again in the twentieth century.

Until recently, it would have been difficult to describe the size and character of the English lexicon accurately, but the availability of standard computerised corpora has changed that. The data presented here rely on three corpora. The Standard Corpus of Present-day Edited American English (the Brown Corpus) comprises 500 text samples, of about 2,000 words each, representing 15 genres of informational and imaginative prose that appeared in print in 1961—about a million words all told. One hundred times that size, the British National Corpus (BNC) contains about 94 million words of British writing and 6 million of transcribed British speech. The Longman Spoken and Written English Corpus comprises about 40 million words in four genres. (See for the Brown Corpus Kučera and Francis (1967) and Francis and Kučera (1982), on which, along with Kučera (1982), we rely in this chapter; for the BNC, Leech et al. (2001) and the references there; for the Longman Corpus, Biber et al. (1999).)

The Brown Corpus contains 61,805 different word forms belonging to 37,851 lemmas. A lemma is a set of word forms, all of which are inflectional or spelling variants of the same base word; thus, the lemma GET comprises the word forms *get* (and *git*), *gets*, *got* (and *gotta*), *gotten, getting* (and *gettin'*). Extrapolating these figures to an infinite sample would yield about 170,000 lemmas in English, excluding proper nouns and highly specialised and technical terms. Remarkably, just 2,124 lemmas (comprising 2,854 word forms) constitute 80 per cent of all tokens in the Brown Corpus. Approximately 22,000 other word forms occur just once each; such *hapax legomena* thus account for 58 per cent of all lemmas. This fact gives some hint as to the range of the lexicon, for the most frequently occurring words are grammatical (i.e., function) words, not lexical (or content) words (cf. Sections 4.3 and 4.4). Because content words are the least predictable textual elements, knowing the 2,124 lemmas that account for 80 per cent of the corpus tokens would fall far short of sustaining comprehension that approximated 80 per cent (Kučera 1982).

The British National Corpus contains 757,087 different word forms, 52 per cent of which (397,041 word forms, according to Leech et al. 2001) occur just once. In any large body of English texts, then, it appears that most words will be used only once or very few times, while relatively few words will be repeated numerous times. Only about 124,000 word forms occur 10 times or more. For example, the BNC's most common lexical verbs are *say* (3,344 occurrences per million words of running text), *get, make, go, see, know, take, think, come, give, look, use, find, want* and *tell* (775); the most common nouns, *time* (1,833), *year, people, way, man* (1,003), *day, thing, child* (710), *government, work, life* and *woman* (631); the most common adjectives, *other* (1,336), *good, new, old, great, high, small, different, large, local, social, important, long, young* and *national* (375); and the most common adverbs, *so* (1893), *up, then, out, now, only, just, more, also, very, well, how, down, back, on, there, still, even* and *too* (701). Frequency lists for prepositions, pronouns, determiners, conjunctions, interjections and discourse markers are also provided in Leech et al. (2001). Strictly speaking, while such quantitative findings are valid only for the corpus on which they are based, the broad outlines and most details are likely to be much the same for comparable corpora. (The distribution of word classes across genres is described in Sections 4.3 and 4.4.)

3.2 Phonology

Throughout its history, English has exhibited striking instability in its system of vowels, while its consonants have remained relatively stable since the fourteenth century. Old English, Middle English and Modern English all exhibit considerable vocalic variation across dialects, while consonants show negligible variation from region to region. Socially significant variation, on the other hand, affects both consonants and vowels, as described in Section 4.2.

The evolution of unstressed vowels has played a pivotal role in the development of English morphology and grammar. The most pregnant phonological feature of the earliest stages of English is the characteristic Germanic stress placement on the first or root syllable. From before the settlement of England, the language of the Angles, Saxons and Jutes suffered certain phonological reductions that differentiate it from High German (e.g. loss of nasals preceding /f/, /θ/, /s/, with compensatory lengthening of the preceding vowel; compare German *Mund* and *Gans* with English *mouth* and *goose*). Such correspondences between the stressed vowels of High and Low German only begin to suggest the wholesale reductions that were to affect English unstressed vowels and consequently the entire inflectional system.

While Gothic (known to us from several centuries earlier than Old English) apparently preserves both long and short vowels in its inflections, Old English exhibits only short vowels there, and syncretism among these inflections is apparent in late Old English, especially in the Northumbrian dialect. While early Old English had a relatively elaborate inflectional system, the characteristic Germanic stress placement began to effect reductions of such magnitude in unstressed vowels that inflectional suffixes in late Old English and Middle English were reduced essentially to the bare system of Modern English. In particular, unstressed /u/, /a/, /e/ and /o/ fell together into *e* [ə]. Coupled with the merging of final /-m/ and /-n/ in /-n/, the collapse of unstressed vowels and subsequent loss of final inflectional /-n/ and of final [ə] led to the virtual elimination of inflectional suffixes except those with final *-s* or *-þ*. This sequence of phonological levellings explains the plural and genitive forms of Modern English nouns, as well as third person singular verbs in orthographic *-s* and past tenses in *-d*.

As to stressed vowels, their history is complicated by the substantial dialectal variation of Old English and the shifting locus of literary standards until the fifteenth century. Still, the extensive diphthongisation and monophthongisation that characterise Old English recur throughout the history of English. When American southerners pronounce *ride* as [raːd], they evidence the same kind of monophthongisation that took place in late Old English when *sēon* became *seen* 'to see' and *heorte* became *herte* 'heart'.

Today, some fourteen to sixteen phonemic vowels and diphthongs exist in the regional varieties of standard English, including /aj/, /aw/ and /ɔj/, the last of which was borrowed from Anglo-Norman. (A more detailed treatment of stressed vowels is available by period in Algeo and Pyles (2004) and by sound in Kurath (1964).) No discussion of English historical phonology can ignore the dramatic shifting of long vowels that occurred mostly between Chaucer's death in 1400 and the birth of Shakespeare in 1564. This so-called Great Vowel Shift altered the pronunciation of the long vowels and diphthongised the high vowels /iː/ and /uː/ to their Modern English reflexes /aj/ and /aw/. Charted in Figure 3.1, this shift is responsible for the discrepancy between English and the Romance languages in the pronunciation of orthographic vowels. Traditional English spellings were propagated with Caxton's introduction of printing into England in 1476, preceding the completion of the shift.

Subsequent to this vowel shift, early ModE /eː/ (< ME /ɛː/) came to be pronounced /i/, thus merging with earlier raised /eː/ and producing two sets of ModE /i/ words, those like *sweet* and *see* from OE /eː/ and those like *sheaf*, *beacon* and *sea* from OE /ɛː/. The raising tendency exhibited in the Great Vowel Shift continues today, where it is sometimes regionally distinctive and sometimes socially marked, as discussed in Section 4.1.

As to consonants, the system has remained relatively stable throughout history, and the inventory of phonemes has changed only slightly since about 1400, although certain allophones have been lost and phonotactic constraints have altered somewhat. The Modern English spelling of *know* and *knife* is indicative of earlier pronunciations in that Old English allowed initial clusters of /hl-/ as in *hlāf* 'loaf', /hr-/ as in *hring* 'ring' and /kn-/ as in *cniht* 'knight', all of which are now prohibited.

Table 3.1 contains a list of Modern English consonant phonemes, followed by exemplars illustrating word-initial, word-medial and word-final occurrence.

Several differences between the consonant systems of Old English and Modern English can be mentioned. The members of the ModE voiced and voiceless fricative

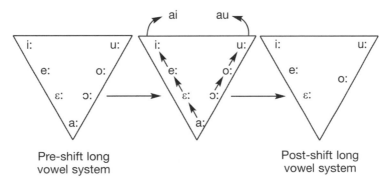

Figure 3.1 The English Vowel Shift (also called Great Vowel Shift).
Source: Bynon 1977.

pairs (/f/-/v/, /θ/-/ð/, /s/-/z/) were allophones of single phonemes in OE, the voiced sounds occurring between other voiced segments, the voiceless sounds occurring initially, finally and in clusters with voiceless obstruents. Relics of the OE allophonic distribution remain in the morphophonemic alternants *wife/wives*, *breath/breathe* and *house/houses*, where the second word in each pair, disyllabic in OE, voiced the intervocalic fricative. Significantly, initial /ð/ is limited in Modern English to the function words *the, this, that, these, those, they* and *them*, *there* and *then, thus, thence, though* and *thither*, with initial voiceless /θ/ in Old English later becoming voiced by assimilation when unstressed, as these words often are. Similarly, /θ/ does not occur medially in any native words, though it can be found in borrowings. During the Middle English period, with the baring of the voiced phones word-finally once the syncreted inflections disappeared, the allophones achieved phonemic status, contrasting in most environments; there may also have been some Anglo-Norman influence.

Modern English /n/ and /ŋ/, non-distinctive variants in Old English, became phonemic during late Middle English or early Modern English. Of the OE allophones of /h/, both [x] and [ç] have disappeared, leaving only [h]. In addition, /g/ had two OE allophones, ModE [g] and a fricative [ɣ] occurring intervocalically but now lost.

Finally, the gap existing in Old English and Middle English where one might expect a voiced palatal fricative /ʒ/ to parallel native /ʃ/ was filled about 1600 when /ʒ/ arose by assimilation of /zj/ from earlier /zi/ (as in *glazier, lesion* and *vision*) and /ziu/ (as in *measure* and *usual*). More recently, word-final /ʒ/ has been borrowed directly from French in words like *mirage, prestige* and *rouge* (though /ʤ/ is also often heard). /ʒ/ is the only

Table 3.1 Modern English Consonants

Phoneme	Initial	Medial	Final
p	pat	caper	tap
b	bat	labour	tab
t	tap	button	bat
d	dad	ladder	pad
k	cad	sicker	talk
g	gab	dagger	gag
f	file	beefy	thief
v	vile	saving	crave
θ	thin	author	breath
ð	then	weather	breathe
s	sin	mason	kiss
z	zebra	posit	pose
ʃ(š)	shame	lashes	push
ʒ(ž)		measure	rouge
tʃ(č)	chin	kitchen	pitch
ʤ(ǰ)	jury	bludgeon	fudge
m	moon	dummy	room
n	noon	sunny	spoon
ŋ		singer	sing
h	hen	ahoy	
j(y)	year	beyond	
r	red	berry	deer
l	lot	silly	mill
w	wind	away	

Modern English consonant not fully native to the English inventory, for the /zj/ cluster from which it arose entered the language mainly in French and Latin loanwords. (This alien sound also developed in American English in words like *Asia(n)*, *emersion* and *version*, where British English has /ʃ/; /ʒ/ sometimes also occurs in American English in words like *transients* and phrases like *as yet* and *all these years*.) The uneven distribution in the pattern of Modern English consonants apparent in the list above reflects the historical development of these sounds.

3.3 Morphology

Old English morphology is considerably more complex than that of Middle English and Modern English. As a consequence of the phonological reductions and mergers described in Section 3.2, extensive syncretism of the OE distinctive inflections occurred, and the inflectional morphology of ModE exhibits only eight inflections. Only pronouns preserve anything resembling their OE complexity; adjectives and the definite article preserve the least. Here we describe the OE and ModE pronominal and adjectival systems, with briefer discussions of nouns, verbs and the definite article.

3.3.1 Nouns

	a-stems		*o-stems*	*athematics*
	M.	*Nt.*	*F.*	*M.*
Singular				
Nominative	stān	dēor	lār	fōt
Accusative	stān	dēor	lāre	fōt
Genitive	stānes	dēores	lāre	fōtes
Dative	stāne	dēore	lāre	fēt
Plural				
Nom./Acc.	stānas	dēor	lāra	fēt
Genitive	stāna	dēora	lāra	fōta
Dative	stānum	dēorum	lārum	fōtum

Old English had several noun declensions, both strong (from Indo-European vowel stems) and weak (from Indo-European consonant, i.e. -*n*, stems). Each noun carried a grammatical gender irrespective of its natural gender (although nouns with human referents show a notable fit between grammatical and natural gender). Nouns were inflected generally for three or four cases in the singular, three in the plural; the nominative and accusative are identical in the plural and also in most singular nouns; paradigms for *stān* 'stone', *dēor* 'animal', *lār* 'learning' and *fōt* 'foot' are illustrative.

From the *stān* declension come the productive Modern English genitive singular in -*s* and all the productive plurals, while the *fōt* declension has yielded the few nouns (like *foot*, *goose* and *tooth*; *louse* and *mouse*; and *man*) whose plurals, generalised from the nominative and accusative, exploit a functional vowel alternation instead of the common suffix in -*s*. This palatal mutation was caused by earlier assimilation of the stem vowels to suffixes. ModE relic phrases like 'a ten-foot pole' derive from the OE genitive plural (translated roughly 'a pole of ten feet'), whose form *fōta* has the reflex *foot*. From the *dēor* declension come ModE uninflected plurals like *deer* and *sheep*.

Other noun declensions in Old English showed variations according to the phonological characteristics of the stems at various periods in their development (and there was considerable dialectal variation). In Modern English the only productive forms of the genitive singular and of the plural are the reduced reflexes of the masculine *a*-stems, like which many older nouns have been analogically reformed and all new nouns are inflected. The plural and genitive morphemes have the same phonologically conditioned allomorphs, which by dissimilation have /-əz/ after stems ending in /s, z, ʃ, ʒ, tʃ, dʒ/, and by assimilation /-s/ after stems ending in other voiceless consonants and /-z/ after voiced segments. The plural and genitive morphemes exhibit syncretism (as in *boys'*) except when the plural noun is marked by a stem change, as in *women's, children's, geese's*. The genitive marker can be attached to such complex nouns as *his father in law's criticism* and *the president of the university's right to consultation* and even to more complex phrases such as *the geek I told you about's blog, one of the buddies I went with's coworkers* and *the person you sent it to's computer screen*.

3.3.2 Verbs

Like the other Germanic languages, Old English and its reflexes exhibit two types of verbs, called strong and weak by Jakob Grimm. While weak verbs (characteristically Germanic) exhibit a dental suffix (/d/ or /t/) in the preterit, strong verbs show an internal vowel change (characteristically Indo-European ablaut). OE had seven classes of strong verbs, with scattered reflexes surviving today, though starting even in OE many strong verbs became weak, while others were reformed analogically. Many OE strong verbs have developed regular ModE forms, with past tense and past participle suffixes in /-t/ or /-d/. Listed here are the principal parts (infinitive, past singular, past plural and past participle) for each OE verb class.

I	rīdan 'ride'	rād/ridon	geriden
II	sēoðan 'boil'	sēað/sudon	gesoden
III	bindan 'bind'	band/bundon	gebunden
IV	beran 'bear'	bær/bǣron	geboren
V	giefan 'give'	geaf/ġēafon	gegiefen
VI	standan 'stand'	stōd/stōdon	gestanden
VII	feallan 'fall'	fēoll/fēollon	gefeallen

From these principal parts can be formed the two tenses (present and preterit) in the indicative and subjunctive moods. A typical weak verb conjugation is provided here, making it apparent that while the present indicative exhibits three singular forms and one plural, the subjunctive contrasts only singular and plural forms. The twelve distinct forms of an OE weak verb have been reduced to four in ModE.

			Indicative	*Subjunctive*
Pres.	Sg.	1	dēme	
		2	dēmst/dēmest	dēme
		3	dēmþ/dēmeþ	
	Pl.		dēmaþ	dēmen
Pret.	Sg.	1	dēmde	
		2	dēmdest	dēmde
		3	dēmde	
	Pl.		dēmdon	dēmden
Gerund			tō dēmenne/dēmanne	
Pres. Part.			dēmende	
Past Part.			dēmed	

The OE verbal system is inflectionally a mere shadow of its Indo-European predecessors. By way of contrast, recall that Latin is inflected for active and passive voice, perfective and imperfective aspects and present, preterit and future tenses, as well as for several moods. On the other hand, the OE verb is a far cry from the periphrastic complexity of its modern counterpart in tense and aspect.

3.3.3 Articles

Though its pragmatically determined use is complicated, the Modern English definite article has only the single orthographic shape *the*, with standard pronunciations [ði] before vowels and [ðə] elsewhere. As shown here, the Old English demonstrative (forerunner of today's definite article) was formally complex, inflected in the singular for five cases (including the instrumental) in the masculine but with fewer distinctive case forms in the feminine and neuter. Neither the neuter singular nor the gender-neutral plural forms differentiated between nominative and accusative case forms.

	Singular			*Plural*
	M.	*F.*	*Nt.*	*M./F./Nt.*
Nom.	sē	sēo	þæt	þā
Acc.	þone	þā	þæt	þā
Gen.	þæs	þǣre	þæs	þāra
Dat.	þǣm	þǣre	þǣm	þǣm
Inst.	þȳ	þǣre	þȳ	

The initial consonant of the nominative masculine singular *sē* and feminine singular *sēo* differed from all other forms, which begin with /θ/, orthographic þ-. Thus, ModE *the* has no direct OE etymon but arose analogically from forms with initial /θ/, influenced by parallel Scandinavian forms introduced in the late eighth and the ninth centuries. By the Middle English period *þe* had become the invariant definite article in the north, whence it soon spread to all dialects. Chaucer uses only *the*. (Customary lack of stress on *the* fostered assimilation of the initial voiceless segment to the vocalic nucleus.)

Such a history is somewhat surprising for what is by far the most common word in Modern English. *The* occurs twice as often as its nearest competitor (*of*) in the British National Corpus and about half again as often as the verb *be* in all its forms combined. Remarkable also is the history of the indefinite article *a/an*, which likewise did not exist as such in Old English. Like ModE indefinite plurals, OE indefinites were frequently unmarked, except that *sum* 'a certain' and *ān* 'one' appear sometimes for emphasis and are declined like adjectives.

3.3.4 Adjectives

Like the definite article, Old English adjectives were formally more complex than those of Modern English. Inflectionally, they agreed with their head noun in gender, number and case in 'strong' and 'weak' declensions. The weak declension (with few distinctions) occurred with the highly inflected demonstratives or possessive pronouns. All other environments, including predicative usage, required the more varied strong declension. Thus, adjective inflections partly compensated for the relative lack of inflections in other parts of the noun phrase. Both strong and weak adjectival declensions are given here.

Strong Declension

| | Singular | | | Plural | | |
	M.	F.	Nt.	M.	F.	Nt.
Nom.	gōd	gōd	gōd	gōde	gōda	gōd
Acc.	gōdne	gōde	gōd	gōde	gōda	gōd
Gen.	gōdes	gōdre	gōdes	gōdra	gōdra	gōdra
Dat.	gōdum	gōdre	gōdum	gōdum	gōdum	gōdum
Inst.	gōde	gōdre	gōde			

Weak Declension

| | Singular | | | Plural |
	M.	F.	Nt.	M./F./Nt.
Nom.	gōda	gōde	gōde	gōdan
Acc.	gōdan	gōdan	gōde	gōdan
Gen.	gōdan	gōdan	gōdan	gōdra (-ena)
Dat.	gōdan	gōdan	gōdan	gōdum

Nothing of the inflectional system of OE adjectives remains in ModE.

3.3.5 Pronouns

Personal Pronouns

The Modern English pronominal paradigm maintains more of its earlier complexity than does any other form class, as can be seen here.

| | Old English | | | | | Modern English | | | | |
| | 1st | 2nd | 3rd Person | | | 1st | 2nd | 3rd Person | | |
			M.	F.	Nt.					
Singular										
Nom.	ic	þū	hē	hēo	hit	I	you	he	she	it
Acc.	mē	þē	hine	hīe	hit	me	you	him	her	it
Gen.	mīn	þīn	his	hiere	his	mine	yours	his	hers	its
Dat.	mē	þē	him	hiere	him	me	you	him	her	it
Dual										
Nom.	wit	git								
Acc.	unc	inc								
Gen.	uncer	incer								
Dat.	unc	inc								
Plural										
Nom.	wē	gē		hīe		we	you		they	
Acc.	ūs	ēow		hīe		us	you		them	
Gen.	ūre	ēower		hiera		ours	yours		theirs	
Dat.	ūs	ēow		him		us	you		them	

A striking difference between Old English and Modern English personal pronouns is the disappearance of the dual number. Further attrition appears in the loss of distinctive singular and plural second person pronouns, where the historical plural forms now serve ambiguously for singular and plural referents; in Middle and early Modern English, *thou*, *thee* and *thine*—reflexes of the OE singulars—developed specialized uses and then disappeared, occurring today only as relics.

With distinct singular and plural forms for first and third person pronouns, the utility of distinct singular and plural second person pronouns is highlighted in vernacular varieties today by several patently plural forms: *yous* in parts of England, Ireland and Australia; also in metropolitan New York City, parts of the northeast, and elsewhere in the United States, though by no means generally; *y'uns* in Western Pennsylvania and the Ohio Valley; and *y'all* in the American South. Recent decades have seen growing use of *you guys*, initially in the United States and increasingly in Britain. While the *OED* recognizes *yous* and *y'all*, it does not yet enter *you guys*, despite a citation from as early as 1896 (albeit with male addressees) and more than a score of subsequent ones pointing to increasingly gender-neutral usage. (Today such possessive forms as *you guys's* and even *your guys's*, though marginal, can be heard.)

Third person pronouns also show interesting developments. *Its*, the Modern English singular genitive neuter form, is not a reflex of Old English *his* but appeared toward the end of the sixteenth century, extended analogically from the nominative and accusative *hit*, thereby leaving the previously ambiguous *his* unambiguously masculine. The source of *she*, not a reflex of its OE counterpart *hēo*, remains puzzling although a probable origin lies in the feminine demonstrative *sēo* (or its variants *sīo*, *sīe*). Strikingly, too, present day plural *th-* forms are not reflexes of their OE counterparts; rather, *they*, *their* and *them* were borrowed from Scandinavian languages in Britain's north and gradually spread south in the course of Middle English.

At the present time, third person singular pronouns are again undergoing adjustment and accommodation. English has shown continuing tension between gender and number in pronoun use for antecedent nominals. Historically the use of inclusive *he* as an epicene pronoun for male and female referents is common, as in Tennyson's *He makes no friend who never made a foe* (from *OED*), as is the use of *he* and *she* in contrast, as in this *OED* 1509 citation: *He or she that mariage doth breke May fere of deth eternall whan they dye.* Commonly, too, a plural anaphoric *they* is used for indefinite singular, as well as plural, antecedents, as in *Evidently someone knows, don't they?* and *Anyone interested in taking up quilling should contact their local library* (from BNC). Prescriptivists as far back as the eighteenth century have objected to plural anaphoric pronouns after formally singular nominals and have privileged number agreement and generic *he*, discounting the socially more salient gender mismatch. Proposals for a gender-neutral third person singular pronoun such as *thon* and *na* have not succeeded (Baron 1986). During the 1970s and 1980s feminist scholars and others recognized that the use of ostensibly gender-neutral *he* often had the effect of erasing women's roles and contributions, and recent decades have seen increased use of *he or she*, as in *It is of little value to a child if he or she can express him or herself in words but is unable to write in a legible hand* (from BNC). Some commentators judge *he or she* to be awkward and instead recommend reformulations such as *It is of little value to children to express themselves in words if they are unable to write in a legible hand.* It is difficult to say whether singular *they* or a new epicene form will eventually succeed; it is probably safe to predict that generic *he* will continue to decrease in use.

Relative Pronouns

In Old English, an invariant particle *þe* served to mark relative clauses; it was often compounded with a form of the demonstrative *sē, sēo, þæt*, as in masculine *sē þe* and feminine *sēo þe* 'who'. The forms of *sē* also occur alone as relatives, as in *ānne æðeling sē wæs Cyneheard hāten* 'a prince who was called Cyneheard'. OE relatives are also sometimes marked by *þe* and a form of the personal pronoun, as in:

nis	nū	cwicra	nān	þe	ic	him	modsefan	minne	durre	āsecgan
there isn't	now	alive	no one	REL	I	him	mind	my	dare	speak

'There is no one alive now to whom I dare speak my mind.'

Middle English favoured solitary *that* as a relative pronoun, the OE indeclinable *þe* surviving only into early Middle English. In the fifteenth century, *which* (from the OE interrogative *hwylc* 'which') appears as a relative, alternating with *that*. Modern English relative *that*, a functionally adapted reflex of the OE demonstrative, is the relative with broadest pronominal application, anaphoric for noun phrases in nominative and oblique cases other than the possessive, though its use is now limited to restrictive clauses. The ModE relatives *who/whom/whose* and *which* derive from OE interrogative pronouns and can be used with restrictive and nonrestrictive clauses. *Whose* (< ME *whōs* by analogy to *whō* < OE *hwā* and to *whōm* < OE *hwām*) ultimately derives from the OE interrogative pronoun *hwæs*. *Who*, *whose* and *whom* are late developments; while Chaucer occasionally used relative *whose* and *whom*, relative *who* did not come into widespread use until the sixteenth century.

3.4 Syntax

Old English is a synthetic language, relying partly on inflectional morphology to indicate grammatical relations of noun phrases and, to a lesser extent, their semantic roles. Its noun phrases exhibit concord in gender, number and case among the demonstrative/ definite article, adjective and noun, with gender a grammatical rather than semantic category. Verbs are inflected for person, number and tense (present and preterit) in indicative and subjunctive moods, the subjunctive occurring far more frequently than in Modern English. Passive voice is signalled periphrastically with *wesan* 'to be' or *weorþan* 'to become' and a past participle; infinitives are sometimes employed passively, and the verb *hātan* 'be called' is generally used with passive force.

As to its word order, late Old English exhibits patterns similar in many respects to those of Modern English. Both show a strong preference for SVO, which ModE exploits in both independent and subordinate clauses, whereas OE, like Modern German, prefers verb-final subordinate clauses. While SOV patterns occur in almost 30 per cent of OE sentences, the twelfth century witnessed the development of an almost exclusively SVO pattern (according to J. Smith, as reported in Hawkins 1983). OE negative sentences introduced by the particle *ne* favour verb-second position, producing a VS order as in the first clause of *ne geseah ic næfre þā burg, ne ic þone sēaþ nāt* 'I have never seen that city, nor do I know the well'. Also apparent in that example is the characteristic negative concord (*ne/næfre* in the first clause; *ne/nāt* in the second, where *nāt* is a contraction of *ne wāt* from *witan* 'to know'). Clauses introduced by *þā* 'then' or *hēr* 'here, in this year' also commonly exhibit verb-second order, as in *þā andswarode Satanas and cwæþ* … 'then Satan answered and said … '; *þā gegaderode Ælfred cyning his fierd* 'then King Alfred gathered his army'; *hēr gefeaht Ecgbryht cyning wiþ fīf and þritig sciphlæsta æt Carrum* 'in this year King Ecgbryht fought against thirty-five shiploads at Charmouth'.

Within Old English noun phrases, the order of elements is usually determiner-adjective-noun, as in Modern English: *sē gōda mann* 'the good man'. Genitives usually precede nouns (far more frequently than in ModE), as in *folces weard* 'people's protector', *mæres līfes man* 'a man of splendid life' and *fōtes trym* 'the space of a foot'. It has been calculated that the percentage of postnominal genitives increased from about 13 per cent in the year 1035 to 85 per cent in 1300 (J. Smith, as reported in Hawkins 1983). Though prepositions usually precede nominals, with pronouns they often follow, as in *sē hālga Andreas him tō cwæþ* ... 'St Andrew said to him ... '. Adjectives too are almost uniformly prenominal (*sē foresprecena here* 'the aforementioned army'), but modifiers can be postnominal, as in these isolated examples cited by Quirk and Wrenn (1955:88–89): *wadu weallendu* 'surging waters'; *ēþel þysne* 'this country'; *wine mīn Unferð* 'my friend Unferð'. Relative clauses generally follow their head nouns.

To a greater degree than Modern English, Old English exhibits a preference for parataxis over hypotaxis. Much OE prose and poetry was written as a series of loosely associated independent clauses, often linked solely by *and*, leaving relationships among succeeding clauses unspecified. While certain genres of informal speech exhibit considerable parataxis in ModE, writing and most spoken genres exploit a high degree of hypotaxis, with logical relationships among clauses marked explicitly by subordinators (*that*, *as*, *if*, *than* and *like* being frequent exemplars).

Denied its earlier inflectional signposts, Modern English developed into an analytical language, more like Chinese than Latin and other early reflexes of Indo-European. With nouns inflected only for possessive case, the chief signal of grammatical relations is now word order, displacing inflectional morphology to such an extent that even the comparatively fuller pronominal inflections are subordinate to the grammatical relations signalled by word order; consequently, an utterance like **her kicked he* may be understood as *she kicked him*.

Why English should have advanced farther along the path to analyticity than other Germanic languages is not altogether clear. A likely basis for explanation lies in the thoroughgoing contact between the Danes and the English after the ninth century, in French ascendance over English for many secular and religious purposes in early Middle English, and in the preservation of the vernacular chiefly in folk speech during the eleventh and twelfth centuries. Decades before the Norman conquest (almost a century earlier in Northumbria), those inflectional reductions started that are everywhere apparent when written English reemerges, and they were doubtless more advanced in speech than extant texts indicate. The syncretism spread as word-order patterns became fixed. Thus, phonological reductions undermined the inflectional morphology and, as flexion grew less able to signal grammatical relations and semantic roles, word order and prepositions (which had somewhat redundantly borne certain aspects of meaning) came to bear those communicative tasks less redundantly. Gradually the freer word order of Old English yielded to the relatively fixed orders of Modern English, whose linear arrangements are the chief carrier of grammatical relations.

Spurred possibly by the virtual absence of inflectional differentiation in its nouns, English syntax has evolved to permit unusually free interplay among grammatical relations and semantic roles. With nouns marked only for genitive case and most pronouns additionally for objective case, Modern English subjects represent a wide range of participant roles. Besides being agents (as in sentence (a)), they may be patients (b), instruments (c), benefactives (d), experiencers (e), locatives (f), temporals (g) and so on; dummy subjects, empty of any semantic content, also occur as in (h):

(a) The janitor (agent) opened the door.
(b) The door (patient) opened.
(c) His first record (instrument) expanded his audiences to thousands of strangers.

(d) The youngest jockey (benefactive) took the prize.
(e) Serge (experiencer) heard his father whispering.
(f) Chicago (locative) is cold in winter.
(g) The next day (temporal) found us on the road to Alice Springs.
(h) It became clear that the government had jailed him there.

In representing pragmatic structure, Modern English exploits neither morphology nor simple fronting to mark focus, leaving sentences like *Nobody expected revolution* focus-neutral. Spoken English exploits sentence stress to signal focus on particular constituents. To carry out pragmatic functions in writing, where intonation is unavailable and the constraints on syntax imposed by real-time processing of speech are reduced, English has a range of syntactic processes, including passivisation, clefting and pseudo-clefting. In the archetypal focusing of noun phrases that is apparent in questions, English does front, as in *What did she win? What did they do?* and *Who(m) did he choose?* Likewise, in relative clauses the relativised noun phrase is fronted irrespective of its grammatical relation within the clause and its participant role in the semantic structure; noun phrases of any grammatical relation can be relativised. In (i) below, the fronted relative pronoun *that* is semantically a recipient functioning grammatically as an oblique; in (j), it is a patient functioning as a direct object.

(i) She's the teacher that I gave the book to.
(j) The president vetoed the bill that his party endorsed.

The flexibility of English syntax in carrying out pragmatic functions permits a high degree of discrepancy between surface form and semantic structure. Thus, the syntactic processes known as subject-to-object raising (illustrated in (k)), subject-to-subject raising (l) and object-to-subject raising (m) all reduce the isomorphism between surface syntactic structure and underlying semantic structure.

(k) The coach wanted her to win the race.
(l) The economy seems to be sluggish.
(m) An incumbent is always tough to beat.

In (k), the underlying subject of the subordinate verb *win* appears as a surface object of the verb *wanted*. In (l), the underlying subject of *to be sluggish* becomes the surface subject of *seems*. In (m), the underlying object of *to beat* serves as the surface subject of the predicate *is ... tough*. As a comparison with the treatments of syntax in the chapters on Russian and German will indicate, English has an exceptionally versatile syntax.

3.5 Orthography

Modern English orthographical practice is more out of harmony with the spoken language than that of many other languages, including Spanish, German and Old English. Today's spelling patterns reflect scribal practices older than the introduction of printing into England by William Caxton in 1476. Since then the relatively static spelling practices have not kept pace with pronunciation despite attempts by reformers like Noah Webster (whose dictionaries popularised many of the characteristic spelling differences between

American and British orthography) and George Bernard Shaw (who famously observed that English permitted *ghoti* to be pronounced *fish*: *gh* as in *cough*, *o* as in *women*, and *ti* as in *nation*). Despite its exaggeration, Shaw's claim highlights the inconsistency in English spelling.

Still, there are advantages to the relative distance between orthography and pronunciation in that written English (but not pronunciation) is strikingly uniform throughout the world, and printed material can be distributed internationally. Further, because English exhibits considerable variation in the pronunciation of a given morpheme in different words, a closer correspondence of written to spoken forms would deprive readers of the manifest association between words like *nation* and *nation+al* (with /e/-/æ/ alternation) and *electric* and *electric+ity* (with /k/-/s/), to cite just a single vowel and a single consonant alternation.

4 Present-day English and its Variation

4.1 Regional and Standard Varieties

As described earlier, English is widely diffused from its earlier home in Britain across the Atlantic to North America and still farther to Australia and New Zealand; it has spread to parts of Asia and Africa and is spoken in isolated enclaves like the Falkland Islands, Bermuda and Tristan da Cunha. Various pidgins, creoles and creole-based varieties also exist, including Krio, spoken as a lingua franca throughout Sierra Leone.

Widely accepted is the view that standard varieties occur roughly in British and (North) American types. To the latter belong the varieties spoken in Canada and the United States, while the British type comprises the varieties principally of England, Wales, Australia, New Zealand and South Africa, with Ireland and Scotland having more complex affiliations. Differences among the standard varieties include some syntactic features but are largely matters of pronunciation and lexicon, although vocabulary differences are not strongly apparent in public discourse. Not governed by uniform standards of pronunciation or vocabulary, speakers throughout the English-speaking world show considerable variation, certainly in their vernaculars but also in standard spoken varieties. National varieties are in the process of codification with dictionaries and usage guides of their own (e.g., Allsopp 1996, Barber 2004, Peters 2007, Ramson 1989).

A good deal about regional features of English, especially in Britain and North America, is known from studies of dialect geography. (See Orton 1962–71 for England and Carver 1987 and Kretzschmar 2004 for references to atlases for the United States and Canada.) *The Atlas of North American English* (Labov et al. 2006) identifies major patterns of vowel shifting, reminiscent of the Great Vowel Shift. Currently underway in the large urban areas on both sides of the U.S./Canada border is the Northern Cities Shift, characterised among other ways by a merger of the low back vowels /ɔ/ and /ɑ/ that makes homonyms of previously distinct pairs like *walk/wok* and *dawn/don*. In the American South, a pattern known as the Southern Shift shows these vowel shifts, among others: the diphthong /aj/ becomes a monophthong in words like *eye* and *time*; the /e/ of *made* and *take* lowers and diphthongises to /aj/; the /ɑ/ of *card* merges with the /ɔ/ of *cord*; the /u/ of *cooed* and /o/ of *code* are fronted; the front lax vowels /ɪ/ and /æ/

are raised and fronted. These extraordinary shifts underscore the continuing instability of the English vowel system.

Excepting principally post-vocalic /r/ and intervocalic /t/, pronunciation of consonants tends to vary socially more than regionally, as we shall see below. There is considerable regional variation in vocabulary especially in folk speech, and regional vocabulary can inspire local pride. With televised speechmaking and press conferences broadcast worldwide, lexical diversity has all but vanished from the public remarks of national leaders, though distinctive national pronunciations remain. Grammatically, few differences in the public speech of political leaders can be noted, and these are typically understood across national boundaries. Vernaculars no doubt tell a very different story.

Quantitative differences in grammar between British and American English are coming to light from corpus studies. Analysis of the Longman Corpus (Biber et al. 1999:216) indicates that interrogative clauses with lexical *have*, as in *Do you have a/ any ... ?*, occur virtually 100 per cent of the time in American conversation, whereas *Have you a/any ... ?* and *Have you got a/any ... ?* account for 80 percent of the British examples. Likewise, British speakers elide initial subjects as much as three times more frequently than American speakers in such replies to questions as *Dunno* and *Depends what you call well off, really* (Biber et al. 1999:1106).

National and regional standards of pronunciation exist but with broad tolerance of variation. RP (Received Pronunciation), until recently associated with the BBC and Britain's prestigious 'public' schools, is spoken only by an estimated three to five per cent of England's population (Trudgill and Hannah 2002:9). Increasingly favoured is an accent varying along a continuum between RP and the regional dialect of London and the Thames estuary and called Estuary English (McArthur 2002). More so in the press than in scholarly venues, considerable ink has been spilled discussing this variety and the appropriateness of its label. The spread of Estuary English transports with it its Cockney echoes, including the glottal stop [?] for intervocalic /t/ in words like *water* and *bitter* and the pronunciation of post-vocalic /l/ as [w] in words like *pool* and *milk*.

In the United States, considerable latitude occurs in standard pronunciations although a 'network standard' (essentially a form of inland northern dialect) dominates broadcasting. Hints of regional origin are heard in the accents of national news broadcasters, and the marked accents of recent American presidents identify their regional origins. Limited ethnic pronunciations can also be heard, not usually in news reports themselves but for example when Latino broadcasters pronounce Latino names.

By contrast, forceful standards of writing permit surprisingly little variation in grammar, lexicon or spelling. In the major centres of publishing within America, as in England, little if any regional variation exists except that, while Canada follows British precedent in certain matters, it increasingly follows American precedent in others. Internationally, some spelling variation exists in, for example, the familiar *-or/-our*, *-er/-re* and *-ize/-ise* distinctions, along with certain matters of punctuation such as the sequencing of periods and commas in relation to quotation marks. As *The New York Times* and *Los Angeles Times*, published 2,500 miles apart, exhibit no regional linguistic differences, so only slight variation in linguistic features arises in the 3,500 mile distance between, say, *The Economist* of London and New York's *Newsweek* magazine. Established printing conventions and a long-standing multinational grammatical and lexicographic tradition combine to mute the variation characteristic of English speechways and keep it from impeding written communication across intra-national or international dialect boundaries.

4.2 Social Variation

Linguistic variation across social groups in English-speaking communities displays highly systematic patterns in morphology, syntax and phonology. In many instances, the same phonological alternants vary in parallel across social groups and across speech styles. For example, the final nasal in the suffix -ing (dancing, teaching) may be pronounced with alveolar /n/ or velar /ŋ/. To illustrate with two widely separated communities, residents belonging to higher ranked socioeconomic status groups in New York City and Norwich, England, pronounce the velar variant /ŋ/ more frequently than do members of successively lower ranked groups. Further, members of all socioeconomic status groups pronounce the velar nasal /ŋ/ with increasing frequency through several graded speech styles (casual speech, interview style and reading passages).

In New York City similar patterns characterise variation of other phonological variables: postvocalic /r/ in the car and beard classes of words; voiceless th in words like thirty and with and voiced th in words like this, brother and breathe (producing the infamous 'dis' and 'dat'); the stressed vowels in the coffee, soft, law and bad, banned, family word sets. For some of these and certain other sounds, similar patterns appear in Norwich (as in many other locales). These sounds and others show systematic variation in which typically standard pronunciations are more frequent both among higher socioeconomic status groups and in styles with increased attention paid to speech (see Labov (1972, 2006) for New York City and Trudgill (1974) for Norwich). In general, then, such phonological variation indexes social group affiliation and social situations.

Table 3.2 shows that alternation between /n/ and /ŋ/ in the suffix -ing for residents of Norwich and New York City reflects socioeconomic status and speaking style. The pronunciation -in' (with alveolar /n/) increases among successively lower ranked status groups (from I through IV or V). To put it the other way around, for each status group the -in' pronunciations decrease from casual speech (A) through careful speech (B) to reading style (C).

Similar patterns of distribution are likely for phonological variables wherever comparable social stratification exists, and further investigation will likely identify similarly patterned morphological and syntactic variation. Such linguistic variation is not semantically significant, but it carries social significance in that it indexes group membership and social situations.

Table 3.2 Per cent of Pronunciation of -ing Suffix as /ɪn/ for Three Styles and Several Socioeconomic Status Groups in Norwich and New York City

	Norwich			New York City		
	A	B	C	A	B	C
I	28	3	0	5	4	0
II	42	15	10	32	21	1
III	87	74	15	49	31	11
IV	95	88	44	80	53	22
V	100	98	66			

Source: Labov 1972: 239; Trudgill 1974: 92.

Notes: A = Casual Speech; B = Careful or Formal Speech; C = Reading Style. Roman numerals refer to socioeconomic groups: Norwich: I = MMC; II = LMC; III = UWC; IV = MWC; V = LWC; New York City: I = UMC; II = LMC; III = WC; IV = LC.

4.3 Variation across Modes: Writing and Speaking

Following conflicting published reports about the linguistic characteristics of written and spoken texts, exploration of large-scale corpora has enabled researchers more systematically to investigate the influence of mode on syntactic complexity, nominal and verbal style, the signalling of pragmatic focus, syntactic constraints imposed by real-time processing and means of establishing coherence, among others. Studies have demonstrated that linguistic differences between speech and writing cannot be adequately characterised using any single dimension such as 'complexity' or 'reliance on context'. Only a multi-dimensional construct can account for the distribution of textual features (Biber 1988), with each dimension defined by a set of co-occurring lexical and syntactic features that vary among texts.

For example, along one dimension (designated 'abstract vs. situated content' by Biber) a text is situated relative to others by the degree to which it exploits the defining features of that dimension: nominalisations, prepositions, passives and *it*-clefts (which mark abstract content) versus time and place adverbs, relative pronoun deletion and subordinator *that* deletion (which mark situated content). That same text would be situated along the 'interactive vs. edited' dimension by the degree to which it exploits a different set of features: *wh*-questions and other questions, *that*-clauses and *if*-clauses, final prepositions, contractions, the pronouns *I*, *you* and *it*, general emphatics (*just, really, so* + adjective), shorter words and a low degree of lexical diversity (characteristic of interactive discourse). A third dimension representing 'reported vs. immediate style' characterises measures of past tense markers, third person pronouns, perfect aspect and an absence of adjectives. The model creates a multi-dimensional space throughout which texts are distributed according to their exploitation of the defining feature sets of each dimension. Texts cannot be differentiated along a single dimension of, say, 'complexity' because the linguistic features commonly taken to represent complexity do not in fact co-occur significantly within texts.

4.4 Register Variation

Computerised corpora have also proven fruitful in the analysis of register variation or variation in linguistic style across situations of use. In the fifteen prose genres (or registers) of the million-word Brown Corpus, the most evenly distributed form classes are function words (articles, coordinating and subordinating conjunctions, infinitival *to*, determiners and prepositions) and the least evenly distributed classes are interjections, personal pronouns, adverbs/particles and past tense in main verbs (Francis and Kučera 1982). With frequent nouns, prepositions and adjectives, informational genres such as press and academic journals are strikingly more nominal than imaginative prose genres such as romantic fiction and science fiction, which are more verbal, exhibiting frequent verbs and adverbs. Similarly, a lopsided representation of pronominal anaphora indicates that imaginative prose genres use that feature as a major device for establishing textual cohesion (Francis and Kučera 1982).

Sentence length, in part because it is assumed to index structural complexity and thus comprehensibility, is a frequent object of analysis. All the informational genres in the Brown Corpus exhibit mean sentence lengths greater than the corpus mean of 18.4 words, while all the imaginative prose genres exhibit sentence lengths less than the corpus mean. That may seem to suggest that informational genres are characterised by sentences of greater complexity than those of imaginative genres, but more refined calculations show that informational prose genres are not structurally more complex than imaginative prose; instead, they deploy more words per predication. The nine informational genres of the Brown Corpus range from 2.59 to 2.93 predications per sentence, with press-reportage, press-reviews and skills/hobbies falling slightly below the corpus mean of 2.64 predications. The imaginative genres, on the other hand, range from 2.23 predications per sentence for science fiction to 2.82 for humour, the latter thus ranking well above the corpus mean. Further, all the informational genres exhibit more words per predication than the corpus mean of 6.96, while all the imaginative genres exhibit fewer, as shown in Table 3.3, with data from Francis and Kučera (1982). (LOB, or the Lancaster-Oslo/Bergen Corpus, a British counterpart to the Brown Corpus, is described in Johansson and Hofland (1989).)

Corpus analysis reveals other differences across registers. The Longman Corpus, comprising 40 million words of conversation, fiction, newspaper texts and academic prose, both British and American, documents just how frequent questions are in conversation, occurring once in every 40 running words, and that they occur in fiction less than a third that often; not surprisingly, questions occur about 50 times more frequently in conversation than in newspaper texts or academic prose (see Biber et al. 1999).

The 100-million-word BNC, containing conversation and task-oriented speech as well as imaginative and informational writing, is being mined for insight. In the BNC, for example, some word classes or subclasses such as proper and common nouns, articles, adjectives, prepositions past-tense lexical verbs (*gave*, *worked*) and coordinating conjunctions occur lopsidedly in writing, whereas others are far more characteristic of speech, including not only interjections and personal pronouns, but singular determiners (*this*, *another*), base form lexical verbs (*give*, *work*), base forms *have* and *do*, modal auxiliaries, adverbs, the negatives *not* and *-n't* and subordinating conjunctions (excluding *than*). More characteristic of task-oriented speech than of conversation are nouns, articles, adjectives, coordinating conjunctions (excluding *but*) and prepositions, while conversation shows significantly higher frequencies of personal pronouns and adverbs, among others. (These and other findings appear in Leech et al. 2001.) Such findings enrich prior descriptions of English and challenge theorists to explain, for example, the relationship between the psychological, or processing, functions of textual features and the social value that attaches to functionally conditioned distributions.

It is too early to assess with confidence the extent and character of any influence on the language that might be prompted or promoted by phenomena such as the Internet, new registers such as instant messaging, and the increase and persistence of international telemarketing. Still, given the distribution of linguistic features apparent across established registers and given the substantial changes occurring in English vocabulary and in English vowels, further and dramatic changes in spoken and written English are highly likely.

Table 3.3 Frequency of Words and Predications in the Brown Corpus

	INFO	*IMAG*	*CORPUS*
Words per sentence	21.06	13.38	18.40
Predications per sentence	2.78	2.38	2.64
Words per predication	7.57	5.62	6.96

Recent decades have also seen increasing attention on 'new' Englishes and 'world' English. The International Corpus of English is being compiled under the auspices of University College London, where million-word corpora of several Englishes are completed and available, including those for Hong Kong, East Africa, India, the Philippines, and Singapore. There can be no doubt that in the decades to come these Englishes and the burgeoning investigations of them will greatly affect English and our perceptions of English. Just what those effects and perceptions will be remains to be seen and heard.

Bibliography

Standard grammars include Quirk et al. (1985), Biber et al. (1999) and Huddleston and Pullum (2002).

Jespersen (1982) is a classic history of English. Algeo and Pyles (2004) and Hogg and Denison (2006) offer balanced treatments of internal and external history; Baugh and Cable (2002) excels at external history; the six volume Cambridge history (Hogg 1992–2001), with four chronological and two topical volumes, is thorough. For vocabulary, see Jespersen (1982) and Baugh and Cable (2002) for French borrowings and Serjeantson (1935) for Latin. Grammars of Old English include Quirk and Wrenn (1955), strong on phonology and morphology, and Mitchell (2006), strong on syntax; Mossé (1968) is a standard work for Middle English. An independent view of the interaction of culture and the history of English, with an attentive eye to the effects of media and corpora, can be found in Knowles (1997).

Detailed studies of sociolinguistic variation and phonological change are available in Labov (2006) and Labov et al. (2006). Mencken (1963) deals with the development of American English; Ferguson and Heath (1981) contains 23 essays taking essentially ethnographic and sociolinguistic approaches to the former and current languages of the USA; Finegan and Rickford complements that volume with analyses principally of English varieties. Comparable volumes are, for the British Isles, Trudgill (1984) and Britain (2007) and, for Canada, Edwards (1998). Changing attitudes towards standard English are discussed by Milroy and Milroy (1999); Trudgill and Hannah (2002) deals with cross-national variation within standard English, especially British versus American; Trudgill (2000) and Hughes and Trudgill (1987) treat traditional and modern dialects of England. For regional variation in England see Orton (1962–71), Orton and Wright (1974) and Orton et al. (1978); for regional variation in the USA see Carver (1989), Cassidy and Hall (1985–), Kurath and McDavid (1962); more recent North American work is readily referenced in Kretzschmar (2004). Lighter (1994–) is a major reference work on American slang. For discussion of gender and epicene pronouns see Baron (1986) and Curzan (2003).

Crystal (2003) discusses global English; McArthur (2002) and Trudgill and Hannah (2002) discuss world Englishes and new Englishes. See also Burchfield (1994), Greenbaum (1996), and the Website for International Corpus of English for more on other Englishes. Crystal (2006) discusses possible effects of the Internet on English and on language more generally.

Among works concerned with computerised corpora and their use in stylistic research, useful references are Francis and Kučera (1982), Johansson and Hofland (1989), and Biber (1988); the quantitative findings from the BNC reported in this chapter come from Leech et al. (2001).

References

Algeo, J. and Pyles, T. 2004. *The Origins and Development of the English Language*, 5th ed. (Heinle, Boston)

Allsopp, R. (ed.) 1996. *Dictionary of Caribbean English Usage* (Oxford University Press, Oxford) (reprinted University of the West Indies, Kingston, Jamaica, 2003)

Barber, K. 2004. *The Canadian Oxford Dictionary*, 2nd edn (Oxford University Press, Toronto)

Baron, D. 1986. *Grammar and Gender* (Yale University Press, New Haven)

Baugh, A. C. and Cable, T. 2002. *A History of the English Language*, 5th edn (Routledge, London)

Biber, D. 1988. *Variation across Speech and Writing* (Cambridge University Press, Cambridge)

Biber, D., Johansson, S. Leech, G. Conrad, S. and Finegan, E. 1999. *Longman Grammar of Spoken and Written English* (Longman, Harlow)

Britain, D. (ed.) 2007. *Language in the British Isles* (Cambridge University Press, Cambridge)

Burchfield, R. W. (ed.) 1994. *The Cambridge History of the English Language. Vol. 5. English in Britain and Overseas: Origin and Development* (Cambridge University Press, Cambridge)

Bynon, T. 1977. *Historical Linguistics* (Cambridge University Press, Cambridge)

Carver, C. 1987. *American Regional English: A Word Geography* (University of Michigan Press, Ann Arbor)

Cassidy, F. G. and Hall, J. (eds.) 1985 –. *Dictionary of American Regional English* (Harvard University Press, Cambridge, MA)

Crystal, D. 2003. *English as a Global Language*, 2nd edn (Cambridge University Press, Cambridge)

—— 2006. *Language and the Internet*, 2nd edn (Cambridge University Press, Cambridge)

Curzan, A. 2003. *Gender Shifts in the History of English* (Cambridge University Press, Cambridge)

Edwards, J. (ed.) 1998. *Language in Canada* (Cambridge University Press, Cambridge)

Ferguson, C. A. and Heath, S. B. (eds) 1981. *Language in the USA* (Cambridge University Press, Cambridge)

Finegan, E. and Rickford, J. R. (eds) 2004. *Language in the USA: Themes for the Twenty-first Century* (Cambridge University Press, Cambridge)

Francis, W. N. and Kučera, H. 1982. *Frequency Analysis of English Usage: Lexicon and Grammar* (Houghton Mifflin, Boston)

Greenbaum, S. (ed.) 1996. *Comparing English Worldwide: The International Corpus of English* (Clarendon Press, Oxford)

Hughes, A. and Trudgill, P. 1987. *English Accents and Dialects: An Introduction to Social and Regional Varieties of British English* (Edward Arnold, London)

Hogg, R. (ed.) 1992–2001. *The Cambridge History of the English Language*, 6 vols. (Cambridge University Press, Cambridge)

Hogg, R. and Denison, D. (eds) 2006. *A History of the English Language* (Cambridge University Press, Cambridge)

Huddleston, R. and Pullum, G. 2002. *The Cambridge Grammar of the English Language* (Cambridge University Press, Cambridge)

Jespersen, O. 1982. *Growth and Structure of the English Language*, 10th edn (University of Chicago Press, Chicago)

Johansson, S. and Hofland, K. 1989. *Frequency Analysis of English Vocabulary and Grammar: Based on the LOB Corpus*, 2 vols. (Clarendon Press, Oxford)

Knowles, G. 1997. *A Cultural History of the English Language* (Hodder Arnold, London)

Kretzschmar, W. A., Jr. 2004. 'Regional Dialects', in Finegan and Rickford, pp. 39–57

Kučera, H. 1982. 'The Mathematics of Language', in *The American Heritage Dictionary*, 2nd college edn (Houghton Mifflin, Boston), pp. 37–41

—— and Francis, W. N. 1967. *Computational Analysis of Present-Day American English* (Brown University Press, Providence, R.I.)

Kurath, H. 1964. *A Phonology and Prosody of Modern English* (University of Michigan Press, Ann Arbor)

Kurath, H. and McDavid, R. I. Jr. 1962. *Pronunciation of English in the Atlantic States* (University of Michigan Press, Ann Arbor)

Labov, W. 1972. *Sociolinguistic Patterns* (University of Pennsylvania Press, Philadelphia)

—— 2006. *The Social Stratification of English in New York City*, 2nd edn (Cambridge University Press, Cambridge)

Labov, W., Ash, S. and Boberg, C. 2006. *The Atlas of North American English: Phonetics, Phonology, and Sound Change* (Mouton de Gruyter, Berlin)

Leech, G., Rayson, P. and Wilson, A. 2001. *Word Frequencies in Written and Spoken English: Based on the British National Corpus* (Longman, Harlow)

Lighter, J. E. (ed.) 1994–. *Historical Dictionary of American Slang* (Random House, New York)

McArthur, T. 2002. *The Oxford Guide to World English* (Oxford University Press, Oxford)

Mencken, H. L. 1963. *The American Language: An Inquiry into the Development of English in the United States*, 4th edn and two supplements, abridged, with annotations and new material by Raven I. McDavid, Jr. (Alfred A. Knopf, New York)

Milroy, J. and Milroy, L. 1999. *Authority in Language*, 3rd edn (Routledge, London)

Mitchell, B. 2006. *A Guide to Old English*, 7th edn (Blackwell, Oxford)

Mossé, F. 1968. *A Handbook of Middle English*, translated by J. A. Walker (The Johns Hopkins Press, Baltimore)

Orton, H. 1962–71. *A Survey of English Dialects* (E. J. Arnold, Leeds)

——, Sanderson, S. and Widdowson, J. (eds) 1978. *The Linguistic Atlas of England* (Routledge, London)

—— and Wright, N. 1974. *A Word Geography of England* (Seminar Press, London)

Peters, Pam. 2007. *The Cambridge Guide to Australian English Usage* (Cambridge University Press, Cambridge)

Quirk, R. and Wrenn, C. L. 1955. *An Old English Grammar* (Methuen, London and Holt, Rinehart and Winston, New York)

Quirk, R., Greenbaum, S. Leech, G. and Svartvik, J. 1985. *A Comprehensive Grammar of the English Language* (Longman, London)

Ramson, W. S. (ed.) 1989. *The Australian National Dictionary: A Dictionary of Australianisms on Historical Principles* (Oxford University Press, Ontario)

Serjeantson, M. S. 1935. *A History of Foreign Words in English* (reprinted Routledge and Kegan Paul, London, 1961)

Silva, P. (ed.) 1996. *A Dictionary of South African English on Historical Principles*. (Oxford University Press: Oxford)

Trudgill, P. 1974. *The Social Differentiation of English in Norwich* (Cambridge University Press, Cambridge)

—— (ed.) 1984. *Language in the British Isles* (Cambridge University Press, Cambridge)

—— 2000. *The Dialects of England* (Blackwell, Oxford)

—— and Hannah, J. 2002. *International English: A Guide to the Varieties of Standard English*, 4th edn (Arnold, London)

4

German

John A. Hawkins

1 Historical Background

German, together with English, Frisian and Dutch (including Afrikaans and Flemish), is a member of the West Germanic group within the Germanic branch of Indo-European. It is currently used by over 90 million speakers in European countries in which it has official national language status (either alone or in conjunction with other languages): the Federal Republic of Germany, united as of 1990 with the former German Democratic Republic (almost 80 million users); Austria (7.5 million); Switzerland (4.2 million); Luxembourg (360,000 users of the Lëtzebuergesch dialect); and Liechtenstein (15,000). Bordering on the official German-language areas there are some sizable German-speaking minorities in Western Europe: Alsace (perhaps 1 million users); Lorraine (some 300,000); South Tirol and other parts of Italy (270,000); and Belgium (up to 90,000). In Eastern Europe there were, until recently at least, as many as two million people with German as their mother tongue: in the former Soviet Union (1.2 million); Romania (400,000); Hungary (250,000); the former Czechoslovakia (100,000); Poland (20,000); and the former Yugoslavia (20,000).

Outside Europe, German is an ethnic minority language in numerous countries to which Germans have emigrated. The extent to which German is still used by these groups varies, and in all cases there is gradual assimilation to the host language from one generation to the next. Nonetheless, there may be as many as nine million people who consider German their mother tongue in countries such as the following: USA (6.1 million according to the 1970 census); Brazil (1.5 million); Canada (561,000); Argentina (400,000); Australia (135,000); South Africa (50,000); Chile (35,000); and Mexico (17,000). Between one and three million of the German speakers outside the official German-speaking countries speak Yiddish, or Judaeo-German, which has undergone strong lexical influence from Hebrew and Slavonic. About half of them live in the USA. Some 300,000 Americans are native speakers of a variant of German called Pennsylvania German or Pennsylvania Dutch.

Map 4.1 gives an indication of the major regional dialects of German within Europe. There are three main groupings of these dialects: Low German in the north (comprising

Map 4.1 Dialects and Dialect Groups.
Source: Adapted from Clyne 1984.

North Lower Saxon, Westphalian etc.); Central German (comprising Middle Franconian, Rhine Franconian, Thuringian etc.); and Upper German in the south (comprising Swabian, Alemannic etc.).

The major basis for the threefold division involves the extent to which the Second Sound Shift of the Old High German period was carried out (cf. below for discussion of the historical periods of German). It changed voiceless stops *p*, *t*, *k* to voiceless fricatives *f*, *s*, *x* ([ç] or [x]) and affricates *pf*, *ts*, *kx*; and voiced stops *b*, *d*, *g* to voiceless stops *p*, *t*, *k*. The Low German dialects (as well as Dutch, Frisian and English) were unaffected by these changes. The Central German dialects carried them out in varying degrees, and Upper German carried them out (almost) completely. The following pairs of words provide examples:

Low German *p*ad, Upper German *Pf*ad (English *p*ath)
Low German ski*p*, Upper German Schi*ff* (English shi*p*)
Low German hei*t*, Upper German hei*ss* (English ho*t*)
Low German i*k*, Upper German i*ch* (English I)
Low German bö*k*, Upper German Bu*ch* (English boo*k*)
Low German, Central German *K*uh, Swiss German *Ch*ue (English *c*ow)
Low German *b*äk, Upper German (Bavarian) *P*ach (English *b*rook)
Low German *d*ör, Upper German *T*ür (English *d*oor)
Low German genuch, Upper German (Bavarian) *k*enug (English enough)

The increasing realisation of these changes within the Central German dialects is illustrated for some representative words involving the *p*, *t*, *k* shifts in Map 4.2.

The gradual conversion of these voiceless stops to the corresponding fricatives or affricates follows the progression shown in Map 4.2, and hence there are dialects of German whose pronunciation of these words corresponds to each of the lines, with Low German shifting at most *ik* to *ich* and Upper German completing all the shifts:

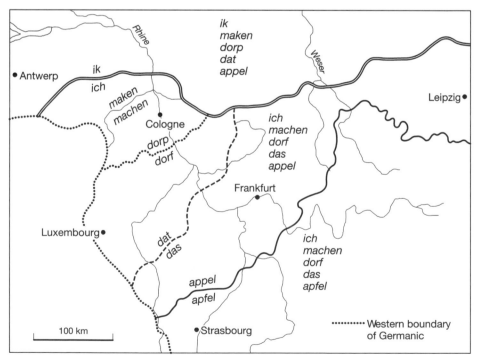

Map 4.2 Isoglosses Resulting from the Second Sound Shift.
Source: Adapted from T. Bynon, 1977, *Historical Linguistics* (Cambridge University Press, Cambridge).

'I'	'make'	'village'	'that'	'apple'	'pound'	
ik	malen	dorp	dat	appel	pund	Low german
ich	maken	dorp	dat	appel	pund	
ich	machen	dorp	dat	appel	pund	
ich	machen	dorf	dat	appel	pund	Central German
ich	machen	dorf	das	appel	pund	
ich	machen	dorf	das	apfel	pund	
ich	machen	dorf	das	apfel	pfund	Upper German

The term High German is used to subsume Central and Upper German (both of which underwent the Second Sound Shift to some extent at least) as opposed to Low German.

There are also numerous other linguistic features which now distinguish the dialects of Map 4.1 (see the references listed in the bibliography for discussion of these). In addition to these regional dialects many scholars now distinguish national varieties of German, corresponding to the major political areas in which German is spoken (Germany, Austria and Switzerland) on account of various supra-regional and supra-dialectal norms that are accepted as standard in each.

This standard language of Germany emerged much later than the corresponding standard languages of England and France, on account of the political and cultural fragmentation of the German-speaking regions of Europe. There was no centre comparable to London or Paris that could impose its variety as the dominant one, so each region employed its own form of German at least until the sixteenth century. Prior to this point there had been a supra-regional 'compromise language' in the south (*das gemeyne Deutsch*), while in the north Low German enjoyed a privileged status until the seventeenth century as the commercial language of the Hanseatic League and was even used as a lingua franca throughout northern Europe. The basis for the emerging standard language in the fifteenth and early sixteenth centuries, however, was East Central German (see Map 4.1). This variety of German was itself a compromise that had arisen as a result of the contact between speakers of numerous dialects following the extensive migration of Germans in the Middle Ages, as they occupied hitherto Slavonic-speaking areas. East Central German was therefore intrinsically well suited to becoming a standard language, and its subsequent acceptance by the remainder of the German-speaking population can be attributed to numerous external factors: the invention of the printing press (1450), which made possible publication on a large scale, the most influential printed work being Luther's translation of the Bible written in East Central German (1522–34) and deliberately intended to be accessible to all German speakers; the use of German instead of Latin for legal records (c. 1400), and the influential and normative role of East Central German legal writing in particular; and the rise of the cities, which attracted people from various regions and increased trade and commerce, making the need for a common language all the more urgent.

The emerging standard gradually permeated both the northern Low German-speaking regions and the south, and during the seventeenth and eighteenth centuries slowly penetrated into Austria and Switzerland as well. However, it was only in the nineteenth century that the phonological norms were finally set. By this time Prussia had become the dominant political force in all the German-speaking areas of Europe except for Switzerland and the Austro-Hungarian Empire, first through a customs union (the *Zollverein*), and then in 1871 through political unification. But prior to its expansion Prussia was originally a northern Low German-speaking state, whose speakers had learnt High German as a second language. With the spread of the emerging High German standard to the north, northern speakers tended to accentuate a close relationship between phonemes and graphemes. And with minor modifications this North German pronunciation of the originally High German standard became the norm for standard German pronunciation or *Bühnendeutsch* (stage German), both in Germany proper, and later in Austria and Switzerland as a result of an agreement concluded between the three countries in 1899. Today, television and radio announcers in Munich, Stuttgart and Baden-Baden sound much the same as their North German counterparts. Despite the 1899 agreement, however, the same does not hold true for Austrian and Swiss announcers. But as far as the written language is concerned, there is now a widespread consensus among the German-speaking countries.

The historical evolution of High German is divided into the following stages: Old High German (OHG), covering the runic inscriptions from the sixth century AD and written texts from the eighth century to 1050; Middle High German (MHG) from 1050 to 1350; Early New High German (ENHG) from 1350 to 1650; and thereafter New High German (NHG) proper.

The Old High German texts are primarily religious writings and translations (from Latin) produced in the monasteries of Central and Upper Germany. Some of the main linguistic changes that separate Old High German from Proto-Germanic are: the Second Sound Shift; numerous vocalic sound changes, including the monophthongisation (in certain environments) of Gmc. *ai* > *ē* and *au* > *ō*, the diphthongisation of Gmc. closed *ē* > *ea* or *ia* and *ō* > *oa*, *ua* or *uo* (depending on the dialect) and the beginnings of *i*-umlaut revealed orthographically in the conversion of *a* > *e* before *i, ī, j*; the development of a definite article out of a demonstrative determiner; and the emergence of new periphrastic verbal constructions for the passive, future, perfect and pluperfect. In late Old High German some morphological syncretism sets in, anticipating Middle High German, but otherwise Old High German contains a very richly differentiated morphology for nouns, adjectives, determiners, pronouns and verbs.

Middle High German is the language of the great German poets of the late Middle Ages (Walther von der Vogelweide, Wolfram von Eschenbach, Gottfried von Strasburg etc.). The two most characteristic phonological differences between Old High German and Middle High German are: the weakening and partial loss of vowels in unstressed syllables; and the spread of *i*-umlaut (or at least of its graphic representation). Both short vowels *a, e, i, o, u* and long vowels *ā, ē, ī, ō, ū* could be reduced to schwa [ə] (orthographic *e*) or lost altogether: compare OHG *wola* 'well' (adv.), *aro* 'eagle', *beran* 'to bear', *salida* 'bliss' with the corresponding MHG *wol(e)*, *ar(e)*, *bërn*, *sælde*. The *i*-umlauting is responsible for the front rounded vowels of Modern German (see Section 2) which became phonemic with the reduction of the *i*-umlaut environment that had triggered their presumably allophonic variation hitherto (e.g. OHG *mūsi* > *MHG miuse* [müsə]). The reduction of unstressed syllables is also responsible for widespread syncretism in morphological paradigms as hitherto distinct vowels became reduced to [ə]. Otherwise the morphological paradigms of Middle High German remain much as they were in Old High German, and retain the lexical members and forms characteristic of the latter. Increasingly, however, the phonologically induced syncretism led to uncertainty as more and more words adopted morphological forms that originally belonged to other paradigms. These analogical formations eventually led to widespread restructuring in the morphology, but only in the Early New High German period. Among syntactic changes in Middle High German the replacement of the Old High German negative morpheme *ne* 'not' by *nicht* (etymologically 'no thing') is one of the more striking, as is the further expansion in the uses of the definite article. And in the area of the lexicon, the strong influence of French courtly society is reflected in numerous loanwords. Some of these were not to survive (e.g. *garzūn* 'page' and *tjost* 'joust') but many have, e.g. *Abenteuer* 'adventure', *fein* 'fine', *Lanze* 'lance', *Melodie* 'melody', *Tanz* 'dance', *Tournier* 'tournament'.

The Early New High German period saw numerous important changes throughout the grammar. In the phonology, short open syllables, for example, underwent either vowel or consonant lengthening (e.g. MHG [ligən] > NHG [liːgən], [hamər] > [hammər]); MHG [ə] was lost altogether in numerous environments (in some dialects much more than others) e.g. *legete* > *legte* 'laid'; the Middle High German diphthongs *ie, üe, uo* became long monophthongs *i:, ü:, u:* (in Central but not Upper German, which retains the diphthongs), MHG *biegen* > [biːgən] 'bend', *küene* > *kühn* 'bold', *ruofen* > *rufen* 'call'; the Middle High German long closed vowels *i:, ü:, u:* were correspondingly diphthongised to *ei, öu (eu), ou* (again subject to dialectal differentiation), MHG *zīt* > *Zeit*, [lütə] > *Leute*, *hūs* > *Haus*. There were profound restructurings in the morphology. For example, new plural paradigms for nouns evolved and expanded to compensate for the vowel reductions in unstressed syllables, particularly umlauted plurals: compare MHG *vogel/vogele* 'bird/birds' with NHG *Vogel/Vögel*. This process went even further in certain dialects with the result that one still hears today *Täg, Ärm, Hünd* in lieu of the standard *Tage* 'days', *Arme* 'arms' and *Hunde* 'dogs', while certain earlier distinct dialectal variants such as *Worte/Wörter* 'words' have both become standard German, though with slightly different meanings (words within a continuous text as opposed to individual words). Another plural suffix that was greatly expanded is *-er*, as in *Kind/Kinder* 'child/children', and also the *-en* suffix. The verb morphology also underwent some reductions, including a certain levelling of alternations in strong verbs (see Section 3) and also a levelling of the Middle High German consonantal alternation between *ich was* 'I was' and *wir wāren* 'we were'. In the syntax, Early New High German was the period in which the characteristic verb position of Modern German was fixed: final position in subordinate clauses, second and first position in main clauses (see Section 4). This had been the basic tendency in earlier periods as well, but there had been much more variation, especially in Middle High German, during which there were numerous postposings of constituents to the right of the verb in hitherto verb-final structures. Prenominal participial relative clause constructions are first attested in this period: *die von dem Bauer geschlachtete Kuh* 'the by the farmer killed cow', i.e. 'the cow which was killed by the farmer'. Certain postposed adjectives and possessive determiners (*den vater almechtigen* 'the father almighty') were replaced by prenominal orders. And there were widespread changes involving subordinate conjunctions: certain conjunctions died out (*wande, wan* 'because'); new ones emerged (e.g. *während* 'while', *falls* 'in the event that'); and the use of *daß* 'that' alone was frequently replaced by more semantically specific and precise forms such as *so daß* 'with the result that', *damit* 'in order that', *weil* 'because', etc.

With the completion of the Early New High German period (1650) we reach what is essentially Modern German. The precise phonological norms of the standard were still to be set (see above), but morphology and syntax now undergo only minor modifications compared with the changes that have been outlined. It is instructive to get a sense of the extent of some of these changes by comparing a short text in Old High German

Table 4.1 The Lord's Prayer

Old High German	Modern German	English
East Franconian, Tatian, c. 830		Authorised Version, 1611
Fater unser thu thar bist in himile,	Vater unser, du bist da im Himmel.	Our father which art in heauen
si giheilagot thin namo,	Geheiligt werde Dein Name.	hallowed be thy name.
queme thin rihhi,	Dein Reich komme.	Thy kyngdome come.
si thin uuillo,	Dein Wille geschehe,	Thy will be done
so her in himile ist so si her in erdu;	wie er im Himmel geschieht, so geschehe er auf Erden.	in earth, as it is in heauen,
unsar brot tagalihhaz gib uns hiutu,	Unser tägliches Brot gib uns heute.	Giue vs this day our daily bread.
inti furlaz uns unsara sculdi	Und vergib uns unsere Sünden,	And forgiue vs our debts,
so uuir furlazemes unsaren sculdigon;	wie wir unseren Schuldigern vergeben.	As we forgiue our debtors.
inti ni gileitest unsih in costunga,	Und du mögest uns nicht in Versuchung führen,	And lead vs not into temptation,
uzouh arlosi unsih fon ubile.	sondern erlöse uns von Bösem.	but deliuer us from euill.

with its Modern German translation. The text is the Lord's Prayer, see Table 4.1, as it appeared in the East Franconian Tatian of c. 830. Alongside it is a New High German translation and also the English of the Authorised Version of 1611.

2 Phonology

The segmental phonemes of Modern Standard German (consonants and vowels) are set out in Table 4.4. Twenty-one consonant phonemes are normally distinguished. Each of these is illustrated in the minimal pairs of Table 4.2, in word-initial, word-medial and word-final position. The blanks in the table indicate that the consonant in question does not occur in the relevant position in a word.

One of the most striking things about the minimal pairs in Table 4.2 is the absence of any voiced obstruents (stops and fricatives) in word-final position, i.e. /b d g v z ž/. This is no accident. Voiced obstruents are regularly converted to their voiceless counterparts in syllable-final position, i.e. before a syllable break. Such syllable breaks occur in three types of positions: at the end of a word, e.g. /liːp/ *lieb* 'dear'; at the end of part of a compound word, e.g. /liːp+oigəln/ *liebäugeln* 'to make eyes at'; and before suffixes beginning with a consonant, e.g. /liːp+liŋ/ *Liebling* 'darling'. By contrast, the voiced /b/ occurs in syllable-initial position in forms such as /liː+bən/ *lieben* 'to love' and /liː +bər/ *lieber* 'rather', and so does not get devoiced. Devoicing also takes place in consonant clusters before /t/ and /s/: /liːpt/ *liebt* 'loves', /liːpst/ *liebst* 'lovest'. Notice that the orthography retains the voiced stop in these examples, thereby representing the morphological relatedness between the different forms of the same stem.

The status of /ç/ and /x/ in German is a matter of some dispute. The velar fricative /x/ occurs only after central and back vowels, and never in initial position. The palatal /ç/

Table 4.2 Minimal Pairs for German Consonant Phonemes

/p/	/pasə/	passe	/raupən/	Raupen	/riːp/	rieb
/b/	/bas/	Baß	/raubən/	rauben		
/t/	/tasə/	Tasse	/baːtən/	baten	/riːt/	riet
/d/	/das/	das	/baːdən/	baden		
/k/	/kasə/	Kasse	/haːkən/	Haken	/ziːk/	Sieg
/g/	/gasə/	Gasse	/haːgən/	Hagen		
/f/	/fasə/	fasse	/höːfə/	Höfe	/raif/	reif
/v/	/vas/	was	/löːvə/	Löwe		
/s/	/sateⁿ/	Satin	/raisən/	reißen	/rais/	Reis
/z/	/zats/	Satz	/raizən/	reisen		
/š/	/šats/	Schatz	/raušən/	rauschen	/rauš/	Rausch
/ž/	/žeːniː/	Genie	/raːžə/	Rage		
/ç/	/çiːna/	China	/raiçən/	reichen	/raiç/	reich
/x/			/rauxən/	rauchen	/raux/	Rauch
/h/	/hasə/	hasse				
/m/	/masə/	Masse	/hemən/	hemmen	/ram/	Ramm
/n/	/nasə/	nasse	/henən/	Hennen	/ran/	rann
/ŋ/			/heŋən/	hängen	/raŋ/	rang
/l/	/lasə/	lasse	/koːlə/	Kohle	/vil/	will
/r/	/rasə/	Rasse	/boːrə/	bohre	/vir/	wirr
/j/	/jakə/	Jacke	/koːjə/	Koje		

occurs after front vowels, after the consonants /n l r/, and in word-initial position. This looks like a classic case of complementary distribution which should lead us to analyse these fricatives as allophones of the same phoneme. But there is an exception. The German diminutive suffix spelled -*chen* occurs as /çən/ in all positions, even after central and back vowels, and hence /ç/ sometimes stands in contrast with /x/: /tauçən/ *Tauchen* ('little rope') versus /tauxən/ *tauchen* ('to dive'); /kuːçən/ *Kuhchen* ('little cow') versus /kuːxən/ *Kuchen* ('cake').

Another problem involves the status of the affricates [pf] and [ts], created by the Second Sound Shift. Are these unit phonemes or clusters of two phonemes? They are historically derived from unit phonemes and minimal pairs are readily found which suggest that they retain this status. Nonetheless, German (like English) has numerous other clusters of stop plus fricative, and there seems to be no clear basis for distinguishing [pf] and [ts] from these: e.g. /ps/ in /gips/ *Gips* 'plaster', /pš/ in /hüpš/ *hübsch* 'pretty', /tš/ in /doitš/ *deutsch* 'German' and /ks/ in /zeks/ *sechs* 'six'.

The phoneme /r/ has a complicated set of allophones and is subject to a certain variation in pronunciation among speakers. When /r/ is followed by a vowel, as in /roːt leːrə besərə/ *rot* 'red', *leere* 'empty', *bessere* 'better' (pl.) (i.e. whether or not it is also preceded by a vowel), most speakers pronounce it as a uvular trill or fricative (phonetic symbol [ʀ]), although some use an apico-alveolar trill or flap (phonetic symbol [ř]). When /r/ is not followed by a vowel, its pronunciation varies depending on whether the vowel which does precede it is long, short or /ə/. After a long vowel, /r/ is always a non-syllabic [ᴧ], much like the /ʌ/ of English *but*. The word *leer* /leːr/ 'empty' is phonetically [leᴧ]. After unstressed /ə/, the /r/ and /ə/ combine to give syllabic [ʌ]. The word *besser* /besər/ 'better' is phonetically [besʌ]. After a short vowel, /r/ may either be a non-syllabic [ᴧ] again or else it may be pronounced as a uvular trill or fricative or as an apico-alveolar trill or fricative, like an /r/ which precedes a vowel. There are therefore three possible pronunciations for a word like *irrt* /irt/ 'errs': [iᴧt] [iʀt] and [iřt].

Table 4.3 Minimal Pairs for German Vowel Phonemes

/iː/	bieten	Stiele	ihn	ihre
/i/	bitten	Stille	in	irre
/üː/	Güte	fühle	kühn	führe
/ü/	Mütter	fülle	dünn	Dürre
/uː/	Rute	Buhle	Ruhm	Fuhre
/u/	Kutte	Bulle	Rum	murre
/eː/	beten	stehle	wen	zehre
/e/	Betten	Stelle	wenn	zerre
/öː/	Goethe	Höhle	tönt	höre
/ö/	Götter	Hölle	könnt	dörre
/oː/	rote	Sohle	Sohn	bohre
/o/	Rotte	solle	Bonn	Lorre
/ɛː/	bäte	stähle	wähne	währe
/ə/	gesagt	bitte	wartete	bessere
/aː/	rate	fahle	Bahn	Haare
/a/	Ratte	falle	Bann	harre
/ai/	leite	Feile	Bein	
/oi/	Leute	heule	neun	eure
/au/	Laute	faule	Zaun	

There are 19 separate vowel phonemes of German (including three diphthongs), exemplified in the minimal pairs of Table 4.3.

The vowels written with umlauts /üː ü öː ö/ are front rounded vowels resulting from *i*-mutation in Old and Middle High German. The colon is a length symbol used for distinguishing the long versus short pairs /iː/ versus /i/, etc. (though see below). There are also articulatory phonetic differences associated with these length distinctions, which are indicated approximately in Table 4.4. The short /i ü u/ are lower and more central than /iː üː uː/, the short /e ö o/ are also lower and more central than /eː öː oː/, and /a/ is higher and more central than /aː/. The three diphthongs involve glides from one tongue position to another: in /ai/ the tongue begins in low central position and glides towards a position which is higher and further front; in /oi/ the tongue begins in lower mid back rounded position gliding also towards a position higher and further front; and with /au/ the tongue begins in low central position and glides towards a position higher and further back.

The important difference between long and short vowels in German is more accurately described as a difference of tense versus lax articulation. Tense vowels are produced with greater muscular energy than lax vowels, and it is this that causes them to be articulated in more extreme positions in the vocal tract. The reason for considering the tense/lax opposition more fundamental is that the additional feature of length is found only in stressed syllables: all the examples in Table 4.3 involve stressed syllables in which the tense vowels are long (those with a colon), and the lax vowels are short (those without). But in unstressed syllables, it is often possible to perceive a tense/lax distinction, and yet both sets of vowels are now short. There are perceptible differences between tense /iː/ in /diːneː/ *Diner* and lax /i/ in /difuːs/ *diffus*, in both of which the

Table 4.4 Segmental Phonemes of German

Consonants

	Bilabial	Labio-dental	Dental-alveolar	Palato-alveolar	Palatal	Velar	Glottal
Stops	p b		t d			k g	
Fricatives		f v	s z	š ž	ç	x	h
Nasals	m		n			ŋ	
Laterals			l r				
Semi-vowels					j		

Vowels

	Front		Central	Back
High	iː	(üː)		(uː)
	i	(ü)	(ü)	(u)
Mid	eː	(öː)		(oː)
	e	(ö)	ɛː ə a	(o)
Low			aː	

Plus: diphthongs ai, oi, au

Note: ( ) designates lip-rounding.

stress falls on the second syllable, and yet both *i* vowels are technically short. Similarly, the unstressed initial syllables of /koːlumbus/ *Kolumbus* and /koleːgə/ *Kollege* differ in tense versus lax articulation of the *o*, but both vowels are again short. In more informal and faster speech, even this tense/lax distinction disappears in unstressed syllables. Nonetheless, the distinctiveness of tense versus lax vowels is not restricted to stressed syllables, whereas the long versus short distinction is. Notice finally that the /ə/ of German occurs only in unstressed syllables.

3 Morphology

Despite the morphological syncretism of the Early New High German period (see Section 1), the inflectional morphology of Modern German is very rich and preserves major features of the Old High German system. Few among the other modern Germanic languages have a morphology of comparable richness. The biggest changes involved the inflectional paradigms for nouns. The Proto-Indo-European and Proto-Germanic system of classification according to the phonology of the stem (which is still evident in, for example, Russian, see Chapter 15 in this volume) was destroyed and new paradigms evolved. Nouns are now classified according to their inherent gender (masculine, feminine or neuter) and according to their plural forms. The major plural allomorphs are: suffixed -*e* (*Tier/Tiere* 'animal'), -*er* (*Kind/Kinder* 'child'), -∅ (*Fenster/Fenster* 'window'), -*en* (*Frau/Frauen* 'woman'), -*s* (*Kino/Kinos* 'cinema'), stem vowel mutation plus -*e* (*Stadt/Städte* 'city'), stem vowel mutation plus -*er* (*Mann/Männer* 'man') and stem vowel mutation alone (*Mutter/Mütter* 'mother'). The noun phrase as a whole distinguishes separate case inflections for nominative, accusative, genitive and dative in both singular and plural, but these are now only residually marked on the noun itself (because of the reduction of unstressed syllables) and are primarily carried by preceding determiners and adjectives. However, the dative plural of all nouns still exhibits an -*(e)n* suffix, the genitive singular of most masculine and neuter nouns an -*(e)s* suffix, and the dative singular of many masculine and neuter nouns an optional -*e* suffix.

The full set of morphological distinctions carried by the German noun phrase (i.e. gender, number and case) can be illustrated by considering the sequence of definite article + noun in the chart given here.

Definite Article and Noun Inflections

	Singular M.	F.	Nt.	*Plural* All genders
Nom.	de*r* Mann	di*e* Frau	da*s* Haus	di*e* Männer
	'the man'	'the woman'	'the house'	'the men'
Acc.	de*n* Mann	di*e* Frau	da*s* Haus	di*e* Männer
Gen.	de*s* Mannes	de*r* Frau	de*s* Hauses	de*r* Männer
Dat.	de*m* Mann(*e*)	de*r* Frau	de*m* Haus(*e*)	de*n* Männer*n*

The definite article assumes just six forms: *der, den, des, dem, das* and *die* (morphologically analysable as two bound morphemes *d+er, d+en* etc.). Since gender distinctions are inherent in the noun, and since plurality is richly marked on the noun itself, the most important function of the determiner is to mark case. Individual definite article forms can be used in more than one case function without risk of intolerable ambiguity: *der* followed by a masculine singular noun is a nominative; followed by a feminine singular noun a genitive or dative; and followed by a noun with plural marking a genitive; etc. The expressive power of these definite article case distinctions is identical to that of all other sequences of determiner + noun, and also to determiner + adjective + noun and ∅ + adjective + noun sequences as well. The weakest distinction is between nominative and accusative, which is marked only by the *der/den* alternation in the masculine singular. However, the nominative is fully distinguishable in all genders and numbers from the genitive, and is also fully distinguishable from the dative. The accusative is also fully distinguishable from both genitive and dative. The genitive is in turn distinct from the dative, except for feminine singular nouns.

An adjective following the definite article receives case inflections according to the weak paradigm, with -*e* or -*en* endings, as shown in the chart of adjective inflections.

Adjective Inflections

Weak Adjective Inflections

	Singular			Plural
	M.	F.	Nt.	All genders
Nom.	der gute Mann	die gute Frau	das gute Haus	die guten Männer
	'the good man'	'the good woman'	'the good house'	'the good men'
Acc.	den guten Mann	die gute Frau	das gute Haus	die guten Männer
Gen.	des guten Männes	der guten Frau	des guten Hauses	der guten Männer
Dat.	dem guten Mann(e)	der guten Frau	dem guten Haus(e)	den guten Männern

Strong Adjective Inflections

	Singular			Plural
	M.	F.	Nt.	All genders
Nom.	guter Wein	gute Milch	gates Obst	gute Äpfel
	'good wine'	'good milk'	'good fruit'	'good apples'
Acc.	guten Wein	gute Milch	gutes Obst	gute Äpfel
Gen.	guten Weines	guter Milch	guten Obstes	guter Äpfel
Dat.	gutem Wein	guter Milch	gutem Obst	guten Äpfeln

Mixed Weak and Strong Adjective Inflections

	Singular			Plural
	M.	F.	Nt.	All genders
Nom.	kein guter Mann	keine gute Frau	kein gutes Haus	keine guten Häuser
	'no good man'	'no good woman'	'no good house'	'no good houses'
Acc.	keinen guten Mann	keine gute Frau	kein gutes Haus	keine guten Häuser
Gen.	keines guten Mannes	keiner guten Frau	keines guten Hauses	keiner guten Häuser
Dat.	keinem guten Mann	keiner guten Frau	keinem guten Haus	keinen guten Häusern

Other determiners requiring weak adjective endings are: *dieser* 'this', *jener* 'that', *welcher* 'which', *jeder* 'each', *alle* 'all'. It will be apparent that these adjective inflections do not increase the expressive power of the German case system, compared with the definite article + noun inflections. When an adjective + noun sequence has no preceding determiner (with indefinite mass nouns and plurals), the same case distinctions can be carried by adjective inflections of the strong paradigm, also shown in the chart of adjective inflections. These strong adjective inflections (-*er*, -*en*, -*es*, -*em*, -*e*) are practically identical in form and distribution to the bound morphemes of the definite article, and the expressive power of the whole paradigm is again identical to the definite article + noun inflections. Indefinite count nouns in the singular require the indefinite article *ein* 'a'. This determiner, together with *kein* 'no' and the possessives *mein* 'my', *dein* 'your', *sein* 'his', etc., is itself inflected more or less like the definite article, but requires accompanying adjective inflections which are a mixture of weak (*-en*, *-e*) and strong (*-er*, *-e*, *-es*). The chart of adjective inflections illustrates this mixed adjective paradigm following *kein*.

Personal Pronouns

Singular

	1st	2nd (familiar)	3rd M.	F.	Nt.
Nom.	ich	du	er	sie	es
Acc.	mich	dich	ihn	sie	es
Gen	meiner	deiner	seiner	ihrer	seiner
Dat.	mir	dir	ihm	ihr	ihm

Plural

	1st	2nd (familiar)	(polite: s. & pl.)	3rd
Nom.	wir	ihr	Sie	sie
Acc.	uns	euch	Sie	sie
Gen.	unser	euer	Ihrer	ihrer
Dat.	uns	euch	Ihnen	ihnen

German personal pronouns exhibit a rich set of case distinctions, as shown in the chart of personal pronouns. All four cases are fully distinct in the singular for first, second (familiar) and masculine third persons, while feminine and neuter third person forms are identical only in the nominative and accusative. In the plural the four cases are on each occasion represented by three separate forms. In the first and second (familiar) persons accusative and dative fall together, and in the second (polite) and third persons nominative and accusative fall together. Relative and interrogative pronouns are also case-marked. The relative pronoun, for example, is identical in form to the definite article, except for all the genitives and the dative plural (the relative pronoun having *dessen* instead of *des*, *deren* instead of *der*, and *denen* instead of *den*).

The existence of a productive case system sets German off from the other modern Germanic languages except for Icelandic and Faroese. As regards the use of the cases, the most important factor which determines the assignment of case to a noun phrase is the nature of the 'governing category', loosely, the category which forms an immediate constituent with this noun phrase and which determines the syntactic type of the resulting phrase. Thus, a preposition combines with a noun phrase to make a prepositional phrase and it assigns a case to this noun phrase; a verb combines with a noun phrase to make a verb phrase and assigns case to this noun phrase; and so on. Different prepositions assign accusative case, dative case or genitive case, as illustrated below:

(a)   durch das Zimmer; für mich (acc.)
      'through the room; for me'
(b)   aus dem Hause; mit mir (dat.)
      'out of the house; with me'
(c)   an die/der Wand; auf den/dem Stuhl (acc./dat.)
      'on the wall; on the chair'
(d)   trotz des Wetters; während des Jahres (gen.)
      'despite the weather; during the year'

The case alternation in (c) carries a difference in meaning: *auf den Stuhl* with an accusative noun phrase signals motion towards the place in question, as in 'the cat jumped on(to) the chair'; *auf dem Stuhl* with a dative designates a location without a change in state, e.g. 'the cat was lying on the chair'.

An adjective within an adjective phrase may also assign case to a noun phrase. Different adjectives assign accusative, dative or genitive case, as in:

(a) Ich bin ihn los. (acc.)
     'I am him rid', i.e. 'I am rid of him.'
(b) Sie ist ihrem Vater ähnlich. (dat.)
     'She is her father similar', i.e. 'similar to her father.'
(c) Er ist dieser Taten schuldig. (gen.)
     'He is these deeds guilty', i.e. 'guilty of these deeds.'

A head noun within a noun phrase assigns genitive case to a modifying possessor noun phrase:

der Hut der Anna; Annas Hut
'the hat of the Anna; Anna's hat'

The most complex governing category is the verb. The single argument of a one-place predicate (verb or predicate adjective) is most typically in the nominative case, as below, though both accusative and dative are found in so-called 'impersonal constructions':

(a) Ich schlafe. Ich friere. (nom.)
     'I am sleeping. I am freezing.'
(b) Mich hungert. Mich friert. (acc.)
     'Me hungers. Me freezes', i.e. 'I am hungry; I am freezing.'
(c) Mir ist warm. (dat.)
     'Me is warm', i.e. 'I am warm.'

These impersonal constructions were more frequent in earlier stages of German, but they still exist in the modern language. With two-place predicates, one argument is in the nominative case (the subject), but the second argument may be accusative, dative or genitive, depending on the choice of verb. Most verbs take the accusative (and these noun phrases then behave syntactically as direct objects), a not inconsiderable number take the dative and just a handful take the genitive (only one or two of which are really productive in modern usage):

(a) Ich liebe dich. Er sieht meinen Vater. (nom.-acc.)
     'I love you. He sees my father.'
(b) Er hilft mir. Sie antwortete ihrem Vater. (nom.-dat.)
     'He is helping me. She answered her father.'
(c) Sie bedarf des Trostes. Er ermangelt der nötigen Kraft. (nom.-gen.)
     'She needs consolation. He lacks the requisite strength.'

In three-place predicate constructions consisting of a verb and three (prepositionless) noun phrases the most common case assignments are nominative–accusative–dative, followed by nominative–accusative–genitive, with just a handful of nominative–accusative–accusative:

(a) Ich schrieb meinem Vater einen Brief. Das rate ich dir. (nom.-acc.-dat.)
    'I wrote my father a letter. That advise I you (to do).'
(b) Man enthob ihn seines Amtes. Er schämt sich seines Sohnes. (nom.-acc.-gen.)
    'One relieved him (of) his office. He shames himself (of) his son.'
(c) Er lehrt mich eine Sprache. Er hieß mich einen Toren. (nom.-acc.-acc.)
    'He is teaching me a language. He called me a fool.'

As in the other Germanic languages, many verbs also take prepositional phrases with characteristic prepositions when expanding on their minimally present argument noun phrases, e.g.:

(a) Ich denke oft *an* dich.
    'I think often *of* you.'
(b) Ich danke dir *für* deinen Brief.
    'I thank you *for* your letter.'

Not all case assignment in German is determined by a governing category in this way. For example, there are productive case contrasts in sentence time adverbials such as those shown below, in which the accusative refers to a specified (definite) time, and the genitive to an unspecified (indefinite) time:

(a) Er kam *letzten Freitag.* (acc.)
    'He came last Friday.'
(b) *Eines Tages* kam er. (gen.)
    'One day came he.'

Finally, the major morphological distinctions carried by the verb are illustrated in the chart of verb inflections.

Verb Inflections

	weak		*strong*	
Infinitive				
	sag+*en* 'to say'		trag+*en* 'to bear'	
Participles				
Present	sag+*end*		trag+*end*	
Past	*ge*+sag+*t*		*ge*+trag+*en*	
Imperative				
2nd Sg. (familiar)	sag+*(e)*		trag+*(e)*	
2nd Pl. (familiar)	sag+*t*		trag+*t*	
Polite form	sag+*en* Sie		trag+*en* Sie	
Present				
	Indicative	*Subjunctive*	*Indicative*	*Subjunctive*
ich (1st)	sag+*e*	sag+*e*	trag+*e*	trag+*e*
du (2nd)	sag+*st*	sag+*st*	träg+*st*	trag+*st*
er, sie, es (3rd)	sag+*t*	sag+*e*	träg+*t*	trag+*e*
wir (1st)	sag+*en*	sag+*en*	trag+*en*	trag+*en*
ihr (2nd)	sag+*t*	sag+*t*	trag+*t*	trag+*t*
sie (3rd), Sie (2nd)	sag+*en*	sag+*en*	trag+*en*	trag+*en*

100

Past

	Indicative	Subjunctive	Indicative	Subjunctive
ich (1st)	sag+*te*	sag+*te*	trug	trüg+*e*
du (2nd)	sag+*test*	sag+*test*	trug+*st*	trüg+*st*
er, sie, es (3rd)	sag+*te*	sag+*te*	trug	trüg+*e*
wir (1st)	sag+*ten*	sag+*ten*	trug+*en*	trüg+*en*
ihr (2nd)	sag+*tet*	sag+*tet*	trug+*t*	trüg+*t*
sie (3rd), Sie (2nd)	sag+*ten*	sag+*ten*	trug+*en*	trüg+*en*

As in all the other Germanic languages, two basic classes of verb need to be distinguished: weak (exemplified by *sagen* 'to say') and strong (exemplified by *tragen* 'to bear'). The strong class undergoes vowel alternations in the stem (so-called 'ablaut') in addition to taking inflectional affixes for person and number agreement, etc. The number of strong verbs has been historically on the decline and there has been a certain levelling and redistribution of vowel alternants among the different tense and person categories that these alternants distinguish (especially in Early New High German), but Modern German still has a large class of strong verbs which includes some of the most common verbs in the language (*geben* 'to give', *essen* 'to eat', *liegen* 'to lie', *sehen* 'to see', *riechen* 'to smell', *gießen* 'to pour', *fliegen* 'to fly', *schreiben* 'to write', *sprechen* 'to speak', *fallen* 'to fall', *fahren* 'to travel', and many others). The weak class does not undergo such vowel alternations and takes (partially different) inflectional affixes for person and number agreement.

Proceeding down the chart of verb inflections, the German infinitive marker is an -*en* suffix attached to the stem. The present participle is formed by adding the suffix -*end*. The past participle consists of a -*t* suffix for weak verbs and an -*en* suffix for strong verbs, with a *ge*- prefix for both in cases where the first syllable of the stem is stressed. If the first syllable is not stressed (e.g. *bemérken* 'to notice'), this initial *ge*- is omitted (*bemérkt* 'noticed' not **gebemérkt*). There are three imperative forms with identical morphologies for weak and strong verbs, as shown. German has only two simple tenses, present and past, both inherited from Proto-Germanic and shared with other Germanic languages. Numerous compound tenses are formed from combinations of *haben* 'to have', *sein* 'to be' and *werden* 'to be/become' plus past participle or infinitive, e.g. the perfect (*ich habe gesagt* 'I have said'), pluperfect (*ich hatte gesagt* 'I had said'), future (*ich werde sagen* 'I will say'), future perfect (*ich werde gesagt haben* 'I will have said') and so on. These compounds were fixed in the Old High German period. The person and number agreement suffixes of the present tense are identical for weak and strong verbs: four suffixes (-*e*, -*st*, -*t*, -*en*) are divided among the six grammatically distinguishable types of subjects that the verb agrees with (first, second and third persons singular, first, second and third persons plural). For stems ending in various (primarily dental) consonants, e.g. -*t* in *wart*+*en* 'to wait', an epenthetic *e* appears before the -*st* and -*t* suffixes (compare *sag*+*st/wart*+*est* and *sag*+*t/wart*+*et*). A special form for the subjunctive exists only in the third person singular (*er sage* as opposed to *er sagt*); otherwise subjunctive and indicative are identical (though productive paradigms for a distinct present subjunctive do exist for *sein* 'to be', the modal auxiliaries and one or two other verbs). The past tense indicative inflections for weak verbs all contain an initial *t*-, and differ in several respects from the corresponding strong verb indicative inflections, as shown. The past subjunctive of weak verbs is identical to the indicative, but the past subjunctive of strong verbs exhibits numerous contrasts with the indicative: first and third persons singular show -*e* rather than -∅ and the stem vowel is umlauted wherever possible.

4 Syntax

One of the most interesting features of Modern German syntax, in comparison with other languages, is its word order (particularly the position of the verb). Within the Germanic language family, German is striking for the extent to which it has remained conservative, preserving structural properties of both Old High German and the Germanic parent language itself. The Scandinavian languages and English, by contrast, have undergone more extensive syntactic changes in the same time period, with Dutch being intermediate between German and English. The present summary will accordingly illustrate some of the basic features of German verb position, and will outline some of the major syntactic differences which now distinguish German from one of the more radical Germanic languages, namely English.

There are three major positions of the verb in German clauses: final position, second position (i.e. the verb is the second clause-level constituent) and first position. The basic rule is: final position in subordinate clauses; second and first position in main clauses. A more precise statement, however, must first distinguish between finite and non-finite (i.e. infinitival and participial) verb forms. In subordinate clauses containing a finite verb (and, optionally, any additional non-finite verbs), all verb forms are final (in the order non-finite before finite), e.g.:

(a) Ich weiß, daß Heinrich die Frau *liebt*.
     'I know that Henry the woman *loves*', i.e. 'loves the woman.'
(b) Ich glaube, daß mein Vater vor einigen Tagen nach London *gefahren ist*.
     'I believe that my father several days ago to London *travelled has*.'

In non-finite subordinate clauses, non-finite verbs are again final:

Ich freue mich darauf, abends in der Wirtschaft Bier *zu trinken*.
'I am looking forward to-it, evenings in the pub beer *to drink*', i.e.
'I am looking forward to drinking beer in the pub in the evenings.'

And so they are even in main clauses, although the finite verb now stands in second position (a–b) or first position (c–d):

(a) Heinrich *liebt* die Frau.
     'Henry *loves* the woman.'
(b) Mein Vater *ist* vor einigen Tagen nach London *gefahren*.
     'My father *has* several days ago to London *travelled*.'
(c) *Liebt* Heinrich die Frau?
     'Loves Henry the woman?' i.e. 'Does Henry love the woman?'
(d) *Ist* mein Vater vor einigen Tagen nach London *gefahren*?
     '*Has* my father several days ago to London *travelled*?'

German verb compounds consisting of a separable element (e.g. an adjective, particle, even a prepositional phrase or a noun phrase) in conjunction with a verb provide further examples of verb-final structures. The separable element assumes the same position as a non-finite verb form, and hence German main clauses frequently end in a verbal satellite constituent, such as *tot* 'dead' from the compound *totschlagen* 'to beat dead':

Der König *schlug* den Feigling *tot*.
'The king *beat* the coward *dead*.'

In subordinate clauses, satellite and verb stand together, and the verb alone, not the whole verbal complex, provides the domain for the attachment of infinitival *zu* 'to':

(a) Ich weiß, daß der König den Feigling *totschlug*.
    'I know that the king the coward *dead-beat*', i.e. 'beat the coward dead.'
(b) Ich freue mich darauf, den Feigling *totzuschlagen*.
    'I look forward to-it, the coward *dead-to-beat*.'

The final position of verbal forms in the above structures is not rigidly adhered to, however. Various constituents can stand to the right of the verb, and the frequency with which they do so is a matter of style: postposings are more frequent in informal, conversational German; and less frequent in formal, written German. There are strict rules governing which constituents can be postposed and which cannot. Direct objects, for example, cannot be postposed over the verbal satellite *über* 'across' (from *übersetzen* 'set across') in the following example, regardless of style:

(a) Man *setzte* die Urlauber in einem Boot *über*.
    'One set the holidaymakers in a boat across.'
(b) *Man *setzte* in einem Boot *über* die Urlauber.
    'One set in a boat across the holidaymakers.'

Nor can obligatory adjuncts (or strictly subcategorised constituents) move to rightmost position, as exemplified in the ungrammatical (b) in which the obligatorily present prepositional phrase has been postposed behind the infinitive *verleiten* 'to lead (astray)':

(a) Die Gelegenheit *wird* ihn bestimmt zu einem voreiligen Schritt *verleiten*.
    'The opportunity will him certainly to a rash move lead', i.e. 'will certainly encourage him to make a rash move.'
(b) *Die Gelegenheit *wird* ihn bestimmt *verleiten* zu einem voreiligen Schritt.
    'The opportunity will him certainly lead to a rash move.'

The constituents which can move are in general: (1) those which are heavy, i.e. which are long in terms of number of words, and complex in their internal structure; and (2) those which are more loosely integrated into the interpretation of the sentence, e.g. optional adverbial constituents which can serve as 'afterthoughts'. With regard to (1), notice that non-subject embedded finite clauses in German *must* be postposed behind a 'final' verb form:

(a) *Er *hatte* daß er nicht lange leben würde *gewußt*.
    'He had that he not long live would known.'
(b) Er *hatte gewußt*, daß er nicht lange leben würde.
    'He had known, that he not long live would.'

With infinitival embeddings (which are typically shorter than finite clauses), the postposing is regularly optional rather than obligatory:

(a) Er *hatte* die Frau zu gewinnen *gehofft.*
     'He had the woman to win hoped', i.e. 'He had hoped to win the woman.'
(b) Er *hatte gehofft*, die Frau zu gewinnen.
     'He had hoped, the woman to win.'

As an example of (2), consider:

(a) Ich erzähle dir gleich, was ich bei Müllers *gehört habe.*
     'I tell you right-away, what I at the Müllers (place) heard have.'
(b) Ich erzähle dir gleich, was ich *gehört habe* bei Müllers.
     'I tell you right-away, what I heard have at the Müllers (place).'

The verb-second structures of the main clauses allow a wide variety of constituents to occupy first position, not just a subject. Some typical examples are given below, involving various fronted adverbials (a–d), non-subject noun phrases (e–f), a verb phrase (g), non-finite verb forms (h–i), an adjective (j) and an embedded clause (k):

(a) Möglicherweise *hat* Heinrich uns *vergessen.*
     'Possibly has Henry us forgotten', i.e. 'Possibly Henry has forgotten us.'
(b) Gestern *sind* wir ins Theater *gegangen.*
     'Yesterday have we to-the theatre gone.'
(c) In München *wohnt* der Mann.
     'In Munich resides the man.'
(d) Schön *singt* die Opernsängerin.
     'Beautifully sings the opera singer.'
(e) Den Hund *sieht* die Katze.
     The dog (acc.) sees the cat (nom.)', i.e. 'The cat sees the dog.'
(f) Dem Mann *habe* ich das Buch *gegeben.*
     'The man (dat.) have I the book (acc.) given.'
(g) Das Auto zu reparieren *hat* der Junge *versucht.*
     'The car to repair has the boy tried,' i.e. 'The boy has tried to repair the car.'
(h) *Gewinnen müssen* wir.
     'Win must we', i.e. 'Win we must.'
(i) *Bestraft muß* er werden.
     'Punished must he be.'
(j) Dumm *bin* ich nicht.
     'Stupid am I not.'
(k) Daß er oft lügt *wissen* wir alle.
     'That he often lies know we all.'

Only one constituent can typically precede the verb in these constructions. A slight exception is provided by structures such as *gestern abend auf der Party fehlte Heinrich* 'yesterday evening at the party was-missing Henry', in which two thematically related constituents precede, *gestern abend* and *auf der Party.* But normally this is not possible. The most normal position for the subject in the above verb-second structures is immediately after the verb, though it can sometimes stand further to the right as well.

All of the structures just given are semantically declarative statements. Verb-first structures, by contrast, occur in a variety of primarily non-declarative sentence types, including yes–no questions (see above). Other verb-first structures are: imperatives (a), exclamations (b), and counterfactual and conditional clauses (c–d):

(a) *Bringen* Sie das Buch herein!
     'Bring you the book in-here.'
(b) *Bist* du aber schmutzig!
     'Are you ever dirty.'
(c) *Hätte* ich nur Zeit, ich würde Ihnen helfen.
     'Had I only time, I would you help.'
(d) *Kommt* er, so sehe ich ihn.
     'Comes he, then see I him', i.e. 'If he comes, then I will see him.'

Modern colloquial German also exhibits a verb-first pattern in 'dramatic' narrative style:

Kommt da plötzlich jemand hereingeschneit.
'Comes then suddenly someone bursting-in',
  i.e. 'Then suddenly someone comes bursting in.'

This pattern was more productive in earlier stages of the language.

The verb-second and verb-first structures of German main clauses have close parallels in all the modern Germanic languages. Even English, which has gone furthest in the direction of fixing SVO, employs a verb-first rule in an almost identical set of environments to German, and it has numerous subject–verb inversion rules creating verb-second structures in a significant number of the environments that we have seen for German (see Hawkins 1986: chs 11 and 12 for a summary).

Before leaving the topic of word order, notice that the positioning of other sentence-level constituents in German apart from the verb is relatively free. Within the other major phrasal categories, however (the noun phrase, the adjective phrase, the prepositional phrase), the ordering of daughter constituents is just as fixed as in English.

With its rich inflectional morphology, verb-final structures and word order freedom, Modern German preserves syntactic features that were common to all the older West Germanic languages. Modern English, by contrast, has essentially lost its case morphology on nouns (as well as other inflectional morphology), has fixed basic SVO word order, and permits less sentence-level word order freedom. Modern English syntax also differs from that of Modern German in other significant ways. Most of these are the result of English having effected changes which were either not carried out, or were carried out to a much lesser extent, in German. We shall conclude with a very brief enumeration of some more of these contrasts.

English has larger and semantically broader classes of subject and direct object noun phrases than German, i.e. the quantity and semantic type of noun phrases that undergo rules sensitive to these grammatical relations is greater in English than in German. For example, many direct objects of English correspond to dative-marked noun phrases in German, which are arguably not direct objects since they cannot be converted to passive subjects. Compare the English sentences below with their German translations and with the corresponding passive sentences:

(a) She loves the man/him.
(b) Sie liebt *den Mann/ihn.* (acc.)

(a) She helped the man/him.
(b) Sie *half dem Mann/ihm.* (dat.)

(a) The man/He is loved.
(b) Der Mann/Er wird geliebt.

(a) The man/He was helped.
(b) *Der Mann/Er wurde geholfen.

The accusative-marked (and semantically prototypically patient) noun phrases of German in these constructions correspond to English direct objects and are also direct objects in German. But the dative (and semantically recipient) argument of *helfen* 'to help' also corresponds to a direct object in English, though it is not itself a direct object in German. The case syncretism of English has collapsed the distinct classes of noun phrases in German into a larger class of direct objects, with consequences for both the productivity of various syntactic operations, and for the semantic breadth or diversity of the direct object relation.

Grammatical subjects in English also constitute a larger and semantically more diverse class. English frequently has subjects with non-agentive semantic roles where these are impossible in German, as the following selection shows:

(a) *The king* visited his people. (Su. = agent)
(b) *Der König* besuchte sein Volk.

(a) *My guitar* broke a string. (Su. = locative; cf. *on my guitar* ...)
(b) *Meine Gitarre* (zer)riß eine Saite.

(a) *This hotel* forbids dogs. (Su. = locative; cf. *in this hotel* ...)
(b) *Dieses Hotel* verbietet Hunde.

(a) *A penny* once bought 2 to 3 pins. (Su. = instrumental; cf. *with a penny* ...)
(b) *Ein Pfennig* kaufte früher 2 bis 3 Stecknadeln.

(a) *This advertisement* will sell us a lot. (Su. = instrumental; cf. *with this ad* ...)
(b) *Diese Anzeige* verkauft uns viel.

Related to this contrast is the existence of a productive set of raising rules in English, creating derived subjects and objects. These operations are either non-existent or extremely limited in German, as the following literal German translations of the English structures show. The English sentences (a–c) exemplify subject-to-subject raising, i.e. *John* is the original subject of *to be ill* and is raised to become subject of *seems*, etc.; (d–e) involve subject-to-object raising, whereby *John* has been raised to become direct object of *believe*, etc.; and (f–h) give examples of object-to-subject raising (or tough movement), in which the original object of *to study* has been raised to become subject of *is easy*, etc.:

(a) John seems to be ill.
(b) John happens to be ill.
(c) John ceased to be ill.

(a) Johann scheint krank zu sein.
(b) *Johann geschieht krank zu sein.
(c) *Johann hörte auf krank zu sein.

(d) I believe John to be ill.
(e) I understand him to be stupid.

(d) *Ich glaube Johann krank zu sein.
(e) *Ich verstehe ihn dumm zu sein.

(f) Linguistics is easy to study.
(g) Literature is pleasant to study.
(h) History is boring to study.

(f) Die Linguistik ist leicht zu studieren.
(g) *Die Literatur ist angenehm zu studieren.
(h) *Die Geschichte ist langweilig zu studieren.

Related to these more productive clause-external raising rules in English is the fact that the extraction of *wh* elements out of subordinate clauses is also more productive in English than in German. For example, German can typically not extract out of finite subordinate clauses:

That is the prize which I hope (that you will win △).

*Das ist der Preis, den ich hoffe (daß du △ gewinnen wirst).

Nor can German extract out of a prepositional phrase, thereby stranding a preposition, whereas such extraction and stranding is typically optional in English:

(a) The woman who I went to the movies PP(with △)

(b) The woman PP(with whom) I went to the movies.

(a) *Die Frau, der ich ins Kino PP(mit △) ging.

(b) Die Frau, PP(mit der) ich ins Kino ging.

The (b) versions of these sentences involve a fronting (or 'pied piping') of the whole prepositional phrase, rather than extraction out of it. German also has a productive verb phrase pied piping rule which is without parallel in English:

(a) *The man $_{VP}$(to kill whom) I have often tried
(b) The man who I have often tried $_{VP}$(to kill △).

(a) Der Mann $_{VP}$(den zu töten) ich öfters versucht habe
(b) Der Mann, den ich $_{VP}$(△ zu töten) öfters versucht habe; OR

   Der Mann, den ich öfters versucht habe $_{VP}$(△ zu töten)

Finally, numerous deletions which are possible in English are blocked in German, in part because the case system of German renders non-identical deletion targets which are identical in English. An example is given below, in which the leftmost occurrence of *the king* can delete in English, whereas the accusative-marked *den König* in German is not identical to the dative *dem König* and cannot be deleted by this latter:

(a) Fred saw *the king* and thanked *the king*.
(b) Fred saw   and thanked *the king*.

(a) Fritz sah *den König* und dankte *dem König*.
(b) *Fritz sah   und dankte *dem König*.

Deletions are also more restricted in German for other reasons as well. For example, deletions, like the extractions discussed above, cannot strand a preposition, even when the relevant noun phrases have identical cases:

(a) He is the father of *the boy* and the friend of *the boy*.
(b) He is the father of   and the friend of *the boy*.

(a) Er ist der Vater von *dem Jungen* und der Freund von *dem Jungen*.
(b) *Er ist der Vater von   und der Freund von *dem Jungen*.

Deletion of a relative pronoun is also impossible in German, but possible in English:

(a) The woman who(m) I love is coming tonight.
(b) The woman   I love is coming tonight.

(a) Die Frau, die ich liebe, kommt heute abend.
(b) *Die Frau   ich liebe kommt heute abend.

Summarising, we have the following overall typological contrasts between English and German:

German	English
More grammatical morphology	Less grammatical morphology
More word order freedom	Less word order freedom
Less semantic diversity of grammatical relations	More semantic diversity of grammatical relations
Less raising	More raising
Less extraction	More extraction
More pied piping	Less pied piping
Less deletion	More deletion

Bibliography

For studies of German written in English, readers may consult Russon (1967) for a concise traditional statement of German grammar. For phonology, reference may be made to Moulton (1962), and to chapters 2 and 3 of König and Gast (2007). König and Gast describe many features of German (phonology, morphology, syntax, semantics and lexicon), with particular reference to their contrasts in English. Hawkins (1986) also contains a survey of the major areas of syntactic and morphological contrast between German and English. Lockwood (1968) presents the major syntactic changes from Old High German to New High German. The papers in Russ (1990) give a summary of the dialects of Modern German. Clyne (1984) discusses the sociolinguistic situation in those countries in which German is the national language or one of the national languages, and Barbour and Stevenson (1990) bring together all aspects of variation (historical change, dialectology and sociolinguistics) in their book on variation in German.

For studies written in German, Eisenberg (1994) gives a single-volume description of German grammar. Althaus et al. (1973a) includes a summary of major areas of German grammar, with extensive further references. For phonology and morphology, see Lessen Kloeke (1982). Bierwisch (1963) is the first detailed generative treatment of the syntax of the German verb and of numerous related rules, and is still considered a classic. See Grewendorf (1988) for a more recent generative syntax of German. The papers in Lang and Zifonun (1996) examine German from a typological perspective, comparing it with other languages and positioning it in relation to current universal generalisations. Bach (1965) is a standard reference work on the history of the German language. Althaus et al. (1973b) gives a summary of dialect differences among the German regions, of major historical changes in the different periods of both High and Low German, and of the current status of German in countries where German is not a national language, with extensive further references throughout.

References

Althaus, H.P., Henne, H. and Wiegand, H.E. 1973a. *Lexicon der germanistischen Linguistik. Studienausgabe I* (Max Niemeyer Verlag, Tübingen)
—— 1973b. *Lexicon der germanistischen Linguistik. Studienausgabe II* (Max Niemeyer Verlag, Tübingen)
Bach, A. 1965. *Geschichte der deutschen Sprache* (Quelle and Meyer, Heidelberg)
Barbour, S. and Stevenson, P. 1990. *Variation in German. A Critical Approach to German Sociolinguistics* (Cambridge University Press, Cambridge)
Bierwisch, M. 1963. *Grammatik des deutschen Verbs*, Studia Grammatica 2 (Akademieverlag, Berlin)
Clyne, M. 1984. *Language and Society in the German-speaking Countries* (Cambridge University Press, Cambridge)
Eisenberg, P. 1994. *Grundriß der deutschen Grammatik*, 3rd edn (Metzler, Stuttgart)
Grewendorf, G. 1988. *Aspekte der deutschen Syntax* (Narr, Tübingen)
Hawkins, J.A. 1986. *A Comparative Typology of English and German: Unifying the Contrasts* (University of Texas Press, Austin; Croom Helm, London)
König, E. and Gast, V. 2007. *Understanding English–German Contrasts* (Erich Schmidt Verlag, Berlin)
Lang, E. and Zifonun, G. (eds) 1996. *Deutsch Typologisch* (de Gruyter, Berlin)
Lessen Kloeke, W. van 1982. *Deutsche Phonologie und Morphologie* (Niemeyer, Tübingen)
Lockwood, W.B. 1968. *Historical German Syntax* (Clarendon Press, Oxford)
Moulton, W.G. 1962. *The Sounds of English and German* (University of Chicago Press, Chicago)
Russ, C.T. (ed.) 1990. *The Dialects of Modern German. A Linguistic Survey* (Routledge, London)
Russon, L.J. 1967. *Complete German Course for First Examinations* (Longman, London)

5

Dutch

Jan G. Kooij

1 Introduction

Modern Standard Dutch is the official language of the Netherlands and one of the official languages of Belgium. In the two countries together, the number of speakers is approximately 17 million. The official Dutch name of the language is *Nederlands*. It is sometimes called *Hollands*, after the most influential province, and the variety of Dutch that is spoken in Belgium is often, incorrectly, referred to as Flemish (*Vlaams*). Frisian (Dutch *Fries*) is a separate language spoken in the north-east of the Netherlands and is in some respects closer to English than to Dutch. *Afrikaans*, the language of part of the white and mixed-race population of the Republic of South Africa, is derived from Dutch dialects but is now regarded as a separate language. Dutch is also the official language of administration in Surinam (formerly Dutch Guyana) and in the Dutch Antilles but it is not widely spoken there. Some Dutch is still spoken in Indonesia. Dutch-based creole languages have never had many speakers, and the language known as *Negerhollands* ('Negro Dutch') on the Virgin Islands has become virtually extinct. Both Sranan, the English-based creole spoken by a large number of inhabitants of Surinam, and Papiamentu, a Spanish-based creole spoken in the Antilles, have been influenced by Dutch, and Sranan increasingly so. Afrikaans also shows definite features of creolisation.

The word *Dutch* derives from Middle Dutch *Diets* or *Duuts*, the name for the (Low) German vernacular; somewhat confusingly for speakers of English, *Duits* is now the Dutch name for (High) German.

Dialect variation in the Dutch language area is considerable, and a number of geographical dialects are not mutually intelligible. Ever since compulsory education was introduced uniformity in speaking and writing has increased, though less so in the Belgian area than in the Netherlands. The process of standardisation still continues. The large majority of inhabitants have a fair command of the standard language, but in some areas in the north, the east and the south a number of people are virtually bilingual. Language variation is politically insignificant in the Netherlands, but the situation in Belgium is more complex. After the establishment of the boundaries of the Dutch Republic in the seventeenth century, the prestige of Dutch in the southern provinces that are now part of Belgium rapidly declined. Its official recognition next to French has been the subject of bitter controversies, and the language situation is still an important factor in political and cultural life. The boundary between the Dutch-speaking area and the French-speaking area runs from west to east just south of Brussels. In the south-east of the country lives a small German-speaking minority. Minority languages in the Netherlands include Chinese (mostly the Cantonese dialect), Bahasa Indonesia and other forms of Malay, Sranan and, more recently, Turkish and North African dialects of Arabic.

2 History and Typology

Dutch belongs to the West Germanic branch of the Germanic languages and is based on Low Franconian dialects spoken in the south of the present language area. Compared to the two other major West Germanic languages, English and German, Dutch is in fundamental respects closer to German. Like English, however, it has lost most of the original Germanic noun morphology, and the proximity of the Romance language area is apparent from the presence of a sizable Romance vocabulary in the Dutch lexicon. Some characteristic differences and similarities among Dutch, English and German are the following.

(a) Germanic [g] went to [x]: Dutch *goed* [xut] vs English *good*, German *gut*,
(b) Short back vowel before [l] plus consonant went to [au]: Dutch *oud* vs English *old*, German *alt*,
(c) Initial [sk] went to [sx]: Dutch *schip* vs English *ship*, German *Schiff*, and in other positions [sk] went to [s]: Dutch *vis* vs English *fish*, German *Fisch* with *[š]*,
(d) Final devoicing of obstruents: Dutch *pond*, German *Pfund* with final [t] vs English *pound*,
(e) Initial voicing of fricatives: Dutch *zien*, German *sehen* with initial [z] vs English *see*,
(f) Predominance of older plural endings over the more recent ending *-s:* Dutch *boeken*, German *Bücher* vs English *books*,
(g) No grammatical umlaut: Dutch *dag–dagelijks*, English *day–daily* vs German *Tag–täglich*,
(h) No initial [š] in consonant clusters: Dutch *steen*, English *stone* vs German *Stein* [štain],
(i) No affricates and fricatives from original plosives [p], [t], [k]: Dutch *pond*, English *pound* vs German *Pfund*; Dutch *tien*, English *ten* vs German *zehn*; Dutch *maken*, English *make* vs German *machen*.

The latter feature Dutch shares with Low German, which was once a major literary language in the German-speaking area (see page 89).

From the period of Old Dutch or Old Low Franconian (*Oud Nederlands*) only a few texts have survived, mainly fragments of psalms translated into the vernacular. From the period of Middle Dutch (*Middelnederlands*, 1100–1500) a considerable number of literary and non-literary texts have been preserved and edited; most of these are written in the dialects of the leading southern provinces, Flanders and Brabant. By the time that Modern Dutch (*Nieuw Nederlands*) developed, the language had already lost most of its case distinctions and flectional morphology, though some of it was still represented in the orthography. The modern standard language is based on the dialects spoken in and around

Amsterdam, since by that time political and cultural leadership had gravitated to the northern provinces; pronunciation was influenced considerably by the speech of immigrants from the Brabant area after the fall of Antwerp in 1585. Typical features of the developing standard pronunciation were the fixation of the diphthongised long [i] as [ɛɪ] rather than [aɪ], Dutch *rijden* vs English *ride* and German *reiten*, and the diphthongisation of original Germanic [u] to [ʌü], Dutch *huis* vs English *house*, German *Haus*. Diphthongisation also affected French loans: compare English *brewery* and Dutch *brouwerij* with final [ɛɪ], English *flute* and Dutch *fluit* with [ʌü]. Another recent feature in the phonology is the weakening of intervocalic [d] to [j] in inflected forms: *goed*, 'good', inflected form *goede* or *goeie*; many of these forms coexist as formal vs informal variants.

As elsewhere in Europe, the writing of grammars in the native language began in the period of the Renaissance; the main focus of the older grammarians was proper usage, standardisation and orthography. The most important early contribution to the scholarly study of Dutch and its relationships with the surrounding languages was made by the Amsterdam linguist Lambert ten Kate (1723). Not until the nineteenth century did Dutch universities introduce chairs for the study of the Dutch language and for Dutch philology and lexicography. There is no Language Academy, but the foundation of a Council for the Dutch Language (Raad voor de Nederlandse Taal) in which the Netherlands and Belgium participate has now been agreed upon.

The uniformisation of the orthography was accomplished in the nineteenth century on the initiative of the central government. The basic rules for the present orthography were laid out in 1863 by De Vries and Te Winkel. They are mildly etymological, for instance the diphthong [ɛɪ] is spelled either *ij* or *ei* according to its history. The spelling of inflected forms of nouns and verbs follows the morphology rather than the phonology. So, the stem *vind* 'find', pronounced [vi̥nt], is spelled with final -*d* because of the infinitive *vinden*, and the form *hij vindt* 'he finds', also pronounced [vi̥nt], is spelled with a final -*dt* paralleling the -*t* in *loop* 'walk', *hij loopt* 'he walks'. This aspect of the system has been challenged but it has never been changed. Otherwise, Dutch orthography follows the principle that distinct sounds are represented by different letters of the Roman alphabet, with the additional convention that a long vowel in closed syllables is represented by two letters and a short vowel by one: *aap* 'monkey' and *stap* 'step'; in open syllables, the difference between long vowels and short vowels is indicated by single and double consonants, respectively: *apen* 'monkeys' vs *stappen* 'steps'. The spelling of vowels is less conservative than in English because the major developments in the standardisation of the pronunciation were taken into account. Peculiar features of Dutch orthography are the use of the letter *ij*, which is considered a single letter, for diphthongised [i] as in *rijden* 'ride', and the use of *oe* for the monophthong [u] as in *boek*, *Oeganda* vs German *Buch*, *Uganda*. The spelling of the Romance vocabulary has been rationalised to some extent, as appears from Dutch *fotografie* vs English *photography*, but proposals for further adaptation, e.g. *k* instead of *c* in *collectie* 'collection' have met with resistance, especially in Belgium.

3 Phonology

Tables 5.1 and 5.2 show the distinctive segmental phonemes of standard Dutch. Dutch has a comparatively simple consonant system. The main distinctive features are place of articulation, manner of articulation and presence vs absence of voicing. The language has no affricates, and no palatal obstruents. Labial fricatives and [ʋ] are labio-dental and all fricatives are strident. Nasals and liquids are never syllabic. [ʀ] is mostly uvular and not often rolled with the tip of the tongue; in most positions, it is distinctly audible: *water* [ʋatəʀ] 'water', *hard* [hɑʀt] 'hard'. The [l] is more velarised than it is in German. In some dialects in the south-west, initial [h] is dropped: *oek* [uk] instead of *hoek* [huk], 'corner'. Palatalisation is mostly restricted to alveolars before [j] or non-syllabic [i̯]: [t̯] in *kat* + *je* 'cat (diminutive)' and [š] in *sociaal* 'social'. Nasalisation of vowels before nasal consonants is absent: *hond* 'dog' is [hɔnt], not [hɔ̃ntə] and *hond* + *je* 'dog (diminutive)' is [hɔnt̯jə] not [hɔ̃nt̯jə]. It is also avoided in French loans: *plafond* 'ceiling' is [plafɔ́n] rather than [plafɔ̃́].

The voiced-voiceless opposition is phonetically quite distinct in plosives, but not in fricatives. For many speakers, the difference between *s/z* and *f/v* is one of tenseness rather than one of voicing. The difference between the voiceless and voiced velar fricatives has become almost allophonic: voiced (or lax) after long vowels word-medially, and voiceless elsewhere. A few exceptions to this regularity are historical and are indicated by the orthography: *lachen* 'laugh' [laxən] vs *vlaggen* 'flags' [ʋlaɣən]. The realisation of the velar fricative as [ç] as in German *ich* 'I', or as voiced [ɣ] in word-initial position is regarded as dialectal, more particularly as 'southern'. In the non-native vocabulary, the word-medial alveolar fricative is predictably voiced after long vowels: *televisie* 'television', *Indonesië* 'Indonesia', *NASA* 'NASA'. Voiced word-initial fricatives are only minimally distinct from the voiceless fricatives that were reintroduced into the language in loanwords: *fier* 'proud' (from French *fière*) [fiːʀ] vs *vier* 'four' [ʋiːʀ]. Voiced [g] is lacking because it changed to [x], also in French loans: *galant* 'gallant' [xalánt].

The vowel system of Dutch is somewhat more complex. The opposition long–short is important in the lexicon and in the morphology: *maan* 'moon' vs *man* 'man'; *boos* 'angry' vs *bos* 'woods'; *veel* 'much' vs *vel* 'skin'; *vies* 'dirty' vs *vis* 'fish'. High vowels

Table 5.1 Vowel Phonemes of Dutch, Schematised

	Front		*Centralised*	*Back*
High	i	ü		u
Mid	e, ɪ	ö	œ, ə	ɔ, o
	ɛ			ɑ
Low			a	
Diphthongs	ɛɪ		ʌü	ɑu

Table 5.2 Consonant Phonemes of Dutch

	Obstruents		*Nasals*	*Liquids*	*Glides*
	Plosive	*Fricative*			
Labial	p, b	f, v	m		ʋ
Alveolar	t, d	s, z	n	l	
Palatal					j
Velar	k,-	x, ɣ	ŋ		
Uvular				ʀ	
Glottal					h

are tense rather than long, but pair with long vowels in the phonological system. Dutch has a full set of rounded front vowels.

Non-low back vowels are rounded. Long [a] is central and very open, but its pronunciation differs considerably across the language area. Long [e] is closed, and diphthongal: [eʲ], but long [o] is markedly less diphthongal than its counterpart in English. Short vowels, except schwa, cannot occur in word-final position. Long variants of the short vowels occur before [R], as in *deur* [dœːR] 'door' vs *deuk* [dök] 'dent', and also in loanwords, e.g. *militair* 'military (adj.)', [militéːR] vs *ver* [vɛR] 'far'. The unstressed vowel and epenthetic vowel [ə] is not always phonetically distinguishable from short [œ] but is clearly a separate phoneme in the system. The pronunciation of the three rising diphthongs varies, but the very open varieties, e.g. [ɑɪ] for [ɛɪ] are socially stigmatised, and so are the non-diphthongised varieties that occur in the larger cities in the western part of the country, e.g. Amsterdam [ɛː] for [ɛɪ] in [fɛːn] *fijn* 'fine', and The Hague [œː] for [ʌü] in [dœːn] *duin* 'dune'.

One of the most typical features of Dutch pronunciation, which it shares with German, is the devoicing of all obstruents in word-final and syllable-final position. This led to morphological contrasts such as *kruis–kruisen* 'cross–crosses' vs *huis–huizen* 'house–houses', *hees–hese* 'husky–id., inflected form' vs *vies–vieze* 'dirty–id., inflected form' and *eis–eisen* 'to demand' vs *reis–reizen* 'to travel'. That the rule is still operative can be seen from the pronunciation of foreign words like *Sidney* [sɪtni], *Rizla* [Rɪsla]. Its effects can be undone through regressive voicing assimilation at morpheme boundaries and in sandhi position: *huisdeur* 'front door' is pronounced [hʌüzdœːR] and *Mazda* is pronounced [mɑzda]. But when the second of two adjacent obstruents is a fricative, voicing assimilation is progressive: *huisvuil* 'garbage' is [hʌüsfʌül], and *badzout* 'bathing salts' is [bɑtsɑut].

Another typical feature is the insertion of [ə] in non-homorganic consonant clusters in word-final position and at morpheme boundaries: *melk* 'milk' [mɛlək], *arm* 'arm' [ɑRəm], *hopeloos* 'hopeless' [hopəlos]. A 'linking phoneme' [ə] also occurs in some compounds: *geitemelk* 'goat milk'. This is a characteristic difference between the pronunciation and the lexicons of Dutch and German: Dutch *mogelijk* 'possible', German *möglich*; Dutch *adelaar* 'eagle', German *Adler*. Glottalisation of initial vowels hardly occurs in Dutch and glides are inserted automatically between vowels except after [a]: *douane* 'customs' [duwánə], *theater* 'theatre' [tejátəR], compare German ['eʔáːtɐ] 'theatre' (Re)syllabification is pervasive, and V(C)C–V sequences will preferably be restructured to V(C) –CV, so that the word *gást* + *àrbeid* + *er* 'immigrant worker' will be pronounced [χɑs-tɑR-béɪ-dəR]. Geminates disappeared from the language, but can occur at morpheme boundaries and in sandhi position: *uit* + *trekken* 'to pull out' [ʌüt:Rɛkən] vs *uit* + *rekken* 'stretch' [ʌütRɛkən]. Word-final *-n* after schwa is dropped in almost all contexts, so that for most speakers the difference between singular and plural has been reduced to a difference between ∅ ending and *-e* ending: *straat–straten* 'street–streets', [stRat]-[stRatə]. This situation has been reinforced by a historical rule that deleted word-final schwa in nouns: Dutch *zon* 'sun', German *Sonne*; as a result of this rule, a large majority of native nouns end in a consonant. That this rule is no longer operative can be seen from the pronunciation of loans like English *score* [skɔːRə] and French elite [elítə]. Deletion of final [t] in consonant clusters is determined by complex morphological, phonological, and stylistic factors, but it is standard in the formation of diminutives: *lucht* + *je* 'smell (diminutive)' is pronounced [lœxjə].

Word stress in Dutch is lexical, which means that the location of main stress is unpredictable to a high degree. In words without internal morphological structure main stress tends to be on the (pre)final syllable, and there is a complex interaction between the distribution of stresses, vowel length and syllable weight. Compare *kóning* 'king' [kónɪŋ] and *koníjn* 'rabbit' [konɛ́ɪn]. All vowels can be stressed except schwa, unstressed vowels are often reduced but not in word-final position: *banáan* 'banana' [banán], [bənán] but *Amérika* 'America' [amɛ́ʀika]. In the Romance vocabulary, Dutch has preserved (pre)final stress; as a consequence, there are systematic differences between the pronunciation of these words in Dutch and the pronunciation of their English cognates: *relátion–relátie* [ʀelátsi] but: *rélative–relatíéf* [ʀèlatíf], *sócial–sociáal* [sošjál]. Most suffixes of Romance origin have kept their stress in Dutch, including the verbal suffix *-eer* that was formed from the original French infinitive ending: *organíseer* 'organise' [ɔʀxanizé·ʀ]. Secondary stress on these words is predictably on the initial syllable when main stress is final. In contrast with the pattern of derived Romance words, most native suffixes and early Latin loans have lost their stress. Main stress in complex native words is usually on the stem: *lángzaam* 'slow' – *lángzaamheid* 'slowness', *árbeid* 'work' – *árbeider* 'worker', *vriend* 'friend' – *vríendelijk* 'friendly'. Nominal and verbal compounds normally have primary stress on the first element and secondary stress on the second element: *húisdeùr* 'front door', *úitvoèr* 'export', *ínleìd* 'introduce'. In some classes of derived forms, especially adjectives, main stress shifts to the last syllable preceding the suffix: *ínleìd–inleídend* 'introductory'.

Sentence intonation in Dutch is more 'flat' than the sentence intonation of (British) English. The typical intonation pattern for the Dutch declarative sentence involves two basic contours: a Low declining contour at the beginning and at the end, and a High declining contour in the middle. What is perceived as 'accent' is the result of either a rise towards the High contour or a fall from the High contour: *die **jongen** schrijft een **brief*** 'that boy is writing a letter'.

4 Morphology

Since Dutch has lost most of its inflectional endings and case endings in the course of its history, its morphology, in that respect, is closer to English than it is to German. Compare the nominal paradigms for the phrase 'the day' in the chart given here.

Nominal Paradigms

		Middle Dutch	Modern Dutch	Modern German
Sg.	Nom.	die dach	de dag	der Tag
	Acc.	dien dach	de dag	den Tag
	Gen.	des daghes	(van) de dag	des Tages
	Dat.	dien daghe	(aan) de dag	dem Tag(e)
Pl.	Nom.	die daghe	de dagen	die Tage
	Acc.	die daghe	de dagen	die Tage
	Gen.	der daghe	(van) de dagen	der Tage
	Dat.	dien daghen	(aan) de dagen	den Tagen

Case distinctions have been preserved to some extent in the forms of pronouns and in some relic forms such as *'s nachts* 'at night'. The basic distinction in both the nominal and the verbal paradigms, however, is the distinction between singular and plural. In the regular (or 'weak') verbal paradigm, singular forms are differentiated for person in the following way: first person stem + ∅, second and third person stem + *t*. As in the nominal paradigms, the contrast between stem-final voiced consonants and stem-final voiceless consonants is neutralised in the singular forms and not consistently represented in the orthography.

Verbal Paradigms

		'travel'	*'demand'*	*'find'*	*'put'*
Stem		reiz	eis	vind	zet
Sg.	1	reis	eis	vind	zet
	2	reist	eist	vindt	zet
	3	reist	eist	vindt	zet
Pl.		reizen	eisen	vinden	zetten
Infinitive		reizen	eisen	vinden	zetten
Past part.		gereisd	geëist	gevonden	gezet

The basic tense opposition in verbs is between past and non-past. Past forms in regular verbs are made by adding *-de/-te* to the stem, and *-den/-ten* for the plural. Like English and German, Dutch has retained a number of 'strong' verbs where the past is formed by vowel change: *ik vond–I found–ich fand*. Regular past participles are formed by adding the prefix *ge-* and the suffix *-d/-t*; strong verbs and a few others have the suffix *-en*. The auxiliaries of the perfect tense are *hebben* 'have' or *zijn* 'be'. Transitive verbs take *hebben*, but intransitives are split into two classes: *ik lach–ik heb gelachen* 'I laugh, I have laughed' and *ik val–ik ben gevallen* 'I have fallen'. The perfect tense is largely aspectual, and the future tense with the auxiliary *zullen* expresses modality rather than tense. The auxiliary of the passive voice is *worden*, but the perfect of the passive takes *zijn* 'be'. The phrase *de deur is gesloten* can be interpreted either as 'the door has been closed (by somebody)' or as 'the door is shut'.

The personal pronouns have subject forms and object forms, and full forms and reduced forms in both categories; see the chart of personal pronouns.

Personal Pronouns

		Subject forms		Object forms	
		Full forms	*Reduced forms*	*Full forms*	*Reduced forms*
Sg.	1	ik	'k	mij	me
	2	jij, u	je,-	jou, u	je,-
	3	hij, zij	-ie, ze	hem, haar	'm, 'r
		(het)	't	(het)	't
Pl.	1	wij	we	ons	-
	2	jullie, u	-	jullie, u	-
	3	zij	ze	(hen), hun	ze

In the spoken language, full forms have become almost emphatic and the reduced forms are commonly used. The neuter pronoun *het* is pronounced [ət]; *het* [hɛt] is used in the orthography. After prepositions, it is obligatorily replaced by the adverbial pronoun *er*: **ik denk aan het/ik denk er aan* 'I think of it'. The clitic pronoun *-ie* and reduced object pronouns cannot be preposed in the sentence: *ik heb 'm niet gezien* 'I haven't seen him', but not *'m heb ik niet gezien*. In the third person, there is strong interaction between personal pronouns and demonstratives, as can be seen from the following sequence of sentences:

Waar is Jan? Die komt vandaag niet. Hij is ziek; ik geloof dat-ie griep heeft.
'Where is John? He is not coming today. He is sick; I think he has the flu.'

The third person plural object pronoun *hen* was artificially introduced into the language and is hardly used; the pronoun *hun* occurs mostly after prepositions: *aan hun* 'to them'. In some dialects it is also used as a subject pronoun: *hun hebben 't gedaan* 'they did it'. A third person reflexive pronoun, *zich*, was introduced under the influence of German. Its syntactic distribution is notoriously complex, and many geographical and social dialects of Dutch still use *hem* instead of *zich: Jan heeft geen jas bij zich/ bij 'm* 'John doesn't have a coat with him'.

The difference between the polite form of address *u* (pronounced [ü]) and the informal forms *jij/jullie* is comparable to the difference between German *Sie* and *du* and French *vous* and *tu*. As everywhere, the sociology of their usage is complicated. Southern forms of Dutch have different forms of address which include the older pronouns *gij/ge*.

In spite of the strong simplification of the nominal and pronominal paradigms, or, maybe, because of these developments, the gender system of Dutch is actually quite complex. Its major features may be summarised as follows:

(1) Nouns are divided into two classes: nouns with common gender, which take the definite determiner *de*, and nouns with neuter gender, which take the definite determiner *het*. In the plural, the determiner is *de* for both classes. In noun phrases with the indefinite determiner *een*, adjectives that modify a *de* word have the inflected form, and adjectives that modify a *het* word have the uninflected form. Compare the chart of gender distinctions in nouns.

Gender Distinctions in Nouns

	'the big city'	'the big house'
Sg. def.	de grote stad	het grote huis
Sg. indef.	een grote stad	een groot huis
Pl. def.	de grote steden	de grote huizen

(2) Nouns belonging to the *de* class are distinguished as masculine and feminine. For instance, words with the ending *-ing* are feminine and require the anaphoric pronoun *zij/ze*. For many speakers in the western area, however, the masculine/feminine distinction is no longer alive, or is felt to be a distinction of natural gender. Anaphoric reference to words denoting a non-human object by the pronouns *hij/hem* or *zij/haar* is sometimes avoided, as in the example: *wat vond je van die lezing? ik vond het vervelend* 'what did you think of that lecture? I found it boring'. In the Belgian area, the masculine/feminine gender distinction is very much alive.

(3) Normally, grammatical gender overrides natural gender, as appears from the usage of the relative pronouns *die* and *dat: de stad, die* 'the town which' vs *het huis, dat* 'the house which' but also *de jongen, die* 'the boy who' vs *het jongetje dat* 'the boy (diminutive) that'. However, when relative pronouns are combined with prepositions, the form of the relative pronoun is determined by the distinction human/non-human and not by the distinction between *de* words and *het* words. Compare: *de man, **wie** ik gesproken heb* 'the man with whom I have been speaking' vs *de stad **waar** ik geen kaart van had* 'the city of which I did not have a map'. In the spoken language, sentences like *de man waar ik mee gesproken heb* are not at all uncommon, and they are another indication that the gender system and the system of pronominal reference are unstable. The adverbial pronouns *er, daar, waar*, which replace the pronouns *het, dat, wat* in combination

117

with prepositions, are the only elements that allow prepositions to be stranded, as appears from the examples above. A sentence like *de man wie ik mee gesproken heb* is incorrect.

Both flection and derivation are predominantly suffixal. With respect to derivation (word formation), many native suffixes were originally elements with independent meanings that they have lost in the course of history, and it would seem that, in the present-day language, some elements are going the same way: *rijk* 'rich', *arm* 'poor'; *zuurstofrijk* 'having much oxygen', *zuurstofarm* 'having little oxygen'. Most native suffixes have also lost their stress, but some have retained their stress and occur in compound-like derivations such as *vriendelijk + heid* 'friendliness' (German *-heit*), *verklaar + baar* 'explainable' (German *-bar*) and *werk + loos* 'unemployed' (German *-los*). Romance suffixes are often fully stressed, as shown in the section on phonology, but the morphological structure of the Romance vocabulary is by and large opaque. The main reason for this is that Dutch formed its own verbal stems on the basis of the original French infinitive: *demonstreer* 'demonstrate'. Consequently, the common element in related nominal and verbal forms is a 'root' that cannot occur as an independent element: *demonstr + eer* 'demonstrate', *demonstr + atie* 'demonstration'. This is atypical for native word formation.

The Romance vocabulary also has a highly involved morphophonology, whereas native word formation in Dutch typically has not. With few exceptions, non-native affixes cannot be attached to native stems, but native affixes can be attached to non-native stems. For instance, a number of Romance verbs ending in *-eer* have both a Romance and a native nominalisation: *realis + atie* as well as *realis + eer + ing* 'realisation'. But a formation like English *reopen* would be totally impossible (the correct form is *heropen*, with the native prefix *her-*) though the prefix *re-* does occur, e.g. in *constructie* 'construction', *reconstructie* 'reconstruction'. All in all, it appears that the Romance vocabulary has been much less integrated into Dutch than it has been into English, and that both phonologically and morphologically it is still very much [–native], in spite of the fact that a number of Romance words are actually quite common, also in the spoken language.

A much discussed feature of Dutch morphology is the system of diminutives. The diminutive suffix is, actually, one of the few really productive derivational suffixes of the modern language. The basic form of the suffix is *-tje*, the variants are *-je* (after obstruents), *-etje* (in some cases after liquids and nasals); *-pje* and *-kje* are assimilated variants of *-tje*. So we have: *ei–eitje* 'egg', *aap–aapje* 'monkey', *man–mannetje* 'man', *maan–maantje* 'moon', *koning–koninkje* 'king' and *raam–raampje* 'window'. Diminutives are very frequent, and semantically they express a whole range of negative as well as positive attitudes and feelings besides the basic meaning of 'small'. A much used variant of the *-je* forms in the spoken language (after consonants except [t]) is *-ie: meisje–meissie* 'girl'. The same paradigm, with the additional ending *-s*, is used to form adverbs from certain adjectives: *zacht* 'soft', *zachtjes* 'softly'; *bleek* 'pale', *bleekjes* 'somewhat pale'.

Prefixation is, generally speaking, more transparent and more productive than suffixation and the phonological boundary between prefix and stem is more distinct as well. The prefix *be-* is used to form transitive verbs from intransitives, as in *spreken* 'speak', *bespreken* 'discuss', and can also be used to form verbs from nouns: *dijk* 'dike', *bedijken* 'to put a dike around'. The prefix *ver-* has a causative meaning in some verbs: *hitte* 'heat (noun)' – *verhitten* 'heat (transitive)', *breed* 'large, broad' – *verbreden* 'enlarge, broaden', but a more complex meaning in other verbs: *draaien* 'turn' – *verdraaien* 'turn into another direction; twist'.

Dutch is like German in that it still exploits a large number of the Indo-European compounding devices. Some of the more familiar types are compounds with nouns as heads: *huisdeur* (noun noun) 'house door; front door', *breekpunt* (verb noun) 'breaking point', *hoogspanning* (adjective noun) 'high voltage' and compounds with verbs as heads: *pianospelen* (noun verb) 'play the piano', *losmaken* (adjective verb) 'make loose, loosen, untie' and *uitvoeren* (particle verb) 'export'. The second group represents the so-called separable compounds. In independent clauses, the complements are separated from the verb as in: *dit land voert bananen uit* 'this country exports bananas'. This type of incorporation, which is actually on the boundary of morphology and syntax, is extremely common and a number of these formations have acquired specialised meanings: *afmaken* 'finish, kill', *zwartmaken* 'blacken, spoil somebody's reputation'. Another special class of compounds are the so-called derivational compounds. On the surface, these formations have the shape of a compound plus derivational suffix, but there is no corresponding non-derived compound, and for some formations, there is no corresponding non-composite derivation either. Some examples: *langslaper* 'somebody who sleeps long' (**langslaap*, but, possibly, *lang* + *slaper*); *werknemer* 'employee' (**werkneem*, and hardly *werk* + *?nemer*); *loslippig* 'talkative' (**loslip*, nor *los* + **lippig*); *driewieler* 'vehicle on three wheels' (**driewiel*, nor *drie* + **wieler*). Here too, it would seem, morphology borders on syntax: one way to account for these words is to assume that they are phrasal at an underlying level: *langslaper* 'somebody who sleeps long'; *loslippig* 'the property of having loose lips', and that they arise through incorporation rather than through simple concatenation of independent elements.

Though some rules of word formation lead to complex forms, it would be wrong to conclude that Dutch is the type of language that allows for fairly unlimited combination of stems and affixes. On the contrary, there are severe, and as yet ill-understood restrictions on affixation and on compounding. Repeated application of compounding rules also has its limitations: compounds of the type *zitkamertafeltje* 'sitting-room-table-diminutive' or *autoverkoopcijfers* 'car-sales-figures' are not very common, and often avoided in favour of more analytical constructions like *cijfers van de autoverkoop*.

5 Syntax

The syntax of Dutch is of the familiar nominative–accusative type. Subject and object are the major grammatical relations. Since the case distinctions have been lost, objects are bare noun phrases and other grammatical relations are expressed by prepositional phrases. Grammatical subjects, including the subjects of passives, agree with the finite verb in person and number and the subject also plays a dominant role in various anaphoric processes, e.g. reflexive pronouns often can only refer to the subject of the sentence. The prominent role of the subject in Dutch is particularly clear from the use of the dummy subject *het* and the use of the dummy subject *er* in impersonal passives, as well as from the fact that subjects in declarative sentences cannot easily be omitted. Compare:

Het is vervelend dat Wim niet komt.	'It is annoying that Bill is not coming'.
Er wordt gedanst.	'There is dancing.'
*(Er) komt niemand.	'(There) comes no one.'

In declarative sentences, the subject precedes the finite verb; in questions, requests and certain types of conditionals the finite verb is sentence-initial: *komt Wim vanavond?* 'Is Bill coming tonight?' Question words are sentence-initial, and when a non-subject is preposed, the subject moves to the position after the finite verb: *wat doe je?* 'what are you doing?'

All this is, indeed, familiar from many other European languages. Nevertheless, Dutch as well as German, Afrikaans and Frisian differ in their surface syntax from both English and, to a lesser extent, the Scandinavian languages in a number of ways, and some of these differences are more than superficial. The prominent features of the Dutch declarative clause can be summarised as follows:

(a) In independent clauses, the finite verb is in second position.
(b) In clauses where the finite verb is an auxiliary, the main verb (whether infinitive or participle) is placed at the end of the clause. The nominal object and any other nominal complement of the verb precede the main verb.
(c) In independent clauses with more than one auxiliary, all verbs except the finite verb are placed at the end of the clause.
(d) In dependent clauses, the finite verb is placed at the end of the clause as well.
(e) In independent clauses, almost any type of constituent can be preposed to sentence-initial position without special emphasis or so-called comma intonation. Compare:

Wim   heeft het boek aan Marietje gegeven.
Het boek   heeft Wim aan Marietje gegeven.
(Aan) Marietje heeft Wim het boek gegeven.
'Bill has given the book to Mary.'

And, with some emphasis:

Mòoi is het níet.
'Beautiful is it not' i.e. 'It is not exactly beautiful.'
Gelàchen hebben we wél.
'Laughed have we modal' i.e. 'We certainly laughed!'

So, it appears that the Dutch independent clause is both verb-second and verb-final. Most grammarians assume that, at a somewhat more abstract level of representation, the Dutch clause is verb-final, and that the second position of the finite verb in the independent clause is 'derived'. It can actually be shown that in the unmarked case, the ordering of constituents proceeds from right to left with the final position of the main verb as the focal point:

Wim heeft   gisteren met een schroevedraaier   het slot opengemaakt.
Bill has   yesterday with a screwdriver   the lock open made
'Bill (has) opened the lock with a screwdriver yesterday'.

Another conclusion is that the Dutch independent clause is not subject-initial but verb-second. The ordering of constituents in those sentences where the subject is not in sentence-initial position is more adequately and more easily accounted for, not by assuming the traditional rule of subject–verb inversion, but by assuming that one constituent has to be preposed to the position before the finite verb. If no other constituent appears in that position, the grammatical subject fills it 'by default'. Preposing is blocked in the dependent clause, but peripheral adverbials can precede the subject in such clauses: *omdat morgen gelukkig de winkels open zijn* 'because tomorrow fortunately the shops open are'.

These constraints on the position of the verb and of its nominal complement developed relatively late in the history of the language and they seem to have been fixed not before the beginning of the period of Modern Dutch. Sentences with a more random word order, including dependent clauses with verb–object order can easily be attested in medieval texts. In the course of the process, Dutch developed another construction that shows a complement ordered to the left of its head, namely, preposed participial modifiers in the noun phrase: *de door de regering genomen beslissing*, 'the by the government taken decision'. The rise of this pattern was probably facilitated by the existence of noun phrases with prenominal adjectives, which is still the basic pattern in all Germanic languages. It should be added that the construction is more typical of the written language than of the spoken language where it can hardly compete with the regular, postnominal relative clause: *de beslissing die de regering genomen heeft* 'the decision that the government has taken'.

As a result of these developments and their codification into the standard language, Dutch, like German, is more of a hybrid in terms of word order typologies than most other Germanic languages are. The noun phrase bears witness to this as well. As we already saw, both prenominal and postnominal modifiers do occur. The genitive construction is predominantly postnominal: *het boek van die man* 'the book of that man', but there is a residue of the prenominal genitive when the 'possessor' is a proper name: *Wim's boek* 'Bill's book', but not **die man's boek*. Interestingly, Dutch developed another genitive construction that is similar to the prenominal genitive, and quite common in the spoken language though not always accepted in the formal style: *die man z'n boek (ligt op tafel)* 'that man his book (is on the table)'. Also adpositions have a somewhat ambiguous position in Dutch syntax. Prepositions are clearly the unmarked case: *in de tuin* 'in the garden'. But postpositions are common, though not always required, when the phrase expresses direction rather than location:

Wim liep de tuin in.   'Bill walked into the garden.'

Here, too, positing a verb-final position at a more remote level of description is of some explanatory value. Compare:

Het regende	toen	Wim de tuin in liep
it rained	as	Bill the garden into walked

'It rained as Bill walked into the garden.'

It is plausible that these postpositions are, at least in origin, complements to the verb. In not a few cases, they can be interpreted both ways. The sentence *Wim zwom de rivier over* 'Bill swam the river across' can be paraphrased both as: 'Bill swam across the river' and as 'Bill crossed the river swimming'. The high frequency of so-called separable verbal compounds, or verb particle constructions, that was noted in the section on morphology may thus be explained through the syntax.

The modal verbs of Dutch are main verbs rather than auxiliaries. They have regular inflection, and they take clausal complements just as other verbs do. In sentences that combine several predicates, all verbs are strung together at the end of the clause. This phenomenon, known as clause union or verb raising, manifests itself in different ways in different West Germanic languages (and is absent in English). Dutch sides with German in the curious fact that the expected past participle of non-finite auxiliaries is replaced with the infinitive. This does not occur in (West) Frisian:

Dutch	dat hij het boek heeft	*kunnen*	lezen
	that he the book has	can	read
	'that he has been able to read the book'		
German	dass er das Buch hat lesen können		
Frisian	dat er it boek lêze *kent* hat		

But Dutch differs from German in that the usual ordering of the modals with respect to the main verb in verbal clusters is the exact mirror image, which is more clear from a comparison of the following sentences:

Dutch	dat hij het boek moet kunnen lezen
	that he the book must can read
	'that he must be able to read the book'
German	dass er das Buch lesen können muss

And the verbal cluster in Dutch can separate the main verb from its complement, something which does not occur in standard German and is also avoided in many varieties of Dutch in Belgium:

dat hij het boek *uit* moet   kunnen   *lezen*
that he the book out must   can   read
'that he should be able to finish reading the book'

The order main verb–auxiliary is to be expected in a language where the verb phrase is basically OV; the reverse ordering in the verbal cluster of Dutch has, consequently, been interpreted as a tendency to move away from OV ordering. In sequences of a single auxiliary and a main verb, Dutch has an option: *omdat hij het boek heeft gelezen/ omdat hij het boek gelezen heeft* 'because he has read the book'. It is a subject of debate among Dutch grammarians and dialectologists whether the main verb–auxiliary order is a Germanism or whether it is the more natural one.

Apart from the fixed positions of the finite verb and the main verb, the Dutch clause shows considerable freedom of constituent ordering. That freedom is exploited for the foregrounding or backgrounding of information and for embedding the sentence in its context. Preposing is one way to achieve this. Calculations on a fair sample of the written language have shown that less than 50 per cent of declarative clauses are subject-initial. Also, definite nominal objects can easily be moved to a position right after the finite verb, and prepositional phrases can be moved to a position after the main verb:

Wim heeft *dat slot* gisteren met een schroevedraaier opengemaakt.
Wim heeft gisteren dat slot opengemaakt *met een schroevedraaier.*

The latter rule also applies to prepositional phrases that are complements of noun phrases:

Ik heb gisteren *een vogel* gezien *met een hele lange staart.*
I have yesterday a bird seen with a very long tail
'I saw a bird with a very long tail yesterday.'

In the German grammatical tradition this phenomenon is known as *Ausklammerung* ('Exbraciation') and it has sometimes been interpreted as a way to avoid difficulties that might be caused by the long distance between the finite verb and its complement in independent clauses. However, the rule applies equally well in dependent clauses where the finite verb and its complement are adjacent. Postposing a nominal complement remains fully ungrammatical and can be achieved only by dislocation and the use of a resumptive pronoun:

Wim heeft *'t* gisteren met een schroevedraaier opengemaakt, *dat slot.*
'Bill has it yesterday with a screwdriver open made, that lock.'

The sentence-initial position is also available for topicalisation of elements from the dependent clause, with more restrictions than in some of the Scandinavian languages but, it would seem, with fewer restrictions than in standard German.

Die man die jij zei dat je niet   kende is de minister-president.
'That man that you said you didn't know – is the prime minister.'

That topicalisation by preposing is a pervasive feature of Dutch syntax also appears from the occurrence, in the spoken language, of an incorrect construction that can be regarded as a form of 'repeated topicalisation':

Toen hebben ze *die man* hebben ze gearresteerd.
then have they that man have they arrested

Sentence-initial anaphoric elements are commonly omitted, as in *waar is Wim? (Dat) weet ik niet*, 'where is Bill? (That) I don't know'. This phenomenon is easiest described as deletion of a topic, which would reinforce the view that the Dutch independent clause is topic-first rather than subject-first.

Summarising, Dutch has an absolute constraint on the order of the verb and its nominal complement, and a strong tendency towards ordering complements to the left of their heads in general, but other features of its syntax indicate that it is, nevertheless, far from being a consistent OV language. It is, therefore, not surprising that the concept of the verb phrase is essential for an adequate description of its syntax, whereas the usefulness of such a concept has been seriously doubted for classical OV languages like Japanese.

Bibliography

Existing grammars of Dutch in English, such as Donaldson (1981) are intended primarily for language learners; the same author's grammar of Afrikaans should also be noted (Donaldson 1993).

Den Hertog (1903–4) is by far the best grammar of the Dutch language, in spite of the fact that it is now more than a hundred years old, and is modern in its treatment of syntax. Geerts et al. (1984) is a practical and descriptive grammar of the present-day language written by a team of Dutch and Belgian linguists; it is meant for the general public, and is important for its wide coverage of facts. Zonneveld et al. (1980) is a collection of articles on various aspects of Dutch phonology, and contains a useful bibliography compiled by Zonneveld.

Franck (1910) is the best available grammar of the older stages of the language. Van Loey (1970) is the standard reference work for the development of Dutch in the context of Germanic, but some sections have been enlarged so often that it would be better if the whole book were rewritten. Van Haeringen (1960) is a critical and comprehensive survey of the study of Dutch in the Netherlands and abroad, by one of the outstanding scholars in the field.

References

Den Hertog, C.H. 1903–4. *Nederlandse Spraakkunst*, 3 vols, 2nd edn (Amsterdam, reprinted with an introduction by H. Hulshof, Versluys, Amsterdam, 1972–3)

Donaldson, B.C. 1981. *Dutch Reference Grammar* (M. Nijhoff, 's-Gravenhage)

—— 1993. *A Grammar of Afrikaans* (Mouton de Gruyter, Berlin)

Franck, J. 1910. *Mittelniederländische Grammatik mit Lesestücken und Glossar* (Tauchnitz, Leipzig, reprinted Gysbers and van Loon, Arnhem, 1967).

Geerts, G., Haeseryn, W., Rooij, J. de and Toorn, M.C. van den (eds) 1984. *Algemene Nederlandse Spraakkunst* (Groningen and Leuven, Wolters)

Van Haeringen, C.B. 1960. *Netherlandic Language Research: Men and Works in the Study of Dutch*, 2nd edn (E.J. Brill, Leiden)

Van Loey, A. 1970. *Schönfeld's Historische Grammatica van het Nederlands*, 8th edn (Thieme, Zutphen)

Zonneveld, W., Coetsem, F. van and Robinson, O.W. (eds) 1980. *Studies in Dutch Phonology* (Martinus Nijhoff, The Hague)

6

Danish, Norwegian and Swedish

Einar Haugen

1 Introduction

Non-Scandinavians are occasionally astonished to hear Danes, Norwegians and Swedes conversing, each in their own language, without interpreters. The fact that some degree of mutual intelligibility exists between these languages, which we shall refer to as the mainland Scandinavian languages, has led some to suggest that together they should really be regarded as only one language. While for some purposes it is convenient to bracket them together, it is hardly correct to speak of only one Scandinavian or Nordic tongue. Such a practice would require a rather restricted definition of the term 'language'. It would neglect those aspects that are not purely linguistic, but are also social and political. To call them 'dialects' is only historically true, i.e. in that they have branched off from a once common Nordic.

In speaking of them as 'languages', we take into account the facts as Scandinavians themselves also see them: that they constitute separately developed norms of writing and speaking. Each language has an officially accepted form, taught in schools, used by journalists and authors, required for government officials, enshrined in grammars and dictionaries and spoken at least by educated members of the nation. They are, in short, what linguists refer to as 'standardised', making them standard languages. This is indisputably true of Danish and Swedish. The fact that Norwegian is spoken and written in two somewhat deviating forms only means that we must distinguish two standard Norwegian languages. These will here be referred to as B-Norwegian (BN), for Norwegian *bokmål* 'book language', formerly *riksmål* 'national language', and as N-Norwegian (NN), for Norwegian *nynorsk* 'New Norwegian', formerly *landsmål* 'country language'. The names used in Norway are misnomers resulting from political conflict and compromise.

In reckoning here with only four mainland languages, we are setting aside what we may call the *insular* Scandinavian languages *Faroese* (in the Faroe Islands) and *Icelandic* (in Iceland). Danish is still one of the two official languages in the Faroes and in Greenland. Swedish is official not only in Sweden, but also alongside Finnish in Finland, although today only 5 or 6 per cent of the population speak it natively. We exclude Finnish from this account, since it is wholly unrelated to the Indo-European languages that surround it. It belongs to the Finno-Ugric family, as does Samic, formerly called Lappish, the dialectally divided speech of the Sami (Lapps), who inhabit the far north of Scandinavia and nearby Russia. Greenlandic, a variety of Eskimo (Inuit), is also spoken within Scandinavia, as are Romany (Gypsy) and along the south Danish border some German. The following account is thus limited to the central, mainland Scandinavian of Indo-European descent, the standard languages of the Scandinavian heartland.

2 Historical Background

The earliest written evidence of language in this area is epigraphic, i.e. consisting of inscriptions from about AD 200, mostly quite short. They were written in an alphabet known as a futhark from the sounds of its first six letters. The letters are called runes and the type of writing is runic. The earliest centres of its use are in the Danish peninsula of Jutland, which may also be its place of origin. The 24 runes of the futhark (also known as the 'older' futhark) are clearly based on a classical alphabet, most likely the Latin, but differently ordered and named. Designed for carving in wood, it is mostly preserved on more permanent objects of stone and metal. It was never used for writing on parchment, although it was in use down to c. AD 800, when it was replaced by a shorter 16-rune 'younger' futhark. Although the latter appeared in several regional variations, it steadfastly maintained the number sixteen well into the modern period.

The Older Futhark

ᚠ	ᚢ	ᚦ	ᚨ	ᚱ	ᚲ	ᚷ	ᚹ	:	ᚺ	ᚾ	ᛁ	ᛃ	ᛇ	ᛈ	ᛉ	ᛊ	:	ᛏ	ᛒ	ᛖ	ᛗ	ᛚ	ᛜ	ᛞ	ᛟ
f	u	þ	a	r	k	g	w	:	h	n	i	j	ė	p	z	s	:	t	b	e	m	l	ng	d	o

The Younger Futhark

ᚠ	ᚢ	ᚦ	ᚬ	ᚱ	ᚴ	:	ᚼ	ᚾ	ᛁ	ᛅ	ᛋ	:	ᛏ	ᛒ	ᛘ	ᛚ	ᛦ
f	u	þ	ą	r	k	:	h	n	i	a	s	:	t	b	m	l	R

The earliest runic material, though scanty, is sufficient to assure us that at this time the inhabitants of Scandinavia were of Germanic speech. These inscriptions are in fact the earliest written evidences of any Germanic language, earlier than the extinct East Germanic Gothic or the West Germanic Old English, Old Saxon, Old High German, Old Low Franconian or Old Frisian. The Proto-Scandinavian of the earliest inscriptions constitutes the North Germanic ancestor of the present-day Scandinavian languages.

The line of descent is best (if somewhat roughly) visualised as a branching tree (Figure 6.1), starting from a hypothetical Common Scandinavian and ending on the bottom line with the present-day languages properly called 'Scandinavian'.

The dates are only approximations. We shall here be dealing with the last four, Danish (Da.), B-Norwegian (BN), N-Norwegian (NN), and Swedish (Sw.). Occasionally it will be convenient to group both Norwegian languages together as 'Norwegian' (Nw.). 'Old Norse' is a commonly used term for a normalised form of Old Icelandic and Old Norwegian, used in the publication of reading texts.

In its medieval, handwritten form there is a large body of Scandinavian writing on parchment or paper. This skill was brought to Scandinavia by Christian missionaries

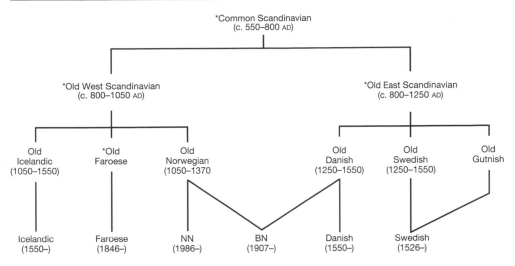

Figure 6.1 The Scandinavian Languages.

and monks at the end of the Viking Age (AD 750–1050), when the Scandinavians were weaned from their worship of Odin and Thor. The missionaries also taught them the Latin alphabet, significantly adapted to suit the language forms then in use. Traditions of writing gradually grew up, reflecting the practices of Latin orthography, but also innovative.

The most extensive, as well as the most notable of this writing, intellectually, historically and as literature, was that part of it produced by Icelanders in the language which Norway and Iceland then still shared. Among its monuments are the collection of pagan mythical and heroic poems called *The Elder Edda*, the handbook of poetics by Snorri Sturluson (1178–1241) known as *The Younger Edda*, and a multitude of so-called *Sagas*, more or less historical tales from Norwegian and Icelandic life in the pagan and post-pagan period. The Icelanders functioned as recorders of tradition for all Scandinavia, and their work is today claimed as part of the heritage of all the Nordic nations. Symbolic is the use of words like 'Viking' and 'Saga', which enter into everyone's stereotyped conceptions of the Scandinavian countries. Today there is a deep cleft between the language of Iceland (and the Faroes) and those of the mainland. Whereas Icelandic and Faroese have retained nearly all the morphological categories of Proto-Germanic, the mainland languages have retained only the genitive as a distinct case (apart from some archaisms), and have gone even further than English by losing verb agreement completely (except for some obsolescent number agreement in Swedish).

As the dates for their standardisation suggest, Danish and Swedish differ from Norwegian in being both unitary and earlier. Their political and cultural development assured their languages of independent status from the time of the Reformation, when the Bible was translated into each. After Sweden won her independence from Danish rule in 1526 under King Gustavus Vasa, a written language in close dependence on the speech of the court in Stockholm and of the whole central Swedish area around it was established, even to some extent deliberately deviant from Danish. When Swedish military power extended to the conquest of former Danish and Norwegian provinces, these also fell under the dominance of Swedish writing. Henceforth Scandinavia was split into two clearly demarcated halves,

Sweden with Finland facing the Baltic, Denmark with Norway and the islands facing the Atlantic.

Denmark, with a language taking shape around Copenhagen (and neighbouring Lund), also got its own Lutheran church and its own Bible, which it succeeded in imposing on Norway as well. Four centuries of Danish dominion (c. 1380–1814) taught Norwegians to write Danish, but not to follow all the newer developments in speech. After an independence gradually won through rupture of the Danish union in 1814 and the Swedish in 1905, the Norwegians found themselves with a cultivated spoken language which, though written like Danish, was spoken with Norwegian sounds and shot through with elements from the folk language. It was a 'Dano-Norwegian' that is still the dominant language, but now written according to its Norwegian pronunciation and known as *bokmål*. The major break with Danish orthography took place in 1907 and was followed by further radical changes in 1917 and 1938. Hence B-Norwegian is shown above as being descended both from Old Norwegian (via speech) and Old Danish (via writing). The father of its spelling reforms was Knud Knudsen (1812–95), schoolmaster and language reformer.

N-Norwegian (known today as *nynorsk*) also goes back to the efforts of a single man, the self-taught linguist and language reformer Ivar Aasen (1813–96). His work was done from 1836 to 1873, including a definitive grammar (1864) and a dictionary (1873). His N-Norwegian was a reconstructed form, a standard based on the spoken dialects, which he was the first to investigate. He was guided also by the Danish and Swedish standards and by Old Norse, which led him to build on the more conservative dialects of western Norway. His norm has been considerably modernised by later users and grammarians, but has won only about one-sixth of the school districts of the country. Even so, it must be taken seriously as the standard of a not inconsiderable section of the Norwegian people, including many authors, scholars and institutions.

The consequence of these historical and social developments has been that the old division of Scandinavia into a western and eastern half has been replaced by a much more complex overlapping. Norwegian has had its form returned to a closer relation to Swedish, geographically natural; while at least B-Norwegian has retained a great deal of its cultivated lexicon from Danish. The present-day relation may be seen as a right triangle, with the hypotenuse between Danish and Swedish. Speaking very generally, B-Norwegian (and to some extent even N-Norwegian) has its lexicon common with Danish, but phonology common with Swedish. When Norwegians and Swedes communicate orally, they can tell what word is being spoken, though they may be uncertain of its meaning. When Norwegians and Danes communicate, they have to listen hard to be sure which word the other is using, but once they get that, they usually know what it means. Or as one wit has put it: Norwegian is Danish spoken in Swedish.

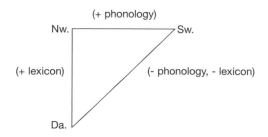

Even though the present-day norms of writing were established with the help of the printing press, at the time of the Reformation, they were not spread to the common people until the nineteenth century, with the establishment of universal public school systems.

3 The Common Heritage

The degree of intelligibility that does exist in Scandinavia today, as well as the obstacles that have led to what I have called 'semi-communication' within the area, have their origin in two major factors: (1) a basic common ancestry in the Old Scandinavian languages; and (2) common influences from outside the area. We do not know how unified Proto-Scandinavian really was; its unity may be an artifact of linguistic reconstruction. There are striking basic similarities that immediately identify the Scandinavian languages, some of them unique, others shared with other Germanic languages. On the other hand, we can follow, at least since the beginning of the manuscript tradition, many of the differential choices made in the course of time. We can also see how the influence of such foreign languages as Greek, Latin, Low German, High German, French, and today English has been incorporated into Scandinavian often giving the same results in each language, but at times also quite different results. Since there has always been some communication within the area, influences of all kinds have spread from one country to the other. It will be noted that the languages listed as providing most of the outside influence are all of the West European type. It is striking that in spite of a certain contact with Celtic languages in the west and with Slavonic languages in the east, very few influences are detectable from these.

The loss of unity in this area is reflected in the growth of dialectal differences both within the countries and between them. Before the standard had been popularised, the mostly rural population split into local and regional dialects. Local communities functioned as closed societies, whether as in Denmark and southern Sweden they were villages, or as in Norway and northern Sweden they were parishes with individual farms. The area turned into a mosaic of dialects, criss-crossed by geographical differences that can be mapped as isoglosses. To this day there are remote areas whose dialects are partly or wholly unintelligible to citizens of the capital, e.g. Jutland in Denmark, Dalecarlia in Sweden, Setesdal in Norway.

For the most part, however, modern mobility and mass media tend to reduce the gap by bringing many rural speakers into contact with urban dialects, often leading to a modification of their own in the direction of the standard. Especially in Norway the dialects are felt to have a national value, a charming and diverting form of local variation to be ecologically protected as part of a vanishing linguistic environment. In each country there are institutes devoted to dialectology. Recent years have seen the growth of a sociolinguistic awareness of speech variation, including the full spectrum from rural dialects and working-class speech to elite and formal varieties.

4 Accent: Stress and Tone

Dynamic stress is distributed over words and sentences in patterns similar to those of other Germanic languages, in degrees varying from primary to weak (also called 'unstressed').

The basic rule of dynamic stress on the first syllable, inherited from Germanic, is still the major rule, but it is now preserved in full only in Icelandic. On the mainland, as in German and English, the rule has been broken to permit a large number of loanwords with stress on the last or penultimate syllable. Post-initial stress may be taken as a marker of 'foreignness' in such words: Da. Nw. Sw. *natu´r* 'nature', *natu´rlig* 'natural'; Nw. *gemytt´lig* 'temper', *gemytt´* 'good natured' (Da. Sw. *gemy´t*, *gemy´tlig* (note that stress is marked with an accent at the end of the stressed syllable). Differences between the languages may require one to check on your neighbours' language with the help of a dictionary: e.g. *egentlig* 'really' is Sw. [ejen´tli], but Nw. [e´gentli], from German *eigentlich*. Verb-particle phrases also have definite, language-specific rules: Danish and Swedish usually stress the particle, Norwegian often the verb, as in Da. *stå opp´/* Sw. *stå upp´/* vs Nw. *stå`-opp* 'get up'.

Compounds usually have primary stress on the first member, secondary or reduced stress on the second, e.g. Da. *kal´veste˛g/* BN *kal`veste˛k/* Sw. *kal`vste˛k* 'veal roast'. Again there are exceptions, as in Da./BN *hushold´ning* Sw. *hu`shållning* 'housekeeping'. Especially confusing are occasional place-names, like Da. *København´n* [-hau´n], Nw. *Kristiansan´d*, Sw. *Drottninghol´m*.

Parallel to similar developments in English and German, the mainland Nordic languages have over the centuries undergone an extensive process of *stress reduction* in the less conspicuous syllables, reflected especially in the quality of vowels and in the inflectional system. While Old Scandinavian regularly had unstressed syllables containing the vowels *-i/-e*, *-u/-o* and *-a*, the modern languages have mostly levelled the three to one, *-e* (pronounced [ə]) in Danish and B-Norwegian, to *-e* and *-a* (and an occasional *-o)* in Swedish and N-Norwegian. It is unclear whether the phonological or the morphological development is primary here, but the result is part of a general trend from a more to a less inflected language, i.e. from a synthetic to an analytic language.

The most striking feature of the Scandinavian accentual system is its preservation of a distinction that probably arose in Common Scandinavian, namely its two contrasting prosodemes, which we shall here designate as 'Accent 1' and 'Accent 2'. In most forms of Norwegian and Swedish and in some Danish dialects, these are realised as tonemes, i.e. musical differences that are regularly associated with the primary dynamic stress and are heard as rising or falling word melodies. The difference is significant in polysyllables, where minimal pairs are common (Accent 1 is marked by an acute, Accent 2 by a grave marker): Nw. *huset* 'the house' [hʉ´sə] vs *huse* 'to house' [hʉ`sə], *fin´ner* '*finds*' vs *fin`ner* 'finder'; Sw. *bu´ren* 'the cages' vs *bu`ren* 'borne', *nub´ben* 'the tack' vs *nub`ben* 'the drink'. The distinction goes back to a difference in Common or Old Scandinavian between monosyllables (with Accent 1) and polysyllables (with Accent 2). Every stressed syllable gets one of the two accents.

In standard Danish the distinction of accent is similar in distribution, but very different in phonetic realisation. Here Accent 1 is realised as a glottal catch or glottalisation, known in Danish as *stød* 'thrust'. It occurs in words that in Old Norse were monosyllables, e.g. *finder* 'finds' [finʔɔ] from ON *finnr*, not in old polysyllables, e.g. *finder* 'finder' from ON *finnari*. There are some special factors in the Danish case, e.g. in the effect of certain consonants in preventing *stød* in monosyllables. While the rules in each case are complex, their similarity to the Norwegian–Swedish situation is so great that scholars agree they are connected. It is not certain which is primary, but most scholars have assumed that the tonemes are primary and the glottalisation secondary.

5 Vowels

Each language has nine basic vowels, the five Latin vowels *a, e, i, o, u* plus four additional ones: *y* (high front round), Da. Nw. *ø*/Sw. *ö* (mid front round), Da. Nw. *æ*/ Sw. *ä* (low front unround) and *å* (mid to low back round; in Da. Nw. formerly written *aa*). The last three are placed at the end of the alphabet: Da. Nw. *æ, ø, å*, Sw. *å, ä, ö*.

All the vowels can be either *long* (tense) or *short* (lax). In Norwegian and Swedish length depends on the following consonant: in stressed syllables vowels are long before short (single) consonants and finally; elsewhere they are short, cf. Nw. Sw. *tak* [taːk] 'roof, ceiling' vs Nw. *takk*, Sw. *tack* [takː] 'thanks'. This inverse syllabic relationship does not apply in Danish, which lacks long consonants. Hence Nw./Sw. *takk/tack* 'thanks' is written *tak* in Danish, but still with a short vowel. Before a vowel the consonant may be written double to mark the preceding vowel as short, but the consonant is pronounced short: *takke* 'to thank' [tagˀə]. In Danish the symbol *ø* has two values, not distinguished in spelling, its usual mid round front value of [ø] and a lower variety, especially before *r:* [œ].

The vowel qualities are less distorted from the old Latin values of the letters than in English, but even so they have done some shifting. If we visualise the relationship in terms of a traditional vowel diagram, we can say that in Danish they have moved clockwise, in Norwegian and Swedish counterclockwise:

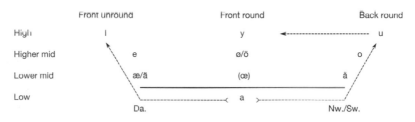

Figure 6.2 Vowel Shifts in Danish, Norwegian and Swedish.

In Danish the *a* has been fronted, bringing it closer to *æ, æ* has moved towards *e* and *e* towards *i*. But in Norwegian and Swedish *a* has moved closer to *å*, being backed and rounded, while *å* has moved toward *o* and *o* to *u*, and *u* has been fronted and rounded to become almost an *y*. To a Norwegian and a Swede the Da. *ja* sounds like *jæ/jä*, while to a Dane the Nw./Sw. *ja* sounds like *jå*.

Only N-Norwegian has retained the Old Norse diphthongs in full, now written *au* [æʉ], *ei* [æi], *øy* [œy]: *laus* 'loose', *bein* 'leg, bone', *løysa* 'loosen'. In Danish and Swedish (and conservative B-Norwegian) these are monophthongs: *løs/lös, ben, løse/ lösa*. B-Norwegian has acquired some diphthongs in recent reforms, e.g. *bein, øy* 'island'. Some are found in loanwords, e.g. BN *feide* 'feud', *mausoleum* 'mausoleum', *føye* 'yield; join'. Others are BN *oi* in *boie* 'buoy', *ai* in *kai* 'quay', *ui* in *hui* 'whee'. In Danish and Swedish these are considered vowel plus consonant, e.g. Da. *fejdel*, Sw. *fejd*, Da. *føje*, Da. *bøje*/Sw. *boj*, Da./Sw. *kaj*, Da./Sw. *huj*. Further examples are:

Da.	BN	NN	Sw.
sten 'stone'	sten/stein	stein	sten
høre 'hear'	høre	høvra	höra
rød 'red'	rød	raud	röd

131

6 Consonants

The symbols of the Latin alphabet are taught in full, but the following are largely limited to proper names, foreign words and place-names: *c q w x z*. In 1801 Sweden adopted a policy of nativising many of these by replacing *c* with *k* (*kapital* 'capital') or *s* (*siffra* 'cipher'), *qu* with *kv* (*kvantum* 'quantity'), *w* with *v* (*valross* 'walrus'), *z* with *s* (*sebra* 'zebra'). Only *x* was regularly retained (*lax* 'salmon'). In 1917 Norway followed suit, going a step further, e.g. adopting *s* for *c* in *sirkus* 'circus' and *sigar* 'cigar' as well as *ks* for *x: laks* 'salmon'. Denmark has been more conservative, except for adopting *ks* for *x* (but keeping *x*, e.g. in *sex*, if only to distinguish it from *seks* 'six').

Certain phonemes are written as clusters (like English *sh, th, ng* etc.). Thus Nw./Sw. [š] may be *sj* (Nw. *sjel*/Sw. *själ* 'soul'), *skj* (Nw. *skjorte*/Sw. *skjorta* 'shirt') or just *sk* before front vowels (Nw./Sw. *ski* [šiː] 'ski', Sw. *sköld* 'shield' but Nw. *skjold*). Similarly [ç] may be spelled *tj* or *kj* (Nw. *tjue*/ Sw. *tjugo* 'twenty', Nw. *kjole* 'dress'/Sw. *kjol* 'skirt') or just *k* before front vowels (BN *kirke*/NN *kyrkje*/Sw. *kyrka* 'church'). These fricatives (or affricates) of Norwegian and Swedish are results of the palatalisation of velar stops, a process not shared by standard Danish, although many Danish dialects have them. Further examples are:

Da.	BN	NN	Sw.
skære 'cut'	skjære	skjera	skära
kysse 'kiss'	kysse	kyssa	kyssa

A feature of modern Scandinavian is the absence of voiced sibilants [z ž dž], lost in Common Scandinavian. But they retain traces of an ancient 'hardening' of the medial sequences *-jj-* and *-ww-*, giving forms like Da. *æg*/ Nw. *egg*/Sw. *ägg* for German *Ei* (English *egg* is a Viking-age borrowing from Norse). A much later development was the trend in Danish and adjacent areas of Norwegian and Swedish to voice short fortis stops *p t k* to *b d g* after vowels. In Danish proper this development went even farther, turning *d* and *g* into spirants or even vocalic glides, a development not reflected in the spelling. The result of this and a general Danish devoicing of the lenis consonants is to make Danish word endings extremely difficult for other Scandinavians to hear correctly:

Da.	BN	NN	Sw.
tabe [taːbə] lose'	tape	tapa	tappa
bide [biːðə] 'bite'	bite	bita	bita
lege [lajə] 'play'	leke	leika	leka

While most of Norwegian and Swedish has retained the Germanic (and Indo-European) *r* as a tongue-tip trill (or tap), Danish has adopted the French and German uvular *r* [ʀ], weakening it usually to a vocalic glide. This insidious sound has spread also into many areas of southern and western Norway and Sweden, still not including either Oslo or Stockholm. But both countries show a widespread weakening of the trills before dentals, resulting in a set of retroflex consonants of Indic type: *rt* [ṭ], *rs* [ṣ], *rl* [ḷ], *rn* [ṇ], *rd* [ḍ]. The same dialects have a so-called 'thick' (cacuminal) flap derived from *rð* and *l*[ɫ] that is virtually unique among the world's languages; though it is universal in the dialects of eastern Norway and north-central Sweden, it is not accepted in elite circles.

7 Morphology

The mainland languages show a parallel and remarkably similar development from the highly synthetic language of Germanic and Old Scandinavian to an analytic, i.e. greatly reduced, formal grammar. Its movement has been in the same direction as Low German and English. The only remaining case is a possessive -*s* that is really a generalised group genitive (see below). Most plural nouns now end in -*r*, and verbs lack markers for person or number of the subject. Definite and indefinite articles, unknown in Proto-Germanic, have developed. Various ways of marking formality of address have arisen, mostly in imitation of German practices.

7.1 Nouns

These still have gender distinction, in which neuter (nt.) is the most stable. In Danish and Swedish and traditional B-Norwegian, masculine (m.) and feminine (f.) have merged into a common (c.) gender having the markers of the masculine. Only in N-Norwegian and folk-oriented B-Norwegian is the feminine retained, in the latter only for certain words or styles. The genders are marked only by accompanying articles, adjectives and referential (anaphoric) pronouns, but are in part also reflected in the forms of the plural.

Plural classes

	Eng.	Da.		BN		NN		Sw.	
m.	'day'	dag	dage	dag	dager	dag	dagar	dag	dagar
	'park'	park	parker	park	parker	park	parker	park	parker
m.f.	'sun'	sol	sole	sol	soler	sol	soler	sol	solar
m.	'shoe'	sko	sko	sko	sko	sko	skor	sko	skor
m.f.	'goose'	gås	gæs	gås	gjess	gås	gjæs	gås	gäss
m.	'brother'	broder	brødre	bror	brødre	bror	brør	bror	bröder
m.	'cock'	hane	haner	hane	haner	hane	hanar	hane	hanar
m.f.	'song'	vise	viser	vise	viser	vise	viser	vise	visor
nt.	'house'	hus	huse	hus	hus	hus	hus	hus	hus
nt.	'kingdom'	rige	riger	rike	riker	rike	rike	rike	riken
nt.	'ear'	øre	ører	øre	ører	øyra	øyro	öra	öron
			(obs. øren)						

N-Norwegian and Swedish show rudimentary remains of older declensions; all four retain old umlaut classes (like English *geese, feet, men* etc.). Possessive -*s* is regularly suffixed (without an apostrophe unless the word ends in *s*): Da. *dags, dagens, dages, dagenes,* but *gås '*. It is often avoided in favour of compounds or prepositional phrases: Da. *dagsverk* 'day's work', *ord for dagen* 'a word for the day, the day's word'. As in English it can be added to any noun phrase (the so-called group genitive), e.g. Da. *kongen af Danmarks brystsukker* 'the King of Denmark's cough drops'. Formal Swedish rejects this genitive, preferring *kungens av Danmark bröstsocker*, but general usage is the same as in Danish and Norwegian.

7.2 Articles

As in English, nouns can appear either with or without articles, depending on context and meaning. The definite articles are historically earlier, and the indefinite articles are a development of the late Middle Ages (that never reached Iceland). Usage is similar to that of English, though for instance abstracts like 'love' and 'hate' usually are definite (Da. *kærligheden/* BN *kjærligheten/*NN *kjærleiken/*Sw. *kärleken* 'love').

The definite article is an interesting and characteristic feature of all Scandinavian languages (aside from some dialects in west Jutland). There are actually two, one suffixed to the noun and one preceding adjectives (which we will discuss below under adjectives). Originally a separate word *inn* m. (*in* f., *it* nt.) 'that, yon', it was already in Old Norse attached to the noun and became a morphological suffix. To illustrate its uses we take some of the same words as in the previous table and include the indefinite article, which is an unstressed form of the word for 'one'; it is used only in the singular, except for an occasional Swedish form *ena* 'some'.

Articles: Indef. Sg., Def. Sg. and Def. Pl.

	Da.		*BN*		*NN*		*Sw.*	
m.	en dag	en park	en dag	en park	ein dag	ein park	en dag	en park
	dag*en*	park*en*	dag*en*	park*en*	dag*en*	park*en*	dag*en*	park*en*
	dag*ene*	park*ene*	dag*ene*	park*ene*	dag*ane*	park*ene*	dag*arna*	park*erna*
m.f.	en gås	en vise	en gås	en vise	ei gås	ei vise	en gås	en vis*a*
	gås*en*	vis*en*	gås*a/-en*	vis*a/-en*	gås*a*	vis*a*	gås*en*	vis*an*
	gæss*ene*	vis*erne*	gjess*ene*	vis*ene*	gj*æsene*	vis*ene*	gäss*ena*	vis*orna*
nt.	et hus	et rige	et hus	et rike	eit hus	eit rike	ett hus	ett rik*e*
	hus*et*	rig*et*	hus*et*	rik*et*	hus*et*	rik*et*	hus*et*	rik*et*
	hus*ene*	rig*erne*	hus*ene*	rik*ene*	hus*a*	rik*a*	hus*en*	rik*ena*

In Norwegian the suffixed *-t* of the neuter singular is silent.

7.3 Adjectives

There are no case endings, but unlike English, there are still gender, definiteness and plurality markers. Gender appears only by the addition of *-t* in the neuter indefinite singular. Definiteness is shown by adding *-e* (Sw. *-a/-e*), plurality by adding *-e* (Sw. *-a/-e*). Definiteness is expressed by the article *den* m.f., *det* nt., *de* (NN *dei*) pl. It may also be dictated by such determiners as the demonstratives *denne* m. f., *dette* nt., *disse* (NN *desse*) pl. 'this, these' and the possessive adjectives (*min* 'my' etc.). The general pattern is displayed in the following chart:

Eng.	*Da.*	*BN*	*NN*	*Sw.*
'a big goose'	en stor gås	en stor gås	ei stor gås	en stor gås
'big geese'	stor*e* gæs	stor*e* gjess	stor*e* gjæser	stor*a* gäss
'a big house'	e*t* stor*t* hus	e*t* stor*t* hus	ei*t* stor*t* hus	et*t* stor*t* hus
'big houses'	stor*e* hus	stor*e* hus	stor*e* hus	stor*a* hus
'the big goose'	den stor*e* gås	den stor*e* gås*en*	den stor*e* gås*a*	den stor*a* gås*en*
'the big geese'	de stor*e* gæs	de stor*e* gjess*ene*	dei stor*e* gjæs*ene*	de stor*a* gäss*ena*
'the big house'	det stor*e* hus	det stor*e* hus*et*	det stor*e* hus*et*	det stor*a* hus*et*
'the big houses'	de stor*e* hus	de stor*e* hus*ene*	dei stor*e* hus*a*	de stor*a* hus*en*

In Swedish *de* is often replaced in speech by *dom*. The suffix *-a* may be replaced by *-e* with masculine nouns, e.g. *min gamle far* (but *min gamla mor*).

In all the languages the definite form (known as 'weak') may be used without a preceding article (a) in set phrases and in place and personal names, e.g. BN *siste natten* 'the last night', Sw. *Stora Torget* 'The Big Market Place', Da./Nw. *lille Harald* 'little Harold'; and (b) as a vocative in phrases of address: Da. *kære ven*/Nw. *kjære venn*/Sw. *kära vän* 'dear friend'.

There is a marked internal difference in the use of what is usually known as the 'double definite', i.e. the use of both definite articles in the same phrase. As shown in the chart above, this usage is avoided in Danish, but is common in Norwegian and Swedish, in N-Norwegian even required.

The definite article with an adjective is used in noun functions: common gender about animates, neuter gender about inanimates: Nw. *den unge* 'the young one (person)', *de unge* 'the young (people)', *det nye* 'the new (idea, thing etc.)'.

Comparison occurs in three degrees: positive, comparative and superlative. It is formed in one of four ways: (a) regular, by adding Da./BN *-ere*, NN/Sw. *-are* to the positive to form the comparative, and Da./BN *-est(e)*, NN/Sw. *-ast(e)* to form the superlative; (b) umlauting, by vowel change and adding *-re* and *-st(e)*; (c) analytic, by using the words for 'more' and 'most' as modifiers (Da./BN *mer*, NN *meir*, Sw. *mer(a)*, and *mest* for all the languages); (d) suppletion, e.g. *mange*/Sw. *många* 'many' – *fler*, NN *fleir* 'more' (in number). Further examples of (a) and (b):

	Da.		BN		NN		Sw.	
Positive	klar	ung	klar	ung	klår	ung	klar	ung
Comp.	klar*ere*	*yngre*	klar*ere*	*yngre*	klår*are*	*yngre*	klar*are*	*yngre*
Sup.	klar*est*	*yngst*	klar*est*	*yngst*	klår*ast*	*yngst*	klar*ast*	*yngst*

7.4 Adverbs

Most of these are morphologically unmarked and may be classed as particles. But two groups are visibly marked: (1) adverbs derived from adjectives; these are always identical with the neuter indefinite singular of the latter, i.e. they (mostly) add *-t*: e.g. *godt*, Sw. *gott* from *god* 'good' means 'well'; *stort* from *stor* 'big' means 'greatly' etc.; (2) adverbs derived from simple adverbs of motion by adding *-e* (Sw. also *-a*), making them adverbs of place (often with a change of stem); the most important are:

Eng.	Da.		BN		NN		Sw.	
'up'	op	opp*e*	opp	opp*e*	opp	opp*e*	upp	upp*e*
'down'	ned	ned*e*	ned	ned*e*	ned	ned*e*	ned	nere
'out'	ud	ud*e*	ut	ut*e*	ut	ut*e*	ut	ut*e*
'in'	ind	ind*e*	inn	inn*e*	inn	inn*e*	in	inn*e*
'home'	hjem	hjemm*e*	hjem	hjemm*e*	heim	heim*e*	hem	hemm*a*
'away'	bort	bort*e*	bort	bort*e*	bort	bort*e*	bort	bort*a*

In their locative sense these can be compared, e.g. Da. *indre* 'inner', *inderst* 'innermost' etc.

7.5 Pronouns

The structure is much the same as in English, aside from the second person and the reflexives. In the following chart only the informal second person is listed; the honorific will be discussed below.

135

Personal Pronouns Synopsis of 1–3 Person Sg. and Pl., Subject and Object

	Da.				BN				NN				Sw.			
1p.	jeg	mig	vi	os	jeg	meg	vi	oss	eg	meg	vi	oss	jag	mig	vi	oss
2p.	du	dig	I	jer	du	deg	dere		du	deg	de	dykk	du	dig	ni	er
3p.m.	han	ham }	de	dem	han	ham }	de	dem	han	honom }	dei		han	honom }	de	dem
3p.f.	hun	hende }			hun	henne }			ho	henne			hon	henne		

The inanimate pronoun is *den* common gender and *det* neuter gender 'it' in all languages; but in N-Norwegian it is replaced in anaphoric use by the appropriate masculine and feminine pronouns (i.e. *han/ho*).

The possessives in the first and second persons are declined like strong adjectives (e.g. for Da. *min* c., *mit* nt., *mine* pl.). Possessive pronouns:

	Da.		BN		NN		Sw.	
1p.	min	vor(es)	min	vår	min	vår	min	vår
2p.	din	jeres	din	deres	din	dykkar	din	er
3p.m.	hans } deres	hans } deres	hans } deira	hans } deras
3p.f.	hendes }	hennes }	hennar }	hennes }
Refl.	sin		sin		sin		sin	

The reflexive pronoun is Da./Sw. *sig*, Nw. *seg* in the third person but identical with the objective form of the pronouns in the first and second persons. Danish restricts the reflexive to the third person singular. It is a peculiarity of Scandinavian that the third person reflexive is in syntactic complementation with the personal. The reflexive is restricted to possessors that are also the subject of the clause in which they occur: *han tok sin hatt* 'he took his (own) hat' vs *han tok hans hatt* 'he took his (somebody else's) hat'.

English 'you' corresponds to *du* in informal conversations, e.g. in families, among friends and close colleagues and among rural people. But in urban settings and between strangers more formal modes of address have been common. In Danish and B-Norwegian the formal pronouns are identical with the third person plural, capitalised when written: *De, Dem, Deres*. In N-Norwegian and Swedish they are identical with the second person plural: NN *Dykk, Dykk, Dykkar*, Sw. *Ni, Er, Er*. However, in Swedish the *ni* has acquired a touch of condescension, and politeness requires the use of the third person, often including the title: *Vad önskar professoren?* 'What does the professor (i.e. you) want?' The awkwardness of this mode of address became obvious after World War II, and the solution has been a general adoption of *du*, followed in part in Norway (less in Denmark).

7.6 Verbs

The mainland languages have developed a common morphology, eliminating person and number while retaining the distinctions of tense, including complex tense forms. A verb is adequately described if we know its 'principal parts', i.e. the infinitive (also used as citation form), the preterit and the perfect participle (used in complex tenses).

Strong verbs are characterised by vowel changes in the stem and the absence of a suffix in the preterit. We list the seven main classes: 1 'bite'; 2 'enjoy'; 3 'find'; 4 'bear'; 5 'give'; 6 'go'; 7 'cry'.

	Da.			*BN*			*NN*			*Sw.*		
1	bide	bed	bidt	bite	bet	bitt	bita	beit	bite	bita	bet	bitit
2	nyde	nød	nydt	nyte	nøt	nytt	nyta	naut	note	njuta	njöt	njutit
3	finde	fandt	fundet	finne	fant	funnet	finna	fann	funne	finna	fann	funnit
4	bære	bar	båret	bære	bar	båret	bera	bar	bore	bära	bar	burit
5	give	gav	givet	gi	gav	gitt	gje	gav	gjeve	giva	gav	givit
6	fare	for	faret	fare	for	faret	fara	for	fare	fara	for	farit
7	græde	græd	grædt	gråte	gråt	grått	gråta	gret	grete	gråta	gråt	gråtit

These are only examples; there is great variation in the verbs of each class. In the infinitive N-Norwegian can have *-e* for *-a*. N-Norwegian forms its present by dropping the final vowel and when possible changing the stem to its umlaut form, e.g. *fer* from *fara*, *kjem* from *koma*. The others add *-(e)r* and change to Accent 1 (fa´rer, kom´mer), except that Swedish drops all suffixes after *r* or *l* (*far* 'go(es)', *stjäl* 'steal(s)'). In the perfect participle N-Norwegian may have *-i* for *-e*; Swedish has *-e-* for *-i-* when the perfect participle is used adjectivally.

Weak verbs form preterits by adding a dental (*-d-*, *-t-*, *-dd-*, lost in N-Norwegian class 1) with a following vowel that is not in the perfect participle. Class 3 is special for Norwegian/Swedish; the Danish verbs of the same type belong to class 1. We list the main classes below: 1 'throw'; 2a 'choose'; 2b 'judge'; 3 'believe'. In Swedish the perfect participle may end in *-d* for *-t* when used adjectivally: *kastad* for *kastat*.

	Da.			*BN*			*NN*			*Sw.*		
1	kaste	kastede	kastet	kaste	kastet	kastet	kasta	kasta	kasta	kasta	kastade	kastat
2a	vælge	valgte	valgt	velge	valgte	valgt	velja	valde	valt	välja	valde	valt
2b	dømme	dømte	dømt	dømme	dømte	dømt	døma	dømde	dømt	döma	dömde	dömt
3	(tro	troede	troet)	tro	trodde	trodd	tru	trudde	trudd	tro	trodde	trott

Modal verbs are a special group by means of which certain nuances of meaning may be signalled when they are used as auxiliaries (usually with an infinitive verb). As elsewhere in Germanic, most of them are preterit-present verbs, i.e. their present forms are old preterits, and their preterits are newly modelled after the weak verbs. We list only 'can', 'must', 'shall' and 'will' in the present and preterit:

Da.		*BN*		*NN*		*Sw.*	
kan	kunne	kan	kunne	kan	kunne	kan	kunde
må	måtte	må	måtte	må	måtte	måste	måste
skal	skulle	skal	skulle	skal	skulle	skall	skulle
vil	ville	vil	ville	vil	ville	vill	ville

The middle voice is a specially Scandinavian form, now signalled by *-s* (NN *-st*) added to many verb forms. Originally a reflexive, it is now used also to form passives, reciprocals and deponents (i.e. active verbs with passive form). An example of each type (here taken from B-Norwegian) follows:

(a) passive: *sangen synges* 'the song is being sung' or 'the song gets sung'
(b) reciprocal: *vi møtes i morgen* 'we will meet tomorrow'
(c) reflexive: *jeg trivs her* 'I enjoy myself here'
(d) deponent: *han synes godt om stedet* 'he thinks well of the place'

These are all in competition with differently structured phrases:

(a) *sangen blir sunget*
(b) *vi møter kl. 10* 'we meet at 10 o'clock'
(c) *jeg liker meg her*
(d) *han tror godt om stedet*

Similar contrasts can be shown for all the languages: the middle voice is highly restricted ('marked'), while the more analytic phrases are relatively unrestricted.

The passive is, as shown above, normally analytic, consisting of an auxiliary (Da. *blive*/BN *bli*/Sw. *bliva*/NN *verta*) plus the perfect participle.

The perfect and the pluperfect are formed by 'have' in the present and preterit tense plus the perfect participle. Except in Swedish (and to some extent in Norwegian) verbs of motion (going, becoming) require the auxiliary 'be'.

Da.	BN	NN	Sw.
har set 'have seen'	har sett	har sett	har sett
havde set 'had seen'	hadde sett	hadde sett	hade sett
er kommet 'have come'	er kommet	er kome	har kommit
var kommet 'had come'	var kommet	var kome	hade kommit

Other verb forms are:

(a) the imperative, formed by dropping the unstressed vowel of the infinitive (except Swedish and N-Norwegian weak class 1: Sw. *kasta!* 'throw!', NN *vakne!* 'awake!');
(b) the present participle, used only adjectivally, formed by adding *-ende* to the verb stem in Danish/B-Norwegian, *-ande* in N-Norwegian/Swedish, except in Swedish after long vowels: *kommande* 'coming', *boende* 'living';
(c) the subjunctive (optative), formed by adding *-e* to the stem of the present, which is used chiefly in set phrases of greeting or cursing: BN *kongen leve* '(long) live the king', *fanden steike* 'may the devil roast (him, me)'. A preterit is found in contrary-to-fact conditional sentences, usually identical in form to the regular preterit: BN *om jeg var* ... 'if I were'. However, Swedish (and N-Norwegian) have certain relic forms of the old subjunctive: *om jag vore* ... 'if I were' (NN *um eg wore* ...). These are also in competition with analytic forms using auxiliaries: *om jag skulle vara* ...

8 Syntax

Only a few of the more significant features will be listed here.

8.1 Basic Word Order

An independent declarative sentence has the same subject–verb–object (SVO) order as English. But the absence of 'do' and 'is' as auxiliaries means that in the present and preterit there are no divided verb forms: Da. *hun kører bilen* 'she drives/does drive/is driving the car'.

8.2 Inversion

In questions the order of subject and verb is simply reversed: Da. *kører hun bilen?* 'does she drive/is she driving the car?'. The same inversion occurs after an initial adverb:

Da. *i kører hun bilen* 'today she is driving the car'. If the adverb is in its usual position, after the object, sentence order is basic: *hun kører bilen i dag* 'she is driving the car today'.

8.3 Sentence Adverbs

An important subgroup of adverbs, which function as modifiers of the whole sentence, follow the verb immediately, usually in the order modals–negatives: Da. *hun kører jo bilen i dag* 'she is, you know, driving the car today'; *hun kører ikke bilen i dag* 'she is not driving the car today'; *hun kører jo ikke bilen i dag* 'she is not driving the car today, you know'. When the sentence is inverted, the negative follows a pronoun subject, but precedes a noun subject: *kører hun ikke bilen i dag?* vs *kører ikke min søster bilen i dag?* 'isn't she driving the car today?' vs 'isn't my sister driving the car today?'

8.4 Subordination

Subordinate clauses have (contrary to German) the same SVO order as independent clauses, except that sentence adverbs then normally precede the verb: *hvis hun ikke kører bilen i dag* ...'if she isn't driving the car today ...' In some cases the same word may be either an adverb or a conjunction, e.g. *da* 'then' or 'when'. In such a case the following word order signals the difference: *da kørte hun bilen* 'then she drove the car' vs *da hun kørte bilen* ... 'when she drove the car ...'

8.5 Relative Clauses

Relative clauses have subordinate order and are usually introduced by *som* (or in Danish also by *der* when it is the subject). This is not a pronoun but a particle, which cannot be preceded by a preposition. Hence prepositions come at the end of the clause, contrary to an English practice consecrated by some English grammarians: *det var bilen (som) hun kørte i* 'that was the car (which) she rode in'. When the relative particle is the object of the subordinate verb, it may be omitted (as in English).

8.6 Imperatives

Imperatives mostly appear without a subject, since this is understood to be 'you'. But the subject may be expressed, as a vocative: *kør bilen ind, Jørgen!* 'drive the car in, Jørgen!' There are of course more polite ways of formulating requests, e.g. with modal auxiliaries or with subjunctives.

8.7 Impersonal Sentences

Impersonal sentences are rather more common than in English, especially in so-called 'cleft' sentences. These have *det* as formal subject, whoever may be the real ('underlying') subject: *det er hun/hende som kører bilen i dag* 'it is she/her who is driving the car today'. 'Cleaving' is used to give emphasis.

8.8 Indefinite Subject

Basically subjectless sentences fill the subject slot with *det* 'it', as in *det regner* 'it's raining', *det sner/snør/snöar* 'it's snowing'. Norwegian and Swedish use *det* also as an equivalent of English 'there', e.g. *det kommer en bil* 'there's a car coming; a car is coming'. Here Danish (and older B-Norwegian) prefers *der*.

8.9 Conditional Clauses

These may be explicitly introduced by *om* 'if' in all languages, Da./BN *dersom, hvis*, Sw. *därest, ifall* 'in case'. But the conjunction may be dropped if the clause inverts subject and verb: *kommer bilen i dag ...* 'if the car comes today ...' One cannot tell if this is a question or a conditional until one hears the conclusion.

8.10 Prepositions

Prepositions can govern clauses and infinitives: Da. *efter at ha kørt bilen ...* 'after having driven the car ...'; *efter at hun hadde kørt bilen ...* 'after she had driven the car ...'

8.11

Norwegian has the option of letting possessives either precede or follow the noun, the latter requiring the definite form of the noun: *min bil* 'my car' (more emphatic) vs *bilen min*.

8.12

Swedish (and some Norwegian dialects) keep the verb together with a conjoined adverbial particle, while Danish and B-Norwegian separate them: Sw. *vill du köra in'bilen* vs Da. *vil du køre bilen ind'* 'will you drive the car in?'.

8.13

Only Swedish can omit the perfect auxiliary in a subordinate clause: *jag vet inte om han (har) lämnat staden* 'I don't know if he has left the city'.

8.14

The inferential perfect is a characteristic Scandinavian construction. Normally the perfect is used as in English, not as in German, to mark past events without specified time, but with ongoing effects. If time is specified, it is implied that the statement is an inference rather than an observed fact: *hun har kørt bilen i går* 'she has driven the car yesterday', i.e. '(I suppose that) she must have, etc.'

8.15 The Exclamatory Preterit

This is a common use of that tense to express a taste or opinion: *det var da en køn bil!* 'that was a lovely car!' i.e. 'that is a lovely car!' This may be said as one is looking at it, but the experience is made more emphatic by placing it in the past.

8.16 Durative Expressions

In the absence of a special 'progressive' verb form like English 'is going', the Scandinavian languages often make use of a verb of motion or position, followed by 'and' and the corresponding tense of the main verb: Da. *jeg sidder og spiser* 'I sit and eat', i.e. 'I am eating'; BN *han stod og spekulerte* 'he stood and speculated', i.e. 'he was speculating (about something)'; Sw. *hon låg och drömde* 'she lay and dreamt', i.e. 'she lay dreaming'. Verbs available for this usage are those that indicate coming, going, sitting, standing and lying.

8.17 Modal Adverbs

Certain adverbs, which have regular meanings when stressed, become vague sentence modifiers when unstressed. The chief examples are Da./BN *da* 'then', *dog* 'yet', *jo* 'yes', *nok* 'enough', *vel* 'well', Da. *nu*/BN *nå*/NN *no*; corresponding to Sw. *då, dock, ju, nog, väl, nu*. They suggest the speaker's degree of assurance or doubt, roughly 'you see', 'after all', 'of course', 'I suppose', 'no doubt', etc.

9 Lexicon

The word stock of any language reflects the needs over time of its speakers and writers and the state of their culture. As suggested above, the similarity and the divergence of the Scandinavian languages mirror their common as well as their separate historical experiences. The lexicon is enshrined in the dictionaries of each language, including massive historical dictionaries. Bilingual dictionaries are also numerous, especially for such familiar languages as English, French and German, and even some intra-Scandinavian.

The origin of the lexicon is multifarious, but overwhelmingly West European, as one can see by consulting the etymological dictionaries. The 'native' stock, i.e. the original Germanic with later native creations, is the bread-and-butter part of the lexicon. The Nordic languages were well equipped to deal with their natural environment of sea, land and mountains in all its variations from the plains of Denmark to the highlands of Norway and the forests of Sweden. Their location as the population closest to the North Pole has left its mark.

The earliest outside influence that is still perceptible was that of the Roman traders who taught them such words as 'buy' (*købe/kjøpe/køypa/köpa*) and 'wine' (*vin*) from Latin *caupo* and *vinum*. They were followed in due course by Roman-trained missionaries who brought them such originally Greek words as 'church' *kirke/kirke/kjørkja/kyrka* and 'priest' (*prest*, Sw. *präst*) from *kuriakon* and *presbuteros* and Latin words like 'dean, provost' (*prost*) and 'mass' (*messe*, Sw. *mässa*) from *prōpositus* and *missa*. Actually, there were various intermediaries, such as Old English and Old High (and Low) German, often hard to distinguish. Scandinavia was at the end of a West European chain of transmission of Catholic Christian vocabulary, most of which was common European property.

But the chief source of Scandinavian loans in the later Middle Ages was northern Germany, where the dominant language was Low German. The distance between Low German and the Nordic languages was small, since both were Germanic and had not undergone the High German Sound Shift. One may even suspect that with a little effort they could converse, at least on everyday topics. In any event, thousands of Low German loanwords flooded the North during the period from 1250 to 1500. Low German was the language not only of the powerful Hanseatic League, the trading towns of northern Germany, but also of the North German princes, who often sat on Scandinavian thrones. Cities like Bergen in Norway, Kalmar and Stockholm in Sweden and of course Copenhagen in Denmark were heavily settled by German merchants and craftsmen.

Some Old Norse words were even displaced by Low German loans, e.g. *vindauga* 'window' in Swedish by LG *fenster* > *fönster*, *vōna* 'hope' by LG *hopen* > Da. *håbe/* BN *håpe/*Sw. *hoppas* (but NN *vona*). Prefixes and suffixes attached to Low German words were also adopted, e.g. *be-, ent-, vor-* and *-heit, -ness, -ske*. Old Scandinavian had a very restricted set of affixes, which were greatly expanded by Low German influence.

At the time of the Reformation (in the sixteenth century) the source of influence changed to High German, the language of Luther's Bible, which became normative for the now converted Scandinavians. Translations of the Bible were modelled on Luther's, giving a heavy freight of German loans. As late as the seventeenth century the Swedish grammarian Samuel Columbus could still write that German and Swedish were sister languages, so that Swedes were justified in taking over words from German. The eighteenth century saw a shift in the direction of French influence, but also a clarification of the independence of the northern languages. A Nordic purism arose, leading to the replacement of French words like *passion* with *lidenskab*, though the latter was ultimately modelled on German *Leidenschaft*. The rediscovery of Old Scandinavian, specifically of Old Icelandic literature, led to a Nordic renaissance.

The nineteenth and even more the twentieth century brought on the Industrial Revolution and with it the rise of English to the status of a world language. Its proximity to Scandinavia and involvement in Nordic affairs made it the source of a new era of influence. Rejection of German led to an adulation of English that changed the attitudes of a whole generation in Scandinavia. An influence already apparent in the 1930s, often transmitted by sailors, merchants and tourists, now led to a flood of military, scientific and literary, as well as generally popular culture, terms. English, once a remote and inaccessible language to most Scandinavians, quickly became a medium not only of information and insight, but a possibly insidious influence on popular thinking and speech.

Only Sweden had a traditional language academy, the Swedish Academy (founded 1786), which still publishes under its ægis a guide to the spelling (and in part the pronunciation) of 'correct' Swedish. But in modern times each country has established special committees or commissions charged with the care of its language. In 1978 a cooperative Nordic Language Secretariat was established under the auspices of the Nordic Council of Ministers. Like its member organisations, the secretariat has only advisory powers. But it is hoped that it will prove to be a useful forum for the discussion of language problems in the area. Aside from issues of correctness, a major concern is for the development and coordination of technical terminology.

Since each language has developed its own lexicon, often along different principles, there are many discrepancies both in words and meanings. These add spice to intra-Scandinavian contacts, but rarely lead to basic misunderstandings.

Differences are either semantic or lexical.

(a) Semantic differences in historically identical words, often called false friends, reflect preferences for one nuance over another. Thus *rar* from Latin *raris*, cognate with English 'rare', means 'good, fine, sweet' in Danish and Swedish, but 'queer, strange' in Norwegian: the 'rare' may be regarded either positively or negatively. *Rolig*, a native word cognate with German *ruhig*, means 'quiet' in Danish and Norwegian, but 'funny, amusing' in Swedish. *Affär*, from French *affaire*, means 'store, place of business' in Swedish, while Danish and Norwegian *affære* means 'affair', as in English. *Anledning*, from German *Anleitung* 'guidance', means 'cause, reason' in Swedish, but 'opportunity, occasion' in Danish/Norwegian. *Blöt* is a native word meaning 'wet' in Swedish (as *blaut* in N-Norwegian), but Da. *blød*/BN *bløt* means 'soft, weak' (with a more recent meaning of 'soft-headed').

(b)   Lexical differences may be due to the extinction of a word in one language or to borrowing from a different source. In Swedish a common word for 'poet' is *skald*, an Old Norse word revived in modern times; in Danish and Norwegian it is used only about Old Norse times, the usual word being *digter/dikter* from German *Dichter* (which Swedish also has as *diktare*). While the words for 'man' and 'woman' are much the same, 'boy' and 'girl' are markedly deviant: Da. *dreng/* BN *gutt*/NN *gut*/Sw. *pojke* 'boy' and Da. *pige*/BN *pike*/NN *jente*/Sw. *flicka* 'girl'. Slang is a part of language that reflects innovation most readily and that is often local; in Swedish it has given rise to terms little known in the other languages, e. g. *kille* 'boy', *kul* 'fun' etc. There are also areas of clothing or vegetation that may surprise neighbours: a '(man's) suitcoat' is Sw. *kavaj*, Da./Nw. *jakke*; an 'overcoat' is Sw. *rock*, Da. *frakke* (Nw. *frakk*). Berries are differently named, e.g. what Swedish calls *hallon* 'raspberry', *smultron* 'strawberry', *hjortron* 'cloudberry', *krushär* 'gooseberry' and *vinbär* 'currant' will be known in Danish and Norwegian as *bringebær, jordbær, multe(r), stikkelsbær* and *ribs/rips*. And so forth.

Bibliography

For more detailed surveys of Scandinavian, with comprehensive bibliographies, the reader is referred to Haugen (1976), a survey of the successive periods of the languages' history with extensive background and illustrative material – an updated German translation by Magnus Pétursson, under the title *Die skandinavischen Sprachen*, has been published by Helmut Buske, Hamburg – and Haugen (1982), a more concentrated survey of the history, organised by linguistic levels and emphasising linguistic rules of historical change. A concise though more up-to-date presentation is provided by Braunmüller (2007).

For descriptive grammars, the best sources are in the original languages: Diderichsen (1962) for Danish; Næs (1972) for B-Norwegian; Beito (1986) for N-Norwegian; Thorell (1973) and Collinder (1974) for Swedish. In English, there are comprehensive grammars for Danish (Allan et al. 1995) and Swedish (Hinchcliffe and Holmes 2003) and a shorter grammar for Norwegian (Strandskogen and Strandskogen 1994).

Haugen (1966) is a detailed account of language planning in relation to Norwegian.

References

Allan, R., Holmes, P. and Lundskaer-Nielsen, T. 1995. *Danish: A Comprehensive Grammar* (Routledge, London)

Beito, O. 1986. *Nynorsk grammatikk*, 2nd edn (Det Norske Samlaget, Oslo)

Braunmüller, K. 2007. *Die skandinavischen Sprachen im Überblick*. 3rd edn (A. Francke, Tübingen)

Collinder, B. 1974. *Svensk språklära* (C.W.K. Gleerup, Stockholm)

Diderichsen, P. 1962. *Elementær dansk Grammatik*, 3rd edn (Gyldendal, Copenhagen)

Haugen, E. 1966. *Language Conflict and Language Planning: The Case of Modern Norwegian* (Harvard University Press, Cambridge, MA)

—— 1976. *The Scandinavian Languages: An Introduction to Their History* (Faber and Faber, London)

—— 1982. *Scandinavian Language Structures: A Comparative Historical Survey* (Max Niemeyer, Tübingen; University of Minnesota Press, Minneapolis)

Hinchcliffe, I. and Holmes, P. 2003. *Swedish: A Comprehensive Grammar.* (Routledge, London)

Næs, O. 1972. *Norsk grammatikk*, 3rd edn (Fabritius, Oslo)

Strandskogen, Å.-B. and Strandskogen, R. 1994. *Norwegian: An Essential Grammar* (Routledge, London)

Thorell, O. 1973. *Svensk grammatik* (Esselte Studium, Stockholm)

7

Latin and the Italic Languages

R.G.G. Coleman

1 Introduction

Latin is the chief representative of the Italic group of Indo-European languages. The most important of the others were Oscan, which was spoken over most of southern Italy in the last four centuries BC and is attested in substantial inscriptions from Avella and Banzi, and Umbrian, which was spoken further north and survives almost exclusively in a series of liturgical inscriptions from Gubbio dating from 350 to 50 BC. A large number of the Oscan and Umbrian texts are in native alphabets, ultimately derived like those of Latin and Etruscan from the Greek alphabet. Some are in the Latin alphabet, and collation of the two graphic systems provides valuable insights into the phonology of the two languages. In this chapter words attested in the native alphabets appear in capitals, those in the Latin alphabet in lower case.

Neither Oscan nor Umbrian is as closely related to Latin as Faliscan, a language attested in a small number of inscriptions from near Città Castellana. Of the non-Italic languages spoken in Italy after 500 BC Venetic in the far north-east was closely related to Italic; Etruscan, which is attested, again epigraphically, over a large area of central and northern Italy, was totally unrelated. Although Oscan was still in use at Pompeii until AD 79, Latin had long since become the written language of all Italy. Some dialects of Latin were partly shaped by the native languages, but it is doubtful whether the latter survived long into the Christian era. In this chapter Oscan and Umbrian phenomena will be treated only in relation to Latin as providing evidence for the Italic complex within which Latin must historically be placed.

For Latin phonology the most valuable source is the spellings, both standard and deviant, and the diachronic changes in spelling that are discernible in the numerous inscriptions recorded from about 500 BC onwards and the manuscripts of contemporary texts written on papyrus and subsequently on other soft materials. The manuscripts of literary texts from antiquity, usually written centuries after their composition, provide fuller testimony for morphology, syntax and lexicon. Among these texts are treatises on the language itself and on rhetoric. These are especially important as revealing the criteria, derived mostly from Greek theory, by which the norms of classical usage were formulated and applied in the period 150 BC–AD 150.

At all periods alongside the formal registers of the written documents there was the Latin spoken by the illiterate majority. Vulgar Latin had of course its own diachrony and, as it spread with the expansion of Roman power, must have acquired the dialectal variations from which the Romance languages emerged. It is partially recoverable from the written documents whose spelling, grammar and lexicon deviate in the direction of Romance from the standard Latin that can be established for the period concerned. Many of these deviations are identifiable with or can be directly linked to the asterisked reconstructions of Proto-Romance. The conservative traditions of the schools of grammar and rhetoric did not entirely immunise classical usage against vulgar infiltration. However, they did ensure that by the ninth century AD written Latin and the diverse spoken forms of Latin had ceased to be registers of one language, coexisting in a state of diglossia like Greek *katharévusa* and *dēmotikḗ*, but were now quite separate, if closely related, languages. ɔ̃Caesar and Livy would have recognised the Latin of Nithard's *Historiae* as a form of their own language; they would have found his citations of the Strassburg oaths as baffling in the *romana lingua* as in the *teudisca*. Latin was to survive for another thousand years after that as a vehicle for liturgy and learned discourse, but in a state of suspended animation dependent upon transfusions from the ancient models. These guaranteed it a homogeneity in time and space, in marked contrast to the independently live and divergent Romance languages.

2 Phonology

The Italic word accent was fixed and not phonemic. In Proto-Italic it is generally thought to have been a stress accent falling on the initial syllable. That this situation continued into the independent history of the languages is confirmed by the fact that both vowel raising ('weakening') in early Latin and syncope in Oscan and Umbrian affected only non-initial syllables. By about 250 BC the rule of the penultimate was established in Latin: in words of more than two syllables the accent was on the penultimate unless it contained a short unchecked vowel (i.e. in an open syllable), in which case the accent retreated to the antepenult. The range of possibilities is illustrated by:

fác 'make!'	fácis 'you make'	fácilēs 'easy' (nom. pl.)
	fē̆cit 'he made'	fēcístis 'you made' (pl.)
	fáctō 'made' (abl.)	factū̆rō 'about to make' (abl.)

The Latin grammarians borrowed from the Greeks the terminology of tonic accentuation, but although some educated native speakers may have affected Greek practice, the frequency of syncope in spoken Latin of all periods and the shortening of the unaccented vowels in *uólō*, *míhī* and later *dícō*, etc. show that the accent remained one of stress (Table 7.1).

The relative frequency and distribution of Latin short vowels had been affected by the raising that took place in non-initial syllables before 250 BC. The raising was higher in unchecked than in checked vowels; e.g. **dēfacites > dēficitis* 'you fail' vs **dēfactos > dēfectus* 'feeble', **homones > hominis* 'of the man' vs **fācondom > fācundum* (acc.) 'eloquent'. /i/ and /u/ became more frequent as a result. Syncope, the terminal point in raising, occurred in all periods of spoken Latin: prehistorically in *reppulī* 'I drove back' (< **repepolai*, cf. *pepulī* 'I drove') and in *mēns* 'mind' (< *mentis*); later in *postus* for *positus* 'placed', *caldus* for *calidus* 'hot', *oclus* for *oculus* 'eye'.

Table 7.1 The Segmental Phonemes of Latin in the Classical Period (c. 150 BC–AD 150)

Vowels:

i		u
e		o
	a	

all ± length

Diphthongs: ae au oe eu ui

Consonants:

	Stop tense	*lax*	*Fricative*	*Nasal*	*Lateral*		*Semi-vowels*
Labial	p	b		m			w
Labio-dental			f				
Dental	t	d		n	l	r	
Alveolar			s				j
Velar	k	g					
Labio-vclar	k^w						
Glottal			h				

Vowel length was phonemic in Latin, e.g. *leuis* 'light', *lēuis* 'smooth'; *rosa* (nom.), *rosā* (abl.) 'rose'. It was never marked systematically in writing, though sporadic devices are found, in Latin (mostly diacritics) as in Oscan (gemination) and Umbrian (addition of *h*). (The long vowels of classical Latin words cited in this chapter are marked diacritically.) /e·/ and /o·/ came to be raised: hence from the first century AD onwards deviant spellings like *filix*, *flus* for *fēlīx*, *flōs*. Eventually the ten vowels were reduced in many areas of Vulgar Latin to seven:

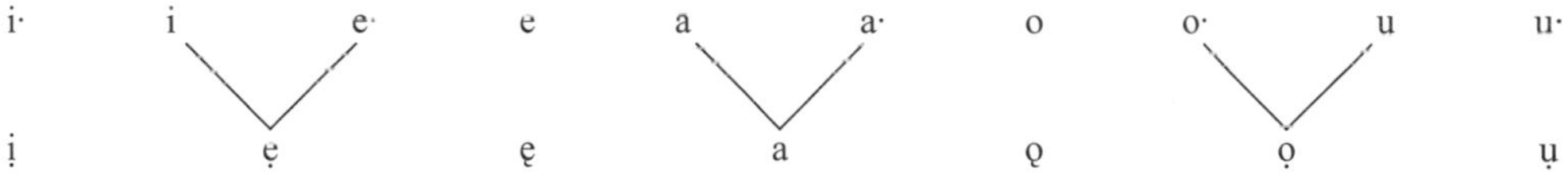

with length merely a concomitant of stress.

There was a general tendency to monophthongise diphthongs: early Latin *deicō* 'I say', *oino(m)* 'one', *ious* 'law' > *dīcō*, *ūnum*, *iūs* by 150 BC. Only /ae/ (< early Latin /ai/), /au/ and the rare /oe eu ui/ survived in the classical period. In some dialects of central Italy /ae/ and /au/ were monophthongised by the second century BC, e.g. *cedre*, *plostrum*, for standard *caedere* 'to cut', *plaustrum* 'cart', and the [ɛ] pronunciation of *ae* was standard by the fourth century AD. The monophthongisation in *cecīdit* (< **cecaidet*) and *accūsō* 'I accuse' (< **adcausō*) implies a form of raising, /ai/ > /ei/, /au/ > /ou/. The result was again to increase the frequency of high vowels, specifically /i·/ and /u·/.

The Oscan vowel system differs in two principal respects from the Latin one. First, it was asymmetrical, with three front vowels /ị į e/ and only two back /ụ ọ/ in addition to /a/. The raising of /e·/ and /o·/, which came relatively late in Latin, had occurred prehistorically in both Oscan and Umbrian. But in Oscan, whereas the resultant /į·/ was distinguished from existing /ị·/, as in *LÍGATÚÍS* 'to the ambassadors' (< **lēgatois)* vs *SLAAGID* 'from the place' (< *stlāgīd), the corresponding raised back vowel merged with /ụụ·/ as in *FRUKTATIUF* 'profit' (< **frūktātiōns*). The raising of /o/ to [ọ] as in PÚD 'which' (< **kʷod*, cf. the allograph *pod*) merely increased the asymmetry of the system.

Second, all but one of the Proto-Italic diphthongs were retained until the latest records of Oscan. Thus *DEÍVAÍ* 'to the goddess', *AVT* 'but', *ÚÍTTIUF* (nom.) 'use', but *LÚVKEÍ* 'in the grove' with /ou/< */eu/; cf. Lat. *dīuae, aut, ūsiō, *lūcī*.

The Umbrian vowel system was more symmetrical. Somewhat like Attic Greek it included two pairs of middle-to-high long vowels, recoverable from the Latin allographs, e.g. *TUTE, tote* 'to the people' with /ọ·/ and /ẹ·/ (< **toutai*) and *HABETU, habitu* 'let him have' with /ẹ·/ and /ọ·/ (< **habētōd*). In monophthongisation Umbrian was further advanced even than Latin, as the following correspondences illustrate: O. *PRAÍ* = Lat. *prae* = U. *PRE* 'before'; O. *DIÚVEÍ* = Lat. *Iouī* = U. *IUVE* 'to Jupiter'; O. *AVT* = Lat. *aut* = U. *UTE* 'but'; u-stem gen. sg. O. *[castr]ous* = Lat. *[trib]ūs* = U. *[trif]or*.

Although neither Oscan nor Umbrian orthography reveals evidence of short vowel raising, the frequency of syncope in non-initial syllables implies its presence; e.g. O. *actud*, U. *AITU* < **agtōd* < **agetōd* 'let him act'; cf. Lat. *agitō*; O. *MEDDÍSS* < **medodikes* (nom. pl.) 'magistrates'. U. *ANTAKRES* < **antagreis* (abl.) 'intact' (cf. Lat. *integrīs*) and similar spellings must be presumed archaisms.

The Oscan and Umbrian consonant systems were very similar to Latin. The chief divergences will be noted in what follows.

The inherited velar stops /k/ and /g/ were retained in Italic generally. In Oscan and Latin palatalisation of [g] before [j] occurred prehistorically; e.g. O. *mais* 'more', Lat. *maiius* 'bigger' < **magjos* (adj. nt.) beside *magis* 'more' < **magios*. Umbrian shows palatalisation before front vowels, e.g. *ṡesna* 'dinner' (the native alphabet has a separate letter, transliterated as *Ç*, representing [tʃ] or [ʃ]), cf. O. *KERSNÚ*, Lat. *cēna*; *muieto*, cf. Lat. *mūgītus* 'a roar'.

The Oscan dialect of Banzi shows palatalisation of [tj] and [dj] (< [ti di]) before vowels: *bansae* 'at Bantia', *zicolom* 'day' < **diēklom*, and it was in this context that the Latin shift began. Lat. *peiius* 'worse' (< **pedjos*) certainly, *Iouī* 'to Jupiter' like O. *IUVEÍ*, U. *IUVE*, (< **djowei*) possibly, provides evidence for a prehistoric tendency. Instances exactly parallel to Oscan are attested in the second century AD: *terciae* for *tertiae* 'third' (Rome), *oze* for *hodiē* 'today' (Algeria). By the fifth century AD the grammarians report the pronunciation of *iūstitia* with [tsia] as normal. Secure Latin examples comparable to U. *ṡesna* do not occur before the fifth and sixth centuries AD: *incitamento* 'encouragement' for *incitāmentō* (Italy), *dissesit* 'left' for *discessit* (Algeria), *septuazinta* 'seventy' for *septuāgintā* (Spain). They are abundant in Lombard and Merovingian documents of the seventh and eighth centuries.

The inherited labio-velars */kʷ/ and */gʷ/ were replaced by /p/ and /b/ in Oscan and Umbrian. In Latin they merged with /kw/ and /gw/. Thus *equus* 'horse' < PIt. **ekwos*, *quid* 'what?' < **kʷid*, cf. O. *PÍD*, U. *PEŘE* < **pid-i* with the distinctive Umbrian affricate reflex of intervocalic /d/. It is probable that Lat. *qu* represents /kʷ/ rather than /kw/, almost certain that *gu* represents [gw]. Inherited */gʷ/ > Lat. /w/ except after a nasal: PIt. **gʷīwos* > *uīuus* 'alive', cf. O. *BIVUS* (nom. pl.), **snigʷm* > *niuem* (acc. sg.) 'snow' but **ongʷen* > *unguen* 'ointment' cf. U. *UMEN* (< **omben*).

The labial glide /w/, which was distinguished graphically from *u* in Oscan and Umbrian, was represented by *u* in Latin. Its phonemic status is guaranteed by rare pairs like *uoluī* with /wi·/ 'I rolled' and *uoluī* with /ui·/ 'I wished'. In some areas /w/ > [β] as early as the first century AD, e.g. *baliat for ualeat* 'farewell!' at Pompeii. By the third century AD consonantal *u*, formerly transliterated as ου in Greek, was frequently rendered by β.

Whereas the earliest Germanic borrowings from Latin show [w], later ones prefer a labio-dental fricative: e.g. OE *win*, *weall* < *uīnum* 'wine', *uallum* 'fence', but *fers* < *uersus* 'verse'. The invention of *double u* in the eighth century AD to represent Germanic [w] indicates that the value of Latin consonantal *u* was now [v]. Hence Latin borrowings from Germanic have *w* or *gu* for Germanic [w], e.g. Go. *wadi* 'pledge' > *wadium* (seventh century AD), OHG *werra* 'strife' > *werra/guerra* (ninth century AD).

The palatal glide /j/ was not distinguished graphically in any Italic language. Its phonemic status is guaranteed not by any minimal opposition with /i/ but by pattern congruity in *iam*, *tam* etc. Intervocalic /j/ was regularly [jj]. Secure evidence of an affricate pronunciation [ʤ] or [ʤ] for /j/ occurs in *Zanuario* (Pozzuoli, fourth century AD) and *Genoarias* (Arles, sixth century AD) for *Ianuar-*.

/f/ and /h/ were more frequent in Oscan and Umbrian than in Latin, often occurring non-initially in uncompounded words. Thus O. *MEFIAÍ* (loc. sg.), cf. Lat. *medius* 'middle' (< *medhio-*); U. *rufru*, cf. Lat. *rubrōs* (acc. pl.) 'red' (< *əₗrudhro-*); U. *VITLAF*, cf. Lat. *uitulās* 'calves' (< *-āns*); O. *FEÍHÚSS* (acc.) 'walls', cf. Lat. *figulus* 'potter' (< *dh(e)igh-*); U. *REHTE*, cf. Lat. *rēctē* 'rightly'. (The diachronic complex that produces the idiosyncratic pattern of reflexes of the Proto-Indo-European voiced aspirates */bh dh gh gʷh/, partially exemplified in some of these forms, is a notable witness to the existence of a unified Proto-Italic.) /h/ was unstable in both Latin and Umbrian. Initially it is ignored in classical versification and there was learned debate about the correct forms of *ūmor* 'moisture' and *harēna* 'sand'; cf. U. *heritu ERETU* 'let him choose'. Medially /h/ is often lost in Latin, e.g. *praehibeō* > *praebeō* 'I provide', *nihil* > *nīl* 'nothing' and, when it remains, it merely marks hiatus, e.g. *ahēnus/aēnus* 'brazen', U. *AHESNES* (abl. pl.); cf. O. *STAHÍNT* 'they stand' (< *stāint*). In Vulgar Latin /h/ disappeared almost completely.

Final /m/ was often omitted in Umbrian and early Latin, e.g. U. *PUPLU* for *PUPLUM* 'people' (acc.), Lat. *oino* for *oinom* 'one' (acc.); rarely in Oscan, except at Pompeii, e.g. *VÍA* for *VÍAM* 'road'. In classical versification it fails to prevent the elision of vowels: *făcĭlem ēssĕ* with [em] > [e]; cf. *făcĭle ēssĕ*. However, *făcĭlēm dărĕ* contrasts with *făcĭlĕ dărĕ*, *which* implies either [em] > [e·] or an assimilation [emd] > [end]. In Vulgar Latin final /m/ was almost totally lost. Hence the homophony of *facilem* and *facile*, *bonum* (acc. sg.) and *bonō* (dat., abl. sg.), with [um] > ų > ǫ.

The frequency of /s/ was much reduced by rhotacism in Latin and Umbrian. In the latter both intervocalic and final /s/ were affected. Thus *FURENT* < *bhusenti* 'they will be', Lat. *foret* but O. *FUSÍD*, both < *bhusēt* (3 sg. subj.); *dequrier* (earlier *TEKURIES* dat. pl.) cf. Lat. *decuria* 'ten-man group'. In Latin final /r/ for /s/ occurs only by paradigmatic analogy; e.g. *honor*, *honōrem* replacing *honōs*, *honōrem* (acc.).

In early Latin final /s/ preceded by a short vowel was apparently lost before consonants but retained before vowels. Together with the normal treatment of final /m/ this would have given the following variants for 'the master's son':

nom.	(fīlius):	fīlius erī,	fīliu dominī
acc.	(fīlium):	fīliu erī,	fīlium dominī

This pattern underlies the graphic and metrical data of the period 250–180 BC. Both -*s* and -*m* were restored in standard orthography by the early second century BC, but final -*s*, unlike -*m*, always counts as a consonant in classical versification: *fīlĭŭs ĕrī*, *fīlĭŭs dŏmĭnī* Vulgar Latin, like Umbrian earlier, shows frequent loss of final consonants, e.g. of

/t/ in VL *ama* 'he loves', U. *HABE* 'he has', but in contrast to e.g. U. *SESTE* for *sestes* 'you set up' it seems to have kept final /s/ in all regions until at least the sixth century AD and only in eighth-century documents from Italy does -*s* begin to disappear on a large scale.

There was a tendency in most periods of Latin to reduce all but a small range of consonant clusters by the assimilation or omission of one or more components or by anaptyxis. Thus */sn/ in *nix* 'snow'< *snigʷs and *cēna* 'dinner', cf. U. *sesna*, O. *KERSNU*; */ns/ in *uiās* 'roads' < *-*āns*, cf. O. *VÍASS*, U. *VITLAF* '*calves*' with /f/ < */ns/, and in *mēnsis* 'month', *sedēns* 'sitting', where early Latin usually has *s*, cf. U. *MENZNE* (< *mensenei loc.) with [ents], *ZEŘEF* (< *sedens). Paradigmatic analogy restored /n/ in *sedens: sedentem* (acc.), and a spelling pronunciation [e·ns] was standard in classical speech; but /n/ was never restored in Vulgar usage and spellings like *mesis* were widespread in late Latin. Initial and final clusters were the more vulnerable, e.g. /gn/ in *nātus*, early Lat. *gnātus* 'son' but *cognātus* 'relative'; */tl/ simplified in *lātus* 'raised', but in *piāculum* 'sacrifice' (cf. U. *pihaclu* (abl.) < *piātlo-) /t/ has been assimilated to the velar allophone of /l/ and resultant /kl/ has undergone anaptyxis; /kt/ simplified in *lac* 'milk' but retained in *lactis* (gen.). As the preceding examples show, Oscan and Umbrian, though they have the same general tendency, often diverge in detail: thus O. *ARAGETU* (abl.) beside Lat. *argentō* 'silver', *ÚPSANNAM* 'which is to be done' beside Lat. *operandam*, *MEDDÍSS* 'magistrate' beside Lat. *iūdex* 'judge', U. *acnu* (acc.) beside O. *AKENEÍ (loc.)*, Lat. *annus* 'year'.

3 Morphology and Syntax

The case system of Italic was typologically close to Proto-Indo-European. The cases were fusional, encoding the categories of case, number and partly gender. The noun morphology was organised in six paradigms, exemplified from Latin in the chart below. All save (4) and (5) are shared with adjectives, and all reflect Proto-Indo-European paradigms except (5), which seems to have developed in Proto-Italic; cf. U. *RI* (dat.-abl.) with Lat. *reī, rē*.

Classical Latin Nominal Paradigms

		1	2	3(a)	3(b)	4	5
Sg. Nom.		ui-a	popul-us	lēx	turr-is	trib-us	r-ēs
		'road'	'people'	'law'	'tower'	'tribe'	'thing'
	Voc.	-a	-e	lēx	-is	-us	-ēs
	Acc.	-am	-um	lēg-em	-im	-um	-em
	Gen.	-ae	-ī	-is	-is	-ūs	-ēī
	Dat.	-ae	-ō	-ī	-ī	-uī	-ēī
	Abl.	-a	-ō	-e	-ī	-ū	-ē
	Loc.	[Rōm-ae 'at Rome']	[hum-ī 'on the ground']	[rūr-e 'in the country']	[Septembr-ī 'in September']	–	[di-ē 'on the day']
Pl.	Nom. } Voc. }	ui-ae	popul-ī	lēg-ēs	turr-ēs	trib-ūs	r-ēs
	Acc.	-ās	-ōs	-ēs	-īs	-ūs	-ēs
	Gen.	-ārum	-orum	-um	-ium	-uum	-ērum
	Dat. } Abl. } Loc. }		-īs	-ibus	-ibus	-ibus	-ēbus

The diachrony of these paradigms as a whole is notable in two respects. Firstly the *i*-stems (3b) became progressively more unlike the *u*-stems (4), to which in Proto-Indo-European they were structurally parallel. This process had not gone so far in Oscan and Umbrian as in Latin, where the cases exhibited for *turris* represent the most conservative form of the paradigm attested, and the distinctive (3b) cases were gradually replaced by those of (3a). Prehistorically assimilation had been in the opposite direction; cf. nom. pl. *hominēs* 'men' for *-ěs*, reflected in O. *HUMUNS*; abl. pl. *legibus*, O. *ligis* as if < *lēg-ifs* < *-ibhos*; cf. U. *homonus* < *-ufs*, with anaptyctic *u*, < *-bhos*.

Second, there were in Latin from an early date doublets belonging to (1) and (5), e.g. *māteria/-ēs* 'timber' and to (2) and (4), e.g. *senātus* 'senate' and *pīnus* 'pine tree'. This led to the wholesale transfer of nouns in Vulgar Latin from (4) and (5) to (2) and (1) respectively and thus to the elimination of the former pair.

The dual number has not survived in Italic noun or verb morphology. The distinction between singular and plural remained systematic.

There are three genders in Italic: masculine, feminine and neuter. The category is systematically encoded in adjectives and partly in pronouns. Hence, while most nouns in (1) and (5) are feminine, (2) and (4) masculine, there are exceptions, and these are recoverable only from concordant pronouns and adjectives, predicative or attributive; e.g. *nauta est ualidus* 'the sailor is strong', *ille diēs* 'that day' (m.); *humus dūra* 'the hard ground', *haec tribus est* 'this is the tribe' (f.). The neuter gender is usually marked in nouns as well as adjectives but only in the nominative and accusative: *bellum* 'war' (sg.), *maria* 'seas' (pl.). Sex is signalled systematically by the gender of adjectives: *rēx bonus* 'the good king', *honestae mulierēs* 'virtuous women', but the masculine acts as common gender: *hominēs sunt ualidī* 'humans are strong'. Inanimate nouns are assigned to all three genders: e.g. *flūmen lātum* (nt.) but *fluuius lātus* (m.) 'broad river', *silua dēnsa* (f.) but *nemus dēnsum* (nt.) 'thick forest'. The neuter is the unmarked form of adjectives and pronouns: *facile est dēscendere* 'to go down is easy', cf. *facilis est dē scēnsus* 'the descent is easy' (m.).

Many of the specific case forms are cognate in the different languages even when sound changes have obscured their identity, as in O. *HÚRZ* 'grove' with /ts/ < *-tos* beside Lat. *hortus* (2 nom. sg.) 'garden' and U. *TRIF* 'three' < *trins* (3b acc. pl.), beside Lat. *trīs*. Divergences occur of course; e.g. in paradigm (2) nom. pl. Lat. *Nōlānī*, *Iguuīnī* with *-ī* < PIE pronominal *-oi* contrast with O. *NÚVLANÚS* 'Nolans', U. *iiouinur* 'Iguvines' < PIE nominal *-ōs*. In addition to the interaction between (3a) and (3b) already noted, (3a) abl. sg. shows Lat. *lēge*, U. *KAPIŘE* 'bowl' with *-e* < PIE loc. *-i* against O. *ligud* < *lēgōd* with the ablative form of (2).

The most remarkable divergence occurs in what is otherwise a very homogeneous paradigm throughout Italic, namely in the genitive singular of (2). PIE *-osio*, reconstructed from Ancient Greek and Indo-Iranian, is directly attested in Faliscan *Kaisiosio* 'Caesius', and in *Valesiosio* 'Valerius' on an inscription, possibly Volscian, from Southern Lazio. Oscan and Umbrian have *-eis*: *SAKARAKLEÍS* 'temple', *popler* 'people'. This was originally the (3b) form, which has also spread to (3a), as in *MEDÍKEÍS* 'magistrate'. Latin *-ī* has cognates in the Venetic and Celtic genitive singular forms, e.g. OIr. *maqi* 'son's'. It reflects either *-ia₂*, for which cf. Vedic *devī́* 'goddess' (< 'belonging to a god, *deváḥ*') or *-ie*, the suffix which was inflected to form adjectives like Latin *patrius* 'belonging to a father, *pater*' and Vedic *divyáḥ* 'belonging to the sky, *dyáuḥ*'.

It will be observed in the chart of nominal paradigms that, although there are fourteen possible cases, no paradigm has more than eight (*populus*, *lēx*) or fewer than six (*rēs*) distinctive forms. The pattern of syncretism, however, varies from one paradigm to another and the only general syncretism is in the dative-locative-ablative plural. This is also one of the maximally differentiated cases, along with the accusative singular and genitive plural, which have distinctive forms in every paradigm. Least marked are the vocative, the case of second person address, and the locative, which signals position in space or time. The vocative is distinguished only in (2) singular, the declension to which most male personal and family names belong. The locative is more distinct morphologically and more active functionally in both Oscan and Umbrian, e.g. O. *AKENEÍ* but Lat. *annō* (abl.) 'in the year'; U. *MANUVE* but Lat. *in manū* (abl.) 'in the hand'; O. *eizeic uincter* 'he is convicted in this', cf. *in hāc rē conuincitur.* In Latin it is reserved for physical location and subject to severe lexical constraints, e.g. *Rōmae* but *in urbe, in Italiā, humī* 'on the ground' but *in solō.*

The syncretism of the Proto-Indo-European case system had already begun in Proto-Italic with the merging of comitative and ablative cases. Thus early Lat. *dedit meretōd* 'he gave with justification', O. *com preiuatud actud* 'let him plead together with the defendant' (Lat. *cum reō agitō*), where the case forms reflect the Proto-Indo-European ablative. In the plural, as we have remarked, this syncretism also absorbed locative and dative functions; e.g. O. *FIÍSÍAÍS* 'at the festival', Lat. *fēriīs, LÍGATÚÍS* 'to the ambassadors', Lat. *lēgātīs.*

A number of Indo-European languages show the apparently independent development of phrases composed of nominal + participle in an appropriate case to signal the temporal location or attendant circumstances of a verbal action or state; e.g. the 'absolute' use of the locative (and genitive) in Sanskrit, and the genitive (and accusative) in Ancient Greek. The corresponding Italic construction has the comitative ablative: O. *lamatir toutad praesentid* 'the penalty is to be exacted with the people being present', Lat. *populō praesente*; U. *ESTE PERSKLUM AVES ANZERIATES ENETU* 'this sacrifice, with the birds having been examined, he is to begin', Lat. *auibus obseruātīs inītō.* Frequent in Latin is the parallel nominal + (predicative) adjective or noun: *auibus secundīs* 'with the birds (being) auspicious', *auibus magistrīs* 'with the birds (being) instructors'. The detachment of the construction from its original comitative meaning is reflected by several developments in the classical period, notably the extension to future participles and to active participles of transitive verbs along with their complements; e.g. *sortītīs cōnsulibus prōuinciās* 'the consuls having been allotted their provinces', *oppugnātūrīs hostibus castra* 'the enemy being about to attack the camp'. The incorporation of pre-positional phrases within the ablative phrase itself, as in *rēbus ad profectiōnem comparātīs* 'things being prepared for the departure', and the replacement of the head noun by a clause or phrase, as in *quor praetereātur dēmōnstrātō* 'why it is omitted having been demonstrated' and *cognitō uīuere Ptolemaeum* 'that Ptolemy was alive having been discovered', also added to the internal complexity of the construction. The term 'ablative absolute' is appropriate once it has become the equivalent of a full adverbial clause, *quom cognōuisset uīuere Ptolemaeum* 'when he discovered that Ptolemy ...', etc. Not surprisingly, once the case orientation was lost, the ablative came to be replaced in Vulgar Latin by the nominative or accusative; cf. *reliquias recollectas tumulum tibi constitui* 'having gathered up your remains, I set up a grave for you' (fourth century AD, Africa), *coiux moriens non fuit alter amor* 'your husband dying, there was no second love' (sixth century AD, Rome).

There are several distinctively Latin idioms in which a case usage is transferred from verbal to nominal dependency. For instance, the purposive use of the dative in *trīs uirōs ēlēgēre lītibus iūdicandīs* 'three men they chose for deciding law suits' → *trēs uirī lītibus iūdicandīs*; *sēmen sātui parāuī* 'I prepared the seed for sowing' → *sātui sēmen* 'seed for sowing'. A halfway stage is the so-called predicative dative, e.g. *auxiliō tibi est* 'he is of assistance (dat.) to you' ← *adest auxiliō tibi* 'he is here for assistance to you'. Similarly the comitative use of the ablative in *singulārī industriā labōrāuit* 'she worked with exceptional industry' → *mulier singulārī industriā* 'a woman of exceptional industry', the so-called ablative of description.

Prepositions originally defined the case meanings more precisely and hence could accompany more than one case, but they came to usurp more and more of the meaning of the phrase and so to be restricted to a single case. Thus the use of the simple accusative with directional verbs survived as an archaism in a few nouns, e.g. Lat. *Rōmam uēnit* 'he came to Rome', *domum rediī* 'I returned home'; but it was generally replaced by prepositional phrases: O. *ANT PÚNTTRAM* 'up to the bridge', cf. Lat. *ante pontem* 'in front of the bridge'; U. *SPINAM-AŘ* 'to the column', cf. *ad spīnam* 'to the spine'.

The encroachment of prepositional phrases on the simple case is well exemplified in the Latin ablative. The ablative functions of the case and those derived from them, e.g. agency, normally have prepositions except with certain words. Thus *parentibus caret* 'of his parents he is deprived' but *ab eīs sēparātus* 'from them separated', *ab eīs dēsertus* 'by them deserted'. Regularly without prepositions are for instance *cōnsule nātus* 'of a consul begotten', *melle dulcius* 'than honey sweeter'. The comitative function normally has prepositions where the accompaniment is physical: *cum agricolīs labōrābat* 'with farmers he was working' vs *magnā (cum) cūrā* 'with great care'. The instrumental function acquires prepositions only in post-classical documents; e.g. *dē gladiō percussus* 'by a sword struck'.

Prepositional phrases also encroached upon the functions of other cases. In Oscan and Umbrian the preposition (or rather postposition) *en* 'in' was sometimes attached to the locative, as in O. *HÚRTÍN* 'in the grove', Lat. *in hortō* 'in the garden', *exaisc-en ligis* 'in these laws', Lat. *in hīs lēgibus*.

By analogy with the plural forms the ablative singular also came to be used in locative functions with prepositions, which were, however, generally omitted when the noun was temporal. Thus O. *ÚP SAKARAKLÚD* 'at the temple' beside *SAKARAKLEÍ* (loc.), *meddikxud* beside *MEDIKKIAÍ* 'in the magistracy'. In Latin, apart from the lexical group referred to above – *Rōmae*, *domī*, etc. – the locative case had been entirely replaced by the ablative: *in templō*, *in magistrātū* and *eō tempore* 'at that time'. In Vulgar Latin even the temporal nouns acquired prepositions.

Prepositional ablative phrases in Latin also encroached upon the genitive case: e.g. *iū dicātus dē capite* for *capitis* 'judged on a capital charge' (cf. O. *dat castrid* for *castrous zicolum deicum* 'for a capital charge the day to name') and especially *maior pars ex hostibus* 'the greater part of the enemy', *dīmidium dē praedā* 'half of the loot' beside the genitives *hostium* and *praedae*. Similarly *ad* + accusative phrases encroached upon the dative. The original distinctions between *ad haec respondit* 'in the face of these (arguments) he replied' and *hīs respondit* 'to these persons he replied' and between *ad rēgem id mīsī* 'to (in the direction of) the king it I sent' and *rēgī id dedī* 'to the king it I gave' became blurred, and in post-classical Latin the Vulgar generalisation of prepositional phrases leads to occasional uses like *ad hōs respondit, ad rēgem id dedī*.

Some of the phonetic changes remarked in Section 2 eroded important distinctions in the Latin case paradigms. Thus the disappearance of final /m/, the loss of distinction between /a/ and /a·/ and the merging of /u/ and /o·/ produced homophony between *lē gem* (acc.) and *lēge* (abl.) in paradigm (3a), between *populum* (acc.) and *populō* (dat., abl.) in (2) and between *u·a* (nom.), *uiam* (acc.) and *uiā* (abl.) in (1). The plural inflections, being more distinctively marked, were less vulnerable. However, the combined effect of grammatical and phonetic changes was a steady reduction of the cases in Vulgar Latin, until of the four surviving paradigms three had three cases, the fourth, (3b), only two:

Sg.	Nom.	*vi̯a	*pǫpǫlǫs	*lẹss	*tǫrrẹs
	Obl.	-a	-ǫ	*lẹ́gẹ̇	-ẹ
Pl.	Nom.	-ẹ	-i̯	-gẹs	-ẹs
	Obl.	-as	-ǫs	-gẹs	-ẹs

(ǵ = a palatalised reflex of /g/)

Pronominal morphology was idiosyncratic to particular languages in both its lexical forms and its inflections, though many of the cases are identical with nouns of (1) and (2). Vulgar Latin developed articles from the deictic pronoun *ille* 'that one' and the cardinal number *ūnus* 'one', the former perhaps partly under Greek influence. This was an innovation in Italic.

The comparison of adjectives was signalled morphologically. Comparatives were formed with inherited *-ios-*; e.g. Lat. *maiior* < **magi̯ōs* (: *magnus* 'big'), O. *mais* < **magi̯os* (nt.), and its allomorph **-is-* + **-tero-* in Oscan and Umbrian, e.g. U. *MESTRU* < **magisterā* (f. nom.), cf. Lat. *magister* 'master'. Superlative forms were more varied. Inherited were **-mo-* in **supmo-* > Lat. *summum*, U. *somo* (acc.) 'highest', **-t(m̥)mo-* in Lat. *ultimam*, O. *ÚLTIUMAM* (f. acc.), **-is(m̥)mo-* in **magism̥mo-* > Lat. *maximās*, O. *maimas* (f. acc. pl.). Unique to Latin is **-is-sm̥mo-* as in *strēnuissimus* 'most vigorous'. The analytic exponents *magis/plūs strēnuus, maximē strēnuus*, etc., encroached, especially in Vulgar Latin.

The Italic verbal inflections too were fusional, encoding the categories of tense, (past, present, future), aspect (imperfective, perfective), mood (indicative, subjunctive, imperative), number (singular, plural), person (first, second, third) and voice (active and medio-passive). Typologically this system was close to Proto-Indo-European. The specific innovations were the creation of a future tense, the merging of perfect and unmarked (aorist) aspectual distinctions in a new perfective, the absorption of optative into subjunctive and of dual into plural, and the decline of the middle functions of the medio-passive.

Minimal oppositions can be illustrated from Latin:

dīcit 'he says' present indicative singular third person active	imperfect:	dīcēbat	'he was saying'
	perfect:	dīxit	'he said'
	subjunctive:	dīcat	'let him say'
	plural:	dīcunt	'they say'
	second person:	dīcis	'you say'
	passive:	dīcitur	'he is said'

all of which are exactly paralleled in Oscan and Umbrian.

There are three Italic participles: (a) the inherited *-nt-* acts as imperfective active; e.g. U. *ZEŘEF* = Lat. *sedēns* 'sitting' (nom. sg.); (b) the inherited *-to-* verbal adjective signalling state, which was originally neutral as to voice, as in U. *TAÇEZ* 'silent' = Lat. *tacitus* beside *tacēre* 'to be silent', *ÇERSNATUR* 'having dined' (nom. pl.), cf. Lat. *cēnāti* beside *cēnāre* 'to dine', became the medio-passive perfect participle; e.g. O. *scriftas* 'written' (nom. pl.), Lat. *scrīptae* beside *scrībere* 'to write', and *indūtus* 'having put on' beside *induere* 'to clothe'; (c) a prospective passive in *-ndo-*, the gerundive, peculiar to Italic; e.g. O. *ÚPSANNAM* 'to be done' (acc. sg.), U. *anferener* 'to be carried about' (gen. sg.); cf. Lat. *operandam, ferendī*. Latin also has a prospective active participle, e.g. *dictūrus* 'about to say'.

There are infinitives, reflecting verbal noun case forms, e.g. *dīcere* < **deikesi* (*s*-stem loc. sg.); *dīcī* < **deikei* (loc. of **deikom* or dat. of **deiks*) and O. *DEÍKÚM* (the corresponding accusative). Latin developed a systematic marking of tense and voice in the infinitives, starting with the arbitrary assignment of **deikesi* to present active, **deikei* to present passive and the extension of **-si* from the present active to form a perfect active **deix-is-si* (> *dīxisse*). The system was completed by an assortment of makeshift analytic formations.

Apart from the verb 'to be' (Lat. *esse*, O. *ezum* U. *erom*) and, at least in Latin, 'to go' (*īre*) and 'to wish' (*uelle*, with its compounds), the Italic verb was organised into four conjugations, classified according to the present infinitive and first person singular present indicative, as in the chart of Latin verb conjugations.

Latin Verb Conjugations

		1	2	3a	3b	4
Infin.		cūrāre	monēre	dīcere	facere	uenīre
		'to care'	'to warn'	'to say'	'to make'	'to come'
Sg.	1	cūr-ō	mon-eō	dīc-ō	fac-iō	uen-iō
	2	-ās	-ēs	-is	-is	-īs
	3	-at	-et	-it	-it	-it
Pl.	1	-āmus	-ēmus	-imus	-imus	-īmus
	2	-ātis	-ētis	-itis	-itis	-ītis
	3	-ant	-ent	-unt	-iunt	-iunt

Conjugation (3a) reflects inherited thematic-stem verbs, e.g. *agere*, O. *acum*, cf. Gk. *ágein* 'to lead', together with a few verbs from the Proto-Indo-European athematic class, e.g. *iungō* 'I join', cf. Ved. *yunájmi*, *sistō* 'I set up', U. *SESTU*, cf. Gk. *hístāmi*. The transfer of the latter probably began in the plural, with the remodelling of **iungmos*, **sistamos* (cf. Ved. *yunjmāḥ*, Gk. *hístamen*) etc. (1) also contains some athematic reflexes, e.g. *fārī* 'to speak', cf. Gk. *phāmí* 'I say', and *stāre* 'to stand', which was formed from the aorist, cf. Gk. *éstān* 'I stood'. But its largest constituency is denominative formations, originally from declension (1), e.g. *cūrāre*, O. *KURAIA* (3 sg. subj.), North O. *coisatens* (3 pl. perf.) all from **koisā* (> Lat. *cūra*), but extended to other declensions, e.g. Lat. *termināre* from the (2)-noun *terminus*, O. *TEREMNATTENS* (3 pl. perf.) from a (3a)-neuter attested in *TEREMENNIÚ* (nom. pl.). In fact it was to this conjugation that all new denominatives and loan-verbs were assigned; e.g. *iūdicāre* from *iūdex* 'judge', cf. O. *medicatud* (abl. part.) 'having been judged', *aedificāre* 'to build' from **aedifex*, *baptizāre* from Gk. *baptizein*, *guardāre/wardāre* from Go. *wardōn* 'to keep watch'.

Conjugation (2) absorbed the Proto-Indo-European stative formant in **-ē-*, e.g. *uidēre* 'to see', the causative **-ejo-*, e.g. *moneō* 'I warn' (cf. *meminī* 'I recall'), and some denominatives from declension (2), e.g. *fatērī* 'to confess', O. *FATÍUM* from **fato-* 'spoken'. (4) has a few denominatives from (3b)-nouns, e.g. *finīre* from *finis* 'finish'. Together with (3b) it also reflects **-jo-* verbs, as in *ueniō* (4) < **gʷnjō*, (3b, cf. O. *FAKIIAD*

155

3 sg. subj) < *dhə₁jō. The distribution between the two conjugations, at first phonologically determined, had long since become more casual. A number of verbs show doublet forms in (3b) and (4), e.g. Lat. *cupiō* 'I desire', U. *HERTER* 'it is required' (< *heri-) but *HERI* 'he wishes' (< *herī-).

Some verbs with long-vowel presents show a different formation in the perfect, e.g. *moneō* : *monu-ī*, *ueniō* : *uēn-ī*, also *iuuō* (1) 'I help' : *iūuī*. Others generalised the long vowel, e.g. *cūrō* : *cūrāuī*, *audio* 'I hear': *audīuī*. This is typical of a general Latin tendency: cf. the spread of the infixed nasal from *iungō* 'I join' to *iunxī* beside the more conservative *rumpō* : *rūpī*.

The most important opposition in the Latin verb was originally between (I) imperfective and (II) perfective aspect. Within each of these two divisions there was a further opposition between (A) the unmarked base form and a pair marked for (B1) prospective and (B2) retrospective tense. The unmarked imperfective form was located in the present tense, the unmarked perfective form was temporally ambivalent between present and past. The following second singular forms of *monēre* illustrate the original distribution of the forms that they reflect:

```
I    A    monē-s
          B1    monē-b-is    B2    monē-b-ās
II   A    monu-istī
          B1    monu-er-is   B2    monu-er-ās
```

This system was not inherited, and the conjugation that is closest to a Proto-Indo-European type, (3), shows a different pattern in IA and B:

```
I    A    dīc-is    B1    dīc-ēs
                    B2    dīcē-bās
```

where *dīcēs* was originally the subjunctive to *dīcis*. This pattern in fact spread via (3b) to (4): *audīs*, *audiēs*. It has a parallel in the relation between U. *PURTUVIS* 'you offer' and *PURTUVIES* 'you will offer'.

The Oscan and Umbrian material is very incomplete; there are no reflexes of II B2, for instance, and only one of I B2. But the following Oscan forms reveal a system, and it is different both from Proto-Indo-European and from Latin:

```
I    A    FAAMA-T(3 sg.)
                    B1    deiua-s-t (3 sg.)
                                   B2    FU-F-ANS (3 pl.)
II   A    PRÚFATT-ENS (3 pl.)
                    B1    TRÍBARAKATT-U-S-ET (3 pl.)
                                   B2    —
```

Here the I B1 form is from *-se-, also attested in early Lat. *faxit*, an infrequent synonym of *faciet* 'he will do', while the unique I B2 form is from *-bhwā-, attested in Lat. *bā-.

Also exemplified in these examples is the diversity of perfective formants: Lat. /w/ in *curā-uī*, *mon-ŭ-ī*, O. /tt/ in *PRÚFATTENS*. There are others too; e.g. U. /l/ in *apelus* 'you will have weighed (< *anpend-luses)*, O. /f/ in *SAKRAFIR* (pass. subj.) 'let there be a consecration'. Some are shared with Latin, e.g. reduplication in U. *DEDE* 'he gave', Lat. *dedit*; long root vowel in O. *hipid* 'he had' (< *hēb- beside Lat. *habuit)*, cf. Lat. *cēpi* 'I took'. The sigmatic formation, productive in Latin, e.g. *dīxī* (cf. Gk. aor. *édeixa*), has no other Italic attestation.

The six tenses had by historical times been reorganised thus:

1 Future (< I B1): monēbis 'you will warn', deiuast 'he will swear'.
2 Past-in-the-Future/Future Perfect (< II B1): monueris 'you will have warned', TRÍBARAKATTUSET 'they will have built'.
3 Present (< I A): monēs 'you warn', FAAMAT 'he orders'.
4 [Past] Imperfect (<I B2): monēbās 'you were warning', FUFANS 'they were'.
5 [Pres.] Perfect/Past Definite (< II A): monuistī 'you warned', PRÚFATTENS 'they approved'.
6 Past-in-the-Past/Past Perfect (< II B2): monuerās 'you had warned'

The original aspectual oppositions survive only in the imperfect and perfect, having become neutralised in the future and present. The temporal relationship between imperfect and past-in-the-past, *monē-b-ās : monu-er-ās*, has been replicated in *monē-b-is : monu-er-is*, with the transfer of the latter from perfective-future to future-perfect function.

The syncretic character of the Italic perfect is reflected in Latin both in its stem classes, which contain inherited perfect (reduplication) and aorist (sigmatic) formants, and in its personal inflections: sg. *uēn-ī, uēn-istī, uēn-it*; pl. *uēn-imus, uēn-istis, uēn-ēre* and *uēnērunt*. This contrasts sharply with the inflections of all the other five tenses, which, apart from first person singular forms in vowel + *m* in the imperfect, past perfect and all subjunctives, are very homogeneous. (In Oscan and Umbrian what can be discerned of the perfect inflections is less idiosyncratic.)

The present-perfect functions of the Latin perfect are well attested, e.g. *nōuī* 'I know', perfect of *nōscō* 'I come to know', *periī* 'I am ruined', perfect of *pereo* 'I perish'. They were especially prominent in the passive, where a stative meaning is predictably more frequent anyway and the analytic exponents had a present orientation: *epistulae scrī ptae sunt* like O. *scriftae set* was originally a present-perfect 'the letters are in a written state', even though it is the regular passive also to the past-definite meaning of *scrīpsī* 'I wrote'.

The ambiguities resulting from the syncretism in the perfect were resolved in the classical period of Latin by the development of two new tenses: an active present-perfect corresponding to *scrīptae sunt* 'they are written' and a passive past-definite for *scrīpsī (epistulās)*:

	Act.		*Pass.*
Perf.	scrīptās habeō (new)	←	scrīptae sunt
			↓
Past Def.	scrīpsī		scrīptae fuērunt (new)

The innovations never established themselves fully in the written language but became current in Post-Classical Vulgar Latin.

The Italic exponents of medio-passive voice are partly reflexes of middle forms in *-r*, which are attested in Hittite and Old Irish, partly the phrases with the *-to-* participle cited above. Thus U. *EMANTUR* 'they are to be taken', Lat. *emantur* 'they are to be

157

bought', U. *screhto est*, Lat. *scriptum est* 'it has been written'. The relation between the medio-passive and active paradigms can be seen in:

	1		3a	
	Sg.	Pl.	Sg.	Pl.
1	cūr-o-r	cūr-ā-mu-r	dīc-o-r	dīc-i-mu-r
2	-ā-ris	-ā-minī	-e-ris	-i-minī
3	-ā-t-ur	-a-nt-ur	-i-t-ur	-u-nt-ur

Most transitive verbs show the live opposition of passive to active. Sometimes the verb is intransitive and the passive therefore subjectless, an impersonal equivalent to an active form, e.g. *pugnātur* 'there is fighting' = *pugnant* 'they (unspecified) are fighting'.

The old middle voice is discernible in occasional uses of these forms, e.g. *mouētur* 'it moves (itself)', *uertitur* 'he turns (himself) around' and more rarely accompanied by a direct object *indūtus tunicam* 'having put on a tunic', cf. *induit tunicam* 'he puts a tunic on (somebody else)'. Sometimes the active and middle forms are synonymous, e.g. *adsentiō/or* 'I agree', *mereō/or* 'I earn'. In a number of verbs, the so-called deponents, only the medio-passive form occurs, either with a middle meaning, e.g. *moror* 'I delay (myself)', O. *KARANTER* 'they enjoy', cf. Lat. *uescuntur*, or more often with a meaning indistinguishable from the active, e.g. *opīnor* 'I believe' beside *crēdō*, *prōgredior* 'I advance' beside *prōcēdō*.

Of the three moods the imperative has only second and third person forms; Lat. *ī* 'go!', *ītō* 'go!' or 'let him go!'< **ei* + *tōd*, cf. U. *ETU*: Lat. *agitō*, O. *actud*, U. *AITU* 'let him act/move' < **age* + *tōd*. Italic subjunctives reflect in form and function both the subjunctive and optative moods of Proto-Indo-European. Thus O. *FUSÍD* = Lat. *foret* 'it was to be' with Proto-Indo-European thematic subjunctive **-ē-*; U. *EMANTUR* 'they are to be taken', cf. Lat. *emantur*, with **-ā-*, a subjunctive formant also found in Celtic, U. *sir* = Lat. *sīs* 'may you be' with *-ī-*, originally the plural allomorph of *-iē-*, the athematic optative formant. The meanings of will (subjunctive) and wish (optative) are illustrated by these examples and by O. *NEP PÚTÍAD* 'nor may he be able', Lat. *nēue possit*, O. *ni hipid* 'let him not hold', with perfect subjunctive as in Lat. *nē habuerit*. Prospective (subjunctive) and hypothetical (optative) meanings are found in Lat. *sī id dī cās, ueniat* 'if you were to say it [in future], she would come' (pres. subj.), *sī id dīcerēs uenīret* 'if you were saying it [now], she would be coming' (imperf. subj.). The introduction into the subjunctive of temporal distinctions modelled on the indicative (*dīcat : dīceret : dīxerit* ← *dīcit: dīcēbat: dīxit*) and the decline of the purely aspectual ones (as in *nē dīxerit* 'he is not to say' vs *nē dīcat* 'he is not to be saying') are notable innovations in Italic.

Sometimes in Latin subordinate clauses the distinction between indicative and subjunctive is neutralised; cf. *currit nē cōnspiciātur* 'he runs in order not to be seen' (volitive: purpose) with *tam celeriter currit ut non cōnspiciātur* 'he runs so fast that he is not seen' (for **cōnspicitur*, declarative); *haec quom dīxisset* (subj.), *ēuāsimus* with *ubi haec dīxit* (indic.), *ēuāsimus* 'when she had said this (declarative), we left'.

In indirect discourse declarative utterances were normally represented by the accusative plus infinitive. It was precisely in order to encode the necessary tense and voice distinctions that Latin developed its heterogeneous collection of infinitives, possibly under the influence of Greek, the only other Indo-European language to employ elaborate forms of accusative plus infinitive. The tense of the direct-discourse verb was reproduced in the infinitive: *uenīs* 'you are coming', *dīcō/dīxī tē uenīre* 'I say you are/ said you were coming'. The construction was very inefficient: the temporal distinctions between *ueniēbās* 'you were coming', *uēnistī* 'you came' and *uēnerās* 'you had come' were lost in *dīcō/dīxī tē uēnisse* 'I say you have/said you had come'; similarly the modal distinction between *ueniās* 'you would come' and *ueniēs* 'you will come' disappears in *tē uentūrum esse*. Eventually the accusative plus infinitive was replaced by *quod* or *quia* + finite verb constructions, perhaps partly under Greek influence, though in contrast to Greek there is a tense shift (see below). The replacement was almost total in Vulgar Latin but only partial in the written language.

In indirect commands, questions, etc. and in all subordinate clauses within indirect discourse finite verbs were used, but with transpositions of mood and tense, the indicative being replaced by subjunctive and the tense being determined not by the tense in direct discourse but by the tense of the governing verb: *imperāuī ut uenīrēs* 'I gave orders for you to come' (← imper. *uenī!*), *rogāuī quor uēnissēs* 'I asked why you had come' (← indic. *quor uēnistī?*). This was almost certainly a native Italic development within the register of laws and edicts: cf. O. *KUMBENED THESAVRÚM PÚN PATENSINS MUINIKAD TANGINÚD PATENSÍNS* 'it was agreed that the treasury, when they opened it, by a joint decision they should open' with Lat. *conuēnit ut thēsaurum cum aperīrent commūnī sententiā aperīrent*; U. *EHVELKLU U FEIA SVE REHTE KURATU SIT* 'a vote he is to hold (as to) whether the matter rightly has been taken care of' with Lat. *sententiam roget num rēctē cūrātum sit*.

The Italic languages had a free word order in the sense that variations from normal patterns did not affect syntactic relationships or make nonsense, but were motivated by pragmatic considerations – topicalisation, emphatic juxtaposition – or by the aesthetics of prose or verse rhythm, etc. However, the unmarked, viz. most frequent, order was SOV. Thus in Latin *informīs hiemēs redūcit Iuppiter*, from a lyric poem by Horace, contrasts with the unmarked classical prose order *Iuppiter hiemēs informīs redūcit* 'Jupiter winters ugly brings back'. The cooccurrence of SOV with noun–adjective patterns generally in Italic characterises the languages as typologically mixed or 'transitional'. Consistent with SOV are: (i) the order genitive-noun attested in O. *SENATEÍS TANGINÚD*, cf. Lat. *senatūs cōnsultō* 'by decision of the senate'; (ii) the anastrophe of prepositions, common in Umbrian but rare in Oscan and Latin, e.g. U. *ASAMAR* = Lat. *ad āram* 'to the altar', U. *FRATRUSPER* = *prō frātribus* 'for the brothers' (cf. O. *censtom-en* = *in cēnsum* 'for the census', Lat. *mēcum* 'with me'); (iii) the early Latin placing of relative clauses before their antecedents. However, none of these was an unmarked order in Latin of the classical period, a fact that confirms its mixed character. The order SOV is overwhelmingly the most frequent in the prose of Cicero and Caesar, and in the post-classical written registers was especially tenacious in subordinate clauses, where it provided a 'punctuating' signal, often combined with rhythmic cadences (*clausulae*). Nevertheless, there are signs in the dialogue of Plautus' comedies (early second century BC) that SVO was becoming established in Vulgar Latin. The reduction of morphological distinctions between nominative and accusative in Vulgar Latin drastically limited the choice of the marked options OSV and OVS. Furthermore the replacement of certain cases by prepositional phrases favoured the fronting of head nouns: *dīmidium praedae* seems to have been replaced by *dīmidium dē praedā* more easily than the marked *praedae dīmidium* by *dē praedā dīmidium*.

A notable feature of the literary register in Classical and Post-Classical Latin was the elaboration of complex and in particular periodic sentence structure. Heavily influenced by Greek rhetoric doctrine and oratorical practice, it became a feature of both formal prose and verse. In a highly inflected language the grammatical concords facilitate the detachment of participial phrases from the nominals on which they depend and enable clausal exponents of subordinate constituents to be embedded without any loss of semantic coherence. The following is typical:

(1)   posterō diē,
(2)   quom per explōrātōres cognōuisset
(3)   quō in locō hostēs
(4)   quī Brundisiō profectī erant
(3)   castra posuissent,
(1)   flūmen trānsgressus est,
(5)   ut hostīs,
(6)   extra moenia uagantēs
(7)   et
(8)   nūllis custōdibus positīs
(7)   incautōs,
(5)   ante sōlis occāsum aggrederētur.

(lit. 'on the next day, | when by reconnaissance patrols he had discovered | in what place the enemy | who from Brindisi had set out | camp had pitched, | the river he crossed | in order that the enemy, | outside the camp wandering and [being] | with no guards posted | unwary, | before the sun's setting he should attack').

This is not strictly a period since a well-formed sentence can be concluded before the final clause, in fact at *trānsgressus est*; but it illustrates the technique very well. (4) is embedded in (3) and the group (2)–(4) in (1); similarly (8) in (7) and (6)–(8) in (5). All the modes of subordination are exemplified: adverbial and relative clauses in (2) and (4), participial and absolute phrases in (6) and (8). The deployment of information in participial exponents ((6)–(8)) dependent on the object of the volitional verb in (5) has both pragmatic significance and the aesthetic effect of contributing variety and balance to the sentence. Latin complex and periodic structure provided the model for similar developments in the formal discourse of later European vernaculars, though none of these possessed the morphological resources to emulate it fully.

4 Lexicon

With so small and specialised a body of data from Oscan and Umbrian it is hazardous to generalise, and we can do no more than note a few specific items in their basic vocabulary. For instance, U. *pir* (cf. O. *PURASÍAÍ* (adj.)) and *UTUR* have widespread Indo-European cognates outside Italic, e.g. *fire*, *water*, but not in Latin (*ignis*, *aqua*); O. *touto*, U. *totam* (acc.) 'community' have specifically West Indo-European cognates, again excluding Latin. On the other hand, some words are peculiar to Italic; e.g. Lat. *cēna*, O. *KERSNU* 'dinner' (the root is Indo-European, meaning 'cut'); *habēre* 'to have', cf. U. *HABIA* (3 sg. subj.); *ūtī* 'to use', cf. O. *ÚÍTTIUF* 'use' (nom. sg.), of no certain etymology; and *familia*, O. *famelo* 'household', probably from Etruscan. Many words attested in Italic generally have of course Indo-European cognates; e.g. *māter* 'mother', O. *MAATREÍS* (gen.); *pēs* 'foot', U. *PEŘI* (abl.); *duodecim*, U. *desenduf* (acc.) 'twelve (two + ten)'; *ferre* 'to bear', U. *FEREST* (3 sg. fut.); *sedēre* 'to sit', U. *ZEŘEF* (pres. part.). A few of these show a semantic specialisation peculiar to Italic; e.g. *dīcere*, O. *DEÍKUM* 'to say'

(< 'to point, show'); *diēs*, O. *zicolom* 'day' (< 'sky'); *agere*, O. *acum* 'to do' (< 'to move along').

In addition to the items just mentioned there are a number of Latin words for which neither cognates nor synonyms happen to be recorded in Italic but which have well-established Indo-European etymologies; e.g. *ego* 'I', *canis* 'dog', *nix* 'snow', *pectus* 'breast', *rēx* 'king', *dūcere* 'to lead', *loquī* 'to speak'. Among the older Indo-European languages Latin's basic vocabulary has closest affinities with Gothic, with which it shares some 38 per cent of items, and Vedic (35 per cent); it has least in common with Old Irish (27 per cent) and Old Armenian (26 per cent). The relatively low percentages and the narrow band within which they cluster indicate a long period of separation between Latin (presumably with Italic) and the rest.

Some frequent Latin words have no etymology even in Italic; e.g. *bonus* 'good', *hīc* 'this', *mulier* 'woman', *omnis* 'all'. Loanwords can be identified at all periods, often by their phonology; e.g. *rosa* 'rose' from an unknown Mediterranean source, *bōs* 'cow' from Sabine, *taberna* 'shop' from Etruscan, *carrus* 'cart' from Celtic, *wadium* 'pledge, wage' from Gothic. By far the largest group is from Greek: not only cultural terms – *balneum* 'bath', *epistula* 'letter', *māchina* 'device', *nummus* 'coin' (all early), *architectus*, *poēta* and Christian terms like *ecclēsia* 'church' and *baptizāre* 'to baptise' – but also more basic items like *āēr* 'air', *bracchium* 'arm', *camera* 'room', *hōra* 'hour' and in Vulgar Latin *colpus* 'blow', *gamba* 'leg', *petra* 'stone', replacing the native words *ictus*, *crūs* and *lapis*. A number of Latin words, especially in the technical registers of philosophy, philology and the arts and crafts, were either created on Greek models, e.g. *quālitās* 'quality' (Gk. *poiótēs*), *indīuiduum* 'the indivisible thing' (Gk. *átomos*), *accentus* 'accent' (Gk. *prosō día* lit. 'a singing in addition'), or semantically adjusted to them e.g. *cāsus* 'a falling' > 'noun case' (Gk. *ptōsis*) and *conclūsiō* 'an enclosing' > 'syllogism' (Gk. *sullogismós*).

The lexical stock was extended by the usual morphological processes. Complex words were created by suffixation. For instance, the diminutive *-lo-* used both literally, e.g. *puella* '(little) girl': **puera* (cf. *puer* 'boy'), *ōsculum* 'kiss' (cf. *ōs* 'mouth'), *articulus* '(small) joint' (cf. *artus* 'joint, limb'), and affectively, e.g. *misellus* 'poor little' (cf. *miser* 'wretched'), *ocellus* 'dear little eye' (cf. *oculus*). In Vulgar Latin some words were displaced by their diminutives, e.g. *culter* 'knife' by *cultellus*, *uetus* 'old' by *uetulus*.

Among the most frequent verbal noun formants in Italic were **-ion-* and **-tion-*, which originally signalled action but were often extended by metonymy to the concrete result of action; e.g. O. *TRÍBARAKKIUF* ('act of building' >) 'a building', *legio* ('act of choosing' >) 'a legion', O. *medicatinom* (acc.) 'judgement' from **medicaum* 'to judge', U. *NATINE* (abl. 'act of birth' >) 'tribe', cf. Lat. *nātiō*. In fact *-tiōn-* was productive at all periods of Latin, e.g. *mentiō* 'an act of reminding' > 'mention' (cf. OIr. *airmitiu* 'respect, honour') beside *mēns* (< *mentis*) 'mind'; *ōrātiō* 'act of pleading' > 'a speech, a prayer' from *ōrāre*; Medieval Lat. *wadiātiō* 'the act of *wadiāre* (to pledge, give security)'. Often associated with *-tiōn-* in Latin is the agent suffix *-tōr-*, e.g. *ōrātor*, *wadiātor*. By contrast *imperātor* (O. *EMBRATUR*) 'commander' is from *imperāre* but the action noun is *imperium*; *auctor* (U. *UHTUR*) 'initiator' from *aug-* 'to enlarge' but *auctoritās*, U. *UHTRETIE* (loc.) 'the status of initiator' with the denominative suffixes in *-tāt-* and *-tiā-* (cf. Lat. *amīc-itia* 'friendship').

Among the productive verb suffixes is *-tā-*, with intensive, in particular frequentative, meanings: *itāre* 'to go often' beside *īre* 'to go' cf. U. *ETAIANS* (3 pl. subj.) < **eitā-*; *habitāre* 'to live' beside *habēre* 'to have'; *tractāre* 'to handle' beside *trahere* 'to drag'. There was a tendency especially in Vulgar Latin for these to replace the simple verbs;

e.g. *spectāre* 'to look at', *cantāre* 'to sing', *iactāre* 'to throw' for *specere* (archaic), *canere, iacere.* This led to greater morphological uniformity; cf. *cantō, cantāuī* and *iactō, iactāuī* with *canō, cecinī* and *iaciō, iēcī.* The intensive meanings themselves came to be hypercharacterised, as *dict-itāre* for *dic-tāre* from *dīcere* 'to say'.

Italic compound words, formed from the stems of two or more distinct lexemes, mostly conform to the OV type. Thus O. *MEDDÍSS* 'magistrate' < **medo-dik-* 'rule-declaring', cf. Lat. *iū-dex* 'judge' < 'law-setting/giving', O. *KÚM-BENN-IEIS* (gen.) 'assembly' < 'a together-coming', cf. Lat. *conuen-tūs*, O. *TRÍB-ARAK-AVÚM* (infin.) 'to build' < 'to house-strengthen', cf. Lat. *aedi-fic-āre*, U. *petur-purs-us* (dat.) 'animals' < 'four-footed', cf. Lat. *quadru-ped-ibus.* Some prefixes acquired intensive force; cf. *cōnficere* 'to complete' with *cōnferre* 'to bring together', *efficere* 'to effect' with *effluere* 'to flow out'. In the literary register compounding was usually a mark of Greek influence. It was associated particularly with high epic, e.g. *caelicola* 'sky-dweller', *suāuiloquēns* 'pleasant-speaking', and parodies thereof, e.g. *dentifrangibulus* 'teeth-breaking'; also with philosophical and philological terminology, where, as we have seen, the precise models were Greek. Latin was never a heavily compounding language like Ancient Greek, Vedic or modern German, and the chief morphological expansions of the lexicon were through the formation of compound-complex words, e.g. **prīmo-cap-* 'first taking' in *prīnceps* 'chief', whence *prīncipium* 'a beginning' (< *-iom*, as in O. *KUMBENNIEÍS*), *principālis* 'primary' (< *-āli-*, as in O. *FERTALIS* 'with sacrificial cakes, *ferta*'), *prīncipātus* 'leadership' (< *-ātu-* (4); cf. *-āto-* (2) reflected in U. *FRATRECATE* < **fratr-ik-ātei* (loc.) 'in the office of the master of the brothers', **frātrik(o)s'*). These processes and many of the actual formants continued in use for as long as Latin survived.

Bibliography

Brief but reliable accounts of the history of Latin are Stolz et al. (1966) and Collart (1967). More detailed, especially on the literary registers, is Palmer (1954). The most comprehensive description of the language is Leumann et al. (1963–72); it is, however, inadequate for Vulgar Latin, for which see Väänänen (1963), and for the written registers of post-classical periods, for which see Löfstedt (1959) and Norberg (1968). An up-to-date linguistic account of the classical language is provided by Pinkster (1990). On particular topics, Kent (1945) on phonology and Kent (1946) on morphology are both predominantly historical, while Woodcock (1958) on syntax is predominantly descriptive; for word order, Adams (1976) is important.

For the other Italic languages, a recent survey is Silvestri (1998); Buck (1928) is still the standard work on Oscan and Umbrian, while Poultney (1959) is comprehensive on Umbrian. Pisani (1964) includes all the Italic languages and also Venetic, Messapic and Etruscan.

References

Adams, J.N. 1976. 'A Typological Approach to Latin Word Order', *Indogermanische Forschungen*, vol. 81, pp. 70–99

Allen, W.S. 1975. *Vox Latina: A Guide to the Pronunciation of Classical Latin* (Cambridge University Press, Cambridge)

Bonioli, M. 1962. *La pronuncia del latino nelle scuole dall'antichità al rinascimento*, vol. 1 (Università di Torino Pubblicazioni, Facoltà di Lettere e Filologia, Turin)

Buck, C.D. 1928. *A Grammar of Oscan and Umbrian* (Ginn, Boston)

Collart, J. 1967. *Histoire de la langue latine* (Presses Universitaires de France, Paris)

Cooper, F.C. 1895. *Word Formation in the Roman Sermo Plebeius* (Trow Directory, New York)

Grandgent, C.H. 1907. *An Introduction to Vulgar Latin* (D.C. Heath, Boston)

Kent, R.G. 1945. *The Sounds of Latin* (Linguistic Society of America, Baltimore)

—— 1946. *The Forms of Latin* (Linguistic Society of America, Baltimore)

Leumann, M., Hoffmann, J.B. and Szantyr, A. 1963–72. *Lateinische Grammatik*, 2 vols (C.H. Beck, Munich)

Löfstedt, E. 1959. *Late Latin* (Aschehoug, Oslo)

Norberg, D. 1968. *Manuel pratique de latin medieval* (Picard, Paris)

Palmer, L.R. 1954. *The Latin Language* (Faber and Faber, London)

Pinkster, H. 1990. *Latin Syntax and Semantics*. London: Routledge

Pisani, V. 1964. *Le lingue dell' Italia antica oltre il latino*, 2nd edn (Rosenberg and Fellier, Torino)

Poultney, J.W. 1959. *The Bronze Tablets of Iguvium* (American Philological Association, Baltimore)

Silvestri, D. 1998. 'The Italic Languages,' in A. Giacalone Ramat and P. Ramat (eds) *The Indo-European Languages* (Routledge, London), pp. 322–44

Stolz, F., Debrunner, A. and Schmid, W.P. (eds) 1966. *Geschichte der lateinischen Sprache* (Walter de Gruyter, Berlin)

Väänänen, V. 1963. *Introduction au latin vulgaire* (Klincksieck, Paris)

Woodcock, E.C. 1958. *A New Latin Syntax* (Methuen, London)

8

Romance Languages

John N. Green

The Romance languages derive, via Latin, from the Italic branch of Indo-European. Their modern distribution is the product of two major phases of conquest and colonisation. The first, between c. 240 BC and c. AD 100 brought the whole Mediterranean basin under Roman control; the second, beginning in the sixteenth century, annexed the greater part of the Americas and sub-Saharan Africa to Romance-speaking European powers. Today, some 665 million people speak, as their first or only language, one that is genetically related to Latin. Although for historical and cultural reasons preeminence is usually accorded to European Romance, it must not be forgotten that European speakers are now outnumbered by non-Europeans by a factor of nearly three to one.

The principal modern varieties of European Romance are indicated on Map 8.1. No uniformly acceptable nomenclature has been devised for Romance and the choice of term to designate a particular variety can often be politically charged. The Romance area is not exceptional in according or withholding the status of 'language' (in contradistinction to 'dialect' or 'patois') on sociopolitical rather than linguistic criteria, but additional relevant factors in Romance may be cultural allegiance and length of literary tradition. Five national standard languages are recognised: Portuguese, Spanish, French, Italian and Rumanian (each treated in an individual chapter below). 'Language' status is usually also accorded on cultural/literary grounds to Catalan and Occitan, though most of their speakers are bilingual in Spanish and French respectively, and the 'literary tradition' of Occitan refers primarily to medieval Provençal, whose modern manifestation is properly considered a constituent dialect of Occitan. On linguistic grounds, Sardinian too is often described as a language, despite its internal heterogeneity. Purely linguistic criteria are difficult to apply systematically: Sicilian, which shares many features with southern Italian dialects, is not usually classed as an independent language, though its linguistic distance from standard Italian is no less than that separating Spanish from Portuguese. 'Rhaeto-Romance' is nowadays used as a cover term for a number of varieties spoken in southern Switzerland (principally Engadinish, Romansh and Surselvan) and in the Dolomites, but it is no longer taken to subsume Friulian. Romansh (local form *romontsch*) enjoys an official status for cantonal administration and so perhaps fulfils the requirements of a language. Another special case is Galician, located in Spain

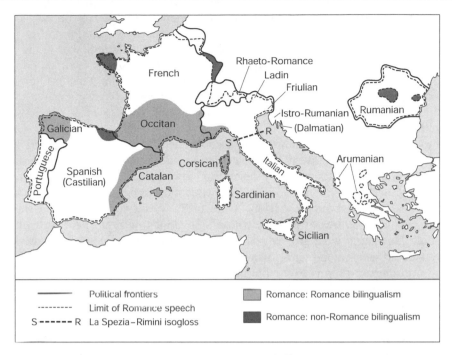

Map 8.1 The territorial extent of Romance as a first language in Europe.

but genetically and typologically very close to Portuguese; in the wake of political autonomy, *galego/gallego* now enjoys protected 'language' status in Spain, although elsewhere it continues to be thought of (erroneously) as a regional dialect of Spanish. Corsican, which clearly belongs to the Italo-Romance group, would be in a similar position if the separatist movement gained autonomy or independence from France.

Outside Europe, Spanish, Portuguese and French, in descending order of native speakers, have achieved widest currency, though many other varieties are represented in localised immigrant communities, such as Sicilian in New York, Rumanian in Melbourne, Sephardic Spanish in Seattle and Buenos Aires. In addition, the colonial era gave rise to a number of creoles, of which those with lexical affinities to French are now the most vigorous, claiming some ten million speakers.

In general, European variants are designated by their geographical location; 'Latin', as a term for the vernacular, has survived only for some subvarieties of Rhaeto-Romance (*ladin*) and for Biblical translations into Judaeo-Spanish (*ladino*). 'Romance' derives, through Spanish and French, from *ROMĀNICĒ* 'in the Roman fashion' but also 'candidly, straightforwardly', a sense well attested in early Spanish. The terminological distinction may reflect early awareness of register differentiation within the language, with 'Latin' reserved at first for formal styles and later for written language and Christian liturgy. The idea, once widely accepted, that Latin and Romance coexisted for centuries as natural, *spoken* languages, is now considered implausible.

Among the chief concerns of Romance linguists have always been: the unity or otherwise of the proto-language, the causes and date of dialect differentiation and the classification of the modern variants. Plainly, Romance does not derive from the polished literary models of Classical Latin. Alternative attestations are quite plentiful, but difficult to interpret. Attempts to echo popular speech in literary works may be suspected of stylistic artifice; inscriptional evidence is formulaic; the abundant Pompeian graffiti may be dialectal, and so on. Little is known of Roman linguistic policy or of the rate of assimilation of new conquests. We may however surmise that a vast territory, populated by widely different ethnic groups, annexed over a period exceeding three centuries, conquered by legionaries and first colonised by settlers who were probably not native speakers of Latin, and never enjoying easy or mass communications, could scarcely have possessed a single homogeneous language.

The social conditions which must have accompanied latinisation – including slavery and enforced population movements – have led some linguists to postulate a stage of creolisation, from which Latin slowly decreolised towards a spoken norm in the regions most exposed to metropolitan influences. Subsequent differentiation would then be due to the loss of administrative cohesion at the break-up of the Empire and the slow emergence of local centres of prestige whose innovations, whether internal or induced by adstrate languages, were largely resisted by neighbouring territories. Awareness of the extent of differentiation seems to have come very slowly, probably stimulated in the west by Carolingian reforms of the liturgical language, which sought to achieve a uniform pronunciation of Church Latin at the cost of rendering it incomprehensible to uneducated churchgoers. Sporadic attestations of Romance, mainly glosses and interlinear translations in religious and legal documents, begin in the eighth century. The earliest continuous texts which are indisputably Romance are dated: for French, ninth century; for Spanish and Italian, tenth; for Sardinian, eleventh; for Occitan (Provençal), Portuguese and Rhaeto-Romance, twelfth; for Catalan, thirteenth; for Dalmatian (now extinct), fourteenth; and for Rumanian, well into the sixteenth century.

Most classifications of Romance give precedence, explicitly or implicitly, to historical and areal factors. The traditional 'first split' is between East and West, located on a line running across northern Italy between La Spezia and Rimini. Varieties to the northwest are often portrayed as innovating, versus the conservative south-east. For instance, West Romance voices and weakens intervocalic plosives: *SAPŌNE* 'soap' > Ptg. *sabão*, Sp. *jabón*, Fr. *savon*, but It./Sard. *sapone*, Rum. *săpun*; *RŌTA* 'wheel' > Ptg. *roda*, Sp. *rueda*, Cat. *roda*, Fr. *roue*, but It./Sard. *rota*, Rum. *roată*; *URTĪCA* 'nettle'> Ptg./Sp./ Cat. *ortiga*, Fr. *ortie*, but Sard. *urtica*, It. *ortica*, Rum. *urzică*. The West also generalises /-s/ as a plural marker, while the East uses vocalic alternations: Ptg. *as cabras* 'the goats', Cat. *les cabres*, Romansh *las chavras*, contrast with It. *le capre* and Rum. *caprele*. In vocabulary, we could cite the verb 'to weep', where the older Latin word *PLANGĔRE* survives in the East (Sard. *pranghere*, It. *piangere*, Rum. *a plînge*) but is completely replaced in the West by reflexes of *PLORĀRE* (Ptg. *chorar*, Sp. *llorar*, Cat. *plorar*, Oc. *ploură*, Fr. *pleurer*). In this classification, each major group splits into two subgroups: 'East' into Balkan-Romance and Italo-Romance, 'West' into Gallo-Romance and Ibero-Romance. The result is not entirely satisfactory. While, for example, Arumanian dialects and Istro-Rumanian group quite well with Balkan-Romance, our scant evidence of Dalmatian suggests it shared as many features with Italo-Romance as with the Balkan group. Catalan is a notorious difficulty, having been subject for centuries to alternating Occitan and Spanish influences. The unity of 'Rhaeto-Romance' also fails to survive closer scrutiny: Ladin groups fairly well with Friulian as part of Italo-Romance, but southern Swiss varieties share many features with eastern French dialects.

'Family-tree' classifications, in which variants are each assigned to a single node, give only a crude indication of relationships in Romance and tend to obscure the convergence brought about by centuries of borrowing from Latin and criss-crossing patterns of contact. This is readily illustrated from the lexicon. The *PLANGĔRE/ PLORĀRE* example, though supportive of the East–West split, is in fact rather atypical. More common are innovations spreading from central areas but failing to reach the periphery. 'To boil' is Ptg. *ferver*, Sp. *hervir*, Rum. *a fierbe* (< *FERVĒRE/FERVĔRE*), but Cat. *bullir*, Oc. *boulí*, Fr. *boullir*, It. *bollire* (< *BULLĪRE*, originally 'to bubble'); 'to request' is Ptg./Sp. *rogar*, Rum. *a ruga* (< *ROGĀRE*), but Cat. *pregar*, Oc. *pregá*, Fr. *prier*, It. *pregare* (< *PRECĀRE*, originally 'to pray'); 'to find' is Ptg. *achar*, Sp. *hallar*, Rum. *a afla*, but Cat. *trobar*, Oc. *trobà*, Fr. *trouver*, It. *trovare* (both forms are metaphorical – classical *INVENĪRE* and *REPERĪRE* do not survive). Among nouns, we may cite 'bird': Ptg. *pássaro*, Sp. *pájaro*, Rum. *pasăre* (< **PASSARE*), versus Oc. *aucèu*, Fr. *oiseau*, Romansh *utschè*, It. *uccello* (< *AUCELLU*); and 'cheese': Ptg. *queijo*, Sp. *queso*, Rum. *caş* (< *CĀSEU*), versus Cat. *formatge*, Oc. *froumage*, Fr. *fromage*, It. *formaggio* (< *[CASEU] FORMATICU* 'moulded [cheese]'). Almost the same distribution is found in a morphosyntactic innovation: the Latin synthetic comparative in *-IŌRE* nowhere survives as a productive form, but peripheral areas have *MAGIS* as the analytic replacement ('higher' is Ptg. *mais alto*, Rum. *mai înalt*) whereas the centre prefers *PLŪS* (Fr. *plus haut*, It. *più alto*).

Despite this differential diffusion and the divergences created by localised borrowing from adstrate languages (notably from Arabic into Portuguese and Spanish, from Germanic into northern French, from Slavonic into Rumanian), the modern Romance languages have a high degree of lexical overlap. Cognacy is about 40 per cent for all major variants using the standard lexicostatistical 100-word list. For some language pairs it is much higher: 65 per cent for French–Spanish (slightly higher if suffixal derivation is disregarded), 90 per cent for Spanish–Portuguese. This is not, of course, a guarantee of mutual comprehensibility (untrained observers are unlikely to recognise the historical relationship of Sp. /oxa/ 'leaf' to Fr. /fœj/), but a high rate of cognacy does increase the chances of correct identification of phonological correspondences. Intercomprehensibility is also good in technical and formal registers, owing to extensive borrowing from Latin, whether of ready-made lexemes (abstract nouns are a favoured category) or of roots recombined in the naming of a new concept, like Fr. *constitutionnel*, *émetteur*, *exportation*, *ventilateur*, etc. Indirectly, coinings like these have fed the existing propensity of all Romance languages for enriching their word stock by suffixal derivation.

Turning to morphosyntax, we find that all modern Romance is VO in its basic word order, though southern varieties generally admit some flexibility of subject position. A much reduced suffixal case system survives in Rumanian, but has been eliminated everywhere else, with internominal relations now expressed exclusively by prepositions. All variants have developed articles, the definite ones deriving overwhelmingly from the demonstrative *ILLE/ILLA* (though Sardinian and Balearic Catalan use *IPSE/ IPSA*), the indefinite from the numeral *ŪNU/ŪNA*. Articles, which precede their head noun everywhere except in Rumanian where they are enclitic, are often obligatory in subject position. Concord continues to operate throughout noun phrases and between subject and verb, though its range of exponents has diminished with the loss of nominal case. French is eccentric in virtually confining plural marking to the determiner, though substantives still show number in the written language. Parallel to the definite articles, most varieties have developed deictic object pronouns from demonstratives. These, like the personal pronouns, often occur in two sets, one free and capable of taking stress, the other cliticised to the verb. There is some evidence of the grammaticalisation of an animate/inanimate distinction, both in the clitic pronouns and in the prepositional marking of specific animate objects. This latter is widespread (using *a* in West Romance and *pe* in Rumanian) but not found in standard French or Italian.

Suffixal inflection remains vigorous in the common verb paradigms everywhere but in French. Compound tense forms everywhere supplement the basic set, though the auxiliaries vary: for perfectives, *HABĒRE* is most common: 'I have sung' is Fr. *j'ai chanté*, It. *ho cantato*, Sp. *he cantado* but Ptg. *tenho cantado* (< *TENĒRE* originally 'to hold') and Cat. *vaig cantar* (< *VĀDO CANTĀRE*) – an eccentric outcome for a combination that would be interpreted elsewhere as a periphrastic future ('I am going to sing'). Most Romance varieties have a basic imperfective/perfective aspectual opposition, supplemented by one or more of punctual, progressive and stative. The synthetic passive has given way to a historically reflexive medio-passive which coexists uneasily with a reconstituted analytic passive based on the copula and past participle. The replacement of the Latin future indicative by a periphrasis expressing volition or mild obligation (*HABĒRE* is again the most widespread auxiliary, but *deppo* 'I ought' is found in Sardinian and *voi* 'I wish' in Rumanian) provided the model for two new synthetic paradigms, the future itself and the conditional, which has taken over a number of functions from the subjunctive. The subjunctive has also been affected by changes in complementation patterns, but a few new uses have evolved during the documented period of Romance, and its morphological structure, though drastically reduced in spoken French, remains largely intact.

In phonology, it is more difficult to make generalisations (see the individual language sections below and, for the development from Latin to Proto-Romance, pages 146–150). We can, however, detect some shared tendencies. The rhythmic structure is predominantly syllable-timed. Stress is dynamic rather than tonal and, on the whole, rather weak – certainly more so than in Germanic; some variants, notably Italian, do use higher tones as a concomitant of intensity, but none rely on melody alone. The loss of many intertonic and post-tonic syllables suggests that stress may previously have been stronger, witness *IŪDĬCE*['i̯u-di-ke] 'judge' > Ptg. *juiz*, Sp. *juez*, Cat. *jutge*, Fr. *juge*; *CUBĬTU* ['ku-bi-tu] 'elbow' > Sp. *codo*, Fr. *coude*, Rum. *cot*. The elimination of phonemic length from the Latin vowel system has been maintained with only minor exceptions. A strong tendency in early Romance towards diphthongisation of stressed mid vowels has given very varied results, depending on whether both higher and lower mid vowels were affected, in both open and closed syllables, and on whether the diphthong was later levelled. Romance now exhibits a wide range of vowel systems, but those of the south-central group are noticeably simpler than those of the periphery: phonemic nasals are found only in French and Portuguese, high central vowels only in Rumanian, and phonemic front rounded vowels only in French, some Rhaeto-Romance and north Italian varieties and São Miguel Portuguese. Among consonantal developments, we have already mentioned lenition, which led to wholesale reduction and syllable loss in northern French dialects. Latin geminates generally survive only in Italo-Romance, and many other medial clusters are simplified (though new ones are created by various vocalic changes). Although Latin is in Indo-European terms a centum language (with *k* for PIE *k̃*), one of the earliest and most far-reaching Romance changes is the palatalisation, and later affrication, of velar and dental consonants before front vowels. Only the most conservative dialect of Sardinian fails to palatalise (witness *kenapura* 'Holy supper = Friday'), and the process itself has elsewhere often proved cyclic.

Developments in phonology illustrate a more general characteristic of Romance: the tendency for a small number of identical *processes* to affect all varieties, though at slightly different rates and with slightly different exponents as the outcome. Whether this is due to directly inherited tendencies, or to analogical development of shared stock, remains a matter of debate – neither standpoint would question the fundamental unity of Romance.

Bibliography

The Romance languages are so richly documented, both synchronically and historically, that relatively few modern works attempt coverage of the whole family. The exception, authoritatively surveying the entire field of Romance linguistics, is Holtus et al. (1988–2006), with hundreds of commissioned articles filling eight volumes; the sheer length of time in publication, however, means that the early volumes are now rather dated. Harris and Vincent (1988) provides detailed typological descriptions of Latin and all principal varieties of modern Romance including the Romance-lexicon creoles. Godard (2003) is a collection of seven articles neatly encapsulating the 'hot' topics of morphosyntactic research: clitics, complex predicates, auxiliaries and transitivity, bare nouns, negation and SV inversion. Cresti and Moneglia (2005) is a valuable resource on modern spoken Romance, with comparable and searchable corpora for standard French, Italian, Portuguese and Spanish.

Vernay (1991–6) is an attractive reference work, grouping selected areas of Romance vocabulary according to semantic field and theme; it can be used both as a comparative dictionary and as an adjunct to dialectological studies. An ambitious project to map the dialectal variety of the Romance languages has been launched (Contini et al., 1996–); meanwhile, Rohlfs (1971) remains the most approachable introduction to dialectology, with some 100 maps showing the diffusion of individual words and expressions, complemented by a further 275 maps in Rohlfs (1986). Posner and Green (1993), the sequel to a four-volume survey of the discipline published in the early 1980s, focuses on theoretical and practical issues of standardisation, diglossia and non-consensual bilingualism when varieties of Romance are in competition.

Posner (1996) is a work of mature synthesis, selective but truly comparative, cutting across traditional modes of presentation; it allocates equal space to similarities and differences, each considered in terms of structural properties and external or sociolinguistic impacts. The papers in Dworkin and Wanner (2000) draw on current theoretical models to scrutinise and rejuvenate some recurrent themes in Romance historical linguistics. The revival of interest in Late Latin and the formative period of Romance is ably represented by Wright (2002), which focuses on the reconceptualisation of Romance as independent of Latin. Earlier still, the heterogeneity of Latin and Proto-Romance is brilliantly documented by Adams (2007).

References

Adams, J.N. 2007. *The Regional Diversification of Latin 200 BC–AD 600* (Cambridge University Press, Cambridge)

Contini, M., Tuaillon, G. et al. (eds) 1996–2002. *Atlas linguistique roman (ALiR)*, 2 vols of projected 12 (Istituto poligrafico e Zecca dello Stato, Rome)

Cresti, A. and Moneglia, M. (eds) 2005. *C-ORAL-ROM. Integrated Reference Corpus for Spoken Romance Languages* (John Benjamins, Amsterdam)

Dworkin, S.N. and Wanner, D. (eds) 2000. *New Approaches to Old Problems. Issues in Romance Historical Linguistics* (John Benjamins, Amsterdam)

Godard, D. (ed.) 2003. *Les langues romanes. Problèmes de la phrase simple* (CNRS Éditions, Paris)

Harris, M. and Vincent, N. (eds) 1988. *The Romance Languages* (Routledge, London; Oxford University Press, New York)

Holtus, G., Metzeltin, M. and Schmitt, C. (eds) 1988–2006. *Lexikon der romanistischen Linguistik*, 8 vols (Niemeyer, Tübingen)

Posner, R. 1996. *The Romance Languages* (Cambridge University Press, Cambridge)

Posner, R. and Green, J.N. (eds) 1993. *Bilingualism and Linguistic Conflict in Romance* (Mouton de Gruyter, Berlin)

Rohlfs, G. 1971. *Romanische Sprachgeographie* (C.H. Beck, Munich)

—— 1986. *Panorama delle lingue neolatine* (G. Narr, Tübingen)

Vernay, H. 1991–6. *Dictionnaire onomasiologique des langues romanes* (Niemeyer, Tübingen)

Wright, R. 2002. *A Sociophilological Study of Late Latin* (Brepols, Turnhout)

9

French

Linda R. Waugh and Monique Monville-Burston

1 Introduction

French is a Romance language descended directly from the (Vulgar) Latin that came to be spoken in what was then Gaul during the period of the Roman Empire. As that Empire crumbled, a number of major dialectal divisions developed, which do not necessarily correspond to present-day political or linguistic frontiers. Such a major division was to be found within medieval France (see Map 9.1), with the dialects of the north and centre (and part of modern Belgium), known collectively as *langue d'oïl*, that are sharply distinguished from those of the south of France, *langue d'oc* (*oïl* and *oc* being the words for 'yes' in the two regions), with a third smaller area in the southeast, known as Franco-Provençal, generally taken to include the French dialects of Switzerland and in the Aosta Valley in Italy. The division between north and south is so marked that it has frequently been argued that, on purely linguistic grounds, the dialects of the south, now generally known collectively as *occitan*, are best not regarded as Gallo-Romance at all, but rather as closely linked with Catalan, the resultant grouping being distinct from Hispano-Romance also.

Within these major dialectal areas, further linguistic fragmentation took place, divergence being strongly abetted by the lack of social cohesion during the so-called Dark Ages. One of the dialects of the *langue d'oïl* that emerged in this way was *francien* (a modern name), the dialect of the Ile-de-France (where Paris is located), and it is from this dialect that, once circumstances arose which facilitated the growth of a national language, modern standard French has developed. (Another northern dialect was Norman, which had a profound influence on the development of English after the Norman invasion of England.) The establishment of a fixed royal court in Paris and the recrudescence of an educational and a legal system there, tended to favour the dialect of Paris and the surrounding area for the status of national language. Since the twelfth and thirteenth centuries, when *francien* gradually came to be accepted as a norm to aim towards, at least in writing and in cultivated speech in northern and central France, progress has been slow but steady. It is worth pointing out, however, that although the literary form of *occitan*, Provençal, never recovered from the devastation caused by the Albigensian

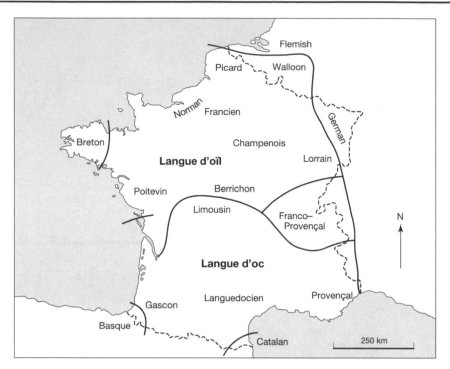

Map 9.1 The Dialect Divisions of Medieval France.

crusade, and although French came to be virtually ubiquitous as the written language after the *Ordonnance* ('Decree') *de Villers-Cotterêts* (1539), it was not until the nineteenth and even the twentieth centuries, particularly in the south, that French came to be wholly dominant within the boundaries of France, at first among the bourgeoisie and in the cities, and later in the more remote rural areas. Indeed, French's long period of predominance as the major international language of culture and diplomacy significantly antedates its general use as a spoken language within France: by the end of the seventeenth century, French had in effect replaced Latin in the former role, to the point that the Berlin Academy was able to ask in 1782, as a matter of fact, *'Qu'est-ce qui a rendu la langue françoise universelle?'* ('What has made the French language universal?'). This situation persisted until the First World War and even beyond.

2 The French-speaking World

It is difficult to evaluate the number of francophones in the world, but it is reasonable to believe that there are presently between 90 and 110 million, 70 million with French as their mother tongue, 20 to 40 million with French as a second language. Hence quantitatively, French ranks eleventh among the world's languages. However, its status is enhanced by other factors. In a number of countries its position is more than that of a foreign language. For example, it is the official language in 28 countries; it is widely used in various major international organisations: it is one of the six official languages of the UN and one of the three 'working languages' of the EU; it is learnt as a foreign language by a large number of students: in Europe, for instance, 9 million study French, i.e. fewer than English (18 million) but more than German (3 million).

Within Europe, French is now spoken by some 60 million people in France (and Monaco), and by some 4 million Walloons in Belgium, principally in the four franco-phone districts of the south, Hainaut, Namur, Liège and Luxembourg. In the bilingual district of Brussels, the Belgian and European capital, French is spoken by 80 per cent of the population. The rivalry between French and Dutch within Belgium, which extends far beyond the linguistic domain, is well known. Around half a million people live in the Grand Duchy of Luxembourg, where the native language of most speakers is a German dialect but where French is the language of education and administration (about 300,000 speakers), while in Switzerland – where French is one of the three official languages with German and Italian – the most recent figures suggest that 20 per cent of a total population of some 7 million are French speakers. Four cantons are francophone (Genève, Vaud, Neuchâtel, Jura) and two are bilingual (Fribourg and Valais). In northern Italy, the Aosta Valley has a French-speaking population of around 90,000, with one-third being regular users of the language.

Outside of Europe, indigenous French speakers are to be found on almost every continent. In Canada 8 million people – about a quarter of the population, descendants of the original French colonists – use French regularly. More than 6.5 million of these live in the province of Quebec where they form over 80 per cent of the total population. Strenuous efforts have been made to preserve and strengthen French, particularly in Quebec, within what has been a bilingual country officially since 1867. In Quebec, Bill 101 – *la loi 101* (1977) – now regulates the use of French in matters of education, commerce and industry, and advertising on the streets and in public places. Descendants of another group of French colonists in Acadia (the easternmost provinces of Canada), driven out in the mid-eighteenth century, carried their language southwards down the eastern seaboard of the United States and into Louisiana. As a result, although there are relatively few French speakers in Acadia today except in New Brunswick (about 240,000), there are significant numbers – about half a million regular speakers of the language – in New England and New York (where there is a major admixture also directly from Quebec), in Florida (almost 340,000), and in Louisiana. In Louisiana, which was French until 1803, the immigrants were primarily from Acadia, and are indeed called 'Cajuns': their form of speech, *français acadien*, is in regular use by around 200,000, alongside a French-based Creole, and also a more or less standard French, the latter spoken by a small elite.

Elsewhere, French is generally in competition not with another European language but with indigenous non-European languages and/or with French-based creoles in former French (or Belgian) colonies. In the West Indies, French is found for instance in Haiti (where it is the official language of some 8 million people but where the great majority actually use Creole, and less than one million are speakers of French) and on islands such as Martinique and Guadeloupe (about 700,000 Francophones). By far the most important areas, however, are the countries of the Maghreb (Algeria, Morocco and Tunisia), where French appears to be holding its own since independence. In Algeria and Tunisia, for example, it is estimated that some 30 per cent of the population can read and write French, with a much higher proportion able to speak it, above all in the cities. In sub-Saharan Africa, there are 16 independent francophone states comprising a great swathe across the west and the centre of the continent from Senegal to the Democratic Republic of Congo, together with Madagascar, and there is a further group of French-creole-speaking islands (Mauritius, Seychelles, Réunion in the Indian Ocean). Being everywhere (except in France) in competition with one or several other languages, French is generally not in a favourable position. However, in many countries where it is used for a variety of official, technical or international purposes, its future as a second language seems relatively secure.

Most countries *ayant le français en partage* ('that share French') are part of *la Francophonie* ('Francophonia', 'the francophone world'). This political, cultural and linguistic organisation was created in the 1960s under the impetus of francophone heads of state, in particular Leopold Senghor (Senegal) and Habib Bourguiba (Tunisia). Its structures and government bodies have evolved greatly over the years. It presently includes 68 member states. *La Francophonie* being now a linguistic community as well as *une communauté de pensée ou de culture* ('a community of thought or culture'), the nature of the membership is varied: countries where French is the vernacular, former colonies, countries with transient historical links with France (e.g. Cambodia, Lebanon, Haiti), neighbours of French-speaking areas (e.g. St Lucia, Guinea-Bissau, Dominica), countries having cultural and/or linguistic affinities with French (e.g. Bulgaria, Romania, Greece). Among Francophonia institutions there are the biennial Summits of heads of states and governments (the first one met in Paris in 1986); the Intergovernmental Agency, which deals with education and culture, and the development of multimedia; the Agence Universitaire de la Francophonie (Association of Francophone Universities), formerly called AUPELF-UREF, which coordinates tertiary education cooperation. *La Francophonie* aims essentially at maintaining French as a global means of communication and at securing cultural and linguistic independence from the English-speaking world. It also functions as a non-aligned political entity (Map 9.2).

3 Variation, Varieties and Variables

Like all languages with any significant degree of diffusion, French is of course not a single homogeneous entity. In the different countries/areas where it is spoken, its status varies and hence its frequency of use and its users' degree of mastery. In some cases, it is the mother tongue of an important part of the population, as in France, Belgium, Quebec, or in some overseas *départements* (e.g. Martinique, Réunion). In diglossic settings, it is a second language (e.g. New Caledonia, Polynesia, former African colonies). Elsewhere, as in the Maghreb, it is purely a vehicular language. Finally, in a number of countries belonging to *la Francophonie*, its use is simply encouraged (Lebanon, Roumania). Even when the same type of situation pertains, there is a great amount of variation, due to factors such as the function of the language (official or administrative), its use in the media and in literary productions, the grade in which it is introduced in schools, etc.

Furthermore, as with any language, French varies with space (regional varieties), speaker characteristics (social position, education, sex, age, urban vs rural habitat, etc.) and usage (different styles for different situations of communication).

In France itself there is in most regions a spectrum of variation from 'pure' patois (the original local dialect, now often moribund) through *français régional* (largely the standard grammar, with a more or less regionally marked phonology and a greater or lesser number of non-standard lexical items) to the standard language (which itself has a wide range of styles and registers). A similar spectrum exists in most if not all of the areas discussed above, often with the added dimension of a French-based creole. In Quebec, for example,

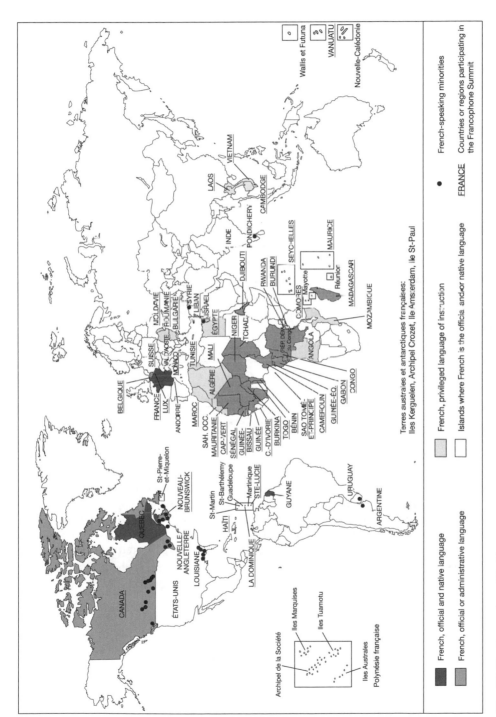

Map 9.2 The Francophone World.

'educated Quebec French' shades imperceptibly through to the fully popular variant known as *joual* (from the local pronunciation of *cheval* 'horse') associated primarily with Montreal. French-based creoles are spoken in Louisiana (alongside Cajun, discussed above), Haiti and various islands mentioned earlier. There is very frequently a continuum from creole to standard, with more educated speakers tending perhaps increasingly towards the 'hexagonal' norms, i.e. the norms applying in France. In parts of Africa, especially in large cities (e.g. Abidjan), similar continua can be observed, from standard French to the local language influenced by French, with various pidginised forms in between.

It is hexagonal standard French (*français courant, commun, standardisé*) that is described in what follows. An attempt will be made however, to indicate major divergences between ordinary, everyday French (*français familier, ordinaire*) and more educated and formal varieties of the language (*français soutenu, cultivé, soigné*), as manifested in its phonology, grammar and lexicon. French being a highly standardised language, differences between the written and the spontaneous oral forms of speech are often substantial. In recent years much attention has been paid by scholars to the spoken language. There is also an increasing interest in urban forms of French, particularly those spoken by young people in the *banlieues* ('outskirts') of large plurilingual French cities, such as Paris, Lyons or Marseilles. This scholarship will be taken into account here.

The standardisation of the language is important in the history of France and the language is a crucial component of national identity. The concept of norm is very strong; prescriptive judgements are easily made, especially by higher social groups. The norm, defined by authorities such as the *Académie française* (French Academy) and transmitted by the schools, takes as its reference point belletristic writing. This engenders puristic attitudes and nourishes the belief that French is threatened from within (by speakers who do not conform to the norm) and from outside (by those who let English invade their vocabulary, for example). As a consequence, the state frequently legislates about linguistic matters and a number of institutions are in place, whose mission is to 'defend' the national language. For example, efforts have been made, first through the *Office du vocabulaire français*, founded in 1957, and thereafter by various government organisations to manage written French vocabulary. Real power in this domain has thus devolved from the *Académie française* to governmental bodies such as the *Délégation générale de la langue française* (*et aux langues de France*) (General Delegation for the French language (and for the languages of France)) and the *Conseil international de la langue française* (International Council for the French Language). Their mission is to deal with gaps in French vocabulary in a wide range of specialist areas by proposing appropriate French words and disseminating official terminology. The *Commission de féminisation des noms de métiers* recently proposed feminine forms for agent nouns in the professions and trades where only masculine forms have traditionally existed, a reform that was, however, less radical in France than in Belgium or Quebec. It should be noted that linguistic legislation is also very important, and constantly updated, in Quebec.

4 Phonology

4.1 Phonology and Orthography

One of the most immediately striking facts about French is the radical nature of the phonological changes that the language has undergone since Vulgar Latin was brought to Gaul by Roman conquerors, changes that differentiate not just French from, say, Spanish or Italian, but also the standard from regional varieties. These changes have led to attempts to use the current 26-letter Latin alphabet along with other means to render the sounds of French: e.g. diacritics (accent marks, plus the cedilla), doubled consonants ('ll' for /j/ as in *fille* 'girl' /fij/), digraphs ('g' before 'n' for the palatal nasal: thus 'gn' for /ɲ/ as in *agneau* 'lamb' /aɲo/, 'ou' for the vowel sound /u/ as in *nous* 'us' /nu/, vowel plus 'n' for a nasalised vowel, as in *an* 'year' /ɑ̃/), Latinised spellings, as in *sept* < *SEPTEM* 'seven' /sɛt/, various distributional rules (e.g. 'c' represents /k/ in certain environments but /s/ in others). The details of French orthography are so many and so complex that we cannot discuss them here. There have been many attempts over the centuries to reform French orthography, most of which have led to small changes but no major overhaul of the system. The last of these was in 1990 but, even though it was approved by the French Academy, most of the 'rectifications' do not seem to be followed. We will use here the current norms according to majority usage.

In the discussion that follows, when we transcribe the sounds of French, we will use the symbols of the International Phonetic Association (IPA) to represent them.

4.2 Syllables and Stress

The functional spoken units in French are phrases, not single words. The tendency in French is to have what is called *enchaînement*: that is, not to make word boundaries within tightly bound groups of words (e.g. the noun phrase, the verb phrase). For example in *On leur a offert | une aide immense |* 'one offered them = they were offered | tremendous help |', only the two phrasal boundaries (marked by | in the examples) are perceived. One of the main ways in which *enchaînement* is accomplished is through syllabification: there is a preference in French for CV syllables (Consonant–Vowel, sometimes called open, or free syllables). So, when a word ending in a consonant precedes a word beginning with a vowel within the same phrasal group, the consonant is syllabified with the next word (in the transcription that follows, syllable breaks are marked by -): *On leur a offert* /ɔ̃-loe-ʁa-ɔ-fɛʁ/ | *une aide immense* /y-nɛ-di-mɑ̃s/. Of course, V (vowel only) and (C)VC (closed, blocked) syllables also occur, as do syllables with more than one consonant before and/or after the vowel (with various restrictions), but they are less frequent and when possible, the syllabification is into CV(C) syllables, as in *énergie* 'energy' /e-nɛʁ-ʒi/. Stress in French is on the vowel in the last syllable of the phrasal group, whether it is a single word or a sequence of tightly bound words. Essentially, therefore, we may say that modern French is a final-stress, phrase-stress language.

4.3 Vowels and Semi-vowels

The vowels and semi-vowels (sometimes called glides) of the French norm are shown in Table 9.1.

There are several points to be noted about this system. The most complex part of the vowel system is the series of higher mid (close, tense) and lower mid (open, lax) vowels (/e/ vs /ɛ/, /o/ vs /ɔ/, /ø/ vs /œ/). This is a common pattern in the languages of the world and is shared with Italian; however, few languages have the /ø/ vs /œ/ opposition. In French, the distribution of the mid vowels is limited according to the type of syllable and its place in the word. When the syllable is word-final, there is a tendency to have

Table 9.1 Vowel and Semi-Vowel Phonemes of the French Norm

	Front	*Rounded*	*Central*	*Back*
High	i j	y ɥ		u w
Higher Mid	e	ø		ʊ
Lower Mid	ɛ ɛ̃	œ œ̃	ə	ɔ ɔ̃
Low	a			ɑ ɑ̃

only the higher vowel (/e, o, ø/) in open syllables. There are two exceptions to this: for /e/ vs /ɛ/, some speakers keep a distinction, as in *piqué* 'stung' /pike/: *piquait* 'was stinging' /pikɛ/, although the distinction is not consistently made. /œ/ also occurs as the highly frequent 'hesitation marker/filler' *euh* 'uh' /œ/. As for word-final closed syllables, only the opposition between /o/ and /ɔ/ is clear and stable (*saute* 'jumps' /sot/: *sotte* 'foolish' (f.) /sɔt/); in the case of /ø/ vs /œ/, there is only one minimal pair and the difference is not made by all native speakers (*jeune* 'young' /ʒœn/ vs *jeûne* 'fasts' /ʒøn/); as for /e/ vs /ɛ/, /e/ does not occur in this position. In non-word-final open syllables, the tendency is to have /e, œ, ɔ/, although there is some variation between these and /ɛ, ø, o/, and in some cases a vowel intermediate between the higher and lower mid vowels is used. The situation is complicated by the possible occurrence of vowel harmony (for example, /ɛ/ can be found in open syllable before /ɛ/ in the next syllable, as in *théière* 'teapot' /tejɛʁ, tɛjɛʁ/, or /e/ before /i/, as in *mairie* 'city hall' /meʁi, meʁi/) in spontaneous speech. In more conservative speech, there may be the influence of derivational morphology: so the verb *rafraîchir* 'refresh', derived from the adjective *frais* (m.), *fraîche* (f.) 'fresh' /fʁɛ/, /fʁɛʃ/, can have two pronunciations depending on whether speakers apply vowel harmony /ʁafʁeʃiʁ/ or keep the stem-vowel of the adjective /ʁafʁɛʃiʁ/.

Another feature of French is its four nasal vowels, /ɛ̃/, /œ̃/, /ɑ̃/ and /ɔ̃/. However, /œ̃/ has a low functional load and is in the process of being absorbed by /ɛ̃/, (*un* 'a, one', rarely /œ̃/, usually /ɛ̃/), though the opposition remains phonemic in some regional varieties; and some speakers/dialects merge /ɔ̃/ with /ɑ̃/. Nasal vowels are infrequent in the languages of the world, and are shared in the Romance family only with Portuguese, although the set of nasal vowels is different. Another facet of the French system which is uncommon (and is found in no other Romance language), is the series of front rounded vowels, /y, ø, œ, œ̃/, although, as said above, the /ø/ vs /œ/ distinction is weak, and /œ̃/ is being lost). In addition, the opposition between front /a/ and more backed /ɑ/ is unstable: for some speakers it is replaced by a length opposition, as in *pâte* 'paste' /pɑːt/ vs *patte* 'paw' /pat/, whereas for others it has been lost.

In addition to these vowels, French has three semi-vowels, corresponding to each of the three high vowels: /j/ (cf. /i/), /ɥ/ (cf. /y/), /w/ (cf. /u/), the most interesting of which is the front rounded [ɥ], which is rare in the languages of the world. Whereas all three semi-vowels can occur in syllable-initial position or after a consonant and before a vowel in the syllable, only /j/ can occur in syllable-final position (as in *paye* 'pays' /pɛj/). There is a high functional link between the vowels and semi-vowels such that /i/, /y/ and /u/ can be /j/, /ɥ/ and /w/ before another vowel: e.g. *tuer* 'to kill' /tɥe/ vs *tue* 'kills' /ty/. Furthermore, while /j/ and /i/ are separate phonemes (e.g. *pays* 'country' /pei/ vs *paye* /pɛj/), and /w/ is distinct from /u/, with some phonemic overlapping (e.g. *loua* 'praised' /lwa/ ~ /lua/ vs *loi* 'law' /lwa/), [y] and [ɥ] are not in contrastive distribution and can be analysed as allophones of the same phoneme.

4.4 Consonants

The consonantal phonemes of the French norm are shown in Table 9.2.

There are few remarks to be made. Among the nasals, the /ɲ/ is unstable for many speakers, who instead use [nj]. In addition, /ŋ/ exists, for certain speakers, in words borrowed from English (*camping* /kãpiŋ/). The /ʁ/ is listed here as uvular and that is the norm, but it varies from velar to uvular to pharyngeal, depending on geographical, social and register conditions and the phonetic environment.

Table 9.2 Consonant Phonemes of the French Norm

	Labial	Dental	(Alveo) Palatal	Velar	Uvular
Stop (Occlusive, Plosive)					
Unvoiced/tense	p	t		k	
Voiced/lax	b	d		g	
Fricative					
Unvoiced/tense	f	s	ʃ		
Voiced/lax	v	z	ʒ		
Nasal	m	n	ɲ		
Liquid (Approximant)		l			ʁ

4.5 Liaison, Elision and 'Mute' (Latent) e

As noted above, in French, syllabification and stress function according to phrases, not according to words. Allied to this, there are two sandhi phenomena that result in the pronunciation or non-pronunciation of some latent sounds within phrases in certain conditions: one is liaison, when a latent consonant is pronounced, the other is elision, when a latent vowel is not pronounced. With liaison, a word-final consonant that would not be pronounced when the next word begins with a consonant, is pronounced when the next word begins with a vowel or semi-vowel. For example (with syllabification, and the liaison consonant underlined), *des amis* 'some friends' /de-za-mi/, *mon école* 'my school' /mõ-ne-kɔl/, *petit ami* 'boy friend' /pə-ti-ta-mi/ (these examples contain the most common liaison consonants: /z, t, n/; /r, p, g/ also occur but less frequently). Liaison consonants are often shown in the orthography (as above); in some adjectives and nouns, they occur as a marker of the feminine and in derived forms, while in the masculine they appear only in liaison (as in *petit* 'small' (m.) /pəti/ vs *petite* (f.) /pətit/ or in derived forms, *petitesse* 'smallness' /pətitɛs/); so which consonant occurs is somewhat predictable. However, the rules are very complex. In general, liaison tends to occur in tightly bound groups like nominal and verbal groups and is more likely before the noun or verb (that is, between the determiner and pre-nominal adjective and the noun, or between the subject and object pronouns and the verb), than after the noun or verb: that is, the more syntactic cohesion there is between words, the more likely liaison is. Liaison also tends to occur more frequently in careful or conservative speech and less in normal speech, e.g. *pas encore* 'not yet' /pa-zã-kɔr/ vs /pa-ã-kɔr/.

In addition to liaison, there is elision, which most affects the vowel written as an *e* and is usually called 'mute e, unstable e', 'schwa' (*e muet, e caduc, e instable, e latent*). This vowel is often transcribed as /ə/, although, when pronounced, it generally is the same as [ø] or [œ]). When a word ending in *e* is followed by a word beginning with a vowel, the /ə/ does not appear. So in *parle à Jean* 'speak to John' the verb is pronounced /paʁl/. In grammatical words like, *je* 'I', *de* 'of', *le* 'the', *que* 'which, that', the *e* is also elided in the spelling: so, *le* 'the' /lə/ plus *ami* 'friend' /ami/, is *l'ami* /la-mi/. In addition, elision occurs with the vowel /a/ in the feminine definite article *la* and the vowel /i/ in *si* 'if'. There is furthermore an ongoing tendency for the high vowels, especially in grammatical words, /i/ as in *qui* 'who' and /y/ as in *tu* 'you (fam.)' to undergo elision, in ordinary conversation (e.g. *tu as* = *t'as* 'you have' /ta/).

Latent /ə/ is also lost in other contexts, when it is in word-final position (even if the next sound is not a vowel), or inside a word. The rules for the loss of /ə/ in these contexts are very complex: in principle the vowel is only kept if it is stressed, if it is needed in order to keep more than three consonants from being sounded together (the so-called *règle des 3 consonnes* 'the rule of the 3 consonants)', or if its elimination would lead to an unacceptable initial consonant cluster (but all of these have to be nuanced in various ways). While in many cases, /ə/ is rendered in the orthography with an 'e', there are times when it can occur without an orthographic equivalent, due to the issue of consonant clusters: e.g. *des contacts pénibles* /de-kɔ̃-tak-tə-pe-nibl/ (mute e underlined, used to break up the consonant cluster /ktp/). Moreover, as with liaison, the rules are influenced by many factors, including speed and register – in general, the faster, more casual the pronunciation, the more elisions, and the more consonant clusters: e.g. *petite amie* 'girl friend' /pə-ti-ta-mi/ (with the latent *e*) vs /pti-ta-mi/ (without the latent *e*).

There are two further complexities in the case of liaison and elision: a number of words that begin with a vowel do not allow either elision or liaison. Many such words begin with an orthographic 'h' and most come from Germanic, where the 'h' was pronounced as /h/. For this reason, it is called the *h aspiré*: so *la hache* 'the axe' /la-aʃ/, *le héros* 'the hero' /lə-e-ʁo/ 'the hero', but *l'héroïne* 'the heroine' /le-ʁo-in/. As the example shows, not all words that begin with an orthographic 'h' have an *h aspiré*; and not all words that block liaison or elision begin with an 'h': *le onze* 'the eleven' /lə-ɔ̃z/. In similar fashion, the semi-vowels sometimes allow elision and liaison and sometimes do not: *l'oie* 'the goose' /lwa/ vs *la ouate* 'cotton wool' /la-wat/.

Liaison, elision, the loss of latent e, *enchaînement*, syllabification without regard to word boundaries – all of these produce many homophones, not only at the level of the word, but also at the level of the phrase or even the sentence. These lead to ambiguities and a host of word games (*Il est tout vert, il est ouvert* 'it's all green, it's open' /ilɛtuvɛʁ/; *c'est assez, c'est tassé, cétacé* 'it's enough, it's firmly packed, cetacian' /setase/). And all of this, in addition to the issue of the relation between sound and letter have led to the famous *dictée* ('dictation exercise') of French classrooms, which has even found its way into popular culture through the media, which often engage the French nation in national *dictées* contests.

5 Morphology and Morphosyntax

French has undergone many changes in its morphosyntax since Vulgar Latin times: to name a few, the loss of the neuter gender, the loss of case and as a compensation the development of prepositional phrases and a marked tendency towards subject–verb–object (SVO) word order, the obligatory expression of subject pronouns, the reorganisation of the verbal system, with in particular the formation of a new future and a conditional as well as compound tenses, the development of new determiners, in particular articles and demonstratives. We refer the reader to historical works in the Bibliography for details, as the approach in what follows will be essentially synchronic in nature.

Just like in Vulgar Latin, and the other Romance languages, grammatical morphology in French is sharply divided between the verb on the one hand, and the noun, adjective and determiners on the other hand. Pronouns are a special case and will be dealt with when we discuss the verb. In addition, there is a clear difference between the morphology of the written language and that of the spoken language. As with phonology, morphology is better understood with respect to the phrase – the verb phrase and the noun phrase, in our case – than to the word. Hence we will consider some details of these phrases in the next sections.

5.1 The Verb Phrase: Written Language

The verb phrase (verbal group, in French terminology) consists of a verb (its only obligatory constituent), which can be accompanied by one or more elements, such as noun phrases and their pronominal equivalents. With certain verbs, some of these are obligatory, such as direct objects (noun phrases or embedded sentences) with transitive verbs (*il lève la main* 'he's raising his hand', *elle pense qu'il viendra* 'she thinks he'll come'), prepositional phrases with verbs that take prepositions (as in *je vais à Paris* 'I'm going to Paris'), adjectives and adjectival phrases (*Jean le croit idiot* 'Jean thinks he's an idiot'), adverbs and adverbial clauses (*il marche lentement* 'he's walking slowly', *je sors quand il fait beau* 'I go out when the weather is good'), etc. In addition, the verb phrase is typically associated with an obligatory subject (noun phrase or its pronominal equivalents), except in the case of imperatives: *marchez!* 'walk!').

The verbal morphology of contemporary French includes tense, aspect, mood, person, and number. Person (first, second, and third) and number (singular, plural) are usually analysed as being properties of the subject, which are also shown by the verb through agreement. The grammatical categories that are proper to the verb and given morphologically (see Table 9.3 for examples) are tense (present, past, future), aspect (imperfective vs perfective) and mood (indicative, subjunctive, imperative), in addition to a conditional that is classified as both a tense and a mood. While tense is a three-way distinction, aspect is only found as a subdivision of past tense: imperfective past (*imparfait*, 'imperfect') vs perfective past (*passé simple*, 'simple past'). The subjunctive mood has a present and an imperfect, and the conditional, only one form. There is as well a full range of *temps composés* ('compound tenses'), formed with the various paradigms of *avoir* 'to have' (or *être* 'to be' in the case of certain intransitive and all reflexive verbs) and the past participle. Thus, each member of the morphological paradigm of present, imperfect, simple past, future, subjunctive, imperfect subjunctive, and conditional has corresponding perfect forms: compound past (*passé composé*), pluperfect (*plus-que-parfait*), anterior past, future perfect, past subjunctive, pluperfect subjunctive, and past conditional, respectively: e.g. for the *passé composé*, *il a donné* 'he has given' (also *il est venu* 'he has come', lit. 'he is come'). There are in addition periphrastic formations that are more or less grammaticalised, in particular the *aller*-future, formed with the present or imperfect form of *aller* 'to go' and the infinitive of the verb (e.g. *il va venir* 'he is going to come', *il allait venir* 'he was going to come').

Table 9.3 Verbal Paradigms for Written French

(a)	Infinitive plus present indicative					Passé composé
	donner *'give'*	finir *'finish'*	être *'be'*	avoir *'have'*	aller *'go'*	avoir donné
	donne	finis	suis	ai	vais	ai donné
	donnes	finis	es	as	vas	as donné
	donne	finit	est	a	va	a donné
	donnons	finissons	sommes	avons	allons	avons donné
	donnez	finissez	êtes	avez	allez	avez donné
	donnent	finissent	sont	ont	vont	ont donné

(b) *Imperfect of all verbs*	(c) *Present subjunctive of all verbs*
donnais (étais, avais, allais)	finisse (sois, aie, aille)
donnais (étais, avais, allais)	finisses (sois, aies, ailles)
donnait (était, avait, allait)	finisse (soit, ait, aille)
donnions (étions, avions, allions)	finissions (soyons, ayons, allions)
donniez (étiez, aviez, alliez)	finissiez (soyez, ayez, alliez)
donnaient (étaient, avaient, allaient)	finissent (soient, aient, aillent)

(d) *Future of all verbs*	(e) *Conditional of all verbs*
finirai (serai, aurai, irai)	finirais (serais, aurais, irais)
finiras (seras, auras, iras)	finirais (serais, aurais, irais)
finira (sera, aura, ira)	finirait (serait, aurait, irait)
finirons (serons, aurons, irons)	finirions (serions, aurions, irions)
finirez (serez, aurez, irez)	finiriez (seriez, auriez, iriez)
finiront (seront, auront, iront)	finiraient (seraient, auraient, iraient)

(f) *Present participle of all verbs*	(g) *Past participle of all verbs*
donnant, finissant, étant, ayant, allant	donné, fini, été, eu, allé

Note: simple past and imperfect subjunctive not included.

Tense, aspect and mood distinctions are given, in some cases, by differences in the verb stem and, in all cases, by characteristic suffixes, which also indicate person and number. Traditionally, there are typically assumed to be three conjugation types: *-er* (*parler* 'speak', *donner* 'give'), *-ir* (*finir* 'finish', *venir* 'come', *ouvrir* 'open'), and *-r/-re* (*voir* 'see', *rompre* 'break'), this latter type having only a few verbs. By far the majority of verbs are in the *-er* (first) conjugation, and almost all new verbs belong to this class, although the *-ir* class will admit new members if there is a strong analogical reason to do so (e.g. *alunir* 'to land on the moon': cf. *atterrir* 'to land', i.e. on earth). Most *-ir* verbs (the regular ones) have two stems, a simple stem, e.g. *fini-*, and a stem with /s/ (written *-iss*), e.g. *finiss-*, as in *(nous) fin-iss-ons* '(we) finish', infinitive *finir*. Furthermore, there are some very frequent 'irregular' verbs: *être* and *aller* are the most anomalous, followed by *avoir* and *faire* 'to make, to do'.

Putting aside the simple past and imperfect subjunctive, which are only found in highly formal written language (with the imperfect subjunctive being very infrequent) and are very idiosyncratic in formation, the suffixes for tense, aspect, mood, person and number can be summarised in the following way (we will give the *-er* suffixes first in each case). In the singular and third plural, the present indicative and present sub-junctive typically have no separate suffix for tense or mood and the person/number suffixes are -e or -s for first sg., -es for second sg., -e or -t in the indicative and -e in the subjunctive for third sg., and -ent for third pl. In the imperfect, the suffix -ai- indicating tense/aspect is followed immediately by -s for first and second sg., -t for third sg., -ent for third pl. The future tense consists of the 'r-form' of the verb, often the same as or based on the infinitive, plus special endings, making it the most distinct form: first sg.: -ai; second sg.: -as; third sg.: -a; third pl.: -ont (these endings are actually the form of the present tense of *avoir*, from which the form of the future is historically derived). The conditional is a combination of the 'r-form' of the verb and the imperfect -ai plus its person/number endings. For all tenses, in the first and second plural, the suffixes are much simpler: first pl.: -ons and second pl.: -ez for present and future, and first pl.: -ions and second pl.: -iez for subjunctive, imperfect and conditional. It should also be added that the present subjunctive forms of the commonest irregular verbs are very distinctive (third sg.: *soit, ait, fasse, vienne, aille, puisse, sache*: 'be', 'have', 'do', 'come', 'go', 'be able', 'know').

A heavily simplified tabulation of an -er verb and a two-stem -ir verb is given in Table 9.3, in addition to the irregular auxiliary verbs *être, avoir, aller* (in parentheses except for the present tense) as well as the *passé composé* of the -er verbs. The forms are in the order: first, second, third sg., first, second, third pl.

The compound verbal forms are complex in their meaning, since, for example, the *passé composé* is both a present perfect and a past tense. They are both a 'perfect', a combination of a prior event with a current relevance, 'prior' and 'current' being defined by the tense of the auxiliary, and a 'perfective' of the corresponding simple tense/aspect/mood. Thus, *passé composé il a donné* could be translated into English as present perfect 'he has given' – where the 'giving' was in the past but has present relevance, or as a perfective past 'he gave' – where the 'giving' was accomplished in the past. In formal written narrative, the simple past (*il donna*, 'he gave') is typically used with past perfective meaning to carry the story line, leaving the *passé composé* for use in dialogue in both of its meanings, since the simple past is not a spoken form. In addition to the special status of the simple past (and imperfect subjunctive), it should be noted that in general, the French subjunctive, unlike the subjunctive in some of the other Romance languages, is typically only found in specifiable subordinate contexts, having been eliminated from main clauses in all but a handful of idioms (e.g. *advienne* (subj.) *que pourra* 'come what may') and the so-called 'jussive' structure (e.g. *qu'il le fasse* (subj.) lit. 'that he may do it' i.e. 'have him do it'). The use of the subjunctive in dependent clauses is determined by the semantics of the main verb (e.g. verbs of 'emotion', 'volition', 'wishing', 'doubt'), thus *je regrette qu'il le fasse* (subj.) 'I'm sorry he's doing so'; *souhaiter* 'wish', for example, requires the subjunctive but *espérer* 'hope' does not, since it suggests a more probable or certain outcome. A small number of minimal pairs however may still be found: e.g. *de sorte que* 'so that' with the indi-cative marks a result (*je l'ai aidé de sorte que le rapport a été* (indic.) *prêt à temps* 'I helped him so that the report was ready in time'), and with the subjunctive a purpose (*aide-le de sorte que le rapport soit* (subj.) *prêt à temps* 'help him so that the report is done in time'); in *dites à Catherine qu'elle vienne immédiatement* 'tell Catherine that she should come immediately' the subjunctive is used to mean a desired event, whereas in *dites à Catherine qu'elle [Marie] vient immédiatement* 'tell Catherine that she [Marie] is coming immediately', the indicative conveys a real event. The conditional, imperfect and future also have important modal uses. The conditional for example can be used: in main clauses (*le roi serait mort*, lit. 'the king would be dead' i.e. 'the king is reputedly dead' – a favourite of journalistic language, so much so that it is sometimes called the journalistic conditional); in apodoses in combination with the imperfect in the protasis with *si* 'if' (*il le ferait si Jacques était avec nous* 'he would do it if Jacques were with us'); and in many subordinate clauses where the subjunctive is required by the rules of prescriptive grammar – hence this is more characteristic of the spoken language (*je cherche une maison qui aurait un jardin* 'I'm looking for a house that would have a garden', the precise identity or location of such a house being at present unknown).

5.2 Pronouns: Written Language

There are two series of pronouns: clitic (conjunctive, dependent) and independent (disjunctive) (Table 9.4). The clitics are typically used only with the verb, cannot occur alone, and cannot be stressed. They are classified into three persons and two numbers, and according to their grammatical function with respect to the verb: subject vs object (direct/indirect) in the first and second person; in the third person, they are split into direct object (DObj) and indirect object (IObj), as well as into masculine and feminine, and reflexive. In addition, there are the adverbial pronouns *y* 'to/about it/them, (to) there' (generally a replacement for complements with *à*) and *en* 'of/from it, them' (generally a replacement for complements with *de*, including its partitive use). The independent pronouns can occur alone, after prepositions, under stress, conjoined with other words, with a relative clause, etc. The two series of pronouns have very different forms for the first, second, third sg. and third pl. while the forms for the first and second pl. are the same. In addition, there are strict rules for ordering of the clitics before the verb: first subject, then object; if more than one object, then in this order: first, second, Refl > third DObj > third IObj > *y* > *en*. *Il se l'est dit* 'he to himself it said = he said it to himself', *il m'en a parlé* 'he me of it spoke = he spoke with me about it', *je la lui donnerai* 'I it (f.) to him will give = I'll give it (f.) to him'. Special rules apply in relation to pronouns co-occurring with imperatives.

Table 9.4 Clitic and Independent Personal Pronouns for Written French

	Clitic				Independent
	Su	*DObj*	*IObj*	*Other*	
1sg	je, j'	me, m'	me, m'		moi
2sg	tu	te, t'	te, t'		toi
3sg					
m.	il	le, l'	lui		lui
f.	elle	la, l'	lui		elle
indef.	on				soi
				y, en	
1pl	nous	nous	nous		nous
2pl	vous	vous	vous		vous
3pl m.	ils	les	leur		eux
f.	elles	les	leur		elles
3sg/pl reflexive		se, s'	se, s'		soi, lui, eux, elle(s)

Note: Alternate forms, like *je, j'* indicate full and elided forms, the latter occurring before a vowel.

5.3 The Verb Phrase and Pronouns: Spoken Language

The everyday spoken language manifests variants affecting the constituents of the verb phrase; some of these have existed for centuries, others are more recent, and still others represent change in progress, making the situation complex. The form *on* has been wholly assimilated into the personal pronoun system as a subject, and its most important use is in the meaning 'we', such that *nous* has virtually ceased to exist in this function (*on part en voyage* 'we're off on a trip'). Since *on* is singular and used with a third person verb, this means that there is a simplification of the verbal paradigm: for *-er* verbs, for example, there is one form for first, second, third sg. (including *on*), and third pl.; only the second pl. is different (and hortative use of the first pl. – *allons-y* 'let's go'). Note that *on* has neither an oblique nor a disjunctive form; within the immediate verb phrase, the third person reflexive form *se* is used (*on se lève de bonne heure* 'we get up early'); elsewhere, the semantically appropriate form appears, thus *nous, on va sortir avec nos amis* 'we're going out with our friends' (lit. 'us, we are going to go out with our friends' – note also the first person plural possessive form *nos* 'our', to the exclusion of the third person singular form *ses* 'one's'). While in the written language, only *on* is used as an indefinite, in the spoken language, both *tu* and *vous* as well as *ils* can take on indefinite meaning, in some contexts.

The relationship between *tu (toi)* and *vous* is not a straightforward singular vs plural one. For much of the twentieth century, it was normal to use *vous* in the case of singular addressees to mark 'respect' or 'distance', *tu (toi)* being limited to intimate contexts (e.g. within a family, between friends) or, more rarely, to mark a superior–inferior relationship (e.g. master using *tu* to servant who uses *vous*). *Vous* used as a 'respectful' singular shows singular concord outside the immediate verb phrase: *vous êtes content, monsieur?* (not *contents*) 'are you satisfied, sir?' However, just as for many other European languages, the intimate forms are tending to gain ground in all but the most formal situations and are losing their strong meaning of 'intimacy', especially for younger speakers.

In addition to these changes, there is an ongoing tendency for the clitic subject forms to become prefixes to the verb (and thus morphemes) in ordinary spoken French. In the first and second person, they are obligatorily present (*Je suis là* 'I'm here') and never occur without the verb (*– Qui est là? – *Je* 'Who's there? – *I'). In the third person, singular and plural, they are also obligatory (*il pleure* 'he's crying') unless the subject is a noun. In that case they are normally present (*mon père il dit que ...* lit. 'my father he says that ...'), but *mon père dit que* 'my father says that ...', is also possible as in the written standard. In addition all of the clitic forms can be shortened through elision even before some consonants, in which case there is also assimilation: e.g. *je* 'I' /ʒə/ reduced to /ʒ/ before vowels and some consonants, as in *j'donne* 'I give' /ʒdɔn/ (/ʃ/ before unvoiced consonants: *j'finis* /ʃfini/ 'I'm finishing'). Impersonal *il* disappears completely in common impersonal expressions such as *(il) faut que* 'it's necessary that' or in the presentative construction *il y a* 'there is/are', which is reduced to /ja/ (although in other cases *il* is kept, as in *il pleut* 'it's raining'). Final consonants tend to occur only in *enchaînement*/liaison contexts: e.g. the /l/ of *il*, and often *elle* (*il veut* /ivø/ 'he wants' vs *il a* /ila/ 'he has' and the /z/ of *ils* and *elles* (*elles veulent* /ɛvœl/ 'they (f.) want' vs *elles ont* /ɛlzɔ̃/ 'they (f.) have'). There is a parallel tendency to reduce the number of preverbal elements. While the subject is almost obligatory, usually there is no more than one of the DObj/IObj/*en*/*y* forms before the verb, so that at most two prefixes are

185

found: *Je (le) lui ai donné* 'I gave (it) to him', which can be further reduced to *j'ui ai donné* or *j'y ai donné*.

A trend to limit the number of grammatical distinctions is to be noted. *En* and *y*, which in the written language are not normally used for humans, can be so used more easily in the spoken language: *je m'en souviens* (i.e. 'I remember it', lit. 'I remind myself of it'; also 'I remember him/her/them'; for *y* see the example above). The independent pronouns *lui* and *elle* (and to a certain extent the clitic subject pronouns *il* and *elle*) are increasingly restricted to animates, in particular to humans, with *ça* and *ce* used for inanimates. Thus *il est beau, lui* 'he's good-looking, him' is naturally interpreted as referring to a man, the corresponding description of an inanimate referent being *c'est beau, ça* 'that's lovely, that'. *Ça* can also be used with a human referent with a generic sense: *ça fait beaucoup de bruit, les enfants* 'children make lots of noise' (lit. 'that makes lots of noise, children').

Another feature of the spoken language is the loss of the preverbal negative marker *ne*. In the written language, negation is composed of two elements: (1) *ne/n'*, which comes after the subject and before either the object clitics or the verb, and (2) another word that follows the verb. The most neutral word is *pas* 'not', others being *plus* 'no longer', *rien* 'nothing', *point* (emphasis), *jamais* 'never', etc.: thus *il ne vient pas* lit. 'he not comes not', i.e. 'he isn't coming', or *il ne l'a jamais fait* 'he not it has never done', i.e. 'he has never done it'. However, in the colloquial language, there is much evidence that the second element of the negation is carrying the negative meaning. So, formal *il ne m'a pas parlé* 'he didn't speak to me' and *je ne sais pas* 'I don't know' tend to become /imapapaʁle/ and /ʃepa/ under the right conditions (e.g. ordinary conversation). There is however much variation in the use of *ne* in colloquial French and certain phonetic, morphosyntactic, social, stylistic, and normative factors have kept *ne* from being eliminated altogether.

Further evidence of the evolution of the verb phrase is given by changes in interrogative constructions. In the written language, questions can be formed by inversion of the clitic pronoun (*vient-il?* 'is he coming?'), especially when there is an interrogative word present before the verb, as in *où vas-tu?* lit. 'where go you?' 'where are you going?'. In addition, there is the *est-ce que* construction, originally a phrase meaning 'is it (a fact) that?' but now better analysed as /ɛsk(ə)/, a question-forming particle (*est-ce que le président vient?* 'is the president coming?', lit. '*question-particle* the president is coming?'). In the spoken language *est-ce que* is very common, including with interrogative words (*où est-ce que tu vas?*, or shortened to *où que tu vas?* in popular speech, 'where are you going?'); more simply, even, the normal SVO word order is maintained and intonation alone makes the sentence interrogative (*Paul est là* 'Paul is there' vs *Paul est là?* 'Paul is there?'). Question words can be added either at the beginning of the question (*où tu vas?* 'where (are) you going?') or in the position where they would stand in an SVO structure (*tu vas où?* 'you're going where?').

The result of all these changes is that the sequence subject clitic + object clitic + verb stem has become a fused unit within which other elements cannot intervene, and no other combination is possible. Put at its simplest, we may regard, for example, *tu l'aimes?* /tylɛm/ with rising intonation 'you love him/her?' as one polymorphemic word (subject-prefix + object-prefix + stem). Furthermore, the compound tenses are widely used and the *aller*-future is preferred over the simple future in many contexts, thus separating out tense–aspect–mood as well as person–number and putting those elements before the verb form, the participle or the infinitive, respectively, which then conveys only lexical meaning. Moreover, there are very few elements that can occur between the auxiliary (*avoir*, *être* or *aller*) and the participle or infinitive.

Hence French in its spoken form seems to be undergoing a typological change from suffixal to prefixal inflection. It is incorporating more grammatical elements in the prefixes, becoming more like some American Indian languages, as pointed out by a French grammarian/linguist many years ago in an article provocatively entitled 'Do You Speak Chinook?', Chinook being an example of a language of this type, i.e. 'polysynthetic'.

In light of these findings, the paradigm for the verb should include the clitics/prefixes at least for the first and second person and as possibilities for the third person. On the other hand, the suffixal paradigm is simpler than for the written language, since the first pl. form is infrequent, and since many of the distinctions made in the written language do not exist. Five of the six possible forms are homophonous (except in the future tense), only -*ez* (/e/) is regularly maintained as a suffix, and there are many homophonous forms across tense/aspect/mood. What is kept is the difference in person – through prefixes, not suffixes. Hence, for -*er* verbs, the forms are as in Table 9.5, with only subject prefixes noted.

The compound tenses, and especially the *passé composé*, deserve special mention with respect to oral speech. As said earlier, the simple past is only used in the written language and one of its major functions is to advance the story line in narratives. In the spoken language, the *passé composé* fulfils this function (although the present tense may also do so). In addition, in the spoken language, there exist *temps surcomposés*, 'double compound' tenses, the one formed on the present tense of the auxiliary being the most frequent: e.g. *il a eu fait* (lit. 'he has had done'). These forms are used by some (but by no means all) native speakers as an optional marker of perfectivity (*quand il a eu payé* ... lit. 'when he has had paid', the sense being 'as soon as he had finished paying').

Table 9.5 Verbal Paradigms for Spoken French: *donner* 'give' with subject prefixes

Simple forms		Prefixed forms	
		3- 1st sg, ɔ̃- 1st pl, ty- 2nd sg, vu- 2nd pl, i- 3rd sg/pl m., ɛ- 3rd sg/pl f.	
Form	*Pers/Numb/Tns/Aspc/Mood*	*Forms*	*Tns/Aspc/Mood*
/dɔn/	2nd sg imperative		
	3rd sg/pl pres ind/subj with N subject	/ʒ-dɔn/, /ɔ̃-dɔn/, /ty-dɔn/, /i-dɔn/, /ɛ-dɔn/	pres ind/subj
/dɔne/	2nd pl imperative	/vu-dɔne/	pres ind
/dɔnɛ/	3rd sg/pl imperfect with N subject	/ʒ-dɔnɛ/, /ɔ̃-dɔnɛ/, /ty-dɔnɛ/, /i-dɔnɛ/, /ɛ-dɔnɛ/	imperfect
(/dɔnje/)		/vu-dɔnje/	imperfect, pres subj
/dɔnʁɛ/	3rd sg/pl conditional with N subject	/ʒ-dɔnʁɛ/, /ɔ̃-dɔnʁɛ/, /ty-dɔnʁɛ/, /i-dɔnʁɛ/, /ɛ-dɔnʁɛ/	conditional
(/dɔnəʁje/)		/vu-dɔnəʁje/	conditional
(/dɔnʁe/)		/ʒ-dɔnʁe/, /vu-dɔnʁe/	future
/dɔnʁa/	3rd sg future with N subject	/ɔ̃-dɔnʁa/, /ty-dɔnʁa/, /i-dɔnʁa/, /ɛ-dɔnʁa/	future
(/dɔnʁɔ̃/)		/i-dɔnʁɔ̃/, /ɛ-dɔnʁɔ̃/	future

Note: Forms in parentheses only exist with a prefix.

5.4 The Noun Phrase

The noun phrase (nominal group, in French terminology) has a canonical minimal form, which includes a determiner and a noun, in that order (*un homme* 'a man'). The extended noun phrase is an expansion of the minimal nominal group with the addition of optional elements, most of which come after the noun, the main exception being a restricted list of pre-nominal adjectives and adjectival phrases that can come between the determiner and the noun (adjectives that can occur both pre- and post-nominally sometimes show a meaning difference in the two positions: *son ancienne école* 'his old/former school' vs *une école ancienne* 'an *ancient/very old* school'). Post-nominal elements include adjectives and adjectival phrases (*un homme sûr de lui* 'a man sure of himself'), prepositional phrases (*un homme de talent* 'a man of talent'), relative clauses modifying the noun (*un homme qui travaille dur* 'a man who works hard'), subordinate clauses or their infinitival equivalents modifying the noun (*la pensée qu'il ne viendra pas la terrifie* 'the thought that he won't come terrifies her'), etc.

With respect to morphology, the most relevant components are the noun, adjective, and determiner, since they evidence the grammatical categories of gender (masculine vs feminine) and number (singular vs plural); however, it is the determiners that are the most consistent indicators of gender and number. Gender is inherent to all nouns, whether animate or inanimate. In nouns referring to human beings and domesticated animals, there is often coincidence between gender and biological sex. This may lead to two different nouns (e.g. *homme* m. 'man', *femme* f. 'woman'; *chien* m. '(male) dog', *chienne* f. '(female) dog') or to one noun with two different genders, which the determiner differentiates (*un Belge* m. 'a (male) Belgian', *une Belge* f. 'a (female) Belgian'; *un enfant* m. 'a (male) child', *une enfant* f. 'a (female) child'). As mentioned earlier, nouns for professional office titles that in the past were only or typically held by men are usually masculine (e.g. *un professeur* 'a teacher') and attempts to create feminine forms of these nouns have been controversial. Most of the time, gender is not shown overtly on the noun, unless the noun includes a derivational suffix that has only one gender (e.g. *-isme* m., as in *pessimisme* 'pessimism', *-tion* f., as in *addition* 'addition'). Many adjectives have the same form for masculine and feminine (e.g. *calme* 'calm', *rapide* 'fast'), although some show gender in the written language through the addition of orthographic *-e* (*joli* vs *jolie* 'pretty'; the same is true for some nouns: *ami* '(male) friend', *amie* '(female) friend'). In the spoken language, this *-e* is not pronounced. Some adjectives have different forms for masculine and feminine: *petit* m., *petite* f. /pti/, /ptit/ 'little', *ancien* m. /ɑ̃sjɛ̃/, *ancienne* f. /ɑ̃sjɛn/ 'former') but, in the spoken language the difference is often not maintained in liaison contexts (cf. *ancien ami/ancienne amie)* 'former male/female friend' /ɑ̃sjɛnami/, *petit(e) ami(e)* 'boy/girl friend' /ptitami/).

In addition to inherent gender, nouns usually carry number. The plural is almost always marked in the written language through the use of suffixal *-s* (of which *-x* is an orthographic variant). However, in the spoken language, this *-s* is not pronounced except in liaison contexts, where it is realised as /z/. Pre-nominal adjectives in liaison contexts indicate plurality, as in *petits éléments* /ptizelemɑ̃/ 'small elements'. Different forms for singular and plural in nouns and adjectives, such as *cheval:chevaux* 'horse:horses' (/ʃəval/:/ʃəvo/) or *banal:banaux* 'banal' (/banal/:/bano/) are very much the exception.

Determiners – which in the articles include a definite vs indefinite vs partitive distinction, based on semantic, pragmatic and discourse criteria – are almost all grouped in sets of three that distinguish a masculine from a feminine in the singular (except in elision and liaison contexts in some cases) and a plural that does not differentiate gender, thus: definite article *le, la, l'* (elision contexts), *les*, e.g. *le pain* 'the bread', *la vie* 'the life', *l'an* (m.) and *l'année* (f.) 'the year'; indefinite article *un, une, des*, e.g. *un verre* 'a glass'; partitive article *du, de la, de l'* (elision contexts), *des*, e.g. *du pain* 'some bread'; demonstrative *ce, cet* (before a vowel), *cette, ces*, e.g. *ces verres* 'these glasses'; possessive, with a different stem depending on the person of the possessor, so *mon, ma* (*mon* in liaison contexts), *mes*, for the first person, etc.: e.g. *ma vie*, 'my life', but *ta vie* 'your life', *sa vie*, 'his/her/its life'. There are a few cases which go against the general rule that the determiner is obligatory and is grouped in sets of three: nouns can occur without a determiner, for example, in fixed phrases, e.g. *avoir faim* 'to have hunger' i.e. 'to be hungry', often after the preposition *en*, or in partitive constructions e.g. *assez de lait* 'enough (of) milk'); and some determiners do not mark gender or plural (*chaque* 'each' and most numerals). Determiners have a range of meanings: the definite article, for example, can be used in a generic sense as well as express definiteness – thus, *j'aime le fromage* can mean either 'I like cheese' or 'I like the (just mentioned) cheese'. Since demonstratives *ce ... -ci* (as in *ce fromage-ci*) and *ce ... -là* (as in *ce fromage-là*) can be utilised to mean 'this ... here' and 'that ... there' respectively, *ce fromage* (with a simple demonstrative) is often best understood as meaning 'the (particular) cheese' rather than 'this' or 'that cheese'.

It is interesting to observe the striking parallelism between the verb phrase and the noun phrase in contemporary French, with respect to the spoken language on the one hand and the written language, and other Romance languages, on the other hand. In the spoken language, in verb phrases, as we saw above, almost all relevant grammatical information is carried by prefixes and by auxiliary verbs, which precede the verbal stem (and not by suffixes, as in the written language). In noun phrases, almost all relevant grammatical information is conveyed by determiners, which precede the nominal stem (and not by suffixes) and it could be argued that these determiners are also prefix-like since they cannot occur by themselves, and tend to be obligatory. The evolution and present-day structures of noun phrases and verb phrases are quite similar, which again shows that there might be a general typological change ongoing in French, at least in the spoken grammar of the language.

6 Syntax and Pragmatics

Sentences can be analysed on the syntactic level into their categorical components: NP subject and VP, i.e. the verb with its complements. On the semantic level, sentences can be analysed in terms of their verbs and the roles of their arguments (agent, patient, beneficiary, location, etc.). They can also be analysed on the pragmatic level. This level is concerned with the type of information being transmitted: something (variously called comment, focus or rheme) is said about someone or something (termed topic, theme or presupposed). Normally the canonical linear order (SVO) reflects the information order (i.e. the topic followed by the comment). Therefore in the sentence *Le président n'a pas répondu au journaliste* ('The president did not answer (to) the journalist'), the NP subject *le président* is the topic, while the rest of the sentence is the comment. Note too that prototypically the topic is represented by a highly determined NP, often animate, with agentive features. But the canonical word order can be disturbed for pragmatic reasons. In *Au journaliste, le président n'a pas répondu – au journaliste* ('to the journalist') is the theme. Because the French language cannot topicalise sentential elements by phonological means (stress may not be used to highlight a sentential element) or by morphosyntactic means (it does not have a case system), it relies on purely structural devices to transmit pragmatic information. Traditionally, a number of these non-canonical constructions were referred to as *syntaxe expressive* ('expressive syntax'). Recently they have ceased to be treated as stylistic variants and are now studied as part of the core syntax of the language.

6.1 Topicalising Structures

French has a number of topicalising structures, i.e. constructions that bring into initial sentence position verb arguments that are not necessarily prototypical (i.e. not necessarily subject, agentive, animate, definite). Some of them are frequent in every speaker's ordinary, unplanned speech, but still not considered as part of the norm. The major topicalising constructions are the following:

(a) focus fronting (placement of non-subject complements to the front of the sentence): *Les montagnes, j'aime* ('Mountains, I like').

(b) segmentation by clefting: in cleft sentences such as *C'est la philosophie qu'il étudie* ('It's philosophy that he studies'), the focus (*la philosophie*) is extracted from the sentence and highlighted by means of *c'est + qui/que/dont*, etc. (relative pronoun forms), while the rest of the sentence constitutes the theme. Subjects can be focalised by clefting when they represent important/new information: *C'est Pasteur qui a mis au point ce vaccin* ('It's Pasteur who perfected this vaccine'). Pseudo-cleft sentences *Ce qu'il étudie, c'est la philosophie* ('What he studies is philosophy') have the reverse effect and relegate new information to the end of the sentence.

(c) 'presentative' segmentation: in ordinary speech, indefinite subjects are rarely found directly at the start of sentences. To *Quelqu'un a téléphoné* ('Someone called') or *Des gens ont tout perdu* ('Some people lost everything') speakers prefer *Il y a quelqu'un qui a téléphoné*; *Il y a des gens qui ont tout perdu*, where the indefinite subjects are framed with *il y a ... qui* ('there is ... who/which'; as said above, *il y a* is often pronounced /ja/).

(d) left dislocation: one or several NPs (including the subject) can be moved to the left periphery of the sentence and repeated by clitic pronouns/prefixes within the core of the sentence (this resumption is called *double marquage*): *Pierre, cette fille, il n'arrête pas de lui téléphoner* ('Peter, this girl, he doesn't stop calling her'). Right dislocations are also possible, the dislocated NP being sometimes referred to as 'antitopic': *Alors tu l'achètes, cette maison?* ('So you're buying it, this house?') The dislocated NP *cette maison* takes up a constituent already salient in earlier discourse.

(e) passive constructions can also be considered as topicalising: they promote to the front of the sentence an argument (the object/patient) which is not a prototypical theme, and by so doing they demote or even cancel the subject/agent of the active sentence. For example the active sentence *Le sénat a voté la loi hier* ('The senate passed the law yesterday') is paralleled by the passive sentence *La loi a été votée (par le sénat) hier* ('The law was passed (by the senate) yesterday') where the agent (*le sénat*) has been demoted in importance or relevance. Passive sentences are not frequent in French, especially in the spoken language. Active structures with impersonal subject pronoun *on* ('one, they') are preferred when the agent is unknown or when its mention or non-mention is of little consequence: *On a voté la loi hier* ('They passed the law yesterday'). In French, as in other Romance languages, the promotion of the theme can also be realised via passive-like (middle) pronominal constructions, for example: *Les appartements ne se vendent pas bien en ce moment* ('Apartments don't sell well presently'). The subject of such structures can never have agentive properties. If it is human/animate, it represents the 'beneficiary/victim' of the process, not the agent. In this case, the verb is in the causative form with *faire*: *Pierre s'est fait voler sa voiture* ('Peter had his car stolen').

6.2 Focalising Procedures

As was said above, normally, the subject in French is placed before the verb (SV) and assumes the function of theme, i.e. represents old, already established information. If, however, the speaker wishes to bring to attention that this constituent provides new or important information, it can be moved after the verb (VS), in focus/rheme position. There are two main focalising procedures (*constructions focalisantes*) in the language:

(a) simple inversion (VS): *Vint la nuit* ('Came the night', i.e. 'Night came'). This construction, which belongs to the literary language, occurs normally when a prepositional or adverbial phrase comes before the verb, but the verb must be intransitive or transitive with no expressed object: *Dans le champ poussaient des oliviers centenaires* ('In the field were growing hundred-year-old olive trees').

(b) impersonal constructions (*Il* VS): The impersonal sentence *Il arrive toujours à mon frère des aventures incroyables* corresponds to *Des aventures incroyables arrivent toujours à mon frère* ('Incredible adventures always happen to my brother'). In an impersonal construction, the subject comes after the verb, but its slot is filled by impersonal pronoun/prefix *il*, with which the verb agrees. The impersonal construction is always more natural with infinitival or sentential subjects. For instance, *Il est important d'être à l'heure* ('It is important to arrive early') is more acceptable than *Être à l'heure est important* ('To be on time is important'). In some cases it is the only grammatically acceptable option: *Il arrive que la porte soit fermée à clé* ('It happens that the door is locked'), to be compared to **Que la porte soit fermée à clé arrive*. A number of constraints regulate the use of impersonal constructions, in particular, the verb must be intransitive and the subject indefinite or quantified: *Il est resté trois gâteaux* ('Three cakes were left'). In addition verbs taking the auxiliary *être* lead to more felicitous sentences.

7 Lexicon

The core vocabulary of French derives in very large measure from the Latin spoken in Gaul, the lexical items in question having in general undergone the phonological changes that so often distinguish a French word sharply from its cognates elsewhere in

Romance. This Latin stock incorporated, before the linguistic fragmentation of the Romance-speaking area, a number of words from other sources, the subsequent development of which has been indistinguishable from that of their indigenous counterparts. Towards the end of the Roman Empire, Greek (e.g. *COLAPHUM* > *coup* 'blow', *CHORDAM* > *corde* 'rope', *PETRAM* > *pierre* 'stone') was particularly important as the source of much specifically Christian vocabulary, some of which later greatly expanded its meaning (*ECCLESIAM* > *église* 'church', *PRESBYTER* > *prêtre* 'priest', but *PARABOLAM* 'parable', now > *parole* 'word'). Equally, among the earliest people whose territory was overrun by the Romans were the Celts, and some Celtic words were borrowed and assimilated into Latin very early: these included, for instance, *CAMISIAM* > *chemise* 'shirt', *CABALLUM* > *cheval* 'horse', and *CAMBIARE* > *changer* 'to change'. The Celtic word *CARRUM* 'cart' underlies not only standard French *char* and (with a diminutive suffix) *charrette* 'cart', but also Norman French *carre*, whence English *car*, a word which has prospered not only in English but once again in French in the sense of '(motor) coach'. More specifically French, however, are around 200 words, which passed into the language from the local form of Celtic, Gaulish, many of them representing the names of plants, birds or other rural objects: e.g. *chêne* 'oak tree', *if* 'yew-tree', *alouette* 'lark', *raie* 'furrow', *soc* 'ploughshare'. The word *grève*, in the sense of 'sandy river bank', is Celtic in origin: on one such bank of the Seine, unemployed workmen gathered, *en grève* thus coming to mean 'out of work' and later 'on strike'. A Celtic vigesimal counting system survives in *quatre-vingts* 'four score' i.e. 'eighty' (*huitante* and similar forms are found in some regional varieties of French: cf. *huit* 'eight').

The Roman occupation of Gaul was ended by the Germanic invasions. Although the conquerors eventually came to be French-speaking, they made a very significant impression on the language. Many words in contemporary French can be traced back either to Frankish or to less specific Germanic sources: of the 1,000 most frequently used words in contemporary French, 35 are from this source, some found also in other Romance languages (e.g. *guerre* 'war', *franc* 'free', *riche* 'rich', *blanc* 'white', *jardin* 'garden'), others only in French (e.g. *bleu* 'blue', *joue* 'cheek'). The fact that many of these words have a direct cognate in English, itself of course a Germanic language, is readily apparent.

The greatest influence on the French lexicon, however, is from Latin (with a not insignificant admixture from Greek). This is because, from the time of the very earliest texts and even more so during and after the Renaissance, the core vocabulary inherited directly via the spoken tradition proved inadequate for the new demands made of it. This process of enrichment has yielded a very large number of 'learned' words in modern French, many of them now 'learned' only in the technical sense that they have not undergone the phonological changes that would have affected truly 'popular' words, thus *nature*, *facile* 'easy', *imaginer.* Indeed, there are many doublets in modern French, that is, a 'popular' and a 'learned' derivative of the same word: for example, *loyal/légal* (< *LEGALEM*); *peser* 'weigh', *penser* 'weigh up mentally', i.e. 'think' (< *PENSARE*); *frêle/fragile* 'breakable'. This last pair, both derived from *FRAGILEM*, shows particularly clearly how much closer phonologically the 'learned' word often is to its etymon.

By far the most significant present-day source of loanwords is English, reflecting at times a genuine cultural or technical innovation, but at times simply a change of fashion. During the eighteenth century, many political and legal terms (*budget*, *vote*, *jury, parlement*) were borrowed, reflecting admiration in France for the form of government in Britain at that time. (Note that many of these had themselves earlier been borrowed into English from (Norman) French, including all of those listed above.) During the nineteenth century, various kinds of sport were emulated, giving words such as *sport, golf, jockey, turf* ('racecourse', 'horseracing'), *boxe* 'boxing', etc., whereas words reflecting England's lead in the Industrial Revolution were also borrowed, particularly in the domain of the railway and textile industries. (Again, many words such as *ticket* and *tunnel* themselves had earlier passed from French to English.) The twentieth century has seen many borrowings which meet a need in this way, but also many which merely reflect either the belief on the part of advertisers and others that an English name or slogan will enhance the product, or simply the willingness of those such as journalists constantly engaged with material in both English and French to use an English word that is readily to hand. (*Pipeline* is a much-quoted example, with the indigenous *oléoduc* now strongly favoured in its place.) Many of the borrowings take the form of closed monosyllables (*cross* 'cross-country race', *test, pull* 'pullover', *spot* 'spot-light', *star*, etc.), or of polysyllables ending in *-ing* (*parking* 'car park', *dumping*) or *-man* (*rugbyman*). As mentioned above, efforts have been made at official level to control the number of borrowings from English, at least in the written language.

The lexicon is the component of language that gets renewed the most rapidly. It is estimated that presently around 25,000 new words come into French every year. Furthermore, usage evolves constantly, words become obsolete while others extend their meanings, and synonyms appear. Lexical variation determined by social and register/style factors is therefore complex. Contemporary dictionaries attempt to capture it by labelling lexical items and their alternatives according to usage range. In *Le Nouveau Petit Robert*, for instance, the following are used: LITTÉR (mainly used in the written elegant language), FAM (used in familiar discourse), POP (belonging to the speech of popular social classes), VULG (shocking, unusable in courteous discourse), VIEILLI (still understandable nowadays, but not used in the current spoken language), TECH (technical), ARG (limited to a group, essentially professional, and unknown to the larger population). For example a dwelling is either a *demeure* (VIEILLI or LITT), a *maison* (neutral) or a *baraque*/a *bicoque*/a *gourbi* (FAM and often pejorative). But dictionaries do not always agree on these usage tags, presumably because of the rapidity of some lexical changes, the difficulty in defining labels, the lexicographer's individual judgement, and the fact that French speakers have become less sensitive to linguistic taboos and do not hesitate to mix formal and informal vocabulary under the right conditions, thus making socio-situational linguistic boundaries hazier. One characteristic feature of twentieth-century and present-day current French is indeed that it is permeable to unconventional usage, even in written forms of the language (such as the press, cartoons, contemporary novels, in particular detective stories).

Lexical items restricted in terms of class, occupation or age group, are often collected in specialised dictionaries: for example, dictionaries of slang, architecture, multimedia, linguistics, didactics, etc. Recently, interest in 'emerging' forms of French has given rise to glossaries of *français branché* (this refers, since the 1970s, to words and expressions promoted by the media and fashionable among people well informed of current affairs) or to lexicons of adolescent language, especially as it is spoken in the *banlieues* (see Section 3 above). In what follows we will develop only two sociologically marked aspects of the French lexicon, as found in *argot* and contemporary youth speech.

Argot was formerly a secretive jargon/code used for several centuries by thieves and other criminals to exclude outsiders, in particular the police, from their communities and to reinforce group cohesion. It has now lost some of its cryptic nature and a number of its words have spread to colloquial French, e.g. *flic* 'policeman', *mouchard* 'police informer', *blase* 'name, nose', *faire gaffe* 'pay attention', *môme* 'child', *se planquer* 'to hide'. However, *argot* remains a way of challenging the establishment and going against its linguistic norms. This includes defacing words through unusual suffixation (e.g. *parigot*, for *parisien* 'Parisian', *pacsif*, *pacson*, for *paquet* 'package'), creating unexpected and often humorous periphrases which metaphorically or metonymically conceal meanings (*mettre la main au panier*, 'to put one's hand in the basket', i.e. 'to attempt to fondle a woman's buttocks') or being provocative: for instance, a number of words referring to sex, death, drinking, can be quite blunt. Besides 'classical' *argot* just described, there are other forms of *argot* (sometimes also called *jargons*) used by occupational groups, all aiming at consolidating group identity and intra-comprehension: *argots* of high-school students, soldiers, musicians, drug traffickers, etc.

In many respects, adolescent speech is argotic in nature, especially *la langue des jeunes*, understood as the variety in use in large cities' high-rise buildings typically on the outskirts of those cities (*langue des cités, des banlieues*). It is group-cohesive, marginalising and often playful and inventive. Youth language is characterised by morphological processes such as truncation of polysyllabic words (either by apocope *dégueu*, for *dégueulasse* 'disgusting' or by aphaeresis *zic*, for *musique*) and the use of certain suffixes, particularly the adjectival suffix *-os*, although it seems to be less fashionable nowadays: e.g. *nullos, chicos, débilos*, based respectively on *nul, chic* and *débile*, 'weak, bad'. To express positive judgement, the younger generation favours hyperbolic prefixes (*hypergentil*, 'very nice', *superclasse*, 'excellent') and over- and understatements: *géant* (lit. 'great', 'giant'). There are many ways of saying 'very good': *sublime, canon* (lit. 'cannon' or 'model'), *génial* (lit. 'of genius, brilliant') on the one hand, and *pas triste* (lit. 'not sad'), *pas sale* (lit. 'not dirty') on the other. Lexical borrowings from English (particularly in the areas of music, clothing and physical appearance, drugs: *hip hop, rap, look, shit, sniffer*, etc.), from migrant languages (African languages, Romani) and from classical *argot* (*thune* 'money', *daube* 'something worthless') are also typical of *la langue des jeunes. Verlan* (*vers l'en* from *l'envers*, 'the reverse'), an old coded process of lexical formation, has been revived in some large urban centres and is considered a distinctive feature of youth language. It consists in switching syllables of existing words, in ways dictated by word and syllable structure: for example *zicmu* from *musique, feubou* from *bouffe* 'food', *reum* from *mère* 'mother'. It should be noted that although the generational variety just described is not used uniformly by all adolescents, some of its features are widely shared and have even made their way into the speech of adults and into dictionaries: e.g. *pas évident* with the meaning of 'not easy'; *beur, chébran, ripou*, which are *verlan* forms for *arabe, branché* 'trendy', and *pourri* 'corrupt policeman'.

French, then, is a language evolving rapidly in all its aspects, particularly in its grammatical system, where the gap between the classical model which is prescribed and what even educated speakers actually do is quite wide at times, and its lexicon. The previous very radical waves of sound change appear to have given way, for the time being at least, to relative stability in phonology. As a world language, French is holding its own surprisingly well in the face of constant competition from English, although only time will tell how long this can be sustained.

Acknowledgement

This chapter includes some material from the chapter on French by Martin Harris in the first edition of *The World's Major Languages*.

Bibliography

Yaguello (2003) contains up-to-date chapters by major scholars on all of the themes mentioned below (except for *Francophonie*). Grevisse and Goosse (2007) is the latest edition of the well-known descriptive/prescriptive grammar of the modern language, often used to answer questions about 'correct usage'. Judge and Healey (1985) is a solid overview of French grammar, written for speakers of English, while Riegel et al. (2004) is a highly readable text, often used by French students, that is regularly updated on the basis of linguistic findings. There are several recent books on French linguistics. Ayres-Bennett and Carruthers (2001) concentrate on interesting or problematic areas pertaining to the phonology, morphology, syntax and lexicon of French. Battye et al. (2000) is a wide-ranging overview, including history, phonology, word formation and sentence patterns, and the stylistic and geographical varieties of French. Fagyal et al. (2006) is a comprehensive guide to the structure of French, including history, phonetics, phonology, morpho-syntax, pragmatics and lexicology. Hawkins and Towell (1996) is an overview of French grammar and its usage. Lodge et al. (1997), meant for students, addresses the varieties of French, the standard parts of French grammar, as well as discourse and everyday conversation. For phonology, Tranel (1994) discusses issues in phonological theory, clearly illustrated with French data. Designed for students, Jones (1996) is a detailed analysis of French grammar combining the insights of generative linguistic theory with those of more traditional grammarians. Rowlett (2007) is an overview of French syntax within current generative theory.

For the history of French, Lodge (1993) offers a very interesting sociolinguistic perspective on the rise of the *francien* dialect to standard French. Chaurand's (1999) treatment combines phonetic, grammatical and lexical history with sociological, political and cultural issues. Picoche and Marchello-Nizia (1994) give equal, and divided, treatment of external history and internal history. Gadet (2003) is an overview of French sociolinguistics within the variationist tradition, while Offord (1990) illustrates how the use of French varies according to a number of different factors (e.g. age, regular residence, subject matter) with special focus on the geographical diversity of French. Sanders (1993) is a profile of French in its social context and addresses a variety of issues: e.g. prescriptivism, gender and language, regional languages and dialects, marginalised language varieties, and the adaptation of French to new uses. In a text meant for students, Walter (1988/1994) discusses French dialects, and 'hexagonal' and global varieties of French.

Gadet (1996) is a study of everyday French, especially its phonology and syntax, taking into account issues of variation. Blanche-Benveniste (2000) examines the difference between spoken and written French and also different registers of spoken French; she then looks at prosody, syntax, 'macro-syntax' and texts.

Ager (1996) is an informative discussion of Francophonie for English-speaking readers. Organisation internationale de la Francophonie (2005) and Poissonnier and Sournia (2006) give up-to-date information about *Francophonie*. Finally, Adamson (2007) traces the long history of language defence in France and examines the multiplicity of official and non-official activities and attitudes, including changing government policy and the work of small private groups.

References

Adamson, R. 2007. *The Defence of French: A Language in Crisis?* (Multilingual Matters, Clevedon)
Ager, D. 1996. *'Francophonie' in the 1990s: Problems and Opportunities.* (Multilingual Matters, Clevedon)

Ayres-Bennett, W. and Carruthers, J. 2001. *Studies in the Modern French Language. Problems and Perspectives* (Longman, London)

Battye, A., Hintze, M.-A. and Rowlett, P. 2000. *The French Language Today: A Linguistic Introduction*, second edition (Routledge, London)

Blanche-Benveniste, C. 2000. *Approches de la langue parlée en français* (Ophrys, Paris)

Chaurand, J. (ed.) 1999. *Nouvelle Histoire de la langue française* (Seuil, Paris)

Fagyal, Z., Kibbee, D. and Jenkins, F. 2006. *French: A Linguistic Introduction* (Cambridge University Press, Cambridge)

Gadet, F. 1996. *Le Français ordinaire*, 2nd edn (Armand Colin, Paris)

—— 2003. *La Variation sociale en français* (Ophrys, Paris)

Grevisse, M. and Goosse, A. 2007. *Le bon usage: grammaire française*, 14th edn (Duculot, Paris)

Hawkins, R. and Towell, R. 1996. *French Grammar and Usage* (Edward Arnold, London)

Jones, M. 1996. *Foundations of French Syntax* (Cambridge University Press, Cambridge)

Judge, A. and Healey, F.G. 1985. *A Reference Grammar of Modern French* (Edward Arnold, London)

Lodge, R.A. 1993. *French: From Dialect to Standard* (Routledge, London)

Lodge, R.A., Armstrong, N., Ellis, Y. and Shelton, J. 1997. *Exploring the French Language* (Hodder Arnold, London).

Offord, M. 1990. *Varieties of Contemporary French* (Macmillan, London)

Organisation internationale de la Francophonie, Haut Conseil. 2005. *La Francophonie dans le monde 2004–2005* (Larousse, Paris)

Picoche, J. and Marchello-Nizia, C. 1994. *Histoire de la langue française* (Nathan, Paris)

Poissonnier, A. and Sournia, G. 2006. *Atlas mondial de la Francophonie* (Editions Autrement, Paris)

Riegel, M., Pellat, J.-C. and Rioul, R. 2004. *Grammaire méthodique du français*, 3rd edn (Presses Universitaires de France, Paris)

Rowlett, P. 2007. *The Syntax of French* (Cambridge University Press, Cambridge)

Sanders, C. (ed.) 1993. *French Today. Language in its Social Context* (Cambridge University Press, Cambridge)

Tranel, B. 1994. *The Sounds of French*, 2nd edn (Cambridge University Press, Cambridge)

Walter, H. 1988. *Le Français dans tous les sens* (Laffont, Paris). English translation: *French Inside Out* (Routledge, London, 1994)

Yaguello, M. (ed.) 2003. *Le Grand Livre de la langue française* (Seuil, Paris)

10

Spanish

John N. Green

1 Introduction

Spanish is by far the most widely spoken Romance language. At a conservative estimate, there are now some 325 million native speakers, scattered through all continents, but most densely concentrated in Central and South America, where Spanish-speaking countries form a great swathe from the United States–Mexico border right to Tierra del Fuego. Spanish is the national language of nineteen countries, in descending order of population: Mexico, Colombia, Spain (including the Balearic and Canary Islands and the enclaves of Ceuta and Melilla on the north African coast), Argentina, Peru, Venezuela, Chile, Ecuador, Cuba, Guatemala, Dominican Republic, Bolivia, El Salvador, Honduras, Paraguay, Nicaragua, Uruguay, Costa Rica, Panama. There are large Spanish-speaking minorities in the United States (including the Commonwealth of Puerto Rico, which is predominantly Spanish-speaking), estimated at 25 million but probably higher and certainly growing rapidly. Spanish is also the official language of Equatorial Guinea, and is spoken by significant minorities in Andorra, Belize, Morocco and Western Sahara, Israel and the Balkan countries, the Philippines and Australia.

Like all pluricentric languages, Spanish is subject to regional and sociolinguistic variation (some specific features are discussed in Sections 3 and 4 below). Despite some well-publicised heterogeneous characteristics, the range of variation is not very great and only rarely disrupts mutual comprehensibility. Difficulties do, however, arise with the Spanish-lexicon creoles of the Philippines and Colombia, and with Judeo-Spanish, the linguistic consequence of the expulsion of Sephardic communities from Spain in 1492. *Sefardí* is reputed to have preserved numerous features of fifteenth-century usage, but the claim is exaggerated: some phonetic traits, like the preservation of initial /f-/, are indeed archaic, but the language has evolved extensively in its morphology and has assimilated large numbers of lexical borrowings. In gradual decline for most of the twentieth century, *sefardí* is now seriously endangered; it has not benefited from migration of the Balkan communities to Israel, where a mildly koineised Latin-American Spanish is thriving and attracting younger speakers.

Natural tendencies towards linguistic divergence are combated by powerful cultural bonds and also by well-developed normative mechanisms, whose antecedents go back several centuries. (One of the earliest and best-known literary examples of linguistic prejudice is the criticism meted out by Juan de Valdés in his *Diálogo de la lengua*, of c. 1535, against Antonio de Nebrija's excellent *Gramática de la lengua castellana*, of 1492, on the grounds that Nebrija, as an Andalusian, could not be expected to know Castilian well enough for the task in hand.) In a puristic context, 'Spanish' almost invariably means 'Castilian', so that *español* and *castellano* remain largely interchangeable as names for the language. In national constitutions, however, *español* and *lengua nacional* are now preferred in Latin America. Since 1714, when it received a royal charter, the Real Academia de la Lengua has had normative authority over the language. Unlike its French counterpart, the Spanish Academy is composed of linguists and philologists, with the result that its decisions, though invariably conservative, command some respect.

In matters of orthography, the Academy has steered a reasonably successful course by dint of approving fairly minor adjustments at regular intervals. Spanish orthography, though popularly reputed to be 'phonetic' (by which is meant 'phonemic'), is in fact quite highly conventionalised. The letter/sound correspondence is skewed. Once the conventions have been mastered, it is relatively easy to pronounce the written language; but transcribing from speech is altogether trickier, as attested by the difficulty Spanish schoolchildren experience with dictation exercises. The main cause is the preservation of etymological spellings. *H* is never sounded, irrespective of origin – *huérfano* 'orphan' = /werfano/, *alhaja* 'jewel' = /alaxa/; *c* and *g* have two pronunciations depending on the following vowel – *cerca* 'near' = /θerka/ or /serka/, *gigante* 'giant' = /xigante/; *b* and *v* correspond to only one phoneme and are not in the same distribution as its two allophones – *beber* 'to drink' = /beber/ [be'βɛɾ], *vivir* 'to live' = /bibir/ [bi'βiɾ]. Words containing *b* and *v* are often misspelled, even on public notices; two observed in Segovia province read *se prohive aparcar* (= *prohibe*) 'no parking' and *coto pribado de caza* (= *privado*) 'private hunting'. Etymological spellings can, of course, be justified on grounds of continuity and cultural relationship, but they are not compatible with phonemic principles. If both French and Spanish were to be spelled phonemically, their visual relatedness would disappear overnight.

2 Historical Background

'Spanish' is conventionally dated to the latter part of the tenth century, the date of a religious text from the monastery of San Millán in the Rioja region, whose scribe openly acknowledged the discrepancy between written Latin and spoken vernacular by annotating the words and phrases he knew would be unintelligible to contemporary hearers with 'translations' or, more likely, prompts for reading aloud. Latin had been introduced into the Iberian peninsula by Roman soldiers and colonists over a period of more than two centuries, beginning during the second Punic War (218–201 BC), when Rome was obliged to subdue the Carthaginians in Spain in order to protect its northern front, and ending in 15 BC, when a long and arduous campaign finally brought the north-west (modern Galicia and Asturias) under Roman rule. Latin took firm enough root in the regions first colonised – the Levant and the Guadalquivir valley – to produce noted centres of learning and some authors celebrated for their style, including Martial and Seneca. By the time of the first Germanic incursions in the third century AD, Latin had long supplanted the indigenous languages of Iberia, with the sole exception of Basque in the north-east. Prolonged contact with Germanic and later Arabic certainly affected its evolution, but at no time does there appear to have been a serious risk that the mass of the population would cease to be Romance-speaking.

In the tenth century there could have been little reason to suppose that Castilian, an obscure dialect of the upper Ebro valley and Cantabria, would become a national, let alone a world, language. The history of its rise is essentially that of the Christian Reconquest, pursued with fluctuating determination and shifting alliances among the medieval kingdoms until the definitive expulsion of the Moorish rulers of Granada in 1492. Though this date is symbolic in Spanish history, the major part of the Reconquest had been achieved much earlier, the first phase culminating in the recapture of Toledo in 1085 by Alfonso VI. This was the king who banished Ruy Diaz, the Cid, and who (according to the epic) had reason to be grateful for the Cid's glorious campaigns against a new wave of Almoravid invaders who at one stage seemed likely to reverse the Christians' recent gains.

The southerly expansion of Castilian has been likened to a wedge driven between the dialects of León to the west and Aragón to the east. Castilian shared many structural properties with its lateral neighbours but differed in a number of salient phonological characteristics that made it sound quite distinct. One of these was the loss from many words of initial /f-/, via an intermediate stage of strong aspiration which is still signalled in the orthography, as in *FACĔRE* 'to do / make' > *hacer* /aθer/. Another was the tendency of the clusters /pl-/, /fl-/ and /kl-/ to palatalise, as in *AFFLĀRE* 'to sniff out' > *hallar* /aʎar/ 'to find'. Castilian also affricated the medial cluster -*CT*-, as in *LACTE* 'milk' > *leche* /letʃe/, Aragonese *leyt*; but failed to diphthongise lower mid vowels before a palatal sound, as in *TENĒO* 'I hold' > *tengo*, Aragonese *tiengo*. There has been intense linguistic debate on whether these and other features should be ascribed to the influence of Basque (the *f-* to *h-* change, for instance, is uncommon in Romance and also happens in parts of south-west France which used to be Basque-speaking). We cannot be certain. Individually, all the changes involve linguistic processes that are well attested. The most we can safely conclude is that prolonged bilingualism with Basque could have reinforced developments that started independently.

Castilian, which had a flourishing tradition of oral literature culminating in the epic *Poema del Mio Cid* (variously dated between c. 1140 and the early thirteenth century), consolidated its national position and its international respectability in the reign of Alfonso X 'El Sabio' 'The Wise', 1252–84. The king, himself a poet and intellectual, assembled a court of international scholars and undertook the translation into Spanish of literary, historical and scientific works written in Latin, Greek, Arabic and Hebrew. Since that time, the pre-eminence of Castilian has never been challenged, though there have always been local norms of pronunciation (see Section 3), and relations with Catalan-speaking areas have not always been easy. Basque, Catalan and Galician, liberated from years of linguistic repression during the Franco era, received a fillip from the regional autonomy policy espoused in the late 1970s, which accorded them official language status within their *autonomía*, but the position of Spanish as the national language is enshrined in the constitution and seems unlikely to be undermined in the long term.

The purely linguistic consequences of this turbulent history are fewer than one might expect. Some phonological changes may be attributable to Basque; one, the velarisation of medieval /ʃ/ to /x/ in a few nouns and southern place names (*SŪCU* 'juice' > *jugo*), can probably be traced indirectly to Arabic via a medieval pronunciation of /s/ as [ʃ] in the southern dialect of Mozarabic. Some syntactic calques from Arabic survive as fossilised expressions and, more importantly, the persistence of VSO word order (which is also common in other southern Romance languages, especially Portuguese) may have been reinforced by Arabic VSO order. No inflectional morphology has been shown to derive from any source but Latin.

This leaves the lexicon (including place and personal names) as the chief repository of historical accretions. A few pre-Roman words are still in use, including *páramo* 'moor', *vega* 'river plain', *pizarra* 'slate', *manteca* 'lard' and perhaps the adjective *gordo* 'fat'; the most frequent is probably *izquierdo* 'left', which has a cognate in Basque, but may be a borrowing there too. Most of the words of Celtic origin, like *cerveza* 'beer', *camisa* 'shirt', *cambiar* 'to change', are widely distributed in western Romance, and it is therefore difficult to decide whether they are survivors of the Celtic substratum in north and central Iberia or were introduced via Latin. A significant number of Germanic words remain in regular use, nearly all shared with French, some of them having probably been diffused via Latin before the main period of invasions. They include military terminology – *guerra* 'war', *guardia* 'guard', *tregua* 'truce', *espuela* 'spur', *estribo* 'stirrup', *yelmo* 'helmet' – but also some everyday words, like *ropa* 'clothing', *falda* 'skirt', *jabón* 'soap', *ganso* 'goose', *ganar* 'to win', together with a set of common adjectives – *rico* 'rich', *blanco* 'white', *gris* 'grey' – and a few abstract concepts: *orgullo* 'pride', *galardón* 'reward' and Old Spanish *fonta/honta* 'shame'. Also Germanic are numerous place and personal names; the common suffix *-ez* of Spanish family names (*López*, *Martínez*, *González*, etc.), though Latin in origin, probably owes its diffusion to the Visigoths.

Approaching 4,000 words can be traced to Arabic, almost all nouns and a high proportion beginning with *a-* or *al-*, representing the agglutination of the Arabic definite article. An important group relates to horticulture and water management: *acequia* 'irrigation channel', *noria* 'water wheel', *aljibe* 'cistern', *aceite* 'olive oil', *alcachofa* 'artichoke', *algodón* 'cotton', *arroz* 'rice', *azafrán* 'saffron', *azúcar* 'sugar', *naranja* 'orange', *zanahoria* 'carrot'. Others concern civil administration – *aduana* 'customs', *alcaide* 'governor/gaoler', *alcalde* 'mayor', *alguacil* 'constable' – and still others have entered international scientific vocabulary: *alcohol*, *algebra*, *cifra* 'figure/cipher', *cenit* 'zenith', *nadir*, etc. For the tourist, some of the most 'typical' features of southern Spain are designated by Arabic words: *azahar* 'orange blossom', *azotea* 'flat roof', *azucena* 'lily', and *azulejo* 'ceramic tile' (so called because the basic colour was a deep blue – *azul*). In categories other than nouns, Arabic has given the adjective *mezquino* 'mean', the verb *halagar* 'to flatter' (both well adapted to Romance grammatical patterns), the preposition *hasta* 'up to' and the exclamative *ojalá* 'would that ...' (literally, 'May Allah grant ...').

Since the Renaissance, Spanish has borrowed extensively from other Romance languages and from Latin; from Amerindian languages spoken in its overseas colonies; and most recently from English (often American rather than British). The borrowings from Latin confront the descriptive linguist with an interesting dilemma. Many of them are related to words which have had a continuous history in the language and have undergone more extensive phonological modification than the latecomers, which were generally admitted in a hispanicised pronunciation of the original spelling. The question is whether these 'doublets' should be related by productive rules to the indigenous items. Consider the twelve examples given here, where a common noun or verb is paired with an adjective of the same root meaning but more elevated register.

hierro 'iron'	:	férrico
hijo 'son'	:	filial
hado 'fate'	:	fatal
hambre 'hunger'	:	famélico
harina 'flour'	:	farináceo
hastío 'distaste'	:	fastidioso
heder 'to stink'	:	fétido
hembra 'female'	:	femenino
hongo 'mushroom'	:	fungoso
hormiga 'ant'	:	fórmico
huir 'to flee'	:	fugaz
hurto 'theft'	:	furtivo

These give an idea of the scale of the phenomenon, being only a subgroup of those involving the phonological change *f- > h- > Ø*. We shall not attempt an answer, but merely observe that any across-the-board solution, whether concrete or abstract, will run foul of mixed derivational sets: *humo* 'smoke' has regular derivatives *humoso* 'smoky' and *ahumar* 'to preserve food by smoking', but is also clearly related to *fumar* 'to smoke' (of fires or of people).

We end this section on a note of optimism. Although purist hackles have been raised by the recent influx of anglicisms (as in France), the productive patterns of the language remain resolutely Romance. Spanish has at all periods created new vocabulary by suffixal derivation. The following selection, all of Latin origin, remain highly productive: the diminutives *-ito*, *illo*, *ino*; the augmentative *-ón*, the agentive *-dor*; the adjectivals *-oso*, *-ero*; the nominals *-aje*, *-ción*, *-miento*. Nor are derivational processes respecters of alien origin: the Germanic borrowings quoted above, *guerra* and *orgullo*, form adjectives *guerrero* and *orgulloso*, and the Arabic *halagar* forms *halagüeño* – a powerful means of integrating the borrowing. Purists can take heart from modern coinings like *urbanización* 'housing development', to be seen on builders' placards all over Spain, and composed of impeccably classical roots. Many other fairly recent inventions which might have attracted foreign labels have in fact been named by compounding indigenous roots: *parachoques* 'bumper bar', *limpiaparabrisas* 'windscreen wiper', *tallalápices* 'pencil sharpener'. Through developments of this kind, Spanish is becoming more, not less, Romance in its structure.

3 Phonology

Like other world languages, Spanish shows a good deal of internal variation. This extends to all linguistic levels but is most noticeable in the phonology. For international trade and diplomacy and for pedagogical purposes, two norms are recognised: either the educated usage of Castile (traditionally identified with Burgos, but now displaced by Madrid) or that of Bogotá, Colombia (itself increasingly eclipsed, both linguistically and culturally, by Mexico City). In the sixteenth and seventeenth centuries, a further model was provided by Seville, which remained a flourishing cultural centre throughout the first period of colonisation of Central and South America. The fact that most of the early settlers were of Andalusian origin and the existence of the Sevillean 'norma culta' are now generally believed to explain the present-day differences between Latin American and Castilian usage, at both popular and educated levels.

The segmental inventory of Castilian is given in Table 10.1. The phonemic consonant system can be presented as neatly symmetrical, with four articulatory positions and five degrees of aperture, but this disguises some interesting irregularities in distribution. While, for instance, the absence of any point-of-articulation opposition between plosives and affricates argues for their merger, they differ in that /ʤ/ is by no means securely established in the system and neither palatal enters into syllable-initial clusters, which plosives do freely. The reintroduction of [ʤ], which was present (probably as an allophone of /ʒ/) in Old Spanish, is comparatively recent and its phonemic status remains doubtful. It represents a strengthened form of certain [j] sounds, some of them apparently determined lexically (especially the personal pronoun *yo* = [ʤo]) and others arising from an earlier weakening of palatal /ʎ/ known as 'yeísmo'. Both innovations are sociolinguistically marked: while the pronunciation of *calle* 'street' as [kaje] is now very widespread in informal speech, the intermediate variant [kaʒe] is often regarded as uneducated and the affricate realisation [kaʤe] is usually stigmatised as vulgar.

The voiceless plosives are all unaspirated. The voiced series is in complementary distribution with a corresponding set of voiced fricatives which occur intervocalically, thus *boca* 'mouth' [boka] but *cabo* 'end' [kaβo], *donde* 'where' [dɔnde] but *nudo* 'knot' [nuðo], *gato* 'cat' [gato] but *lago* 'lake' [laɣo]. In indigenous words neither /b/ nor /g/ occurs word finally; orthographic -*d* is weakened to [θ] or lost completely. It has traditionally been assumed that the fricatives are the subordinate members of these pairs, since the weakening of the plosives in some environments is well attested as a historical process. Research on language acquisition among Mexican children, however, seems to show that the fricatives are acquired first and remain dominant.

Table 10.1 Segmental Sounds of Castilian

Consonants				
	Bilabial	*Dental*	*Palatal*	*Velar*
Plosives [-voice]	p	t		k
[+voice]	b	d		g
Affricates			tʃ (ʤ)	
Fricatives [-voice]	f	θ	s	x
Nasals [+voice]	m	n	ɲ	
Laterals [+voice]		l	ʎ	
Vibrants [+voice]		r/r̄		

Vowels			Semi-vowels	
High	i	u	j	w
Mid	e	o		
Low	a			

The voiceless fricatives represent the remnants of a much larger set of sibilants in Old Spanish, including a phonemic voiced series whose demise is still not wholly explained. The absence of phonemic voiced sibilants now sets Spanish apart from most other Romance varieties; [z] occurs infrequently as an allophone of /s/ before voiced obstruents, but not intervocalically, thus *desde* 'from/since' [dɛzde] but *esposa* 'wife' [ɛsposa] – compare Portuguese [ʃpozɐ], Italian [spɔːza] and French [epuz]. American Spanish and most varieties of Andalusian lack the distinctive Castilian opposition between /θ/ and /s/, as in *cima* 'summit' /θima/: *sima* 'abyss' /sima/, *caza* 'hunt' /kaθa/: *casa* 'house' /kasa/, *haz* 'bundle' /aθ/: *as* 'ace' /as/. Throughout South America and in most of Andalucía, only [s] is found – a feature popularly called 'seseo'. In a few parts of Andalucía, [θ] alone is used – labelled 'ceceo'. It is probably not true that American Spanish *lost* the /θ:s/ opposition; more likely it was not present in the language of the first colonists. The merger, whatever its exact date, seems to have led to some vocabulary changes in order to avoid ambiguity: the Castilian minimal pair *coser* 'to sew' /koser/ : *cocer* 'to cook' /koθer/ poses no problem in America, where *coser* is maintained, but *cocinar* /kosinar/ is the verb 'to cook'.

The three nasals contrast intervocalically, where there are numerous permutations of minimal pairs and a few triads: *lama* 'slime' /lama/ : *lana* 'wool' /lana/ : *laña* 'clamp' /laɲa/. Elsewhere, the opposition is incomplete. Word-initially, /ɲ-/ is very rare, confined to a few affective coinings and Amerindian borrowings; among Latinate items, only /m-/ and /n-/ are possible. Nasals combine freely with obstruents to form heterosyllabic clusters, in which seven or more phonetic variants can be detected, always homorganic with the following consonant and therefore neutralising the opposition *infeliz* 'unhappy' [iɱfeliθ], *incierto* 'uncertain' [inθjɛrto], *incapaz* 'unable' [iŋkapaθ], etc. The opposition is also neutralised in word-final position, where only /-n/ occurs. A variant pronunciation, previously common in Andalucía and parts of Latin America, is now spreading rapidly in Spain though it remains sociolinguistically marked: word-final and sometimes syllable-final /-n/ is realised as [-ŋ]. Some phoneticians believe this may be the prelude to phonemic nasalisation of the preceding vowel, a development Spanish has so far resisted.

Turning to the liquids, we find /l/ is pronounced either dental or alveolar but never velar, and /ʎ/, as we noted above, is tending to lose its lateral element. /r/ and /r̄/ are unique in contrasting at the same point of articulation, but the opposition is only intervocalic – *caro* 'expensive' /karo/ : *carro* 'cart' /kar̄o/; elsewhere the two sounds are in complementary distribution. In standard Castilian the difference seems to be one of tenseness rather than length: /-r-/ is usually a flap and /-r̄-/ a full-bodied alveolar trill. But in some central American dialects /-r̄-/ is realised as a weaker sound with palatal friction [ɼ]. This development suggests an intriguing historical parallel with the palatals /ʎ/ and /ɲ/ which also had their principal source in Latin intervocalic geminates and appear to have evolved via a stage of tenseness.

Before passing on to vowels, we should say a few words about prosodic features, both for their intrinsic interest and because vocalic structure cannot be examined in isolation from stress and rhythm. Spanish has often been quoted as a textbook example of a syllable-timed language, with a delivery sometimes likened to a recalcitrant machine-gun. A newer proposal suggests Spanish would be more accurately described as 'segment timed' since the delivery, though perceptually regular, does not always produce isochronous syllabification *or* isochronous stress intervals. The rhythmic pattern, naturally, has implications for intonation, which tends to avoid abrupt changes and readily accommodates melodic units of ten to fifteen syllables. Castilian, whose every-day register is confined to little more than an octave, has a basic rise–fall for simple declaratives, a sustained rise for most yes–no questions, and the characteristic western Romance level or rising tone to mark enumerations and sentence-medial clause boundaries. A prominent feature of Castilian is its 'dynamic' or intensity accent, which is noticeably free from tonal modulation. Most writers also comment on the resonant quality that Castilians and northern dialect speakers impart to their everyday speech. This has been variously ascribed to an unusual articulatory setting, to the rhythmic structure, to the predominance of low, open vowels, and to the stability of vowel sounds in both stressed and unstressed positions. Though all these factors may be contributory, the principal cause must be articulatory setting, since many other regional varieties of Spanish are produced with a less marked resonant quality despite sharing the other structural features of Castilian.

As will be apparent from Table 10.1, the five simple vowels form a classic symmetrical triangle. Their frequency of occurrence in running prose also follows a regular pattern: low vowels are more frequent than high, front more so than back (hence in ascending order, /u, i, o, e, a/). All five occur as independent words, with /e/ and /a/ both representing homophones. All occur both stressed and unstressed, in open and closed syllables, though /i/ and /u/ are rare in word-final position. As we noted above, there is little tendency to weakening or centralisation in unstressed syllables, a feature which sets Spanish clearly apart from its peninsular neighbours Portuguese and Catalan. Regardless of the presence or absence of stress, however, all vowels are represented by laxer variants in closed syllables; the high and mid series are lowered slightly and /a/, which in citation has a central low articulation, may be displaced forward or backward depending on the adjacent consonant: *presté* 'I lent' /pres'te/ [pɾɛs'te], *cortó* 'it cut' /kor'to/ [kɔɾ'to], *jaulas* 'cages' /'xaulas/ ['χɑwlas̞].

This unexceptional laxing has paved the way for a change in Andalusian and some Latin American varieties which may have far-reaching consequences for the vowel system and for plural marking. In the singular, most Spanish nouns end in open /-a/, /-o/ or /-e/, but the addition of the plural marker /-s/ closes the syllable and produces the regular allophonic variation in the vowel:

hermano(s) 'brother(s)'	/ermano/ [ɛɾ'mano]	+ /s/ = [ɛɾ'manɔs]
hermana(s) 'sister(s)'	/ermana/ [ɛɾ'mana]	+ /s/ = [ɛɾ'manæs]
madre(s) 'mother(s)'	/madre/ ['maðɾe]	+ /s/ = ['maðɾɛs]

In Andalusian, syllable-final /-s/ often weakens to an aspiration [-h], so *los hermanos* becomes [lɔʰ ɛɾmanɔʰ], etc. This substitution, though phonetically salient, does not affect the phonemic status of the vowels. In a more 'advanced' variety of Andalusian, however, the aspiration is lost altogether and with it the conditioning factor for the vowel alternation. Now [la maðɾe] contrasts functionally with [læ maðɾɛ], and we are obliged to recognise a new system of plural marking – not too different from the vocalic alternations of Italian – and with it three new vowel phonemes.

Table 10.1 shows no diphthongs or triphthongs. On the phonetic level, combinations of vowels and vowel-like elements are common, but their phonemic status has always been among the most controversial areas of Spanish linguistics. Eighteen monosyllabic combinations can be distinguished, eight with a glide onset /ja, je, jo, ju, wa, we, wi, wo/, six with an off-glide /aj, aw, ej, ew, oj, ow/, and a further four with both on- and off-glides /waj, wej, jaw, waw/ of which the last two are very rare. The analyst's task is complicated by the existence of numerous other combinations, both within and across word boundaries, of vowels 'in hiatus' – pronounced as two syllables in careful speech but readily coalescing into monosyllables in rapid or informal delivery.

To explain the controversy, we must make a brief foray into stress assignment. Stress in Spanish is usually predictable and is not used as the sole means of differentiating lexical items. Stress position is calculated from the end of the word: those ending in a consonant other than /-n/ or /-s/ (which are mostly morphological endings) are stressed on the final syllable, while almost all others are stressed on the penultimate. It follows that nearly all plural forms are stressed on the same syllable as the corresponding singular. A few words, mainly borrowings, are stressed on the antepenultimate – a feature known by the convenient mnemonic of *esdrújulo*. These are not predictable (except as plurals maintaining the pattern of proparoxytone singulars, like *jóvenes* 'youths'); they all have an open penultimate syllable but this is a necessary, not sufficient, condition. Stress can only move further back than the third syllable if the word is clearly compound: *entregándomelo* 'handing it to me', *fácilmente* 'easily', though the latter has a secondary stress in the expected position. This fairly straightforward account of stress is complicated when we turn to verb inflection. Here, stress operates functionally to differentiate otherwise identical forms of the same lexeme – *hablo* 'I speak': *habló* '(s)he spoke', *¡cante!* 'sing!': *canté* 'I sang', *tomara* '(s)he might/would take': *tomará* '(s)he will take'. It follows that an analysis wishing to view stress as generally predictable must make reference to morphological information. Some theories, of course, rule this out by axiom.

Returning to what we earlier labelled 'semi-vowels', we can now appreciate the problem. At first sight, [j, w] appear to be in complementary distribution with the vowels /i, u/ respectively (a pattern which holds good even for the speakers who regularly substitute [j] for /ʎ/). The economical analysis requires prior knowledge of stress position: /i/ is realised as [j] (or becomes [-syllabic] in feature phonology) if and only if it is unstressed and adjacent to some other vowel. Now, some linguists have hankered after the neatest solution, that both semi-vowels and stress assignment are predictable. Can it be done? Consider these examples:

amplio ['am.pljo]	: amplío [am.'pli.o]	: amplió [am.'pljo]
'ample'	'I broaden'	'(s)he broadened'
continuo [kɔn.'ti.nwo]	: continúo [kɔn.ti.'nu.o]	: continuó [kɔn.ti.'nwo]
'continuous'	'I continue'	'(s)he continued'

Here, the occurrence of the full vowel or glide is predictable, once stress is known. But the converse is not true: stress cannot be predicted using only the phonological information given here. Nor can it be made predictable by including general morphological conditions, since other verbs behave differently in the middle form of the series: *cambiar* 'to change' and *menguar* 'to lessen' give respectively ['kam.bjo] and ['mɛŋ.gwo] not *[kam.'bi.o] or *[mɛŋ.'gu.o]. For reductionists, the consequences are uncomfortable: neither semi-vowels nor stress assignment can be predicted on strictly phonological criteria.

An allied debate has raged around the predictability or otherwise of the verb stem alternations traditionally called 'radical changes'. The two most frequent ones involve semi-vowels and stress assignment. The verb *poder* 'to be able' has two stems: /pod-/

when the following vowel is stressed and /pwed-/ when the stem itself is stressed. This results in a heterogeneous paradigm, very striking in the present indicative, with 1 sg. *puedo* alongside 1 pl. *podemos*. Similarly, *helar* 'to freeze', has the stressed stem *hielo* /jelo/ alongside *helamos* /elamos/. Some 400 verbs follow these two patterns, far more than one would normally wish to describe as 'irregular'. In any event, the observable changes are perfectly regular once one knows the stress assignment. But the interesting question is whether membership of the radical changing pattern is itself predictable. It used to be. Most western Romance dialects inherited a seven-term vowel system /i, e, ɛ, a, ɔ, o, u/ in which the mid vowels /e : ɛ/ /o : ɔ/ were phonemically distinct. In northern Spain, /ɛ/ and /ɔ/ diphthongised when stressed. This was a regular phonological change, affecting all word classes equally and all types of syllable (in northern French, the same vowels diphthongised only in open syllables). So, Spanish verbs with /ɛ/ or /ɔ/ as their stem vowel were regularly subject to diphthongisation under stress, stress in turn being positioned according to the number of syllables in the inflection.

What has changed between early and modern Spanish is the loss of the phonemic opposition between the mid vowels in favour of an allophonic variation predictable from syllable structure (see above). It is no longer possible to tell, from an infinitive, whether a verb will be radical changing or not: the stem vowel of *podar* 'to prune' is identical to that of *poder* but does not diphthongise; neither does the *e* of *pelar* 'to peel', although it is phonetically indistinguishable from that of *helar*. Some linguists, arguing that so common an alternation must be produced by regular rule, have postulated underlying vowels /ɛ, ɔ/ for radical changing verbs and thus claim the synchronic process is identical to the historical change. Others reject this abstract analysis, but point out the alternation is almost wholly predictable if the stressed diphthongal forms like *puede* are taken as basic rather than the infinitive. Yet others believe that Spanish speakers cannot predict these alternations at all, and must learn them as inherent features of the individual verb (rather like learning the gender of a noun). This last group point to two pieces of evidence. First, derivational processes have destroyed the earlier phonological regularity of diphthongisation: *deshuesar* 'to remove bones/pits' is a verb coined from the noun *hueso*, but the diphthong which regularly occurs under stress in the noun is irregular in the infinitive, where it is unstressed. Parallel examples are *ahuecar* 'to hollow out' from *hueco*, or *amueblado* 'furnished' from *mueble*. Second, speakers of some varieties stigmatised as substandard, especially Chicano, regularly keep the diphthongised stem throughout a paradigm regardless of stress placement, saying *despiertamos*, *despiertáis* for *despertamos*, *despertáis* 'we/you awaken'. All told, it looks as though a process which at first was phonologically regular has passed through a stage of morphological conditioning and is now giving way to lexical marking on individual words. As often happens in linguistic change, this will preserve analogical relationships at the expense of phonological regularity.

4 Morphology

It is well known that the Romance languages have, over the centuries, eliminated much of the inflectional morphology that characterised formal Latin. Spanish is no exception to the general trend away from synthetic towards more analytic forms of expression. At the same time, historical accounts, by concentrating on what has been eliminated, tend to exaggerate the extent to which Spanish has abandoned inflection. True, the declension system for nouns and related forms has been radically simplified, and some extensive areas of verbal inflection (including the entire morphological passive) have been lost without trace. Nevertheless, the most frequently occurring forms of the verb remain highly synthetic in structure, and derivational patterning has always been a favoured and vigorous means of enriching the vocabulary. In consequence, Modern Spanish is far from being an isolating language: very few words consist of only one morph and the 'synthesis index' for running prose has been calculated at between 1:1.9 and 1:2.2 depending on the complexity of the register.

We begin with the simple tense-forms of the verb. Spanish verbs are traditionally said to belong to one of three conjugations, with infinitives in -ar, -er and -ir. The -ar group, deriving from the Latin first conjugation in -ĀRE, is by far the largest and the one which accommodates almost all new coinings (compare *alunizar* 'to land on the moon' with French *alunir*). The distinction between the -er and -ir patterns is more apparent than real: aside from the future and conditional paradigms (which necessarily diverge since they take the infinitive as their stem) their endings are identical in all but four instances. We shall therefore distinguish only two basic conjugations for regular verbs, as set out in the chart given here.

The Simple Tense-forms of Regular Verbs,
Showing the Stress and a Possible Morphological Analysis

Conjugation I: tomar 'to take'   Conjugation II: comer 'to eat'

(a) *Present*

Indicative	Subjunctive		Indicative	Subjunctive
tóm-∅-o	tóm-e-∅		cóm-∅-o	cóm-a-∅
tóm-a-s	tóm-e-s		cóm-e-s	cóm-a-s
tóm-a-∅	tóm-e-∅		cóm-e-∅	cóm-a-∅
tom-á-mos	tom-é-mos		com-é-mos	com-á-mos
tom-á-is	tom-é-is		com-é-is	com-á-is
tóm-a-n	tóm-e-n		cóm-e-n	cóm-a-n

(b) *Imperfect*

Indicative	Subjunctive (1) or	(2)	Indicative	Subjunctive (1) or	(2)
tom-á-ba-∅	-á-se-∅	-á-ra-∅	com-í-a-∅	-ié-se-∅	-ié-ra-∅
tom-á-ba-s	-á-se-s	-á-ra-s	com-í-a-s	-ié-se-s	-ié-ra-s
tom-á-ba-∅	-á-se-∅	-á-ra-∅	com-í-a-∅	-ié-se-∅	-ié-ra-∅
tom-á-ba-mos	-á-se-mos	-á-ra-mos	com-í-a-mos	-ié-se-mos	-ié-ra-mos
tom-á-ba-is	-á-se-is	-á-ra-is	com-í-a-is	-ié-se-is	-ié-ra-is
tom-á-ba-n	-á-se-n	-á-ra-n	com-í-a-n	-ié-se-n	-ié-ra-n

(c) *Preterit or simple past (indicative only)*

tom-∅-é	(? = á+i)	com-∅-í	(? = í+i)
tom-á-ste		com-í-ste	
tom-∅-ó	(? = á+u)	com-i-ó	
tom-á-mos		com-í-mos	
tom-á-ste-is		com-í-ste-is	
tom-á-ro-n		com-ié-ro-n	

(d) *Future indicative (all verbs)*   *Conditional (all verbs)*

tom-a-r-é	com-e-r-ía
tom-a-r-ás	com-e-r-ías
tom-a-r-á	com-e-r-ía
tom-a-r-émos	com-e-r-íamos
tom-a-r-éis	com-e-r-íais
tom-a-r-án	com-e-r-ían

As in Latin, each paradigm consists of six forms representing three grammatical persons in both singular and plural. In general, all six forms are distinct, though there is some syncretism in first and third persons singular (and more in dialects which have lost final /-s/). As we noted earlier, stress operates functionally to differentiate otherwise identical forms. The unmarked paradigm is the present indicative and the unmarked person the third singular, which is the morphological shape assumed by the handful of verbs that do not accept animate subjects (*nieva* 'it is snowing', *tronó* 'it thundered'). It is useful to distinguish a 'theme vowel' after the lexical stem, /-a-/ for the first conjugation and for the second /-e-/ or /-i-/, in a rather complicated phonological distribution. It can then be seen that the distinction between the present indicative and subjunctive rests on a reversal of the theme vowel.

The order of morphemes is fixed: lexical stem + theme vowel + tense marker (sometimes including an empty morph) + person marker. Some forms, however, have fused in the course of history and a neat segmentation is not always possible. The preterit is the most difficult paradigm to analyse, since the theme vowel is sometimes indistinguishable, and segmenting the plural person markers in the regular way, /-is-,-n/, leaves an awkward residue which occurs nowhere else in the system. (We should perhaps add that the Latin perfect, from which this paradigm is derived, is scarcely more amenable to segmentation.) The future and conditional pose a rather different problem: both have evolved during the history of Spanish (see below) from combinations of the infinitive with either the present or imperfect of the auxiliary *haber* 'to have', and despite considerable phonetic reduction the 'endings' still contain traces of this verb's lexical stem. This secondary derivation explains the identity of the conditional endings with those of the second conjugation imperfect.

Spanish is in the unusual position of having alternative forms for the imperfect subjunctive, neither of which is a reflex of the Latin. The *-se* series derives from the Latin pluperfect subjunctive, and the *-ra* from the pluperfect indicative. In northwestern dialects of Spain and in parts of Latin America, *-ra* is still used as a pluperfect. In standard Spanish, the two forms are not quite interchangeable: in the 'attenuating' sense, *quisiera* 'I should like' and *debiera* 'I really ought' cannot be replaced by the *-se* counterparts, and elsewhere their distribution may be determined by considerations of symmetry or by sociolinguistic factors.

By the strictest criteria, almost 900 Spanish verbs are irregular in one or more of the simple tense-forms. This disconcerting figure contains a very few with anomalies in their endings; all the others are subject to alternations in the stem, with varying degrees of predictability. (The total, incidentally, excludes numerous other verbs which, though perfectly regular in their morphology, undergo orthographic changes and which are misguidedly classified as irregular in some manuals.) Over half the total are 'radical changing', of the types discussed above or of a minor type affecting only *-ir* verbs; some others, like *huir* 'to flee', insert a glide under predictable conditions. A significant minority retain the Latin opposition between primary and historic stems; those which do, have their preterit and both imperfect subjunctives built on a different stem from all other paradigms (see the chart of irregular verbs). Some twenty verbs of conjugation II modify their infinitival stem in the future and conditional. Finally, a handful of very frequent verbs are totally eccentric and even undergo stem suppletion.

Five Irregular Verbs Used as Auxiliaries, Given in Standard Orthography

	ser	estar	haber	tener	ir
	'to be'	'to be'	'to have'	'to have'	'to go'

(a) *Present indicative*

ser	estar	haber	tener	ir
soy	estoy	he	tengo	voy
eres	estás	has	tienes	vas
es	está	ha	tiene	va
somos	estamos	hemos	tenemos	vamos
sois	estáis	habéis	tenéis	vais
son	están	han	tienen	van

(b) *Present subjunctive (endings regular, same stem throughout)*

sea	esté	haya	tenga	vaya

(c) *Imperfect indicative (endings regular, same stem throughout)*

era	estaba	había	tenía	iba

(d) *Future indicative (endings regular, same stem throughout)*

seré	estaré	habré	tendré	iré

(e) *Preterit indicative (endings slightly irregular, same stem throughout)*

fui	estuve	hube	tuve	fui
fuiste	estuviste	hubiste	tuviste	fuiste
fue	estuvo	hubo	tuvo	fue
fuimos	estuvimos	hubimos	tuvimos	fuimos
fuisteis	estuvisteis	hubisteis	tuvisteis	fuisteis
fueron	estuvieron	hubieron	tuvieron	fueron

(f) *Imperfect subjunctive (endings regular, same stem throughout)*

	ser	estar	haber	tener	ir
(1)	fuese	estuviese	hubiese	tuviese	fuese
(2)	fuera	estuviera	hubiera	tuviera	fuera

One class, amounting to some 200 including compounds, deserves special mention. Polysyllabic verbs which end in *-cer* or *-cir* preceded by a vowel, like *conocer* 'to know' or *relucir* 'to flaunt', have an extra velar consonant before non-front vowels, *conozco* being pronounced [ko.'noθ.ko] in Castilian and [ko.'nos.ko] in 'seseo' districts of Andalucía and throughout Latin America. The intriguing question is: where does the velar come from? Is it part of the underlying stem but lost before front vowels? Or is it epenthetic, and if so under what conditions? The first answer is historically correct: all these verbs contain an originally inchoative infix *-SC-* whose velar remained intact before low or back vowels but regularly palatalised before a front vowel and then assimilated to the preceding sibilant. Even so, it seems unlikely that contemporary speakers recapitulate this process to produce the less frequent of the two alternants. If the velar is regarded as epenthetic (though phonetically unmotivated), it remains predictable in Castilian but only by reference to the phoneme /θ/. In 'seseante' dialects which lack the /θ : s/ opposition, the alternation is unpredictable: speakers cannot know from the phonological structure that *reconocer* 'to recognise' [re.ko.no.'sɛɾ] requires [-k-] while *recoser* 'to sew up' [re-ko-'sɛɾ] does not. They must, in other words, learn the alternation as an inherent lexical feature of the verb. Castilians, too, may do this; but they appear to have a choice.

In addition to its simple paradigms, Spanish is particularly well endowed with compound or periphrastic forms, more so than any other standard Romance language. Usually, these consist of an inflected auxiliary followed by a non-finite form of the lexical verb (an infinitive or participle), but more complex combinations are also possible. Virtually all are Romance creations, though some embryonic models are attested in Latin. The most far-reaching innovation was the compounding of *HABĒRE*, originally meaning 'to possess', with a past participle. *HABEŌ CĒNA(M) PARĀTA(M)* first meant 'I have the supper here, already prepared', but with increased use and a change of word order, it soon came to mean simply 'I've prepared the supper'. The new construction provided a powerful model: in principle, any paradigm of *HABĒRE* could be combined with the past participle to make a new tense-form. This remains true in Modern Spanish: all eight simple paradigms of *haber*, including the rare future subjunctive, can be compounded (their meanings are discussed in Section 5). Although the compounds were flourishing in Old Spanish, they could only be used with transitive verbs, a direct consequence of their etymology. Intransitives were conjugated with *ser*, rather as in Modern French. It was only at the end of the fifteenth century that *haber* ousted *ser* for all verbs, and the past participle became invariable. In Spanish, *tener* can also be used as an auxiliary: *tengo preparada la cena*, with agreement, means the same as the Latin expression from which we set out.

The chart of irregular verbs, detailing the most common auxiliaries, shows two verbs 'to be', a notorious difficulty for foreign learners of Spanish. At some risk of over-simplification we shall say that *ser* is the normal copula, denoting inherent qualities, while *estar* focuses on resultant states; compare *la pimienta es picante* 'pepper is hot' (inherently) with *la sopa está fría* 'the soup's cold' (because it's cooled down). Both verbs can be used as auxiliaries, in conjunction with a past participle, to make analytic passives. This results in a plethora of forms, since any paradigm of *ser* or *estar* can be used, including those which are already compound. Nor are the two passives synonymous: *ser* denotes the action or process, as in *el dinero ha sido robado (por un atracador)* 'the money has been stolen (by a gangster)', whereas *estar* denotes the subsequent state, as in *la tienda está abierta* 'the shop's open' (because it has been opened). *Estar* also combines with a present participle to create a range of progressive forms. In turn, these may combine with other compounds, without grammatical restriction. Nevertheless, three-term compounds like *había estado andando* 'I'd been walking' are not frequent, and monsters like *ha estado siendo construído* 'it's been being built' are usually avoided in compassion for the listener.

By comparison with the verb, the Spanish noun and its related forms have a very simple inflectional structure. This is mainly due to the complete elimination of the Latin declension system, from a very early date and well before the emergence of vernacular texts in the tenth century. Nonetheless, as we hinted earlier, the effect of vigorous derivational processes has been to create large numbers of nouns whose overall morphological structure, while reasonably transparent, can hardly be described as simple. An abstract nominal like *desaprovechamiento* 'negligence' probably consists of six synchronic morphemes, with a further historical division fossilised in the root *-pro (-vech)-*. The majority of nouns consist of at least two morphemes, a root and a gender marker, to which a plural marker is affixed if need be.

The categories of number and gender inherited from Latin are for the most part overtly marked on determiners, demonstratives, pronouns and adjectives of all kinds, as well as nouns. In Castilian, all plural substantives and determiners end in /-s/, though the derivation of plurals from singulars is not quite so straightforward as this implies, since a sizeable minority adds the full syllable /-es/ and a few already ending in /-s/ remain unchanged. We have already seen the drastic effect on plural marking in those dialects which have lost final /-s/. Modern Spanish has only two genders, which normally respect the sex of animate beings, but must be regarded as inherent and semantically arbitrary for inanimate nouns. The Latin neuter was eliminated from sub-stantives, usually in favour of masculine, before the Old Spanish period, but faint traces of it persist in the pronoun system. Thanks to the frequency of the markers -a (over-whelmingly feminine) and -o (almost exclusively masculine) the gender of a high pro-portion of nouns is immediately apparent, though predictability for other endings is much lower. Curiously, -a and -o derive from Latin suffixes whose primary purpose was to mark not gender, but declension membership, from which gender was only partially predictable.

The demonstratives form a three-term system which correlates with grammatical person: *este* 'this (of mine)': *ese* 'that (of yours)': *aquel* 'yonder (of his/hers/theirs)'. One set of forms doubles up for adjectives and pronouns (the latter take an ortho-graphic accent) and the system is essentially identical to its Latin forerunner, though with different exponents. In European Spanish, person is undoubtedly a three-term system if approached via verbal inflection, but there are in fact eleven pronouns to distribute among the inflectional endings, and it is the third person which proves obli-gingly polysemous. Since the late sixteenth century, the physical distance encoded in the person category (and in demonstratives) has been exploited metaphorically as a marker of social distance. Thus the 'polite' forms *usted/ustedes* colligate with third person endings, emphasising the differential status accorded by the speaker to the addressee. The minor semantic clash of second person referent with third person verb is resolved in West Andalusian and Canary Island dialects by colligating *ustedes* with second person morphology: *ustedes sois*, etc. In Latin America, the position is more complicated. *Vosotros*, the familiar plural form, has given way to *ustedes*, used with third person inflection, as a generalised plural. *Vos*, which in medieval Spanish had been used as a polite singular (just as Modern French *vous*), has taken over in many varieties as the generalised singular, colligating with inflections which are historically both singular and plural, sometimes even blends. 'Voseo' is not a recent phenomenon; its roots must be sought in the colonial period, and recent archival research has revealed that it was well established in educated Buenos Aires usage by the beginning of the nineteenth century.

5 Syntax

Spanish is sometimes described as having free, or relatively free, word order. Without qualification, this is misleading. What is usually meant is that subject noun phrases are not fixed by grammatical requirements at a particular point in the sentence. This is a salient characteristic, one which differentiates Spanish from French (in its formal reg-isters) and more so from the major Germanic languages, but which is less unusual among the southern Romance group. At the same time, Spanish has strong constraints on word order *within* the main syntactic constituents and even the theoretical freedom available elsewhere is subject to pragmatic conventions. As a general rule, themes precede rhemes and new information is located towards the end of the utterance.

To characterise the purely syntactic constraints, we must recognise the categories of subject, verbal unit, object and complement (abbreviated as S, V, O, C). Within the simple declarative sentence, object and complement phrases follow the verb: *Elena compró un coche* 'Helen bought a car', *el libro parecía interestante* 'the book seemed interesting'. In everyday language, the VO/VC order is fixed; objects cannot precede their verbs – *Elena un coche compró*. It is certainly possible to topicalise an object consisting of a definite noun phrase or proper noun by moving it to the front of the sentence, but when this happens there is an intonation break after the topic, and an object clitic is obligatorily inserted before the verb: *el coche, lo compró Elena* '(as for) the car, Helen bought it'. The result of this 'clitic-copying' is no longer a simple sentence: *lo compró Elena* is a complete structure in its own right.

Subject phrases are harder to pin down. Because of the marked tendency for the topic to coincide with the grammatical subject in spoken language, SVO/SVC order is very frequent, especially where the subject consists of a single proper noun or very short phrase. So *?compró Elena el coche* would sound very odd, and *compró el coche Elena* would tend to be reserved for contradiction or contrast – 'it was Helen (not Jane) who bought the car'. Nevertheless, in more formal registers VSO order is common, and in all registers unusually long or 'heavy' subject phrases appear to the right of the verb: *han llegado todos los transeuntes de la Compañía X* 'all passengers travelling with Company X have now arrived'. VS order is the norm in many types of subordinate clause even when the subject consists of a single word: *no vi lo que leía Juana* 'I didn't see what Jane was reading'. VS is also obligatory in existentials, *hay varios rascacielos en Madrid* 'there are several skyscrapers in Madrid', and in questions beginning with an interrogative word: *¿qué quieren ustedes?* 'what would you (pl) like?', but not *¿qué ustedes quieren?* Interrogatives of this kind should not be assumed to entail syntactic inversion since VS, as we have seen, frequently occurs in statements and conversely yes–no questions may show either VS or SV order, relying entirely on the intonation to differentiate questions from corresponding statements.

On most of the criteria favoured by typological theory, Modern Spanish is a consistent VO language. Briefly: in simplex sentences VO/VC order is obligatory; noun phrase relationships are expressed exclusively by prepositions; genitives follow their head noun; the standard follows the comparative; most adjectives and all attributive phrases and relative clauses follow their head noun; most adverbs follow the verb they modify; auxiliaries are frequent and always precede the lexical stem; quantifiers and negatives precede the item they qualify and have only forward scope; interrogative words are always phrase-initial. Needless to add, there are some complications. Among the adjectives, some of the most common always precede their noun, most others may precede if used figuratively, and a few are polysemous according to position: *un pobre pueblecillo* 'a miserable little town', *un aristócrata pobre* 'an impoverished aristocrat'. Adverbs usually occupy initial position when acting as sentential modifiers, *Desgraciadamente, ...* 'Unfortunately, ...'; adverbs modifying adjectives almost always precede whereas those modifying verbs just as regularly follow, so that scope (for manner adverbials at least) is pivotal.

The most serious discrepancy for VO typology, however, is the vigour of suffixal inflection in the verb system, a feature little modified by the development of auxiliaries, since auxiliaries themselves are both frequent and highly inflected. Verbal inflection has two important syntactic functions. In conjunction with the concord system (see below) it guarantees the freedom of movement of subject phrases. It also tends to preserve the optionality of subject pronouns, permitting many grammatical sentences of V(S)O form with no overt subject nominal. Spanish, as we have seen, shows little syncretism in its inflections and, unlike French, rarely needs subject pronouns to avoid syntactic ambiguity, though they are regularly used for emphasis and contrast. At the same time, any move to increase the use of personal pronouns (and there is some evidence this is happening in colloquial registers) would undermine the necessity to preserve verbal inflection.

212

Spanish has a fully explicit concord system which marks number and gender on all modifiers within the noun phrase, and number and person (and occasionally gender too) between the subject and verb. There is no concord between verb and object. In most cases, concord unambiguously assigns a subject to a verb, and any ambiguity arising in this relationship (if, for instance, both subject and object are third person singular) is usually resolved by syntactic differences between subjects and objects. They differ in two important ways, both connected with specificity. The first is illustrated in *el hombre compra huevos* 'the man is buying (some) eggs'. The subject phrase in Spanish – whether definite, indefinite or generic – requires a determiner, but the object does not. In this respect Spanish differs considerably from Latin, which had no articles and did not require determination of either subjects or objects, but has evolved less far than French, which requires both. The second distinction is illustrated in *vi a tu hermana* 'I saw your sister', where the specific, animate object is introduced by the preposition *a* (popularly known as 'personal *a*'). At first sight, this looks like a nominative:accusative opposition, and it may indeed represent a remnant of the defunct case system. In fact, the opposition is between particularised animate beings, and all other object phrases (with a little latitude for metaphorical extension). Moreover, this distinction is preserved at the expense of another: since *a* is also the preposition used to introduce datives, there is no overt difference between the majority of direct and indirect objects. Whether the categories have genuinely fused or are merely obscured by surface syncretism is hard to say. Most Latin American varieties preserve a distinction between third person direct and indirect pronominal objects, but this too has been lost in much of Spain.

Curiously, voice is the verbal category with which pronominals have been most closely linked during the history of Spanish. The connection, brought about by cliticisation of part of the pronoun system, seems likely to result in the evolution of a new set of medio-passive paradigms. Whereas Latin pronouns were free forms not necessarily positioned adjacent to the verb, in most Romance varieties they have become clitic, sometimes resulting in differentiated sets of free and bound forms. In Spanish, clitics may appear alone or supported by a corresponding free form, but the converse is not true: *te vi* 'I saw you', *te vi a ti* 'I saw *you*', but not **vi a ti*. Enclisis, which was frequent in older stages of the language, has been virtually eliminated from contemporary spoken Spanish, where clitics 'climb' from a lower clause to the front of the main verb – compare formal *tiene que traérmelo* 'he must bring it for me' with colloquial *me lo tiene que traer*. As we noted earlier, clitics show a direct:indirect opposition only in the third person, and not always there. Reflexivity is distinguished, if at all, only in third person *se*, which neutralises not only direct:indirect, but also number and gender.

Se and its congeners in other Romance languages have been the focus of intense linguistic debate. The problem is whether *se* should be treated as one single morpheme or a set of homophonous forms. Traditional accounts distinguish four or more functions: a true reflexive or reciprocal pronoun – *se lavaron* 'they washed themselves/one another'; a passive marker – *el congreso se inauguró* 'the congress was opened'; an impersonal marker – *se habla inglés* 'English spoken'; and a substitute form of *le/les* when used with another deictic pronoun – *se lo dio* 'she gave it to him', not **le lo dio*. (The latter usage is peculiar to Spanish and is known to have a different historical origin from the others.) These functions, however, seem to be semantically compatible, yet Spanish never permits more than one *se* per verb phrase. Combinations of, for instance, an 'impersonal' *se* with a 'reflexive' verb are ungrammatical – **se se esfuerza por* ... 'one struggles to ...' – as are many other apparently reasonable pairs. If *se* were only one morpheme, the problem would not arise; but can such disparate meanings be reconciled? Two accounts are now available which solve most of the problems. In one, *se* is viewed as a pronoun with very little inherent meaning ('third person, low deixis'), which acquires significance from contextual inferences. In the other, *se* is seen as part of a new medio-passive paradigm, its third person impersonal use paralleling that of Latin: *VĪVITUR* = *se vive* = 'one lives'. These treatments share an intuition that runs counter to tradition, namely that *se* is not a reflexive pronoun.

If Spanish is indeed creating new inflectional morphology, it would not be the first time. The clearest example is the new future paradigm we mentioned above, a compound of the lexical verb plus *HABĒRE* (/kantar + 'abjo/ > /kanta're/, etc.), which originally expressed mild obligation 'I have to sing' and whose component parts were still separable in Old Spanish. Another example would be the adverbials in -*mente*, compounded from the ablative of the feminine noun *MĒNS* 'mind/manner' with a feminine adjective, thus *STRICTĀ MĒNTE* > *estrechamente* 'narrowly' (notice the Latin adjective position); here the two components remain separable. But is Spanish really in need of a new passive when it already has a plethora of compound forms with *ser* and *estar*? All we can reply is that they have discrete functions: only the *ser* passive is acceptable to most speakers with an explicit agentive phrase; only the 'reflexive' passive is used in an inchoative sense (*se vio obligado a* ... 'he (just) had to …') or with deontic modality (*eso no se hace* 'that isn't done/you shouldn't do that'). But the major difference is one of register: *ser* passives, though common in journalistic and technical writing, have been virtually ousted from speech and from literary styles to the advantage of the clitic forms, which may eventually generalise to all contexts.

We have so far said little on the verbal categories of tense, aspect and mood, and will devote our remaining space to them. The first two are inextricably bound up with the evolution of auxiliaries, in which Spanish is particularly prolific. Auxiliaries usually derive from full lexical verbs whose semantic content is progressively 'bleached' as they become grammaticalised. By the strictest definition – a verb with no independent lexical meaning – Spanish has only one auxiliary: *soler*, as in *Juan suele madrugarse* 'John habitually gets up at dawn'. *Haber*, *ser* and *estar* come close behind, having only remnants of lexical meaning: *yo soy* 'I exist', *Ana no está* 'Anne's not at home'. After that comes a continuum of more than fifty verbs, ranging from *tener* and *ir* which have important auxiliary functions, to those like *caminar* 'to walk/journey' which in expressions like *camina enlutada* 'she goes about in mourning' contrive to support the past participle while preserving most of their lexical content. True auxiliaries carry tense and aspect information for the main verb and this is clearly one reason for the grammaticalisation of *HABĒRE*. The Latin system opposed three time values to two aspects, imperfective and perfective, giving a six-cell structure; but one paradigm, usually called 'perfect', was bivalent between present perfective and past punctual meaning. The development of *HABĒRE* compounds not only preserved the morphological marking of aspect (previously perfective was signalled by a stem alternation) but also resolved this bivalency, *VĪDĪ* in the sense of 'I have seen' being replaced by *HABEŌ VĪSU(M)* > *he visto*, leaving the original to mean 'I caught sight of'. In the 'core' system of Modern Spanish this opposition is maintained, though in Castilian the perfect *he visto* is beginning to encroach on contexts previously reserved for the preterit *vi*. It is not yet clear whether Spanish is moving towards the pattern of Modern French, but certainly the elimination of the preterit paradigm would provoke a major realignment of functions.

All varieties of Spanish preserve a vigorous subjunctive mood (see the charts of regular and irregular verbs for the morphology). Opinion is divided, however, on whether the subjunctive – which does not occur in declarative main clauses – should be viewed as a 'mere' marker of subordination or as a meaningful category. In many contexts, its use seems to be grammatically determined; *querer* 'to want', for instance, when followed by a clause always takes a subjunctive – *quiero que lo hagas/*haces* 'I want you to do it'. In others, the conditioning is more subtle: *busco a un amigo que puede ayudarme* 'I'm looking for a (particular) friend to help me' alternates with *busco un amigo que pueda ayudarme* 'I'm looking for a (= any) friend to help me', but the subjunctive may still be grammatically conditioned by the indeterminacy of the object noun phrase. There are a few instances, however, where a genuine alternation is possible: *¿crees que vendrá?* and *¿crees que venga?* can both be translated as 'do you think he'll come?', but the first is neutral in implicature while the second conveys the speaker's belief that he won't. If such examples are taken as criterial, the 'grammatical marker' hypothesis cannot be maintained. In any event, the complementiser *que* is a much more efficient marker of subordination, and most complement clauses dependent on verbs of saying, thinking or believing require an indicative rather than a subjunctive. Nevertheless, it remains very difficult to find a single, uniform meaning for the subjunctive, the traditional suggestions of 'doubt' or 'uncertainty' being only partially accurate. The most we can say is that the 'meaningful' uses of the subjunctive, though rather few, are Romance creations and appear to be increasing rather than decreasing.

Bibliography

Since the 1990s, there has been a huge upsurge of interest in the linguistics of Spanish, with many of the one-volume classics superseded by longer, more accurate, and often more technical reference works. Authoritative dictionaries include Real Academia Española (2001) and the revised electronic version of Moliner (2001–2). Davies (2006) is on a smaller scale and has the backing of a large corpus of usage; it is useful for language learners. The best descriptive grammar is Bosque and Demonte (1999); this three-volume collaborative work has the imprimatur of the Spanish Academy, which has not issued a recent edition of its own normative grammar. Zagona (2002) is a more theoretical introduction to Spanish syntax. Descriptive studies that focus on aspects of contemporary usage include: Clements and Yoon (2005); Márquez Reiter and Placencia (2004); and Silva-Corvalán (2001), which also has coverage of some sociolinguistic issues in the United States. Hualde (2005) is the most accessible recent treatment of Spanish phonology and pronunciation.

Roca (2000) gives a good coverage of Spanish as spoken in the United States, including research on mixed varieties and code-switching. Lipski (1994) offers a very fair overview of Spanish in Latin America, complemented by the more traditional dialectological articles in Alvar (1996). For a well-documented study of the current position of Judeo-Spanish, see Quintana (2006). For the internal history of Spanish, Penny (2002) is highly acclaimed, complemented by Pharies (2002) on the history of suffixation, while Cano (2004) is a larger collaborative undertaking which also covers external history. Finally, Del Valle and Gabriel-Stheeman (2002) offer an interpretation of the historical sociology of Castilian, showing how the language has been standardised and 'commodified' for hegemonic purposes.

References

Alvar López, M. (ed.) 1996. *Manual de dialectología hispánica. I. El español de España. II. El español de América*, 2 vols (Ariel, Barcelona)

Bosque, I. and Demonte, V. (eds) 1999. *Gramática descriptiva de la lengua española*, 3 vols (Real Academia Española and Espasa-Calpe, Madrid)

Cano, R. (ed.) 2004. *Historia de la lengua española* (Ariel, Barcelona)

Clements, J.C. and Yoon, J. (eds) 2005. *Functional Approaches to Spanish Syntax: Lexical Semantics, Discourse and Transitivity* (Palgrave-Macmillan, London)

Davies, M. 2006. *A Frequency Dictionary of Spanish* (Routledge, New York and London)

Del Valle, J. and Gabriel-Stheeman, L. (eds) 2002. *The Battle over Spanish between 1800 and 2000* (Routledge, New York and London)

Hualde, J.I. 2005. *The Sounds of Spanish* (Cambridge University Press, Cambridge)

Lipski, J.M. 1994. *Latin American Spanish* (Longman, London and New York)

Márquez Reiter, R. and Placencia, M.E. (eds) 2004. *Current Trends in the Pragmatics of Spanish* (John Benjamins, Amsterdam)

Moliner, M. 2001–2. *Diccionario de uso del español*, revised CD-Rom edn (Gredos, Madrid)

Penny, R. 2002. *A History of the Spanish Language*, 2nd edn (Cambridge University Press, Cambridge)

Pharies, D. 2002. *Diccionario etimológico de los sufijos españoles y de otros elementos finales* (Gredos, Madrid)

Quintana Rodríguez, A. 2006. *Geografía lingüística del Judeoespañol* (Peter Lang, Bern and Frankfurt-am-Main)

Real Academia Española. 2001. *Diccionario de la lengua española*, 22nd edn (Espasa-Calpe, Madrid)

Roca, A. (ed.) 2000. *Research on Spanish in the United States* (Cascadilla Press, Somerville, MA)

Silva-Corvalán, C. 2001. *Sociolingüística y pragmática del español* (Georgetown University Press, Washington DC)

Zagona, K. 2002. *The Syntax of Spanish* (Cambridge University Press, Cambridge)

11

Portuguese

Stephen Parkinson

1 Introduction

Portuguese, the national language of Portugal and Brazil, belongs to the Romance language group. It is descended from the Vulgar Latin of the western Iberian Peninsula (the regions of Gallaecia and Lusitania of the Roman Empire), as is Galician, often wrongly considered a dialect of Spanish.

Portugal originated as a county of the Kingdom of Galicia, the westernmost area of the Christian north of the peninsula, the south having been under Arabic rule since the eighth century. Its name derived from the towns of Porto (Oporto) and Gaia (< *CALE*) at the mouth of the Douro river. As Galicia was definitively incorporated into the Kingdom of Castile and León, Portugal achieved independence under the Burgundian nobility to whom the county was granted in the eleventh century. Alfonso Henriques, victor of the battle of São Mamede (1128), was the first to take the title of King of Portugal. Apart from a short period of Castilian rule (1580–1640), Portugal was to remain an independent state.

The speed of the Portuguese reconquest of the Arabic areas played an important part in the development of the language. The centre of the kingdom was already in Christian hands, after the fall of Coimbra (1064), and many previously depopulated areas had been repopulated by settlers from the north. The capture of Lisbon in 1147 and Faro in 1249 completed the Portuguese Reconquest, nearly 250 years before its Spanish counterpart, bringing northern and central settlers into the Mozarabic (arabised Romance) areas. The political centre of the kingdom also moved south, Guimarães being supplanted first by Coimbra, and subsequently by Lisbon as capital and seat of the court. The establishment of the university in Lisbon and Coimbra in 1288, to move between the two cities until its eventual establishment in Coimbra in 1537, made the centre and south the intellectual centre (although Braga in the north remained the religious capital). The form of Portuguese which eventually emerged as standard was the result of the interaction of northern and southern varieties, which gives Portuguese dialects their relative homogeneity.

For several centuries after the independence of Portugal, the divergence of Portuguese and Galician was slight enough for them to be considered variants of the same language. Galician–Portuguese was generally preferred to Castilian as a medium for lyric poetry until the middle of the fourteenth century. Portuguese first appears as the language of legal documents at the beginning of the thirteenth century, coexisting with Latin throughout that century and finally replacing it during the reign of D. Dinis (1279–1325).

In the fifteenth and sixteenth centuries the spread of the Portuguese Empire established Portuguese as the language of colonies in Africa, India and South America. A Portuguese-based pidgin was widely used as a reconnaissance language for explorers and later as a lingua franca for slaves shipped from Africa to America and the Caribbean. Some Portuguese lexical items, e.g. *pikinini* 'child' (*pequeninho*, diminutive of *pequeno* 'small'), *save* 'know' (*saber*), are common to almost all creoles. Caribbean creoles have a larger Portuguese element, whose origin is controversial – the Spanish-based Papiamentu of Curaçao is the only clear case of large-scale relexification of an originally Portuguese-based creole. Brazilian Portuguese (BP), phonologically conservative, and lexically affected by the indigenous Tupi languages and the African languages of the slave population, was clearly distinct from European Portuguese (EP) by the eighteenth century. Continued emigration from Portugal perpetuated the European norm beside Brazilian Portuguese, especially in Rio de Janeiro, where D. João and his court took refuge in 1808. After Brazil gained its independence in 1822, there was great pressure from literary and political circles to establish independent Brazilian norms, in the face of a conservative prescriptive grammatical tradition based on European Portuguese.

With approaching 200 million speakers in the eight member states of the Comunidade dos Países de Língua Portuguesa (CPLP), Portuguese is reckoned to be the sixth most widely spoken language in the world. It is spoken by 10 million people in Portugal and over 180 million in Brazil (following estimates based on the 2000 census figure of 170 million), and is the official language of Angola, Mozambique, Guiné-Bissau, São Tomé-Príncipe, Cape Verde and East Timor. It is spoken in isolated pockets in Goa, Malacca and Macau, and in expatriate communities in Europe and North America. Portuguese-based creoles are widely found in W. Africa and the Caribbean; Cape Verdean creole notably has official status beside Portuguese.

The standard form of European Portuguese is traditionally defined as the speech of Lisbon and Coimbra. The distinctive traits of Lisbon phonology (centralisation of /e/ to /ɐ/ in palatal contexts; uvular /ʀ/ in place of alveolar /r/) have more recently become dominant as a result of diffusion by the mass media. Unless otherwise stated, all phonetic citation forms are of European Portuguese.

Of the two main urban accents of Brazilian Portuguese, Carioca (Rio de Janeiro) shows a greater approximation towards European norms than Paulista (São Paulo). While the extreme north and south show considerable conservatism, regional differences in Brazilian Portuguese are still less marked than class-based differences; non-standard varieties and informal speech show considerable simplification of inflectional morphology and concord, which has invited comparison with creoles.

2 Phonology

Portuguese orthography (summarised in Table 11.1) is phonological rather than narrowly phonemic or phonetic, assuming knowledge of the main phonological and morphophonemic processes of the language. It also uses a variety of devices to indicate

Table 11.1 Portuguese Orthography

a		/a ɐ/*		lh		/ʎ/
á		/a/ (stressed) *		m	(final)	nasality of preceding vowel*
ã		/ɐ̃/			(elsewhere)	/m/
â		/ɐ/ (stressed) *		n	(final)	nasality of preceding vowel*
ãe		/ɐ̃ĩ/			(elsewhere)	/n/
ão		/ɐ̃ũ/		nh		/ɲ/
b		/b/		ó		/ɔ/(stressed) *
c	(+a, o, u)	/k/		ô		/o/ (stressed) *
	(+i, e)	/s/		o		/o ɔ u/*
ç		/s/		ou		/o/
ch		/ʃ/		õe		/õĩ/
d		/d/		p		/p/
e		/e, (ɐ), ɛ, ɨ, i/*		qu	(+a, o)	/kw/
é		/ɛ/ (stressed) *			(+i, e)	/k/
ê		/e/ (stressed) *		r		/r, ʀ/*
f		/f/		rr		/ʀ/
g	(+a, o)	/g/		s	(final)	/z ʃ ʒ/*
	(+i, e)	/ʒ/			(intervocalic)	/z/
gu	(+a, o)	/gw/			(elsewhere)	/s/
	(+i, e)	/g/		t		/t/
h		silent (but cf. ch, lh, nh)		u		/u/
				v		/v/
i		/i, j/*		x		/ʃ/
j		/ʒ/		z	(final)	/z ʃ ʒ/*
l		/l/			(elsewhere)	/z/

Notes: This table represents European Portuguese pronunciation.

* Marks points (including Brazilian Portuguese variants) explained in the text. ai, au, ei, éi, eu, éu, u, oi, ói, ui represent falling diphthongs. k,w are only found in foreign words. final = word- and syllable-final.

word stress. Final stress is regular (i.e. orthographically unmarked) in words whose final syllable either (a) contains an oral diphthong, one of the nasal vowels /ã õ ĩ ũ õĩ/ or orthographic *ão, i, u, ãe* (as opposed to *am, e, o, em* (*en*), which indicate unstressed final syllables); or (b) ends in *r, l* or *z* (but not *s*, which generally indicates inflectional endings). Otherwise, penultimate stress is regular. Any irregular stress pattern, including all cases of antepenultimate stress, is marked by a written accent. These accents also indicate vowel quality (often redundantly). The circumflex accent ˆ indicates closed vowels [ɐ e o], while the acute accent ´ indicates open vowel qualities [a ɛ ɔ] and is also used to mark stress on *i, u*, which are deemed to have no 'closed' phonetic values. In a few cases these two accents are still used to indicate vowel quality in regularly stressed words (e.g. *três* 'three', *pôde* '(s)he could' vs *pode* '(s)he can', *pó* 'dust') and to distinguish stressed monosyllables from clitics, e.g. *dê* [de] 'give (3-sg. pres. subj.)' vs -*de* [dɨ] 'of'. The grave accent has a very limited use to indicate unreduced atonic vowels (usually /a/). Nasality is indicated either by the til ˜ or by a nasal consonant following the vowel.

Brazilian and Portuguese orthographies have been progressively harmonised by agreements between the respective governments and academies, latterly in 1971 decrees in both countries, in which the distinctively Brazilian convention of marking unpredictable closed mid vowels with the circumflex was abandoned, as part of a rationalisation of the use of accents. The orthographic differences that remain reflect phonological differences between European and Brazilian Portuguese. The most recent agreement on orthographic harmonisation, still to be accepted by all CPLP states, was ratified by the Portuguese government in 2008, amid some controversy.

The vowel system of Portuguese (Tables 11.2 and 11.3) is one of the most complex of the Romance family. Portuguese is rich in monophthongs and (falling) diphthongs, as a result of two developments which set it off from Castilian. There was no diphthongisation of Vulgar Latin /ɛ ɔ/ (compare Cast. *nueve*, Ptg. *nove* < *NOVEM* 'nine', Cast. *diez*, Ptg. *dez* < *DECEM* 'ten'), with the result that the seven-vowel system inherited from Vulgar Latin remains complete. Intervocalic /l/ was effaced, and /n/ fell after nasalising the preceding vowel: these two processes, in addition to the deletion of intervocalic /d g/, resulted in Old Portuguese being characterised by large numbers of sequences of vowels in hiatus: e.g. *BONUM* > *bõo* 'good', *MALUM* > *mao* 'bad', *MOLINUM* > *moĩo* 'mill', *PEDEM* > *pee* 'foot'. Many of these hiatuses were resolved as monophthongs or falling diphthongs: *pee* > *pé*; *bõo* > *bõ*; *mao* > *mau*. Nasal vowels in unresolved hiatuses were denasalised (*BONAM* > *bõa* > *boa* 'good (f.)'; **PANATARIUM* > *pãadeiro* > *paadeiro* > *padeiro* 'baker') except for the sequences [ĩo], [ĩa] where the hiatus was broken by a palatal nasal glide [j̃] which subsequently developed into the nasal [ɲ], e.g. *moinho* [muˈiɲu] < *moĩo*. The effacement of intervocalic /l n/ has been morphologised, in the inflection of nouns and adjectives with root-final /l/ e.g. *azul* 'blue', plural *azuis*, and in derivational morphology, partly as

Table 11.2 Portuguese Vowels

Monophthongs						
i	ĩ	(ɨ)	u	ũ		High
e	ẽ		o	õ		High mid
ɛ		(ẽ) ɐ	ɔ			Low mid
		a				Low

Diphthongs	Front			Central			Back		
iu							ui		ũĩ
eu	(ei)	ẽĩ				(ou)		oi	õĩ
ɛu	(ɛi)		ɐi	ẽĩ				ɔi	
			ai	au	ẽũ				

Table 11.3 Atonic Vowel Systems

	EP			BP		
Final (including clitics)						
	ɨ	u		i		u
	ɐ				a (= [ɐ])	
Non-final	i	ɨ	u	i		u
		(o)		e		o
	(ɛ)	ɐ	(ɔ)			
	(a)				a	

the result of the introduction of unevolved forms: *céu* 'heaven, sky' (< *CAELUM*) corresponds to *celeste* 'heavenly'; *fim* [fĩ] 'end' (< *FINEM*) to *final* 'final'; beside *irmão* 'brother' there is a familiar form *mano* (borrowed from Castilian *hermano*).

The phoneme /ɐ/ is only found in the European Portuguese system, and there in a marginal role. In Brazilian Portuguese, [ɐ] represents a range of allophones of /a/ in post-tonic position and in nasal contexts; in European Portuguese, [ɐ] is likewise tied to atonic and nasal contexts, but the exclusion of [a] from the same contexts is not absolute, leading to occasional contrasts not found in Brazilian Portuguese, e.g. *nação* [nɐ'sẽu] 'nation' vs *ação* [a'sẽũ] 'action'; *a* (preposition, f. sg. def. art.) [ɐ] vs *à* (*a* + *a*) [a]; *-amos* (1 pl. pres. indic., 1st conjug.) -['ɐmuʃ] vs *-ámos* (ibid., pret.) -[amuʃ]; *casa suja* ['kazɐ'suʒɐ] 'dirty house' vs *casa azul* ['kaza'zul] 'blue house'. In Lisbon, [ɐ] is found preceding the palatal consonants [ʃ ʒ ʎ ɲ] where other accents have /e/, and the diphthongs /ɐi/ and /ẽĩ/ correspond to /ei ɛi/ and /ẽĩ/ in other accents.

Of the large inventory of phonemic diphthongs (ignoring those phonetic diphthongs arising by vowel contraction) most have a limited distribution. /ũĩ/ is found only in *muito* 'much, many' (and is often realised as [wĩ]); /iu/ is only found in preterit forms of third conjugation verbs; /ɛu/, /ɛi/, ẽĩ/, /ẽũ/, /ẽĩ/, /ui/, /õĩ/ and /ɔi/ are found almost exclusively in stem-final position, and are closely associated with inflectional patterns. /ẽĩ/ (Lisbon /ẽĩ/) is a word-final variant of /ẽ/, as can be seen from the doublet *cento* 'hundred' [sẽtu], *cem* 'hundred' [sẽĩ], and also occurs preceding inflectional *-s: nuvem* 'cloud' ['nuvẽĩ] plural *nuvens* ['nuvẽĩʃ]. (The orthographic change of *m* to *n* is without phonetic significance.) In many dialects there is a distinction between /ẽĩ/ and the relatively uncommon /ẽĩ/: *quem* 'who' /kẽĩ/ vs *cães* 'dogs' /kẽĩʃ/. In Lisbon the centralisation of /ẽ/ eliminates the distinction by realising all cases of /ẽĩ/ as /ẽĩ/. Some dialects retain the diphthong /ou/ distinct from /o/ (European Portuguese has evidence for a morphophonemic /ou/, in cases of unreduced atonic /o/). In Brazilian Portuguese, the vocalisation of postvocalic /l/ creates a new series of falling diphthongs, e.g. *sol* 'sun' [sɔu] (BP) [sɔl] (EP).

The vowel system is further complicated by a regular alternation of high vowels (/i u/), low mid vowels (/ɛ ɔ/) and high mid vowels (/e o/) inside verbal paradigms. The alternation is found in the second and third conjugations, where root-final mid vowels are realised as /e o/ (2nd conjug.) or /i u/ (3rd conjug.) in the first person singular present indicative, and the whole of the present subjunctive (which always takes its stem form from the first person singular present indicative) but as /ɛ ɔ/ in the remaining root-stressed forms of the indicative (2 sg., 3 sg., 3 pl.). Thus *meter* 'put' (see the chart of verb forms) has present indicative forms ['metu] (1 sg.), ['mɛtɨ] (3 sg.), and *servir* 'serve' ['sirvu] (1 sg.), ['sɛrvɨ] (3 sg.). This alternation is known as 'metaphony' in token of its origin in an assimilation of the open root vowel to the theme vowel in the first person singular, where the theme vowel was semi-vocalised and lost, e.g. *SERVIO* > **sirvjo* > *sirvo*. The process has long been morphologised, but can still be analysed as an assimilation in a relatively abstract morphophonemics. It was extended by analogy to some third conjugation verbs where the root vowel was originally a high /i u/ e.g. *fugir* 'to flee'. Vowel alternation is found in a more restricted domain in adjectives and nouns, where it is less easily explicable as assimilation. Adjectives with stem-final /o/, particularly those ending in *-oso* (f. *-osa*) have a closed /o/ in the masculine singular form and open /ɔ/ elsewhere, e.g. *formoso* 'beautiful' [fur'mozu] f. sg. *formosa* [fur'mɔzɐ], pl. [fur'mɔzuʃ], [fur'mɔzɐʃ]. A similar alternation is found in a restricted set of nouns such as *ovo* 'egg', sg. ['ovu] pl. ['ɔvuʃ].

221

Nasal vowels are in contrast with the corresponding oral vowels in open syllables (medial and final): e.g. *mudo* ['mudu] 'dumb' – *mundo* ['mũdu] 'world'; *ri* [ʀi] 'laugh' – *rim* [ʀĩ] 'kidney'. There is no contrast between nasal vowels and sequences of vowel + nasal consonant in this position, nasal vowels being very frequently followed by a more or less consonantal nasal off-glide, e.g. ['mũdu] = [ˈmũndu], so that it is frequently argued that nasal vowels can be analysed phonologically as vowel + nasal consonant sequences. (This analysis is problematic because it cannot easily accommodate nasal diphthongs, and is not easily reconciled with morphophonemic rules relating nasal vowels and nasal consonants.) There is a general phonetic tendency for nasal consonants to cause nasalisation of preceding and following vowels; in Brazilian Portuguese the resulting nasality can be as strong as phonemic nasality. (Historical progressive nasalisation accounts for the nasal vowels of *mãe* 'mother' (< *MATREM*); *muito* (< *MULTUM*); *mim* 'me' (< *MIHI*), *nem* 'nor' (< *NEC*) and for the palatal nasals of *ninho* 'nest' ['niɲu] < *nĩo* < **nio* < *NIDUM* and *nenhum* 'no, not any' < *nẽ ũu* < *NEC UNUM*.)

The open vowels /a ɛ ɔ/, absent from the nasal series, are also excluded from contexts where a nasal consonant follows. This restriction is absolute in Brazilian Portuguese; in European Portuguese it is overridden by morphophonemic processes leading to open vowels (notably metaphony) and by antepenultimate stress. A verb such as *comer* 'eat' shows metaphonic alternations in European but not in Brazilian Portuguese; BP *tônico* 'tonic' corresponds to EP *tónico*.

The morphophonemics of nasal vowels were complicated by a series of changes resulting in the syncretism of the old Portuguese word-final nasal vowels -[ã], -[õ], with -[ãũ] (> [ẽũ]) leading to alternations such as *cão* (sg.) 'dog' (< *cã*) – *cães* (pl.); *razão* (sg.) 'reason' (< *razõ* – *razões* (pl.); *fala* (3 sg. 'speak') – *falam* ['falẽũ] (3 pl.). This phonological change was effectively morphologised when it was obscured by the subsequent reintroduction of final -*õ* and -*ã* by the contraction of -*õo* and -*ãa: bom* < *bõo*, *irmã* < *irmãa* in the fifteenth century.

Stress, (or more precisely, lack of stress) is a major conditioning factor in vowel quality, the range of atonic vowel contrasts being systematically limited, as shown in Table 11.3. There is large-scale neutralisation of vowel quality contrasts in the front and back vowel series, most of all in final syllables, where each series is represented by a single vowel: the front vowels by EP [ɨ], BP [i], the back vowels by /u/. (In European Portuguese atonic final [i] is very rare, and can usually be replaced by [ɨ]: *táxi* 'taxi' ['taksi], ['taks(ɨ)].) Portuguese [ɨ] is a 'neutralisation vowel' rather than an independent phoneme. In this respect it is similar to English [ə]. (The symbol [ə] was once widely used for the Portuguese neutralisation vowel.)

In European Portuguese (and to a lesser extent in Brazilian Portuguese) the rules relating tonic and atonic systems are the source of widespread allomorphic variation in inflectional and derivational morphology: e.g. casa ['kazɐ] 'house', *casinha* [kɐ'ziɲɐ] 'little house', *mora* ['mɔrɐ] '(s)he lives', *morara* [mu'rarɐ] (BP [mo'rarɐ]) '(s)he had lived', *bate* ['batɨ] '(s)he hits', bater [bɐ'ter] 'to hit', *peso* ['pezu] 'weight', *pesar* [pɨ'zar] (BP [pe'zax]) 'to weigh'. In some accents of Brazilian Portuguese similar effects result from a rule of vowel harmony by which pretonic /e o/ are raised to /i u/ when a high vowel (usually /i/) follows, e.g. *dormir* [dux'mix] 'to sleep', *medir* [mi'dʒix] 'to measure'. In European Portuguese there are many 'irregular' forms in which pretonic /a o ɛ ɔ/ appear (hence their appearance in parentheses in Table 11.3). Most are explicable as originating in vowel sequences or diphthongs which were not subject to atonic vowel reduction (as diphthongs and nasals are still exempt): e.g. *pregar* 'preach' [prɛ'gar] <

preegar < *PREDICARE*; *corado* 'red, blushing' [kɔ'radu] < *coorado* < *COLORATUM*; *roubar* 'steal' [ʁo'bar] (EP), [xou'bax] (BP) < OPtg. *roubar*. Other cases of pretonic /ɛ ɔ a/ occur in syllables closed by plosives, e.g. *secção* [sɛk'sẽũ], *optar* [ɔp'tar] 'to choose', where Brazilian Portuguese has open syllables and atonic /e o/: [se'sẽũ], [opi'tax].

Atonic vowels are also involved in a major feature of phrasal phonetics, the contraction of vowels across word boundaries. This most typically takes the form of the fusion of word-final atonic vowels or clitic articles with word-initial vowels or clitics, and results in a wide range of diphthongs and monophthongs: *o uso* 'the custom' /u uzu/, [u:zu]; *uma amiga* 'a friend' /umɐ ɐ'migɐ/, [uma'migɐ]; *é o Pedro* 'it's Pedro' /ɛ u 'pedru/ [ɛu'pedru].

Like English, Portuguese is nominally a free-stress language, with stress being nonetheless predictable in the majority of words, by a complex of grammatical and morphophonological factors. Stress generally falls on the penultimate syllable (or the final syllable, if it is strong, that is, closed by any consonant except inflectional /z/ or containing as its nucleus a diphthong or nasal vowel); in verbs (simple forms) stress falls on the final vowel of the stem, unless this vowel is word-final, when penultimate stress is the rule. It should be noted that the (morpho)phonological regularities of stress placement do not always agree with the orthographic rules previously given. European Portuguese is a clear case of a stress-timed language. Atonic syllables are considerably shorter than tonic ones, the vowels being centralised and raised; [ɨ] and [u] are frequently effaced or reduced to secondary articulation of preceding consonants. Brazilian Portuguese has considerable reduction of atonic final vowels, but otherwise is mainly syllable-timed. This difference in timing is related to syllable structure. Brazilian Portuguese tends towards a simple consonant–vowel structure, allowing few syllable-final consonants, weakening syllable-final /l r/, and breaking medial clusters by vowel epenthesis, e.g. *advogado* 'lawyer' EP [ɐdvu'gadu], BP [adʒivo'gadu]. The epenthetic vowels are often counted as full syllables for metrical purposes. European Portuguese allows more syllable-final consonants (compare EP *facto* 'fact' ['faktu] BP *fato* ['fatu]; EP *secção* [sɛk'sẽũ] BP *seção* [se'sẽũ]) and freely uses them in acronyms (e.g. *CUF* [kuf] *Companhia União Fabril* compared to BP *PUC* ['puki] *Pontifícia Universidade Católica*); large numbers of clusters and syllable-final consonants result from the effacement of European Portuguese atonic [ɨ].

The consonant system, displayed in Table 11.4, is less complex. As in Spanish the contrast between the two 'r' phonemes is neutralised in all except intervocalic position. Elsewhere, /ʁ/ is always found in syllable-initial position; in many Brazilian Portuguese accents /ʁ/ also fills syllable-final positions, invariably filled by /r/ in European Portuguese. This is closely connected to the phonetic realisations of /ʁ/. In European Portuguese /ʁ/ is a strong uvular or post-alveolar trill, its distribution following a well-known Hispanic pattern of strengthening of sonorants in 'strong' syllabic contexts; in Brazilian Portuguese /ʁ/ is realised as a fricative or frictionless continuant, the range of phonetic variants including [h x χ ʁ], and thus occupies the 'weak' syllable-final contexts originally filled by /r/. In both languages syllable-final *r* is subject to further weakening; EP /r/ may be an approximant [ɹ] while BP /ʁ/ is frequently effaced.

The sibilants /s z ʃ ʒ/ are only in contrast intervocalically (inside the word) and word-initially (where /ʃ/ derives mainly from palatalised plosive + lateral clusters, e.g. *chama* 'flame' < *FLAMMA*, *chuva* 'rain' < *PLUVIA*); elsewhere they are subject to complex distributional (or morphophonemic) rules. Before a voiceless consonant or pause, only /ʃ/ (EP) or /s/ (BP) is found; before a voiced consonant only /ʒ/ (EP) or /z/ (BP); before

Table 11.4 Portuguese Consonants

	Bilabial (and Labio-dental)	Dental	Palatal (Palato-alveolar)	Velar	Uvular
Plosives	p	t		k	
	b	d		g	
Fricatives	f	s	ʃ		
	v	z	ʒ		
Nasals	m	n	ɲ		
Laterals		l	ʎ		
Vibrants		r[ɾ]			ʀ
Semi-vowels	(w)		(j)		

a word initial vowel only /z/ (EP and BP). Northern dialects of European Portuguese retain an apico-alveolar series of fricatives (the 's beirão') which was originally distinct from the dental and palato-alveolar series. In all except the most northerly dialects this three-way contrast has been reduced to a binary contrast, between dentals and palato-alveolars in the south and between apico-alveolars and palato-alveolars in the centre, together with the loss of the contrast between palato-alveolar affricate /tʃ/ and the corresponding fricative [ʃ]. Northern dialects show their affinity to Galician by having no contrast between /b/ and /v/.

In many Brazilian Portuguese accents the dental plosives /t d/ are realised as palato-alveolar affricates [tʃ dʒ] when followed by /i/: *o tio de Dino vende um lote* 'Dino's uncle sells a piece of land' [u tʃiu dʒi dʒinu vẽdʒi ũ lɔtʃi].

The semi-vowels /j w/ are marginal phonemes. In most cases [j w] result from the semi-vocalisation of atonic /i u/ in hiatus: *diário* ['djarju] (= [di'ariu]) 'daily', *suar* 'to sweat' [swar] (= [su'ar]), except for a few borrowings (e.g. *iate* 'yacht' [jatɨ]) and /kw gw/ in *quando* 'when', *guarda* 'policeman', which are perhaps best analysed as labialised velars /kʷ gʷ/.

3 Morphology

The basic morphological structure of Portuguese simple verb forms is stem + tense/aspect/mood + person/number. For the present, imperfect and pluperfect indicatives, and the future subjunctive and (regular) imperfect subjunctive, the stem is made up of the root and the theme (conjugation class) vowel (first conjugation /a/; second /e/; third /i/ subject to some morphophonemic variation); the present subjunctive has the same structure with mood indicated by reversed theme vowels (first conjugation /e/, second/third /a/); the remaining tenses employ special stem forms (basic stem + r for the future group; suppletive stem forms for irregular preterits) and idiosyncratic person–number morphs. (It is possible, but not always plausible, to devise abstract underlying forms of a uniform morphological structure for all synthetic forms.) There is a nucleus of irregular verbs resisting easy incorporation in any conjugation; *ser* 'to be', *ir* 'to go', which incorporate forms from more than one Vulgar Latin verb, and *ter* 'to have', *vir* 'to come', *pôr* 'to put', (OPtg. *têer* < *TENERE*, *vĩir* < *VENIRE*, *põer, poer* < *PONERE*) which incorporate nasal root vowels with a variety of realisations. Regular and irregular paradigms of the types described are displayed in the chart of verb forms, tentatively segmented.

Alongside the synthetic past tenses (imperfect, preterit, pluperfect) there exists a series of analytic forms, made up of the auxiliary *ter* and the past participle: perfect, pluperfect and future perfect tenses (indicative and subjunctive) are formed using the present, imperfect and future tense forms of *ter*. (*Ter* has replaced *haver* < *HABERE* not only as auxiliary but also as the verb of possession; in Brazilian Portuguese even the existential *há* 'there is', *havia* 'there was', etc. has been taken over by forms of *ter: tem* (present), *tinha* (imperfect). Only in the pluperfect are the synthetic and analytic forms equivalent, though the former is rarely used in colloquial registers.) The (synthetic) preterit is aspectually complex. It is a non-durative past tense, in opposition to the durative imperfect; it can also have the value of a present perfect (*o que se passa? – morreu o meu pai* 'what's the matter? – my father has died') because the (analytic) perfect tense represents only continued or repeated action in the near past (*tenho tomado banho todos os dias* 'I've been bathing every day'). The perfect subjunctive, however, is a genuine present perfect: *não é possível que ele tenha feito isso*, 'he cannot have done that' (lit. 'it is not possible that he has done that'). The perfect and pluperfect subjunctives have no synthetic form. There is a wide range of periphrastic verbal expressions (which traditional grammar does not clearly distinguish from verb complementation structures) expressing temporal, modal and aspectual values: *estar* + *-ndo* (present participle) (progressive); *ir* + infinitive (future); *haver de* + infinitive (predictive/obligative); *ter que* + infinitive (obligative); *ficar* + present participle (resultative). In European Portuguese the constructions with the present + participle are interchangeable with constructions with *a* + infinitive.

The future and conditional still retain a mark of their origin in analytic forms incorporating the auxiliary *(h)aver*; clitic pronouns are mesoclitic – affixed between stem and ending – e.g. *amar-me-á* '(s)he will love me'. (This feature is not found in Brazilian Portuguese, where either the pronoun is proclitic to the whole verb form or an alternative verb form is used.)

Two noteworthy morphological peculiarities of Portuguese are the retention of a future subjunctive form and the appearance of an infinitive inflected for person/number. (In neither is it unique in the Romance sphere: Old Castilian had the former, and Sardinian is reported to have the latter. Only in Portuguese do both appear, with a close link between them.) In regular verbs the forms are identical (though possibly of different structure, cf. the chart of verb forms). In irregular verbs the future subjunctive uses the strong preterit stem, instead of the infinitive stem, betraying its origin in the Latin future perfect indicative (*FABULARINT* > *falarem: DIXERINT* > *disserem*). The origin of the personal infinitive is less clear: its form derives from the Latin imperfect subjunctive (*FABULARENT* > *falarem, DICERENT* > *dizerem*), but its use (see Section 4) is a Galician–Portuguese innovation.

Gender and number are the only two grammatical categories relevant to noun and adjective inflection. Singular number is unmarked; plural is marked by *-s* (morphophonemic /z/ realised as /s z ʃ ʒ/ according to the sibilant system) with a number of consequent stem alternations in roots with final consonants (e.g. *flor-flores* 'flower(s)'; *raiz–raízes* 'root(s)'; *sol–sóis* 'sun(s)'; *pão–pães* 'loaf, loaves'). Nouns are classified by gender as masculine or feminine, grammatical gender usually correlating with natural gender, with a few exceptions, e.g. *cônjuge* (m.) 'spouse'; *criança* (f.) 'child'. Stem-final /u/ usually corresponds to masculine gender, stem-final /a/ to feminine; other endings

225

can correspond to either gender, e.g. *amor* (m.) 'love', *cor* (f.) 'colour'; *rapaz* (m.) 'lad', *paz* (f.) 'peace'; *estudante* (m. and f.) 'student'. Similar patterning is found in adjectives, except that the lack of a gender suffix is more frequently a mark of masculine gender, in opposition to the regular feminine suffix /a/: e.g. *inglês–inglesa* 'English', as it is in animate nouns, e.g. *professor–professora* 'teacher'. (There is a tendency to extend this pattern to nouns ending in *-e:* in popular speech the feminine counterpart of *estudante* is *estudanta*, following the pattern of *monge* (m.) 'monk' *monja* (f.) 'nun'.)

Portuguese Verb Forms
Regular verbs

	falar 'speak'		*meter 'put'*		*partir 'depart'*	
Present indicative	fal-o (a+u)	fala-mos	met-o (e+u)	mete-mos	part-o (i+u)	parti-mos
	fala-s	(fala-is)	mete-s	(mete-is)	parte-s	(partís (i+i))
	fala	fala-m	mete	mete-m	parte	parte-m
Imperfect indicative	fala-va	falá-vamos	meti-a	metí-amos	parti-a	partí-amos
	fala-vas	etc.	meti-as	etc.	parti-as	etc.
Pluperfect indicative	fala-ra	falá-ramos	mete-ra	metê-ramos	parti-ra	partí-ramos
	fala-ras	etc.	mete-ras	etc.	parti-ras	etc.
Imperfect subjunctive	fala-sse	falá-ssemos	mete-sse	metê-ssemos	parti-sse	partí-ssemos
	etc.		etc.		etc.	
Present subjunctive	fal-e (a+e)	fal-emos	met-a (e+a)	met-amos	part-a (i+a)	part-amos
	fal-es	(fal-eis)	met-as	(met-ais)	part-as	(part-ais)
	fal-e	fal-em	met-a	met-am	part-a	part-am
Future subjunctive	fala-r	fala-rmos	mete-r	mete-rmos	parti-r	parti-rmos
	fala-res	(fala-rdes)	mete-res	(mete-rdes)	parti-res	(parti-rdes)
	fala-r	fala-rem	mete-r	mete-rem	parti-r	parti-rem
Infinitive	falar	falar-mos	meter	meter-mos	partir	partir-mos
	falar-es	(falar-des)	meter-es	(meter-des)	partir-es	(partir-des)
	falar	falar-em	meter	meter-em	partir	partir-em
Future	falar-ei	falar-emos	meter-ei	meter-emos	partir-ei	partir-emos
	falar-ás	(falar-ais)	etc.		etc.	
	falar-á	falar-ão	etc.		etc.	
Conditional	falar-ia	falar-íamos	etc.		etc.	
Present participle	fala-ndo		mete-ndo		parti-ndo	
Past participle	fala-do		meti-do		parti-do	
Preterit (regular)	falei (a+i)	fala-mos	meti (e+i)	mete-mos	parti (i+i)	parti-mos
	fala-ste	(fala-stes)	mete-ste	(mete-stes)	parti-ste	(parti-stes)
	falou (a+u)	fala-ram	mete-u	mete-ram	parti-u	parti-ram

Irregular verbs

	estar 'be'		*dizer 'say'*		*poder 'be able'*	
Preterit	estive	estive-mos	disse	disse-mos	pude	pude-mos
	estive-ste	(estive-stes)	disse-ste	(disse-stes)	pude-ste	(pude-stes)
	esteve	estive-ram	disse	disse-ram	pôde	pude-ram
Pluperfect	estive-ra	estivé-ramos	disse-ra	dissé-ramos	pude-ra	pudé-ramos
Future subjunctive	estive-r	estive-rmos	disse-r	disse-rmos	pude-r	pude-rmos
		etc.		etc.		etc.
Imperfect subjunctive	estive-sse	estivé-ssemos	disse-sse	dissé-ssemos	pude-sse	pudé-ssemos
		etc.		etc.		etc.

The determiner system includes definite and indefinite articles (the former identical to weak direct object pronouns (see the chart of pronouns), the latter, *um*, f. *uma* identical in the singular to the numeral *um* '1') and a three-term demonstrative system, *este* 'this' (first person) *esse* 'that' (second person) *aquele* 'that' (third person) parallel to the adverbs *aqui*, 'here' *aí*, 'there', *ali* 'over there', and containing a separate series of indefinite (but not, strictly speaking, neuter) demonstrative pronouns *isto*, *isso* and *aquilo*.

The Portuguese pronoun systems are displayed in the chart given here. Modern Portuguese distinguishes weak (clitic) pronouns from strong pronouns: the former are used as verbal objects, the latter as subjects or prepositional objects. The pronoun system has been radically affected by the development of the address system.

Portuguese Pronouns

	Strong Pronouns		*Weak Pronouns*	
	Subject	Object	Dir. Obj.	Indir. Obj
1 sg.	eu	mim (OPtg. mi)	me	me
2 sg.	tu	ti	te	te
3 sg. (address)	ele (m.), ela (f.)	ele, ela	o (m.), a (f.)	lhe
	você	você, si		
	o senhor (etc.)	o senhor		
1 pl.	nós	nós	nos	nos
(2 pl.	vós	vós	vos	vos)
3 pl. (address)	eles, elas	eles, elas	os, as	lhes
	vocês	vocês, si		
	os senhores	os senhores		

Portuguese maintains a highly structured system of address forms which has been compared to the honorific systems of oriental languages. Second person plural forms are no longer used except in a religious or highly formal ceremonial context (and accordingly appear in parentheses in the charts of verb forms and pronouns). Second person singular forms are used for familiar address in European Portuguese (and conservative Brazilian Portuguese dialects): otherwise, third person verb forms, with the pronoun *você(s)* or the partly pronominal *o senhor* (m.), *a senhora* (f.) are used for all formal (and plural) address in European Portuguese and all address in Brazilian Portuguese. In addition, a wide range of titles can be used as address forms, e.g. *o pai* 'father', *o senhor doutor* 'Doctor', *a avó* 'grandmother', etc., with third person verb forms. Accordingly, third person object pronouns *o(s)*, *a(s)*, have also acquired second person reference. Brazilian Portuguese has been resistant to this: there is a tendency for *lhe*, exclusively used as an indirect object in European Portuguese, to be used for second person functions. Alternatively, the second person object pronoun *te* is used even where the corresponding subject pronoun and verb forms are missing, or else weak forms are avoided altogether: *eu vi ele* 'I saw him', *eu vi você* 'I saw you'.

4 Syntax

The basic word order of Portuguese simplex sentences is subject–verb–object (SVO): *o gato comeu a galinha* 'the cat ate the hen'. (All of the features of VO typology identified in the chapter on Spanish (page 212) are equally applicable to Portuguese.) In the absence of any morphological case marking, word order indicates grammatical subjects and objects, and is little varied. The order VS is very common with intransitive verbs, especially those of temporal or locative content: *chegou o domingo* 'Sunday came'; *apareceu um homem no jardim* 'a man appeared in the garden', reflexives, *libertaram-se os escravos* 'the slaves freed themselves' (or 'the slaves were freed'), and in sentences with heavy subject clauses, *entraram dois homens gordos e um rapaz loiro* 'two fat men and a fair-haired boy came in'. This is closely related to the principle of thematic organisation which specifies that new information is placed at the end of sentences for maximum prominence. Noun phrases may be dislocated for the purposes of topicalisation: *comeu a galinha, o gato* (VOS), though objects cannot be preposed without a pronoun copy (cf. the discussion in the chapters on French and Rumanian, page 190): *a galinha, o gato comeu-a* (OSVPron), *a galinha, comeu-a o gato* (OVPronS). Topicalisation is more usually by varieties of cleft or pseudo-cleft constructions: *foi a galinha que o gato comeu, foi o gato que comeu a galinha* (clefting); *o que comeu a galinha foi o gato*; *o que o gato comeu foi a galinha* (normal pseudo-cleft); *o gato comeu foi a galinha* (elliptical pseudo-cleft) including the emphatic use of *é que: o gato é que comeu a galinha*.

Word order changes are not greatly used for other grammatical functions. Interrogation is by intonation (*o seu pai está aqui?* lit. 'your father is here?'), or by tag question (*o seu pai está aqui, não é?* 'your father is here, isn't he?'). In non-polar questions inversion is the rule in EP after non-pronominal interrogatives: *quando morreu o seu pai?* lit. 'when died your father?', *onde mora você?* 'where live you?' (the same order being possible in noninterrogative subordinate clauses: *quando morreu o seu pai, o que é que você fez?* 'when your father died, what did you do?'); normal SVO order can still be preserved by use of the *é que* periphrasis: *quando é que o seu pai morreu?* BP more generally preserves SVO order: *quando seu pai morreu? onde você mora?* As the interrogative pronouns *quem* 'who(m)', *o que* 'what' have no case marking, inversion is avoided and the *é que* form used in object interrogation: *o que (é que) matou a galinha?* 'what killed the hen?', *o que é que o gato matou?* 'what did the cat kill?'. Replies to yes–no questions take the form of an echo of the main verb: *(você) tem lume? – tenho (sim)/ não tenho*, 'do you have a light?' – '(yes) I have/no I have not' (the appropriate response to an *é que* question being *é* or *não é*.)

The principal means of negation is the negative particle *não* inserted before the verb (or the auxiliary, in the case of an analytic form). Multiple negation occurs with additional negative elements following the verb: when they precede it, *não* is not inserted: *não veio ninguem = ninguem veio* 'nobody came'; *não fiz nada = nada fiz* 'I did nothing'. The indefinite *algum* 'some' may be used as an emphatic negative; *não vi nenhum homem* 'I didn't see any man', *não vi homem algum* 'I didn't see any man whatsoever'. (*Nada* is rarely used as a subject, and may be used as an adverb *não gostei nada da comida* 'I didn't like the meal at all'.)

Aspectual contrasts are behind the distinction between the copular and auxiliary verbs *ser* and *estar* (see Chapter 10, page 264). *Ser* (< *ESSERE/SEDERE*) is used in non-progressive (stative) expressions and *estar* (< *STARE*) in progressive expressions (including its use as the auxiliary for progressive verb forms). In the majority of cases the aspectual value is expressed by (or inherent in) the context, so that the choice of verb is conditioned rather than contrastive: *o João é bombeiro* 'João is (**ser**) a fireman', *o Pedro está zangado* 'Pedro is (**estar**) angry'; *o João é um desempregado* 'João is (permanently) unemployed', *o Pedro está desempregado* 'Pedro is unemployed'; *o João é esquisito* 'João is an awkward person', *o Pedro está (sendo) esquisito (hoje)* 'Pedro is (being) awkward (today)'. For expressing location, the aspectually neutral verb *ficar* is more often used: *onde fica o Turismo?* 'where is the Tourist Office?'

Ser functions as auxiliary for the passive construction: *a casa foi construída por J.Pimenta*, 'the house was built by J. Pimenta'. There is a good case for analysing the passive as a copula + adjective (passive participle) construction. The alternative copula can be used to form passives, *a casa está cercada por soldados* 'the house is surrounded by soldiers'. Where verbs maintain two forms of the past participle, e.g. *prendido, preso* from the verb *prender* 'to arrest', the strong form is usually used as passive participle and the weak form as an active participle. Frequently used alternatives to the passive are the reflexive passive (common in the Romance languages), *aqui alugam-se quartos* 'rooms are let here', and the impersonal construction using *se* as marker of an indefinite subject, with third person singular verb forms, *aluga-se quartos aqui* (cf. the discussion in the chapter on Spanish, page 213–214).

The extensive set of verb forms outlined in Section 3 is rarely utilised in spoken forms of Portuguese. The present indicative is used in place of the future (*se tiver tempo, falo com você* 'if I have time I (will) talk with you'). The imperfect indicative replaces the conditional both in temporal and modal functions: *eu disse que vinha* … 'I said I would come', *eu queria perguntar* … 'I would like (lit. 'wanted') to ask …'.

As in Spanish, the subjunctive mood occupies a less central position, especially in spoken registers. Its use is determined by a complex of grammatical and semantic factors, so that any attempt to define its 'meaning' must come to terms with the fact that it is rarely independently meaningful. The subjunctive is used to the exclusion of the indicative in a wide range of subordinate clauses: *se ele viesse, não o cumprimentaria* 'if he came, I would not greet him', *que os meninos bebam vodka não me aflige* 'I'm not worried about the children drinking vodka', *chamei para que ela me ajudasse* 'I called for her to help me', *grito sem que me ouçam* 'I shout without them hearing me'. The indicative only appears in subordinate clauses expressing real events: the subjunctive has thus been characterised negatively as the mood of suspension of reality. Only in a few rather recondite cases, however, does the context permit a contrast of indicative and subjunctive, so that the subjunctive form can carry all the connotations of irreality. Contrasts like *gritei de maneira que me ouviram* 'I shouted so that they heard me' vs *gritei de maneira que me ouvissem* 'I shouted so that they should hear me' are not the stuff of normal colloquial speech. In spoken Portuguese the present subjunctive is frequently replaced by the indicative.

The most vital subjunctive form is the one whose use is most restricted, namely the future subjunctive. It is used in temporal or conditional clauses with future reference (not necessarily expressed by a main verb in the future tense): *quando vier o pai, teremos comida* (future)/*avisa-me* (imperative)/*vou-me embora* (present), 'when Father comes we will have some food/tell me/I'll go away'. In some registers it is the only non-past verb form used with *se* and *quando*.

One of the main functions of the personal infinitive is to circumvent problems of mood. Being a verb form marked only for person/number it is used where contrasts of tense and mood are (or can be) neutralised, but where the non-identity of the subjects of the main and subordinate clauses would otherwise require a finite verb form (and the selection of an appropriate tense/mood). Many of the preceding examples can be recast using the personal infinitive: *não me aflige os meninos beberem vodka*; *chamei para vires*; *grito sem me ouvirem*; *gritei de maneira de eles me ouvirem*. The usage of the personal infinitive (vis-à-vis the plain infinitive) cannot be precisely defined because of a tendency to use personal and impersonal infinitives indiscriminately with overt subjects, following the widespread belief that extensive use of the personal infinitive is a mark of good style. (The fact that in the first and third persons singular the forms are identical is an additional problem for description.)

In EP subject pronouns are duplicated by verb inflection and are frequently omitted, especially in the unambiguous first and second person forms. Third person forms are more ambiguous. The use of third person grammatical forms as the main form of address restricts the omission of pronouns to clear cases of anaphora or address. Otherwise, subjectless third person verbs are interpreted as having indefinite subjects *é horrível* 'it is terrible', *dizem que é proibido* 'they (people) say that it is forbidden'. In BP subject pronouns are more frequently included, and subjectless verbs can be interpreted as medio-passives: *ele é horrível* 'it (he) is terrible', *diz que é proibido* 'it is said to be forbidden'.

Weak object pronouns are usually enclitic to the verb in European Portuguese and proclitic in Brazilian Portuguese: *o pai deu-me um bolo* (EP), *o pai me deu um bolo* (BP) 'Father gave me a cake'. In written Brazilian Portuguese, as in European Portuguese, sentence-initial clitics are excluded, but this does not hold for spoken Brazilian Portuguese. In both varieties the clitic will invariably precede the verb if any item except a lexical subject noun phrase precedes; negatives, subordinating conjunctions, notably *que*, relative pronouns, interrogative pronouns and (in literary language) preposed adverbs all trigger clitic attraction, e.g. *não me deu o bolo* 'he did not give me the cake', *se me der o bolo* 'if he gives (fut. subj.) me the cake', *quero que me dê o bolo* 'I want him to give me the cake'.

5 Lexicon

The main body of the Portuguese lexicon is predictably of Latin origin, either by direct transmission through Vulgar Latin or as a result of borrowing at some stage of the language's history. The same Latin etymon can thus surface in several different phonetic and semantic guises: *ARTICULUM* was the source for OPtg. *artelho* 'ankle', modern *artigo* (< *artigoo*) 'article' and *artículo* 'joint'; in the fifteenth century *flor* 'flower' was reborrowed to replace the older *frol* and *fror* (< *FLOREM*).

Portuguese shows a typical Iberian conservatism of vocabulary, preserving Latin terms which French and Italian replaced: *queijo* 'cheese' < *CASEUM* (cf. Castilian *queso*, Rumanian *caş*); *uva* 'grape' (cf. Fr. *fromage*, *raisin*). Portuguese is alone in maintaining unchanged the old Christian denominations of days of the week: after *domingo* 'Sunday', first day of the week, come the weekdays numbered two to six: *segunda-feira* (< *FERIAM SECUNDAM*), *terça-feira*, *quarta-feira*, *quinta-feira*, *sexta-feira* until *sábado* ushers in the weekend. (The weekdays are often reduced to their number, *chegará na quinta* 'he will arrive on Thursday'.)

Portuguese shares the common Romance and Ibero-Romance heritage of pre-Roman Celtic and post-Roman Germanic vocabulary: *barro* 'mud', *veiga* 'plain', *manteiga* 'butter' are Celtic terms shared with Castilian; *guerra* 'war', *guardar* 'guard', *roubar* 'steal', *branco* 'white' are common Germanic items. The Arabic adstrate of the South contributed some 1,000 words to Portuguese, such as *alface* 'lettuce', *arroz* 'rice', *armazém* 'store', *azulejo* 'glazed tile', and many placenames, e.g. *Alfama*, *Algarve*.

The African element is fairly strong in Brazilian Portuguese, particularly in those areas of popular culture and belief with strong African roots: *macumba* 'voodoo ritual', *samba*, *marimba*; *cachimbo* 'pipe' has passed into common European Portuguese usage.

Tupi contributes a large vocabulary of Brazilian Portuguese flora and fauna: *maracujá* 'passion-fruit', *piranha* 'piranha fish'. Contacts with the Far East contributed *chá* 'tea' (borrowed from Mandarin: English *tea* is the Min form); *mandarim* 'mandarin' from Malay *mantri* contaminated by Ptg. *mandar* 'to order'.

Portuguese makes extensive use of derivational suffixes. As well as the common stock of noun- and verb-forming suffixes derived and borrowed from Latin (e.g. *-izar* (verb-forming), *-ismo*, *-ista* (noun-forming), *-ção* (< *-TIONEM*) (nominalising)) there is a large stock of productive and semi-productive suffixes with semantic (rather than grammatical) content, frequently involving emotive as well as referential meaning. Prominent among these are diminutive and augmentative suffixes. The most productive diminutives are *-(z)inho* (feminine *-(z)inha)* and *-(z)ito* (*-(z)ita*): *pedra* 'stone', *pedrinha* 'pebble', *pedrazinha* 'small stone'; *casa* 'house', *casita* 'little house'. These diminutives have connotations of endearment or disparagement (according to situational context) which become prominent when they are applied to humans: *mulher* 'woman', *mulherinha* 'scheming woman'; *avó* 'grandmother', *avozinha* '(dear old) granny', and especially when used to modify adverbs or interjections: *adeus* 'goodbye', *adeusinho* 'bye-bye' (familiar), *devagar* 'slowly', *devagarinho* 'little by little'. Augmentative suffixes have strong pejorative overtones: *mulher* 'woman', *mulherona* 'stout woman'.

A further set of suffixes has a very wide range of meanings (including augmentatives, collectives and instrumentals) such that the suffix can only be taken as signalling the morphological link between the derived form and the base, while the precise meaning of the word is an independent lexical unit: the suffix *ada* is identifiable in *palmada* 'slap' (*palma* 'palm of hand'); *colherada* 'spoonful' (*colher* 'spoon'); *rapaziada* '(gang of) kids' (*rapaz* 'boy'); *marmelada* 'quince conserve' (source of Eng. *marmelade*) from *marmelo* 'quince'; *noitada* 'night out' (*noite* 'night').

In those suffixes with alternative forms incorporating the augment *-z-* (e.g. *-(z)inho*), the unaugmented variant functions as an internal suffix, forming a complex stem which is stressed like simple forms, while the augmented suffix functions as an external suffix, forming compounds in which the base and the suffix both have gender and number markers (the latter being overt only when plural number is realised by stem mutations as well as suffixes, e.g. *pãozinho* 'bread roll', plural *pãezinhos*) and are both stressed. (Similar structure is found in the adverbs formed with *-mente*, e.g. *novamente* [nɔvɐ'mẽtɨ] 'recently, newly' where the suffix is affixed to the feminine form of the adjective *novo* 'new' and the base vowel quality is preserved.) The augmented suffixes thus give a morphological transparency, which is matched by a semantic transparency: forms incorporating internal suffixes are more likely to have unpredictably restricted meanings, e.g. *folha* 'leaf, sheet of paper', *folhazinha* 'small leaf', *folhinha* 'calendar'.

Bibliography

Câmara (1972) is a synchronic and diachronic description by a revered Brazilian linguist. Among reference grammars, Cunha and Cintra (1984), Cuesta and Luz (1971), and Teyssier (1976) are reliable, and Perini (2002) gives good coverage of written and spoken Brazilian Portuguese. Azevedo (2005) is a competent linguistic manual, and Mateus et al. (2003) is a comprehensive linguistic account, weighted towards modern syntax and semantics. Mateus and Andrade (2000) is an eclectic account of Portuguese phonetics and phonology. Teyssier (1982) is a concise history of the language.

References

Azevedo, M.M. 2005. *Portuguese: A Linguistic Introduction* (Cambridge University Press, Cambridge)

Câmara, J. Mattoso. 1972. *The Portuguese Language*, translated by A.J. Naro (University of Chicago Press, Chicago)

Cuesta, P.Vázquez and Luz, M. 1971. *Gramática portuguesa*, 3rd edn, 2 vols (Gredos, Madrid)

Cunha, C. and Cintra, L.F.L. 1984. *Nova gramática do português contemporâneo* (João Sá da Costa, Lisbon)

Mateus, M.H.M.M. and Andrade, E. 2000. *The Phonology of European Portuguese* (Oxford University Press, Oxford)

Mateus, M.H.M.M., Brito, A.M., Duarte, I. and Faria, I.H. 2003. *Gramática da língua portuguesa*, 5th edn (Caminho, Lisbon)

Perini, M.A. 2002. *Modern Portuguese: A Reference Grammar* (Yale University Press, New Haven and London)

Teyssier, P. 1976. *Manuel de langue portugaise (Portugal-Brésil)* (Klincksieck, Paris)

—— 1982. *História da língua portuguesa* (Sá da Costa, Lisbon)

12

Italian

Nigel Vincent

1 Introduction

'Italy', in the words of Count Metternich, 'is a geographical expression.' He might with equal truth have added that Italian is a linguistic expression. While there is now, almost a century and a half after political unification, a fair measure of agreement on the grammar and the morphology and, to a lesser extent, on the phonology and lexis of the standard language as used in the written and spoken media and as taught in schools and to foreigners, it is still far from being the case that Italians speak only, or in many instances even principally, Italian. It is appropriate, therefore, to begin this chapter with a general survey in two dimensions, historical and geographical.

Historically, Italian is clearly one of the modern-day descendants of Latin, but the line of descent is not altogether direct. With the dismemberment of the Roman Empire, the spoken Latin of everyday usage – what has come to be called Vulgar Latin – gradually split into a series of regional vernaculars, whose boundaries are identifiable by bundles of isoglosses in a linguistic atlas. The most important of these, which separates Western (French, Spanish, Portuguese, etc.) from Eastern (Italian, Rumanian, etc.) Romance, cuts right across peninsular Italy to form the so-called La Spezia–Rimini line. Dialects to the north of the line are divisible in turn into Gallo-Italian (Piedmontese, Ligurian, Lombard and Emilian) and Venetian, with the latter sharing some of the properties of other northern dialects and some of the properties of Tuscan. Typical northern traits include the loss of final vowels (*pan* vs st. It. *pane* < Lat. *PANEM* 'bread'), often with devoicing of the resultant final obstruents and velarisation of a nasal; lenition or even loss of intervocalic stops (*-ado* or *-ao* vs *-ato* < *-ATUM* 'past participle suffix'); palatalisation of *-kt-* clusters (*lač* vs *latte* < *LACTEM* 'milk'), and of Cl-clusters (*čatsa* vs *piazza* < *PLATEAM* 'square'); development of front rounded vowels (*čöf* vs *piove* < *PLUIT* 'it rains'), frequent use of subject pronouns, usually derived from the Latin accusative; loss of the synthetic preterit in favour of the present perfect periphrasis; a two-term deictic system; etc. These dialects, then, are often structurally closer to French and Occitan than to the dialects south of the line. The latter may in turn be further subdivided into Tuscan, central (Umbrian and the dialects of northern Lazio and the

Marches) and southern dialects (Abruzzese, Neapolitan, Pugliese, Calabrese, Sicilian). Relevant southern features here are NC > NN (*monno* vs *mondo* < *MUNDUM* 'world', *piommo* vs *piombo* < *PLUMBUM* 'lead'); characteristic patterns of both tonic and atonic vowel development; use of postposed possessives (*figliomo* vs *mio figlio* 'my son'); extensive use of the preterit; etc. A number of features mark off Tuscan from its neighbours: absence of metaphony (umlaut); -V*ri*V- > -V*i*V- (*IANUARIUM* > *gennaio*, cf. *Gennaro*, patron saint of Naples); fricativisation of intervocalic voiceless stops – the so-called *gorgia toscana* 'Tuscan throat' – which yields pronunciations such as [la harta] *la carta* 'the paper', [kaφo] *capo* 'head', [lo θiro] *lo tiro* 'I pull it'; etc.

Such divisions reflect both geographical and administrative boundaries. The La Spezia–Rimini line corresponds very closely both to the Apennine mountains and to the southern limit of the Archbishopric of Milan. The line between central and southern dialects approximates to the boundary between the Lombard Kingdom of Italy and the Norman Kingdom of Sicily, and to a point where the Apennines broaden out to form a kind of mountain barrier between the two parts of the peninsula. The earliest texts are similarly regional in nature. The first in which undisputed vernacular material occurs is the Placito Capuano of 960, a Latin document reporting the legal proceedings relating to the ownership of a piece of land, in the middle of which an oath sworn by the witnesses is recorded verbatim: *sao ko kelle terre, per kelle fini que ki contene, trenta anni le possette parte Sancti Benedicti* 'I know that those lands, within those boundaries which are here stated, thirty years the party of Saint Benedict owned them.' The textual evidence gradually increases, and by the thirteenth century it is clear that there are well-rooted literary traditions in a number of centres up and down the land. These are touched on briefly by the Florentine Dante (1265–1321) in a celebrated section of this treatise *De Vulgari Eloquentia*, but it is the poetic supremacy of his Divine Comedy, rapidly followed in the same city by the achievements of Petrarch (1304–74) and Boccaccio (1313–75), which ensured that literary, and thus linguistic, pre-eminence should go to Tuscan.

There ensued a centuries-long debate about the language of literature – *la questione della lingua* 'the language question', with Tuscan being kept in the forefront as a result of the theoretical writings of the influential Venetian (!) Pietro Bembo (1470–1547), especially his *Prose della volgar lingua* (1525). His ideas were adopted by the members of the Accademia della Crusca, founded in Florence in 1582–3, which produced its first dictionary in 1612 and which still survives as a centre for research into the Italian language. Meanwhile, although the affairs of day-to-day existence were largely conducted in dialect, the sociopolitical dimension of the question increased in importance in the eighteenth and nineteenth centuries, assuming a particular urgency after unification in 1861. The new government appointed the author Alessandro Manzoni (1785–1873) – himself born in Milan but yet another enthusiastic non-native advocate of Florentine usage – to head a commission, which in due course recommended Florentine as the linguistic standard to be adopted in the new national school system. This suggestion was not without its critics, notably the great Italian comparative philologist, Graziadio Ascoli (1829–1907), and a number of the specific recommendations were hopelessly impractical, but in any case the core of literary usage was so thoroughly Tuscan that the language taught in schools was bound to be similar. Education was, of course, crucial since the history of standardisation is essentially the history of increased literacy. On the most conservative estimate only 2.5 per cent of the population would have been literate in any meaningful sense of the word in 1861, although a more recent and more generous estimate would go as high as 12.5 per cent. The figure had increased to about 91.5 per cent by 1961, the centenary of unification and the thousandth anniversary of the first text. Even so, there is no guarantee that those who can use Italian do so as their normal daily means of communication, and it was only in 1982 that opinion polls recorded a figure of more than 50 per cent of those interviewed claiming that their first language was the standard rather than a dialect. Yet the opposition language/dialect greatly oversimplifies matters. For most speakers it is a question of ranging themselves at some point of a continuum from standard Italian through regional Italian and regional dialect to the local dialect, as circumstances and other participants seem to warrant. Note too that the term dialect means something rather different when used of the more or less homogeneous means of spoken communication in an isolated rural community and when used to refer to something such as Milanese or Venetian, both of which have fully fledged literary and administrative traditions of their own, and hence a good deal of internal social stratification.

Another significant factor in promoting a national language was conscription, first because it brought together people from different regions, and second because the army is statutorily required to provide education equivalent to three years of primary school to anyone who enters the service illiterate. Indeed, it is out of the analysis of letters written by soldiers in the First World War that some scholars have been led to recognise *italiano popolare* 'popular Italian' as a kind of national substandard, a language which is neither the literary norm nor yet a dialect tied to a particular town or region. Among the features which characterise it are: the extension of *gli* 'to him' to replace *le* 'to her' and *loro* 'to them', and, relatedly, of *suo* 'his/her' to include 'their'; a reduction in the use of the subjunctive in complement clauses, where it is replaced by the indicative, and in conditional apodoses, where the imperfect subjunctive is replaced by the conditional, and the pluperfect subjunctive is replaced by either the conditional perfect or the imperfect indicative (thus standard *se fosse venuto, mi avrebbe aiutato* ('if he had come he would have helped me') becomes either *se sarebbe venuto, mi avrebbe aiutato* or *se veniva, mi aiutava*, the latter having an imperfect indicative in the protasis too; the use of *che* 'that' as a general marker of subordination; plural instead of singular verbs after nouns like *la gente* 'people'. Some of these uses – e.g. *gli* for *loro*, the reduction in the use of the subjunctive and the use of the imperfect in irrealis conditionals – have also begun to penetrate upwards into educated colloquial usage, and it is likely that the media, another powerful force for linguistic unification, will spread other emergent patterns in due course. Industrialisation, too, has had its effect in redrawing the linguistic boundaries, both social and geographical.

In addition to the standard language, the dialects and the claimed existence of *italiano popolare*, there are no less than eleven other languages spoken within the peninsula and having, according to one recent but probably rather high estimate, a total of nearly 2.75 million speakers. Of these, more than two million represent speakers of other Romance languages: Catalan, French, Friulian, Ladin, Occitan and Sardinian. The remaining languages are: Albanian, German, Greek, Serbo-Croat and Slovene. Amidst this heterogeneity, the Italian national and regional constitutions recognise the rights of four linguistic minorities: French speakers in the autonomous region of the Valle d'Aosta (approx. 75,000), German speakers in the province of Bolzano (approx. 225,000), Slovene speakers in the provinces of Trieste and Gorizia (approx. 100,000), Ladin speakers in the province of Bolzano (approx. 30,000). Yet French (and Occitan – approx. 200,000) and German speakers outside the stated areas are not protected in the same way. Nor paradoxically are the nearly 800,000 speakers of Friulian, very closely related to Ladin, the two in turn being sub-branches of the Rhaeto-Romance group. The recognised linguistic minorities are, not surprisingly, in areas where the borders of the Italian state(s) have oscillated historically. In contrast, the southern part of the peninsula is peppered with individual villages which preserve linguistically the traces of that region's turbulent past. It is here that we find Italy's 100,000 Albanian, 20,000 Greek and 3,500 Serbo-Croat speakers, as well as a number of communities whose northern dialects reflect the presence of mediaeval settlers and mercenaries.

Sardinia too contains a few Ligurian-speaking villages and 20,000 Catalan speakers in the port of Alghero as evidence of former colonisation. More importantly, the island has almost 1,000,000 speakers of Sardinian, a separate Romance language which has suffered undue neglect ever since Dante said of the inhabitants that they imitated Latin *tanquam simie homines* 'as monkeys do men'. What he was referring to was the way in which Sardinian, both in structure and vocabulary, reveals itself to be the most conservative of the Romance vernaculars. Thus, we find a vowel system with no mergers apart from the loss of Latin phonemic vowel length; an absence of palatalisation of *k* and *g*; preservation of final *s* (with important morphological consequences); a definite article *su*, *sa*, etc. which derives from Latin IPSE rather than ILLE. Old Sardinian also maintained direct reflexes of the Latin pluperfect indicative and imperfect subjunctive. and the language is one of the few not to retain a future periphrasis from Latin infinitive + *HABEO*, using instead a reflex of Latin *DEBERE* 'to have to', e.g. *des essere* 'you will be'. On the lexical side we have *petere* 'to ask', *imbennere* 'to find' (cf. Lat. *INVENIRE*), *domo/domu* 'house', *albu* 'white', etc. (contrast It. *chiedere*, *trovare*, *casa*, *bianco*).

The presence of Italian outside the boundaries of the modern Italian state is due to two rather different types of circumstance. First, it may be spoken in areas either geographically continuous with or at some time part of Italy, as in the independent Republic of San Marino (population 30,000), enclosed within the region of Emilia-Romagna, and in Canton Ticino (population approx. 325,000), the entirely italophone part of Switzerland. Both have local dialects, Romagnolo in San Marino and Lombard in Ticino, as well as the standard language of education and administration. Elsewhere, the historical continuity is reflected at the level of dialect, but with the superimposition of a different standard language. Thus, in Corsica (population approx. 280,000) the dialects are either Tuscan (following partial colonisation from Pisa in the eleventh century) or Sardinian in type, but the official language has since 1769 been French. The same situation obtains for those Italian dialects spoken in the areas of Istria and Dalmatia now part of Slovenia and Croatia.

The second circumstance arises when Italian, or more often Italian dialects, has been carried overseas, mainly to the New World. In the USA about one million Italian speakers constitute the second largest linguistic minority (after Hispano-Americans). They are concentrated for the most part either in New York, where they are mainly of southern origin and where a kind of southern Italian dialectal koine has emerged, and in the San Francisco Bay area, where northern and central Italians predominate, and where the peninsular standard has had more influence. Italian language media include a number of newspapers, radio stations and television programmes. The current signs of a reawakening of interest in their linguistic heritage amongst Italo-Americans are paralleled in Canada and Australia, each with about half a million Italian speakers according to official figures. There were also in excess of three million émigrés to South America, mostly to Argentina, and this has led, on the River Plate, to the development of a contact language with Spanish known as 'cocoliche'. If Italian in the Americas and Australia had its origins in the language of an underprivileged and often uneducated immigrant class, in Africa – specifically Ethiopia and Somalia and until recently Libya – Italian survives as a typical relic of a colonial situation. Ethiopia also has the only documented instance of an Italian-based pidgin, used not only between Europeans and local inhabitants but also between speakers of mutually unintelligible indigenous languages. The position of Italian in Malta is similarly due to penetration at a higher rather than a lower social level. Research is only now beginning into the linguistic consequences of the postwar migration of, again mainly southern, Italian labour as 'Gastarbeiter' in Switzerland and Germany. Finally, two curiosities are the discovery by a group of Italian ethnomusicologists in 1973 in the village of Štivor in northern Bosnia of a community of 470 speakers of a dialect from the northern Italian province of Trento, and the case of a group of émigrés from two coastal villages near Bari in Puglia, who settled in Kerch in the Crimea in the 1860s and whose dialectophone descendants died out only in the late twentieth century.

2 Phonology

One of the consequences of the chequered and fragmented linguistic and political history outlined in the previous section is that at the phonetic and phonological level there has been even less uniformity of usage than at other levels. The conventional starting point for any treatment of Italian phonology is the speech of educated Florentines. Incidentally, most of the letters of the Italian alphabet correspond closely to the IPA value of that symbol, but the following exceptions should be noted: *-gl-* = /ʎ/, *-gn-* = /ɲ/, *sc(i)* = /ʃ/, *s* = /s/ or /z/ (see below on the status of /z/), *z* = /ts/ or /dz/, *c*, *g* = /k, g/ before *a*, *o* and *u*, and /tʃ, dʒ/ before *i* and *e*. The digraphs *ch*, *gh* represent /k, g/ before *i*, *e*, and *ci*, *gi* represent /tʃ, dʒ/ before *a*, *o* and *u*. No orthographic distinction is made between /e/ and /ɛ/ or between /o/ and /ɔ/ although in stressed final position /e/ is represented normally by *é* and /ɛ/ by *è*. Stress is marked only when final, usually by a grave accent (except on /e/); other accent marks used in this chapter are for linguistic explicitness and are not part of the orthography.

Table 12.1 sets out the consonant phonemes usually recognised in the Florentine system. Some comments on points of detail are in order. First, note that for the vast majority of speakers [s] and [z] do not contrast: in initial position before a vowel all speakers have [s], including after an internal boundary as in *ri*[s]*aputo* 'well known' – cf. [s]*aputo* 'known'; [s]*taccato*[s]*i* 'having detached oneself – cf. [s]*taccare* 'to detach'

Table 12.1 Italian Consonant Phonemes

	Bilabial	Labio-dental	Dental	Alveolar		Palato-alveolar	Palatal	Velar
Stop	p b		t d					k g
Affricate				ts dz	tʃ	dʒ		
Fricative		f v		s (z)	ʃ			
Nasal	m			n			ɲ	
Lateral				l			ʎ	
Trill				r				

and [s]*i* '3rd pers. refl. pron.'. Preconsonantally the sibilant takes on the value for voicing of the following segment. Intervocalically, when no boundary is present, northern speakers have only [z] and southern speakers only [s]. However, in parts of Tuscany, including Florence, it is possible to find minimal pairs: *chie*[s]*e* 'he asked' vs *chie*[z]*e* 'churches'; *fu*[s]*o* 'spindle' vs *fu*[z]*o* 'melted'. The opposition between /ts/ and /ʣ/ is also somewhat shaky. In initial position, although both are found in standard pronunciation – /ts/ in *zio* 'uncle', *zucchero* 'sugar', and /ʣ/ in *zona* 'zone', *zero* 'zero', there is an increasing tendency due to northern influence for /ʣ/ to be used in all words. Medially, the two sounds continue to exist side by side, and a few genuine minimal pairs can be found, e.g. *ra*[tts]*a* 'race' vs *ra*[dʣ]*a* 'ray fish'. /ts, ʣ/ share with /ʃ, λ, ɲ/ the property of always occurring long intervocalically, an environment in which for all other consonants there is an opposition between short and long (or single and double): e.g. *copia* 'copy' vs *coppia* 'couple'; *beve* 'he drinks' vs *bevve* 'he drank'; *grato* 'grateful' vs *gratto* 'I scratch'; *vano* 'vain' vs *vanno* 'they go'; *serata* 'evening' vs *serrata* 'lock-out'; etc.

The vowel system is displayed in Table 12.2. /i, u/ have allophones [j, w] in non-nuclear position in the syllable: *più* ['pju] 'more', *può* ['pwɔ] 'he can'.

Table 12.2 The Vowels of Italian

The oppositions /e~ɛ/ and /o~ɔ/ are neutralised outside stress, but even allowing for this their status is problematic, since, although most speakers have the four sounds, the lexical classes and phonological rules which govern their distribution vary widely.

Another important type of neutralisation in Italian phonology is that which affects nasals before consonants and ensures that the whole cluster is homorganic. This is only reflected orthographically in the case of bilabials – hence *campo* 'field', *impossibile* 'impossible', etc., but labio-dentals, dentals, etc., are always spelt *nC*: *inferno* [iɱfɛrno] 'hell', *indocile* [iṇdɔtʃile] 'unmanageable', *incauto* [iŋkauto] 'incautious'. The same process also operates across word boundaries in a fully productive manner: *con Paolo* 'with Paul' [... mp ...] vs *con Carlo* 'with Charles' [... ŋk ...], etc. A morphophonemic process of more limited applicability is the synchronic residue of Romance palatalisation, which is revealed in alternations such as *amico* 'friend (m. sg.)' with *c* = [k] and *amici* 'friends (m. pl.)' with *c* = [tʃ], and *vin*[k]*o* 'I win' but *vin*[tʃ]*i* 'you win'. Note that the *e* which marks feminine plural (< Latin *AE*) does not trigger this process nor does plural *-i* in most nouns, and hence the spellings *amiche* 'friends (f.)', *buchi* 'holes'. *e* as a thematic vowel (see page 241), a direct reflex of the Latin thematic *e*, does; thus *vincere* 'to win', *vince* 'he wins', *vinceva* 'he was winning', all with [tʃ]. The same patterning is also found with the voiced congeners of [k, tʃ], namely [g, ʤ] in the paradigm of a verb such as *volgere* 'to turn'. A further synchronic residue is observable in what are traditionally called *dittonghi mobili* 'mobile diphthongs', as in *buono* 'good' but *bontà* 'goodness', *viene* 'he comes' but *venire* 'to come'. They are the result of a historical process causing the diphthongisation of Latin Ĕ, Ŏ in stressed, open syllables. The pattern is, however, being gradually eroded away by analogical generalisations in both directions, e.g. *suono* 'I play' had a past participle *sonato* but one now more commonly finds *suonato*, whereas *provo* 'I try' has replaced an earlier *pruovo*.

Italian words may consist of one or more syllables and are subject to a general constraint that they be vowel-final. Exceptions to this are certain loanwords (*sport*, *boom*, *slip*, *camion*, etc.), a handful of Latinisms (*lapis* 'pencil', *ribes* 'blackcurrant') and an increasing number of acronyms (*Agip*, *Fiat*). Some grammatical words – e.g. the masculine singular of the definite article *il*, the prepositions *in*, *con*, *per*, the negative particle *non* – have final consonants, but the rules of the syntax will never allow them to appear in sentence-final position. Similarly, there is a vowel truncation rule which deletes final /e/ after /l, r, n/, but only between words in a close syntactic nexus: *volere dire* 'to mean' (lit. 'to want to say') may become *voler dire* but not *volere dir*, even though the latter sequence is possible with a different constituency, e.g. *volere (dir bene di qualcuno)* 'to want (to speak well of someone)'.

Words may begin with either a consonant or a vowel. A word-initial single consonant may be any of those given in Table 12.1, though initial /ɲ/ is rare (*gnomo* 'gnome', *gnocco* 'a kind of dumpling' and a few others) and initial /ʎ/ non-existent in lexical words. However, since the form *gli* /ʎi/ occurs both as the masculine plural of the definite article before vowel-initial nouns (*gli amici* 'the friends') and as the masculine singular dative unstressed pronoun (*gli dissi* 'I said to him'), /ʎ/ in utterance-initial position is very common.

Apart from in borrowings and in technical terms, two-member initial clusters are limited to the following types:

(i)   /p b t d k g f/ + r
(ii) /p b k g f/ + l
(iii) s + /p b t d k g tʃ dʒ f v l r m n/

(Note that /s/ is realised as [z] before voiced consonants – hence not just [zb] in *sbagliare* 'to make a mistake' or [zdʒ] in *sgelo* 'thaw', but also [zl] in *slitta* 'sledge', [zn] in *snello* 'slim', etc. It should also be noted that purists do not admit [stʃ], but it is regularly heard in words where there is a clear morphemic boundary, e.g. *scentrato* 'off centre'.)

Three-member clusters can only consist of /s/ plus any of the possible two-member clusters under (i) or (ii). A non-final syllable may end in /l, r, s/ or a nasal. Examples of such clusters can be created productively by juxtaposing forms such as *il*, *per*, *bis* and *in* with a noun or an adjective, although only a subset of the possible clusters generated in this fashion are attested internally in existing lexical items. An intervocalic cluster may also consist of a geminate consonant, with a syllable boundary between the two: *piop-po* 'poplar', *gof-fo* 'clumsy', *cad-de* 'he fell', *bel-lo* 'beautiful'. Indeed, the evidence of syllable division is one of the principal reasons for treating them as geminates rather than long consonants. Note that in such groups, if the first member is a stop or affricate, it is unreleased, hence such transcriptions as [pat-tso] for *pazzo* 'mad', [fat-tʃa] for *faccia* 'face'.

Tautosyllabic vowel sequences all conform to the pattern of a nuclear vowel followed or preceded, or both, by [j] or [w]: *piano* 'flat' [pjano], *sai* [saj] 'you know'. Otherwise, vowel sequences involve a hiatus between two syllables: *teatro* 'theatre', *poeta* 'poet'. We have both in *laurea* 'university degree' ['law-re-a].

Primary or lexical stress is not predictable on phonological grounds alone, hence such minimal pairs as *princìpi* (plural of *princìpio* 'principle') and *prìncipi* (plural of *prìncipe* 'prince'), or *càpito* 'I turn up', *capìto* 'understood', *capitò* 'he turned up'. There are, however, a number of morphological cues to stress. A third person singular preterit verb form is always final-stressed, while all second person plural forms are penultimately stressed. Such patterns are best described by distinguishing in the morphology between stress-neutral and stress-attracting suffixes. The lexical bases which receive these suffixes may be either penultimately or antepenultimately stressed: *cànta* 'sing' vs *fàbbrica* 'make'. A stress-neutral suffix attached to the latter produces stress four syllables from the end: *fàbbricano* 'they make'. If clitics are attached post-verbally, stress may be made to appear even farther from the end of the word: *fàbbricalo* 'make it', *fàbbricamelo* 'make it for me', *fàbbricamicelo* 'make it for me there'. Underived words, however, can only have stress on one of the last three syllables: *ànima* 'soul', *lèttera* 'letter', *perìodo* 'period'; *radìce* 'root', *divìno* 'divine', *profòndo* 'deep'; *virtù* 'virtue', *caffè* 'coffee', *velleità* 'wish'. Final-stressed words are either loanwords, often from French, or the results of a diachronic truncation: *virtù* < Old Italian *virtude* < Lat. *VIRTUTEM*. Secondary stress is not in general contrastive, but is assigned rhythmically in such a way as to ensure that (a) the first syllable, if possible, is stressed; (b) there are never more than two unstressed syllables in sequence; (c) there are never two adjacent stressed syllables. Apparent minimal pairs have, nonetheless, been adduced such as: ˌauto-reattòre 'auto-reactor' vs *auˌtore-attòre* 'author-actor' (contrasting position of secondary stress); *procùra* 'he procures' vs ˌpró-cùra 'for-care' (two stresses vs one).

Stress interacts with vowel length and the distribution of geminate consonants. Vowels are always short if not primarily stressed, or if followed by a consonant in the same syllable. They are long, therefore, in stressed, open syllables: *ànima* ['aː-ni-ma], *lèttera* ['lɛt-te-ra], *divino* [di-'viː-no], *profondo* [pro-'fon-do]. Final vowels are always short, so that if stressed and in close nexus with a following word, they ought to create a violation of our previously stated principle. Such a situation, however, is avoided by so-called *raddoppiamento sintattico* 'syntactic doubling', whereby the initial consonant of the following word is geminated: *parlò chiaro* 'he spoke clearly' [par-'lɔk-'kjaː-ro]. The double consonant here also seems to act as sufficient barrier to permit two adjacent main stresses. It has recently been pointed out that in the north, where the doubling effect is not found, the first of the two stresses is retracted instead. This doubling also takes place after a number of words which have lost the final consonant they had in Latin: *tre* 'three' < Lat. *TRES*, *a* 'to' < Lat. *AD*, though again this effect is only found south of the La Spezia–Rimini line. *Raddoppiamento*, then, is typical of central and southern speech, and the failure of northern speakers to adopt it mirrors its absence from their own dialects, and explains their tendency to produce only those geminates which the orthography indicates. Indeed, it can be argued more generally that there is emerging in Italy a kind of standardised spelling pronunciation based on the interaction of northern phonetic habits and an orthography which reflects the Florentine origin of the standard language.

3 Morphology

In morphology Italian exhibits a typically Indo-European separation of verbal and nominal inflection, the latter also encompassing pronouns, articles and adjectives.

3.1 The Noun

Nouns inflect for gender – masculine and feminine – and number – singular and plural – according to the following patterns:

Singular	Plural	Gender	
-o	-i	m.	*libro* 'book'; exception *mano* f. 'hand' (< Lat. MANUS f.)
-a	-e	f.	*casa* 'house', *donna* 'woman'
-e	-i	m. or f.	*monte* m. 'mountain', *mente* f. 'mind'
-a	-i	m.	*problema* 'problem' and other words of Greek (*sistema*, *programma*, etc.) or Latin (*artista*, *poeta*, etc.) origin.

Such a system of plural by vowel alternation rather than by suffixing of *-s* is one of the features which marks Italian off from Western Romance languages such as French, Spanish and Portuguese. Nouns which in the singular end in *-i*, e.g. *crisi* 'crisis', in stressed vowels, e.g. *città* 'town', *tribù*, 'tribe' and in consonants, e.g. *sport, camion* 'lorry', are unchanged in the plural. A small class of nouns – e.g. *dito* 'finger', *uovo* 'egg', *lenzuolo* 'sheet' – distinguish between a collective and a non-collective plural: *osso* 'bone', *le ossa* 'bones (together, as in a skeleton)', *gli ossi* 'bones (scattered)'. The synchronically unusual *-a* in the collective plural is a residue of the Latin neuter plural. Note that articles and adjectives going with such nouns are masculine in the singular and feminine in the plural.

Adjectives fall into two principal classes, having either four forms. *buono, -i, -a, -e* 'good' or two: *felice, -i* 'happy' (with a few like *rosa* 'pink' that are uninflected). The four-form pattern also shows up in the unstressed pronoun system: *lo/la/li/le*. In Old Italian these were also the forms of the definite article, but the modern language has a more irregular pattern: m. sg. *lo* only before /ʃ/, s + consonant, and certain other groups, *il* elsewhere; m. pl. *gli* corresponding to *lo* and *i* to *il*; f. sg. *la*; f. pl. *le*. In the case of both articles and pronouns the vowels of the singular forms commonly delete before an initial vowel in the following word.

3.2 The Verb

The chart of verb forms represents the paradigmatic structure of three typical regular verbs exemplifying the three traditional conjugations, each of which is marked by a characteristic thematic vowel, *a, e* or *i*. The chart is organised in such a way as to bring out the four classes of elements in the verbal structure – stem, thematic vowel, tense/aspect/mood markers and person/number markers – whose linear relations are schematically displayed as: STEM + TV + (T/A/M) + P/N. The use of curly brackets seeks to highlight some of the patterns of overlap between the traditional conjugations (at the expense of some non-traditional segmentations), and the numbers here and throughout this section refer to the six grammatical persons, three singular and three plural.

However, a classification of this kind is inadequate in two apparently contradictory respects. On the one hand, it does not allow for a number of further classes which seem to be necessary, for instance to distinguish between two types of *e*-verb according to whether they have stem or ending stress in the infinitive: *crèdere* 'to believe' and *vedère* 'to see' do not rhyme. Historically, in fact, the stem-stressed verbs have in some cases even undergone loss of the theme vowel in the infinitive with attendant consonant deletion or assimilation: Lat. *PONERE, DICERE, BIBERE* > It. *porre, dire, bere.* We also

Finite Forms of Italian Regular Verbs

	1	2	3	4	5	6
Present indicative	cant / tem / sent -o	-i	canta / tem / sent -e	cant / tem / sent -iamo	canta / teme / senti -te	canta / tem / sent -no / -ono
Imperfect	canta / teme / senti -v -o	-i	canta / teme / senti -va / ∅	-mo	-te	-no
Present subjunctive	cant / tem / sent -i / -a	-i / -a	-i / -a	cant / tem / sent -iamo	-iate	cant / tem / sent -i / -a -no
Preterit	canta / teme / senti -i	-sti	cantò / temè / senti	-canta / teme / senti -mmo	-ste	-rono
Past subjunctive	canta / teme / senti -ss -i	-i	-e	-imo	canta / teme / senti -ste	-ss -ero
Future	canter / temer / sentir -ò	-ai	-à	-emo	-ete	-anno
Conditional	-ei	-esti	-ebbe	-emmo	-este	-ebbero

need to recognise two types of *i*-verb, one with the stem augment *-isc-* in persons 1/2/3/6 of the present and one without: *capisco* 'I understand' but *servo* 'I serve', and *partisco* 'I divide' as against *parto* 'I leave'. These latter two verbs have a number of homophonous forms elsewhere in the paradigm: *partiamo, partire, partivo*, etc. On the other hand, a basically tripartite classification fails to capture the generalisation that *e*- and *i*-verbs are a good deal more similar to each other morphologically than either is to *a*-verbs (which constitutes the main open class for new coinings and borrowings). This relationship is particularly noticeable in forms 3/6 of the present indicative, and in the reversal effect whereby the present subjunctive vowel is *-i-* for *a*-verbs and *-a-* for *i/e*-verbs. Hence a better representation of Italian conjugational structure might be as in Figure 12.1.

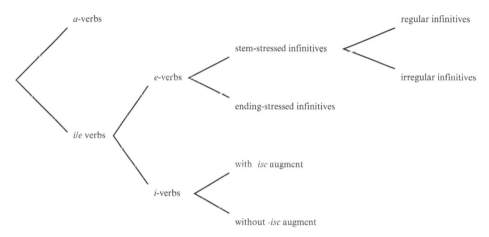

Figure 12.1 A Model of Italian Conjugation Structure

In addition to these finite forms, each verb has a past participle (*cant-a-to, tem-u-to, sent-i-to*) and a gerund (*cant-a-ndo, tem/sent-e-ndo*), which are used both independently and in a number of verbal periphrases (see Section 4 for details of these and of the grammar and meaning of the various finite forms). The present participle formation (*-a/e/ie-nte*) is of more equivocal status since the possibilities for its use are grammatically very circumscribed.

As in any language, there are a number of verbs which fail to conform to the schemata established above, but it would be neither possible nor helpful in the present context to list all such idiosyncrasies. It is, however, of interest to note the ways in which patterns of irregularity intersect with the regular verb paradigms. For example, no verb has any irregularity in the imperfect (except *essere* 'to be', which seems to stand outside all such generalisations), and, again excluding *essere*, only *dare* 'to give' and *stare* 'to be, stand' have irregular past subjunctives (*dessi, stessi* for the expected **dassi, *stassi*). Discrepancies in the future and the conditional (and no verb is irregular in one without having the same irregularity in the other) are due either to the verb already having an exceptional infinitive – *porrò, dirò, farò* – or to the historical effects of syncope on the periphrases from which they derive: *VENIRE + HABEO > verrò, VOLERE + HABUIT > vorrebbe*, etc.

By far the largest number of exceptions, however, are to be found in three parts of the paradigm: the present (indicative and subjunctive), the preterit and the past participle. Of these, the latter two are closely related: very few verbs have an irregular preterit and a regular past participle, and even fewer have an irregular past participle and a regular preterit. The characteristic perturbation in both cases is a reduced stem, which appears in persons 1/3/6 and the participle: e.g. for *prendere* 'to take', we have *preso* (past part.) and *presi* (1), *prese* (3), *presero* (6) vs *prendesti* (2), *prendemmo* (4), *prendeste* (5). The patterns are best accounted for by assuming a base form with no theme vowel (hence no stress on the ending) but in its place a sigmatic preterit marker (ultimately of Indo-European origin but considerably generalised in its applicability in Vulgar Latin). This form, *prend-s-i*, etc., can then be converted into the surface forms by a set of phonotactically motivated rules of consonant cluster reduction and assimilation. The sigmatic form in the participle (e.g. *preso*) is less common, but the regular suffix *-to* will trigger the same effects if not preceded by a theme vowel: e.g. for *assumere* 'to take on', *assumesti* (2), but *assunsi* (1) and *assunto* (past part.). Where the irregular preterit base is due to the Latin *-u-* [u~w] perfect marker (which occurs in the regular participial formation *temuto*, and which also extended considerably in Vulgar Latin), subsequent sound changes have produced a geminate consonant from the earlier [Cw] sequence: *HABUI* > *ebbi* (1) 'I had' (cf. *avesti* (2)), **CADUIT* > *cadde* (3) 'he fell' (cf. *cadesti* (2)). Such verbs, as might be expected, have regular participles: *avuto, caduto.*

There are perhaps 200 verbs whose only irregular formations are in the preterit and the past participle, almost without exception members of the class of *e*-verbs. On the other hand, there are fewer than 50 which are irregular in the present, and they are spread throughout the conjugation classes. We cannot characterise all the patterns here, but once again it is worth noting how the incidence of stress was one of the principal determining factors for these alternations in the diachronic perspective (we have added the accent marks for clarity here, although the normal orthography does not use them). Thus, we find *uscìre* 'to go out' has *èsco* (1), *èsci* (2), *èsce* (3), *èscono* (6), and *èsca (no)* (subj.), but *usciàmo* (4), *uscìte* (5) and *uscìvo* (imperf.), *uscìi* (pret.), etc. For *avère* 'to have', we find (and the *h* here is purely orthographic) *hò* (1), *hài* (2), *hà* (3), *hànno* (6), but *àbbia(no)* (subj.), *abbiàmo* (4) and *avète* (5), *avèvo* (imperf.). Notice too how a verb like *andàre* 'to go' may be suppletive in the stem-stressed forms: *vàdo* (1), *vài* (2), *và* (3), *vànno* (6), *vàda(no)* (subj.), but almost entirely regular elsewhere: *andiàmo* (4), *andàte* (5), *andàvo* (imper.), *andài* (pret.), *andàto* (past part.) – but note the minor irregularity in the future and conditional: *andrò, andrei,* etc. This is also a good example of the way in which a verb may be irregular to the point of suppletion in the present and show few or no ill effects elsewhere in its paradigm.

A number of other exceptional formations involve the morphophonemic processes of diphthongisation and palatalisation discussed in Section 2. Thus, *sedère* 'to sit': *sièdo* (1), *sièdi* (2), *sliède* (3), *sièdono* (6) vs *sediàmo* (4), *sedète* (5); *morìre* 'to die': *muòio* (1), *muòri* (2), *muòre* (3), *muòiono* (6) vs *moriàmo* (4), *morìte* (5) exhibit clearly the effects of the so-called *dittonghi mobili*. Palatalisation is to be seen in *dico* 'I say' where *c* = [k] vs *dici* 'you say' where c = [tʃ].

The conjugation of *essere* is as follows: Present 1 *sono*, 2 *sei*, 3 *è*, 4 *siamo*, 5 *siete*, 6 *sono*. Imperfect 1 *ero*, 2 *eri*, 3 *era*, 4 *eravamo*, 5 *eravate*, 6 *erano*. Present subjunctive 1, 2, 3 *sia*, 4 *siamo*, 5 *siate*, 6 *siano*. Preterite 1 *fui*, 2 *fosti*, 3 *fu*, 4 *fummo*, 5 *foste*, 6 *furono*. Past subjunctive 1, 2 *fossi*, 3 *fosse*, 4 *fossimo*, 5 *foste*, 6 *fossero*. Future 1 *sarò*, etc. Conditional 1 *sarei*, etc. Present participle *essendo*. Past participle *stato*.

Finally with regard to the verb, mention must be made of the system of address. Like many languages, Standard Italian distinguishes between a familiar and a polite style. The former is expressed through the use of the second person singular forms *tu*, *ti*, *tuo* and the imperatives *canta*, *temi*, *senti* (note again the formal overlap of the *i/e*-verbs). The latter requires the deferential pronoun *Lei*, which is grammatically third person singular and is therefore accompanied by clitic *si* and possessive *Suo*. In lieu of the imperative the present subjunctives *canti*, *tema*, *senta* are used. The use of *Lei* goes back to Late Latin, and became widespread due to Spanish influence in the Renaissance. Until quite recently the same distinction could be regularly maintained in the plural with *voi*, *vi*, *vostro* for familiar usage and *Loro* (lit. 'they') as the polite form. The latter is becoming increasingly rare and is now only used in the most formal circumstances – otherwise *voi* serves both functions. *Voi* as a polite singular, on the other hand, is still common in parts of southern Italy, particularly amongst older speakers.

3.3 Suffixes

Italian has an unusually rich range of affective suffixes relating to the size and the speaker's (dis)approval of the object in question. Thus, from *ragazzo* 'boy', we have *ragazzino*, *ragazzetto*, *ragazzuccio* 'little boy', *ragazzone* 'big lad', *ragazzaccio* 'nasty boy, lout', *ragazzotto* 'sturdy lad'. The chief analytical problem is that not all suffixes combine with all nouns, yet no clear rules are discernible for predicting the possible combinations: *-ello* is a diminutive but **ragazzello* cannot be used for 'little boy'. Sometimes too a noun plus suffix has acquired independent status as a lexical item: *pane* 'bread', *panetto* 'small loaf', *panino* 'bread roll' and *panettone* (etymologically containing two contradictory suffixes *-ett-* 'small' and *-one* 'large') refers to a special kind of fruit cake eaten at Christmas. This process is reminiscent of the way certain items of Italian vocabulary are derived from Latin diminutives – e.g. Lat. *AURIS* 'ear', but It. *orecchio < AURICULUM*. These suffixes are most commonly attached to nouns, but can also be used with other categories: adjectives – *facile* 'easy', *facilino* 'quite easy', *caro* 'dear', *caruccio* 'quite expensive' (but note *carino* 'pretty'); adverbs – *bene* 'well', *benone* 'very well', *benino* 'quite well'; verbs – *dormire* 'to sleep', *dormicchiare* 'to snooze', *sputare* 'to spit', *sputacchiare* 'to splutter'.

4 Syntax

We shall concentrate here on aspects which either seem to typify Italian as opposed to other languages, or which have aroused interest amongst syntactic theorists, the two naturally not being unconnected.

4.1 The Nominal Group

Nouns in Italian may be accompanied by articles, definite or indefinite, numerals and quantifiers, demonstratives, possessives and adjectives. Of these, demonstratives and articles have parallel distribution and may be united in a single class of determiners. It is worth noting that only a two-term deictic opposition survives in modern usage, *questo* 'this' vs *quello* 'that'. The often cited third term, *codesto* 'that by you' (cf. Spanish *ese)*, is now limited to Tuscany, and is archaic even there. Possessives behave distributionally more like adjectives than determiners and, except in the case of nouns for close members of the family, never occur unaccompanied by an article or demonstrative: *mio zio* 'my uncle', *la mia macchina* 'my car', *un tuo cugino* 'one of your cousins' (lit. 'one your cousin'), *questi suoi libri* 'these books of his' (lit. 'these his books'). Quantifiers such as *alcuni* 'some', *parecchi* 'several', *pochi* 'few' may also precede the possessive: *parecchi nostri amici* 'several (of) our friends'. This class includes some words which in a different sense follow the noun as independent adjectives: *certe persone* 'a certain number of people' and *certi miei colleghi* 'some of my colleagues', but *persone certe* 'people who are certain', *diversi tuoi professori* 'several (of) your teachers' but *due caratteri diversi* 'two different characters'.

Examples such as these in turn raise one of the central issues of the syntax of the noun phrase in Italian: the function and position of the adjective. It is clear that there are independent pre- and post-nominal positions: *una breve visita* 'a short visit', *una visita turistica* 'a sightseeing visit', *una breve visita turistica* 'a short sightseeing visit'. Three questions arise: are there any constraints on how the two positions may be filled? Can a systematic meaning be attached to each position? Is one position dominant, such that it would make sense to say that Italian had noun-adjective order, say, in the way that typological cataloguing seems to require? Note first that although there is a small class of adjectives where a change of position corresponds to a quite discernible change of meaning, cf. the above examples and others: *un semplice soldato* 'a mere soldier' vs *un soldato semplice* 'a private soldier', *numerose famiglie* 'many families' vs *famiglie numerose* 'large families', most adjectives can occur in either position. Nor is length a decisive factor: the heptasyllabic *interessantissimo* 'very interesting' frequently precedes the noun in the speech of the more gushing interviewers and journalists! What distinguishes the two positions rather is the function of the adjective: if it is used in a distinguishing or restrictive sense, it follows; if the use is descriptive, rhetorical, emphatic or metaphorical, it precedes. *Pietre preziose* are 'precious stones' as opposed to ordinary ones, but one would refer to *i preziosi gioielli della contessa* 'the countess's precious jewels', where the value is taken for granted. Similarly, courtesy would require one to thank a friend for *il suo prezioso aiuto* 'his valuable help'. Hence, whether an adjective precedes or follows will depend on how easily its inherent meaning lends itself to one or other or both types of use. Adjectives of place and nationality are normally contrastive and therefore tend to follow: *i turisti inglesi* 'English tourists', *l'industria settentrionale* 'northern industry'. To distinguish Florentine literature from that of Rome or Venice one would talk of *la letteratura fiorentina*, but since everybody knows that the *Divine Comedy* is by a Florentine, the adjective has a more rhetorical function and precedes in *la fiorentina Divina Commedia*. A postposed adjective would suggest Dante had a rival elsewhere!

We are, then, required to say that Italian has two equal but different adjective positions. The opposition having thus been grammaticalised, the typological parameter of adjective-noun order in such a language is rendered irrelevant.

4.2 The Verbal Group

We begin with some remarks on the meaning and use of the verbal forms set out in Section 3, paying particular attention to mood, aspect, valency and voice.

The subjunctive mood is clearly identifiable both in terms of its morphological marking and its grammatical and semantic role. The latter emerges perhaps most evidently in pairs of the following kind: *Pietro vuole sposare una ragazza che ha* (indic.)/*abbia* (subj.) *studiato l'astrofisica* 'Peter wants to marry a girl who has (indic./subj.) studied astrophysics'. The indicative verb tells us there is a particular girl, one of whose attributes is that she has studied astrophysics; with the subjunctive we know only what Peter considers to be the desirable quality in a future wife, but not whether such a person exists. The function of the subjunctive, then, is to deny, put in doubt or suspend judgement on the question of the independent existence of the state of affairs referred to in the relevant proposition. Hence it is mandatory in the complement clauses of verbs which express attitudes towards possible, desired, feared, etc. situations rather than assert that such situations actually obtain: *voglio/temo/spero che il treno sia* (subj.) *in ritardo* 'I want/fear/hope that the train is late.' With other verbs a contrast emerges: *se pensi che ha* (indic.) *soltanto dodici anni* 'if you think (= bear in mind) that he is only twelve' vs *se pensi che abbia* (subj.) *soltanto dodici anni* 'if you think (= believe) that he is only twelve'. Likewise, the subjunctive is also appropriate after a negated verb: *capisco perché l'ha* (indic.) *fatto* 'I understand why he did it' but *non capisco perché l'abbia* (subj.) *fatto* 'I don't understand why he did it'; and after conjunctions that introduce an element of doubt or futurity: *prima che il gallo canti* (subj.) 'before the cock crows', *benché Giorgio sia* (subj.) *partito* 'although George has left', *lavora sodo perché lo si paga* (indic.) *bene* 'he works hard because they pay him well' vs *lavora sodo perché lo si paghi* (subj.) *bene* 'he works so that they will pay him well'. Similar factors are involved in the use of the subjunctive with *se* in conditionals, but space prohibits even a cursory treatment of this complex area. Nor indeed has it been possible to survey all other uses of the subjunctive, but the foregoing should suffice to demonstrate that the category is semantically productive in the modern language. We may note finally that the subjunctive is less widely used in some colloquial registers, including so-called *italiano popolare*, and in some regions. On the other hand, in Sicilian and some other southern dialects where a conditional verb form has not emerged historically, the subjunctive has an even wider range of functions.

The central issue regarding aspect is the relation between the imperfect (*cantava*), the preterit (*cantò*), and the present perfect (*ha cantato*) (see Section 3 for a full list of forms). The conventional view is that the first of these expresses an incomplete or a habitual action – 'he was singing' or 'he used to sing' – while the latter two refer instead to single completed actions. The difference between them in turn involves the recentness and the relevance of the events described to the current situation. Hence, in native grammatical terminology, *ha cantato* is dubbed the *passato prossimo* 'near past' and *cantò* the *passato remoto* 'distant past'. However, the imperfect is often found, particularly with verbs of mental state – *non sapeva cosa dirmi ieri* 'he didn't know what to say to me yesterday' – and in journalism and less formal writing where traditional usage might require one of the other two forms. Hence it has recently been argued that the imperfect is the unmarked past tense, deriving its precise value from the context, whereas both the perfect and the preterit have an inbuilt aspectual value. One advantage of this view is that it more easily accommodates the common, though by no means obligatory, progressive periphrasis *stava cantando* (cf. the present *sta cantando* 'he is singing'). In the case of the preterit and the present perfect, the issue is further complicated by the fact that spoken usage varies considerably up and down the peninsula. Northern speakers rarely utter the preterit, so the perfect subsumes both functions (cf. the discussion of French on page 183), while southern speakers often use only the preterit, reserving the reflex of the Latin HABEO + past participle periphrasis for a sense more like that in English 'I have the letter written'. The traditional distinction lives on in Central Italian (including Florentine and Roman) speech, but northern influence is strong even here and may eventually come to predominate.

One question not treated in the preceding discussion concerns the choice of auxiliary verb in constructing the perfect periphrasis. There are four possibilities: (a) some verbs always take *avere* 'to have' – *ho pensato* 'I have thought', *ha viaggiato* 'he has travelled', *abbiamo letto il libro* 'we have read the book'; (b) others always take *essere* 'to be' – *è uscita* 'she has (lit. is) gone out', *è morto* 'he has died'; (c) some take either auxiliary, but with more or less discernible differences of sense – *hanno aumentato il prezzo* 'they have increased the price', but *è aumentato il prezzo* 'the price has gone up'; *ha corso* 'he has run (= done some running)' vs *è corso* 'he has run (= gone by running)'; (d) a very small number of verbs, particularly weather verbs, take either auxiliary with no difference of meaning – *è/ha piovuto* 'it has rained'. Crucial to an understanding of the process of auxiliary selection is an appreciation of the semantic relation between the subject and the verb. If the subject is the agent or experiencer (for a verb of mental state), then the auxiliary is *avere*; hence type (a) regardless of whether the verb is transitive or intransitive. If the subject is more neutrally involved in the activity or state defined by the verb – in traditional terms a patient, then the auxiliary is *essere*. Such verbs will by definition be intransitive – *andare* 'to go', *salire* 'to go up' (contrast *arrampicare* 'to climb' with *avere*), *morire* 'to die', *ingiallire* 'to turn yellow, wither'. If a verb can take two different types of subject – *aumentare* 'to increase', *correre* 'to run', *crescere* 'to grow', *procedere* 'to proceed' (with patient subject and *essere)* vs *procedere* 'to behave' (with agent subject and *avere)*, then it can take both auxiliaries. If the distinction between agent and patient is not valid for certain types of activity/state, then either auxiliary may be chosen indifferently – *piovere* 'to rain', *vivere* 'to live'. A final point to note here is that if the infinitive following a modal verb would independently take *essere*, then by a process of auxiliary attraction the modal itself, which would normally take *avere*, may take *essere:* either *ho dovuto uscire* or *sono dovuto uscire* 'I had to go out'.

Patient as subject not only identifies *essere*-taking verbs but is of course the time-honoured way of characterising the passive voice, and it is not coincidental that *essere* is also the auxiliary in passive constructions – *gli svedesi vinceranno la battaglia* 'the Swedes will win the battle', *la battaglia sarà vinta dagli svedesi* 'the battle will be won by the Swedes'. In fact, if we regard the subject of *essere* as itself being a patient (i.e. having a neutral role as the person/thing/etc. about which predications are made), then we can achieve a unified explanation of why (a) it takes *essere* as its own auxiliary; (b) it is the active auxiliary of the appropriate subclass of intransitives and the passive auxiliary of all transitives; (c) the other two verbs which enter into passive periphrases are also patient subject verbs. The first of these is *venire* 'to come', which may be regularly substituted for *essere* to distinguish an 'action' from a 'state' passive. Thus, *la bandiera veniva/era issata all'alba* 'the flag was hoisted at dawn', but only *essere* in *in quel periodo la bandiera era issata per tutta la giornata* 'at that time the flag was hoisted (i.e. remained aloft) all day'. The second is *andare* 'to go', which combines with the past participle to express the meaning 'must be V-ed', e.g. *questo problema va risolto subito* 'this problem must be solved at once'. One interesting morphosyntactic restriction is that neither *andare* nor *venire* can occur in these functions in their compound forms, whereas *essere* of course can. Curiously, *andare* does occur as a compound auxiliary in *la casa è andata distrutta* 'the house was (lit. is gone) destroyed', but then there is no sense of obligation and the construction is limited to verbs of loss and destruction.

Essere is also the auxiliary for all reflexives: *Maria si è criticata* 'Mary criticised herself.' Since a reflexive is only a transitive verb where agent and patient happen to be identical, one might expect to find *avere*, as indeed one sometimes does in Old Italian and in some, notably southern, dialects. However, another very frequent use of the reflexive construction is as a kind of passive. Thus, in *le finestre si sono rotte* 'the windows got broken' (lit. 'broke themselves') the sentence is formally reflexive but the subject is patient rather than agent (contrast the non-reflexive in *Giorgio ha rotto le finestre* 'George has broken the windows'). Furthermore, since patient-subject verbs and constructions in Italian frequently have post-verbal subjects (see below), we also have the possibility of *si sono rotte le finestre*, a structure which is susceptible to an alternative analysis, viz.: *si* (su.) V *le finestre* (obj.). Evidence that such a reanalysis has taken place comes from the fact that, colloquially at least, such sentences often have a singular verb: *si parla diverse lingue in quel negozio* 'several languages are spoken in that shop', and from the extension of the construction to intransitive verbs of all kinds: *si parte domani* 'one is leaving tomorrow', *si dorme bene in campagna* 'one sleeps well in the country'. Indeed, it is even possible to have the so-called impersonal *si* in combination with a reflexive verb: *ci si lava(no) le mani prima di mangiare* 'one washes one's hands before eating' (where *ci* is a morphophonemic variant of *si* before *si*).

These two *si*s (impersonal and reflexive) take different positions in clitic sequences: *lo si dice* 'one says it', *se lo dice* 'he says it to himself' (*se* for *si* before *lo* is a consequence of a regular morphophonemic adjustment), and hence with both present we find *ce lo si dice* 'one says it to oneself'. Notice too that if *si* in impersonal constructions is taken as subject, then examples like *si rilegano libri* 'one binds books' have to be construed as involving object agreement on the verb. Subject *si* is also unusual in that in predicative constructions while the verb is singular, following adjectives, participles and predicate nominals are plural: *si è ricchi* (m. pl.) 'one is rich', *si è usciti* 'one has gone out', *quando si è attrici* (f. pl.) 'when one is an actress'. Compare in this regard the plural with other impersonal verbs; *bisogna essere sicuri* 'it is necessary to be safe'. On the other hand if impersonal *si* is found with a verb which normally requires *avere*, the auxiliary becomes *essere*, as with reflexive *si*, but the past participle does not agree; *si è partiti* 'one has left' vs *si è detto* 'one has said'.

As the preceding examples have shown, one feature of the Italian verbal group is the possible presence of clitic pronouns, whose categories and basic order are set out in the following table:

1st sg.	3rd sg. dative	2nd pl.	2nd sg.	1st pl.	Refl.	3rd sg./pl. accusative	Imp.	Partitive
mi	gli (m.) le (f.)	vi	ti	ci	si	lo (m. sg.) la (f. sg.) li (m. pl.) le (f. pl.)	si	ne

Note, however, that combinations of *ne* and the third person accusative forms are rare, but when they do occur, *ne* precedes: *ne la ringrazierò* 'I'll thank her for it.' In clitic clusters there is a morphophonemic adjustment of /i/ to /e/ before sonorants. Hence *me lo*, *te ne*, etc. Standard too in such clusters is the replacement of *le* 'to her' by its masculine congener *gli*, so that *gliene* translates as 'of it to him/her'. *Gli* for *le* in isolation is becoming increasingly common, but is still regarded as non-standard. Much more acceptable is *gli* for *loro*, the latter being anomalous in occurring post-verbally: *ho detto loro* 'I said to them.' Likewise, *suo* 'his/her' is extending ground to replace *loro* 'their' in the possessive. In *italiano popolare* and in many dialects the whole system *gli/le/loro* merges with the neuter *ci*, which thus becomes an omni-purpose indirect object clitic. Note that, whereas in modern Italian, unlike in earlier stages of the language, the past participle in the perfect does not normally agree with its object, clitic objects do trigger agreement: *ho trovato Maria* 'I found Mary' vs *l'ho trovata* 'I found her.' *Ne* also causes agreement (contrast French *en*): *ne hanno mangiati tre* 'they have eaten three of them'.

A further complication arises in the rules for placement of the clitics or clitic clusters. The general principle is that they precede finite verb forms but follow non-finite ones: *me lo darà* 'he will give it to me', *deve darmelo* 'he must give it to me', *avendomelo dato* 'having given it to me'. Certain verbs, however, which take a dependent infinitive allow the latter's clitics to 'climb' and attach to the governing verb: *vuole parlarti* or *ti vuole parlare* 'he wants to speak to you', *volendo parlarti* or *volendoti parlare* 'wanting to speak to you'. Such clitic-climbing is obligatory with the causative *fare: me lo farà dare* 'he will have it given to me', even if this formally converts the causative into a reflexive and provokes an attendant auxiliary change: *si è fatto dare un aumento di stipendio* 'he got himself given a rise'. Furthermore, if the clitics climb (and in a cluster they must all move or none), then the phenomenon of auxiliary attraction mentioned earlier becomes obligatory: *non ho/sono potuto andarci* 'I couldn't go there' but only *non ci sono potuto andare*.

4.3 The Sentence

We conclude with some brief remarks relating to overall sentence structure, beginning with the question of word order. Assuming a traditional division of the sentence, we find both the orders subject-predicate and predicate-subject attested: *Pietro fumava una sigaretta* 'Peter was smoking a cigarette', *è arrivato il treno* 'the train has arrived'. To understand what distinguishes the two orders we need to add the concepts of theme (= what is being talked about) and rheme (= what is said about the theme), and the ordering principle 'theme precedes rheme'. In the unmarked case, a subject which identifies the agent-experiencer of the activity/state expressed by the verb will constitute the theme, and will accordingly come first. The rheme will consist of the verb plus, where appropriate, an object whose interpretation follows directly from the meaning of the verb, what we have earlier called a patient. Thus, SV(O) is a natural order for sentences with any transitive and some intransitive verbs in Italian. If we extend the notion object to include the sentential complements of verbs of saying, thinking, etc. and also allow for indirect objects and prepositional objects, we can say that the rheme consists of the verb followed by its complement(s). If, however, the subject is rhematic with respect to its verb, as it will be if its semantic role is patient, then it will normally follow. Hence the characteristic post-verbal subjects in the *essere*-taking constructions discussed above: *verrà Giorgio* 'George will come' (taking the 'mover' as patient with a verb of motion), *domani saranno riaperti il porto e l'aeroporto* 'tomorrow the docks and the airport will be reopened', *si svolgeva il dibattito* 'the debate took place'. In appropriate circumstances and with suitable intonation the basic patterns can be reversed, but that does not alter the fact that the position of the subject in Italian is not fixed but depends on its semantic relation to the verb. Moving the object from its post-verbal position is, by contrast, less easy and normally requires a pronominal copy: *quel libro, non lo legge nessuno* 'that book nobody reads'. Similarly, it is rare and decidedly rhetorical for the subject to be interposed between verb and object. Adverbs and subcategorised adjectives on the other hand regularly separate verb and noun: *parla bene l'italiano* 'he speaks Italian well', *il professore ha fatto felici gli studenti* 'the teacher made the students happy'.

The possibility of post-verbal subjects with *essere*-taking verbs and the general optionality of pronominal subjects have been linked in the recent generative literature with another detail of Italian syntax, namely the fact that sentences such as *chi credi che verrà?* 'who do you think will come?' are grammatical (contrast the ungrammaticality of the literal English rendering *who do you think that will come?*). If such an example was derived from an intermediate structure like *credi che verrà chi*, then Italian and English both agree in being able to extract from a post-verbal position (cf. English *who do you think that Fred saw?*), but differ in what may occupy such a position. The preverbal subject is treated throughout as a dummy category licensed by the putatively universal Empty Category Principle (ECP), and languages like Italian have thus become known as pro-drop or null-subject languages. In addition to the properties already mentioned, such languages are claimed to have rightward agreement of the copula (*sono io* 'it's me'), so-called 'long' wh-movement of the subject (*l'uomo che mi domando chi abbia visto* 'the man that I wonder who he saw' cf. the ungrammaticality of the English translation) and the possibility of an empty resumptive pronoun in embedded clauses (*ecco la ragazza che mi domando chi crede che vincerà* vs English '*there's the girl that I wonder who believes that she will win'). Unfortunately, there is not room here to examine in more detail these fascinating insights into Italian syntax.

Acknowledgement

I am grateful to Joe Cremona, Martin Harris, Giulio Lepschy, Žarko Muljačić and Donna Jo Napoli for their comments on an earlier version of this chapter.

Bibliography

Lepschy and Lepschy (1977) is an excellent general manual which is refreshingly up-to-date and unprescriptive in its approach to points of grammar. Muljačić (1982) is a very handy one-volume bibliographical guide.

Among descriptive grammars, Renzi et al. (2001) now occupies pride of place, while Maiden and Robustelli (2007) is an excellent resource in English. Chapallaz (1979) is a good traditional account of the phonetics of the standard language; Muljačić (1972) is a useful survey of work done on Italian phonology from a variety of theoretical viewpoints; Bertinetto (1981) is an excellent study of the suprasegmental phonology of Italian. Rizzi (1982) is a collection of articles by the leading figure in the investigation of Italian in the light of recent generative theory.

Rohlfs (1966–69) is a classic historical grammar with very generous attention to the dialects; Tekavčić (1980) is an indispensable manual combining factual detail on the history of the language and largely structuralist methods of analysis and interpretation. Migliorini and Griffith (1984) is the best external history of the language.

De Mauro (1983) is the standard account of the changes in the linguistic situation in the peninsula since unification in 1861. Two volumes out of four have so far appeared of Cortellazzo (1969–), one of Italy's leading dialectologists; unfortunately, we still await the main descriptive volume. Albano Leoni (1979) is a wide-ranging set of conference proceedings which give a clear picture of the current linguistic complexity of the peninsula.

References

Albano Leoni, F. (ed.) 1979. *I dialetti e le lingue delle minoranze di fronte all'italiano*, 2 vols (Bulzoni, Rome)

Bertinetto, P.M. 1981. *Strutture prosodiche dell'italiano* (Accademia della Crusca, Florence)

Chapallaz, M. 1979. *The Pronunciation of Italian* (Bell and Hyman, London)

Cortelazzo, M. 1969–. *Avviamento alla dialettologia italiana*, 4 vols (Pacini, Pisa)

De Mauro, T. 1983. *Storia linguistica dell'Italia unita*, 8th edn (Laterza, Bari)

Lepschy, A.L. and Lepschy, G.C. 1977. *The Italian Language Today* (Hutchinson, London; revised Italian edition: *La lingua italiana*, Bompiani, Milan, 1981)

Maiden, M. and Robustelli, C. 2007. *A Reference Grammar of Modern Italian*, 2nd edn (Arnold, London; McGraw-Hill, New York)

Migliorini, B. and Griffith, T.G. 1984. *The Italian Language*, 2nd edn (Faber and Faber, London; translation and adaptation of B. Migliorini, *Storia della lingua italiana*, 5th edn, Sansoni, Florence, 1978)

Muljačić, Ž. 1972. *Fonologia della lingua italiana* (Il Mulino, Bologna)

—— 1982. *Introduzione allo studio della lingua italiana*, 2nd edn (Einaudi, Turin)

Renzi, L., Salvi, G. and Cardinaletti, A. (eds) 2001. *Grande grammatica italiana di consultazione*, 3 vols, rev. edn (Il Mulino, Bologna)

Rizzi, L. 1982. *Issues in Italian Syntax* (Foris Publications, Dordrecht)

Rohlfs, G. 1966–69. *Grammatica storica della lingua italiana e dei suoi dialetti*, 3 vols (Einaudi, Turin; translation and revision of *Historische Grammatik der italienischen Sprache und ihrer Mundarten*, 3 vols, Francke, Bern, 1949–54)

Tekavčić, P. 1980. *Grammatica storica della lingua italiana*, 2nd edn, 3 vols (Il Mulino, Bologna)

13

Rumanian

Graham Mallinson

1 Introduction

The relative neglect of Balkan Romance by linguists in favour of the Western Romance languages is attributable in part to the geographical isolation of the country where most Rumanian speakers live. Rumania has a population of over 22 million, of which some 90 per cent have Rumanian as their first language. A further 2½ million speakers constitute about 60 per cent of the population of Moldova. Including speakers in other neighbouring countries brings the total number of speakers to about 23½ million. This failure of linguistic and national borders to coincide reflects the fluid political history of the Balkans. Rumania itself is host to several minority language groups, including German-speaking Saxons (though recent emigration to Germany has reduced their number from over half a million to under 50,000) and Hungarians (about one and a half million). Both these minorities are concentrated in Transylvania, the presence of so many Hungarian speakers resulting from the acquisition by Rumania of the province from Hungary at the end of the First World War.

A number of features at all linguistic levels serve to highlight the differences between Rumanian and the Western Romance languages, many being attributable to its membership of the Balkan Sprachbund. In each of the four main sections which follow, reference will be made to such features in describing the divergence of Rumanian from mainstream Romance evolution.

The form of Balkan Romance to be discussed is Daco-Rumanian, so named because it is associated with the Roman province of Dacia, on the north bank of the lower Danube (part of the Empire for a relatively short period from the first decade of the second century to AD 271). The wider term Balkan Romance includes three other varieties: Arumanian, spoken in northern Greece, Albania, Serbia and Macedonia; Megleno-Rumanian, spoken in a small area to the north of Salonika; Istro-Rumanian, spoken in the Istrian peninsula of Croatia. All four varieties are deemed to have a common origin, with the initial split dating from the second half of the first millennium. Because the earliest extant Rumanian texts date from as late as the beginning of the sixteenth century, the history of Balkan Romance involves a great deal of speculation (compare the dates of early extant texts for Old French).

Besides the question of dating the break-up of Common Rumanian, other controversies include the problem of whether the original centre of dispersion was north of the Danube in Dacia, or south of the Danube in Moesia; also, whether Arumanian, Megleno- and Istro-Rumanian are dialects of Rumanian or constitute separate languages. In the latter case, one can say that the four varieties are very closely related but that the three minor varieties have each been heavily influenced by the national languages of the countries in which they are spoken. Mutual intelligibility between Daco-Rumanian and Arumanian would be at a very low level on first contact but would increase dramatically in a very short period. However, in this area of Europe it is extra-linguistic factors such as nationalism that are more pertinent to the perception of linguistic identity (compare the discussion in Chapter 18 about the relations between Serbian and Croatian). In the case of Balkan Romance I will leave this sensitive question open, since I will be concentrating on Daco-Rumanian (henceforth simply 'Rumanian'), the national language of Rumania.

Finally, Rumanian is also spoken by a considerable number of immigrants to the New World. Even in Australia there are enough Rumanian speakers to warrant a weekly one-hour programme in both Sydney and Melbourne on ethnic radio, though not enough to have given rise to discernible, institutionalised features of Antipodean Rumanian such as one finds in the larger Italian and Greek communities.

Rumanian proper can be divided into several (sub)dialects. The major forms are Moldavian and Muntenian, spoken in the former principalities of Moldavia (northeast) and Muntenia, or Wallachia (southeast), though several other minor dialects can be discerned within present-day Rumania. These are spoken in the north and west of the country,

Map 13.1 Areas of Rumanian Dialects.

including much of Transylvania. Despite its political history in relative isolation from the two principalities, it is, however, inaccurate to speak of a Transylvanian dialect as such. Both Moldavian and Muntenian cover parts of Transylvania, and there is, as one would expect, overlap between dialects spoken in adjoining regions.

During the course of the nineteenth century, Muntenian was gradually adopted as the national and literary standard, the final step in this process being the union of the principalities in 1859 as an independent state with Bucharest as the capital. The use of Muntenian as the point of entry into Rumanian of Western Romance vocabulary and morphosyntactic innovations over the last 150 years (a period marked at times by what has been described as 'Gallomania') has served to set this dialect off from the others. However, communication and education in modern society have allowed many innovations to filter through and dilute other dialects, including the original spoken Muntenian on which the national standard is based and which was itself left behind by the developing literary language.

Even so, spoken Muntenian was already somewhat more innovative than the other spoken dialects. For example, it showed a greater tendency to fricativise voiced dental plosives before front vowels: Lat. *DĪCO* > zic /zik/ 'say', compared with Moldavian affrication in /dʑik/. Muntenian has also gone further towards complete elimination of the high, back vowel /u/ from Latin words ending in -*o* (+C) and -*u* (+C): *AMĀRU-* > *amar* /amar/ 'bitter', compared with Moldavian /amarʲ/. Both /dʑ/ for /z/, and final /u/ are also typical of Arumanian.

The 'reromancing' tendency of the last two centuries has gone some way towards countering the specifically Balkan character of earlier Rumanian development. Such Western Romance influence was by no means accidental, however, and groups of writers during the late eighteenth and early to mid-nineteenth centuries made positive efforts to import French- and Italian-based vocabulary to fill gaps in the native lexical stock. The Transylvanian School made the first real attempt to replace the Cyrillic orthography with a Roman one, as well as engineering Rumanian vocabulary to substitute Romance for Slavonic. However, they had only limited success in each case, their main fault being an overzealous desire to hark back to the Latin origins of the language. Their etymological spelling system (that rendered /tʃintʃ/ 'five' by *quinqui* – compare the modern spelling *cinci*) could serve only to confuse the populace whom they wished to educate.

It was the mid-nineteenth-century writers of Muntenia, with their less extreme attitude towards renewing the language, who had the greatest influence in resurrecting its Romance character. Yet one should point out also that political developments helped to bring to prominence the dialect in which they wrote. One can only speculate on the likelihood of some Transylvanian-based form of Rumanian having come to the fore had that province not been isolated from the two principalities. And if some other dialect had been adopted as the national standard, one might also ask how great a difference there would have been today between the other three varieties of Balkan Romance and a national language of Rumania based on a more conservative form.

2 Orthography and Phonology

The Cyrillic writing system was introduced into the area occupied by the modern language when Old Church Slavonic (see page 269) became the medium for religious texts. Given the absence of contact between Rumanian and Latin in medieval times (compare the situation in the west of Romania), it was inevitable that when Rumanian words and names of places and people began to appear sporadically in Old Church Slavonic texts from the thirteenth century, they too should be written in Cyrillic script. The first extant texts wholly in Rumanian merely followed this tradition so that a non-Roman alphabet was dominant for the greater part of the four and a half centuries since then.

Two clear factors led to dissatisfaction with this system and thus to the eventual adoption of a Roman script: the practical problem of adapting the Cyrillic system to match phonemes found in Rumanian and those introduced with Romance loans from the west; and the growing feelings of national awareness that increased as contact with the Western Romance languages grew and brought widespread recognition of linguistic ties with Latin, Italian and French. Nevertheless, it was not until the union of the principalities in the late nineteenth century that the Cyrillic system was finally replaced by a Roman one. During the nineteenth century, various attempts were made to adapt the Roman alphabet to Rumanian, including systems of a transitional nature with a largely Roman alphabet but with Cyrillic symbols for those sounds not represented orthographically in Western Romance – for example, the middle vowel /ə/ was represented by ъ and the post-alveolar fricative /ʃ/ by /ш/.

Today Rumanian is written and printed in a wholly Romanised alphabet with three diacritics. Because it is a relatively short time since the current Rumanian alphabet was instituted, there has been little opportunity for the spoken and written languages to diverge. For this reason, Rumanian examples will normally be given in their orthographic form. The phonemic values of the letters are shown in Table 13.1, with some oddities discussed in the remarks which follow it. One value of using the orthography is that, as with French, it provides some insight into the history of the language, because of the method used for representing final palatalised consonants.

Table 13.1 Orthographic System of Modern Rumanian

a	/a/	m	/m/
ă	/ə/	n	/n/
b	/b/	o	/o/
c(+h)	/k/	p	/p/
c (+i/e)	/tʃ/	r	/r/
d	/d/	s	/s/
e	/e/	ş	/ʃ/
f	/f/	t	/t/
g(+h)	/g/	ţ	/ts/
g(+i/e)	/dʒ/	u	/u/
h	/h/	v	/v/
i	/i/*	#w	/v/ or /w/
î/â	/ɨ/	x	/ks/
j	/ʒ/	y	/j/
k	/k/	z	/z/
l	/l/		

Notes:
* *i* is the most troublesome orthographic symbol in Rumanian. The phoneme equivalent given here relates to full vowels. See the text for comments on other values.
\# Used for common international terms only, e.g. *weekend, watt*.

256

Among the vowel symbols, *â* and *î* are allographs, originally used following etymological principles, but with the current distribution (after some vacillation) being *î*
word-initially and -finally, *â* word-medially. A limited number of words beginning with
e- are pronounced /je-/, this ioticisation apparently a Slavonic inheritance. More recent
loans from Western Romance are unaffected, giving rise to the occasional doublet: *era*
/éra/ 'the era' but *era* /jerá/ 'was'. Initial *i-* before another vowel is also pronounced /j-/:
iute /jute/ 'quick'; *iar* /jar/ 'again'. Final *-i* normally represents palatalisation of the
preceding consonant: *lup* /lup/ 'wolf' but *lupi* /lupʲ/ 'wolves'. However, this does not apply
when the preceding consonant cluster is consonant + liquid: *tigri* /tigri/ 'tigers'. Final *-ii*
represents a full /i/ and so the system allows for the differentiation of some masculine
nouns into three forms. Thus, the singular *lup* /lup/ 'wolf' is made plural by the palatalisation of the final plosive: *lupi* /lupʲ/ 'wolves', and definite plural by addition of a full
/i/: *lupii* /lupi/ 'the wolves'. This can be alarming when the stem of the noun ends in *-il*.
The noun *copil* 'child' has a plural *copii* /kopi/ 'children' (the final /l/ is palatalised out
of existence) and a definite plural *copiii* /kopʲi/ 'the children'. The three major diphthongs /eɑ/, /oɑ/ and /eo/ are represented by their starting and finishing points – *ea*, *oa*
and *eo*. The sequence *au* is pronounced as two separate vowels, as normally is *ău* too.

Among the consonant symbols, *k* is a comparative rarity (being reserved for international terms such as *kilogram, kilometru*) and the voiceless velar plosive is represented by *c* (*ch* before front vowels). Similarly, the voiced velar plosive is represented
by *g* (*gh* before front vowels). The post-alveolar affricates /tʃ/ and /dʒ/ are also represented by *c* and *g*, but by the digraphs *ci* and *gi* (sometimes *ce* and *ge*) before back and
middle vowels (see Italian, Chapter 12, page 237). The fronting of velar plosives before
front vowels is a characteristic Rumanian shares with Western Romance, and is discussed
later in this section.

Standard Rumanian has 32 phonemes (or more, depending on the method of pho
nological analysis employed – the series of palatalised consonants being treated either
as a distinct set or as the non-palatal series plus a recurring palatal off-glide). The
neatest system identifies 7 simple vowels, 3 diphthongs and 22 consonants, which
include two semi-vowels. The number of diphthongs is increased substantially if the
semi-vowel /j/ is treated as a vowel unit rather than as a consonant (thus /je/ would be a
diphthong, but is treated here as a consonant-vowel sequence). The phoneme inventory
is set out in Figures 13.1 and 13.2, and Table 13.2.

There is some symmetry within the consonant system, most obstruents being in
voiced/voiceless pairs. Voiced and voiceless plosives alike are unaspirated. Unpaired
are the glottal fricative /h/ (often pronounced with audible friction) and the dental
affricate /ts/ – though in more conservative dialects this too is matched with the voiced

Table 13.2 Consonants

	Bilabial		Labio-dental		Dental		Post-alveolar		Palatal	Velar		Glottal
Stops	p	b			t	d				k	g	
Affricates					ts		tʃ	dʒ				
Fricatives			f	v	s	z	ʃ	ʒ				h
Nasals		m				n						
Liquids					l	r						
Semi-vowels		w							j			

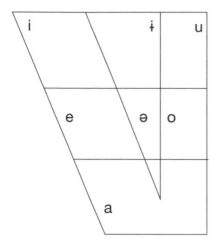

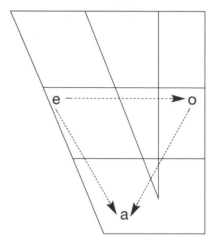

Figure 13.1 Vowels.
Note: The two back vowels are rounded, the remainder are unrounded.

Figure 13.2 Diphthongs.
Note: All three diphthongs are rising, with stress on the second element.

equivalent /ʤ/. There are only two nasals, the gap in the system being the velar nasal, which occurs only as an allophone of /n/ before velar plosives. There are two liquids, /r/ being a lingual flap or light roll, and the dental lateral /l/ being consistently clear.

As mentioned earlier, Rumanian has followed the normal Romance path of fronting velar plosives before front vowels, giving rise to the post-alveolar affricates. However, /k/ and /g/ also occur slightly fronted as an allophonic variation before front vowels: *chema* 'call' and *ghetou* 'ghetto'. The failure of the velar plosives to front all the way to post-alveolar affricates in many words reflects the distinct treatment of words inherited directly from Latin and those borrowed from other languages at later dates, e.g. from Slavonic: *chilie* '(monk's) cell' (from *kelija*) or from Hungarian: *chip* 'face, facial expression' (from *kép*).

Among consonants also attributable to contact with other languages is /ʒ/. This derives from Latin *-di-* sequences: *DEORSUM* > *jos* 'down'; *ADJŪTO* > *ajut* 'help'; but also from Latin *j* + back vowels: *JUGUM* > *jug* 'yoke'; *JOCUM* > *joc* 'game'. Its presence in Slavonic-based words (*grajd* 'stable'; *jar* 'live coals') testifies to its reinforcement through contact with Southern Slavonic if it is not actually a Slavonic-induced development.

The glottal fricative /h/ has an uncertain history, some linguists claiming it was reintroduced after its loss in Vulgar Latin in order to bring symmetry back to the plosive/fricative system (thus: p~f; t~s; k~h). Again this development was reintroduced, if not necessarily induced, by languages Rumanian came into contact with: from Slavonic, *duh* 'soul' and *hrană* 'food, fodder'; from Hungarian, *hotar* 'border' and *hârdău* 'bucket'; from Turkish, *hamal* 'porter' and *huzur* 'leisure'.

A substratum influence from Dacian/Thracian has been suggested for some distinctive phonological developments in Balkan Romance, though this is highly speculative, given the dearth of extant material from such a substratum. Comparison with Albanian shows some parallels: /ə/ from unstressed /a/ is found in both Rumanian and Albanian, as well as Bulgarian; Rumanian /ɨ/ from /a/ before nasals in closed syllables:

Latin *CAMPUM* > *câmp* 'plain', but not in open syllables: Latin *ANNUM* > *an* 'year' (-*nn*- appears to have become a long, rather than geminate, consonant and was grouped with the following vowel); labialisation of velars in velar + dental clusters: Latin *COXAM* > *coapsă* 'thigh' (Albanian *kofshë*). Treatments like this last one also provide useful patterns for comparison between Balkan and Western Romance:

Latin	Rumanian	French	Italian	Spanish
FACTUM	fapt	fait	fatto	hecho
LACTEM	lapte	lait	latte	leche

Like Italian, however, Rumanian inherits vowel-final plurals from Latin, with loss of final -*s: FLŌRES* > *flori* 'flowers' (though, of course, final -*i* now represents palatalisation of the final consonant).

In some instances there was substitution of one liquid for the other: *CAELUM* > *cer* 'sky'; *MELLEM* > *miere* 'honey'; *SALEM* > *sare* 'salt'. Later loans from Western Romance thus gave rise to doublets: *ceresc~celest* 'celestial/of the sky'. Sixteenth-century texts of the north Transylvania area of Maramureş also show evidence of rhotacism, with intervocalic /n/ becoming /r/: *lumiră* for *lumină* 'light'; *tire* for *tine* 'you'. This is a feature also of Istro-Rumanian: *pliră* for *plină* 'full'; *lâră* for *lână* 'wool'.

Consonant clusters also show differences between Rumanian and Western Romance. Matching the voiceless /str/ and /skl/ are the voiced /zdr/ and /zgl/; /zb/ and /zg/ match /sp/ and /sk/; /zv/ matches /sf/; /zm/ and /zl/ also occur; while the presence of post-alveolar /ʃ/ leads to the existence of clusters such as /ʃt(r)/ and /ʃp(1~r)/. While all these clusters fill natural gaps in the Romance system, phonotactically much more unexpected are: /hl/, /hr/, /ml/ and /mr/ as well as word-initial /kt/.

Finally, stress is free and variable, giving rise to doublets: *módele* 'the fashions' but *modéle* 'models'; *cấntă* 'sings, sing!' but *cântắ* 'sang'. Rumanian orthography does not regularly mark stress but it will be marked here whenever it is relevant to the discussion.

3 Morphology

As in Western Romance, the Latin declension system for nouns and adjectives was reduced in Balkan Romance through phonetic attrition. However, Rumanian is more conservative to the extent that it retains three distinct case forms: nominative/accusative, genitive/dative, vocative. It has also reintroduced what has been described as a neuter gender. This diversity of case forms is most evident among feminines, but also with masculines when the noun is definite. A characteristic that Rumanian shares with Bulgarian and Albanian is the use of suffixes to mark definiteness: Latin *HOMO ILLE* > *omul* 'the man', with fusion of the demonstrative (compare the normal pattern in the West from *ILLE HOMO*). Indefinites follow the normal Romance pattern: *un om* 'a man'.

The representative sample in the chart of nouns demonstrates the greater variation in form within the feminines in the non-definite paradigms. Vocatives are discussed separately, as they are irregular and relatively infrequent. It will be seen that morphologically the neuters are masculine in the singular and feminine in the plural. They have also been described as *ambigeneric* for this reason. Syntactically, it is difficult to choose between the two labels, the only relevant data, involving the agreement between adjectives and conjoined nouns of different genders, being highly unreliable.

Nouns

(a) some typical masculine nouns

(i) lup 'wolf'

		Sg.	Pl.
Nom./acc.	−def	lup	lupi
	+def	lupul	lupii
Gen./dat.	−def	lup	lupi
	+def	lupului	lupilor

(ii) arbore 'tree'

		Sg.	Pl.
Nom./acc.	−def	arbore	arbori
	+def	arborele	arborii
Gen./dat.	−def	arbore	arbori
	+def	arborelui	arborilor

(iii) codru 'forest'

		Sg.	Pl.
Nom./acc.	−def	codru	codri
	+def	codrul	codri
Gen./dat.	−def	codru	codri
	+def	codrului	codrilor

Note: Some further sg./pl. alternations: *om-oameni* 'man'; *împărat-împărați* 'emperor'; *băiat-băieți* 'boy'; *cal-cai* 'horse'; *fiu-fii* 'son'; *brad-brazi* 'fir tree'.

(b) some typical feminine nouns

(i) casă 'house'

		Sg.	Pl.
Nom./acc.	−def	casă	case
	+def	casa	casele
Gen./dat.	−def	case	case
	+def	casei	caselor

(ii) stea 'star'

		Sg.	Pl.
Nom./acc.	−def	stea	stele
	+def	steaua	stelele
Gen./dat.	−def	stele	stele
	+def	stelei	stelelor

(iii) câmpie 'plain'

		Sg.	Pl.
Nom./acc.	−def	câmpie	câmpii
	+def	câmpia	câmpiile
Gen./dat.	−def	câmpii	câmpii
	+def	câmpiei	câmpiilor

Note: Some further sg./pl. alternations: *basma-basmale* 'kerchief'; *viață-vieți* 'life'; *carte-cărți* 'book'; *fată-fete* 'girl'; *dovadă-dovezi* 'proof'; *bară-bări* '(metal) bar'.

(c) some typical 'neuter' nouns

(i) studiu 'study(ing)'

		Sg.	Pl.
Nom.acc.	−def.	studiu	studii
	+def	studiul	studiile
Gen./dat.	−def	studiu	studii
	+def	studiului	studiilor

(ii) oraș 'town'

		Sg.	Pl.
Nom./acc.	−def.	oraș	orașe
	+def	orașul	orașele
Gen./dat.	−def	oraș	orașe
	+def	orașului	orașelor

(iii) deal 'hill'

		Sg.	Pl.
Nom./acc.	−def	deal	dealuri
	+def	dealul	dealurile
Gen./dat.	−def	deal	dealuri
	+def	dealului	dealurilor

Note: Some further sg./pl. alternations: *tablou-tablouri* 'picture'; *nume-nume* 'name'; *templu-temple* 'temple'.

The examples in the chart of nominal paradigms show that masculines and neuters are invariable without the definite suffix, in both singular and plural paradigms. In the indefinite system it is only feminines that show a distinction between nominative/accusative and genitive/dative, the feminine genitive/dative singulars normally coinciding in form with the plural. It is the suffixal nature of the definite marker that has contributed most to the apparent conservative nature of the Rumanian case system.

The vocative case is defective, being reserved mainly for animates, especially humans. It also usually occurs in the definite form: *om* 'man' → *omule* 'o man'; *cumătru* 'godfather' → *cumătrule* 'o godfather' (but also *cumetre* – the use of kin terms without possessives or definite determiners being common in Rumanian, as in other languages).

Proper names also occur as vocatives, the use of the definite suffix depending on the stem termination: *Radu* → *Radule* but *Gheorghe* → *Gheorghe* (not *Gheorghele*); *Ana* → *Ana, Ană* or *Ano*.

The vocative is under very heavy pressure and is likely to disappear. Its occurrence in the modern language, as limited as it is, is felt to be a Slavonic legacy – in particular, feminines in *-o* (*Ano*; *vulpe* 'vixen' → *vulpeo* 'o vixen' – though this latter is admittedly rare). This directly reflects a Slavonic termination and cannot readily be accounted for by normal evolution from the Latin vocatives.

Adjectives follow the same morphological pattern as nouns, with which they agree in gender, number and case. There are some less variable adjectives which do not distinguish masculine and feminine in the indefinite form of the nominative/accusative: *mare* 'big' (m./f. sg.) ~ *mari* 'big' (m./f. pl.), but genitive/dative feminine singular follows the same pattern as the nouns in matching the plural forms: *unui om mare* 'of/to a big man', *unei fete mari* 'of/to a big girl'. Normal adjectives inflect like the noun they agree with: *om bun* 'good man', *fată bună* 'good girl'; feminine/neuter plural adjectives take the *-e* form, not *-uri*. Finally, it is also possible for adjectives to take definite suffixes: *omul bun* 'the good man' and *bunul om* 'the *good* man'.

The personal pronoun system derives directly from Latin. The chart of personal pronouns shows cliticised and free forms for nominative, accusative and dative.

Personal Pronouns

		1st sg.	2nd sg.	3rd sg. (m.)	3rd sg. (f.)	1st pl.	2nd pl.	3rd pl. (m.)	3rd pl. (f.)
Nominative	Cliticised								
		eu	tu	el	ea	noi	voi	ei	ele
	Free								
Accusative	Cliticised	mă	te	îl	o	ne	vă	îi	le
	Free *pe* +	mine	tine	el	ea	noi	voi	ei	ele
Dative	Cliticised	îmi	îţi	îi	îi	ni	vi	le	le
	Free	mie	ţie	lui	ei	nouă	vouă	lor	lor

Note: The cliticised forms are the full forms. Syncope takes place depending on environment: for example, *îmi dau cadoul* 'they give the present to me' but *mi-l dau* 'they give it to me'.

The preposition *pe* is an accusative marker – its distribution is dealt with in Section 4.

There are from three to five verb conjugations, depending on how strong is the linguist's desire to relate them to the classical Latin system. The infinitive and present indicative and subjunctive of the different types, together with *have* and *be*, are given in the chart of verb forms. The greatest controversy is whether verbs like *vedea* 'see' (from Latin second conjugation verbs like *VIDĒRE* and *MONĒRE*) are in the process of being absorbed into the larger pattern represented by *face* 'do, make'. Following the chart there is some discussion of the forms of the various tenses, moods and voices, with comments on their origins.

The future in Rumanian is periphrastic, and appears to have been so throughout its history. The more literary form is *voi cânta*, deriving from Vulgar Latin forms of *VOLEO* 'wish' (*voi, vei, va, vom, veţi, vor*) + infinitive. The selection of 'wish' as the auxiliary is characteristic of Balkan languages. Periphrastic too is the spoken future: *am să cânt* (lit.) 'have to sing' – formed from the auxiliary 'have' from *HABEO* + subjunctive; the invariable particle *o* also occurs in a similar structure: *o să cînt* 'I will sing', *o să cânţi* 'you will sing'.

The imperfect is a direct development from Latin-*BAM* forms: *cântám, cântái, cântá, cântám, cântáţi, cântáu* 'I etc. was singing/used to sing'. The perfect derives from the Latin perfect: *CANTĀVĪ* > *cântái, cântáşi, cântắ cântárăm, cântáráţi, cântárắ* 'I, etc., sang'. However, this is normal only in Oltenia, the western region of Muntenia (as well as in Arumanian, where its use matches that of the Greek aorist). Normally in Rumanian the compound perfect is used: *am, ai, a, am, aţi, au cântat* 'I, etc., sang/have sung' (based on *HABEO* + past participle). Conversely, in Rumanian the compound pluperfect does not exist, the synthetic forms deriving from Latin pluperfect subjunctives: *cântásem, cântáseşi, cântáse, cântáserăm, cântáserăţi, cântáseră* 'I, etc., had sung' (while in Arumanian, Greek contact is again reflected in the use of a compound pluperfect).

Present Indicative and Subjunctive

	Type I (a)	Type II	Type IV (a)	Type V(a)	Irregulars	
	cântá 'sing'	vedeá 'see'	*dormí 'sleep'	omorí 'kills'	aveá 'have'	
1 sg.	cânt	văd	dórm	omór	am	
2 sg.	cấnţi	vézi	dórmi	omóri	ái	
3 sg.	cấntă	véde	doárme	omoáră	are	
1 pl.	cấnắm	vedém	dormím	omorấm	avém	
2 pl.	cântáţi	vedéţi	dormíţi	omorấţi	avéţi	
3 pl.	cấntă	văd	dórm	omoáră	áu	
3 subj.	să cấnte	să vádă	să doármă	să omoáre	să aíbă	

	Type I(b)	Type III	Type IV (b)	Type V(b)		
	lucrá 'work'	fáce 'make/do'	*zidí 'build'	urí 'hate'	fi 'be'	
					Indicative	Subjunctive
1 sg.	lucréz	fác	zidésc	urắsc	sânt	să fiu
2 sg.	lucrézi	fáci	zidéşti	urấşti	éşti	să fii
3 sg.	lucreáză	face	zidéşte	urấşte	é(ste)	să fie
1 pl.	lucrắm	fácem	zidím	urắm	sấntem	să fim
2 pl.	lucráţi	fáceţi	zidíţi	urắţi	sấnteţi	să fiţi
3 pl.	lucreáză	fác	zidésc	urắsc	sânt	să fie
3 subj.	să lucréze	să fácă	să zideáscă	să urắscă		

Notes: Stress is shown on all forms, though it is normally unmarked in written Rumanian. Comparison between types II and III shows that type II has stress on the termination in 1 and 2 plural; in type III, stress is consistently on the stem.

* Orthography is irregular here – consistent system would show full vowel value of -*i* by -*ii*.

Morphologically, the present subjunctive has been all but neutralised with the indicative being differentiated from the present indicative only in the third person, except for the irregular *fi*. The remaining forms of the verb paradigm are periphrastic, with combinations of *voi* (future marker), *să* (subordinating particle) or *aş* (conditional particle) followed by the BE infinitive *fi* and then either the past participle (*chemat*) or the gerundive (*chemînd*). That is:

$$\begin{Bmatrix} \text{voi} \\ \text{să} \\ \text{aş} \end{Bmatrix} \qquad \text{fi} \qquad \begin{Bmatrix} \text{chemat} \\ \text{chemând} \end{Bmatrix}$$

for example: *să fi chemat* (perfect subjunctive); *aş fi chemând* (conditional presumptive).

Most notable of the periphrastic forms is the conditional: *aş, ai, ar, am, aţi, ar cânta* 'I, etc., would sing'. This seems to represent the unusual process of a synthetic form being reinterpreted diachronically as an analytic construction, i.e. from original *cântarcaş*, the *-re* termination having been lost after the periphrastic form came about, in line with the general loss of the *-re* termination on all infinitives.

The morphological material on which the numeral system is based is predominantly Latin (with the exception of *sută* 'hundred', from Old Slavonic *sŭto*). There has, however, been a calquing on the Slavonic pattern for the teens and multiples of ten: *QUATTUOR SUPER DECEM > patrusprezece* 'fourteen'; *QUATTUOR + DECEM > patruzeci* 'forty'. Arumanian is more conservative in retaining the Latin 'twenty' (/jingits/, from *VĪGINTI*), but less conservative in following the Slavonic pattern for 'twenty-one' to 'twenty-nine' as well as for 'eleven' to 'nineteen' (/patrusprejingits/ 'twenty-four').

4 Syntax

The basic order of major constituents is: subject–verb–object (SVO), though variations occur under a variety of circumstances. Yes–no questions are normally represented by a change in intonation but inversion of subject and (part of the) verbal complex is an option, and normal with *wh-* questions: *când a venit Ion?* 'when did Ion come?' Heavy constituents also may result in a change of word order, with long noun phrases containing embedded clauses being extraposed: *Merită să fie notate în această ordine încercările scriitorului de a găsi un echivalent sunetelor ă şi î* lit. 'deserve to be noted in this respect the attempts of the writer to find an equivalent for the sounds *ă* and *î*'. Pronouns also complicate discussion of word order. They can occur in different positions as clitics from their full noun phrase equivalents: *bărbatul a dat carnetul copilului* 'the man gave the notebook to the child', but *(el) i l-a dat* lit. '(he) to him it gave'. Along with most other Romance languages Rumanian subject personal pronouns can be dispensed with, there being sufficient morphological differences between the personal verb forms to make them redundant, except for emphasis or contrast.

OVS is also a common alternative to SVO, as in other Balkan languages such as Greek. The ability to distinguish subject from object morphologically increases the incidence of this reversed order. The preposition *pe* (normally 'on') acts as an accusative marker for all pronouns but also for full noun phrases high in animacy (and thus to some extent corresponds to Spanish *a* – see page 213). It can thus decode noun phrase-verb-noun phrase structures and is assisted in this by the use of reduplicative pronouns. *Ion a văzut-o pe Maria* lit. 'Ion saw her Maria' occurs as an alternative to *Ion a văzut Maria* 'Ion saw Maria', but both *pe* and the clitic must appear when the order is OVS: *pe Maria a văzut-o Ion* lit. 'Maria saw her Ion'. Resumptive pronouns also occur as a cross-reference for lower items on the animacy hierarchy when these occur as initial objects (though *pe* is not obligatory under these circumstances): *singura menţiune a acestei părţi de cuvânt o găsim în ...* lit. 'the only mention of this word part (we) it find in ...'; and in relative clauses, a relativised object must be represented by both decoding methods: *acesta e carnetul pe care l-am furat* lit. 'this is the notebook which (I) it stole'.

Variability in the use of *pe* as an object marker (it is a feature more of formal than of informal language) leads to hypercorrection. The Rumanian linguist Graur notes examples such as: *îmi trebuie pe cineva care ...* lit. 'to me is necessary someone who ...', where speakers have treated the grammatical subject *cineva* as an object.

Within noun phrases the normal order is:

(a)	Determiner	–	Noun	–	Adjective
	Un/acest		copil		bun
	'A/this good child'				
(b)	Noun + def	–	Demonstrative + def	–	Adjective
	Copilul		acesta		bun
	'This good child'				
(c)	Adjective + def	–	Noun		
	Bunul		copil		
	'The good child'				

Thus, indefinite determiners precede the noun, while adjectives (and relative clauses) follow it, except for contrastive use, as in (c); when demonstratives follow the noun (as in (b)), both are marked for definiteness.

Definiteness on nouns is unmarked when the noun is part of a prepositional phrase (*cu* 'with' is an exception), unless the noun is further modified: *masă* 'table'; *masa* 'the table'; *sub masă* 'under the table'; *sub masa pe care ai construit-o* 'under the table that you constructed (it)'. This phenomenon provides a useful method of distinguishing restrictive and non-restrictive relative clauses. Compare the following *non*-restrictive example, where the head noun is *not* marked for definiteness: *sub masă, pe care ai construit-o* 'under the table, which you constructed (it)'.

Rumanian retains the reflexive *se*, but with an increase in its use. In addition to its true reflexive sense (*se bate* 'beat oneself'), it has semi-fossilised to form verbs without a reflexive interpretation (*se duce* '(he) goes, to go'); it is used as an impersonal (*se spune* 'it is said') and as a passive (*aici se vând cărţile* 'here are sold books').

Features shared with other Balkan languages include the periphrastic future, with 'wish' as the auxiliary; the use of a suffixal definite marker (found not only in Rumanian and Albanian, but also in Bulgarian/Macedonian, unusual among the Slavonic languages in having the equivalent of the definite article in English); the use of cliticised resumptive pronouns (these occur in Western Romance but are usually part of a dislocated structure); and a severe decline in the use of the infinitive.

Like Western Romance, Rumanian inherited an infinitival complement clause structure in addition to indicative and subjunctive structures. However, where French and Italian would now use an infinitive Rumanian is more likely to use a subjunctive: Fr. *je veux chanter*; It. *volo cantare*; Rum. *vreau să cânt* 'I want to sing'. Within the auxiliary system one can see retention of the short infinitive: *voi cânta* 'I will sing'; *aş cânta* 'I would sing'. Many speakers also use *pot cânta* for *pot să cânt* 'I am able to sing'. Given the modal value of verbs representing ability or possibility, such an option is not surprising – the short infinitive can be seen as a stem form of the verbal complex and *pot* straddles the boundary between main verb and auxiliary verb.

The decline of the infinitive appears to be relatively recent. It is used as a complement clause marker in regular alternation with the subjunctive in a mid-eighteenth century grammar: *se cuvine a păzi/se cuvine să păzească* 'it is proper to be on guard'. Hand in hand with the reduction in use of the infinitive went its truncation (by loss of its Latin *-re* termination). In the modern language, *-re* forms are now clearly established as nominals and correspond closely to gerunds or derived nominals in English: *se întoarce* 'to return, he returns'→*întoarcerea lui neaşteptată* 'his unexpected return'.

Despite these Balkan characteristics, there has been some tendency during the last 150 years for the language to move towards the mainstream Romance pattern in syntax. The infinitive has begun to appear more regularly as a complement clause marker, and the periphrastic passive has made great inroads into the area occupied by the reflexive passive: *a fost furat* lit. 'was stolen' is more common than *s-a furat* lit. 'stole itself'. The regional use of a preposition to mark possession or indirect objects has found some currency in the spoken standard language, rather than the genitive/dative case marking. A much-cited example of a prepositional indirect object marking is: *dă apă la vite* instead of *dă apă vitelor* 'give water to the cattle', and street vendors in Bucharest were noted between the wars as using the prepositional *planul de Bucureşti* in place of *planul Bucureştiului* 'plan of Bucharest'. In Arumanian it is normal to find the *la* 'to' + nominative/accusative structure with full noun phrases instead of the dative case, since Greek also has a prepositional construction: *ðíno ta práγmata stin yinéka* 'I give the things to the woman.'

It is, of course, impossible to predict how far this reromancing tendency will go in morphosyntax but it is certainly the case that in some areas of structure change is unlikely. Thus, while there has been a resurgence in the use of the infinitival future (*voi cânta*) rather than the subjunctive alternative (*o să cânt*) in literary texts, it is hard to imagine Rumanian adopting a future based on infinitive + 'have' in line with Western Romance. Indeed, it would appear that in Western Romance a periphrastic future is also on the increase.

5 Vocabulary

Since vocabulary is more readily borrowed than other linguistic features, it is in its lexical stock that Rumanian has shown the greatest tendency to reromance during the last 150 years. For the same reason, however, the language had also had its original Latin lexical base diluted by contact with other languages in the Balkans, not least Slavonic. The total Slavonic element in Rumanian has been put as high as 40 per cent, though recent borrowings of international vocabulary have reduced this overall proportion considerably. It is in any case misleading to give a single figure for the language as a whole, since no speaker will use, or even know, all the words in the language. In everyday conversation the proportion of words from one source may well differ from the overall proportion in the language of material from that source. Using a basic 100- or

200-item word list relating to everyday life, it can be shown that Rumanian has a Latin lexical base of well over 90 per cent.

Nevertheless, the overall Slavonic element in Rumanian cannot be ignored, even if the Romance structure of the language has been left relatively unaffected. For the remainder of this section I give a brief résumé of the various lexical influences Rumanian has undergone, with examples from the major sources.

There is little evidence of substratum influence in Balkan Romance. Latin appears to have replaced the local Thracian language to such an extent that only a few words can even be considered Thracian in origin. Some of these are cognate with Albanian words and it is possible that they represent the remains of some Thraco-Illyrian language base. The following words are possible candidates, though it cannot be ruled out that they are indigenous Albanian words borrowed from Albanian by Rumanian: Rum. *abure* 'steam' (Alb. *avull*); Rum. *brad* 'fir' (Alb. *bredhi*); Rum. *mal* '(river) bank' (Alb. *mat*); Rum. *vatră* 'hearth' (Alb. *vatrë*).

Slavonic vocabulary in Rumanian can be divided into two main groups: popular, borrowed from the time of earliest contact between Balkan Romance and South Slavonic (approximately from the sixth century onwards); and technical or literary borrowings, from the thirteenth century onwards. This gave rise to doublets: from Old Slavonic *sŭvŭršiti* came popular *sfîrşi* and literary *săvîrşi* 'finish, complete'. Borrowing was not always direct and calques can be found. One much-cited example: on the basis of the two meanings of the South Slavonic *světŭ* 'light' and 'world', Latin *LŪMEN-LŪMINIS* 'light' had two derivations in Rumanian – *lume* 'world' and *lumină* 'light'.

Much religious vocabulary in Rumanian has a Slavonic character – as pointed out in Section 2, Old Church Slavonic was the official language of the Orthodox Church in what is now Rumania. When the vernacular became the norm, much of the Old Church Slavonic terminology was taken over. At the same time, it should be appreciated that an original source of much of this vocabulary was Greek, Old Church Slavonic merely being the vehicle for its transfer to Rumanian. The word *chilie* 'cell' attributed in Section 2 to Slavonic was in fact borrowed originally by Old Church Slavonic from Greek *kéllion*. It is partly for this reason that Greek influence on Balkan Romance was much greater than on Western Romance. Greek words also found their way into Rumanian via popular Slavonic language: *broatec* 'toad' derives via Slavonic from Greek *brotachos*, with cognate forms in Albanian and Arumanian. However, the early borrowing *drum* 'way, road' via Bulgarian from Greek *ðrómos* is not found in the Arumanian of present-day Greece, where a derivative of Latin *CALLEM* 'track' is used instead (Arumanian /kale/; Rum. *cale* does exist but has a more restricted sense than the general word *drum*).

During the Phanariot period (1711–1821), when the principalities of Moldavia and Wallachia were administered for the Turks by Greek princes, many words were borrowed from Greek by Rumanian, though it has been calculated that of the more than 1,200 words borrowed in this period only 250 are left in the modern language (e.g. *stridie* 'oyster' from *strídi*; *aerisi* 'air, ventilate, fan' from the aorist of *aerízo*). During this period too, Turkish words found their way into Rumanian but many of these have also disappeared from use. Perhaps 3 per cent of Rumanian vocabulary is Turkish in origin, and relatively common words include: *duşman* 'enemy' (Tk. *duşman*) and *chior* 'one-eyed' (Tk. *kör*).

Over the last 200 years the influence of Western Romance and Latin on Rumanian has been substantial. The Transylvanian School began importing Western Romance loans from the late eighteenth century, but interest was more in the Latin origins of the language than in Romance relationships. Consequently, not only did they etymologise their writing system (see Section 1), but they also set about purging the language of Slavonic loans and creating new Latin-based vocabulary. Some portmanteau words were created: from Slavonic-based *război* 'war' and Latin *BELLUM* was created *război*, which has not survived into the modern language; on the other hand, the combination of Slavonic-based *năravuri* 'customs' and Latin *MŌRES* gave *moravuri* 'customs, morals', which is in common use today. The desire to 'improve' and 'purify' Rumanian on the part of the Transylvanian School has complicated considerably the already difficult task of carrying out research on the origins of Rumanian vocabulary.

It was the rise of France and French as cultural models during the nineteenth century that did most to change the overall pattern of the Rumanian word stock. French became the source of much new vocabulary but also the vehicle for the entry of words from other languages. For example, a modern dictionary attributes *miting* '(political) meeting' and *dumping* '(trade) dumping' to 'French (from English)'. On the other hand, some French vocabulary entered Rumanian via Russian. As Russian influence increased during the second half of the nineteenth century, military and administrative terms were introduced: *infanterie* 'infantry', *cavalerie* 'cavalry', *parlament* 'parliament' and *administrație* 'administration' all appear to have followed this route.

There were two distinct attitudes among writers of the Muntenian school towards the treatment of Romance loans. There were those who, like the Transylvanian School, wanted to modify considerably in line with what were felt to be normal Rumanian developments. This gave rise to linguistic terms such as *obiept* and *subiept* in place of *obiect* and *subiect* (though the *-pt-* form reflects the *CT > pt* pattern discussed in Section 2, it was the *-ct-* form that survived). Other writers took a more realistic approach and, while only using words for which there was not already an adequate native Rumanian equivalent, embraced the imported vocabulary without amendment. Nevertheless, the lack of a clear relationship between French spelling and pronunciation has meant that, for example, Fr. *réveillon* is rendered in Rumanian today as both *reveion* and *revelion* 'New Year celebration'. Finally, French loans also gave rise to doublets as Latin-based words came face to face again. In addition to the example in Section 2, *sentiment* was imported alongside the more native *simțământ* 'feeling, sentiment'.

Today, the effect of American economic power and technological growth can be felt in the importing of many English technical and commercial terms into Rumanian, their fate regulated to some extent by the Rumanian Academy, which began to unify the treatment of neologisms (choosing, for example, the appropriate gender and plural forms) from 1940 onwards. The irony is, of course, that much of this new vocabulary from English has itself Latin and Romance origins, thus adding yet another layer onto what was already a very complex foundation.

Bibliography

Much of the material on Rumanian is written in that language, but Mallinson (1986) is a thorough reference grammar in English.

Agard (1958) is a short volume in structuralist mould, concentrating on phonology and morphology, while Lombard (1974) is a detailed structural description, fuller than Agard but more difficult to find one's way around. Deletant (1983) is a very good introduction to the language for those wishing to speak it. The Academy grammar, Graur (1963), is very thorough and better than many academy grammars, though it has the usual slightly prescriptive bias. Sandfeld and Olsen (1936–62) is a full description of the syntax of the written language, with many examples, in the style of Lombard; a transformational description of the major syntactic structures, in the framework of Chomsky's Standard Theory, is provided by Vasiliu and Golopenţia-Eretescu (1969).

For the history of the language, Rosetti (1968) gives a wealth of detail on the development of the language from Latin and its contact with other languages, and is well worth the effort for those with an interest in Romance languages; Rosetti (1973) is a brief summary of this magnum opus. Close (1974) is an excellent discussion of the rise of the Muntenian dialect as the standard language, with great detail on the nineteenth-century vogue for Romance and particularly French linguistic culture.

References

Agard, F.B. 1958. *Structural Sketch of Rumanian* (Linguistic Society of America, Baltimore)

Close, E. 1974. *The Development of Modern Rumanian – Linguistic Theory and Practice in Muntenia 1821–1838* (Oxford University Press, Oxford)

Deletant, D. 1983. *Colloquial Romanian* (Routledge and Kegan Paul, London)

Graur, Al. 1963. *Gramatica limbii romîne*, 2 vols (Academy of Sciences, Bucharest)

Lombard, A. 1974. *La Langue roumaine – une presentation* (Klincksieck, Paris)

Mallinson, Graham. 1986. *Rumanian* (Routledge, London)

Rosetti, Al. 1968. *Istoria limbii române de la origini pînă in secolul al XVII-lea* (Bucharest)

—— 1973. *Brève histoire de la langue roumaine des origines à nos jours* (Mouton, The Hague)

Sandfeld, Kr. and Olsen, H. 1936–62. *Syntaxe roumaine*, 3 vols (Droz, Paris)

Vasiliu, E. and Golopenţia-Eretescu, S. 1969. *Sintaxa transformaţională a limbii române* (Bucharest; also available in an irritatingly poor English translation, *The Transformational Syntax of Romanian*, Mouton, The Hague, 1972)

14

Slavonic Languages

Bernard Comrie

The approximate present distribution of the Slavonic (or Slavic) languages can be seen from the attached sketch-map. The languages currently spoken, according to their genetic relations within Slavonic (see below) are: South Slavonic: Bulgarian, Macedonian, Serbian/Croatian/Bosnian, Slovene; West Slavonic: Czech, Slovak, Polish, Upper and Lower Sorbian (Lusatian); East Slavonic: Russian, Ukrainian, Belarusian (Belorussian). In addition, some speech varieties have an official status on the border between language and dialect, such as Kashubian (Cassubian) in Poland. Finally, two extinct Slavonic languages are known from texts: Polabian (a West Slavonic language spoken in northern Germany until around 1700) and Old Church Slavonic (Old Bulgarian) (a South Slavonic language attested by a huge volume of texts starting in the ninth century). In phonological and morphological structure the Slavonic languages are very close to one another, more so than the Romance languages. The same applies to their basic lexicon; for more abstract and technical vocabulary, however, there is considerable language diversity, reflecting different national policies towards loanwords and use of native word-forming techniques: thus Russian and Polish use the international word *teatr* 'theatre', while Czech uses *divadlo* (from a root meaning 'look'), and Serbian/Croatian/Bosnian has two words, Croatian preferring *kazalište* (from a root meaning 'show'), Serbian *pozorište* (from a root meaning 'see').

The earliest Slavonic texts are from the ninth century (though extant copies are later), in Old Church Slavonic. Since the final break-up of Common Slavonic unity is dated not much earlier than this, Old Church Slavonic is very close to Late Common Slavonic, although Old Church Slavonic does have distinctive South Slavonic (more specifically, Bulgarian-Macedonian) features. Two alphabets were in use in the early period, both providing a good fit to the phonemic system of Old Church Slavonic: Glagolitic and Cyrillic. Glagolitic is usually considered the older; the forms of its letters are quite distinctive, although similarities to the alphabets of other important Christian languages of the period are detectable. The Cyrillic alphabet is more closely modelled on Greek (see Chapters 15 and 18 for two modern Cyrillic alphabets). The Cyrillic alphabet continues in use among Slavonic peoples of traditional Orthodox religion (i.e. for the East Slavonic languages, Bulgarian, Macedonian and the Serbian variety of Serbian/Croatian/Bosnian), while the others use the Latin alphabet.

Map 14.1 Approximate Distribution of Slavonic Languages in Europe.

Within the Indo-European family, the Slavonic languages are satem languages, with sibilant reflexes of Proto-Indo-European $\hat{k}$, e.g. PIE *$de\hat{k}m$ 'ten', OCS *desętъ*. An interesting development in the vowel system, of major importance for the later development of Slavonic, is the shift of PIE *i, *u to reduced vowels (jers), symbolised ь, ъ, e.g. OCS *mьgla* 'mist' (cf. Lith. *miglà*), OCS *snъxa* 'daughter-in-law' (cf. Skt. *snuṣā́*). Two main sets of sound changes separate Proto-Indo-European from Common Slavonic. One is a tendency for sounds within the syllable to be arranged in order of increasing sonority (i.e obstruents, then liquids and semi-vowels, then vowels). Particular changes instantiating this tendency are:

270

(a) loss of syllable-final consonants, e.g. OCS *synъ* (cf. Lith. *sūnùs*);
(b) the development of certain sequences of vowel plus nasal within the syllable to nasalised vowels, of which Common Slavonic has back *ǫ* and front *ę*, e.g. OCS *svętъ* 'holy' (cf. Lith. *šveñtas*), OCS *pǫtь* 'way' (cf. Lat. *pons*, gen. *pontis* 'bridge');
(c) the monophthongisation of diphthongs, e.g. OCS *iti* 'to go' (cf. Lith. *eĩti*), OCS *suxъ* 'dry' (cf. Lith. *saũsas*);
(d) the development of sequences of **o* or **e* plus a liquid within the syllable (symbolised **tort*) either by metathesis (South and West Slavonic) or by insertion of a vowel after the liquid (East Slavonic), e.g. OCS *glava*, Cz. *hláva*, Po. *głowa*, Rus. *golova* 'head' (cf. Lith. *galvà*).

The second major set of sound changes is a series of palatalisations. By the first palatalisation, **g*, **k*, **x* become, respectively, *ž*, *č*, *š* before original front vowels, e.g. OCS *živъ* 'alive' (cf. Lith. *gývas*). By the second palatalisation, the same three consonants become, respectively, *ʒ* (a voiced dental affricate, subsequently de-affricated to *z* in most languages), *c* (voiceless dental affricate) and *s* (but *š* in West Slavonic) before front vowels newly arisen from monophthongisation, e.g. OCS *cěna* 'price' (cf. Lith. *káina*). Thus the first palatalisation took place before monophthongisation occurred, the second palatalisation after. The third palatalisation has the same effect as the second, but occurs after front vowels, e.g. OCS *kъnęʒь* 'prince', a loan from Common Gmc. **kuningaz* 'king'. Since a given morpheme can occur sometimes before a back vowel, sometimes before a front vowel, the palatalisations give rise to synchronic morphophonological alternations, e.g. OCS *mǫka* 'torment', *mǫčiti* 'to torture'; *noga* 'leg', locative singular *noʒě* (where *ě* is from **ai*). In addition to the three palatalisations, Common Slavonic also developed palatal consonants *nj*, *lj*, *rj* from sequences of sonorant plus semivowel; despite the usual transcription, these are unit phonemes. Finally, sequences of dentals plus **j* also gave rise to palatal consonants, e.g. OCS *šyti* 'to sew' (cf. Lith. *siúti*).

In terms of nominal declension, the oldest Slavonic languages are conservative Indo-European languages. Three numbers are distinguished (singular, dual, plural), as are three genders (masculine, feminine, neuter) and seven cases (nominative, vocative, accusative, genitive, dative, instrumental, locative). The distinct declension classes and the distinction between substantival and pronominal declension are retained, though there are many analogies leading to the combination of similar declension classes (for instance, of masculine *o*-stems and *u*-stems, see below). An important innovation of the Common Slavonic period is the relevance of animacy to declension, whereby certain animate nouns (originally only some masculine singulars) replace the accusative by the genitive, e.g. OCS *bogъ* 'God', accusative *boga*, but *gradъ* 'city', accusative *gradъ*. An innovation within the morphology of adjectives is the development of pronominal adjectives, initially used only attributively and indicating a definite noun phrase, e.g. OCS *dobryjь člověkъ* 'the good man', cf. *dobrъ člověkъ* 'a good man'; Common Slavonic, like most of the modern languages (except Bulgarian and Macedonian), has no articles.

The verbal morphology of Common Slavonic represents a more radical departure from Proto-Indo-European. The morphological encoding of person and number in finite verbs is retained, as is the present/imperfect/aorist opposition. Morphologically expressed voice and mood distinctions are lost, except for that between indicative and imperative. There is no morphologically expressed future. The aspectual opposition between imperfective and perfective, so characteristic of the modern Slavonic languages (see further Chapter 15, pages 283–284), is already present, at least in embryonic form, from the earliest Slavonic texts. Various periphrastic verb constructions are found: the perfect, formed with the auxiliary 'be' and the past participle, occurs in all the languages, while the auxiliaries used for the future vary considerably from language to language.

Within the Indo-European family, the Slavonic languages are particularly close to the Baltic languages (Lithuanian, Latvian, Old Prussian), whence the frequent use of Lithuanian in this section for comparison with Slavonic. One particularly striking parallelism is the above-mentioned development of pronominal adjectives, cf. Lithuanian *geràsis žmogùs* 'the good man', *gēras žmogùs* 'a good man'. These similarities are sometimes taken as evidence for a single Balto-Slavonic branch of Indo-European, sometimes to reflect close contact between the two branches rather than a period of common development.

As indicated above, the Slavonic languages subdivide into three groups, which can be identified on the basis of phonological criteria. The most salient characteristic of East Slavonic is the already mentioned insertion of an extra vowel in **tort* sequences (*polnoglasie*), as in Rus. *golova* 'head'. One salient characteristic of West Slavonic is the development of **tj* to *c* and of **dj* to *ʒ* (later de-affricated in most languages to *z*), e.g. PIE **medhios*, Po. *miedza*, Cz. *meze*, cf. Rus. *meža*, OCS *mežda*, SCB *mèđa*, Slovene *méja* 'boundary'; another is the development of **x* to *š*, rather than *s*, under the second and third palatalisations, e.g. Po. *szary*, Old Cz. *šěrý*, cf. Old Rus. *sěr*, Slovene *ser* 'grey'. South Slavonic is a less homogeneous grouping, and the only clear common phonological innovation is the development of Early Common Slavonic **jōns* (which occurs in a few morphological forms) to *ę* rather than *ě*; indeed, the apparent unity of South Slavonic may well be in large measure an artefact of its physical separation from the other Slavonic languages, in particular Slovak, by the incursion of Hungarian and the expansion of Rumanian.

It is more difficult to say much that is interesting and reliable about Common Slavonic syntax. Most of the earliest texts are rather literal translations, especially from Greek, and it therefore difficult to know to what extent word order, for instance, follows native Slavonic preferences or is calqued directly from the original. On the basis of the early textual evidence and comparison with later stages of the Slavonic languages, one can, however, state two generalisations that tie in intimately with the rich morphological system. Word order is grammatically free, i.e there is no fixed order among subject, predicate, objects, adverbial modifiers, etc.; the case inflections are usually sufficient to retrieve these grammatical relations, and variation in word order correlates primarily with pragmatic distinctions such as that between topic and comment (see further Chapter 15, pages 287–288). The rich morphological system also provides rich possibilities for agreement: thus, the verb agrees in person and number with its subject, and adjectives agree in gender, number and case with their head noun.

Later phonological, morphological and syntactic developments belong properly to the histories of the individual Slavonic languages, but the seeds of some of these later developments can already be seen in the Late Common Slavonic period but then took somewhat different paths in the different languages. Above, we have already discussed the different details of palatalisation and of **tort* sequences in different branches of Slavonic. One major innovation of the early literary period that unites the Slavonic languages in type but divides them in detail is the subsequent development of the jers. In all Slavonic languages, a distinction is made between strong and weak jers, where in general a weak jer is one in word-final position or in a syllable preceding a full vowel, while a strong jer is one in a syllable preceding a weak jer. Weak jers are lost, while strong jers are strengthened to full vowels, but the precise full vowel to which each of the two jers is strengthened varies from language to language. In Common Slavonic **sъnъ* 'sleep', the first jer is strong, the second weak. In Russian, strong jer gives *o*, i.e *son*; in Polish, it gives *e*, i.e *sen*. The loss of the jers has a major effect on the phonological structure of words in Slavonic languages, since it leads to syllable-final consonants and consonant clusters that were previously impossible: thus Common Slavonic nominative singular **мъхъ* 'moss' and instrumental singular **мъхъмь* give Russian *мох* and *мхом* respectively, the latter contracting from three syllables to one.

Another phonological development that characterises much of the Slavonic domain, especially East Slavonic and Polish, is the further development of a systematic opposition between plain and palatalised consonants. Weak ь, though lost as a segment, palatalises a preceding consonant, e.g. Russian *pjat'* 'five', cf. OCS *pętь*. In common Slavonic, there is no possible palatalisation opposition before *o*, whereas languageparticular developments in Russian and Polish give rise to just this contrast: from the Common Slavonic stem **nes-* 'carry' Russian has *nës* (phonemically /ńos/) '[he] carried' (cf. *nos* 'nose'), while Polish has *niosę* (phonemically /ńosẽ/) 'I carry'.

The rich nominal morphology of Common Slavonic is remarkably stable over most of the Slavonic territory. Only Bulgarian and Macedonian have lost morphological case. The dual has been lost in all Slavonic languages except Slovene and Sorbian. Most languages have undergone some simplification of the remaining distinctions, the main line of innovation being the loss of minor declension types in favour of the three main declension classes (*o*-stems, *a*-stems, *i*-stems), though in some instances the actual surviving inflection is taken from the minor class (e.g. the most common Polish suffixes for genitive and dative of masculine *o*-stems are -*u* and -*owi*, originally from the *u*-stems).

The morphology of the verb has undergone more radical shifts. Here, Bulgarian and Macedonian prove to be most conservative in retaining the rich Common Slavonic system, although both have also innovated in the development of special periphrastic verb constructions to indicate events not directly witnessed by the speaker (*preizkazvane*), e.g. Bulgarian *toj bil peel* 'he was (they say) singing', cf. *toj peeše* 'he was singing'. The aorist and imperfect have been ousted by the originally compound perfect in most Slavonic languages: apart from Bulgarian and Macedonian, these verb forms survive only in Sorbian and in literary Serbian/Croatian/Bosnian. The aspectual opposition between imperfective and perfective has developed in all Slavonic languages (including Bulgarian and Macedonian) into a fully fledged morphological opposition.

Bibliography

Comrie and Corbett (1993) provides a detailed survey of the Slavonic languages, emphasising the structure and history of the individual languages, while Sussex and Cubberley (2006) is organised primarily by topic. Schenker (1995) emphasises Common Slavonic and the period of the earliest written records.

References

Comrie, Bernard and Corbett, Greville (eds) 1993. *The Slavonic Languages* (Routledge, London)
Schenker, Alexander M. 1995. *The Dawn of Slavic: An Introduction to Slavic Philology* (Yale University Press, New Haven)
Sussex, Roland and Cubberley, Paul (2006). *The Slavic Languages* (Cambridge University Press, Cambridge)

15

Russian

Bernard Comrie

1 Historical Background

Russian, together with Ukrainian and Belarusian (Belorussian), is a member of the East Slavonic group within the Slavonic branch of Indo-European. Although the three languages are now considered distinct literary languages, they are very close to one another, with a high degree of mutual intelligibility. At the time of the emergence of writing in East Slavonic, around the year 1000, there was just a single language, conventionally called Old Russian. In terms of the development of Russian as a modern literary language and of the separation of Ukrainian and Belarusian, there are two strands that must continually be borne in mind: the relation between native East Slavonic forms and forms borrowed from South Slavonic, and the relations among regional variations within East Slavonic.

Although there is some controversy concerning the possible independent, native development of writing in Russian, it is generally agreed that writing was introduced to Russia together with Christianity towards the end of the tenth century. The liturgical language that was introduced in this process was Old Church Slavonic, a South Slavonic language. At this period Old Church Slavonic and Old Russian were presumably readily mutually intelligible, yet still there were clear differences between them, namely the criterial differences between East and South Slavonic (see page 272). At this early period, much of the writing was of religious content (biblical and liturgical translations, saints' lives) or was written by monks (for instance, historical chronicles), and in such writing the attempt was made to write Church Slavonic, avoiding local East Slavonic peculiarities. In practice, the Russian monks writing these manuscripts often erred by allowing East Slavonic forms to creep into their texts, but many of the religious texts of this time are very close to canonical Old Church Slavonic. Parallel to this writing in Church Slavonic, secular writing also developed, in particular for legal purposes (law codes, contracts, wills, treaties), later also personal messages. The language of these secular documents is much closer to the East Slavonic of the time, although inevitably, since any scribe was trained in Church Slavonic, numerous Church Slavonic forms crept into secular texts. Thus Old Russian of this early period was characterised by something akin to diglossia between native East Slavonic (the low variety) and Church Slavonic (the high variety).

With the passage of time, the divergence between the two varieties became gradually less, in particular with many Church Slavonic forms gaining acceptance into even the lowest forms of language. A break in this process was marked by the Second South Slavonic influence. The capture of Constantinople by the Turks in 1453 led to the immigration of a large number of South Slavonic clerics to Russia, and one effect of their immigration was a return, in religious writing, to a more correct imitation of canonical Old Church Slavonic. While South Slavonic forms already accepted into lower styles remained, the higher styles now followed an archaic Church Slavonic language far removed from the spoken language of the period.

By the eighteenth century, in particular through the modernisation and secularisation efforts of Peter the Great, need was felt for a written language that would be closer to the educated spoken norm. The brilliant polymath M.V. Lomonosov, in his *Russian Grammar* (1755), set out a theory of three styles. According to this theory, there should be a high style, i.e. Church Slavonic, which would be used (in addition to religious purposes) for high poetic genres; a low style, almost purely East Slavonic (except for fully assimilated Church Slavonic features), to be used for personal correspondence and low comedy; and a middle style, to be used for lyric poetry, literary prose and scientific treatises. This middle style, which combined features of both East Slavonic and Church Slavonic, is the style which soon came to form the basis of the modern standard language. By the time of A.S. Pushkin (1799–1837), the first of the great writers of Russia's nineteenth century, this middle style is already established as the literary language. (Some influence of French, spoken fluently by Russia's ruling class in the nineteenth century, is now widely acknowledged, but remains to be studied in detail.) Although the language has continued to develop during the intervening two centuries, which have included the major social upheavals of the October Revolution (1917) and the collapse of the Soviet Union (1991), the modern Russian literary language is still defined chronologically as the language from Pushkin to the present day.

The coexistence of East Slavonic and South Slavonic forms from the earliest Old Russian to the present day is one of the salient characteristics of the language. It may be compared with the coexistence of Anglo-Saxon and Norman French elements in English, with the exception that East and South Slavonic are much closer to one another genetically than are English and French. In modern Russian, it is common to find doublets, i.e. derivatives of the same Common Slavonic root in both East Slavonic and Church Slavonic forms, the Church Slavonic form usually having a more abstract or learned connotation. One of the main differences between East Slavonic and South Slavonic is the treatment of Common Slavonic sequences of *o/e* followed by a liquid between consonants, symbolised *tort*. In East Slavonic, this sequence yields *torot*, while in South Slavonic it yields *trat*. In modern Russian, alongside East Slavonic *golová* 'head', there is also South Slavonic *glavá* 'chief; chapter'. (Note that in English *head* is of Anglo-Saxon origin, whereas *chief* and *chapter* are of Romance origin.) Another distinction between the two groups of Slavonic languages is the treatment of Common Slavonic *tj*, *dj*, which give East Slavonic *š*, *ž*, but South Slavonic *šč* (more accurately: *št*, but pronounced *šč* in Russian Church Slavonic), *žd*: contrast the East Slavonic form *gorjáčij* 'hot' with the present participle *gorjáščij* 'burning', which, like all modern Russian present participles, is of Church Slavonic origin. Since Common Slavonic had, within the paradigm of the same verb, some forms with just *t* and others with *t* followed by *j*, this gives rise to morphophonological alternations in modern Russian, either between *t* and *č* (East Slavonic forms, e.g. *platít'* 'to pay', *plaču* 'I pay') or between *t* and *šč* (Church Slavonic forms, e.g. *sokratít'* 'to abbreviate', *sokraščú* 'I shall abbreviate'). In addition to East Slavonic and Church Slavonic doublets of the above kinds, there are also some instances where the Church Slavonic form has completely supplanted the native form, e.g. *sládkij* 'sweet', cf. Old Russian *solodъkъjь*.

At the time of the oldest Russian texts, the main dialect division was between Northern and Southern Russian, the dividing line running approximately along the latitude of present-day Moscow. The cultural centre of the south was Kiev; the north had several centres, the most important being Novgorod. In texts from the northern area, a number of regional features occur, one of the most salient being the neutralisation of *c* and *č* into a single affricate, usually *c*. It is probable that at this early period north and south were already divided by what is still one of the major dialect divisions in Russian, namely the pronunciation of Common Slavonic *g*, the north having a plosive [g], the south a fricative [ɣ]; the age of this feature is suggested, among other things, by the fact that modern Ukrainian and Belarusian share this feature with South Russian dialects. Unfortunately, the Cyrillic alphabet has no way of distinguishing between the plosive and the fricative sounds, so textual evidence is inconclusive.

The linguistic separation of Ukrainian and Belarusian runs parallel to their political separation. In the mid-thirteenth century, Russia fell under Tatar domination, and subsequently what are now Ukraine and Belarus fell under Lithuanian, subsequently Polish hegemony. The distinctive features of Ukrainian are most marked, with Belarusian often occupying an intermediate position between the other East Slavonic languages. During the period of political separation, innovations that began in Ukraine were in general unable to penetrate Russian, and vice versa. One of the main characteristics of Ukrainian is the development of Common Slavonic *ě*, which in standard Russian ultimately merged with *e*, to *i*, e.g. Old Russian *lěto*, Russian *léto*, Ukrainian *líto* 'summer'. Another characteristic of Ukrainian is that consonants lose their palatalisation before reflexes of Old Russian *e* (Ukrainian *e*) and *i* (Ukrainian *y*). Belarusian has fewer unique characteristics, one being the affrication of palatalised *t*, *d* to *ć*, *ʒ́*, just as in Polish.

Meanwhile, in Russian proper, another phonological development of major importance for the dialectal composition of the language was taking place, namely *ákan'e*. This refers to the pronunciation of Old Russian unstressed *o* as *a*, e.g. of *vodá* as [vadá]. This change probably started somewhere in the south of Russia, but spread rapidly to cover the whole of the south, some central areas, and also Belarus (but not Ukraine, further evidence of its greater separateness). Lack of *ákan'e* is usually referred to as *ókan'e*. This phonological development ties in with a crucial political development. In the struggle against the Tatars, a key role came to be played by Muscovy, the area around Moscow, leading to the independence and unification of Russia (minus Ukraine and Belarus) under Moscow by the late fifteenth century. Although Moscow seems originally to have been part of the *ókan'e* dialect area, the city and surrounding area succumbed to the spread of *ákan'e*. Moscow's central position, coupled with the fact that it combined features of Northern dialects (in particular, the plosive pronunciation of *g*) and of Southern dialects (in particular, *ákan'e*), led to the formation of a new intermediate dialect grouping, the Central dialects, which lie at the basis of the modern standard language. The main dialect areas in Russian are thus: Northern (*ókan'e*, plosive *g*), Central (*ákan'e*, plosive *g*) and Southern (*ákan'e*, fricative *g*), with the standard language following the compromise Central dialect distribution of these features. Despite the huge area over which Russian is spoken, dialect differences, whether regional or social, are remarkably small and are, as in many other countries, becoming ever smaller with the spread of education.

The number of native speakers of Russian in 2006 is around 145 million, the overwhelming majority in Russia, although there are also substantial Russian-speaking populations in some other parts of the former Soviet Union, especially Ukraine, Kazakhstan, Belarus, Uzbekistan, Moldova and Kyrgyzstan. Russian is the official language of the Russian Federation. (In ethnically based republics and other administrative areas, this is typically alongside the local language.) It is also a co-official language of Belarus. While the situation regarding co-official use of Russian is somewhat fluid in Central Asia, with decisions having gone back and forth since the break-up of the USSR, in 2006 Russian is a co-official language of Kazakhstan and Kyrgyzstan. It is also widely used elsewhere in Central Asia and in Azerbaijan, Moldova and Ukraine.

2 Phonology

The segmental phonemes of Russian (stressed vowels, consonants) are set out in Table 15.1; certain minor phonemes, which occur only in the speech of some speakers of the standard language, have been omitted. One striking feature of this phoneme inventory is the richness of the consonant system, in large measure due to the almost completely systematic opposition of palatalised and non-palatalised consonants, as in *brat'* 'to take' [brat] versus *brat* 'brother' [brat]. The only non-palatalised consonants to lack palatalised counterparts are [c], [š], [ž]. Conversely, a few consonants are always palatalised with

Table 15.1 Segmental Phonemes of Russian

Vowels			
	i	ɨ	u
	e		o
		a	

Consonants	*Plain stop*		*Affricative*	*Fricative*		*Nasal*	*Lateral*	*Trill*	*Semi-vowel*
Bilabial	p	b				m			
	ṕ	b́				ḿ			
Labio-dental				f	v				
				f́	v́				
Dental	t	d	c			n	l		
	t́	d́				ń	ĺ		
Alveolar				s	z			r	
				ś	ź			ŕ	
Palato-Alveolar				š	ž				
			č́	ś:					j
Velar	k	g		x					
	ḱ	ǵ		x́					

277

no non-palatalised counterpart: [č], [š:], [j]. (The functional yield of palatalisation with the velars is, however, minimal.)

The vowels represented in Table 15.1 are those found in stressed syllables. In Russian, stress is free (can occur in principle on any syllable of a word) and mobile (different forms of the same word can have different stresses). Thus lexical items can be distinguished solely by stress, e.g. *muká* 'flour', *múka* 'torment', as can morphological forms of the same lexical item, e.g. genitive singular *rukí*, nominative plural *rúki*, from *ruká* 'hand'. Although there are some principles of accentuation (e.g. perfective verbs with the prefix *vy-* always stress this prefix), there is much that is purely conventional, and even within the standard language there are many instances of alternative stresses. Within the stressed vowel system, the phonemic status of the *i/ɨ* alternation is debatable: in general, *ɨ* occurs only after non-palatalised consonants, *i* only after palatalised consonants and word-initially. One of the main characteristics of Russian phonology is that the vowel system of unstressed syllables is radically different, because of a number of vowel neutralisations affecting, for many speakers, all vowels except *u*. By the phenomenon of *ákan'e*, the *o/a* opposition is neutralised in unstressed syllables (for the position after a palatalised consonant, see below); word-initially and in the immediately pretonic syllable, both vowels appear phonetically as [ʌ], elsewhere as [ə], e.g. *golová* 'head' [gəlʌvá], *magazín* 'shop' [məgʌźin]. After palatalised consonants, all of *a/e/o*, for some speakers also *i*, are neutralised to give [ɪ], e.g. *mestá* 'places' [ḿɪstá], *časý* 'clock' [čɪśɨ]' (this phenomenon is referred to as *íkan'e*; the precise nature of *íkan'e* is subject to a number of more specific constraints and also to some variation, even within the standard language).

The Russian writing system uses the Cyrillic alphabet (Table 15.2). The writing system is based, like the Greek and Roman alphabets, on the alphabetic principle, with as a basic rule one letter per phoneme. To assist the reader in converting the transliterations used in this section to a reasonably accurate phonetic representation, some details of divergences beween phoneme and letter sequences will be noted. Although stress is phonemic in Russian, it is not usual to mark it in writing; in this chapter, however,

Table 15.2 Russian Alphabet

Cyrillic		Transliteration	Cyrillic		Transliteration
А	а	a	Р	р	r
Б	б	b	С	с	s
В	в	v	Т	т	t
Г	г	g	У	у	u
Д	д	d	Ф	ф	f
Е	е	e	Х	х	x
Ё	ё	ë	Ц	ц	c
Ж	ж	ž	Ч	ч	č
З	з	z	Ш	ш	š
И	и	i	Щ	щ	šč
Й	й	j	Ъ	ъ	″
К	к	k	Ы	ы	y
Л	л	l	Ь	ь	′
М	м	m	Э	э	è
Н	н	n	Ю	ю	ju
О	о	o	Я	я	ja
П	п	p			

stress is always marked by an acute accent. Likewise, the diacritic on *ë*, which is always stressed, is usually omitted in writing Russian. Otherwise, for vowels, it should be noted that Russian orthography does not represent the effects of *ákan´e* and similar phenomena: thus the unstressed vowels of голова (*golová*) 'head' and магазин (*magazín*) 'shop' are distinguished orthographically, but not phonetically.

In pronunciation, Russian word-final obstruents are always voiceless, but orthographically voiced and voiceless obstruents are distinguished: thus рот (*rot*) 'mouth' and род (*rod*) 'birth' are both pronounced [rot]. Similarly, in Russian, sequences of obstruents assimilate in voicing to the last obstruent, but this is not shown in the orthography, e.g. гибкий (*gíbkij*) 'flexible' [gípkij]. The main complication in relating spelling to pronunciation, however, is the representation of palatalisation. It will be seen from comparison of Tables 15.1 and 15.2 that Russian has no special letters for palatalised consonants. Rather, palatalisation is indicated by modifying the non-palatalised consonant letter as follows. Word-finally or before a consonant, palatalisation is indicated by adding the letter ь after the non-palatalised consnant, as in брать (*brat´*) 'to take' [brat], тьма (*t´ma*) 'mist' [tma]. Before a vowel, different vowel symbols are used to distinguish palatalised and non-palatalised consonants. After a non-palatalised consonant, the vowel letters а, э, ы, о, у (*a, è, i, o, u*) are used; after a palatalised consonant я, е, и, ё, ю (*ja, e, i, ë, ju*) are used; e.g. мать (*mat´*) 'mother' [mat], мять (*mjat´*) 'to crumple' [mat]. The unpaired consonants ц, ч, ш, щ, ж (*c, č, š, šč, ž*) are treated differently: after them one always writes а, е, и, у (*a, e, i, u*), which thus have no effect on the palatalisation status of the preceding consonant (both *o* and *ë* are used; after *c, y* is written in native words). thus: шить (*šit´*) 'to sew' [šit], час (*čas*) 'hour' [čas]. The representation of the phoneme /j/ is also complex and intertwined with the representation of palatalisation. In syllable-final position, the special letter й (*j*) is used, e.g. мой (*moj*) 'my' [moj], война (*vojná*) 'war' [vʌjná]. Word-initially and after a vowel, the special letters я, е, и, ё, ю (*ja, e, i, ë, ju*) represent the sequence of /j/ plus vowel, e.g. яма (*jáma*) 'pit' [jámə], союз (*sojúz*) 'union' [sʌjús]. After a consonant, /j/ is represented by using the letter ь (´) (across prefix-stem boundaries, ъ (˝)) followed by я, е, и, ё, ю (*ja, e, i, ë, ju*), e.g. пьяный (*p´jányj*) 'drunk' [pjánɨj], муравьи (*murav´í*) 'ants' [murʌvjí]. Although the representation of palatalisation in Russian may seem complex, it does, given the richness of the consonant system and the relative poverty of the vowel system, enable the full range of phonemic oppositions to be maintained orthographically with a restricted set of distinct letters.

It will now be useful to consider some of the main historical phonological processes that have affected Russian in its development from Common Slavonic, in particular as these relate to the morphophonological alternations to be discussed below. The Common Slavonic nasal vowels, as in most Slavonic languages except Polish, were lost in Russian (before the earliest written texts), *ǫ becoming *u* and *ę becoming *a* with palatalisation of the preceding consonant, e.g. Common Slavonic *pǫtь 'way', *pętь 'five', Russian *put´, pjat´*. The Common Slavonic (and Old Russian) reduced vowels (jers) are lost in Russian as in the other Slavonic languages. In Russian, strong ъ and ь give *o* and *e* respectively; the weak jers are lost, but ь causes palatalisation of the preceding consonant, e.g. Old Russian *sъnъ*, genitive *sъna* 'sleep', modern *son, sna*; Old Russian *dьnь* 'day', genitive *dьnja*, modern *den´, dnja*.

Another innovation in Russian is the shift of Old Russian *e* to *o* before nonpalatalised consonants, but with retention of palatalisation in the preceding consonant. Thus Old Russian *nesъ* 'carried' gives modern *nës* [nos]. The effect of this change, like some of those already discussed (loss of *ę, loss of ь) is to increase the domain of the palatalisation opposition, since *nës* contrasts with *nos* 'nose'. One of the latest changes in the vowel system, and one not shared by all dialects of Russian, is the merger of Old Russian *ě* and *e* (of which the former probably had a closer pronunciation in Old Russian, as still in those dialects that retain it) to *e*. (Distinct orthographic symbols were retained until 1918.) This shift of *ě* to *e* post-dates the shift of *e* to *o* noted above and is thus not subject to it, thus further reinforcing the phonemic distinctiveness of the palatalisation opposition: modern Russian has the triple *voz* (Old Russian *vozъ*) 'cart', *vëz* (Old Russian *vezъ*) 'transported', *ves* (Old Russian *věsъ*) 'weight'.

Other changes in the vowel system already referred to are *ákan'e* and related phenomena (e.g. *íkan'e*), leading to neutralisation of unstressed vowels. In the obstruent system, the voice opposition was neutralised word-finally by the devoicing of voiced obstruents, leading to the merger of Old Russian *rъtъ* 'mouth' and *rodъ* 'birth' in modern pronunciation as [rot], and by assimilation of obstruents to the voice of a following obstruent, so that Old Russian *gibъkъjь* 'flexible' gives the modern pronunciation [ɡípkij].

One of the main characteristics of modern Russian is the large number of morphophonological alternations. Indeed, it is perhaps not accidental how much of modern morphophonological theory has been developed by Russian phonologists and by phonologists working on Russian, such as Trubetzkoy, Jakobson and Halle; since Polish shares this typological feature with Russian, one can enlarge the list to include Baudouin de Courtenay. Some of the alternations are inherited from Indo-European, in particular ablaut (see pages 14–15), as in the alternation between the stem vowels of *tekú* 'I flow' and *tok* 'current' (Indo-European *e/o* ablaut). The more systematic alternations, however, are those that have arisen through innovatory sound changes in Common Slavonic or Russian. The main Common Slavonic innovations relevant here are the palatalisations and other processes leading to the development of palatalised consonants. Thus the first palatalisation gives rise to the modern Russian *k/č* alternation in *pekú* 'I bake', *pečëš'* 'you bake': the original segment is **k*, retained before the back vowel (Common Slavonic **ǫ*) in the first member of the pair, but palatalised before the front vowel (Common Slavonic *e*) in the second item. The shift of **sj* to **š* in Common Slavonic turns up in modern Russian in the alternation found in *pisát'* 'to write', *pišú* 'I write', where the second item in early Common Slavonic was, with morpheme breaks, **pis-j-ǫ*.

Post-Common Slavonic innovations that have given rise to morphophonological alternations include the loss of the jers. Since strong jers develop to full vowels while weak jers are lost, and since a given Old Russian jer might be strong in some morphological forms of a word but weak in others, the Old Russian predictable alternation of strong and weak jers gives rise in the modern language to alternation between a full vowel and zero, as in *son* 'sleep', genitive *sna*, *den'* 'day', genitive *dnja*.

Ákan'e and related phenomena give rise to vowel alternations, given the mobile stress. Thus we find nominative singular *golová* 'head' [ɡəlʌvá], nominative plural *gólovy* [ɡóləvɨ], genitive plural *golóv* [ɡʌlóf], with alternation of the vowels in the first two syllables, and alternation of the first vowel in nominative singular *seló* 'hamlet' [śiló], nominative plural *sëla* [śólə]. In morphophonological transcription, the stems of these two words would be {golov-} and {śol-}. Lastly, final devoicing and consonant voice assimilation give rise to morphophonological alternations. Final devoicing gives rise to alternations because in different morphological forms of the same word a consonant can appear now word-finally, now followed by a vowel, as in *rod* 'birth' [rot], genitive *róda* [ródə]. Voicing assimilation gives rise to alternations because of the alternation between vowel and zero resulting from the loss of the jers, as in *pryžók* 'jump' [pr_ižók], genitive *pryžká* [pr_išká].

3 Morphology

Russian nominal morphology is illustrated in the chart of declension types (Table 15.3), with examples of the four major types of noun declension and of adjective declension. The nominal morphology turns out to be typologically very close to that of the oldest Indo-European languages. In particular, the morphology is fusional: thus, in the declension of nouns, it is not possible to segment one inflection encoding number and another encoding case, rather these two categories are encoded by a single formative, so that the final *-u* of dative singular *stolú* represents 'dative singular', rather than part of it representing 'dative' and some other part 'singular'. In the adjective declension, the inflections are fusional for gender as well as for number and case, so that the inflection of *stár-uju* encodes the complex 'feminine singular accusative'. In fact, with nouns,

Table 15.3 Russian Declension Types

Noun	a-*stem*	Masculine o-*stem*	Neuter o-*stem*	i-*stem*
Singular:				
Nominative	straná	stol	mésto	brov´
Accusative	stranú	stol	mésto	brov´
Genitive	straný	stolá	mésta	bróvi
Dative	strané	stolú	méstu	bróvi
Instrumental	stranój	stolóm	méstom	bróv´ju
Locative	strané	stolé	méste	bróvi
Plural:				
Nominative	strány	stolý	mestá	bróvi
Accusative	strány	stolý	mestá	bróvi
Genitive	stran	stolóv	mest	brovéj
Dative	stránam	stolám	mestám	brovjám
Instrumental	stránami	stolámi	mestámi	brovjámi
Locative	stránax	stoláx	mestáx	brovjáx

Adjective	Masculine		Neuter	Feminine
Singular:				
Nominative	stáryj		stároe	stáraja
Accusative	stáryj		stároe	stáruju
Genitive		stárogo		stároj
Dative		stáromu		stároj
Instrumental		stárym		stároj
Locative		stárom		stároj
Plural:				
Nominative			stárye	
Accusative			stárye	
Genitive			stáryx	
Dative			stárym	
Instrumental			stárymi	
Locative			stáryx	

there is fusion of yet another category, namely that of declension type: thus in the *a*-stems
-*u* indicates 'accusative singular', whereas in the *o*-stems it indicates 'dative singular'.
Although there is a high correlation between gender and declension type, it is not absolute:
most *a*-stem nouns are feminine, but those with clear male reference are masculine;
nearly all *i*-stem nouns are feminine, but *put'* 'way' is an isolated exception, being masculine; a masculine noun with male reference might be either an *o*-stem or an *a*-stem,
while a feminine noun might be either an *a*-stem or an *i*-stem. In addition to the major
declension types, there are also minor types represented by just a handful of nouns (e.g.
ten neuter nouns follow the pattern of *ímja* 'name', genitive *ímeni*), in addition to
idiosyncratic irregularities, including in particular the personal pronouns (e.g. *ja* 'I',
genitive *menjá*).

One important parameter in Russian nominal declension not revealed by the table is
animacy. In Russian, animate nouns (i.e. nouns referring to humans or animals), as well
as attributive adjectives (including demonstrative and possessive adjectives) accompanying them, have the accusative case like the genitive rather than the form given in
Table 15.3 if they are either masculine *o*-stems or plural (of any gender or declension
type). Thus *stáryj stol* 'old table' has accusative *stáryj stol*, but *stáryj slon* 'old elephant' has *stárogo slóná*; likewise nominative-accusative plural *stárye stolý*, but nominative plural *stárye slóný* and accusative-genitive *stáryx slonóv*. An animate noun not
belonging to the *o*-stems, such as *žába* 'toad', has accusative singular *žábu*, nominative
plural *žáby*, accusative plural *žab*.

Although Russian nominal morphology may look complex in comparison with, say,
English, it reflects a number of significant simplifications relative to Old Russian or
Common Slavonic. Few categories have been lost altogether, these being the dual
number and the vocative case. However, several Common Slavonic declension types
have been lost through merger with the more common types, such as *u*-stems with
o-stems, most consonant stems with one of the other declension types. In addition, there
has been some neutralisation (syncretism) leading to simplification, the most noticeable
such effect being the loss of gender distinctions in the plural: thus the modern nominative plural *stárye* represents the merger of three distinct Old Russian forms: masculine
starii, feminine *staryě*, neuter *staraja*. In addition to the overall pattern of simplification,
there has also been some complication. For instance, some masculine *o*-stems have a
partitive genitive in -*u* distinct from the regular genitive in -*a*; some masculine *o*-stems
form the nominative (and inanimate accusative) plural in -*á* rather than -*y*, e.g. *gorodá*,
plural of *górod* 'city'. In addition, some forms continuing Old Russian types have been
retained as idiosyncratic irregularities (e.g. the endingless genitive plural of masculine
o-stems in *glaz* 'eye', genitive plural also *glaz*).

In Common Slavonic, there were two declensions of adjectives, the so-called simple
declension (identical to noun declension) and the pronominal declension. In attributive
usage, they were distinguished in terms of definiteness, e.g. Old Russian *starъ gorodъ* 'an
old town', *starъjь gorodъ* 'the old town'. In modern Russian, only the pronominal adjective survives in attributive usage, as in *stáryj górod* '(the/an) old town', and it is this
form, conventionally termed the long form, that is given in the table of declensions. In
predicative usage, either the long form or the so-called short form, continuing the Old
Russian simple declension of adjectives, may be used, i.e. *górod stáryj/star* 'the town is
old', *straná krasívaja/krasíva* 'the country is beautiful'. Since the short form is only used
predicatively, it does not decline, but does distinguish gender and number (singular
masculine *star*, feminine *stará*, neuter *stáro*, plural for all genders *stáry* or *starý*).

Russian verbal morphology is rather less like that of the older Indo-European languages. Inflectionally, only a small number of categories are distinguished, as represented in the chart of conjugation types. Among the finite forms, the only mood distinct from the indicative is the imperative. Within the indicative, there is a binary morphological opposition between non-past (i.e. present-future) and past. In the non-past, verbs agree with their subject in person and number; in the past, they agree in gender and number. Of the non-finite forms, the infinitive is in common use, in particular after certain finite verbs, e.g. *ja xoču čitát'* 'I want to read'. Modern Russian also has participles (verbal adjectives) and converbs (verbal adverbs, conventionally called gerunds in English grammars of Russian), but use of these is primarily restricted to literary and scientific writing.

In addition to the categories represented in Table 15.4, Russian has a further category, that of aspect, with an opposition between imperfective and perfective. The general morphological principle is as follows. Simple verbs without a prefix are usually imperfective, e.g. *pisát'* 'to write'. Attachment of a prefix to such a verb makes it perfective, e.g. *na-pisát'* 'to write', *o-pisát'* 'to describe'. Usually, for a given simple verb there is one (unpredictable) prefix which adds no semantic component other than that of perfectivity, so that *pisát'- napisát'* (likewise *čitát'- procitát'* 'to read') can be considered an imperfective–perfective pair. Other prefixes do make other semantic modifications, e.g. *opisát'* means 'to describe', not just 'to write', but such verbs can be given imperfective counterparts by suffixation, thus giving a pair *opísyvat' – opisát'*. In addition, there are less common ways of forming aspectual pairs, such as suffixation of nonprefixed verbs, e.g. perfective *rešít'*, imperfective *rešát'* 'to decide'. In general, then, Russian verbs come in imperfective–perfective pairs, but it is often impossible to predict what the perfective counterpart of a given imperfective verb will be or vice versa.

While the meaning of tense is to locate a situation (action, event, state) in a certain time (for instance, past tense in the time before the present moment), the meaning of aspect is concerned rather with the subjective way of viewing the internal temporal structure of the situation. More particularly, the perfective views a situation as a single

Table 15.4 Russian Conjugation Types

		I Conjugation	II Conjugation
Infinitive		čitát'	govorít'
Non-past:			
Singular	1	čitáju	govorjú
	2	čitáeš'	govoríš'
	3	čitáet	govorít
Plural	1	čitáem	govorím
	2	čitáete	govoríte
	3	čitájut	govorját
Past:			
Singular	masculine	čitál	govoríl
	feminine	čitála	govoríla
	neuter	čitálo	govorílo
Plural		čitáli	govoríli
Imperative:			
Singular 2		čitáj	govorí
Plural 2		čitájte	govoríte

whole, effectively as a point, while the imperfective views a situation as having internal structure, effectively as a line. This distinction can be clarified by some actual examples. In a narrative, one normally presents a series of events each of which is viewed as complete in itself, and here the perfective is appropriate, as in *ja vošël v kómnatu, sel i vzjal knígu* 'I entered the room, sat down and took a book'. In background description, however, one presents situations that are on-going throughout the whole of the narrative sequence, and here the imperfective is appropriate, as in *pápa sidél v zelënom kreslé i spal* 'Father was sitting in the green arm-chair and was sleeping' (sc. when I entered the room). The imperfective is thus also ideal for habitual situations, which serve as a potential background to individual events, as in *kogdá ja byl mál'čikom, ja sobirál poctóvye márki* 'when I was a boy I used to collect postage stamps'. Although there are differences of detail, the distinction between imperfective and perfective in Russian can be compared to that between the imperfect and preterit in Romance languages; in nonhabitual, non-stative meaning, the opposition can be compared to that between progressive and non-progressive in English. All of these are aspectual oppositions.

In Russian, this aspectual opposition applies throughout the verb system, in particular in the infinitive (e g. *čitát' pročitát'*), in the non-past (e.g. *čitáju pročitáju*; here the imperfective has present meaning, the perfective future meaning), in the past (*čitál pročitál*) and in the imperative (*čitáj pročitáj*).

In addition to morphological forms, Russian also has a small number of periphrastic verb forms. The conditional is formed by attaching the invariable clitic *by* to the past tense, e.g. *ja čitál by* (perfective: *ja pročitál by*) 'I would read'. The imperfective future uses the auxiliary *búdu* 'I will be' in the appropriate person and number with the imperfective infinitive, e.g. *on búdet čitát'* 'he will read, he will be reading'. (Only the verb *byt'* 'to be' has a morphological future, namely *búdu* itself.) There is thus a certain discrepancy between the tense-aspect correlation in form and meaning in the non-past. In form, *čitáju* and *pročitáju* go together in contrast to the periphrastic *búdu čitát'*, which has no perfective counterpart; in meaning, however, *čitáju* is the isolated form. Russian has no perfective present, while *búdu čitát'* and *pročitáju* form an aspectual pair.

Historically, this represents a considerable simplification of the Old Russian verb system, virtually the only complication being the fully fledged development of the aspectual system. Gone completely are, in addition to the dual number, the Old Russian simple past forms (imperfect and aorist) inherited from Common Slavonic. The modern Russian past tense derives from an Old Russian perfect, somewhat similar to English 'I have read', except that the auxiliary 'be' rather than 'have' is used with the past participle. Thus Old Russian has a present perfect *jazъ esmь čitalъ* 'I have read', and also equivalent forms in other tenses, e.g. pluperfect *jazъ běxъ čitalъ* 'I had read'. Of these, only the present perfect survives to modern Russian; as elsewhere in Russian, the copula is lost in the present tense, giving rise to modern Russian *ja čitál*, which, with the loss of all the other past tenses, now survives as the basic and only past tense. The fact that the form *čitál* is etymologically a participle (i.e. a verbal adjective) accounts for why it agrees in gender and number rather than in person and number with its subject.

4 Syntax

In this brief discussion of Russian syntax, attention will be focused on two features: agreement and word order. In order to follow the example sentences, two particular features of Russian syntax should be noted in advance. Russian lacks equivalents to the English definite and indefinite articles, so that a noun phrase like *sobáka* will sometimes be translated as 'a dog', sometimes as 'the dog'. In copular constructions in the present tense, there is usually a zero copula, so that corresponding to English 'Viktor is a student' we have *Víktor studént*. In other tenses, however, there is an overt copula, as in *Víktor byl studéntom* 'Viktor was a student'; this overt copula usually governs the instrumental case of a predicate noun, although the nominative is also possible.

In Russian, most predicates must agree, in some combination of person, gender and number, with their subject; the only exceptions are adverbial predicates and predicate nouns (or noun phrases) with the zero copula, as in *Víktor/Léna zdes'* 'Viktor/Lena is here'. Finite verbs in the non-past tense agree with their subject in person and number, e.g. *ja čitáju* 'I read', *on/oná čitáet* 'he/she reads', *oní čitájut* 'they read', *mál'čiki čitájut* 'the boys read'; despite the rich agreement morphology on the verb, it is not usual in Russian to omit unstressed subject pronouns (in this respect Russian differs from many other Slavonic languages, including Polish, Czech and Serbian/Croatian/Bosnian). Finite verbs in the past tense agree with their subject in gender and number, e.g. *ja/on čitál* 'I (male referent)/he read', *ja/oná čitála* 'I (female referent)/she read', *oní čitáli* 'they read'. Predicate adjectives agree in gender and number with their subject, whether there is an overt or a zero copula, e.g. *Víktor glup* 'Viktor is stupid', *Léna glupá* 'Lena is stupid', *Víktor i Léna glúpy* 'Viktor and Lena are stupid', *Víktor byl glúpym* 'Viktor was stupid', *Léna bylá glúpoj* 'Lena was stupid', *Víktor i Léna býli glúpymi* 'Viktor and Lena were stupid' (the adjectives in the past-tense sentences are in the instrumental case, although the nominative or the short form would also be possible).

Attributive adjectives (including possessive and demonstrative adjectives) agree in number, gender and case with their head noun. Thus from nominative singular *bédnyj mál'čik* 'poor boy' we can form genitive *bédnogo mál'čika*, nominative plural *bédnye mál'čiki*, dative plural *bédnym mál'čikam*; taking a feminine noun, we have nominative singular *bédnaja dévuška* 'poor girl', genitive *bédnoj dévuški*, nominative plural *bédnye dévuški*; taking a neuter noun, we have *bédnoe seló* 'poor hamlet', genitive *bédnogo selá*. Agreement of possessive and demonstrative adjectives can be illustrated by: *tot mál'čik* 'that boy', genitive *togo mál'čika*; *ta dévuška* 'that girl', genitive *toj dévuški*; *náše seló* 'our hamlet', genitive *nášego selá*.

One particularly complex area of Russian syntax, reflecting an unusual interplay of agreement and government, is the syntax of noun phrases involving numerals. In Russian, the numeral 'one' is an adjective, agreeing in case, gender and number with its head noun, e.g. *odín mál'čik* 'one boy', genitive *odnogó mál'čika*; *odná bédnaja dévuška* 'one poor girl'; the plural form is used with nouns that occur only in the plural but refer to a single object, e.g. *odní nóžnicy* 'one (pair of) scissors'. The numerals 'two', 'three' and 'four' in the nominative-accusative govern a noun in the genitive singular, while an accompanying adjective may stand in either the nominative plural or the genitive plural (usually the latter), e.g. *dva mál'čika* 'two boys', *dve bédnye/bédnyx straný* 'two poor countries', *tri/četýre mál'čika/straný/selá* 'three/four boys/countries/hamlets'; note that of these numerals, 'two' distinguishes masculine-neuter *dva* from feminine *dve*. In the other cases, these numerals agree in case with their head noun (and show no gender distinction, as is usual in Russian in the plural), e.g. dative *dvum/trëm/četyrëm mál'čikam/stránam/sëlam*. Numerals from 'five' up to 'nine hundred' in the nominative accusative govern a following noun (with attributes) in the genitive plural, e.g. *pjat' bédnyx mál' čikov/dévušek/sël* 'five poor boys/girls/hamlets'; in other cases, they agree with the head noun, e.g. dative *pjatí bédnym mál'čikam/dévuškam/sëlam*. The numeral 'thousand' and higher numerals take a following genitive plural irrespective of case, e.g. *millión bédnyx dévušek* 'a million poor girls', dative *milliónu bédnyx dévušek*.

Apart from the idiosyncrasy of the genitive singular after the numerals 'two' to 'four' (with nominative or genitive plural attributes), the other patterns can all be described in terms of the interaction of attributive adjective syntax (attributive adjectives agree with their head) and measure-noun syntax (nouns of measure govern a following count noun in the genitive plural, e.g. *vedró červéj* 'a bucket of worms'): thus, the numeral 'one' behaves consistently as an adjective, while the numerals from 'nine hundred' on behave consistently as measure nouns, the numerals from 'five' to 'thousand' combining aspects of adjective and measure-noun syntax. The synchronically unusual system can best be understood in terms of its historical origin. In Old Russian, 'one' is an adjective, while all numerals from 'five' on are measure nouns; diachronically, adjective properties have been creeping up the number scale. In Old Russian, the numeral 'two' derives etymologically from a nominative dual, i.e. originally this was an instance of agreement; for a few nouns, the genitive singular and the form used after 'two' still differ in stress, e.g. *čas* 'hour', genitive *čása*, but *dva časá* 'two hours'. The use of the erstwhile dual, now genitive singular, after 'three' and 'four' is a later analogical development.

Turning now to word order, we may distinguish between word order within the noun phrase and word order within the clause (i.e. the order of major constituents within each clause). Within the noun phrase, word order is fairly rigid in Russian, in particular the written language, especially in scientific writing. Adjectives, including demonstrative and possessive adjectives, precede the head noun, as in *stáraja sobáka* 'old dog', *mojá sobáka* 'my dog', *ta sobáka* 'that dog'. Genitives, on the other hand, follow the head noun, as in *sobáka Víktora* 'Viktor's dog'. Relative clauses follow the head noun, e.g. *sobáka, kotóruju ja vídel, ukusíla tebjá* 'the dog that I saw has bitten you'; this reflects the general tendency in Russian for non-adverbial subordinate clauses to follow main clauses (i.e. Russian, like English, is a right-branching language). We may also note at this point that Russian has prepositions rather than postpositions, e.g. *v dóme* 'in the house', *péred dómom* 'in front of the house'; prepositions govern various cases, other than the nominative.

With respect to the order of major constituents within the clause, Russian is often referred to as a free word order language. This means that, in general, any permutation of the major constituents of the clause produces a grammatical sentence with essentially the same meaning as the original order (in particular, with the same truth conditions). Thus alongside *Víktor vstrečáet Lénu* 'Viktor meets Lena', one can also say: *Víktor Lénu vstrečáet*; *Lénu Víktor vstrečáet*; *Lénu vstrečáet Víktor*; *vstrečáet Víktor Lénu*; *vstrečáet Lénu Víktor*. In Russian, the morphology is nearly always sufficient to provide unique recovery of the grammatical relations of the various major constituents: in these examples, the nominative *Víktor* is unambiguously subject, while the accusative *Lénu* is unequivocally direct object. To say 'Lena met Viktor', one would have to change the cases to give *Léna vstrečáet Víktora* (or any permutation of these three words). In some instances, agreement may reveal the grammatical relation, as in *mat' vstrečáet avtóbusy* 'the mother meets the buses', where the singular verb *vstrečáet* allows *mat'* 'mother', but disqualifies *avtóbusy* 'buses' as subject. It is actually quite difficult to construct sensible sentences where the morphology is insufficient to disambiguate, e.g. *mat' vstrečáet doč'*, literally 'mother meets daughter', where both nouns happen to have the same form for nominative and accusative and are of the same person and number. In such sentences, the most salient interpretation is 'the mother meets the daughter', one of the pieces of evidence suggesting that the basic word order in Russian, as in English, is subject–verb–object. But whereas in English departures from this order produce either nonsense or sentences with different meanings (*Viktor Lena meets*; *Lena meets Viktor*), in Russian the main clue to grammatical relations is the morphology, giving rise to the phenomenon of free word order.

This does not mean, however, that there are no principles of word order in Russian. Word order of major constituents within the clause is governed by two main principles. The first is that the topic of the sentence, i.e. what the sentence is about, comes initially. The second is that the focus of the sentence, i.e. the essential new information communicated by the sentence, comes last. Thus word order in Russian is largely pragmatically determined. (A further pragmatic principle, this time shared with English, is that interrogative pronouns and relative pronouns occur clause-initially, as in *kogó ty vídel?* 'whom did you see?'; *mál'čik, kotórogo ja vídel* 'the boy whom I saw'.) One way of illustrating these principles is to produce miniature dialogues where the choice of topic and focus in the final sentence is forced by the context. Imagine that we have a discourse about meeting. If we ask *who met X?* then in the answer *Y met X, Y* must be the focus, since it is the new information communicated. Conversely, given the question *what about Y?*, in the answer the topic must be *Y*, since any reasonable answer to a question about *Y* must have *Y* as its topic. The following miniature dialogues illustrate pragmatic word order in Russian, in each case the relevant sentence being the last one of the discourse:

(a) Víktor vstrétil Lénu   Viktor met Lena
     A Róbert, kogó on vstrétil?   And what about Robert, whom did he meet?
     Róbert vstrétil Mášu   *Róbert* met Másha
(b) Víktor vstrétil Lénu   Viktor met Lena.
     A Mášu, kto vstrétil eë?   And as for Masha, who met her?
     Mášu vstrétil Róbert   Róbert met *Masha*

In each example, the topic is italicised and the focus marked with the diacritic on the stressed vowel. In English, the final turns in (a) and (b) are distinguished by sentence stress, this stress falling in each case on the focus. In Russian, too, the sentence stress falls on the focus, but there is the added differentiation brought about by the word order, which can thus be used to indicate topic and focus even in writing, where sentence stress is not indicated. (In the spoken language, for emotive effect, departures from the 'focus-last' principle are possible, but such deviations would be quite out of place in scientific writing.)

Freedom of word order in Russian applies primarily to major constituents of the clause. Under certain circumstances it is, however, possible to extract constituents of major constituents for purposes of topic or focus, as in *knígi u menjá xoróšie*, literally 'books at me good', i.e. 'I have good books'.

In English, the variation in word order that is possible directly in Russian can sometimes be achieved by less direct means. Thus one of the differences in English between the active voice, as in *Viktor met Lena*, and the passive voice, as in *Lena was met by Viktor*, is topicalisation of the patient in the passive. In English, the order subject–verb–object is fairly rigid, but since the passive voice presents the direct object of the active sentence as subject of the passive sentence, this change in voice effectively allows one to prepose the patient to give a close equivalent to Russian *Lénu vstrétil Víktor*. Russian does have a passive similar in form to that of English, e.g. *Léna bylá vstréčena Víktorom*, but this construction is much less frequently used in Russian than in English – it serves primarily as an indicator of literary style – and, moreover, given the free word order of Russian it is possible to invert the order of the noun phrases to have the agent, though not subject, as topic, i.e. *Víktorom bylá vstréčena Léna!*

This infrequent use of the passive in Russian as compared to English is a particular case of a general phenomenon distinguishing the two languages. English has a wide range of possibilities for the link between the grammatical relations of a sentence and its semantic roles. Thus the subject is agent in *Viktor met Lena*, but patient in *Lena was met by Viktor*; in *lightning killed the soldier*, the subject is a natural force. In Russian, the fit between semantic roles and grammatical relations is much closer. As already indicated, avoidance of the passive is one instance of this. The most natural Russian translation of *lightning killed the soldier* (and equally of *the soldier was killed by lightning*) is impersonal (subjectless), with neither 'lightning' nor 'soldier' as subject: *soldáta* (accusative) *ubílo* (neuter singular) *mólniej* (instrumental), literally (apart from word order) 'it killed the soldier with lightning'. In yet further instances where English allows a given predicate to take grammatical relations with different semantic roles, Russian allows this only if the predicate is marked overtly to indicate the difference in semantic roles. Thus, in English the verb *close* can take an agentive subject transitively in *Lena closed the door* and a patient subject intransitively as in *the door closed*; in Russian, the second usage must be overtly distinguished by the reflexive clitic *-sja/-s'*: *Léna zakrýla dver'*; *dver' zakrýlas'*. In English, the same verb can be used in *the farmer sowed maize in the field* and in *the farmer sowed the field with maize*, while Russian requires different prefixes on the verbs: *férmer poséjal kukurúzu v póle*; *férmer zaséjal póle kukurúzoj*. The interaction among morphology, word order, grammatical relations, semantic roles and pragmatic roles is one of the major typological differences between the grammars of Russian and English.

Bibliography

For a more detailed discussion of the range of topics covered here, reference may be made to Cubberley (2002). The best overall descriptive grammar of Russian from a linguistic perspective is Timberlake (2004); for a verbal aspect, the wide coverage in Forsyth (1970) remains unparalleled in English. A more detailed traditional history of the Russian language is provided in Vlasto (1986), while Comrie, Stone and Polinsky (1996) cover the twentieth century up to the beginning of *glasnost'* (i.e. roughly the Soviet period) and Ryazanova-Clarke and Wade (1999) the period from *glasnost'*.

References

Comrie, Bernard, Stone, Gerald and Polinsky, Maria 1996. *The Russian Language in the Twentieth Century* (Clarendon Press, Oxford)

Cubberley, Paul 2002. *Russian: A Linguistic Introduction* (Cambridge University Press, Cambridge)

Forsyth, J. 1970. *A Grammar of Aspect: Usage and Meaning in the Russian Verb* (Cambridge University Press, Cambridge)

Ryazanova-Clarke, Larissa and Wade, Terence 1999. *The Russian Language Today* (Routledge, London)

Timberlake, Alan 2004. *A Reference Grammar of Russian* (Cambridge University Press, Cambridge)

Vlasto, A.P. 1986. *A Linguistic History of Russian to the End of the Eighteenth Century* (Clarendon Press, Oxford)

16

Polish

Gerald Stone

1 Historical Background

The West Slavonic languages include a subgroup, known as 'Lechitic', comprising Polish (its easternmost variety) and the other Slavonic languages once spoken throughout what is now north Germany as far west as the Lüneburg Heath. Most of the dialects of Lechitic were extinct by the late Middle Ages and are attested only by fragmentary evidence, principally in the form of place names; but its westernmost variety, which has been given the name 'Polabian' by philologists, survived until the eighteenth century and is recorded in a number of substantial texts. Unless we bestow separate status on Cassubian, a variety of Lechitic still spoken by a population whose size is estimated variously at a few thousand to half a million near the Baltic coast to the west of the Bay of Gdańsk, Polish is the only Lechitic language which survives to the present day. Cassubian, despite features testifying to its former independence, is now generally regarded as a dialect of Polish. Within West Slavonic the Lechitic subgroup on the one hand and the Czecho-Slovak on the other constitute the two extremities. A link between them is provided by Sorbian.

Our earliest evidence of the Polish language comes in the form of place names, tribal names, and personal names recorded in medieval Latin documents going back to the ninth century AD. Among the most useful records of this kind are the Papal Bull of Gniezno (1136) which contains 410 names and the Bull of Wrocław (Breslau) (1155) containing about 50 more. The same kind of evidence becomes even more plentiful in the thirteenth century, by which time we also find isolated words other than proper nouns imbedded in Latin texts and accompanied by Latin explanations. In about 1270 the Cistercian monks of Henryków, near Wrocław, wrote a history of their monastery (in Latin) and included several Polish words. Their history also contains the first known Polish sentence: '*daj ać ja pobruczę a ty poczywaj*' ('Let me grind and you rest'), which is quoted to explain the etymology of the place name Brukalice.

It is only in the fourteenth century that we find entire Polish texts consisting of many sentences. The earliest of these are the undated *Kazania Świętokrzyskie* ('Holy Cross Sermons'), which are attributed to the middle of the century or a little later. A translation of the Book of Psalms into Polish, known as the *Psałterz Floriański* ('St Florian Psalter'), is reckoned to date from the end of the century, as are the *Kazania Gnieźnieńskie* 'Gniezno Sermons'. There are also court records, dating from 1386 onwards, in which the main account is written in Latin, but the actual words of depositions sworn by witnesses and litigants are in the original Polish. The number of such depositions dating from before 1500 exceeds 8,000 and collectively they constitute one of our main sources for the state of medieval Polish. There are, however, many other sources, mostly of a devotional and literary kind, dating from this period. They include a manuscript of the greater part of the Old Testament, known as *Biblia królowej Zofii* ('Queen Sophia's Bible'), dating from around 1455.

The spelling in these early texts is far from systematic and it is consequently, in particular, almost impossible to distinguish between the three series of sibilants: /tɕ/, /ɕ/, /ʑ/ : /tʃ/, /ʃ/, /ʒ/ : /ts/, /s/, /z/, which in modern Polish are written respectively: *ć, ś, ź : cz, sz, ż : c, s, z* (see Section 2). However, the local features in most of these texts are far less prominent than one might expect them to have been in the speech of the areas they came from. Clearly, certain standardising processes had been at work. Nevertheless, some local features may be detected in almost any medieval text of reasonable size. To a large extent the medieval dialectal features can be correlated with those observed in modern dialects. For example, the feature *chw → f* (e.g. *chwała* 'glory' pronounced as *fała*) is known to most modern dialects with the exception of that of Great Poland (Wielkopolska). Therefore, medieval spellings with *f* (such as *fala* 'glory') indicate that the text in question could not have originated in Great Poland. The reconstruction of medieval dialectal divisions is greatly helped by the forensic records owing to the fact that they almost always include the exact date and place of origin. Most of the devotional texts can be assigned either to Little Poland (Małopolska) (e.g. the St Florian Psalter) or to Great Poland (e.g. the Gniezno Sermons). The centre of gravity of the Polish state is known to have been in Great Poland until the reign of Kazimierz the Restorer (reigned 1034–58), but in 1037 the capital was moved to Cracow, and the position of importance consequently acquired by Little Poland was maintained until, and even after, the further transfer of the capital to Warsaw in 1596.

The modicum of standardisation exhibited by fourteenth- and fifteenth-century manuscripts attracted a lot of interest among Polish scholars in the first half of the twentieth century. It was asserted by one faction that the standard must have been based on the dialect of Great Poland, which even after 1037 retained the seat of the archbishop (at Gniezno) and exerted great authority. Others claimed that the new capital Cracow must have provided the variety on which the standard was based. (No one doubted that Mazovia, which with its capital, Warsaw, was united to Poland only in the sixteenth century, could have had no influence in the matter.) One of the crucial features in this argument was that known as *mazurzenie*, i.e. the neutralisation of the distinction between *c, s, z* and *cz, sz, ż* respectively. It was held that deliberate avoidance of this feature in the language of many scribes and later in printed books meant that the standard was based on a variety unaffected by *mazurzenie*. Dialectologists were able to show that Great Poland did not have *mazurzenie*, whereas (by the time dialectologists enquired, at least) Little Poland did. The question now turned on dating the arrival of *mazurzenie* in Little Poland. But the controversy was never settled.

The arrival of printing in Poland (the first book in Polish was printed in 1513) put an end to the untidy spelling system used by the scribes. The printers aimed for less ambiguity and more standardisation. The sixteenth century, known as the Golden Age of Polish literature, was also the age in which the first dictionaries and grammars appeared. The most

Map 16.1 Traditional Regions of Poland.

important of these are Jan Mączyński's *Lexicon latinopolonicum* (Königsberg 1564), which contains 20,700 Polish words, and the *Polonicae grammatices institutio* (Cracow 1568) of Piotr Statorius (Stojeński). Also, at least five different treatises on spelling were published.

Towards the end of the fifteenth century the Polish vocalic system underwent a great change. It had hitherto involved the opposition of long and short vowels, but now vocalic quantity ceased to be a relevant phonemic distinction. The long vowels, in losing their length, acquired a new quality. At the beginning of the fifteenth century only the vowels /i/ and /u/ were unaffected by a quantitative distinction. Short /a/, /ɛ/, /ɔ/ and /ã/ were distinguished from long /aː/, /ɛː/, /ɔː/ and /ãː/. But by the sixteenth century there were ten qualitatively distinguished vowel phonemes: /a/, /ɑ/, /ɔ/, /o/, /u/, /i/, /e/, /ɛ/, /ɛ̃/, and /ɔ̃/. Books printed in the sixteenth century and later frequently made use of the acute accent to distinguish between /a/, and /ɑ/, /ɔ/ and /o/, /e/ and /ɛ/. In standard pronunciation, however, the ten-vowel system was eventually reduced to seven vowels, as the distinction between /a/ and /ɑ/, /o/ and /u/, and /e/ and /ɛ/ was neutralised. The last relic of the ten-vowel system is in the modern spelling system, which still uses *ó* for reasons of tradition (as in *wóz* 'cart, car', *gród* 'castle', etc.), though this letter now represents the same sound as the letter *u*.

With the First Partition of Poland in 1772 the Polish language entered a period of trial that was to last until the restoration of independence after the First World War. After 1795, when Poland disappeared from the map altogether, there were attempts by all the partitioning powers (Prussia, Austria and Russia) at one time or another to reduce the social functions of Polish and replace it with German or Russian. After 1848, however, language policy in the Austrian partition was modified to the advantage of the Poles and their language was henceforth able to thrive here. In the other two partitions users of Polish suffered numerous indignities. As a result of its prohibition from the schools a clandestine system of Polish instruction grew up to ensure the language's survival. Matters came to a head in May 1901 in a school in Września (Posnania), where the compulsory use of German during religious instruction led to a riot which attracted the attention of world public opinion.

By this time, owing to the practical advantages of knowing German or Russian and the influence of military service on the male population, a large proportion of educated Poles were bilingual. Bilingualism was most common in the Prussian partition, where educational standards were higher than in Russia or Austria. The existence of three separate administrations fostered the Polish language's existing tendency to regional variation. Some of the regional features first observed then have survived until recent times even in educated usage: e.g. *kurczak* 'chicken' (Warsaw) corresponding to *kurczę* elsewhere; *na polu* 'outside' (Cracow) corresponding to *na dworze* (Poznań) and *na dworze* or *na dworzu* (Warsaw); *listonosz* 'postman' (Cracow) corresponding to *listowy* (Poznań) and *listonosz* or *bryftrygier* (Warsaw).

After the First World War Polish was restored to its position as the language of the Polish state, but there were also many speakers of other languages living in Poland. At the 1931 census a population of 32,107,000 was recorded, of whom only 21,993,000 gave Polish as their native language. This situation was completely changed in the upheaval brought about by the Second World War. The population according to the first census held within the post-war frontiers (1946) was 23,930,000. Since then it has expanded to over 38 million, of whom almost all have Polish as their native language. The national minorities total about one per cent of the population. At the same time, there are millions of Polish speakers living outside Poland, including over 300,000 in the former USSR and perhaps as many as six million in the USA.

2 Phonology

The segmental phonemes of Polish are set out in Table 16.1. As in the case of Russian, the richness of the consonant system is striking. However, certain Russian oppositions between palatalised dentals (t:ţ; d:ḍ; r:ṛ) have no counterpart in Polish. On the other hand, Polish has an additional type of opposition, viz. that between ʧ and tɕ, ʤ and ʥ, ʃ and ɕ, ʒ and ʑ. This distinction depends less on the precise portion of the roof of the mouth involved in the articulation than on the fact that ʧ, ʤ, ʃ and ʒ are articulated with the tip of the tongue, whereas tɕ, ʥ, ɕ and ʑ are produced with the middle of the tongue.

The functional load of ʤ is very light, since it is largely restricted to loanwords, but the rest of these oppositions have a substantial yield. Some have a role in the morphological system, e.g. *duży* /duʒi/ 'big' (masculine nominative singular): *duzi* /duʑi/ 'big' (masculine personal nominative plural); *lepszy* /lɛpʃi/ 'better' (masculine nominative singular): *lepsi* /lɛpɕi/ 'better' (masculine personal nominative plural).

Double consonants are not uncommon in Polish and their phonological function is well attested, e.g. *lekki* /lɛkki/ 'light' (masculine nominative singular): *leki* /lɛki/ 'medicines'. Phonetically they may be double or long, but there are no cases of the opposition of morphologically indivisible long and short consonants. The example given breaks

Table 16.1 Segmental Phonemes of Polish

Vowels	Oral				Nasal				
	i		u						
	ɛ	ɔ			ɛ̃	ɔ̃			
		a							

Consonants	Plain stop		Affricate		Fricative		Nasal	Lateral	Trill	Semi-vowel
Bilabial	p	b					m			w
	pʲ	bʲ					mʲ			
Labio-dental					f	v				
					fʲ	vʲ				
Dental	t	d	ts	dz	s	z	n	l		
Alveolar			tʃ	dʒ	ʃ	ʒ			r	
Pre-palatal			tɕ	dʑ	ɕ	ʑ	ɲ			
Post-palatal	kʲ	gʲ								j
Velar	k	g			x					

down into *lek-* (stem) and *-ki* (ending). Loss of this distinction (e.g. the pronunciation of *lekki* as /lɛki/) is a regional feature of Great Poland (Wielkopolska) and Silesia.

The distribution of the nasal vowels is restricted. They may only occur at the end of a word or before fricatives, e.g. *chodzę* /xɔdʑɛ̃/ 'I walk', *gęś* /gɛ̃ɕ/ 'goose', *mąż* /mɔ̃ʃ/ 'husband'. (The nasal vowel letters, however, appear before consonants of all kinds and are therefore phonetically misleading.) In addition to /ɛ̃/ and /ɔ̃/ other nasal vowels may occur, but only before fricatives, e.g. *tramwaj* [trãvaj] 'tram', *inspektor* [ĩspɛktɔr] 'inspector', *triumf* [triũf] 'triumph'. Before fricatives the vowels /ɛ̃/ and /ɔ̃/ may be spelled *en*, *em*, *on* or *om*, e.g. *sens* /sɛ̃s/ 'sense', *konferencja* /kɔ̃fɛrɛntsja/ 'conference'. Before plosives and affricates, however, only the sequence oral vowel (abbreviated as V) plus nasal consonant (phonemes /n/, /ɲ/ and /m/) (abbreviated as N) may occur. Therefore, with the exception /ɛ̃/ and /ɔ̃/ at the end of a word, nasal vowels are positional variants of VN. Clearly, [ĩ], [ã], [ũ] are not phonemes, and even the phonemic status of /ɛ̃/ and /ɔ̃/ depends solely on their occurrence at the end of a word before a pause, e.g. *tą* /tɔ̃/ 'that' (instrumental feminine singular) is distinct from *to* /tɔ/ 'that' (nominative neuter singular), *ton* /tɔn/ 'tone' and *tom* /tɔm/ 'volume'; *listę* /listɛ̃/ 'list' (accusative singular) is distinct from *listem* /listɛm/ 'letter' (instrumental singular); *piszę* /piʃɛ̃/ 'I write' is distinct from *pisze* /piʃɛ/ 'he writes'. However, no one, not even actors, consistently pronounces /ɛ̃/ at the end of words. *Piszę* 'I write', for example, may be realised as /piʃɛ/, in which case it becomes indistinguishable from *pisze* 'he writes'. On the other hand, no speaker of the standard language consistently denasalises final /ɛ̃/ and the possibility of making the distinction always exists. Therefore /ɛ̃/ is a phoneme. There is even less doubt in the case /ɔ̃/ since denasalisation of final /ɔ̃/ is less common.

The distinction between voiced and voiceless paired consonants (i.e. between /b/ and /p/, /d/ and /t/, /v/ and /f/, /dz/ and /ts/, /z/ and /s/, /dʒ/ and /tʃ/, /ʒ/ and /ʃ/, /dʑ/ and /tɕ/, /ʑ/ and /ɕ/, /g/ and /k/) is neutralised at the end of a word. Thus, for example, *Bóg* /buk/ 'God' and *buk* /buk/ 'beech' are homophones. At the end of a word only the voiceless member of the pair can occur, but this feature is not reflected in the spelling, as we may see from such examples as *ząb* /zɔmp/ 'tooth', *nóg* /nuk/ 'feet' (genitive plural), *mosiądz* /mɔɕɔnts/ 'brass', *mąż* /mɔ̃ʃ/ 'husband', *ród* /rut/ 'breed'.

With few exceptions, Polish words are stressed on the penultimate syllable. Thus, for example, *ziemia* 'earth' is pronounced as ['ʑɛm‚a], *sprawiedliwość* 'justice' as [spraʋɛ-'dlivɔɕtɕ] and *sprawiedliwości* 'justice' (genitive, dative or locative singular) as [spraʋ-ɛdli'vɔɕtɕi]. The exceptions are mainly words of Greek origin, such as *muzyka* ['muzika] 'music', or of Latin origin, such as *uniwersytet* [uɲi'vɛrsɨtɛt] 'university', but even a few Slavonic words are irregular, such as *rzeczpospolita* [ʒɛt͡ʃpɔ'spɔlita] 'commonwealth'. In addition, the first and second persons plural of the past tense of verbs have antepenultimate stress, e.g. *byliśmy* ['biliɕmi] 'we were', *wiedzieliście* [ʋɛ'dʑɛliɕtɕɛ] 'you knew' (masculine personal plural).

The Polish writing system uses an alphabet based on Latin, making liberal use of digraphs and diacritics (Table 16.2). The Latin language and its alphabet were introduced to Poland simultaneously with Christianity in the tenth century AD. Gradually the alphabet was adapted to make it fit Polish.

The vowel letters *i* and *y* do not represent separate phonemes. They both stand for the phoneme /i/, but have separate functions in reflecting the quality of the consonant

Table 16.2 The Polish Alphabet

A	a	M	m
Ą	ą	N	n
B	b	Ń	ń
C	c	O	o
Ć	ć	Ó	ó
D	d	P	p
E	e	R	r
Ę	ę	S	s
F	f	Ś	ś
G	g	T	t
H	h	U	u
I	i	W	w
J	j	Y	y
K	k	Z	z
L	l	Ź	ź
Ł	ł	Ż	ż

Note: In addition to the 32 letters shown above, Q q, V v and X x may occasionally be found in foreign words, e.g. *Quebec*, *vademecum*, *Pax*. The digraphs *ch*, *cz*, *rz*, *sz*, *dz*, *dź*, *dż*, for the purpose of alphabetic order, are treated as sequences of separate letters.

immediately preceding. Thus, for example, the written sequences *ci*, *dzi*, *si*, *zi*, *pi*, *bi*, *mi*, *fi*, *wi*, *ni* correspond respectively to /tɕi/, /dʑi/, /ɕi/, /ʑi/, /pʲi/, /bʲi/, /mʲi/, /fʲi/, /ʋʲi/, /ɲi/, whereas *cy*, *dzy*, *sy*, *zy*, *py*, *by*, *my*, *fy*, *wy*, *ny* represent /tsi/, /dzi/, /si/, /zi/, /pi/, /bi/, /mi/, /fi/, /vi/, /ni/. Except in words of foreign origin or in onomatopoeic words, the letter *i* is rarely or never written after the letters *d*, *t*, *cz*, *dz*, *sz*, *ż*, *ch*, *ł*, *r*. Subject to exceptions of the same kind, the letter *y* does not occur after *k*, *g*, or *l*.

The phoneme /tɕ/ is represented by *ć* or *ci*, the phoneme /dʑ/ by *dź* or *dzi*, the phoneme /ɕ/ by *ś* or *si*, the phoneme /ʑ/ by *ź* or *zi*, and the phoneme /ɲ/ by *ń* or *ni*. There is an orthographical convention whereby *ć*, *dź*, *ś*, *ź* and *ń* are written only at the end of a word (as in *być* /bitɕ/ 'to be') or immediately before another consonant (as in *ćma* /tɕma/ 'moth'). Elsewhere (i.e. before a vowel), *ci*, *dzi*, *si*, *zi* and *ni* are used (as in *ciemny* /tɕɛmni/ 'dark', *siano* /ɕanɔ/ 'hay', and *ziarno* /ʑarnɔ/ 'grain'). If the vowel following is /i/, it is not shown separately in the spelling. For example, *ci* /tɕi/ 'to you', *nikt* /n̦ikt/ 'nobody', *musi* /muɕi/ 'he must', *zima* /ʑima/ 'winter'. In such cases the letter *i* has a double function: it participates with the consonant letter in the representation of the consonant and also stands for the vowel /i/. Any other vowel, however, is shown separately in the spelling. In our examples *ciemny*, *siano* and *ziarno* (see above) the letter *i* is relevant only to the representation of the consonant.

The bilabial and labio-dental consonants /p̦/, /b̦/, /m̦/, /f̦/ and /v̦/ can only occur immediately before a vowel, e.g. *biały* /b̦awi/ 'white'. In the sixteenth century they could occur at the end of a word and their palatalised quality was then sometimes indicated by means of a diacritic. The gradual process whereby they were replaced in this position by their non-palatalised counterparts was complete by the nineteenth century. As a result, we sometimes find palatalised and non-palatalised labials alternating in the stems of certain nouns, e.g. *gołąb* (nom. sg.) 'dove': *gołębia* (gen. sg.); *Wrocław* (nom. sg.): *Wrocławia* (gen. sg.). This tendency has gone even further in the north-east, including Warsaw, where even before vowels the palatalised labials are often replaced by the sequence non-palatalised labial + /j/, e.g. not /b̦awi/ but /bjawi/.

The following are some of the less obvious graphemic-phonemic correspondences:

Grapheme		Phoneme
ą		finally and before fricatives: /ɔ̃/ e.g. *mąż* /mɔ̃ʃ/ 'husband', *idą* /idɔ̃/ 'they go'
		before dental plosives and affricates: /ɔn/ e.g. *kąt* /kɔnt/ 'angle', *zając* /zajɔnts/ 'hare'
		before /k/ and /g/: /ɔŋ/ (phonetically [ɔŋ]) e.g. *łąka* [wɔŋka] 'meadow'
		before /p/ and /b/: /ɔm/ e.g. *dąb* /dɔmp/ 'oak'
		before /w/: /ɔ/ e.g. *wziął* /vʑɔw/ 'took'
ę	(i)	finally and before fricatives: /ɛ̃/ e.g. *chcę* /xtsɛ̃/ 'I want', *często* /tʃɛ̃stɔ/ 'often'
	(ii)	finally (colloquially): /ɛ/ e.g. *chcę* /xtsɛ/ 'I want'
	(iii)	before dental plosives and before dental and alveolar affricates: /ɛn/ e.g. *okręt* /ɔkrɛnt/ 'ship', *nędza* /nɛndza/ 'poverty', *tęcza* /tɛntʃa/ 'rainbow'
	(iv)	before pre-palatal affricates: /ɛn/ e.g. *pięć* /pɛn̦tɕ/ 'five'
	(v)	before /k/ and /g/: /ɛn/ (phonetically [ɛŋ]) e.g. *ręka* [rɛŋka] 'hand'
	(vi)	before bilabial plosives: /ɛm/ e.g. *postęp* /pɔstɛmp/ 'progress'
	(vii)	before /w/ and /l/: /ɛ/ e.g. *wzięli* /vʑɛli/ 'they took'
c		/ts/ e.g. *noc* /nɔts/ 'night'
ch } h		/x/ e.g. *suchy* /suxi/ 'dry', *błahy* /bwaxi/ 'trivial'
ć } ci		/tɕ/ e.g. *być* /bitɕ/ 'to be', *ciemny* /tɕɛmni/ 'dark'
cz		/tʃ/ e.g. *czas* /tʃas/ 'time'
ł		/w/ e.g. *łapać* /wapatɕ/ 'to catch'
rz } ż		/ʒ/ e.g. *rzeka* /ʒɛka/ 'river', *żagiel* /ʒagɛl/ 'sail'
ś } si		/ɕ/ e.g. *oś* /ɔɕ/ 'axis', *siano* /ɕanɔ/ 'hay'
sz		/ʃ/ e.g. *szok* /ʃɔk/ 'shock'
ó } u		/u/ e.g. *róg* /ruk/ 'corner', *mur* /mur/ 'wall'
w		/v/ or /v̦/ e.g. *kawa* /kava/ 'coffee', *wiara* /v̦ara/ 'faith'
ź } zi		/ʑ/ e.g. *luźny* /luʑni/ 'loose', *zima* /ʑima/ 'winter'

In the speech of a rapidly diminishing minority of Poles the archaic variant [ł] in place of normal [w] may be heard. The articulation of this dental lateral involves raising the back of the tongue. It is similar to the Russian non-palatalised /l/. Until recently Polish [ł] was obligatory in stage-pronunciation and it is still used by many actors. Regionally, it is mainly associated with the speech of Poles from the eastern areas now in Belarus and Ukraine, but it may also be encountered as a dialectal feature in the Tatra Mountains. The change [ł] > [w] began several centuries ago, but is still not complete.

Another feature characteristic of speakers from the eastern parts of the Polish speech area is the distinction of two separate phonemes /h/ and /x/, whereas most speakers have only one, viz. /x/. The phoneme /h/, which is a voiced laryngeal fricative, usually corresponds to the letter *h*. It is consequently possible in this type of pronunciation to make distinctions such as that between *hełm* [hɛłm] 'helmet' and *Chełm* [xɛłm] (a town in eastern Poland). For the vast majority of Poles these two words are homophones, both being pronounced [xɛwm].

The distinction between voiced and voiceless consonants is often neutralised as a result of assimilation, but the effects of assimilation are not always shown in the orthography. The orthography reveals that there was a time in the past when assimilation could operate progressively (i.e. towards the end of the word), e.g. *przy* /pʃi/ 'near'; but the active processes of assimilation are now only regressive (i.e. towards the beginning of the word), e.g. *prośba* /prɔʑba/ 'request'. Regressive assimilation may take place not only within the body of a word but also at the boundary between words. For example, *jak dobrze* 'how good' is pronounced /jag dɔbʒɛ/, *naród polski* 'the Polish nation' is pronounced /narut polski/. This kind of assimilation is found on all social levels in all parts of Poland. However, if the second word begins with a vowel or a sonant (/m/, /n/, /r/, /l/, /w/), the presence or absence of assimilation by voicing is a regional feature distinguishing the north-east (including Warsaw) from the south and west (including Cracow and Poznań). In the north-east voicing is absent, e.g. *tak mało* 'so little' is pronounced /tak mawɔ/, *róg ulicy* 'the corner of the street' is pronounced /ruk ulitsi/. The corresponding variants in the south and west are /tag mawɔ/ and /rug ulitsi/. This variable is unaffected by social level. (Prepositions ending in a voiced consonant, however, are not affected by this type of variation. Their final consonants remain voiced before vowels and sonants in all parts of Poland.)

The results of the historical progressive assimilation of /v/ within the body of the word also varies regionally regardless of social factors. The pronunciation of such words as *twój* 'your', *kwiat* 'flower' with /f/ or /f̣/ (/tfuj/, /kf̣at/) is found in all parts of Poland except the eastern borderlands, Great Poland and Pomerania, where we hear /tvuj/, /kv̝at/, etc.

We now come to consider some of the sound changes which have taken place in Polish and which distinguish it from the other Slavonic languages:

(i)   The Common Slavonic nasal vowels were inherited by Polish and wherever the letters *ę* and *ą* are written today we may conclude that there was once a nasal vowel. However, as we have seen, these letters nowadays represent phonetically nasal vowels only in certain positions. The earliest records indicate that the Common Slavonic nasal vowels *ę* and *ǫ* were still distinguished in Polish until the beginning of the fourteenth century. During the course of this century, however, they appear to have coalesced as a single nasal vowel, written with the letter ǫ. Depending on prosodic factors, however, this single nasal underwent new changes, so that by the beginning of the sixteenth century (or perhaps even earlier) there were again two nasals (now written ę and ą). The present-day spelling system still reflects the state of the nasals in the sixteenth century. Of course, there is no correlation between the Polish letter ę and Common Slavonic ę, nor between Polish ą and Common Slavonic ǫ. For example, Polish ręka 'hand', zięć 'son-in-law', rząd 'row', ząb 'tooth' correspond to Common Slavonic *rǫka, *zętь, *rędъ, *zǫbъ, respectively.

(ii) The Common Slavonic reduced vowels or *jers* (ъ and ь) in strong positions give Polish e. In weak positions they are lost. The distinction between ъ and ь whether strong or weak, survives in the quality of the preceding consonant. For example, *pьsъ > pies 'dog', but *vьsь > wieś 'village'; *sъnъ > sen 'sleep', but *dьnь > dzień 'day'.

(iii) In early Polish consonants located immediately before the front vowels (e, i, ě, ь, ę) were palatalised. In the case of the labials and labio-dentals this has resulted in the existence of pairs of consonants distinguished from each other solely by the feature 'palatalised' (i.e. the raising of the middle of the tongue to the hard palate). This is the only feature distinguishing /b̦/ from /b/, /p̦/ from /p/, /v̦/ from /v/, /f̦/ from /f/ and /m̦/ from /m/. In the case of the dentals s, z, t, d and n, however, the change eventually involved more than the addition of the feature 'palatalised': /s/ > /ç/, /z/ > /ʑ/, /t/ > /tç/, /d/ > /dʑ/, /n/ > /ɲ/ For example, *osь > oś 'axis', *zemja > ziemia 'earth', *tęžьkъjь > ciężki 'heavy', *kъdě > gdzie 'where', *dьnь > dzień 'day'. In each case the place of articulation of the resultant sound is entirely different from that of its origin (see Table 16.1). Nevertheless, the native speaker, owing mainly to morphological alternations, feels that the relationship between the members of these pairs is the same as that between the non-palatalised and palatalised members of the labial and labio-dental pairs. The same is true of the pairs /w/ : /l/ and /r/ : /ʒ/, in each of which the phonological distinction also originally stems from the palatalisation of the second member before front vowels. Nowadays, however, neither member of either pair is palatalised.

(iv) Polish, in common with the other Lechitic languages, is affected by changes in certain Common Slavonic vowels if they were followed by the dental consonants s, z, t, d, r or l, and these consonants were themselves not followed by a front vowel. Thus, in this position, e > 'o (i.e. o with palatalisation of the preceding consonant), e.g. *sestra > siostra 'sister', *berǫ > biorę 'I take'. In the same conditions, ě > 'a (i.e. a with palatalisation of the preceding consonant), e.g. *lěsъ > las 'forest', *větrъ > wiatr 'wind'. In all other positions e and ě coalesced as e, e.g. *večerъ > wieczór 'evening', *běgati > biegać 'to run'. This is one of several sound changes that have led to morphophonemic vowel alternations.

3 Morphology

Polish nominal morphology is illustrated in the chart of declension types, with examples of the four main types of noun declension and of adjective declension. Although there is a high correlation between gender and declension type, it is not absolute: most a-stems are feminine, but those with clear male reference are masculine, e.g. mężczyzna 'man'. There are, in addition, subsidiary types such as that exemplified by *żrebię* 'foal', which has genitive singular *żrebięcia* and nominative plural *żrebięta*. The only noun belonging to this declension which is not neuter is *książę* 'prince'.

Polish Declension Types

Singular:	a-*stem*	Masculine o-*stem*	Neuter o-*stem*	i-*stem*
Nominative	głowa	ptak	słowo	noc
Vocative	głowo	ptaku	słowo	nocy
Accusative	głowę	ptaka	słowo	noc
Genitive	głowy	ptaka	słowa	nocy
Dative	głowie	ptakowi	słowu	nocy
Instrumental	głową	ptakiem	słowem	nocą
Locative	głowie	ptaku	słowie	nocy
Plural:				
Nominative	głowy	ptaki	słowa	noce
Vocative	głowy	ptaki	słowa	noce
Accusative	głowy	ptaki	słowa	noce
Genitive	głów	ptaków	słów	nocy
Dative	głowom	ptakom	słowom	nocom
Instrumental	głowami	ptakami	słowami	nocami
Locative	głowach	ptakach	słowach	nocach

Adjective

Singular:	Masculine		Neuter	Feminine
Nominative	stary		stare	stara
Vocative	stary		stare	stara
Accusative	stary		stare	starą
Genitive		starego		starej
Dative		staremu		starej
Instrumental		starym		starą
Locative		starym		starej

Plural:	
Nominative	stare
Vocative	stare
Accusative	stare
Genitive	starych
Dative	starym
Instrumental	starymi
Locative	starych

Two important interrelated distinctions in Polish nominal declension not revealed by the table are animate/non-animate and masculine personal/non-masculine personal. Masculine *o*-stem nouns and adjectives referring to human beings and other animals (and their attributes) in the singular have an accusative case coinciding in form with the genitive singular. This is demonstrated by the example *ptak* 'bird' in the chart of declension types. In all other cases, the accusative singular of masculine *o*-stems coincides with the nominative singular. Thus, for example, *stary dom* 'an old house' has accusative singular *stary dom*, but *stary Polak* 'an old Pole' has *starego Polaka*. Masculine *a*-stems, such as *kolega* 'friend', like all other *a*-stems, have an accusative singular ending in -*ę*, e.g. *kolegę*. But adjectives agreeing with such nouns have an accusative singular coinciding with the genitive, e.g. *starego kolegę*. The masculine adjectival forms shown in the chart of declension types are those appropriate to a non-animate noun.

In the plural, however, the criterion is not whether the noun is animate, but whether it refers to a group embodying the two features 'masculine' and 'human'. If it does, the accusative plural has the same form as the genitive plural. If not, the accusative plural is the same as the nominative plural. Thus, for example, the accusative plural of *stary Polak* is *starych Polaków*, whereas the accusative plural of *stara Polka* 'an old Polish woman' is *stare Polki*, coinciding with the nominative plural. The masculine personal subgender is also manifested in the endings of the nominative plural. Some masculine personal nouns have the nominative plural ending -*owie*, e.g. *synowie* (nom. pl. of *syn* 'son'). Others have an ending which has evolved from the Common Slavonic nominative plural ending -*i*, but which in Polish is written -*i* or -*y*, depending on the nature of the preceding consonant, e.g. *chłopi* (nom. pl. of *chłop* 'peasant'), *Polacy* (nom. pl. of *Polak* 'Pole'). Masculine personal adjectives in the nominative plural can have only the -*i*/-*y* ending, e.g. *słabi* (from *słaby* 'weak'). This ending, whether used with nouns or adjectives, involves stem-consonant alternations, most of which result from the Common Slavonic second palatalisation of velars (see page 271) or from the Polish palatalisation of consonants before front vowels, but some of which are the result of analogy. Thus, for example, *k* alternates with *c* (e.g. *Polak:Polacy*), *g* with *dz* (e.g. *szpieg* 'spy' : *szpiedzy*), *s* with *ś* (e.g. *prezes* 'chairman' : *prezesi*), and (in adjectives only) *ż* with *ź* (e.g. *duży* 'big' : *duzi*), *sz* with *ś* (e.g. *lepszy* 'better': *lepsi*).

Polish Conjugation Types

			Conjugation 1	Conjugation 2	Conjugation 3	Conjugation 4
Infin.			pisać 'to write'	lubić 'to like'	padać 'to fall'	jeść 'to eat'
Non-past:						
Sg.		1	piszę	lubię	padam	jem
		2	piszesz	lubisz	padasz	jesz
	2 or 3		pisze	lubi	pada	je
Pl.		1	piszemy	lubimy	padamy	jemy
		2	piszecie	lubicie	padacie	jecie
	2 or 3		piszą	lubią	padają	jedzą
Imperative:						
Sg.		2	pisz	lub	padaj	jedz
Pl.		2	piszcie	lubcie	padajcie	jedzcie
Past:			Masculine	Neuter	Feminine	
Sg.		1	pisałem		pisałam	
		2	pisałeś	pisałoś	pisałaś	
	2 or 3		pisał	pisało	pisała	
			Masculine personal		Non-masculine personal	
Pl.		1	pisaliśmy		pisałyśmy	
		2	pisaliście		pisałyście	
	2 or 3		pisali		pisały	

However, the masculine personal/non-masculine personal distinction is not shown in the ending of most nouns whose stem ends in *c, ć, dź, j, ń, ś, ź, l, cz, dż, dz, rz, sz,* or *ż*. Thus, for example, the nominative plural *żołnierze* 'soldiers' is not morphologically distinct from *kołnierze* 'collars'. Masculine personal nouns ending in the nominative singular in -*ec* have nominative plural -*cy*, e.g. *chłopiec* 'boy': *chłopcy*. They are thus morphologically distinguished from non-masculine personal nouns like *dworzec* 'station': *dworce*. But other nouns ending in -*c* are not distinguished, e.g. *szlachcic* 'nobleman': *szlachcice*, cf. *szkic* 'sketch': *szkice*.

Polish verbal morphology is in many ways similar to that of Russian, but conventionally four conjugational types are distinguished (as opposed to two in Russian), principally on the basis of the vowel occurring in the endings of the middle four members of the paradigm (*-e-*, *-i-* or *-a-*) of the present tense. Conjugation 4 scarcely deserves separate status, as it includes only four verbs (viz. *umieć* 'to be able', *śmieć* 'to dare', *wiedzieć* 'to know', and *jeść* 'to eat') and their derivatives. Even these four differ in the third person plural (*umieją, śmieją, wiedzą, jedzą*). The paradigm of *być* 'to be' in the present tense is unique.

The Verb 'To Be' in Polish

Infinitive   *być* 'to be'

Present:

Sg.	1	jestem
	2	jesteś
	2 or 3	jest
Pl.	1	jesteśmy
	2	jesteście
	2 or 3	są

Imperative:

Sg.	2	bądź
Pl.	2	bądźcie

Past:

		Masculine	*Neuter*	*Feminine*
Sg.	1	byłem		byłam
	2	byłeś	byłoś	byłaś
	2 or 3	był	było	była

		Masculine personal	*Non-masculine personal*
Pl.	1	byliśmy	byłyśmy
	2	byliście	byłyście
	2 or 3	byli	były

Future:

Sg.	1	będę	Pl.	1	będziemy
	2	będziesz		2	będziecie
	2 or 3	będzie		2 or 3	będą

Most finite verbal forms are unambiguously first, second or third person, singular or plural, and it is consequently not usual for them to be accompanied by personal pronouns, except for the purpose of emphasis. Exceptions to this rule, however, are the honorific second person pronouns *pan* (masculine singular), *pani* (feminine singular), *panowie* (masculine plural), *panie* (feminine plural), *państwo* (mixed gender plural). They are used with forms of the verb which are identical with those used in the third person. Therefore, unless the pronouns are expressed, the meaning is unambiguously third person. For example, *panowie piszą* 'you (m. pl.) are writing', but *piszą* 'they are writing'. These non-familiar address pronouns are all gender-specific and thus inevitably involve sexual discrimination.

The Polish personal pronouns (apart from the second person honorifics *pan* etc., already mentioned) are: *ja* 'I', *ty* 'you' (singular familiar), *on* 'he, it' (m.), *ona* 'she, it' (f.), *ono* 'it' (nt.), *my* 'we', *wy* 'you' (plural, familiar; or singular, honorific), *oni* 'they' (masculine personal), *one* 'they' (non-masculine personal). The most widespread type of non-familiar address is with one of the pronouns, *pan, pani*, etc. (see above) in conjunction with a verb in the same form as for the third person, e.g. *pan pisze* 'you are writing', but *wy* with forms of the second person plural is used to address one person by peasants. Most Poles address older kin with *ty* and the corresponding verbal forms, but in the country *wy* often has this function, e.g. *coście powiedzieli, matko?* 'what did you say, Mother?' In this type of address masculine personal forms are used, even if the addressee is a female. In some families kinship terms are used as second person pronouns to address older kin in conjunction with verbs in the same form as the third person, e.g. *co mama powiedziała?* 'what did you say?' (lit. 'what did Mummy say?').

The past tense (as may be seen from the chart of conjugation types) is derived from the same stem as the infinitive, e.g. *pisa-*, to which are added *-ł-* or *-l-* (denoting 'past'), a vowel (including zero) denoting gender and number and an ending (including a zero ending) denoting person. Historically, the form ending in *ł/l* is a participle; the ending is part of the present tense of the auxiliary *być* 'to be'. The erstwhile independence of the ending is demonstrated by the fact that it need not follow the *ł/l* participle, but may appear elsewhere in the sentence, e.g. *gdzieście byli?* or *gdzie byliście?* 'where have you been?'.

The aspectual system is similar to that of Russian (see pages 283–284). Non-past imperfective verbs (e.g. those in the chart of conjugation types) have present meaning. Non-past perfective verbs have future meaning, e.g. *napiszę* 'I shall write'. The imperfective future is expressed periphrastically using the auxiliary *będę* 'I shall be' in the appropriate person and number with the imperfective infinitive, as in Russian, e.g. *będzie pisać* 'he will write, be writing', or with the *ł/l* participle, e.g. *będzie pisał*. The participle agrees in number and gender with the subject.

The conditional is formed by the addition of the invariable clitic *by* to the past tense. Most commonly it is inserted between the *ł/l* participle and the personal ending, e.g. *pisałbym* 'I should write', *panowie pisaliby* 'you would write' (m. plural). There is also a past conditional formed by the addition of the present conditional of the verb *być* 'to be' to the *ł/l* participle, e.g. *byłbym pisał* 'I should have written', *byłabyś pisała* 'you would have written' (familiar, feminine singular).

The pluperfect also exists, though it is extremely rare and is found only in a formal literary style. The *ł/l* participle of the auxiliary *być* is added to the past tense, e.g. *pisałem był* 'I had written, been writing'.

There are two declined participles (one active, one passive). The active declined participle is derived from the present stem of imperfective verbs by means of the morpheme *-ąc-* to which the adjectival endings are added, e.g. *piszący* 'writing' (masculine nominative singular). The passive declined participle, which may be formed from both imperfective and perfective verbs, is derived from the past (or infinitive) stem by means of the morpheme *-t-* or *-n-* followed by the adjectival endings, e.g. *kryty* 'hidden', *pisany* or *napisany* 'written'. The present undeclined (adverbial) participle is identical with the active declined participle minus the adjectival endings, e.g. *pisząc* 'writing'. There is also a past undeclined (adverbial) participle, which is derived from the past stem by the addition of *-wszy*, e.g. *napisawszy* 'having written'. It may be formed only from perfective verbs.

The passive need not involve the use of the passive participle. It may also be expressed by means of a finite form of the verb accompanied by the reflexive particle *się*, e.g. *książka się drukuje* 'the book is being printed' (lit. 'the book prints itself). Such expressions may also be impersonal, e.g. *mówi się* 'it is said', *drukuje się książkę* (accusative). There are, in addition, impersonal constructions involving the use of special forms of the passive participle ending in *-no* or *-to*, e.g. *zaczęto taniec* 'the dance has been begun', *zamknięto okno* 'the window has been shut', *podano herbatę* 'tea is served'. As in the personal counterparts of these constructions (*podali herbatę* 'they served tea' etc.) the object is in the accusative.

The morphology of numerals in Polish is complicated by the fact that their gender system is different from that of nouns. In particular, the numeral 'two' manifests a fourfold distinction between *dwa* (masculine non-personal and neuter), *dwie* (feminine), *dwaj* (or *dwóch* or *dwu*) (group consisting exclusively of male persons), and *dwoje* (one man and one woman). (However, *dwoje* is also used with nouns which exist only in the plural or denote young creatures, including children.) Although this degree of subtlety is restricted to this numeral and words for 'both', the morphological specification of groups consisting exclusively of male persons is characteristic of numerals generally and in contradistinction to nominal gender, which only specifies groups containing at least one male person.

4 Syntax

Main verbs agree in number and person with their subjects. For example, *urzędnik pisze* 'the official is writing' (3 singular), *urzędnicy piszą* 'the officials are writing' (3 plural). Past tense verbs, in addition, agree in gender with their subject. For example, *urzędnicy pisali* 'the officials were writing' (3 plural, masculine personal), *nauczycielki pisały* 'the teachers (feminine) were writing' (3 plural, non-masculine personal), *koty siedziały* 'the cats were sitting' (3 plural, non-masculine personal). In the case of composite subjects the two features 'masculine' and 'personal' may be supplied separately by two nouns one of which is masculine (but not human) and the other of which is human (but not masculine). Thus: *nauczycielka i kot siedzieli* 'the teacher (feminine) and the cat (masculine) were sitting'.

Adjectives agree in number, case and gender with the nouns they modify, e.g. *Jadwiga jest chora* 'Jadwiga is ill' (feminine nominative singular), *mam młodą córkę* 'I have a young daughter' (feminine accusative singular). Nouns which refer to male human beings may, for expressive purposes (positive or negative), be used in the non-masculine personal form, e.g. *morowe chłopy* 'fine lads' (instead of masculine personal *morowi chłopi*). In such cases, both adjectives and past tense verbs may agree with the expressive form, e.g. *jakieś idioty to wymyśliły* 'some idiots have dreamed that up' (rather *than jacyś idioci to wymyślili*). Certain essentially expressive words hardly ever or never appear in the masculine personal form, e.g. *Szwab* 'German' (derogatory) always has plural *Szwaby*. (*Szwabi* or *Szwabowie* means 'Swabians' i.e. 'inhabitants of Swabia'.)

From some masculine nouns referring to professional posts and titles it is possible to derive feminine counterparts, e.g. from *nauczyciel* 'teacher' (masculine) we derive *nauczycielka* 'teacher' (feminine). Words like *nauczycielka* are straightforward feminine nouns and take normal feminine agreement. In some other cases, however, particularly those of professions which until recently were mainly the preserve of men, there is no feminine form. Therefore, the originally masculine noun is now usually of common gender, i.e. it is masculine when referring to a man and feminine when referring to a woman. This is so, for example, in the case of *doktor* 'doctor', *inżynier* 'engineer', *ambasador* 'ambassador', *architekt* 'architect'. It is possible, when referring to a woman, to retain masculine agreement, e.g. *nasz doktor wyjechał* 'our doctor has gone away' *may* refer to a woman. But in practice the predominant tendency is to avoid ambiguity by using feminine agreement, e.g. *nasza doktor wyjechała*. Similarly, when the syntax demands an oblique case, it is permissible to decline such nouns according to the masculine paradigm, but a sentence such as *oddałem książkę redaktorowi* 'I returned the book to the editor' will normally be taken to imply that the editor is a man. Therefore, the usual practice, if one of these nouns refers to a woman, is to leave it undeclined, e.g. *oddałem książkę redaktor*, thereby leaving no room for doubt as to the editor's sex.

Some collective nouns ending in *-stwo*, e.g. *państwo* 'ladies and gentlemen', *wujostwo* 'uncle and aunt', decline as singular nouns, but take plural, masculine personal agreement. For example, *Doktorostwo Kowalscy byli u nas wczoraj* 'Doctor and Mrs Kowalski were visiting us yesterday', *ci państwo przyszli* 'that lady and gentleman have arrived'. This syntactic property is one of the features distinguishing *państwo* 'ladies and gentlemen, Mr and Mrs, etc.' from *państwo* 'state', which takes neuter singular agreement.

The numeral 'one' takes agreement in the singular, e.g. *jeden dzień* 'one day', *jedna kobieta* 'one woman', and itself agrees in gender and case with the noun it modifies. It also has a plural form *jedne/jedni* meaning 'some' or 'certain'. In compound numerals ending in 'one' *jeden* is invariable, e.g. *kupiliśmy dwadzieścia jeden książek* 'we bought twenty-one books'. The numerals 'two', 'three' and 'four' take the plural and agree in gender and case with the noun they modify, e.g. *dwa konie* 'two horses' (masculine non-personal nominative and accusative), *dwie książki* 'two books' (feminine nominative and accusative). The masculine personal category (i.e. exclusively masculine) is expressed by means of the forms *dwaj* 'two', *trzej* 'three', *czterej* 'four', e.g. *czterej urzędnicy pisali* 'four officials were writing', or by means of a genitive subject, e.g. *czterech urzędników pisało* 'four officials were writing'. The current tendency is for the latter type to become increasingly common at the expense of the former type. In the case of numerals from 'five' upwards, if the subject is masculine personal (exclusively) it *must* be in the genitive, e.g. *osiemdziesięciu czterech robotników pracowało* 'eighty-four workmen were working'. If the subject is not exclusively masculine personal, numerals from 'five' upwards are followed by the genitive plural, e.g. *dwadzieścia ptaków odleciało* 'twenty birds flew away', unless they are composite and end in one of the numerals 'two' to 'four', in which case the form of the noun is determined by the last component, e.g. *dwadzieścia trzy ptaki odleciały* 'twenty-three birds flew away'.

The collective numerals *dwoje*, *troje*, *czworo*, *pięcioro* etc. have among their functions the possibility of referring to groups containing, but not consisting exclusively of, male persons. Thus, for example, the phrase *ich czworo* '(there are) four of them' (if it refers to adult human beings), reveals that there is at least one man and at least one woman in the group. When in the subject, the collective numerals are always followed by the genitive plural of the noun they modify.

One of the striking features of the Polish system of gender and agreement is the high degree of redundancy. The same information on gender and number may be repeated several times in the sentence. Even more striking, however, is the lack of non-specific forms. It is difficult to make any observation about any plural entity without sizing up its human or non-human and sexual properties. The word *osoba* 'person', which is always feminine, is a boon to those wishing to be non-specific about human groups. But from the problem of deciding whether one's interlocutor (even on the telephone) is male (requiring the address pronoun *pan* + masculine agreement) or female (requiring the address pronoun *pani* + feminine agreement) there is no escape.

Bibliography

Szober (1968) is a standard reference grammar in Polish, while Brooks (1975) is the best reference grammar available in English, and Bielec (1998) provides a briefer statement; Urbańczyk et al. (1978) is an encyclopedia covering all aspects of Polish. For pronunciation, Karaś and Madejowa is a dictionary of Polish pronunciation using the International Phonetic Alphabet, with an introduction in English; Puppel et al. (1977) is the only book of its kind presenting Polish pronunciation in English.

The standard history of the Polish language is Klemensiewicz (1974), while Klemensiewicz et al. (1965) is the standard historical grammar. For historical phonology, Stieber (1973) is a classic work, better than anything in Polish on this subject (including Stieber's own work). Westfal (1985) is a useful account of the language with historical explanations.

References

Bielec, D. 1998. *Polish: An Essential Grammar* (Routledge, London)

Brooks, M.Z. 1975. *Polish Reference Grammar* (Mouton, The Hague)

Karaś, M. and Madejowa, M. 1977. *Słownik wymowy polskiej PWN* (Państwowe Wydawnictwo Naukowe, Warsaw and Cracow)

Klemensiewicz, Z. 1974. *Historia języka polskiego* (Państwowe Wydawnictwo Naukowe, Warsaw)

Klemensiewicz, Z., Lehr-Spławiński, T. and Urbańczyk, S. 1965. *Gramatyka historyczna języka polskiego*, 3rd edn (Państwowe Wydawnictwo Naukowe, Warsaw)

Puppel, S., Nawrocka-Fisiak, J. and Krassowska, H. 1977. *A Handbook of Polish Pronunciation for English Learners* (Państwowe Wydawnictwo Naukowe, Warsaw)

Stieber, Z. 1973. *A Historical Phonology of the Polish Language* (Carl Winter Universitätsverlag, Heidelberg)

Szober, S. 1968. *Gramatyka języka polskiego*, 10th edn (Państwowe Wydawnictwo Naukowe, Warsaw)

Urbańczyk, S. (ed.) 1978. *Encyklopedia wiedzy o języku polskim* (Ossolineum, Wrocław, Warsaw, Cracow and Gdańsk)

Westfal, S. 1985. *The Polish Language*, 2nd edn (Veritas Foundation Publication Centre, London)

17

Czech and Slovak

David Short

1 Introduction

On purely statistical grounds, Czech and Slovak are by no means major languages, with around 9.5 and 4.5 million speakers in the Czech and Slovak republics respectively, whereas Ukrainian, for example, has around 40 million speakers. Since the break-up of Czechoslovakia, about half a million Slovaks elected to move to or stay in the Czech Republic. Both Czechs and Slovaks are, however, to be found scattered worldwide, either diffused or in close-knit villages and some larger communities in Romania, Croatia, Hungary, Poland and the Ukraine, due to local, mainly nineteenth-century, small-scale migrations or the vagaries of political frontiers, or in Canada, the USA and South America owing to the modern tradition of political or economic migration. Since the fall of Communism, some Volhynian Czechs have 'returned' from the Ukraine and a number of post-World War II émigrés have also returned from the West; conversely, since their home countries joined the European Union, increasing numbers of Czechs and Slovaks have arrived in Britain and Ireland, many intending to stay. The historical pockets of extra-territorial populations add several thousand to the total numbers of speakers; their languages, however, necessarily differ, through physical separation and the external influence of dominant languages in the alien environment, from the Czech and Slovak to be described in the following pages.

If not on statistical grounds, then historically Czech at least does have a claim as a major language: the Kingdom of Bohemia controlled, in the Middle Ages, a much vaster area than just the Lands of the Bohemian Crown (Bohemia and Moravia) that still constitute the core of the Czech Republic; Bohemian kings have been Holy Roman Emperors, and twice there have been, among other international arrangements, Anglo-Bohemian dynastic links through marriage. More recently, Czechoslovakia was, between the wars, a major economic force in Europe (mineral extraction, iron and steel, armaments, footwear), and its sportsmen have never been far to seek in many disciplines at international level (football, ice hockey, athletics, tennis).

By contrast, until 1993 Slovakia had hardly ever enjoyed independence, coming closest to it briefly during the Second World War as a client state of Germany; between

1968 and 1992 it was one of the two federated republics of former Czechoslovakia. As a separate economic power it has only begun to assert itself in the twenty-first century, attracting much inward investment in, for example, the automotive, electronics and confectionery industries; surprisingly to many, it now leads Europe in per capita car production.

The two languages are taken together in this volume because, despite the natural processes of divergence brought about by geography, geopolitical separation and exposure to different influences of neighbouring languages (Czech is heavily influenced by German, Slovak by Hungarian; since the fall of Communism, both are, in the view of some, creaking under the impact of global English), they have a great deal in common and traditionally have been held to be about 90 per cent mutually intelligible. When they shared a common state, Czechs and Slovaks were each constantly exposed to the other language and mutual intelligibility was reinforced by, for example, labour mobility, military service and the media. Since the countries split, such reinforcement has been lost almost totally and the youngest generation sometimes claims to understand the other language no better than, say, Polish. Slovak post-independence language legislation also contributed to the decline.

The similarities between the languages are highest at the lexical level (and new lexical developments continue to show them evolving in tandem), though some of the most striking differences are also in this area. Phonologically and morphologically the differences between the standard forms of the two languages affect most words, though often not enough to impede comprehension. The overall distinctiveness between Czech and Slovak is, however, great enough for translations between the literatures to be a meaningful exercise, though such a view is not held universally.

2 The Historical Background

The written tradition in what was Czechoslovakia goes back to the ninth century, with the Christian mission of Saints Cyril (Constantine) and Methodius to Great Moravia, where they prepared Slavonic translations of the central religious texts. At the time, the Macedonian dialect of Slavonic that they used was readily comprehensible to all other Slavs. Although used for centuries afterwards in Eastern Orthodox Christianity, in the west it fell into disuse after the Slavonic monks were driven from the Sázava monastery in Bohemia in 1097. The existence of this standardised literary language undoubtedly contributed to the general stability of the early literary tradition in Bohemia; however, the Slavonic alphabets used in it, the Glagolitic created by St Cyril and the Cyrillic as still used by Bulgarian, Macedonian and Serbian and the East Slavonic Languages, were not widely employed. Czech and Slovak used a modified Latin alphabet, possibly because Cyril and Methodius were actually preceded by western missionaries from Italy, Bavaria and Ireland. The earliest texts show developing refinements of the Latin alphabet as it was adapted to express the non-Latin sounds of Czech, and the first attempt to systematise the orthography is generally attributed to the religious reformer and competent 'general linguist' Jan Hus (1373–1415). Among many other linguistic guidelines, Hus introduced a system of diacritics to replace the many cumbersome digraphs in use until then. His system was not adopted universally or immediately, but a version of it became generalised when adopted by the Czech Brethren, whose authority and literary output guaranteed its ultimate acceptance. This sixteenth-century

'Brethren' orthography differed from the modern in the use of *g*, *ğ*, *j*, *w*, *v* and *au* for *j*, *g*, *í*, *v*, *u* and *ou* respectively, and critically in the distribution of *i* and *y*. The modern values of the letters were established fairly painlessly in a sequence of nineteenth-century reforms, except in the case of *i/y*, which underlay a major controversy. The distinction between *i* and *y* as accepted in the modern orthographies is on etymological or morphological grounds and represents the victory of the 'iotist' camp in the nineteenth-century debate. The 'ypsilonists' gave precedence to phonetic considerations in certain critical environments. The iotist victory was assured once Josef Jungmann (1773–1847) and Josef Dobrovský (1753–1829) firmly adopted the new conventions, the matter being essentially settled about 1817–19. It was not laid to rest completely, however, until the death of the chief ypsilonist, Jan Nejedlý (1776–1834), though Jiří (Juraj) Palkovič (1769–1850) continued with the *y*-convention in Slovakia until his death.

Since the nineteenth-century there have been further minor reforms, notably in the distribution of *s* and *z* medially and as prefixes, the two languages being not quite in step here; Slovak has generally adhered to the phonetic principle. In the twentieth century, the old *i/y* problem resurfaced. Early in 1984 it seemed quite likely that *y* would be eliminated altogether in favour of *i* in Czech, except after *d*, *t* and *n*, which as hitherto would represent palatal stops before *i* and alveolar before *y*, and also that *ů* would be replaced by *ú*. However, the public outcry over the consequences for language study and language learning, not to mention the continuing need to be able to read with ease texts in the pre-reform orthography which were unlikely to be reprinted, meant that the proposal was dropped. That is not to say it may not be resurrected at some future date.

The father of Slavonic studies, Josef Dobrovský, produced the first scholarly modern grammar of Czech, at a time when the French Enlightenment and Austrian responses to it (the reforms of Josef II) had spurred on the National Revival and a new interest in the Czech nation and language. As his sources Dobrovský took both the best of the humanist tradition, associated with the name of Jan Blahoslav (1523–71), the Kralice Bible (1579–93) and the printer Daniel Adam z Veleslavína (1546–99), and the living language of the rural Czech populace. The resultant grammar, still the basis of modern Czech, contained perforce many archaic features, and Dobrovský himself was not convinced that the language could be fully revived. It fell largely to Josef Jungmann to demonstrate, through translations of, among others, Milton's *Paradise Lost* and Goethe's *Hermann und Dorothea*, that Czech was capable of high-style verse, and to provide Czech with a complete lexicon, his Czech–German dictionary of 1834–9. Czech was no longer a vehicle with limited capacity for expressing the full breadth of human communicational needs. Jungmann himself, and those who followed in the provision of technical terminologies, drew on some of the earlier vocabularies and on knowledge of other Slavonic languages as a source for rationally motivated loan-neologisms.

Meanwhile in Slovakia the language situation was also evolving. As part of Hungary, its official language had been Latin or Hungarian, while the Protestant liturgy continued to use Czech, the Czech of the Kralice Bible. The first attempt at codification of Slovak was by Anton Bernolák (1762–1813), a Catholic priest, who produced a grammar based on a Western Slovak dialect, and a six-volume dictionary published posthumously in 1825–7. Bernolák's version of literary Slovak failed to gain wide approval, unlike the second attempt, by Ľudovít Štúr (1815–56), whose 1846 work, based on Central Slovak, found immediate favour. There have been changes since, in both the morphology and the lexicon of the standard, but the modern language still owes most to Štúr. Before Štúr and Bernolák there had been writing in 'Slovak' – various hybrids of Czech and local dialects written according to a variety of spelling conventions. It has become the practice to refer to these pre-standardisation versions of the language as 'cultured (*kultúrna*) western/central/eastern Slovak'. Throughout the gestation and parturition of Slovak as an independent literary language there was also a continuous current which favoured the use of Czech, either as such, or in a mutation of a common Czechoslovak; the latter survived as a linguistic myth right through the First Republic (1918–38).

In many ways Slovak is more modern than Czech, especially morphologically, for it has far fewer surviving redundant distinctions. Czech has more later phonological innovations, and more still in its most progressive form, 'Common Czech', based on the Central Bohemian dialect. This has evolved into a remarkably distinctive version – lexically and morphologically – of the national language.

Although there has been a strong tendency in the past to keep Slovak maximally distinct from Czech and free of Bohemicisms, there have at times been signs of a reverse tendency, due in part to the shift of the languages' centres of gravity away from the high literary towards the technical. Both languages resort to neologisms, and standardisation to international norms often means coincidence rather than further division. Added to that, Slovak, despite the opposition of purists, remained, within Czechoslovakia, open to influences from Czech; Slovak influence on Czech was much slighter, though not fully appreciated. Since the break-up in 1993, the two populations have had far fewer opportunities for day-to-day contact with the other language and assertive Slovak language legislation has inhibited influences further. The youngest generation admits freely to finding the other language hard to understand.

3 The Alphabets, Orthography and Phonology of Czech and Slovak

Typographically similar letters given on the same line in Table 17.1, e.g. *a*, *á*, have no effect on ordering in the dictionary, while those on separate lines, e.g. Slovak *a*, *ä*, are ordered separately. The three digraphs *ch*, *dz*, *dž* are treated in every respect as single letters. Although *d/ď*, *t/ť*, *n/ň* and *l/ľ* are ordered indiscriminately in accordance with the following letter, i.e. *ťuhýk* will always precede *tuk*, the sounds represented by each member of the pairs are phonetically and phonologically distinct, as alveolar and palatal respectively. But because of certain spelling conventions a *d*, *t*, *n* or *l* may have the palatal values of a *ď*, *ť*, *ň* and *ľ*, notably before *ě* and *i* in Czech and (in most cases) *e* and *i* in Slovak. Note also the conventions whereby *ď* and *ť* use the hook ˇ instead of the apostrophe on capitals and in handwriting; in the past this also occurred on the typewriter keyboard, though while the computer keyboard uses the symbol as a dead key for building up letters that are too scarce to have a key of their own, the software will interpret whether the hook or apostrophe is required (i.e. *Ť* and *ť*). Of the other consonants, *h* is a voiced glottal fricative, *c* and *dz* represent alveolar affricates, *č* and *dž* palato-alveolar affricates, *š* and *ž* palato-alveolar fricatives, and *ř* a rolled post-alveolar fricative (never the sequence of [r] + [ʒ] commonly attempted by non-Czechs in the name *Dvořák*). The letters *q*, *w* and *x* are confined to loanwords, though for obvious reasons only *x* is particularly common. In Slovak *g* is marginally more common than in Czech, thanks to a number of words containing /g/ that are not merely

Table 17.1 The Alphabets of Czech and Slovak

Czech	Slovak	Czech	Slovak
a, á	a, á	m	m
	ä	n, ň	n, ň
b	b	o, ó	o, ó
c	c	p	p
č	č	q	q
d, ď	d, ď	r	r, ŕ
	dz	ř	
	dž	s	s
e, é, ě	e, é	š	š
f	f	t, ť	t, ť
g	g	u, ú, ů	u, ú
h	h	v	v
ch	ch	w	w
i, í	i, í	x	x
j	j	y, ý	y, ý
k	k	z	z
l	l, ľ, ĺ	ž	ž

loans or onomatopoeic. By contrast *f* is more domesticated in Czech, having evolved as the voiceless counterpart of /v/, though it too is most frequent in loanwords. In circumstances parallel to the Czech devoicing of /v/ to /f/, Slovak has the bilabial /w/, not represented orthographically other than as *v* after any vowel or syllabic /r/; the same sound occurs as *u* after *o* in morphologically conditioned positions. The remaining consonant symbols have values similar to English, but the voiceless plosives represented by *p*, *t* and *k* are not aspirated.

Of the vowel symbols, *ě* signals that a preceding *d*, *t* or *n* is to be pronounced as the appropriate palatal counterpart, or that preceding *b*, *p*, *f*, *v* or *m* is to be pronounced [bj], [pj], [fj], [vj] or [mɲ]. Slovak *ä* represents a sound between /a/ and /e/, but is often indistinguishable from the latter, which the orthoepic standard allows. Slovak *ô* represents the diphthongal phoneme /uo/, and the circle on the Czech *ů* is an historical convention appearing in circumstances where a long /u/ has evolved from a long /o/. Length in a vowel and Slovak syllabic /l/ and /r/ is otherwise marked by the 'acute accent'. Long *ó* occurs only in loanwords. Any occurrences of 'accented' letters from other languages (*è*, *ö*, *å*, *ş* etc.) are not accorded special treatment in terms of ordering.

In addition to /uo/ (*ô*) Slovak has three other diphthongs represented by *ia*, *ie* and *iu*. Czech has one diphthong /ou/, spelled *ou* (contrast the Slovak *ou* sequence as [ow]).

Voice assimilation in clusters of consonants is important in both Czech and Slovak, but is only sporadically reflected in the spelling. Voice assimilation in consonant clusters works right through both languages where consonants present in voiced–voiceless pairs are involved, e.g. *bt* and *tb* will be pronounced /pt/ and /db/ respectively, and in Slovak also before (non-paired) *r*, *l*, *ľ*, *m*, *n*, *ň* and *j* at word and some morpheme boundaries. Czech and Slovak spelling is thus morphophonemic rather than phonetic.

One phonetic difference, not reflected in the orthography, is the presence and absence of the glottal stop in Czech and Slovak respectively; it appears in Czech between vowels and before words beginning with a vowel.

Both languages have fixed stress, on the first syllable, and this usually passes forward onto a preceding monosyllabic preposition.

4 The Evolution of Czech and Slovak

Among the early dialect divisions of Slavonic are the different resolutions of the *tort formula, as indicated on page 272. Importantly, Czech and Slovak here share the South Slavonic resolution, namely *trat, unlike Polish *trot; the only Czech/Slovak inconsistencies here are in variations of vowel length, brought about by different patterns of accent-shifting or the workings of analogy. Where they are distinct is in the related word-initial *ort formula: Central Slovak (the basis of the standard language) has fairly consistently *rat, while Czech has *rat or *rot according to whether the original tone had been rising or falling. Slovak is thus united to South Slavonic by an extra isogloss, cf. Cz. *role* 'field', *rádlo* 'plough', Slk. *raľa, radlo*, Serbo-Croat *ral, ralo*.

The palatalisations (see page 271) produced two Czech/Slovak distinctions. Under the second palatalisation of velars *ch* yielded *š* in Czech as in West Slavonic generally, but *s* in Slovak (another feature shared with South Slavonic), hence *Češi/Česi* 'Czechs'. The affricate *dz* had two origins: from *g* by the second and third palatalisations, and from *d + j*. Whereas in Czech *dz* of either origin de-affricated to *z* (see page 272), suggesting near simultaneity of the two processes, in Slovak they must have been separated in time, since de-affrication only affected *dz < g*. The change of *d + j* to *dz* came about only after de-affrication was completed, leaving this second appearance of *dz* unchanged as the source of this Slovak-only phoneme.

To the Slavist knowing, say, Russian or Polish, a striking feature of Czech and Slovak is the absence of *g* from the native word stock and its replacement by *h*. This is a consequence of the realignment of consonantal parallelisms after the de-affrication of *dž* to *ž*. Prior to that there was symmetry between *k:g* (voiceless and voiced velar plosives) and *č:dž* (their post-palatalisation corresponding palatal affricates), with *ch* and its counterpart *š* standing to one side. Subsequently a voiced/voiceless relationship emerged between *ž* and *š*, not matched by *g:ch*. This led to the change *g > h*, leaving *h:ch* as a nearly matching pair of fricatives, differing slightly in the place of articulation (glottal and velar respectively). Before and after the de-affrication the picture was thus:

Before: k:g   ch   After: k   h:ch
         č:dž   š   č   ž:š

The resolution of the jers (see pages 272–273) is another area in which Czech and Slovak differ. Czech has all strong jers vocalised to *e*, while Slovak has essentially followed the Russian pattern, i.e. *e* for ь, *o* for ъ. Slovak also uses *a*, for which many conflicting theories have been advanced, as also for the explanation of the not infrequent cases of *o* for ь and *e* for ъ.

One of the most striking differences between Czech and Slovak (along with the easternmost dialects of Czech itself) is the outcome of the processes known in Czech as *přehláska* (approximately 'umlaut'), whereby the back vowels *a/á, u/ú* and *o/ó* underwent a forward shift to *ě/ie, i/í* and *ě/ie*. The three sets of changes were not quite simultaneous, nor did they happen under exactly the same circumstances. The common factor was basically the influence of a preceding soft (palatalised) consonant, and although later developments, especially the effect of analogy, have 'undone' some of the effects, the consequences have been far-reaching phonologically (in the range of new syllable types), morphemically (in the increased incidence of root-vowel alternation, as in *pět/pátý* 'five/fifth' or *přítel/přátel* 'friend (nom. sg./gen. pl.)', instances where for *a* > *ě*, *á* > *ie* > *í* the nature of a following consonant was also relevant), and morphologically. Here it led on the one hand to a proliferation of hard/soft oppositions in the declensional paradigms: *žena:duše* 'wife:soul', acc. sg.: *ženu:duši*; *oknům:mořím* 'window:sea' dat. pl. (*ů* < *ó*, *í* < *ie* < *ó*); and on the other hand it led, after the change of *ie* > *í*, to the obliteration of case-distinct forms in one particular, large neuter paradigm (the contemporary *í*-declension, in which the only distinctively marked cases are those commonly associated with a consonant). Slovak was quite untouched by *přehláska*.

Czech and Slovak both possess syllabic liquids. The original **trt*, **tlt* have survived with fewer innovations in Slovak, while Czech has, in different circumstances, supporting vowels after *č* and *ž* with *r*, hence *čerpat* 'draw (water)', *žerď* 'pole' to Slovak *črpať*, *žrď*, and after all consonants with *l*, except after labials where the *l* was of the soft variety, hence *žlutý* 'yellow', *dlouhy* 'long' to Slovak *žltý*, *dlhý*, but *vlk* 'wolf' and *plný* 'full' in both languages. As a consequence of the loss of the weak jers, many new consonantal clusters arose, often containing liquids. The picture is a complex one, with up to five different solutions to the problem, varying with position in the word and geographical distribution. Of most significance here are the initial and final positions, since this time it is Slovak which evolves supporting vowels, hence *luhat* 'lie, fib', *ľahostajný* 'indifferent', *ruvat* 'tear', *ruman* 'chamomile', *eržat* 'neigh' correspond to the Czech *lhát*, *lhostejný*, *rvát*, *rmen*, *ržát* (where the initial liquids are only semi-syllabic, that is, they do not attract the stress), and *niesol* 'he carried', *myseľ* 'mind', *vietor* 'wind' to the Czech *nesl*, *mysl*, *vítr* (where the liquids are syllabic and indistinguishable from original syllabic *l* and *r*). The failure of Slovak to evolve secondary final syllabic liquids underlies one of the contrasts in the absorption of loanwords in the two languages (there are of course others). Where Czech spelling and pronunciation have here too a syllabic *l* or *r*, as in *manšestr* 'corduroy', *metr* 'metre' or *triangl* 'triangle' – the instrument, Slovak has *menčester*, *meter* and *triangel*, and the orthoepic pronunciation of foreign toponyms, etc., is analogously distinct (/menčestr/ vs /menčester/ 'Manchester').

In any account of the Czech consonant system mention must be made of the almost uniquely Czech phoneme represented by *ř*, a fully palatalised historically soft *r*.

This background account of the history of distinctive phonological features is by no means exhaustive, but there remains one more which cannot be overlooked, namely the so-called rhythmical law of Slovak. In essence this states that where two (historically) long syllables appear in succession, the second one shortens. This is most conspicuous in adjectival endings, which by the process of contraction were long. Contraction operated in most cases where there were two vowels in sequence separated by a jot, hence in the adjectives **krásnъjь*, **krásnaja*, **krásnoje* 'beautiful (nom. sg. m., f., nt.)' gave *krásný*, *krásná*, *krásné*. By the rhythmical law the second long vowels shortened, hence modern Slovak *krásny*, *krásna*, *krásne*; this does not apply if the preceding syllable is short, as in *pekný* 'nice' (Cz. *pěkný*). Forms such as *krásne* are ambiguous in Slovak (on paper) as between some case-forms of the adjective (e.g. neuter singular nominative/accusative) and the adverb (equivalent to Czech *krásně*), but there is a pronunciation difference, the *n* of the adverb being palatal, that of the adjectival forms being alveolar. No Slovak *e* that has shortened in this manner causes prepalatalisation. The rhythmical law can be seen operating on various suffixes, such as *-ník*, as in *strážnik* 'policeman', cf. Czech *strážník*, as opposed to Slovak/Czech *hutník* 'smelter', or in diminutive formation, as in *národík*, *králiček*, from *národ* 'nation', *králik* 'rabbit' respectively, cf. Czech *nárůdek, králíček*. The Slovak rhythmical law is consistent throughout the word, that is, it is not confined to shortening of final syllables, but there are some half-dozen morphologically conditioned circumstances when it is not observed. These include the third person plural of *í*-conjugation verbs, e.g. *chvália* 'praise' (*ia* is a diphthong and therefore long; diphthongs are generally covered by the rhythmical law otherwise), the genitive plural of some noun types, e.g. *piesní* 'songs', and adjectives formed from the names of animals, e.g. *vtáčí* 'birds'.

Both languages have evolved fixed stress, on the first syllable; this contrasts with Polish, where it is fixed on the penultimate, and Russian or Serbo-Croat, where it is mobile.

5 Morphology

Like most of the Slavonic languages, Czech and Slovak have been fairly conservative in their morphology, although they are by no means identical. They both have three genders and a fully developed case system. There are two differences here, however: (a) Slovak has lost the vocative (remnants survive); (b) the animate/inanimate opposition within the masculine gender (only) applies in Czech absolutely, from *prvok* 'protozoon' to *Bůh* 'God', singular and plural, whereas in Slovak it applies in the singular only. In the plural in Slovak the opposition is human/non-human, animal names (with few exceptions) being aligned with inanimates. The number system has become bipartite, singular and plural, with just a few remnants in Czech of the old dual declension surviving as anomalous plurals, chiefly associated with names for parts of the body. Standard literary Czech is the most conservative, Slovak and Common Colloquial Czech having proceeded further in the direction of eliminating redundant distinctions, notably in having a near-universal instrumental plural ending in *-mi* and *-ma* respectively (with an appropriate linking vowel where relevant). The latter *-ma* ending is a curiosity in that it comes from the instrumental dual, although the dual survives 'legitimately' only in the remnants mentioned.

The main distinctions between the two languages in noun morphology have come about because of *přehláska* changes which affected Czech, while a not unimportant difference comes in the feminine hard *a*-declension where the more conservative Czech retains the products of palatalisation in the dative and locative singular, Slovak having evolved, like Russian, with forms that eliminate stem alternation; thus to the words *matka* 'mother', *kniha* 'book', *socha* 'statue' the dative/locative singular forms are Cz. *matce, knize, soše* and Slk. *matke, knihe* and *soche*.

Animacy, as a subcategory of the masculine gender (only) in Czech and Slovak, shows some further important differences. The singular of the masculine nouns central to the inanimate–animate distinction is fairly similar, in having *-a* for the animate genitive singular and *-ovi* for the animate dative/locative singular, compare, e.g. *pána, pánovi, pánovi* 'mister' to *hradu* (gen.), *hradu* (dat.) and *hradě* (loc.). (In Czech alone the soft animate genitive, dative and locative forms coincide with those of the inanimate declension.) In common with general practice in the Slavonic languages, the animate genitive form is also used in the animate accusative. In the plural, however, the two languages differ in their expression of animacy: in Slovak it (as human animate) operates in a manner similar to the singular, that is, the genitive form in the accusative, but in Czech it is expressed through the survival of the ancient nominative–accusative

Table 17.2 Czech and Slovak Noun Declensions Compared

(a) Masculine Hard Declension – Animate

		Czech	Slovak
Sg.	Nom.	chlap 'fellow'	chlap
	Voc.	chlape, synu 'son', bože 'god'[1]	
	Acc.	chlapa	chlapa
	Gen.	chlapa	chlapa
	Dat.	chlapovi, -u[2]	chlapovi
	Inst.	chlapem	chlapom
	Loc.	chlapovi, -u	chlapovi
Pl.	Nom.	chlapi, sousedé 'neighbour', filologové 'philologist'	chlapi, občania 'citizen', filologóvia
	Voc.	*as nom.*	
	Acc.	chlapy	chlapov
	Gen.	chlapů	chlapov
	Dat.	chlapům	chlapom
	Inst.	chlapy	chlapmi, majordómami 'butler'
	Loc.	chlapech, soudruzích 'comrade'	chlapoch

Notes:
1 Subclasses of all paradigms may vary in one or more case.
2 Alternative forms exist and may vary functionally.

(b) Masculine Hard a-Declension – Animates Only[1]

		Czech	Slovak
Sg.	Nom.	hrdina 'hero'	hrdina
	Voc.	hrdino	
	Acc.	hrdinu	hrdinu
	Gen.	hrdiny	hrdinu[2]
	Dat.	hrdinovi	hrdinovi
	Inst.	hrdinou	hrdinom
	Loc.	hrdinovi	hrdinovi
Pl.	Nom.	hrdinové, houslisté/-sti 'violinist'	hrdinovia, húslisti
	Voc.	*as nom.*	
	Acc.	hrdiny	hrdinov
	Gen.	hrdinů	hrdinov
	Dat.	hrdinům	hrdinom
	Inst.	hrdiny	hrdinami, husitmi 'Hussite'
	Loc.	hrdinech, sluzích 'manservant'	hrdinoch

Notes:
1 Compare and contrast these forms with (a) above and (g) below.
2 The acc./gen. syncretism based elsewhere on gen. is here uniquely based on acc. The same distribution of endings in Slk. also applies to most native names ending in *-o*, e.g. *Botto, Bottu, Bottu.*

opposition, lost in the singular, cf. Czech *páni* (nom. pl.), *pány* (acc.), *pánů* (gen.) and Slovak *páni, pánov, pánov.* A uniquely Slovak feature is the treatment of animacy in the peripheral masculine *a*-declension, which, other differences apart, has produced syncretism between the accusative and the genitive singular, as one expects, but based on the accusative form. In Czech this declension retains most of the case distinctions of the central feminine *a*-declension; compare Tables 17.2a, 17.2b and 17.2g.

Table 17.2 continued

(c) Masculine Soft Declension – Animate

		Czech	Slovak
Sg.	Nom.	muž 'man', otec 'father'	muž *declined as (a) above*
	Voc.	muži, otče	
	Acc.	muže	muža
	Gen.	muže	muža
	Dat.	muži, Lubošovi	mužovi
	Inst.	mužem	mužom
	Loc.	muži, Lubošovi	mužovi
Pl.	Nom.	muži, otcové, učitelé 'teacher', rodiče 'parent'	muži, otcovia, učitelia, rodičia
	Voc.	*as nom.*	
	Acc.	muže	mužov
	Gen.	mužů	mužov
	Dat.	mužům	mužom
	Inst.	muži	mužmi
	Loc.	mužích	mužoch

Note: The -*ovi* ending in Czech is confined to proper names only.

(d) Masculine Soft a-Declension – Animate Only

		Czech	Slovak	
Sg.	Nom.	správce 'administrator, caretaker'	správca	
	Voc.	správce		
	Acc.	správce	správcu	*Slovak sg. declined like (b)*
	Gen.	správce	správcu	
	Dat.	správcovi	správcovi	
	Inst.	správcem	správcom	
	Loc.	správcovi	správcovi	
Pl.	Nom.	správci, správcové	správci, správcovia	
	Voc.	*as nom.*		
	Acc.	správce	správcov	*Slovak pl. declined mostly like (c)*
	Gen.	správců	správcov	
	Dat.	správcům	správcom	
	Inst.	správci	správcami	
	Loc.	správcích	správcoch	

The basic neuter declensions in both languages are highly conservative. On the Slovak side, however, there are three innovations worthy of mention: lengthening of the ending of the nominative/accusative plural, unless inhibited by the rhythmical law, e.g. *mesto* (nom./acc. sg.) but *mestá*, cf. Czech *město, města*; the extending of the feminine *a*-declension locative ending -*ách/-iach* to the neuters, e.g. *ženách/dušiach* (f.) and *mestách/poliach*, in contrast to Czech *městech/polích*, which retain their affinity with the masculine (there is some penetration of *a*-declension endings into the neuter in Czech in the case of velar stems, e.g. *kolečkách* 'wheel' (diminutive), which avoids stem alternation of the type **kolečcích*); and vowel lengthening before the zero ending of the genitive plural if not inhibited by the rhythmical law, e.g. *mesto* (nom. sg.), *miest*. This last is another feature shared with the *a*-declension, cf. *žena/žien*, and an

Table 17.2 continued

(e) Masculine Hard Declension – Inanimate

		Czech	Slovak
Sg.	Nom.	hrad 'castle'	hrad
	Voc.	hrade	
	Acc.	hrad	hrad
	Gen.	hradu, lesa 'forest'	hradu, duba 'oak'
	Dat.	hradu	hradu
	Inst.	hradem	hradom
	Loc.	hradě, rohu 'corner, horn'	hrade, rohu, mieri 'peace'
Pl.	Nom.	hrady	hrady
	Voc.	hrady	
	Acc.	hrady	hrady
	Gen.	hradů	hradov
	Dat.	hradům	hradom
	Inst.	hrady	hradmi, listami 'leaf; letter'
	Loc.	hradech, stolcích 'table' (dimin.)	hradoch

Note: The ending -a in gen. sg. is confined in Czech to a fairly small number of nouns; in Slovak it is the preferred ending for concreta

(f) Masculine Soft Declension – Inanimate

		Czech	Slovak
Sg.	Nom.	stroj 'machine'	stroj
	Voc.	stroji	
	Acc.	stroj	stroj
	Gen.	stroje	stroja, čaju 'tea'
	Dat.	stroji	stroju
	Inst.	strojem	strojom
	Loc.	stroji	stroji
Pl.	Nom.	stroje	stroje
	Voc.	*as nom.*	
	Acc.	stroje	stroje
	Gen.	strojů	strojov, dní 'day'
	Dat.	strojům	strojom
	Inst.	stroji	strojmi
	Loc.	strojích	strojoch

interesting aspect of it is that it applies equally to a true stem vowel and any fill-vowel which might appear, e.g. *okno/okien* 'window'. (Note that vowel lengthening often, as in these examples, means diphthongisation.)

Apart from the above, Czech noun morphology is generally more conservative than Slovak in the greater degree of preservation of the effects of the second palatalisation of velars, in the locative plural masculine (*jazycích* 'tongue', Slovak *jazykoch*) and the nominative plural animate, where it affects all three velar consonants: *žák/žáci* 'student', *Čech/Češi, vrah/vrazi* 'murderer'; in Slovak this only applies to the first two, hence: *žiak/žiaci, Čech/Česi,* but *vrah/vrahovia* (*-ovia,* like Cz. *-ové,* is an alternative nominative plural masculine animate ending used with specific subclasses of nouns; a third is *-ia,* Cz. *-é*).

315

Table 17.2 continued

(g) Feminine Hard Declension

		Czech	Slovak
Sg.	Nom.	žena 'woman'	žena
	Voc.	ženo	
	Acc.	ženu	ženu
	Gen.	ženy	ženy
	Dat.	ženě, dceři 'daughter'[1]	žene
	Inst.	ženou	ženou
	Loc.	ženě, dceři[1]	žene
Pl.	Nom.	ženy	ženy
	Voc.	*as nom.*	
	Acc.	ženy	ženy
	Gen.	žen, povídek 'short story'	žien, záhrad 'garden', budov 'building', sestier 'sister'...[2]
	Dat.	ženám	ženám
	Inst.	ženami	ženami
	Loc.	ženách	ženách

Notes:

1 An isolated anomaly with roots in the consonantal declension (cf. Table 17.2n, page 319).

2 The final, pre-zero-ending, syllable, whether a root syllable or containing a fill-vowel, is lengthened in Slk., except before -v, after -j- or where lengthening is inhibited by the rhythmical law. In Cz. the fill-vowel in gen. pl. is always -e-, whereas in Slk. there are several possibilities: *hradieb* < *hradba* 'rampart', *vojen* > *vojna* 'war', *kvapôk* < *kvapka* 'drop, drip', *sestár* (alternative to *sestier*), *látok* < *látka* 'material'. Increasingly, -ie- is becoming the fill-vowel of choice, even in defiance of the rhythmical law, hence, for example, *čísiel* has largely replaced *čísel*.

(h) Feminine Soft Declension – Basic Type

		Czech	Slovak
Sg.	Nom.	duše 'soul', ulice 'street', chvíle 'moment'	duša, dielňa 'workshop', ulica, chvíľa
	Voc.	duše	
	Acc.	duši	dušu
	Gen.	duše	duše
	Dat.	duši	duši
	Inst.	duší	dušou
	Loc.	duši	duši
Pl.	Nom.	duše, housle 'violin'	duše, husle
	Voc.	*as nom.*	
	Acc.	duše	duše
	Gen.	duší, houslí, ulic, chvil	duší, dielní, ulíc, chvíľ, husieľ/huslí
	Dat.	duším	dušiam
	Inst.	dušemi	dušami
	Loc.	duších	dušiach

Notes: The zero ending in gen. pl. is confined in Cz. to native words ending in -ice and a small number of others ending in -le. In Slk. there is a slightly higher preference for zero; lengthening of the final syllable follows patterns similar to those noted in (g). The case of Slk. *dielní* is one of the standard deviations from the rhythmical law.

Table 17.2 continued

(i) Feminine Soft Declension – Mixed Type

		Czech	Slovak
Sg.	Nom.	dlaň	dlaň
	Voc.	dlani	
	Acc.	dlaň	dlaň
	Gen.	dlaně	dlane
	Dat.	dlani	dlani
	Inst.	dlaní	dlaňou
	Loc.	dlani	dlani
Pl.	Nom.	dlaně	dlane
	Voc.	*as nom.*	
	Acc.	dlaně	dlane
	Gen.	dlaní	dlaní, piesní 'song'
	Dat.	dlaním	dlaniam
	Inst.	dlaněmi	dlaňami
	Loc.	dlaních	dlaniach

(j) Feminine i-Declension

		Czech	Slovak
Sg.	Nom.	kost	kosť
	Voc.	kosti	
	Acc.	kost	kosť
	Gen.	kosti	kosti
	Dat.	kosti	kosti
	Inst.	kostí	kosťou
	Loc.	kosti	kosti
Pl.	Nom.	kosti	kosti
	Voc.	*as nom.*	
	Acc.	kosti	kosti
	Gen.	kostí	kostí
	Dat.	kostem	kostiam
	Inst.	kostmi	kosťami
	Loc.	kostech	kostiach

Adjective declension is typified by the presence of long vowels in the ending (unless inhibited by the rhythmical law in Slovak as in the example following) as a result of contraction, cf. the disyllabic endings, in the nominative at least, in Russian, where contraction did not occur: Czech *krásný* 'beautiful' (m. sg.), *krásná* (f. sg.), *krásné* (n. sg.), *krásní* (m. anim. pl.), *krásné* (m. inanim. and f. pl.) and *krásná* (n. pl.); Slovak *krásny* (m. sg.), *krásna* (f. sg.), *krásne* (n. sg.), *krásni* (m. hum. pl.), *krásne* (all other plurals), Russian *krasnyj* (m. sg.), *krasnaja* (f. sg.), *krasnoje* (n. sg.) and *krasnyje* (all plurals).

Apart from the operation of the rhythmical law in Slovak the other main differences between the Czech and Slovak adjectival declensions can be explained by the relative conservatism of Slovak phonology, notably the absence of *přehláska* and the non-monophthongisation of *ie*, both affecting the soft adjectives and illustrated in, for example, the feminine and neuter singular forms *cudzia*, *cudzie*, Czech *cizí* 'alien, someone else's'.

Table 17.2 continued

(k) Hard Neuter Declension

		Czech	Slovak
Sg.	Nom.	město 'town, city', sucho 'drought', dobro 'good'	mesto, sucho, dobro, vnutro 'inside', nebo 'heaven'
	Voc.	město	
	Acc.	město	mesto
	Gen.	města	mesta
	Dat.	městu	mestu
	Inst.	městem	mestom
	Loc.	městě, suchu, dobru[1]	meste, suchu, dobre, vnutri, nebi[1]
Pl.	Nom.	města	mestá
	Voc.	as nom.	
	Acc.	města	mestá
	Gen.	měst	miest
	Dat.	městům	mestám
	Inst.	městy	mestami
	Loc.	městech, ložiskách[2] 'deposit, bearing'	mestách

Notes:

1 The loc. sg. ending -u is preferred with abstracts in Cz., with velar stems in Slk.; the -i ending in Slk. is associated with stem-final -r or items once in a different class.

2 The loc. pl. ending -ách in Cz. applies chiefly to stems ending in a velar consonant; its high incidence is due in particular to that of diminutive forms in -ko.

(l) Neuter Soft Declension – Equivalent of Foregoing

		Czech	Slovak
Sg.	Nom.	srdce	srdce
	Voc.	srdce	
	Acc.	srdce	srdce
	Gen.	srdce	srdca
	Dat.	srdci	srdcu
	Inst.	srdcem	srdcom
	Loc.	srdci	srdci
Pl.	Nom.	srdce, letiště 'airport'	srdcia
	Voc.	as nom.	
	Acc.	srdce	srdcia
	Gen.	srdcí, letišť	sŕdc, polí
	Dat.	srdcím	srdciam
	Inst.	srdci	srdcami
	Loc.	srdcích	srdciach

Both languages show full adjective–noun agreement in case, number and gender, including animacy. A curiosity on the Czech side is the special form of the instrumental plural in -*ýma*, used in agreement with the handful of nouns which retain -*ma* in that case – one of the dual remnants referred to earlier, occurring in *ruce–rukama* 'hands, arms', *nohy–nohama* 'feet, legs', *uši–ušima* 'ears', *oči–očima* 'eyes'.

It is worth noting that Czech retains a number of so-called short adjectives, e.g. *zdráv* 'healthy', *živ* 'alive', *jist* 'sure', *zvědav* 'curious', *vědom* 'aware', *bos* 'barefoot', which only occur in the predicate and in a narrow range of essentially idiomatic usages. Both

Table 17.2 continued

(m) Neuter Long Soft Declension

		Czech	Slovak
Sg.	Nom.	vysvědčení 'certificate'	vysvedčenie
	Voc.	*as nom.*	
	Acc.	vysvědčení	vysvedčenie
	Gen.	vysvědčení	vysvedčenia
	Dat.	vysvědčení	vysvedčeniu
	Inst.	vysvědčením	vysvedčením
	Loc.	vysvědčení	vysvedčení
Pl.	Nom.	vysvědčení	vysvedčenia
	Voc.	*as nom.*	
	Acc.	vysvědčení	vysvedčenia
	Gen.	vysvědčení	vysvedčení
	Dat.	vysvědčením	vysvedčeniam
	Inst.	vysvědčeními	vysvedčeniami
	Loc.	vysvědčeních	vysvedčeniach

(n) Neuter '-nt-' Declension[1]

		Czech		Slovak	
Sg.	Nom.	děvče 'little girl', kníže (m.) 'prince'		dievča, holúbä 'squab'; knieža (m., n.)	
	Voc.	děvče			
	Acc.	děvče, knížete		dievča; kniežaťa	
	Gen.	děvčete		dievčaťa	
	Dat.	děvčeti		dievčaťu	
	Inst.	děvčetem		dievčaťom	
	Loc.	děvčeti		dievčati	
Pl.	Nom.	děvčata, knížata (m., n.)	dievčatá		dievčence, holúbätá
	Voc.	*as nom.*			
	Acc.	děvčata	dievčatá		dievčence
	Gen.	děvčat	dievčat		dievčeniec, holúbät
	Dat.	děvčatům	dievčatám		dievčencom
	Inst.	děvčaty	dievčatami		dievčencami
	Loc.	děvčatech	děvčatech		dievčencoch
			↑		↑
			alternative plurals		

Note:

1 So-called on historical grounds; the alternating *a/e* before *-t-* originated in a nasal vowel, in turn from *-Vn-*.

Czech and Slovak have the short adjective *rád/-a/-o* which has no long counterpart and serves in conjunction with any verb to express the meaning 'like-ing'.

Possessive adjectives represent a survival of the full short adjectival declension. They may be formed from one-word singular possessor nouns, common or proper, denoting humans, masculine or feminine. (It follows that possessive nouns are not formed from neuters, multi-word possessor phrases, plurals, names of animals, but also nouns/names that are already adjectival in form, such as Czech *pokojská*, Slovak *chyžná* 'chambermaid', Czech *vrátný* 'doorman' and others, including many surnames.) They are formed

Table 17.3 Adjective Declension

Hard Adjectival Declension

		Czech			Slovak		
Sg.	Nom.	dobrý 'good'	-á	-é	dobrý	-á	-é
	Voc.	dobrý	-á	-é			
	Acc.	{ dobrý / dobrého	-ou	-é	{ dobrý / dobrého	-ú	-é
	Gen.	dobrého	-é	-ého	dobrého	-ej	-ého
	Dat.	dobrému	-é	-ému	dobrému	-ej	-ému
	Inst.	dobrým	-ou	-ým	dobrým	-ou	-ým
	Loc.	dobrém	-é	-ém	dobrom	-ej	-om
Pl.	Nom.	{ dobré / dobří	-é	-á	{ dobré / dobrí	-é	-é
	Voc.	{ dobré / dobří	-é	-á			
	Acc.	dobré	-é	-á	{ dobré / dobrých	-é	-é
	Gen.		dobrých			dobrých	
	Dat.		dobrým			dobrým	
	Inst.		dobrými			dobrými	
	Loc.		dobrých			dobrých	

Soft Adjectival Declension

		Czech			Slovak		
Sg.	Nom.	cizí 'alien'	-í	-í	cudzí	-ia	-ie
	Voc.	cizí	-í	-í			
	Acc.	{ cizí / cizího	-í	-í	{ cudzí / cudzieho	-iu	-ie
	Gen.	cizího	-í	-ího	cudzieho	-ej	-ieho
	Dat.	cizímu	-í	-ímu	cudziemu	-ej	-iemu
	Inst.	cizím	-í	-ím	cudzím	-ou	-ím
	Loc.	cizím	-í	-ím	cudzom	-ej	-om
Pl.	Nom.		cizí		{ cudzie / cudzí	-ie	-ie
	Voc.		*as nom.*				
	Acc.		cizí		{ cudzie / cudzích	-ie	-ie
	Gen.		cizích			cudzích	
	Dat.		cizím			cudzím	
	Inst.		cizími			cudzími	
	Loc.		cizích			cudzích	

Notes: Pairs of forms joined by braces indicate variation by animacy, inanimate above, animate below. The masculine plural animate ending -í causes palatalisation of dental and velar stems in Czech, but not in Slovak.

Table 17.4 Declension of Possessive Adjectives

		Czech				Slovak		
Sg.	Nom.	Petrův 'Peter's'	-ova	-ovo		Petrov	-ova	-ovo
	Voc.	Petrův	-ova	-ovo				
	Acc.	{ Petrův / Petrova	-ovu	-ovo	{	Petrov / Petrovho	-ovu	-ovo
	Gen.	Petrova	-ovy	-ova		Petrovho	-ovej	-ovho
	Dat.	Petrovu	-ově	-ovu		Petrovmu	-ovej	-ovmu
	Inst.	Petrovým	-ovou	-ovým		Petrovým	-ovou	-ovým
	Loc.	Petrově/-u	-ově	-ově/-u		Petrovom	-ovej	-ovom
Pl.	Nom.	{ Petrovy / Petrovi	-ovy	-ova	{	Petrove / Petrovi	-ove	-ove
	Voc.	{ Petrovy / Petrovi	-ovy	-ova				
	Acc.	Petrovy	-ovy	-ova	{	Petrove / Petrových	-ove	-ove
	Gen.		Petrových				Petrových	
	Dat.		Petrovým				Petrovým	
	Inst.		Petrovými				Petrovými	
	Loc.		Petrových				Petrových	

Note: As in the preceding table, the lower member of braced pairs of forms are animate (human in Slovak).

by means of the suffixes -ův/-ov for masculine possessors, -in for feminine possessors, with additional case, gender, number endings; in Czech this suffix causes pre-palatalisation, but not in Slovak, hence from *matka* 'mother' the possessive adjective 'mother's' is *matčin* and *matkin* respectively. Whichever suffix applies, the declension is the same. Note that in the singular and nom./voc./acc. pl. the Czech forms are close to those of the core noun classes (inst. sg. and the plural oblique cases are akin to the main adjectival pattern), while in Slovak there is closer approximation to adjectival or pronominal patterns.

An interesting morphological innovation is to be found in the declension of numerals in Slovak. The core system is as in Czech: *jeden* 'one' varies by gender and has case (and number) agreement – it actually declines in Czech like the demonstrative pronoun *ten*; *dva* 'two' has a special form *dve* (*dvě* in Czech) for feminine and neuter (contrast Russian, where *dve* is feminine only, with *dva* for masculine and neuter); *dva/dve, tri* 'three', *štyri* 'four' (*tři, čtyři* in Czech) all agree with their noun; *päť* (*pět*) 'five' and higher numerals take the genitive plural of the counted noun when the entire phrase is in any nominative or accusative slot in the sentence, otherwise there is case agreement (marked only rudimentarily in Czech) except after prepositions, when *päť* etc. do not decline in Slovak. Slovak's main innovation is in the possession of forms of *dvaja, tvaja, štyria, piati* and onwards for use with animates; all such forms show agreement with the counted noun. The genderless *päť* and above may be used instead of *piati* etc., but the survival of the latter is ensured through the Slovak mutation of the expression of animacy, which has consistently distinctive forms in the nominative and the genitive-accusative. Hence not only *krásni muži–krásnych mužov*, but also *dvaja–dvoch, traja–troch, štyria–štyroch* and *piati–piatich*.

Verbal morphology in Czech and Slovak differs basically in consequence, again, of *přehláska* in Czech and the rhythmic law in Slovak. Slovak has, however, gone further than Czech in having consistent person markers, notably in having *-m* as the universal marker of the first person singular. In both languages this has spread from a minor conjugation, the so-called athematic verbs (with the meanings 'be', 'have', 'know', 'eat' and 'give'), which formed a distinctive group in Proto-Slavonic and continue to exhibit various anomalous features, especially in Czech. Where Czech has not evolved the *-m* first person marker is in the conjugations here described as *e-*, *ne-*, *uje-* (the same endings also shared by the *je*-type): *e-*: *nést–nesu* 'carry', *brát–beru* 'take', *mazat–mažu/-i* 'smear', *péci–peču*, 'bake', *umřít–umřu* 'die'; *ne-*: *tisknout–tisknu* 'print', *minout–minu* 'pass', *začít–začnu* 'begin'; *je-*: *krýt–kryji/-u* 'cover'; *uje-*: *kupovat–kupuji/-u* 'buy'. The original ending in these classes was *-u* (from the nasal *ǫ*), which has since given *-i* in cases where *přehláska* operated. The tolerance which the standard language has shown for a reversal of this *i*-ending to *-u*, by analogy with the majority, has varied from type to type, coming latest with those classes containing a final *-j-* in the present tense stem.

Slovak has long had *-ť* as the sole infinitive marker, whatever the shape of the remainder of the infinitive stem: *niesť*, *brať*, but also *piecť*, while in the latter type Czech has had an anomaly in *-ci* (*péci*, *říci*, *moci*, etc.), with forms in *-t* only in Common Czech. By a recent reform, however, the compelling force of analogy has led to a degree of upward mobility of the forms in *-t* (*péct*, *říct*, *moct*) towards their acceptance in the more colloquial version of the standard language.

Czech and Slovak, like Russian, but unlike Serbo-Croat, have moved right away from a complex tense system, still alive in Old Czech, to an aspect-based system, with pairs of verbs for all meanings that are acts, and single verbs for activities and states. The two members of the aspect category (perfective and imperfective) are much the same as for the other Slavonic languages: perfective for a single action seen as a whole, completed and potentially having consequences for subsequent actions, imperfective for an action in progress, repetition or to name the action *per se*, which may be completed but where consequence is immaterial. Differences of detail between Czech/Slovak and Russian relate in particular to the aspect form used in certain cases with explicitly expressed repetition; in Czech/Slovak the choice often hinges on the semantics of specific conjugations and adverbs. The specific consequence for Czech/Slovak is the use of the perfective present (formally the same as the perfective future) in certain general or non-actual present time contexts, whereas it is normally the case that the only aspect in the present is the imperfective.

Having an aspect-based system, Czech and Slovak overcome the impoverishment of the tense system and the general Slavonic lack of sequence-of-tense rules by expressing anteriority, posteriority and simultaneity, in certain important subordinate clause types, e.g. after *verba dicendi*, by past, future and present tense forms, whatever the tense of the main clause: Czech *řekl/říká/řekne, že přijde* 'he said/is saying/will say that he would/will come', *řekl/říká/řekne, že tam byl* 'he said/is saying/will say that he had/has been there', *řekl/říká/řekne, že nekouří* 'he said/is saying/will say that he did/does not smoke'.

Both Czech and Slovak, unlike Russian, use auxiliary verbs in the past tense (omitted in the third persons), while in the conditional the auxiliary (evolved out of the aorist of *být* 'be') conjugates. A difference between Czech and Slovak is that the plural forms of the past *l*-participle do not mark gender in Slovak (cf. Russian), a simplification present only in colloquial Czech. Another difference of detail is in the greater refinement of the expression of the second person in the past tense in Czech, which can discriminate

Table 17.5 Conjugation[1]

	Czech	*Slovak*
e-conjugation		
Infinitive	nést 'carry'	niesť
Present sg.	nesu neseš nese	nesiem neseš nesie
pl.	neseme nesete nesou	nesieme nesiete nesú
Imperative	nes nesme neste	nes nesme neste
Past	nesl	niesol
Transgressive	nesa nesouc nesouce[2]	nesúc
Pfv. Transgressive	(do-)nes, -nesši, -nesše[2]	(do-)nesúc
Pass. participle	nesen/-ý[3]	nesený
ne-conjugation		
Infinitive	vadnout 'fade, wilt'	vädnúť
Present sg.	vadnu vadneš vadne	vädnem vädneš vädne
pl.	vadneme vadnete vadnou	vädneme vädnete vädnú
Imperative	vadni vadněme vadněte	vädni vädnime vädnite
Past	vadl	vädol
Transgressive	vadna vadnouc vadnouce	vädnúc
Pfv. Transgressive	(u-)vadnuv, -vadnuvši, -vadnuvše	(u-)vädnúc
Pass. participle	tištěn/-ý, tisknut/ý[4]	-tisnutý[4]
uje-conjugation		
Infinitive	kupovat 'buy'	kupovať
Present sg.	kupuji/-ji kupuješ kupuje	kupujem kupuješ kupuje
pl.	kupujeme kupujete kupují/ jou	kupujeme kupujete kupujú
Imperative	kupuj kupujme kupujte	kupuj kupujme kupujte
Past	kupoval	kupoval
Transgressive	kupuje kupujíc kupujíce	kupujúc
Pfv. Transgressive	(na-)kupovav, -vši, -vše	(na-)kupujúc
Pass. participle	kupován/-aný	kupovaný
i-conjugation		
Infinitive	prosit 'ask for'	prosiť
Present sg.	prosím prosíš prosí	prosím prosíš prosí
pl.	prosíme prosíte prosí	prosíme prosíte prosia
Imperative	pros prosme proste	pros prosme proste
Past	prosil	prosil
Transgressive	prose prosíc prosíce	prosiac
Pfv. Transgressive	(po-)prosiv, -ivši, -ivše	(po-)prosiac
Pass. participle	prošen/-ý	prosený
a-conjugation		
Infinitive	volat 'call, phone'	volať
Present sg.	volám voláš volá	volám voláš volá
pl.	voláme voláte volají	voláme voláte volajú
Imperative	volej volejme volejte	volaj volajme volajte
Past	volal	volal
Transgressive	volaje volajíc volajíce	volajúc
Pfv. Transgressive	(za-)volav, -vši, -vše	(za-)volajúc
Pass. participle	volán/-aný	volaný

Notes:

1 This summary of the basic conjugational types cannot show the imbalance brought about by *přehláska* on the Czech side, particularly in the distribution of verbs among the *a*- and *i*-conjugations, or by the operation of the rhythmical law on the Slovak. Each class has various subclasses in both languages.

2 The present (imperfective) and perfective transgressives (the traditional term in Czech and Slovak

grammars) are the gerunds of other Slavonic languages. The three forms in Czech are for masculine, feminine/neuter and plural, agreement being governed by the subject of the main clause.

3 The two forms of the Czech passive participle are described as 'short' and 'long' respectively. The short form occurs in higher styles only, in combination with the verb 'to be' as auxiliary to form the periphrastic passive. The long form may appear both attributively and predicatively.

4 Forms from the transitive verb *tisknout* 'print' / *tisnúť* 'press'; *vadnout/vädnúť* is intransitive and therefore has no passive participle.

between not only the sex (gender) of the addressee, but also number and degree of familiarity, hence *byl jsi* 'you were' is singular familiar masculine, *byla jsi* singular familiar feminine, *byl jste* singular formal masculine, *byla jste* singular formal feminine, *byli jste* plural masculine or mixed, *byly jste* plural feminine (in speech the last distinction is not heard, thanks to the phonetic equivalence of *i* and *y*). Slovak distinguishes gender in the familiar singular: *bol si/bola si*, but all other forms are *boli ste*.

6 Syntax

A complete description of Czech and Slovak syntax is beyond the scope of the present outline, but some features are worthy of special mention. These include the use and position of enclitics (mostly the auxiliary verbs and pronouns) and the expression of the passive. Both have a bearing on word order, on which more will be said in the concluding sentences.

Czech, and to a lesser degree Slovak, has quite strict rules on word order with enclitics. In a nutshell, these say that any enclitic will appear in the second grammatical slot (not merely second word) in the sentence, that is, there must be at least one stressed word at the beginning of a sentence on which the stressless enclitics can lean. The critical first slot may be occupied by the subject, object, an infinitive or other main form of a verb, an adverb or conjunction (but not the weak coordinating conjunctions *a* 'and', *i* 'and even' or *ale* 'but'; this last constraint applies much less in Slovak). It may also be occupied by a subject pronoun, which will be there for emphasis, since subject pronouns are not normally required, person being adequately expressed in the verb, even in the past tense, thanks to the use of auxiliaries (unlike in Russian). Within the second, enclitic slot the ordering is also fixed: an auxiliary verb in the past tense or conditional (but not the imperfective future auxiliary) will always take precedence, followed by any reflexive pronoun, then any dative, then accusative (occasionally genitive) object pronouns, and finally certain enclitic adverbs or particles. Hence, in Czech, for example:

Včera	jste	mi	ji	však	nedal.
Yesterday	2nd pers. aux.	me (dat.)	it (f.)	though	not gave

'But yesterday you did not give it to me.'

The only refinements to this rule in Czech relate to the use of the reflexive pronouns *se/si* (accusative and dative respectively) either of which takes precedence over all other pronoun objects, and to the referentially vague *to* which, whether subject or object, that is, nominative or accusative, stands in the accusative/genitive enclitic slot: *včera jste mi to neřekl* 'you did not tell me (it) yesterday', *Petrovi by se to* (subject) *nelíbilo* 'Peter would not like it/that' (*líbit se* 'be pleasing'). The situation as described is beginning to break down, the enclitics, especially *se*, showing a tendency to be more closely associated with the verb phrase wherever it may stand. In Slovak the process has gone slightly further.

The passive in Czech and Slovak is only rarely expressed by the periphrastic form analogous to the English passive, although it is quite common in technical and some journalistic and official texts. Instead, the shift of emphasis, or perspective, from 'Peter killed Paul' to 'Paul was killed by Peter' is carried by simple inversion of subject and object: *Petr zabil Pavla, Pavla zabil Petr*, an obvious possibility in a language where syntactic relations are explicit in their morphology and where there are relatively few constraints on word order. Very widespread in both languages are passive, quasi-passive and impersonal constructions, comparable to many passive-like constructions in English, based on verb phrases with *se*, here best interpreted as a passivising or intransitivising particle. They are used typically where no agent is (or can be) named (*talíř se rozbil* 'the plate broke/got broken'), in the language of instructions (*cibule se tam dá nejdřív* 'the onion is put in first', *tato samohláska se vyslovuje dlouze* 'this vowel is pronounced long'), and in depersonalised accounts of events (*pivo se pilo, písničky se zpívaly a okna se rozbíjela* 'beer was drunk, songs were sung and windows were broken'); in this last type the same construction is available with instransitive verbs, always in the third person singular neuter (*nepracovalo se a šlo se domů brzy* 'no work was done and people went home early', lit. 'it was not worked and it was gone home early').

Word order in Czech and Slovak, as was hinted above, is governed primarily by functional sentence perspective. That element which carries most emphasis, or most new information, is reserved to the end of the sentence. In general terms, the 'communicative dynamism' of an utterance builds up from low to high as the sentence unfolds. This allows maximum exploitation of 'free word order', which of course does not mean random word order. A great deal of work has been done on the subtleties of word order, ever since Vilém Mathesius and the Prague Linguistic Circle, and new theories and descriptions continue to appear. It has also been an area of study in contrastive, comparative and confrontational linguistics.

7 The Contemporary Language Situation

As with any modern language, Czech and Slovak show much variation in regional and social dialects. Czech divides into four main regional dialect groupings, Slovak into three.

The Czech macrodialects are: Bohemian, Central Moravian (Haná), Eastern Moravian or Moravian Slovak, and Silesian (Lach). The dialect differences have evolved in fairly recent times, mostly since the twelfth century, but particularly during the fourteenth to sixteenth centuries. Some prehistoric differences are also present, in the distribution of some lexical items, suffixes and vowel quantity in certain prosodically distinct word types: long in Bohemian *práh* 'threshold', *bláto* 'mud', *žába* 'frog', *bříza* 'birch', *moucha* 'fly', *vítr* 'wind', short in Central Moravian *prah*, *blato*, *žaba*, *březa*, *mucha*, *vjetr*.

One of the most important sound changes in the history of Czech was, as mentioned earlier, *přehláska*. That of *a* to *ě* was carried through in a decreasing number of

325

environments the further east one goes through Moravia, while *u* > *i* is practically unknown anywhere in Moravia. One consequence of this is the much greater degree of similarity between 'soft' and 'hard' declensional paradigms than in standard Czech and a measure of interchange between them, words in *-sa*, *-za* and *-la* with originally hard *s*, *z* and *l* tending to shift to the equivalent soft paradigm.

The Lach dialects separated from the rest of Czech by the retention of softness in the syllables *ďe*, *ťe*, *ňe*, the loss of distinctions of vowel quantity, and the development, as in Polish, of fixed stress on the penultimate.

Typical of the Bohemian dialects are the changes of *ý* into *ej* and *ú* into *ou*, which took over two centuries to complete, peaking in the sixteenth century. Eastern Moravian and the Lach dialects show no sign of this shift, cf. for *strýc* 'uncle' Cent. Boh. *strejc*, E. Mor. *strýc*, Lach *stryc*, and for *múka* 'flour' Cent. Boh. *mouka*, E. Mor. *múka*, Lach *muka*. (Note that the forms used in standard Czech are *strýc* and *mouka* respectively, though *strejc* is colloquial; few words with *ej* < *ý* have passed into the standard language whereas *ou* < *ú* is the norm except initially.) The same dialects were also unaffected by the Central Bohemian change from *aj* to *ej* in closed syllables and *é* to *í*, hence *daj* 'give (sg. imper.)' for Central Bohemian and standard Czech *dej* and *dobré mléko* 'good milk' for Central Bohemian *dobrí mlíko*. (Here the standard Czech has the 'conservative' *dobré mléko*, one of the reasons why Moravians are often heard to assert that they speak a 'better' Czech than the Bohemians.)

Eastern Bohemian was once distinguished by the loss of softness from labials before *e*, giving rise to syllables *pe*, *be*, *me*, *ve*, where elsewhere Czech has /pje/, /bje/, /mňe/ and /vje/, though this feature has largely yielded to the more universal version of these syllables. By contrast, one of the features marking out the south-west group of Bohemian dialects is the survival of softness, again expanded to a *j*, even before *i*, as in *pjivo* 'beer'.

These days the most typical features of north-east Bohemian are the bilabial pronunciation of *v* in closed syllables, much as in Slovak, and, in morphology, the spread of the ending *-ej* in the instrumental singular of soft feminine nouns. The Giant Mountains area is renowned for the appearance of *e* before syllabic *r*: *perší* '(it) rains', *perkno* 'board' for standard *prší*, *prkno*.

The last major contributor to the distinctness of the Moravian centre, the Haná and related dialects, is a change of *ej* to *é* and from *ou* to *ó*. The former is very widespread, since it affects *ej* from *ý*, *ej* from *aj* and cases where the *e* and the *j* straddle a morpheme boundary, hence Central Bohemian *dobrej strejc* 'good uncle' (from *dobrý strýc*), *dej* (from *daj*) and *nejsem* '(I) am not' (from *ne* + *jsem*) correspond to Haná *dobré stréc*, *dé* and *nésem*. Related changes in the short vowels produce so many local variants that the Moravian dialect area is fragmented on this basis alone into dialects with five-, six- or seven-member vowel systems in various combinations.

From all the foregoing it follows that the East Moravian dialects have been the more conservative, untouched by many of the sound changes mentioned. In this, and in certain other respects, they represent a transition to Slovak.

The dialect situation in Slovakia is even more complex than in the Czech-speaking areas. Three macrodialects are usually pinpointed, but each has numerous subdivisions, partly understandable from a glance at the country's physical geography.

Since Central Slovak became the basis for the Slovak literary language, it is usually taken as the reference point against which to describe the other main dialect groupings. Not all of the features typical of the central dialects have been adopted by the standard. Some of the distinctive Central Slovak features are as follows:

- The reflexes of the jers and the so-called fill-vowels vary more than in any other Slavonic language or dialect, with *e*, *o* or *a* in short syllables and *ie*, *uo* (orthographically *ô*) or *á* in long syllables; in Western Slovak, as in Czech, it is always *e*, and in Eastern Slovak predominantly so, with sporadic instances of *o*.
- The *ä* of the standard language (where /e/ is a tolerated alternative pronunciation) is replaced after labials by *e*, alternating with *ia* in cognate long syllables; in Western Slovak the alternation is between *a* and *á*, and in Eastern between *e* and *ia*.
- There are the four diphthongs of the standard language, with none in Western Slovak, and local survivals of *ie* and *uo* in Eastern dialects.
- The syllabic liquids occur in long and short syllables, but in Western Slovak they are only short as in Czech. In Eastern Slovak they have not even survived as syllabic and are always accompanied by a vowel, with considerable local variation.
- The standard language owes its rhythmical law to Central Slovak, since Western Slovak reveals no such vowel shortening, and phonological quantity has totally disappeared from Eastern Slovak.
- Central Slovak morphological features include the long *á* or *ia* ending in the neuter plural of nouns, the *e*-ending of soft neuter nouns in the nominative singular (*o* in Western and Eastern Slovak, hence *vreco* 'sack', *ojo* 'shaft' to Central and standard Slovak *vrece*, *oje*), the instrumental singular feminine endings *-ou* (*-ú* in the west, *-u* in the east), and two very distinctive adjectival endings: nominative neuter singular in *-uo*, contrasting with *-é* in the west and *-e* in the east, and the locative singular masculine and neuter ending *-om* as against *-ém* in most of the west and *-im* in the east. The third-person plural of the verb 'to be' is generally *sa*, which also occurs in parts of the west, but the standard form has adopted *sú*, the Western Slovak form, comparable also with *su* in the east.

Two important Western Slovak features not mentioned (and there are others of course) are the absence of the soft /ľ/ phoneme, and the curious extension of the third person singular of the verb *byť* 'to be' in the negative (*neni*) into the function of simple negator, hence *neni som* 'am not', originally 'isn't am'.

Additional distinctive Eastern Slovak features include: stress on the penultimate, as in Polish, complete absence of phonological quantity, a change of *ch* [x] to *h*, and the adoption of a universal genitive and locative plural ending for all genders, usually *-och* (*bratoch* 'brother', *ženoch* 'woman', *mestoch* 'town', etc.) and locally *-of*.

The foregoing are only a sample of the most striking features and those which cover most of the respective macrodialect areas. What they do not reveal immediately is something which has provided material for numerous books and papers, namely that there are a number of similarities between Western and Eastern Slovak which make them jointly distinct from the Central macrodialect. It is now generally accepted that this is a consequence of the different route and chronology in the arrival of the Slavonic-speaking population of the area. A number of features which Central Slovak shares with South Slavonic suggests a period of contiguity with the South Slavs and that colonisation of Central Slovakia proceeded from the south. The full details of this prehistory are still the subject of debate.

In addition to the horizontal (geographical) division of Czech and Slovak into dialects, there is a vertical division into a more or less conventional range of styles, registers, social dialects, slangs and so forth. On the whole it is probably safe to say that Slovak is the less interesting of the two, though not for any lack of richness or variety. There is indeed a full range of linguistic variation, much of it still being described for the first time. The slightly greater interest of Czech stems from the fact, already mentioned, of a literary standard language rich in essentially archaic features, some of which are jettisoned in the colloquial (*hovorový*) versions of it, and the parallel existence of Common Czech, or Common Colloquial Czech (*obecná čeština*). This is phonologically and morphologically closely related to the Central Bohemian dialect, syntactically to the less strict versions of Colloquial Czech, with some other features often ascribed to the influence of German, and lexically often quite distinct, that is, there are many lexical items peculiar to Common Czech which have to be 'translated' into standard Czech, e.g. *táta* = *otec* 'father'. Although rooted in Central Bohemia, Common Czech has spread well beyond the frontiers of that dialect area, especially from the urban areas and then outward from them. However, with this spread it is also ceasing to be a universal koine and other versions are being observed to arise, especially in Moravia. Here the influence of the distinctive local dialects proper has given rise to the fairly recent conception of a Common Moravian Czech. A great deal of work has been conducted in recent decades on analyses of urban speech (*městská mluva*) in a number of large towns, and this has shown how Common Czech is contributing to the disappearence of local dialects while taking on specific local variations of detail from them.

Czech and Slovak are both rich in slangs, and although there are large areas of difference, it is interesting to note that here, as with the standard languages, there has been a degree of convergence. This was understandable when one appreciates the cross-mobility, within the unitary Czechoslovak state, of such groups as students, members of the armed forces or those involved in pop music and other subcultures. Even since the countries have split, there remains considerable similarity in patterns of slang neologising. This is not to suggest that here, or at any other level, the process of convergence will ever be more than partial, indeed since the split it is decelerating, as each side has less and less daily exposure to the other's language. Actual divergence may come as the young (in particular) find it progressively more difficult to understand the other language, especially in spoken registers.

The most striking feature of both languages is the rampant and unfettered intrusion of anglicisms into the vocabulary of every sphere of life, from popular culture to high science and especially business.

Bibliography

Janda and Townsend (2000) and Naughton (2005) are recent reference grammars of Czech, while Townsend and Komar (2000) serve a similar purpose on a contrastive basis. Potentially contrastive, thanks to the common section layout within the volume, is Short's discursive description of the language (2003a) in Comrie and Corbett (paperback edition of an earlier work). Still key works on the syntax and phonetics/phonology of Czech are Grepl and Karlík (1998) and Palková (1994), respectively. The standard Czech reference grammar (the 'academy grammar') is Petr *et al.* (1986–7), whose three volumes deal respectively with phonetics, phonology, morphemics and word-formation (1), morphology (2), and syntax (3). Bermel (2000) is the best recent study of all aspects of the coexistence of a standard language and the fairly clearly contoured everyday language, Common Czech.

Pauliny (1981) and Mistrík (1988) remain the main reference grammars of Slovak, while Short (2003b) gives a discursive account of the language in English. The other major study in English is Rubach (1993). Slovak linguists are much concerned with contemporary language change, hence such works as Dvonč (1984) and Horecký *et al.* (1989) on the dynamism of Slovak morphology and the lexicon, respectively.

References

Bermel, N. 2000. *Register Variation and Language Standards in Czech* (Lincom Europa, Munich)

Dvonč, L. 1984. *Dynamika slovenskej morfológie* (Veda, Bratislava)

Grepl, M. and Karlík, P. 1998. *Skladba češtiny* (Votobia, Olomouc)

Horecký, J., Buzássyová, K. and Bosák, J. 1989. *Dynamika slovnej zásoby súčasnej slovenčiny* (Veda, Bratislava)

Janda, L.A. and Townsend, C.E. 2000. *Czech* (Lincom Europa, Munich)

Mistrík, J. 1988. *A Grammar of Contemporary Slovak*, 2nd edn (Slovenské pedagogické nakladateľstvo, Bratislava)

Naughton, J. 2005. *Czech. An Essential Grammar* (Routledge, London and New York)

Palková, Z. 1994. *Fonetika a fonologie češtiny* (Univerzita Karlova, Prague)

Pauliny, E. 1981. *Slovenská gramatika* (Slovenské pedagogické nakladateľstvo, Bratislava)

Petr, J., Marek, N. and Rusinova, Z. 1986–7. *Mluvnice Češtiny*, 3 vols (Academia, Prague)

Rubach, J. 1993. *The Lexical Phonology of Slovak* (Clarendon Press, Oxford)

Short, D. 2003a. 'Czech', in B. Comrie and G.G. Corbett (eds), *The Slavonic Languages* (Routledge, London and New York), pp. 455–532

—— 2003b. 'Slovak', in B. Comrie and G.G. Corbett (eds), *The Slavonic Languages* (Routledge, London and New York), pp. 533–92

Townsend, Charles E. and Komar, Eric S. 2000. *Czech through Russian*, revised and expanded edn (Slavica, Bloomington)

18

Serbo-Croat

Bosnian, Croatian, Montenegrin, Serbian

Greville Corbett and Wayles Browne

1 Historical Background

The Serbo-Croat (or Serbo-Croatian) area is a striking example of mismatching between dialect differentiation and the rise of standard languages.

The line which divided Europe into east and west, Orthodox and Catholic, runs right through this part of South-east Europe. Various states have prospered at different times in this region, such as the Serbian medieval kingdom under rulers like Stefan Nemanja and Stefan Dušan and the unique city-state of Dubrovnik (Ragusa). Parts of the territory have been under Venice, Austro-Hungary and the Turks. We can only hope to hint at the complex and turbulent history of the area.

The ancestors of the South Slavs arrived in the Balkans during the sixth and seventh centuries and within the next two centuries the first Slav states of the area sprang up. By this time too the main linguistic divisions were evident. There were two main sets of dialects: East South Slavonic would later develop into Bulgarian and the closely related Macedonian, while West South Slavonic was the basis for Slovene and Serbo-Croat. From the ninth century the Slovenes in the north-west were ruled by Bavarian and Austrian princes and so were separated from their Slavonic neighbours. In the remaining area, roughly equivalent to modern Bosnia-Hercegovina, Croatia, Montenegro and Serbia (or former Yugoslavia excepting Slovenia and Macedonia), a range of dialects developed.

Christianity was accepted in the ninth century, with certain political repercussions. The tenth-century Croatian kingdom looked to Rome in matters of religion. Serbia's adoption of Orthodoxy meant that it looked first to Constantinople and later, after the fall of Constantinople, to Moscow for support. Montenegro was also Orthodox. The picture was complicated by the invasion of the Turks, who defeated the Serbs at Kosovo in 1389, and by the resulting migrations of population. In the next century the Turks occupied Bosnia and Hercegovina, where a large proportion of the population adopted Islam, and parts of Montenegro. By the time the Turks were finally removed (1878), Croatia was part of the Austro-Hungarian Empire, which took over Bosnia-Hercegovina. It was not until 1918 that the different groups were united into one state –

the Kingdom of Serbs, Croats and Slovenes, soon officially renamed Yugoslavia (from *jug* 'south' and *Slav*).

Three main dialect groups had emerged, which take their names from the interrogative pronoun 'what?': Čakavian (*ča?* 'what?'), Kajkavian (*kaj?*) and Štokavian (*što?*). Kajkavian was spoken in the north, Čakavian in the west and Štokavian in the east, centre and south-west. However, the dialectal, political and religious boundaries did not match in a straightforward way, particularly after Štokavian speakers, escaping the Turks, moved north and west, confining Čakavian to the Croatian coastal area and Kajkavian to north-west inland Croatia. Despite this troubled history there have been some remarkable flowerings of literature. When the Serbian Kingdom was at its height during the twelfth to fourteenth centuries, literature flourished, written not in the vernacular but in the Serbian version of Church Slavonic. In the west too, Croatian Church Slavonic was used at first, but by the sixteenth century major writers like Marulić, Hektorović, Zoranić and Lucić were using Čakavian. The rise of Dubrovnik brought Štokavian to the fore also in the sixteenth century. And in the eighteenth century, Kajkavian was widely written in Croatia around Zagreb.

This diversity of literary tradition, mirroring the tri-dialectal fragmentation of the area, naturally impeded the development of a common literary language for Croatians. In the east, Turkish domination had severely hampered the development of the Serbian Church Slavonic tradition. Russian Church Slavonic was adopted in the eighteenth century and a hybrid language (Slavenoserbian) evolved, with elements of Russian Church Slavonic and vernacular Serbian. Its artificiality, contrary both to the aspirations of intellectuals influenced by the Enlightenment and to the needs of modern society, led to a movement towards a more popular language, which was brought to fruition by Vuk Karadžić (1787–1864). Karadžić rejected Slavenoserbian, insisting that the new literary language must be based on the vernacular and on a single dialect, the Štokavian dialect of East Hercegovina. He made his revolutionary proposals in his dictionary (1818), which also contained a grammar of the language. There had already been some movement in the west towards basing the literary language on Štokavian – spoken by the majority of Croats, though not native to the cultural centres of Zagreb and the coast. The Zagreb editor Ljudevit Gaj (1809–72) and other intellectuals helped accelerate this trend. In 1850 the Literary Accord between Croats and Serbs was signed in Vienna. It justified the use of Štokavian (Hercegovinian dialect) as the literary language and gave rules for writing it. Reactions to the Accord varied; not surprisingly it aroused a great deal of hostility, but gradually it gained support. Yet the centuries of division between different dialects, religions, cultures and political groups could not be removed by such an agreement. In any case, the major task of adapting the chosen variant to all the functions of a modern literary language had still to be faced. Nevertheless the Accord crystallised a unifying trend. A major success associated with this trend was the reform of the writing system.

2 Writing Systems

The original alphabet for South Slavonic was Glagolitic. In the eastern, Serbian Orthodox area this was replaced from the twelfth century on by Cyrillic. In the west, the Latin alphabet was introduced in the fourteenth century, under Catholic influence. However, Glagolitic remained in use in the west, particularly among priests of the Dalmatian coast and islands, even into the twentieth century. From the sixteenth century until the Second World War, some Moslem writers in Bosnia used the Arabic script.

Neither in the east nor in the west was the writing system satisfactory. The version of the Cyrillic alphabet employed was appropriate for Church Slavonic but not for the contemporary language, while the use of the Latin alphabet in the west was influenced by Italian or Hungarian practice (depending on the area), neither of which was a suitable model for a Slavonic language. In his dictionary of 1818, Vuk Karadžić justified and used a new version of Cyrillic. This was a major reform involving simplifying the alphabet, using a single letter per sound and adopting a phonemically based orthography. He eliminated several unnecessary letters and introduced six new ones. Despite initial angry opposition, his alphabet was adopted and, with one minor modification, is in use today.

The equivalent reform for the Latin alphabet was carried out a little later by Ljudevit Gaj, using diacritic symbols on the Czech model. With minor modifications, Gaj's alphabet is the present one. Unlike the Cyrillic alphabet it includes digraphs: *lj*, *nj* and *dž* (also *dj* though this latter is usually written *đ*). Single symbols exist for these but their use is restricted to certain academic publications. The digraphs cause little problem; the combination *l+j* does not occur, while *n+j* and *d+ž* are rare; an example is *nadživjeti/nadživeti* (Cyrillic надживјети/надживети) 'to outlive', where *d+ž* represent separate sounds. The two modern alphabets are given in Table 18.1.

Table 18.1 The Alphabets of Serbo-Croat

Latin		Cyrillic		Latin		Cyrillic	
A	a	А	а	L	l	Л	л
B	b	Б	б	Lj	lj	Љ	љ
C	c	Ц	ц	M	m	М	м
Č	č	Ч	ч	N	n	Н	н
Ć	ć	Ћ	ћ	Nj	nj	Њ	њ
D	d	Д	д	O	o	О	о
Dž	dž	Џ	џ	P	p	П	п
Đ	đ	Ђ	ђ	R	r	Р	р
E	e	Е	е	S	s	С	с
F	f	Ф	ф	Š	š	Ш	ш
G	g	Г	г	T	t	Т	т
H	h	Х	х	U	u	У	у
I	i	И	и	V	v	В	в
J	j	Ј	ј	Z	z	З	з
K	k	К	к	Ž	ž	Ж	ж

The characters are arranged in the Latin order; the Cyrillic order is: А, Б, В, Г, Д, Ђ, Е, Ж, З, И, Ј, К, Л, Љ, М, Н, Њ, О, П, Р, С, Т, Ћ, У, Ф, Х, Ц, Ч, Џ, Ш. This Cyrillic list includes six characters not found in Russian Cyrillic; conversely, Russian has nine characters not used in Serbo-Croat. Note from the table that there is an exact correspondence, letter for letter, between the two alphabets of Serbo-Croat. The digraphs in the Latin version function as autonomous letters. This means that in a dictionary, all words beginning with *lj* are grouped together after all those with initial *l* (unlike English, where *thin* comes before *tin*); in a crossword, *lj* occupies a single square. The exact correspondence between the two alphabets means that transliteration is automatic; a typescript may be submitted in the Latin alphabet though it is to be printed in Cyrillic. This parallel use of the alphabets is found in Serbia and Montenegro, while elsewhere the Latin alphabet is found almost exclusively. In the twentieth century there was a trend in the east towards greater use of the Latin alphabet. In present-day Belgrade the two coexist with no apparent confusion: one sees shop windows with notices in both alphabets side by side, or a lecturer may begin labelling a diagram in one alphabet and then continue in the other.

The orthography of Serbo-Croat is based on the phonemic principle. Assimilations are indicated in spelling, for example, *gladak*/гладак (masculine singular) 'smooth' but *glatka*/глатка (feminine singular); *top*/топ 'gun' but *tobdžija*/тобџија 'gunner'. If a consonant is dropped it is omitted in spelling, for example, *radostan*/радостан (masculine singular) 'joyful' but *radosna*/радосна (feminine singular). Though there are rare exceptions, this phonemic principle is applied (at the expense of the morphological principle) with unusual consistency.

3 The Contemporary Situation: Dialects and Standard Languages

While Yugoslavia existed, Serbo-Croat was its major language, being spoken in the Yugoslav republics of Bosnia-Hercegovina, Croatia, Montenegro and Serbia, by a total of over 17 million according to the 1981 census. Slovenia and Macedonia have their own languages but many Slovenes and Macedonians knew Serbo-Croat (as did large numbers of the sizable populations of Albanians and Hungarians living in Yugoslavia and of the smaller groups of Bulgarians and Rumanians). Many hundreds of thousands of Serbo-Croat speakers lived abroad, notably in the United States and Australasia, and in West Germany and Sweden.

When Yugoslavia broke up (1991–5), four countries were formed, each with its own standard, as we shall see below. The number of speakers living abroad increased greatly as people fled the destructive wars and ruinous economic conditions.

As stated earlier, there are three dialect groups: Čakavian, Kajkavian and Štokavian. Each of these is in fact a set of related dialects. In contrast to their earlier importance, Čakavian and Kajkavian are spoken in relatively small areas, so we shall discuss them briefly. Čakavian survives along the Dalmatian coastal fringe, on the Adriatic islands, in Istria and in a small part of northern Croatia. As we shall see in the next section, it preserves an interesting accentual system; in morphology too it is more conservative than Štokavian. Kajkavian is spoken around Zagreb in the north-west of Croatia, bordering on Slovenia. It shares several features with Slovene. Like Čakavian, in the plural it retains distinct dative, instrumental and locative endings, which are merged in Štokavian; another interesting archaic feature is the preservation of the supine to express purpose.

The main dialect, Štokavian, is spoken over the remainder of the Serbo-Croat area. It is divided first into New Štokavian (the innovating dialects, typically those which underwent the stress shift described in the next section) and Old Štokavian (those which did not). The most important of the Old Štokavian dialects are the Prizren–Timok dialects, which are spoken in the south-east of Serbia, bordering on Bulgaria and Macedonia. They have lost the infinitive and reduced the case system to three cases only and are therefore clearly transitional to Bulgarian and Macedonian. The Kosovo–

Resava dialects run in a band from south-west to north-east, between the Prizren–Timok dialects and the rest of the Štokavian dialects, and share features with both.

Within New Štokavian, the traditional feature for distinguishing between dialects is the reflex of the Common Slavonic vowel *ě* (named *jat'*), which may be *i*, *e* or *ije/je*. This gives three dialect groups: Ikavian, Ekavian and Ijekavian, in which the word, say, for 'child' is *dite*, *dete* and *dijete* respectively. The Ikavian dialect is found in Dalmatia, the west of Bosnia-Hercegovina and parts of Lika and Slavonia. It is no longer used as a literary standard language (though certain Ikavian features are established in the standard languages). This leaves the two major dialects of New Štokavian: Ekavian is spoken in most of Serbia; Ijekavian is found in the western part of Serbia, Montenegro, the east of Bosnia-Hercegovina and in those parts of Croatia not previously mentioned. Ekavian is the basis of the standard Serbian of Serbia, which has Belgrade and Novi Sad as its centres; Ijekavian is the foundation of standard Croatian, whose focal point is Zagreb, even though Zagreb is in a traditionally Kajkavian area. The Ijekavian of Bosnia-Hercegovina can be seen as transitional between the two, but has some characteristics of its own. Montenegro is particularly interesting in that it is Ijekavian, but in terms of lexis goes together with Serbian.

It is worth looking in a little more detail at the differences between the two most highly standardised languages – Croatian and the Serbian of Serbia. As previously mentioned, Croatian uses Ijekavian pronunciation. This means that Common Slavonic *ě* is represented as *ije*, in long syllables, e.g. *snijeg* 'snow', and as *je* in short syllables: *snjegovit* 'snowy'. In Serbian (Ekavian), *e* is found in both cases: *sneg*/снег, *snegovit*/снеговит. Croatian is written in the Latin alphabet, Serbian traditionally in Cyrillic, but now also in the Latin alphabet. The other most obvious area of difference is in lexis. Several very common objects are referred to by different words in the two standards: 'bread' is *kruh* in Croatia, but *hleb*/хлеб in Serbia; a 'train' is *vlak* in the west, but *voz*/воз in the east. Technical terminology also differs, having been formed separately: Croatian *dušik* but Serbian *azot*/азот 'nitrogen'. There are fewer borrowings in Croatian and correspondingly more calques and neologisms; we find, for example, *sveučilište* 'university' (based on *sve* 'all' and the root *uč-* 'teach, learn') whereas Serbia has *univerzitet*/универзитет. Those words which have been borrowed into Croatian come predominantly from German, Latin and also Czech, while borrowings from Turkish, Greek and Russian are more common in Serbian. Words borrowed into both standards may show differences in derivational morphology. Thus *student*/студент 'male student' is found in both; 'female student' is *studentica* in Croatian, *studentkinja*/студенткиња in Serbian. Salient differences in inflectional morphology and in syntax will be pointed out in the appropriate sections.

We specified 'Serbian of Serbia' above, because many Serbs living outside Serbia use Ijekavian pronunciation, though otherwise following the Serbian standard as described. So they may say and write *snijeg*/снијег, *snjegovit*/сњеговит, *hljeb*/хљеб and the like.

While noticeable differences exist between Croatian and Serbian standards, some of them are not absolute but are a matter of frequency of usage. Many features often quoted as characteristic of one actually occur in the other, though they are less common there. The whole question of the status of the two standard forms is very sensitive, because of the cultural and political implications. To the outside linguist, the numerous shared features, added to the ease of mutual comprehension, suggest one language with multiple varieties. This was official policy during the Yugoslav period, and many Yugoslavs concurred. But at present neither independent Croatia nor independent Serbia wants input from the other country in questions of standardisation. The official language of Croatia, with its ca. 4.5 million inhabitants, is officially termed Croatian, and is regulated by spelling dictionaries (*pravopis*) and grammars published in Zagreb. The language of Serbia, with more than 6.6 million speakers (plus ca. 200,000 in Kosovo) and many second-language speakers, is referred to as Serbian.

Matters are more complicated in the other two new countries. In Bosnia-Hercegovina, with ca. 4.25 million inhabitants, the largest single group is Bosniaks (*Bošnjak*, meaning Bosnian of Muslim heritage), and these mostly call their language Bosnian. A Bosnian *pravopis* and grammars exist but usage does not always follow them strictly. Croatians living in Bosnia-Hercegovina claim the right to follow the Croatian standard, and the Serbs of the Republika Srpska subpart prefer the Serbian standard, although mainly keeping the local Ijekavian pronunciation.

The standard of Montenegro (population ca. 600,000) is Serbian with Ijekavian pronunciation. As in Serbia, the Cyrillic alphabet is felt to be a national symbol but Latin is used side by side with it.

In each country language questions kindle heated polemics in the press. In Croatia these concern the desirability of replacing foreign words – including those thought to be Serbian – with new coinages; the merits of competing *pravopisi*; and the custom of having a *lektor* 'language corrector' read any text that is to be published. Serbia debates the need to favour Cyrillic over Latin, and also has competing *pravopisi*. In Bosnia, ethnic Croats and Serbs defend their 'own' standards, and some claim that standard Bosnian should be renamed *Bošnjak* because only Bošnjaks adhere to it. In Montenegro the name of the language is debated (Montenegrin or Serbian?), a point connected with the wider issue of whether Montenegrins are a subpart of the Serbian nation or a group unto itself. Some adherents of separate Montenegrin identity have published a *pravopis* adding three extra letters for local sounds (palatals *ś* and *ź* as in Polish, and *3* for the affricate *dz*), but this has not been officially adopted.

Few people in the countries involved identify their own language as 'Serbo-Croat' nowadays, though many scholars outside the region still find it useful. As used in the present chapter, 'Serbo-Croat' does not deny the differences between the standard languages, but is a cover term referring to the many features they have in common. In what follows, we will cite Ijekavian and Ekavian pronunciations side by side, but in the Latin alphabet.

4 Phonology

Serbo-Croat's inventory of segmental phonemes is one of the smallest in the Slavonic family, since it does not have the range of palatalised consonants found, say, in Russian. Generally 25 consonants are recognised. Of these *r*, which is trilled, can be syllabic (= a vowel), as in *trg* 'square'. In addition there is a straightforward five-vowel system. The phonemes are presented in Table 18.2, using the normal orthography, which does not distinguish syllabic *r* and which includes digraphs for single sounds.

The vowel system provides the most interesting feature of Serbo-Croat phonology, namely accentuation. The classical account goes back to Karadžić and his follower Daničić and is that found still in most modern descriptions. In this analysis, vowels (including syllabic *r*) vary according to length and pitch. Vowels may be long or short, both in stressed position and in positions after the stress. Pitch is differentiated only in initial stressed position, where there is an opposition between rising and falling tone. These possibilities are indicated using the symbols given in Table 18.3. The top four symbols indicate the position of the stress, tone and length. Thus *govòriti* 'to talk' is stressed on the second syllable, where there is a short vowel with rising tone. On unstressed syllables length is indicated; the absence of a marker, as on the other three vowels of this example, indicates an unstressed short vowel. Thus in *glȅdalācā* (genitive plural) 'of the spectators' the first vowel is stressed and has falling tone and is short; the second is unstressed and short; the other two are unstressed and long.

These symbols are used in dictionaries and grammars but are not printed in ordinary texts. We shall include them when discussing phonology and morphology but not in the syntax section. An indication is given in texts to avoid confusion, notably for the genitive plural, which in many nouns is identical to the singular, apart from vowel length. For example, *rȉbāra* (genitive singular) 'fisherman', *rȉbārā* (genitive plural). The first would be printed without accent, the second as *ribarâ*, using the circumflex. (This actually retains Karadžić's usage; the macron ‾, given in our table, is a twentieth-century innovation in linguistic usage.) While the opposition of genitive singular to genitive plural is the most crucial distinction which depends on the accentual system, other morphological distinctions rest on it in some words. Furthermore, there is a small number of frequently quoted minimal pairs: *grâd* 'city', *grȁd* 'hail'; *pâs* 'belt', *pȁs* 'dog'; *kúpiti* 'to buy', *kȕpiti* 'to collect'; *pàra* 'para' (unit of currency), *pȁra* 'steam'.

Table 18.2 Segmental Phonemes of Serbo-Croat

Vowels

	i	r	u
	e		o
		a	

Consonants

	Plain stop		Affricate		Fricative		Nasal	Lateral	Trill	Semi-vowel
Bilabial	p	b					m			
Labio-dental					f	v				
Dental	t	d	c				n	l		
Alveolar					s	z			r	
Palato-alveolar			č	dž	š	ž				
Palatal			ć	đ			nj	lj		j
Velar	k	g			h					

Table 18.3 Serbo-Croat Accentuation

		long	short
stressed syllables	falling tone	∩	\\\\
	rising tone	/	\\
unstressed syllables		‒	

There are severe restrictions on the distribution of tone and length, which are best understood in terms of historical development. Falling tone is found only on initial syllables and monosyllables always have falling tone. Apart from monosyllables, and a few recent borrowings, stress is never on the final syllable of a word. Long vowels occur in stressed position or after the stress. When we compare the position of the stress in Serbo-Croat with that of the other Slavonic languages which have free stress and which, in the main, preserve the Common Slavonic stress position (the East Slavonic languages and Bulgarian), we find that normally the Serbo-Croat stress is one syllable nearer the beginning of the word, for example *sèstra* 'sister', as compared to the Russian *sestrá*.

Serbo-Croat had inherited a long–short opposition in vowels; of the other Slavonic languages only Slovene, Czech and Slovak preserve this opposition. There was also an opposition, for long vowels, between acute (/) and circumflex (∩) intonations; the origin of this opposition is open to debate, many claiming it is of Indo-European origin, others believing it dates only from Common Slavonic times. In very broad outline the development was as follows. The acute was replaced by a short vowel with falling pitch. A special rising tone, however, had arisen when the ultra-short vowels (jers) could no longer carry stress: *krāljь* > *krãljь* 'king'. This long rising accent, denoted ˜ and called the 'neo-acute', is preserved in Čakavian and Kajkavian dialects. In Štokavian, with the exception of some dialects in Slavonia, the neo-acute became identical with the long falling accent. At this stage, then, vowels were opposed in length (long or short only, after the loss of the jers). As a result of various changes, this opposition occurred in stressed position, immediately before the stress and in all post-tonic positions.

The crucial development took place around the fourteenth century in the central Štokavian dialects. The stress moved one syllable towards the beginning of the word, creating new rising tones If the stress moved on to a long vowel, long rising tone resulted (/), and short rising (\) if the vowel was short. The modern restrictions on tone and length are explicable in terms of this change. Falling tone is found only on initial syllables since stress moved from all other syllables to produce rising tone. Monosyllables have falling tone because they were not involved in stress shifts. Stress is not found on final syllables because, of course, it has moved leftward. Finally, length is found in stressed and post-tonic positions only, because the earlier additional position (immediate pre-tonic) was covered by the accentual shift.

This, then, is the classical account of Serbo-Croat accentuation and its development. However, an extensive survey by Magner and Matejka revealed that the Karadžić–Daničić system is not so well preserved in towns as in rural areas. The influx of population to urban centres with the resultant mixing of dialects has led to a less clear situation. In particular, many speakers in Serbia and Croatia do not distinguish length on unstressed (post-tonic) vowels.

5 Morphology

Serbo-Croat has been generally conservative, maintaining most of the categories of Common Slavonic and changing some of the actual forms remarkably little. However, there have also been some surprising innovations. Seven cases have been preserved, together with three genders, which are distinguished in the plural as well as the singular (unlike Russian). The dual number has been lost, but it has left its mark on the plural oblique case forms (a Serbo-Croat innovation). The chart given here shows the main types of noun declension, corresponding to those given for Russian.

Serbo-Croat Nominal Declension

	a-*stem*	Masculine o-*stem*	Neuter o-*stem*	i-*stem*
Singular:				
Nom.	žèna 'woman'	zákon 'law'	sèlo 'village'	stvâr 'thing'
Voc.	žȅno	zákone	sèlo	stvâri
Acc.	žènu	zákon	sèlo	stvâr
Gen.	žènē	zákona	sèla	stvâri
Dat.	žèni	zákonu	sèlu	stvâri
Inst.	žènōm	zákonom	sèlom	stvârju/stvâri
Loc.	žèni	zákonu	sèlu	stvári
Plural:				
Nom.	žène	zákoni	sȅla	stvâri
Voc.	žȅne	zákoni	sȅla	stvâri
Acc.	žène	zákone	sȅla	stvâri
Gen.	žénā	zákōnā	sêlā	stvárī
Dat.	žènama	zákonima	sȅlima	stvárima
Inst.	žènama	zákonima	sȅlima	stvárima
Loc.	žènama	zákonima	sȅlima	stvárima

In broad typological terms, the picture is similar to that of Russian: the morphology is fusional, and there is a high, but not absolute, correlation of gender with declensional class. When we look in more detail, however, we find interesting differences as compared to Russian. The vocative case is preserved, requiring a mutation of consonants for many masculine nouns. Thus *Bôg* 'God', vocative singular *Bȍže*, *prèdsjednīk/prèdsednīk* 'chairman', vocative singular *prèdsjednīče/prèdsednīče*. These mutations go back to the first palatalisation (see page 310). The second palatalisation is well preserved too. It is found in the singular of feminine *a*-stems: *knjȉga* 'book', dative and locative singular *knjȉzi*; *rijéka/réka* 'river', dative and locative singular *rijéci/réci*. In addition, it occurs in the plural of masculine nouns: *ìzlog* 'shop window', nominative plural *ìzlozi*, dative, instrumental and locative plural *ìzlozima*; *tèpih* 'carpet', nominative plural *tèpisi*, dative, instrumental and locative plural *tèpisima*. The innovatory mutation *l/o* also affects nominal paradigms: *pèpeo* 'ash', genitive singular *pèpela*. When combined with a fleeting *a*, the reflex of both jers in 'strong' position, it can make forms from a single paradigm sound very different: *čìtalac* 'reader', vocative singular *čìtaoče*, accusative singular *čìtaoca*, genitive singular *čìtaoca*. These last examples illustrate the genitive–accusative syncretism found with animate nouns. In Serbo-Croat this is much more restricted than in Russian, being limited to masculine singular nouns. Note, however, that masculine plurals have an accusative form distinct from both nominative and genitive. While Serbo-Croat preserves the vocative, it has all but lost the distinction between dative and locative. Probably the major innovation in the nominal paradigms is the genitive plural -*ā*, for most nouns except *i*-stems. The origin of this form is still subject to debate. An *ā* may also be inserted to avoid consonant clusters before this ending, for example, *stùdent* 'student', genitive plural *stùdenātā*.

There are various smaller declensional classes which complicate the picture: some consonant stems are preserved, though with regularised endings, and certain suffixes may be added or lost in the declension of masculine nouns. And as the first noun in our chart shows, the length and tone of the stressed syllable may change within a paradigm; furthermore, as in Russian, the position of the stress may move as well. Before leaving the declension of nouns, it is interesting to note that, with a very few exceptions, all Serbo-Croat nouns are declinable. Even borrowings ending in a vowel decline: *bìrō* 'office', genitive singular *biròa*, unless they are feminine. This contrasts with Russian, where nouns whose stem ends in a vowel (a considerable number) are normally indeclinable. On the other hand, most of the numerals in Serbo-Croat no longer decline, while in Russian they decline fully.

Many of the adjectival endings (as shown in the chart of adjectival declension) are similar to those of Russian, though contraction has applied to a greater extent. The accusative singular masculine form depends on the animacy of the noun. The forms given in brackets are optional additions; thus the genitive singular masculine and neuter is *mlâdōg* or, less usually, *mlâdōga*. Note that the three genders are distinguished in the direct cases of the plural. The forms given in the chart are the definite (pronominal, long) forms. Serbo-Croat retains indefinite forms, though these are distinguished by inflection in the masculine singular only; elsewhere the difference is normally one of length, the definite endings including a long vowel and the indefinite endings typically a short one. The distinction is best preserved in the nominative singular masculine: *dòbrī čòvjek/čòvek* 'the good man' contrasts with *dòbar čòvjek/čòvek* 'a good man'. Thus noun phrases are clearly marked for definiteness providing they include an attributive adjective and a masculine singular noun in the nominative case (or accusative–nominative). As in other Slavonic languages, though later than in most, the indefinite forms are being lost. The main reason they are best preserved in the nominative is that when the adjective is used predicatively it stands in the nominative and the indefinite form is used. Definite forms are therefore attributive; indefinites could be attributive or predicative and are increasingly a sign of predicative usage. A secondary reason for the retention of the opposition in the masculine concerns case-marking. Subjects and direct objects are clearly distinguished for animate nouns since, as mentioned earlier, animates have accusative forms identical to the genitive. For inanimates, however, nominative and accusative are identical. In actual text, a high proportion of subjects is definite, while most direct objects are indefinite. Therefore, for inanimate masculine nouns, the opposition of definite and indefinite forms helps to mark case.

Serbo-Croat Adjectival Declension (Definite)

	Masculine		*Neuter*	*Feminine*
Singular:				
Nom.-Voc.	mlâdī 'young'		mlâdō	mlâdā
Acc.	as nom. or gen.		mlâdō	mlâdū
Gen.		mlâdōg(a)		mlâdē
Dat.		mlâdōm(e)		mlâdōj
Inst.		mlâdīm		mlâdōm
Loc.		mlâdōm(e)		mlâdōj
Plural:				
Nom.-Voc.	mlâdī		mlâdā	mlâdē
Acc.	mlâdē		mlâdā	mlâdē
Gen.			mlâdīh	
Dat.			mlâdīm(a)	
Inst.			mlâdīm(a)	
Loc.			mlâdīm(a)	

When we move to verbal morphology, we find a plethora of forms. Serbo-Croat is moving from a system based on tense to one in which aspect has a central role, but it has not lost the redundant tense forms as most other Slavonic languages have. A concomitant change involves greater use of compound tenses. We start, however, with simple forms. The main conjugations are given in the chart of conjugation types (there are several variations on these forms which will be omitted).

Serbo-Croat Conjugation Types

		I Conjugation	*II Conjugation*	*III Conjugation*
Infinitive		čìtati 'to read'	nòsiti 'to carry'	trésti 'to shake'
Present:				
Singular	1	čìtām	nòsīm	trésēm
	2	čìtāš	nòsīš	trésēš
	3	čìtā	nòsī	trésē
Plural	1	čìtāmo	nòsīmo	trésēmo
	2	čìtāte	nòsīte	trésēte
	3	čìtajū	nòsē	trésū
Imperative:				
Singular	2	čìtāj	nòsi	trési
Plural	1	čìtājmo	nòsimo	trésimo
Plural	2	čìtājte	nòsite	trésite

Similarities with the present tense forms in the other Slavonic languages already given are evident. The main innovation is in the first person singular. The *-m* has spread from the very small group of athematic verbs to all the verbs in the language (with two exceptions: *mòći* 'to be able', first person singular *mògu*, and *htjèti/htèti* 'to want', first person singular *hòću* or *ću*). As stated earlier, long vowels after the stress, which occur in all persons in the present tense, are shortened by many speakers. Serbo-Croat preserves two more simple tenses, the imperfect and the aorist, illustrated in the charts displaying these forms. Note that in the imperfect the stem may show a consonant mutation, as in the case *nòšāh* from *nòsiti*; several verbs have two possible forms, while *ìmati* 'to have' has three: *ìmāh*, *imàdijāh* and *imađāh*. The imperfect indicates action in process in the past. It contrasts with the aorist, which is normally used for a completed single action in the past. Both tenses are particularly used for events witnessed by the speaker.

The Imperfect Tense in Serbo-Croat

		I Conjugation	*II Conjugation*	*III Conjugation*
Infinitive		čìtati 'to read'	nòsiti 'to carry'	trésti 'to shake'
Imperfect				
Singular	1	čìtāh	nòšāh	trésijāh/trésāh
	2	čìtāše	nòšāše	trésijāše/trésāše
	3	čìtāše	nòšāše	trésijāše/trésāše
Plural	1	čìtāsmo	nòšāsmo	trésijāsmo/trésāsmo
	2	čìtāste	nòšāste	trésijāste/trésāste
	3	čìtāhu	nòšāhu	trésijāhu/trésāhu

The Aorist Tense in Serbo-Croat

		I Conjugation	*II Conjugation*	*III Conjugation*
Infinitive		sàznati 'to find out'	kúpiti 'to buy'	istrésti 'to shake out'
Aorist				
Singular	1	sàznah	kúpih	istrésoh
	2	sàzna	kûpī	ìstrēse
	3	sàzna	kûpī	ìstrēse
Plural	1	sàznasmo	kúpismo	istrésosmo
	2	sàznaste	kúpiste	istrésoste
	3	sàznaše	kúpiše	istrésoše

In the aorist of third conjugation verbs, a mutation of velar consonants may occur in the second and third persons singular (first palatalisation), for example, *rèći* 'to say', first singular aorist *rèkoh*, second and third singular aorist *rèče*. In the first conjugation, some forms coincide with the imperfect – apart from post-accentual length. There is, however, little possibility of confusion, since the imperfect is formed only from imperfective verbs and the aorist usually, but not exclusively, from perfectives (hence the different illustrative verbs given in the chart of aorist tense forms). The notion of aspect is discussed in the chapter on Russian (pages 283–284). In broad outline, the aspectual system is similar in Serbo-Croat in both morphology (perfectives are typically derived from imperfectives by prefixation, and imperfectives from perfectives by suffixation) and semantics (the perfective views a situation as a single whole, the imperfective views a situation as having internal subdivisions). Given the basic aspectual meanings, it is not surprising that the imperfect is found with imperfective verbs and the aorist typically with perfectives. However, the increasing importance of the aspectual opposition imperfective–perfective, which duplicates the imperfect–aorist opposition, is leading to the supplanting of both tenses by a compound past tense, which can be formed from verbs of either aspect. We shall refer to it simply as the 'past tense'; it is sometimes referred to as the 'perfect'. For many speakers, particularly outside Bosnia-Hercegovina, the past tense is replacing both the imperfect and aorist, the aorist being the better preserved.

Before going on to the past and other compound tenses, we should return for a moment to the present tense. Whereas in Russian only imperfectives have a present tense (forms with the morphological appearance of the present formed from perfective verbs are future perfective), in Serbo-Croat there is a present perfective, distinct from the future. It is formed identically to the examples given in the chart of conjugation types, but from perfective verbs. Thus *istrésti* 'to shake out', first person singular present *istrésēm*. The perfective present has a range of uses, but is not used for events occurring at the moment of speech. In the example: *štò nè sjednēš/nè sednēš* (perfective present) 'why don't you sit down?', the addressee is evidently not actually doing so. This tense is frequently used in subordinate clauses; examples will be given in the syntax section.

Of the compound tenses, the past is easily the most important. It is formed using the past participle of the verb. This participle agrees in gender and number, as is illustrated using the verb *znàti* 'to know'.

Forms of the Past Participle

	Masculine	*Feminine*	*Neuter*
Singular	znäo < znäl	znäla	znälo
Plural	znäli	znäle	znäla

The other component of the past tense consists of the present tense forms of the auxiliary verb *bìti* 'to be'. These agree in person and number, and they are enclitic (see Section 6), though there are also long forms used for emphasis and in questions. Subject personal pronouns are normally omitted in Serbo-Croat unless they are under contrastive or emphatic stress. If there is no nominal subject or other preceding word in the sentence, the participle precedes the enclitic, which, as we shall see in Section 6, cannot stand in first position. The past tense paradigm is therefore as that given for *znàti* 'to know'. The past tense can be formed from imperfective verbs, like *znàti*, and such forms have largely supplanted the imperfect tense. The past tense can also be formed from perfectives in just the same way: *sàznati* 'to find out', *sàznao sam* 'I found

341

out' (such forms replace the aorist). Compare *písala je písmo* (imperfective) 'she was writing a letter', *napísala je písmo* 'she wrote a letter'.

The Past Tense in Serbo-Croat

Infinitive		znàti 'to know'
Past Tense		
Singular	1	znào/znàla sam
	2	znào/znàla si
	3	znào/znàla/znàlo je
Plural	1	znàli/znàle smo
	2	znàli/znàle ste
	3	znàli/znàle/znàla su

While the past is easily the most common tense for reference to past events, there is in addition a pluperfect tense. This can be formed from the imperfect of *bìti* plus the past participle, for example Ijek. *bìjāh* / Ek. *bèjāh čìtao* 'I had been reading'. As elsewhere, the past can replace the imperfect, so a more frequent alternative formation with the past tense of *bìti* is *bìo sam čìtao*. The pluperfect occurs infrequently. If the aorist of *bìti* is combined with the past participle, then the conditional results: *čìtao bih* 'I would read'. These auxiliary forms are again enclitics. The inflections of the aorist are being lost in this usage and the uninflected form *bi* is taking over (as has happened in Russian, see page 284). There is also a past conditional: *bìo bi rèkao* 'he would have said'. This tense is found in the western varieties but has practically died out in the east.

All the compound tenses discussed so far use the auxiliary *bìti*. In contrast, the future tense is formed with the verb *htjèti/htèti* 'to want' together with the infinitive. Normally the short forms of *htjèti/htèti* are used (singular *ću, ćeš, će*, plural *ćemo, ćete, ćē*), for example, *žèna će znàti* 'the woman will know'. These short forms are enclitic, so that if no subject is expressed the infinitive is likely to precede: *dóći ću* 'I will come'. If an infinitive in *-ti* precedes the auxiliary, the *-ti* is not pronounced. This is reflected in the spelling in Serbia and Montenegro: *znàću* 'I will know'; the pronunciation is the same in Croatia, but only the *i* is dropped in the spelling: *znàt ću*. (Bosnian uses both spellings.) The long forms of *htjèti/htèti* can be used for emphasis: *hòću dóći* 'I **will** come', and in questions: *hòću li dóći?* 'shall I come?' As our examples show, the future is formed with verbs of both aspects: *znàti* is imperfective and *dóći* is perfective. Particularly in the east, the infinitive is frequently replaced by *da* plus verb in the present tense; we return to this topic in the next section.

A further tense, sometimes called the 'future exact', is formed from a second set of present tense forms of *bìti* 'to be' (singular: *bùdēm, bùdēš, bùdē*; plural: *bùdēmo, bùdēte, bùdū*) plus the past participle. It is used only in subordinate clauses, especially those introduced by *àko* 'if' and temporal conjunctions such as *kàd* 'when': *àko bùdēš dòšao* 'if you (in the future) come'. It can be used with verbs of either aspect. In the case of perfective verbs, the present perfective can be used instead: *àko dôđēš*, and this is regarded as more proper in Croatian.

Of all the tenses described, the ones which form the backbone of the system in the modern language are the present, the past (*znào sam/znàla sam* 'I knew') and the future (*znàt ću/znàću* 'I will know'). Each of these can be formed from perfective and imperfective verbs, giving six possibilities, which cover most situations. As aspect has gained in significance, tenses other than the main ones have been reduced to marginal status. It will be interesting to observe how many of them survive and for how long.

In contrast to the wealth of tense forms, the inventory of non-finite verbal forms is limited. There are two indeclinable adverbs, termed 'gerunds'. The present gerund is formed from imperfective verbs (*čìtati* 'to read' gives *čìtajūći* 'reading') and denotes action contemporaneous with that of the main verb. The past gerund, normally formed from perfective verbs (*sàznati* 'to find out': *sàznāvši* 'having found out'), is for an action prior to that of the main verb. There is also the passive participle in *-n/-en/-t*, formed more frequently from perfective verbs than imperfectives, for example, *kúpiti* 'to buy' *kûpljen* 'bought'. The passive participle takes adjectival endings and, with *bìti* 'to be' as auxiliary, forms the passive voice.

6 Syntax

Two particularly interesting aspects of Serbo-Croat syntax (enclitics and the replacement of the infinitive by a subordinate clause) have already been mentioned and will be described in more detail. In addition, we shall give brief consideration to questions and to agreement.

Serbo-Croat enclitics are already familiar to many non-Slavists through the work of W. Browne, who showed the problems they posed for transformational theory. Enclitics must come in second position in a clause. There are six 'slots', each of which may be filled by one enclitic, in the strict order given in Table 18.4. As examples, consider the following: *gdje/gde ste me našli?* (enclitics II, V) 'where did you find me?'; *želim mu ih dati* (III, V) 'I wish to give them to him'; *našao ga je* (V, VI) 'he found it'; *sjećate/ sećate li me se?* (I, IV, V) (*sjećati se/sećati se* is a reflexive verb which governs the genitive) 'do you remember me?'

Table 18.4 Serbo-Croat Enclitics

I	Interrogative particle: li
II	Verbal auxiliaries: sam, si, smo, ste, su (but not 3.sg. *je*)
	ću, ćeš, ćé, ćemo, ćete, će
	bih, bi, bi, bismo, biste, bi
III	Dative pronouns: singular: mi, ti, m. nt. mu, fem. joj (reflexive *si* in west only)
	plural: nam, vam, im
IV	Genitive pronouns: singular: me, te, m. nt. ga, fem. je
	plural: nas, vas, ih
V	Accusative pronouns: identical to the genitive pronouns; also the reflexive *se*
VI	Third singular form of *biti*: je

There are two special rules concerning *je*, the third person singular of *biti*. If the combination *se je* is expected, then *je* is dropped. *Vratiti se* 'to return' is a reflexive verb; the expected third singular masculine of the past tense would be *vratio se je*, but we find *vratio se* 'he returned'. This is now an absolute rule in the east but occasional forms with *se je* occur in the west. The other special rule prohibits the combination **je je*, where the first is the accusative case of the personal pronoun (third singular feminine) and the second is the third singular of *biti*. Instead, the first is replaced by the form *ju*, for example, *našao ju je* 'he found her'.

Earlier it was stated that enclitics stand in 'second' position. The expected interpretation of this statement might be after the first accented constituent. This interpretation would fit the examples given so far, as well as sentences like: *taj student mi je napisao pismo* 'that student wrote me a letter'. If an initial constituent is separated by a pause, enclitics will then occur in second position counting from the pause: *početkom ove godine, taj student mi je napisao pismo* 'at the beginning of this year, that student wrote me a letter'. In some cases an initial long constituent is disregarded though there is no pause. More surprisingly, the enclitics may stand after the first accented word, even though by doing so they split a constituent: *taj mi je student napisao pismo* (lit. 'that to me is student written letter') 'that student wrote me a letter'.

Enclitics are found in the other Slavonic languages, though Serbo-Croat has preserved them particularly well and has created new ones, such as the clitic forms of *htjeti/hteti*. Our next point of interest, however, is unusual in Slavonic (being found only in Bulgarian and Macedonian in addition to Serbo-Croat) but shared with other languages of the Balkans (e.g. Rumanian and Greek – see pages 264–265 and 366–367). Mainly in the eastern varieties, Serbo-Croat tends to replace the infinitive by a construction consisting of the conjunction *da* plus a verb in the present tense. The infinitive with purposive meaning is most likely to be replaced, so that examples like: *Marija je došla da kupi knjigu* (lit. 'Mary came that she buys a book') 'Mary came to buy a book', occur freely in the west as well as in the east. With verbs like *željeti/želeti* 'to wish', both constructions occur: *Marija želi da kupi knjigu/Marija želi kupiti knjigu* 'Mary wishes to buy a book', but the first is more likely in the east and the second in the west. The construction with *da* has spread into the ordinary future: *Marija će da kupi knjigu* 'Mary will buy a book'. This is common in the east, much less so in the west, where one would expect the infinitive: *Marija će kupiti knjigu*. Broadly speaking, as one moves eastwards, so the infinitive becomes rarer, though there is considerable variation even among individuals. In eastern dialects transitional to Bulgarian and Macedonian the infinitive is effectively excluded.

Questions often contain multiple interrogative words, and all are moved towards the beginning of their clause: *Koga ste gdje/gde našli?* Or *Gdje/gde ste koga našli?* 'Whom did you find where? Where did you find whom?' As we see, one or another of the interrogatives is moved 'more' to the left, so that the enclitic *ste* follows it. A classic article by C. Rudin (1988) contrasts Serbo-Croat with Bulgarian, in which the mutual ordering among interrogative words is fixed. Recent work (Ž. Bošković, S. Stjepanović) has however shown that interrogatives in subordinate clauses require a more fixed order even in Serbo-Croat.

The last area to consider is agreement. Like the other Slavonic languages described, Serbo-Croat shows agreement of attributive modifiers with their head nouns in gender, number, case and, to a limited extent, in animacy. Main verbs agree in person and number with their subjects, participles in gender and number. There are various complications. For example, a few nouns are of different gender in the singular and the plural: *to* (nt. sg.) *oko* 'that eye'; *te* (f. pl.) *oči* 'those eyes'. Then there is a class of nouns ending in -*a*, which have the appearance of feminines but refer to males. In the singular, these are masculine: *naš gazda* 'our master'. In the plural, both masculine and feminine agreements are found: *naši/naše gazde* 'our masters'. Furthermore, a small group of nouns, instead of having a normal plural paradigm, takes another singular. Thus *dijete/ dete* (nt. sg.) 'child' has the form *djeca/deca* 'children', which declines like the feminine singular noun *žena* in the chart of nominal declension. Agreement with *djeca/deca* is singular or plural, depending on the construction: *majka ove* (gen. sg. f.) *djece/dece* 'the mother of these children'; *djeca/deca spavaju* (pl.) 'the children are sleeping'.

Since Serbo-Croat retains the original gender distinctions in the plural, there are rules for agreement with conjoined noun phrases, which may be of different genders. If all conjuncts are feminine, then feminine agreements are found (all these examples are from works by the Nobel prize-winning novelist, Ivo Andrić): *nad njim su stajale* (f. pl.) *Jelenka* (f.) *i Saveta* (f) 'over him were standing Jelenka and Saveta'. In all other cases, the masculine plural is used even though no masculine is present: *znanje* (nt. sg.) *i intuicija* (f. sg.) *su kod njega sarađivali* (m. pl.) … 'knowledge and intuition worked together in him …' Conjoined neuter singulars similarly require a masculine plural predicate. Comparable rules are found in Slovene. However, Serbo-Croat has made an interesting innovation. If the conjuncts are all of feminine gender, but they refer to inanimates, then masculine agreements may be found: *službena revnost* (f. sg., -*i* declension) *i lična sujeta* (f. sg.) *zanosili* (m. pl.) *su ih* … 'professional zeal and personal vanity carried them away …' It appears, therefore, that Serbo-Croat is moving towards a position in which the feminine plural will be required for agreement with conjoined nouns referring to females, the feminine will be optional for other feminine nouns and the masculine will be used under all other circumstances.

This last construction typifies the particular interest of Serbo-Croat for the linguist. The preservation of the original gender distinctions in the plural is an example of its conservatism; there are, as we have seen, various forms still found in Serbo-Croat which have been lost in most of the other Slavonic languages. On the other hand, the innovation permitting masculine agreement with feminine nouns (depending on their type) is, like other innovations we have noted, a surprise and a challenge for the linguist.

Acknowledgement

We are very grateful to all of the following for helpful comments on the draft of the first edition: P.V. Cubberley, P. Herrity, Milka and Pavle Ivić, D.J.L. Johnson, Lj. Popović and R.D. Sussex. Theresa Alt was very helpful in preparing the present revision.

Bibliography

Alexander and Elias-Bursać (2006) is a solid grammar in textbook form, covering Bosnian, Croatian, and Serbian, with an accompanying reference grammar Alexander (2006). Descriptive grammars include Meillet and Vaillant (1969), with thorough coverage of morphology but somewhat dated, and Leskien (1914), a landmark in its time. Browne (1993) and Kordić (1997) may be consulted with profit for the present-day situation. The following deal with accent: Lehiste and Ivić (1963 and 1986), extensive acoustical studies; Magner and Matejka (1971), a challenge to traditional accounts, perhaps overstated, though a good entry point to the extensive literature on the subject; Gvozdanović (1980), an acoustical study, with a useful introduction to the phonology of Serbo-Croat. The *Publications of the Yugoslav Serbo-Croatian–English Contrastive Project* (1968–) contain papers covering a range of topics, especially in syntax and lexicon; for instance, *Contrastive Analysis of English and Serbo-Croatian*, vol. 1 (1975) includes a paper by W. Browne giving a detailed account of clitics. Progovac (2005) treats syntax extensively. Greenberg (2004) interprets the sociolinguistic situation before and after the break-up of Yugoslavia. Benson (1990 and later reprints) remains the most informative dictionary for the English-speaking reader.

For the history of the language, Naylor (1980) provides a clear account of the external history of Serbo-Croat; Popović (1960) lays particular emphasis on the early period and on contacts with other languages; while Vaillant (1928–79) is a historical grammar of wider scope than its title suggests. Ivić (1958) provides a survey of Serbo-Croatian dialects by one of Yugoslavia's foremost linguists.

Nearly every annual issue of *Formal Approaches to Slavic Linguistics* includes recent research on Bosnian, Croatian or Serbian.

References

Alexander, R. 2006. *Bosnian, Croatian, Serbian: A Grammar* (University of Wisconsin Press, Madison)

Alexander, R. and Elias-Bursać, E. 2006. *Bosnian, Croatian, Serbian: A Textbook* (University of Wisconsin Press, Madison)

Benson, M. with Šljivić-Šimšić, B. 1990. *SerboCroatian–English Dictionary* (Cambridge University Press, Cambridge)

Browne, W. 1993. 'Serbo-Croat', in B. Comrie and G.G. Corbett (eds) *The Slavonic Languages* (Routledge, London and New York), pp. 306–87

Greenberg, R.D. 2004. *Language and Identity in the Balkans: Serbo-Croatian and Its Disintegration* (Oxford University Press, Oxford)

Gvozdanović, J. 1980. *Tone and Accent in Standard Serbo-Croatian (with a Synopsis of Serbo-Croatian Phonology)* (Österreichische Akademie der Wissenschaften, Vienna)

Ivić, P. 1958. *Die serbokroatischen Dialekte: ihre Struktur und Entwicklung, I: Allgemeines und die štokavische Dialektgruppe* (Mouton, The Hague)

Kordić, S. 1997. *Serbo-Croatian* (Lincom Europa, München and Newcastle)

Lehiste, I. and Ivić, P. 1963. *Accent in Serbocroatian: An Experimental Study* (University of Michigan, Ann Arbor)

—— 1986. *Word and Sentence Prosody in Serbocroatian* (MIT Press, Cambridge, MA)

Leskien, A. 1914. *Grammatik der serbokroatischen Sprache, I: Lautlehre, Stammbildung, Formenlehre* (Carl Winter, Heidelberg)

Magner, T.F. and Matejka, L. 1971. *Word Accent in Modern Serbo-Croatian* (Pennsylvania State University Press, University Park and London)

Meillet, A. and Vaillant, A. 1969. *Grammaire de la langue serbo-croate*, 2nd edn (Champion, Paris)

Naylor, K.E. 1980. 'Serbo-Croatian', in A.M. Schenker and E. Stankiewicz (eds) *The Slavic Literary Languages: Formation and Development* (Yale Concilium on International and Area Studies, New Haven, CT), pp. 65–83

Popović, I. 1960. *Geschichte der serbokroatischen Sprache* (Otto Harrassowitz, Wiesbaden)

Progovac, Lj. 2005. *A Syntax of Serbian: Clausal Architecture* (Slavica, Bloomington)

Publications of the Yugoslav Serbo-Croatian–English Contrastive Project (1968–) (Institute of Linguistics, University of Zagreb, Zagreb)

Vaillant, A. 1928–79. *La Langue de Dominko Zlatarić, poète ragusain de la fin du XVIe siècle*, 3 vols (Institut d'Études Slaves, Paris and Serbian Academy of Sciences, Belgrade)

19

Greek

Brian D. Joseph

1 Historical Background

The Greek language forms, by itself, a separate branch of the Indo-European family. It is one of the oldest attested Indo-European languages, being attested from c. 1400 BC in the Mycenaean Greek documents found on Crete (and from somewhat later, on the Greek mainland) written in the Linear B syllabary. Except for a break in attestation between the end of the Mycenaean empire (c. 1150 BC) and roughly 800 BC, a period sometimes referred to as the 'Dark Ages' of Greek culture, Greek presents a continuous record of attestation for the linguist, right up to the present day.

Commonly called *Greek* in English, based on the term *Graeci* used by the Romans to label all the Greeks (though originally the name may have properly applied only to a tribe in the north-west of Greece), the language is also referred to as *Hellenic*, from the Greek stem Ἑλλην-*,[1] used in the *Iliad* to refer to a Thessalian tribe but in Herodotus (and elsewhere) to designate the Greeks as a whole as opposed to barbarians; indeed, the Greeks themselves have generally referred to their language as ἑλληνική, though contemporary Greeks also use the designation ρωμαίικα, an outgrowth of their connection historically with the Eastern Roman Empire based in Constantinople.

Using a somewhat outmoded but nonetheless still widely cited putative dialect division within Indo-European, one can classify Greek as a 'centum' language, for it shows a distinct set of reflexes for the Indo-European labio-velars, opposed to a single set of reflexes for the Indo-European palatals and velars combined; thus, Greek shows a root πρια- 'buy' (cf. also Mycenaean *qi-ri-ja-to* 'bought' showing the labio-velar preserved as < q >) from Proto-Indo-European *k^wriH₂-* (cf. Sanskrit root *krī-* 'buy'), a noun κρέας 'meat' from Proto-Indo-European *$krewH_2s$* (cf. Sanskrit *kravis-* 'raw flesh'), and a root κει- 'lie (down)' from Proto-Indo-European *$\hat{k}ei$-* (cf. Sanskrit root *śī-* 'lie'), in which the plain *k* of the proto-language and the palatal *$\hat{k}$* show a merger while the labio-velar *k^w* is kept distinct. Greek also shows some particular affinities with Armenian and Indo-Iranian, sharing with these branches, for example, the past-tense morpheme *e-* (the 'augment'), and the use of the negator *$m\bar{e}$* (Greek μή), and with Armenian alone the vocalisation of the Indo-European 'laryngeal' consonants in initial

347

position, and some notable parallels in vocabulary (e.g. ἀλώπηξ 'fox' = Arm. *aluēs*, where no other Indo-European language has precisely this form, or πρωκτός 'anus' = *erastank* 'buttocks'). Moreover, Greek preserves the Indo-European vowel system (with long and short *a* *e* *i* *o* *u*) more faithfully than any other language in the family.

Differentiating Greek from the other members of the Indo-European family, though, are several particular features. In morphology, Greek innovated a (past and future) passive marker -θη- and elaborated the infinitival system. With regard to phonology, Greek alone in Indo-European shows voiceless aspirates (in the ancient language) as the continuation of the Indo-European voiced aspirate consonants (e.g. φερ- 'carry' from **bher-*, cf. Sanskrit *bhar-*); in addition, Greek lenited Indo-European **s* to *h* in many environments, ultimately losing it intervocalically (e.g. ἑπτά 'seven' from **septm*, cf. Latin *septem*, or γένε-ι 'in, at, to a race, kind (dat. sg.)' from **genes-i*, cf. Sanskrit *janas-i* 'in the people (loc. sg.)'). Also, Greek deleted original word-final stops (e.g. μέλι 'honey' from **melit*, cf. Hittite *milit* 'honey').

Moreover, although Common Greek preserved the Indo-European labiovelars as such, to judge in part from their preservation in Mycenaean (cf. *qi-ri-ja-to* above), the ancient language is characterised by a number of complex dialectal developments with **kʷ*, **gʷ* and **gʷh*. Labial reflexes occur in some environments and in some dialects (e.g. pan-Greek interrogative stem πο- from **kʷo-*, Aeolic (Boeotian) πέτταρες 'four' from **kʷetwr̥-*), dental reflexes in other environments, also dialectally conditioned (e.g. τίς 'who' from **kʷis*, and non-Aeolic (Attic) τέτταρες 'four'), and even velar reflexes in some dialects when adjacent to **u* or **w* (e.g. εὐχ-'wish' from **ewgʷh-*). Further Greek-particular developments setting the language off from other Indo-European languages include a number of complex treatments of clusters of obstruent + **y* and of clusters of resonant *(*r *l *m *n *y *w)* + **s* (examples below in Section 4.1). A final diagnostic feature for Greek within Indo-European is a three-way distinction in reflexes of the laryngeal consonants, represented by ε, α and o in Greek; this feature is likely to represent the continuation of a three-way Proto-Indo-European contrast in the laryngeals, but by some accounts it is a significant Greek innovation (perhaps morphologically induced).

The early attestation of Greek and the archaic nature of the Homeric epic corpus together serve to make Greek extremely important for the understanding and reconstruction of all aspects of Proto-Indo-European language and culture. In addition, the literary output of writers of Greek has throughout the ages been of utmost importance to Western culture so that Greek has a special place in a variety of humanistic pursuits, including the history of linguistics because of the native Greek grammatical tradition developed by the Alexandrians in the Hellenistic era. Finally, the long and relatively continuous attestation of the Greek language gives it a significance for general historical linguistics, as it offers a 'window' on the nature of language change which few other languages can provide.

With such a long historical record for the language, it is convenient, as well as conventional, to break the span up into several major periods of development. These periods are defined in part by external, especially political and historical, factors, but also reflect real linguistic developments. These periods are:

(a) Mycenaean Greek (c. 1500–1150 BC)
(b) Classical Greek, including Homeric Greek (c. 800–300 BC)

(c) Hellenistic Greek, including New Testament Greek and the Roman period (c. 300 BC–AD 300)

(d) Middle Greek, comprising Byzantine Greek (c. AD 300–1100) and Medieval Greek (c. AD 1100–1600)

(e) Modern Greek (c. AD 1600 to the present), actually covering the early Modern era (c. AD 1600–1800) and contemporary Greek.

With such a long period of attestation for Greek, it is of course natural to find that there are some significant differences between Greek of the fourteenth century BC and Greek of the twenty-first century AD, and these differences are chronicled in the sections to follow. At the same time, though, there are some aspects of the language, occasionally isolated ones though some fit into a system, which show remarkable continuity and stability over some 3,500 years. Among these are the past tense augment ε-, still found in stressed positions in the modern language, the personal endings in the present active and medio-passive present and past (excepting the third person plural), the general structure of the nominal and verbal systems, and numerous lexical items, including some which have changed neither phonetic form (excepting the realisation of accent) nor meaning, e.g. ἄνεμος 'wind'.

2 Greek in its Geographic and Social Context

Greek has been spoken in the southern Balkans since early in the second millennium BC, according to conventional accounts of the coming of the Greeks to the area. Arriving most likely in waves of different tribes over a period of several centuries, the Greeks absorbed some autochthonous groups, traces of whose language(s) can probably be seen in numerous place names and terms for native flora and fauna containing the sequences -νθ- and -σσ-, among others (e.g. Κόρινθος 'Corinth', μίνθη 'mint', Παρνασσός 'Parnassus', etc.), and possibly also in Indo-European-like words with a somewhat aberrant phonology if natively Greek (e.g. ἀλείφω 'I anoint' with a prefixed ἀ- and a voiceless aspirate consonant, both unexpected if the word were inherited directly from Proto-Indo-European into Greek, versus inherited Greek λίπος 'fat', from an Indo-European root *leip-). Greek has remained in the Balkans since that early period, although it has spread to other areas as well.

In ancient times, Greek colonies were established in Cyprus (perhaps as early as the twelfth century BC) and southern Italy (c. eighth century BC), and there have been Greek speakers continuously in these places up to the present day. Similarly, colonies established in western Asia Minor were continuously peopled by Greek speakers up to the beginning of the twentieth century, when population exchanges in the 1920s between Greece and Turkey led to the relocation of most of the Greeks back to Greece. All of these settlements were renewed with further Greek speakers throughout the Hellenistic period, when Greek spread as the lingua franca for all of the eastern Mediterranean, the Middle East and into Central Asia as far east as Persia and India. Some of the pockets of Greek speakers established in that period have remained into the contemporary period, for example in Alexandria (Egypt).

In the Middle Greek period, the geographic domain of Greek became somewhat more restricted, with important centres still in Constantinople, Asia Minor in general, Alexandria, Cyprus and elsewhere in the general eastern Mediterranean area, including

349

Ukraine. The modern era has seen the reduction in the number of Greek speakers in all these areas except Cyprus, but also the expansion of Greek into the 'New World'. There are now significant Greek-speaking communities in America (especially the urban centres of the East), in Canada, in Britain and in Australia. The speakers in Greece, Cyprus and elsewhere in the Mediterranean together with those in the 'Hellenic diaspora' number some 12 million today (c. nine million in Greece).

Despite the rather widespread geographic distribution of Greek throughout its history, it is Balkan Greek, i.e. Greek of the southern Balkans together with the islands of the Ionian Sea and the Aegean Sea, including Crete, that is of primary importance here. The dialect diversity in ancient times, with four main dialect groups (Attic-Ionic, Aeolic, Arcado-Cyprian and West Greek (comprising Northwest Greek and Doric)) as well as the earlier Mycenaean Greek (problematic in terms of its connections with these dialect groups), centred more on matters of detail in phonological and morphological development rather than on broad structural aspects. Thus, Attic, the dialect of Athens and the pre-eminent dialect from a cultural and political standpoint, and more generally the Attic-Ionic branch of Greek, constitute the primary and certainly best-known representative of Ancient Greek. Moreover, Attic-Ionic provided the basis for the Hellenistic koine (ἡ κοινὴ διάλεκτος 'the common dialect'), which showed considerable uniformity across the whole area of its use. This koine, in turn, provided the basis for the Middle and Modern Greek dialects, with the exception of Tsakonian, spoken in the eastern part of the Peloponnesus, which derives directly from the ancient Doric dialect. Finally, the language of the modern Hellenic diaspora, while incorporating features, mainly lexical items, from the local dominant languages, has nonetheless remained true to its Attic-Ionic origin in terms of general structural characteristics.

Focusing on Balkan Greek is important for another reason. This particular geographic setting is crucial for understanding the development of the language in the late Middle Greek and early Modern Greek periods, and especially for understanding many of the differences, to be discussed in more detail below, between these later stages of the language and its earlier stages. Greek in these later stages shows numerous linguistic features that are found as well in other languages of the Balkans, such as Albanian, Aromanian, Rumanian, Macedonian, Bulgarian, Romany and, to a somewhat lesser extent, Serbian. These features include various mergers of nominal case functions, especially possessive and indirect object functions in a single form, the formation of a future tense with a form of the verb 'want' (e.g. Modern Greek θά from earlier impersonal θέλει 'wants' + subjunctive marker νά), the widespread use of finite complement clauses where many other languages (and indeed, earlier stages of the languages in question, for the most part) would use non-finite forms, and others of a more particular nature.

The exact nature of the relation between developments of this sort in Greek and parallel developments in the other Balkan languages is disputed; some scholars argue that Greek underwent the changes as part of its natural development and that (many of) these changes spread to the other languages from Greek, while others argue that their appearance in Greek is the result of the importation of foreign features into the language through contact with the other Balkan languages. It is more likely, though, that no single explanation can be found to be valid for all of these common features, and that some may have begun in Greek and spread from there, others may have made their way into Greek from elsewhere, and others may even be the result of a combination of Greek-internal developments enhanced or guided along a particular path through language contact.

One final aspect of the social setting of Greek that is vital to an understanding of the language concerns the extent to which a high- versus low-style distinction, inherent, probably, in all languages, has come to pervade Greek language use. In Ancient Greek, there is evidence for a distinction at least between the literary language in which most of the classical works (drama, poetry, philosophy, etc.) were written and the colloquial language as evidenced in numerous inscriptions; investigations in the 1970s into the inscriptions of the Athenian ἀγορά ('marketplace') indicated that colloquial usage was marked by pronunciations which came to be more current in later stages of the language, e.g. [iː] for [eː] and a spirantal pronunciation of the voiced stops, and observations contained in Plato's dialogue *Cratylus* provide confirmation of this point. Similarly, the Greek of the non-literary papyri of Hellenistic Egypt gives a good indication of what must have been true colloquial usage through numerous hypercorrections and mistakes in approximating 'correct', i.e. high-style, Attic Greek.

In later stages of Greek, though, a consciously archaising tendency on the part of many Middle Greek writers to 'Atticise', i.e. emulate Classical Attic Greek spelling, morphology, syntax and usage, served to create a large stylistic rift in the language. Consequently, there were writers in the Middle Greek era who wrote in a language not unlike Classical Attic Greek (though it must be noted that mistakes abound!), while others wrote in a form more in line with colloquial usage of the day, the result of several centuries of natural linguistic development from the Hellenistic koine. Even in such a speech form, though, numerous learned borrowings occur, owing to the prestige enjoyed by the archaising style. Accordingly, even 'pure' colloquial Greek, what has come to be called Demotic (Greek: δημοτική), at all times in the post-classical period has incorporated many historically anomalous and anachronistic elements; this is, of course, an expected development in a language with a long literary history available to speakers and writers at all times (compare the situation in India with regard to Sanskrit and the modern Indic languages, the Romance languages and Latin, and the Slavonic languages and Old Church Slavonic).

In the case of Greek, though, with the founding of the Greek national state in the 1820s and the desire at the time for a unified form of a national language, this stylistic rift became institutionalised and politicised. The debate over which form of Greek to use in this context, the consciously archaising so-called 'puristic' Greek (Greek: καθαρεύουσα 'purifying') or the form more based in the colloquial developments from the koine, the Demotic Greek, has occupied much of the linguistic and political energy of the Greeks since the 1820s; the current official position on the 'language question' (Greek: τὸ γλωσσικὸ ζήτημα) is in favour of the Demotic, with the now-standard language being based generally on the southern (i.e. Peloponnesian) dialect.

3 Writing Systems for Greek

Greek has been written in a variety of writing systems throughout its history. The earliest written Greek is found in the syllabic system known as Linear B, in which Mycenaean Greek documents were written, generally on clay tablets. A syllabic system, related in some way to that of Linear B (though the exact details of the relationship are controversial) was also used in Cyprus in ancient times to write many of the ancient Cyprian dialect inscriptions. In addition, Greek Muslims in Crete occasionally used the Arabic alphabet to write Greek, and Greek Jews in the sixteenth century in Constantinople used the Hebrew alphabet for the same purpose.

The most enduring writing system for Greek, though, is the Greek alphabet. Adapted from the old North Semitic alphabet (traditionally, according to the Greeks themselves, transmitted through the Phoenicians) and embellished with separate signs for vowel sounds, the Greek alphabet has served the Greek language well for some 2,800 years since its introduction into Greece in the tenth or ninth century BC.

The system is basically a one-letter-to-one-phoneme system, though there are some 'double letters' representing clusters and at all stages some distinctive oppositions are either not represented at all (e.g. [a] versus [aː] in Ancient Greek) or represented only secondarily via clusters of letters (as with [d] versus [ð], spelled < ντ > and < δ >, respectively, in Modern Greek). Also, diacritics to represent pitch accent in Ancient Greek were not introduced until Hellenistic times (c. 200 BC) by the Alexandrian grammarians, and changes in the accentual system, from a pitch accent to a stress accent, left the writing system with more diacritics than needed for Middle and Modern Greek (though in 1982 an official orthography was adopted with but a single accentual diacritic). Moreover, the phonetic values of the letters have changed over time, so the current orthography is not as well matched with the phonological system as in earlier stages. Table 19.1 gives the information about the former and current phonetic values and transcriptions of the letters of the Greek alphabet.

4 Structural Features of Greek

Although five different periods were distinguished for the purposes of outlining the internal and external history of the Greek language over the approximately 3,500 years of its attestation, for the purpose of giving the major structural features of the language,

Table 19.1 The Greek Alphabet, with Transliteration and Pronunciation for Ancient (Attic) Greek and (Standard) Modern Greek, plus Diphthongs and Clusters

Capital letter	Small Letter	Ancient phonetics	Usual transliteration	Modern pronunciation	Usual transliteration
A	α	[a]	a	[a]	a
B	β	[b]	b	[v]	v
Γ	γ	[g]	g	[j](/—i, e) [ɣ] (elsewhere)	y g(h)
Δ	δ	[d]	d	[ð]	d(h)
E	ε	[ɛ]	e	[ɛ]	e
Z	ζ	[zd]	z	[z]	z
H	η	[ɛː]	eː, ē	[i]	i
Θ	θ	[tʰ]	th	[θ]	th
I	ι	[i]	i	[i]	i
K	κ	[k]	k	[k]	k
Λ	λ	[l]	l	[l]	l
M	μ	[m]	m	[m]	m
N	ν	[n]	n	[n]	n
Ξ	ξ	[ks]	x	[ks]	ks, x (as in *box*)
O	o	[o]	o	[o]	o
Π	π	[p]	p	[p]	p

Table 19.1 continued

Capital letter	Small letter	Ancient phonetics	Usual transliteration	Modern pronunciation	Usual transliteration
P	ρ	[r]	r	[ɾ]	r
Σ	σ(ς ##)	[s]	s	[s]	s
T	τ	[t]	t	[t]	t
Y	υ	[y]	y, u	[i]	i
Φ	φ	[pʰ]	ph	[f]	f
X	χ	[kʰ]	ch, kh	[χ]	h, x (IPA value)
Ψ	ψ	[ps]	ps	[ps]	ps
Ω	ω	[ɔ:]	o:, ō	[o]	o
	αι	[aj]	ai	[ɛ]	e
	αυ	[aw]	au	[av] (/___+voice)	av
				[af] (/___-voice)	af
	ει	[e:]	ei	[i]	i
	ευ	[ew]	eu	[ev] (/___+voice)	ev
				[ef] (/___- voice)	ef
	οι	[oj]	oi	[i]	i
	ου	[o:]	ou	[u]	u
	υι	[yj]	yi, ui	[i]	i
	γ before γ χ ξ	[ŋ]	n (g, kh, x/ks)	[ŋ]	n(g, h, x/ks)
	γκ	[ŋk]	nk	[(ŋ)g] (medially)	(n)g
				[g] (initially)	g
	μπ	[mp]	mp	[(m)b] (medially)	(m)b
				[b] (initially)	b
	μβ	[mb]	mb	[mv]	mv
	ντ	[nt]	nt	[(n)d] (medially)	(n)d
				[d] (initially)	d
	νδ	[nd]	nd	[nð]	nd(h)
	τζ			[dz]	dz
	(##)ʻ	[h]	h	Ø	Ø
	(##)ʼ	Ø (absence of #h)		Ø	Ø

it is more useful to examine the ancient language in contrast with the modern language. In general, then, the relevant distinction is between Classical Greek and Post-Classical Greek, for most of the changes which characterise the difference between these two stages of the language were already under way and evident in the koine of the Hellenistic period. Similarly, the differences between Middle Greek and Modern Greek are not great, and some scholars even date the beginning of the modern era to around the tenth or eleventh centuries AD. Accordingly, the whole post-classical period can be treated in a unified fashion, with the understanding that what is described in the modern language is the end-point of a long period of development from the classical language, and the stages of Hellenistic and Middle Greek defined earlier represent way stations on the road to Modern Greek; references to individual stages in particular developments, though, are made whenever necessary or appropriate.

4.1 Phonology

The consonant inventory of Ancient Greek included three distinctive points of articulation – labial, dental and velar – and three distinctive manners of articulation among the stops – voiced, voiceless unaspirated and voiceless aspirated. As noted above, in Common Greek (c. 1800 BC) and in Mycenaean Greek, there were also labio-velar consonants, which later merged with the labial, dental and velar stops under the conditions alluded to earlier. In addition, Greek had a single sibilant [s] (with [z] as an allophone before voiced consonants), the resonants [r] (with a voiceless allophone [r̥] in initial position) and [l], the nasals [m] and [n] (with [ŋ] as an allophone before velar consonants) and the glottal fricative [h]. There may have been an affricate [dᶻ], though most of the evidence concerning the pronunciation of the letter < ζ > suggests it represented a true cluster of [z+d] not a unitary affricated segment (cf. spellings such as Διόζοτος for *Διὸς δοτός, literally 'by-Zeus given'). The Common Greek [j] and [w] had been eliminated in many positions by Classical Greek, though they did remain as the second element of several diphthongs in the classical language; moreover, [j] is found in Mycenaean in several positions (e.g. *jo-i-je-si* 'so they send', interpretable 'alphabetically' as ὡς ἱενσι), and [w] occurs in many of the dialects (e.g. Mycenaean *wo-i-ko*, Doric, Thessalian and Arcadian ϝοικος, where the letter < ϝ > ('digamma') represents [w], to be compared with Attic οἶκος 'house').

By contrast to this relatively straightforward and simple consonant inventory, the vowel system of Ancient Greek was most complex. Length was distinctive and several degrees of height were distinguished as well; moreover, there were numerous diphthongs. The system of monophthongs is summarised in Table 19.2 and the diphthongal system is given in Table 19.3. It should be noted that the front rounded vowels ([y] and [yː] of Table 19.2) are characteristic of the Attic-Ionic dialect only; the other dialects had back [u] and [uː] corresponding to these Attic-Ionic vowels. Furthermore, the gaps in the short diphthongs (absence of [ej] and [ow]) are the result of early sound changes by which *ej became [eː] and *ow became [oː]. Finally, the long diphthongs were somewhat rare and had a very low functional load; in fact, early on in the classical period, [eːj], [aːj], [oːj] lost their off-glide and merged with the corresponding long pure vowels.

Although there are dialectal differences in the consonants, these tend not to be in the consonantal inventory but rather have to do more with the outcome of the Common Greek labio-velars (e.g. labials generally in Aeolic versus conditioned (before front

Table 19.2 Ancient (Attic) Greek Monophthongs (IPA Symbols)

i iː y yː				
e eː			o oː	
ɛː			ɔ	
		a aː		

Table 19.3 Ancient (Attic) Greek Diphthongs (IPA Symbols)

	ew	yj	eːj	eːw
aj	aw		aːj	aːw
oj			oːj	

vowels) dental reflexes or (elsewhere) labial reflexes in other dialects, as in πέτταρες/ τέτταρες 'four' cited above), and the outcome of complex cluster developments involving obstruent plus glide combinations and resonant or nasal plus *s*. For example, generally speaking – there are several exceptional cases – *t+y* yielded a geminate *-ss-* (graphic < σσ >) in Ionic, Doric in general, Arcadian and part of Aeolic, a geminate *-tt-* (graphic < ττ >) in Attic and part of Aeolic (Boeotian), and various spellings < ζ >, < ττ >, < θθ >, which may represent developments of something like [ts]), in Central Cretan (Doric), as in the feminine adjectival ending (from *-e(n)t-ya*) (χαρί-)εσσα (Ionic), (Παδο-)εσσα (Arcadian), (οἰνοῦ-)ττα (Attic), (χαριϝ-)ετταν (Boeotian), (ἐα-)σσα (Doric), (ια-)τταν (Central Cretan). Similarly, for certain classes of words and with some obscuring of dialect distribution due to analogies and some borrowings, there is a major split in the Greek dialects concerning the outcome of *t* before the vowel *i*, with West Greek and part of Aeolic (Thessalian and Boeotian) preserving *t* in this context and the other dialects assibilating it to *s*, as in Doric εἶτι '(s)he goes' versus Attic-Ionic εἶσι.

The vowel systems of the ancient dialects, however, show considerable variation, with alternations of length and quality and the outcome of various contractions serving to distinguish the dialects from one another. Particularly notable is the raising and fronting of Common Greek *a:* to [æː] and ultimately [εː] in the Attic-Ionic dialect; thus one finds Attic-Ionic μήτηρ 'mother' versus Doric (for example) μάτηρ from Common Greek *ma:te:r*. The fronting of [u] to [y] in Attic-Ionic has already been noted. Lengthening (often due to the loss of *s* or *y* in a cluster with a resonant) and contraction (of combinations of *e* and *o*) gave rise in Attic-Ionic to the long closed ([eː] and [oː]) vowels and likewise in parts of Doric (e.g. Corinthian and Delphian) and Thessalian and Boeotian (both Aeolic), while in Lesbian (Aeolic) and Arcadian and the rest of Doric (e.g. Cretan, Laconian) long open vowels ([εː] and [ɔː]) are found as the corresponding elements. For example, Attic-Ionic has εἰμι [eːmi] 'I am' from Common Greek *esmi*, while Doric has ἠμί [εːmi]; similarly, Attic-Ionic has τρεῖς [treːs] 'three' from Common Greek *treyes*, while Doric has τρης.

Among the peculiarities of Ancient Greek phonotactics, the following are to be noted: [r] could not occur in initial position; one finds instead the unvoiced allophone [r̥] (which has sometimes been described as an aspirated *r*). In final position, only [r], [s], [n] and vowels were permitted. Geminate consonants were permitted, though geminate labial and velar stops occur most often in onomatopoeic, nursery and expressive words. Lastly, Ancient Greek tolerated numerous consonant clusters, including a variety of initial clusters: any stop plus *r* or *l* is permitted (including #τλ-); all but *βν-, *βμ-, *γμ-, *θμ-, *πμ-, *τν-, *φμ- and *χμ- are found for stop plus nasal clusters, though φν- occurs only in a single onomatopoeic form, and τμ-, δν- and κμ- are quite rare; two stops are permitted initially if they differ in point of articulation but agree in manner and the second stop is a dental, though the voiced such clusters (βδ- and γδ-) were found in only a small number of words; and clusters of σ plus as many as two consonants occur (e.g. σχίζω 'cut', σπλάγχνα 'innards', σκνίπτω 'pinch, nip', etc.).

The Ancient Greek accentual system was based on a pitch accent. There were a high pitch (the acute, Greek ὀξύς, marked with the diacritic < ´ >), a low pitch (the grave, Greek βαρύς; marked with the diacritic < ` >), and a contour pitch (the circumflex, Greek περισπομένος, marked with the diacritic < ˜ >) which consisted of an acute plus a grave on the same syllable and occurred only on long vowels or diphthongs. At most, one high pitch, either an acute or circumflex, occurred per word (except for some special developments with enclitics), and all non-high syllables were considered grave.

Accent placement was predictable (for the most part – some exceptions exist) only in finite verb forms and in declined forms of certain nouns, e.g. those with antepenultimate accent in their lexical form; for such forms, the accent is said to be 'recessive', i.e. as far from the end of the word as permitted. Also, the placement of accent was predictable in certain morphologically definable formations, e.g. compounds with εὐ- 'well, easy' had recessive accent, verbal adjectives in -τος were accented on the final syllable, etc. In other contexts, accent placement was unpredictable and was therefore an element of the underlying (lexical) form of the word in question, though there were some regularities in the realisation of the accent (e.g. circumflex if the accent fell on a long penultimate syllable when the ultima was short). Thus, accent was distinctive in the Ancient Greek phonological system, for some words were distinguished only by the type of accent on a given syllable (e.g. locative adverbial οἴκοι 'at home' versus nominative plural οἶκοι 'houses') and others only by the placement of the accent (e.g. τιμά 'two honours' versus τίμα '(you) honour!').

An overriding principle in the placement of the pitch accent in Ancient Greek is the so-called 'Dreimorengesetz' (Law of Three Morae, more usually referred to in English as the 'Law of Limitation'), by which the accent could only occur on the antepenultimate, penultimate or ultimate syllable and never earlier in the word than that. With a few exceptions, this restriction can be stated in terms of morae (hence the name 'Dreimorengesetz'), so that Ancient Greek was probably a mora-timed language (note also that syllable quantity mattered for purposes of the ancient poetic metres). This restriction gave rise to certain of the predictable aspects of the placement of accent, especially in those forms which had recessive accent. For example, a noun such as θάλαττα 'sea' was lexically accented on the antepenultimate syllable, as indicated by the citation form (nominative singular); in the genitive singular, though, the final syllable is long (θαλάττης) and as a result, the accent cannot stand on the antepenultimate syllable. Instead, it predictably is pulled forward to the penultimate, so that it does not stand more than three morae from the end. Similarly, a finite verb form such as κελεύω 'I order' was predictably accented on the penultimate syllable because the ultima is long and finite forms have recessive accent; the first person plural present form κελεύομεν and the first person singular past form ἐκέλευσα, however, are both accented on the antepenultimate syllable because the ultima is short. By contrast, the perfect middle participle of this verb, a non-finite form, had penultimate accent (e.g. in the nominative singular masculine form) even though the ultima was short, i.e. κεκελευμένος. In this way, therefore, accent placement in the verb serves also as a correlate of the morphosyntactic category of finiteness; recessive accent correlates with the presence of person and number markings on the verb, but not with the absence of such markings, in general.

With regard to the morphophonemics of Ancient Greek, three types of alternations must be distinguished: vowel alternations that represent a remnant – by then fully morphologically conditioned – of the Indo-European ablaut patterns (see pages 14–15), alternations caused by the sound changes that separate Greek from Proto-Indo-European and that distinguish the individual dialects of Greek itself, and alternations due to natural processes such as assimilation.

Within paradigms, except for a few irregular verbs (e.g. εἶ-μι 'I go' versus ἴ-μεν 'we go') with alternations between *e*-grade and zero-grade retained from the proto-language, the vowel alternations one finds in Greek are those of length. This situation occurs in a few verbs (e.g. δί-δω-μι 'I give' versus δί-δο-μεν 'we give', actually a remnant of Proto-Indo-European full-grade/zero-grade ablaut transformed in Greek into simply a length distinction) and in a large number of nominal forms of the consonant stem declension (e.g. nominative singular τέκτων 'carpenter' versus genitive singular τέκτονος, nominative singular ποιμήν 'shepherd' versus genitive singular ποιμέν-ος, masculine adjective ἀληθής 'true' versus neuter ἀληθές, etc.).

Across paradigms, between derivationally related forms of the same root, one finds alternations in vowel quality as well as quantity. For example, the inherited *e/o*-ablaut is found in numerous Greek pairs of related forms, such as λέγ-ω 'I say' versus λόγ-ος 'word', φέρ-ω 'I bear' versus φόρ-ος 'tribute, (tax) burden' (and compare also the related form φώρ 'thief (i.e. one who bears off something)' for a length alternation; moreover, it has a grammatical function still in forms such as present tense λείπω 'I leave' versus perfect λέ-λοιπ-α 'I have left' (and note the zero-grade reflex in past ἔ-λιπ-ον 'I did leave'). This *e/o*-ablaut interacts with the development of the labio-velars to give etymologically related (but probably synchronically unrelated) pairs such as θείνω 'I strike' from *g^when-yo:* versus φόνος 'murder' from *g^whon-os*. Transformations of the Indo-European ablaut due to sound changes are also to be found, such as in the masculine stem τέκτον- 'carpenter' versus the feminine τέκταινα 'carpentress', where the -o-/-αι- alternation results from an alternation which in pre-Greek terms would have been *-on-∅* versus *-n̥-ya* (with -αιν- from *-n̥y-*).

Among the sound changes that left traces in morphophonemic alternations, one noteworthy one that operates in noun paradigms is the loss of final stops. Thus one finds such alternations as γάλα 'milk' (nominative singular) versus γάλακτος (genitive singular), or λέων 'lion' (nominative singular) versus λέοντος (genitive). Similarly, the loss of medial *s* created paradigmatic alternations such as γένος-∅ 'race, kind' (nominative singular) versus γένε-α (nominative plural), from *genes-a*. Across paradigms, the developments of clusters with *y* gave rise to derivational alternations, since *-ye/o-* was an especially common present tense formative – compare ταραχ-ή 'trouble, disorder' with the related verb ταράττ-ω (Ionic ταράσσ-ω) 'disturb, trouble' from *tarakh-yo:*, for example – and since *-y-* figured in other derivational processes, as with the formation of certain comparative adjectives (e.g. μέγ-ας 'big' versus μείζων 'bigger' from *meg-yo:n*). Furthermore, in dialects with the assibilation of *t* to *s* before *i*, one finds such alternations as πλοῦτ-ος 'wealth' versus πλούσ-ιος 'wealthy' (and note the predictable accent-realisation difference, with circumflex in the noun versus acute in the adjective, due to the distance of the (long) accented syllable (the root) from the end of the word). In addition, the *-s-* formative, which appeared in some past tense forms, created alternations in vowel quality with the dialectal resolution of resonant plus *s* clusters, e.g. νέμ-ω 'I distribute' ἔ-νειμ-α versus 'I distributed' (Doric ἔ-νημ-α, both from *e-nem-s-a*).

Finally, many morphophonemic alternations result from more or less natural processes that take effect when certain segments come together as the result of word formation processes. For example, assimilation in voicing is common, as seen in the pair ἄγ-ω 'I lead' versus ἄξ-ω (i.e. *ak-s-o:*) 'I will lead' where -s- is the marker for future tense, or in the pair κρύπ-τω 'I hide' versus κρύβ-δην 'secretly'. Similarly, deaspiration before -s- occurs, as in γράφ-ω 'I write' versus γράψ-ω (i.e. *grap-s-o:*) 'I will write', and assimilation in aspiration to a following aspirate is found as in τρίβ-ω 'I rub' versus ἐ-τρίφ-θην 'I was rubbed' (cf. also τρίψ-ω 'I will rub').

The phonology of Ancient Greek has been described in such detail here because it provides the appropriate starting point for a discussion of Post-Classical Greek phonology. The relation is not merely chronological here, for in Post-Classical Greek and on into Modern Greek, one finds that many of the same general phonological characteristics occur in the language, but with different realisations. For example, by the Hellenistic period, systematic shifts in the consonant inventory were under way – to be completed later in Post-Classical Greek – which nonetheless preserved the earlier three-way contrast but with new distinctive oppositions established. The voiced stops became voiced spirants and the voiceless aspirates became voiceless spirants, while the voiceless plain stops remained the same (in general). Thus one finds in Post-Classical Greek the system:

v	p	f
ð	t	θ
γ	k	χ

replacing the earlier *b p pʰ/d t tʰ/g k kʰ* system. In addition, *z* became a distinctive sound (with phonemic status) and *h* was lost.

A [j] reentered the language, originally as an allophone of [γ] before front vowels and of unstressed [i] before vowels, but now it (probably) has phonemic status in the modern language and in any case is more fricated than the simple glide it presumably once was. Similarly, throughout the post-classical period, new voiced stops (*b, d, g*) arose, first as allophones of voiceless (and original voiced) stops after homorganic nasals, and later as distinctive segments (although their synchronic status is still somewhat controversial) through further sound changes that obscured the original conditioning factors. Thus the verb ἐντρέπομαι 'I feel misgivings about' has yielded Modern Greek ντρέπομαι [drɛpomɛ] 'I feel ashamed' through the stages *endrep-* > *edrep-* (with reduction of nasal-plus-stop clusters, a process still present in the standard language but now sociolinguistically and stylistically conditioned, and still found in many of the regional dialects) > *drep-* (with loss of unstressed initial vowels, a sound change of Middle Greek), though conceivably the sequence was *endrep-* > *ndrep-* > *ⁿdrep-* > *drep-*. In addition, borrowings have provided new instances of voiced stops in the language (e.g. more recently μπάρ 'bar', ντάμα 'queen (in cards)', γκαράζ 'garage', etc., but some even as early as Hellenistic times).

Finally, in Middle Greek a *ts* and a *dz* were added to the language, partly through dialectal affrications and borrowings from other languages. These sounds probably represent unitary sounds (affricates) in the modern language, but a cluster analysis cannot be ruled out entirely for them.

The major changes in the vowel system were also beginning in the Hellenistic period, though, as noted above, some of the innovative pronunciations may have been associated with an originally non-standard sociolect of Attic Greek in the late classical period. The principal changes are as follows: length became non-distinctive; the diphthongs monophthongised, with [aj] becoming [ɛ], [yj] and [oj] becoming [i] (presumably through a stage of [y], still present probably as late as the tenth century AD), and the off-glide in [e(:)w] and [aw] becoming fully consonantal, realised as [f] before voiceless sounds and as [v] before voiced ones; and several of the height distinctions were neutralised with a tendency for vowels to move to [i]. The result is that the Modern Greek vowel system (and that of late Middle Greek as well) consists of five short 'pure' vowels: *i e a o u*. Sequences which are diphthong-like, though perhaps still to be analysed as true sequences of vowels, have arisen through the loss of intervening consonants, as with λέει ([leï]) '(s)he says' from Ancient Greek λέγει through the Middle (and careful Modern) Greek pronunciation [léji], and through borrowings (e.g. τσάï 'tea', λαούτο 'lute', etc.). Nonetheless, there are some words that are probably best analysed as having underlying diphthongs, e.g. γάϊδαρος 'donkey', which would underlyingly violate the modern equivalent of the 'Dreimorengesetz' if it were /γáiδaros/.

Since the vowel length came to be non-distinctive in the later stages of Greek, it is not surprising that the principles upon which accent placement was based would change, inasmuch as vowel quantity mattered for Ancient Greek accent placement. Modern Greek generally has accent placed in the same positions in words as Ancient Greek, and the 'Dreimorengesetz' still holds now though as a 'three-syllable rule'. The realisation of accent has changed, though, and Modern Greek now has a stress accent, not a pitch accent, with prominent stress corresponding to the earlier high (acute or circumflex) pitch (and note that by Middle Greek, the basis for poetic metre was syllable counting, with a 15-syllable line being the preferred metrical pattern). Modern Greek thus has some of the same accent shifts as Ancient Greek, as for example in άνθρωπος 'man' (nominative singular) versus ανθρώπου (genitive), but because of the absence of a phonological motivation for them, numerous levellings have occurred, resulting in stable stress throughout a paradigm (as in πράσινος 'green' (nominative singular masculine) versus πράσινου (genitive) from Ancient Greek πράσινος/ πρασίνου, and in dialectal forms such as άνθρωπου for standard ανθρώπου). The recessive accent rule for finite verb forms no longer holds in general, but is valid for the simple past and imperfect tenses of verbs which are stem-stressed (as opposed to end-stressed) in the present (e.g. νομίζω 'I think' versus νόμιζα 'I was thinking', νομίζαμε 'we were thinking', νόμισα 'I thought', νομίσαμε 'we thought'). Stress placement, though, is distinctive, as shown by pairs such as κοπή 'cutting' – κόποι 'troubles, reward', κύριος 'master' – κυρίως 'above all, chiefly', among others.

The major change in phonotactics concerns new final sequences which have entered the language through borrowings (e.g. final [l] in γκόλ 'goal' from English, final [z] in γκαράζ 'garage' from French, final [p] in (the perhaps now somewhat dated) πίκ-απ 'record-player' from French, etc.). One noteworthy change in allowable clusters, though, affected combinations of voiceless stops and combinations of Ancient Greek voiceless aspirated stops. Both types of clusters, e.g. πτ and φθ, have converged, through what has been described as a manner dissimilation, on the combination of voiceless fricative plus voiceless (unaspirated) stop. Thus earlier πτ has yielded φτ [ft], as in πτερόν 'feather' > φτερό (with regular loss of final *n* as well), and earlier φθ has also yielded [ft], through a stage of [fθ], as in φθάνω > φτάνω 'I arrive'. The effects of the diglossia alluded to above can be seen especially clearly in this aspect of the phonology, for in many words of learned origin, the non-dissimilated clusters remain and both cluster types occur as stylistic variants within one and the same speaker's idiolect even, because of the stylistic mixing induced by the diglossic situation.

For the most part, the later stages of Greek preserved the same types of morphophonemic alternations as Ancient Greek, though again with different phonetic realisations. Thus one now finds alternations such as γράφ-ομε 'we write' versus γράψ-αμε 'we wrote' with an *f/p* alternation (Ancient Greek *pʰ/p* alternation), ανοίγ-ω 'I open' versus άνοιξ-α 'I opened' with a *γ/k* alternation (Ancient Greek *g/k* alternation), where the structure of the alternations is the same but the segments involved have changed in part. Various morphological changes in the noun in particular have undone many of the Ancient Greek nominal alternations, as with Ancient Greek φλέψ (i.e. [pʰlep-s]) 'vein' (nominative singular) versus φλέβα (accusative) being remade to a paradigm with φλέβα [fleva], the continuation of the old accusative form, serving as the nominative and accusative form. One can still find the Ancient Greek alternations preserved relatively intact, though, in the archaising linguistic forms of early Post-Classical Greek on through Middle Greek and into Modern Greek; such forms are not – and probably never were – in current colloquial usage, however.

A final point about Post-Classical Greek phonology concerns some of the major differences that characterise the Modern, and to a large extent the Middle, Greek dialects. Characteristic of the northern dialect zone (north of Attica on the mainland, though excluding the urban Thessaloniki dialect, and the islands of the northern Aegean including Thasos, Samothraki, Lemnos and Lesbos, and also the more southerly Samos) is the raising of unstressed mid vowels and the deletion of unstressed high vowels. Thus one finds paradigms such as present [pirmén] '(s)he waits' (cf. standard περιμένει), imperfect [pirímini] '(s)he was waiting' (cf. standard περίμενε). This syncope has also given rise in these dialects to consonant clusters not found in the standard language and the more southerly and eastern dialects (e.g. [éstla] 'I sent' for standard έστειλα). Another isogloss distinguishing the regional dialects is the presence of palatalisations (especially [č] for [k] before front vowels) in the southeastern dialects (of Chios, the Dodekanese islands including Rhodes, and Cyprus), in Cretan and in Old Athenian (the dialect of Attica before the establishment of the standard language in the 1820s, which survived into the early twentieth century in a few isolated pockets in Euboea and elsewhere), but not in the northern dialects (in general, though [š] for [s] before front vowels is common) nor in the standard language, based as it is on the Peloponnesian-Ionian (Island) dialect.

4.2 Morphology

It is safe to say that the general character of Greek morphological structure has remained fairly stable over the 3,500 years of our knowledge of the language, though, of course, there have been numerous significant changes as well. Greek has been a fusional language throughout all stages in its development; in Middle and Modern Greek, though, there is a distinct tendency in the direction of analytic expressions, examples of which are given below *passim*. To illustrate the fusional character of the language, one need only consider the nominal ending -ους (Ancient Greek [-oːs], Modern Greek [-us]), for it marks accusative case, plural number and masculine gender, all in a single unanalysable unit, for the so-called *o*-stem nouns. Moreover, even though there is a nominal ending -ου and another nominal ending -ς, so that one might attempt to analyse -ους as -ου plus -ς, such an analysis cannot work: -ου marks genitive singular for masculine *o*-stem nouns and -ς marks nominative singular for certain masculine and feminine consonant stem nouns in Ancient Greek and for masculine nouns in general in Modern Greek.

The relevant morphological categories for the Greek nominal system, comprising nouns, adjectives and pronouns, are as follows. In Ancient Greek, there were five cases (nominative, accusative, genitive, dative and vocative), three numbers (singular, dual and plural), and three genders (masculine, feminine and neuter). In Modern Greek, by contrast, there are four cases (nominative, accusative, genitive and vocative), two numbers (singular and plural), and the same three genders. The loss of the dative began as early as Hellenistic Greek, though this change was not completed until well into the Middle Greek era (in part because of the pressure from the learned language in which the dative was retained). In Modern Greek, the genitive case has assumed some of the typical functions of the earlier dative case, e.g. the expression of indirect objects, but one also finds, in keeping with the analytic tendency noted above, indirect objects expressed in a prepositional phrase (σ(έ) 'in, at, to', from Ancient Greek εἰς 'in, into', plus accusative). It is worth noting as well that the genitive plural is obsolescent in Modern Greek for many nouns and for many speakers, with periphrases with prepositions, especially ἀπό 'from', plus accusative generally being used instead.

In both Ancient and Modern Greek, these nominal morphological categories were realised in different ways depending on the class of noun involved. In Ancient Greek, the assignment to inflectional class was based on phonological characteristics of the nominal stem, so that one finds o-stem nouns, a:-stem nouns and consonant stem nouns (including i- and u-stems as consonantal); within these stem classes, all three genders were represented, though feminine o-stems were rare as were masculine a:-stems (and neuter a:-stems were non-existent). In Modern Greek, the assignment to inflectional class is by and large based on gender, not phonological stem shape, so that in general, the masculine nouns are inflected alike, especially in the singular, with -s in the nominative singular versus -∅ in the accusative singular and -∅ in the genitive singular, and the feminines are inflected alike, again especially in the singular, with a -∅ ending in the nominative and accusative singular versus -s in the genitive singular. As with most changes between Ancient and Modern Greek, the beginnings of this shift in inflectional class assignment can be seen early in the post-classical period. In the chart given here the inflection of six nouns is given for Ancient and Modern Greek by way of illustrating the basic patterns for these stages and of highlighting the differences between the two.

Nominal Inflection in Ancient and Modern Greek

		Feminine a:-*stem*	*Masculine* o-*stem*	*Neuter* o-*stem*	*Feminine*	*Masculine* Consonant stem	*Neuter*
		γνωμα:- 'opinion'	λόγο- 'word'	δῶρο- 'gift'	φλέβ- 'vein'	φύλακ- 'watchman'	σωματ- 'body'
Ancient Greek							
Nom.	sg.	γνώμη	λόγος	δῶρον	φλέψ	φύλαξ	σῶμα
Acc.	sg.	γνώμην	λόγον	δῶρον	φλέβα	φύλακα	σῶμα
Gen.	sg.	γνώμης	λόγου	δώρου	φλεβός	φύλακος	σώματος
Dat.	sg.	γνώμηι	λόγωι	δώρωι	φλεβί	φύλακι	σώματι
Voc.	sg.	γνώμη	λόγε	δῶρον	φλέψ	φύλαξ	σῶμα
Nom.	du.	γνώμα:	λόγω	δώρω	φλέβε	φύλακε	σώματε
Acc.	du.	γνώμα:	λόγω	δώρω	φλέβε	φύλακε	σώματε
Gen.	du.	γνώμαιν	λόγοιν	δώροιν	φλεβοῖν	φυλάκοιν	σωμάτοιν
Dat.	du.	γνώμαιν	λόγοιν	δώροιν	φλεβοῖν	φυλάκοιν	σωμάτοιν
Voc.	du.	γνώμα:	λόγω	δώρω	φλέβε	φύλακε	σώματε
Nom.	pl.	γνῶμαι	λόγοι	δῶρα	φλέβες	φύλακες	σώματα
Acc.	pl.	γνώμα:ς	λόγους	δῶρα	φλέβας	φύλακας	σώματα
Gen.	pl.	γνωμῶν	λόγων	δώρων	φλεβῶν	φυλάκων	σωμάτων
Dat.	pl.	γνώμαις	λόγοις	δώροις	φλεψί	φύλαξι	σώμασι
Voc.	pl.	γνῶμαι	λόγοι	δῶρα	φλέβες	φύλακες	σώματα

		Feminine	Masculine	Neuter	Feminine	Masculine	Neuter
Modern Greek							
Nom.	sg.	γνώμη	λόγος	δῶρο	φλέβα	φύλακας	σῶμα
Acc.	sg.	γνώμη	λόγο	δῶρο	φλέβα	φύλακα	σῶμα
Gen.	sg.	γνώμης	λόγου	δῶρου	φλέβας	φύλακα	σώματος
Voc.	sg.	γνώμη	λόγε	δῶρο	φλέβα	φύλακα	σῶμα
Nom.	pl.	γνώμες	λόγοι	δῶρα	φλέβες	φύλακες	σώματα
Acc.	pl.	γνώμες	λόγους	δῶρα	φλέβες	φύλακες	σώματα
Gen.	pl.	γνωμών	λόγων	δῶρων	φλεβών	φυλάκων	σωμάτων
Voc.	pl.	γνώμες	λόγοι	δῶρα	φλέβες	φύλακες	σώματα

Notes: Accentuation in Modern Greek forms follows current official monotonic orthography, with a single accentual diacritic. The colon (:) for length in the Ancient Greek forms is given here only to indicate pronunciation; it was not a part of the Ancient Greek orthography.

Although the nominal system of Greek, especially the ancient language, shows a goodly number of inflectional categories and markers, it is the verbal system that presents the greatest morphological complexity in the language. Moreover, despite a number of reductions in this complexity between Ancient and Modern Greek, especially in the realm of non-finite verbal forms, Modern Greek still has a verbal system that is, in basic character, very like its ancient source.

Ancient Greek, for instance, distinguished three persons in verbal inflection, and three numbers (singular, dual and plural), although the combination of first person with dual number was not generally realised inflectionally in the language at all (being restricted to a handful of middle voice forms only). A significant distinction was made in the verbal system between finite and non-finite forms, with the relevant morphological distinction for finiteness being the presence of person and number markings; as noted above in the section on accentuation, though, recessive accent placement also served to distinguish finite from non-finite forms. Among the non-finite forms were several different infinitives and several different participles, as enumerated below, differing in voice, aspect and tense, and two verbal adjectives (denoting capability and obligation, respectively).

As indicated, there were inflectional categories for voice, with active, passive and middle voice being distinguished. The middle voice indicated reflexive action (though there were also available in the language overt reflexive pronominal forms), or more generally, action one undertook on one's own behalf or to one's own benefit. For example, the active βουλεύω means 'to take counsel' while the middle βουλεύομαι means 'to take counsel with oneself, to deliberate', and the active λούω means 'to wash' while the middle λούομαι means 'to wash oneself, to bathe'. The passive was formally distinct from the middle only for future tense and simple past (aorist) forms. In addition, there were four moods, an indicative, a subjunctive, an optative (used in the expression of potentiality and for past time in indirect discourse, for example) and an imperative, all fully inflected for all the voice, number and person categories, as well as most of the temporal/aspectual categories described below.

Finally, Ancient Greek is usually described as having seven 'tenses', a present, a future, a (present) perfect, a pluperfect, a future perfect (which is usually passive), an imperfect past and a simple past (known as the aorist). In actuality, these 'tense' forms encoded two different types of distinctions – a purely temporal one of present time versus future time versus past time, and an aspectual one of action that is continuous (imperfective) versus action that is completed (perfective) versus action that is simply taking place (aoristic). The three-way distinction is realised fully in past time forms only, incompletely in the present, and via a formal merger of two categories in the future. These relations are summarised in Table 19.4 below (adapted from Goodwin and Gulick 1958).

Illustrative examples are: present γράφω 'I am writing', perfect γέγραφα 'I have written', imperfect ἔγραφον 'I was writing', aorist ἔγραψα 'I did write, I wrote', pluperfect ἐγεγράφη 'I had written', future γράψω 'I will be writing (continuous aspect), I will write (simple occurrence)', and future perfect γεγράψεται 'it will have been written'.

The non-finite forms show the aspectual nature of the category oppositions especially clearly, for one finds a present infinitive and participle, an aorist infinitive and participle, and a perfect infinitive and participle, corresponding to the continuous, simple and completed aspectual distinctions in the finite verbal system. In addition, though, there is a future infinitive and participle, so that the non-finite system too shows some purely temporal as well as aspectual distinctions. As with the different moods, the non-finite forms occur in all voices, so that there are 11 different infinitival types and a like number of participles.

Many of the complexities of this system are retained in Post-Classical Greek and on into Modern Greek, though in some instances, there is only apparent, and not actual, continuity. Some of the differences are the result of responses to system-internal pressures, as for example, with the changes in the voice and aspect categories, while others may have been, at least in part, induced by external factors, as with the changes in the non-finite system and the future tense. Many, however, are in keeping with a tendency towards analytic expressions where Ancient Greek had synthetic ones.

The only difference in person and number categories is that, as in nominal inflection, the dual number category has been eliminated, its demise evident as early as Hellenistic Greek. The moods too have been altered. The optative began to fall into disuse in the Koine period, partly as a result, no doubt, of sound changes leading to partial homophony (in four of eight forms) with the subjunctive and (less so) with the indicative. Similarly, it is a matter of some debate even today as to whether Greek now has a distinct subjunctive mood, for there is no formal difference between the continuation of the old present indicative and present subjunctive due to various sound changes, and virtually all 'subjunctive' uses are marked with the element νά, giving an analytic counterpart to the Ancient Greek synthetic subjunctive (e.g. να γράψεις versus ancient γράψῃις 'that you (might) write'). Finally, where Ancient Greek had synthetic forms for non-second person imperatives, Modern Greek has, again, analytic forms, marked by the particle ἄς, though distinct (synthetic) second person imperative forms remain.

Table 19.4 Ancient Greek Tense Aspect Relations

Aspect \ Tense	Present	Past	Future
Continuous	present	imperfect	future
Simple occurrence	(no realisation)	aorist	future
Completed	perfect	pluperfect	future perfect

Post-Classical Greek maintains an opposition among active, middle and passive voices, though from a formal standpoint, the middle voice and passive voice are never distinct; the cover term medio-passive or even nonactive is thus perhaps more appropriate. This development seems to be a natural outgrowth of the Ancient Greek system in which the distinction was realised formally only in the aorist and future tenses but in no others. Thus in Modern Greek, and earlier stages of Post-Classical Greek as well, a form such as πλύθηκα, a medio-passive aorist of the verb πλύνω 'wash', can mean 'I was washed (by someone)' or 'I washed myself', with the context of the utterance generally being the only determinant of which of these interpretations is preferred.

The Ancient Greek tenses all remain in Modern Greek, but here the continuity is apparent only. In the Koine period, the perfect tense system was eliminated, with the simple past (aorist) taking over some of the old perfect functions and various peri-phrastic (i.e. analytic) constructions (e.g. εἰμί 'be' plus the perfect participle) taking over other of its functions. Thus there was a period in the post-classical language in which there was no formal perfect tense system. By the middle of the Middle Greek period, approximately the tenth century, though, a pluperfect arose, formed with the aorist of 'have' plus one continuation of the Ancient Greek infinitive (e.g. εἶχα γράψαι 'I had written', later εἶχα γράψει); this construction was originally used, in late Hellenistic and early Middle Greek, as a conditional but later passed over into a true pluperfect meaning. The relation between it and the *habeō* + infinitive/participle for-mations found in Vulgar Latin and Romance (see page 168) is uncertain, but some influence through Balkan Romance cannot be discounted. From that pluperfect, a new perfect system, with the full range of inflectional categories, was spawned; a present perfect was created consisting of the present of 'have' plus this continuation of the old infinitive, and later a future perfect was formed with the Middle and Modern Greek future formants, an imperative perfect arose, etc. The Modern Greek perfect system, therefore, represents a considerable elaboration within the Post-Classical Greek verbal system, and though only indirectly connected with them, parallels the Ancient Greek perfect system forms.

Similarly, Modern Greek has a future tense, just as Ancient Greek had, but again one finds an analytic expression in place of the earlier synthetic one, with only an indirect connection between the two forms. In the case of the future, though, as opposed to the perfect, there seems never to have been a period in which the future tense failed to exist as a formal category in the language. Within the Hellenistic period, the use of the older synthetic future, e.g. γράψω 'I will write', became obsolescent, with various peri-phrases arising to compete with it, including the present of 'have' plus a continuation of the infinitive and other quasi-modal constructions (e.g. μέλλω 'be about to' plus infinitive). With the passage of the 'have' forms into the incipient perfect system, as just described, a new future periphrasis arose, by the tenth century, completely ousting the earlier synthetic form. This was a future based on the verb 'want' (θέλω); as with the perfect, the relation between this form and similar ones found in virtually all the Balkan languages is controversial. In the medieval period, an unusual variety of future formations with this verb can be found, consisting of combinations of inflected forms of θέλω plus uninflected (infinitival) main verbs, uninflected (i.e. invariant third person singular) forms of θέλω plus inflected forms of main verbs, inflected forms of θέλω plus inflected forms of a main verb, the optional use of the subordinating marker νά and so forth; representative examples of these patterns would be θέλω γράψει(ν) (infinitive), θέλει (invariant) (νὰ) γράψω, θέλω (νὰ) γράψω, all meaning 'I will write'. Ultimately, the formation of the type θέλει (νὰ) γράψω won out, and through various reductions involving regular sound changes and various analogies, the modern standard and widespread dialectal future marker θα (e.g. θα γράψω 'I will write') was created.

Going along with these future formations were parallel conditional formations consisting of a past tense of the auxiliary-like verb plus a form of the main verb (compare the ἔχω 'have' plus infinitive future and εἶχα plus infinitive conditional of early Post-Classical Greek). These conditional formations have no formal category correspondent in Ancient Greek (the modal particle ἄν with the optative mood is the Ancient Greek potential/conditional expression), so that here too one finds an elaboration within the earlier tense/mood system.

The aspectual system too has undergone various rearrangements from the Ancient Greek system. In this case, the internal pressures within the system, partly as a result of the incomplete realisation of the aspect system within the tense system (see Table 19.4) were a major factor in the developments. The basic opposition of continuous versus punctual aspect has been maintained throughout the development of Post-Classical Greek and, with the new periphrastic formations, has been extended to the future tense as well (e.g. θα γράφω 'I will be writing' versus θα γράψω 'I will write', in Modern Greek, or θέλω γράφει(ν) versus θέλω γράψει(ν) in Middle Greek). The completed aspect category now finds expression in the new perfect system, though one can still find uses of the simple past (aorist) which signal completed action as opposed to simply past action, as with the 'pro futuro' use of the aorist (e.g. ἔφυγα 'I'm about to leave' lit. 'I (have) left; my leaving is over and done with').

Finally, Modern Greek, as well as Post-Classical Greek in general, maintains the Ancient Greek distinction of finite versus non-finite forms, though this opposition has undergone perhaps the greatest series of restructurings of any part of the verbal system. In particular, the realisation of the opposition has changed considerably. In Ancient Greek the imperative patterned with the finite forms in terms of accent placement and person/number markings, while in Modern Greek it patterns instead with the non-finite forms; like the participles (and unlike, for example, the indicative), the imperative allows only postposed weak object pronouns and not preposed ones, and like the participles (and again unlike the indicative), it is arguably marked only for number and not for person (cf. singular δές '(you (alone)) see!' versus plural δέσ-τε '(you (all)) see!' where the only formal difference is -∅ versus -τε and the only semantic difference singular versus plural) – recall that non-second person imperative forms of Ancient Greek gave way to analytic expressions with the marker ας in later Greek. Moreover, the number of participles has been reduced, so that Modern Greek has only a present (continuous aspect) medio-passive participle (e.g. γραφόμενος 'being written') and a present (continuous aspect) active participle, also called a gerundive, which generally serves only as an adverbial adjunct modifying the surface subject of a sentence (e.g. γράφοντας '(while) writing').

Similarly, the category of *infinitive* has been eliminated entirely from the language, although the indications are that it was maintained until approximately the sixteenth century as at least a marginal category. The details of this development are discussed more in the following section on syntax. The only remnant of the earlier infinitive is in the new perfect system, for the second part of the perfect periphrasis (γράψει in ἔχω γράψει 'I have written') continues a Middle Greek analogical replacement for the Ancient Greek aorist infinitive (so also in the medio-passive, e.g. ἔχει γραφθεῖ 'it has

been written' from Middle Greek ἔχει γραφθῆν(αι)). There is no synchronic justification, though, for treating these remnants as categorically distinct within the morphology, and they perhaps are to be considered now as the punctual aspect counterparts to
the continuous aspect participles (thus γράψει versus γραφθεῖ as γράφοντας versus
γραφόμενος). In both the case of the reduction of the participle and the case of the
demise of the infinitive, the Modern Greek situation represents the end-point of a long
and gradual process whose roots are to be found in Hellenistic Greek usage of the
non-finite forms.

4.3 Syntax

A considerable amount of space has been spent on the phonology and morphology of
Greek, both from a synchronic standpoint for relevant periods and from a diachronic
standpoint, in part because it is possible to give a fairly complete picture of these
components of a language in a relatively short space. With regard to the syntax, it is of
course impossible to do justice to any stage of the language in anything less than a full-
sized monograph (and it is worth noting that there are numerous lengthy works dealing
with individual constructions in single periods of the language). Nonetheless, a few of
the especially noteworthy aspects of the syntactic combinations of the language can be
mentioned, along with a sketch of their development over the centuries.

Perhaps one of the most elaborate parts of the Ancient Greek syntactic system was
the system of verbal complementation. Not only were there so many non-finite forms –
infinitives and participles – available which were utilised in forming complements to
main verbs, but there were also a goodly number of finite forms, differing, as has been
described, in aspect and mood, which could combine with a variety of subordinating
conjunctions to form verbal complements. Thus a major part of the description of
Ancient Greek syntax must deal with the question of how the moods, aspects and non-
finite forms were actually used. Not surprisingly, there is a fairly complex set of sequence
of tense conditions governing allowable combinations of main verb and dependent verb,
especially in indirect discourse and in conditional sentences.

One significant development in the verbal complementation system in later stages of
Greek is the demise of the infinitive, mentioned above in its purely morphological
context. From as early as Hellenistic Greek, finite clause complements can be found in
places in which Classical Greek had used an infinitive (or even participle). For example, in the New Testament, a finite clause complement competes with an infinitival
complement with the adjective ἄξιος 'worthy, deserving', a context in which only an
infinitive could appear in Classical Greek:

(a) οὗ   οὐκ εἰμὶ ἄξιος τὸ ὑπόδημα τῶν ποδῶν λῦσαι
(Acts 13.25)
whose not am/1sg. worthy the-sandal the-feet/gen. loosen/infin.
'(One) of whom I am not worthy to loosen the sandal from his feet'

(b) οὗ οὐκ εἰμὶ ἐγὼ ἄξιος ἵνα λύσω αὐτοῦ τὸν ἱμάντα τοῦ ὑποδήματος
(Jo. 1.27)
I/nom.   that loosen/ his   the-thong/acc. of-the-sandal
1sg. subj.

The spread of finite complementation, most usually introduced by the subordinating conjunction ἵνα (later Greek νά through an irregular stress shift and regular sound changes) but also with the true complementisers such as the neutral ὅτι (comparable to English *that*), at the expense of infinitival complements continued throughout the post-classical era, working its way through syntactically defined classes of construction type (e.g. like-subject complements versus unlike-subject complements) and within each such class diffusing across the range of governing lexical items. By Middle Greek, the only productive uses of the infinitive were with the verbs ἔχω and θέλω in the perfect and future periphrases, respectively, though a few sporadic uses of the infinitive with other verbs (e.g. (ἠ)μπορῶ 'can') and as an adverbial adjunct are to be found as well.

The spread of finite complementation is complete, though, in Modern Greek, and there are no instances of non-finite complementation remaining. Thus from the standpoint of typology, Modern Greek, unlike its predecessors, is a language in which all complement verbs are fully finite, marked for person, number and tense/aspect. Greek thus now diverges considerably from the Indo-European 'norm', but interestingly, as noted earlier, converges on this point with the other languages of the Balkans; in fact, Greek, along with Macedonian, shows the greatest degree of infinitive loss among all the Balkan languages. As with the other Balkan areal features, the extent to which the developments with the infinitive represent an internal development in Greek (and the other languages) or a contact-induced one is debated; in this case, a combination of internal and external factors seems to provide the best account for this phenomenon within each language, Greek included, and within the Balkans as a whole.

It is to be noted, moreover, that the replacement of the infinitive by finite expressions with a verbal marker ties in with the general trend towards analytic constructions seen in the morphology. Other syntactic reflexes of this move towards analysis include comparison productively via the particle πιό with an adjective in Modern Greek versus a bound suffix -τερος in Ancient Greek (e.g. ἀξιώτερος 'more worthy' > πιό ἄξιος), and the expression of indirect objects with a prepositional phrase (σ(ε) plus accusative) versus the Ancient Greek dative case alone.

The developments with the moods and the tenses and the infinitive between Ancient and Modern Greek show also a trend towards the development of a system of preverbal markers, especially, for the future θά, for the subjunctive and infinitival replacement νά, and for non-second person imperatives ας (from earlier ἄφησε 'let', itself an imperative). A further reflection of this development is to be seen in the pronominal system of Modern Greek as compared with that of Ancient Greek. While Ancient Greek had both strong forms of the personal pronouns and weak forms, the weak forms were restricted to the oblique (non-nominative) cases only, and use of the weak genitive forms in the expression of possession was somewhat limited; true possessive adjectives were substitutable for the weak forms in all persons and numbers and were the preferred variant in the first and second person plural. In Modern Greek, by contrast, there is now a set of nominative weak pronominal forms (though they are restricted just to the third person and just to use with the deictic predicate νά 'here (is)!' and the interrogative predicate πού(ν) 'where (is)?'), and the primary means of expressing possession is with weak genitive forms of the personal pronouns for all persons and numbers. Thus in Ancient Greek one finds both ὁ σὸς ἀδελφός (lit. 'the your brother') and ὁ ἀδελφός σου (lit. 'the brother of you') for 'your brother', while Modern Greek has only the latter type.

Similarly, the weak object pronouns (both accusative and genitive) of Ancient Greek have been expanded in use in Modern Greek. In particular, they are now quite commonly used to cross-index definite and specific objects, as in:

(a) τον   είδα   τον Γιάννη
     him/acc. clit. saw/1 sg.   the-John/acc.
     'I see John.'

(b) του   (το)   έδωσα   του Γιάννη   το βιβλίο
     him/gen. clit. it/acc. clit. gave/1 sg.   the-John/gen. the-book/acc.
     'I gave the book to John.'

This feature represents another way in which Modern Greek diverges from Ancient Greek in the direction of the other Balkan languages (though again the causes for the divergence and convergence are subject to debate). For some speakers of Greek, this pronominal doubling is obligatory at least for indirect objects, while for others it is an optional process with an emphatic function.

All of these preverbal markers are amenable to analysis as prefixes (and not more independent elements), though this is controversial. Under such an analysis, the grammatical apparatus of the modern language has expanded considerably and the nature of the grammatical marking has changed from that found in earlier stages.

Two relatively stable elements of the syntax of Greek over the centuries are to be found in the syntax of the nominal system – the use of the definite article and adjectival position. The development of a definite article took place within the history of Greek, for in Homeric Greek, the form which became the Classical definite article is generally used as a demonstrative pronoun, and a few traces of this usage survive in the classical language. The definite article in classical times came to be used also as a means of substantivising virtually any part of speech or phrasal category, including adverbs (e.g. τοῖς τότε 'to the (men) of that time' (lit. 'the (dat. pl. masc.) then'), infinitives, whether alone or in a verb phrase (e.g. τὸ δρᾶν 'the acting, action', τὸ βίαι πολίτων δρᾶν 'acting in defiance of citizens'), and so on. Moreover, virtually any type of modifier, whether adverb, prepositional phrase, noun phrase or adjective, could be placed between the article and a modified noun. This construction with the definite article and modified nominals is to be found throughout the history of Greek, so that in Modern Greek in place of the 'articular infinitive' one finds nominalised finite clauses (e.g. το να είναι Έλληνας 'the (fact of) being a Greek'), extended prenominal modifiers (though these can have a bookish feel, e.g. ὁ μορφομένος στό Παρίσι γειτονάς μου 'my educated-in-Paris neighbour'), etc.

As just noted, adjectives could in Ancient Greek, and still can in Modern Greek, appear prenominally. Throughout the history of Greek, there has been an important contrast in the position of an adjective based on its function. An adjective standing outside the article had, and still has, a predicative function, determining a clause without the necessity for an overt copular verb, e.g.:

(a) καλὸς   ὁ ἀδελφός   (b)   ὁ ἀδελφὸς καλός
     good (nom. sg. m.)   the-brother (nom. sg.)
     'The brother is good.'

When the adjective occurs between the article and the noun or if no article is present, then the adjective has attributive function, and a noun phrase is determined:

(a) ὁ καλὸς ἀδελφός   (b) καλὸς ἀδελφός
     'the good brother'   'a good brother'

For the most part, other aspects of Greek word order have remained more or less stable throughout its development. In particular Greek has always enjoyed a relatively free ordering of the major constituents of a sentence, with grammatical relations and relations among constituents being encoded in the inflectional morphology, although certain patterns seem to be preferred in particular contexts (e.g. verb–subject–object order in the modern language in sentences presenting wholly new information). One area of difference, however, is in the placement of weak object pronouns, which were positioned relative to the clause in Ancient Greek (generally in second position) but are now positioned relative to the verb (with finiteness of the verb apparently mattering for pre- versus post-positioning).

4.4 Lexicon

At all points in its history, the Greek lexicon has incorporated a large number of native (inherited) lexical roots and stems. As noted earlier, some of these have remained more or less intact over the years, e.g. ἄνεμος 'wind', ἄλλος 'other'; more usually, though, words in Modern Greek show the effects of regular sound changes, e.g. γράφω 'I write' (with [γ] and [f] for earlier [g] and [pʰ]), μέρα 'day' (Ancient Greek ἡμέρα), changes in form and meaning, e.g. χῶμα 'bank, mound (Ancient Greek); soil (Modern)' and morphological reshapings (e.g. φύλακας versus φύλαξ – see the chart of nominal inflection). Finally, many words in the later language are built up out of native elements but with no direct ancestor in the ancient language, e.g. πιστοποίηση 'guarantee', and the many modern scientific terms built out of Greek morphemes by non-Greek speakers and reborrowed back into Greek, e.g. ατμοσφαίρα 'atmosphere'.

At the same time, though, there has always been also in Greek a significant number of foreign elements. Ancient loans from Semitic (e.g. χιτών 'tunic', σαγήνη 'large drag-net'), Anatolian (e.g. κύανος 'dark blue enamel', κύμβαχος 'crown of a helmet'), and other languages of the ancient Near East can be identified, and as noted in Section 2 above, there may be numerous words in Ancient Greek taken over from the languages indigenous to Greece before the arrival of the Greeks proper. During the Hellenistic period, a major source of loanwords into Greek was Latin. During the later periods, one finds first an influx of Venetian (Italian) words and somewhat later an admixture of some Slavonic and Albanian words but mainly Turkish lexical items and phrases. More recently, loans from French and especially English have entered the language in great numbers. One final important source of borrowings in Greek has always been Greek itself; due to the long literary record of the language and the importance placed from a sociolinguistic standpoint on the literary language (recall the discussion of Greek diglossia in Section 2), there has always been pressure to borrow from the literary language into the colloquial language, so that Modern Greek now has an internal lexical stratification parallel to what is found in Slavonic or Romance.

Bibliography

With the possible exception of English, there has probably been more written on the Greek language than on any other language. Consequently, giving references for information on Greek in its various aspects is difficult. Nonetheless, it is possible to identify a number of basic and representative works on the language.

Mention must be made first of the monumental comprehensive encyclopedic volume covering the history of the language up through ancient times, Christides 2007.

Specifically for the Ancient language, grammars abound, and the most detailed available, though a bit difficult to use because of a somewhat odd arrangement of facts, is Schwyzer (1939) and Schwyzer and Debrunner (1950). This work, moreover, contains much information on the historical development of the language and on the ancient dialects. For practical purposes, the more pedagogically oriented grammars of Smyth (1920) or Goodwin and Gulick (1958) contain sufficient information for the understanding of the structure of the language. Vilborg (1960) offers a grammatical sketch of Mycenaean Greek, as does Ventris and Chadwick (1973). More specialised works include Lejeune (1972) (on the historical phonology in general, including Mycenaean), Sommerstein (1973) (a generative treatment of Attic phonology), Teodorsson (1974) (also on Attic phonology), Chantraine (1973) (on the morphology, especially diachronically), and Rijksbaron (2002) (on the syntax and semantics of the verb). The basic treatment in English of the dialects is Buck (1955).

For the Hellenistic period, the best grammars available are Moulton (1908) and Blass and Debrunner (1961), both of which deal primarily with New Testament Greek.

For Greek of the Byzantine and Medieval periods, unfortunately no standard grammar is currently available. Perhaps the best general statements on Greek of that period are the (relatively brief) description found in Browning (1982) and the somewhat more comprehensive Tonnet (1993) and Horrocks (1997). Note also specialised studies such as Pappas (2003) on weak pronouns in the Medieval period. More is available on the modern language, and many of the historically oriented works fill in some of the gaps in the literature on Middle Greek. Mirambel (1939, 1959) are standard structuralist treatments of Modern Greek, and Householder et al. (1964) provides a useful account in English. More recently, there are general grammatical descriptions, following modern linguistic principles, such as Joseph and Philippaki-Warburton (1987) and Holton et al. (1997), and two large dictionaries, by Babiniotis (1998) and by the Triandafilidi Instituto (1998). Though now a bit outdated, however, Thumb (1964) is the best general work available in English, providing much on the dialects and general historical development of Modern Greek. as well as numerous sample texts. Newton (1972) is a study within the generative framework of Greek dialect phonology, including, to a certain extent, the dialect bases of the standard language, and Tzitzilis (2007) offers a fine survey of the different dialects of the modern language. Warburton (1970) and Sotiropoulos (1972) provide a modern treatment of the verb and noun respectively. As yet there is no full-length generative study of Greek syntax and semantics, though there is a growing body of such literature (especially in the pages of the *Journal of Greek Linguistics*, where other relevant studies are to be found as well; see Kalmoukos and Phillipaki-Warburton (1982) for some references, many in English, and Alexiadou and Anagnostopoulou 2000 for an updated survey). Joseph 2000 offers an annotated bibliography of important works in Greek linguistics written in English up to the mid-1990s.

Finally, there are several general surveys of the Greek language, covering all or most of the stages in its development. Meillet (1920) and Palmer (1980) focus more on the earlier stages, though both treat Middle and Modern Greek as well. Browning (1982) focuses primarily on the later stages, but gives the necessary background on the early stages too. Mention can also be made of Costas (1936), Atkinson (1933), Thomson (1966) and Householder and Nagy (1972).

Note

1 Greek forms are cited throughout in the Greek alphabet. See Table 19.1 for the pronounciation of the letters.

References

Alexiadou, A. and Anagnostopoulou, E. 2000. 'Greek Syntax: A Principles and Parameters Perspective', *Journal of Greek Linguistics*, vol. 1, pp. 171–222

Atkinson, B.F.C. 1933. *The Greek Language* (Faber and Faber, London)

Babiniotis. G. 1998. *Λεξικό της νέας ελληνικής γλώσσας*. Athens: Kendro Leksilogias

Blass, F. and Debrunner, A. 1961. *A Greek Grammar of the New Testament and Other Early Christian Literature* (Cambridge University Press, Cambridge; translated and revised by R. Funk from the 9th–10th edn of *Grammatik des neutestamentlichen Griechisch*, Vandenhoeck and Ruprecht, Göttingen)

Browning, R. 1982. *Medieval and Modern Greek* (Cambridge University Press, Cambridge)

Buck, C.D. 1955. *The Greek Dialects*, revised edn (University of Chicago Press, Chicago, reprinted 1973)

Chantraine, P. 1973. *Morphologie historique du grec*, 2nd edn (Klincksieck, Paris)

Christides, A.-Ph. (ed.) 2007. *History of the Greek Language: From the Beginnings to Late Antiquity* (Cambridge University Press, Cambridge)

Costas, P. 1936. *An Outline of the History of the Greek Language with Particular Emphasis on the Koine and the Subsequent Periods* (reprinted by Ares Publishers, Chicago, 1979)

Goodwin, W. and Gulick, C. 1958. *Greek Grammar* (Blaisdell, Waltham, MA)

Holton, D., Mackridge, P. and Philippaki-Warburton, I. 1997. *Greek: A Comprehensive Grammar of the Modern Language* (Routledge, London)

Horrocks, G. 1997. *Greek. A History of the Language and its Speakers* (Longman, London)

Householder, F. and Nagy, G. 1972. *Greek. A Survey of Recent Work* (Mouton, The Hague)

Householder, F., Kazazis, K. and Koutsoudas, A. 1964. *Reference Grammar of Literary Dhimotiki* (Mouton, The Hague)

Joseph, B. 2000. 'Selected Titles on Language and Linguistics', in S. Constantinidis (ed.) *Greece in Modern Times (An Annotated Bibliography of Works Published in English in 22 Academic Disciplines during the Twentieth Century)* (Scarecrow Press, Lanham, MD), pp. 441–74

Joseph, B. and Philippaki-Warburton, I. 1987. *Modern Greek* (Croom Helm, London)

Kalmoukos, X. and Philippaki-Warburton, I. 1982. 'Βιβλιογραφικό σημείωμα των εργασιών σχετικά με την σύνταξη και την μορφολογία της Νέας Ελληνικής που έχουν εκπονηθεί κατά το πρότυπο της γενετικής μετασχηματιστικής γραμματικής' ('Bibliographic Notice of Works Concerning the Syntax and Morphology of Modern Greek which have been Produced According to the Model of Generative-Transformational Grammar'), *Mantatoforos*, vol. 20, pp. 8–17

Lejeune, M. 1972. *Phonétique historique du mycénien et du grec ancien* (Klincksieck, Paris)

Meillet, A. 1920. *Aperçu d'une histoire de la langue grecque*, 2nd edn (Hachette, Paris)

Mirambel, A. 1939. *Précis de grammaire élémentaire du grec moderne* (Société d'Édition 'Les Belles Lettres', Paris)

——1959. *La Langue grecque moderne: description et analyse* (Paris)

Moulton, J. 1908. *A Grammar of N.T. Greek* (T. and T. Clark, Edinburgh)

Newton, B. 1972. *The Generative Interpretation of Dialect: A Study of Modern Greek Phonology* (Cambridge University Press, Cambridge)

Palmer, L. 1980. *The Greek Language* (Humanities Press, Atlantic Heights, NJ)

Pappas, P. 2003. *Variation and Morphosyntactic Change in Greek. From Clitics to Affixes* (Palgrave Macmillan, Houndmills)

Rijksbaron, A. 2002. *The Syntax and Semantics of the Verb in Classical Greek: An Introduction*, 3rd edn (University of Chicago Press, Chicago)

Schwyzer, E. 1939. *Griechische Grammatik, I: Lautlehre, Wortbildung, Flexion* (C.H. Beck, Munich)

Schwyzer, E. and Debrunner, A. 1950. *Griechische Grammatik, 2: Syntax und syntaktische Stilistik* (C.H. Beck, Munich)

Smyth, H. 1920. *A Greek Grammar for Colleges* (American Book Co., New York)

Sommerstein, A. 1973. *The Sound Pattern of Ancient Greek* (Basil Blackwell, Oxford)

Sotiropoulos, D. 1972. *Noun Morphology of Modern Demotic Greek* (Mouton, The Hague)

Teodorsson, S.-T. 1974. *The Phonemic System of the Attic Dialect, 400–340 BC* (= Studia Graeca et Latina Gothoburgensia XXXVI, Göteborg)

Thomson, G. 1966. *The Greek Language*, 2nd edn (Heffer, Cambridge)

Thumb, A. 1964. *A Handbook of the Modern Greek Language: Grammar, Texts, Glossary* (Argonaut, Chicago; translated from the 2nd edn of *Handbuch der neugriechischen Volkssprache. Grammatik. Texte. Glossar*, Karl I. Trübner, Strassburg)

Tonnet, H. 1993. *Histoire du grec moderne. La formation d'une langue* (Éditions L'Asiathèque, Paris)

Triandafilidi Instituto. 1998. *Λεξικό της κοινής νεοελληνικής* (Idrima Manoli Triandafilidi, Thessaloniki)

Tzitzilis, C. (ed.) 2007. *Handbook of Modern Greek Dialects* (Centre for the Greek Language, Thessaloniki)

Ventris, M. and Chadwick, J. 1973. *Documents in Mycenaean Greek*, 2nd edn (Cambridge University Press, Cambridge)

Vilborg, E. 1960. *A Tentative Grammar of Mycenaean Greek* (= Studia Graeca et Latina Gothoburgensia IX, Göteborg)

Warburton, I. 1970. *On the Verb in Modern Greek* (Mouton, The Hague)

20

Indo-Aryan Languages

George Cardona

Revised by Silvia Luraghi

1 Introduction

Indo-Aryan languages, the easternmost group within Indo-European, are spoken by approximately five hundred million persons in India, Pakistan, Bangladesh, Nepal and other parts of the Himalayan region, as well as in Sri Lanka. Gypsy (Romany) dialects of the USSR, the Middle East and North America are also of Indo-Aryan origin. Indo-Aryan is most closely related to Iranian, with which it forms the Indo-Iranian subgroup, speakers of which shared linguistic and cultural features, including a name they called themselves (Sanskrit *ārya-*, Avestan *airya-*). Among the innovations that characterise Indo-Iranian is the merger of Proto-Indo-European ĕ, ŏ, ă into ă: Skt. *asti* 'is' *pati-* 'master, husband', *ajati* 'leads', *dadhāti* 'puts, makes', *dadāti* 'gives', *mātr̥-* 'mother': Av. *asti, paiti-, azaiti, dadāiti* ('puts, makes, gives'), *mātar-*: Gk. *estí, pósis, ágei, títhēsi, dídōsi, mátēr* (Dor.). Two major phonological features distinguish Indo-Aryan from the rest of Indo-European, including Iranian. One of these is an inherited property: Indo-Aryan retains voiced aspirated stops, as in Skt. *gharma-* 'warmth', *dadhāti, bharati* 'carries'. The other is an innovation: Indo-Aryan languages distinguish dental and retroflex stops. Originally, retroflex *-ḍ-, -ḍh-* arose through sound changes, as in Skt. *nīḍa-* 'resting place, nest', *mīḍha-* 'reward', with *-īḍ-, -īḍh-* from *-iẓḍ-, iẓḍh-* (< *-izd-, -izdh-*). Such developments resulted in contrastive retroflex stops, albeit restricted, and the compass of such consonants was extended through borrowings from Dravidian languages. Most Indo-Aryan languages still have voiced aspirates and retroflex stops, although in certain ones, abutting on non-Indo-Aryan languages, these contrasts have been reduced: Sinhalese (Sinhala) has no aspirated stops, Kashmiri lacks voiced aspirates and Assamese (Asamiya) has no retroflex stops.

Old Indo-Aryan is represented in numerous sources (see Chapter 21). The earliest preserved Middle Indo-Aryan documents are Aśoka's edicts (third century BC), in various dialects. Middle Indo-Aryan languages were also used for other literary, philosophical and religious works. The Buddhist canon and later treatises of Theravada Buddhism are in Pāli, the Jaina canon in Ardhamāgadhī; Jainas also used Jaina Māhārāṣṭrī and Śaurasenī in works. The literary exemplar of Middle Indo-Aryan, however, is Māhārāṣṭrī and the most advanced stages of Middle Indo-Aryan developments are found in Apabhraṁśa dialects, used as literary vehicles from before the sixth century. All Middle Indo-Aryan varieties can be subsumed under the label Prakrit (Skt. *prākṛta* Pkt. *pāia*- 'stemming from the original, natural'), referring to vernaculars in contrast to the polished language called *saṁskṛta*. Traditionally, most Indian commentators and grammarians of Prakrits derive these from Sanskrit, but there are formations in Prakrits found in Vedic sources but not in Classical Sanskrit. Thus, as Classical Sanskrit is not derivable from a single attested Vedic dialect, so the Prakrits cannot be derived from Classical Sanskrit. In the present sketch, I use *Prakrit* in a narrow sense, of Middle Indo-Aryan languages other than Aśokan dialects, Pāli or Apabhraṁśa. There are abundant literary sources for New Indo-Aryan languages from the twelfth century on, some materials from earlier times.

Several scripts have been and currently are used for Indo-Aryan languages. In ancient times, two major scripts were used on the subcontinent: Kharoṣṭhī written from right to left, was predominantly used in the north-west, Brāhmī, written from left to right, elsewhere. Most scripts used for Indo-Aryan languages stem from Brāhmī, including Devanāgarī (see Chapter 21, Section 2), widely employed for Sanskrit and now the official script for Hindi, Marathi, Nepali. The Arabic script, with modifications, is used for some Indo-Aryan languages, including Urdu.

2 Phonological and Grammatical Developments

In the following, I sketch major phonological and grammatical developments that characterise Middle and New Indo-Aryan, using Old Indo-Aryan as a point of reference (see Chapter 21, Sections 1.2 and 2).

2.1 Phonology

In Middle Indo-Aryan, word-final consonants other than -*m*, which developed to -*ṁ* with shortening of a preceding vowel, were lost: Skt. *putrāt* (abl. sg.) 'son', *putrās* (nom. pl.), *putram* (acc. sg.): Pāli *puttā*, *puttaṁ*. Interior clusters of dissimilar consonants were generally eliminated through assimilation (as in *puttā*) or epenthesis: Skt. *sakthi*- 'thigh', *varga*- 'group', *agni* 'fire', *śukla*- 'white', *pakva*- 'cooked, ripe', *satya*- 'true', *adya* 'today': Pāli *satthi*-, *vagga*-, with assimilation of the first consonant to the second, *aggi*-, *sukka*-, *pakka*-, with the second consonant assimilated to the first, and *sacca*-, *ajja*-, with palatalisation; similarly, Skt. *rājñā* (inst. sg.) 'king', *rājñas* (gen. sg.): *rāññā*, *rāñño* in the Girnār version of Aśoka's first rock edict, but *lājinā*, *lājine*, with epenthesis, in the Jaugaḍa version. Generally, a nasal remains unassimilated before an obstruent: Skt. Pāli *danta*- 'tooth'. Metathesis applies in clusters of *h* with nasals or *y*, *v*: Skt. *cihna*- 'mark', *sahya*- 'to be endured', *jihvā*- 'tongue': Pāli *cinha*-, *sayha*-, *jivhā*-. Clusters of voiceless spirants with obstruents develop to obstruent sequences with aspiration: Skt. *paścāt* 'afterwards', *hasta*- 'hand': Pāli *pacchā*, *hattha*-. Further, clusters with voiceless spirants and nasals show voice assimilation and metathesis, resulting in nasals followed by *h*: Skt. *tṛṣṇā*- 'thirst, longing': Pāli *taṇhā*-. Initial clusters changed in the same ways, with subsequent simplification: Skt. *prathama*- 'first', *tyajati* 'abandons', *skandha*- 'shoulder', *snāti* 'bathes': Pāli *paṭhama*-, *cajati*, *khandha*-, *nhāyati*. In compounds and preverb-verb combinations where the assimilated cluster was intervocalic, it was retained, resulting in alternations such as Pāli *pamāṇa* 'measure':

appamāṇa- 'without measure, endless' (Skt. *pramāṇa-, apramāṇa-*). In early Middle Indo-Aryan, word-internal single consonants were retained, as shown in examples cited. Later, as exemplified in Māhārāṣṭrī, non-labial non-retroflex unaspirated obstruents were generally deleted, and *p, b* changed to *v: loa-* 'world, people', *naa-* 'mountain', *paura-* 'ample', *gaa* 'elephant', *viāṇa-* 'awning', *savaha-* 'oath': Skt. *loka-, naga-, pracura-, gaja-, vitāna-, śapatha-*. Presumably, an intermediate step prior to loss involved the voicing of consonants, and some dialects reflect this; for example, in Śaurasenī intervocalic dentals were voiced (*ido* 'hence', *tadhā* 'thus': Skt. *itas, tathā*), and *thūbe* 'stupa' (Skt. *stūpas*) occurs in Aśokan. The loss of consonants resulted in word-internal sequences of vowels that were not found in Old Indo-Aryan, though such vowels were separated by *y, v* in some dialects. Intervocalic non-retroflex aspirates generally changed to *h*, but *-ṭ-, -ṭh-* were voiced, and *-ḍ-* developed to *-ḷ-* whence *-l-*: Pkt. *sāhā-* 'branch', *meha-* 'cloud', *naḍa-* 'actor', *maḍha-* 'cloister' (Skt. *śākhā-, megha-, naṭa-, maṭha-*), Skt. *krīḍati* 'plays': Pāli *kīḷati*, Pkt. *kīlai*. The spirantal system of Old Indo-Aryan was also generally simplified. On the evidence of Aśokan documents, dialects of the extreme north-west retained *ś ṣ s*, as in Shāhbāzgaṛhī *paśucikisa* 'medical treatment for cattle', *vaṣeṣu* (loc. pl.) 'years'. But elsewhere the sibilants merged to *s*, and later in the east, as represented by Māgadhī, one has *ś* (e.g. *keśeṣu* (loc. pl.) 'hair', *śuhaśśa-* 'thousand': Skt. *keśeṣu, sahasra-*). In Apabhraṁśa, *-s(s)-* developed to *-h-*, as in *taho* 'of that' (Pāli *tassa*, Skt. *tasya*), and intervocalic nasals lost their occlusion, resulting in nasalisation, as in *gāũ* 'village' (Pkt. *gāmo*, Skt. *grāmas*), *pasāẽ* 'through the grace of' (Pkt. *pasāeṇa*, Skt. *prasādena*).

The Middle Indo-Aryan vowel system also shows major developments. As shown, word-internal vowel sequences not permitted earlier now occurred. Conversely, over-heavy syllables – with long vowels followed by consonant clusters – permissible in Old Indo-Aryan, were eliminated, through shortening of vowels or reduction of clusters. Moreover, as -V̄C- and -V̆CC- were prosodically equivalent, one has either as reflex of earlier -V̄C-, -V̆CC-. For example: Skt. *lākṣā-* 'lac', *dīrgha-* 'long', *śvaśrū-* 'mother-in-law', *sarṣapa-* 'mustard seed': Pāli *lākha-, dīgha-, sassū-, sāsapa-*: Pkt. *lakkhā-, diggha-/dīgha-, sāsū-, sāsava-*. In addition, vocalic *ṛ* is replaced by various vowels, *ai, au*, were monophthongised to *e, o; -aya-, -ava-* developed to *-e-, -o-*; and short *ĕ, ŏ* arose through shortening before clusters: Skt. *ṛkṣa-* 'bear', *vṛścika* 'scorpion', *pṛcchati* 'asks', *taila-* 'oil', *jayati* 'is victorious', *prekṣate* 'looks', *aurasa-* 'legitimate', *bhavati* 'is', *maulya-* 'price': Pāli *accha-, vicchika-, pucchati, tela, jeti, pekkhati, orasa-, hoti, molla-*. Moreover, many of the complex morphophonemic alternations that applied in Old Indo-Aryan across word boundaries (see Chapter 21, Section 1.2) were eliminated. Certain phonological developments also characterised major dialect areas. As noted, the extreme north-west retained different sibilants. In addition, at Aśoka's time the extreme west and east respectively were characterised by having *r*, consonant assimilation and *-o* for earlier *-as* and its variants as opposed to *l*, a tendency to epenthesis and *-e: rāñño* versus *lājine*.

Some of the tendencies observed earlier continue in evidence into New Indo-Aryan. Thus, the resolution of -V̆CC- to *gacchantānaṁ* takes place in some areas: Gujarati *pākū* 'ripe', *lāḍū* 'a sweet': Hindi *pakkā, laḍḍu*. Though *ai, au* are retained well into the modern period and still found, they are also monophthongised, as in Hindi *hɛ* 'is', *cɔthā* 'fourth' (spelled *hai, cauthā*). Middle Indo-Aryan *ḍ, ḍh* develop to flaps (but the etymological spellings are retained) except in initial position and after nasals, e.g. Hindi *sāḍī* 'sari' (Pkt. *sāḍiā-*). In the north-west, assimilation affects a sequence of a nasal with an obstruent: Panjabi *dand* 'tooth' versus Hindi *dā̃t*. On the other hand, the widespread loss of earlier final vowels results in word-final consonants, although in certain areas the final vowels are retained; e.g. Panjabi *dand*, Hindi *dā̃t*, but Sindhi *Dandu*. The last has an initial imploded stop, characteristic of Sindhi and some adjacent languages. Dialectal developments have resulted in other phonological features not found in Middle Indo-Aryan. For example, Panjabi developed a tonal system; Kashmiri has developed pharyngealised consonants; in languages of the south-west there are two sets of affricates, as in Marathi *c* (= *ts*) versus *č*; and languages of the extreme east have rounded the vowel *a*, as in Bengali (Bangla), where one also finds limited vowel harmony.

2.2 Morphology and Syntax

The grammatical system of Middle Indo-Aryan is characterised by a general reduction of complexities in comparison with Old Indo-Aryan. The dual is eliminated as a category distinct from the plural. The trend to replace variable consonant stems with single stems ending in vowels, already evident in Old Indo-Aryan (e.g. Skt. *danta-* 'tooth', earlier *dant-/dat-*), continues: Pāli *gacchanta-* 'going' (masc. nom. sg. *gacchanto*, gen. pl. *gacchantānaṁ*) as against Skt. *gacchant-/gacchat-* (see Chapter 21, Section 2.2.2). The loss of final consonants also contributed to the steady elimination of consonant stems, e.g. Pāli *āpā-* 'emergency', *sappi-* 'butter': Skt. *āpad-*, *sarpis-*. The nominal case system too is reduced. At an early stage, the dative is replaced by the genitive except in expressing a goal or purpose: Pāli *etesaṁ pi abhayam dammi* 'I grant (*dammi*) them too (*etesaṁ pi*) security' has a genitive *etesaṁ* construed with *dammi*, and Jaina Māhārāṣṭrī *namo tāṇaṁ purisaṇṇaṁ* 'homage to those men' has a genitive in construction with *namo*. Formal datives occur in examples like Aśokan *etāya atthāya idaṁ lekhāpitaṁ* 'this (*idaṁ*) has been caused to be written (*lekhāpitaṁ*) for this purpose (*etāya atthāya*)', Pāli *jhassu rūpaṁ apunabbhavanāya* 'give up (*jhassu*) your body (*rūpaṁ*) so as not to be born again (*apunabbhavanāya*)'. In addition, nominal and pronominal types are less strictly segregated, as can be seen from *etāya*, *tāṇ aṁ* (Skt. *etasmai*, *teṣām*) in examples cited.

Although early Middle Indo-Aryan retains middle forms, the contrast between active and medio-passive in the verb system is generally obliterated. Thus, Pāli has *maññati* 'thinks', *jāyati* 'is born' and passives of the type *vuccati* 'is said', with etymologically active endings; contrast Skt. *manyate*, *jāyate*, *ucyate*. The contrast between two kinds of future formations is absent in Middle Indo-Aryan, which has the type Pāli *hossati* 'will be'. Further, the distinction among aorist, imperfect and perfect is obliterated. With few exceptions, the sigmatic aorist supplies the productive preterit. Thus, Pāli has several preterital formations, but the productive one is sigmatic and based on the present stem, not on the root as in Old Indo-Aryan: *ahosi* 'was' (3 sg.), *ahosisuṁ* 'were' (pres. *hoti honti*), *agacchi*, *agacchisuṁ*, (*gacchati*, *gacchanti*). In later Middle Indo-Aryan, verbally inflected preterits are generally given up in favour of participial forms, as in Śaurasenī *mahārāo viāado* 'the king (*mahārāo*) also (*vi*) has arrived (*āado*)', where *āado* agrees in case, number and gender with *mahārāo*. The participle of a verb that takes a direct object shows object agreement: in Jaina Māhārāṣṭrī *teṇa vi savvaṁ siṭṭhaṁ* 'he too has told everything', *teṇa* (inst. sg.) refers to the agent, and *siṭṭhaṁ* 'told' agrees with *savvaṁ* (nom. sg. nt.) 'everything'. If no object is explicitly referred to, the neuter nominative singular of a participle is used, e.g. Jaina Māhārāṣṭrī *pacchā raṇṇā cintiyaṁ* 'afterwards, the king (inst. sg. *raṇṇā*) thought (*cintiyaṁ*)'.

Alternations of the type Skt. *asti-santi* (see Chapter 21, Section 2.2.3) are eliminated in Middle Indo-Aryan, where the predominant present formation involves a single stem: Pāli *eti* 'goes' *enti* 'go', *sakkoti-sakkonti* (*sak* 'be able'), *chindati-chindanti* (*chid* 'cut'). Stems like *chinda-* reflect a generalisation, based on a reanalysis of third plural forms, of stems with *-a*. The elimination of strictly athematic presents with variable stems allowed the use of the second singular imperative *-hi* in a domain wider than this had in Old Indo-Aryan, e.g. Pāli *jīvāhi* 'live' (Skt. *jīva*). Similarly, optatives with *-e-* and *-yā-* are not sharply segregated; a form like Pāli *bhaveyya* (3 sg.) shows a blend of the two. Middle Indo-Aryan continues to use morphological causatives with *-i-/-e-* (Pāli 3 sg. pres. *kāreti*), but the type in *-āpe-* (Pkt. *-āve-*) is extended beyond its earlier domain, as in Pāli *vasāpeti* 'has … stay'.

Nominal forms of the Middle Indo-Aryan verb system are of the same types as in Old Indo-Aryan: present and past participles (see above), gerundives (Pāli *kātabba-* 'to be done', *dassanīya-* 'worthy of being seen'), gerunds, infinitives, with some innovations. For example, Pāli *nikkhamitvā* 'after leaving' has *-tvā-* after a compound, and *pappotuṁ* has *-tuṁ* added to the present stem, not the root.

The late Middle Indo-Aryan stage represented in Apabhraṁśa foreshadows New Indo-Aryan in several ways. Forms of the nominal system with *-au*, *-aū*, *-ī* presage the modern oppositions among masculine, neuter and feminine types such as Gujarati *navo*, *navū*, *navī* 'new', Hindi *nayā*, *naī* (m., f.). The case system of Apabhraṁśa is at a more advanced stage of disintegration than found earlier. For example, instrumental and locative plurals are now formally identical, and etymologically instrumental singular forms like *dāhiṇabhāē* are used in locatival function: *dāhiṇabhāē bharuhu thakku* 'Bharata is located (*thakku*) in the southern division'. The paucity of distinct forms is evident in personal pronouns, where, for example, *maī*, *paī* (1st, 2nd person sg.) have functions equivalent to older accusative, instrumental and locative forms. Although Apabhraṁśa has some presents like *hoi* 'is', stems in *-a* of the type *kara-* 'do, make' (3 sg. *karai*) predominate. The Apabhraṁśa causative type *karāva-(karāvai)* is comparable to New Indo-Aryan formations (e.g. Gujarati *karāve che* 'has … do'). Moreover, Apabhraṁśa has causative formations found in modern languages but not attested earlier in Middle Indo-Aryan; e.g. *bhamāḍ-a-* 'cause to turn' (Gujarati *bhamāḍ-*).

The gender system of earlier Indo-Aryan is retained in some modern languages (e.g. Gujarati, see above), but is reduced in others (e.g. Hindi, with masculine and feminine only); some languages (e.g. Bengali) have eliminated systematic gender distinctions. Various inflectional forms are retained (e.g. Gujarati agentive *mē* 'I'), but the prevalent modern nominal system involves stems and postpositions or, much less commonly, prepositions. Over a large area of New Indo-Aryan, one finds variable nominals with direct and oblique forms, the former used independently, the latter with postpositions and other clitic elements. For example, Gujarati has singular direct forms in *-o* (m.), *-ū* (nt.), *-ī* (f.), oblique forms in *-ā* (m. -nt.), *-ī*. Some languages (e.g. Hindi) distinguish direct and oblique in the plural, others (e.g. Gujarati) do not. There are also nominals without these variations. Combinations of stems and postpositions serve the functions of inflected forms in earlier Indo-Aryan. Different languages have different postpositions for the same functions; e.g. Hindi *-ko*, Gujarati *-ne* mark definite direct objects, regularly animate, and indirect objects. Adjectives in general are formally like nouns, which they regularly precede in attributive constructions, and, with few exceptions, postpositions follow such phrases, not individual components; e.g. Gujarati *mē tamārā dikrā-ne joyo* 'I saw your son'. Second person pronouns in New Indo-Aryan are differentiated essentially according to distinctions of deference, distance and familiarity, not according to number; e.g. Hindi *āp* has plural agreement but can refer to one person. Languages of the south-west also distinguish between first person inclusive and exclusive forms; e.g. Gujarati *ame* (exclusive), *āpṇe*. In demonstrative and relative pronouns, languages differ with regard to gender distinctions made; e.g. Marathi relative singular *jo* (m.), *je* (nt.), *ji* (f.), Gujarati *je* for all genders. They also differ in the deictic distinctions made.

The tendency to incorporate nominal forms in the verb system, evident in earlier times, continues into New Indo-Aryan. For example, Hindi has a contrast comparable to that of Bengali *korchi* 'am doing', *kori* 'do', both verbally inflected, but instead uses nominally inflected forms: *kar rahā/rahī hū* 'am doing', *kartā/kartī hū* 'do'. Gujarati lacks the contrast, but has verbally inflected presents (*karū chū* 'do, am doing') and nominally inflected preterits (*karto hato*, *kartī hatī*). Temporal auxiliaries like Hindi *hū*, Gujarati *chū* show verbal inflection, as do imperatives and some other forms. Person–number distinctions accord with the use of pronouns, but some languages (e.g. Bengali) have given up number distinctions in the verb. Future formations also show areal differences. Some languages have futures with -*š*- or -*h*- (e.g. Gujarati *kariš* 'I will do'), but -*b*- is characteristic of the east (e.g. Bengali *jabe* 'will go') and there are future formations that include gender distinctions, as in Hindi *jāegā* 'he will go', *jāegī* 'she will go'. The perfective of many New Indo-Aryan languages is semi-ergative, reflecting earlier participial constructions. For example, Gujarati *ghɛr gayo/gaī* 'he/she went home' has masculine *gayo*, feminine *gaī*, depending on whether the agent is a man or a woman, but in *mɛ̃ tamārā dīkrā-ne joyo* 'I saw your son' agreement (m. sg. *joyo*) is determined by the object (*dīkrā-ne* 'son'). Some languages (e.g. Hindi) suspend agreement if an object nominal takes a postposition, so that the construction is no longer strictly passive. A formal passive such as *nahī bulāyā jāegā* (m. sg.) 'will not be invited' in an example like Hindi *baccõ-ko nahī bulāyā jāegā* 'children will not be invited' is also construed with a noun phrase containing an object marker (*baccõ-ko*), so that this construction too is different from the passive of earlier Indo-Aryan. Moreover, formal passives normally are used in sentences without agent expressions except under particular semantic conditions; e.g. Gujarati *mārā-thī nahi jawāy* 'I (agentive *mārā-thī*) won't be able to go', with the passive *jaw-ā-y* (3 sg. pres.). As shown, formal passives are also not restricted to transitive verbs, and in some languages they are formed with a suffix, in others they are periphrastic formations.

Examples cited illustrate the usual unmarked word order of most New Indo-Aryan languages: subject (including agentive forms), object (with attributive adjectives, including number words, before this and preceded by possessives), verb (with auxiliaries). Adverbials can precede sentences or the verb. Relative clauses generally precede correlative clauses. A notable exception to the above, at least in its superficial order, is Kashmiri, where the verb occurs in second position.

Bibliography

Cardona and Emmerick (1974) contains a survey of Indo-Aryan on pages 439b–57a, including a table of languages and a map. Bloch (1965) is a general and masterful survey of the historical developments, while Varma (1972–6) is a handy summary of Grierson's survey of the modern languages, still valuable, though in serious need of updating. Turner (1966–9) is an indispensable reference work for lexicon, and includes an index by D.R. Turner. Masica (1991) is a comprehensive description of the

Modern Indo-Aryan languages organised by linguistic levels; it also includes information regarding language history. Cardona and Jain (2003) is a description of all Indo-Aryan languages, including Sanskrit and Middle Indo-Aryan Prakrits, organised by language.

References

Bloch, J. 1965. *Indo-Aryan from the Vedas to Modern Times* (Adrien-Maisonneuve, Paris; translation by A. Master, with revisions, additions and an index, of *L'Indo-Aryen du véda aux temps modernes*, Adrien-Maisonneuve, Paris, 1934)

Cardona, G. and Emmerick, R.E. 1974. 'Indo-Aryan Languages', in *The New Encyclopaedia Britannica: Macropaedia*, 15th edn (Encyclopaedia Britannica, Chicago), pp. 439b–57a

Cardona, G. and Jain, D. (eds) 2003. *The Indo-Aryan Languages* (Routledge, London and New York)

Masica, Colin P. 1991. *The Indo-Aryan Languages* (Cambridge University Press, Cambridge)

Turner, R.L. 1966–9. *A Comparative Dictionary of the Indo-Aryan Languages*, 2 vols (Oxford University Press, London)

Varma, S. 1972–6. *G.A. Grierson's Linguistic Survey of India, a Summary*, 3 vols (Vishveshvaranand Institute, Panjab University, Hoshiarpur)

21

Sanskrit

George Cardona

Revised by Silvia Luraghi

1 Background

1.1 Introduction

Sanskrit (*saṃskṛta-* 'adorned, purified') refers to several varieties of Old Indo-Aryan, whose most archaic forms are found in Vedic texts: the *Rigveda* (*Ṛgveda*), *Yajurveda*, *Sāmaveda*, *Atharvaveda*, with various branches. Associated with these are groupings of explicatory and speculative works (called *brāhmaṇas*, *āraṇyakas*, *upaniṣads*) as well as texts concerning the performance of rites (*kalpa-* or *śrauta-sūtras*), treatises on phonetics, grammar proper, etymological explanations of particular words, metrics and astrology. Early Vedic texts are pre-Buddhistic – the composition of the *Rigveda* is plausibly dated in the mid-second millennium BC – although their exact chronology is difficult to establish. Brāhmaṇas and early sūtra works can properly be called late Vedic. Also of the late Vedic period is the grammarian Pāṇini (not later than early fourth century BC), author of the *Aṣṭādhyāyī* who distinguishes between the language of sacred texts (*chandas*) and a more usual language of communication (*bhāṣā* from *bhāṣ* 'speak'), tantamount to Classical Sanskrit. Epic Sanskrit is so called because it is represented principally in the two epics, *Mahābhārata* and *Rāmāyaṇā*. The date of composition for the core of early epic is considered to be in the first centuries BC. It is in the *Rāmāyaṇā* that the term *saṃskṛta-* is encountered probably for the first time with reference to the language. Classical Sanskrit is the language of major poetical works, dramas, tales and technical treatises on grammar, philosophy and ritual. It was not only used by Kalidasa and his predecessors but continued in use after Sanskrit had ceased to be a commonly used mother tongue. Sanskrit is a language of learned treatises and commentaries to this day. It has also undergone a literary revival, and original works are still being composed in this language. Indeed, Sanskrit is used as a lingua franca by paṇḍitas from different parts of India, and several thousand people claim it as their mother tongue.

1.2 Diachronic Changes within Sanskrit

Linguistic changes are discernible in Sanskrit from earliest Vedic down to the language Pāṇini describes. The nominative plural masculine in -āsas (devāsas 'gods'), which has a counterpart in Iranian, is already less frequent in the Rigveda than the type in -ās (devās), and continues to lose ground; in Brāhmaṇas, -ās is the norm. The Rigveda has examples of an archaic genitive plural in -ām to a-stems, but the form in -ānām prevails here and is the only one used later. The instrumental singular of a-stems has both -ā and -ena (originally a pronominal type) in the Rigveda vīryā/vīryeṇa 'heroic might, act', but the latter is already prevalent and becomes the norm later. The Rigvedic nominative-accusative dual masculine of a-stems ends in -ā or -au (mitrāvaruṇā/-varuṇau 'Mitra and Varuṇa'), distributed according to phonological environments in early parts of the Rigveda, but -au steadily gains the upper hand and finally ousts -ā completely. For the nominative-accusative plural of neuter a-stems, the Rigveda has forms in -ā and -āni: bhīmāni āyudhā 'fearful weapons'. The former predominates in the Rigveda, but the situation is reversed in the Atharvaveda; later, -āni is the norm. Early Vedic had derivate ī-stems of two types, as in vṛkīs 'she wolf', devī 'goddess' (nom. sg.), vṛkyas, devīs (nom. pl.). The type vṛkī- is gradually eliminated as an independent formation, but leaves traces incorporated into the devī type (e.g. nom. pl. devyas). Rigvedic feminine i- and u-stems have instrumental singular forms of the type ūtī 'with, for help', jātū 'by nature' in addition to forms with -ā (ūtyā, dhenvā 'cow'). Even in the Rigveda, u-stems usually have forms of the type dhenvā, and the type ūtyā also becomes the norm later. Masculine and neuter stems in -i, -u have Rigvedic instrumental singulars with -ā (pavyā, paśvā to pavi- 'felloe', paśu- 'animal') and -nā (agninā 'fire, Agni', paśunā). The latter predominate in the Atharvaveda and ultimately take over except for a few nouns (patyā 'husband', sakhyā 'friend'). The Rigveda has avyas, madhvas, genitive singulars of avi- 'sheep', madhu- 'honey'; the regular later forms are aves, madhunas (also madhos in Vedic). Endingless locatives like ahan (ahan- 'day') are also gradually eliminated in favour of forms with the ending -i: ahani/ahni. Early Vedic has pronominal forms not found in Classical Sanskrit: asme, yuṣme (loc. pl.) from the first and second person pronouns, replaced by asmāsu, yuṣmāsu; āvos (1st person gen.-loc. du.), mahya (1st person dat. sg.), replaced by āvayos, mahyam. Pāṇini expressly classes such earlier Vedic forms as belonging to the language of sacred texts.

The verbal system shows comparable differences. Early Vedic had modal forms from several stems: present, aorist, perfect. For example, the Rigvedic imperatives śṛṇudhi, śṛṇuhi, śṛṇu (2 sg.) and the Atharvavedic optative śṛṇuyāt (3 sg.) are formed to the present stem śṛṇu- of śru 'hear, listen', but the Rigvedic imperative śrudhi (2 sg.) and optative śruyās (3 sg.) are formed to the aorist stem. In later Sanskrit, imperatives and optatives regularly are formed from present stems. The first plural primary active ending -masi (bharāmasi 'we carry'), which has an equivalent in Iranian, predominates over -mas in the Rigveda, but not in the Atharvaveda, and later -mas is the rule. Early Vedic forms like ās 'was' (3 sg. imperfect of as) and avāṭ (3 sg. aorist of vah 'transport') show the effects of the simplification of word-final clusters. Such forms are replaced by the types āsīt, avākṣīt with -it (2 sg. -īs), in which endings are clearly shown. Aorist forms made directly from verb roots are also replaced by forms from stems in -a or sigmatic stems, the latter especially in the medio-passive. Thus, the Rigveda has 1 sg. akaram, 2 sg. akar (< akar-s), 3 sg. akar (< akar-t), but the Atharvaveda has 2 sg. akaras, 3 sg. akarat, from kṛ 'make, do', and the Rigveda has not only a root aorist third plural middle *ayujran* but also a sigmatic form *ayukṣata* 'they yoked'. Commentators like Patañjali (mid-second century BC) and the etymologist Yāska before him used the sigmatic form *akṛṣata* (3 pl. middle) in paraphrasing a Vedic verse with the root aorist form *akrata*. Early Vedic forms of the type *śaye* 'is lying' are gradually replaced by the type *śete*, with *te*, which is explicitly marked for person.

Early Vedic distinguishes among the aorist, imperfect and perfect. The aorist is commonly used to refer to something that has recently taken place, and the imperfect is a narrative tense form used of acts accomplished or states prevailing at a past time not close at hand. For example, *úd u jyótir ... savitā́ aśret* 'Savitṛ has set up (*úd ... aśret*) the light (*jyótis*)', spoken at dawn, has the aorist *úd ... aśret*, but *ná mṛtyúr āsīd amṛ́tam ná tárhi ná rā́tryā áhna āsīt praketáḥ* 'then (*tárhi*) was there (*āsīt*) not (*ná*) death (*mṛtyús*) or deathlessness (*amṛ́tam*) nor was there the mark (*praketás*) of night (*rā́tryās*) or day (*áhnas*)' has the imperfect *āsīt*. The perfect originally signified, as in early Greek, a state of being; e.g. *bhī* 'fear': *bibhāya* '... is afraid'. From the earliest Vedic texts, however, this is not always the use of the perfect, which came to be used as a narrative tense. For example, the following Brāhmaṇa passage has both perfect and imperfects: *yajño vai devebhya ud akrāman na vo'ham annaṁ bhaviṣyāmīti/neti devā abruvan annam eva no bhaviṣyasīti/taṁ devā vimethire ... te hocur devā na vai na itthaṁ vihṛto'laṁ bhaviṣyati hantemaṁ yajñaṁ bharāmeti/tatheti taṁ sam jabhruḥ* 'the sacrifice (*yajñas*) fled (*ud akrāmat*) from the gods (*devebhyas*), saying (citation particle *iti*), "I will not be (*na bhaviṣyāmi*) food (*annam*) for you (*vas*)"; the gods (*devās*) said (*abruvan*), "No, you will be (*bhaviṣyāsi*) food for us (*nas*)"; the gods tore it apart (*taṁ vi methire*) ... the gods said (*ūcus*), "Truly (*vai*), it will not be sufficient (*na ... alaṁ bhaviṣyāti*) for us thus (*ittham*) torn apart (*vihṛtas*), so let us put this sacrifice together (*imaṁ yajñaṁ sam bharāma*)"; they agreed (*tatheti* "yes") and put it together (*taṁ sam jabhrus*).' The imperfect *ud akrāmat, abruvan* and the perfect *vi methire, saṁ jabhrus* occur in similar contexts. This passage also illustrates the normal later combination of preverbs and verbs: preverbs immediately precede the verb stems with which they are connected; in earlier Vedic, tmesis was common – as in *úd ... aśret* of the Rigvedic passage cited earlier. In addition, the augment became obligatory, as it had not been before, in imperfect and aorist forms.

The Brāhmaṇa passage just quoted also contains the future forms *bhaviṣyāmi, bhaviṣyasi, bhaviṣyati*, from the verb *bhū*, with the augmented suffix *-iṣya*. This and the unaugmented suffix *-sya* (*dāsya-* 'will give') are used from earliest Vedic on, but there is also a composite type, originally formed from an agent noun of the type *kartṛ-* (nom. sg. *kartā*) followed, except in the third person, by forms of the verb 'be': *kartāsmi* 'I will do', *kartāsi* 'you will do', *kartā* 'he will do'. This formation, which was in common use at Pāṇini's time, was rare in early Vedic. The perfect also has a periphrastic formation, for derived verbs such as causatives; e.g. *gamayāñ cakāra* (3 sg.) 'made to go' (3 sg. present *gamayati*), formed with the accusative singular of an action noun (*gamayā-*) and the perfect of *kṛ* 'do'. This type first appears in the *Atharvaveda* (form cited), and gains currency; Pāṇini recognises it not only as the regular perfect for derived verbs but also for some primitive verbs. Corresponding to future forms such as *bhariṣyati* 'will carry', there were, from earliest Vedic, secondary augmented forms like *abhariṣyat* 'was going to carry', and these are later to become the regular verbal constituents in contrary-to-fact conditional sentences.

Early Vedic has a category that goes out of use later: the injunctive, formally an unaugmented secondary form; for example, *bhūt, carat* are third person singular injunctives corresponding to the aorist *abhūt* and the imperfect *acarat*. In a Rigveda passage such as *agníḥ sáptiṁ vājambharáṁ dadāti* ... *agní ródasī ví carat* 'Agni (*agnís*) gives (*dadāti*) a horse (*sáptim*) that carries away prizes (*vājambharám*) ... Agni wanders through (*ví carat*) the two worlds (*ródasī*)', the injunctive *ví carat* and the present *dadāti* are juxtaposed, both used of general truths. In such statements, Vedic also uses subjunctives, characterised by the vowel *-a-* affixed to a present, aorist or perfect stem, as in Rigvedic *ná duṣṭutī́ mártyó vindate vásu ná śrédhantaṁ rayír naśat* 'a mortal (*mártyas*) does not find (*ná vindate*) treasure (*vásu*) through bad praise (*duṣṭutī́*) nor does wealth (*rayís*) come to (*naśat*) one who falters in the performance of rites (*śrédhantam*)', where the present *vindate* is juxtaposed with the aorist subjunctive *naśat* 'reach'. In addition, subordinate clauses such as *pūṣā́ no yáthā* ... *ásad vṛdhé* 'so that (*yáthā*) Pūṣan be (*ásat*) our protector in order that we might grow (*vṛdhé*)' use the subjunctive, which also occurs in requests; e.g. *devó devébhir ā́ gamat* 'may the god come (*ā́ gamat*) with the gods (*devébhis*)'. In negative commands, the injunctive is used with the particle *mā*, as in *mā́ no vadhīḥ* ... *mā́ párā dāḥ* 'do not kill (*mā́ vadhīs*) us (*nas*), do not forsake (*mā́ párā dās*) us', with the second person singular aorist injunctives *vadhīs, párā dās*. The regular negative particle used with a subjunctive, however, is *na*: e.g. *sá júno ná reṣan máno yó asya* ... *ā́ vívāsāt* 'that person (*sá jánas*) does not suffer ill (*ná reṣat*), who seeks to win (*yás ā́ vívāsāt*) his (*asya*) spirit (*mánas*)' has the aorist subjunctive *reṣat* and the subjunctive of the present desiderative stem *ā́ vívāsa-* (*-sāt* < *-sa-a-t*). Later, the injunctive is retained only in negative commands of the type *mā vadhīs*, 3 sg. *mā vadhīt*. The subjunctive also steadily loses ground until it is no longer current; for Pāṇini subjunctive forms belong to the language of sacred texts. Only the first person type *karavāṇi* 'I may do, let me do', incorporated into the imperative system, is retained. The functions of the subjunctive are taken over by the optative and the future. For example, in Vedic a subordinate clause introduced by *yathā* may have a subjunctive or an optative, but *yadi* 'if' is regularly used with a subjunctive in early Vedic. Thus, a passage cited above has *yathā* ... *asat*, and *yáthā bhávema mīḷhúṣe ánāgāḥ* 'that we may be (*yáthā bhavema*) sinless (*ánāgās*) towards the gracious one (*mīḷhúṣe*)' has the optative *bhavema*, but *ā́ gha gamad yádi śrávat* 'let him come (*ā́* ... *gamat*) if he hear (*yádi śrávat*)' has the aorist subjunctive *śravat*. In later Vedic, however, *yadi* is used with an optative, as in *yádi bibhīyád duścármā bhaviṣyāmī́ti somapauṣṇáṁ śyāmám ā́ labheta* 'if he fear (*yádi bibhīyát*) that he might be' (*bhaviṣyāmī́ti* "I will become") stricken by a skin disease (*duścármā* "bad-skinned"), let him immolate (*ā́ labheta*) a black goat (*śyāmám* "black") dedicated to Soma and Pūṣan'.

Nominal forms within the verbal system of early Vedic are numerous. The *Rigveda* has derivatives with *-ya, -tva* that function as gerundives: *vācya-* 'to be said' (root *vac*), *kartva-* 'to be done' (*kṛ*). In addition, the *Atharvaveda* has forms with *-(i)tavya, -anīya*: *hiṁsitavya-* 'to be harmed', *upajīvanīya-* 'to be subsisted upon'. By late Vedic, the type with *-tva* has lost currency, and for Pāṇini the regular formations are of the types *kārya-, kartavya-, karaṇīya-*. In Indo-Aryan from Vedic down to modern times, gerunds are used with reference to the earlier of actions performed in succession, usually by the same agent ('after doing A, ... does B', '... does A before doing B'); e.g. *yuktvā́ háribhyāṁ úpa yāsad arvā́k* 'let him yoke his bay horses to his chariot (*yuktvā* "after yoking") and come hither (*upa yāsad arvāk*) with them (*haribhyām* "with two bay horses")', *gūḍhvī́ támo* ... *abodhi* '(dawn) has awakened (*abodhi*) after hiding away (*gūḍhvī*) the darkness (*támas*)', *piba niṣadya* 'sit down (*niṣadya* "after sitting down") and drink (*piba*)'. The Rigveda has gerunds with *-tvā, -tvāya-tvī, -(t)ya*, but these are ultimately reduced to two main types: *-tvā* after simple verbs or verbs with the negative prefix *a(n)-*, *-ya* after compounds with preverbs. Early Vedic uses a variety of case forms of action nouns, including root nouns, as what western grammarians traditionally call infinitives; e.g. dat. sg. *vṛdhe* (root noun *vṛdh-* 'growing'), *-tave* (*dātave* 'to give'), gen. sg. *-tos* (*dātos*), the last two from a derivative in *-tu* which also supplies the accusative *-tum* (*dātum*). There are other Vedic types, but nouns in *-tu* are noteworthy in that for later Vedic the accusative with *-tum* and the genitive in *-tos*, the latter construed with *īś* or *śak* 'be able', become the norm. According to Pāṇini forms in *-tum* and datives of action nouns are equivalent in sentences like *bhoktum/bhojanāya gacchati* '... is going (*gacchati*) in order to eat'.

1.3 Sanskrit Dialects

That some formations fell into disuse in the course of Old Indo-Aryan is no surprise: the developments sketched above represent chronological and dialectal changes. Such changes were recognised by grammarians who spoke the language. Patañjali notes that second plural perfect forms like *cakra* or *ūṣa* (*vas* 'dwell') were not used in his time; instead, one used participial forms such as *kṛtavantas*, *ūṣitās* (nom. pl. m.). Grammarians also recognised that various dialects existed. Pāṇini takes note of forms used by northerners, easterners and various dialectal usages described by other grammarians. The etymologist Yāska notes, as does Patañjali, that finite forms of the verb *dā* 'cut' were used in the east, while in the north the verb occurred in the derivative *dātra-* 'sickle'. Earlier documents also afford evidence of dialect differences. The major dialect of the *Rigveda* is one in which Proto-Indo-European *l* merged with *r* (e.g. *pūrṇa-* 'full'), but other dialects developed *l*, and one finds doublets such as *rohita-/lohita-* 'red'. The development of retroflex liquids *-ḷ-*, *-ḷh-* from intervocalic *-ḍ-*, *-ḍh-* is another characteristic of some areas, among them the major dialect of the *Rigveda*.

1.4 Sanskrit and Other Languages

Classical Sanskrit represents a development of one or more such Old Indo-Aryan dialects, accepted as standard, at a stage when archaisms such as those noted (Section 1.2) had largely been eliminated. It is plausible to accept that both Classical Sanskrit and earlier dialects of Indo-Aryan coexisted with vernaculars that were removed from these by changes which characterise Middle Indo-Aryan, just as in later times Sanskrit and vernaculars were used side by side under particular circumstances. There is evidence to support this view, particularly in Patañjali's *Mahābhāṣya*, where he discusses the use of 'correct speech forms' (*śabda*) and 'incorrect speech forms' (*apaśabda*), considered corruptions (*apabhraṃśa*) of the former. Patañjali speaks of *śiṣṭas*, model speakers, who are characterised as much by moral qualities as by their speech. They are Brāhmaṇas who reside in Āryāvartta, the land of the Āryas in north-central India, who at any time have only as much grain as will fit in a small pot, who are not greedy, who behave morally without ulterior motives and who attain full knowledge of traditional learning with consummate ease, not having to be taught. These model speakers are those one should imitate and, it is assumed, the models Pāṇini followed in composing his grammatical rules. However, even learned men did not avoid vernaculars, as Patañjali also points out. He remarks that a restriction such that correct speech forms should be used to the exclusion of others is absolute only in respect of rituals. To illustrate, Patañjali speaks of sages who said *yar vā naḥ* 'what is ours', *tar vā naḥ* 'that is ours' instead of *yad vā naḥ, tad vā naḥ* but did not use such forms in the course of ritual acts. Now, forms like *yar* instead of *yad* reflect an Indo-Aryan tendency to eliminate obstruence for non-initial retroflex and dental stops; the particular change in question is seen also in Prakrit *bāraha* as opposed to Sanskrit *dvādaśa* 'twelve'. Moreover, Patañjali must have been, if not a native speaker of Sanskrit in the strictest sense, at least one fully fluent in the language, with authority concerning its usage. For he explicitly distinguishes between what is desirable – that is, what is required by accepted usage – and what obtains by grammatical rules. At Patañjali's time, then, Sanskrit must have been a current vehicle of communication in certain circles and under particular social and religious conditions, used concurrently with vernaculars. Much the same picture is painted for later periods, when Sanskrit was doubtless revived. Thus, in his *Kāmasūtra*, Vātsyāyana notes that to be held in high esteem a man-about-town should use neither Sanskrit nor a local language exclusively. Indeed, the coexistence of Middle Indo-Aryan and Sanskrit speech is to be envisaged even for the time when very early texts were given their final redactions. The *Rigveda* has forms like *vikaṭa-* 'deformed' and *jyotis-* 'light'. The former is a Middle Indo-Aryan form of *vikṛta-* with *-aṭ-* for *-ṛt-*, comparable to Aśokan *kaṭa-* 'made' (Skt. *kṛta*), and the latter had *jy-* for *dy-*. It has been suggested, plausibly in my estimation, that there was an archaic Middle Indo-Aryan contemporaneous with early Vedic.

Sanskrit was also subject to non-Aryan influence from early on. In the sixth century BC Darius counted Gandhāra as a province of his kingdom, and Alexander the Great penetrated into the north of the subcontinent in the fourth century. From Iranian come terms such as *lipi-* 'writing, script', *kṣatrapa-* 'satrap', and Greek is the source of such words as *kendra-* 'centre', *jāmitra-* 'diameter', *horā-* 'hour'. At a later time borrowings entered from Arabic and other sources. But long before this Sanskrit was influenced by Dravidian, from which it borrowed terms such as *kāla-* 'black', *kuṭī-* 'hut' (cf. Tamil *kar* 'blackness', *kuṭi*) and the influence of which contributed to the spread of retroflex consonants (see Chapter 20, Section 1). It is not certain in every instance, however, that borrowing proceeded from Dravidian to Indo-Aryan, since Dravidian languages also freely borrowed from Indo-Aryan. For example, some scholars maintain that Skt. *kaṭu-* 'sharp, pungent' is a Dravidian borrowing, but others treat it as a Middle Indo-Aryan development of *kṛtu-* 'cutting' (root *kṛt* 'cut'). Whatever be the judgement on any individual word, nevertheless, it is clear that Sanskrit and other Indo-Aryan dialects borrowed from Dravidian sources.

2 Brief Description of Classical Sanskrit

2.1 Sound System and Script

The sounds of Sanskrit are shown in Table 21.1. In the present context, it is not necessary to take a particular stand about which sounds should be considered 'basic', 'underlying' or 'phonemic'. Suffice it to note that sounds of Table 21.1 within square brackets have restricted distributions. *r̄* occurs only in accusative or genitive plurals of *pitṝn* *ṛ*-stems (*pitṝn* 'fathers', *mātṝs* 'mothers', gen. pl. *pitṝṇām*, *mātṝṇām*, rare nom.-acc. pl. nt. *kartṝṇi* 'which do'); *ḷ* is found only in forms of *kḷp* 'be fit, arrange, imagine' (past participle *kḷpta-*). Due to the reduction of word-final clusters, *-ṇ* occurs in words such as *prāṅ* (nom. sg.) 'directed forward, toward the east', but otherwise *ṇ* and *ñ* are found before velar and palatal stops, respectively, though not necessarily as replacements of *n* or *m* at morph boundaries. The nasal off-glide *ṁ* occurs word-internally before spirants at morph boundaries as the final segment of items that have *-n* or *-m* before vowels and in word-final position before spirants and semi-vowels or stops, where it varies with nasalised semi-vowels and nasal stops homorganic with following stops. *ḥ* is a word-final segment in prepause position or before voiceless spirants, velars, and labials. *χ φ* are alternants to *-ḥ* before velars and labials. Like *ṅ* and *ñ*, *ṇ* is not the initial sound of lexical items. It occurs in word-final position, though rarely except before nasals as the final sound of a morph that has a non-nasal retroflex stop before vowels, but intervocalic *-ṇ-* is found in words like *kaṇa-* 'grain, atom', that do not contain sounds which condition retroflexion.

The vowels *i, u* and *ī, ū* differ essentially in duration: short vowels last one mora (*mātrā*), long vowels two morae; however, in accepted modern pronunciations, *i* and *u* can be lower than their long counterparts. *e, o* are monophthongs of two morae, though they derive historically from diphthongs and alternate with *ay, av* before vowels. *ai, au* are diphthongs for which ancient phoneticians and grammarians recognised dialect variants: for example, the first segment of each was a closer vowel in some dialects than in others. Prosodically, however, *ai, au* behave in the manner of simple long vowels, and there are good reasons for not treating them as combinations of *ā* with *i, u*. *ṛ* is also a complex sound, consisting of *r* surrounded by vowel segments, according to a fairly old description, but this also behaves prosodically as a single vowel. In north-central India, *ṛ* is pronounced as *r* followed by short *i*. *a, ā* behave as a pair of short and long vowels, but they are also qualitatively different, as shown. Vowels can be unnasalised or nasalised. They also have pitch differences such that they are called *anudātta, udātta* and *svarita*. Pāṇini's statements concerning these are best understood as reflecting a

Table 21.1 The Sounds of Sanskrit

Vowels					
	i	ī		u	ū
		e			o
			a		
			ā		
	ṛ [r̄]	[ḷ]		ai	au

Consonants	*Obstruents* Voiceless	Voiced	*Nasals*	*Semi-vowels*	*Liquid*	*Tap*	*Spirants* Voiceless	Voiced
Pharyngeal							[h]	h
Velar	k kh	g gh	[ṅ]				[χ]	
Palatal	c ch	j jh	[ñ]	y			ś	
Retroflex	ṭ ṭh	ḍ ḍh	ṇ			r*	ṣ	
Alveolar						r*		
Dental	t th	d dh	n		l		s	
Labio-dental				v				
Labial	p ph	b bh	m [ṁ]				[φ]	

Note: * Some ancient authorities say *r* is retroflex, others say it is alveolar.

system in which an anudātta vowel is low-pitched, an udātta vowel is high-pitched, and a svarita vowel has a combination of both pitches: *a, á, à*. According to Pāṇini, a svarita vowel is high-pitched for the duration of half a mora from its beginning, low-pitched for its remainder, but there were dialectical variations, as can be seen from other ancient descriptions. There are also differences in Vedic traditions of recitation concerning the relative pitches of the vowels in question.

Sanskrit generally does not allow word-final clusters, although -*r*C is permitted if both consonants belong to the same element; e.g. *ūrk* (nom. sg.) 'strength' (acc. sg. *ūrj-am*). Sanskrit also has a fairly complex system of morphophonemic adjustments (*sandhi*) across grammatical boundaries, at word boundaries if the items in question are pronounced

Table 21.2 Devanāgarī Symbols and Their Transliterations

Vowels (*svarāḥ*)

अ	आ	इ	ई	उ	ऊ	ऋ	ॠ	ऌ	ए	ऐ	ओ	औ
a	ā	ɪ	ɪ	u	ū	ṛ	ṝ	ḷ	e	ai	o	au

Consonants (*vyañjanāni*)

Stops (*sparśāḥ*)					Semi-vowels (*antaḥsthāḥ*)	Spirants (*ūṣāāṇaḥ*)	Others
क	ख	ग	घ	ङ		ह	ः
k	kh	g	gh	ṅ		ḥ	ḥ
च	छ	ज	झ	ञ	य	श	
c	ch	j	jh	ñ	y	ś	
ट	ठ	ड	ढ	ण	र	ष	ॐ
ṭ	ṭh	ḍ	ḍh	ṇ	r	ṣ	ḻ
त	थ	द	ध	न	ल	स	
t	th	d	dh	n	l	s	
प	फ	ब	भ	म	व		
p	ph	b	bh	m	v		

Examples of combinations

का	कों	कि	की	कु	कू	कृ	कॄ	कॢ	क्त	क्र	क्ष	ज्ञ	त्र	त्व	द्य
kā	kāṃ	ki	kī	ku	kū	kṛ	kṝ	kḷ	kta	kra	kṣa	jña	tra	tva	dya

द्र	द्व	प्त	ब्द	र्क	र्कं	श्च	श्र	श्व	स्त	स्य	स्र	स्व	ह्म
dra	dva	pta	bda	rka	rkaṃ	śca	śra	śva	sta	sya	sra	sva	hma

ह्य	ह्र	ह्ल	ह्व	र्त्स्न्य
hya	hra	hla	hva	rtsnya

Numerals

१	२	३	४	५	६	७	८	९	०
1	2	3	4	5	6	7	8	9	0

Note: I have adopted the most generally accepted order of symbols and the subgroupings most widely accepted traditionally; the usual Sanskrit terms for sound classes are given in parentheses.

in close juncture (*saṃhitāyām*). Some of these adjustments are illustrated in examples given; e.g. in the Bhāhmaṇa passage cited in Section 1.2: *yahño vai ← yajnas vai, devebhya ud ← devebhyas ud, akrāman na ← akrāmat na, voham ← vas aham, annaṃ bhaviṣyāmīti ← annam bhaviṣyāmi iti, neti ← na iti, devā abruvan ← devās abruvan, no bhaviṣyasi ← nas bhaviṣyasi, taṃ devā vi methire ← tam devās vi methire, hocur devās na ← ha ūcus devās na, tatheti ← tathā iti, taṃ saṃ jabhruḥ ← tam sam jabhrus*, the last with *-ḥ* instead of *-s in pausa*. These adjustments also affect vowel pitches. The particular place of a high-pitched vowel in an underived base is not predictable. In general, a syntactic word has one high-pitched vowel only – but may have none – and a finite verb form following a term that is not a finite verb has no high-pitched vowel except in particular collocations. Further, a low-pitched vowel following a high-pitched one shifts to a svarita vowel, as in *ā gàmat ← ā gamat*. There are other accentual adjustments that involve considerable complexity and dialectal variation.

Sanskrit was and continues to be written in various scripts in different areas, but the most widely recognised is the Devanāgarī script, the symbols of which are shown in Table 21.2. These are traditionally arranged as follows: symbols for vowels, then for consonants; the latter are subdivided into: stops (five groups of five), semi-vowels, voiceless spirants, *h*. In addition, there are symbols for *ḷ* and *ḥ*. *ṃ* is designated by a *dot* (*bindu*) over a consonant or a vowel symbol, nasalisation by a dot within a half-moon (*ardhacandra*) over a symbol; χ φ are designated by ː before symbols for voiceless velars and labials.

In referring to vowels, one pronounces the sounds in question; e.g. '*a*' denotes the vowel *a*. Consonants in general are referred to by a combination of the sounds and a following *a*, e.g. '*ka*' denotes *k*. In addition, a sound name is formed with suffixed *-kāra*, e.g. '*akāra*', '*kakāra*' refer to *a, k*. Certain sounds, however, have particular names: *r ḥ ṃ χ φ*, respectively, are called *repha, visarjanīya* (or *visarga*), *anusvāra, jihvāmūlīya, upadhmānīya*.

Consonant symbols, except those for *ḥ ṃ χ φ*, without any appended element, denote consonants followed by *a*. Other consonant-vowel combinations are designated by consonant symbols with appended vowel symbols, which may precede, follow, or come under the former, as illustrated in Table 21.2. There are also ligatures for consonant combinations, some of which are illustrated in Table 21.2. Finally, there is a set of Devanāgarī numerals. Variants of symbols are found in different areas.

2.2 Grammar

2.2.1 Introduction

Although many archaic features of earlier Vedic dialects have been eliminated in Sanskrit, the grammatical system nevertheless remains quite rich. Singular, dual and plural forms are distinguished in both the nominal and the verbal systems, and ablaut variations are maintained in many types of formations.

2.2.2 Nominal System

Eight cases can be distinguished, although the vocative does not have a syntactic status comparable to the others: nominative (nom.), vocative (voc.), accusative (acc.), instrumental (inst.), dative (dat.), ablative (abl.), genitive (gen.), locative (loc.), according to traditional western terminology. All eight are formally distinguished in the singular of masculine a-stems; e.g. *deva-* 'god': nom. *devas*, voc. *deva*, acc. *devam*, inst. *devena*, dat. *devāya*, abl. *devāt*, gen. *devasya*, loc. *deve*. Otherwise, there are homophonous forms as follows. All stems: dual nom.-voc.-acc., inst.-dat.-abl., gen.-loc.: *deva-*: *devau*, *devābhyām*, *devayos*; *phala-* (nt.) 'fruit': *phale*, *phalābhyām*, *phalayos*; *senā-* (f.) 'army': *sene*, *senābhyām*, *senayos*; *agni-* (m.) 'fire': *agnī*, *agnibhyām*, *agnyos* (similarly *kṛti-* (f.) 'deed'); *vāri-* (nt.) 'water': *vāriṇī*, *vāribhyām*, *vāriṇos*; *vāyu-* (m.) 'wind': *vāyū*, *vāyubhyām*, *vāyvos* (similarly *dhenu-* (f.) 'cow'); *madhu-* (nt.) 'honey': *madhunī*, *madhubhyām*, *madhvos*; *devī-* 'goddess': *devyau*, *devībhyām*, *devyos*; *vadhū-* 'bride': *vadhvau*, *vadhūbhyām*, *vadhvos*; *sakhi-* (m.) 'friend': *sakhāyau*, *sakhibhyām*, *sakhyos*; *pitṛ-* 'father': *pitarau*, *pitṛbhyām*, *pitros* (similarly *mātṛ-* 'mother'); *kartṛ-* 'doer, maker': *kartārau* (m.) *kartṝṇī* (nt.), *kartṛbhyām*, *kartros*; *go-* 'ox, cow': *gāvau*, *gobhyām*, *gavos*; *rājan-* 'king': *rājānau*, *rājabhyām*, *rājños*; *vāc-* (f.) 'voice, speech': *vācau*, *vāgbhyām*, *vācos*; *sraj-* (f.) 'garland': *srajau*, *sragbhyām*, *srajos*; nom.-voc. pl.: *devās*, *phalāni*, *senās*, *agnayas*, *kṛtayas*, *vārīṇi*, *vāyavas*, *dhenavas*, *madhūni*, *devyas*, *vadhvas*, *sakhāyas*, *pitaras*, *mātaras*, *kartāras*, *gāvas*, *rājānas*, *vācas*, *srajas*. All stems except personal pronouns: dat.-abl. pl.: *devebhyas*, *phalebhyas*, *senābhyas*, etc. (with *agni-*, etc., and *-bhyas*), *rājabhyas*, *vāgbhyas*, *sragbhyas*, but dat. *asmabhyam* 'us', *yuṣmabhyam* 'you', abl. *asmat*, *yuṣmat*. Nom.-acc. of all numbers for neuter stems: sg. *phalam*, *vāri*, *madhu*, *kartṛ* for dual and plural see above. Abl.-gen. sg. except for masculine and neuter a-stems and personal pronouns: *senāyās*, *agnes*, *kṛtes/kṛtyās*, *vārīṇas*, *dhenos/dhenvās*, *madhunas*, *devyās*, *vadhvās*, *sakhyus*, *pitus*, *mātus*, *kartus*, *gos*, *rājñas*, *vācas*, *srajas*, but *devāt devasya* (similarly for *phala-*), *mat mama*, *tvat tava*. The accusative plural of feminine *ā*-stems and consonant stems is homophonous with the nominative and vocative plural (see above), but other stems make a distinction: *devān*, *agnīn*, *kṛtīs*, *vāyūn*, *dhenūs*, *devīs*, *vadhūs*, *sakhīn*, *pitṝn*, *mātṝs*, *rājñas*. In the singular, a few stems make no distinction between nominative and vocative (e.g. *gaus*, *vāk*, *śrīs* 'splendour, wealth'), but the two are usually distinguished: *devas*, *deva*; *senā*, *sene*; *agnis*, *agne*; *kṛtis*, *kṛte*, *vāri*, *vāre/vāri*; *vāyus*, *vāyo*; *dhenus*, *dheno*; *madhu*, *madho/madhu*; *devī*, *devi*; *vadhūs*, *vadhu*; *sakhā*, *sakhe*; *pitā*, *pitar*, *mātṛ*, *kartṛ rājā*, *rājan*. As can be seen, certain endings have variants according to stems, and this is true of the genitive plural, which has *-ām* after consonant stems (*rājñām*, *vācām*, *srajām*) and some vowel stems (e.g. *śriyām*, *gavām*) but *-nām* after most vowel stems, with lengthening of short vowels before this ending: *devānām*, *phalānām*, *senānām*, *agnīnam* etc.; however, personal pronouns have *-kam* (*asmākam*, *yuṣmākam*), and other pronominals have *-sām* (e.g. *teṣām* 'of them').

Endings are divisible into two groups with respect to phonological and grammatical alternations; nominative, vocative, accusative singular and dual and nominative plural for non-neuter stems as well as the nominative and accusative plural for neuter stems are strong endings, others are weak endings. Consonant-initial weak endings behave phonologically as though they were separated from stems by a word boundary; for example, *as*-stems have variants with *-o* before *-bhyām* (inst.-dat.-abl. du.), *-bhis* (inst. pl.), *-bhyas* (dat. -abl. *-aḥ* pl.), *-aḥ* before *-su* (loc. pl.): *manas-* 'mind, spirit': nom.-acc. sg. *manas*, inst. sg. *manasā* but *manobhyām*, *manobhis*, *manaḥsu*.

Stems show variation that in part reflects Proto-Indo-European ablaut alternation. For example: *agni-/agne-* (*agnay-* before vowels), *vāyu-/vāyo-*(*vāyav-*), *sakhi-/sakhe-/sakhāy-/sakhā-*, *pitṛ-/pitar-/pitā-*, *kartṛ-/kartar-*, *kartār-/kartā-*, *rājan-/rājān-/rājā-/rājñ-* (before vocalic weak endings)/*rāj*-; (before consonantal weak endings). There are also heteroclitic stems such as *asthi-/asthan-* (nt.) 'bone': nom.-acc. sg. *asthi*, du. *asthinī*, pl. *asthīni*, inst.-dat.-abl. du. *asthibhyām*, etc., with *asthi*- before consonantal weak endings, but inst. sg. *asthnā* etc., with *asthn*- before vocalic weak endings, and loc. sg. *asthani/ asthni*. Due to the palatalisation of *k*, *g* to *c*, *j* before front vowels prior to the merger of *ĕ* with *ă* and to analogic realignments, there are stems with palatals before vocalic endings and velars elsewhere; e.g. *vāc-*, *sraj-* (see above).

Adjectives generally pattern in the manner of comparable nouns. For example, *śukla-*, *śuklā-* 'white', *śuci-* 'bright', *guru-* 'weighty, heavy', *paṅgū-* 'lame' inflect in the same way as noun stems in -*a*, -*ā*, -*i*, -*u*, -*ū*. There are also consonant stem adjectives with ablaut alternation; e.g. *sant-/sat-* 'being' (m. nom. sg. *san*, nom.-acc. du. *santau*, nom. pl. *santas*, acc. sg. *santam*, acc. pl. *satas*, inst. sg. *satā*, inst.-dat.-abl. du. *sadbhyām*, etc.), *gacchant-/gacchat-* 'going' (*gacchan*, *gacchantau*, *gacchantas*, *gacchantam*, *gacchatas*, *gacchatā*, *gacchadbhyām*, etc.), *vidvans-/vidvāns-/viduṣ-/vidvad-* 'one who knows' (*vidvān*, *vidvan* (voc. sg.), *vidvāṃsau*, *vidvāṃsas*, *vidvāṃsam*, *viduṣā*, *vidvadbhyām*, etc.). In addition, there are adjectives that inflect pronominally. For example, nom. pl. *sarve*, dat. sg. *sarvasmai* (m.-nt.), *sarvasyai* (f.), gen. pl. *sarveṣām*, *sarvāsām*, from *sarvă-* 'whole, all', are comparable to *te*, *tasmai*, *tasyai*, *teṣām*, *tāsām* from *tă* 'this, that'.

Personal pronouns not only have variants but also distinguish between independently accented and enclitic forms: acc. sg. *mā tvā*, dat. sg. *me te*, acc.-dat.-gen. du. *nau vām*, acc.-dat.-gen. pl. *nas vas* are enclitics corresponding to sg. acc. *mām tvām*, dat. *mahyam tubhyam*, gen. *mama tava*, du. acc. *āvām yuvām*, dat. *āvābhyām yuvābhyām*, gen. *āvayos yuvayos*, pl. acc. *asmān yuṣmān*, dat. *asmabhyam yuṣmabhyam*, gen. *asmākam yuṣmākam*. Demonstrative pronouns distinguish various degrees of proximity and distance: *etad* 'this here', *idam* 'this', *tad* 'this, that', *adas* 'that yonder' (all nom.-acc. sg. nt.). Interrogative and relative pronouns respectively have *kă-*, *yă-*, which inflect like pronominal *a*-stems except in the nominative and accusative singular neuter of the former (*kim yad*).

The Sanskrit system of number words is a familiar Indo-European one in that terms for 'one' to 'four' show inflectional and gender variation, but it also differs from the system of other ancient Indo-European languages in that higher number words also inflect; e.g. inst. pl. *pañcabhis* 'five', *ṣaḍbhis* 'six', *saptabhis* 'seven', *aṣṭābhis* 'eight', *navabhis* 'nine', *daśabhis* 'ten'.

Sanskrit is also like other older Indo-European languages in using suffixes for deriving what are traditionally called comparatives and superlatives, with two kinds of suffixes. For example, *garīyas-* 'quite heavy', *gariṣṭha-* 'exceedingly heavy' have -*īyas* and -*iṣṭha* following *gar-*, a form of the base that appears in the adjectival derivative *guru-*, but -*tara* and -*tama* follow adjectival stems, as in *madhumattara-* 'quite sweet', *madhumattama-* 'exceedingly sweet', from the stem *madhumat-*. It is noteworthy that -*tara*, -*tama* are used not only in derivates like *uttara-* 'upper, superior', *uttama-* 'highest', from *ud* 'up', but also in derivates from terms like *na* 'not' and finite verb forms: *natarām* 'the more not so (in view of an additional argument)', *natamām* 'all the more not so', *pacatitarām* 'cooks quite well', *pacatitamām* 'cooks exceedingly well'.

Derived nominal bases formed directly from verb roots include action nouns like *gati-* 'going', *pāka-* 'cooking', agent nouns such as *kartṛ-*, *kāraka-* 'doer, maker', object nouns like *karman-* 'deed, object', instrument nouns such as *karaṇa-* 'means', participles like *gata-* 'gone', *kṛta-* 'done, made', gerunds, gerundives and abstract nouns that function as infinitives (see Section 1.2). Bases with secondary derivate affixes (*taddhita* affixes) are of several types. There is a large group of derivates that correspond to phrases of the type *X-E Y-*, with which they alternate, where the values of *X-E* are case forms of particular nominals and *Y* stands for a nominal whose meaning is attributable to the derivational affix. For example, there are patronymics such as *dākṣi-* 'son of Dakṣa': any case form of *dākṣi-* corresponds to and alternates with a phrase containing the genitive *dākṣasya* 'of Dakṣa' and a form of *putra-* 'son' or a synonym. Other derivatives are formed from a more restricted set of nominals – predominantly pronominals – and correspond to particular case forms; e.g. *tatas* 'from that, thence', *tatra* 'in that, there' correspond respectively to ablative and locative forms of *tad-* 'this, that', with which they alternate. There are also redundant affixes. For example, *aśvaka-* 'nag' differs in meaning from *aśva-* 'horse', but *avika-* and *avi* 'sheep' show no such semantic difference. Moreover, some taddhita affixes form derivates which do not alternate with forms or phrases containing items to which they are added. Thus, *kṛtrima-* 'artificial' has a suffix *-ma*, but *kṛtrima-* does not alternate with a phrase containing a form of *kṛtri-* since there is no such action noun: once *-tri* is affixed to *kṛ*, then *-ma* is obligatory.

Compounds are of four general types: tatpuruṣa (determinative), dvandva (copulative), bahuvrīhi (exocentric) and a type that is usually invariant (avyayībhava). The first member of a tatpuruṣa compound is generally equivalent to a case form other than a nominative. For example, *tatpuruṣas* (nom. sg. m.) 'his man, servant' is equivalent to *tasya puruṣas*, with which it can alternate. Similarly, *grāmagatas* 'gone to the village' is equivalent to *grāmaṁ gatas*, with the accusative *grāmam* 'village'. There is a subtype of tatpuruṣa compounds in which the first member is coreferential with the second, which it modifies, as in *nīlotpalam* 'blue (*nīla-*) lotus', equivalent to *nīlam utpalam*, with two nominatives. Copulative compounds are equivalent to phrases with *ca* 'and'; e.g. *mātāpitarau* 'mother and father' alternates with *mātā pitā ca*. The term *bahuvrīhi* is an example of a bahuvrīhi compound: *bahuvrīhis* is equivalent to *bahur vrīhir asya*, used with reference to someone who has (*asya* 'of this') much (*bahus*) rice (*vrīhis*); similarly: *prāptodaka-* '(somewhere) that water (*udaka-*) has reached (*prāpta-*)', *ūḍharatha-* '(an animal) by which a chariot (*ratha-*) has been drawn (*ūḍha-*)'. There are also exocentric compounds which, for technical reasons, belong to the tatpuruṣa group; e.g. *pañcagava-* 'a group of five cows', a member of the subgroup of tatpuruṣas called dvigu. Avyayībhava compounds are generally, though not always, invariant; e.g. *upāgni* 'near the fire', *anujyeṣṭham* 'according to (*anu*) seniority (*jyeṣṭha-*"oldest")'. Compounds like *upāgni* do not have alternative phrases containing the members of the derivate.

2.2.3 Verbal System

The basic elements on which the Sanskrit verbal system is built are the verb base or root, either primary or derived, and the present-imperfect stem. The root is the base for the present-imperfect stem, for various aorist stems and future formations, the perfect, the conditional and the precative. The present-imperfect stem is the basis not only for present and imperfect forms but also for imperative and optative forms. Although Sanskrit has eliminated quite a few complexities found in Vedic, its verbal system is still varied.

There is a systematic contrast between active and medio-passive. Some verbs take only active endings in agentive forms, others only middle endings. For example, the present *asmi, asi, asti* (1, 2, 3 sg.), *svas, sthas, stas* (1, 2, 3 du.), *smas, stha, santi* (1, 2, 3 pl.) and the imperfect *āsam āsīs āsīt, āsva āstam āstām, āsma āsta āsan* have only active

391

endings with *as* 'be', and *āse āsse āste, āsvahe āsāthe āsāte, āsmahe ādhve āsate, āsi āsthās āsta, āsvahi āsāthām āsātām, āsmahi ādhvam āsata* have middle endings with *ās* 'be seated'. Other verbs take either active or middle endings in agentive forms, depending on a semantic contrast: if the result of the act in question is intended for the agent, middle endings are used, if not, active endings occur. For example, *kurute* is used with reference to someone making something for himself, *karoti* of one making something for another. Medio-passive endings alone are used in passives; e.g. *kaṭaḥ kriyate* 'a mat (*kaṭas*) is being made', with *-te* after the passive stem *kriya-*. Sanskrit also has formally passive forms comparable to the impersonal middle found in other Indo-European languages (the type Latin *itur* 'it is gone' i.e. 'one goes'), but it allows an agent to be signified with an instrumental in construction with such forms; e.g. *devadattena supyate* 'Devadatta is sleeping', with the formally passive *supyate* (act. *svapiti*) and the agentive instrumental *devadattena*. In both active and middle sets, three groups of endings are distinguished, which, following usual western terminology, I shall call primary, secondary and perfect endings. Although comparative evidence shows that certain primary endings were originally complexes with a particle, analogic developments have obscured this relation in some instances. The contrast between primary and secondary endings has been illustrated above: primary active: *-mi, -si (asi < as-si), -ti; -vas, -thas, -tas; -mas, -tha, -anti/ati* (e.g. *juhvati* 'they offer oblations'); secondary active: *-am, -s, -t* (augmented *-is -īt*); *-va, -tam, tām; -ma, -ta, -ant/us* (e.g. *ajuhavus* 'they offered oblations', *adus* 'they have given', *akārṣus* 'they have made'); primary medio-passive: *-e, -se, -te; -vahe, -āthe, -āte; -mahe, -dhve (ādhve < ās -dhve), -ate/ ante* (e.g. *edhante* 'they thrive'); secondary medio-passive: *-i, -thās, -ta; -vahi, -āthām, -ātām; -mahi, -dhvam, -ata/anta*. Certain endings are particular to the perfect, as can be seen from the following (*kṛ*): active: *cakā̆r-a, cakartha, cakār-a; cakṛ-va, cakr-athus, cakr-atus; cakṛ-ma, cakr-a, cakṛ-us*; medio-passive: *cakr-e, cakṛ-ṣe, cakr-e; cakṛ-vahe, cakr-āthe, cakr-āte; cakṛ-mahe, cakṛdhve, cakr-ire*.

There is also a contrast between augmented and unaugmented stems. Indicative imperfect and aorist forms, as well as those of the conditional, have augmented stems. The augment is *a* for consonant-initial bases, *ā* for vowel-initial bases; e.g. imperfect *akarot*, aorist *akārṣīt*, conditional *akariṣyat* from *kṛ* imperfect *āsit* (3 pl. *āsan*) from *as*.

Present-imperfect stems may be considered according to two major criteria. Some stems consist simply of verb roots, others have affixes; some stems exhibit grammatical alternation (ablaut), others do not. Stems that do not show grammatical alternation regularly have suffixes with *-a*: root-accented *bhav-a-* 'be, become' (*bhavāmi, bhavasi, bhavati; bhavāvas, bhavathas, bhavatas; bhavāmas, bhavatha, bhavanti*), *edh-a-* 'thrive' (*edhe, edhase, edhate; edhāvahe, edhethe, edhete; edhāmahe, edhadve, edhante*); *dīv-ya-* 'gamble' (*dīvyāmi*, etc.); suffix-accented *tud-a-* 'goad, wound' (*tudāmi* etc.), passive *kri-ya-*. Such stems have *-ā* (< **o* by 'Brugmann's Law') before *-v-, -m-* of endings and *-e-* in second and third dual medio-passive forms. Root presents generally exhibit ablaut variation: full-grade in the singular active indicative, zero-grade elsewhere. For example: *as-ti, stas, s-anti; han-ti, ha-tas, ghn-anti* (*han* 'kill'); *dveṣ-ṭi, dviṣ-ṭas, dviṣ-anti; dviṣ-ṭe, dviṣ-āte* (*dviṣ* 'hate') *dog-dhi, dug-dhas, duh-anti; dugdhe, duh-āte, duh-ate* (*duh* 'milk'). On the other hand, *ad* 'eat' has an invariant root stem (*at-ti at-tas ad-anti*) due in the first instance to phonologic developments (e.g. 3 du. **tas < ttas < d-tas*) that led to remodelling, and bases in *-ā* generalised this vowel in root presents, as in *yāti, yātas, yānti* (*yā* 'go, travel'). Moreover, there are some verbs with inherited invariant root presents, such as *ās, vas* 'have on, wear' (*vas-te, vas-āte, vas-ate*), *śī* 'lie, recline' (*śe-te,* *śay-āte, śe-rate*). Further, root presents of verbs in *-u* have *-au* instead of *-o* in alternation with *-u*, e.g. *stau-ti, stu-tas, stuv-anti* (*stu* 'praise'). There are also reduplicated stems, as in *juho-ti, juhu-tas, juhv-ati* (*hu* 'offer oblations'). In addition, ablauting present-imperfect stems are formed with suffixes and an infix. Thus, *śakno-/śaknu-* (*śak* 'be able'), *cino-/cinu-* (*ci* 'gather, heap'), *suno-/sunu-* (*su* 'press juice out of something') have a suffix *-no-/-nu-* (*-nv-* before vowels, *-nuv-* if the root ends in a consonant): *śaknoti, śaknutas, śaknuvanti; cinoti, cinutas, cinvanti, cinute, cinvāte, cinvate; sunoti, sunute*, etc. But *chi-na-d-/chi-n-d-* (*chinatti, chinttas, chindanti; chintte, chindāte, chindate*) shows an infix *-na-/-n-* added to *chid* 'cut'. Stems such as *pu-nā-/pu-nī-/pu-n-* 'purify' (*punāti, punītas, punanti, punīte, punāte, punate*), with short root vowels (contrast *pū-ta-* 'purified'), reflect an inherited formation with an infix added to a laryngeal base (Proto-Indo-European *-ne-H-/-n-H-*), but the types *krī-ṇā-* ... 'buy' (*krīṇāti, krīṇite* etc.), *badh-nā-* ... 'tie up' (*badhnāti*, etc.), with *-nā* etc. after a long vowel (cf. *krī-ta-* 'bought') or a consonant, show that this has been reanalysed as a suffix comparable to *-no-/-nu-*. Historical developments led to the creation of a stem *karo-/kuru-* (*karoti, kurutas, kurvanti, kurute, kurvāte, kurvate*) from *kṛ*, in addition to the earlier *kṛṇo-/kṛṇu*, which allowed the abstraction of a suffix *-o-/-u-*, as in *tano-/tanu-* (*tanoti, tanute*, etc.), comparable to *śakno-/śaknu-*, from *tan* 'stretch', although originally this was the same suffix as in the type *śakno-/śaknu-*, only with bases in *-n* (*tano-/tanu- < *tṇ-neu-/yṇ-nu-*).

Third person active and medio-passive imperative forms respectively have *-u, ām* instead of *-i, -e* of present indicatives; c.g. *as-tu, s-antu; ās-tām, ās-ātām, ās-atām*. However, second singular active imperatives of stems in *-a* have no overt ending: *bhav-a, dīv-ya, tud-a*. The same is true of the type *cinu*. However, if *-u* of the suffix *-nu-* follows a cluster, the imperative retains the ending *-hi*: *śaknuhi*; and this ending has a variant *-dhi* after *juhu-* and consonant-final stems: *juhudhi, chindhi* (< *chinddhi*). In addition, following consonant-final stems one has *-āna-* for presents with *-nā-*: *punīhi, krīṇīhi*, but *badhāna*. Second singular middle imperatives have a suffix *-sva*; *āssva, edhasva, cinuṣva*. First person imperative forms are historically subjunctives (see Section 1.2): *bhavāni, bhavāva, bhavāma; edhai, edhāvahai, edhāmahai*. Other forms simply have secondary endings. In addition, there is an imperative with *-tāt* for both second and third singular, which, according to Pāṇini's description, was used in wishing someone well, as in *jīvatāt* 'may you/he live long'.

Stems in *-a* form optatives with *-ī-/-īy-*; other stems have optatives with *-yā-/-y-* in active forms and *-ī-/-īy-* in medio-passive forms. Optatives have the usual secondary endings except for active third plural *-us*, middle first singular *-a*, third plural *-ran*. For example: *bhaveyam, bhaves, bhavet, bhaveva, bhavetam, bhavetām, bhavema, bhaveta, bhaveyus; edheya, edhethās, edheta, edhevahi, edheyāthām, edheyātām, edhemahi, edhedhvam, edheran; syām, syās, syāt, syāva, syātam, syātām, syāma, syāta, syus* (as 'be'); *āsīya, āsīthās, āsīta, āsīvahi, āsīyāthām, asīyātām, āsimahi, āsīdhvam, āsīran*. Although synchronically the types *bhavet, edheta* are analysable as containing *-īy-/-ī-* (*-ey- < -a-īy-,-e- < -a-ī-*), these correspond to optatives elsewhere in Indo-European that point to *-oi-*. In addition, the use of *-yā-* in active and *-ī-* in medio-passive forms represents a redistribution of ablaut variants of an original single affix.

Aorists are either radical or formed with suffixes. Unreduplicated root aorists are rare in Classical Sanskrit as compared with earlier Vedic. Except for the third person singular passive aorist type *akāri* 'has been made' – which is freely formed to any verb, but is not necessarily to be analysed as a root aorist – only active forms of bases in *-ā* (e.g. *dā* 'give': *adāt, adātām, adus*) and of *bhū* 'be, become' (*abhūt, abhūtām, abhūvan*) regularly belong to this type, although some middle forms of root aorists have been incorporated into the sigmatic system. There are also stems in *-a*, such as *agama-* (*agamat, agamatām, agaman*: *gam* 'go'), *aghasa-* (*ghas* 'eat'), *aśaka-* (*śak* 'be able'). In addition, a reduplicated stem in *-a* regularly corresponds to a causative (see below) and supplies aorist forms to a few other verbs; e.g. *adudruva-* (*dru* 'run'). However, the productive Sanskrit aorist formation is sigmatic, of four subtypes: *-s-, -iṣ, -siṣ-, -sa-*. The last developed from the middle of the *s*-aorist of *duh* (e.g. 1 sg. *adhukṣi*, 3 sg. du. pl. *adugdha, adhukṣātām, adhukṣata*), as can be seen from the earliest usage in Vedic, from the fact that *s*-forms are indeed incorporated into the *sa*-paradigm (e.g. mid. 1 sg. *adhukṣi*, 3 sg. *adugdha/adhukṣata*), and from the fact that this aorist is formed only with verbs that have penultimate *i, u, ṛ* and final consonants which give *-kṣ-* in combination with the *-s-* of the suffix. The *s*-aorist itself is characterised by particular variants of roots preceding the suffix. Verbs with *-ĭ-, -ŭ-, -ṛ-* have alternants with *-ai, -au, -ār* before *-s-* in active forms, and verbs with *-ĭ, -ŭ* have variants with *-e, -o* in mediopassive forms, e.g. *ci*: *acaiṣīt, acaiṣṭām, acaiṣus, acaiṣṭa, acaiṣātām, acaiṣata*; *hu*: *ahauṣīt, kṛ*: *akārṣīt* (but middle *akṛta akṛṣātām akṛṣata*). Verbs with medial vowels also have alternants with vṛddhi vowels in active forms, but they have mediopassives with *-a-, -i-, -u-, -ṛ-*, e.g. *pac* 'cook': *apākṣīt, chid*: *achaitsit, rudh* 'obstruct': *arautsit, mṛṣ* 'suffer, allow': *amārṣīt* versus *apakta, achitta, aruddha, amṛṣṭa*. Forms such as *akṛta, adita* (*dā* 'give') beside *alṛṣātām, adiṣātām* etc. and active *adāt*, etc. reflect the incorporation of root aorist forms into the productive sigmatic system. The *iṣ*-aorist is probably best considered originally an *s*-formation to verbs with *-i* from a laryngeal, then spread well beyond these limits. This also has vṛddhi vowels in forms such as *apāvīt, apāviṣṭām, apāviṣus* (*pū*), but in general not for consonant-final bases; e.g. *div* 'gamble': *adevīt*. The *siṣ*-aorist obviously a combination of *-s-* and *-iṣ-*, is of very limited compass, predominantly from verbs in *-ā*; e.g. *ayāsīt*(*yā*).

Although scholars disagree concerning the historical origins of the precative, the place of the forms in question within the Sanskrit system viewed synchronically is fairly clear. The active precative type *bhuyāt, bhuyāstām, bhuyāsus* 'may ... be, prosper' is radical, and the middle type *edhiṣīṣṭa, edhiṣīyāstām*, 'may ... thrive' is sigmatic.

The semantically unmarked future of Sanskrit has a suffix *-(i)ṣya* after a root. In addition, there is a future used with reference to a time beyond the day of reference. In origin, this is a periphrastic formation (see Section 1.2), but synchronically it cannot be treated as such in view of forms like *edhitāhe, edhitāsve, edhitāsmahe* (1 sg. du. pl. mid.), since *as* does not regularly have middle inflection. The future in *-(i)ṣya* (e.g. *bhaviṣyati, edhiṣyate*) is the basis for the Sanskrit conditional, of the type *abhaviṣyat, aidhiṣyata* – with augment and secondary endings – used in both the protasis and the apodosis of contrary-to-fact conditional sentences.

The Sanskrit perfect is generally characterised not only by particular endings but also by reduplication (see above). Yet one inherited perfect, which in Sanskrit functions as a present, lacks reduplication: *veda, vidatus, vidus* 'know(s)'. As can be seen, perfect stems show the same kind of grammatical alternation as found in present and aorist stems. However, for verbs of the structure *CaC*, in which *-a-* is flanked by single consonants the first of which is not subject to modification in a reduplicated syllable, instead of *-CC-* preceded by a reduplicated syllable, one has *CeC* alone; e.g. *tan*: *tatāna, tenatus, tenus*; *śak*: *śaśāka, śekatus, śekus* (contrast *gam*: *jagāma, jagmatus, jagmus*). This represents the spread of a particular form from verbs like *yam* 'extend' (*yayāma, yematus*

($< ya$-*ym*-) ...), *sad* 'sit' (*sasada, sedatus* ($<$ *sa-zd-*) ...). There is also a periphrastic perfect, which in Sanskrit has been extended to some primary verbs; e.g. *hu: juhavāñ cakāra* beside *juhāva.*

As can be seen from what has been said, it is not possible in Sanskrit to predict an aorist formation from the present-imperfect stem of a verb. There are instances where totally separate roots are used suppletively in different formations. Thus, *as* supplies only a present-imperfect stem; other forms are from *bhū* 'be, become': aorist *abhūt*, future *bhaviṣyati*, perfect *babhūva*, infinitive *bhavitum*, past participle *bhūta*-, etc. Similarly: *han* 'strike, kill': aorist *avadhīt*, precative *vadhyāt*, *ad* 'eat': aorist *aghasat*, *i*: aorist *agāt*.

Derived verbs are deverbative or denominative. Causatives are formed with -*i*-/-*e*-, e.g. *kṛ: kār-i* 'have ... do, make'(*kār-ay-a-ti, kār-ay-ate*), *pac: pāc-i, chid: ched-i, yuj-* 'connect, yoke': *yoj-i.* Certain verbs have augmented variants before the causative suffix. For example, many verbs with -*ā* take the augment -*p*, as in *dāp-i* 'have ... give' (*dā*). The causative is also connected with a particular active aorist formation, a reduplicated *a*-aorist; e.g. *kār-i: acīkarat*, etc. (but medio-passive *akārayita, akārayiṣātām*, etc.). Desideratives are formed with -*sa*-, which conditions reduplication; e.g. *kṛ: cikīṣṣati*, etc.). Desiderative forms alternate with phrases consisting of a verb meaning 'wish' and infinitives; e.g. *cikīrṣati = kartum icchati* '... wishes to do, make'. Intensives are formed with -*ya*-, which also conditions a particular type of reduplication; further, intensives have middle inflection; e.g. *kṛ: cekrīya-* (*cekrīyate*) 'do intensely, repeatedly', *chid: cechidya-, yuj: yoyujya-, pac: pāpacya-.* Derived verbs form periphrastic perfects, as *gamayāñ cakāra, cekrīyāñ cakre.* Moreover, such deverbative formations can involve suppletion; e.g. *ad:* desiderative *jighatsa-, i: jigamiṣa-.* Denominatives are formed with several suffixes, principal among which is -*ya*-, and have a broad range of meanings. For example, *putrīyati* (*putrīya-*) corresponds to *putram icchati* '... desires a son', *putram ivācarati* '... behaves (*ācarati*) towards ... as though he were his son (*putram iva*)'; *śyenāyate* corresponds to *śyena ivācarati* 'behaves like a falcon (*śyena iva*)', *tapasyati* is equivalent to *tapaś carati* 'carries out (*carati*) ascetic acts (*tapas*)'. Especially noteworthy in view of the later Indo-Aryan causative type in -*āv-e*- (see Chapter 20, Section 2.2) is the denominative type *satyāpi-* (*satyāpayati*) 'say something is true (*satya*)', known already to Pāṇini which involves -*āp*- and the suffix -*i*-/-*e*-.

2.2.4 Syntax

In major aspects of syntax Sanskrit is a fairly conservative Indo-European language, although it exhibits specifically Indic features. Examples given in the following sketch are based on Pāṇinian sources, reflecting usage that antedates classical literary works, but every construction illustrated has a counterpart in Vedic (see Section 1.2) and literary texts of later times.

The seven cases of the nominal system excluding the vocative (Section 2.2.2) are used with reference to various roles participants play in respect of what is signified by verbs in general or by particular verbs. Typical roles and case forms linked with them are illustrated by the following. In *devadattaḥ kaṭaṁ karoti* 'Devadatta is making (*karoti*) a mat (*kaṭam*)' *devadatto grāmaṁ gacchati* 'Devadatta is going (*gacchati*) to the village (*grāmam*)', the accusatives *kaṭam, grāmam* refer to objects, the latter specifically to a goal of movement. Such a goal is alternatively signified by a dative: *devadatto grāmāya gacchati.* In addition, an object can be designated by a genitive in construction with an agent noun; e.g. *sa kumbhānāṁ kartā* 'he (*sa*) (is) a maker (*kartā*) of pots (*kumbhānām*)'. In the passive sentence *devadattena kaṭaḥ kriyate* 'a mat is being made (*kriyate*) by Devadatta', the instrumental *devadattena* refers to an agent, as does the same form in *devadattena supyate* (Section 2.2.3). The instrumental *dātreṇa* 'sickle' of *dātreṇa lunāti* '... cuts (*lunāti*) with a sickle', on the other hand, refers to a means of cutting. A dative can be used with references not only to a goal of movement but also to a desired object, in construction with *spṛh* 'yearn for': *puṣpebhyaḥ spṛhayati* '... yearns for flowers (*puṣpebhyas*)'. More generally, dative forms designate indirect objects, as in *māṇavakāya bhikṣāṃ dadāti* '... gives (*dadāti*) alms (*bhikṣām*) to the lad (*māṇavakāya*)'. Ablatives can be used to signify points of departure, as in *grāmād ā gacchati* '... is coming (*ā gacchati*) from the village', but they have other functions as well; for example, in *vṛkebhyo bibheti* '... is afraid (*bibheti*) of wolves', *vṛkebhyas* refers to wolves as sources of fear. Locative forms are used of loci where agents and objects are while they are involved in whatever a verb signifies; e.g. *devadattaḥ sthālyāṃ gṛha odanaṃ pacati* 'Devadatta is cooking (*pacati*) rice (*odanam*) in a pot (*sthālyām*) in the house (*gṛhe*)'.

There are also relations that do not directly involve verb meanings, so that syntactically one has nominals directly linked with each other. The typical case form for such relations is the genitive; e.g. *vṛkṣasya śākhā-* 'branch (*śākhā-*) of a/the tree (*vṛkṣasya*)' in *vṛkṣasya śākhāṃ paraśunā chinatti* '... is cutting a branch (*śākhām*) of the tree with an axe (*paraśunā*)'. Particular nominals, however, co-occur with other case forms. For example, *namo devebhyaḥ* '(let there be) homage (*namas*) to the gods' has the dative *devebhyas* in construction with *namas*. Moreover, pre- and postposed particles take part in such constructions: *sādhur devadatto mātaraṃ prati* 'Devadatta (is) good (*sadhus*) towards his mother (*mātaraṃ prati*)', *putreṇa sahāgataḥ* 'he came (*āgatas*) with his son (*putreṇa saha*)', *māṣān asmai tilebhyaḥ prati dadāti* '... gives (*dadāti*) this man (*asmai*) māṣa-beans (*māṣān*) in exchange for sesame seeds (*tilebhyaḥ prati*)', *ā pāṭaliputrād varṣati* 'it is raining (*varṣati*) up to Pāṭaliputra (*ā pāṭaliputrāt*)' have the accusative *mātaram* linked to *prati*, the instrumental *putreṇa* connected to *saha*, and the ablatives *tilebhyas*, *pāṭaliputrāt* construed with *prati* and *ā*.

There are different kinds of complex sentences. Some involve related finite verb forms, others finite forms connected with particular nominal derivates, infinitival and participial. For example, optatives are used in conditional sentences such as *mriyeya ... na syas tvaṃ yadi me gatiḥ* 'I would die (*mriyeya*) if (*yadi*) you (*tvam*) were (*syās*) not (*na*) my (*me*) refuge (*gatis*)', but *edhān āhartum gaccha ti* ' ... is going (*gacchati*) in order to fetch (*āhartum*) firewood (*edhān*)' has *gacchati* linked to the infinitive *āhartum*, itself connected with the accusative *edhān*. There is an elliptical version of the second sentence type, with a dative referring to the direct object in question: *edhebhyo gacchati* '... is going for firewood'. Present participle forms occur in complex sentences such as *pacantaṃ devadattam paśyati* '... is watching (*paśyati*) Devadatta cook', in which *pacantam* 'cooking' agrees with *devadattam*, or *grāmaṃ gacchatā devadattena bhuktam* 'Devadatta ate on his way to the village', where the participial form *gacchatā* 'going' agrees with the agentive instrumental *devadattena*, both construed with *bhuktam* 'eaten'. In addition, Sanskrit has absolute constructions, the prevalent one being a locative absolute, as in *goṣu duhyamānāsu gataḥ* 'he left (*gatas*) while the cows were being milked': the present participle *duhyamānāsu* (loc. pl. f.) agrees with *goṣu* 'cows', both used absolutely. Where two or more verbs signify sequentially related acts or states, Sanskrit subordinates by using gerunds; e.g. *bhuktvā vrajati* '... eats before going out', with the gerund *bhuktvā* 'after eating', *piba niṣadya* (see Section 1.2).

Examples cited illustrate the agreement features of Sanskrit. Finite verb forms – which themselves signal person and number differences – agree in person and number with nominals that function as grammatical subjects used in referring to agents or objects. Participial forms and other adjectivals, whether attributive or predicative, agree in gender and number with the nominals to which they are complements. The examples also illustrate the most common aspects of Sanskrit word order. What may be called the neutral word order in prose, where metrical constraints are not at play, generally has the verb in last position. However, a sentence does not necessarily have an overt verb: Sanskrit has nominal sentences, in which a third person present form of a verb meaning 'be' is not overtly expressed. There are few restrictions on word order that are strictly formal, but the position of certain particles is fixed: particles like *vai* 'as is known, truly', *ced* 'if' occupy second position, as does *ca* 'and' used as a sentence connective. Similarly, the enclitic pronouns *mā*, *tvā*, etc. (Section 2.2.2) are excluded from sentence-initial position.

An aspect of overall sentence prosody is worth noting in this context. A sentence-internal vocative generally has no high-pitched vowel. Under certain conditions, however, the vowels of an utterance are all pronounced monotone, except for the last vowel, which is then not only high-pitched but also prolated. For example, in *ā gaccha bho māṇavaka devadatta* 'come along (*ā gaccha*), Devadatta my boy (*bho māṇavaka devadatta*)', used in calling Devadatta from afar, all the vowels up to the *-a* of the vocative *devadatta* are uttered without pitch variations, but this last vowel is prolated and udātta.

Bibliography

Burrow (1965) is a summary of the prehistory and history of Sanskrit, including Vedic, with references to Middle Indo-Aryan; somewhat personal views are given in places, but the work remains valuable. For a good summary of views on the dialects of Old Indo-Aryan, with discussion of theories proposed and references, see Emeneau (1966).

The standard reference grammar is Whitney (1889). Renou (1956) is an insightful summary of the grammar, vocabulary and style of different stages of Sanskrit, including Vedic, with text selections and translations. Wackernagel (1896–) is the most thorough reference grammar of Sanskrit, but remains incomplete: the published volumes are: I (*Lautlehre*), reissued with a new 'Introduction générale' by L. Renou and 'Nachträge' by A. Debrunner (1957); II, 1 (*Einleitung zur Wortlehre, Nominalkomposition*), 2nd edn with 'Nachträge' by A. Debrunner (1957); II, 2 (*Die Nominalsuffixe*), by A. Debrunner (1954); III (*Nominalflexion – Zahlwort-Pronomen*) (1930); there is also a *Register zur altindischen Grammatik von J. Wackernagel und A. Debrunner* by R. Hauschild (1964). Lazzeroni (1998) is a brief introductory survey of the Sanskrit language from the vantage point of Indo-European comparative linguistics. Cardona (2003) is a description of Sanskrit, based on the Indian tradition of grammatical description.

References

Burrow, T. 1965. *The Sanskrit Language*, 2nd edn (Faber and Faber, London)
Cardona, G. 2003. 'Sanskrit', in G. Cardona and D. Jain (eds) *The Indo-Aryan Languages*, (Routledge, London and New York), pp. 104–60.
Emeneau, M.B. 1966. 'The Dialects of Old Indo-Aryan', in H. Birnbaum and J. Puhvel (eds.), *Ancient Indo-European Dialects* (University of California Press, Berkeley and Los Angeles), pp. 123–38.

Lazzeroni, R. 1998. 'Sanskrit', in A. Giacalone Ramat and P. Ramat (eds) *The Indo-European Languages* (Routledge, London and New York), pp. 98–124

Renou, L. 1956. *Histoire de la langue sanskrite* (IAC, Paris)

Wackernagel, J. 1896–. *Altindische Grammatik* (Vandenhoek and Ruprecht, Göttingen)

Whitney, W.D. 1889. *Sanskrit Grammar, Including Both the Classical Language and the Older Dialects, of Veda and Brahmana*, 2nd edn (Harvard University Press, Cambridge, MA)

22

Hindi-Urdu

Yamuna Kachru

1 Introduction

Hindi is a New Indo-Aryan language spoken in the north of India. It belongs to the Indo-Iranian branch of the Indo-European family of languages. It is spoken by more than three hundred million people either as a first or second language in India, and by peoples of Indian origin in Trinidad, Guyana, Fiji, Mauritius, South Africa and many other countries. It is the official language of India, and English is the associate official language. In addition, Hindi is the state language of Bihar, Chattisgarh, Haryana, Himachal Pradesh, Jharkhand, Madhya Pradesh, Rajasthan, Uttarkhand (formerly, Uttaranchal) and Uttar Pradesh.

Urdu, a language closely related to Hindi, is spoken by twenty-three million people in India and approximately eight million people in Pakistan as a mother tongue. It is the official language of Pakistan. In India it is the state language of the states of Jammu and Kashmir, and in Uttar Pradesh, it shares that status with Hindi.

Hindi and Urdu have a common form known as Hindustani which is essentially a colloquial language (Verma 1933), adopted by Mahatma Gandhi and the Indian National Congress as a symbol of national identity during the struggle for freedom. It, however, never became a language of literature and high culture (see Bhatia 1987 and Rai 1984 for details of Hindi-Urdu–Hindustani controversy).

2 Background

It is difficult to date the beginnings of the New Indo-Aryan languages of India. Scholars generally agree that the development of Indo-Aryan languages of India took place in three stages. The Old Indo-Aryan stage is said to extend from 1500 BC to approximately 600 BC. The Middle Indo-Aryan stage spans the centuries between 600 BC and AD 1000. The Middle Indo-Aryan stage is further subdivided into an early Middle Indo-Aryan stage (600–200 BC), a transitional stage (200 BC–AD 200), a second Middle Indo-Aryan stage (AD 200–600), and a late Middle Indo-Aryan stage (AD 600–1000). The period from AD 1000–1200/1300 is designated the Old New Indo-Aryan stage because it is at this stage that the changes that began at the Middle Indo-Aryan stage became established and the New Indo-Aryan languages such as Hindi, Bengali, Marathi, etc., assumed distinct identities.

Before proceeding with a description of Hindi-Urdu, it may be useful to sketch the outline of the sociolinguistic situation of Hindi-Urdu in the Indian subcontinent (Rai 1984). The name Hindi is not Indian in origin; it is believed to have been used by the Persians to denote the peoples and languages of India (Verma 1933). Hindi as a language is said to have emerged from the patois of the market place and army camps during the period of repeated Islamic invasions and establishment of Muslim rule in the north of India between the eighth and tenth centuries AD. The speech of the areas around Delhi, known as *khari boli* [k'həṛī bolī], was adopted by the Afghans, Persians and Turks as a common language of interaction with the local population. In time, it developed a variety called Urdu (from Turkish *ordu* 'camp'). The term Urdu was not used for the language before the end of the eighteenth century, as Faruqi, Rai and others agree. Hindustani as a label for language was used at least since the time of the Mughal Emperor Babur (ruled 1526–30) and even before that (Srivastava 1994: 90). The most common names used by Amir Khusrau (1253–1325) and other writers were Hindi, Hindvi or Rexta (mixed language), and later Dakhini. The early form of the language developed at the market place and the army camps, naturally, had a preponderance of borrowings from Arabic and Persian. Consequently, it was also known as *Rexta* 'mixed language'.

The speech of the indigenous population, though influenced by Arabic and Persian, remained relatively free from large-scale borrowings from these foreign languages. In time, as Urdu gained some patronage at Muslim courts and developed into a literary language, the variety used by the general population gradually replaced Sanskrit, literary Prakrits and Apabhramshas as the literary language of the midlands (*madhyadesha*).[1] This latter variety looked to Sanskrit for linguistic borrowings and Sanskrit, Prakrits and Apabhramshas for literary conventions. It is this variety that became known as Hindi. Thus, both Hindi and Urdu have their origins in the *khari boli* speech of Delhi and its environs although they are written in two different scripts (Urdu in Perso-Arabic and Hindi in Devanagari). The two languages differ in minor ways in their sound system, morphology and syntax. These differences are pointed out at appropriate places below.

Both Urdu and Hindi have been in use as literary languages since the twelfth century. The development of prose, however, begins only in the eighteenth century under the influence of English, which marks the emergence of Hindi and Urdu as fully fledged literary languages.

3 Phonology

The segmental phonemes of Hindi-Urdu are listed in Table 22.1. The phonemes that occur only in the highly Sanskritised or highly Persianised varieties are given in parentheses. The two noteworthy features of the inventory of consonant phonemes are the following: Hindi-Urdu still retains the original Indo-European distinction between aspirated and unaspirated voiced plosives (cf. Indo-European *ghṛdho* and Hindi g'ər 'house'). It retains the distinction between aspirated and unaspirated voiceless plosives that emerged in Indo-Aryan, i.e. the distinction between *kal* 'time' and k'al 'skin'. Another Indo-Aryan feature, that of retroflexion, is also retained in Hindi-Urdu, cf. *tota* 'parrot' and *ṭoṭa* 'lack'. These two features, i.e. those of aspiration and retroflexion, are mainly responsible for why Hindi-Urdu sounds so different from its European cousins.

Table 22.1 Phonemes of Hindi-Urdu

Vowels		Front	Central	Back
High		ī		ū
		ɩ		u
Mid high		e		o
Mid low		ɛ	ə	ɔ
Low			ɑ	

Consonants			Labial	Dental	Retroflex	Alveo-Palatal	Velar	Back Velar
Stop	vls.	unasp	p	t	ʈ	c	k	(q)
		asp	p′	t′	ʈ′	c′	k′	
	vd.	unasp	b	d	ḍ	j	g	
		asp	b′	d′	ḍ′	j′	g′	
Nasal			m	n	ṇ	ɲ	ŋ	
Flap	vd.	unasp			ɽ	r		
		asp			ɽ′			
Lateral						l		
Fricative	vl.		(f)	s	ṣ	ʃ	(x)	
	vd.			(z)		(ʒ)	(ɣ)	
Semi-vowels			w (v)			y		

Oral and nasal vowels contrast, e.g. *ak* 'a plant' and *ãk* 'draw, sketch'; hence, nasalisation is distinctive. Short and long consonants contrast, e.g. *pəta* 'address', *pətta* 'leaf'; hence, length is distinctive.

The contrast between aspirated and unaspirated consonants is maintained in all positions, initial, medial and final. The distinction between tense *ī* and lax *i* and tense *ū* and lax *u*, however, is lost in the final position except in very careful and formal speech in the highly Sanskritised variety.

Stress is not distinctive in Hindi-Urdu; words are not distinguished on the basis of stress alone. For instance, a word such as *kəla* 'art', whether stressed *kə́la* or *kəlá*, means the same. The tense vowels are phonetically long; in pronunciation the vowel quality as well as length is maintained irrespective of the position of the vowel or stress in the word. For instance, the word *muskərahət* 'smile' can either be stressed as *múskərahət* or *muskəráhət*, in either case, the vowel quality and length in the syllable-*ra*-remain unaffected. Words such as *jamata* 'son-in-law' are pronounced with three successive long vowels although only the first or the second syllable is stressed. Stressing and de-stressing of syllables is tied to syllable weight in Hindi-Urdu. Syllables are classified as one of the three measures of weight: light (syllables ending in a lax, short vowel), medium (syllables ending in a tense, long vowel or in a lax, short vowel followed by a consonant) and heavy (others). Where one syllable in a word is of greater weight than others, the tendency is to place the word stress on it. Where more than one syllable is of maximum weight in the word (i.e. there is a succession of medium or heavy syllables), usually the last but one bears the word stress. This stress pattern creates the impression of the staccato rhythm that speakers of English notice about Hindi-Urdu.

The predominant pattern of penultimate stress in Hindi-Urdu is inherited from an earlier stage of Indo-Aryan, i.e. the Middle Indo-Aryan stage. Old Indo-Aryan had phonemic accent of the pitch variety and there is evidence for three pitches in Vedic: *uddātta* 'high, raised', *anudātta* 'low, unraised' and *svarita* 'high falling, falling'. At a later stage of Old Indo-Aryan, Classical Sanskrit does not record accent. By late Old Indo-Aryan, pitch accent seems to have given way to stress accent. There are different opinions about stress accent in Middle Indo-Aryan. It is generally believed that stress occurred on the penultimate syllable of the word, if long, or on the nearest preceding syllable if the penultimate was not long; in words with all short syllables, stress occurred on the initial syllable.

Syllable boundaries in Hindi-Urdu words fall as follows: between successive vowels, e.g. *pa-e* 'legs', *a-I-e* 'come' (hon.), *nə-ī* 'new' (f.), *so-i-e*, 'sleep' (hon.); between vowels and following consonants, e.g. *ro-na* 'to cry', *pə-ta* 'address', *ũ-ca* 'tall, high'; between consonants, e.g. *səɽ-kẽ* 'roads', *pət-la* 'thin', *hin-dī* 'Hindi language'.

As has already been said, Hindi is written in the Devanagari script, which is the script used by Sanskrit, Marathi and Nepali also. On the basis of the evidence obtained from the ancient inscriptions, it is clear that Devanagari is a descendant of the Brahmi script. Brahmi was well established in India some time before 500 BC. Despite some controversy regarding the origin of the Brahmi script, it is generally believed that its sources lie in the same Semitic script which later developed into the Arabic, Hebrew, Greek, Latin, etc. The scripts used for the New Indo-Aryan and the Dravidian languages of India are believed to have developed from the northern and southern varieties of Brahmi.

There are minor differences between the scripts used for Hindi, Sanskrit, Marathi and Nepali. For instance, Hindi does not have the retroflex lateral ळ /ḷ/ or the retroflex vowels ऋ, ऌ /ṛ, ḷ/ and their tense counterparts. It uses the retroflex vowel symbol ऋ /ṛ/ and the symbol for weak aspiration /:/ only in words borrowed from Sanskrit. Although written as ऋ /ṛ/, the vowel is pronounced as a combination of /r/ and /i/.

In general, there is a fairly regular correspondence between the script and the pronunciation. The one notable exception is the pronunciation of the inherent vowel ə. The Devanagari script is syllabic in that every consonant symbol represents the consonant plus the inherent vowel ə, thus, क represents the sound *k* plus ə, or *kə*. Vowels are represented differently according to whether they comprise entire syllables or are parts of syllables, i.e. are immediately preceded by a consonant: thus, the symbol इ represents the syllable *i* but in the syllable *ki*, it has the shape ि, which is adjoined to the symbol for *k*, resulting in कि. Even though each consonant symbol represents a consonant plus the inherent vowel, a word written as कल, i.e. *kələ*, is not pronounced as such, it is pronounced as *kəl* 'yesterday, tomorrow'. That is, all the final inherent vowels are dropped in pronunciation. The rules regarding the realisation of the inherent vowel in pronunciation are as follows; in two or three syllable words, the penultimate inherent vowel is pronounced when the final one is dropped, and in words of four syllables, both the final and the antepenultimate inherent vowels are dropped while the others are pronounced. Thus, *səməjʼə* is pronounced as *səməjʼ* 'understanding', *mehənətə* is pronounced as *mehnət* 'hard work'. These general principles, however, do not apply to words containing medial *h*, loanwords, compounds and words formed with derivational suffixes. For instance, *səmajh* with the inflectional suffix of perfective *-a* is pronounced as *səmjha* 'understood', but with the derivational agentive suffix *-dar* is pronounced *səməjʼdar* 'sensible' (see Ohala 1983 for details of ə-deletion).

Although most derivational and inflectional morphology of Hindi is affixal in nature (i.e. Hindi mostly utilises prefixes and suffixes), there are remnants of the morphophonemic

Table 22.2 Devanagari Script

Vowels
Independent

अ	आ	इ	ई	उ	ऊ	ऋ
ə	ɑ	i	ī	u	ū	ṛ

ए	ऐ	ओ	औ	अं	अः
e	ɛ	o	ɔ	əm	əh

Following Consonants

ा	ि	ी	ु	ू	े	ै	ो	ौ	ं	:
ɑ	i	ī	u	ū	e	ɛ	o	ɔ	əm	əh

Consonants

क	ख	ग	घ	ङ		
kə	k'ə	g'ə	g'ə	ŋə		
च	छ	ज	झ	ञ		
cə	c'ə	jə	j'ə	ɲə		
ट	ठ	ड	ढ	ण	ड़	ढ़
ṭə	ṭ'ə	ḍə	ḍ'ɔ	ṇə	ṛə	ṛ'ə
त	थ	द	ध	न		
tə	t'ə	də	d'ə	nə		
प	फ	ब	भ	म		
pə	p'ə	bə	b'ə	mə		
य	र	ल	व	श	ष	स	ह
yə	rə	lə	və	ʃə	ṣə	sə	hə
क़	ख़	ग़	ज़	फ़		
qə	xə	ɤə	zə	fə		

ablaut alternation of vowels of the *guṇa* and *vṛddhi* types in a substantial number of verbal roots and nominal compounds in Hindi. These are the most frequent and regular of vowel changes for derivation as well as inflection in Sanskrit. A *guṇa* vowel differs from a simple vowel as it results from a vowel combining with another according to the usual rules given below; a *vṛddhi* vowel, by a further lengthening of a *guṇa* vowel. ə is its own *guṇa* and *a* remains unchanged for both *guṇa* and *vṛddhi*. The series of corresponding degrees is as follows (Kellogg 1875):

Chart of *guṇa* and *vṛddhi* Increments[2]

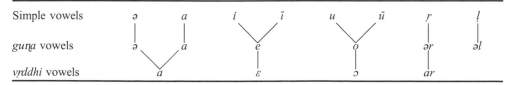

The *guṇa* increment is an Indo-European phenomenon, the *vṛddhi* increment is specifically Indian in origin. These processes are still utilised to some extent in coining new compounds of borrowings from Sanskrit for modernising Hindi. Some examples of the verbal roots that exemplify these processes are pairs such as *kʹul* 'open' (intr.) and *kʹol* 'open' (tr.); *kəʈ* 'cut' (intr.) and *kaʈ* 'cut' (tr.); *dɪkʹ* 'be visible' and *dekʹ* 'see'; and some examples of nominal compounds are *pərəmə* + *īʃvər* = *pərmeʃvər* 'Supreme God'; *məha* + *īʃə* = *maheʃ* 'Great God' (a name of Lord Shiva); *səda* + *evə* = *sədɛv* 'always'. Some examples of modern vocabulary coined on the same principles are *sərvə* + *udəy* = *sərvodəy* 'universal welfare', *mətə* + *ɛky* = *mətɛky* 'unanimity of opinion', *ʃulbʹə* + *iccʹu* = *ʃubʹeccʹu* 'well-wisher'.

To the extent that it shares a basic vocabulary with Hindi, the *guṇa* and *vṛddhi* phenomena are applicable to Urdu as well. The Urdu writing system, however, is based on the Perso-Arabic script. As is clear from Table 22.3, the script lacks adequate vowel symbols but has an overabundance of consonant symbols for the language. Table 22.3 lists the independent forms only.[3]

Table 22.3 The Urdu Alphabet

Letter	Pronunciation	Urdu Name
ا	a*	əlyf
ب	b	be
پ	p	pe
ت	t	te
ٹ	ṭ	ṭe
ث	s	se
ج	ǰ	ǰim
چ	č	če
ح	h	he [/bəṛi he/]
خ	x	xe
د	d	dal
ڈ	ḍ	ḍal
ذ	z	zal
ر	r	re
ڑ	ṛ	ṛe
ز	z	ze
ژ	ž	že
س	s	sin
ش	š	šin
ص	s	swad
ض	z	zward
ط	t	to, toe
ظ	z	zo, zoe
ع	*	əyn
غ	γ	γəyn
ف	f	fe
ق	q	qaf
ک	k	kaf
گ	g	gaf
ل	l	lam
م	m	mim
ن	n	nun
و	v	vao
ە	h	he [/choṭi he/]
ی	y	ye

4 Morphology

A brief description of Hindi-Urdu nominal and verbal morphology follows (for a detailed discussion of derivational and inflectional morphology, see Bailey (1956, 1982), Bhatia (1996), Y. Kachru (2006), McGregor (1972), Russell (1980), Schmidt (1999), Sharma (1958) and Singh and Agnihotri (1997)).

4.1 Nominal

Forms of Hindi-Urdu nouns undergo changes in order to indicate number, gender and case. There are two numbers, singular and plural; two genders, *masculine* and *feminine*; and three cases: *direct*, *oblique* and *vocative*.

Nouns are declined differently according to the gender class and the phonological property of the final segment in the word. Given here are paradigms of the major classes of masculine and feminine nouns.

Paradigm of masculine nouns ending in -a

	Sg.	*Pl.*
Dir.	ləɽka 'boy'	ləɽke
Obl.	ləɽke	ləɽkõ
Voc.	ləɽke	ləɽko

Masculine nouns ending in - i

Dir.	malī 'gardener'	malī
Obl.	malī	mliyõ
Voc.	malī	maliyo

Nouns ending in -ū

Dir.	saɽʹū 'wife's sister's husband'	saɽʹū
Obl.	saɽʹū	saɽʹuõ
Voc.	saɽʹū	saɽʹuo

Nouns ending in a consonant

Dir.	nɔkər 'servant'	nɔkər
Obl.	nɔkər	nɔkrõ
Voc.	nɔkər	nɔkro

Certain masculine nouns ending in -*a* such as such as *raja* 'king', *pita* 'father', *caca* 'father's younger brother', *mama* 'mother's brother' are exceptions in that they do not change for direct plural and oblique singular.

Paradigm of feminine nouns ending in -ī

	Sg.	*Pl.*
Dir.	ləɽkī 'girl'	ləɽkiā̃
Obl.	ləɽkī	ləɽkiyõ
Voc.	ləɽkī	ləɽkiyo

Nouns ending in -a

Dir.	mata 'mother'	mataẽ
Obl.	mata	mataõ
Voc.	mata	matao

Nouns ending in -ū

Dir.	bəhū 'daughter-in-law'	bəhuẽ
Obl.	bəhū	bəhuõ
Voc.	bəhū	bəhuo

Nouns ending in a consonant

Dir.	bəhən 'sister'	bəhnẽ
Obl.	bəhən	bəhnõ
Voc.	bəhən	bəhno

In Perso-Arabic borrowings, High Urdu keeps the Perso-Arabic plural markers, e.g. *kaɣəz* 'papcr', *kaɣzat* 'papers'.

The oblique case forms are used whenever a noun is followed by a postposition, e.g. *ləɽke ko* 'to the boy', *g'ərõ mẽ* 'in the houses', *ləɽkiyõ ke sat'* 'with the girls', etc.

The adjectives occur before the noun and agree with their head noun in number, gender and case. They do not, however, exhibit the full range of forms. This can be seen in the paradigm of *əcc'A* 'good' (A is a cover symbol for the various inflections).

Adjective *əcc'A* 'Good'

Masculine	*Sg.*	*Pl.*
Dir.	əcc'a	əcc'e
Obl.	əcc'e	əcc'e
Voc.	əcc'e	əcc'e

Feminine	*Sg.*	*Pl.*
Dir./ Obl./ Voc.	əcc'ī	əcc'ī

The adjectives that end in a consonant, e.g. *sundər* 'beautiful', and in a vowel other than -*a* e.g. *nəklī* 'false, artificial', are invariant, e.g. *sundər ləɽka/ləɽkī* 'handsome boy/beautiful girl', *nəklī dãt (m.)/bãh (f.)* 'artificial teeth/arm'.

The main postpositions that indicate case relations such as accusative, dative, instrumental, etc., are the following: *ne* 'agentive, marker of a transitive subject in the perfective', *ko* 'accusative/dative', *se* 'instrumental/ablative/comitative', *mẽ, pər* 'locative', *kA* 'possessive/genitive', and *ke liye* 'benefactive'. There are several other postpositions that indicate location, direction, etc., such as *ke pas* 'near', *kī or* 'towards', *ke samne* 'in front of', *ke pīc'e* 'behind', *ke bahar* 'out (of)', *ke əndər* 'inside', *ke par* 'across', *ke bina* 'without', *ke sat'* 'with' and *ke hat'/dvara* 'through'.

The pronouns have more case forms than the nouns, as is clear from the following paradigm:

	1st		*2nd*		*3rd*	
	Sg.	*Pl.*	*Sg.*	*Pl.*	*Sg.*	*Pl.*
Dir.	mɛ̃	həm	tū	tum	yəh/vəh	ye/ve
Obl.	muj'	həm	tuj'	tum	is/us	in/un
Poss.	merA	həmərA	terA	tumhərA	iskA/uskA	inkA/unkA

The third person pronominal forms are the same as the proximate and remote demonstratives, *yəh* 'this' and *vəh* 'that', and their inflected forms.

The possessive form of the pronouns behaves like an adjective and agrees with the possessed noun in number, gender and case, e.g. *mere beṭe ko* 'to my son', *tumharī kıtabõ mẽ* 'in your books', *unkī bəhnõ ke sat'* 'with their sisters', etc. The oblique forms are used with the postpositions except that the first and second person pronouns are used in their direct case forms with the agentive postposition *ne*. The third person plural pronouns have special combined forms when they are followed by the agentive postposition, e.g. *in + ne = inhõne* and *un + ne = unhõne*. All the pronouns listed above have special contracted forms when followed by the accusative/dative postposition, e.g. *muj' + ko = muj'e, tuj' + ko = tuj'e, is/us + ko = ise/use, həm + ko = həmẽ, tum + ko = tumhẽ, in/un + ko = inhẽ/unhẽ*.

In addition to the pronouns listed above, Hindi-Urdu has a second person honorific pronoun *ap* which is used with both singular and plural reference for both male and female addressees. The honorific pronoun has the same form in all numbers and cases, i.e. it is invariant. The possessive is formed by adding the postposition *kA* to *ap*. To make the plural reference clear, the item *səb* 'all' or *log* 'people' may be added to the form *ap*, e.g. *ap səb/log*.

Hindi-Urdu also has a reflexive pronoun *ap* 'self' which has an oblique form *əpne* and a possessive form *əpnA*. The form *ap* is used for all persons. There is a reduplicated form of *ap*, i.e. *əpne ap*, which is also used as the reflexive pronoun in Hindi-Urdu, e.g. *ram ne əpne ko/əpne ap ko ʃiʃe mẽ dek'a* 'Ram looked at himself in the mirror.'

The two interrogative pronouns, *kɔn* and *kya* are used for human and non-human respectively. The oblique forms of these pronouns are *kis* in the singular and *kin* in the plural. The possessive is formed by adding the possessive postposition *kA* to the oblique. Similar to the third person pronouns, these pronouns also have combined forms such as *kinhõne, kise* and *kinhĩ*.

The devices of reduplication and partial reduplication or echo-compounding are used for expressing various meanings. For instance, reduplication of adjectives has either an intensive or a distributive meaning, e.g. *lal-lal saṛi* 'very red saree', *taza-taza dud'* 'very fresh milk', *kale-kale bal* 'jet-black hair', *ũce-ũce pəhaṛ* 'tall mountains', etc. Echo-compounding of adjectives, nouns and verbs has the meaning 'and the like', e.g. *sundər-vundər* 'pretty and such', *cay-vay* 'tea and other such things', *milna-vilna* 'meeting and other such things', etc. The echo-compounding usually tones down the meaning of the adjective; however, it adds to the meaning of other words; for instance, *cay-vay* means not only tea but snacks that go with it. Another device used extensively is that of compounding two words with related meanings: *hə̃si-xuʃi* 'laughter and happiness' (pleasant state or occasion), *duk'-təklif* 'sorrow and pain' (state full of sorrow), *ʃadi-byah* 'wedding', etc. Note that in all these examples, one item is from Indic sources, the other from Perso-Arabic sources. This is extremely common, though not absolutely obligatory.

In Hindi-Urdu, the possessor normally precedes the possessed and the possessive postposition *kA* agrees with the possessed in number, gender and case, e.g. *ləṛke ki kitab* 'the boy's book', *ləṛke ke sir pər* 'on the boy's head', etc. (the postposition *ka* agrees with the following noun, namely, 'book' and 'head', respectively). High-Urdu has an alternative construction where the possessed precedes the possessor following the convention of the *ezafe*-construction in Persian, e.g. *ʃer-e-kəʃmir* 'the lion of Kashmir', *qəvaid-e-urdu* 'grammar of Urdu', etc.

4.2 Verbal

Two most noticeable things about Hindi-Urdu verbs are their occurrence in morphologically related sets and in series. The first phenomenon is known as causal verbs and the second as compound verbs. Whereas the causative is inherited from Old Indo-Aryan, the development of compound verbs in New Indo-Aryan is recent – it became frequent only in the period between AD 600 and 1000.

Some examples of causal verbs can be seen in the chart given here.

Causal verbs

Intr.	Tr.	Dbl. tr.	Caus.
uʈʰ 'rise'	uʈʰa 'raise'	–	uʈʰva
kəʈ 'be cut'	kaʈ 'cut'	–	kəʈva
–	suna 'hear'	suna	sunva
–	kʰa 'eat'	kʰila	kʰilva

Examples of compound verbs are *gir jana* 'fall go = fall down', *kʰa lena* 'eat take = eat up', *pəʈʰ lena* 'read take = read to oneself', *pəʈʰ dena* 'read give = read out loud to someone'.

Hindi-Urdu verbs occur in the following forms: root, e.g. *likʰ* 'write', *cəl* 'move', imperfect stem, e.g. *likʰtA*, *cəltA*, perfect stem, e.g. *likʰA*, *cəlA*, and infinitive, *likhnA*, *cəlnA*. The stems behave like adjectives in that they agree with some noun in the sentence in number and gender. The imperfect and perfect participles, which are made up of the imperfect and perfect stems followed by the perfect stem of the verb *ho* 'be', i.e. *huA*, agree in case also. This means that the stem final *-A* changes to *-e* or *-i* for agreement. Whereas the imperfect and perfect aspectual distinction is expressed by suffixation, the continuous aspect is indicated by an independent lexical item, *rəhA*. This marker follows the root and behaves like the imperfect and perfect stems with regard to gender and number agreement.

The tense distinction of present versus past is expressed with the forms of the auxiliary verb, the present auxiliary *hE* and the past auxiliary *tʰA*. These are the present and past forms of the stative verb *honA* 'be'. As in all Indo-European languages, the verb 'be' is irregular in Hindi. It has the following forms: root *ho*, imperfect stem *hotA*, perfect stem *huA*, infinitive *honA*, stative present *hE*, stative past *tʰA*. The stem-final -A changes to *-e*, *-i* or *-ĩ* for number and gender agreement and the final -E changes to various vowels to indicate person, number and gender agreement. The forms of the verb *honA* in stative present are as follows: 1st person sg. *hũ*, 2nd and 3rd person sg. *hɛ*, 2nd person pl. *ho*, and 1st and 3rd person pl. and 2nd hon. *hɛ̃*.

In addition to tense and aspect distinctions, the verbal forms express mood distinctions as well. There is no distinction made between indicative and interrogative, i.e. in assertions as well as questions, the verbal forms are made up of the stems and auxiliaries described above. Historically, Old Indo-Aryan did not make a distinction between these two moods either. The moods in Old Indo-Aryan were indicative, imperative, optative and subjunctive. In Hindi-Urdu, the optative forms are made up of the root and the following suffixes: 1st person sg. *-ũ*, 2nd and 3rd person sg. *-e*, 1st and 3rd pl. and 2nd honorific *-ẽ*, and 2nd pl. *-o*. The future tense is formed by adding the suffix *-gA* to the optative forms, e.g. *ja-ũ̃-ga* 'I (m.) will go', *jaogī* 'you (f.) will go', etc. The following are the imperative forms: root form of the verb (intimate or rude), 2nd pl. optative (familiar), root with the suffix *-iye* (honorific, polite), root with the suffix *-iye* followed by the suffix *-ga* (remote, therefore, extra polite) and the infinitive form of the verb (remote imperative, therefore even when used with second plural, polite). Thus, the imperative forms of the verb *soc* 'think' are *(tū) soc* 'you (intimate) think', *(tum) soco* 'you (familiar) think', *(ap) sociye* 'you (honorific) think', *(ap) sociyega* 'you (honorific) please think (perhaps a little later?)', *(tum) socna* 'you (familiar, polite) think' or 'you (familiar) think (perhaps a little later?)'.

The paradigm of the verb *gʰūmna* 'to take a walk' illustrates the full range of the forms discussed above.

Paradigm of verb forms

Root: g′ūm 'take a walk'
Imperfect stem: g′ūmtA
Perfect stem: g′ūmA
Optative: g′ūmũ (1st sg.), g′ūmo (2nd pl.), g′ūme (2nd and 3rd sg.), g′ūmẽ (1st and 3rd pl., 2nd honorific)
Imperative: g′ūm (2nd sg., intimate/rude), g′ūmo (2nd pl., familiar), g′ūmiye (2nd honorific, polite), g′ūmiyega (2nd honorific, extra polite)

Future

	1st		*2nd*		*3rd*	
	M.	*F.*	*M.*	*F.*	*M.*	*F.*
Sg.	g′ūmũga	g′ūmũgī	g′ūmega	g′ūmegī	g′ūmega	g′ūmegī
Pl.	g′ūmẽge	g′ūmẽgī	g′ūmoge	g′ūmogī	g′ūmẽge	g′ūmẽgī
Hon.			g′ūmẽge	g′ūmẽgī	g′ūmẽge	g′ūmẽgī

Present imperfect

	Sg.	*Pl.*	*Hon.*
1st M.	g′ūmta hũ	g′ūmte hẽ	
1st F.	g′ūmtī hũ	g′ūmti hẽ	
2nd M.	g′ūmta hɛ	g′ūmte ho	g′ūmte hẽ
2nd F.	g′ūmtī hɛ	g′ūmtī ho	g′ūmtī hẽ
3rd M.	g′ūmta hɛ	g′ūmte hẽ	
3rd F.	g′ūmtī hɛ	g′ūmtī hẽ	

The past forms are: past imperfect: *g′ūmta t′a, g′ūmte t′e, g′ūmtī t′ī, g′ūmtī t′ĩ*, etc.; present perfect: *g′ūma hũ, g′ūmī hũ*, etc.; past perfect: *g′ūma t′a, g′ūme t′e, g′ūmī t′ī*, etc.; present continuous: *g′ūm rəha hɛ, g′ūm rəhe hɛ, g′ūm rəhī hɛ*, etc.; past continuous: *g′ūm rəha t′a, g′ūm rəhe t′e, g′ūm rəhī t′ī*, etc.

In general, Urdu speakers use the masculine plural form as undifferentiated for gender in the first person, e.g. *həm kəl kəlkətte ja rəhe hẽ* 'We (m./f.) are going to Calcutta tomorrow.'

The contingent, past contingent and presumptive tenses are formed with the imperfect and perfect stems and the continuous form followed by the auxiliaries *ho* 'contingent', *hotA* 'past contingent' and *hogA* 'presumptive'. Roughly, these three are translatable into English as follows: *pīta ho* '(he) may be drinking', *piya ho* '(he) may have drunk', *pīta hota* 'had (he) been drinking', *piya hota* 'had (he) drunk', *pīta hoga* '(he) must be drinking', *piya hoga* '(he) must have drunk'.

Hindi-Urdu verbs are very regular, which means that once we know the infinitive form of the verb, we can isolate the root and derive the imperfect and perfect stems by suffixing -*tA* and -*A* respectively. Thus, from *hə̃sna* 'laugh', we get the imperfect stem *hə̃stA* and perfect stem *hə̃sA*. Note that when the root ends in a vowel and the perfect stem-forming suffix -*A* is added to it, a semi-vowel is inserted to separate the two vowels. If the root ends in *ī*, -*a* or -*o*, a -*y*- is inserted, if the root ends in -*ū*, a -*v*- is inserted, e.g. *ga* + -*A* = *gaya* 'sang (m.)', *ro* + -*A* = *roya* 'cried (m.)', *pī* + -*A* = *piya* 'drank (m.)', *c′ū* + -*A* = *c′uva* 'touched (m.)'.

One verb, *cahiye*, is completely irregular in that it is invariable, i.e. it occurs only in this form. It takes dative subject and means 'to need' or 'want'. The following verbs have irregular perfect stems: *kər* 'do' – *kiya*, *le* 'take' – *liya*, *de* 'give' – *diya*, *ja* 'go' – *gəya*. The following verbs have irregular polite imperative forms: *kər* 'do' = *kījiye*, *le* 'take' = *lījiye*, *de* 'give' = *dījiye*, *pī* 'drink' = *pījiye*.

Hindi-Urdu has two types of compound verbs: those that involve verbs in a series and those that involve a nominal and a verbal. Some examples of the former have already been given (see the beginning of this section), a few examples of the latter are: *svīkar kərna* 'acceptance do' or 'to accept', *pəsənd hona* 'liking be' or 'to like' (non-volitional), *pəsənd kərna* 'liking do' or 'to like' (volitional), *təng ana* 'torment come' or 'to be fed up'.

In the verbs-in-series type of compound verbs, usually the meaning of the whole is derived from the meaning of the first, or main, verb; the second, or explicator, verb performs the function of either restricting, or adding some specific shade of meaning to the meaning of the main verb. Additionally, the explicator verb necessarily expresses the meaning 'a one-shot action or process'. For instance, *marna* can mean either 'hit' or 'kill', *mar ḍalna* 'hit/kill pour' means only 'kill'; *likʰna* means 'write', *likʰ marna* 'write hit' means 'to dash off a few lines in a hurry/thoughtlessly'; *rəkʰna* means 'keep, put', *rəkʰ choṛna*, 'keep leave' means 'save'. The main explicator verbs are the following and they roughly signify the meanings described below:

ana 'come': occurs with intransitive verbs of motion and indicates that the action of the main verb is oriented towards a focal point which may be a person or which may be set in time or space; e.g. *vəh sīṭʰiyã cəṭʰ ai* 'she came up the steps' and *vəh sīṭʰiyã utər ai* 'she came down the steps'.

jana 'go': occurs with intransitive verbs of motion and other change-of-state verbs and indicates motion away from the focal point; with dative subject verbs, it indicates definitive meaning; and with transitive verbs, it indicates hurried, compulsive action; e.g. *vəh sīṭʰiyã cəṭʰ gəi* 'she went up the steps', *rəjū ko kitab mil gəi* 'Raju got the book', *vəh gusse mẽ jane kya kya likʰ gəya* 'who knows what he dashed off in his anger.'

lena 'take': occurs with affective (transitive) verbs and indicates completive meaning; with other transitive verbs, it indicates a self-benefactive meaning; and with certain intransitive verbs, it indicates internal expression; e.g. *usne kam kər liya* '(s)he completed (his/her) job', *mẽ ne ṭʰīk soc liya hɛ* 'I have made a decision'.

dena 'give': occurs with transitive verbs other than affective verbs and indicates that the action is directed towards a beneficiary other than the agent of the action denoted by the main verb; and with intransitive verbs of expression, it indicates external expression; e.g. *usne sara rəhəsy bəta diya* 'he divulged the whole secret', *sīma zorõ se hãs dī* 'Sima laughed loudly'.

uṭʰna 'rise': occurs with intransitive and transitive verbs of punctual action and indicates suddenness; e.g. *vəh mujʰe dekʰte hī ro uṭʰī* 'she suddenly began to cry when she saw me'.

bɛṭʰna 'sit': occurs with certain verbs and indicates impudence; e.g. *vəh əpne 'bas' se ləṛ bɛṭʰa* 'he fought with his boss'.

pəṛna 'fall': occurs with intransitive change-of-state verbs, and certain verbs of expression, and indicates suddenness; e.g. *bəcca dʰəmaka sun kər cõk pəṛa* 'the child was startled to hear the big noise'.

ḍalna 'pour': occurs with transitive verbs that express violent action and certain transitive verbs (*kər* 'do', *pəṭ* 'read', *likʰ* 'write') and indicates violence; e.g. *jəldī se pətr likʰ ḍalo!* 'write the letter quickly (get it over with)!'

rəkʰna 'keep': occurs with certain transitive verbs and indicates a temporary state resulting from the action of the main verb; e.g. *mɛ̃ ne kəmīzẽ dʰo rəkʰī hɛ̃* 'I have washed (and kept ready) the shirts'.

cʰoṛna 'leave': occurs with certain transitive verbs and indicates dissociation of the agent with the result of the action; e.g. *pitajī ne merī pəṛʰaī ke liye pɛse rəkʰ cʰoṛe hɛ̃* 'father has put aside money for my education'.

marna 'hit': occurs with very few verbs and indicates rash action; e.g. *kucʰ bʰī likʰ maro!* 'just write something!'

dʰəməkna 'thump': occurs with *ana* 'come' and *jana* 'go' and indicates unwelcome arrival; e.g. *vəh subəh-subəh a dʰəmka, mujʰe cay pīne tək tək ka məka nəhĩ mila* 'he showed up very early, I did not even have time to have a cup of tea.'

pəhũcna 'arrive': occurs with *ana* 'come' and *jana* 'go' and indicates arrival rather than motion; e.g. *ʃyam dillī a pəhũca* 'Shyam arrived in Delhi'.

nikəlna 'emerge': indicates sudden emergence from some enclosed space – real or imaginary; e.g. *uskī ãkʰõ se ãsū bəh nikle* 'Tears began to flow from her eyes'.

There are verbs-in-series constructions in which the stem of the main verb is in a participial form; these, however, participate in the tense-aspect system in terms of their meaning. For instance, the following have inceptive, continuative and frequentative import: *pita jī dəftər jane ləge* 'Father began to go to (his) office'; *ramū der tək gata rəha* 'Ramu continued to sing for a long time'; and *nīna əksər film dekʰne jaya kərti hɛ* 'Nina frequently goes to the movies.'

5 Syntax

In this brief section on syntax, I will discuss mainly the verbal syntax of Hindi-Urdu after a few remarks on word order. The reason for this will become clearer as the discussion progresses.

Hindi-Urdu is a verb-final language, i.e. the order of words in a sentence is subject, object and verb. Actually, the position of the verb is relatively more fixed than the position of any other constituent. Since most grammatical functions of nouns are indicated by the postpositions following them, the nominal constituents can be moved around freely for thematic purposes. The position of the verb is changed only in poetic or extremely affective style. Historically, word order was relatively free in Old Indo-Aryan, but became more fixed in Middle Indo-Aryan between AD 200 and 600.

In existential sentences, the locational/temporal adverbial comes first: *mez pər kitab hɛ* 'there is a book on the table', *kəl bəṛī ṭʰənd tʰī* 'it was very cold yesterday'. The verb agrees with the unmarked noun in the sentence. In intransitive and non-perfective

411

transitive sentences, where the subject is unmarked, the verb agrees with the subject, e.g. *ləṛke bɛʈʰe* 'the boys sat', *ləṛkī səmacar sun rəhī hɛ* 'the girl is listening (f.) to the news (m.)', *rajū cay pīta hoga* 'Raju (m.) must be drinking (m.) tea (f.)'. In transitive sentences in the perfective, where the subject is followed by the postposition *ne*, the verb does not agree with the subject. It agrees with the object if it is unmarked; if the object is followed by the postposition *ko*, the verb remains in its neutral form, i.e. third person singular masculine: cf. *rajū ne kitab pəṛʰī* 'Raju (m.) read (f.) the book (f.)', *əfsərõ ne əpnī pətniyõ ko bulaya* 'the officers called (3rd sg. m.) their wives'. Not all transitive verbs require that their subjects be marked with the agentive postposition *ne*: e.g. *bolna* 'speak', *lana* 'bring' do not take *ne*, *səməjʰna* 'understand' can occur either with or without *ne*: *mɛ̃ apkī bat nəhĩ səmjʰa* 'I do not understand you', *ap ne kya səmjʰa?* 'what did you understand?' In the case of compound verbs, only if both the main and the explicator verbs require *ne* does the compound verb require *ne*: *ʃīla ne dū dʰ piya* 'Sheila drank the milk', *ʃīla ne dūdʰ liya* 'Sheila took the milk', *ʃīla ne dūdʰ pī liya* 'Sheila drank up the milk', but *ʃīla dūdʰ pī gəī* 'Sheila drank up the milk' since the intransitive verb *ja* 'go' is not a *ne* verb.

Semantically, Hindi-Urdu makes a distinction between volitional versus non-volitional verbs and affective versus non-affective verbs. A verb is volitional if it expresses an act that is performed by an actor/agent. A verb is affective if the act expressed by the verb is directed towards the actor/agent, i.e. it is self-benefactive. Ingestive verbs such as *kʰana* 'eat', *pīna* 'drink', etc., are good examples of affective verbs in that it is the actor/agent of eating, drinking, etc., who benefits from these acts. Verbs such as 'work', 'write', etc., on the other hand, may be either self-benefactive or directed towards some other beneficiary. Typically, the explicator verb *lena* 'take' occurs with an affective verb, the explicator *dena* 'give' does not, i.e. sentences such as the following are ungrammatical in Hindi-Urdu: **usne kʰana kʰa diya* 'he/she ate for someone else' because *kʰana* 'eat' is an ingestive verb whereas the explicator *dena* 'give' indicates that the beneficiary is someone other than the actor/agent of the main verb. Verbs such as *girna* 'fall', *jana* 'go', etc., express self-directed actions, hence are affective. These distinctions are important for the verbal syntax of Hindi-Urdu. Transitivity, volitionality and affectiveness do not necessarily coincide. For instance, *sona* 'sleep' is intransitive, volitional and affective, *sīkʰna* 'learn' is transitive, volitional and affective, *girna* 'fall' is intransitive, non-volitional and affective, *jana* 'go' is intransitive, volitional and affective. Only the affective verbs participate in the compound verbal construction with *lena* 'take' as the explicator; only volitional verbs occur in the passive construction (Kachru 1980, 2006).

In many cases, verbs in Hindi-Urdu come in related forms so that the stative versus active and volitional versus non-volitional meanings can be expressed by varying the syntactic constructions. For instance, the verb *milna* can mean both 'to run into someone' (accidental meeting) or 'to go to see someone' (deliberate meeting). In the first case, the verb is used with a dative subject and the object of meeting is unmarked; in the second case, the subject is unmarked and the object is marked with a comitative postposition *se*, e.g. *kəl bazar jate hue mujʰe ram mila tha* 'yesterday while going to the market I ran into Ram', *kəl mɛ̃ ram se uske dəftər mɛ̃ mila tʰa* 'yesterday I met Ram in his office'. In a large number of cases, the intransitive verb denotes non-volitional action and if the actor is to be expressed, it is expressed with the instrumental postposition *se*, e.g. *apka ʃīʃa mujʰse ṭūṭ gəya* 'your mirror got broken by me'. The deliberate action is expressed with the related transitive verb in the agentive construction, e.g. *is ʃərartī bəcce ne apka pyala toṛ ḍala* 'this naughty child broke your cup'. Most intransitive and all dative subject verbs are either stative or change-of-state verbs and are non-volitional. Hindi-Urdu has sets of stative, change-of-state and active verbs of the following types:

Stative	Change-of-state	Active
kʰula hona 'be open'	kʰulna	kʰolna
kruddʰ hona 'be angry'	krodʰ'ana	krodʰ' kərna
yad hona 'remember'	yad ana	yad kərna
pəsənd hona 'like'	pəsənd ana	pəsənd kərna

The stative verbs are usually made up of an adjective or past participle and the verb 'be', the change-of-state verbs are either lexical verbs or compounds made up of a nominal and the verb 'become' or 'come', and the active is either a causal verb morphologically derived from the non-causal or a compound made up of a nominal and the verb 'do' (or a set of other active transitive verbs).

This, however, does not mean that all intransitive verbs in Hindi are of the above types. There are active intransitive verbs such as the verbs of motion *cəl* 'move', *bʰag* 'run', etc., verbs of expression (*hə̃s* 'laugh', *ro* 'cry', etc.) and others. Verbal compounding is also exploited to reduce the volitionality of verbs, e.g. *ro pəṛna* 'cry + fall = to burst out crying', *bol uṭʰna* 'speak + rise = to blurt out', etc.

The non-volitional intransitive sentence above *apka ʃīʃa mujʰse ṭūṭ gəya* 'Your mirror got broken by me' has been translated into English with the passive; it is, however, not a passive construction in Hindi-Urdu. The passive in Hindi-Urdu is formed by marking the agent of the active sentence, if retained, with the instrumental postposition *se* and using the perfect stem of the verb and the auxiliary *ja* 'go' which takes all the tense-aspect endings: e.g. *ram ne kʰana nəhī̃ kʰaya* 'Ram did not eat' vs *ram se kʰana nəhī̃ kʰaya gəya* 'Ram was not able to eat'. The translation equivalent of the Hindi-Urdu passive in English points to an interesting fact about this construction. If the agent is retained and marked with the instrumental postposition, the passive sentence is usually interpreted as a statement about the capability of the agent; if, however, the agent is deleted, the passive sentence has a meaning similar to that of English. That is, the sentence is interpreted as being about the object in the active sentence and the agent is either unknown or not important enough to be mentioned (Y. Kachru 1980, 2006).

In addition to the present and past participles, there are two other participles in Hindi which are used a great deal: the conjunctive participle which is formed by adding the form *kər* to the root of the verb and the agentive participle which is formed by adding the suffix *-vala* to the oblique form of the verbal noun, e.g. *likʰnevala* 'writer', *janevala* 'one who goes', *sonevala* 'one who sleeps', *ugnevala* 'that which rises or grows', etc. This suffix has become a part of the English lexicon in the form *wallah* and is used extensively in Indian English and the native varieties of English, especially in the context of topics related to India, Forms such as *Congresswallah* ('one belonging to the Indian National Congress'), *Bombaywallah* ('one from Bombay') are common in literature dealing with India.

The syntax of Hindi-Urdu differs from that of English most noticeably in the use of the participles. For instance, the preferred constructions for modifying nouns or conjoining clauses are the participles: the present, past and agentive for modifying nouns and the conjunctive participle for conjoining clauses. Compare the following Hindi sentences with their English translations: *vah gʰər se bahər nikəltī huī ɔrtõ ko dekʰ raha tʰa*

413

'he was observing the women (who were) coming out of the house'; *muj'e məhadevī jī kī lik'ī huī kəvitaẽ bəhut pəsənd hẽ* 'I like the poems written by Mahadevi ji very much'; *usko bat bat par ronewale bəcce bilkul əcc'e nəhĩ ləgte* 'he does not like children who cry at the smallest provocation'; *vəh g'ər a kər so gəya* 'he came home and went to sleep'. Both the present and the past participles are used adjectivally as well as adverbially, cf. *mā ne rote hue bəcce ko god mẽ ut'a liya* 'Mother picked up the child who was crying' vs *vəh rote hue b'ag gəya* 'he ran away, crying' and *mẽ vəhā bɛt'ī huī ləṛkī ko nəhĩ jantī* 'I don't know the girl seated over there' vs *ləṛkī vəhā bɛt'ī (huī) pətr lik' rəhī hɛ* 'the girl is writing a letter sitting there'. The agentive participle is used both as an agentive noun, e.g. *(gəṛī) cəlanevala* 'driver (of a vehicle)' and as an adjective, e.g. *b'arət se anevale c'atr* 'the students who come from India'. The conjunctive participle is used to express the meanings of sequential action, related action, cause–effect relationship and purpose adverbial, e.g. *vəh hindī pəṛ' kər k'elne jaega* 'he will go to play after studying Hindi', *vəh kūd kər ūpər a gəī* 'she jumped and came up', *həm ne use pɛse de kər xuʃ kər liya* 'we pleased him by giving him money', *jəldīse panī gərm kərke nəha lo* 'heat the water quickly and take a bath' (Kachru, 1980, 2006).

Although the participial constructions are preferred in Hindi-Urdu, there are linguistically determined environments where full relative and other types of subordinate and conjoined clauses are used. The relative clause, unlike in English, is not a constituent of the noun phrase. It may either precede or follow the main clause as in the following: *jo ərtẽ gana ga rəhī hẽ ve merī səheliyā hẽ* or *ve ərtẽ merī səheliyā hẽ jo gana ga rəhī hẽ* 'the women who are singing are my friends'. Note that, depending upon the order of the relative and the main clause, either the noun in the subordinate or the main clause is deleted, i.e. the above are the results of deleting the noun in parentheses in the following: *jo ərtẽ gana ga rəhī hẽ ve (ərtẽ) merī səheliyā hẽ* or *ve ərtẽ merī səheliyā hẽ jo (ərtẽ) gana ga rəhī hẽ*. The relative marker *jo* (obl. sg. *jis*, obl. pl. *jin*, special forms with *ne* and *ko*, *jinhõne* and *jinhẽ*) and the correlative marker *vəh*, which is identical to the remote demonstrative/third person pronoun, function like a determiner to their respective head nouns. Both the head nouns may be retained in the case of an emphatic construction; in normal speech/writing, however, the second instance is deleted. Under the influence of Persian and later, English, the relative clause is sometimes positioned following the head noun, e.g. *ve ərtẽ jo gana ga rəhī hẽ merī səheliyā hẽ*; in this case, the second instance of the noun (following *jo*) must be deleted.

Earlier, it has been said that the nominal constituents of a sentence in Hindi-Urdu can be moved around freely for thematic purposes. Usually, the initial element in a sentence in Hindi coincides with the theme. The focus position in Hindi is identified with the position just before the main verb. In addition to manipulating the word order, heavy sentence stress and certain particles are used to indicate focus (heavy sentence stress indicated by capitalisation), e.g. RAM *ne mohən ko pīṭa* 'it was Ram who hit Mohan', *ʃīla ne hī yəh bat kəhī t'ī* 'it was Sheila who had said this', where the item in capital letters in the first sentence and the item followed by the particles *hī* in the second is under focus. In addition to the initial position, the particle *to* indicates the theme, e.g. in *sīma to cəlī gəī* 'as for Sima, she has left', where the item followed by *to* is thematic. As moving elements to the initial position is not the favoured device for indicating focus, the interrogative pronouns in Hindi-Urdu do not necessarily occur sentence-initially; compare the Hindi-Urdu sentences with their English equivalents, *ap kya pəṛ' rahe hẽ?* 'what are you reading?', *vəh kəl kəhā gəya t'a?* 'where did he go yesterday?', *in mẽ se ap ko kɔn sī kitab pəsənd hɛ?* 'which of these books do you like?'

6 Regional and Style Variation

In addition to the distinction between Hindi (Sanskritised variety), Urdu (Persianised variety) and Hindustani (neutral, colloquial variety), both Hindi and Urdu have regional varieties as well throughout the Indian subcontinent. Broadly speaking, these are Western, Eastern and Southern in India, whereas in Pakistan the varieties are with reference to the substratum languages of the provinces, e.g. Panjabi, Sindhi, Balochi, etc., in contrast to the language of the population that migrated from India, especially Bihar and United Provinces, following the formation of Pakistan. The three varieties in India, Eastern, Western and Southern (Dakhni) Hindi, differ in phonology, morphology, lexicon and syntax (for examples, see Kachru 2006).

In the past two centuries, Hindi has developed several registers, or functionally defined varieties, e.g. newspaper Hindi, legal Hindi, official Hindi, scientific-technical Hindi, etc. As the use of Hindi in new domains increases, new registers develop rapidly, and as they replace the use of Persian or English in these domains, they assimilate some features of these languages. Thus, Hindi has developed, in addition to a Sanskritised form, a Persianised and an Englishised form as well (for examples, see Kachru 2006).

7 Conclusion

In conclusion, Hindi-Urdu differs from its European cousins typologically in several respects. Phonologically, aspiration, retroflexion, nasal vowels and lack of distinctive stress mark Hindi-Urdu as very different from English. Morphologically, the gender and case distinctions and the devices of reduplication and echo-compounding exemplify the major differences between the two languages. Syntactically, the word order differences are striking. So is the fact that Hindi-Urdu makes certain semantic distinctions which are not made as clearly in English, viz. volitionality and affectiveness. These distinctions result in a closer correspondence between semantic and syntactic grammatical roles that nominal constituents have in a sentence, e.g. all agentive (-ne-marked) subjects are agents, all dative (ko-marked) subjects are experiencers, and so on. The extent of mixing with other languages that Hindi tolerates, resulting in Sanskritised, Persianised and Englishised styles, is also unique to the South Asian multilingual context. Many of these characteristics of Hindi-Urdu are shared by not only the other Indo-Aryan but also the Dravidian and other languages of India.

Notes

1 A recent book by Faruqi (2001) claims that Urdu was never a court language and expresses doubt that a form of Hindi devoid of Arabic-Persian influence was ever the common language of the so-called Hindi area. Faruqi's claims are puzzling in view of the fact that Urdu replaced Persian as the court language of the last Mughal Emperor Bahadur Shah Zafar, himself a well-known poet of Urdu (see Abidi and Gargesh in Kachru et al. 2008), and a form of Hindi devoid of Persianisation and Sanskritisation is attested in many of the poets of medieval period, including Amir Khusrau (1253–1325), Kabir (fifteenth century) and Abdul Rahim Khankhana (sixteenth century).

2 In Indo-European linguistics, *vṛddhi* has become a term for the lengthened grade of the ablaut vowel gradation, a well-known characteristic of the Indo-European languages.

3 *alyf* is pronounced as *a* following a consonant; *ayn* is either not pronounced at all or given the value of *ə* or *a* following a consonant. It is pronounced as a glottal stop only in High Urdu.

Bibliography

Among the literature in English, Kachru (2006) and Montaut (2004) are solid descriptive grammars of Hindi, while Schmidt (1999) provides an overview of Urdu grammar. More pedagogically oriented works include Bhatia (1996) for Hindi and Bailey (1956, 1982) for Urdu. For particular aspects, reference may be made to Ohala (1983) on phonology, Singh and Agnihotri (1997) on morphology, and Kachru (1980) on syntax. For details of the relation between Hindi and Urdu, see Rai (1984).

References

Bailey, Thomas Grahame. 1956. *Teach Yourself Urdu* (English Universities Press, London)

—— 1982. *Learn Urdu: For English Speakers*, ed. J.R. Firth and A.H. Harley (Saphrograph, Brooklyn, NY)

Bhatia, T.K. 1987. *A History of the Hindi Grammatical Tradition* (Brill, Leiden)

—— 1996. *Colloquial Hindi: The Complete Course for Beginners* (Routledge, London)

Faruqi, Shamsur Rahman. 2001. *Early Urdu Literary Culture and History* (Oxford University Press, Delhi)

Kachru, B.B., Kachru, Y. and Sridhar, S.N. (eds) 2008. *Language in South Asia* (Cambridge University Press, Cambridge)

Kachru, Yamuna. 1980. *Aspects of Hindi Grammar* (Manohar Publications, New Delhi)

—— 2006. *Hindi* (Oriental and African Language Library, London; John Benjamins, Amsterdam)

Kellogg, S.H. 1875. *A Grammar of the Hindi Language* (Routledge and Kegan Paul, London)

McGregor, R.S. 1972. *Outline of Hindi Grammar* (Oxford University Press, London)

Montaut, Annie. 2004. *A Grammar of Hindi*, LINCOM Studies in Indo-European Linguistics 02 (Lincom GmbH, München)

Ohala, Manjari. 1983. *Aspects of Hindi Phonology* (Motilal Banarsidass, Delhi)

Rai, Amrit. 1984. *A House Divided: The Origin and Development of Hindi/Hindavi* (Oxford University Press, Delhi)

Russell, Ralph. 1980. *A New Course in Hindustani for Learners in Britain* (School of Oriental and African Studies, London)

Schmidt, Ruth Laila. 1999. *Urdu, an Essential Grammar* (Routledge, London)

Sharma, Aryendra. 1958. *A Basic Grammar of Modern Hindi* (Government of India, Ministry of Education and Scientific Research, Delhi)

Singh, R. and Agnihotri, R.K. 1997. *Hindi Morphology: A Word-based Description* (Motilal Banarsidass, Delhi)

Srivastava, Ravindra Nath. 1994. *Hindi bhasha ka samaj shastr*, compiled and ed. Mahendra Beena Srivastava and Dilip Singh (Radhkrishna Parkashan, New Delhi)

Verma, Dhirendra. 1933. *Hindi bhasa ka itihas* (Hindustani Academy, Allahabad)

23

Bengali

M.H. Klaiman

1 Historical and Genetic Setting

Bengali, together with Assamese and Oriya, belongs to the eastern group within the Magadhan subfamily of Indo-Aryan. In reconstructing the development of Indo-Aryan, scholars hypothetically posit a common parent language from which the modern Magadhan languages are said to have sprung. The unattested parent of the Magadhan languages is designated as Eastern or Magadhi Apabhraṁśa, and is assigned to Middle Indo-Aryan. Apart from the eastern languages, other modern representatives of the Magadhan subfamily are Magahi, Maithili and Bhojpuri.

Within the eastern group of Magadhan languages, the closest relative of Bengali is Assamese. The two share not only many coincidences of form and structure, but also have in common one system of written expression, on which more details will be given later.

Historically, the entire Magadhan group is distinguished from the remaining Indo-Aryan languages by a sound change involving sibilant coalescence. Specifically, there occurred in Magadhan a falling together of three sibilant elements inherited from common Indo-Aryan, dental /s/, palatal /š/ and retroflex /ṣ/. Among modern Magadhan languages, the coalescence of these three sounds is manifested in different ways; e.g. the modern Assamese reflex is the velar fricative /x/, as contrasted with the palatal /š/ of Modern Bengali.

The majority of Magadhan languages also show evidence of historical regression in the articulation of what was a central vowel /ă/ in common Indo-Aryan; the Modern Bengali reflex is /ɔ/.

Although the Magadhan subfamily is defined through a commonality of sound shifts separating it from the rest of Indo-Aryan, the three eastern languages of the subfamily share one phonological peculiarity distinguishing them from all other modern Indo-Aryan languages, both Magadhan and non-Magadhan. This feature is due to a historical coalescence of the long and short variants of the high vowels, which were distinguished in common Indo-Aryan. As a result, the vowel inventories of Modern Bengali, Assamese and Oriya show no phonemic distinction of /ĭ/ and /ī/, /ŭ/ and /ū/. Moreover, Assamese and Bengali are distinguished from Oriya by the innovation of a high/low distinction in the mid vowels. Thus Bengali has /æ/ as well as /e/, and /ɔ/ as well as /o/. Bengali differs phonologically from Assamese principally in that the latter lacks a retroflex consonant series, a fact which distinguishes Assamese not just from Bengali, but from the majority of modern Indo-Aryan languages.

Besides various phonological characteristics, there are certain grammatical features peculiar to Bengali and the other Magadhan languages. The most noteworthy of these features is the absence of gender, a grammatical category found in most other modern Indo-Aryan languages. Bengali and its close relative Assamese also lack number as a verbal category. More will be said on these topics in the section on morphology, below.

Writing and literature have played no small role in the evolution of Bengali linguistic identity. A common script was in use throughout eastern India centuries before the emergence of the separate Magadhan vernaculars. The Oriya version of this script underwent special development in the medieval period, while the characters of the Bengali and Assamese scripts coincide with but a couple of exceptions.

Undoubtedly the availability of a written form of expression was essential to the development of the rich literary traditions associated not just with Bengali, but also with other Magadhan languages such as Maithili. However, even after the separation of the modern Magadhan languages from one another, literary composition in eastern India seems to have reflected a common milieu scarcely compromised by linguistic boundaries. Although vernacular literature appears in eastern India by AD 1200, vernacular writings for several centuries thereafter tend to be perceived as the common inheritance of the whole eastern area, more so than as the output of individual languages.

This is clearly evident, for instance, in the case of the celebrated Buddhist hymns called the *Caryāpada*, composed in eastern India roughly between AD 1000 and 1200. Though the language of these hymns is Old Bengali, there are reference works on Assamese, Oriya and even Maithili that treat the same hymns as the earliest specimens of each of these languages and their literatures.

Bengali linguistic identity is not wholly a function of the language's genetic affiliation in the Indo-Aryan family. Eastern India was subjected to Aryanisation before the onset of the Christian era, and therefore well before the evolution of Bengali and the other Magadhan languages. Certain events of the medieval era have had a greater significance than Aryanisation in the shaping of Bengali linguistic identity, since they furnished the prerequisites of Bengali regional and national identity.

Among these events, one of the most crucial was the establishment of Islamic rule in the early thirteenth century. Islamisation led to six hundred years of political unity in Bengal, under which it was possible for a distinctly national style of literary and cultural expression to evolve, more or less unaffected by religious distinctions. To be sure, much if not all early popular literature in Bengali had a sacred basis; the early compositions were largely translations and reworkings of Hindu legends, like the Krishna myth cycle and the *Rāmāyaṇa* religious epic. However, this material seems to have always been looked upon more as a product of local than of sectarian tradition. From the outset of their rule, the Muslim aristocracy did little to discourage the composition of literature on such popular themes; on the contrary, they often lent their patronage to the authors of these works, who were both Muslim and Hindu. Further, when in the sixteenth and seventeenth centuries Islamic writers ultimately did set about creating a body of sectarian, didactic vernacular literature in Bengali, they readily adapted the originally Hindu motifs, themes and stories that had become part of the local cultural tradition.

The relative weakness of religious identity in Bengali cultural institutions is perhaps best interpreted in light of a major event which occurred concomitant to the rise of Islamic rule. This event was a massive shift in the course of the Ganges River between the twelfth and sixteenth centuries AD. Whereas it had earlier emptied into the Bay of Bengal nearly due south of the site of present-day Calcutta, the river gradually approached and eventually became linked with the Padma River system in the territory today called Bangladesh. The shift in the Ganges has been one of the greatest influences upon material history and human geography in eastern India; for, prior to the completion of the river's change of course, the inhabitants of the eastern tracts had been virtually untouched by civilisation and sociocultural influences from without, whether Islamic or Hindu. Over the past four centuries, it is the descendants of the same people who have come to make up the majority of speakers of the Bengali language; so that the basis of their Bengali identity is not genetic and not religious, but linguistic. That the bulk of the population perceives commonality of language as the principal basis of its social unity is clear from the name taken by the new nation-state of eastern Bengal following the 1971 war of liberation. In the proper noun *Bangladesh* (composed of *bāṅglā* plus *deśa*, the latter meaning 'country'), the first part of the compound does not mean the Bengali people or the territory of Bengal; the term *bāṅglā* specifically refers, rather, to the Bengali language.

The Muslim aristocracy that ruled Bengal for some six centuries was supplanted in the eighteenth century by new invaders, the British. Since the latter's withdrawal from the subcontinent in 1947, the community which identifies itself as Bengali has been divided between two sovereign political entities. However, the Bengali language continues to be spoken throughout Bengal's traditional domains, and on both sides of the newly imposed international boundary. Today, Bengali is one of the official regional speeches of the Indian Union, a status which is also enjoyed by the other eastern Magadhan languages, Oriya and Assamese. Among the three languages, the one which is currently in the strongest position is Bengali, since it alone also has the status of a national language outside India's present borders. With over 70 million native speakers in India and over 100 million in Bangladesh, Bengali has perhaps the sixth largest number of native speakers among the languages of the world, considerably more than such European languages as Russian, German and French.

2 Orthography and Sound System

The writing system of Modern Bengali is derived from Brāhmī, an ancient Indian syllabary. Brāhmī is also the source of all the other native Indian scripts (including those of the modern South Indian languages) as well as of Devanāgarī, a script associated with classical Sanskrit and with a number of the modern Indo-Aryan languages.

The scripts of the modern eastern Magadhan languages (Oriya, Assamese and Bengali) are based on a system of characters historically related to, but distinct from, Devanāgarī. The Bengali script is identical to that of Assamese except for two characters; while the Oriya script, though closely related historically to the Bengali-Assamese script, is quite distinctive in its appearance.

Like all Brāhmī-derived scripts, Bengali orthography reads from left to right, and is organised according to syllabic rather than segmental units.

Accordingly, a special diacritic or character is employed to represent a single consonant segment in isolation from any following vowel, or a single vowel in isolation from any preceding consonant. Furthermore, the writing system of Bengali, like Devanāgarī, represents characters as hanging from a superimposed horizontal line and has no distinction of upper and lower cases.

Table 23.1 sets out the Bengali script according to the traditional ordering of characters, with two special diacritics listed at the end. Most Bengali characters are designated according to the pronunciation of their independent or ordinary form. Thus the first vowel character is called ɔ, while the first consonant character is called kɔ. The designation of the latter is such, because the corresponding sign in isolation is read not as a single segment, but as a syllable terminating in /ɔ/, the so-called 'inherent vowel'. Several Bengali characters are not designated by the pronunciation of their independent or ordinary forms; their special names are listed in the leftmost column of Table 23.1. Among the terms used in the special designations of vowel characters, *hrɔsso* literally means 'short' and *dirgho* 'long'. Among the terms used in the special designations of consonant characters, *talobbo* literally means 'palatal', *murdhonno* 'retroflex', and *donto* 'dental'. These terms are used, for historical reasons, to distinguish the names for the three sibilant characters. The three characters (transliterated *ś*, *ṣ* and *s*) are used to represent a single non-obstruent sibilant phoneme in Modern Bengali. This phoneme is a palatal with a conditioned dental allophone; further discussion will be given below. It might be pointed out that another Bengali phoneme, the dental nasal /n/, is likewise represented in orthography by three different characters, which are transliterated *ñ*, *ṇ* and *n*.

In Bengali orthography, a vowel sign normally occurs in its independent form only when it is the first segment of a syllable. Otherwise, the combining form of the vowel sign is written together with the ordinary form of a consonant character, as illustrated in Table 23.1 for the character kɔ. There are a few exceptional cases: for instance, the character *hɔ* when written with the combining form of the sign *ri* appears not as হৃ but as হ (pronounced [hri]). The character *rɔ* combined with *dirgho u* is written not as রূ but as রু [ru]. The combination of *talobbo sɔ* with *hrɔsso u* is optionally represented either as শু or as শু (both are pronounced [šu]), while *gɔrɔ* and *hɔ* in combination with *hrɔsso u* yield the respective representations গু [gu], রু [ru], and হু [hu].

Table 23.1 Bengali Script

Vowel segments			
Special name of character, if any	*Independent form*	*Combining form* (*shown with the sign kɔ*)	*Transliteration*
	অ	ক	ɔ
	আ	কা	a
hrɔsso i	ই	কি	i
dirgho i	ঈ	কী	ī
hrɔsso u	উ	কু	u
dirgho u	ঊ	কূ	ū
ri	ঋ	কৃ	ri
	এ	কে	e
	ঐ	কৈ	oy
	ও	কো	o
	ঔ	কৌ	ow

Table 23.1 continued

Consonant Segments	Ordinary form	Special form(s)	Transliteration (so-called 'inherent vowel' not represent)
	ক		k
	খ		kh
	গ		g
	ঘ		gh
	ঙ	ং	ṅ
	চ		c
	ছ		ch
	জ		j
	ঝ		jh
	ঞ		ñ
	ট		ṭ
	ঠ		ṭh
	ড		ḍ
	ড়		ṛ
	ঢ		ḍh
	ঢ়		ṛh
	ণ		ṇ
	ত	ৎ	t
	থ		th
	দ		d
	ধ		dh
	ন		n
	প		p
	ফ		ph
	ব		b
	ভ		bh
	ম		m
ɔntostho jɔ	য		j
ɔntostho ɔ	য়	্য	y, w
	র	্ ্র	r
	ল		l
talobbo sɔ	শ		ś
murdhonno sɔ	ষ		ṣ
donto sɔ	স		s
	হ	ঃ	h
Special diacritics			-
cɔndrobindu	ঁ		
hɔsonto	্		

Several of the consonant characters in Bengali have special forms designated in Table 23.1; their distribution is as follows. The characters ṅɔ and tɔ occur in their special forms when the consonants they represent are the final segments of phonological syllables. Thus /baṅla/ 'Bengali language' is written বাংলা while /šɔt/ 'true' is written সৎ.

The character ɔntostho ɔ has a special form listed in Table 23.1; the name of this special form is jɔ phɔla. Generally, jɔ phɔla is the form in which ɔntostho ɔ occurs when combined with a preceding ordinary consonant sign, as in ত্যাগ [tæg] 'renunciation'. When combined with an ordinary consonant sign in non-initial syllables, jɔ phɔla tends to be realised as gemination of the consonant segment, as in গ্রাম্য [grammo] 'rural'. The sign ɔntostho ɔ in its ordinary form is usually represented intervocalically, and generally realised phonetically as a front or back high or mid semi-vowel. Incidentally, the character ɔntostho ɔ in its ordinary form is not to be confused with the similar looking character that precedes it in Table 23.1, the ɔntostho jɔ character. This character has the same phonemic realisation as the consonant sign jɔ (listed much earlier in Table 23.1), and is transliterated in the same way. While jɔ and ɔntostho jɔ have the same phonemic realisation, they have separate historical sources; and the sign ɔntostho jɔ occurs today in the spelling of a limited number of Bengali lexemes, largely direct borrowings from Sanskrit.

The sign rɔ exhibits one of two special forms when written in combination with an ordinary consonant sign. In cases where the ordinary consonant sign represents a segment which is pronounced before /r/, then rɔ appears in the combining form rɔ phɔla; to illustrate: প্রেত [pret] 'ghost, evil spirit'. In cases where the sound represented by the ordinary consonant sign is realised after /r/, rɔ appears in the second of its combining forms, which is called reph; as in অর্থ [ɔrtho] 'value'.

The sign hɔ has a special form, listed in Table 23.1, which is written word-finally or before a succeeding consonant in the same syllable. In neither case, however, is the special form of hɔ very commonly observed in Bengali writing.

Two special diacritics are listed at the end of Table 23.1. The first of these, cɔndrobindu represents the supersegmental for nasalisation, and is written over the ordinary or combining form of any vowel character. The other special diacritic, called hɔsonto is used to represent two ordinary consonant signs as being realised one after another, without an intervening syllabic, in the same phonological syllable; or to show that an ordinary consonant sign written in isolation is to be realised phonologically without the customary 'inherent vowel'. Thus: বাক্ [bak] 'speech', বাক্শক্তি [bakšokti] 'power of speech'. In practice, the use of this diacritic is uncommon, except where spelling is offered as a guide to pronunciation; or where the spelling of a word takes account of internal morpheme boundaries, as in the last example.

Table 23.1 does not show the representation of consonant clusters in Bengali orthography. Bengali has about two dozen or so special soṅjukto (literally 'conjunct') characters, used to designate the combination of two, or sometimes three, ordinary consonant signs. In learning to write Bengali, a person must learn the soṅjukto signs more or less by rote.

Before considering the sound system of Bengali, it should be mentioned that the spelling of Bengali words is well standardised, though not in all cases a strict guide to pronunciation. There are two especially common areas of inconsistency. One involves the representation of the sound [æ]. Compare the phonetic realisations of the following words with their spellings and transliterations: [æto] এত (transliterated etɔ) 'so much, so many'; [bæsto] ব্যস্ত (transliterated byɔstɔ) 'busy'; and [læj] ল্যাজ (transliterated lyajɔ) 'tail'. The sound [æ] can be orthographically represented in any of the three ways illustrated, and the precise spelling of any word containing this sound must accordingly be memorised.

Another area of inconsistency involves the realisation of the 'inherent vowel'. Since, as mentioned above, the diacritic *hɔsonto* (used to indicate the absence of the inherent vowel) is rarely used in practice, it is not always clear whether an unmodified ordinary consonant character is to be read with or without the inherent vowel. Compare, for example, [kɔto] কত (transliterated *kɔtɔ*) 'how much/how many' with [mɔt] মত (transliterated *mɔtɔ*) 'opinion'. This example makes it especially clear that Bengali spelling is not an infallible guide to pronunciation.

The segmental phonemes (oral vowels and consonants) of the standard dialect of Bengali are set forth in Table 23.2. As Table 23.2 makes clear, the feature of aspiration is significant for obstruents and defines two phonemically distinct series, the unaspirates and the aspirates. Though not represented in the table since it is non-segmental, the feature of nasalisation is nonetheless significant for vowels and similarly defines two phonemically distinct series. Thus in addition to the oral vowels as listed in Table 23.2, Bengali has the corresponding nasalised vowel phonemes /ɔ̃/, /ã/, /æ̃/, /õ/, /ẽ/, /ũ/ and /ĩ/.

The phonemic inventory of modern standard Bengali marks it as a fairly typical Indo-Aryan language. The organisation of the consonant system in terms of five basic points of articulation (velar, palatal, retroflex, dental and labial) is characteristic, as is the stop/flap distinction in the retroflex series. (Hindi-Urdu, for instance, likewise has several retroflex stop phonemes and a retroflex flap.) Also typically Indo-Aryan is the distinctive character of voicing in the Bengali obstruent inventory, along with the distinctive character of aspiration. The latter feature tends, however, to be suppressed preconsonantally, especially in rapid speech. Moreover, the voiced labial aspirate /bh/ tends to be unstable in the pronunciation of many Bengali speakers, often approximating to a voiced labial continuant [v].

Table 23.2 Segmental Phonemes of Bengali

Consonants	*Labial*	*Dental*	*Retroflex*	*Palatal*	*Velar*	*Post-velar*
Obstruents						
voiceless:						
unaspirated	p	t	ṭ	c	k	
aspirated	ph	th	ṭh	ch	kh	
voiced:						
unaspirated	b	d	ḍ	j	g	
aspirated	bh	dh	ḍh	jh	gh	
Nasals	m	n	ṇ		ṅ	
Flaps		r	ṛ			
Lateral		l				
Spirants				s		h

Vowels	*Front*		*Back*	
High	i		u	
High mid	e		o	
Low mid	æ		ɔ	
Low		a		

In the consonant inventory, Bengali can be regarded as unusual only in having a palatal sibilant phoneme in the absence of a dental sibilant. The historical background of this has been discussed in the preceding section. The phoneme in question is realised as a palatal [š] in all environments, except before the segments /t/, /th/, /n/, /r/, and /l/, where it is realised as a dental, i.e. as [s]. For simplicity, this Bengali sibilant is represented as *s* in the remainder of this chapter.

Nasalisation as a distinctive non-segmental feature of the vowel system is typical not only of Bengali but of modern Indo-Aryan languages generally. In actual articulation, the nasality of the Bengali nasalised vowel segments tends to be fairly weak, and is certainly not as strong as the nasality of vowels in standard French.

The most interesting Modern Bengali phonological processes involve the vowel segments to the relative exclusion of the consonants. One process, Vowel Raising, produces a neutralisation of the high/low distinction in the mid vowels, generally in unstressed syllables. Given the stress pattern of the present standard dialect, which will be discussed later, Vowel Raising generally applies in non-word-initial syllables. Evidence for the process is found in the following alternations:

mɔl	'dirt'	ɔmol	'pure'
sɔ	'hundred'	ækso	'one hundred'
æk	'one'	ɔnek	'many'

A second phonological process affecting vowel height is very significant because of its relationship to morphophonemic alternations in the Bengali verbal base. This process may be called Vowel Height Assimilation, since it involves the assimilation of a non-high vowel (other than /a/) to the nearest succeeding vowel segment within the phonological word, provided the latter has the specification [+ high]. Outside the area of verbal morphophonemics, the evidence for this process principally comes from the neutralisation of the high/low distinction in the mid vowels before /i/ or /u/ in a following contiguous syllable. Some alternations which illustrate this process are:

æk	'one'	ekṭi	'one' (plus classifier -ṭi)
lɔjja	'shame'	lojjito	'ashamed'
nɔṭ	'actor'	noṭi	'actress'
æk	'one'	ekṭu	'a little, a bit'
tɔbe	'then'	tobu	'but (then)'

At this point it will be useful to qualify the observation drawn earlier that Bengali is – phonologically speaking – a fairly typical Indo-Aryan language. It is true that most of the segments in the Modern Bengali sound system can be traced more or less directly to Old Indo-Aryan. However, the retroflex flap /ṛ/ of the former has no counterpart in the latter, and its presence in modern standard Bengali (and in some of its sisters) is due to a phonological innovation of Middle Indo-Aryan. Furthermore, while the other retroflex segments of Modern Bengali (/ṭ/, /ṭh/, /ḍ/, /ḍh/) have counterparts in the Old Indo-Aryan sound system, their overall frequency (phonetic load) in Old Indo-Aryan was low. On the other hand, among the modern Indo-Aryan languages, it is Bengali (along with the other Magadhan languages, especially the eastern Magadhan languages) which demonstrates a comparatively high frequency of retroflex sounds. Some external, i.e. non-Aryan influence on the diachronic development of the

Bengali sound system is suggested. Such a hypothesis ought logically to be tied in with the observation in the earlier section of this essay that the numerical majority of Bengali speakers represents what were, until recent centuries, culturally unassimilated tribals of eastern Bengal, about whose prior linguistic and social history not much is known.

Further evidence of probable non-Aryan influence in the phonology is to be found in the peculiar word stress pattern of Modern Bengali. Accent was phonemic only in very early Old Indo-Aryan, i.e. Vedic (see pages 386–387). Subsequently, however, predictable word stress has typified the Indo-Aryan languages; the characteristic pattern, moreover, has been for the stress to fall so many morae from the end of the phonological word. Bengali word stress, though, is exceptional. It is non-phonemic and, in the standard dialect, there is a strong tendency for it to be associated with word-*initial* syllables. This pattern evidently became dominant after AD 1400, or well after Bengali acquired a linguistic identity separate from that of its Indo-Aryan sisters. What this and other evidence may imply about the place of Bengali within the general South Asian language area is an issue to be further pursued toward the end of this essay.

3 Morphology

Morphology in Modern Bengali is non-existent for adjectives, minimal for nouns and very productive for verbs. Loss or reduction of the earlier Indo-Aryan adjective declensional parameters (gender, case, number) is fairly typical of the modern Indo-Aryan languages; hence the absence of adjectival morphology in Modern Bengali is not surprising. Bengali differs from many of its sisters, however, in lacking certain characteristic nominal categories. The early Indo-Aryan category of gender persists in most of the modern languages, with the richest (three-gender) systems still to be found in some of the western languages, such as Marathi. Early stages of the Magadhan languages (e.g. Oriya, Assamese and Bengali) also show evidence of a gender system. However, the category is no longer productive in any of the modern Magadhan languages. In Modern Bengali, it is only in a few relic alternations (e.g. the earlier cited pair *nɔṭ* 'actor'/*noṭi* 'actress') that one observes any evidence today for the system of nominal gender which once existed in the language.

The early Indo-Aryan system of three number categories has been reduced in Modern Bengali to a singular/plural distinction which is marked on nouns and pronouns. The elaborate case system of early Indo-Aryan has also been reduced in Modern Bengali as it has in most modern Indo-Aryan languages. Table 23.3 summarises the standard Bengali declension for full nouns (pronouns are not given). Pertinent parameters not, however, revealed in this table are animacy, definiteness and determinacy.

Table 23.3 Bengali Nominal Declension

	Singular	Plural
Nominative	∅	-ra/-era; -gulo
Objective	-ke	-der(ke)/-eder(ke); -guloke
Genitive	-r/-er	-der/-eder; -gulor
Locative-Instrumental	-te/-e *or* -ete	-gulote

Generally, the plural markers are added only to count nouns having animate or definite referents; otherwise plurality tends to be unmarked. Compare, e.g. *jutogulo dɔrkar* 'the (specified) shoes are necessary' versus *juto dɔrkar* '(unspecified) shoes are necessary'. Further, among the plurality markers listed in Table 23.3, -*gulo* (nominative), -*guloke* (objective), -*gulor* (genitive) and -*gulote* (locative-instrumental) are applicable to nouns with both animate and inanimate referents, while the other markers co-occur only with animate nouns. Hence: *chelera* '(the) boys', *chelegulo* '(the) boys', *jutogulo* 'the shoes', but **jutora* 'the shoes'.

The Bengali case markers in Table 23.3 which show an alternation of form (e.g. -*r/-er*, -*te/-e* or -*ete*, -*der(ke)/-eder(ke)*, etc.) are phonologically conditioned according to whether the forms to which they are appended terminate in a syllabic or non-syllabic segment respectively. Both -*eder(ke)* and -*ete* are, however, currently rare. The usage of the objective singular marker -*ke*, listed in Table 23.3, tends to be confined to inanimate noun phrases having definite referents and to definite or determinate animate noun phrases. Thus compare *kichu (*kichuke) caichen* 'do you want something?' with *kauke (*kau) caichen* 'do you want someone?'; but: *pulis caichen* 'are you seeking a policeman/ some policemen?' versus *puliske caichen* 'are you seeking the police?'.

Bengali subject-predicate agreement will be covered in the following section on syntax. It bears mentioning at present, however, that the sole parameters for subject–verb agreement in Modern Bengali are person (three are distinguished) and status. Inflectionally, the Bengali verb is marked for three status categories (despective/ordinary/honorific) in the second person and two categories (ordinary/honorific) in the third. It is notable that the shapes of the honorific inflectional endings are modelled on earlier Indo-Aryan plural inflectional markers. Table 23.4 lists the verbal inflection of modern standard Bengali.

The most interesting area of Bengali morphology is the derivation of inflecting stems from verbal bases. Properly speaking, a formal analysis of Bengali verbal stem derivation presupposes the statement of various morphophonological rules. However, for the sake of brevity and clarity, the phenomena will be outlined below more or less informally.

But before the system of verbal stem derivational marking can be discussed, two facts must be presented concerning the shapes of Bengali verbal bases, i.e. the bases to which the stem markers are added.

First, Bengali verbal bases are all either monosyllabic (such as *jan-* 'know') or disyllabic (such as *kamṛa-* 'bite'). The first syllabic in the verbal base may be called the root vowel. There is a productive process for deriving disyllabic bases from monosyllabics by the addition of a stem vowel. This stem vowel is -*a-* (post-vocalically -*oa-*)

Table 23.4 Bengali Verbal Inflection

	1st person	2nd person despective	2nd person ordinary	3rd person ordinary	Honorific (2nd, 3rd persons)
Present imperative	–	∅	-o	-uk	-un
Unmarked indicative and -*(c)ch*- stems	-i	-is	-o	-e	-en
-*b*- stems	-o	-i	-e	-e	-en
-*t*- and -*l*- stems	-am	-i	-e	-o	-en

as in *jana-* 'inform'; although, for many speakers, the stem vowel may be *-o-* if the root vowel (i.e. of the monosyllabic base) is [+ high]; e.g. *jiro-*, for some speakers *jira-* 'rest'. Derived disyllabics usually serve as the formal causatives of their monosyllabic counterparts. Compare: *jan-* 'know', *jana-* 'inform'; *oṭh-* 'rise', *oṭha-* 'raise'; *dækh-* 'see', *dækha-* 'show'.

Second, monosyllabic bases with non-high root vowels have two alternate forms, respectively called low and high. Examples are:

	Low alternate base	High alternate base
'know'	jan-	jen-
'see'	dækh-	dekh-
'sit'	bɔs-	bos-
'buy'	ken-	kin-
'rise'	oṭh-	uṭh-

When the root vowel is /a/, /e/ is substituted to derive the high alternate base; for bases with front or back non-high root vowels, the high alternate base is formed by assimilating the original root vowel to the next higher vowel in the vowel inventory (see again Table 23.2). The latter behaviour suggests an extended application of the Vowel Height Assimilation process discussed in the preceding section. It is, in fact, feasible to state the rules of verb stem derivation so that the low/high alternation is phonologically motivated; i.e. by positing a high vowel (specifically, /i/) in the underlying shapes of the stem-deriving markers. In some verbal forms there is concrete evidence for the /i/ element, as will be observed below. Also, Vowel Height Assimilation must be invoked in any case to account for the fact that, in the derivation of verbal forms which have zero marking of the stem (that is, the present imperative and unmarked (present) indicative), the high alternate base occurs before any inflection containing a high vowel. Thus *dækh-* 'see', *dækho* 'you (ordinary) see', but *dekhi* 'I see', *dekhis* 'you (despective) see', *dekhun* (honorific) 'see!', etc. That there is no high–low alternation in these inflections for disyllabic bases is consistent with the fact that Vowel Height Assimilation only applies when a high syllabic occurs in the immediately succeeding syllable. Thus *oṭha-* 'raise (cause to rise)', *oṭhae* 'he/she raises', (**uṭhai*) 'I/we raise', etc.

The left-hand column of Table 23.4 lists the various Bengali verbal stem types. Two of the verbal forms with ∅ stem marking, the present imperative and present indicative, were just discussed. It may be pointed out that, in this stem type, the vowel element /u/ of the third person ordinary inflection *-uk* and of the second/third person honorific inflection *-un*, as well as the /i/ of the second person despective inflection *-is*, all disappear post-vocalically (after Vowel Height Assimilation applies); thus (as above) *dekhis* 'you (despective) see' but (from *hɔ-* 'become') *hok* 'let him/her/it/them become!'; *hon* 'he/she/you/they (honorific) become!'; *hos* 'you (despective) become'.

A verbal form with ∅ stem marking not so far discussed is the denominative verbal form or verbal noun. The verbal noun is a non-inflecting form and is therefore not listed in Table 23.4. In monosyllabic bases, the marker of this form is suffixed *-a* (*-oa* post-vocalically); for most standard dialect speakers, the marker in disyllabics is *-no*. Thus *oṭh-* 'rise', *oṭha* 'rising', *oṭha-* 'raise', *oṭhano* 'raising'; *jan-* 'know', *jana* 'knowing', *jana-* 'inform', *janano* 'informing'; *ga-* 'sing', *gaoa* 'singing', *gaoa-* 'cause to sing', *gaoano* 'causing to sing'.

Continuing in the leftmost column of Table 23.4, the stem-deriving marker *-(c)ch-* signals continuative aspect and is used, independent of any other derivational marker, to derive the present continuous verbal form. The element (*c*) of the marker *-(c)ch-* deletes post-consonantally; compare *khacche* 'is eating' (from *kha-*) with *anche* 'is bringing' (from *an-*). In forming the verbal stem with *-(c)ch-* the high alternate base is selected, unless the base is disyllabic or is a monosyllabic base having the root vowel /a/. Compare the last examples with *uṭhche* 'is rising' (from *oṭh-*), *oṭhacche* 'is raising' (from *oṭha-*). In a formal treatment of Bengali morphophonemics, the basic or underlying form of the stem marker could be given as *-i(c)ch-*; in this event, one would posit a rule to delete the element /i/ after Vowel Height Assimilation applies, except in a very limited class of verbs including *ga-* 'sing', *sɔ-* 'bear' and *ca-* 'want'. In forming the present continuous forms of these verbs, the element /i/ surfaces, although the element (*c*) of the stem marker tends to be deleted. The resulting shapes are, respectively: *gaiche* 'is singing' (*gacche* is at best non-standard); *soiche* (**socche*) 'is bearing'; *caiche* 'is wanting' (*cacche* does, however, occur as a variant).

The stem-deriving marker *-b-* (see Table 23.4) signals irrealis aspect and is used to derive future verbal forms, both indicative and imperative (except for the imperative of the second person ordinary, which will be treated after the next paragraph). In Bengali, the future imperative, as well as the present imperative, may occur in affirmative commands; however, the future imperative, never the present imperative, occurs in negative commands.

In forming the verbal stem with *-b-*, the high alternate base is selected except in three cases: where the base is disyllabic, where the monosyllabic base has the root vowel /a/ and where the monosyllabic base is vowel-final. Thus: *uṭhbo* 'I/we will rise' (from *oṭh-*), but *oṭhabo* 'I/we will raise' (from *oṭha-*); *janbo* 'I/we will know' (from *jan-*), *debo* 'I/we will give' (from *de-*). Compare, however, *dibi* 'you (despective) will give', where Vowel Height Assimilation raises the root vowel. It is possible, again, to posit an underlying /i/ in the irrealis stem marker's underlying shape (i.e. *-ib-*), with deletion of the element /i/ applying except for the small class of verbs noted earlier; thus *gaibo* (**gabo*) 'I/we will sing', *soibo* (**sobo*) 'I/we will bear', *caibo* (**cabo*) 'I/we will want'.

The future imperative of the second person ordinary takes the termination *-io*, which can be analysed as a stem formant *-i-* followed by the second person ordinary inflection *-o* (which is also added to unmarked stems, as Table 23.4 shows). When combining with this marker *-i-*, all monosyllabic bases occur in their high alternate shapes; e.g. *hoio* 'become!' (from *hɔ-*). The *-i-* marker is deleted post-consonantally, hence *uṭho* 'rise!' (from *oṭh-*); it also deletes when added to most monosyllabic bases terminating in final /a/, for instance: *peo* 'get!' (**peio*) (from *pa-* 'receive'); *geo* 'sing!' (from *ga-* 'sing'). Bengali disyllabic bases drop their final element /a/ or /o/ before the future imperative stem marker *-i-*. Vowel Height Assimilation applies, hence *uṭhio* 'you must raise!' (from *oṭha-*), *dekhio* 'you must show!' (from *dækha-*), *kamṛio* 'you must bite!' (from *kamṛa-*).

Continuing in the left-hand column of Table 23.4, the stem-deriving marker *-t-* signals non-punctual aspect and appears in several forms of the Bengali verb. The Bengali infinitive termination is invariant *-te*, e.g. *jante* 'to know' (from *jan-*) (as in *jante cai* 'I want to know'). The marker *-t-* also occurs in the finite verbal form used to express the past habitual and perfect conditional, e.g. *jantam* 'I/we used to know' or 'if I/we had known'. The high alternate of monosyllabic bases co-occurs with this marker except in those bases containing a root vowel /a/ followed by a consonant. To illustrate, the infinitive of *oṭh-* 'rise' is *uṭhte*; of *oṭha-* 'raise', *oṭhate*; of *de-* 'give', *dite*; of *hɔ-* 'become', *hote*; of *kha-* 'eat', *khete*; of *an-* 'bring', *ante* (**ente*). Similarly, *uṭhtam* 'I/we used to rise' or 'if I/we had risen'; *oṭhatam* 'I/we used to raise' or 'if I/we had raised', etc. As before, evidence for an /i/ element in the underlying form of the marker *-t-* (i.e.

-it-) comes from the earlier noted class of verbs 'sing', etc.; for example, *gaite* (*gate*) 'to sing', *gaitam* (*gatam*) 'I/ we used to sing' or 'if I/we had sung'; *soite* (*sote*) 'to bear', *soitam* (*sotam*) 'I/we used to bear' or 'if I/we had borne'; *caite* (*cate*) 'to want', *caitam* (*catam*) 'I/we used to want' or 'if I/we had wanted', etc.

The stem-deriving marker -*l*- signals anterior aspect and appears in two verbal forms. The termination of the imperfect conditional is invariant -*le*, e.g. *janle* 'if one knows' (from *jan*-). The marker -*l*- also occurs in the ordinary past tense verbal form, e.g. *janlam* 'I/we knew'. The behaviour of monosyllabic verbal bases in co-occurrence with this marker is the same as their behaviour in co-occurrence with the marker -*t*- discussed above. Thus *uthle* 'if one rises', *othale* 'if one raises', *dile* 'if one gives', *hole* 'if one becomes', *khele* 'if one eats', *anle* 'if one brings'; *uthalam* 'I/we rose', *othalam* 'I/ we raised'; and, again, *gaile* (*gale*) 'if one sings', *soile* (*sole*) 'if one bears', *caile* (*cale*) 'if one wants'; *gailam* 'I/we sang', and so on.

To complete the account of the conjugation of the Bengali verb it is only necessary to mention that certain stem-deriving markers can be combined on a single verbal base. For instance, the marker -*l*- combined with the uninflected stem in -*(c)ch*- yields a verbal form called the past continuous. Illustrations are: *uthchilam* 'I was/we were rising' (from *oth*-), *othacchilam* 'I was/we were raising' (from *otha*-), *khacchilam* 'I was/we were eating' (from *kha*-).

It is also possible to combine stem-deriving markers on the Bengali verbal base in the completive aspect. The marker of this aspect is -*(i)e*-, not listed in Table 23.4 because it is not used in isolation from other stem-forming markers to form inflecting verbal stems. Independently of any other stem-forming marker it may, however, be added to a verbal base to derive a non-finite verbal form known as the conjunctive participle (or gerund). An example is: *bujhe* 'having understood' from *bujh*- 'understand' (note that the element (*i*) of -*(i)e*- deletes post-consonantally). When attached to the completive aspect marker -*(i)e*-, all monosyllabic bases occur in their high alternate shapes; disyllabic bases drop their final element /a/ or /o/; and in the latter case, Vowel Height Assimilation applies. Thus: *uthe* 'having risen' (from *oth*-); *jene* 'having known' (from *jan*-); *diye* 'having given' (from *de*-); *uthie* 'having raised' (from *otha*-), *janie* 'having informed' (from *jana*-). Now the stem-deriving marker -*(c)ch*- may combine with the verbal stem in -*(i)e*-, yielding a verbal form called the present perfect; the combining shape of the former marker in such cases is invariably -*ch*-. This is to say that the element (*c*) of the marker -*(c)ch*- not only deletes post-consonantally (see the earlier discussion of continuous aspect marking), but also following the stem-deriving marker -*(i)e*-. Some examples are: *dekheche* 'has seen' (from monosyllabic *dækh*-), *dekhieche* 'has shown' (from disyllabic *dækha*-), *diyeche* 'has given' (from *de*- 'give'). The verbal stem in -*(i)e*- followed by -*(c)ch*- may further combine with the anterior aspect marker -*l*- to yield a verbal form called the past perfect; e.g. *dekhechilam* 'I/we had seen', *dekhiechilam* 'I/we had shown'.

Examples of conjugation for four Bengali verbal bases are given in the chart of verbal conjugation types. The inflection illustrated in the chart is the third person ordinary.

4 Syntax

The preceding discussion of declensional parameters (case and number for nouns, person and status for verbs) ties in naturally with the topic of agreement in Bengali syntax.

Bengali Verbal Conjugation Types

	pa- 'receive'		*an-* 'bring'		*bɔs-* 'sit'		*bɔsa-* 'seat'	
Verbal noun	paoa	'receiving'	ana	'bringing'	bɔsa	'sitting'	bɔsano	'seating'
Present indicative	pae	'receives'	ane	'brings'	bɔse	'sits'	bɔsae	'seats'
Present imperative	pak	'let him/her/them receive!'	anuk	'let him/her/them bring!'	bosuk	'let him/her/them sit!'	bɔsak	'let him/her/them seat!'
Present continuous	pacche	'is receiving'	anche	'is bringing'	bosche	'is sitting'	bɔsacche	'is seating'
Future indicative/future imperative	pabe	'will receive'/'must receive!'	anbe	'will bring'/'must bring!'	bosbe	'will sit'/'must sit!'	bɔsabe	'will seat'/'must seat!'
Infinitive	pete	'to receive'	ante	'to bring'	boste	'to sit'	bɔsate	'to seat'
Perfect conditional/past habitual	peto	'would receive'	anto	'would bring'	bosto	'would sit'	bɔsato	'would seat'
Imperfect conditional	pele	'if one receives'	anle	'if one brings'	bosle	'if one sits'	bɔsale	'if one seats'
Ordinary past	pelo	'received'	anlo	'brought'	boslo	'sat'	bɔsalo	'seated'
Past continuous	pacchilo	'was receiving'	anchilo	'was bringing'	boschilo	'was sitting'	bɔsacchilo	'was seating'
Conjunctive participle	peye	'having received'	ene	'having brought'	bose	'having sat'	bosie	'having seated'
Present perfect	peyeche	'has received'	eneche	'has brought'	boseche	'has sat'	bosieche	'has seated'

A number of modern Indo-Aryan languages (see, for example, the chapter on Hindi-Urdu) demonstrate a degree of ergative patterning in predicate–noun phrase agreement; and Bengali, in its early historical stages, likewise showed some ergative patterning (i. e. sentential verb agreeing with subject of an intransitive sentence but with object, not subject, of a transitive sentence). However, this behaviour is not characteristic today of any of the eastern Magadhan languages.

Thus in Modern Bengali, sentences normally have subjects in the nominative or unmarked case, and the finite predicates of sentences normally agree with their subjects for the parameters of person and status. There are, however, two broad classes of exceptions to this generalisation. The passive constructions exemplify one class. Passive in Modern Bengali is a special variety of sentence nominalisation. When a sentence is nominalised, the predicate takes the verbal noun form (discussed in the preceding section) and the subject is marked with the genitive case. Under passivisation, a sentence is nominalised and then assigned to one of a small set of matrix predicates, the most common being *hɔ-* 'become' and *ja-* 'go'; and when the latter is selected, the subject of the nominalised sentence is obligatorily deleted. Examples are: *tomar jɔthesṭo khaoa hoyeche?* (your enough eating has-become) 'have you eaten enough?' (i.e. has it been sufficiently eaten by you?) and *oke paoa gælo* (to-him getting it-went) 'he was found' (i.e. him was found). In a passive sentence, the matrix verb (*hɔ-* or *ja-*) lacks agreement with any noun phrase. In particular, it cannot agree with the original subject of the active sentence – this noun phrase has become marked with the genitive case under nominalisation, or deleted altogether. This is to say that the Modern Bengali passive construction lacks a formal subject; it is of a type referred to in some grammatical literature as the 'impersonal passive'. These constructions form one class of exceptions to the characteristic pattern of Bengali subject–verb agreement.

The other class of exceptions comprises certain expressions having subjects which occur in a marked or oblique case. In Bengali there are a few complex constructions of this type. Bengali also has several dozen predicates which regularly occur in non-complex constructions with marked subjects. These constructions can be called indirect subject constructions, and indirect subjects in Modern Bengali are invariably marked with the genitive case. (At an earlier historical stage of the language, any of the oblique cases could be used for the marking of the subject noun phrase in this sort of construction.) In the Modern Bengali indirect subject construction, the finite predicate normally demonstrates no agreement. An example is: *maer tomake pɔchondo hɔy* (of-mother to-you likes) 'Mother likes you'. Bengali indirect subject predicates typically express sensory, mental, emotional, corporal and other characteristically human experiences. These predicates constitute a significant class of exceptions to the generalised pattern of subject–finite predicate agreement in Modern Bengali.

The remainder of this overview of Bengali syntax will be devoted to the topic of word order, or the relative ordering of major constituents in sentences. In some literature on word order types, Bengali has been characterised as a rigidly verb-final language, wherein nominal modifiers precede their heads; verbal modifiers follow verbal bases; the verbal complex is placed sentence-finally; and the subject noun phrase occupies the initial position in a sentence. In these respects Bengali is said to contrast with earlier Indo-Aryan, in which the relative ordering of sentential constituents was freer, notwithstanding a statistical tendency for verbs to stand at the ends of their clauses.

It is true that the ordering of sentential elements is more rigid in Modern Bengali than in Classical Sanskrit. However, the view that Bengali represents a 'rigid' verb-final language does not adequately describe its differences from earlier Indo-Aryan word order patterning.

Word order within the Modern Bengali noun phrase is, to be sure, strict. An adjective or genitive expression is always placed before the noun it modifies. By contrast, in earlier Indo-Aryan, adjectives showed inflectional concord with their modified nouns and consequently were freer in their positioning; more or less the same applied to the positioning of genitive expressions with respect to nominal heads. Not only is the ordering of elements within the noun phrase more rigid in Modern Bengali, but the mutual ordering of noun phrases within the sentence is strict as well, much more so than in earlier Indo-Aryan. The subject noun phrase generally comes first in a Modern Bengali sentence, followed by an indirect object if one occurs; next comes the direct object if one occurs; after which an oblique object noun phrase may be positioned. This strictness of linear ordering can be ascribed to the relative impoverishment of the Modern Bengali case system in comparison with earlier Indo-Aryan. Bengali case markers are, nonetheless, supplemented by a number of postpositions, each of which may govern nouns declined in one of two cases, the objective or genitive.

We will now consider word order within the verb phrase. At the Old Indo-Aryan stage exemplified by Classical Sanskrit, markers representing certain verbal qualifiers (causal, desiderative, potential and conditional) could be affixed to verbal bases, as stem-forming markers and/or as inflectional endings. Another verbal qualifier, the marker of sentential negation, tended to be placed just before the sentential verb. The sentential interrogative particle, on the other hand, was often placed at a distance from the verbal complex.

In Modern Bengali, the only verbal qualifier which is regularly affixed to verbal bases is the causal. (See the discussion of derived disyllabic verbal bases in Section 3 above.) The following pair of Bengali sentences illustrates the formal relationship between non-causative and causative constructions: *cheleṭi ciṭhiṭa poṛlo* (the-boy the-letter read) 'the boy read the letter'; *ma cheleṭi-ke diye ciṭhiṭa pɔralen* (mother to-the-boy by the-letter caused-to-read) 'the mother had the boy read the letter'. It will be noted that in the second example the non-causal agent is marked with the postposition *diye* 'by' placed after its governed noun, which appears in the objective case. Usually, when the verbal base from which the causative is formed is transitive, the non-causal agent is marked in just this way. The objective case alone is used to mark the non-causal agent when the causative is derived either from an intransitive base, or from any of several semantically 'affective' verbs — transitive verbs expressing actions whose principal effect accrues to their agents and not their undergoers. Examples are: 'eat', 'smell', 'hear', 'see', 'read' (in the sense of 'study'), 'understand' and several others.

It was mentioned above that the modalities of desiderative and potential action could be marked on the verbal form itself in Old Indo-Aryan. In Modern Bengali, these modalities are usually expressed periphrastically; i.e. by suffixing the infinitive marker to the verbal stem, which is then followed by a modal verb. To illustrate: *uṭhte cae* 'wants to rise', *uṭhte pare* 'can rise'.

Conditional expressions occur in two forms in Modern Bengali. The conditional clause may be finite, in which case there appears the particle *jodi*, which is a direct borrowing from a functionally similar Sanskrit particle *yadi*. To illustrate: *jodi tumi kajṭa sarbe (tɔbe) eso* (if you the-work will-finish (then) come) 'if/when you finish the work, (then) come over!'. An alternate way of framing a conditional is by means of the non-finite conditional verbal form (imperfect conditional), which was mentioned in

Section 3. In this case no conditional particle is used; e.g. *tumi kajṭa sarle (tɔbe) eso* (you the-work if-finish (then) come) 'if/when you finish the work, come over!'.

The particle of sentential negation in Bengali is *na*. In independent clauses it generally follows the sentential verb; in subjoined clauses (both finite and non-finite), it precedes. Thus: *boslam na* (I-sat not) 'I did not sit'; *jodi tumi na bɔso* (if you not sit) 'if you don't sit'; *tumi na bosle* (you not if-sit) 'if you don't sit'. Bengali has, it should be mentioned, two negative verbs. Each of them is a counterpart to one of the verbs 'to be'; and in this connection it needs to be stated that Bengali has three verbs 'to be'. These are respectively the predicative *hɔ-* 'become'; the existential verb 'exist', having independent/subjoined clause allomorphs *ach-/thak-*; and the equational verb or copula, which is normally ∅ but in emphatic contexts is represented by *hɔ-* placed between two arguments (compare, for example, non-emphatic *ini jodu* (this-person ∅ Jodu) 'this is Jodu' versus emphatic *ini hocchen jodu* (this-person is Jodu) 'this (one) is Jodu'). While the predicative verb 'to be' has no special negative counterpart (it is negated like any other Bengali verb), the other two verbs 'to be' each have a negative counterpart. Moreover, for each of these negative verbs, there are separate allomorphs which occur in independent and subjoined clauses. The respective independent/subjoined shapes of the negative verbs are existential *nei/na thak-* (note that the verb *nei* is invariant) and equational *nɔ-/na hɔ-*. It bears mentioning, incidentally, that negative verbs are neither characteristic of modern nor of earlier Indo-Aryan. They are, if anything, reminiscent of negative copulas and other negative verbs in languages of the Dravidian (South Indian) family, such as Modern Tamil.

The Modern Bengali sentential interrogative particle *ki* is inherited from an earlier Indo-Aryan particle of similar function. The sentential interrogative *ki* may appear in almost any position in a Bengali sentence other than absolute initial; however, sentences vary in their presuppositional nuances according to the placement of this particle, which seems to give the most neutral reading when placed in the second position (i.e. after the first sentential constituent). To illustrate, compare: *tumi ki ekhane chatro?* (you interrogative here student) 'are you a student here?'; *tumi ekhane ki chatro?* (you here interrogative student) 'is it here that you are a student?'; *tumi ekhane chatro (na) ki?* (you here student (negative) interrogative) 'oh, is it that you are a student here?'.

To complete this treatment of word order, we may discuss the relative ordering of marked and unmarked clauses in Bengali complex sentences. By 'marked clause' is meant either a non-finite subordinate clause or a clause whose function within the sentential frame is signalled by some distinctive marker; an instance of such a marker being *jodi*, the particle of the finite conditional clause. As a rule, in a Bengali sentence containing two or more clauses, marked clauses tend to precede unmarked. This is, for instance, true of conjunctive participle constructions; e.g. *bari giye kapor chere ami can korlam* (home having-gone clothes having-removed I bath did) 'going home and removing my clothes, I had a bath'. Relative clauses in Bengali likewise generally precede main clauses, since they are marked (that is, with relative pronouns); Bengali, then, exhibits the correlative sentential type which is well attested throughout the history of Indo-Aryan. An illustration of this construction is: *je boiṭa enecho ami seṭa kichu din rakhbo* (which book you-brought I it some days will-keep) 'I shall keep the book you have brought for a few days'. Finite complement sentences marked with the complementiser *bole* (derived from the conjunctive participle of the verb *bɔl-* 'say') likewise precede unmarked clauses; e.g. *apni jacchen bole ami jani* (you are-going complementiser I know) 'I know that you are going'.

An exception to the usual order of marked before unmarked clauses is exemplified by an alternative finite complement construction. Instead of clause-final marking (with *bole*), the complement clause type in question has an initial marker, a particle *je* (derived historically from a complementiser particle of earlier Indo-Aryan). A complement clause marked initially with *je* is ordered invariably after, not before, the unmarked clause; e.g. *ami jani je apni jacchen* (I know complementiser you are-going) 'I know that you are going'.

5 Concluding Points

In this final section the intention is to relate the foregoing discussion to the question of Bengali's historical development and present standing, both within the Indo-Aryan family and within the general South Asian language area. To accomplish this, it is useful to consider the fact of lectal differentiation in the present community of Bengali speakers. Both vertical and horizontal varieties are observed.

Vertical differentiation, or diglossia, is a feature of the current standard language. This is to say that the language has two styles used more or less for complementary purposes. Of the two styles, the literary or 'pundit language' (*sadhu bhasa*) shows greater conservatism in word morphology (i.e. in regard to verbal morphophonemics and the shapes of case endings) as well as in lexis (it is characterised by a high frequency of words whose forms are directly borrowed from Sanskrit). The less conservative style identified with the spoken or 'current language' (*colti bhasa*) is the everyday medium of informal discourse. Lately it is also gaining currency in more formal discourse situations and, in written expression, has been encroaching on the literary style for some decades.

The institutionalisation of the *sadhu–colti* distinction occurred in Bengali in the nineteenth century, and (as suggested in the last paragraph) shows signs of weakening today. Given (1) that the majority of Bengali speakers today are not Hindu and cannot be expected to maintain an emotional affinity to Sanskritic norms, plus (2) the Bangladesh government's recent moves to enhance the Islamic character of eastern Bengali society and culture and (3) the fact that the colloquial style is overtaking the literary even in western Bengal (both in speech and writing), it remains to be seen over the coming years whether a formal differentiation of everyday versus 'pundit' style language will be maintained.

It should be added that, although throughout the Bengali-speaking area a single, more or less uniform variety of the language is regarded as the standard dialect, the bulk of speakers have at best a passing acquaintance with it. That is, horizontal differentiation of Bengali lects is very extensive (if poorly researched), both in terms of the number of regional dialects that occur and in terms of their mutual divergence. (The extreme eastern dialect of Chittagong, for instance, is unintelligible even to many speakers of other eastern Bengali dialects.) The degree of horizontal differentiation that occurs in the present Bengali-speaking region is related to the ambiguity of Bengali's linguistic affiliation, i.e. areal as contrasted with genetic. It is to be noted that the Bengali-speaking region of the Indian subcontinent to this day borders on or subsumes the domains of a number of non-Indo-Aryan languages. Among them are Malto (a Dravidian language of eastern Bihar); Ahom (a Tai language of neighbouring Assam); Garo (a Tibeto-Burman language spoken in the northern districts of Bengal itself); as well as several languages affiliated with Munda (a subfamily of Austro-Asiatic), such as Santali and Mundari (both of these languages are spoken within as well as outside the Bengali-speaking area).

It has been pointed out earlier that modern standard Bengali has several features suggestive of extra-Aryan influence. These features are: the frequency of retroflex consonants; initial-syllable word stress; absence of grammatical gender; negative verbs. Though not specifically pointed out as such previously, Bengali has several other formal features, discussed above, which represent divergences from the norms of Indo-Aryan and suggest convergence with the areal norms of greater South Asia. These features are: post-verbal negative particle placement; clause-final complement sentence marking; relative rigidity of word order patterning in general, and sentence-final verb positioning in particular; proliferation of the indirect subject construction (which was only occasionally manifested in early Indo-Aryan).

In addition to the above, it may be mentioned that Bengali has two lexical features of a type foreign to Indo-Aryan. These features are, however, not atypical of languages of the general South Asian language area (and are even more typical of South-East Asian languages). One of these is a class of reduplicative expressives, words such as: *kickic* (suggesting grittiness), *mitmit* (suggesting flickering), *tɔlmɔl* (suggesting an overflowing or fluid state). There are dozens of such lexemes in current standard Bengali. The other un-Aryan lexical class consists of around a dozen classifier words, principally numeral classifiers. Examples are: *du jon chatro* (two human-classifier student) 'two students'; *tin khana boi* (three flat-thing-classifier book) 'three books'.

It is probable that the features discussed above were absorbed from other languages into Bengali after the thirteenth century, as the language came to be increasingly used east of the traditional sociocultural centre of Bengal. That centre, located along the former main course of the Ganges (the present-day Bhagirathi–Hooghley River) in western Bengal, still sets the standard for spoken and written expression in the language. Thus standard Bengali is defined even today as the dialect spoken in Calcutta and its environs. It is a reasonable hypothesis nevertheless, as suggested above in Section 1, that descendants of non-Bengali tribals of a few centuries past now comprise the bulk of Bengali speakers. In other words, the vast majority of the Bengali linguistic community today represents present or former inhabitants of the previously uncultivated and culturally unassimilated tracts of eastern Bengal. Over the past several centuries, these newcomers to the Bengali-speaking community are the ones responsible for the language's having acquired a definite affiliation within the South Asian linguistic area, above and beyond the predetermined and less interesting fact of its genetic affiliation in Indo-Aryan.

Bibliography

Chatterji (1926) is the classic, and indispensable, treatment of historical phonology and morphology in Bengali and the other Indo-Aryan languages. A good bibliographical source is Čižikova and Ferguson (1969). For the relation between literary and colloquial Bengali, see Dimock (1960).

The absence of a comprehensive reference grammar of Bengali in English is noticeable. Ray et al. (1966) is one of the better concise reference grammars. Chatterji (1939) is a comprehensive grammar in Bengali, while Chatterji (1972) is a concise but thorough treatment of Bengali grammar following the traditional scheme of Indian grammars. Two pedagogical works are also useful: Dimock et al. (1965), a first-year textbook containing very lucid descriptions of the basic structural categories of the language, and Bender and Riccardi (1978), an advanced Bengali textbook containing much useful information on Bengali literature and on the modern literary language. For individual topics, the following can be recommended: on phonetics–phonology, Chatterji (1921) and Ferguson and Chowdhury (1960); on the morphology of the verb, Dimock (1957), Ferguson (1945) and Sarkar (1976); on syntax, Klaiman (1981), which discusses the syntax and semantics of the indirect subject construction, passives and the conjunctive participle construction in modern and earlier stages of Bengali.

References

Bender, E. and Riccardi, T. Jr 1978. *An Advanced Course in Bengali*, South Asia Regional Studies (University of Pennsylvania, Philadephia)

Chatterji, S.K. 1921. 'Bengali Phonetics', *Bulletin of the School of Oriental and African Studies*, vol. 2, pp. 1–25

—— 1926. *The Origin and Development of the Bengali Language*, 3 vols (Allen and Unwin, London)

—— 1939. *Bhāṣāprakāśa bāṅgālā byākaraṇa* (Calcutta University, Calcutta)

—— 1972. *Sarala bhāṣprakāśa bāṅgālā byākaraṇa*, revised edn (Bāk-sāhitya, Calcutta)

Čižikova, K.L. and Ferguson, C.A. 1969. 'Bibliographical Review of Bengali Studies', in T. Sebeok (ed.) *Current Trends in Linguistics*, vol. 5: *Linguistics in South Asia* (Mouton, The Hague), pp. 85–98

Dimock, E.C., Jr 1957. 'Notes on Stem-vowel Alternation in the Bengali Verb', *Indian Linguistics*, vol. 17, pp. 173–7

—— 1960. 'Literary and Colloquial Bengali in Modern Bengali Prose', *International Journal of American Linguistics*, vol. 26, no. 3, pp. 43–63

Dimock, E.C., Battacharji, S. and Chatterji, S. 1965. *Introduction to Bengali*, part 1 (East–West Center, Honolulu; reprinted South Asia Books, Columbia, MO, 1976)

Ferguson, C.A. 1945. 'A Chart of the Bengali Verb', *Journal of the American Oriental Society*, vol. 65, pp. 54–5

Ferguson, C.A. and Chowdhury, M. 1960. 'The Phonemes of Bengali', *Language*, vol. 36, pp. 22–59

Klaiman, M.H. 1981. *Volitionality and Subject in Bengali: A Study of Semantic Parameters in Grammatical Processes* (Indiana University Linguistics Club, Bloomington)

Ray, P.S., Hai, M.A. and Ray, L. 1966. *Bengali Language Handbook* (Center for Applied Linguistics, Washington, DC)

Sarkar, P. 1976. 'The Bengali Verb', *International Journal of Dravidian Linguistics*, vol. 5, pp. 274–973

24

Iranian Languages

J.R. Payne

Revised by Behrooz Mahmoodi-Bakhtiari

1 Overview and Historical Background

Iranian Languages form a branch of the Indo-Iranian group of the Indo-European family, which are probably spoken by more than 80 million people in a wide area from Turkey (with Zaza, as the westernmost) to China (with Sarikoli, as the easternmost Iranian language), and mainly cover the whole of Iran, Afghanistan, and Tajikistan. The development of the Iranian languages may be studied within three major historical periods: Old Iranian (up to the fourth/third centuries BC), Middle Iranian (from the fourth/third centuries BC to the eighth/ninth centuries AD), and New Iranian.

Among the Old Iranian languages, two are known and attested, Avestan and Old Persian. However, the Middle Iranian languages (*c.* 300 BC–AD 950) are much more numerous; they are divided into two major groups, western and eastern. Modern Iranian languages fall into two major 'eastern' and 'western' groups, with 'northern' and 'southern' subgroups for each.

Within the Indo-European family, the Iranian languages are satem languages, e.g. Proto-Indo-European *$\hat{k}m̥tom$ 'hundred', Avestan *satəm*, and show a very close relationship to the Indo-Aryan (and Dardic) branches. There are three common phonological developments which separate Iranian and Indo-Aryan from the rest of Indo-European: (1) the collapse of Proto-Indo-European *a, *e, *o, *$n̥$, *$m̥$ into *a*, and correspondingly of *$\bar{a}$, *$\bar{e}$, *$\bar{o}$, *$n̥̄$, *$m̥̄$ into *$\bar{a}$*, e.g. Proto-Indo-European *$dek̂m̥$ 'ten' > Avestan *dasa*, Sanskrit *dáśa*, but Old Church Slavonic *desętъ* Latin *decem*; (2) the development of Proto-Indo-European *$ə$ into *i*, e.g. Proto-Indo-European *$pət\bar{e}(r)$ 'father' > Old Persian *pitā*, Sanskrit *pitá*, but Latin *pater*; (3) the development of Proto-Indo-European *s into *$š$ or *$ṣ$ after *i, *u, *r, *k, e.g. Proto-Indo-European *$ueks$ 'grow' > Old Persian and Avestan *vaxš-*, Sanskrit *vakṣ-* but German *wachs-*, English *wax*; Proto-Indo-European *sed- 'sit' > Old Persian *ni-šad-*, Sanskrit *ni-ṣīd-* (with additional prefix), but Latin *sed-*, English *sit*. In addition, Iranian and Indo-Aryan inherit from Proto-Indo-European strikingly similar verbal conjugations and nominal declensions. Compare for example the following forms of the first person singular pronoun 'I': (a) nominative: Old Persian *adam*, Avestan *azəm*, Sanskrit *ahám*; (b) accusative: Old Persian *mām*, Avestan *mām*,

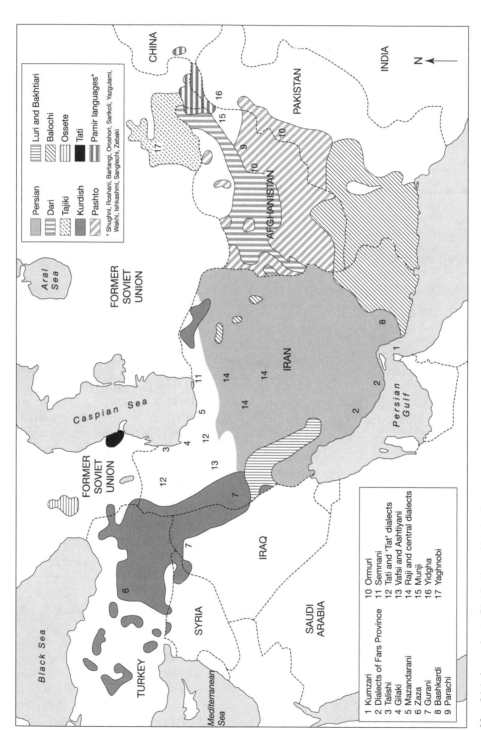

Map 24.1 Approximate Distribution of Iranian Languages.
Source: Map compiled by J. R. Payne.

The following labels and legend appear within the map:

Legend:
- Persian
- Dari
- Tajiki
- Kurdish
- Pashto
- Luri and Bakhtiari
- Balochi
- Ossete
- Tati
- Pamir languages*

* Shughni, Roshani, Bartangi, Oroshori, Sarikoli, Yazgulami, Wakhi, Ishkashmi, Sanglechi, Zebaki

1 Kumzari
2 Dialects of Fars Province
3 Talishi
4 Giliaki
5 Mazandarani
6 Zaza
7 Gurani
8 Bashkardi
9 Parachi
10 Ormuri
11 Semnani
12 Tati and 'Tat' dialects
13 Vafsi and Ashtiyani
14 Raji and central dialects
15 Munji
16 Yidgha
17 Yaghnobi

CHINA
INDIA
PAKISTAN
AFGHANISTAN
FORMER SOVIET UNION
Aral Sea
Caspian Sea
IRAN
Persian Gulf
IRAQ
SYRIA
SAUDI ARABIA
TURKEY
Black Sea
Mediterranean Sea

N

Sanskrit *mā́m*; (c) genitive: Old Persian *manā*, Avestan *mana*, Sanskrit *máma*; (d) enclitic accusative: Old Persian *-mā*, Avestan *-mā*, Sanskrit *-mā*; (e) enclitic genitive: Old Persian *-maiy*, Avestan *-mōi*, Sanskrit *-mē*; (f) enclitic ablative: Old Persian *-ma*, Avestan *-maṯ*, Sanskrit *-mát*.

All Iranian languages of the Middle and Modern periods exhibit some common characteristics. The unmarked word order is typically verb-final, and the tense system is invariably based on two verb stems, present and past. Whereas the present stem continues the Old Iranian present, inherited directly from Indo-European, the past stem is based on a participial form of the verb ending in *-ta*. This participle had an active orientation for intransitive verbs, but was originally passive in the transitive paradigm, as in Old Persian *hamiçiyā hagmatā* (rebels (nom.) assembled (nom. m. pl.)) 'the rebels assembled', *ima tya manā kartam* (this what me (gen.) done (nom. nt. sg.)) 'this is what was done by me'. The subsequent reanalysis of the passive participle as an active verb leads to ergative past tenses, preserved in a number of languages including Kurdish and Pashto, e.g. Kurdish (Kurmanji dialect) *ez ket-im* (I (abs.) fell (1 sg.)) 'I fell', but *min çîrok xwend* (I (obl.) story (abs.) read (3 sg.)) 'I read a story'. The majority of the modern Iranian languages exhibit various stages in the decay of the past tense ergative system into a nominative one, as preserved in the tenses based on the present stem. Modern Persian is typical here of the final stage, with no traces of ergativity except the form of the first person singular pronoun *man* 'I' (< Old Persian genitive *manā*). In the following sections, the three stages of the development of Iranian languages will be briefly discussed.

2 Old Iranian Languages

The oldest attested forms of Iranian are Old Persian, known from the cuneiform inscriptions of the Achaemenid emperors, in particular Darius the Great (521–486 BC) and Xerxes (486–465 BC), and Avestan, the language of the *Avesta*, a collection of sacred Zoroastrian texts. The oldest parts of the *Avesta*, the Gathas or songs attributed to the prophet Zoroaster himself, reflect a slightly more archaic stage of development than the Old Persian inscriptions, and must therefore be dated to the sixth century BC or earlier, although the first manuscripts are from the thirteenth and fourteenth centuries AD.

Genetically, Old Persian can be clearly associated with the South-West Iranian group, the Achaemenid empire being centred on the province of Fârs in the south-west of modern Iran, and must be considered a direct precursor of forms of Middle and Modern Persian. The position of Avestan is, however, complex and disputed, although the Gathas represent some clear east Iranian characteristics, notably a tendency to voice clusters which appear as *-ft-* and *-xt-* in West Iranian. However, it is clear that Avestan shows none of the features characteristic of South-West Iranian.

From archaeological and textual evidence, it can be deduced that Iranian languages at the time of the Achaemenid empire had a wider geographical distribution than at present, extending from the steppes of southern Russia in the west to areas of Chinese Turkestan (Xinjiang) in the east. Although Old Persian and Avestan are the main linguistic sources from this period, some proper names and toponyms, provide some information about Median, the language of the province of Media centred on Ecbatana (modern Hamadan in north-west Iran), and about the language of the Scythian and Sarmatian tribes of the south Russian steppes. The Median language, which belongs genetically to the North-West group, was originally the language of the Median empire (eighth to sixth centuries BC), and some of its influence can be seen in the Old Persian inscriptions.

3 Middle Iranian Languages

Middle Iranian is the phase in the development of the Iranian languages that roughly coincides with late antiquity and the early Islamic period. It represents a larger number of languages, as well as providing a wealth of materials. It is during this stage that classification of the Iranian languages into Western and Eastern groups becomes more meaningful, as a larger number of distinct languages are attested during this period. Western Middle Iranian is represented by Middle Persian and Parthian, and the major Eastern Middle Iranian languages are Khotanese and Tumshuqese, Sogdian, Khwarezmian, and Bactrian.

Middle Persian (or Pahlavi), is the best-known literary language among the Middle Iranian. It belongs to the South-West group, and is almost the direct descendant of Old Persian and the precursor of Modern Persian. Although the earliest documents, inscriptions on coins, date from the second century BC, the main corpus illustrates the language of the Sassanid empire (third to seventh centuries AD), centred on the province of Fars (ancient Persis), but by the time of the Arab conquest (seventh/eighth centuries AD) extending over a wide area of present-day Iran, Afghanistan and Central Asia. It includes both secular and Zoroastrian documents written in the Pahlavi script, which is based on the Aramaic and does not show short vowels. The term *Pahlavi* itself is the adjective from the noun *Pahlav* < *Parθava* 'Parthia'. Middle Persian is also represented by a large corpus of Manichean texts found in Turfan, Chinese Turkestan (Xinjiang), and dating mainly to the eighth and ninth centuries AD, although the earliest documents go as far back as the time of Mani (AD 216–74), the founder of the religion. These latter are written mostly in the Manichean script, another derivative of Aramaic, but are also found in Sogdian and Runic Turkic forms.

On the other hand, Parthian belongs to the North-West group. It is more sparsely documented than Middle Persian, but was the language of the province of Parthia which flourished at the time of the Arsacid dynasty (third century BC) to the south-east of the Caspian Sea. It is known through Parthian versions of Sassanid inscriptions and Manichean texts, as well as through minor documents from the first century BC and ostraca from ancient Nisa, located near Ashgabat in Turkmenistan.

Sogdian is perhaps the most important member of the middle North-East group, as it was the lingua franca of an extensive area centred on Samarqand and the silk route to China. There are some letters left from the fourth century AD in the Sogdian script, as well as some secular documents dating to the eighth century AD from Mt Mugh in the Zeravshan (Zarafshan) area of Tajikistan, beside a number of Buddhist texts of the same period. The modern descendant of Sogdian is Yaghnobi, spoken by a small group in Tajikistan.

Another important representative of Middle North-East Iranian is Khwarezmian, located in a region centred on modern Khiva, and attested in documents and inscriptions in a type of Aramaic script dating mainly to the third to eighth centuries AD. Later fragments of Khwarezmian have survived in Islamic texts of the eleventh to fourteenth centuries AD.

Finally, to the South-East group belong Saka languages (Khotanese and Tumshuqese), the languages of eastern Scythian tribes from Khotan (Xinjiang), and Bactrian, the language of the Kushan kingdom of Bactria, which has an intermediate position between Western and Eastern Iranian. The former is known through an extensive corpus of Buddhist texts in the Brahmi script, and dating primarily to the fifth to tenth centuries AD, while the latter is represented mainly by an inscription of twenty-five lines in a variant of the Greek script, found at the temple of Surkh Kotal in northern Afghanistan.

4 New Iranian Languages

The New Iranian languages are those used mainly after the emergence of Islam in the Iranian region. Like their Middle and Old ancestors, the New Iranian languages fall within two major Eastern and Western groups, a distinction which is the most fundamental division in Iranian dialectology.

The distinction of the Eastern and Western Iranian languages lies in the basic geographical distribution of the main speakers of these languages, on the east or the west of the Kavir and Lut deserts in Iran. The languages spoken inside today's Iran (like Balochi, Zaza, Persian, Kurdish and Gorani) are regarded as the Western Iranian languages, and the languages spoken towards the east in Tajikistan, Afghanistan and Western China (like Yaghnobi, Shughni and Wakhi) are Eastern languages.

This geographical distinction, although convincing and easy at first sight, is also misleading, as such conventional terms do not always correspond to the present real geographical situation of the languages. The Tajiki and Dari dialects of Persian, for example, are Western, although geographically to the east. Ossetian, on the other hand, which belongs to the North-East group, is spoken in the Caucasus, which represents the north-west of the present Iranian language area.

However, some clear phonological features characterise the basic division between East and West Iranian. These features are:

1 West Iranian preserves *b*, *d*, *g*, but these are mainly converted in East Iranian into the corresponding voiced fricatives *β* (*v*, *w*), *δ*, *γ*, e.g. Old Persian *brātar* 'brother', Modern Persian *barādar*, Balochi *brās*, but Sogdian *βr't*, Yaghnobi *virōt*; Avestan *dasa* 'ten', Modern Persian *dah*, Bakhtiari *deh*, Zaza *däs*, but Sogdian *δs'*, Shughni *δīs*; Old Persian *gauša* 'ear', Modern Persian *gūš*, Gurani *goš*, Kurdish *goh*, but Sogdian *γwš*, Ossetian *γos*, Bartangi *γu*.

2 West Iranian preserves *č*, but this is mainly converted into *c* in East Iranian, e.g. Middle Persian *čahār* 'four', Balochi *čār*, but Khwarezmian *cf'r/cβ'r*, Shughni *cavōr*.

3 The consonantal clusters -*ft*- and -*xt*- are preserved in West Iranian, but converted into the voiced counterparts -*vd*- and -*γd*- in East Iranian; equally, originally voiced clusters of this type tend to be preserved in East Iranian but devoiced in West Iranian, e.g. *hafta 'seven' > Middle Persian *haft*, Kurdish *häft*, but Khwarezmian *'βd*, Ossetian *avd*, Yazgulami *uvd*; *duγdar 'daughter' > Modern Persian *doxtar*, Gilaki *duxtə*, but Avestan *dugədā*, Khwarezmian *δyd*, Wakhi *δəγ̈d*.

Each of these Eastern and Western languages has its own subgroups, dividing them into Northern and Southern classes. Each of these classes has some specific distinctive features.

4.1 New West Iranian Languages

Geographically, the New West Iranian languages and dialects may be divided into eight subgroups: the Central dialects, Caspian dialects, North-Western dialects, South-Western dialects, South-Eastern dialects, Kurdic languages and dialects, Zaza-Gorani languages, and the different dialects of Baluchi.

In historical and typological terms, the New West Iranian languages are divided into two Northern and Southern subgroups. North-Western Iranian dialects are those dating back to the languages spoken in the northern and north-western parts of the Iranian plateau. North-Western Iranian languages, to which most of the West languages belong, are now found in Kurdestan and Azarbaijan in north-west of Iran, as well as around the Caspian Sea and central Iran, together with Baluchi in the southeast of Iran. Needless to say, this change of location is mostly due to the migration of these people from their original places.

There are some phonological characteristics which separate the South-West and North-West groups. In the North-Western languages, we may notice:

1. Preserving the Old Iranian *z*, as opposed to the change of *z* into *d* in the South-Western languages, such as NW *zumâ* or *zâmâ* 'bridegroom, son-in-law' vs SW *dâmâd*. Other examples are Avestan *zān-* 'know', Parthian *z'n-*, Gurani *zān-*, Kurdish *zan-*, but Old Persian *dān-*, Modern Persian *dān-* and Tati *dan-*.

2. Preserving the Old Iranian *s*, as opposed to the change of *s* into *θ* or *h* in the SW languages (such as the Old Persian word *θata-* 'hundred' vs the Median **sata-*).

3. The change of the OIran. *-θr* into *-hr* and, later on, *r*; as opposed to the change of *-θr* into *-s* in the SW, like the NW *pur* and the SW *pus(ar)* 'son'.

4. Maintenance of the cluster *-sp* as in NW *asp* 'horse' (OP *asa-*).

5. Change of the initial cluster *dv-* into *b-* (and *d-* in SW), such as NW *bar* vs SW *dar* 'door' from the OIran. **dvara-*. The Parthian is *br*, Zaza *bär*, but Middle Persian and Modern Persian *dar*.

6. Preserving the OIran. initial *v-* (vs the transition of *b < v* in the SW) such as NW *vid* vs SW *bid* 'willow'.

7. Change of the intervocalic OIran. **-č-* into *-j-*, such as *rij* (present stem of the verb) for the OIran. ** raičaya-* > 'to pour'.

8. Later changes *j* > NW *ǰ-/ž-* SW *z-*, and *dv-* > NW *b-*, SW *d-*, also clearly differentiate the groups, e.g. Parthian *ǰn* 'woman', Zaza *ǰan*, but Middle Persian *zan*, and Modern Persian *zan*.

9. Change of the OIran. **-xt-* into *-t-*, such as *sut-* 'burned', from the OIran. ** suxta-*.

Beside these phonological features, many of the NW Iranian languages are also syntactically different from the SW in the sense that they have preserved the split ergativity of the Middle Western Iranian languages. Persian and most of the SW languages are now nominative-accusative languages.

North-West Iranian languages are very numerous, but the major ones may be named as follows: Kurdish (Turkey, Iran, Iraq, Syria, and some parts of the Caucasus); Taleshi (Iran, Azarbaijan); Balochi (Iran, Pakistan Afghanistan, Turkmenistan, and the Persian Gulf); Gilaki (Iran); Mazandarani (Iran); Zaza (Turkey); Gurani (Iran, Iraq); Bashkardi (Iran); Parachi (Afghanistan); Ormuri (Afghanistan, Pakistan); Semnani and related dialects (Iran); 'Tat' dialects, centred on Tabriz, Zanjan, Qazvin and Saveh (Iran); Vafsi and

Ashtiyani (Iran); dialects of central Iran, centred on Kashan, Esfahan, Yazd, Kerman and the Dashte-Kavir (Iran).

The best-known SW Iranian languages are Persian (Iran, Persian Gulf) with its Dari and Tajiki variants; Luri and Bakhtiari (western Iran); Kumzari (Persian Gulf); non-Persian dialects of Fars province, centred on Shiraz, Kazerun, Sivand and Lar (Iran); Judeo-Tati (in the Republic of Azerbaijan).

Among all these languages, Persian is no doubt the best-attested language. The official language of Iran, it developed as early as in the ninth century, and is a continuation of Middle Persian. However, it is now remarkably simpler in terms of formal grammar. Many inflectional systems such as gender distinction, noun inflection, adjectival agreement, and some irregularities in verbal conjugation have disappeared. Possession is shown by a suffix called *ezafeh*, and tense, mood, voice and negative are likewise indicated by a series of affixes. See also Chapter 25.

4.2 New East Iranian Languages

The modern Eastern Iranian languages are numerous and varied, with two major sub-groups: Northern and Southern, and most of the Eastern languages belong to the North-Eastern subgroup.

The subdivision of the Eastern Iranian group into South-East and North-East Iranian is based on both phonological and morphological features. The morphological features characterising the North-East group are:

1 In the North-East group, the development of a plural marker in *-t* form is found. Examples of this marker are Sogdian *'wt'k* 'place', plural *'wt'kt*, Yaghnobi *pōda* 'foot', plural *pōdō-t* and Ossetian *sər* 'head', plural *sər-tə*.

2 The South-East group, on the other hand, shows a variety of voiced continuants in place of intervocalic *-š-*, e.g. Yaghnobi *γuš* 'ear', but Shughni *γŭγ̌*, Munji *γūy*, as well as a tendency to develop retroflex consonants (though these are lacking in the Shughni-Roshani subgroup of Pamir languages). Within the South-East group, Shughni, Roshani, Bartangi, Oroshori and Sarikoli (and more distantly Yazgulami) form a genetic subgroup, as do Ishkashmi, Zebaki and Sanglechi, and Munji and Yidgha. Munji and Yidgha share with Pashto the development of *d > l*.

Among the Eastern Iranian languages, Ossetian (Georgia) and Yaghnobi (Tajikistan) are the major North-Eastern ones; and the rest, containing the 'Shughni' group which consists of Shughni, Roshani, Khufi, Bartangi, Roshorvi (in Tajikistan and to a lesser extent in Afghanistan) and Sarikoli (in China), Ishkashmi (in Afghanistan and Tajikistan); Sanglechi (Afghanistan); Zebaki (Afghanistan); Wakhi (Afghanistan, Tajikistan, Pakistan, China); Munji (Afghanistan); Yidgha (Afghanistan and Pakistan), and Pashto (in Afghanistan), are South-Eastern languages.

Bibliography

The fullest and most detailed general survey available is Rastorgueva (1979–), planned in five volumes. Three have appeared so far: 1 *Drevneiranskie jazyki* on Old Iranian (1979), 2 *Sredneiranskie jazyki* on Middle Iranian (1981), 3 *Novoiranskie jazyki: zapadnaja gruppa*, *prikaspijskie jazyki* on the

South-West Iranian and Caspian languages (1982). Spuler (1958) is the only comprehensive handbook in a language other than Russian, although Payne (1981) gives a short survey of linguistic properties of Iranian languages of the former Soviet Union. Oranskij (1963) includes annotated specimens of many of the languages and a useful map. Schmitt's (1989) edited volume is an extremely useful survey of the three stages of the Iranian languages, with detailed bibliographies at the end of each chapter. Among bibliographical resources, MacKenzie (1969) is a short survey of Iranian studies and full basic bibliography; while Sims-Williams (1998) may also be used a general overview of the field. Oranskij (1975) is a very thorough bibliographical guide to the Iranian languages of Tajikistan; Redard (1970) is also comprehensive survey of the study of minor Iranian languages, with full bibliography. But for those interested in the New Eastern Iranian languages, Morgenstierne's publications are the best references. Linguistic articles in *Encyclopedia Iranica* provide more detailed information about the dialects, all with extensive bibliographies.

References

MacKenzie, D.N. 1969. 'Iranian Languages', in T.A. Sebeok (ed.) *Current Trends in Linguistics*, vol. 5 *Linguistics in South Asia* (Mouton, The Hague), pp. 450–77

Morgenstierne, G. 1926. *Report on a Linguistic Mission to Afghanistan* (Oslo).

—— 1927. *An Etymological Vocabulary of Pashto* (Oslo).

—— 1929–389. *Indo-Iranian Frontier Languages; I: Parachi and Ormuri, II: Iranian Pamir Languages* (Oslo)

Oranskij, I.M. 1963. *Iranskie jazyki* (Izd-vo Vostočnoj Literatury, Moscow)

—— 1975. *Die neuiranischen Sprachen der Sowjetunion*, 2 vols (Mouton, The Hague)

Payne, J.R. 1981. 'Iranian Languages', in B. Comrie (ed.) *The Languages of the Soviet Union* (Cambridge University Press, Cambridge), pp. 158–79

Rastorgueva, V.S. (ed.) 1979–. *Osnovy iranskogo jazykoznanija* (Nauka, Moscow)

Redard, G. 1970. 'Other Iranian Languages', in T.A. Sebeok (ed.) *Current Trends in Linguistics*, vol. 6 *Linguistics in Southwest Asia and North Africa* (Mouton, The Hague), pp. 97–135

Schmitt, R. (ed.) 1989. *Compendium Linguarum Iranicarum* (Wiesbaden)

Sims-Williams, N. 1998. 'The Iranian Languages,' in A. Giacalone Ramat and P. Ramat (eds) *The Indo-European Languages* (Routledge, London), pp. 125–53

Spuler, B. (ed.) 1958. *Handbuch der Orientalistik. Abt. I, Bd. IV, I, Iranistik* (Brill, Leiden)

25

Persian

Gernot L. Windfuhr

1 Historical Background

Persian has been the dominant language of Iranian lands and adjacent regions for over a millennium. From the tenth century onward it was the language of literary culture, as well as the *lingua franca*, in large parts of West, South and Central Asia until the mid-nineteenth century. It began with the political domination of these areas by Persian-speaking dynasties, first the Achaemenids (c. 558–330 BCE), then the Sasanids (224–651 CE) which resulted in the establishment of Persian-speaking colonies throughout the empire and beyond, which contributed to the spread of the political-cultural complex and ideology constructed first under the Achaemenids, most importantly for the course of the development of Persian, in the northeast, i.e. in what is now Khorasan, northern Afghanistan and Central Asia. It is documented, for example, by the Middle Persian texts of the Manicheans found in the oasis city of Turfan in Chinese Turkistan (Sinkiang). This process led to increasing regionalisation.

1.1 Dialectology

Persian is the only Iranian language which is documented for two and a half millennia, from the Old Persian of the Achaemenids, to the Middle Persian of the Sasanids; to New Persian (since the eighth century). It originates in the southwestern Iranian province of *Fārs*, earlier *Pārs* (Old Persian *Pārsa*, hence Greek *Persis*), and is a member of the Southwestern group within the Iranian branch of the Indo-Iranian languages (as opposed to the Northwestern group, which includes Kurdish and Balôchi as the most prominent members). Most closely related are Luri-Bakhtiāri, then the Fārs dialects, and more distantly the Lārestān dialects, and smaller dialects of southern Iran.

Regionally, Persian has three major varieties, each with its own dialectal subgroups, and symbiotic with other Iranian and non-Iranian languages: (1) the Persian of Iran in the west, where it is the official language; (2) the Persian of Afghanistan, now called Dari, in the east, where it is the official language besides East Iranian Pashto; and, separated by Turkmen and Uzbek-speaking areas, (3) the Persian spoken in Tajikistan in Central Asia in the northeast, where it is the official language. Smaller varieties of Persian outside Iran proper include Muslim and Jewish Tat in the southeastern Caucasus, and others.

All Iranian-speaking regions continue to be multilingual. Thus, while Persian is the official language of Iran, it is the mother tongue of only about 60 percent of the population. Most widely spoken in Iran besides Persian are Turkic languages and dialects. Bilingualism and multilingualism are widely found. The approximate numbers of native speakers of the three major varieties of Persian are: Iran, 42 million; Afghanistan, 15.5 million; Tajikistan, 6 million (total populations 70, 31, and 7.5 million, respectively).

1.2 Origin of Literary Persian

The advent of Islam (since 651 CE) represents a crucial cultural break in the history of Iran and thus of Persian. It brought not only the adoption of the Arabic script, but also an increasing infusion of Arabic, mainly vocabulary and phonology (comparable to the absorption of the Norman component into English). Literary New Persian as the language of administration, culture and commerce evolved out of a variety of Late Middle Persian. It is first documented in texts originating not from the southwestern, but from the eastern regions. That variety was recognised by contemporary Arab and Iranian authors as *Pārsi-ye dari* 'Court Persian' already in the ninth and tenth centuries. It appears that it originated in a form of Late Middle Persian spoken at the court (*dar*) in Ctesiphon in Mesopotamia, the capital of the Sasanids, and formerly of the Parthians (c. 247 BCE– 224 CE). It had presumably spread from Ctesiphon through administration and commerce across the northern half of Iran to the east, and in return had spread from there westward across Iran and beyond. It was recognisably distinct from *Pārsi* proper, the 'pure' southern variety of Persian, by the admixture of a considerable number of Northwest Iranian features, as well as by the loss of certain morphological and syntactic features of Late Middle Persian, and, after Islamisation, by the increasing admixture of Arabic.

The reasons for the rise of Literary New Persian in the east are still being debated, but the following considerations appear to be plausible. One explanation widely accepted is the rise of pro-Iranian sentiments in the east, at a long distance from the Arab-speaking Abbasid caliphate in Baghdad (758–1258). The other, quite plausible explanation for the use of Dari, even before Islam, points to the multilingual situation in Central Asia, rather than the politics of the west. It recognises that Dari had already become the regional *koine* in the eastern regions and *lingua franca* spoken along the Silk Road up to the borders of China. Being particularly suited for this function due to the minimally inflectional characteristics of this vernacular, it was adopted as the language of written communication for practical purposes, as opposed to high-register Arabic, by the new Arab-Muslim administration, and subsequently by religious propagandists during the rapid expansion of Islam. Persian increasingly regained prestige both as the spoken and the literary medium of the Iranian and Iranised elite, the latter including foremost Turkic speakers, and rapidly superseded the indigenous Iranian languages, first Parthian, and then the East Iranian languages such as Bactrian (modern Balkh region), Khwarezmian (southern Aral Sea region), Khotanese and Tumshuqese (Chinese Turkistan/Sinkiang), and Sogdian which until then had been the long-standing *lingua franca* in Central Asia and along the Silk Road.

In the south of Iran, from Khuzistan in the west to Sistan in the east, the Arabic script had also been adopted during the same early period by Zoroastrians, and by new

Muslims, for their own spoken variety, Pārsi. It directly continued spoken Late Middle Persian of the formerly prestigious south, and was characterised by the retention of distinct features such as the morphological passive marked by *-ih* (which had been replaced by analytical passive construction in the Dari variety). By the end of the eleventh century, this southern literary variety was superseded by Dari. Written in Hebrew characters, this southern spoken variety was also used for the Early Judaeo-Persian texts. In fact, the first preserved documents of New Persian are three brief inscriptions dating from the middle of the eighth century found in eastern Afghanistan. They were written in Hebrew characters, indicating the early use of the new vernacular by minorities less dominated by the written standards of the time.

1.3 Phases of Literary Persian

There do not yet exist comprehensive historical grammars of Persian. Lazard (1963) is a comprehensive study of the texts of the tenth and eleventh centuries. For historical phonology, Pisowicz (1985) comprehensively covers both Middle and New Persian. Accordingly, the delimitation of phases remains tentative. In approximation, the phases are: Early New Persian (tenth/eleventh cent.); a transitional phase (twelfth cent.), leading to the so-called 'Classical' Persian phase, with internal sub-phases (thirteenth–sixteenth cent.); a further transitional phase (seventeenth cent.) to Early Modern Persian, leading to Modern Persian (mid-nineteenth cent. to present). However, the texts attest to the gradual evolution of Persian throughout its history, different for each item and in frequency of use.

Most of the preserved early texts originate in the eastern regions, and as such exhibit a fair degree of linguistic homogeneity. Nevertheless, the peculiarities of the eastern poets, especially in their Iranian vocabulary, led to the compilation of dictionaries explaining those in 'common' Persian, such as the dictionary by Asadi of Tus from the middle of the eleventh century. The major document of the formative phase, which in effect consolidated the new literary Persian, is the *Shāh-nāmeh* 'The Book of Kings', the monumental epic by Ferdowsi (d. 1019 or 1025) of Tus in Khorasan which recounts Iranian history from creation to the Muslim conquest. Linguistically it retained many features of late Middle Persian. Considerably less retention is found in examples of the scholarly use of the new literary language, prominently by the philosopher Ebn-e Sinā, Latinised Avicenna (d. 1047) who, while mostly writing in Arabic, chose Persian for his *Metaphysics*, for which he also created new Persian terminology.

Until the Mongol conquests in the middle of the thirteenth century, the northeast, with cultural centres such as Samarkand, Bukhara, Balkh, Merv, Herat and Nishapur, continued to be the major area of New Persian and its literature. By that time, the regionally marked features had largely disappeared in both poetry and prose. This process is concomitant not only with the expansion of Persian, but also with the shift of cultural centres to the west, specifically to Fars, a major centre being the city of Shiraz with its most famous poets Sa'di (d. 1292) and Hāfiz (d. 1390). From there the centre shifted to the north, first to Isfahan, the splendid capital of the Safavids (1501–1731), then, from the first half of the nineteenth century, to Tehran, the new capital of the Qajars (1779–1924).

The dominance of the Persian of the classics continued to a considerable degree until the beginning of the nineteenth century. At that time new political, economic and cultural conditions, not least under influence from Europe, sponsored gradual simplifications of style. With it came the acceptance in writing of features of the educated spoken language that had developed in the capital Tehran, at first in journalism, then in prose and finally in poetry. Thus emerged the contemporary Standard Persian of Iran. At the same time, by linguistic engineering Tajikistan under Russian and Soviet rule developed its own literary language which is based on local dialects, and written in the Russian alphabet, but formal Persian is regaining attention, and is still the high register medium in Afghanistan, albeit with local features, particularly in the vocabulary, as opposed to Kaboli, the regional vernacular used throughout by speakers of most of the some 30 languages of that country, including Pashto.

1.4 Colonial Persian

Persian was cultivated at the courts of the Ottoman rulers (1299–1922), several of whom are known for composing Persian poetry. Probably best known is Jalāl al-din Rumi (d. 1273), the most cherished Persian mystic poet who had come to Konya from Wakhsh near Balkh in Afghanistan. Literary Ottoman Turkish is a virtual amalgam of Turkish and Persian (with all of the latter's Arabic loan elements). In the east, Urdu '(language of the) military camp', developed under heavy Persian influence. Persian first entered India with the conquest of northwest India by Ghaznavid armies in the eleventh century. Four centuries later, Persian was chosen as the court language of the Mogul kings (1530–1857), who were major patrons of Persian literature and poets from Iran, unlike the contemporary Safavids in Iran. It was at the courts of India and Turkey where many of the major traditional dictionaries of Persian were compiled from the fifteenth to the eighteenth centuries, many with grammatical treatises. Simultaneously, there developed in India a Persian vernacular, and it was from the Indian scribes and secretaries that the English officers of the East India Company, many of whom wrote grammars of Persian, learned their Persian, with all its local idiosyncrasies. Persian was abolished in its last official bastion – the courts of law – in 1837 by the authorities of the East India Company.

2 Phonology

2.1 Sound System

The sound system of contemporary standard Persian is quite symmetric. Its 29 segmental phonemes consist of four pairs of stops and four pairs of fricatives, two nasals, liquid and trill, three glides, and three pairs of vowels. This is given in Table 25.1.

Table 25.1 The Persian Phoneme System

Stops and Affricates	tense/voiceless	p	t	č	k
	lax/voiced	b	d	j [dž]	g
Fricatives	tense/voiceless	f	s	š	x
	lax/voiced	v	z	ž	q [γ]
Nasals		m	n		
Liquid and Trill		l	r		
Glides		y	h	'	
Vowels	tense/long (stable)	i	ā	u	
	lax/short (unstable)	e	a	o	

2.2 Writing System

The Persian writing system uses the Arabic alphabet, which is a consonantal system (see Chapter 33). Vowels are written as follows: the three long vowels are represented by the letter of the consonant nearest in pronunciation. Thus, the letter <y> represents both /y/ and /i/, <w> both /v/ and /u/, and <alef> both the glottal stop /'/ and /ā/. The three short vowels may be, but are usually not, represented by diacritics which ultimately derive from the same letters <w>, <y> and <alef>. The main innovations in Persian are two: additional letters were created for the four Persian consonants /p/, /č/, /g/, /ž/ by adding three dots to the 'Arabic' letters <b> <j> <k> <z> (the dots merged into an oblique stroke in the case of <g>. Unlike Arabic, in final position, short vowels are always represented by consonantal letters, final /o/ by <w> and both final /e/ and /a/ by <h>. The Persian alphabet is given in Table 25.2.

The Arabic orthography is retained, distinctly by the subset of letters marked A in Table 25.2. They represent pharyngeals, a pair of non-strident interdental fricatives, and the voiceless stop *q*, which in Persian phonemically merged with the corresponding plain and strident consonants, respectively, except *ẓ* > *z*, while *q* merged with voiced *ġ*. Otherwise, the orthography is basically phonemic in the representation of the consonants and long vowels, but does not represent short vowels other than in final position. In rare instances, an Arabic pharyngeal letter is used, such as <ṣ> in <ṣad> for *sad* 'hundred'.

2.3 Features

In spite of systemic simplicity, there remains considerable debate about the features of certain individual phonemes and of sets of phonemes.

The phoneme *q* has triple origins: the inherited voiced fricative *γ*; the Arabic voiceless stop *q* and the voiced fricative *γ*; and the Turkic voice-neutral velar stop *k* before back vowels. While systemically a voiced fricative in the Persian system, its peculiar articulation appears like a virtual compromise of its origins: intervocalically it is a voiced fricative; in initial and final position it is partially or fully devoiced, following the devoicing rule, and may have an affricate-like voiced release before vowels (varying with the speaker and speech-situation).

The vocalic onset in Persian is an automatic feature before initial vowels and in hiatus, e.g. *in* / 'in/ 'this', hiatus *pā 'iz* 'autumn', affixal *xāné-'i* 'a house', and as such was originally not phonemic. Arabic has a phonemic glottal stop and a pharyngeal stop both of which may occur in any position. Their merger with the Persian onset made their distribution unconditioned and thus a phonemic glide.

Together with the glide *h*, the glottal stop is considerably unstable. In other than high register or slow articulation they tend to result in compensatory lengthening of the preceding short vowel, e.g. *ba 'd* > *ba:d* 'bad', to be lost in postconsonantal and final position, *sobh* > *sob* 'morning', *sob-e zud* 'early morning', with occasional compensatory germination of continuants, e.g. *jom 'é* > *jom(:)é* 'Friday'.

Gemination is a distinctive characteristic of Arabic, whereas in Persian it is a marginal feature. While retained in high registers and slow speech, it is eliminated in contemporary standard pronunciation, e.g. Persian *mat(t)é* 'drill', Arabic *talaf(f)óz* 'pronunciation'.

The issue whether the feature that distinguishes the pairs of stops and fricatives in contemporary standard Persian is voice or tenseness continues to be debated. Less debated is the feature that distinguishes the pairs of vowels. While the original opposition was

Table 25.2 The Persian Alphabet

Position in Letter Group

final	medial	initial	Separate	Name		Phonemic
ا			ا		ʾalef	'
ا			ا			ā
ـب	ـبـ	بـ	ب		be	b
ـپ	ـپـ	پـ	پ	P	pe	p
ـت	ـتـ	تـ	ت		et	t
ـث	ـثـ	ثـ	ث	A	ṣe	s
ـج	ـجـ	جـ	ج		jim	j
ـچ	ـچـ	چـ	چ	P	če	č
ـح	ـحـ	حـ	ح	A	ḥe-ye jim	h
ـخ	ـخـ	خـ	خ		xe	x
ـد			د		dāl	d
ـذ			ذ	A	ẕāl	z
ـر			ر		re	r
ـز			ز		ze	z
ـژ			ژ	P	že	ž
ـس	ـسـ	سـ	س		sin	s
ـش	ـشـ	شـ	ش		šin	š
ـص	ـصـ	صـ	ص	A	ṣād	s
ـض	ـضـ	ضـ	ض	A	żād	z
ـط	ـطـ	طـ	ط	A	ṭā	t
ـظ	ـظـ	ظـ	ظ	A	ẓā	z
ـع	ـعـ	عـ	ع	A	ʿeyn	'
ـغ	ـغـ	غـ	غ		ġeyn	q
ـف	ـفـ	فـ	ف		fe	f
ـق	ـقـ	قـ	ق	A	qāf	q
ـک	ـکـ	کـ	ک		kāf	k
ـگ	ـگـ	گـ	گ	P	gāf	g
ـل	ـلـ	لـ	ل		lām	l
ـم	ـمـ	مـ	م		mim	m
ـن	ـنـ	نـ	ن		nun	n
ـو			و		vāv	v/u/ow/final o
ـه	ـهـ	هـ	ه		he	h/final e, a
ـی	ـیـ	یـ	ی		ye	y/i

Notes: A = letters occurring mostly in Arabic loanwords; P = letters found in Persian only.
The basic shapes و ز ر د ا do not connect to the left.

one of length, the contemporary feature is stability, in part indicated by the lengthening of *e a o* (< *i a u*) when stressed and their shortening and partial conditioned assimilation when unstressed.

Of the two diphthongal sequences *ey* and *ow* (< *ai, au*), the latter increasingly tends to be contracted to *o:*, even in higher registers.

2.4 Syllable Structure

There are no initial consonant clusters. Clusters inherited from Middle Persian began to be broken up in Early New Persian by the insertion of a vowel, either between the consonants or before them, the latter mostly with an initial sibilant, a pattern that is still active, e.g. MPers *brādar* > NPers *barādár* 'brother', MPers *brū-g* > NPers *abrú* 'brow', modern loans *perofesór* 'professor', *estudiyó* 'studio'. This pattern thus agreed with that of both the Arabic and the Turkic loan component.

Vowels may be followed by none, one or two consonants, including the glottal stop: CV, CVC, CVCC, e.g. *do* 'two', *dud* 'smoke', *'abr* 'cloud'. Accordingly, diphthongs have no independent phonemic status, just as in Arabic, e.g. *dowr* 'turn'.

2.5 Stress

The basic stress pattern of Persian is predictable and non-phonemic. Word stress is progressive, i.e. on the last non-enclitic syllable, in nominals, including nominal verb forms; verbal prefixes (*mí-*, *bé-*, *ná-*) are always stressed. Phrase stress is regressive. This is evident in pseudo-pairs such as *bāz-kón* 'opener' vs *báz kon* 'open!' (*bāz* 'open', *kon-* 'to make, do'). The third rule, continued from Indo-European, is vocative stress on the first syllable, e.g. *xānandé-ye azíz > xánandè-ye azìz* 'Dear reader!'

2.6 Morphophonemic Alternation

Unlike Eastern Iranian languages such as Pashto, the rules of Indo-European quantitative ablaut alternation still productive in Old Iranian had been reduced or lost already by the end of the Achaemenid period (c. fourth century BCE). This alternation is fossilised in the present and past stems of the so-called irregular verbs and in root nouns, e.g. the New Persian noun *bār* 'load', the present stem *bar-* 'to carry away, bear', and the corresponding past stem *bord* reflect the long, full, and zero grades, respectively, of the Old Iranian root *bar-* 'carry, bear' (cf. English *bear, bore, borne*).

The massive Arabic loan component in the Persian lexicon (about 50 per cent) reflects the complex morphophonology of Arabic, e.g. loans based on the root *n-z-r* 'to see, watch' include *nazar* 'view', *nazir* 'similar, like', the passive participle *manzur* 'considered, intended', also 'viewpoint, opinion', the verbal noun of the Arabic eighth formation *entezār* 'expectation' with the participle *montazer* 'expecting, waiting'.

Probably most conspicuous is the retention of the morphophonology of the Arabic plural formations (which occasionally was applied to Persian), e.g. *vazir*, pl. *vozarā* 'vizier', including some borrowed early into Arabic, e.g. *gauhar* > Ar. *jawhar* 'essence, jewel', pl. *jawāhir*, and were borrowed back as new items with slightly shifted connotations without replacing the original term (see the discussion of plural morphology below).

3 Morphology

3.1 Pronouns and Endings

In terms of morphology Persian with its dialects may be called the most atypical Iranian language. It is to Iranian what English is to Germanic. Unlike East Iranian Pashto and many smaller dialects, it has almost completely lost the inherited synthetic nominal and verbal inflection and their inflectional classes, and thus the *inflectional* distinction of case, number and gender as well as of aspect, mood and tense, and voice. This process began already in late Old Persian times. Three persons in singular and plural are, however, still distinguished in pronouns and personal endings (see Section 3.3 below), as shown in the chart given here.

Endings and Pronouns

	Singular			Plural		
Endings	*1*	*2*	*3*	*1*	*2*	*3*
Present stem	*-am*	*-i*	*-ad*	*-im*	*-id*	*-and*
Imperative		∅			*-id*	
Past stem	*-am*	*-i*	*-∅*	*-im*	*-id*	*-and*
Perfect stem/Copula	*-am*	*-i*	*ast*	*-im*	*-id*	*-and*
Existential verb	*hast-am*	*hast-i*	*hast-∅*	*hast-im*	*hast-id*	*hast-and*
Pronouns						
Independent	*man*	*to*	*u*	*mā*	*šomā́*	*išā́n*
Suffixed	*-am*	*-at*	*-aš*	*-emā́n*	*-etā́n*	*-ešā́n*

Demonstratives				*Interrogatives*	
Singular		*Plural*			
that	this	those	these	who	what
ān	*in*	*ān-hā́*	*in-hā́*	*ki*	*če*

The independent pronouns contrast with the unstressed pronominal suffixes, which function as non-topical oblique cases (possessor, direct and indirect object).

Animacy is minimally retained. Both third person pronouns refer only to humans, *u* 'he/she' and *išān* 'they' (mostly), which latter also refers to individuals in polite phraseology. With verbs, animacy is retained by the optional use of the third singular endings with inanimate plural subjects.

3.2 Nouns and Noun Phrases

3.2.1 Nominal Morphology

Any unmodified noun may be used generically, or imply single or more items, whether subject, predicative complement, direct object, or other, e.g. *man ketāb lāzem dār-am* 'I need a book/books', *ketāb mofid ast* 'a book is/books are useful', *mā dānešju hast-im* 'we are students'.

The plural markers are stressed *-hā* and *-ān*. The latter shows restricted use: it is obligatory in elliptic adjectival plurals referring to humans, e.g. *bozorg-ān* 'the elder (people), leaders', and *digar-ān* 'the others', but optional, besides *-hā*, in literary registers for humans and for a small set of body parts and plants. The modern partial distinction of animacy reflects the situation in Early New Persian, where *-hā* marked inanimate and *-ān* animate, originating in an Old Iranian abstract suffix and the genitive plural ending, respectively. The basic function of *-hā* is amplification, including count nouns, mass nouns, and adverbials, e.g. *ketāb-hā* 'books', *āb-hā* 'waters, all kinds of waters, plenty of water', *[in taraf]-hā* 'hereabouts' (these sides). In addition, there are the multiple plural formations of the Arabic loan component which tend to function as markers of complex entities. Thus, the loaned feminine-abstract plural ending *-āt* generalises, e.g. *deh-āt* 'the rural area' vis-à-vis the Persian plural *deh-hā* 'villages'. So do broken plurals, e.g. *atrāf* 'hereabouts' (sing. *taraf* 'direction').

Adjectives are unmarked. The comparative and superlative are marked by *-tár* and *-tarín*, e.g. *bozorg/bozorg-tar/bozorg-tar-in* 'big/bigger/biggest'.

Ordinal numbers are marked by *-óm* and *-om-ín*, e.g. *sāl-e dah-om/dah-om-in sāl* 'the tenth year', the latter with focus on the number.

3.2.2 Noun Phrase Syntax

Persian is a right-branching language. The unstressed particle *-e* connects any attributive constituent (adjectives, nouns, noun phrases, etc.) to the head noun in the so-called *ezāfe*-construction ('addition'), e.g. *pesar-(hā-y)e xub* 'good boy(s)', *pesar-e dust-e man* 'my friend's son'.

Basic Possessive Paradigms

	Independent	*Suffixed (non-topical)*	
1s	*ketāb-e man*	*ketāb-am*	'my book'
2s	*ketāb-e to*	*ketāb-at*	'your (sg.) book'
3s	*ketāb-e u*	*ketāb-aš*	'his/her book'
1p	*ketāb-e mā*	*ketāb-emān*	'our book'
2p	*ketāb-e šomā*	*ketāb-etān*	'your (pl.) book'
3p	*ketāb-e išān*	*ketāb-ešān*	'their book'

In its basic function the *ezāfe*-construction identifies characteristics and class and item, including species, names, and numbers, e.g. *gol-e roz* 'the rose(-flower)', *xānom-e javādi* 'Mrs Javadi', *sā'at-e se* 'three o'clock'.

In the extended noun phrase, demonstrative, number (and classifier), and kind, directly precede the noun, e.g. *se (tā) otobus* 'three (items of) busses', *in do now' qāli* 'these two kinds of carpet'. Personal suffixes as well as indefinite *-i* attach to the adjective, if present, e.g. *dast-aš* 'his hand', *[taraf-e čap]-aš* '(on) its left side', *so'āl-i, [so'āl-e xub]-i* 'a question, a good question'. Schematically, the patterns are (N = noun, A = adjective):

Demonstrative – Number – (Classifier) – (Kind) – Head
NN: N(A) *-e* N(A)
NA: [Noun-*e* Adjective]-*i*/personal suffixes/-*e* NA/NN

Dependent nouns and noun phrases can be topicalised by inversion and anaphoric suffix, e.g. *pedar-e man* > *[man] pedar [-am]* 'my father', which has become the unmarked construction in Tajik under the influence of Turkic syntax.

Indefiniteness is marked by *-i* in both singular and plural, both non-specific (any) and specific (certain, some), e.g. *so'āl-i/so'āl-hā-i* 'a question/questions', *[ketāb-e gerān]-i* 'an expensive book'.

Specificity, both definite and indefinite, is marked in direct object phrase by the clitic *-rā*, e.g. *ketāb(-hā)-rā* 'the book(s)', *ketāb(-hā)-i-rā* 'a certain book/certain books', *[ketāb-e gerān-e kelās-e fārsi-y-e u]-rā* 'the expensive book of the Persian class of him/her'.

3.2.3 Diachrony

The history of the noun phrase morphosyntax is the history of the foregrounding of genericity, indefiniteness and specificity. Already in Old Persian, the singular could be used generically, though restricted to non-human. This still held in Early New Persian which shows number agreement in predicative position, e.g. *havā-šenās-ān bud-and* 'they were meteorologists'. In contemporary Persian, genericity is generalised.

The indefinite marker *-i* originates in the Old Iranian prenominal number *aiwa* 'one'. In Middle Persian it developed the secondary function of indefiniteness if following the noun. In Early New Persian this use was generalised to singular and plural nouns, but it

453

was still immediately attached to the noun. Today, it generally follows the adjective with a few marked exceptions.

The history of *rā* and of the pronominal suffixes is the coming into syntactic-semantic prominence of the direct object and specificity. *Rā* originates in the Old Persian postposition *rādi* 'by reason of, concerning' (cf. Latin *ratione*). In Middle Persian, *rāy* expressed cause, purpose and reference (partially like English '(as) for'). By extension of the implicit directional meaning its range began to include occasional use with indirect and direct objects in Late Middle Persian.

In Early New Persian, *rā* had a similar range, but was not obligatory with either direct or indirect objects. Its function is preserved in *barā-ye* 'for' (the sake of, < MPers *pad rāy ī*).

The function of nominal subordination to express class-item, among which possession is only one, continues verbless appositional phrases in Old Iranian introduced by the generalised relative pronoun OPers *haya*/Avestan *yat* > *-e*. This progressive sub-ordination, NN[1]-*e* NN[2], is typically Southwestern Iranian in terms of dialectology. The marked topical inversions in Persian are the unmarked ones in Northwestern Iranian, and can in part be understood as originally marked borrowed features.

3.3 Verb Morphology

3.3.1 Stems

Verbs have two basic stems, present and past, and a perfect stem derived from the latter by *-é*; further a verbal noun, or infinitive, ending in *-án*. Regular verbs have the formant *-id*; irregular verbs show either various forms of other past formants, or subsets with morphophonological changes between the two basic stems (inherited from Old Iranian); e.g. *bus/bus-íd/busidan* 'to kiss'; *riz/rix-t/rixt-é/rixtan* 'to fall, drop', *kon/kard/kard-é/kardan* 'to do, make'. Since Early New Persian, many irregular past stems have been replaced by regular stems.

Causative stems are derived from the present stem by *-ān* of limited productivity (though including a few Arabic bases), e.g. *xor/xor-ān-* 'to eat/feed'. There is no morphological passive, which is expressed periphrastically by the perfect participle and the paradigm of *šodan* 'to become', e.g. *sāxte mi-šav-ad* 'it is being built' (cf. English *to get built*). It is an agentless construction and utilised pragmatically to avoid mention of the agent, in bureaucratic jargon and in the elaborate polite phraseology typical for Persian.

A distinct feature of contemporary Persian, which is increasingly the focus of syntactic and semantic research, is the extraordinary number of so-called compound verbs vis-à-vis simple verbs. These consist of a limited set of simple verbs with nominal components, which may be of considerable syntactic and semantic complexity. They often form pairs of transitivity, causation, and voice, e.g. *bidār šodan/kardan* 'to wake up' (become/make awake), *(be) harakat oftādan/andāxtan* 'to get moving/ (make) move' (fall/throw to movement). A good number express basic concepts, having replaced earlier simple verbs, e.g. *dust dāštan* 'to love, like', lit. 'to have (as) friend', *kār kardan* 'to work', lit. 'to do work'. Of the some 700 verbs still occasionally found, particularly in high registers and writing, and poetic diction, only some 150 are in frequent use, while the number of compound verb constructions probably exceeds 2000.

3.3.2 Verb System

The identification of the categorial vectors defining the verb system continues to present considerable problems. It appears that the primary parameter in contemporary Persian is aspect, which intersects with tense and mood.

Imperfective forms, traditionally called present and imperfect, are marked by the prefix *mí-*. The aorist, traditionally called preterit or simple past due to its primary contextual use, is the unmarked or neutral central member, simply conveying the action or event as completed. The resultative forms, traditionally called present perfect and past perfect, consist of the perfect participle plus forms of *budan* 'to be', with focus on near vs remote deixis (as in the corresponding perfect subjunctive and conditional with regard to potentiality). All three aspects have evidential forms (see further below), which are derived resultative forms confined to past contexts.

The subjunctive and imperative are marked by the prefix *bé-*; the resultative subjunctive consists of the perfect participle plus the prefixless present stem of 'to be', *bāš-*. The imperfective and resultative conditional (counterfactual) forms are identical with the corresponding indicative forms. In addition, there is an isolated definite future construction with the modal *xāh-* 'to wish, want' followed by the plain past stem. The absence of the future paradigm further shows that tense is not the primary vector. The basic verb system and inflection may be as given in the charts using the verb *rav/raft* 'to go, leave' in the third person singular. Note that three forms have double function.

Aspects, Moods, and Tenses: *raftan* 'to go, leave'

	Indicative	*Non-Indicative*	
Imperfective:			
		bé-row	Imperative (2 sing.)
Present	*mí-rav-ad*	*bé-rav-ad*	Subjunctive
Imperfect	*mí-raft*	*mí-raft*	Conditional
Evidential	*mí-raft-e ast*		
Aorist:			
Preterit	*raft*		
Evidential	*raft-é ast*		
Resultative:			
		raft-é bāš	Imperative (2 sing.)
Present Perfect	*raft-é ast*	*raft-é bāš-ad*	Subjunctive
Past Perfect	*raft-é bud*	*raft-é bud*	Conditional
Evidential	*raft-é bud-è ast*		
Affirmative Future:		*xāh-ád raft*	

Note: Negation is marked by the prefix *ná-* which precedes the entire verb form, and replaces *bé-*.

Basic Paradigms: *raftan* 'to go, leave'

	Present	*Preterit*	*Imperfect*	*Present Perfect*	*Past Perfect*
1s	*mi-rav-am*	*raft-am*	*mi-raft-am*	*raft-e am*	*raft-e bud-am*
2s	*mi-rav-i*	*raft-i*	*mi-raft-i*	*raft-e i*	*raft-e bud-im*
3s	*mi-rav-ad*	*raft*	*mi-raft*	*raft-e ast*	*raft-e bud*
1p	*mi-rav-im*	*raft-im*	*mi-raft-im*	*raft-e im*	*raft-e bud-im*
2p	*mi-rav-id*	*raft-id*	*mi-raft-id*	*raft-e id*	*raft-e bud-id*
3p	*mi-rav-and*	*raft-an*	*mi-raft-and*	*raft-e and*	*raft-e bud-and*

Notes: Present subjunctive: *be-rav-am, -i, -ad, -im, -id, -and* 'that I, you, he/she, we, you, they go'. Perfect subjunctive: *raft-e bāsh-am, -i, -ad, -im, -id, -and* 'that I, you, he/she, we, you, they may have gone'.

The basic function of the subjunctive is to express potential action, and it is typically used as adhortative, e.g. *be-rav-ad* 'he should go/let him go'. It is obligatory after modal verbs and expressions with potential connotations, e.g. *bāyad al'ān bé-rav-ad* 'he must go now (*al'ān*)'. The function of the counterfactual is typically to express unlikely situations, including wishes, e.g. *kāš mi-raft* 'if he would only go/had only gone'.

The three evidential forms convey second-hand knowledge, conclusion and reminiscence, e.g. past perfective-resultative, *zāheran xod-aš-rā košte bude ast* 'he apparently (*zāheran*) had killed himself'.

3.3.3 Diachrony

The functions of the three stems of the verb reflect their history. Present stems originate in the Old Persian 'present', i.e. imperfective, stems (e.g. OPers *bar-a-* > NPers *bar-* 'to carry, bear', *da-dā* > NPers *deh-* 'to give', *k-r̥-nu* > NPers *kon* 'to do, make'); past stems originate in the Old Persian perfect participle in *-tá* (e.g. OPers *dā-tá* > NPers *dād*), from which the imperfective past came to be differentiated; and perfect stems originate in Middle Persian participles in *-t-ag* (< *-taka*, extended Old Persian participles).

The history of the prefix *mi-* reflects the coming into prominence of imperfective aspect. It derives from the Early New Persian adverb *hamē*, MPers *hamē(w)* 'always', which was used to express iterative action (< OPers **hama-aiwa-da* 'at the same time/place'), and in the form *mē* had absorbed the habitual, as well as counterfactual, function of the optative clitic *-ē(d)* (< OPers *hait* 'it may be') by the fourteenth century.

3.3.4 Aktionsart

Standard colloquial Persian has developed a progressive-incipient construction by preposing *dāštan* 'to keep, hold, have' to the indicative imperfective forms, e.g. *dār-ad al'ān kār mi-kon-ad* 'he is now working/is about to work'. It is confined to positive statements, and not yet literary standard. The appearance of this innovative construction was triggered by corresponding locative progressive constructions both in several Persian varieties and non-Persian languages of Iran, and in Turkic.

4 Syntax

4.1 The Sentence

Persian is an SOV language. Interrogatives do not trigger inversions. Subjects are unmarked, indirect objects are marked by the preposition *be*, and direct objects by the postposition *rā* if specific. Adverbial phrases are marked by the prepositions, including *barā-ye* 'for', *be* 'to', *az* 'from, by, than', *bā* 'with', *tā* 'till, than (comparing clauses)', *dar* 'in/into', and by adverbial phrases, e.g. *(be) ru-ye* 'on(to)' (*ru* 'face').

4.2 Subordinate Clauses

The general subordinator is *ke*. It originates in *kē* 'who, which', and the latter's absorption of the functions of Middle Persian *kā* 'when' and *kū* 'that; where'.

Relative clauses are postnominal and introduced by the general subordinator *ke* (comparable to English *that*). The head of restrictive clauses is marked by the particle *-i*, which is lacking with non-restrictive clauses (similar to nominal attributes vs appositions, respectively). Within the clause, agreement with the head noun is marked by an anaphoric pronoun, optionally if subject or object, e.g. *ān mard ke māšin-rā az u xarid-i* 'that man – (that) from him you bought the car', *ān mard-i ke māšin-rā az u xarid-i* 'thát man from whom you bought the car' (not the other one etc.). Complement clauses are similarly introduced by *ke*, while adverbial clauses are introduced either by *ke* or specific conjunctions and conjunctional phrases.

The basic rule for the sequence of main and subordinate clauses in contemporary Persian may be stated as follows: subordinate clauses with actions or states which logically or temporally precede others, i.e. cause, time and condition, precede the main clause; those whose actions and states logically or temporally follow others, i.e. explanation, sudden interruption, time of potential or factual completion and exception, follow the main clause. This basic rule is seen in the pattern of the most frequent adverbial clauses.

Preceding			*Following*		
Cause	*čun*	'because'	Explanation	*zi-rā*	'(that is) because'
Time	*vaqt-i*	'when'	Interruption	*ke*	'when (suddenly)'
Point/	*tā*	'as soon as'	End point	*ta*	'until, so that'
Stretch		'as long as'			
Condition	*agar*	'if'	Exception	*magar*	'unless, if not'

The use of tense and mood is strict and predictable: factual situations are in the indicative, e.g. *agar mi-xāh-i, mi-rav-im* 'if you (really) want to, we will go', potential situations are in the subjunctive, e.g. *raft, tā az u be-pors-ad* 'he went in order to ask him', and unlikely ones in the counterfactual. Similarly, the use of aspect is predictable, notably the use of the perfective aorist expressing prior completion, which in English corresponds to a present form, e.g. *agar u-rā did-i, zang be-zan* 'If you see him, call me'.

5 Comparative Dialectology

The three main dialects of Persian in Iran, Afghanistan and Tajikistan have diverged in their phonology, most prominently in their vocalic systems. The development in their morphosyntax is the history of the increasing differentiation particularly in their verb systems by the development of new formations expressing aktionsarten, mood and causation, partially under the influence of Turkic.

The development of the vowels is shown in the diagram given here.

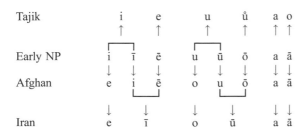

Compared with Early New Persian, Afghan Persian is the least changed, lowering the short high vowels as in Iran to mid vowels, which are now opposed to the retained long mid vowels. Tajik is the most changed, losing the length distinction, most likely under the influence of Turkic, by the merger of the short and long high vowels and the rounding of long *a*.

Evidentiality, also called non-witnessed mode, while found in both Iranian and Afghan Persian, is fully developed in Tajik, again clearly by interference from Turkic (see the discussion of Turkish *-mIş*, page 528). While restricted to past contexts in the other two varieties, in Tajik the imperfective and resultative forms have come to apply to present contexts as well, and a new evidential progressive has developed: *me-karda ast* 'he is/ was (evidently) doing, will/would do'; *karda ast* 'he (evidently) is (now)/has done/did'; *karda buda ast* 'he (evidently) had done'; *karda istoda ast* 'he is/was (evidently) doing'.

Just as the verb forms of Turkic are mostly based on participles, so in Tajik one finds the development of participial formations with so-called converbs, where the participial main verb is followed by a varied set of verbs whose meaning is generalised to express various aktionsarten. For example, *šudan* 'to become' expresses completion, *bar-omad-an* 'to come out' expresses thorough completion, and *guzaštan* 'to pass through, by' expresses completion after prolonged action, e.g. *[kitob-ro xond-a] šud bar-omad/ guzašt* 'he completed reading the book/he completed reading through the book/he completed the book after prolonged reading'.

Similarly, in Tajik the progressive is a participial formation with *istodan* 'to stand', e.g. *[kitob-ro xond-a] istod-a ast* 'he is reading the book'. This development has progressed less in Afghan Persian, which has developed two participial formations, the progressive marked by the con-verb *raft-an* 'to go', e.g. *[ketāb-ra xānd-a] mē-rav-ad* 'he is reading the book', and the dubitative based on the particle *xāt < xāh-ad* 'it will/may (be)', e.g. *[zad-a] xat bud-om* 'I might hit'. In fact, constructions with the perfect participle are a distinct feature already of Early New Persian texts, most of which originate in the east, but they were eliminated in the course of standardising literary Persian, except for the standard passive construction with *šodan* (see above).

Bibliography

Windfuhr (1979) is the 'state-of-the-art' concise survey of the study of Persian grammar, theoretical approaches and analyses, including new insights into syntax, semantics and phonology with extensive references, together with the most comprehensive alphabetical and topical bibliographies. Lazard (1957, Eng. tr. 1992) is an excellent detailed descriptive-structuralist grammar of contemporary Persian. Lazard (1963) provides an abundantly documented analytic description of Early New Persian prose texts of the eleventh and twelfth centuries, with historical and dialectal discussion. Farhadi (1975) remains the most inclusive description of Dari Persian. Perry (2005) is the most comprehensive description of Tajik Persian, and implicitly of Standard Persian given that most of its linguistic features are shared with Standard Persian. Ahadi (2001) is the first comprehensive study of the syntax and semantics of the verb phrase in Standard Persian.

References

Ahadi, S. 2001. *Verbergänzungen und zusammengesetzte Verben im Persischen: eine valenztheoretische Analyse* (Reichert, Wiesbaden)

Farhadi, R. A. G. 1975. *Le Persan parlé en Afghanistan. Grammaire du kâboli accompagnée d'un recueil de quatrains populaires de la région de Kâbol.* (Klincksieck, Paris)

Lazard, G. 1957. *Grammaire du persan contemporain* (Klincksieck, Paris); English translation: *Grammar of Contemporary Persian* (Mazda Publishers, Cosa Mesa, CA, 1992)

―― 1963. *La Langue des plus anciens monuments de la prose persane* (Klincksieck, Paris)

Mahootian, S. 1997. *Persian* (Routledge, London)

Paul, L. 2000. 'The language of the Shahnameh in historical and dialectal perspective', ILEX Foundation, Papers Presented at the Second Ferdowsi Conference, Center for the Great Islamic Encyclopedia, Tehran, Iran, August 21–28, 2000; http://www.ilexfoundation.org/pdf/ferdowsi_2/ludwigpaul300.pdf

Perry, J. R. 2005. *A Tajik Persian Reference Grammar* (Brill, Leiden-Boston)

Pisowicz, A. 1985. *Origins of the New and Middle Persian Phonological Systems* (Nakł. Uniwersytetu Jagiellońskiego, Cracow)

Utas, B. 2006. 'A multiethnic origin of Persian?', in Lars Johanson and Christiane Bulut, eds. *Turkic-Iranian Contact Areas: Historical And Linguistic Aspects* (Harrassowitz, Wiesbaden), pp. 241–51.

Windfuhr, G. L. 1979. *Persian Grammar. History and State of its Study* (Mouton, The Hague, Paris and New York)

26

Pashto

D.N. MacKenzie

1 Introduction

Long recognised as the most important language of the North-West Frontier Province of British India, now Pakistan, where it is spoken by 90 per cent of the population, Pashto was by royal decree of 1936 also declared to be the national language of Afghanistan in place of 'Dari' Persian. This official pre-eminence was artificial, however, and it now shares the honour with Persian. The areas of Afghanistan to which Pashto is native are those in the east, south and south-west, bordering on Pakistan, but in recent years Pashto speakers have also settled in parts of the northern and eastern provinces of the country. Pashto is estimated to have about 10 million native speakers in Pakistan (mainly in the North-West Frontier Province, also some in Baluchistan) and to be spoken natively by perhaps half of Afghanistan's population of over 30 million, though the figure for Afghanistan may include second-language speakers. Pashto is in any event the second most widely spoken Iranian language after Persian.

The name of the language, properly *Paxto*, also denotes the strong code of customs, morals and manners of the Pashtun (*Paxtun*, Indianised as *Paîhān*) nation, also called *Paxtunwālay* – whence the saying *Paxtun haγa nə day če Paxto wāyi lekin haγa če Paxto lari* 'A Pashtun is not he who speaks Pashto, but he who *has* Pashto.'

2 History

Pashto belongs to the North-Eastern group within the Iranian branch of Indo-European. The relationship can best be demonstrated by two phonological features characteristic of most members of this branch, viz. the development of the Old Iranian initial voiced plosives *b*, *d*, *g* and of the dental groups *-ft-*, *-xt-*. Initial *b*, *d*, *g*, preserved in Western Iranian, regularly became the voiced fricatives *β*, *γ*, *δ* in Khwarezmian and Sogdian. For example, Old Iranian *brātar-* 'brother', **buza-* 'goat', **duγdar-* 'daughter', *dasa-* 'ten', *gauša-* 'ear', **gari-* 'mountain' yield Sogdian *βr'ι*, *'βz-*, *δwγt'*, *δs'*, *γwš*, *γr-*, Khwarezmian *βr'd*, *'βz*, *δγd*, *δs*, *γwx*, *γryck*. Pashto shows the same development of *g-*, in *γwaǧ* 'ear', *γar* 'mountain'; *b-*, however, has passed through *β-* to the labial continuant *w-*, *wror* 'brother', *wəz* 'goat', and *d-* through *δ-* to *l-*, *lur* 'daughter', *las* 'ten'.

The dental group *-ft-*, also preserved in Western Iranian, becomes voiced in Eastern Iranian to [*-βd-*]: e.g. Old Iranian **hafta-* 'seven', **tafta-* 'heated', **xšwifta-* 'milk' give Sogdian *'βt*, *tβt*, *xšyβt*, Khwarezmian *'βd*, —, *xwβcy* [**xuβji]. In Pashto the group has been simplified either to *-(w)d-* (cf. Khotanese Saka: *hauda*, *ttauda*, *svīda*), as in *tod*, feminine *tawda* 'hot', *šodə/e* 'milk', or to *-w-*, as in *owə* 'seven'. *-xt-* coincides with *-γd-* in Eastern Iranian, e.g. *suxta-* 'burnt', *baxta-* 'shared', *duγdar-* 'daughter' give Sogdian *swγt*, *βγt-*, *δwγt'*, Khwarezmian —, *βγd*, *δγd*. Just as *-γd-* was reduced in Khotanese, via [*-d-*], to a hiatus-filling [*-w-*] (*sūta* [**sūda-*] > *-suva*, *būta* [**būda*] > *būva*, *dūta* [**dūda*] > *dūva*), so in Pashto it has either become *w* or, finally, dropped without trace: *səway* 'burnt', *su*, feminine *swa* 'it burnt', *tə* 'went' < **taxta-*, *tar-lə* 'father's brother's daughter' < **-duγda-*.

The change of *d* to *l*, already mentioned, is found in other neighbouring languages: there is evidence for it having occurred in at least some Sogdian dialects and in Bactrian (e.g. *Βαγολαγγο* < **bagadānaka-*, the modern Baghlan), and it is normal in modern Munji (where *luγda* 'daughter', *pāla* 'foot' < **pādā-*). Pashto goes further, however, in that all dentals, *t*, *θ*, *d*, become *-l-* post- or intervocalically; e.g. OIran. *pitar-* 'father', *sata-* 'hundred', *paθana-* 'broad', **čaθwar-* 'four', **gada-* 'robber', **wadi-* 'stream', yield Pashto *plār*, *səl*, *plən*, *calor*, *γal*, *wāla*. In other contexts, though, the dentals were often preserved, e.g. *tə** 'thou' < *tú*, *dre* 'three' < **θrayah*, *atə* 'eight' < *ašta*, (*γaw-*, etc.) *wišt* 'twenty (-one, etc.)' < **wīsati* (contrast *šəl* 'twenty' alone < **wīsáti*).

Only a few other sound changes can be mentioned. Perhaps the most striking in Pashto, as in the Pamir languages, are those undergone by some *r*-groups. Both *-rt-* and *-rd-* changed into the retroflex *-ṛ-* and *-rn-* into its nasalised counterpart *-ñ-* e.g. **ārta-* 'milled' > *oṛə* 'flour', *mṛta-* 'dead' > *məṛ*, **zṛdya-* 'heart' > *zṛə* **amarnā-* > *mañá* 'apple', **karna-* 'deaf' > *kuñ*. The presence of a sibilant complicated matters. *sr* and *rš* became *x̌* and *ǧ* respectively (on the phonemes written *x̌*, *ǧ*, see below), e.g. **hwasrū-* 'mother-in-law' > *xwáx̌e*, **ṛša-* 'bear' > *yaǧ*, and in *-str-*, *-štr-*, *-ršt-* the *-t-* was lost, leaving *x̌*, e.g. *uštra-* 'camel' > *ux̌*, *wāstra-* 'grass' > *wāx̌ə*, **hṛštaka* 'left' > *ix̌ay*. *-rs-*, on the other hand, coincided with *-rst-* to yield *-x̌t-*, and *-rz-* similarly gave *-ǧd-*, e.g. **uz-kṛstaka-* 'cut out' > *skáx̌tay*, *pṛsa-* 'ask' > *pux̌t-*, **warsya-* 'hair' > *wex̌tə*, **bṛz-* > *uǧd* 'long', **arzana-* 'millet' > *ǧdən*. It is an example of this development of *-rs-* that has given *Pax̌to* its name, from an original **Parsawā-* closely akin to the old names of the Persians and Parthians, respectively *Pársa-* (< **Parswa-* ?) and *Parθawa-*. *Pax̌tun* probably continues an old **Parswāna-*.

The Pashto lexicon is as fascinating as an archaeological museum. It contains side-by-side words going back to the dawn of Iranian, neologisms of all ages and loanwords from half a dozen languages acquired over a couple of millennia. The oldest of these loans date from the Greek occupation of Bactria in the third century BC, e.g. *mečə́n* (feminine) 'hand-mill, quern' taken over from *mēkhanḗ* at a time when *kh* was still an aspirated *k*, or *mačóyna*, *mačnóyza*, *mačlóyza* 'sling', which may be evidence for a weapon called *manganiká* (cf. Arabic *manǰanīq* 'mangonel') already at the same period. No special trace of a Zoroastrian or a Buddhist past remains, but the Islamic period has brought a great number of Arabic and Persian cultural words. Throughout the centuries everyday words also have been borrowed from Persian in the west and from Indo-Aryan neighbours in the east. Usually it is difficult to establish when: *marγalára* 'pearl', for example, could be from Greek *margarítēs*, or like it from an Old Persian **margāritā-*, or later from a Parthian or Sogdian form. Irregular assimilation makes it hard to decide when, say, *blárba* 'pregnant', *cerá* 'face, picture', *ǰalá* 'separate', *pex̌* 'happening' were acquired from Persian *bārbar*, *čihra*, *ǰudā*, *peš*, but it was long ago. The different stages of assimilation show that *žranda* 'water-mill' and *ǰandra* 'padlock' have been borrowed at different times from Lahnda (Western Panjabi) *ǰandar* 'mill' and *ǰandrā* 'padlock'. The sources of the many such Indian loanwords are particularly hard to distinguish. It is only when we come to *ǰarnáyl* 'general', *lāt̂* 'lord', *palt̂án* 'platoon, regiment', *t̂ikás* 'ticket, stamp' and *t̂wal* 'towel' that we are on firm ground again. The greater part of the basic vocabulary is nevertheless inherited Eastern Iranian. Still it is noteworthy how many original words have given way to neologisms. Most striking among these are some words for parts of the body: *γāx̌* 'tooth' (< **gaštra-* *'biter'), *stárga* 'eye' (< **str̥kā* *'little star'), *tandáy* or *wačwúlay* 'forehead' (the *tánda* 'thirsty' or *wač* 'dry' part), *tóray* 'spleen' (the *tor* 'dark, black' organ), and several of unknown origin, such as *šā* 'back', *xwla* 'mouth'.

3 Phonology

The maximum inventory of segmental phonemes in Pashto is set out in Table 26.1. Besides the common consonant stock of most modern Iranian languages, it comprises the dental affricates *c*, *j* [ts dz] and, thanks to its neighbourhood to Indo-Aryan languages, a set of retroflex, or cerebral, sounds. While the retroflex stops *t̂*, *d̂* occur only in loanwords, the *r̂* has, as we have seen, also developed within Pashto. In distinction from the alveolar trill *r* and from the dental (or alveolar) lateral *l*, it is basically a

Table 26.1 The Segmental Phonemes of Pashto

Vowels

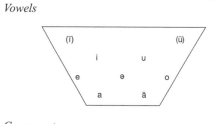

Consonants

	Plosive		Affricate		Fricative		Nasal	Lateral	Trill	Semi-vowel
Bilabial	p	b					m			w
Labiodental					(f)					
Dental	t	d	c	j			n	l		
Alveolar					s	z			r	
Retroflex	t̂	d̂			(x̌	ǧ)		ṅ	r̂	
Postalveolar			č	ǰ	š	ž				y
Velar	k	g			x	γ				
Uvular	(q)									
Glottal	(')				h					

retroflexed lateral flap. Its nasal counterpart *n̂* which does not occur word-initially, is a nasalised *r̂* – the nasalisation often extending to the preceding vowel – and not simply a retroflex nasal (which latter only occurs as an allophone of dental *n* before *t̂, d̂*).

The bracketed *f, q* and ' occur only in the elegant pronunciation of unassimilated loan-words from Persian and Arabic. Generally *f* is replaced by *p* (occasionally by *w*) and *q* by *k*, e.g. *fatīla > palitá* 'wick', *tafaḥḥuṣ > tapós* 'enquiry', *lafz > lawz* 'word, promise', *qiṣṣa > kisá* 'story', *qawm > kām* 'tribe'. The glottal stop (representing both Arabic *hamza* ' and *'ayn* ') is usually dropped, either without trace, e.g. *mas'ala > masalá* 'question, matter', or having widened the adjacent vowel, as in *šar' > šára* 'holy law', *ma'mūr > māmúr* 'official', *šurū' > šuró* 'beginning', *mawẓi' > mawzé* 'place'. This resembles the treatment of word- and syllable-final *h, ḥ* in loanwords, e.g. *ṣaḥīḥ > sahí* 'correct', *fatḥ > fáta* 'victory', *iḥtirām > etarā́m* 'respect', *makrūh > makró* 'abominable'.

Characteristic of Pashto are the two phonemes written *x̌, ǧ*. These developed originally as retroflex spirants [ṣ̂ ẑ] and continue generally as such in the south-western dialects, particularly the prestigious one of Qandahar, where they contrast with the post-alveolar *š, ž*. In the south-eastern dialects this contrast has been lost. In most central dialects these phonemes are still realised distinctly, but as palatal spirants [x̌ γ̌]. In the north-east, however, they have coincided entirely with velar *x* and *g* (not *γ*!). The non-phonetic symbols *x̌ ǧ* thus represent a compromise between [ṣ̂/š/x̌/x] and [ẑ/ž/γ̌/g] respectively. This wide and striking variation between south-western [pašto] and north-eastern [paxto] accounts for the description of the different dialects as 'soft' and 'hard' Pashto. It is noteworthy that the hard dialects, most directly exposed to Indo-Aryan influence, have also abandoned the dental affricates *c, j* (which lose their plosive element, to coalesce with *s, z*) and *ž* (which joins the affricate *j*) in other words, with the exception of *x, γ* and *z*, their phonemic system has largely been Indo-Aryanised.

A notable feature of Pashto phonology, in which it differs from most other modern Iranian languages, is its toleration of groups of two or (including *w*) three consonants in word-initial position. Some hundred such groups occur, e.g. eleven with *š-* alone: *šp-, št-, šk-, šx-, šxw-, šm-, šn-, šl-, šr-, šr̂-, šw-*. Such initial groups are particularly unstable, being subject to various metatheses, assimilations and dissimilations. Thus *pxa* 'foot', *kx̌əl* 'pull' and *psarláy* 'spring' become hard *xpa, xkəl* and *sparláy* respectively; *nwar* 'sun' occurs in different dialects as *nmar* and *lmar*, *rwaj* 'day' as *wraj*, *ǧmənj* 'comb' as *g(u)manj, mangáz*, and so on.

The vowel phonemes in Table 26.1 are the stressed ones of standard Pashto, stress also being phonemic. The following diphthongs also occur: *ay, əy, āy, oy, uy; aw, āw*. The phonemic status of the historically long vowels *ī, ū* is questionable. In most dialects they have been reduced to coincide with *i, u*; i.e. length is here, as in the case of *e, o*, no longer significant but depends on position and stress. Stressed *a, ə*, are entirely distinct, e.g. *bal* 'alight': *bəl* 'other', *γla* 'female thief': *γlə* 'male thieves'. In unstressed position, however, they are usually in free variation. It is convenient to regard unstressed [a ə] both as allophones of *a*, i.e. to regard *ə* only as a strong- or weak-stressed phoneme. Otherwise (as is unfortunately the case in some modern works on Pashto, both Afghan and foreign) there are some dangers of confusion, for example in writing the diphthongs unstressed *ay* [~ əy] and stressed *-áy*. In fact there is an important morphophonemic distinction between final *-áy, '-ay* and *-ə́y*. In the hard dialects *-ay* is generally monophthongised to an open [ε(:)], allowing *-əy* to shift and take its place at [εi]. In all dialects, but especially those of the south-west, there is a tendency towards regressive vowel harmony, in that the middle vowels *e, o* in syllables preceding high vowels *i, u* are themselves raised. Also in the south-west unstressed final *e, o* often coalesce with *i, u*, but not to the extent that morphological distinctions are lost. Thus *óse* 'you dwell' remains, in contrast to *ósi* 'he dwells'. *mor*, oblique *móre* 'mother', however, becomes *móri* [muːri], though still without rhyming with *lur*, obl. *lúre* 'daughter' > *lúri*. In some non-standard mountain dialects of the Afghan–Pakistan borderland, particularly of the Afridi and Wazir tribes, there is a vowel shift of *ā* to [ɔː] *o* to [œː > ɛː], and *ū* to [iː] (but not *u* > *i*); e.g. Waziri [plɔːr] 'father', [mɛːr] 'mother', [liːr] 'daughter'.

Three degrees of stress can be recognised: strong, medium and weak. Strong stress is comparatively free, in that it can occur on any syllable of a word, but it is mainly restricted to the first, last or penultimate syllables. It can also, particularly in verbal inflection, be mobile, though the shifts involved follow regular patterns, e.g. from *prewatə́l* 'to fall', also 'they (masculine) were falling', *préwatəl* 'they fell' and *prewátay* 'fallen (masculine singular)'. Occasionally lexical items may be distinguished solely by stress, e.g. *áspa* 'mare': *aspá* 'spotted fever', *gorá* 'fair-skinned, European': *góra* 'look!', *palitá* 'wick': *palíta* 'indecent woman', *wārə́* 'small (masculine plural)': *wā́ra* [-ə] 'all'.

4 Script

The earliest authenticated records of Pashto as a literary language date from the late sixteenth century, at a time when the whole area was, if turbulently, a part of the Mogul empire. The language has always been written in the Perso-Arabic script (see the

Table 26.2 Pashto Alphabet, with Transliteration

*	ا		ā medial		س	ـس	s
	آ		ā initial		ش	ـش	š
ب	ـب		b		ښ	ـښ	x̌
پ	ـپ		p		[ص]	ـص	ṣ]
ت	ـت		t		[ض]	ـض	ẓ]
ټ	ـټ		ṭ (P also Urdu ٹ)		[	ط	ṭ, occasionally for ṭ]
[ث]	ـث		s̱]		[	ظ	ẓ]
ج	ـج		ǰ		[ع]	ع	ʿ]
ځ	ـځ		č		غ	ـغ	γ
څ	ـڅ		{ ǰ (A ج) / c		ف	ـف	f
[ح]	ـح		ḥ]		[ق]	ـق	q]
خ	ـخ		x		ک	ک	k
	د		d		گ	ـگ	g
	ډ		ḍ (P also Urdu ڈ)		ل	ل	l
[	ذ		ẕ]		م	ـم	m
	ر		r		ن	ـن	n
	ړ		ṛ (P alo Urdu ڑ)			ڼ	ñ (A ن ڼ)
	ز		z	*		و	w
	ژ		ž	*		ه	h
	ږ		ǵ	*	ی	ـی	y

Notes: * On the function as vowel carrier of ا and ه in word-initial and final position respectively, and of و and ی medially and finally, see the discussion in the chapters on Arabic and Persian and Table 26.3.

464

Table 26.3 Vowel Representation

	Initially	*Medially*	*Finally*	
a	آ	َ	ﺣ	
ā	آ	ا	ﺍ	
ə	-	ُ	ﺣ	(P ﮥ)
e	ایِ	ﹷ	ي	(P ﮯ)
			(P - in particles)	
ay	اَی	ﹶ	ي	(P ﮯ)
əy	-	-	ئ	(A ی nominal, ئ verbal)
			-	
i	اِ	ﹻ (A ﮭ)	-	
ī	ایِ	ﹻ	ي	
o	او	و	و	
aw	او	و	و	
u	اُ	ﹹ (A و)	و (P ﮫ)	
ū	او	و	و	

discussion of script in Chapters 25 and 33), with the addition of certain modified letters to represent the peculiar consonant phonemes of Pashto. In the earliest manuscripts, from the late seventeenth to early eighteenth century, there is considerable variety in the representation of these consonants, but later a standard system emerged which persisted until recently. Since the adoption of Pashto as a national language in Afghanistan a number of innovations have been introduced into the script, which in the main make for more clarity. In Pakistan, on the other hand, there have been some tendencies, e.g. the occasional use of Urdu forms of letters and the phonetic representation of hard dialect forms (*ǧ* as *g*, *x̌* as *x*, *j* as *z*, etc.), causing a departure from the classical standard. In Table 26.2 the standard alphabet is given, with the modern Afghan (A) and Pakistani (P) forms as variants. The letters in square brackets occur only in unassimilated Arabic loanwords and the diacritics used in the transliteration are merely for mnemonic purposes, and have no phonetic significance. Thus ذ *ẓ*, ض *ẓ*, ظ *ẓ* are all pronounced [z], i.e. are all allographs of the phoneme *z*, usually written ز.

The Perso-Arabic script is by nature a consonantal one. The means by which the relatively simple vowel systems of Arabic and Persian are represented in it are inadequate for Pashto, where vowel representation is thus somewhat complicated: see Table 26.3. The short vowels *a*, *ə* are not normally written, but are represented notionally by the superscript signs ˊ *zwar* for *a*, ˉ *zwar-akay* for *ə*. In standard script the latter is sometimes represented by the sign ء *hamza*, e.g. زﮤ *zə́* 'I'. The signs ˏ *zer* and ˈ *peš* can represent *i* or *e* and *u* respectively, though all these vowels may also (particularly in Afghan practice) be written *plene* with the appropriate semi-vowel letters ی and و respectively; e.g. *injór* انخر or اینﺨُر 'fig', *kisá* قصه or کیسه 'story', *de* دﮤ or دﻱ 'your', *gul* ﮐل or ﮔول 'flower'.

5 Morphology

Although it has departed considerably from the morphological patterns of Old and even Eastern Middle Iranian (as evidenced, for example, by Sogdian and Khotanese Saka)

Pashto has nevertheless a remarkably complex nominal and verbal morphology. Two grammatical genders (masculine and feminine) and two numbers (singular and plural) are distinguished in both noun and, in part, verb. Although the nominal case system has essentially been reduced to a contrast between direct and oblique, there is in the singular also a vocative and a second oblique case used in conjunction with certain prepositions. Moreover the formatives used are not, as in practically all other still inflectional Iranian languages, restricted to suffixes. Alterations of stem vowels and stress and the substitution of endings also come into play.

Old Iranian masculine stems in -a, -i, (-u) have generally lost their final vowel, to appear in Pashto as consonant stems: kāra- > kor 'house, family', gauša- > ɣwaǧ 'ear', *gari- > ɣar 'mountain'. The old feminine stems in -ā alone have survived practically unscathed as -a stems: aspā- > áspa 'mare', uštrā- > úxa 'she-camel', wanā- > wə́na 'tree', xšapā- > špa 'night'. Old -an- stems similarly preserved their nominative singular -ā to emerge as masculine nouns in -a: *maiθman- > melmá 'guest'. Feminine stems in -ī, (-ū) also lost their final vowel, e.g. hapaθnī- > bən 'co-wife', *raθī- > lār 'way, road', *witasti- > wlešt 'span', but generally they adopt an -a from the general feminine form: *sraunī- > xn-a 'buttock, leg', *strī-čī- > xə́j-a 'woman', *wahunī- > *wēn > wín-a 'blood', *zanu- > zə́n-a 'chin'. Neuter stems joined either masculine or feminine, in the latter case also generally adopting a final -a: raučah- > rwaj f. 'day', *asru- > óx-a 'tear', *gauna- > ɣún-a 'colour', *parna- > pán̂-a 'leaf'. Only rarely do old masculines become feminine, e.g. angušta- > gút-a 'finger', safa- > sw-a 'hoof'. Several forms in -ya-, nominal or adjectival (including the comparative in -yah-) yield Pashto -ə: *(p)tr̥wya- > trə 'paternal uncle', *t(a)igriya- > terə́ 'sharp', srayah- 'better' > xə 'good', *abrya- > orə́ 'cloud'. A more common formative, however, as in Sogdian and Khotanese Saka, was the suffix -ka-. The resulting stems in -aka-, -ika-, -uka- became, via nominative or genitive *-ai (as in Khotanese), either stressed or unstressed -ay. The feminine equivalent, originally *-akī-, became -ə́y when stressed but -e when not: *daru-ka-ka- > largáy 'wood', *sarda-ka- > sar̂áy 'man', *spaka- > spay 'dog': *spakī- > spə́y 'bitch', *āsu-kī- > (h)osə́y 'deer', *náwa-ka- > nə́way m. 'new' : *náwa-kī- > nə́we f. 'new'. The result of these far-reaching changes was three main masculine stem-types, ending in a consonant, stressed -áy or unstressed -ay respectively, and three corresponding feminine stem-types, ending in (generally unstressed) -a, stressed -ə́y or unstressed -e. There are also several exceptions which fit into this scheme as best they can, e.g. masculines ending in -ə, -ā, -ū and feminines in a consonant, -ā, -e, -o, all unchanged in the singular but approximating to the masculine consonant or feminine -a declension in the plural, or again masculines (professions) and feminines (abstracts) in -i joining the -áy and -ə́y stems respectively. The stem-types pair up in the case of adjectives to form the three declensions numbered 1, 4, 5 in the chart of adjectival declension. In all adjectival declensions the oblique singular forms are identical with the direct plural. Only nouns generally distinguish plural forms by plural markers, of bewildering variety. The 'prepositional' case is marked in the masculine by an unstressed -a, which probably represents an old ablative ending -āt, added to the direct case stem. In the feminine it coincides with the direct case. The vocative coincides in most, but not all, masculine singulars with the prepositional form and in most feminines with the oblique. The oblique, and also vocative and prepositional, plural marker -o (in soft dialects, stressed -ó, unstressed -u) is common to all declensions.

Adjectival Declension

	1 'other'	2 'ripe, cooked'	3 'bitter'	4 'thin, narrow'	5 'new'
Masculine					
Singular					
Direct	bəl	pox	trix	naráy	nə́way
Vocative	bə́la	póxa	tríxa	naráya	nə́we
Prepositional	bə́la	póxa	tríxa	naráya	nə́wi
Oblique	bəl	pāxə́	tarxə́	narí	nə́wi
Plural					
Direct	bəl	pāxə́	tarxə́	narí	nə́wi
Oblique					
(Voc., Prepl.)	bə́lo[2]	paxó	tarxó	narío[2]/naró	nə́wyo[2]/nə́wo[2]
Feminine					
Singular					
Direct	bə́la	paxá	tarxá	narə́y	nə́we
Vocative	bə́le[1]	paxé	tarxé	narə́y	nə́we[1]
Prepositional	bə́la	paxá	tarxá	narə́y	nə́we[1]
Oblique	bə́le[1]	paxé	tarxé	narə́y	nə́we[1]
Plural					
Direct	bə́le[1]	paxé	tarxé	narə́y	nə́we[1]
Oblique					
(Voc., Prepl.)	bə́lo[2]	paxó	tarxó	narə́yo[2]/naró	nə́wyo[2]/nə́wo[2]

Notes: Qandahari:
1 bə́li, nə́wi.
2 bə́lu, naríu, nə́w(y)u.

There are also two further types of consonant stem (declensions 2, 3), represented among both nouns and adjectives, in which stress and vowel changes occur which may go back to a very early stage of the language. In the first type, comprising some (but not all) monosyllabic nouns and adjectives with the stem vowel *o* or *u* and some nouns with final -*un*, the oblique singular and direct plural masculine substitute the vowel -*ā*-, and the oblique plural and entire feminine the vowel -*a*-, all with additional stressed endings. In the other type the same stressed endings occur with a stem either unchanged or with the stem vowel reduced to an -*a*- or nil. Thus *kuŋ* 'deaf' has the plural *kāŋə́* and feminine *kaŋá* but *ruŋ* 'light' plural *ruŋə́* feminine *ruŋá*; *soŗ* 'cold', plural *sāŗə́* but *sur* 'red' plural *srə*. Similarly declined are a few words ending in stressed -*ə*: *xə* 'good', singular and plural masculine, *xa* feminine singular, *xe* plural. A last set of adjectives comprises all those which end in any other vowel – *a, ā, e, i, o, u*. These are indeclinable for number, gender or case, except that they may take the universal oblique plural -*o*.

The plural of masculine nouns of the first declension, which also includes those ending in -*ə*, -*a*, -*u*, is generally -*úna*, oblique -*úno*, e.g. *lās* 'hand', *lāsúna*, *zŗə* 'heart' *zŗúna*. Animate nouns take the suffix -*ā́n*, borrowed from Persian, oblique -*ā́no* e.g. *ux̌* 'camel', *ux̌ā́n*, *lewə́* 'wolf', *lewā́n*; before this suffix a -*y*- is inserted after -*ā*, e.g. *mullāyā́n* 'mullahs', or a -*g*- after other vowels, e.g. *nikəgā́n* 'ancestors'. Inanimate nouns in -*u* take the same ending: *bāŋugā́n* 'eye-lashes'. Feminine nouns of this declension ending in a consonant or -*a* behave like adjectives even in the plural, e.g. *lār* 'road', plural *lā́re*, *xwla* 'mouth', *xwle*. Animate ones ending in -*o*, however, take the mixed Persian and Pashto suffix -*gā́ne*, e.g. *pišogā́ne* 'cats', and those in -*e* change this to -*yā́ne*, e.g. *xwā́x̌e* 'mother-in-law', *xwāx̌yā́ne*. Inanimate feminine nouns in -*ā*, -*o* on the other hand take an unstressed plural ending -*we*, e.g. *mlā́we* 'waists'. Nouns of declension 2 generally

467

follow the adjectival pattern, e.g. *sor* 'rider', direct *swārə́*, oblique *swaró*, *paχtún* 'Pashtun', plural *paχtānə́*, feminine *paχtaná* 'Pashtun woman', etc. Some such nouns, however, follow declension 1 in the plural, e.g. *žwandún* 'life, livelihood', oblique singular *žwandānə́*, plural *zwandunúna*. This is also the case with declension 3: *γar* 'mountain', plural *γrə* or *γrúna*, *trə* 'paternal uncle', *trə* or *trúna*. A number of nouns which only modify the vowel of their final syllable can also be classed here: *melmá* 'guest', plural *melmə́* (or *melmānə́*), *duχmán* 'enemy', *duχmən*. A few nouns ending in *-ba* (sometimes alternating with *-bun*) follow declension 3 in the singular and 2 in the plural, e.g. *γobá* (or *γobún*) 'cowherd', oblique singular *γobə́* (*γobānə́*) plural *γobānə́*, *γobanó*. Nouns of declensions 4 and 5 also follow the adjectival pattern, except that animates may also take the appropriate *-ān* ending, e.g. *spay* 'dog', plural *spi* or *spiā́n*, *spəy* 'bitch', *spəy* or *spiā́ne*, *budəy* 'old woman', *budəygā́ne* or *budyā́ne*. Even this catalogue does not exhaust the full variety of plural forms. The class of nouns of relationship is particularly rich in irregularities, as the following list will show: *plār* 'father', plural *plā́rúna*; *mor* 'mother', *máynde* (*mándi*); *xor* 'sister', *xwáynde* (*xwāndi*); *tror* 'aunt', *tráynde* (*trándi*)*, troryā́ne*; *yor* 'husband's brother's wife', *yúñe*; *lur* 'daughter', *lúñe*; *wror* 'brother', *wrúña*; *wrārə* 'brother's son', *wrerúna*; *zoy* (*zuy*) 'son', *zāmə́n*.

Several nouns, particularly those denoting substances, occur only in the plural, whether masculine, e.g. *čars* 'hashish', *γanə́m* 'wheat', *γwaří* 'cooking oil', *māγzə́* 'brain', *ořə́* 'flour', *tambākú* 'tobacco', *wāχə́* 'grass', or feminine, e.g. *čāy* 'tea', *obə́* 'water', *orbə́še* 'barley', *šomlé* 'buttermilk'. To these may be added words with a collective meaning, such as *xalk* 'people', onomatopoeics ending in *-ahā́r* denoting noises, e.g. *šrapahā́r* 'splashing' and all verbal infinitives used as nouns. A last quirk of nominal declension concerns masculine consonant stems, mostly inanimate, when qualified by and directly following a cardinal number higher than 'one', or a similar adjective such as *co* 'several, how many?'. Instead of appearing in the plural, as all other nouns then do, they take a 'numerative' ending *-a* in the direct case. This also affects the higher numbers (*šəl* 'score', *səl* 'hundred', which then takes the form *saw*, *zər* 'thousand') and the enumerative words which frequently appear between number and noun: *co jə́la* 'how many times?', *dre kā́la* 'three years', *calór sáwa saří* 'four hundred men', *pinjə́ zə́ra míla* 'five thousand miles', *atə́ kitā́ba* or *atə ǔuka kitābúna* 'eight (volumes) books'. This numerative ending may well be a last relic of the ancient dual.

The direct case of nouns serves both for the grammatical subject and direct object of verbs. Case relationships are all expressed by pre- and postpositions or a combination of both, used with one of the oblique cases: an oblique form alone may have adverbial sense, e.g. *yáwa wrə́je* 'one day'. The simple prepositions are *da* 'of', which provides the only means of expressing a genitive or possessive relationship, *la* 'from', *pa* 'in, at, etc.', *tar* 'to, from': postpositions, appearing independently or in combination with prepositions, are *na* 'from', *ta* 'to', *bā́nde* 'on', *cáxa* and *jə́ne* 'from', *kče* (generally reduced to *ke*, *ki*) 'in', *lā́nde* 'under', *lará* 'for', *pās* 'above', *pasé* 'after', *póre (púri)* 'up to', *sará* 'with'. Combinations of pre- and postpositions vary somewhat from dialect to dialect: common examples are *da ... na* 'from', *la ... sará* 'with', *pa ... kče* 'in', *pa ... bā́nde* 'on', *tar ... póre* 'up to, till'. Most pre- and all postpositions take the main oblique case. The second oblique case, which as it serves no other function can for convenience be called the 'prepositional' case, is as a rule taken only by the simple prepositions *be* 'without', *la* and *tar* and by *pa* (*... kče*) but this last, remarkably, with feminine nouns only.

With pronouns things are somewhat different. Pashto has, in fact, comparatively few independent pronouns. Besides those for the first and second persons, singular and plural, there are proximate and remote demonstrative pronouns, which double for the third persons, and a few indefinite and interrogative forms. For the rest paraphrase is used, much as in English. e.g. *jan* 'body, self' for 'my-, your-, himself, etc.', *yaw ... bəl* 'one ... other' for 'each other'. The place of a relative pronoun is taken by the conjunctive particle *če* 'that', '(the man) who came' being expressed as 'that he came', and 'whose house ...' as 'that his house ...' and so on.

Pronouns

	Singular		Plural			'who?,	'what?,
	1	*2*	*1*	*2*		somebody'	something'
Direct	zə	tə	muǧ¹	t̃áso	t̃ási	cok	cə
Oblique	mā	tā	muǧ	t̃áso	t̃ási	ča	cə
Possessive	jmā	stā	jmuǧ¹	stáso	stási	da čā	

	'this'					'that'
Masculine						
Direct		day	dáɣa			háɣa
Oblique		də	dáɣə			háɣə
Feminine						
Direct		dā	dáɣa			háɣa
Oblique		de	dáɣe			háɣe
Plural						
Direct		duy	dáɣa			háɣa
(Personal)			dáɣuy			háɣuy
Oblique		duy, dío	dáɣo			háɣo

Note:
1 Hard dialects, mung, zmung.

Of those pronouns which show a difference, the first and second person singular ones are unique in that the direct forms act only as subject, the oblique case forms (distinct only in the singular) being used both for the direct and a prepositional object. The personal pronouns also have distinct possessive forms, combining the old preposition *hača* 'from' in the form *j-*, *(z-)*, *s-*, which may also occur with postpositions usually combined with *da*, e.g. *jmā na* 'from me'. There are also two kinds of pronominal particle, one independent and one enclitic. The enclitics are only incompletely distinguished for person and number: 1st singular *me*, 2nd singular *de*, 3rd singular and plural *(y)e*, 1st and 2nd plural *mo*. They fulfil all the oblique functions of the pronouns except that of prepositional object, though even in this case there are traces of the third person form to be seen in combinations of the sort of English 'therefrom, -on, -in', Pashto *tre < *tar-e*, *pre < *par-e*, *pakše < *pa kšé-ye*. The independent forms, *rā*, *dar*, *war*, are by origin local adverbs 'hither, thither' and 'yonder' and still act as such when no person is involved. They come to act as pseudo-pronouns, however, distinguishing only person, neither number nor gender. Thus they may be governed by post- but not prepositions, e.g. *dar sara* 'with you', or serve as a prepositional object with certain verbs: *war ba nənawózəm* 'I shall enter therein' or 'go in to him', according to context.

The verbal morphology of Pashto, as with all other modern Iranian languages, is based on the opposition between two stems, one present and one past. Present stems are either simple (inherited or borrowed ones) or secondary (made with the formatives *-eǧ-* intransitive or *-aw-* transitive and causative). These latter both generally form denominatives (*num-eǧ-* 'be named') or serve to assimilate loan-words (*bah-eǧ-* 'flow', from Hindi *bahnā*), but in some cases -*eg̊*- also distinguishes a continuous sense from a timeless or habitual one: *dəlta ḍera wāwra óri* 'here much snow falls (lit. rains)': *orég̊i* 'it is raining'. The past stems are essentially old perfect passive participles in -*ta*-, though more often than in any other Iranian language phonetic developments have disguised the characteristic dental ending. In contrast, for example, to Persian *sūz-ad*, *sūxt* 'it burns, burnt', Pashto has *swaj-i*, *su*. A dental may even arise in the present and disappear from the past, e.g. *təxt-* 'flee' < *ṭrsa-* against *təx̌* 'fled' < *ṭṛšta-* or the two stems may coincide, as in *ačaw-* 'throw' < **ā-škaba-* and -*škafta-*. As a result a new past marker has emerged, a stressed -*ə́l*- identical with the infinitive ending -*ə́l* (< **-ati*-), which is added to the past stem whenever the need is felt to arise. Corresponding to the intransitive present formative -*eg̊*-, and generally but not always paired with it, there is a past formative -*ed*-.

On the basis of these two stems simple tenses are formed by the addition of personal endings, stressed or not according to the stem, which distinguish first and second persons singular and plural, but third person only, without difference of number. Thus, from *lwedə́l* 'fall' and *ačawə́l* 'throw' are formed the present and past paradigms shown here.

		Present		Past	
Singular	1	lwég̊-əm	acaw-ə́m	lwéd-əm	ačaw-ə́l-em
	2	lwég̊-e	acaw-é	lwéd-e	ačaw-ə́l-e
	3 m.	lwég̊-i	acaw-í	lwéd(-ə́)	ačawə́
	3 f.			lwed-ə́la	ačaw-ə́la
Plural	1	lwég̊-u	acaw-ú	lwéd-u	ačaw-ə́l-u
	2	lwég̊-əy[1]	acaw-ə́y[1]	lwéd-əy[1]	ačaw-ə́l-əy[1]
	3 m.	lwég̊-i	acaw-í	lwed-ə́l	ačaw-ə́l
	3 f.			lwed-ə́le	ačaw-ə́le

Note:
1 Qandahari, 2nd plural -*āst*, thus lwég̊-*āst,* etc.

The original composition of the past tense, from a passive participle and the copula, is still clear in the third person, where the copula is lacking and the forms are declined like adjectives, though frequently with an irregular masculine singular form in which a stem vowel -*a*- is lengthened to -*ā*- or changed to -*o*- (*xatə́l* 'rise', *xot* 'rose'). Moreover the old participle of transitive verbs, as past stem, retains its passive meaning throughout: *ačawə́m* 'I throw', but *ačawə́ləm* 'I was being thrown'. This is also true of the modern past participle, a regular adjective of declension 5, e.g. *lwedə́lay* 'fallen', *ačawə́lay* '(having been) thrown', which with the auxiliary verb 'be' forms periphrastic tenses. The modern copula similarly betrays the probable pronominal origin of its third person forms. The simple perfect, for example, is formed as in the chart given here.

		Masculine	Feminine	M./F.
Singular	1	lwedə́lay yəm	lwedə́le yəm	ačawalay/e yəm
	2	lwedə́lay ye	lwedə́le ye	ačawalay/e ye
	3	lwedə́lay day	lwedə́le da	ačawalay/e day/da
Plural	1	lwedə́li yu	lwedə́le yu	ačawali/e yu
	2	lwedə́li yəy	lwedə́le yəy	ačawali/e yəy
	3	lwedə́li di	lwedə́le di	ačawali/e di

'I have fallen' etc., but 'I have been thrown', etc. In contrast to the present tenses, 'I throw it', etc., there is thus no means of expressing the active non-present tenses of the transitive verbs by forms in concord with a logical subject or agent in the direct case. Instead of

'I threw it', therefore, an ergative construction is obligatory, which – to avoid the passive 'it was thrown by me' – can only be expressed in English as 'me thrown it'. In Pashto the logical object but grammatical subject, inherent in the verb, may of course be expressed by an independent form, but if it is pronominal it need not be. The agent, however, must appear, in the oblique case. A personal pronoun may then be represented either by an independent form (*mā*, etc.), which then generally precedes the grammatical subject, or by an enclitic (*me*, etc.). Various different possible paradigms thus arise (a matter to which we shall return), e.g.:

mā kāñay...	or *kāñay me ačawə́lay day*	'I have thrown a stone',
tā zə...	or *zə de ačawə́lay yəm*	'you have thrown me',
hayəačawə́lay day	or *ačawə́lay ye day*	'he has thrown it'.

In contrast to this a real passive usually only occurs when the agent is unknown or at least not expressed. Such a passive is formed by the past participle, or in soft dialects the 'old past participle', i.e. the third person past forms, with the auxiliary verb *kedəl/ šwəl* 'become': *ačāwə́/ačawə́lay keğəm* 'I am being thrown', *ačawə́la/ačawə́le šwa* 'she was thrown', *ačawə́l/ačawəli šə́wi di* 'they have been thrown'. A full passive, with the agent expressed by a prepositional phrase like 'by means of', as in *kāle če da nāwe la xwā roγ šəwe wi* 'clothes which will have been made by (lit. from the side of) the bride', is a rarity.

Pashto employs two further means, besides the different temporal stems, for distinguishing a series of forms which intricately mark differences of mood and aspect. The one means is to provide each verb with secondary stems, present and past II. This is mostly done by means of a stressed separable prefix *wə́* (eastern *(w)u*), e.g. *wə́lweğ-, wə́lwed-*. With an initial *a-* the prefix forms *wā-*, which then makes itself independent of the verb as a pseudo-preverb, e.g. *wā́čaw-, wā́čawal-*. True preverbs, like *kše* and *nə́na* 'in', *póre* 'to, across', *pre* 'off, from', exclude the prefix *wə́*. Instead they attract the stress to themselves, e.g. from *kšewatə́l* 'enter', present stem I *kšewə́z-*, II *kšéwəz-*, past II *kšéwat-*. Half a dozen of the commonest verbs combine stems of widely different origins, so that the I and II stems are sufficiently distinct to dispense with the help of *wə*. Among these *kedə́l* 'become', present I *kéğ-*, II *š-*, past II *šw-*; *kawə́l* 'do, make', present I *kaw-'*, II *k(ṛ)-'*, past II *kṛ-* and the particularly complicated *tləl* 'go', present I *j-*, II *wlāṛ š-*, past II *wlāṛ-* but *rā-tlə́l* 'come (hither)', present I *rā-j-'*, II *rā́-š-*, past II *rā́-γl-* which follows the same pattern with alternative prefixes in *dar-tlə́l* 'come, go to you', *war-tlə́l* 'go to him'. Denominative verbs distinguish their I and II stems in yet another way. Here the composite primary stems are opposed to secondary stems in which the independent inflected nominal form is compounded with the secondary stems of *kedəl* or *kawal*: thus from *joṛ* 'well, ready, agreeable', *joṛedə́l* 'get well, be made, made ready, agree', present I *joṛéğ*, II *joṛ š-*, past II *joṛ šw-*. The contrast is even more marked with words of declension 2 or 3, since they form denominatives from the 'weak' feminine stem, e.g. from *pox* 'cooked', *paxawə́l* 'cook', present I *paxaw-'*, II *póx kṛ-*, past II *póx kṛ-*.

The other means is a movable enclitic particle *ba*. Its positioning will be described below, but for the moment we shall consider it in relation to the finite verb alone. It remains only to mention the distinctive endings of the imperative (singular *-a*, plural *-əy*) and of the conditional mood (*-āy*, eastern *-ay*, for all persons) and we have all the ingredients for the first part of the verbal system sketched in Table 26.4. The lower part

Table 26.4 The Verbal System

Present I	Present II	Future I	Future II
lwéǧi	wə́lweǧi	lwéǧi ba	wə́-ba-lweǧi
Imperative I	Imperative II		
lwéǧa	wə́lweǧa		
Past I	Past II	Past III	Past IV
lwedə́	wə́lwed	lwedə́ ba	wə́-ba-lwed
Conditional I	Conditional II	Conditional III	
lwedā́y	wə́lwedā́y	lwedā́y ba	
Perfect I	Perfect II		Future Perfect
lwedə́lay day	lwedə́lay wi		lwedə́lay ba wi
Past Perfect I		Past Perfect III	
lwedə́lay wə		lwedə́lay ba wə	
Perfect Conditional		Perfect Conditional III	
lwedə́lay wā́y		lwedə́lay ba wā́y	
Potential Present		Future	
(wə́)lwedā́y ši		(wə́)lwedā́y ba ši	
Past		Past III	
(wə́)lwedā́y šu		(wə́)lwedā́y ba šu	
Conditional			
(wə́)lwedā́y šwā́y			

comprises both the periphrastic tenses, formed from the past participle, and the forms expressing the potential mood, which are compounded of the simple conditional form and the auxiliary verb *šwəl* (Qandahari *swəl*) 'be able', the forms of which chance to be identical with the secondary ones of *kedəl* 'become'. Here the prefix *wə* seems to have lost its significance, to become facultative.

Between the present I and II there is a difference of mood, I being indicative, 'falls, is falling', II subjunctive, '(that, if) it fall'. In the corresponding future forms, however, with the addition of the particle *ba*, there is a distinction of aspect, I being durative, 'will be falling', II perfective, 'will fall'. This holds good also in part for the imperative, I 'keep on falling', II 'fall'. But the prohibitive, with the particle *ma* 'not', cuts across this. It is normally only formed from stem I, regardless of aspect: *mā lwéǧa* 'do not fall'. The past II is again perfective, 'fell', in contrast to the past I with durative sense, 'was falling', or occasionally inchoative, 'was about to fall'. The addition of *ba* in this case, although giving a sense of customariness, does not entirely remove the aspectual distinction: III 'used to fall, be falling, continuously': IV 'used to fall repeatedly'. With the conditional forms I and II no aspectual difference can be seen: both can express present or future conditions, '(if) it were falling' or *'were to fall', the possible consequences '(then) it would fall' being expressed either by the past III or IV, or the conditional III (IV being unusual). The periphrastic tenses are by nature all perfective. With the perfect forms the sense follows that of the auxiliary verb, i.e. between perfect I and II there is a difference of indicative, 'has fallen', and subjunctive, '(if) it (should) have fallen', in the third person only, as the other persons of the copula have common forms for both I and II. The future perfect only occurs in the II form, there being no durative future form of the copula. It has both senses of the corresponding English tense, 'it will (i.e. must) have fallen (by now, or some past time)', or 'it will have fallen (by some future time)'. The perfect conditional I expresses no longer possible conditions, '(if) it had fallen', and the past perfect III or the perfect conditional III the consequence, '(then) it would have fallen'.

6 Syntax

The first important syntactic feature to be considered is word order, which, starting from the noun phrase, is fairly inflexible in Pashto. All qualifiers precede the head of a noun phrase. The English freedom to say 'that man's hand' or 'the hand of that man' is denied a Pashto-speaker, who has only *da haγ̂ə sar̂i lās* 'of that man hand'. Missing is an article in Pashto, though this lack may occasionally be made up by the use of a demonstrative or the word *yaw* 'one'. Combining *yaw zor̂ kə́lay* 'an old village' and *tange kucé* 'narrow streets' yields *da yawə zār̂ə tange kucé* 'an old village's narrow streets'. Only the personal possessive forms can precede the *da* group: *stā́so da kə́lo kucé* 'your villages' streets'. The apparent parallelism breaks down, however, when the noun phrase is governed by a pre- or postposition. The postposition appears at the end of the entire phrase, but a lone or accompanying preposition must be placed immediately before the head and its attributes. Thus 'from the very narrow streets of your old villages' can only be *stā́so da zar̂o kə́lo lu êro tango kucó na* 'your of-old-villages from very-narrow-streets-from'.

Since both subject and direct object of a non past transitive verb appear in the direct case, only a fixed word order can disambiguate them. Pashto has therefore become an inflexible subject–object–verb language: *sar̂áy xə́ja wíni* 'man woman sees' can only mean 'the (a) man sees the (a) woman'. The positioning of adverbial phrases is freer. The order of the following sentence seems to be the most natural one: *(A: hara wraj) (B: pa kum waxt če kə́li ta ji) yaw sar̂áy (C: pa êer tā́jub) yawa barbanд̂a xə́ja (D: pa lāra kx̌e) wini* '(every day) (at what time he goes to the village) a certain man (to his great surprise) sees a naked woman (on the road)'. But an alternative arrangement *(A) (C) yaw sar̂áy (B) (D) yawa barbanд̂a wini* is just as thinkable as the English '(A), (C), a certain man, (B), sees (D) a naked woman'. Given the inflexibility of the SOV order in the non-past, it is not surprising that the ergative construction of the past parallels it. With independent forms the necessary word order is agent–patient–verb or, translated into terms of grammatical concord, agent (oblique)–subject (direct)–verb (concord): *mā sar̂ay wə́lid* 'I saw the man', *sar̂í xə́ja wə́lidəla* 'the man saw the woman', *zar̂o kə́lo ba tange kucé larə́le* 'old villages used to have narrow streets'. This simple rule is disturbed, however, by the fact already noted that a pronominal agent may be expressed by an enclitic form, and enclitics are a law unto themselves in Pashto.

Besides those already met, pronominal *me, de, (y)e, mo* and verbal *ba*, Pashto has a few more enclitics. *de (di)* may lose its original pronominal force and, as an ethic dative, simply give the present II (subjunctive) form a jussive sense: *kitābúna da r̂áwr̂i* 'let him bring the books'. Then there are the conjunction *xo* 'but' and the adverb *no* 'so, then, still, yet', which can be used encliticaliy. Two or three of these may occur together, when they have the following fixed pecking order:

xo / ba / me, de, ye, mo / no

pré-xo-ba-ye-nə́-ǧdəm 'but I shall not leave it', *dā́-xo-ba-me nə́ kāwə* 'but this I used not to do'. As a group they always seek the earliest possible support in a clause, namely the first syntagm, be it word, phrase or more, bearing at least one main stress. In short, when the agent is expressed by an enclitic pronoun its position is not relative to the grammatical subject at all, but is governed by the word order of the clause as a whole: *šikāyát-ye wə́kəř* 'complaint him made', i.e. 'he complained', *(da xéṯe la xwə́ǧ cəxa)-ye šikāyát wə́kəř* '(of stomach from pain-from) him complaint made', i.e. 'he complained of stomach ache', *hálta-ye (da ... cəxa) šikāyát wə́kəř* 'there he complained (of stomach-ache)'. Conversely as the content of a sentence is reduced an enclitic agent is forced back until it may be supported by parts of the verb, including a preverb, alone: *paroskā́l-ba-mo xar rā́wost/xár-ba-mo rā́wost/rā́-ba-mo-wost* '(last year) we used to bring (the donkey) it'. All this is equally true of the enclitic pronouns in their other functions, as direct object or possessive: *nə́-ye wažni* 'he does not kill it', *magar wažnə́ y-ba-ye nə́* 'but kill them you shall not'; *(stā da xeîe ilā́j kawa* or) *da xeîe ilā́j-de kawa* 'have your stomach treated', *xayrāt pradáy wə, no xéîa-xo-de xpə́la wa* 'the free food was provided by somebody else, but the stomach was your own'. Even poetic licence and transpositions *metri causa* cannot affect the rule. Instead of prosaic **mine-ba-me larγun da tan kor səway wə, ka-me žařā́ pa himāyat nə rātlay* 'love would long since have burnt the house of my body, if weeping had not come to my support (in dousing it)', the poet 'Abdul Hamid Mohmand has:

da tan kór-ba-me larγún wə mine sə́way
ka-me nə́ rātlay žařā́ pa himāyát.

The only constituent that can hold an enclitic back from its natural support is a relative clause immediately following it. A clause is clearly felt to be too diffuse to support enclitics, which are forced to attach themselves to the next best, i.e. following, syntagm: *haγa nǰələ́y-me māx̌ā́m simemā́ ta byāyi* 'that girl is taking me to the cinema this evening', *haγa nǰələ́y, če os-mo wə́lidəla, māx̌ā́m-me sinemā́ ta byāyi* 'that girl we just saw is taking me to the cinema this evening'. Sometimes, however, an enclitic may burst the bounds of its own subordinate clause to move to the front of the main clause, e.g. instead of *har sabā če γrə-ta-ba tə,* 'every morning, when he would go to the mountain', we find *har sabā-ba če γrə-ta tə*; instead of *pa har jāy-kx̌e če mumí-ye,* 'in whatever place he finds it' – *pa har jāy-kx̌e-ye če mumi.*

Of agreement in Pashto there is little to be said except that, where the forms permit it, it is all-pervading. Adjectives, whether attributive or predicative, agree in number, gender and case with their head nouns or subjects respectively: *zmā grā́na aw mehrabā́ na plā́ra* 'my dear and kind father!' (masculine singular vocative), *klā́ka zmə́ka* 'firm earth', *zmə́ka klā́ka da* 'the earth is hard' (feminine singular direct), *če stā mlā sáma ši yā da nóro xálko mlāgā́ne kubə́y ši* (they asked a hunchback whether he wanted) 'that your back should become straight (feminine singular direct) or other people's (masculine plural oblique) backs should become hunched (feminine plural direct)'. This agreement extends to adjectives used adverbially, e.g. *ḍer* 'much, many' but also 'very', *hawā́ ḍéra tawdá wi* 'the climate is (always) very hot' (feminine singular direct), *kix̌tə́y-e klā́ka wə́niwəla* 'he seized hold of the boat firmly' (feminine singular direct). While the agreement of subject and verb is normally restricted to person and number (note *Tor zə aw tə botlu* 'Tor took (1st plural) me and you'), with the third person singular copula gender also comes into play: *ā́s day* 'it is a horse', *áspa da* 'it is a mare'. In the ergative construction, with all third person forms both gender and number are marked throughout: *xə́je ās wə́wāhə* 'the woman struck the horse', *áspe-ye wə́wahəla* 'he/she/they struck the mare', *āsúna-ye wə́wahəl* '... struck the horses', *áspe-ye wə́wahəle* '... struck the mares'. In the perfective forms of denominative verbs, in which the nominal element is free, agreement is naturally to be expected: *zə bāyad γwáxe paxé kəm* 'I must cook some meat (feminine plural direct of *pox*)'. More unexpectedly, even nouns forming denominatives become adjectivised in this context: thus from the Persian loanword *yād* 'memory', forming *yādedə́l* 'be remembered', we find *haγa xə́ja-me yə́da šwa* 'I remembered that woman'.

If we compare the archaic structure of Pashto with the much simplified morphology of Persian, the leading modern Iranian language, we see that it stands to its 'second cousin' and neighbour in something like the same relationship as Icelandic does to English.

Bibliography

The best modern study in English is Penzl (1955), despite minor errors; it is based on the work of Afghan grammarians. Trumpp (1873) remains, despite its age, the best grammar based on classical Pashto literature. For syntax, Lorimer (1915) is an amateur study, but a mine of information. Morgenstierne (1942) is a unique historical study, by the leading specialist.

References

Lorimer, D.L.R. 1915. *(A) Syntax of Colloquial Pashtu* (Oxford University Press, Oxford)
Morgenstierne, G. 1942. 'Archaisms and Innovations in Pashto Morphology', *Norsk Tidskrift for Sprogvidenskap*, vol. XII, pp. 87–114
Penzl, H. 1955. *A Grammar of Pashto* (American Council of Learned Societies, Washington, DC)
Trumpp, Ernest. 1873. *Grammar of the Paṣ̌tō or Language of the Afghans* (Trübner, London)

27

Uralic languages

Robert Austerlitz

The term 'Uralic' refers to a language family with one large branch, Finno-Ugric, and one smaller one, Samoyedic. Each branch is further subdivided into sub-branches and these into individual languages. *Finno-Ugric* is often used in its wider meaning of Uralic. Though this is sanctioned by usage, it will be avoided here.

The best-known Uralic languages are Hungarian, with some fourteen million speakers, Finnish with some five million, and Estonian with about one million. These are also the populations which are most thoroughly integrated into the European cultural and economic community.

Hungarian and Finnish are related only remotely, while Finnish and Estonian are related much more intimately. The network which unites the entire family genetically can be seen in Figure 27.1.

In terms of numbers of speakers of the remaining Uralic languages, Mordva is the largest, followed by Mari and Udmurt.

Most Uralic languages are spoken in the Russian Federation, the main exceptions being Hungarian, Finnish, Estonian and the majority of the Saami (Lappish) languages; Livonian recently became extinct in Latvia.

In terms of very broad cultural features, the Hungarians are Central Europeans, the Finns, and to some extent the Saamis, are Fenno-Scandians, the Estonians and the other Baltic-Finnic speakers are Balts. The Mari, Mordva and Udmurt are agrarian populations. Komi culture occupies an intermediate position between that of the central-Russian agrarians and a sub-Arctic form of living. The Ob-Ugrians and the Samoyeds were, until this century, sub-Arctic peoples, as were the northernmost Saami.

The family tree of the Uralic languages (Figure 27.1) shows that this is a closely knit family in the accepted sense. Only two questions are still awaiting resolution:

(1) The precise position of Saami within the family. This group of languages has been considered Baltic-Finnic (node α), Finno-Ugric (node β), a separate branch of Uralic (node γ) and a 'mixed language', a vague term which generates further questions.
(2) The precise relationship between Mordva and Mari.

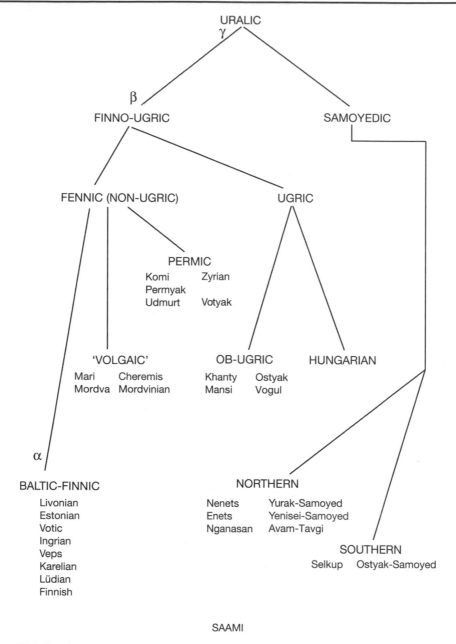

Figure 27.1 The Uralic Language Family.

The Uralic languages can also be plotted along an ear-shaped geographical arc extending from Fenno-Scandia and the Baltic in the West, extending eastward over the Kola peninsula into the basins of the Pechora, Ob and Yenisei rivers. At that point the arc is broken. It begins again in the Volga–Kama basin and ends, after another break, in the Carpathian basin (see Figure 27.2). The model of this arc can also serve as a device for visualising the order in which the forebears of the speakers of today's Uralic languages separated

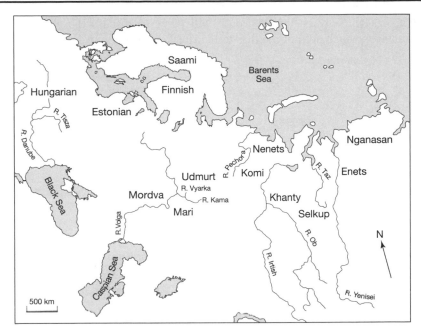

Map 27.1 Location of Uralic Languages.

out of early family groupings and ultimately out of the original proto-language. The generally accepted order is: Samoyed (estimates of the date of separation range from the fourth to the second millennium BC); Ugric, which split into an early form of Hungarian on the one hand and the language which later developed into Khanty and Mansi on the other. The last group to split up was Permic, around the seventh or eighth century AD. Hypothetical dates for the formation of the individual Baltic-Finnic languages as well as the proto-history of the Mari and the Mordva remain in dispute.

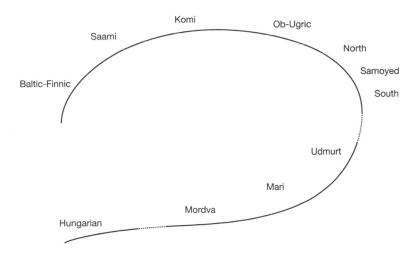

Figure 27.2 Schematic Location of Uralic Languages.

479

Another arc will now be introduced. It will serve to discuss those features of the Uralic languages which are not familiar to the speakers of western European languages.

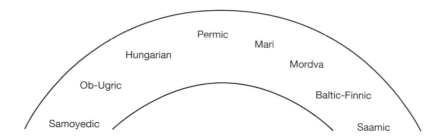

Consonant gradation is a prominent phenomenon in Baltic-Finnic and Saami. Thus, *-nt-* (strong grade) in Finnish *anta-vat* 'they give' alternates with *-nn-* (weak grade) in *anna-n* 'I give'. Originally, the strong–weak opposition correlated with open versus closed syllable, as in this Finnish example. Traces of this phenomenon can be found in Mordva and Mari. It is absent from the other languages.

The only typically Uralic grammatical feature found in the Permic languages is the so-called negative conjugation: Komi *o-g mun* 'I do not go', *o-z mun* 'you (sg.) do not go', *e-g mun* 'I did not go'. In this construction it is not the main verb (*mun* 'to go'), but the auxiliary negative verb (present *o-*, past *e-*) which is conjugated (*-g* 'I', *-z* 'you (sg.)'). Mari, Mordva, some of the Baltic-Finnic languages and the Samoyedic languages (except Selkup) also have such a device for negating the verb.

Vowel harmony occurs in Hungarian, in some of the Baltic-Finnic languages and in various degrees of development elsewhere (Mordva, Mari, Khanty, Samoyedic). It is absent from Permic and Saami. The rules of vowel-harmony require that only specific subclasses of vowels coexist in a non-compounded word. Thus, in Finnish, the sign of the third person plural is *-vat* and *-vät* as in *anta-vat* 'they give' and *kyntä-vät* 'they plough' (read *y* as *ü*); cf. Hungarian *lop-nak* 'they steal' vs *tör-nek* 'they break'. The vowel of the suffix adjusts to the vowels contained in the stem. The specific subclasses of vowels are determined by physiological factors, basically the position of the tongue (front/back) and of the lips (rounded/unrounded).

The grammatical category of the dual ('two of a kind') plays an important role in Ob-Ugric, in Samoyedic and in Saami. The following Mansi example will also illustrate the possessive suffix of the third person singular, *-et-* 'his/her', and the instrumental case, *-l* 'with': *aamp-aγ-et-l* 'with his two dogs' (*-aγ-* is the dual, 'two'). In Saamic, the dual occurs only in pronouns and in the verb. The dual, then, is found only in the languages at the two extremes of the arc and can be thought of as closing the circle.

Another typological feature, reference to a specific object within the verbal complex (also called the objective conjugation) is more difficult to place on the arc: it predominates on the left (Ugric, Samoyedic) but is also found in Mordva. The details of this feature differ strongly from one subgroup to another. Essentially, it signals the presence of a specific object, e.g. Hungarian *lop-j-uk* 'we steal it' as against *lop-unk* 'we steal' (without reference to a specific third-person object in the latter).

Mordva and Hungarian also have a definite article. In Hungarian *a ház* 'the house' the article *a* precedes the noun and is separable from it (*a kék ház* 'the blue house'), as in English. In Mordva *kudo-ś* 'house-the' the article is suffixed, as in the Scandinavian languages and some Balkan languages (e.g. Rumanian).

The basic and still prevalent rule of word order in the Uralic languages is subject–object–verb (SOV). However, this rule is rigid only in Ob-Ugric and in Samoyedic – on the left side of the arc – while Baltic-Finnic languages are basically SVO. The other languages have so-called free word order. Thus, in Hungarian, all permutations are possible: *A fiúk krumplit lopnak* 'the boys are stealing potatoes' (lit. 'the boys potato[-object] steal'), *krumplit lopnak a fiúk*, *lopnak a fiúk krumplit*, *lopnak krumplit a fiúk*, *a fiúk lopnak krumplit* and *krumplit a fiúk lopnak* can all occur under specific circumstances. The nuances of meaning expressed are in the areas of emphasis and focus. Those languages which lack this sort of syntactic elasticity have other ways of expressing emphasis and focus, generally particles which attach to specific parts of the sentence.

All of the Uralic languages have a set of spatial cases which convey such meanings as 'in', 'from', 'to', etc. The languages richest in this respect are Hungarian and Permic. In Baltic-Finnic and Saami one such local case, the partitive, which originally meant 'from', has acquired the additional function of partitive object, as in French, e.g. Finnish *juo-n maito-a* 'I am drinking milk' (lit. in French, *bois-je lait-du*) as against *juo-n maido-n* 'I am drinking (the) (entire quantity of) milk (which has already been specified in the discourse)'. The *-n* in *maido-n* is the accusative case marker. The more archaic function of the partitive (*-a*) can be seen in *taka-a* '(movement) from behind (something)'; contrast *taka-na* '(which is) behind'. Also in Finnish, all negative objects must be in the partitive, e.g. *e-n juo maito-a* 'I do not drink milk'; a sentence such as **e-n juo maido-n* (with the object in the accusative) is impossible.

Some of the salient features of the sound systems of the Uralic languages are: (1) word stress on the first vowel of the word, with the notable exception of Udmurt, where it falls on the last (and less striking exceptions in Mordva, Mari, Komi and Permyak); (2) vowel systems with reduced vowels: Mari, Ob-Ugric, Northern Samoyedic; (3) vowel systems with front rounded vowels (*ü*, *ö*): Baltic-Finnic, Mari, Hungarian (and, in a less developed form, in Khanty). Vowel systems with back unrounded vowels: Estonian (and some other Baltic-Finnic languages), Permic. A vowel system with both front rounded and back unrounded vowels is found in Selkup. (4) A correlation of palatalisation: Mordva, Permic, Samoyedic. (5) Rich systems of affricates: Hungarian, Permic, Selkup. (6) A correlation of voice in the obstruents: Hungarian, Permic, Saami (rudimentary in Mordva).

Each Uralic language has a constellation of typological features of the kind discussed above which is unique unto itself and which lends it its own particular profile. The features themselves evolved and crystallised during the historical development of each individual language for a variety of reasons – the economy of the phonology and grammar of each language, stimuli from other, related or unrelated, languages or combinations of the two. One task of the specialist is to peel off the layers of each Uralic language and to find correspondences among subsets of related languages. Such correspondences eventually permit the reconstruction of a parent language. By the same token, it is the task of the specialist to identify innovations in each language.

One tractable approach to the history of each of the Uralic languages is the study of loanwords – vocabulary items which entered each individual language in the course of its history as a result of contact with other languages and cultures. All of the Uralic languages have loanwords from Slavonic, acquired relatively recently. All of the Finno-Ugric languages have loans from Iranian or perhaps even Indo-Iranian, acquired so long ago that it is thought that they entered the proto-language and were passed on to its descendants along with the native vocabulary. One such item is Finnish *sata*, Hungarian *száz* 'hundred', an item which has implications for early commercial contacts between the two parties.

Table 27.1 gives a synoptic view of the lending and the borrowing parties.

The systematic comparison of the Finno-Ugric languages amongst themselves has provided a glimpse into both the structure of an earlier, hypothetical Proto-Finno-Ugric language and, through it, of some aspects of the culture of the population which spoke this language. Analogously, the same has been done for the Samoyedic languages. The comparison of Proto-Finno-Ugric with Proto-Samoyedic, then, affords an insight into the still earlier Proto-Uralic hypothetical language. Table 27.2 displays the data on which such a step-by-step comparison is carried out. The word in question is thought to have meant 'vein' but may also have meant something like 'sinew' and thus carries

Table 27.1 Loanwords in Uralic Languages

	Later Iranian	East Turkic	West Turkic	Baltic	Germanic		Slavonic
					Older	1200–	
Samoyedic	+	+					+
Ob-Ugric	+	+					+
Hungarian	+	+	+			+	+
Permic	+	+	+				+
Mari	+	+	+				+
Mordva	+	+	+	+ ?			+
Baltic-Finnic				+	+	+	+
Saami				+	+	+	+

Table 27.2 A Proto-Uralic Reconstruction

URALIC								
	SAMOYEDIC		South	Kamassian Selkup	t'en čɔt, tən	Proto-Samoyedic: *cən		Proto-Uralic: *sәne
			North	Nganasan Enets Nenets	taŋ ti/tino- teʔ/ten-			
	FINNO-UGRIC	UGRIC	Ob-Ugric	Khanty Mansi Hungarian	ton, lan, jan taan, tən ín/ina-		Proto-Finno-Ugric: *sone, *soone, *sәne	
			Permic	Udmurt Komi	sən sən			
		FENNIC	(Volgaic)	Mari Mordova	šün, śün san			
			Balto-Finnic	Livonian Estonian Finnish	suón/suonә- soon/soone- suoni/suone-			
	SAAMIC			Saami	suodnâ/suonâ-			

suggestions about the use of the objects denoted – archery, fishing equipment and the like. What can be reconstructed in the area of vocabulary has analogues in grammar. Proto-Uralic probably had a nominative (or absolute case, with no overt marker), an accusative, a genitive, at least three local cases (locative, allative, ablative), adverbial cases (with such meanings as 'with'), aspect (or tense) in the verb, an imperative and possibly an impersonal form of the verb.

Bibliography

Abondolo (1998) provides a detailed introduction to the Uralic languages, with chapters on the individual languages or groups of languages, and references to the earlier and more detailed literature.

References

Abondolo, D. (ed.) 1998. *The Uralic Languages* (Routledge, London)

28

Hungarian

Daniel Abondolo

1 Introduction

Hungarian (native name *magyar*) is the only Uralic language spoken in central Europe. Hungarian has a total of about 14 million native speakers, with over 10 million in Hungary, about one and a half million in Rumania, and smaller numbers in other neighbouring countries and elsewhere, mainly in the USA and Canada.

Because it is a Uralic language, Hungarian is typologically unlike the majority of European languages. But paradoxically, Hungarian is also atypical among the Uralic family. It is by far the largest, disproportionately so, in the sense that more than half of all speakers of Uralic languages speak Hungarian. It has both a rich vocalism (14–15 vowels) and a rich inventory of voiced/voiceless oppositions in its consonantism (which includes four affricates). Most of its inflectional morphemes are innovations. Its syntax boasts an impressive set of coordinating conjunctions. The array of foreign elements in its lexicon rivals that of Gypsy (Romany). Unlike Finnish, Hungarian has no close relatives; the Ob-Ugric languages, traditionally bundled together with Hungarian into the Ugric subgroup of the Uralic family, are radically different from Hungarian in their phonology, syntax and vocabulary.

This singular character is due to one decisive difference: migration by the Proto-Hungarians, first southward from the Uralic Urheimat into the maelstrom of cultures in the South Russian steppe, then westward into the heart of Roman Christian Europe.

This rudimentary sketch outlines only a few of the more salient features of Hungarian grammar and lexicon. In order to compress the presentation without sacrificing accuracy of detail, the following typographic conventions have been observed: suffixes are written to the right of a hyphen (-) if inflectional, of an equals sign (=) if derivational. A double equals sign (= =) marks a coverb to its left.

2 Sounds and Orthography

2.1 Vowels

The short vowels are *i, e, a, o, u* and the front rounded *ü, ö*, marked with umlaut as in German. These seven vowels are sounded much as in German, with two important

Table 28.1 Hungarian Vowel Phonemes

i	ü	u		í	ű	ú	
(ë)	ö	o		é	ő	ó	
e		a					á

exceptions: *e*, which is an open vowel resembling the *a* of English *mat*; and *a*, which is pronounced with a slight rounding of the lips, as in English *chalk*.

Nearly one half of Hungarian speakers distinguish an eighth, short *e*-type vowel like that of English *met*; this sound is written throughout this chapter (and in Hungarian dialectology) as *ë*, for example: *szëg* 'carpenter's nail' (rhymes with English *beg*). For speakers who distinguish this sound, this word differs in pronunciation from the verb *szeg-* 'break' somewhat as English *set* differs from *sat* (in the Hungarian words, however, both vowels are equally short).

The long vowels are indicated in the orthography with an acute accent (*í, é, á, ó, ú*) or, if marked with umlaut when short, with a double acute accent, a diacritic unique to Hungarian (*ű, ő*). Phonetically, these seven long vowels are simply longer versions of their short counterparts, again with two important exceptions: (1) *é* is *not* a long version of *e* (which would be the *ä* of literary German *gäbe*), but rather a long high *e*-sound similar to the first *e* of German *gebe*; and (2) *á* is not a long version of *a*, which would have lip-rounding as in English *caught*, but rather is a long open unrounded *a*-sound as in German *Gabe*. The vowel system of Hungarian is set out in Table 28.1.

The salient assimilatory phenomenon associated with the Hungarian vowels is called vowel harmony. This is a mechanism which, at one time, regulated the quality (front vs back) of vowels within the word, but which today affects only suffixal vowels. Oversimplifying, we may state that stems containing only front vowels select front vowel variants of suffixes (e.g. *szűr-tök* 'you (pl.) strain'), while other stems select back vowel variants (e.g. *szúr-tok* 'you (pl.) pierce'). An important exception is the class of verb roots whose sole vowel is *i* or *í*, most of which take back vowel suffix forms (e.g. *ír-tok* 'you (pl.) write'). Note also that oblique stem vowels of nouns (see Section 3.2) play a decisive role in suffix vowel selection, e.g. *híd-ról* 'off (the) bridge' (and not **híd-ről*: this noun has an oblique stem *hida-* with back vowel *a*).

Vowel harmony also affects the roundedness of vowels in certain suffixes. For example, the second person plural suffix (*-tök/-tok* above) is *-tëk* after unrounded front vowels: *ér-tëk* 'you (pl.) arrive'.

Another prevalent vowel alternation is that of the short mid vowels (*o, ö, ë*) with zero. This alternation is evident in allomorphy such as that of the accusative suffix, which is *-ot/-öt/-ët* (according to vowel harmony, cf. above) after labials, velars, apical stops and affricates and consonant-final oblique stems, but *-t* after vowels and apical continuants (*r, l, ly/j, n, ny, sz, s, z, zs*). Sample accusative forms:

ostrom-ot	'siege'
hercëg-ët	'duke'
ökr-öt	'ox' (citation form *ökör*)
korbács-ot	'scourge'
lakat-ot	'(pad)lock'
ládá-t	'crate'
hajó-t	'ship'

jege-t	'ice' (citation form *jég*)
mája-t	'liver' (citation form *máj*)
lakáj-t	'lackey'
gúny-t	'mockery'

2.2 Consonants

The consonant system and its regular orthographic representations are given in Table 28.2.

In modern Hungarian, *j* and *ly* (originally a palatal lateral) are pronounced alike. Noteworthy are the oppositions palatal vs non-palatal among the oral and nasal stops (t vs t́, d vs d́, n vs ń) and sibilant vs shibilant among the apical fricatives and affricates (s vs š, z vs ž, c vs č, ӡ vs ӡ̌). From the historical point of view, the development of the opposition of voice (p vs b, f vs v, etc.) is particularly striking (within Uralic, it is developed fully only in the rather distantly related Permic languages – see Chapter 27).

The most conspicuous assimilatory phenomena affecting the consonants centre on the above-outlined three oppositions. Thus: (1) unpalatalised /t/ followed by palatal /ń/ yields the palatal sequence /t́ń/ e.g. *cipő-t nyer* /cipőt́ńer/ 'wins (a pair of) shoes'; (2) sibilant /z/ followed by shibilant /ž/ yields the shibilant sequence /žž/, e.g. *tíz zsaru* /tī žžaru/ 'ten cops'; (3) distinctively voiced /z/ followed by distinctively voiceless /s/ yields the voiceless sequence /ss/, e.g. *tíz szarka* /tīssarka/ 'ten magpies'.

Other assimilatory phenomena include (a) combinations of the above three types; thus (1 + 3) /t/ + /d́/ yields /d́d́/ e.g. *cipő-t gyárt* /cipőd́d́árt/ 'manufactures shoes', (2 + 3) /z/+/š/ yields /šš/, e.g. *tíz saru* /tīššaru/ 'ten (pairs of) sandals'; and (b) adaffrication, e. g. /t/+/š/ yields /čč/, e.g. *rét=ség* /réččég/ 'meadow + (collective/abstract suffix)' = 'meadowlands'.

Table 28.2 Hungarian Consonantism

Phonemes					Orthography			
		r					r	
	l	j				l	j, ly	
m	n	ń			m	n	ny	
p	t	t́	k		p	t	ty	k
b	d	d́	g		b	d	gy	g
f	s	š	h		f	sz	s	h
v	z	ž			v	z	zs	
	c	č				c	cs	
	ӡ	ӡ̌				dz	dzs	

3 Inflection

3.1 Conjugation

Every Hungarian conjugated verb form may be analysed as consisting of three parts: (1) a stem, followed by (2) a tense/mood suffix, followed by (3) a person-and-number suffix. The four forms of the verb *mën-* 'go' listed below, all with second person plural subject, illustrate the four tenses/moods occurring in the present-day language:

present	mën-∅-tëk	'you (pl.) go'
past	mën-te-tëk	'you (pl.) went'
conditional	mën-né-tëk	'you (pl.) would go'
subjunctive	mën-je-tëk	'you (pl.) should go; go!'

The suffix of the present tense is zero (-∅-). The suffixes of the past, conditional and subjunctive are subject to considerable formal variation, conditioned by the phonological and grammatical make-up of the morphemes which flank them. Compare the various shapes of the subjunctive suffix (*-ja-*, *-je-*, *-já-*, *-j-*, *-zé-*, *-s-*, *-∅-*) in the following forms (the list is not exhaustive):

vár-ja-tok	'you (pl.) should wait'
mér-je-tëk	'you (pl.) should measure'
vár-já-l	'you (sg.) should wait'
vár-j-on	'(s)he/it should wait'
néz-zé-l	'you (sg.) should watch'
mos-s-on	'(s)he/it should wash'
mos-∅-d	'you (sg.) should wash if'

The person suffixes present a complex and intriguing picture. Each person suffix refers not only to the person and number of the subject (as, for example, in Latin, Russian or Finnish), but also to the person – but not the number – of the object. Certain suffixes are explicit and unambiguous with regard to the person of the object; for example, the first person singular suffix $-l^e_ak$ refers explicitly, and exclusively, to a second person object: *lát-lak* 'I see you' (more precisely, *lát-∅-lak* 'see-present-I/you'). On the other hand, certain other suffixes are ambiguous with regard to object person and indeed need not refer to any object whatsoever. For example, the form *lát-∅-nak*, built with the third person plural suffix $-n^e_ak$ may be translated as 'they see me', 'they see you', 'they see us', or simply 'they (can) see (i.e. are not blind)'. The form *lát-∅-nak* is explicit with regard to object person only in a negative sense: the object cannot be a specific third person object known from the context; that is, this form cannot mean 'they see him/her/it/them'.

One way to think about object-person marking in Hungarian is to arrange the persons (first, second, and third) on a concentric model with first person (the speaker) at the centre (Figure 28.1). A form such as *lát-∅-lak* 'I see you' may then be plotted on the model as an arrow which starts at the centre (subject = first person) and points outward (object = second person); see arrow *a* in Figure 28.1. All forms having such centrifugal orientation on the model are unambiguous with regard to object person. It follows, therefore, that there is a separate form meaning 'I see him/her/it/them', namely *lát-∅-om*, symbolised by arrow *b* in Figure 28.1.

Similarly, the form *lát-∅-ja* '(s)he/it sees him/her/it/them' is also unambiguous with regard to object person, since the object is invariably third person. Such a form is also centrifugal in orientation, since there is an unlimited supply of potential third person subjects. The arrow representing this form points outward into the realm of other third person objects, schematically *3a* in Figure 28.2. Conversely, suffixes which are ambiguous with regard to object person show only inward-pointing arrows on the concentric model and may therefore be termed centripetal. For example, the form *lát-∅-nak* cited above may refer to a first or a second person object (arrows *a* and *b* in Figure 28.3) or to no object at all (point *c* in Figure 28.3).

487

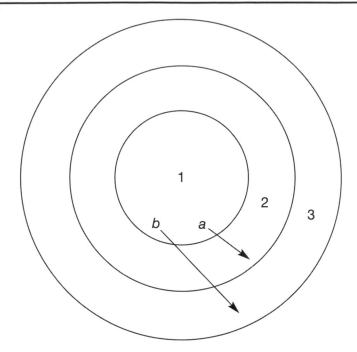

Figure 28.1

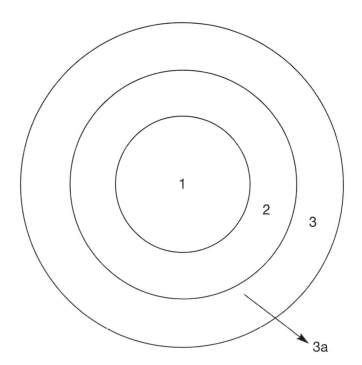

Figure 28.2

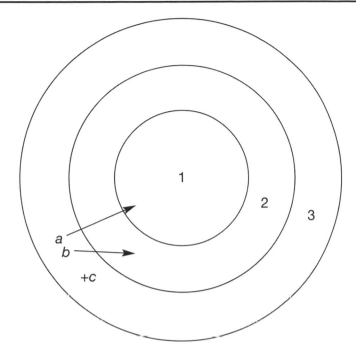

Figure 28.3

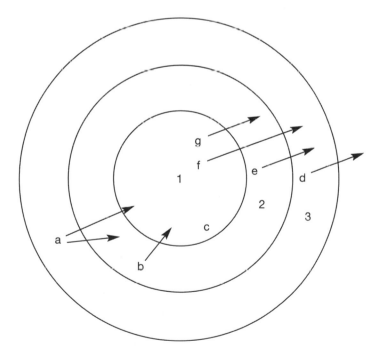

Figure 28.4

The seven singular forms of the present tense of the verb *lát-* 'see' may therefore be presented synoptically as in Figure 28.4. These forms (*a* to *g* in Figure 28.4) are:

	Centripetal		Centrifugal
(a)	*lát-∅-∅*	(d)	*lát-∅-ja*
(b)	*lát-∅-sz*	(e)	*lát-∅-od*
(c)	*lát-∅-ok*	(f)	*lát-∅-om*
		(g)	*lát-∅-lak*

All Hungarian verb stems end in a consonant or a consonant cluster. Alternations characteristic of verb stems are (1) syncope, which deletes a short mid vowel to the left of a stem-final *z*, *l*, *g* or *r*, yielding stem alternates such as *rögtönöz-/rögtönz-* 'improvise', *hízelëg-/hízelg-* 'flatter'; and (2) *v*-stem alternations, in which a stem-final *v* is either deleted or assimilates to a following consonant. Stems exhibiting the latter type of alternation are characterised by other peculiarities as well, such as stem extension (with = *sz* or = V*d*) or stem vowel alternations (*o ö ë* with *ó ő é*), or both.

Below, three verb stem types are contrasted. They are represented by (a) *ver-* 'beat', a non-alternating stem, (b) *pëdër-/pëdr-* 'twirl', a syncopating stem and (c) *tëv-* 'do, make, put', a *v*-stem.

	a	*b*	*c*
1	ver=és	pëdr=és	tëv=és
2	ver-∅-tëk	{ pëdr-∅-ëtëk / pëdër-∅-tëk }	të=sz-∅-tëk
3	ver-né-tëk	{ pëdr-ené-tëk / pëdër-né-tëk }	tën-né-tëk
4	ver-je-tëk	pëdër-je-tëk	tëgye-tëk
5	ver-j-∅	pëdër-j-∅	tégy-∅

Form 1 is a nominal derivate: 'beating', 'twirling', 'doing'. Forms 2, 3 and 4 are present, conditional and subjunctive, respectively, second person plural; form 5 is the imperative (singular). Note the parallel forms (b2, b3). In forms c4 and c5, segmentation of the stem from the mood suffix is impossible at the phonemic level.

3.2 Noun inflection

Every Hungarian noun may be analysed as a stem followed by three inflectional slots, i.e. positions in which inflectional suffixes may occur. The first slot indicates number (singular vs plural), the second slot indicates person (possessor) and the third slot indicates case (direct object, indirect object and some fifteen others). Thus the form *hajóimon* 'on my ships' may be seen as consisting of the sequence *hajó-i-m-on* 'ship-s-my-on'.

Any or all of these three slots may be occupied by a zero suffix. According to its position in the chain of inflectional suffixes appended to the noun stem, this zero suffix denotes either singular number (first position), absence of possessor (second position) or nominative case (third position). Thus we have: *hajó-∅-m-on* 'ship-∅-my-on'='on my ship', *hajó-k-∅-on* 'ship-s-∅-on'='on ships', *hajó-i-m-∅* 'ship-s-my-∅'='my ships'. Notice that the plural suffix is *-i-* when second position is occupied by a person/possessive suffix but *-k-* when second position is occupied by zero (i.e. no possessor).

Table 28.3 Locative Cases

		Stationary		Moving			
				Approach		Depart	
Interior		1	-b^e_an	2	-b^e_a	3	-b^ő_ol
	Surface	4	-n	5	-r^e_a	6	-r^ő_ol
Exterior	Proximity	7	-n$^é_á$	8	-h^ö_oz	9	-t^ő_ol
	Terminus			10	-ig		

The case suffixes may be classified into two basic groups, local and non-local. The local cases form a neat system defined by concrete spatial and kinetic oppositions such as interior vs exterior, stationary vs moving, etc., shown schematically in Table 28.3.

A few concrete examples will illustrate the meanings of these cases. Within the category 'moving/approaching' (the middle column in Table 28.3) four degrees of intimacy are distinguished: suffix 2 (illative) indicates movement into an interior, e.g. *fal-ba* 'into (the) wall'; suffix 5 (sublative) indicates movement onto a surface, e.g. *fal-ra* 'onto (the) wall'; suffix 8 (allative) indicates movement into an immediate proximity, e.g. *fal hoz* '(moving) over to the space immediately next to (the) wall'; and suffix 10 (terminative) indicates movement as far as, but no farther than, a point in space, e.g. *fal-ig* 'as far as (the) wall but no farther'.

The non-local cases normally express primary syntactic or adverbial functions, e.g. subject, direct and indirect object, possessor or instrument. The traditional names of these cases can be quite misleading; the so-called dative (-n^e_ak) for example, may mark not only the indirect object, but also the possessor or a predicate construed with an infinitive. Note the dative form of the noun *katona* 'soldier' in the sentences:

(1) Odaadta a katonának. 'He gave it *to the soldier.*'
(2) A katonának nehéz az élete. *'A soldier's* life is difficult.'
(3) Katonának lenni nehéz. 'To be *a soldier* is difficult.'

The other non-local cases are: nominative (-$\emptyset$); accusative (-*t*); essive (-^ü_ul e.g. *cél-ul* '(considered) as a goal'); causal/final (-*ért*, indicating the efficient or final cause, e.g. *hazá-ért* '(sacrificed his life) for (the) fatherland'); instrumental (-v^e_al e.g. *olló-val* 'with (a pair of) scissors'); and translative (-v$^é_á$, indicating transformation into another state, e.g. *só-vá* '(turned) into salt'). The *v*-initial in the last two suffixes assimilates to a preceding consonant, e.g. *olló-m-mal* '(pair of) scissor(s)-my-with'='with my scissors', *kenyér-ré* '(turned) into bread'.

In contrast to verb stems, noun stems may end in either a consonant or a vowel. The vowel may be any save *o, ö, ë* or *á*; the consonant may be any save *dz*, but *dzs, zs, ty, ʃ* and *h* are rare.

All stems with final *a* or *e* exhibit lengthening of this vowel before most suffixes, whether declensional or derivational. Examples: *alma/körte* 'apple'/'pear', *almá-m/körté-m* 'my apple'/'my pear', *almá=s/körté=s* 'containing apples'/'containing pears'. This is by far the largest class of vowel-final noun stems. It contains more than 1,200 underived stems (like *alma* and *körte* above) and thousands of derivates such as *jár=da* 'sidewalk' (from the verb *jár-* 'be in motion, walk'), *cukor=ka* 'bonbon' (from *cukor* 'sugar'), *pëng=e* 'blade' (from the verb *pëng-* 'ring, clang').

There is also a closed set of nearly 500 stems which exhibit a special stem form only when followed by certain suffixes. This special stem form, termed here for convenience the 'oblique stem', differs from the nominative singular (citation form) by the presence of a stem-final *a* or *e*, the absence of a stem-penultimate *o*, *ö* or *ë* or both. For example: from their nominative singular forms, it would appear that the nouns *dal* 'song' and *fal* 'wall' are parallel in shape and, presumably, inflectional pattern. This is not so, however, because *fal*, unlike *dal*, has an oblique stem with final *a*, namely *fala-*; compare the accusative forms *dal-t*, *fala-t*. Similarly, *nyomor* 'misery' and *gyomor* 'stomach' display different inflectional patterns because the latter noun has an oblique stem which lacks the penultimate *o*, namely *gyomr-*; compare the accusative forms *nyomor-t*, *gyomr-ot*. Finally, some noun stems (about 115) exhibit both types of alternation simultaneously, e.g. *sátor* 'tent', in the oblique stem of which we find at once the absence of the penultimate *o* and the presence of final *a*; contrast *sátra-m* 'my tent' with *mámor-om* 'my rapture'.

Nouns whose oblique stems have final *a* or *e* may be subclassified according to additional alternations. For example, it was noted above that the oblique stem of the noun *fal* 'wall' differs from its nominative singular only by virtue of a stem-final *a*; this is not the case with the noun *falu* 'village', whose oblique stem has not only a final *a* but also *v* instead of *u*, namely *falva-*, as in the form *falva-k* 'villages'. Contrast a stem such as *kapu* 'gate', which has no oblique stem and therefore forms its plural simply as *kapu-k* 'gates'. Another characteristic subtype of oblique-stem alternation involves the long vowels *á* and *é*, which when penultimate in the oblique stem occur as short *a* and *e*, e.g. *madár* 'bird', oblique stem *madara-*, thus: *madara-k* 'birds'.

Broadly speaking, the oblique stem of a noun occurs only to the left of derivational suffixes and older declensional suffixes. This distribution in the present-day language reflects the historical fact that most nouns which now exhibit oblique stems date from at least Ugric and often Finno-Ugric or even Uralic times. An important exception to this distribution is the derivational suffix=*i*, which normally requires the nominative singular form of the stem, e.g. *madár=i* 'avian', *fal=i* 'wall-' as in *fal=i óra* 'wall-clock'.

4 Derivation

Both the verb and the nominal are capable of extensive derivation. Examples of nominal derivation: *ház* (oblique stem *háza-*) 'house'; *ház=i* 'domestic'; *háza=s* 'married'; *ház=i=as* 'homely'; *háza=tlan* 'houseless', especially in the construction *háza=tlan csiga* 'houseless snail'='slug'; *háza=cska* 'cottage'; *ház=beli* 'tenant'. Examples of verbal derivation: *fog-* 'seize, grasp'; *fog=ad-* 'accept'; *fog=an-* 'become pregnant, conceive'; *fog=dos-* 'handle, paw at'; *fog=lal-* 'occupy'; *fog=lal=koz-* 'occupy oneself'.

Combined verbal and nominal derivatives are extremely common, e.g. *öle=l=és* 'embrace (noun)', cf. *öle=l-* 'embrace (verb)' and *öl/öle-* 'lap, space between shoulders and knees'; *ad=ag=ol-* 'measure out', cf. *ad=ag* 'portion' and *ad-* 'give'.

Verbal derivation is especially enriched by the coverbs, which are a special class of adverb-like forms. Like preverbs in Slavonic languages, Hungarian coverbs are connected with aspect; like verbal prefixes in German, they are not always to be found in preverbal position (see Section 6). The change in meaning effected by the addition of a coverb may be obvious (e.g. *jön* 'comes': *vissza==jön* 'comes back') or less than obvious (e.g. *meg==jön* 'comes (back) to one's proper place (as was hoped/expected)').

Often, the role played by a coverb (or by its absence) is entirely outside the limits of the sentence in which it occurs/is lacking; for example, in the sentence pair

(1) Mikor vetted meg   azt a cipőt?
(2) Mikor vetted ∅   azt a cipőt?

both translatable as 'when did you buy those shoes?', sentence (1) is a sincere request for information, while sentence (2) may veil criticism of the shoes' appearance.

5 Lexicon, History

The existence of Hungarian independent of its closest congeners Mansi and Khanty is reckoned to be some 2,500 to 3,000 years old. Evidence of early forms of Hungarian may be found in documents only for the last millennium of this period. The earliest such documents are Arab, Persian and Byzantine political and geographical tracts in which Hungarian personal and tribal names are cited in isolation. While extremely useful as historic and linguistic sources, such documents contain no connected passages of Hungarian. The oldest source to contain a running text in Hungarian is the *Halotti Beszéd* (Funeral Oration), c. 1200, a free – and elegant – translation of a Latin text contained in the same codex.

The first 1,500 to 2,000 years of the Hungarian language can be studied only indirectly, through the historiography of neighbouring peoples and with the aid of the tools of archaeology, philology and linguistics. For example, the frequent denomination of the Hungarians as 'Turks' in various early sources (e.g. *toúrkoi* in the mid-tenth century *De Administrando Imperio* of Constantinos Porphyrogennetos) suggests that from the seventh to the ninth centuries at least a part of the Hungarians were under Turkic dominance.

It is the evidence of loanwords, however, which paints the most vivid picture of this long period in Hungarian chronology and culture. The trajectory of migration, first southward, then westward, from the Urals to the Carpathian basin, can be traced in reverse by unpeeling, one by one, the layers of foreign elements in the Hungarian lexicon.

Immediately beneath the rich top layer of pan-Europeanisms such as *atléta* 'athlete', *pësszimista* 'pessimist' are hundreds of loans originating in or mediated through German. Thus, from the eighteenth and nineteenth centuries: *copf* 'braid; pigtail', *púdër* '(cosmetic) powder', *fasírt* 'ground meat' (*falschiert(es Fleisch)*), *vigéc* 'commercial traveller (slang)' (*wie geht's*), *priccs* 'cot'; from the sixteenth and seventeenth centuries: *lakáj* 'lackey', *prés* 'wine-press', *tucat* 'dozen', *pisztoly* 'pistol'. Older still (twelfth to fifteenth centuries) are such loans as *hercëg* 'duke', *kastély* 'castle', *tánc* 'dance', *céh* 'guild', *polgár* 'Bürger', *ostrom* 'siege, attack' (*Sturm*).

Of loanwords from the Romance languages, the most recent (and thinnest) layer is borrowed from Rumanian. Although the oldest known Rumanian loanword in Hungarian, *ficsúr* 'dandy, fop', dates from the fourteenth century, most are from the sixteenth to the eighteenth centuries: *cimbora* 'pal, crony', *poronty* 'brat', *málé* 'polenta, corn-cake', *tokány* 'a kind of ragoût', *cujka* 'a kind of fruit brandy'.

The richest stock of Romance vocabulary is from Italian. Hungarian–Italian contacts grew in breadth and intensity from military then trade contacts with Venice in thirteenth-century Dalmatia through the Angevin dynasty (1308–86), culminating in the decidedly Tuscan-oriented rule of Mathias I, 'Corvinus' (ruled 1458–90). Examples:

dús 'luxurious' (from Venetian *dóse* 'doge', probably by way of Croatian), *paszomány* 'braiding, piping', *piac* 'market-place', *lándzsa* 'lance', *pálya* 'course, track'.

There is also a small set of loanwords from Old French and Provençal dating from the twelfth and thirteenth centuries (later French influence, in the eighteenth and nineteenth centuries, was filtered through Vienna and therefore through German; cf. *púdër* above). Although the earliest French contacts were monastic (Benedictines, Cistercians, Premonstratensians), the earliest Old French loanwords are secular in meaning, e.g. *lakat* '(pad)lock' (*loquet*), *mécs* 'wick' (*mèche*), *kilincs* 'latch' (*clinche*).

Religious vocabulary, not surprisingly, is overwhelmingly Latin in origin, e.g. *templom* 'house of worship', *mise* 'mass', *ostya* 'Host', *angyal* 'angel'. The list extends even to terms exclusively Protestant in implementation, e.g. *ëklézsia* 'congregation', *kollégium* 'dormitory' (originally 'seminary'). Although Latin loanwords belong primarily to the area of Christian terminology, numerous other semantic areas may also be cited, e.g. schooling (*tinta* 'ink', *tábla* 'blackboard', *lénia* 'ruler'), medicine and horticulture (*kúra* 'course of treatment', *petrezselyëm* 'parsley') or jurisprudence (*juss* 'patrimony' from Latin *ius*). Even a few Latin adverbs survive in present-day colloquial Hungarian: *persze* 'of course' (*per sē*), *plánë* 'especially' (*plānē* 'smoothly; really'); note also *ipse* 'fellow, chap' (*ipse* 'he himself'). The time-frame for Latin influence on the Hungarian lexicon is extremely broad: Latin was (at least nominally) the official language of the Kingdom of Hungary from its inception (1001) until the mid-nineteenth century. On the other hand, direct ties to the Christian East were tenuous and short-lived, a fact reflected in the very small number of words borrowed directly from the Byzantine Greek: *paplan* 'quilt', *iszák* 'knapsack', *katona* 'soldier' and perhaps a few others.

The two largest and most important sets of loanwords are those from Slavonic and Turkic languages. It is not surprising, given the geographical location of Hungary, that loans from the Slavonic languages are both numerous (c. 500) and central to basic vocabulary. Examples drawn only from the Hungarian word stock beginning with *p*- are *pad* 'bench', *palack* 'bottle', *pálinka* 'distilled spirits', *pap* 'clergyman', *pëcsënye* 'roast', *patak* 'brook', *pëlënka* 'diaper', *poloska* 'bedbug', *pók* 'spider', *puszta* 'bare, deserted'. Slavonic languages served as mediators for terminology of both Byzantine (-Christian) and Roman Christian culture. Examples of the former: *terëm* '(large public) room', *pitvar* 'porch', *palota* 'palace', *kërëszt* 'cross'; of the latter: *malaszt* 'grace', *apáca* 'nun'. The intensity and variety of contact with different forms of Slavonic may be inferred from doublets internal to Hungarian such as *vacsora* 'evening meal', *vëcsërnye* 'Vespers'; *rozsda* 'rust', *ragya* 'mildew; rust (on plant)'; *mëgye* 'county', *mezsgye* 'boundary-mark between ploughed fields'; *család* 'family', *cseléd* 'servant'.

The Turkic component of the Hungarian lexicon is a unique amalgam of elements borrowed from several different Turkic peoples over a span of some 1,500 years. The most recent layer dates from the Ottoman (Osmanli) occupation (sixteenth and seventeenth centuries); this layer is quite thin (about 30 words), e.g. *zseb* 'pocket', *findzsa* 'demi-tasse', *korbács* 'scourge', *kávé* 'coffee'. An earlier layer, also quite thin, of Turkic loanwords dates from the two or three centuries following the arrival of the Hungarians in Europe (tenth to thirteenth centuries). The words of this layer are borrowed from the languages of the Pechenegs and the Cumans, e.g. *csősz* 'fieldguard', *koboz* 'a type of lute', *orosz* 'Russian'.

By far the most numerous and culturally significant, however, are the loanwords taken from Turkic languages during the Hungarian migration westward across southern Russia. Some 300 such loanwords entered during this period (roughly fifth to ninth centuries). A small sampling reveals the cultural breadth and depth of this Old Turkic component of the Hungarian lexicon: *dél/dele-* 'south, noon', *idő* 'time', *szél/szele-* 'wind', *szám* 'number', *ok* 'cause', *tanú* 'witness', *ír-* 'write', *bocsát-* 'forgive', *sátor/sátra-* 'tent', *sëprő* 'broom', *szék* 'chair', *gyümölcs* 'fruit', *szőlő* 'grape', *bor* 'wine', *bika* 'bull', *ökör/ökr-* 'ox', *borjú/borja-* 'calf', *ünő* 'heifer', *disznó* 'pig', *gödény* 'pelican', *kar* 'arm', *boka* 'ankle', *gyomor/gyomr-* 'stomach', *köldök* 'navel', *szakáll/szakálla-* 'beard', *szeplő* 'freckle'.

Older still are three thin layers of Iranian loanwords acquired at the earliest stages of the Hungarian migration. To the most recent of these three layers belong *vám* 'tithe, toll, customs-station' and *vásár* 'bazaar' from Persian; older are *híd/hida-* 'bridge' and *asszony* 'woman (as opposed to girl)', from Alanic (= Old Ossete); and oldest are *tehén/tehene-* 'cow', *tej/teje-* 'milk', *nemez* 'felt', and perhaps *vászon/vászna-* 'linen', from an Iranian language which cannot be precisely identified.

But the oldest layers of the Hungarian vocabulary are of course not borrowed at all; rather, they are descended from the common Ugric, Finno-Ugric or Uralic lexical stock. To these layers belong hundreds of basic vocabulary items from such semantic domains as kinship (*fiú/fia-* 'son', *mëny/mënye-* 'daughter-in-law', *vő/veje-* 'son-in-law', *öcs/öccs(é)-* 'younger brother'); parts of the body (*fej/feje-* 'head', *szëm* 'eye', *nyelv/nyelve-* 'tongue', *ín/ina-* 'tendon', *epe* 'gall', *máj/mája-* 'liver'); natural phenomena (*ég/ege-* 'sky', *hajnal* 'dawn', *tél/tele-* 'winter', *jég/jege-* 'ice', *tó/tava-* 'lake'); animals, hunting and fishing (*fogoly/fogly-* 'partridge', *fajd* 'grouse', *íj/íja-* 'bow', *nyíl/nyila-* 'arrow', *hal/hala-* 'fish', *háló* 'net'); and primary functions and activities expressed by monomorphemic verbs (*lësz/lëv-* 'become', *él-* 'live', *hal-* 'die', *öl-* 'kill', *mëgy/mën-* 'go', *jön/jöv-* 'come', *ëszik/ëv-* 'eat', *iszik/iv-* 'drink').

The statistically preponderant component of the Hungarian lexicon is neither borrowed nor inherited. These words are constructions built from mostly native elements during the independent existence of Hungarian; they range in age and type from unconscious and doubtless quite old onomatopoeic and affective vocabulary (e.g. *rëcs=ëg* 'creak, squeak', *krák=og* 'caw', *mëk=ëg* 'bleat', *hömpöly=ög* 'billow, surge') to conscious creations which often can be attributed to a particular language reformer who either sired or fostered them, for example *vissz + hang* 'back + sound' = 'echo' (Dávid Baróti Szabó, 1739–1819), *könny + elmű* 'light + minded' = 'heedless' (Ferenc Kazinczy, 1759–1831). Thousands of such new terms survived but briefly, e.g. *ibl=any* 'violet + (suffix)' = 'iodine' (Pál Bugát, 1793–1845); in this and countless similar instances, the Hungarian term which prevailed is the Europeanism (*jód* 'iodine').

The creation of new vocabulary of this sort, termed language renewal (*nyelvújítás*), was practised by even its harshest critics, e.g. Ferenc Verseghy (1757–1822) who, on the analogy of verb/noun pairs such as *tag = ol-/tag* 'dismember/member', introduced such new coinages as *gúny* 'mockery', *pazar* 'spendthrift', by subtracting the final *ol*-sequence from the verbs *gúnyol* 'mock' and *pazarol* 'squander'.

6 Syntax

In the noun phrase, demonstratives alone agree in number and case with their head, e.g. *ez-ek-ben a nagy görög ládá-k-ban* 'in these large Greek crates', where *nagy* 'large' and *görög* 'Greek' lack the plural and inessive suffixes *-(ë)k* and *-b^e_an*. Cumulative plural subjects are usually construed with a singular predicate, especially if they are members of a coherent semantic set, e.g. *a só mëg a bors itt van a ládá-ban* 'the salt and pepper are (lit. is) here in the crate'.

The elements of a Hungarian sentence are ordered according to the textually and contextually determined factors of topic (what is assumed) and focus (the central component of the comment about the topic). Focus position is immediately to the left of the finite verb; topic position is normally sentence-initial. Thus in the sentence *a pék elfutott* 'the baker ran away', the baker (*a pék*) is the topic and 'away' *(el)* is the focus of the comment about him. By relocating the coverb *el*, the baker can be made into the focus: *a pék futott el* 'it is the baker who ran away'. The coverb can also be placed in sentence-initial position and thus be topicalised: *el a pék futott* 'as for (running) away, it is the baker (who did that)'.

The situation is much more complex, however, since certain grammatical and semantic categories are inherently associated with focus, for example negation in the examples *a pék nem futott el* 'the baker did not run away', *nem a pék futott el* 'it is not the baker who ran away', *el nem a pék futott* 'as for (running) away, it is not the baker (who did that)'. Different stress patterns produce different types of contrastive focus, e.g. *a pék nem 'elfutott, hanem 'befutott* 'the baker didn't run *away*, he ran *in*', or *a pék nem el'futott, hanem el'sétált* 'the baker didn't *run* away, he *sauntered* away'. For many speakers, stress also plays a role in the rendering of aspect. Thus if both verb and coverb receive stress in the sequence *a pék futott el* cited above, the meaning is something like 'the baker was (in the act of) running away'.

Bibliography

Three general works on Hungarian can be recommended: Simonyi (1907) is still the best introduction, encyclopaedic and circumstantial; Sauvageot (1971) is an insightful overview, primarily historical; Benkő and Imre (1972) is a general work, whose best chapters are those by Hajdú and Imre. The standard grammar in Hungarian is the three-volume Kiefer (1992–2000). Lotz (1939) is an unsurpassed reference grammar in English, to which can now be added Kenesei et al. (1998) in the Routledge Descriptive Grammars series and the briefer statement in Rounds (2001). Abondolo (1988) provides an account of Hungarian inflectional morphology, while Kiss (2002) is a generatively oriented but broadly accessible account of syntax. Given the importance of derivation in Hungarian, the reverse-alphabetised dictionary by Papp (1969) is indispensable.

References

Abondolo, D. 1988. *Hungarian Inflectional Morphology* (Akadémiai Kiadó, Budapest)

Benkő, L. and Imre, S. (eds) 1972. *The Hungarian Language* (Mouton, The Hague and Paris)

Kenesei, I., Vago, R.M. and Fenyvesi, A. 1998. *Hungarian* (Routledge, London)

Kiefer, F. (ed.) 1992–2000. *Strukturális magyar nyelvtan*, 3 vols (Akadémiai Kiadó, Budapest)

Kiss, K. 2002. *The Syntax of Hungarian* (Cambridge University Press, Cambridge)

Lotz, J. 1939. *Das ungarische Sprachsystem* (Ungarisches Institut, Stockholm)

Papp, F. 1969. *A magyar nyelv szóvégmutató szótára/Reverse-Alphabetized Dictionary of the Hungarian Language* (Akadémiai Kiadó, Budapest)

Rounds, C. 2001. *Hungarian: An Essential Grammar* (Routledge, London)

Sauvageot, A. 1971. *L'Edification de la langue hongroise* (Klincksieck, Paris)

Simonyi, S. 1907. *Die ungarische Sprache* (Karl J. Trübner, Strassburg)

29

Finnish

Michael Branch

1 Introduction

Finnish (native name *suomi*) is one of a group of closely related and to some extent mutually intelligible languages, known collectively as Baltic-Finnic. They are spoken mainly in the Republic of Finland, Republic of Karelia (Russian Federation), Estonia, and adjacent areas of Russia and Latvia. According to the 1979 Soviet census figures the number of speakers of Karelian was 138,400; Vepsian, 8,100; Ingrian, 700. In 2005 about two-thirds of the population of Estonia (1,345,000) spoke Estonian as their first language. Of historical interest, but almost extinct, are Votic and Livonian. Of the present-day population of Finland (5,274,820), the majority speak Finnish as their first language. An estimated 263,700 Finnish citizens speak Finland-Swedish as their first language, and in 2005 approximately 8,000 spoke Saami (formerly Lapp). Most speakers of Finland-Swedish and the Saami dialects of Finland are competent in Finnish. Finnish and Estonian are also spoken by migrants and their descendants in Sweden, Norway, northwest Russia and North America.

The relationship of Finnish to the other major Finno-Ugric language, Hungarian, is described elsewhere in this book (see pages 477–480). Attempts to reconstruct anything more than a relative chronology of the two languages' separate development from ancient Finno-Ugric origins are inevitably speculative, and indeed there remain many uncertainties even about the historical development of the Baltic-Finnic languages. Until recently, scholars had assumed that speakers of a language of Finno-Ugric origin, 'Pre-Finnic', had migrated from regions to the east and southeast, reaching the area of present-day Estonia about 500 BC. There they were thought to have lived for several centuries in close contact first with Ancient Balts and then with groups of East Germanic peoples. According to this theory, about two thousand years ago a group of people speaking 'Proto-Finnic' – a development of 'Pre-Finnic' – was thought to have divided into smaller units which slowly migrated in various directions: south and southeast, north across the Gulf of Finland into Finland proper, and northeast

497

around the Gulf into Ladoga Karelia and thence into eastern Finland or further north and northeast into Olonets and Archangel Karelia. It was further thought that the northern lands into which these groups had migrated were largely empty of population apart from groups of Saami, who had moved north ahead of the Baltic-Finnic new-comers and who spoke a language that derived, probably through borrowing, from 'Pre-Finnic'.

In recent years, comparative multidisciplinary research has led to substantial revision of this theory. Archaeologists have shown that Finland has been continuously inhabited for at least 8,000 years; comparative linguists and ethnographers now believe that speakers of Germanic and Baltic languages have inhabited various parts of the lands now occupied by speakers of the Baltic-Finnic languages for at least the last 3,500 years. Thus the early theory of a clearly stratified hierarchy of language contact and development has given way to one of a mosaic of sporadic contacts over a far longer time and probably of greater influence in shaping the grammar, syntax and lexicon of the Baltic-Finnic languages than had earlier been thought possible.

A number of dialects, from which present-day Finnish took shape, were probably being spoken in southern and western Finland in the early centuries AD. The available evidence indicates an area of small, isolated settlements, inhabited by hunters and fishermen; wandering northwards they began to combine pastoralism with food gathering and then slowly adapted to a primitive agricultural way of life, largely dependent on burn–beat cultivation. In the southern coastal regions contacts were formed with traders coming from the east and Vikings from the west. Although fragments of Christianity began to penetrate from the east during the late dark ages, the inhabitants' religious world-view appears to have been animist, and it was not until the twelfth century, with the Swedish Crusades, that efforts were made to replace this ancient world-view with that of Roman Catholic Christianity. At the same time a centrally based system of government was instituted which demanded faith in the Christian deity, loyalty to a ruler, service to those in authority and the payment of taxes. The confluence in Finland of influences from various directions and their impact on Arctic and sub-Arctic cultures accounts for the present-day east–west distribution of linguistic, anthropological and ethnographical distinctive features along an axis running northwest from the region of Viipuri in the south to Oulu in the north; historically and politically this division was fixed by the Treaty of Schlüsselburg signed between Sweden and Novgorod in 1323. Although there have been various changes in the frontier since then (notably in 1595, 1617, 1721, 1743, 1809 and 1944), none of these has altered in any significant way the east–west linguistic, anthropological and ethnographical division.

Since the late middle ages the dominant political and cultural influences that have shaped – and preserved – Finnish were religion and nationalism. The earliest written record known to survive in a Baltic-Finnic language is a spell written in a Karelian dialect, and dated to the thirteenth century. Although there is sufficient evidence from secular and non-secular sources to show that Finnish was in use as a written language during the late middle ages, when the Church of Rome was still dominant, the earliest surviving specimens of continuous passages in Finnish date from the 1540s with the publication in 1542 of Bishop Mikael Agricola's *Abckiria* ('ABC book'), the first known printed book to appear after the declaration of the Reformation in Finland in 1527. This was followed by various liturgical and biblical works written or translated in a literary language which was codified from dialects spoken in southwest Finland and which was to remain the canonical form of Finnish until the early nineteenth century.

The growth of a national consciousness that began at the end of the eighteenth century awoke among a small but influential number of intellectuals a desire to cultivate a distinctive Finnish national identity rooted in the Finnish language. This ideal gained powerful momentum early in the nineteenth century when Finland became a Grand Duchy in the Russian Empire, and the following generation of nationalists took as their aim the elevation of Finnish to equal standing with Swedish as a language of government, trade, commerce, education and culture. This aim was achieved in 1863 with the issue of the Language Edict. A literary language, codified in the course of the nineteenth century, retained much of the old canon, although its structure and lexicon were revised and standardised to take account of the dialects of Eastern Finland that had acquired prominence through the publication in 1835 and 1849 of Elias Lönnrot's compilation of oral epic poems, *Kalevala*.

Finnish shares with Hungarian a rich vocalism, but unlike Hungarian it has relatively few consonant phonemes. It is an agglutinative language with a complex but consistent regularity in its morphophonology; inflectional suffixes, of which a large number have cognates in most other Finnic-Ugric languages, account for a wide range of grammatical functions, while a large stock of derivational suffixes provides a productive source of word creation. Of particular interest in the structure of Finnish is the case system and the variety of finite and non-finite verbal categories. (In the present description of the characteristic features of Finnish, the typographic conventions used in the chapter on Hungarian have been observed (i.e. suffixes are written to the right of a hyphen (-) if they are inflectional, or to the right of an equals sign (=) if they are derivational).) (See Table 29.1.)

2 Phonology and Orthography

The orthography of standard Finnish is for the most part phonetic. With three exceptions each letter represents a single phoneme; with two exceptions all sounds are marked orthographically. If a letter is written twice, it indicates that quantity is double the length of a single sound.

Table 29.1 Finnish Vowel Phonemes

Monophthongs	i		y		u	ii		yy		uu
	e		ö		o	ee		öö		aa
		ä		a			ää		aa	
Diphthongs	ei		äy		eu					
	äi									
	ui									
	ai				au					
	oi				ou					
	öi		öy							
	yi									
	ie									
			yö		uo					
					iu					

2.1 Vowels

Finnish has eight monophthong phonemes and 16 diphthong phonemes. The short front vowels are *ü* (*y* in orthography), *ö* and *ä*; *i* and *e* are regarded as 'neutral' vowels in respect of vowel harmony; the back vowels are *u*, *o* and *a*. The front vowel *ä* is pronounced as in English *bad*; the other two front vowels are pronounced as in German. The back vowels are pronounced as in English *pull*, *hot* and *father*. The neutral vowels *i* and *e* are as in English *hit* and *pet*. Each of these sounds can be pronounced long, doubling the quantity but not changing the quality.

With the exception of certain recent loanwords, the vowels in a Finnish word are subject to partial assimilation. This phenomenon, known as *vowel harmony*, requires that all the vowels of a word are front or back depending on the category of the vowel in the first syllable of the word. In compound words vowel harmony affects each lexical component separately, e.g. *työaika: työ* 'work' + *aika* 'time'. This assimilatory phenomenon determines suffix–vowel selection in those inflectional and derivational suffixes which allow front/back vowel opposition: e.g. *pöydä-llä* 'on the table' but *tuoli-lla* 'on the chair'. In compound words vowel harmony in suffixes is determined by the vowel category of the final lexical component. Each neutral vowel word has a fixed requirement for front or back suffixal forms determined on historical grounds: e.g. *silmä-llä* 'with an eye' but *silla-lla* 'on the bridge'; *elä-mä-llä-än* 'by his/her life' but *ehdo-i-lla-an* 'on his/her conditions'. On the basis of such oppositions some scholars classify the neutral vowels as each having front and back allophones: the /e/ opposition has a cognate in Estonian front -*e*- and back -*õ*-, while the /i/ variation can be compared with a similar phenomenon in Hungarian (see page 485).

2.2 Consonants

The consonant system has 15 phonemes and 13 letters. Letters preceded by an asterisk (*) occur only in foreign toponyms and commercial brand names or in very recent loans; for many speakers the pronunciation of these sounds will vary between the non-Finnish sound and an assumed Finnish correspondent. A hyphen to the right of a consonant (e.g. h-) indicates that it occurs only in syllable-initial position, to the left (-h) only in syllabic-final positions; hyphens on either side (-d-) indicate that the sound can occur only in a word-medial position. Underlining indicates that the item also occurs as a long sound and in orthography is written twice (Table 29.2).

Table 29.2 Finnish Consonant Phonemes

Phonemes					Orthography				Recent loans		
	r̲					r̲					
	l̲	j				l̲	j				
m̲	n̲	-ŋ-/-ŋŋ-			m̲	n̲	nk/ng				
p̲	t̲	k̲	-ʔ		p̲	t	k̲	Ø	*b	*d-	*g-
	-d-					d					
	s̲	h-	-h			s̲	h	h	*f	*š	
v̲					v(w)						*z
									*ts/*c	*tš	

The pronunciation of the consonant phonemes is close to that of English. The lack of voiced/unvoiced opposition among the stops, of an apical sibilant *s* (Finnish *s* is more palatalised than general European *s*) and of an unvoiced labio-dental *f*, however, results in less marked opposition between the distinctive categories. Thus Finnish *v* is more labialised than in English. The final-position glottal stop /ʔ/ represents a former /k/ that occurred word-finally after /e/ and as a component of suffixes marking the final sound of the short infinitive (e.g. *haluta* 'to want') and certain negative and imperative forms. In spoken Finnish the glottal can be heard if followed by a vowel sound; otherwise it assimilates with a following consonant to form a long sound: e.g. *perhe saapuu* pronounced /perhessaapuu/ 'the family arrives'; *en käytä maitoa* /enkäytämmaitoa/ 'I don't take milk'. Partial assimilation occurs at word juncture where a final dental nasal is followed by a bilabial stop, e.g. *talonpoika* /talompoika/ 'farmer'.

2.3 Quantity and Syllable Structure

Opposition between a long and short sound is an important distinctive feature (e.g. *tapan* 'I kill', but *tapaan* 'I meet'; *tuli palaa* 'the fire burns' but *tuuli palaa* 'the wind returns'). A syllable may have only one vowel sound. The minimum component of a syllable is a vowel (i.e. a short or long monophthong or a diphthong). A syllable ending in a vowel is classified as 'open': e.g. *vai/ke/a* 'difficult', *sa/no/a* 'to say', both of which have three syllables. The second syllable type, classified 'closed', comprises [vowel + consonant] or [consonant + vowel + consonant]: e.g. *Hel/sin/ki/in* 'to Helsinki', which has four syllables. Variation in the 'open' or 'closed' status of a syllable is determined by the addition of inflectional and derivational suffixes and frequently causes a phonological change at the word stem (see Sections 3.1.1 and 3.1.2).

2.4 Stress

The main stress falls on the first syllable of a word, with decreasing secondary stress on the third and fifth syllables; similarly, sentence intonation is generally falling, although there may be a small rise at the beginning of the final word or constituent.

3 Inflection

3.1 The Word Stem

Morphophonemic alternation at the juncture of the word stem is a characteristic feature of Finnish. It is determined by the phonology and environment of derivational and inflectional suffixes and accounts for the 85 declension classes and 45 conjugation classes identified in the definitive dictionary of Finnish, *Nykysuomen sanakirja*. In respect of morphophonemic alternation this classification into nominal and verbal categories is functional, serving the purpose of convenient grammatical description. In effect, the 130 classes listed in the *Nykysuomen sanakirja* represent the narrow realisation of regular phonemic change conditioned by specific morphological and phonemic environments.

The phonemic features underlying this complex set of realisations at the end of the word stem are consonant gradation, total or partial consonant assimilation, vowel mutation, and vowel loss (Holman's terminology). They can operate either singly or in various combinations. The environment in which they operate is determined by stress, which varies according to the syllable in which the stem juncture is located (see Section 2.4), and by the phonology of the set of suffixes added to the word. In distinguishing between various forms of the narrow realisation account must also be taken of the historical development of Finnish and in certain cases of the irregular selection of alternative forms to avoid ambiguity. An example of this is the change, or lack of change, in situations where the sounds /t/+/i/ combine, yielding either -*si*- at a very early period (e.g. *ves-i-llä* 'on the waters', *halus-i* 'wanted') but -*ti*- at a later period (e.g. *tina* 'tin', *vuot-i* 'leaked'). The difference between the noun forms is explained by historical period (i.e. the change *ti* > *si* had ceased to be effective by the time the Germanic *tina- had entered Finnish), but it is the need to avoid homonymic clash that accounts for the variation in the verbal forms (*vuosi would conflict with the noun *vuosi* 'year').

Suffixes are added to an oblique stem. Every Finnish word has an oblique stem ending in a vowel. In many words this is the only stem and for nominals it is often identical with the nominative case which is also the dictionary referent (e.g. *yö* 'night', *talo* 'house', *asema* 'station', *ruskea* 'brown'). For those verbs which have only one oblique stem the stem is identified by removing the infinitive marker from the dictionary referent, i.e. the short 1st infinitive (e.g. *syödä* → *syö*- 'eat', *sanoa* → *sano*- 'say', *lähteä* → *lähte*- 'depart'). In certain nominals, however, the vowel of the oblique stem differs from that of the nominative: e.g. *järve*- 'lake' but nominative *järvi*, *suure*- 'large' but nominative *suuri*. In such cases the stem vowel should be considered primary and the vowel of the nominative stem as the result of sound change in final, unmarked positions. As with the /t/+/i/ feature discussed above, such change is historically determined, as can be seen from comparison of *risti* 'cross', which has the oblique stem *risti*- (a Slavonic loan adapted to the prevailing phonological system of early Finnish by simplification of the initial consonant cluster through consonant loss and of the final cluster through the addition of -*i*). Since *risti* entered Finnish at a time when the -*e* > -*i* change in final unmarked position was no longer operative on new items, the nominative form also functions as the oblique stem.

Several classes of Finnish nominals have, in addition to an oblique stem ending in a vowel, a second oblique stem that ends in a consonant; the stem to which suffixes are added is determined by the morphophonemic environment. Nominals of this type fall into two main categories: those in which the nominative ends in a vowel and those in which it ends in a consonant; in each sub-category the stem to be used is environmentally determined. Examples of the first category are: *tuli* 'fire', vowel stem *tule*- (e.g. genitive *tule-n*), consonant stem *tul*- (e.g. partitive *tul-ta*); *pieni* 'small', (*piene*-, gen. *piene-n*, partitive *pien-tä*); *lumi* 'snow', vowel stem *lume*- (e.g. gen. *lume-n*), consonant stem *lun*- (e.g. partitive *lun-ta*). Examples of consonant-ending nominatives are *sydän* 'heart', vowel stem *sydäme*- (e.g. gen. *sydäme-n*), consonant-stem *sydän*- (partitive *sydän-tä*); *punainen* 'red', vowel stem *punaise*-, consonant *stem punais*- (e.g. *punaise-n*, *punais-ta*).

Reference has already been made to verbs that have only one oblique stem. Similarly, however, there are categories of verbs which also have vowel and consonant stems, whose selection is determined by comparable morphophonemic environmental features. An example of the verb type with a single oblique stem is *puhua* 'to speak' (e.g. *puhu-n* 'I speak', *puhu-kaamme!* 'let us speak!'). Sub-categories of the two-stem type are illustrated by *ansaita* 'to earn' and *levätä* 'to rest': vowel stems *ansaitse*- (e.g. *ansaitse-n* 'I earn'), *lepää*- (e.g. *lepää-t* 'you. (sg.) rest'); consonant stems *ansait*- (e.g. *ansait-kaa!* '(you pl.) earn!'), *levät*- (e.g. *levät-kööt!* 'let them rest!').

3.1.1 Consonant Gradation

Alternation caused by consonant gradation affects the stops /k/, /p/ and /t/. The type of alternation depends on the length of the stop and on whether it occurs alone and intervocalically or as the first or second component of an intervocalic cluster of which the other consonant is /m/, /n/, /ŋ/, /l/, /r/, or /h/. Alternation is classed as qualitative or quantitative; a qualitative alternation changes the sound, whereas in a quantitative alternation it is the length of the stop that changes. The operation of alternation is dependent on the status of the stem syllable as determined by the morphophonemic environment: an open syllable requires the strong grade of the alternation, a closed syllable the weak grade, though subsequent changes have sometimes obscured the original environment. Thus there is in Finnish a strong/weak gradation correlation with open/closed syllable form (see page 501). The most common examples of gradation are illustrated in Table 29.3.

Less frequent forms of gradation in standard Finnish are *ht~hd*, *lke~lje*, *rke~rje*, *hke~hje*; further variations occur in dialects.

3.1.2 Other Changes at the Stem

Partial consonant assimilation affects intervocalic *-t-* and causes the change *-t-* → *-s-* in an environment in which it is followed by *-i-* (allowing for the variation described in Section 3.1). In nominals this environment arises most commonly from the change of final *-e*, *-i* and from the suffixing of the oblique plural marker, e.g. stem *käte-* 'hand', nominative singular *käsi*, adessive plural *kas-i-lla* 'with the hands'. In verbal forms the environment usually arises from the suffixing of the imperfect *-i-* marker to those categories of verbs that have a consonant stem (see Section 3.1), e.g. consonant stem *levät-* 'rest', imperfect *lepäs-i* 'rested'.

Total consonant assimilation at the stem occurs only in verbal morphology and affects the consonant stems ending in *-t-*, *-n-*, *-l-* and *-r-* when suffixes are added to

Table 29.3 Finnish Consonant Gradation

			Strong		*Weak*	
Quantitative						
kk	~	k	akka	~	akassa	(inessive 'old woman')
pp	~	p	piippu	~	piipusta	(elative 'pipe')
tt	~	t	matto	~	maton	(genitive 'mat')
Qualitative						
t	~	d	vete	~	vedestä	(elative 'water')
k	~	∅	ruoka	~	ruoan	(genitive 'food')
k	~	v	suku	~	suvulla	(adessive 'family')
p	~	v	lupa	~	luvatta	(abessive 'promise')
mp	~	mm	kampa	~	kamman	(genitive 'comb')
nt	~	nn	tunte	~	tunnen	('I feel')
nk	~	nŋ	hanke	~	hangella	(adessive 'snow crust')
lt	~	ll	multa	~	mullassa	(inessive 'soil')
rt	~	rr	saarta	~	saarramme	('we surround')

mark the active indicative past participle (*-nut/-nyt*), the active potential mood suffix (*-ne-*), the 1st short infinitive *-ta/-tä* suffix type, and the passive-impersonal present voice of verbs of the same category. In the case of past participles and the potential, total assimilation also occurs in *-s-* consonant stems. The influence of total assimilation in these occurrences is either regressive or progressive. In the case of *-t-* stems, assimilation is regressive after suffixing of the past participle and potential markers (e.g. *levät-* → *levän-nyt*, *levän-ne-*) but is progressive in its influence on the infinitive and passive-impersonal forms (e.g. *levät-ä*, *levät-ään*). Total assimilation is progressive in all four verbal forms where the stem consonant is *-n-*, *-r-* or *-l-* (e.g. *pan-* 'put, place', *pan-nut*, *pan-ne-*, *pan-na*, *pan-naan*', *kuul-* 'hear', *kuul-lut*, *kuul-le-*, *kuul-la*, *kuul-laan*; *sur-* 'grieve', *sur-rut*, *sur-re-*, *sur-ra*, *sur-raan*) and in the two forms affecting consonant stems in *-s-* (e.g. *pes-* 'wash', *pes-syt*, *pes-se-*).

Vowel mutation or vowel loss at the word stem is caused by the suffixing of *-i-*; in nominals this arises most commonly from the oblique plural suffix, in verbs the *-i-* sound functions as the imperfect tense suffix and as a component of the conditional mood suffix (*-isi-*). In most instances the result of this suffixing is phonemically determined irrespective of nominal or verbal categories. The short stem vowels subject to loss or mutation are *-a-*, *-ä-*, *-e-* and *-i-*. In two-syllable words stem *-a-* labialises if the vowel of the first syllable is *-a-*, *-e-* or *-i-* (e.g. *kirja-* 'book', inessive plural *kirjo-i-ssa*; *maksa-* 'pay', 3rd person singular imperfect *makso-i*); if the vowel of the first syllable is labial (*-o-* or *-u-*), the stem vowel is lost (e.g. *kunta-* 'group(ing), region', inessive plural *kunn-i-ssa*; *osta-* 'buy', imperfect *ost-i*). Where the stem vowel of a two-syllable word is *-e-* or *-ä-*, the vowel is always lost (e.g. *isä-* 'father', adessive plural *is-i-llä*; *kiittä-* 'thank, praise', imperfect *kiitt-i*, *saare-* 'island', adessive plural *saar-i-lla*; *näke-* 'see', imperfect *näk-i*).

In nominals only a stem *-i-* mutates to *-e-* (e.g. *viini-* 'wine', inessive plural *viine-i-ssä*). In verb forms only, stem vowels *-a-* and *-ä-* mutate to *-e-* in the formation of the stem form of the passive-impersonal voice (e.g. *hoita-* 'care for', passive-impersonal present *hoide-taan*; *estä-* 'prevent', passive-impersonal *este-tään*). Both these features also occur in all other syllables of nominals and verbs respectively in the specific categories described. Apart from these specific categories, the short stem vowels discussed above are normally lost in words of more than two syllables when an *-i-* is added; the only exception is *-a-* which in certain vowel and consonant environments may labialise (e.g. *asia-* 'thing', adessive plural *asio-i-lla*).

The result of suffixing *-i-* markers to a long monophthong or diphthong is shortening of the monophthong or mutation of the diphthong. In the case of all long monophthongs, irrespective of the syllable in which the stem is located, the *-i-* sound becomes the second component of the resulting diphthong (e.g. *maa-* 'land', inessive plural *ma-i-ssa*; *saa-* 'obtain', imperfect 3rd person singular *sa-i*; *saappaa-* 'boot', inessive plural *saappa-i-ssa*; *pelkää-* 'fear', conditional present 3rd person singular *pelkä-isi*; *venee-* 'boat', inessive plural *vene-i-ssä*; *kaunii-* 'beautiful', adessive plural *kauni-i-lla*; *talkoo-* 'group work', adessive plural *talko-i-lla*). A diphthong can occur as a stem vowel in monosyllabic words only. From a synchronic point of view the effect of an *-i-* marker on such stems (unless the second component of the diphthong is also *-i-*) appears to work differently, causing loss of the first component of the diphthong (e.g. *yö-* 'night', inessive plural *ö-i-ssä*; *luo-* 'create', imperfect 3rd person singular *lo-i*; *tie-* 'road, way', adessive plural *te-i-llä*). As each of these diphthongs has evolved from a long monophthong, however (i.e. **öö*, **oo*, **ee* respectively, cf. Estonian cognates *öö, loo-, tee*), the effect of suffixing the *-i-* sound is historically consistent with the long-monophthong examples. Where diphthong stems end in *-i-*, the stem *-i* can be assumed to have been lost (e.g. *voi-* 'be able', imperfect 3rd person singular *vo-i*). In dialects, alternative realisations of these sound changes are common. A rare example of an alternative realisation becoming established as the canonical form is the imperfect and conditional present of *käy-* 'go, visit' (e.g. 3rd person singular *kävi, kävisi*). More common is the destabilising influence of alternative realisations on the standard language, illustrated by the variants *myi-* and *möi-* as acceptable forms for many speakers of the imperfect of *myy-* 'sell'.

3.2 Verbal Morphology and Usage

The finite forms of the Finnish verb comprise two voices, active and passive-impersonal. Each voice has four moods: indicative, potential, conditional and imperative. The indicative mood has four tenses, two primary and two secondary. The primary tenses are the present-future (non-preterite in Holman's classification) and the imperfect; the secondary tenses, formed with the auxiliary *olla* 'to be' and a past participle, are the perfect and pluperfect. The potential, which conveys the possibility of something happening, and the conditional each have one secondary form based on the auxiliary *olla* and a past participle. Apart from certain fixed forms of expression, the potential mood has fallen out of common use in the modern spoken language and occurs with decreasing frequency in modern written usage. Various secondary forms of the imperative can also be construed but their realisation in normal usage is very rare; the use of the imperative in certain specific situations is also decreasing (see Section 3.2.2).

3.2.1 Active Voice

In the active voice an inflected verb form can comprise up to four components in fixed sequence. Slot 1: *stem* (including any embedded derivational suffix). Slot 2: *tense/mood suffix*. Slot 3: *number-and-person suffix* (historically both items are present but have undergone partial fusion in the 1st and 2nd persons). Slot 4: *enclitic suffixes*. Back/front variation occurs in vowel components as a result of vowel harmony. Depending on the particular emphasis of a statement and the syntactic environment, the 1st or 2nd personal pronoun can also be used as a separate item in other parts of the sentence either before or after the verb, depending on the nature of the emphasis required. When the subject of the 3rd person is the personal pronoun *hän* 'he, she' or *he* 'they (animate)', the pronoun must be used (except in the imperative mood). The variation in the use of the personal pronouns is probably explained by the fact that the suffixes of the 1st and 2nd persons evolved from suffixing pronominal items to the verb, whereas 3rd person forms of the active voice appear to derive from an active present participle suffix. Some scholars argue that the [verb + personal suffix] structure of the 1st and 2nd person markers has its realisation in the 3rd person in the passive-impersonal voice, and would prefer to classify the latter as the 4th person of the active voice (see Section 3.2.2).

The basic verbal morphological structure, excluding Slot 4, is illustrated in the chart given here, in which the present-future tense of the verb *puhua* 'to speak' is conjugated.

The Present-future Tense of *puhua*

Personal pronoun	Slot 1 Stem	Slot 2 Tense/mood suffix	Slot 3 Number/person suffix	Example
[minä]	puhu	∅	-n	puhun
[sinä]			-t	puhut
hän			stem vowel lengthens	puhuu
[me]			-mme	puhumme
[te]			-tte	puhutte
he			-vat/-vät	puhuvat

This paradigm structure applies to all verb types in the present-future tense with variation only in the formation of the 3rd person singular. Instead of lengthening the stem vowel, verbs with long-vowel or diphthong stems mark the 3rd person singular by -∅ (e.g. stems *jää-* 'remain', *syö-* 'eat', *luetteloi-* 'classify', 3 sg. *jää, syö, luetteloi*).

In the imperfect, the tense suffix (Slot 2) is *-i-*, in the potential present the mood suffix (Slot 2) is *-ne-*, and in the present conditional it is *-isi-* , e.g.

imperfect:	*puhu-i-n, puhu-i-t, hän puhu-i*, etc. ('I spoke', etc.). In all forms of the imperfect the 3rd p. singular marker is -∅ (see Section 3.1.2).
potential:	*puhu-ne-n, puhu-ne-t, hän puhu-ne-e*, etc. ('I might speak', etc.). As discussed above (see Section 3.1.2), a morphophonemic feature of the potential in certain verb types is the use of a consonant stem with regressive or progressive assimilation at the stem juncture (e.g. *tule-* 'come', potential *tullen; nouse-* 'rise', *nousset*).
conditional:	*puhu-isi-n, puhu-isi-t, hän puhu-isi*, etc. ('I should speak', etc.).

The secondary forms of the active indicative, potential and conditional are formed with the appropriate tenses or moods of the auxiliary *olla* and an active past participle formed from [verb stem + suffix *-nut/-nyt*, plural *-neet*]. Where the participle is formed from a consonant stem, regressive or progressive assimilation at the stem juncture occurs in specific morphophonemic environments (e.g. *ole-* 'be', *ollut*, plural *olleet* 'been', see Section 3.1.2). The conjugation of the auxiliary *olla* follows the above pattern but with two differences: the 3rd person forms of the present-future tense are *on* and *ovat* respectively, and in the potential mood the auxiliary is the cognate *liene-* 'might be', e.g.

perfect: *olen, olet, hän on puhu-nut, olemme, olette, he ovat puhu-neet*;
pluperfect: *olin puhunut*, etc.; potential perfect: *lienen puhunut*, etc.;
conditional perfect: *olisin puhunut*, etc.

Negation in all the above forms is based on a negative auxiliary: [*e-* + person marker] (i.e. *en, et, hän ei, emme, ette, he eivät*). Tense or mood is indicated by the form of the principal verb. In the present tense this is [verb stem + orthographically unmarked glottal] (e.g. *en puhu*). The imperfect negative is indicated by [negative verb + past participle of the principal verb] (e.g. *en puhunut, emme puhuneet*). In the potential and the conditional it is the mood stem that follows the negative auxiliary verb (e.g. potential *hän ei puhune, he eivät puhune*; conditional *en puhuisi, emme puhuisi, he eivät puhuisi*).

Structurally the fourth mood, the imperative, comprises similar components although they have a different morphophonemic realisation. Thus *sano-* 'say' has the forms: 2nd person singular [*sano-* + orthographically unmarked glottal]; 3rd person singular *sano-koon*; plural *sano-kaamme, sano-kaa, sano-koot* (front vowel variants: *-köön, -käämme, -kää, -kööt*). Similarly, the negative employs an auxiliary *äl-* (thus *äl-ä, äl-köön*, etc.) followed by a form of the principal verb, e.g. [*sano-* + orthographically unmarked glottal], in the 2nd person singular, and by the form [principal verb + *-ko/-kö*] (e.g. *sanoko*) in all other forms, e.g. *älä sano* but *älkäämme sanoko*). The function of the imperative tends to be instructional in the 1st person plural and in the 2nd persons, but exhortative in the 3rd persons. In normal modern speech the use of the passive-impersonal voice is more common for the persuasive or exhortative imperative in the 1st person plural. Thus the grammatical imperative *menkäämme!* 'let's go!' is likely to be used in situations where orders are expected to be given and obeyed, whereas in ordinary social situations the passive-impersonal *mennään!* is preferred.

3.2.2 Passive-impersonal

The morphological structure of the passive-impersonal voice has the same pattern as the active voice forms; morphological differences concern the stem (Slot 1) and the number–person suffix (Slot 3). Historically the stem appears to have embedded in it a derivational suffix which once generated a reflexive or medio-passive function. The mood and tense markers are identical with those of the active voice. According to some scholars the person component of the number–person suffix consists of items cognate with the historical form of the 3rd person singular pronoun *hän*. The passive-impersonal verb paradigm is illustrated by *sanoa* 'to say' and *lähteä* 'to depart'.

The Passive-impersonal Voice of *sanoa* and *lähteä*

Present/future	sano-taan	lähde-tään
Imperfect	sano-ttiin	lähde-ttiin
Potential	sano-tta-neen	lähde-ttä-neen
Conditional	sano-tta-isiin	lähde-ttä-isiin
Past participle	sano-tt-u	lähde-tt-y

The negative auxiliary is the 3rd person singular *ei*, while the mood and tense are marked by the appropriate passive-impersonal stem (e.g. present-future *ei sanota*, conditional *ei lähdettäisi*). Regular variation in stem forms and in the length and form of vowels and consonants is explained by the working of consonant gradation, various forms of assimilation, mutation and loss of vowels and consonants (see Sections 3.1.1, 3.1.2).

All verbs can occur in the passive-impersonal voice irrespective of their transitivity or intransitivity. In modern literary Finnish a very common function of this voice is to express impersonal general statements of the kind introduced in German by *man* or in French by *on* (e.g. *täällä puhutaan suomea* 'Finnish spoken here'). In modern collo-quial language, the use of the passive-impersonal in sentence-initial position is the usual way of expressing the 1st person plural imperative (e.g. *syödään!* 'let's eat!'). When preceded by the personal pronoun *me* 'we', a passive-impersonal form com-monly – and in some social groups, always – replaces the active 1st plural forms (e.g. *me lähdetään kotiin junalla* 'we shall go home by train', *me oltiin siellä kaksi viikkoa* 'we were there for two weeks'). In active functions of this kind the object of a transitive verb is also marked (e.g. *me nähtiin sinut koulussa* 'we saw you in school', *me ei osteta omenia* 'we shall not buy any apples').

There is a restricted use of the passive-impersonal voice that corresponds to English passive usage. This is found in statements about an action which is performed intentionally by an inferred but unspecified human agent, e.g. *mies pelastettiin merestä* 'the man was rescued from the sea', i.e. the man was saved by some human intervention. If there had been no information about how the man survived or if his escape had been by his own efforts, Finnish would require the use of an appropriately derived verb in the active voice, e.g. *mies pelastui merestä* 'the man saved himself from the sea'.

3.3 Nominal Morphology and Usage

The morphology of the Finnish noun and adjective provides for the expression of five functions. The noun has five slots in fixed sequence. Slot 1: *stem* (including any embedded derivational suffix). Slot 2: *number* (singular vs plural). Slot 3: *case suffix*. Slot 4: *personal possessor suffix*. Slot 5: *enclitic suffixes*. Demonstratives and adjectives used attributively precede the noun and there is concord in Slots 2 and 3, but they have no marking in Slot 4. Demonstratives and adjectives may have enclitic suffixes independently of the head word.

In Slots 2, 3, 4 and 5, function is indicated by the opposition zero vs suffix. In Slot 2 zero marks singular. Grammatical plurality is marked by *-t* in the nominative and accusative cases, by *-t-*, *-i-* or both in the genitive case, and by *-i-* in all other cases. If a personal possessor suffix is added to the nominative or accusative plural, the *-t* suffix is not used and plurality is indicated by context or syntax, or both, e.g. *poikani on täällä* 'son-my is here', but *poikani ovat täällä*, where the plural verb *ovat* signifies the plural number of homonymic *poikani*.

3.3.1 The Case System

In Slot 3 a zero suffix indicates nominative singular. All other cases are marked. Back/front variation occurs in the vowel component of certain case suffixes as a result of vowel harmony. In the chart showing the case system the front vowel form follows the stroke in the suffix column; in the partitive, genitive and illative cases, variation in the phonemic structure of the suffix is dependent on the class of word stem (see Sections 3.1, 3.1.2). The two examples in the chart, *mies* 'man' and *kirja* 'book' illustrate, in addition to vowel harmony and phonemic structure variation, two stem types: *mies* represents one of the types of word that has a consonant and a vowel stem (e.g. *mies-*, *miehe-*), while *kirja* is typical of words that have only a vowel stem (*kirja-*). Where more than one realisation of a suffix occurs, the form most common in standard usage is given. The accusative case has two suffixes in the singular; *-n* marks the accusative of all nouns and adjectives, *-t* that of the personal pronouns (i.e. *minu-t* 'me', *sinu-t* 'you (familiar)', *häne-t* 'him/her') and the interrogative pronoun *kuka* (accusative *kene-t*) 'who'. In the illative case -V- is identical with the stem vowel subsequent to the marking of number; the bracketed form in the translative is used when a personal possessor suffix follows in Slot 4; the bracketed form in the comitative marks attributive adjectives.

The Case System of *mies* and *kirja*

Case	Suffix	Singular	Plural
Nominative	-Ø; -t	mies; kirja	miehet; kirjat
Accusative	-n (-t); -t	miehen; kirjan	miehet; kirjat
Genitive	-n	miehen; kirjan	miesten; kirjojen
General local cases			
Essive	-na/ä	miehenä; kirjana	miehinä; kirjoina
Partitive	-a/a; -t/ä; -tta/ä	miestä; kirjaa	miehiä; kirjoja
Translative	-ksi (→-kse-)	mieheksi; kirjaksi	miehiksi; kirjoiksi
Interior local cases			
Inessive	-ssa/ä	miehessä; kirjassa	miehissä, kirjoissa
Elative	-sta/ä	miehestä; kirjasta	miehistä; kirjoista
Illative	-Vn; -hVn; -sVVn	mieheen; kirjaan	miehiin; kirjoihin
Exterior local cases			
Adessive	-lla/ä	miehellä; kirjalla	miehillä; kirjoilla
Ablative	-lta/ä	mieheltä; kirjalta	miehiltä; kirjoilta
Allative	-lle	miehelle; kirjalle	miehille; kirjoille
Instructive	in	miehin; kirjoin	miehin; kirjoin
Comitative	-ineen (-ine)	miehineen; kirjoineen	miehineen; kirjoineen
Abessive	-tta/ä	miehettä; kirjatta	miehittä; kirjoitta

There are marked differences in the productivity of the various cases. Apart from the nominative, the cases in most common use are the accusative, genitive, the three so-called general 'local' cases (essive, partitive, translative) and the six specific 'local' cases, which are subdivided into interior (inessive 'in', elative 'from (outside)', illative 'into') and exterior (adessive 'at or near', ablative 'from (outside)', allative 'to, towards'). Certain cases, such as the instructive (e.g. *kyns-in hampa-in* 'with nail and tooth', *kaik-in voim-in* 'with all one's might') and comitative (e.g. *äiti perhe-ineen* 'the mother accompanied by her family'), are only productive nowadays in very restricted areas of usage. The abessive (e.g. *raha-tta* 'moneyless'), for example, occurs productively mainly in non-finite verbal constructions (see Section 5.3); used with nominals it has largely given way to prepositional *ilman* (e.g. *ilman rahaa* 'without money'). In addition to its function as the subject of a sentence the nominative singular stands in certain specific environments as object. The most common of these environments is in marking nouns and adjectives which are the direct object in affirmative sentences of monopersonal (i.e. 3rd person singular) verbs of obligation (e.g. *meidän täytyy ostaa kirja* lit. 'us-to it is necessary buy-to the book'), the 2nd persons and the 1st person plural of the imperative mood (e.g. *osta kirja!* 'buy the book!'), and verbs in the passive-impersonal voice (e.g. *me ostetaan kirja* 'we buy the book'). If the object is a personal pronoun or the interrogative pronoun *kuka*, however, it is marked in all these forms by the *-t* accusative suffix.

In modern Finnish the accusative of nouns and adjectives is marked in the singular by the same suffix as the genitive singular. Historically, however, they are of different origin (acc. *-n* < **-m*). In affirmative sentences the accusative denotes the object of a resultative action (e.g. *hän osti kirjan* 'he/she bought the book') and an object that is in itself definite and total (e.g. *hän joi maidon* 'he/she drank (all) the milk', cf. partitive object *maitoa* denoting that only some of the milk was drunk). In normal usage the difference in accusative and genitive function of the *-n* suffix is made clear by the contextual and syntactic environment. In the genitive case nominal items precede the constituent they govern (e.g. *nuoren tytön musta koira* 'the young girl's black dog'). The second major area of usage of the genitive case is in the headwords of postpositions (e.g. *talon takana* 'behind the house', *mäen päällä* 'on top of the hill'). In certain constructions the genitive has a dative function. This is most apparent in fixed expressions such as *Jumalan kiitos* 'God-to thanks', i.e. 'thanks be to God', and in statements of state or condition of the kind *minun on jano* 'me-to is thirst', i.e. 'I am thirsty'. The dative function in the expression of obligation occurs with monopersonal verbs (e.g. *minun pitää äänestää* 'I must vote') and in various constructions based on the verb *olla* (e.g. *minun on mentävä* 'I have an obligation to go').

Comparison with other Finno-Ugric languages and the evidence of certain historically fixed forms indicate that the components of the general local case suffixes once denoted various perceptions of location and movement. The essive case appears to have indicated a stationary location (cf. fixed forms *kaukana* 'far away', *ulkona* 'outside'). The partitive marked separation, movement away from the main body or substance (cf. *kaukaa* 'from afar', *ulkoa* 'from outside'). The translative, which historically is much younger than the essive or partitive, appears to have indicated movement towards an object, a function still found in such forms as *lähemmäksi* 'coming closer', *rannemmaksi* 'moving closer to the shore' (e.g. a boat). While comparable spatial and kinetic features underlie certain of the present-day functions of these cases, the specific oppositions of location and movement are expressed with greater precision by the six interior and exterior local cases, in which some features of the morphology of the general local cases are embedded. Adessive *-ssa/-ssä*, for example, is thought to derive from internal location marker *-s* + *n*V, elative *-sta/-stä* from *-s-* + separation marker *-t*V. Similarly the *-n*V and *-t*V components have been identified in the adessive *-lla/-llä* and ablative *-lta/-ltä* with the initial *-l-* thought to derive from an exterior locative.

While retaining certain features of their original spatial and kinetic functions all the general local cases have developed additional temporal, syntactic and adverbial functions. The essive denotes various static positional and temporal states, e.g. *hän on opettajana siellä* 'he/she is (in employment as) a teacher there', cf. *hän on opettaja* 'he/she is a teacher (but may not be employed as such)'; *pidän häntä hyvänä opettajana* 'I consider him/her a good teacher', *hän opetti siellä kolmena vuotena* 'he/she taught there for three years'.

In modern Finnish the main function of the partitive case is the marking of various categories of the direct object. The object of any verb in the negative is always in the partitive. In affirmative statements several categories of verbs govern a partitive object (e.g. emotive usage: *hän kaipaa lomaa* 'he/she is longing for a holiday'). In opposition with the accusative object, the partitive denotes an incomplete or continuing action (e.g. *Mikko söi kanaa* (partitive object) 'Mikko ate some chicken' but *Mikko söi kanan* (accusative object) 'Mikko ate all the chicken'). Other functions of the partitive include that of subject and direct object, where an indefinite divisible quantity is denoted (e.g. *lasissa on maitoa* 'there is some milk in the glass', *tulta* 'some fire'). Of the secondary functions performed by the translative, the three most productive are those denoting change of form (e.g. *poika kasvoi mieheksi* 'the boy grew into a man'), time (e.g. *menin sinne kolmeksi kuukaudeksi* 'I went there for three months') and the expression of purpose or intention (e.g. *poika aikoo lääkäriksi* 'the boy intends to become a doctor').

Schematically the oppositions of exterior and interior space and direction of movement can be represented in part by the same model as for the corresponding cases in Hungarian (Table 29.4, and see page 491, Table 28.3).

Table 29.4 The Finnish Interior and Exterior Local Cases

	Stationary	*Moving*	
		Approaching	*Departing*
Interior	-ssa/ä	-Vn -hVn -sVVn	-sta/ä
Exterior	-lla/ä	-lle	-lta/ä

Lacking from the Finnish scheme, compared to that of Hungarian, is the closer definition of exterior location and movement in terms of the oppositions of surface, proximity and terminus. In Finnish such distinctions are either contextually determined or require the use of specific postpositions or, less commonly, prepositions.

The range of spatial, temporal and syntactic functions performed by the interior and exterior local cases can be illustrated by the example of the adessive. Spatially it refers to static position on the surface of an object, e.g. *pöydällä* 'on the table', *seinällä* 'on the wall'. In denoting geographic location it functions often in opposition with the static interior case, the inessive, e.g. *maa* 'earth; land; countryside': inessive *maassa* 'in the earth; in the country' but *maalla* 'in the countryside'; *koulu* 'school': *koulussa* 'in school' but *koululla* 'somewhere on the school premises (inside or outside)'. In temporal expression the adessive denotes time when or during which an action takes place, e.g. *kesällä voimme uida meressä* 'in summer we can swim in the sea', *ensi viikolla olen ulkomailla* 'next week I shall be abroad'. A third area of function is instrumental, denoting the means of performing an action, e.g. *kaadoin koivun kirveellä* 'I felled the birch with an axe', *kuljen Helsinkiin autolla* 'I shall go to Helsinki by car'. A major area of usage is the expression of ownership corresponding to that of English 'have', e.g. *isällä on suuri saari* 'Father has a large island', *lehmällä on vasikka* 'the cow has a calf'.

3.3.2 Personal Possessor Suffixes

The fourth slot in the morphology of the noun is occupied by the suffix of personal possessor. The item possessed and its attributes can be preceded by the genitive of the personal pronoun in the 1st and 2nd persons if particular emphasis is required; in the 3rd person the preceding pronoun in the genitive is necessary (cf. use of personal pronouns in the verbal system, Section 3.2.1):

Personal Possessor Suffixes

Personal pronoun	*Possession suffix*	*Example*		
[minun]	-ni	inessive	veneessäni	'in my boat'
[sinun]	-si	elative	kirjoistasi	'about your books'
hänen	-nsa/ä	nominative	talonsa	'his/her house(s)'
	-Vn	ablative	ystäviltään	'from his/her friends'
		allative	sisarelleen	'to his/her sister'
[meidän]	-mme	adessive	kirkollamme	'at our church'
[teidän]	-nne	elative	kirjeestänne	'from your letter'
heidän	-nsa/ä	illative	kotiinsa	'to their home(s)'
	-Vn	adessive	saarellaan	'on their island'

In modern Finnish the use of the 3rd person suffix *-nsa/ä* is mainly used to mark the singular and plural of the nominative and accusative, when it is added to the vowel stem, and of oblique cases which end in a consonant. The *vowel + n* suffix marks possession in oblique cases ending in a vowel; the vowel component is the same as that of the case suffix vowel, thus generating a long vowel. Possession in the oblique cases ending in a vowel may also be marked by the *-nsa/ä* suffix, although this is becoming less frequent.

Where a case suffix ends in a consonant, that consonant is totally assimilated regressively by the adjacent consonant of the person suffix (e.g. *talo* 'house', illative *taloon*, *taloosi* 'into your house', *taloomme* 'into our house'). Assimilation of this kind leads to homonymic conflict: *taloni* can be the singular or plural of the nominative or accusative, or it can be the singular genitive of *talo*; function is defined by context and syntax. This same assimilation process also produces forms in which consonant gradation is expected but does not occur (e.g. *puku* 'suit', nom. plural *puvut*, gen. singular *puvun* produce, for example, *hänen pukunsa* 'his/her suit', *pukumme* 'our suit', pukunne 'your suit/suits'). The explanation for this homonymic clash and the absence of consonant gradation rests on a theory of the historical fusion of embedded case and plural markers. Comparison with other Baltic-Finnic languages in which the same feature occurs suggests that, at an ancient period before the fusion of the markers was complete, the strong grade in the personal possessor forms occurred as part of the language's normal morphophonemic variation. As the fusion process produced various realisations, analogy and levelling focused on the present strong grade forms which have remained fixed.

4 Lexicon

The vocabulary of modern Finnish has several sources. A large stock of words for which no loan source can be identified dates from an ancient Finno-Ugric phase and from the subsequent era lasting until the division of the Baltic-Finnic languages into their present groups. For the sake of reference this part of the lexicon may conveniently be called 'indigenous'. Throughout this era and subsequently the vocabulary has been extended both by loans and by the spontaneous and conscious operation of the language's derivation mechanisms on indigenous and loan materials alike. In particular, conscious derivation, compounding and calquing have played an important role in the generation of Finnish since the Reformation; and in the past one hundred and fifty years, with the planned cultivation of Finnish, these mechanisms have enabled the language to handle change and innovation in the modern world.

Examples of words belonging to the oldest Finno-Ugric layers of indigenous vocabulary refer to such categories as parts of the body (*käsi* 'arm, hand', *pää* 'head', *silmä* 'eye'), gender differentiation and kinship (*uros* 'male animal', *naaras* 'female animal', *isä* 'father', *emo* 'mother', *miniä* 'daughter-in-law'), environment and survival (*vesi* 'water', *joki* 'river', *kala* 'fish', *kuu* 'moon', *kota* 'shelter, house', *talvi* 'winter', *jää* 'ice', *lumi* 'snow'), and verbs denoting numerous basic activities (*elä-* 'live', *kuole-* 'die', *kaata-* 'fell', *mene-* 'go', *otta-* 'take', *teke-* 'do, make', *näke-* 'see', *tietä-* 'know').

The oldest layer of loanwords shows the influence of Indo-European languages during the Finno-Ugric period (*mesi* 'honey', *sata* 'hundred') and intermittently thereafter. Vocabulary sheds very little light on the nature of the contacts between the ancestors of the speakers of Finnish during the thousands of years separating the Finno-Ugric period and the earliest documentation of their location in the Baltic-Finnic region in the last centuries BC. Loans dating from the so-called Pre-Finnic and Proto-Finnic periods suggest the existence of contacts concurrently with speakers of Ancient Baltic and Germanic over at least one millennium in various areas north, east and south of the Gulf of Finland. Lexical materials from this phase indicate development in social organisation with some evidence of pastoralism and simple agriculture in addition to improved techniques of food gathering. In each set of examples, words of Ancient Baltic origin are given first, with examples of East or North Germanic origin following the semicolon. The main areas of borrowing represent experience and perception of nature (*meri* 'sea', *routa* 'permafrost'; *aalto* 'wave', *kallio* 'rock, cliff', *turska* 'cod'), parts of the body (*hammas* 'tooth'; *maha* 'stomach', *kalvo* 'membrane'), technology (*aisa* 'harness shaft', *kirves* 'axe', *tuhat* 'thousand'; *airo* 'oar', *satula* 'saddle', *keihäs* 'spear', *rauta* 'iron'), dwellings (*lauta* 'plank', *tarha* 'enclosure'; *ahjo* 'forge', *porras* 'step', *tupa* 'hut, room'), livelihood (*ansa* 'trap', *lohi* 'salmon', *herne* 'pea'; *leipä* 'bread', *sima* 'mead', *seula* 'sieve'), social organisation (*heimo* 'tribe', *seura* 'group', *talkoot* 'group labour'; *kuningas* 'king', *kauppa* 'trade', *hallitse-* 'rule, govern'), belief (*virsi* 'sacred song', *perkele* 'devil'; *pyhä* 'sacred', *runo* 'poem', *vihki-* 'make sacred').

As the ancestors of the Finns became established in the area of present-day Finland and the neighbouring regions, new vocabulary was borrowed from both western and eastern sources. Early Slavonic materials entered by various routes. Certain Slavonic loans appear to have been borrowed by Finnish as early as the fifth or sixth century to denote early Christian concepts (e.g. *pappi* 'priest', *pakana* 'pagan') and various features of domestic life (e.g. *palttina* 'linen', *saapas* 'boot'). During the middle ages and later the largest number of Slavonic and, more specifically, Russian loans was borrowed by Karelians who lived under Russian rule and belonged to the Russian Orthodox Church. Some of these loans entered Finnish much later in the eighteenth and nineteenth centuries as a result of closer contacts between Karelians and speakers of the eastern Finnish dialects, and in the late nineteenth and twentieth centuries as Finnish language reformers combined features of western and eastern dialects in their shaping of Finnish into a language of culture, business, government and administration.

For almost a thousand years, from the early middle ages until the present century, Swedish was the largest source of loans. As Finland evolved into a modern European society, Swedish loans were adapted to the phonological system of Finnish to convey new and more precise concepts of religion, government, domestic and economic life, and culture. Much of the vocabulary acquired in this way was not in itself native Swedish but was transmitted in its Swedish form from other languages, most importantly from Latin, Greek, German and French, but also from Italian, Arabic, Spanish and English. It was only in the twentieth century that English and German on any significant scale began to reach Finnish directly, and it was not until after the Second World War that English rivalled Swedish as an intermediate source of new loans.

A complex system of derivational suffixes has always provided a very productive source of new vocabulary. Nominal and verbal forms are generated from either nominal or verbal base forms: 85 suffixes create nominals from nominal forms, and 21 create verbs from nominals; from verbs, 44 suffixes generate nominals and 34 generate verbs. An example of how nouns and adjectives are generated can be seen in the following illustration: noun *usko* 'belief', adj. *usko=ll=inen* (stem: *uskollis-*) 'faithful, loyal', noun *usko=ll=is=uus* 'fidelity, loyalty'; verb *syö-* 'eat', noun *syö=minen* 'eating'. The great flexibility that exists between the verb and nominal categories in derivation is apparent from the analysis of the Finnish word for 'invincibility', *voi=tta=ma=ttom=uus*, which comprises five components: (1) verb stem *voi-* 'to be able'; (2) causative suffix *-tta-'* 'to beat, conquer'; (3) *-ma-* noun formative, 'beating, conquering'; (4) *-ttom-* negating adjectival suffix, 'non-beaten, non-conquered'; (5) *-uus* abstract noun suffix.

A distinctive feature of Finnish is the productivity of the language's stock of verbal derivational suffixes. With these the main verb can be adapted to perform several specific verbal functions. Although the examples given below are all well established in the language, the pattern of derivation illustrated is commonly used by native speakers to produce new and immediately intelligible items: *seiso-* 'stand', momentaneous *seis=ahta-* 'halt'; *pure-* 'bite', momentaneous *pur=aise-* 'take a bite'; *sylke-* 'spit', frequentative *sylje=ksi-* 'spit habitually'; *ui-* 'swim', frequentative *ui=skentele-* 'float'; *hake-* 'fetch', causative *ha=etta-* 'have fetched', *siirtä-* 'move, shift (causative)', intransitive *siirt=y* 'move, shift'; *maista-* 'taste' (transitive), *maist=u-* 'taste of'.

During the past 150 years all the above methods of vocabulary generation have been cultivated by linguists in their development of Finnish as a national language. Nowadays the government funds a language office to advise on the generation of new items and to monitor linguistic usage generally. Yet despite the numerous layers of loans and later creations that make up the lexicon of Finnish, frequency analyses show that some 60–70 per cent of any modern Finnish text is likely to consist of words belonging to the indigenous lexicon or generated from lexical, morphological and derivational items within that lexicon.

5 Syntax

In view of the morphosyntactic character of Finnish, various features of syntax have already been touched upon in the sections on verbal and nominal morphology. The present section will concern itself with four features of Finnish syntax: concord, numerals, non-finite verbal forms and word order.

5.1 Concord

There are no lexical items in Finnish equivalent in function to the English definite or indefinite article, but various degrees of definiteness can be denoted, where this is not already contextually defined, by the use of three degrees of demonstratives (*tämä* 'this', *tuo* 'that', *se* 'further away (either spatially or figuratively)'); similarly, indefiniteness can be marked by two degrees (*eräs* 'a certain', *yksi* 'one').

In noun phrases, there is concord in number and case of demonstratives and adjectives with their head noun. In the standard literary language there will also be concord in number between a nominative subject and the verb (except where the subject is an accumulation of singular items). In normal spoken language, however, the singular form of the 3rd person usually occurs; in sentences where the use of the singular creates ambiguity (e.g. *poikani on täällä* 'my son is here' or 'my sons are here') the speaker will frequently seek periphrastic ways of conveying plurality rather than use the verb in the plural.

5.2 Numerals

In noun phrases containing numerals and certain measure words, concord and government work differently. The numeral *yksi* 'one' functions as an adjective in concord with the head word (e.g. *yksi kirja jäi pöydälle* 'one book remained on the table', *yhdestä kirjasta en pidä* '(there is) one book I do not like', *hän näki yhden kirjan pöydällä* 'he/she saw one book on the table'). All other numerals and most measure words in the nominative and accusative cases (the ∅-marked accusative is used in such occurrences) govern a noun and its attributes in the partitive singular; in all other cases the numeral governs singular number, but there is concord of case between the numeral and head word (e.g. *kaksi nuorta miestä istui huoneessa* 'two young men were sitting in the room', *huomasin kaksi nuorta miestä huoneessa* 'I noticed two young men in the room', but *kahden nuoren miehen avulla maalasin huoneen* 'with the help of two young men I painted the room').

5.3 Non-finite Verbal Forms

Finnish grammarians have traditionally described as infinitives and participles a complex system of forms that 'function as nouns and noun-like words, adjectives, and adverbs with various shades of verbal meaning' (Holman 1984: 27). Attention will be drawn here to several of these forms that are productive and determine a range of syntactic relations. The first infinitive has a short and long category. The short category, which serves as the verb referent in dictionaries, functions in much the same way as the English verb infinitive as the complement of an auxiliary (e.g. *haluan laula-a* 'I want to sing'); in certain environments the infinitive can also function as a coverb (e.g. *tyttö juosta viipotti* 'the girl ran daintily').

The long form of the first infinitive and the two forms of the second infinitive are close in structure to the short first infinitive but carry case suffixes and in certain circumstances personal possessor suffixes. The long infinitive is in the translative case and person is marked by the nominal personal possessor markers (e.g. short infinitive *tul-la* 'to come', long form *tulla-kse-ni*, *tullaksesi*, etc.), and expresses purpose (e.g. *ostin karttakirjan suunnitellakseni automatkan* 'I bought an atlas in order to plan a car journey'). The second infinitive is marked by the inessive and a historically fixed singular form of the instructive (*-en*). The function of the second infinitive is adverbial, indicating simultaneity (inessive) or manner of action (instructive) (e.g. *auringon paistaessa söimme ulkona* 'while the sun was shining we ate outside'; *hän löi lasta kaikkien nähden* 'he/she beat the child as all were watching').

The most complex of the infinitives is the third. Its base form is marked by *-ma/mä* and the lexicon includes a stock of nouns formed in this way which are no longer perceived by speakers as non-finite verbal forms (e.g. *kuolema* 'death', *kuolla* 'to die', *sanoma* 'message', *sanoa* 'to say'). An important function of the third infinitive is as 'agential participle' (Holman) (e.g. *isän rakentama talo* lit. 'Father's the building house', i.e. 'the house built by Father'); where the agent is a personal pronoun, there is suffix concord with the participle (e.g. *minun rakentamani talo* 'the house built by me'). Concord also exists between the categories of singular and plural and case (e.g. *paljon ihmisiä asui isän rakentamissa taloissa* 'many people lived in the houses built by Father').

The second area of usage is after a coverb when the third infinitive occurs in the singular illative, inessive, elative, adessive or abessive cases. In the inessive case the infinitive functions with the coverb *olla* 'to be' to express continuity of action (e.g. *äiti oli lukemassa sanomalehtiä kun saavuin* 'Mother was reading the newspapers when I arrived'; *sunnuntaina olen hoitamassa pihaani* 'on Sunday I shall be tending my garden'; *koko perhe oli keittiössä juomassa kahvia* 'the whole family was in the kitchen drinking coffee').

515

The illative usage, which is also very common, denotes that an action is about to take place (e.g. *hän tuli syömään lounasta* 'he/she came to eat lunch'; *lähdemme nyt juoksemaan* 'we are going to (start) run(ning) now'). The frequency of usage is also to some extent explained by the fact that a large number of verbs, and also adjectives taking a complement, govern this non-finite form of the verb (e.g. *ruveta* 'to begin', *pyytää* 'to ask, request', *oppia* 'to learn'; *halukas* 'keen, willing', *valmis* 'ready'). A similar pattern of development characterises the elative case, which as part of the third infinitive usually conveys separation (e.g. *tulin taloon sisään hoitamasta pihaani* 'I came into the house after tending my garden'; *perhe tuli juomasta kahvia* 'the family came (once they had finished) from drinking coffee'), but is governed as complement by specific verbs (e.g. *lakata* 'to stop, cease', *kieltää* 'to forbid'). In adessive usage it is the instrumental function of the case which is represented, indicating how the action of the finite verb is accomplished (e.g. *lukemalla kirjallisuutta oppisit maailman menosta* 'by reading literature you would learn about the ways of the world'; *maalaamalla talomme itse säästimme paljon rahaa* 'by painting our house ourselves we saved a lot of money'). As mentioned in Section 3.3.1, the use of the abessive third infinitive accounts largely for the productive use of this case in the modern language. Its function is to show that an action does not take place (e.g. *työt jäivät tekemättä* 'the jobs remained undone'; *hän asui Helsingissä kaksi vuotta oppimatta suomea* 'he/she lived in Helsinki for two years without learning Finnish').

5.4 Word Order

Word order in a noun phrase constituent is fixed: demonstrative–numeral–adjective(s)–noun. Within the clause the normal order of constituents is subject–verb–object. This order remains in the type of questions that require the addition of a question word at the beginning of the clause (e.g. *sinä odotat meitä kotona* 'you will wait for us at home', but *missä sinä odotat meitä?* 'where will you wait for us?' or *miksi sinä odotat meitä kotona?* 'why are you waiting for us at home?'). Where a question word is not used, as in the clause 'are you waiting for us at home?', Finnish preposes the focus of the question to which the particle *ko/kö* is suffixed: *odotatko sinä meitä kotona?* 'will you wait for us at home?' Since the morphosyntactic system usually makes the grammatical, syntactic and semantic functions of each constituent in the clause unambiguous, considerable flexibility is possible within the general SVO framework, allowing shifts of emphasis and focus to be marked by word order variation. When special emphasis or change of focus is required, word order is usually pragmatically determined in order to place the focus as the first or final constituent of a clause.

Bibliography

A. Hakulinen *et al.*'s (2004) recent survey of the contemporary use of Finnish is the current authoritative reference work in Finnish on the subject. Sulkala's and Karjalainen's descriptive grammar (1992) presents an informative and well-codified overview in English of Finnish suitable both for language specialists and as a supplementary source for students learning Finnish. Among grammars of Finnish in English, Atkinson (1977) is a succinct introduction to Finnish morphology and syntax, while Karlsson (1983) is an intelligent presentation of the morphology of Finnish for the adult student, including useful sections on pronunciation and the differences between the colloquial and literary languages. Holman (1984) provides a concise linguistic analysis of the finite and non-finite categories of the Finnish verb. Denison (1957) describes the form and numerous functions of the partitive case in all the Baltic-Finnic languages. A. Hakulinen and Karlsson (1979) offer informative insights on Finnish syntax with their rationalisation of many of the complications of Finnish by the application of modern linguistic methodology. L. Hakulinen (1979) surveys the development of Finnish in the context of other Baltic-Finnic languages and the Finnish dialects; particular attention is paid to derivation and loanwords. Tuomi (1972) is an indispensable tool in studying derivation. Saukkonen *et al.*'s (1979) frequency dictionary, based on usage in the 1960s, is a broad analysis of vocabulary frequency in various registers of Finnish.

References

Atkinson, J. 1977. *A Finnish Grammar* (Suomalaisen Kirjallisuuden Seura, Helsinki)

Denison, N. 1957. *The Partitive in Finnish* (Finnish Academy of Sciences, Helsinki)

Hakulinen, A. and Karlsson, F. 1979. *Nykysuomen lauseoppia* (Suomalaisen Kirjallisuuden Seura, Jyväskylä)

Hakulinen, A., Vilkuna, M., Korhonen, R., Koivisto, V., Heinonen, T.R. and Alho, I. 2004. *Iso suomen kielioppi* (Suomalaisen Kirjallisuuden Seura, Helsinki)

Hakulinen, L. 1979. *Suomen kielen rakenne ja kehitys*, 4th edn (Otava, Helsinki). An abridged English version, *The Structure and Development of the Finnish Language* (trans. J. Atkinson), of the 1st edition (1941, 1946) was published in 1961 (Indiana University Press, Bloomington)

Holman, E. 1984. *Handbook of Finnish Verbs* (Suomalaisen Kirjallisuuden Seura, Vaasa)

Karlsson, F. 1983. *Finnish Grammar* (Werner Söderström, Juva)

Kulonen, U.-M., Seurujärvi-Kari, I. and Pulkkinen R. 2005. *The Saami* (Suomalaisen Kirjallisuuden Seura, Vammala)

Nykysuomen sanakirja. 2002, 15th edn (WSOY, Helsinki)

Saukkonen, P., Haipus, M. Niemikorpi, A. and Sulkala H. 1979. *Suomen kielen taajuussanasto* (Werner Söderström, Porvoo)

Sulkala, H. and Karjalainen, M. 1992. *Finnish* (Routledge, London)

Tuomi, T. (ed.) 1972. *Suomen kielen käänteissanakirja/Reverse Dictionary of Modern Standard Finnish* (Suomalaisen Kirjallisuuden Seura, Hämeenlinna)

30

Turkish and the Turkic languages

Jaklin Kornfilt

1 General and Historical Background

A strict terminological distinction should be drawn between Turkic, the name of a language family, and Turkish, the name of a language. Although Turkish is by far the largest language (in terms of number of speakers) in the Turkic family, it accounts for only some 30 per cent of the total number of speakers of Turkic languages. The main geographic locations of Turkic languages are: (1) Turkey (Turkish), (2) the former USSR and Iran: the Caucasus and northwestern Iran (e.g. Azerbaijani), formerly Soviet Central Asia, Kazakhstan and southern Siberia (e.g. Uzbek, Kazakh, Turkmenian, Kirghiz) and on the Volga (e.g. Tatar). One Turkic language (Yakut, or Sakha, as it is called by its native speakers) is spoken in northern Siberia. (More than one inhabitant in ten of the formerly Soviet areas is a native speaker of a Turkic language.) In addition, there are substantial Turkic-speaking communities in northwestern China (especially Uighur, and also Kazakh).

In terms of linguistic structure, the Turkic languages are very close to one another, and most of the salient features of Turkish described below (e.g. vowel harmony, agglutinative morphology, verb-final word order, nominalised subordinate clauses) are true of nearly all Turkic languages, with only minor modifications. This similarity of structure makes it difficult to determine the precise number of Turkic languages and their boundaries and to sub-classify them, since one typically finds chains of dialects, with adjacent dialects in essence mutually intelligible and mutual intelligibility decreasing as a function of distance, rather than clear language boundaries. Only one Turkic language, Chuvash, spoken on the middle Volga, is radically different from all its relatives.

The external genetic relationships of the Turkic family remain controversial. The most widely accepted affiliation is with the Mongolian languages (in Mongolia, northern China and parts of the former USSR) and the Tungusic languages (Siberia and northeastern China), to form the Altaic phylum; the typological similarities among these three families, though striking (e.g. vowel harmony, SOV word order typology) are not proof of genetic relationship, while even the shared vocabulary has been argued to be the result of intensive contact rather than common ancestry. Bolder hypotheses would extend the Altaic phylum eastwards to include Korean, perhaps even Japanese; or northwards to include the Uralic family (to give a Ural-Altaic phylum).

Turkish is the official and dominant language of Turkey (Turkish Republic), where it is the native language of over 90 per cent of the population, i.e. some 70 million people. (The largest linguistic minority in the Turkish Republic is formed by Kurdish speakers, mainly in southeastern Turkey; small minority language communities are formed by speakers of Arabic, of some Caucasian languages, and, especially in the European part of the country, by speakers of Gagauz, a closely related Turkic language primarily spoken in Moldova.) Turkish is also a co-official language (with Greek) in Cyprus, where it is spoken by 18–19 per cent of the population, or about 140,000 people. But the largest number of Turkish speakers outside Turkey, perhaps close to one million, is to be found in the Balkans, especially in Bulgaria, but also in the former Yugoslavia (particularly in Macedonia) and in Greece.

Although there is no general agreement in Turkological literature on the most adequate geographic grouping of the Turkic languages, we shall go along with those sources that classify the contemporary language spoken in the Turkish Republic within a South-West (or Oγuz) group, together with Gagauz, Azerbaijani and Turkmenian, the latter forming the eastern component of the group. Within this group, some sources differentiate a subgroup called *Osman* (i.e. Ottoman), which would consist of the following dialects: Rumelian, Anatolian and South Crimean. Modern standard Turkish represents a standardisation of the Istanbul dialect of Anatolian.

The question of the ancestor language of this group is not settled, either. It seems established, however, that the language of the oldest documents (i.e. the Orkhun inscriptions and the Old Uighur manuscripts) is the ancestor of another group, namely of the Central Asiatic Turkic languages; the South-West languages are presumably descendants of the language of the 'Western Türküt' mentioned in the Chinese Annals.

The ancient languages of this group would be Old Anatolian and Old Osman. These labels themselves are misleading, however, and have more political and historical justification than linguistic motivation, since there are no clear-cut criteria to distinguish the languages they represent from one another – while there might be more reason to distinguish Old Osman (which is usually claimed to extend until the fifteenth century, ending with the conquest of Constantinople) from Ottoman proper; but, even there, no justification exists for a strict cut-off point.

The first Anatolian Turkish documents date from the thirteenth century and show that the literary tradition of Central Asia was only very tenuously carried over by the Turkish people (who had been converted to Islam earlier) after invading Anatolia from the east in the late eleventh century. It is clear that these tribes were influenced heavily by both Persian and Arabic from the very beginnings of their settling down in Anatolia, given the higher prestige and development of the culture and literature of these neighbouring Muslim nations. The number of works in Turkish written by the Turks of Anatolia (as opposed to those written by them in Arabic and Persian and even Greek) greatly increased in the fourteenth century, together with the Selĵuqi period of feudalism in Anatolia. The gap between the eleventh and thirteenth centuries with respect to the lack of written documents can probably be explained by assuming that the Turkish leaders used Arabic and Persian, not finding a local Turkic language in their new surroundings and not having a strong literary tradition to fall back on – given that these Turkish tribes (to a large extent belonging to the Oγuz) were not among the culturally more advanced Turkic groups and, moreover, were geographically separated at that time from the Central Asian centres of Turkic literature.

From the very beginning of its Anatolian period, Turkish was written in the Arabic script, until the Latin script was adopted in the course of the so-called 'writing reform' of 1928 (put into force in 1929), one of the various reforms introduced after the founding of the Turkish Republic with the aim of westernising the country. However, the Uighur script was also employed by the Anatolian Turks up to the fifteenth century, which might explain some features of the Arabic script as used by the Turks of that period and which differ from standard Arabic usage, e.g. vowels are written out in Turkish words. This point, incidentally, has often been brought up to motivate the so-called 'writing reform', arguing that the multiple ambiguities that arise in Turkish within a non-vocalised orthography made the Arabic system highly inadequate for Turkish.

The dialect of the earliest Anatolian texts has various features in common with the Oɣuz dialect as documented for the eleventh century, before the migration to Anatolia, and with Qïpchaq (an ancient language of the Northwestern group) and Turkmenian. Some of these are listed below:

(1) *d* for *t* in Old Turkic. (A number of these *d*s became devoiced again through assimilation in the fifteenth century.)
(2) Initial *b* changes to *v: bar-* > *var-* 'to go; to arrive'; *ber-* > *ver-* 'to give'
(3) Suffix-initial *ɣ*, *g* disappears (in most instances; there are some surviving suffixes such as *-gil*, *-gen*, but those aren't productive).
(4) Word-final *ɣ*, *g* disappears in polysyllabic words.
(5) Instead of the second person plural imperative ending *-ler*, *-lar* in Old Turkic, the forms *-nüz*, *-nuz*, *-niz*, *-nız* are found (and remain until today).

Forms which are limited to Anatolian Turkish are the following:

(1) The suffix *-ecek*, *-acaq* appears for the first time in the thirteenth century (but is used as a participle and not yet as a finite verb, as is also possible in Modern Turkish).
(2) The suffix *-iser*, *-ïsar* is the most widely used suffix for the future tense in Anatolian Turkish between the thirteenth and fifteenth centuries and is seen only very infrequently in some Turkmenian and Qïpchaq works.

However, the differences between Old Turkic and early Anatolian Turkish must not have been great and their phonology essentially identical. The vocabulary is also similar to a large extent, although obviously many borrowings from Islamic sources are seen in the realm of religious-mystical concepts.

In the works of the fourteenth century and afterwards, peculiarities of Eastern Turkic, which had crept into Anatolian Turkish because of the Eastern origins of some authors, disappear almost completely, while the component of Arabic and Persian words and forms increases; such Eastern Turkic features include: initial *m* instead of *b* in words containing a nasal: *men* instead of *ben* 'I'; *min-* instead of *bin-* 'to ride'; initial *b*, which, as mentioned above, changed to *v* in Anatolia and neighbouring areas, remained unchanged in Eastern Turkic and is also sporadically found in early Anatolian works: *ber-* instead of *ver-* 'to give'; and, as another example for a different feature, *bol* instead of *ol* 'to be'.

In the literature written for scholarly, administrative and literary purposes, the Persian and Arabic components became so prevalent that 'Ottoman' became a mixed language, having lost some of its characteristic Turkic properties to the point of not being usable as a medium of communication common to all social classes. During the same time, however, there also was a considerable production of mystical literature and folk poetry which was written for the less educated classes, in the language used by those segments of the population, namely Anatolian Turkish as influenced very little by Persian and Arabic. These works are very close to the 'Republican Turkish' of today and can essentially be understood without too much difficulty. Among the authors of the 'court literature' there were, time and again, also some who called for a purification of the language and ultimately, starting in the eighteenth century, there was a general movement towards a language with local (rather than foreign) features.

The culmination of such movements was reached after the turn of the century. In 1909, a 'Turkish Club' (*Türk Derneği*) was founded in Istanbul and started publishing a journal, proclaiming its aims for a simpler Turkish. Similar movements and journals followed soon and literary works written in a 'purified' Turkish were produced (see, for instance, the works of Ömer Seyfettin and Ziya Gökalp). Conscious and systematic efforts to establish criteria for maintaining the vocabulary as well as the structural properties of Turkish were continued through the 'War of Liberation' (after World War I) into the founding of the Republic and the reform movements. The language reform, which can be said to have started with the 'writing reform', should therefore be viewed within a tradition of a search for a national identity, combined with a general campaign for westernisation. A Turkish Language Academy was founded in Ankara, with the tasks of etymological research and creation of new words, the latter in accordance with the Turkish rules of word formation and using Turkic roots, where the 'purification' of the language from Arabic and Persian vocabulary had created gaps which could not be filled with current synonyms. Although some of these new creations were judged to be just as foreign to the current colloquial language as the borrowed vocabulary and dropped out of usage almost as soon as they were introduced, the work of the Academy can be viewed as having been essentially successful in creating a widely understood language with a transparent morphological component and its own, typologically consistent syntax.

2 Phonology and Orthography

The vowel inventory of Turkish is very symmetric. The eight phonemic vowels are grouped into foursomes with respect to the features of height, backness and rounding, as in Table 30.1.

All vowels of the native vocabulary are underlyingly (or, say, phonemically) short. There is, however, vocalic length on the surface, having various sources: (1) borrowings with unpredictably long vowels; e.g. *ha:dise* 'event, happening'; *ma:zi:* 'past';

Table 30.1 Turkish Vowels

	[−back] [−*round*]	[+*round*]	[+back] [−*round*]	[+*round*]
[+high]	i	ü	ɨ	u
[−high]	e	ö	a	o

(2) compensatory lengthening in words of Turkic origin, where an original voiced velar fricative (which is no longer part of the *surface* inventory of segments in modern standard Turkish) used to follow a vowel. There are some arguments that show this segment to be part of the *phonemic* inventory, since it behaves like a consonant in stem-final position with respect to allomorphy choice of following suffixes. For example, the accusative and dative suffixes are: *-I* and *-A* after a consonant, but *-yI* and *-yA* after a vowel, respectively. (For the notation with capital letters, see page 526.) After a stem-final phonetically long vowel due to 'compensatory lengthening' (but not after an *inherently* long vowel), the allomorph regularly chosen by consonant-final stems appears; e.g. orthographic *dağ* 'mountain', pronounced *da:*, accusative *daɨ*, dative *daa*. Compare these forms with: *araba* 'car', accusative *arabayɨ*, dative *arabaya*, and *bina:* 'building', accusative *bina:yɨ*, dative *bina:ya*. Where that segment (which is, as shown in the examples above, rendered by the sign *ğ* in Turkish orthography and can never occur word-initially – see also the section on the historical background of Turkish) is in either word-final or pre-consonantal (i.e. in syllable-final) position, the preceding vowel is lengthened; e.g. orthographic *çağ* 'era', pronounced *ča:*, locative *çağda*, pronounced *ča:da*. Note that length doesn't necessarily lead to word-level stress; thus, the last example is stressed on its final, short, vowel, while the long vowel remains without stress: [*ča:dá*]. The same is true when vowel length is due to inherent length in borrowings, rather than to compensatory lengthening: [*bina:yá*].

Another peculiarity of Turkish vowels is that non-high vowels cannot be round, unless they are in a word-initial syllable. While many borrowed stems are exceptional in this respect (e.g. *dekor* 'stage design'; *pilot* 'pilot'), there is only one affix that is exceptional: the progressive suffix *-(I)yor*.

Perhaps the most prominent property of the Turkish vowels is the fact that they undergo vowel harmony with respect to backness and rounding. We shall discuss this issue in more detail later on, when the phonological rule system of the language is investigated.

The consonant inventory of Turkish is given in Table 30.2. The consonants *k*, *g* and *l* have two forms: palatal and velar. Their distribution is, in general, determined by the backness versus frontness of the tautosyllabic vowel, e.g. *čök* 'collapse' versus *čok* 'many; very'; *bel̡* 'waist' versus *bal* 'honey'; *k̡ör* 'blind' versus *kor* 'ember'; *il̡ik̡* 'marrow' versus *ilik* 'luke-warm'. (x̠ denotes a palatal consonant.) These assimilative changes are not always predictable, however; there are some borrowings where the

Table 30.2 Turkish Consonants

		Bilabial	Labio-dental	Dental, Alveolar	Palato-alveolar	Palatal	Velar	Glottal
Stop	voiceless	p		t	č		k	
	voiced	b		d	ǰ		g	
Fricative	voiceless		f	s	š			
	voiced		v	z	ž			
Nasal		m		n				
Lateral approximant				l				
Central approximant				r		y		h

palatal variant precedes or follows a tautosyllabic back vowel; e.g. *ka̲lp* 'heart'; *k̲ar* 'profit'. (Where a palatal velar stop precedes a back vowel, a palatal glide is inserted after the palatal velar stop; cf. the section on orthography further below.)

The Latin alphabet used for modern standard Turkish is, both in its printed and hand-written versions, the familiar system used in more familiar European languages – as, for example, in English. The diacritics used for less common sounds make some of the signs very similar to some versions of the phonetic script; for instance, the phonetic symbols for vowels given in Table 30.1 are also the ones used in Turkish orthography, with one exception: Instead of *i*, the sign used for the high back non-round vowel, we find *ı*, i.e. a dotless *i*. The difference between the two non-round high vowels is signalled in the same way for capital letters: *İ* for the front, *I* for the back, high non-round vowel. As for the consonants, we have commented on the 'silent' *ğ* earlier. Other letters that don't correspond to the familiar phonetic symbols are the following: *c* for [ǰ], *ç* for [č], *ş* for [š], *j* for [ž].

The orthographic conventions correspond roughly to those of a broad phonetic transcription. Predictable alternations (e.g. those due to syllable-final oral stop devoicing, to voicing assimilation or to vowel harmony) are written out, differing in this respect from, say, the German orthography. Other predictable alternations are not signalled, however: since there are no special signs for the palatal versus velar *k*, *g* and *l*, the alternations that these segments undergo remain unexpressed by the orthography. Unpredictable occurrences of the palatal variants of these consonants with back vowels *is* sometimes shown, however, by placing a circumflex on the vowel: *kâr* [k̲yar]. (A front glide is inserted when the consonant in question is a *k̲*.) Inherent vowel length is not shown by the writing, although it is unpredictable.

With the exception of some learned words and the borrowed vocabulary of native speakers who either have some knowledge of European languages or live in big cities with extensive western influence, Turkish does not allow consonant clusters in initial position. In standard pronunciation (and increasingly also in the orthography) such clusters that enter the language via borrowings are broken up by an epenthesised high vowel, which – in general – harmonises with the following vowel(s) in backness and rounding, e.g. learned *k̲lūp* 'club', colloquial *kulüp*; learned *kral* 'king', colloquial *kı̇ral*.

Turkish is somewhat more tolerant of syllable-final consonant clusters. Three types of clusters are allowed as a coda: (a) sonorant + obstruent: *k̲ent* 'city', *harf* 'letter'; (b) voiceless fricative + oral stop: *çift* 'couple', *şevk̲* 'fervour' (note that the *v* is pronounced [f] and thus fits this characterisation involving a voiceless fricative); (c) *k* + *s*: *raks* 'dance', *boks* 'boxing'. Where a stem has a consonant cluster in syllable-final position that does not fall under any of the permissible sets, again a high vowel is epenthesised which undergoes harmony, e.g. 'forehead' accusative *aln* + *ı*, nominative *alın*; 'nose' accusative *burn* + *u*, nominative *burun*; 'city' accusative *şehr* + *i*, nominative *şehir*; 'time' accusative *vakt* + *i*, nominative *vakit*.

A subcase of syllable-final consonant clusters are geminate consonants. While Turkish does tolerate geminate consonant sequences when their members are hetero-syllabic (e.g. *et* + *te* 'meat + loc.'), it does not allow them to occupy syllable-final position. Rather than breaking up such clusters by epenthesis, however, the language has a rule of degemination, e.g. 'feeling' accusative *hiss* + *i*, nominative *his*; 'line' accusative *hatt* + *ı*, nominative *hat*.

In addition to the rules discussed above (i.e. vowel epenthesis, consonant degemination), there are a few other important phonological rules that were mentioned in passing and which will receive further attention below.

Syllable-final oral stop devoicing: similar to the more general obstruent devoicing rule in languages like German and Russian, Turkish has a rule that devoices oral non-continuants (i.e. regular stops as well as affricates) in syllable-final position, e.g. *kitap* 'book', accusative *kitab* + *ı*, locative *kitap* + *ta*; *kireç* 'lime', accusative *kirec* + *i*, locative *kireç* + *te*.

The *k/∅* alternation: the final *k* of a polysyllabic word is deleted phonetically in intervocalic position, where the preceding vowel is short. This *k/∅* alternation is orthographically rendered as a *k/ğ* alternation, e.g. *kabak* 'pumpkin', accusative *kabağı* [kabaɨ]; *kabuk* 'crust', accusative *kabuğu* [kabuu]. It is possible to view this phenomenon as a subcase of the voiced/voiceless alternation discussed in the previous section. If it is assumed that the alternating *k*s are derived from underlying *g*s as a result of syllable-final stop devoicing and if a rule of intervocalic fricativisation is posited for the voiced velar stop, the data are essentially covered.

Word-final liquid devoicing: another striking phenomenon somewhat related to stop devoicing is the word-final devoicing of liquids, especially common in the Istanbul dialect and in the speech of educated speakers in the other big cities: *ka̯r* 'snow', *bakı̯r* 'copper', *ke̯l* 'bald'. It should be noted, however, that this is not a completely unified phenomenon; some speakers devoice only the palatal *l*, while other speakers do not make a distinction between the two variants of the lateral. (The *r* is devoiced by all speakers who observe the liquid devoicing rule.) It should also be pointed out that liquid devoicing differs from oral stop devoicing in applying at word boundary rather than at syllable boundary; e.g. while the underlying stem-final *b* devoices in: *kitap* + *lık* 'object designated for books; bookshelf', the stem-final *r* remains voiced in a similar environment: *kar* + *lı* 'with snow; snowy' (and not: **ka̯rlı*).

Morpheme-initial voicing assimilation: a morpheme-initial obstruent assimilates in voicing to the preceding segment within the word. This rule has to apply after syllable-final stop devoicing has taken place, e.g. (a) *gemi* + *ci* 'sailor' (cf. *gemi* 'ship'), *iz* + *ci* 'boy-scout' (cf. *iz* 'track, trace'), *bakır* + *cı* 'coppersmith' (cf. *bakır* 'copper'); (b) *kitap* + *çı* (cf. *kitap* 'book', underlyingly /kitab/), *şarap* + *çı* 'wine maker, wine seller' (cf. *şarap* 'wine', underlyingly /şarab/).

Vowel harmony: perhaps the most striking property of Turkish phonology is the fact that the distribution of vowels within a word is governed by vowel harmony, i.e. vowels share the specification for the feature [back] and, if they are high, they also share the specification for [round]: *bülbül* + *ümüz* + *ün* 'nightingale + 1 pl. + gen.', 'belonging to our nightingale'; *bülbül* + *ler* + *imiz* + *in* 'nightingale + pl. + 1 pl. + gen.', 'belonging to our nightingales'; *kol* + *umuz* + *un* 'arm + 1 pl. + gen.', 'belonging to our arm'; *kol* + *lar* + *ımız* + *ın* 'arm + pl. + 1 pl. + gen.', 'belonging to our arms'. Note that the [–high] vowel of the plural morpheme, while undergoing vowel harmony for backness, does not undergo rounding harmony. Moreover, since there is a condition (mentioned earlier in this section) on [–high] vowels to the effect that they have to be [–round] if they are in a non-initial syllable, the negative specification of this vowel for rounding is fully determined. Note also that once a non-round vowel follows a round vowel (as in the second and fourth examples above) all vowels to the right of that non-round vowel will be non-round as well, irrespective of their height.

This situation can be characterised in more general terms: where a vowel does not share the specification for a harmony feature with preceding vowels, it will create its own harmony domain, in the sense that it will determine the specification with respect to that particular feature for the following vowels. This description also characterises the application of vowel harmony where an exceptional vowel occurs. As mentioned before, many stems have exceptional vowels that violate either backness or rounding harmony or both at once; the second vowel of the progressive marker -*(I)yor* is also exceptional in this respect and never alternates. (Capital letters denote archiphonemes whose missing feature values are predictable by rule. In the case of vowels, *I* stands for a [+high], *A* for a [–high] vowel before application of vowel harmony. In the case of consonants, a capital letter stands for a segment which may undergo syllable-final stop devoicing, morpheme-initial voicing assimilation or intervocalic *k*-deletion. Symbols in parentheses denote affix allomorphy in those instances where the segment in question deletes after a 'like' segment (i.e. a vowel after a vowel, a consonant after a consonant).) In such cases, it is the exceptional vowel (or, if there is more than one, the last exceptional vowel) that determines what kind of vowel harmony the following vowels will undergo. Observe the following examples: *dekor* + *un* + *u* 'stage design + 3 sg. + acc.', 'his stage design, acc.', *otobüs* + *ün* + *ü* 'bus + 3 sg. + acc.', 'his bus, acc.'; *buket* + *in* + *i* 'bouquet + 3 sg. + acc.', 'his bouquet, acc.'; *Macar* + *istan* + *ın* + *ı* 'Hungarian + country + 3 sg. + acc.', 'his Hungary, acc.'.

Sometimes, however, a consonant rather than a vowel can determine (backness) harmony. This happens when a palatal consonant unpredictably follows a back vowel in the same syllable and where that consonant is in stem-final position (or a member of a stem-final consonant cluster). In such cases the following vowels will exhibit *front* harmony; i.e. the 'trigger' of vowel harmony will be the exceptional consonant rather than the regular vowel, e.g. *petrol* 'petrol, gasoline', accusative *petrol* + *ü*; *kalp* 'heart', accusative *kalb* + *i*; *vals* 'waltz', accusative *vals* + *i*.

Labial attraction: there are a number of stems with a vowel sequence of *a* ... *u* and an intervening labial consonant (the latter can also be part of a consonant cluster). Since the second vowel, being high, should undergo rounding harmony, it should surface as an *ı*. Its rounding has traditionally been ascribed to the preceding labial consonant. Some examples are *karpuz* 'watermelon', *kavun* 'melon'. The status of this observation in terms of a rule (of assimilation) in modern standard Turkish has been challenged more recently. While such an assimilatory process might have been productive in Early Anatolian Turkish (and could even have been a feature common to the Southwestern Turkic group), it seems that it is less general in the contemporary language; there are a number of examples where the sequence *a* ... *ı* shows up in spite of an intervening labial consonant, e.g. *çarmıh* 'cross', *sabır* 'patience', *kapı* 'door' (but note that, interestingly, this item is pronounced as [*kapu*] in some dialects). Furthermore, an even larger number of stems exhibit *a* ... *u* sequences without any intervening labial consonant; e.g. *ka:nun* 'law', *arzu* 'desire', *fasulya* 'bean'.

Turkish has in general word-final stress: *kitáp* 'book'; *gör* + *ebil* + *ecek* + *lerin* + *i* 'see + abilit. + fut. + 3 pl. + acc.' 'that they will be able to see'. Some suffixes are exceptional, however, in: (a) rejecting stress when in word-final position: *gör* + *ecék* + *ti* 'see + fut. + past' 'he was going to see'; (b) dividing the word into stress domains where not word-final: *gör* + *é* + *me* + *yecek* + *lerin* + *i* 'see + abilit. + neg. + fut. + 3 pl. + acc.' 'that they will not be able to see'. Under both circumstances, the vowel preceding the exceptional morpheme receives primary stress. More recent literature has attempted to predict exceptionality of stress by applying syntactic criteria; e.g. -*ti*, the past tense morpheme in *gör* + *ecék* + *ti* 'see + fut. + past' is not inherently exceptional, but only if it follows another tense morpheme, as is the case in this example, where it follows the future suffix and thus functions as a perfective marker. If this morpheme is analysed as a copular past tense with the preceding future morpheme as a (future) participle marker that 'closes off' a 'small word' domain, then that domain receives regular final stress, and this example stops being an exception. Other exceptional suffixes may be less amenable to such an account, but other syntactically based accounts are possible nonetheless.

A rule that applies within a phrase or a compound to reduce stresses left-to-right is needed independently: *dérs kitab + i* 'course book + compound marker', 'textbook'. This rule can be used to account for the stress in words like *górémeyeceklerinì* which consist of more than one stress domain and exhibit word-final non-primary stress.

Exceptionality with respect to stress is also exhibited by some unsuffixed stems. Such items do not fall into one clearly and independently defined set. Many (but not all) borrowed stems and almost all place names fall under this group, within which there are subregularities: they are stressed on the antepenultimate syllable, if it is the first non-final closed syllable; otherwise, the penultimate syllable is stressed. Some illustrative examples follow: *Istánbul, Ánkara, Izmir, Zongúldak, Adána, fasúlya* 'bean', *lokánta* 'restaurant'.

3 Morphology

Turkish morphology is agglutinative and suffixing; there are only very few exceptions to the one-to-one relationship between morpheme and function and only one process that is prefixing rather than suffixing, namely reduplication of the first syllable (with an inserted consonant) in intensifying adjectives and adverbs; e.g. *beyaz* 'white', *bembeyaz* 'completely white'; *çabuk* 'fast', *çarçabuk* 'very fast'. The nature of the inserted consonant is hard to predict fully; the general consensus in the literature is that the phonological features of the consonant are based on a dissimilation process.

In the following, a brief survey will be given of the most productive suffixes and some restrictions will be stated that govern their occurrence and the ordering among those morphemes that can co-occur; later on, specific categories of special interest will be discussed. Inflectional suffixes will be referred to as 'verbal' or 'nominal' according to the category of the stem they attach to. By 'nominal stems' are meant nouns, adjectives and adverbs. (Participials and gerundives will fall under the 'nominal' group in this respect.)

As to be expected, derivational suffixes precede inflectional ones. Not surprisingly, among those morphemes that derive nominals, those that attach to verbal stems precede those that attach to nominal ones, where the two types co-occur: *ver + im* 'give + abstr. n.', 'profit'; *ver + im + li* 'give + abstr. n. + with (adj.)' 'profitable'; *ver + im + li + lik* 'give + abstr. n. + with (adj.) + abstr. n.', 'profitability'. The suffixes exemplified in the last two examples can attach to underived nominals, as well: *balkon + lu* 'with a balcony; balconied'; *dürüst + lük* 'honest + abstr. n.', 'honesty'. Both groups are productive; two other productive members of the first group are the action/manner suffix *-(y)Iş*, the result/action morpheme *-mA* and the infinitive marker *-mAK*. In the second group, we find *-CI*, deriving nouns meaning 'professional', and *-sIz*, deriving adjectives meaning 'without'.

The first member of a sequence of nominal inflectional suffixes and hence immediately following derivational morphemes, if present, is the plural marker *-lAr: gül + üş + ler* 'laugh + act. n + pl.', 'laughters; manners of laughing'; *at + lar* 'horse + pl.', 'horses'.

Next come nominal agreement suffixes. These are often referred to as 'possessive suffixes' in traditional literature, the reason being that the nominal stem they attach to is often, if not always, interpreted as possessed by a noun phrase within the clause or phrase. The reason they are referred to as 'agreement suffixes' here is that they express the person and number features of their 'possessors'. A more detailed account of these suffixes will be offered in the next part of this section which will be devoted to issues of special interest.

Case morphemes occur last, e.g. *üstün* + *lüğ* + *ümüz* + *ü* 'superior + abstr. n. + 1 pl. + acc.' 'our supremacy (accusative)'. The group of agreement morphemes will be discussed in more detail in the second part of this section. It should be mentioned here, however, that not more than one case morpheme can occur within an immediate sequence of suffixes.

There is only one completely productive morpheme that derives verbs from nominals: *-lA*, which has a meaning related to the causative; e.g. *karşı* + *la* + *mak* 'opposite + deriv. morph. + infin.', 'to go to meet; to respond; to reply to'; *kara* + *la* + *mak* 'black + deriv. morph. + infin.', 'to blacken'. This morpheme can then be followed by the various verbal suffixes which we shall briefly discuss according to the sequential order in which they occur within the word.

The leftmost productive class in the string of verbal suffixes is the category often called 'voice' by traditional grammars. This group consists of the middle/reflexive (*-(I)n*), the reciprocal (*-(I)ş*), the passive *(-Il/n)* and the causative *(-DIr/t)*. (The *-Il* allomorph of the passive follows consonants, the *-n* allomorph follows vowels. *-DIr* is the basic allomorph of the causative; *-t* occurs after polysyllabic stems which end in a vowel or in the oral sonorants *r* and *l*.) The middle/reflexive and the reciprocal cannot co-occur; where the passive co-occurs with either one, it has to follow them. In the very few examples where the causative can co-occur with the middle/reflexive and the reciprocal it has to follow them, and, while it can co-occur with the passive, it has to precede it; e.g. *tanı* + *ş* + *tır* + *ıl* + *dı* + *lar* 'know + recip. + caus. + pass. + past + 3 pl.' 'they were caused to know each other; they were introduced to each other'.

Suffixes of this group can be followed by the verbal negation marker *-mA*, which is one of the suffixes that are exceptional from the point of view of word stress in rejecting word-final stress and causing the preceding vowel to be stressed. This suffix, in turn, is followed either by one of the various mood markers or by purely verbal or gerundive/participial forms, the latter expressing tense in varying degrees of differentiation. The mood markers are: the desiderative *-sA*, the necessitative *-mAlI* and the optative *-(y)a;* e.g. *gör* + *üş* + *me* + *meli* + *yiz* 'see + recip. + neg. + necess. + 1 pl.', 'we shouldn't/mustn't see each other'. The suffixes of the mood category are mutually exclusive.

The tenses are: definite past: *-DI*; reported past: *-mIş*; aorist: *-(A)r*; future: *-(y)AcAK*; present progressive: *-(I)yor*. These forms have also aspectual connotations: the past tenses denote accomplished actions and the aorist actions that are either extended or repeated over a period of time. The present progressive is similar to its English equivalent in denoting an action that, roughly speaking, takes place at the time of the utterance. One difference is that stative verbs, unlike those in standard English, can take the progressive in Turkish:

ev	+	e	git +	mek	isti +	*yor*	+	um
home	+	dat.	go +	infin.	want +	pres. prog.	+	1 sg.

'I want (*am wanting) to go home'

The main participial forms are those used in relative clauses: -(y)An and -DIK, and they will be discussed in Section 4. Also in this group (from the point of view of positional slots within the morphological word) are so-called verbal nouns and converbs (these are terms often used in traditional literature). The 'verbal nouns' consist mainly of the infinitive suffix -mAK and the result/action noun marker -mA and were also listed among the derivational morphemes that convert verbs into nominals. -DIK is a general factive nominaliser that corresponds rather closely to the English gerundive -ing. It has non-future temporal value; for future, the suffix -(y)AcAK is used, which doubles as a finite future marker. Converbs (or gerundives, as they are also called) are suffixes that yield adverbial forms. Some examples are the manner suffix -(y)ArAk, the conjunction adverbial -(y)Ip which denotes close successions of actions and the time adverb suffix -(y)IncA. In general, only one of the suffixes in this group can occur at a time. In other words, within the morphological sequence, the various gerundive, participial and nominal markers take the place of the tense or mood markers, whether they have tense connotations themselves or not.

However, two tense markers (as well as a tense and a mood marker) *can* co-occur in immediate succession to form complex tenses; in such examples, it might be appropriate to view the second marker as a copula carrying the main tense or mood and the preceding sequence as a participial:

imtihan + ım   + a   başlı + *yor* + *du* + m
exam   + 1 sg. + dat. start + prog. + past + 1 sg.
'I was starting my exam (when...)'

Note that in such sequences, the present progressive marker -(I)yor retains its aspectual meaning.

The reported past marker -mIş is used as a perfective aspect marker in such sequences (i.e. when it is the first member of the sequence):

imtihan + ım   + a   başla + *mış* + *tı* + m
exam   + 1 sg. + dat. start + perf. + past + 1 sg.
'I had started my exam (when...)'

All tense and some mood markers can occur as the first members in these sequences; however, only the two past tense markers and the mood marker for the desiderative (the latter as a conditional) can occur as the second member, i.e. as the main tense or modality marker. However, all the tenses can be used as a main tense or modality within a periphrastic construction with an auxiliary verb. The most widely used auxiliary is the verb *ol-* 'be, become'; e.g.

imtihan + ım + a   başlı + *yor* ol + *acağ* + ım
exam + 1.sg. + dat. start + prog. be + fut.   + 1 sg.
'I shall be starting my exam...'

imtihan + ım + a   başla + *mış* ol + *acağ* + ım
exam + 1.sg. + dat. start + perf. be   fut.   1.sg.
'I shall have started my exam'

This mixed positional group is followed by agreement markers, wherever such markers are possible. (Among the suffixes that cannot be followed by agreement markers are the infinitive marker -*mAK*, the participial marker -*(y)An* (unless it functions as a verbal noun) and the gerundive marker -*(y)Ip*.)

Now that we have looked at the most productive morphemes and some regularities of their distribution, let us discuss some typological characteristics of the morphological system.

Gender is neither overtly expressed in nouns (or pronouns), nor does it affect agreement. Agreement itself (by which term we shall mean agreement of the verbal or nominal head of a construction with its subject (or possessor) in terms of the features of person and number) can be either verbal or nominal; in other words, there are two basic slightly different paradigms, given in Table 30.3. (Additional, partly defective, paradigms are not included here, due to their more peripheral status.)

The verbal paradigm appears with the predicates of main clauses and of 'direct complements' (for discussion of the latter, see Section 4); the nominal paradigm is used on the head nouns of possessive noun phrases as well as on the nominalised verbs of gerundive and participial complements. Some illustrative examples follow:

Verbal agreement used with a main clause predicate verb:

(Ben) bu   makale + yi   yarın   bitir + eceğ + *im*
I   this   article + acc. tomorrow   finish + fut. + 1 sg.
'I shall finish this article tomorrow'

(Biz) her   akşam   çok   çalış +   ır + *ız*
we   every   evening a lot   work +   aor. + 1 pl.
'We work a lot every evening'

Verbal agreement used with a main clause predicate adjective:

(Ben) bugün   çok   yorgun + *um*
I   today   very   tired + 1 sg.
'I am very tired today'

(Siz) çok   güzel + *siniz*
you   very   pretty + *2pl.*
'You are very pretty'

Table 30.3 Agreement Markers

	Verbal	Nominal
1 sg.	-Im	-(I)m
2 sg.	-sIn	-(I)n
3 sg.	-∅	-(s)I(n)
1 pl.	-Iz	-(I)mIz
2 pl.	-sInIz	-(I)nIz
3 pl.	-lAr	-lArI(n)

Notes: As before, the suffix-initial vowels in parentheses are deleted after a stem-final vowel; the suffix-initial consonant in parentheses is deleted after a stem-final consonant. The suffix-final consonant in parentheses is deleted in word-final position.

Nominal agreement in a possessive noun phrase:

(Biz-im)   heykel + *imiz*
we-gen.   statue + *1pl.*
'our statue'

Ayşe-nin   araba + *sı*
Ayşe-gen.   car + *3sg.*
'Ayşe's car'

Nominal agreement used in a gerundive complement:

Herkes   [(biz + im) heykel + i   kır + dığ +   *ımız*] + ı
everybody   we + gen.   statue + acc. break + fact.n. + *1pl.* +acc.
                         bil   + iyor
                         know   + pres.prog.
'Everybody knows that we broke the statue'

Herkes   [Ayşe + nin heykel + i   kır + ma   + *sın*] + ı   isti + yor
Everybody   Ayşe + gen. statue + acc. break + act.n. + *3.sg.* +acc. want I pres.prog
'Everybody wants Ayşe to break the statue'

Another property of Turkish agreement worth remarking on is the lack of it where modifiers are concerned. This means that neither singular/plural properties of a noun nor its case marking will 'spread' onto its adjective modifier(s) or any of its determiners. As a matter of fact, another striking property of Turkish in this respect is the lack of overt plural marking on a noun where its quantifier clearly expresses plurality; this generalisation holds irrespective of the grammatical relation of the noun phrase involved. The following examples will illustrate this point:
      Subject noun phrase:

Beş   adam   (*adam + *lar*)   heykel + i   kır + dı
five   man   (man + pl.)   statue + acc. break + past
'Five men broke the statue'

Indirect object noun phrase:

Beş   adam + a   (*adam + *lar* + a)   yardım   et + ti + m
five   man + dat. (man + pl. + dat.)   help   do + past + 1 sg.
'I helped five men'

Let us now return to subject-head agreement. The two paradigms in Table 30.3 might be slightly misleading in that the suffixes for plural subjects are presented as unanalysed morphemes. However, especially the nominal paradigm in Table 30.3 can substantiate a possible claim that, at least for the first and second person plural forms, those suffixes consist of two morphemes: 1 sg. -*(I)m*, 2 sg. -*(I)n*, 1 pl. -*(I)m* + *Iz*, 2 pl. -*(I)n* + *Iz*. Hence, it would make sense to view the suffix -*Iz* as a plural marker. (This plurality would have to be confined to subject agreement, however, since the general plurality morpheme, -*lAr*, is different.)

The same analysis carries over to the verbal paradigm, if it is assumed that the suffix for person is, idiosyncratically, unrealised in the first person plural agreement form: 1 sg. -*Im*, 2 sg. -*sIn*, 1 pl. -*∅* + *Iz*, 2 pl. *sIn* + *Iz*. The agreement suffixes for third person plural subjects do not seem to fall under this generalisation, simply because their shape is rather different from those of the first and second person plural agreement morphemes. However, we would like to claim that there, too, a further analysis into a person morpheme, distinct from a number morpheme, is possible. Once again, we shall start with the nominal paradigm, which is more perspicuous than the verbal paradigm, since all morphemes are overtly realised: 3 sg. -*(s)I(n)*, 3 pl. -*lAr* + *I(n)*. Two factors are worth noticing: in comparison with the agreement forms for first and second person plural subjects, the order between the person and number suffixes is switched around, i.e. the number morpheme precedes the person morpheme. In addition, the number morpheme itself is suppletive. Instead of the form -*Iz*, the agreement morpheme for (plural) number exhibited elsewhere in both paradigms, we see here the general plurality morpheme -*lAr*. (Note, incidentally, that the suffix for third person appears in a perfectly regular shape: we know that the parenthesised initial *s* of that morpheme is deleted after a consonant. Since, within the third person plural agreement form, the third person suffix always follows the plural number suffix – and hence an *r* – that suffix will always surface without that *s*.)

Once again, the analysis carries over to the verbal paradigm. The agreement form for third person plural exhibits the suppletive morpheme -*lAr* for plural number. Since the third person morpheme remains unexpressed in the verbal paradigm, nothing else but the plural -*lAr* is included in the total form of the third person plural morpheme, as the last line of Table 30.3 shows.

Yet another peculiarity of the third person plural morpheme is that, under some circumstances, it can be omitted. Essentially, when the subject noun phrase is overtly present (as we shall see in Section 4, subjects can be omitted), the plural 'submorpheme' is optional (and, as a matter of fact, its omission is stylistically preferred):

Adam + lar   heykel + i   kır + dı (+ *lar*)
man + pl.   statue + acc.   break + past *(+3pl.)*
'The men broke the statue'

Hasan [adam   + lar + ın   heykel + i   kır + dık + *lar* + ın + ı/
Hasan man   + pl. + gen.   statue + acc.   break + fact.n. + *pl.* +*3pers.*
                                                    + acc./

                             kır + dığ + ın + ı]   bil + iyor
                             break + fact.n. + *3pers.*   know + pres. prog.
                             + acc.
'Hasan knows that the men broke the statue'

None of the other agreement morphemes exhibits this freedom of partial occurrence.

Yet another property that determines the occurrence of the plural 'submorpheme' of third person plural agreement is the animacy of the subject noun phrase. The stylistic preference we mentioned in favour of omitting the morpheme in question strengthens to the point of almost a grammatical prohibition against its occurrence when the subject is inanimate:

Kitap + lar   masa + dan yer + e   düş + tü   (??/* + *ler*)
book + pl.   table + abl. floor + dat.   fall + past   (*3pl.*)
'The books fell from the table to the floor'

Let us now turn to the case system in Turkish. It is a matter of some controversy how many cases Turkish has. Traditional Turkish grammars usually assume five cases: nominative: not marked overtly; accusative: *-(y)I*; dative: *-(y)A*; locative: *-DA*; ablative: *-DAn*. It is a fairly well-known phenomenon that the two 'structural' (i.e. non-oblique) cases, the accusative and the genitive, don't show up when the constituent in question (i.e. the direct object or the subject of a nominalised clause, respectively) is non-specific (non-referential):

Ali kitab + *ı*   oku + du
Ali book + *acc.*   read + past
'Ali read the book'

Ali bir   kitab + *ı*   oku   + du
Ali a   book   + *acc* read   + past
'Ali read a (particular, specific) book'

Ali bir   kitap oku + du
Ali a   book   read + past
'Ali read a (non-specific) book'

Ali kitap   oku + du
Ali book   read + past
'Ali read books' ['Ali book-read']

[Ali + yi   bir   arı   + *nın* sok + tuğ + un] + u   duy   + du + m
Ali + acc. a   bee   + *gen.* sting + fact.n. + 3.sg. + acc. hear + past + 1.sg.
'I heard that a (particular) bee stung Ali'

[Ali + yi   (bir) arı   sok   + tuğ + un] + u   duy   + du + m
Ali + acc. (a)   bee   sting + fact.n. + 3.sg. + acc. hear + past + 1.sg.
'I heard that (a) bee (non-specific) stung Ali' ['I heard that Ali got bee-stung']

The non-specific constituents that lack morphological case marking are quite rigidly limited to immediate pre-verbal position – a rather striking observation, given the otherwise rather free word order in Turkish (to be addressed in the next section on syntax). In this context, some of the relevant literature has analysed such non-specific constituents lacking structural case morphemes as 'incorporated' into the verb. It has become a matter of controversy in some literature what the nature of this incorporation is. The morphological incorporation found in polysynthetic languages is clearly different from the Turkish type, as in Turkish, the verb doesn't change its valency. I will not take a stand here on this matter.

Turkish has also a genitive: *-(n)I(n)*, and an instrumental: *-(y)lA*. It is probably because the genitive is not 'governed' by verbs, but is rather a structural property of the subjects of nominal phrases or clauses, that many grammarians were reluctant to recognise it as a regular case. As for the instrumental, it is a cliticised form of a formerly unbound morpheme; from the synchronic point of view, there are two criteria that could argue against viewing it as a case morpheme: (a) it is exceptional from the point of view of stress (as are all other cliticised morphemes), while all other case morphemes (including the genitive) are regular; (b) it follows the genitive when it is suffixed to a personal pronoun and hence behaves like a postposition that governs a case – namely the genitive in this instance – and not like a regular case morpheme, which can never immediately follow another case suffix, as was mentioned earlier. We shall not take a stand here on this issue.

In conjunction with the discussion about the status of the instrumental, it should be mentioned that various postpositions 'govern' certain cases, similarly to verbs. The point of interest within the context of morphology is that regular nouns are treated differently from pronouns in this respect by those postpositions that take objects in the nominative. Specifically, while full nouns appear in the nominative in those contexts, pronouns have to be marked with the genitive: *kadın gibi* 'like a woman', *Ahmet kadar* 'as much as Ahmet'; but: *ben + im gibi* 'I + gen. like', 'like me', *ben + im kadar* 'I + gen. as much as', 'as much as I'.

4 Syntax

Turkish is a perfect example of a left-branching type of language where governed elements precede their governors, i.e. objects precede the verb, the postpositional object precedes the postposition and the (adjective, genitive, or quantificational etc.) modifier precedes the modified head.

The unmarked word order in sentences is SOV; if there is more than one object, and if one of them is a direct object, the order with the indirect object closer to the verb seems less marked than others, at least with certain verbs:

Hasan   kitab + ı   çocuğ + a   oku + du
          book + acc.   child + dat read + past
'Hasan read the book to the child'

However, other orders are possible, as well. As a matter of fact, Turkish is rather free in its word order. Often (but not always), the divergences from the unmarked order have a pragmatic, discourse-oriented function, in that the position immediately preceding the verb is the preferred focus position and the sentence-initial position is the preferred topic position. New information and material stressed for emphasis appear in focus position and, in addition to being syntactically marked in this way, also receive intonational stress. The topic, i.e. the material that the sentence is about, is placed at the beginning of the sentence and is often separated from it – orthographically by a comma and by a slight pause in speech.

Differently from other SOV languages (e.g. Japanese), Turkish is so lenient about non-canonical word orders that it even permits non-verb-final constructions. Such sentences arise when material is added as an afterthought or when the speaker assumes the hearer to know about it: *Hasan çocuğ + a ver + di elma + yı* 'Hasan child + dat. give + past apple + acc.', 'Hasan gave the apple to the child'. For this example to be felicitous, it must be clear within the discourse that something happened to the apple or even that Hasan gave the apple to somebody. Some recent literature claims that such post-verbal, backgrounded constituents have the same pragmatic as well as structural properties as topicalised constituents. This claim has been successfully contested on structural grounds, showing that post-verbal constituents have different syntactic behaviour from pre-verbal ones. On the other hand, the pragmatic aspect of this issue is still being debated in relevant literature.

An embedded sentence takes up the same position that the corresponding noun phrase with the same grammatical relation would and can move around within the main clause with the same ease as a regular noun phrase:

Hasan ban + a	[imtihan + ı	geç + tiğ + in] + i	anlat + tı
Hasan I + dat.	exam + acc.	pass + fact. nom. + 2 sg. + acc.	tell + past

'Hasan told me that you passed the exam'

Hasan ban + a	anlat + tı	[imtihan + ı geç + tiğ + in] + i

The constituents of the embedded sentence are somewhat less free in their word order. While they can still successfully violate the canonical SOV order within their own clause, they have to move to the right of the highest sentence when they cross the boundary of their own clause and cannot 'scramble into' higher material; thus, compare the following examples with the last set of examples above:

Ahmet ban + a	[— geç + tiğ + in] + i	anlat + tı imtihan + ı
*Ahmet ban + a	[— geç + tiğ + in] + i	imtihan + ı anlat + tı

(The original site of the 'scrambled' constituent is marked with a —.)

In possessive noun phrases, the possessor precedes the head noun; in 'regular' noun phrases, modifiers precede the head. Where there is both an adjectival modifier and an article (only the indefinite article is overtly expressed in Turkish), the adjective precedes the article; where there is both a numeral and an adjective, the unmarked order is for the numeral to precede the adjective:

Ahmed	+ in	kitab + ı	
Ahmet	+ gen.	book + 3 sg.	'Ahmet's book'
ilgi	+ nç	bir kitap	
interest	+ ing	a book	'an interesting book'
üç	ilginç	kitap	
three	interesting	book	'three interesting books'

The genitive-marked possessor can 'scramble' in either direction, while the article and numerals cannot. The adjective is not free to move, either, as far as spoken language and written prose are concerned. In poetry, however, an adjective can occur to the right of its head. Let us also mention, without going into details, that parts of nominal compounds cannot scramble and that postpositions cannot be stranded.

One striking characteristic of Turkish is that a subject can be left unexpressed in finite clauses (i.e. those exhibiting some type of subject-predicate agreement) as well as in possessive noun phrases:

— okul + a	gid +	eceğ + im
school + dat	go +	fut. + 1 sg.

'I shall go to school'

Ahmet	[— kitab + ım] + ı	kayb + et + miş
	book + 1 sg. + acc.	loss + do + rep. past

'It is said that Ahmet lost my book'

535

(The sites of the missing constituents are marked with a —.) This possibility has been traditionally linked to the rich agreement morphology of Turkish, i.e. to the fact that agreement suffixes will uniquely 'identify' the person and number of the subject which is unexpressed.

Although Turkish has no agreement markers for non-subjects, it is also possible to 'drop' such constituents; e.g. *bul* + *du* + *m* 'find + past + 1 sg.' 'I found (it)'. Such examples are more restricted, however, than 'subject-drop' examples. They can never start a discourse, while 'subjectless' finite sentences can. Such constructions are felicitous only if the antecedent of the 'dropped' constituent has been mentioned in the discourse or has somehow been made clear by a pragmatic act.

As we saw before, passive is marked by the morpheme -*Il* (with a morphophonemic alternant -*n*) on the verbal stem. From the syntactic point of view, there are two types of passive constructions; they will be referred to as 'transitive passive' and 'intransitive passive'; the former type is derived from transitive verbs, the latter from intransitive ones. By 'transitive verb' we mean verbs that take direct objects (noun phrases that are marked accusative when they are specific), and by 'intransitive verbs' we mean verbs that do not take such objects (i.e. that either lack objects altogether or take only indirect or oblique objects). The two constructions exhibit the following surface differences: the patient of the action (or, in other words, the direct object of the corresponding active sentence) is the subject of the transitive passive construction. This claim is substantiated by the fact that these subjects exhibit syntactic properties typical of subjects in general: they appear in the nominative case, and in sentence-initial position when the word order is unmarked; the verb agrees with these constituents, as it does with subjects in general; these constituents can show up as the accusative-marked subjects of clauses that act as complements to 'believe-type' verbs (see page 540); they can correspond to the understood subjects of infinitivals; and the agent of the action can appear in an agentive phrase. However, the non-accusative objects that an intransitive verb might co-occur with are not surface subjects in an intransitive passive construction (in the sense that they do not exhibit the criteria just enumerated), and agentive phrases are judged to be awkward at best, if not completely ungrammatical. Some illustrative examples for these differences follow:

(*Biz*)	döv + *ül* + dü + *k*
we	hit + pass. + past + 1 pl.
'We were hit'	

Biz + *e*	yardım ed + *il* + di
we + dat.	help do + pass. + past
'We were helped'	

*biz(+ e)	yardım ed + il + di + *k*
We (+ dat.)	help do + pass. + past + *1.pl.*
Intended reading: 'We were helped'	

(*Biz*)$_i$	[PRO$_i$	döv + ül + mek] iste + mi + yor + uz
we		hit + pass. + infin. want + neg. + pres. prog. + 1 pl.
'We don't want to be hit'		
*(biz$_i$)	[PRO$_i$	yardım ed + il + mek] iste + mi + yor + uz
	help	do + pass. + infin. want + neg. + pres. prog. + 1 pl
Intended reading: 'We don't want to be helped'		

Obviously, verbs that do not take any objects at all can also appear in impersonal passive constructions:

Koş +   ul   + du
run +   pass.   + past
'It was run (i.e. running took place)'

Eğlen +   il   + di
amuse +   pass.   + past
'Fun was had'

Agentive phrases are ungrammatical in such objectless constructions.

It has been claimed in some relevant literature that only verbs with agentive semantics can enter the intransitive passive construction, but that stative verbs cannot. While this generalisation does hold for most cases in Turkish, it is possible to find examples where non-agentive verbs can successfully enter the construction. Such examples are best when combined with a 'tense' that has an aspectual connotation of duration (rather than, say, momentary or completed action):

Böyle   bir   hava + da   iyi   uyu + n + ur
such   a   weather + loc.   good   sleep + pass. + aor.
'One sleeps well in such a weather'

Compare this quite acceptable sentence with the following ungrammatical ones:

*şimdi   iyi   uyu + n + uyor
now   good   sleep + pass. + pres. prog.
'Now it is being slept well (i.e. one is sleeping well now)'

*Dün   bütün gün   uyu + n + du
yesterday   wholeday   sleep + pass. + past
'Yesterday it was slept the whole day (i.e. one slept the whole day yesterday)'.

Turkish has various wh-question particles most of which are morphologically derived from the particle *ne* 'what': *ne* 'what', *neden* 'why', *niçin* 'why', *niye* 'why', *hangi* 'which', *kim* 'who'. These elements, which are inherently focused, can be found in various positions, as focused constituents can in general. However, again similarly to focused elements in general, they are preferred when they immediately precede the verb. Some relevant literature calls the latter type of focus 'presentational focus', and focused constituents elsewhere in the sentence 'contrastive focus'.

Çocuğ + a   kitab + ı   kim ver + di
child + dat. book + acc.   who give + past
'Who gave the book to the child?'

Yes–no questions are formed by suffixing the particle *-mI* to the constituent questioned; if the whole sentence is questioned, the particle is attached to the verb, preceding the subject agreement markers in simple tense/aspect forms (with the exception of the simple past and the conditional, where -mI follows the agreement marker) and preceding the copula and its tense and agreement markers in complex forms:

(Sen)   çocuğ + a   kitab + ı   ver + di + n + mi
you   child + dat.   book + acc.   give + past + 2 sg. + mI
'Did you give the book to the child?'

(Sen) çocuğ + a   kitab + ı   ver   + ecek + mi + y + di + n
you   child + dat.   book + acc.   give   + fut. + mI + cop. + past + 2 sg.
'Were you going to give the book to the child?'

It should be noted that the particle -mI exhibits dual behaviour with respect to the phonology of the language: it is exceptional from the point of view of word stress (rejects domain-final stress), but regular with respect to vowel harmony.

A few examples follow where -mI takes a constituent into its scope:

Çocuğ + a   kitab + ı   sen + mi   ver + di + n
child + dat.   book + acc.   you + mI   give + past + 2 sg.
'Was it you who gave the book to the child?'

(Sen)   kitab + ı   çocuğa + a + mı   ver + di + n
'Was it the child that you gave the book to?'

(Sen)   çocuğ + a   kitab + ı + mı   ver + di + n
'Was it the book that you gave to the child?'

The translations show that such constituent questions correspond to clefted questions in English. (Turkish has also a cleft construction which can enter yes–no questions; formally, the construction consists of a relative clause lacking a head noun.) Note that the questioned constituent is located in the (presentational – see above) focus position.

One general property of embedded sentences in Turkish is that they lack complementisers that introduce (or terminate) clauses, as say the complementisers *that* or *for ... to* in English. But a perhaps even more striking characteristic feature of such clauses is exhibited by their predicates: rather than being fully finite in exhibiting the various tense and aspect markers and their combinations as is the case with verbs of main clauses, the predicates of embedded clauses are 'nominalised' with the help of various morphemes (as we saw in the section on morphology). We also saw that the subject agreement markers on these 'nominalised' predicates come from the nominal rather than the verbal paradigm; one additional criterion for calling these clauses 'nominalised' is that their predicates carry overt case markers:

[Ahmed + in   ben + i   sev + diğ + in] + *i*
Ahmet   + gen.   I + acc.   love + fact. nom. + 3 sg. (nom.) + *acc.*
bil + iyor + um
know + pres. prog. + 1 sg.
'I know that Ahmet loves me'

[Ahmed + in   ben + i   sev + me + sin] + *i*   isti +   yor +   um
Ahmet + gen. I + acc. love + act.n. + 3 sg. (nom) + *acc.* want + pres.prog. + 1.sg.
'I want Ahmet to love me'

The two 'nominalisation' morphemes (i.e. *-DIK*, the 'factive nominalisation', and *-mA*, the non-factive 'action nominalisation') exhibited above are the forms exhibited by embedded clauses that function as arguments of the verbs of the higher clause. The semantics of that higher verb and the propositional properties of the clause determine which one of the two morphemes will be chosen, as illustrated by the examples above and their translations.

A subset of the verbs that take clauses with the 'action' (or non-factive) nominal marker also take clauses that are marked with the infinitive suffix *-mAK*. These are comparable to English infinitivals in that they necessarily lack overt subjects; note also that they do not carry agreement morphology:

Ben [sev + il + mek]   isti + yor + um
I   love + pass. + infin. want + pres. prog. + 1 sg.
'I want to be loved'

Infinitivals can take case markers, too, and are thus shown to be genuine nominalised clauses, as well:

Ahmet [ben + i   sev + meğ] + *e*   başla + dı
Ahmet I + acc.   love + infin. + *dat.*   start + past
'Ahmet has started loving me'

Clauses which are postpositional objects and adverbial clauses are also nominalised; in part, their morphology and syntax are similar to those of argument clauses as illustrated above and in part somewhat different. But to discuss these details would go beyond the scope of this chapter. A brief overview follows.

The most typical adverbial clauses are ones where the predicate bears a special, non-finite morphological form that has no morphological subject agreement suffix and which is traditionally called a 'converb'. The subject is typically (and, in manner adverb clauses, obligatorily) omitted; where the subject does show up, it is in the nominative (rather than in the genitive, as might be expected in a non-finite clause):

Ali oda   + ya   [— gül + *erek*]   gir   + di
Ali room + dat. laugh + manner conv. enter + past
'Ali entered the room laughingly' (The 'silent' subject is represented with a — space.)

Ali [—   yorul   + *unca*]   ev   + e   dön   + dü
Ali   tire   + temp. conv. home + dat. return + past
'Ali returned home when (he) got tired' (The 'silent' subject is represented with a — space.)

Ali [Oya   yorul   + *unca*]   ev   + e   dön   + dü
Ali Oya (nom.) tire   + temp. conv. home + dat. return + past
'Ali returned home when Oya got tired'

Adverbial clauses can also bear the factive and the non-factive (= action) nominalisation markers:

[[Oya + nın yemek pişir + me   + si]   için] (ben) ev + de   kal + dı + m
Oya + gen. food   cook + act.n. + 3.sg. for   I   home + loc.stay + past + 1.sg.
'I stayed home so that Oya should/could cook' (' ... for Oya to cook')

[[Oya   yemek pişir + diğ   + i]   için] (ben) ev + de   kal + dı + m
Oya (nom.) food   cook + fact.n. + 3.sg. for   I   home + loc. stay + past + 1.sg.
'I stayed home because Oya cooked'

Note that the subject of the non-factive 'action' adverbial clause is in the genitive, just as it is also in the corresponding argument clauses. However, the subject of the factive adverbial clause is in the nominative, in contrast to the corresponding argument clause, but patterning with 'converb' clauses, as illustrated above. There is a body of recent literature that addresses these properties and contrasts.

A very small subset of embedded clauses exhibits verbal morphology and syntax identical to that of main sentences. Such clauses occur with verbs of belief and are, essentially, interchangeable with corresponding -*DIK* clauses (i.e. factive nominals) which can also be taken by verbs of belief. In some of the few instances where these constructions have been noted, they have been called 'direct complements'. They are of two types:

(a) the embedded subject is marked nominative; the embedded verb exhibits regular verbal subject agreement marking:

Herkes   [(ben)   üniversite + ye   başla + *yacağ* + *ım*]   san +   ıyor
everybody I (nom.) university + dat. start +   fut. +   1 sg. believe + pres. prog.
'Everybody believes that I shall start university'

(b) the embedded subject is marked accusative; the embedded verb exhibits only tense/aspect marking, but no agreement marking:

Herkes   [ben + *i* üniversite +   ye   başla + yacak]   san +   ıyor
everybody I + acc. university +   dat.   start   + fut.   believe + pres. prog.
'Everybody believes me to be starting university'

In addition, there are speakers who also accept a hybrid form where the embedded subject is accusative, but where the embedded verb exhibits regular verbal agreement markers:

Herkes   [ben + *i* üniversite +   ye   başla +   yacağ + ım]   san +   ıyor
everybody. I + acc. university +   dat. start +   fut. +   1 sg. believe + pres. prog.
(Same translation as the previous example.)

Note that no speakers accept such tensed 'direct' complement clauses, when the embedded verb doesn't exhibit subject agreement marking and when the embedded subject is in the nominative:

*Herkes   [ben   üniversite +   ye   başla +   yacak]   san +   ıyor
everybody I (nom.)   university +   dat. start +   fut.   believe + pres. prog.
Intended reading: 'Everybody believes me to be starting university'

Like all modifiers in the language, relative clauses in Turkish precede their heads. The verbs of such clauses are nominalised, and just as is the case with all regular embedded clauses, they lack complementisers. There is a gap in the position of the constituent within the clause that corresponds to the head.

The factive nominal marker -*DIK* is the basic type of morphology in these constructions; -*mA*, the 'result action' nominal, never occurs, and neither does the infinitive. -*DIK* is replaced by the morpheme -*(y)An* where the 'relativised' constituent is a subject, part of a subject or a non-subject of a clause that lacks a subject (e.g. of an intransitive passive construction as in the last example below); yet another difference between the two constructions follows from this last property: -*DIK* is, as usual, followed by nominal agreement morphology; -*An* never is:

[Ahmed +   *in*   git +   *tiğ* +   *i*]   okul
Ahmet +   gen.   go +   *DIK* +   3 sg.   school
'the school that Ahmet goes to'

[okul +   a   gid +   *en*]   çocuk
school +   dat.   go +   (y)*An*   child
'the child that goes to school'

[[oğl + u]   okul +   a   gid +   en]   adam
son + 3 sg.   school + dat.   go +   (y)*An*   man
'the man whose son goes to school'

[gid + *il* +   en]   okul
go + pass. +   (y)*An*   school
'the school that is gone to'

Embedded questions have essentially the shape of regular embedded clauses: they are nominalised. Only -*DIK*-clauses can be embedded questions; -*mA*-clauses cannot. (This probably goes together with the fact that -*DIK*-clauses are independent from the main clause with respect to tense and aspect, since they are overtly marked for at least the future/non-future distinction; -*mA*-clauses lack tense completely and are dependent on the main clause for tense and aspect.) This does not mean that *wh*-elements cannot occur within -*mA*-clauses; when they do, however, the main clause is interpreted as a question rather than the embedded clause, while with -*DIK*-clauses either interpretation is possible:

Ahmet [okul + a   kim + in   git + tiğ + in] + i   duy + du
Ahmet school + dat. who + gen. go + fact.n. + 3 sg. + acc. hear + past

This has the embedded question reading: 'Ahmet heard who went to school' and the main clause question reading: 'Who did Ahmet hear goes to school?' (i.e. 'about whom did Ahmet hear whether he goes to school?'). (These two interpretations are distinguished intonationally, with falling intonation on the main clause verb for the former and slightly rising intonation for the latter.) This ambiguity disappears when the question element occurs with a *-mA*-clause:

Ahmet [okul + a   kim ı in   git + me + sin] + i   isti + yor
Ahmet school + dat who + gen. go + act.n. + 3 sg. + acc. want + pres. prog.
'Who does Ahmet want to go to school?'

The embedded question reading is not possible: '*Ahmet wants whom to go to school.'

Yes–no questions are also basically similar to regular embedded clauses, particularly where constituents of the embedded clause are questioned; however, where the whole embedded clause is questioned, and where attachment of the question particle *-mI* is expected on the embedded verb, a periphrastic construction in the shape of a participial coordinate structure is found instead (sometimes referred to as an 'A-not-A construction'):

Ahmet   [(ben + im) okul + a   gid + ip   git + me + diğ + im] + i
Ahmet   I + gen. school + dat   go + and   go + neg. + fact.n. + 1 sg. + acc.
                                                        sor + du
                                                        ask + past
'Ahmet asked whether I go/went to school (or not)'

It is ill-formed to say, with this meaning,

*Ahmet [(ben + im) okul + a git + tiğ + im + i + mi] sor + du,

although this is grammatical with the interpretation 'is it about my going to school that Ahmet asked?'

One more construction with a main/embedded clause asymmetry in the sense that a given constraint holding of the embedded structure does not hold of the main clause is verb-gapping in coordinate structures. In main clause coordinate structures with identical verbs, either the first or the second conjunct can lack its verb:

Ahmet   balığ + ı   pişir + di,   Mehmet   + te ıstakoz + u
Ahmet   fish + acc.   cook + past   Mehmet   + and lobster + acc.
'Ahmet cooked the fish and Mehmet (cooked) the lobster'

Ahmet balığ + ı, Mehmet + te ıstakoz + u pişir + di
'Ahmet (cooked) the fish, and Mehmet cooked the lobster'

Most SOV languages (e.g. Japanese) do not allow 'forward gapped' structures like the first one above. Interestingly enough, Turkish itself does not allow such structures when they are embedded:

(Ben) [Ahmed + in balığ + ı,   Mehmed + in + de ıstakoz + u
                                            pişir + diğ + in] + i bil + iyor + um
'I know that Ahmet (cooked) the fish and Mehmet cooked the lobster'

*(Ben) [Ahmed + in balığ + ı   pişir + diğ + in + i, Mehmed + in + de
ıstakoz + u] bil + iyor + um
'I know that Ahmet cooked the fish and Mehmet (cooked) the lobster'

This concludes our overview of the syntax of Turkish.

Bibliography

For the classification of the Turkic languages, reference may be made to the contributions in Deny et al. (1959), to Johanson (1998), and to Schönig (1997). The following works are useful for the historical background to Turkish: Karamanlıoğlu (1972) – an overview of some historical literature, offering the author's own views on the development and geographical typology of the Turkic languages, especially those closely related to Turkish, and a discussion of the language reform – Von Gabain (1963) and Mansuroğlu (1954). Lewis (1999) is a perceptive, interesting and somewhat controversial account of the language reform.

Lewis (2000) is a revised and enlarged edition of the original grammar published in 1967. It is a comprehensive and detailed treatment of Turkish grammar with useful quotations from contemporary literature and the press. Göksel and Kerslake (2005) is in a similar vein, but more extensive, with a somewhat more pedagogical focus, and with attention to intonation. Underhill (1976) is a semi-pedagogical grammar, written in an informal early generative framework. Kornfilt (1997) is a reference grammar published in a descriptive grammars series, under the general editorship of Bernard Comrie, that uses a questionnaire common to the entire series and is thus intended primarily for use by typological and theoretical linguists.

Turkish phonology (and not only vowel harmony) has proved of continual interest to generative phonologists, starting with Lees' (1961) pioneering treatment, and new solutions to various problems continue to appear regularly in the generative phonological literature.

The fullest account of the pragmatic functions of Turkish word order is Erguvanlı (1984).

Useful overview articles on basic aspects of Turkish, i.e. on its syntax, semantics, pragmatics and phonology, can be found in Boeschoten and Verhoeven (1991). Of those, Kornfilt (1991) offers discussion of generative studies on syntactic aspects of Turkish, in addition to a description of Turkish syntax. Underhill (1986) consists of brief capsules on studies in English on numerous aspects of Turkish. Johanson and Csató (1998) consists of useful overview articles on Turkic as a language family as well as on individual Turkic languages.

References

Boeschoten, H. and Verhoeven, L. (eds) 1991. *Turkish Linguistics Today* (E.J. Brill, Leiden)

Deny, J., Grønbech, K., Scheel, H. and Togan, Z.V. (eds) 1959. *Philologiae Turcicae Fundamenta*, vol. 1 (Steiner, Munich)

Erguvanlı, E.E. 1984. *The Function of Word Order in Turkish Grammar* (University of California Press, Berkeley, Los Angeles and London)

Göksel, A. and Kerslake, C. 2005. *Turkish: A Comprehensive Grammar* (Routledge, London and New York)

Johanson, L. 1998. 'The History of Turkic', in L. Johanson and É.Á. Csató (eds) *The Turkic Languages* (Routledge, London and New York), pp. 81–125

Johanson, L. and Csató, É.Á. (eds) 1998. *The Turkic Languages* (Routledge, London and New York)

Karamanlıoğlu, A. 1972. *Türk Dili – Nereden Geliyor, Nereye Gidiyor* (= Hareket Yayınları, no. 46, Istanbul)

Kornfilt, J. 1991. 'Some Current Issues in Turkish Syntax', in H. Boeschoten and L. Verhoeven (eds), *Turkish Linguistics Today* (E.J. Brill, Leiden), pp. 60–92.

—— 1997. *Turkish* (Routledge, London and New York)

Lees, R.B. 1961. *The Phonology of Modern Standard Turkish* (Indiana University Press, Bloomington)

Lewis, G.L. 1999. *The Turkish Language Reform: A Catastrophic Success* (Oxford University Press, Oxford)

—— 2000. *Turkish Grammar*, 2nd revised edn (Oxford University Press, Oxford)

Mansuroğlu, M. 1954. 'The Rise and Development of Written Turkish in Anatolia', *Oriens*, vol. 7, pp. 250–64

Menges, K.H. 1959. 'Classification of the Turkic Languages, II', in J. Deny, K. Grønbech, H. Scheel and Z.V. Togan (eds) *Philologiae Turcicae Fundamenta*, vol. 1 (Steiner, Munich), pp. 5–10

Schönig, C. 1997. 'A New Attempt to Classify the Turkic Languages', *Turkic Languages* vol. I, pp. 117–33.

Slobin, D.I. and Zimmer, K. (eds) 1986. *Studies in Turkish Linguistics* (John Benjamins, Amsterdam and Philadelphia

Underhill, R. 1976. *Turkish Grammar* (MIT Press, Cambridge, MA)

—— 1986. 'Bibliography of Modern Linguistic Work on Turkish', in D.I. Slobin and K. Zimmer (eds), *Studies in Turkish Linguistics* (John Benjamins, Amsterdam and Philadelphia), pp. 23–51

Von Gabain, A. 1963. 'Die Südwest-Dialekte des Türkischen', in *Handbuch der Orientalistik*, I Abt., 5 Band, 1 Abschn (E.J. Brill, Leiden), pp. 174–80

31

Afroasiatic Languages

Robert Hetzron

1 Introduction

The approximately 250 Afroasiatic languages, spoken by about 340 million ethnically and racially different people, occupy today the major part of the Middle East, all of North Africa, much of North-East Africa and a considerable area in what may roughly be defined as the northwestern corner of Central Africa. Though the distribution and spread of the specific languages was substantially different, about the same area was covered by Afroasiatic languages in antiquity. In the Middle Ages, Sicily and the southern half of Spain were also conquered by those who were to become the largest Afroasiatic-speaking people, the Arabs. Today, only Maltese represents this family as a native language in Europe.

The term 'Semitic' was proposed in 1781 for a group of related tongues, taken from the Bible (Genesis 10–11) where Noah's son Shem is said to be the ancestor of the speakers of these languages – showing, incidentally, awareness of linguistic relationships at this time. When it was realised that some other languages were further related to this group, the term 'Hamitic', based on the name of Shem's younger brother Ham (Cham), the biblical ancestor of Egypt and Kush, was coined for the entire family. Later the composite term Hamito-Semitic (sometimes Semito-Hamitic) was introduced. However, this created the wrong impression that there exists a 'Hamitic' branch opposed to Semitic. Of all the other terms proposed (Erythraic, Lisramic, Lamekhite), 'Afroasiatic' has been gaining ground. Even this name has the inconvenience of being misinterpreted as a group including all the languages of Africa and Asia. To dispel this, a further contraction, Afrasian, has also been used.

2 Division

Afroasiatic is composed of several branches. Various proposals have been made concerning the internal relationship between the branches, but none of these subdivisions are convincing enough to be adopted. The main branches are the following.

(a) **Egyptian** is the extinct language of one of the major civilisations of antiquity, that of Pharaonic Egypt (in today's Egypt, Arabic is spoken). This language can boast the longest continuous history. Its earliest documentations are from 3000 BC. From AD 300 on, the term 'Coptic' is used for the Egyptian idiom of monophysite Christians. It was spoken till the sixteenth century, perhaps even later; it is still used as a liturgical language.

(b) **Semitic** (see Chapter 32).

(c) **Cushitic** consists of about 40 languages, spoken by perhaps 40 million people in Ethiopia, Somalia, northwestern Kenya and adjacent areas. Beja (of eastern Sudan and northern Ethiopia), with about a million Muslim speakers, has been classified as North Cushitic, but there is some likelihood that it constitutes a separate branch of Afroasiatic. Central Cushitic or Agaw used to be the major language of Ethiopia before the Semitic conquest. It has split into a number of languages and is still spoken, by few, in scattered enclaves. Rift Valley (or Highland East) Cushitic is spoken by nearly two million people around the Ethiopian Great Rift Valley. Its best known representative is Sidamo. Lowland (East) Cushitic is numerically the most important group. Among others, it comprises Afar-Saho (Dankali) along the Red Sea, Oromo (formerly Galla), spoken by 20 million or more people, Somali, the official language of the Republic of Somalia and the vehicle of about 12 million Muslims, the Dullay languages, etc. The status of South Cushitic is debated; many consider it a separate main branch, but it may also be a southern offshoot of Lowland Cushitic. The oldest Cushitic texts are from the eighteenth century. Note that the term 'Cush' was originally applied to an unrelated country and civilisation: Meroë.

(d) **Omotic** is the name of a group of about 40 languages in the Omo Valley of southern Ethiopia, with about 1,500,000 speakers. It used to be classified as West Cushitic. Yet the great divergences led scholars to list it as a separate branch. On the other hand, since the divergences mainly consist of absence of some typical Cushitic features, Omotic may also be a simplified, pidginised offshoot of some branch of Cushitic.

(e) **Berber** is a cluster of closely related yet not always mutually intelligible dialects. Once the major language of all of North Africa west of Egypt, it still has between 14 and 20 million (or even more) speakers, with the heaviest concentration in Morocco. The earliest documentation is provided by the Lybian inscriptions (the only one dated is from 139 BC). The major dialects are Tuareg, Tamazight, Tshalhit, Tirifie, Kabyle, Chawiya and Zenaga. An old consonantal alphabet, the *tifinagh*, has survived among the Tuareg. The extinct language of the Canary Islands, Guanche, may have also been a Berber tongue.

(f) **Chadic** (see Chapter 36).

3 Problems of Relationship

The assertion that certain languages are related means that it is assumed that they are descended from a single common ancestor. Naturally, this is not necessarily true of the speakers themselves. It often happens that the same sedentary population switches language, adopting, with a certain degree of modification, the type of speech that has been imported by a relatively small, yet dominant group of newcomers. Thus, it could be just the language that wanders, whereas the people remain stationary and only change linguistic allegiance. This explains why so many anthropological types are found in this family: the brown-skinned Mediterranean Semites, the white-skinned Berber, the black-skinned, yet in many ways still different, Cushites and Chadic speakers.

Since Semitic, a linguistically fairly homogeneous group, seems to have had its major branches already established at least 5,000 years ago, and further, taking into consideration the great internal heterogeneity of Cushitic and Chadic, the period when the putative ancestral common Afroasiatic language was spoken must be placed at a much earlier period than the previously assumed sixth millennium BC. The location of this hypothetical tongue has been assumed to have been in North Africa, perhaps in the area which is now the Sahara Desert, and the various branches must have diffused from there.

Theories have been advanced about further relationships of Afroasiatic with other languages, especially with Indo-European within a wide superfamily, Nostratic, also including Uralic, Altaic, Kartvelian, Dravidian, etc. In view of the enormous time-depth that has to be accounted for, it is extremely hard to form any critical opinion of the reconstructions proposed to support this or other such proposals.

4 On Afroasiatic Comparison

In view of the great diversity among the branches of Afroasiatic, one should not expect many features in common that are to be found everywhere. Some such features do exist, such as gender distinction with *t* as a mark of the feminine, an element *k* as a mark of the second person, some vocabulary items such as the root **mut* 'die'. Otherwise, we have to content ourselves with features that are found in several, but not all, branches, yielding an intertwined system that ultimately makes the unity of the family quite obvious. Thus, the root **šim* 'name' is found everywhere but in Egyptian, the prefix conjugation is attested in Semitic, Cushitic and Berber, the stative suffix conjugation in Semitic, Egyptian, Berber and possibly Cushitic, etc. Naturally, for comparative purposes, it is sufficient for an item to be attested in at least one language of a branch to be used as an isogloss, e.g. the suffix conjugation only in Kabyle within Berber, the root **mut* clearly only in Rendille within Cushitic.

Because of the fact that Semitic exhibits such a great deal of regularity and also because of its being the best known branch, some of the reconstructions have been strongly inspired by phenomena of Semitic. The opposite attitude, rejecting Semitic phenomena in reconstruction in order to avoid bias, has also been seen. Other disturbing factors are: lack of knowledge of Egyptian vowels (only Coptic provides clues about them), quite recent attestation and no ancient documents of most Cushitic, Omotic and Chadic languages, contrasting with millennia-old Semitic and Egyptian data. Nevertheless, one should not dogmatically believe that older data necessarily reflect a more archaic situation. Some phenomena found in recently discovered languages may be direct survivals from the oldest times.

5 Some Afroasiatic Features

The following is a brief listing of linguistic features that may be original Afroasiatic.

547

5.1 Phonetics

All branches except Egyptian exhibit a special set of consonants, besides voiced and voiceless pairs, the 'emphatic' series, realised as pharyngealised (velarised) in Arabic and Berber, glottalised (ejective, explosive) in South Arabian, Ethiopian and Cushitic and glottalised (explosive or implosive) in Chadic; Egyptian, incidentally, also lacked voiced consonants (*d* stands for /t/, *t* for /tʰ/, in the standard transliteration). There is evidence for several lateral consonants in Proto-Semitic; they are still used in modern South Arabian, South Cushitic and some Chadic languages (e.g. *balsam* ultimately comes from the Semitic root *bśm* where *ś* must have been a lateral fricative). Laryngeal sounds ', *ḥ* and *x* are found in Egyptian, Cushitic, Berber and Semitic. A prenasalised phoneme *^{m}b* has also been reconstructed.

The original vowel system is assumed to be long and short *a*, *i*, *u*, as still in Classical Semitic. Cushitic, Omotic and Chadic have tonal systems, e.g. Awngi (Cushitic, Agaw) *aqá* '(turn) into a man', *aqâ* 'I have been' and *áqâ* 'I have known'; *a* represents mid tone, *á* high tone, *à* low tone and *â* falling tone.

5.2 Morphology

In the pronominal system, **an* for 'I' in Semitic and Cushitic vs **ana:ku* 'I' with a further velar in Egyptian and marginally in Semitic (perhaps also in the Berber suffix *-γ*), or *ka* for masculine 'thee, thy' in Semitic and Chadic vs *ku* in Cushitic and marginally in Semitic (unclear for Egyptian) with different vowels, may represent original dialectal variations in Afroasiatic. The opposition *u/i* for masculine/feminine, especially in third person singular pronouns, seems to be original as well: Akkadian (Semitic) *šu:/ ši:*, Somali (Cushitic) *-uu/-ay* 'he/she', Omotic: *-o/-e* gender markers in Kafa, parts of the third person singular masculine/feminine verb endings in Dizi, noun gender markers in Mubi (Chadic) (e.g. *mùndúró/mìndíré* 'boy/girl') and perhaps Egyptian *-f/-s* 'his/her' (from **hʷ/hʸ*?).

In the demonstrative system the following gender-and-number markers are found: m. sg./f. sg./pl. *n/t/n* (Semitic, Chadic, traces in Berber), *ku/ti/hu* (Cushitic, also Chadic: Mubi *g-/d-/h-*), *p/t/n* (Egyptian) and for m./f. *w/θ* (in Berber). It is possible that both *p* and *w* come from **ku*.

Two verbal conjugation systems are found in more than one branch. One, found in Semitic, Cushitic and Berber, operates with the prefixes: *ʔ-* or *a-* for first person singular, *n-* for first person plural, *t-* for second person and for third person singular feminine and *y-* for the other third persons. Further suffixes added to the second and third person plurals and, in Semitic and Beja, to the second person singular feminine make up the full conjugations. Note the homonymy of second person singular masculine and third person singular feminine. The Cushitic languages have all switched to suffix conjugations by means of prefix-conjugated postposed auxiliaries, though a few of them have maintained the original conjugation for a limited number of verbs. This suffix conjugation is not to be confused with the original Afroasiatic suffix conjugation which can be reconstructed for predicates expressing a state, rather than an action, and is attested in Semitic (with the original value in Akkadian), Egyptian, Kabyle (Berber, for predicative adjectives) and probably in Cushitic.

In spite of its absence from Egyptian, Omotic and Chadic, it is likely that the prefix conjugation harks back to Proto-Afroasiatic.

Internal inflection, i.e. internal vocalic changes within a consonantal root to express tense, mood and other categories (the *root-and-pattern* system) is an operative principle in Semitic (Akkadian *i-prus* 'he divided', *i-parras* 'he divides', root *p-r-s*), less systematically in Berber (*-θ-lal* 'she (will) be born', *θ-lula* 'she was born'), in traces in Cushitic (Beja *ʔadanbíil* 'I collect', *ʔadbìl* 'I collected', root *d-b-l*). In Chadic, where the person of the subject is expressed by means of preposed particles which are very similar in shape to the oblique pronouns of other branches and where other categories like tense, mood, etc., are expressed either by elements attached to these particles or, in part at least, by the stem form of the verb, alternations like Mubi *nítúwà* 'I (will) *nə́-tì* 'I ate' have been considered traces of the Afroasiatic internal inflection by some scholars, while others have attributed them to independent developments. It is likely that an internal *a* is to be posited to mark the non-past in Afroasiatic. Internal *a/u* for non-past/past is attested in Semitic, Berber and Cushitic.

The verbal derivation system plays an important part in Afroasiatic vocabulary. Verbal roots are subject to modification; new verbs are created by the addition of derivative affixes. The element *s* produces a causative, the addition of *t* or *n* makes the verb intransitive (passive or reflexive). Repetition of the root or part of it or mere consonantal gemination expresses repeated action. Berber: *aɣəm* 'to get water', *ss-iɣəm* 'cause to get water', *ttuy-uɣəm* '(water) be drawn'; Beja *tam* 'eat', *tamtam* 'gobble'.

Classical Semitic and Egyptian used to have a dual in their nominal system, e.g. Egyptian *sn* 'brother', *sn.wy* 'two brothers', *sn.w* 'brothers'. For plural marking, several devices are found. The endings *-u:/-w* and *-n* seem to be attested all over. Repetition of the last consonant is found in Cushitic (Somali *miis/miisas* 'table/tables') and Chadic (Mubi *lísí/lésas* 'tongue'). In Cushitic and Chadic, one finds singulative systems where the basic form is a collective and the addition of a suffix makes it singular, e.g. Mubi (Chadic) *mándàr* 'boy(s) (in general)'/*mùndúrò* 'boy'. Yet the most interesting plural formation is what has been called the broken plural, based on internal inflection, *sinn-/asna:n-* in Arabic (Semitic), *sini/san* in Logone (Chadic) for 'tooth/teeth', Xamta (Agaw, Cushitic) *gezéŋ/agzéŋ* 'dog/dogs', Berber *ikərri/akrarən* (with a further *-n*) 'ram/rams'. Though the basic principle seems to be the infixation of an *a*, the broken plural forms cannot be predicted automatically from the singular. This is also an argument in favour of their archaic character. Thus, some form of internal inflection *must* have existed indeed in Afroasiatic. The Afroasiatic noun also distinguished between the genders masculine and feminine. The latter is used not only for female animates, but often also for derivatives such as diminutives, e.g. Berber *axam* 'tent' – *θaxamθ* 'small tent'. Furthermore, Semitic and Cushitic have traces of polarity whereby a noun changing number may also change its gender, e.g. Sidamo (Cushitic) *ko beetti* 'this boy'/*te ooso* 'these boys' vs *te seemo* 'this girl'/*ko seenne* 'these girls' (m. *ko*, f. *te*).

In nominal derivation, the prefix *ma-* plays an important role to form agent, locative or instrumental nouns.

5.3 Word Order

Classical Semitic, Egyptian and Berber are VSO languages, Cushitic is almost all SOV, while Chadic is mainly SVO. The reconstruction of Proto-Afroasiatic word order is open to speculation.

Bibliography

Diakonoff (1965) is a short yet highly informative comparative presentation, the best so far in the field. Hodge (1971) is a collection of chapters from the Current Trends in Linguistics series, somewhat uneven, partly inevitably obsolete, but still an important research tool. Cohen (1947) is a pioneering work in comparative Afroasiatic, but restricted to vocabulary and with only few references to Chadic. Bender (1976) provides concise yet comprehensive sketches of the structure of the major Cushitic languages, with state-of-the-art introductions, and is a ground-breaking publication. Greenberg (1963) includes a valuable discussion of Afroasiatic. Reference should be made to Hayward (2000) for an up-to-date current appraisal.

References

Bender, M.L. (ed.) 1976. *The Non-Semitic Languages of Ethiopia* (Michigan State University, East Lansing)

Cohen, M. 1947. *Essai comparatif sur le vocabulaire et la phonétique du chamitosémitique* (Champion, Paris)

Diakonoff, I.M. 1965. *Semito-Hamitic Languages* (Nauka, Moscow)

Greenberg, J.H. 1963. *The Languages of Africa* (Indiana University, Bloomington; Mouton, The Hague)

Hayward, R.J. 2000. 'Afroasiatic', in B. Heine and D. Nurse (eds) *African Languages: An Introduction* (Cambridge University Press, Cambridge), pp. 74–98

Hodge, C.T. (ed.) 1971. *Afroasiatic: A Survey* (Mouton, The Hague)

32

Semitic Languages

Robert Hetzron

Revised by Alan S. Kaye

1 Introduction

Originally limited to the area east of the Mediterranean, the Semitic languages spread into North Africa, southern Europe and the Horn of Africa. In antiquity, the Assyrian and Babylonian Empires were major centres of civilisation. Phoenician traders were establishing colonies all over the Mediterranean basin. Hebrew culture, through its monotheistic religion, Judaism, has exerted an exceptional influence, directly or indirectly (through the two religions that followed it: Christianity and Islam), on all of humankind. Arabic, in addition to being the carrier of an important medieval civilisation, has become one of the world's major languages.

While the ancestor of Semitic, Proto-Afroasiatic, is assumed to have originated in Africa, the homeland of Semitic itself, i.e. the area where, having arrived from Africa, the different branches started to split off, may have been approximately the region where the Arabic peninsula reaches the continental bulk of the Near East. In all likelihood, however, Proto-Afroasiatic and Proto-Semitic contained dialectal variation.

2 Division

The following is a listing of the Semitic languages according to the latest classification, with summary information on the speakers.

(A) East Semitic: Akkadian was the language of ancient Mesopotamia (approximately today's Iraq), the carrier of a grandiose civilisation from c. 3000 BC to the beginnings of the Christian era. Akkadian gradually replaced the unrelated linguistic isolate Sumerian, which had greatly influenced it. It was soon divided into Assyrian (northern) and Babylonian (southern) branches, corresponding to a political division. The last written documents date from the first century AD. Afterwards, Akkadian was completely forgotten and had to be rediscovered, and its writing system deciphered, in the nineteenth century. The

Akkadian script, usually written from left to right, is called cuneiform, i.e. 'wedge-shaped', because of the graphic components of the symbols written on clay tablets. The recently discovered language of Ebla (modern Tell el-Mardikh in Syria; third millennium BC), usually called Eblaite, is related to Akkadian in East Semitic.

(B) West Semitic, the other major branch of Semitic, is divided into two sub-branches.

    (a) South Semitic is composed of three groups, the exact relationship of which has not yet been determined.

        (i) Epigraphic South Arabian (attested from the ninth century BC to the sixth century AD) is known only from short inscriptions written in a consonantal script. Its dialects were Sabaean (of Sheba), Minean, Awsani, Qatabani and Hadramauti. Once spoken in the southern half of the Arabian peninsula, they were completely replaced by Arabic.

        (ii) Modern South Arabian, a group of non-Arabic languages (which are in all likelihood not the descendants of Epigraphic South Arabian), is still spoken by perhaps 200,000 people in Dhofar (Oman) and Yemen: Šheri, Mehri, Harsusi and, on the island of Socotra, Soqotri. Serious investigation of some of them has started only recently.

        (iii) Ethiopian. Speakers of Old South Arabian crossed the Red Sea millennia ago – much earlier than the usually given date of the fourth century BC – into the highlands of Ethiopia and mixed with the local Cushitic population, who gradually adopted their language and modified it to a significant extent. The Ethiopian Semitic (Ethio-Semitic) languages can be divided into two main branches:

            (α) North Ethiopic comprises the following: the now extinct Ge'ez, attested between the fourth and ninth centuries AD, was the language of the Axumite Empire. It is still used as the liturgical language of the Ethiopian Coptic Church, occasionally also for literature. Almost all the Ge'ez material comes from a period when it was no longer in everyday use, which makes the data less reliable. Tigrinya has over four million speakers in Eritrea and Tigray Province, Ethiopia. Tigré is spoken by about 800,000 Muslims in Eritrea and neighbouring Sudan.

            (β) South Ethiopic has two branches: (I) Transversal South Ethiopic, which comprises Amharic, the dominant language of modern Ethiopia, the native language of about 18 million Coptic Christians and the second language of about as many more; the nearly extinct Argobba; Harari (Adare), the language of the Muslim city of Harar; and East Gurage (Zway or Zay and the Selti–Wolane–Ulbarag cluster), a practically undescribed unit. (II) Within Outer South Ethiopic, the recently extinct Gafat, Soddo (the language of about 250,000 Christians) and Goggot constitute the *n*-group; Muher and Western Gurage (Masqan, the 'Central' Ezha–Gumer–Chaha–Gura cluster and the 'Peripheral' Gyeto–Ennemor–Endegeñ–Ener cluster) make up the *tt*-group. 'Gurage' is, incidentally, not a valid linguistic unit; it designates a number of Semitic languages belonging to different branches, spoken in one specific area.

(b) Central Semitic comprises the following languages and groups:

(i) Aramaic is the label for a group of related dialects, originally spoken in what is today Syria. It is attested from the beginning of the first millennium BC. It later spread throughout the Near East, replacing Akkadian, Hebrew and other languages, only to be replaced, in turn, by Arabic after the rise of Islam in the seventh century AD. Major parts of the biblical books of Ezra and Daniel are in Aramaic. Jesus' native tongue was Palestinian Aramaic. Nabatean was spoken by ethnic Arabs around the beginning of the Christian era. The Babylonian Talmud was written in Eastern Aramaic, a language close to Syriac, the language of the Christian city of Edessa (till the thirteenth century AD), still the liturgical language of the Nestorian and Jacobite Christian Churches. Classical and Modern Mandaic are associated with a Gnostic sect. Today, a variety of Western Aramaic is on the verge of extinction in Syria, but Eastern Neo-Aramaic (Modern Syriac) is still vigorous in Christian communities in northwestern Iran and adjacent areas in Iraq, Georgia and in scattered communities around the world. The speakers (about 500,000) are sometimes inappropriately called Chaldean or (Neo-)Assyrian. The consonantal Aramaic square script is used for Hebrew today (see Chapter 34).

(ii) South-Central Semitic

(α) Arabic (see Chapter 33; the traditional assignment of Arabic to South Semitic is untenable).

(β) Canaanite. Ancient Canaanite inscriptions of Byblos are from the sixteenth and fifteenth centuries BC. Moabite (ninth century BC) is known from one fairly long inscription. One ancient, long-extinct language may also be Canaanite, though further study is needed: Ugaritic, the language of the city-state of Ugarit (now Ras Shamra, Syria, on the Mediterranean) around the fourteenth/thirteenth century BC, with an impressive literature written in a cuneiform consonantal script. The poorly attested Amorite (first half of the second millennium BC) is considered to be West Semitic, though its precise position requires further research.

Phoenician was originally spoken in the coastal areas of today's Lebanon and is attested through inscriptions (from the twelfth century BC to AD 196). Phoenician merchants, however, established settlements all over the Mediterranean area: Cyprus, Greece, Malta, Sicily, Sardinia, southern France, southern Spain and, above all, North Africa. In the latter area, the city of Qart Ḥadašt 'new city', known in Europe as Carthage, founded in 814 BC, developed into a large empire after the fifth century BC. It was destroyed, under the rule of Hannibal, in 146 BC by the Romans. Their variety of late Phoenician is called Punic, attested till the fifth century AD.

The Phoenician consonantal script of 22 letters, written from right to left, practically identical to the old Hebrew script, is probably of Egyptian origin. It is the direct ancestor of the Greek and Latin alphabets. The Arabic, South Semitic (including Ethiopian) and Syriac scripts also come from the Canaanite writing system. Furthermore, the writing systems of Central Asia (e.g. Mongolian writing) and India (the Devanāgarī script) are also descended from the Syriac one.

For the historically most important Canaanite language, Hebrew, see Chapter 34.

3 The Structure of Semitic

3.1 Phonology

The original vowel system consisted of long and short *a*, *i* and *u*. Consonants occurred simple or doubled (geminated). A typical feature of the consonant system is the existence of 'triads', groups of three consonants with the same point of articulation: voiced (e.g. *d*), voiceless (*t*) and 'emphatic' (*ţ*). The latter are pronounced pharyngealised ('dark') in Arabic, as glottalised ejectives (where the glottal closure is maintained till high pressure is achieved, then the closure in the oral cavity is released with an explosion) in Ethiopian and Modern South Arabian (though the two do not sound the same) and dropped in Modern Hebrew (where they are pronounced voiceless, but note *ş* > *ts*). The nature of the articulation is unknown in the extinct languages. The original set of laryngeals, *ʔ*, *ʕ* (voiced pharyngeal constriction), *ħ* (voiceless pharyngeal constriction) and *x* (voiceless uvular constriction) has been maintained in full in Arabic only. Ethiopian script still marks them, but of all the living languages, only Tigrinya and Tigré kept all but *x* (but a new *x* was secondarily developed). Akkadian had lost all of them (former *ħ* and *ʕ* left their trace in changing a neighbouring *a* into *e*).

In the causative prefix, in the third person independent pronouns, in the archaic dative endings and in some other cases, one finds an alternation across languages *š* (e.g. Akkadian) ~ *h* (Hebrew), etc. This may go back to an old phoneme *ś which merged with other phonemes in different ways, possibly an originally voiceless lateral or palatal fricative. There is strong evidence for Arabic *ḍ* and Hebrew *ś* once having been lateral; Modern South Arabian still has the laterals *ś* and *ź*.

In Arabic and South Semitic, old *p* became *f*, and in most Arabic dialects, *g* became *ǰ* or *ž*. In Aramaic, Hebrew and several Ethiopian languages, a morphophonemic process of spirantisation took place, leading to alternations in different forms of the same root. Post-vocalic non-geminate stops of Hebrew (see pages 584–585): *p*, *t*, *k*, *b*, *d*, *g* became *f*, *θ*, *x*, *β*, *ð*, *γ* respectively. In modern North Ethiopic, only *k* and *q* were spirantised (the latter yielding a curious spirant ejective sound). In Outer South Ethiopic *tt*-languages, complicated spirantisation processes, also depending on position in the root, took place, *k~h* being the most basic. In some of these languages, all geminate consonants became voiceless and simple. Thus, Ezha has *bäkkʸä-*, Chaha *bäkʸä-* 'he cried', but both have *yəβähʸ* 'he cries' (note the spirantisation *b~β* as well, root *b-k-y*). For 'he broke/breaks', Ezha has *säbbärä-/yəsäbər*, Chaha *säpärä-/yəsäβər* (root *s-b-r*).

3.2 Morphology

In the noun, there was a distinction between masculine and feminine genders (the latter marked by *-(a)t*), e.g. Ge'ez *nəgus* 'king'/*nəgəst* 'queen'; for number: a singular, a dual (for two units; alive in Arabic, Epigraphic and Modern South Arabian, only in traces in Akkadian and Hebrew, lost in Ethiopian; marked by *-a:/-ay*) and a plural. For plural marking, the suffixal ('sound') plural had, as its markers: lengthening of the last vowel most often followed by *-n(a)* in the masculine and *-t* (i.e. *-a:t*) in the feminine, but most frequently the plural was formed by internal vocalic changes (the so-called 'broken plural'). Examples (sg./pl.): Akkadian *šarr-/šarr* + long vowel or *šarra:n* 'king', Ge'ez *nəgəst/nəgəstat* 'queen' (sound), *ləbs/albas* 'clothing', *nəgus/nägäst* 'king' (broken). The *-t* of the latter is the trace of an interesting phenomenon, polarity, whereby in changing number nouns also change gender. Hence the feminine ending after the plural of a masculine. For the opposite direction, much rarer, see Ge'ez *təʔ mərt/təʔamər* 'miracle', where the plural loses its feminine ending. Polarity is never a truly consistent principle in any Semitic language, but it left its traces in plural formation, in the Arabic agreement rules (see page 572) and in the numeral system (see below).

The type of vocalisation assumed by the broken plural form is predictable from the singular in a minority of cases only. Usually, it has to be memorised separately. One noun may have several broken plural forms, e.g. Ge'ez *kälb* 'dog', pl. *käläbat, akləbt* or *aklab* (cf. *kalb/kila:b* in Arabic), sometimes with differences in meaning, e.g. Classical Arabic *ʔamr* has two plurals, *ʔumu:r* 'matters' and *ʔawa:mir* 'orders'. Broken plurals are widely used in Arabic, Modern South Arabian and North Ethiopic, with some traces in South Ethiopic and Hebrew (e.g. *kɛlɛb/klåbīm* 'dog/dogs', with a further sound plural ending), but none in Akkadian.

A further morphological category applying to nouns is 'state': the construct state (a phonetically shortened form in Hebrew, with an ending *-ä* in Ge'ez) is for the noun attached to a genitival noun; the pronominal state is used before possessive suffixes; the predicative state in Akkadian is the shape of a predicative noun, containing also a subject ending; in Aramaic, the emphatic state (suffix *-å*) refers to a definite noun; otherwise, the noun is in the absolute state (with an ending *-m* in the singular in Akkadian and *-n* in Classical Arabic).

The basic case system consists of a nominative case and an oblique one. In the singular, the latter is subdivided into an accusative and a genitive. Construct state nouns have only a 'genitive/all the rest' opposition in Akkadian and no case in Ge'ez. In the singular, the endings are nom. *-u*, acc. *-a*, gen. *-i*; in the dual nom. *-a:*, obl. *-ay*; in the plural nom. *-u:*, obl. *-i:*. Prepositions combine with the genitive/oblique case. Proto-Semitic probably had a richer case system, as suggested by the evidence of some traces. The above system is found in Akkadian and Classical Arabic only; Ge'ez has acc. *-ä* vs *-∅* in the singular only (and East Gurage has *-ä* for a definite accusative). The prepositional system that had been the mainstay of case marking since Proto-Semitic has completely taken over everywhere else (for dual and plural marking, the oblique forms were generalised), with further prepositions (forming circumpositions) developing in modern Ethiopian, and with postpositions only (some of which used to be prepositions) in Harari (e.g. Proto-Semitic **bi-bayt-i* 'in-house-gen.', Ge'ez *bä-bet*, East Gurage *bä-gar wəst* (= 'inside'), Harari *gar-be* for 'in (a/the) house').

In the pronominal and verbal system, no distinction of gender is made in the first person, but the second and third persons have both a masculine and a feminine, in the singular everywhere, but no longer in the plural in modern Eastern Aramaic, Transversal South Ethiopic and Gafat (and some modern Arabic dialects).

There are three basic sets of personal pronouns: independent ones for subject and predicate functions, possessive pronouns suffixed to nouns (Amharic *bet-e* 'house-my') or to prepositions (Hebrew *b-ī* 'in my' for 'in me') and object pronouns attached to verbs.

Beside basic adjectives, nouns may be adjectivalised by means of the suffix *-i:/-iyy* (the so-called nisba), e.g. Arabic *bayt-iyy-* 'domestic, home-made'.

Numerals from 'three' to 'ten' (with some complications, from 'eleven' to 'nineteen' as well in South-Central Semitic) show clear traces of polarity. Numerals with a feminine ending precede masculine nouns and those without such an ending occur with feminine nouns. This harks back to a prehistoric period when the plural of a masculine was indeed a feminine and vice versa.

The centrality of the verb has always been pointed out in the description of Semitic. Verbal morphology is an essential part of grammar. Most nouns are derived from verbs and, conversely, most nouns that seem to be basic may be the sources of verbal roots (e.g. Arabic *ba:ta* 'spend the night' from *bayt-* 'house'). And it is here that the most important feature of Semitic morphology, the root-and-pattern system (see broken plurals above) ought to be properly introduced.

The Semitic root consists of a set of consonants, ideally three, but sometimes four, e.g. Akkadian *p-r-s* 'divide, decide, etc.' There is strong evidence that pre-Semitic may have had also biconsonantal roots that were later made triconsonantal by the addition of another consonant; cf. the Hebrew roots *p-r-d* 'divide', *p-r-m* 'open, seam', *p-r-s* 'break up, divide up', suggesting an old root **p-r*. Roots that behave regularly are called 'sound' roots, as opposed to 'weak roots' which have a weak root consonant, such as a semi-vowel *y* or *w*, which may be reduced to a vowel (*i/u* respectively) or disappear, for Akkadian and Hebrew also *n*, which may assimilate to the subsequent consonant; or else, to be 'weak', the last two consonants may be identical, like *p-r-r* 'annul', which may be subject to contractions through the conjugation.

Such roots are combined with patterns made up of vowels and often also consonants in a prefixal, suffixal or, more rarely, infixal position. Thus, in Akkadian, the pattern CCuC yields *-prus*, the past tense 'divided', whereas the present has CaC:aC, leading to *-parras* (where the gemination is part of the pattern); Ca:CiC is the active participle: *pa:ris-* 'divider'; CtaCaC is the perfect theme *-ptaras* 'has divided'; šaCCVC is the causative stem, where the value of V depends on tense: *-šapras* for the present and *-šapris* for the past; with a further *mu-*, we obtain an active participle *mušapris-* 'the one who makes divide'; some nominal patterns: CiCiCt- (*t* for feminine) *pirist-* 'decision', CaCC *pars-* 'part', etc.

There are two sets of basic conjugations in Semitic, one called 'prefixal', in reality a combination of four prefixes and, in seven cases out of twelve, further suffixes, and one purely 'suffixal'. Table 32.1 gives the forms that may be reconstructed for Proto-Semitic. (There are uncertainties about the first person dual. In the prefix conjugation, note the identity of second person singular masculine and third person singular feminine and, more puzzling, of the dual and feminine plural. The first person plural typically has no suffix.)

These affixes are attached to various stem forms to create verbal words. Stem forms (as the term is used here) consist of the verbal root and the pattern expressing tense, mood and type of derivation (see below). In the following, the root *p~f-r-s* (Akkadian 'divide', Arabic 'make a kill (of a predatory animal)', Ge'ez 'destroy') is used to illustrate the forms. For Proto-Semitic we reconstruct:

Non-past (= present or future) **-parrVs*	Prefix
Past **-prVs* ~ jussive (imperative-like) **-prVs*	Prefix
Stative (see below) **parVs*	Suffix

The stative originally referred to the state in which the object, or sometimes the subject, finds itself as a lasting result of a previous action (e.g. Akkadian *parsa:ku* 'I have been cut away'). The past and the jussive were almost homophonous but, most probably, distinguished by the stress: on the prefix for the past and on the stem for the jussive

Table 32.1 Person Markers of the Verb

	Prefix			Suffix		
	M.	Common	F.	M.	Common	F.
Singular						
1st		a-...			...-ku	
2nd	ta-...		ta-...-i:	...-ta		...-ti
3rd	ya-...		ta-...	...-∅		...-at
Dual						
2nd		ta-...-a:			...-tuma:	
3rd		ya-...-a:		...a:		
Plural						
1st		ni-...			...-nu/na:	
2nd	ta-...-u:		ta-...-a:	...-tumu:		...-tinna(:)
3rd	ya-...-u:		ya-...-a:	...-u:		...-a:

(*y'iprus* 'he divided', *yipr'us* 'let him divide!'). 'V' above refers to the 'thematic vowel', *a*, *ı* or *u*, specified for each verb in the lexicon, but not necessarily the same in the three basic forms of the same verb. It is most probably the remnant of an old semantic distinction between active and stative (transitive and intransitive?) verbs. *a* is still often associated with passive-intransitive.

The above system is more or less valid for Akkadian, which, however, had in addition a resultative-perfect (with an infix *-ta-* after the first root consonant: *-ptaras*). West Semitic dropped the old prefix-conjugated past (which, however, left some traces) and promoted the original stative into a past tense. Furthermore, South Semitic replaced the *-t-* of the second person suffixes by *-k-*, whereas Central Semitic changed the first person singular to *-tu*. Central Semitic underwent a radical change. It dropped the original non-past forms (*-parras*) and adopted the jussive forms followed by indicative endings as a new non-past. The vocalisation of the prefixes was also reorganised. Some examples of non-past/past (2 sg. f.): Akkadian *taparrasi:/taprusi:*, Ge'ez *təfärrəsi/färäski*, Arabic *tafrisi:-na/farasti*.

The verbal derivational system is of great importance in Semitic. The above samples represent the 'basic' form ('stem' in the traditional terminology). Derivation is made through root-internal and prefixal modification. A gemination of the middle radical throughout creates an 'intensive' form, mainly for repeated action. A long vowel after the first radical produces the 'conative' form, comparable to what is called 'applicative' in other language families (e.g. Bantu), i.e. with the function of making an indirect object into a direct object. This system of three units, basic–intensive–conative, is but one axis of the derivation. Prefixed *ni-* or *ta-* (the latter sometimes infixed) forms an intransitive – passive or reflexive. The prefix *ša-/ha-/ʔa-* produces a causative. A compound *a/ista-* is a causative or reciprocal or has other values. Originally, all of these prefixes (questionable for *ni-*, which may have been restricted to the basic form) could be combined with any of the root-internally distinguished forms (Ge'ez is still closest to this), but now combinations are strictly limited according to the language. Moreover, the meanings attributed to them above are actually true in part only. Only some of the derivations are free, only some of the meaning modifications may be predicted. The actual occurrences of a verb in various forms are defined by the lexicon. Thus, 'causative' is to be understood more as a morphological label than a semantic one, though many causative-prefixed verbs are indeed the causatives of the corresponding basic forms. Derived forms have no special thematic vowels and the internal and prefix vocalisation is also different.

In the South-Central Semitic languages 'internal passives' are also found. The introduction of an *u* after the first consonant makes a form passive: Arabic *tufrasi:-na/furisti* 'you (f. sg.) were killed (as prey by an animal)'. Modern South Arabian Śheri *yə'rɔfɔs/rə'fɔs* has an internal passive *yər'fɔs/rə'fis* 'he is/was kicked', but the latter may be the remnant of the old thematic vowel change making a verb stative-intransitive.

3.3 Notes on Syntax

Proto-Semitic word order is assumed to have been VSO, still so in Classical Arabic, to a decreasing extent in Biblical Hebrew and, less clearly, in Ge'ez. Akkadian was SOV under the influence of the Sumerian substratum, as is modern Ethiopian, copying the Cushitic system. Later Hebrew and Arabic are basically SVO. The adjective, however, always follows the noun, except in modern Ethiopian (and partly in Ge'ez). Numerals most often precede the noun. Demonstratives follow, except in Arabic (though Egyptian and Sudanese dialects are exceptions to the usual Arabic pattern) and parts of modern Ethiopian. Residual case endings aside, case marking is predominantly prepositional (see above). Subordinate clauses follow their head, except in modern Ethiopian.

Adjectives agree with the noun they qualify in gender and number and, when used attributively, also in suffixal case and definiteness/state (e.g. Akkadian *umm-a-m damiq-t-a-m* 'the good mother' lit. 'mother-acc.-abs. good-f.-acc.-abs.', Aramaic *yamm-å rabb-å* 'sea-the big-the'. For numeral agreement, see 'polarity' above. For Arabic subject–verb agreement, see page 576.

There are usually two genitive constructions, one using the construct state, one with a genitive particle, e.g. Ge'ez *betä nəguš* or *bet zä-nəguš* 'the king's house' (*bet* 'house', *zä-* 'of'). Except in modern Ethiopian, the order is always possessed–possessor (cf. Amharic *yä-nəgus bet* for the opposite order).

In Akkadian and Ethiopian (and originally in Aramaic), the 'of' particle also serves as a relative particle. The function of the head noun is marked by a pronoun next to the verb, as a suffix: *awi:l-a-m ša šarr-u-m bi:t-a-m iddin-u-šu amur* 'man$_i$-acc.-abs. that king-nom.-abs. house-acc.-abs. he+gave-subordinate him$_i$ I+saw', Amharic *nəgus bet-u-n yä-sättu-t-ən säw ayyähu-t* 'king house-the-acc. that-he+gave-him$_i$-acc. man$_i$ I+saw-him' for 'I saw the man to whom the king gave the house'; with an independent prepositional pronoun: Akkadian *ša ittišu tuššabu*, Amharic *kəssu gar yämməttənoralläh*, 'that with him you live', i.e. 'with whom you live', etc. As can be seen, the Akkadian verb has a special suffix for the subordinate verb (here *-u*).

Subordinating particles are clause-initial, except in modern Ethiopian, where they are affixed to the clause-final verb. Another example of the latter in Tigré: *dərho Ɂət bet kəm Ɂatrafawo* 'chicken in house as they+left+him' for 'as they left the chicken at home'.

3.4 Conclusion

For the comparative linguist, the Semitic languages exhibit a great deal of similarity. The family is much more uniform than, say, Indo-European. Yet, from a practical point of view, these languages are very different, there being no mutual comprehensibility even between close relatives. On the other hand, however compact the family, scholars do not always agree on matters of reconstruction. Semitic scholarship is a very active field, further enlivened by the recent involvement of other branches of Afroasiatic.

Bibliography

There is a serious need for an up-to-date manual on comparative Semitic. Brockelmann (1908–13) is the classical work in the field. Gray (1934) is a useful, but outdated, introduction. Moscati et al. (1964) is the result of cooperation between specialists of the main branches; it is conservative in approach and to be used with caution. Bergsträsser (1983) is a collection of sample texts preceded by sketch grammars; while still valuable in many details, it is now altogether obsolete, in spite of attempts at updating by the translator. Lipiński (2001) contains a wealth of information and Haelewyck (2006) is a short textbook for intermediate students.

References

Bergsträsser, G. 1983. *Introduction to the Semitic Languages* (Eisenbrauns, Winona Lake IN; translated by P.T. Daniels from the German original, *Einführung in die semitschen Sprachen*, Max Hueber, Munich, 1928, 2nd edn 1963)

Brockelmann, C. 1908–13. *Grundriß der vergleichenden Grammatik der semitischen Sprachen* (Reuther und Reichard, Berlin; reprinted G. Olms, Hildesheim, 1961)

Gray, L.H. 1934. *Introduction to Semitic Comparative Linguistics* (Columbia University Press, New York)

Haelewyck, J.-C. 2006. *Grammaire comparée des langues sémitiques: Éléments de phonétique, de morphologie et de syntaxe* (Éditions Safran, Brussels)

Lipiński, E. 2001. *Semitic Languages: Outline of a Comparative Grammar* 2nd edn (Peeters, Leuven)

Moscati, S. (ed.) 1964. *An Introduction to the Comparative Grammar of the Semitic Languages, Phonology and Morphology* (O. Harrassowitz, Wiesbaden).

33

Arabic

Alan S. Kaye

1 Arabic and the Semitic Languages

Arabic is by far the Semitic (or indeed Afroasiatic) language with the greatest number of speakers, probably now in excess of 200 million, although a completely satisfying and accurate estimate is lacking. It is the major language throughout the Arab world, i.e. Egypt, Sudan, Libya, the North African countries usually referred to as the Maghrib (such as Tunisia, Morocco and Algeria), Saudi Arabia, Iraq, Jordan, the Gulf countries, etc., and it is even the major language of non-Arab countries such as the Republic of Chad in central Africa (i.e. more Chadians speak Arabic as their mother tongue than any other language).

Arabic is also a minority language in other countries such as Nigeria, Iran (Khuzistan), and former Soviet Central Asia (though these Central Asian varieties of Arabic are heavily endangered). Furthermore, Arabic is in wide use throughout the Muslim world as a second language (e.g. in Somalia, a member of the Arab League) and as a learned, liturgical language (e.g. in Pakistan, India, Indonesia). Indeed, among orthodox Muslims Arabic is *luɣat almalāʔikah* 'the language of the angels', and the language *par excellence* in the world since Allah himself speaks Arabic and has revealed his Holy Book, the Koran (*qurʔān*), in the Arabic language. One can also easily comprehend that the Arabs are very proud of their (most beautiful) language, since there is even a verb *ʔaʕraba* 'to speak clearly and eloquently' from the root *ʕRB*, also occurring in the word *alʕarabiyyah* 'the Arabic language' or *lisān ʕarabī* 'the Arabic language' in the Koran.

There is even a historical dialect of Arabic, Maltese, sometimes, although erroneously, called Maltese Arabic, which, through its isolation from the rest of the so-called Arab world, developed into a new Semitic language in its own right (a similar, but weaker, argument could be made for Cypriot Maronite Arabic). The two major reasons for my claiming that Maltese is not to be regarded synchronically as a dialect of Arabic are: (1) Maltese, if an Arabic dialect today, would be one without diglossia, i.e. it does not have Classical Arabic as a high level of language (more on this important topic later); and (2) it would be the *only* Arabic dialect normally written in the Latin Script.

560

2 Arabic as Central Semitic

According to the new classification of the Semitic languages proposed by R. Hetzron (see Chapter 32), there is evidence that Arabic shares traits of both South Semitic and North-West Semitic. Arabic preserves Proto-Semitic phonology almost perfectly (Epigraphic South Arabian is even more conservative), except for Proto-Semitic $*p > f$ and Proto-Semitic $*\acute{s} > s$. But Arabic also shares features with Hebrew, Ugaritic and Aramaic, such as the masculine plural suffix -īna/-īma and the internal passive, e.g. Arabic qatala 'he killed' vs qutila 'he was killed' and Hebrew hilbīš 'he dressed (someone)' vs hulbaš 'he was dressed (by someone)'.

The morphology of the definite article in Hebrew (ha- + gemination of the following consonant if that consonant is capable of gemination) and Arabic (ʔal-, which assimilates before dentals or sibilants, producing a geminate) also points to a common origin and so on. The Hebrew ha-, in fact, also shows up in the Arabic demonstratives hāðā 'this, m. sg.' hāðihi 'f.' and hāʔulāʔi 'pl.'. Even the broken plurals of Arabic may be compared with Hebrew segholate plurals such as kəlāvīm 'dogs' (cf. sg. kɛlɛv + -īm 'm. pl.'), where one can easily see the vocalic change in the stem (cf. Arabic kilāb).

There are some other very striking morphological affinities of Arabic with Hebrew such as the ancient dialectal Arabic relative particle ðū, cf. Biblical Hebrew zū, while the Western form ðī occurred in Arabic ʔallaðī 'who, m. sg.' and Aramaic dī. Some Eastern dialects also reflected Barth's Law, i.e. they had i as the imperfect preformative vowel with a of the imperfect system like the Canaanite dialects.

3 Some Characteristics of Arabic and the Designation 'Arabic'

Arabic sticks out like a sore thumb in comparative Semitic linguistics because of its almost (too perfect) algebraic-looking grammar, i.e. root and pattern morphology (sometimes known as transfixation). (It is so algebraic that some scholars have accused the medieval Arab grammarians of contriving some artificiality around it in its classical form.) For instance, the root KTB has to do with 'writing'. In Form I (the simple form of the verb corresponding to the Hebrew qal stem), kataba means 'he wrote', imperfect yaktubu 'he writes', with three verbal nouns all translatable as 'writing' – katb, kitāba and kitba. In Form II (the exact nuances of the forms will be discussed in Section 9), kattaba, imperfect yukattibu means 'to make write'; form III kātaba, imperfect yukātibu means 'to correspond'; Form IV ʔaktaba, imperfect yuktibu 'to dictate'; Form VI takātaba, imperfect yatakātabu 'to keep up a correspondence'; Form VII ʔinkataba, imperfect yankatibu 'to subscribe'; Form VIII ʔiktataba, imperfect yaktatibu 'to copy'; Form X ʔistaktaba, imperfect yastaktibu 'to ask to write'. There are ten commonly used forms of the verb (five others occur but are very uncommon); the root KTB does not occur in Form V, which is often a passive of Form II ('to be made to write'?), or Form IX, which is a very special form reserved only for the semantic sphere of colours and defects (so we would not expect it to occur in this form). The linguists who have seen a much too regular Systemzwang in this particular case have doubted the authenticity of some of the forms with this root and have asked about an automatic plugging in of the root to obtain a rather forced (artificially created) meaning.

There are also many other words derivable from this triconsonantal root by using different vocalic patterns. For instance, kitāb 'book' (vowel pattern = $C_1iC_2\bar{a}C_3$) with its plural *kutub* ($C_1uC_2uC_3$), *kutubī* 'bookseller', *kuttāb* 'Koranic school', *kutayyib* 'booklet', *kitābī* 'written', *katība* 'squadron' – it is difficult, if not impossible, to see how this word fits into the semantic sphere of 'writing' – *maktab* 'office', *maktaba* 'library', *miktāb* 'typewriter', *mukātaba* 'correspondence', *ʔiktitāb* 'registration', *ʔistiktāb* 'dictation', *kātib* 'writer', *maktūb* 'letter, note', etc.

The Arabic dictionary lists words under their respective roots, thus all of the above are found under the root *KTB*. However, in most native but older dictionaries, a word is listed by what it ends with, so that all of the above words would be listed under /b/. The reason that this was done was to make life easier for the poets (who were the real inventors of the classical language), since the usual state of a traditional Arabic poem was that it would have only one general rhyming pattern (Arabic poetry is also metrical).

It is very important to keep in mind that one must sharply distinguish what is meant by the term 'Arabic' language. Our preceding examples have all come from modern standard Arabic, sometimes called modern literary Arabic or modern written Arabic, which is essentially a modernised form of Classical Arabic. All of these three designations just mentioned are known as *ʔalʕarabiyya alfuṣḥā* or *ʔalʕarabiyya alfaṣīḥa* (the 'pure' or 'clear' language). On the other side of the coin is a language which many Arabs think is devoid of grammar, the colloquial language, *luɣat alʕāmma* or *ʔalluɣa alʕāmmiyya* or *addārija* or *lahaǧāt*.

ʔalʕarabiyya alfuṣḥā originated from the ancient poetic language of the Arabs in pre-Islamic Arabia, which was a period of idol worship (known in Arabic as *ʔalǧāhiliyya* 'the period of ignorance'). The linguistic situation in ancient Arabia was such that every tribe had its own dialect, but there evolved a common koine used by the *rāwīs* (the ancient poets), which helped the preservation of the language and assisted in its conservatism. The Holy Koran, written in this dialect (of course it was at first oral) but with linguistic features of Muhammad's speech (the Meccan dialect), eventually became *the* model for the classical language. Surprisingly enough, due principally to Islam, the classical language has changed in grammar very little since the seventh century AD. In fact, most students are amazed at the easy transition between reading a modern novel and a *sūra* of the Koran (vocabulary and stylistics are other matters, however).

The colloquial dialects number in the thousands. The number reported in an ever-growing literature runs in the hundreds. There are many remarkable parallels in the development of the modern Arabic dialects and the development of the Romance languages from a Latin prototype, the most notable of which is a general grammatical simplification in structure (i.e. fewer grammatical categories). Three such simplifications are: (1) loss of the dual in the verb, adjective and pronoun; (2) loss of case endings for nouns and adjectives; and (3) loss of mood distinctions in the verb. In addition to a demarcation of the colloquial dialects of various countries, cities, towns and villages, there are many sociolects which can be observed. Educated speech is, of course, quite distinct from that of the *fallāḥīn* (peasants). In terms of comparative Arabic dialectology, more is known about urban dialects than rural or nomadic (Bedouin) counterparts.

One should also keep in mind that the differences between many colloquials and the classical language are so great that a *fallāḥ* who had never been to school could hardly understand more than a few scattered words and expressions in it without great difficulty. One could assemble dozens of so-called Arabs (*fallāḥīn*) in a room, who have never been exposed to the classical language, so that not one could properly understand the other. One should also bear in mind that educated Arabs use their native dialect in daily living and have all learned their colloquial dialects first. Indeed, all colloquial Arabic dialects are acquired systems but the classical language is always formally learned. This has probably held true from the beginning.

4 The Influence of Arabic on Other Languages

As Islam expanded from Arabia, the Arabic language exerted much influence on the native languages with which it came in contact. Persians and speakers of other Iranian languages such as Kurdish and Pashto, Turkic-speaking peoples, Indians, Pakistanis, Bangladeshis and many speakers of African languages such as Hausa and Swahili (this list is by no means exhaustive) used the Arabic script to write their own native languages and assimilated a tremendous number of Arabic loanwords. One did not have to become a Muslim to embrace Arabic, as Judeo-Arabic proves (Jews in Arabic-speaking countries, who spoke Arabic natively, wrote it in Hebrew characters with a few diacritical innovations). Words of ultimate Arabic origin have penetrated internationally and interlingually. A recent study turned up 400 'common' Arabic loanwords in English based on the *Random House Dictionary of the English Language, Webster's Third New International Dictionary* and the *Shorter Oxford English Dictionary*. A few examples will illustrate: the *al-* definite article words such as *algebra, alkali, alcohol, alcove* and many other famous ones such as *Allah, artichoke, assassin, Bedouin, cadi, cipher, emir, gazelle, giraffe, harem, hashish, imam, Islam, lute, mosque, mullah, Muslim, nadir, saffron, sheikh, sherbet, syrup, talc* and *vizier*.

It is important to point out that some of the loanwords mentioned earlier have as many as five alternate spellings in English due to transliteration differences and preferences, so that a word such as *cadi* (Arabic *qāḍin* 'judge', *ʔalqāḍī* 'the judge' – there is no Classical Arabic word *qāḍī*) can also be spelt *kadhi, kadi, qadi* and *qazi* (this latter pronunciation reflects a Perso-Indian influence since in those languages /ḍ/ > /z/); *emir* can also be spelt as *ameer, amir* or *emeer*.

5 Phonology

The consonantal segments of a fairly typical educated pronunciation of modern standard Arabic can be seen in Table 33.1 (of course, there can always be debate about the exact meaning of 'fairly typical').

The symbols are IPA or quasi-IPA symbols (as used by linguists who specialise in Arabic and in the other Semitic languages). The Arabic alphabet is a very accurate depiction of the phonological facts of the language; however, it should be noted that there are some pronunciations different from the ones presented in Table 33.1. For instance, /q/ is voiced in many dialects, both ancient and modern, i.e. [ɢ], especially the Bedouin ones, which probably reflects its original pronunciation; the *jīm* (the name of the letter represented by the grapheme ǰ) corresponds to many pronunciations such as [dʸ], [gʸ], [g] or [ž], even [j] as in English *yellow*, stemming from a Proto-Semitic */g/.

Every consonant may be geminated, in contradistinction to Hebrew, for example, which cannot geminate the so-called 'gutturals' (ʔ, ʕ, h, ħ and r).

Classical Arabic does not have a /p/, but standard pronunciations tend to devoice a /b/ before a voiceless consonant, e.g. /ħabs/ → [ħaps] 'imprisonment' or /ħibs/ → [ħips] 'dam'. Some modern Arabic dialects, notably those in Iraq, have both /p/ and /p̣/ (emphatic);

Table 33.1 Arabic Consonant Phonemes

	Bilabial	Labio-dental	Inter-dental	Dental	Emphatic	Palatal	Velar	Uvular	Pharyngeal	Laryngeal
Stops	b			t d	ṭ ḍ		k	q		ʔ
Affricates						ǰ				
Fricatives		f	θ ð	s z	ṣ ọ̈ (ẓ)	š		x ɣ	ħ ʕ	h
Nasals	m			n						
Laterals				l	ḷ					
Trill				r						
Approximants	w					y				

however, the great majority of Arabic speakers will produce English /p/s as /b/ due to interference modification (one Arab asks another, 'Which Bombay are you flying to? Bombay, India or Bombay (Pompei), Italy?'). Incidentally, Persian, Urdu and other languages which have /p/ have taken the grapheme for /b/ = ب and made پ by placing three dots underneath its basic configuration. This grapheme, in turn, has been reborrowed by some Iraqi Arabs.

Classical Arabic does not have a /v/, but phonetically, due to regressive assimilation, a [v] might occur as in /ħifð/ → [ħivð] 'memory'. /n/ also assimilates regressively, i.e. nb → mb, and nk → ŋk as in /bank/ → [baŋk] 'bank'.

The 'emphatic' consonants, often misleadingly called velarised-pharyngealised, are depicted with a dot underneath the particular consonant. Perhaps nowhere else in Arabic linguistic literature is there more controversy and more debate than in this area of the emphatics and how they are to be described and how they function. The vowels around an emphatic consonant tend to become lower, retracted or more centralised than around corresponding non-emphatics (the very back consonants /x, ɣ, q, ħ, ʕ/ have a similar effect on vowels), which is why the vowel allophonics of Arabic are much more cumbersome and intricate than the consonantal allophonics.

In Old Arabic, the primary emphatics were, in all likelihood, voiced, i.e. /ḍ/ < [ẓˡ] (lateralised), /ṭ/ < [ḍ], [ð̣] or [ẓ] < [ð̣] and /ṣ/ < [ẓ].

W. Lehn reviewed much of the previous literature including Arabic grammatical thought and concluded, at least for Cairo Arabic, that the minimum domain of emphasis is the syllable and the maximum domain is the utterance. Lehn has suggested that emphasis not be treated as a distinctive feature of the consonant or vocalic system but as a redundant feature of both. In later works Lehn underscores all emphatic syllables.

The /ḷ/, which occurs only in the name of God, /ʔaḷḷāh/ (but not after /i/ as in /bismillāh/ 'in the name of Allah'), was shown to be a phoneme in Classical Arabic by C.A. Ferguson. Some modern Arabic dialects have many more examples of /ḷ/, especially those spoken in the Gulf countries.

Arabic is perhaps the best known of the world's languages to linguists for its vowel system. It has the classical triangular system, which preserves Proto-Semitic vocalism:

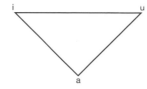

For Classical and modern standard Arabic, these may be short or long (geminated). Many modern Arabic dialects have, however, developed other vowels such as /ə/, /e/, /o/ etc., just as the other Semitic languages had done centuries earlier through the general process of 'drift' (i.e. parallel development).

The vowel allophonics are much richer than the consonantal allophonics chiefly because vowels take on the colouring of the adjacent emphatic and emphatic-like consonants (including /r/), while the non-emphatic consonants push the vowels to higher and less centralised qualities. What is important to keep in mind is that the pronunciation of the standard language or any oral interpretation of the classical language is all directly dependent on the nature of one's native colloquial dialect.

The vowel allophonics have been accurately described on the basis of detailed spectrographic analysis for the modern standard as used in Iraq. The rules may be stated as follows:

(1)　/ī/　→　[ɨ̄]/ – [+ emphatic] – (except /l/)
　　　　→　[ī̱]/ – {ʕ, ɣ} –
　　　　→　[ī]/ ...

(2)　/i/　→　[ɨ]/ – [+ emphatic] –
　　　　→　[I]/ – {ʕ, ɣ} –
　　　　→　[i]/ ...

(3)　/ū/　→　[ʊ̄]/ – [+ emphatic] – (except /l/)
　　　　→　[ū]/ ...

(4)　/ū/　→　[ʊ]/ – [+ emphatic] –
　　　　→　[u]/ ...

(5)　/ā/　→　[ā]/ – {+ emphatic, q, r} –
　　　　→　[ʌ̄]/ – {ʕ, ɣ} –
　　　　→　[ǣ]/ ...

(6)　/a/　→　[ə]/ _____ # (but not next to q, ʕ, r and ɣ)
　　　　→　[a]/ – {+ emphatic, q, r} –
　　　　→　[ʌ]/ – {ʕ, ɣ} –
　　　　→　[æ]/ ...

What tends to happen in modern Arabic dialects is that the short vowels are more susceptible to change than the long ones. Thus Classical /i/ and /u/ in Damascus Arabic, for instance, both merge into /ə/. Indeed /a/ can usually be regarded as the most stable and conservative of the three short vowels, yet it too is now becoming subject to change or deletion in many dialects; /yā/+/maħammad/ → /yamħammad/ 'Oh Muhammad!' Classical Arabic knows many doublets in its short vowel configuration such as /ħubs/ ~ /ħibs/ 'inalienable property, the yield of which is devoted to pious purposes' or /lass/ ~ /liss/ ~ /luss/ 'thief' (a triplet!).

Diphthongs are two in number: /aw/ and /ay/ as in /θawr/ 'bull' and /bayt/ 'house', respectively. In most of the colloquial dialects, diphthongs have monophthongised into /ē/ and /ō/, respectively (and /ī/ and /ū/ in Moroccan dialects – usually just written /i/ and /u/ – a development which occurred in Akkadian centuries before and is another good attestation of 'drift' in the Semitic languages).

There are two well-known phonological processes which deserve mention. The first is called *ʔimāla* (lit. 'inclination'), which refers to /ā/-raising, usually due to the umlauting influence of /i/, which means that words such as *ʕibād* 'slaves' could have had a dialectal (peculiar, at first, perhaps) pronunciation *ʕibēd* or *ʕibīd*. *ʕimāla* has produced the very distinctive high vowel pronunciations of /ā/ in many Syro-Lebanese dialects giving for /bāb/ 'door': [bēb] or [bīb] or phonetic qualities in between those or adjacent to them, which may be compared with Maltese *bieb* 'door'. (Maltese has for Arabic *kalimāt* 'words' *kelmiet* and for Arabic *kitāb* 'book' *ktieb*.)

The second process is known as *ʔišmām* ('delabialisation'), which explains /ū/ → /ī/ (through an intermediate stage of [ü]) as in *rūm* ~ *rīm* 'Rome' or some dialectal pronunciations of /rudda/ as /rüdda/ 'it was returned' or /qūla/ for /qīla/ 'it was said', which derives from /quwila/, the passive form I of the root *QWL*. This phonological process may also explain why *ū* rhymes with *ī* in Koranic Arabic.

Stress is one of the most involved topics in Arabic phonology (even for the Nigerian dialect of Arabic I researched at first hand, stress was the most intricate part of the entire phonology). The Arab grammarians never mentioned it, and therefore the modern-day pronunciation of the standard (classical) language is directly dependent on the stress rules of the native colloquial dialect counterpart. Thus for the word 'both of them (f.) wrote', segmentally /katabatā/, graphemically /ktbtʔ/, which of the four possible syllables receives the stress? Indeed some native Arabic speakers say (1) /kátabatā/ (Iraqis); others (2) katabátā/ (Egyptians); still others (3) /katabatá/ (many Syrians and Lebanese); and others may say: (4) katábatā/. Thus it is possible to stress any of the four syllables and still be correct. This is one of the reasons why I consider modern standard Arabic an ill-defined system of language, whereas I deem all colloquials well-defined.

One set of rules for the assignment of lexical stress are:

(1) When a word is made up of CV syllables, the first syllable receives the primary stress, e.g. /kátaba/ 'he wrote'.
(2) When a word contains only one long syllable, that long syllable receives the primary stress, e.g. /kātib/ 'writer, clerk'.
(3) When a word contains two or more long syllables, the long syllable nearest to the end of the word receives the primary stress, e.g. /raʔīsuhúnna/ 'their (f. pl.) chief'.

There are, however, rules of syllabicity that can be described with a greater degree of accuracy. Long vowels are shortened in closed syllables, which explains why one says /yákun/ 'let him be' (jussive of /yakūnu/ 'he will be') instead of the expected (apocopated imperfect) */yakūn/. The only exception is that /ā/ may appear in a closed syllable, but it is not necessary to enter into the details of this here. Also, syllable-initially and -finally, only single consonants occur. Thus the borrowing from Latin *strāta* 'path' is /ṣirāṭ/ (the *str*- consonant cluster was first simplified to *sr*- and then an anaptyctic vowel /i/ was inserted between the /ṣ/ and the /r/; further, the emphatic /ṣ/ and /ṭ/ are typical of what Arabic does in its loanword phonology).

The normal use of modern standard Arabic requires an understanding of pausal forms. When a pause occurs in speech (reflected in reading as well), speakers drop final short vowels (case and mood markers) and drop or shorten case endings. For example, Arabic marks indefiniteness by what is called nūnation (named after the Arabic letter *nūn*): *-un* for nominative, *-in* for genitive and *-an* for accusative (there are only three cases). At the end of an utterance (i.e. sentence, breath group), a word such as /mudarrisun/ 'a teacher' → /mudarris/, /mudarrisin/ → /mudarris/ but /mudarrisan/ →

/mudarrisā/ (note that Arabic words are usually cited with nūnation, called in Arabic *tanwīn*), and /mudarrisatun/ /mudarrisah/ 'a teacher (f.)'.

6 Morphophonemic Changes

We shall not list all occurrences because that would require more space than allotted to us. We will rather present a few of the most common changes occurring in Classical Arabic.

(1) *awa* → *ā*, e.g. *qamawa* → *qāma* 'he stood up'
(2) $C_1aC_2aCa_2$ → $C_1aC_2Ca_2$, e.g. *radada* → *radda* 'he returned'
(3) *ʔ{a, i, u}ʔ* → *ʔ{ā, ī, ū}*, e.g. *ʔaʔlām* → *ʔālām* 'pains'
(4) *uw* → *ū*, e.g. *suwdun* → *sūdun* 'black' (m. pl.)
(5) *ūy* → *ī*, e.g. *būyḍun* → *bīḍun* 'white' (m. pl.), *mudarrisūya* → *mudarrisīya* 'my teachers' (m., all cases)
(6) *yw* → *yy*, e.g. *ʔaywāmun* → *ʔayyāmun* 'days'
(7) haplology, e.g. *tataqataluna* → *taqātalūna* 'you are fighting each other'
(8) dissimilation, e.g. *madīnīyun* → *madanīyun*
(9) *āw* → *āʔ*, e.g. *qāwilun* → *qāʔilun* 'speaker'

7 The Arabic Alphabet

The Latin script is used by more languages than any other script ever invented (and it is used for languages as diversified in structure as Polish, English and Vietnamese). After Latin, the Arabic alphabet is number two because it was or is used to write a vast number of different languages such as Persian, Urdu, Pashto (all Indo-Iranian), Hausa (the Chadic sub-branch of Afroasiatic), Swahili (Bantu), Turkish (Altaic), Malay (Austronesian) and over a hundred others. The reason for this diversity is undoubtedly the spread of Islam.

The earliest Arabic inscription is dated AD 512. According to an early Arabic scholar, Ibn Khaldūn, the Arabic alphabet had evolved from the Epigraphic South Arabian script; however, we know that it was borrowed from the Nabatean alphabet (which was, in turn, borrowed from the Aramaic), which consisted of twenty-two consonantal graphemes. The Nabateans added six more graphemes representing phonemes that did not occur in Aramaic (the oldest Nabatean inscription dates from AD 250, found at Umm al-Jimāl): ت, ذ, ض, ظ, خ, and غ. The oldest Arabic inscription written in the Nabatean script is the Namāra inscription, a grave inscription of seventy-one lines found in south-eastern Syria, which dates from AD 328 (the inscription was discovered in 1902).

Like Phoenician, Hebrew, Ugaritic and other Semitic alphabets (or syllabaries), the adapted Nabatean system used by the pre-Islamic Arabs represents only consonants, which is appropriate to the root structure of Semitic.

The invention of diacritical marks to indicate vowels was borrowed from Syriac in the eighth century AD. In fact, the invention is attributed to Al-Khalil ibn Ahmad. Arabic's written development can be explained as follows. The Arabs grew tired of fifteen basic letter shapes for twenty-eight phonemes (the confusion must have been overwhelming), so dots were invented above and below the letters in groups of one to three to distinguish the underlying grapheme. The process of using dots (inserting the diacritics) is called *ʔiʕjām* and although it is used for Aramaic, the Arabs began to use it very systematically.

Arabic calligraphy is truly an art. There are many styles of the script, and Table 33.2 presents the *nasxī* one, commonly used for print. Column 5 presents the final unconnected allograph of the grapheme. The script is written, like Hebrew, from right to left, and tends to be very cursive (although the Persians and Ottoman Turks have gone even further), especially in handwritten forms. All the graphemes can be attached to preceding ones, but six never connect to what follows: *ʔalif, dāl, ðāl, rāʔ, zāy* and *wāw*. There are no capital letters and Table 33.2 presents the graphemes and their allographs as well as their older Semitic numerical values (the so-called *ʔabjad*).

Handwriting generally shortens the strokes and replaces the three dots with ^ and two dots with –, allowing it to be written very quickly in comparison to the painstaking effort required for the printed forms.

Table 33.2 The Arabic Alphabet

Transliteration	Final	Medial	Initial	Alone	Name	Numerical value
ā	ﺎ			ا	ʔalif	1
b	ﺐ	ﺒ	ﺑ	ب	bāʕ	2
t	ﺖ	ﺘ	ﺗ	ت	tāʔ	400
θ	ﺚ	ﺜ	ﺛ	ث	θāʔ	500
ǰ	ﺞ	ﺠ	ﺟ	ج	jīm	3
ħ	ﺢ	ﺤ	ﺣ	ح	ħāʔ	8
x	ﺦ	ﺨ	ﺧ	خ	xāʔ	600
d	ﺪ			د	dāl	4
ð	ﺬ			ذ	ðāl	700
r	ﺮ			ر	rāʔ	200
z	ﺰ			ز	zāy	7
s	ﺲ	ﺴ	ﺳ	س	sīn	60
š	ﺶ	ﺸ	ﺷ	ش	šīn	300
ṣ	ﺺ	ﺼ	ﺻ	ص	ṣād	90
ḍ	ﺾ	ﻀ	ﺿ	ض	ḍād	800
ṭ	ﻂ	ﻄ	ﻃ	ط	ṭāʔ	9
ð̣	ﻆ	ﻈ	ﻇ	ظ	ð̣āʔ	900
ʕ	ﻊ	ﻌ	ﻋ	ع	ʕayn	70
ɣ	ﻎ	ﻐ	ﻏ	غ	ɣayn	1000
f	ﻒ	ﻔ	ﻓ	ف	fāʔ	80
q	ﻖ	ﻘ	ﻗ	ق	qāf	100
k	ﻚ	ﻜ	ﻛ	ك	kāf	20
l	ﻞ	ﻠ	ﻟ	ل	lām	30
m	ﻢ	ﻤ	ﻣ	م	mīm	40
n	ﻦ	ﻨ	ﻧ	ن	nūn	50
h	ﻪ	ﻬ	ﻫ	ه	hāʔ	5
w	ﻮ			و	wāw	6
y	ﻰ	ﻴ	ﻳ	ى	yāʔ	10

The vowel diacritics are: *fatha* ´ /a/; *damma* ' /u/; *kasra* ˌ /i/; and *sukūn* ° for zero (no vowel). Long vowels are represented thus: /ā/ by *ʔalif* or *ʔalif madda* (آ, in initial position), /ī/ by *yāʔ*; and /ū/ by *wāw*.

There are other details such as ligatures, nūnation, stylistic variations etc., for which the reader should refer to Mitchell (1953).

8 Diglossia

A very interesting and relatively rare linguistic phenomenon has developed in Arabic, called diglossia, which is often confused with bilingualism. There can be no doubt that it is an old phenomenon going back, in all likelihood, to the pre-Islamic period, although J. Blau states it arose as late as the first Islamic century in the towns of the Arab empire as a result of the great Arab conquests (I do not agree with Blau that there was no intermediary of the Arabic koine). Diglossia involves a situation in which two varieties of the same language live side by side, each performing a different function. It involves the use of two different variants of a single language, whereas bilingualism definitely involves two different languages. The two variants are: (1) a 'high' one used in relatively formal situations; and (2) a 'low' one used colloquially and usually informally. Although the term was coined by the Arabist W. Marçais in 1930 (*diglossie*), it was C.A. Ferguson who brought it to the attention of general linguistics and ethnology.

'High' Arabic, which we have been calling modern standard Arabic, and 'Low' Arabic, a colloquial dialect which native speakers acquire as a mother tongue, have specialised functions in Arab culture. The former is learned through formal education in school like Latin, Sanskrit and Biblical Hebrew and would be used in a sermon, university lecture, news broadcast and for mass media purposes, letter, political speech (except, perhaps, after an informal greeting or the first few sentences, as was typical of the speeches of Gamal Abdul Nasser), while the latter is always an acquired system (no formal learning ever takes place to learn anyone's native tongue) and is the native language used at home conversing with family or friends or in a radio or television soap opera. It is important to realise that a small elite has developed in the Arab countries very proud of their skills in the standard language (Modern Classical Arabic). There have even been reports that certain individuals have adopted the standard language as their exclusive means of oral communication, yet I have reservations about this.

Many native speakers, regardless of the level of education, maintain a set of myths about the 'high' language: that it is far more beautiful than any dialect (colloquial), far more logical, more elegant and eloquent, has much more vocabulary available to it, especially for the expression of philosophical ideas, and is far better able to express all the complex nuances of one's thoughts. Arabs also believe (and other Muslims too) that Arabic is the most perfect of all languages since God speaks it and has revealed his message in the Holy Koran in it. If asked which dialect is closest to the classical, many Arabs will respond that their own dialect is! Of course, this may be a relative answer depending on who else is present and where the question is asked – another common answer is that the Bedouin in the desert speaks a dialect nearest to the classical. In fact, the Bedouin has often been called upon to settle linguistic arguments of all kinds.

Classical Arabic has always had situations where its use was required and it was never acquired by all members of the particular society in question. Modern standard Arabic continues the tradition and unifies the Arab world linguistically as it is the official language of Iraq, Jordan, Egypt, Sudan, Tunisia, Algeria, Morocco, Mauritania, Kuwait, Saudi Arabia, Lebanon, Libya, Yemen, Oman, the Gulf countries, etc. It is the mark of ʕurūba or Arabism (pan-Arabism), since there can be a high degree of mutual unintelligibility among the various colloquial dialects, where a Syrian Arabic-speaking friend of mine once heard a tape of a Nigerian speaking Nigerian Arabic and confessed he understood almost nothing in it. Recently, a Jordanian friend had similar sentiments when listening to a short monologue in Moroccan Arabic.

There is also a tremendous amount of sociological concern about the language, dialect and variety in the Arab world. Let me illustrate what I mean by relating a true story. I once participated in a long conversation one entire afternoon in a Beirut coffee house with two other gentlemen. One was Lebanese, but he did not want to appear uneducated so he spoke French, a language he knew quite well and which he had studied for years formally. The other was French, but he did not want to come off as any sort of colonialist so he was speaking colloquial Lebanese Arabic, which he knew beautifully. I, as an American-trained linguist who had studied a variety of modern dialects, spoke modern standard Arabic, since I knew that language better than the other two choices represented. And the conversation was delightful, each of us taking turn in this trialogue about all sorts of subjects.

It is important to realise that there are a few Arabic speech communities where diglossia is unknown. Cypriot Maronite Arabic spoken in Kormakiti, Cyprus, by about 1,300 people is one such example, as are most dialects of Nigerian and Chadic Arabic.

Perhaps the most striking feature of diglossia is the existence of many paired vocabulary items (the examples are from C.A. Ferguson).

Classical Arabic	Gloss	Egyptian colloquial Arabic
raʔā	'he saw'	šāf
ħiðāhun	'shoe'	gazma
ʔanfun	'nose'	manaxīr
ðahaba	'he went'	rāħ
mā	'what'	ʔē(h)
ʔalʔāna	'now'	dilwaʔti

To demonstrate how different the modern dialects can be, consider 'now'. In addition to the words cited above, Moroccan has *dába*, Algerian *delwóq* or *druk*, Tunisian *tawwa*, Saudi Arabian *daħħīna*, Hassaniyya (Mauritania) *dark*, Syrian *hallaʔ*, Nigerian *hatta* or *hassa* or *dātēn*; consider also 'good, well': Moroccan *mizyán* or *wáxxa*, Algerian *mlīeħ*, Syrian-Lebanese *mnīħ*, Libyan and Tunisian *bāhi*, other Tunisian *ṭayyab*, some Sudanese *samiħ*, Chadian *seme*, Yemeni *ʕīs*, Nigerian *zēn* or *ṭayyib* and Egyptian *kuwayyis*. Finally, consider 'nothing': Moroccan *wálu*, Algerian *ši*, Libyan *kān lbarka*, Tunisian *šay*, Saudi Arabian *walašay*, Nigerian *še*. Indeed, sometimes it is in the basic everyday vocabulary that one can most easily spot such major distinctions.

To give the linguist somewhat of a feel for this, Ferguson cites the nearest English parallel such as *illumination* vs *light*, *purchase* vs *buy*, and *children* vs *kids*. I should also mention the elegance one can immediately feel when one is invited to *dine* vs plain ol' *eat*. The verb *dine* certainly involves higher cost as well as getting dressed up and lovely and expensive surroundings (tablecloth, utensils, décor, etc.). 'High' Arabic gives one the feeling of dining at a fine restaurant, whereas 'Low' Arabic is eating the same old thing day in and day out. In addition to the lexical distinctions, there are also different grammatical systems involved in diglossia.

In support of the hypothesis that modern standard Arabic is ill defined is the so-called 'mixed' language or 'Inter-Arabic' used in the speeches of, say, former President Bourguiba of Tunisia, noting that very few native speakers of Arabic from any Arab country can really ever master the intricacies of Classical Arabic grammar in such a way as to extemporaneously give a formal speech in it. This may best be illustrated in the use of the Arabic numerals, in which the cardinal numbers from 'three' to 'ten' govern the indefinite genitive plural, but from 'eleven' to 'nineteen' govern the indefinite accusative singular (in addition to being indeclinable, with the exception of 'twelve'), whereas cardinal numbers such as 'one thousand', 'two thousand', 'three thousand', 'million', etc., take the indefinite genitive singular. Another good illustration is in the use of the classically prescribed 'pausal' forms, especially for feminine singular nouns.

9 Nominal Morphology

Modern standard Arabic nouns are inflected for case, determination, gender and number. The function of the noun is usually indicated by short vowel suffixes – /u/ marking nominative, /i/ genitive and /a/ accusative (with added nūnation marking indefiniteness). Thus /kitābun/ 'a book' (nom.), gen. /kitābin/ and acc. /kitāban/ (this is an example of a triptote since it takes all three case endings). Determination is normally handled by the definite article which is /ʔal-/, but it assimilates before the so-called 'sun' letters (t, d, θ, ð, s, z, ṭ, ḍ, ṣ, ̣ n, l, r, š) (they are called this because the word /šams/ 'sun' begins with one; all the others are called 'moon' letters because the word /qamar/ 'moon' begins with one). When /ʔal-/ prefixes a noun, there is no longer any need to have the nūnation since it marks the indefinite, thus /ʔalkitabu/ 'the book' (nom.), with /ʔalkitābi/ (gen.) and /ʔalkitāba/ (acc.). (The /ʔ/ and initial vowel are subject to the rules of elision after vowels.)

The diptote noun, which is in the minority when one compares to triptotes, does not take nūnation and merges the accusative -a with the genitive, e.g. /ʔaḥmadu/ 'Ahmad' (nom.), with gen.-acc. /ʔaḥmada/. Many broken (internal) plural patterns are diptotic, as are many proper names, elatives (i.e. comparatives and superlatives), colours and other forms.

Dual and so-called 'sound' (i.e. no morphophonemic alternation) plural suffixes also do not differentiate the genitive and accusative (called 'oblique'). 'Teachers' (m.) is /mudarrisūna/, obl. /mudarrisīna/, f. /mudarrisātun/, obl. /mudarrisātin/. The masculine forms remain the same with the article, but the nūnation is lost with the feminine. The dual is marked by /-āni/, obl. /-ayni/; thus 'two teachers' (m.) is /mudarrisāni/, obl. /mudarrisayni/; feminine counterparts are /mudarrisatāni/ and /mudarrisatayni/, respectively.

Gender and number are obligatory grammatical categories. Feminine nouns take feminine concord and government and tend to be overtly marked with /-at/ followed by the case marker, e.g. /mudarrisatun/, pausal form /mudarrisah/ 'teacher'. Very few feminine-marked nouns are masculine, e.g. /xalīfatun/ 'caliph'. Many nouns which are not overtly marked feminine are so, e.g. body parts which occur in pairs (this is common Semitic) such as /rijlun/ 'foot, leg' and the names of most countries and cities; in addition, plurals of irrational beings are treated as feminine singulars.

Mention has already been made of the dual number and the 'sound' masculine and feminine endings. All lose nūnation in the construct state (*status constructus*), which is the normal means of expressing the possessum in a possessive (genitive) relationship (e.g. /kitābu lmaliki/ 'the book of the king' or 'the king's book' – the first member of this construction (called in Arabic /iḍāfa/) has neither the article nor nūnation, e.g. 'the teachers of the school' can be dual /mudarrisā lmadrasati/, f. /mudarrisatā lmadrasati/, obl. /mudarrisatay lmadrasati/, m. pl. /mudarrisū lmadrasati/, obl. /mudarrisī lmadrasati/, f. /mudarrisātu lmadrasati/, obl. /mudarrisāti lmadrasati/.

Most Arabic nouns do not take sound plurals but have a broken (*ablaut*) plural, which can also involve the addition of prefixes and/or suffixes. There are several dozen possible patterns in common usage and very few are predictable. The three most common broken (sometimes also called 'inner') plural patterns, based on data in the Lane Lexicon, are: (1) $ʔaC_1C_2āC_3$, e.g. /lawḥun/ 'blackboard', pl. /ʔalwāḥun/; (2) $CiC_2āC_3$, e.g. /raǧulun/ 'man', pl. /riǧālun/; (3) $C_1uC_2ūC_3$, e.g. /baytun/ 'house', pl. /buyūtun/.

There are many prefixes and suffixes in derivational morphology such as the *nisba* /-īyun/, colloquial /-i/, which forms relative adjectives (it is well known since so many other languages have borrowed it, e.g. *Kuwait*, *Kuwaiti*), such as /lubnānīyun/ '(a) Lebanese', colloquial /lubnāni/, f. /lubnānīyatun/, m. pl. /lubnānīyūna/, obl. /lubnānīyīna/, f. pl. /lubnānīyātun/, obl. /lubnānīyātin/. Among the most common (and recognisable, due to loanwords such as *Muslim*) is /m-/, marking nouns of time or place, instruments, active and passive participles and verbal nouns, e.g. /maktabun/ 'office', /maktabatun/ 'library', related to /kataba/ 'he wrote', /maktūbun/ 'written', coming to mean 'anything written' or 'letter' (passive participle of Form I), /miftāḥun/ 'key', related to /fataḥa/ 'he opened'. (Incidentally, since a language like Persian, of the Indo-Iranian family, has borrowed so many Arabic loanwords and since a Persian dictionary is arranged alphabetically and not on the basis of a triconsonantal root, it is safe to say that, due to the statistically high occurrence of /m-/ from Arabic loanwords, /m-/-initial words make up the largest section in a Persian dictionary; thus in F. Steingass, *A Comprehensive Persian–English Dictionary* (Routledge and Kegan Paul, London, 1863) the letter *mīm* (i.e. < m >) runs from p. 1,136 to p. 1,365 – the entire dictionary has 1,539 pages.

10 Verbal Morphology

Some preliminary information on the algebraically predictable verbal system has been mentioned in Section 3. Person, mood and aspect are marked by prefixes and suffixes. There are nine derived themes (forms) or stems of the verb plus the basic one, i.e. Form I, yielding a total of ten verbal forms (and five more that are archaic or very rare), each with a 'normal' range of semantic value, e.g. intensivity, causativity, reflexivity, etc. Each form has its own set of active and passive participles and verbal nouns (sometimes called 'verbal abstracts'). Further, there is an internal passive for each of the forms, formed by vocalic change from its corresponding active.

Form I verbs are of three types depending on the second vowel of the perfect: /qatala/ 'he killed', /ʕalima/ 'he knew' and /ḥasuna/ 'he was good'. /i/ in the perfect usually marks an intransitive verb, denoting often a temporary state; /u/ in the perfect usually marks an intransitive verb expressing a permanent state.

Form II is formed by geminating the second radical of the root so that the verb functions like a quadriradical (statistically these are in the very small minority of roots, e.g. /tarǧama/ 'he translated'), e.g. /ʕallama/ 'he taught'. Among the meanings of Form II are: (1) intensiveness, /kasara/ 'he broke' vs /kassara/ 'he smashed'; (2) iterative, /qataʕa/ 'he cut' vs /qattaʕa/ 'he cut up'; (3) causativity, /ʕallama/ 'he taught' is the causative of /ʕalima/ 'he knew', i.e. 'to cause to know'; (4) estimation, /kaðaba/ 'he lied' vs /kaððaba/ 'he considered (someone) a liar'; (5) denominative function, /xaymatun/ 'a tent' yields

/xayyama/ 'he pitched a tent', and (6) transitivity, /nāma/ 'he slept' produces /nawwama/ 'he put to sleep' or 'he anaesthetised'.

Form III is formed by lengthening the first /a/. The meanings are: (1) reciprocity (directing an action towards somebody), e.g. /kātaba/ 'he corresponded with', /qātala/ 'he fought with and tried to kill'; and (2) the attempt to do something, e.g. from /sabaqa/ 'he preceded' one forms /sābaqa/ 'he competed with' (i.e. 'he attempted to precede').

Form IV is formed by prefixing a glottal stop (= Hebrew /h-/ and Ancient Egyptian /s-/) followed by /a/ and making the first radical vowel-less, e.g. /jalasa/ 'he sat down' has /ʔajlasa/ 'he seated' as its causative. In addition to the (primary) causative meaning, one encounters (1) a declaration (used with /mā/ 'how; what' in the third person perfect only), e.g. /mā ʔaħsanahu/ 'how handsome he is!' There are often Form IV verbs with the meaning 'became', e.g. /ʔaṣbaħa/ 'he became' (also /ʔamsā/ and /ʔaḍħā/). Also one finds denominatives of place names, e.g. from /najdun/ 'Najd' (north-central Saudi Arabia) one obtains /ʔanjada/ 'to go to Najd'.

Forms V and VI are passives and reflexives of Forms II and III, respectively, and are both formed by prefixing /ta-/ to those forms. From /ʕallama/ 'he taught' one obtains /taʕallama/ 'he taught himself', i.e. 'he learned' or 'he was taught' (one can understand the verb both ways in terms of English). From /qātala/ and /kātaba/ one obtains /taqātala/ 'to fight each other' and /takātaba/ 'to correspond with each other', respectively. Form VI also denotes a pretence, e.g. from /mariḍa/ 'he was sick' one obtains /tamāraḍa/ 'he pretended to be sick', or from /nāma/ 'he slept' one obtains /tanāwama/ 'he pretended to be asleep' (this latter is a good example of what is called a 'hollow' verb because a morphophonemic //w// occurs in the root, which manifests itself in Form VI but not in Form I).

Form VII is formed by prefixing a vowel-less /n-/ to Form I. As no word can begin with a vowel-less consonant, an anaptyctic vowel /i/ is inserted and, initially, a prothetic /ʔ/ precedes the /i/ since no word can begin with a vowel. (This is true of Hebrew too, with only one exception.) It is usually the passive or reflexive of Form I, e.g. Form I /kasara/ 'he broke' (transitive) forms Form VII as /ʔinkasara/ 'it broke' (intransitive).

Form VIII, the only infixing form, infixes /-ta-/ between the first and second radicals. As the first radical is vowel-less, it uses the anaptyctic /i/ rule and glottal insertion, as did Form VII (see above). It is usually the reflexive of Form I, but contrary to Form VII, it may take a direct object. As examples, one notes: /ʔiktataba/ 'he was registered' and /ʔiqtatala/ 'to fight with one another'. Occasionally, there is no difference in meaning between Forms I and VIII, e.g. /šarā/, imperfect /yašrī/ 'he bought' (Form I) = /ʔištarā/, imperfect /yaštarī/.

Form IX is very restricted semantically, the meaning revolves around a colour or a physical defect, e.g. /ʔiswadda/ 'he became black' or /ʔiʕwajja/ 'he became bent'. It is made by geminating the third radical of the root and deleting the vowel of the first radical with the appropriate anaptyctic /i/ and glottal stop insertion (see the remarks for Form VII).

Form X is formed by making the first radical of the root vowel-less and prefixing /sta-/. Like the preceding forms, there is anaptyxis and glottal stop insertion (see the remarks for Form VII). It is the reflexive of Form IV or has to do with asking someone for something (for oneself) in terms of the basic sememe of the root. Also, there is a meaning of consideration. From /ʔaʕlama/ 'he informed' one obtains /ʔistaʕlama/ 'he enquired' (i.e. 'he asked for information for himself'); from /kataba/ 'he wrote' one obtains /ʔistaktaba/ 'he asked someone to write'; from /ħasuna/ 'he was good' one obtains /ʔistaħsana/ 'he considered (as) good'.

The conjugation of a regular verb in the perfect and imperfect (Form I) is shown in the chart given here, for the verb 'kill', in the perfect ('he killed') and imperfect 'he kills'):

	Perfect	Imperfect
1 sg.	qataltu	ʔaqtulu
2 sg. m.	qatalta	taqtulu
2 sg. f.	qatalti	taqtulīna
3 sg. m.	qatala	yaqtulu
3 sg. f.	qatalat	taqtulu
2 du.	qataltumā	taqtulāni
3 du. m.	qatalā	yaqtulāni
3 du. f.	qatalatā	taqtulāni
1 pl.	qatalnā	naqtulu
2 pl. m.	qataltum	taqtulūna
2 pl. f.	qataltunna	taqtulna
3 pl. m.	qatalū	yaqtulūna
3 pl. f.	qatalna	yaqtulna

There are five forms of the imperative of the regular verb: *ʔuqtul* 'kill' (m. sg.), f. sg. *ʔuqtulī*, m. pl. *ʔuqtulū*, f. pl. *ʔuqtulna* and du. *ʔuqtulā*.

There are three moods of the imperfect: the indicative (given in the chart of regular verb forms), the subjunctive and the jussive. To form the subjunctive, the basic change is to replace the final *-u* of the indicative with *-a*. Indicative forms ending in *-na/-ni* after a vowel drop *-na/-ni*. The second and third person feminine plural forms are the same in all three moods.

The jussive is formed by dropping the final *-u* of the indicative. Forms not ending in *-u* in the indicative have the jussive identical to the subjunctive.

The conjugation of a hollow verb (i.e. one with *w* or *y* as middle radical) is as shown in the following chart (Form I).

	Perfect	Imperfect
1 sg.	qultu	ʔaqūlu
2 sg. m.	qulta	taqūlu
2 sg. f.	qulti	taqūlīna
3 sg. m.	qāla	yaqūlu
3 sg. f.	qālat	taqūlu
2 du.	qultumā	taqūlāni
3 du. m.	qālā	yaqūlāni
3 du. f.	qālatā	taqūlāni
1 pl.	qulnā	naqūlu
2 pl. m.	qultum	taqūlūna
2 pl. f.	qultunna	taqulna
3 pl. m.	qālū	yaqūlūna
3 pl. f.	qulna	yaqulna

The forms of the imperative are: *qul*, *qūlī*, *qūlū*, *qulna* and *qūlā*.

11 Verbal Aspect

Many Semitists agree that the semantic system of the Arabic verb is very difficult to examine from an Indo-European perspective. Arabic has a *māḍī* ('past' or 'perfect' or 'perfective') or suffixed conjugation and a *muḍāriʕ* ('similar to the triptote noun in taking three endings'; 'imperfect' or 'imperfective' or 'non-past') or prefixed conjugation. The imperfect can refer to present, but also to future and past; the perfect can refer to past, but also to future or present. The fact that the perfect can refer to the present is illustrated by the following. In a buying–selling transaction, once the event is regarded (in the mind of the speaker) as completed (or 'manifest', to use a Whorfian term), one may say *biʕtuka hāðā* lit. 'I sold (perfect) you this', which means 'I sell you this' or 'I am (now) selling you this'. No money has yet exchanged hands, though. That the imperfect can express a past action is illustrated by the following: *jāʔū ʔābāhum yabkūna* lit. 'they came to their father – they cry', which means 'they came to their father crying' or *ʔatā ḷayna yašrabu* lit. 'he came to the well – he drinks', which means 'he came to the well to drink'.

Few Arabic verbs embody unambiguous time. The great majority of Arabic verbs can be either static or dynamic. In English this will often be reflected in a different verb. From the verbal nouns *rukūbun*, the static value is 'ride' – dynamic 'mount'; *ʔiḥmirārun*, static 'be red' – dynamic 'turn red'; *ʔiqāmatun* 'reside' and 'settle', respectively; *ḥukmun* 'govern' and 'decree', respectively; *ʕilmun* 'know' and 'get to know', respectively.

The colloquial Arabic dialects have felt the need for finer tense distinctions, in addition to the opposition perfect/imperfect, and have developed overt tense markers such as /ḥ-/ or /h-/ marking future in Egyptian and other colloquial dialects.

The problem of aspect and tense in Arabic (and in Semitic in general) is one on which much has already been written, but much more research needs to be accomplished before the final answer is in. It remains one of the most debated and hotly contested facets of Semitic linguistics. Surely both aspect and (relative) tense are involved.

12 Syntax

Arabic uses a non-verbal construction for some verbs in English, the most notable of which is 'have'. Arabic uses the preposition /li-/ 'to, for' or /ʕinda/ 'with (Fr. *chez*)' for 'have', e.g. /lī kitābun/ or /ʕindī kitābun/ 'I have a book'.

English is more analytical than is Arabic. Thus in English one needs three words to say 'I killed him'. In Arabic, one word renders this sentence, /qataltuhu/. English again needs three words to way 'he is sad', Arabic /ḥazina/, or 'he makes (someone) sad', /ḥazzana/ or /ʔaḥzana/.

The basic word order for Classical Arabic is VSO, e.g. 'Muhammad went to school' is rendered *ðahaba* ('he went') *muḥammadun* ('Muhammad') *ʔilā* ('to') *l-madrasati* ('the school', gen. sg.). It is possible to begin the sentence with the subject for stylistic reasons; however, if this is done, it is usual to precede the subject with *ʔinna* 'indeed', which then forces the subject to be in the accusative, i.e. *ʔinna muḥammadan ðahaba ʔilā l-madrasati*.

Colloquial Arabic dialects are basically SVO (although I think most are, I refrain from saying 'all') and there is now convincing evidence that modern standard Arabic has become SVO as well. D.B. Parkinson has investigated this by examining newspapers such as *Al-Ahrām* and *Al-Akhbār* from 1970 to 1978 and the conclusion is that this change is still in progress. There is evidence that SVO is the more archaic word order since proverbs may still preserve this Proto-Arabic stage, e.g. *ʔaljāhilu yaṭlubu lmāla walʕāqilu yaṭlubu lkamāla* 'the fool seeks wealth, the wise man seeks perfection'.

If the verb precedes its subject, usually it is in the singular (Classical Arabic is more rigid than modern standard Arabic), but if it follows the subject there must be agreement in number (as well as gender), e.g. 'the two men bought a book' may be *ʔištarā rrajulāni kitāban* (VSO, singular verb) or *ʔinna rrajulayni štarayā kitāban* (SVO, dual verb).

Interrogatives arc placed at the beginning of the sentence, e.g. 'where did the teacher study?' *ʔayna* ('where') *darasa* ('he studied') *lmuʕallimu* ('the teacher', nom. sg.).

Two types of clauses have been studied in detail and the first is a hallmark of Arabic. The *ħāl* or circumstantial clause is usually introduced by /wa-/ 'and', which translates into English as 'while' or 'when', e.g. 'he wrote a letter while he was sick' – *kataba* ('he wrote') *maktūban* ('a letter', acc. sg.) *wahuwa* ('and he') *marīḍun* ('sick', nom. sg.) or 'he killed him while/when she was pregnant' – *qatalahu* ('he killed him') *wahiya* ('and she') *ħāmilun* ('pregnant', nom. sg.). The second is the relative clause, which contains a pronominal reference to the modified noun, but no relative pronoun occurs if the modified noun is indefinite, e.g. 'he wrote a book which I read' – *kataba* ('he wrote') *kitāban* ('a book', acc. sg.) *qaraʔtuhu* ('I read it', m. sg.) vs 'he wrote the book which I read' – *kataba* ('he wrote') *lkitāba* ('the book', acc. sg.) *llaðī* ('which', m. sg.) *qaraʔtuhu* ('I read it').

Arabic sentence structures may be divided into the nominal sentence (usually also referred to as the equational sentence or zero copula or *ʔaljumlatu lismiyya* in Arabic) and the verbal sentence. The equational sentence is a favourite sentence type of Arabic. It consists of two parts: a topic or subject (Arabic *mubtadaʔ*) and a comment or predicate (Arabic *xabar*). The subject is usually a noun or pronoun (or a phrase derived thereof) and the predicate is a nominal, pronominal, adjectival, adverbial or prepositional phrase. Consider 'the university library is a beautiful building' – *maktabatu* ('library' in the construct state, nom. sg. indefinite) *ljāmiʕati* ('the university', gen. sg. definite) *bināʔun* ('building, nom. sg. indefinite) *jamīlun* ('beautiful', m. sg. nom. indefinite). Negation of the equational sentence is formed by the irregular verb *laysa* 'not to be', which governs a predicate in the accusative (as any other verb does). The negative of the above illustrative sentence is *laysat maktabatu ljāmiʕati bināʔan jamīlan*.

When the predicate of an equational sentence is an adverb or a prepositional phrase and there is an indefinite subject, the normal word order is predicate-subject, e.g. '(there is) a book on the table' = *ʕalā* ('on') *lmāʔidati* ('the table', definite gen.) *kitābun* ('a book', indefinite nom.).

With non-present time reference, one finds equivalent verbal sentences. The verb 'to be', *kāna* in the perfect, *yakūnu* in the imperfect, occurs in the past and future and governs, like any other verb, the accusative case. The Arab grammarians also put the verb *laysa* 'not to be' into this same category (called 'the sisters' of *kāna*) along with *mā zāla* 'continue to be', *mā ʕāda* 'no longer to be', *kāda* 'be on the verge of'. The following verbs all mean 'to become': *ṣāra*, *ʔaṣbaħa*, *bāta*, *ʔamsā* and *ʔaḍħā* and verbs meaning 'remain' such as *baqiya* also belong to this verbal group.

To illustrate, consider that *kāna tājiran* 'he was a merchant' has *tājiran* in the indefinite accusative singular; its plural is *kānū tujjāran* (*tujjār* is the broken plural of *tājir*). *Kāna tājirun* means 'there was a merchant'.

A major characteristic of *kāna*-type verbs is that they can govern a following imperfect instead of a noun in the accusative. Thus one can say *lā ʔadrī* 'I do not know' or *lastu* (< *laysa*) *ʔadrī* (lit. 'I am not – I know').

Bibliography

For classical Arabic, Fleisch (1956) is a solid overview, while Wright (1955), though originally published more than a century ago, remains a superbly documented grammar. Bravmann (1953) and Badawi et al. (2004) are among the best syntaxes available, while for phonetics Gairdner (1925) is probably one of the finest works ever written on the subject, dealing primarily with Koranic Arabic. Fück (1955) is a most important treatise on the history and development of Classical Arabic, while Owens (2006) is the first basic linguistic history of Arabic. Holes (2004) is a survey of language structure and language varieties.

Pellat (1956) is a very good learner's manual for modern standard Arabic, while Stetkevych (1970) is a solid and thorough investigation of lexical and stylistic developments.

For the modern vernaculars, there are three superb grammars in the same series; Cowell (1964) on Syrian Arabic, Erwin (1963) on Iraqi Arabic and Harrell (1962) on Moroccan Arabic. Mitchell (1956), on Egyptian Arabic, is one of the finest pedagogical grammars ever written, while Woidich (2006) is a detailed descriptive grammar. Qafisheh (1977), on Gulf Arabic, is a fine grammar, based on fieldwork in the Gulf countries, and deals with the vernacular dialects of important emerging countries. For Nigerian Arabic, references may be made to Kaye (1982), a dictionary of 6,000 lexemes with illustrative sentences and a linguistic introduction.

Mitchell (1953) is a fine treatise on the writing system.

References

Badawi, E., Carter, M. G. and Gully, A. 2004. *Modern Written Arabic: A Comprehensive Grammar* (Routledge, London)

Bravmann, M.M. 1953. *Studies in Arabic and General Syntax* (Imprimerie de l'Institut d'Archéologie Orientale, Cairo)

Cowell, M.W. 1964. *A Short Reference Grammar of Syrian Arabic* (Georgetown University Press, Washington DC)

Erwin, W.M. 1963. *A Short Reference Grammar of Iraqi Arabic* (Georgetown University Press, Washington DC)

Fleisch, H. 1956. *L'Arabe classique: esquisse d'une structure linguistique* (Imprimerie Catholique, Beirut).

Fück, J. 1955. *Arabiya: Recherches sur l'histoire de la langue et du style arabe* (Marcel Didier, Paris; translated by C. Denizeau, with an introduction by J. Cantineau, from the German original, *Arabiya: Untersuchungen zur arabischen Sprach- und Stilgeschichte*, Akademie-Verlag, Berlin, 1950)

Gairdner, W.H.T. 1925. *The Phonetics of Arabic* (Oxford University Press, London)

Harrell, R.S. 1962. *A Short Reference Grammar of Moroccan Arabic* (Georgetown University Press, Washington DC)

Holes, C. 2004. *Modern Arabic: Structures, Functions, and Varieties* (Georgetown University Press, Washington DC)

Kaye, A.S. 1982. *A Dictionary of Nigerian Arabic* (Undena, Malibu, CA)

Mitchell, T.F. 1953. *Writing Arabic: A Practical Introduction to the Ruq'ah Script* (Oxford University Press, London)

—— 1956. *An Introduction to Colloquial Egyptian Arabic* (Oxford University Press, London)

Owens, J. 2006. *A Linguistic History of Arabic* (Oxford University Press, Oxford)

Pellat, C. 1956. *Introduction à l'arabe moderne* (Adrien-Maisonneuve, Paris)

Qafisheh, H.A. 1977. *A Short Reference Grammar of Gulf Arabic* (University of Arizona Press, Tucson)

Stetkevych, J. 1970. *The Modern Arabic Literary Language: Lexical and Stylistic Developments* (University of Chicago Press, Chicago)

Woidich, M. 2006. *Das Kairenisch-Arabische: eine Grammatik* (Harrassowitz, Wiesbaden)

Wright, W. 1955. *A Grammar of the Arabic Language*, 3rd edn (Cambridge University Press, Cambridge)

34

Hebrew

Robert Hetzron

Revised by Alan S. Kaye

1 Introduction

The importance of the Hebrew language is not to be measured by the number of its speakers at any time in its history. It is the language of the Jewish Bible, the Old Testament of Christians. It also has a very long continuous history. Kept in continuous use by Jews from antiquity to modern times, its reformed version, in an unprecedented process of revival, became the official language of the modern state of Israel.

It is futile to ask whether Modern Hebrew is the same language as the idiom of the Hebrew Bible. Clearly, the difference between them is great enough to make it impossible for the person who knows one to understand the other without effort. Biblical scholars have to study the modern language if they want to benefit from studies written in Hebrew today and Israelis cannot properly follow Biblical passages without having studied them at school. Yet a partial understanding is indeed possible and the similarities are so obvious that calling them separate languages or two versions of the same tongue would be an arbitrary, purely terminological decision.

Impressive as the revival of Hebrew as a modern language may be, one ought not to have an exaggerated impression of its circumstances. Since Biblical times, Hebrew has never been a dead language. True, it ceased to be a spoken language used for the 'pass me the salt' type of everyday communication, but it has been cultivated – applied not only to liturgy and passive reading of old texts, but also to correspondence, creative writing and, occasionally, conversation. Actually, it was so extensively used for writing that the language, through this medium, underwent all the changes and developments that are characteristic of a living language. The revival in Israel made it again an everyday colloquial tongue.

2 The Script

Hebrew is written from right to left. This is essentially a consonantal script. (In the following, capital letters will be used for transliteration of Hebrew words.) A word like *šibbōlɛṯ* (*shibboleth*) 'ear of corn' is written in four letters *ŠBLT*. Yet long *ū* and *ī* (but not long *ā* > *ō*) are indicated by the letters otherwise marking semi-vowels: *W* and *Y* respectively. Moreover, the original diphthongs **aw* and **ay*, which were legitimately represented by *W* and *Y* in the consonantal transcription, were mostly reduced to *ō* and *ē*, yet they kept their *W* and *Y* symbols, making these trivalent symbols for semi-vowels and both closed and mid labial and palatal vowels respectively. Thus, the word which was originally **hawbi:lu:* 'they carried', Biblical *hōʷḇīʸlūʷ*, modern /hovʼilu/, is written *HWBYLW*. Two more factors need to be added. The *aleph*, originally a symbol for the glottal stop *ʔ*, has been maintained in the orthography even after the *ʔ* ceased to be pronounced. Word-final *-H* was pronounced in a few cases only; otherwise the letter stands as a dummy symbol after a final vowel *-ɛ/-ē* or, more frequently, after final *-ā̊*. This latter is most often a feminine ending. The use of *-H* here preserves the second stage of the phonetic development of this ending: **at* > *-āh* > *-ā̊*.

These originally consonantal letters used for partial vowel marking are traditionally called *mātrēs lectiōnis* 'mothers (= helping devices) of reading'. I transcribe them with raised letters.

The old Hebrew consonantal script, practically identical with the Phoenician one, was gradually replaced, beginning at the end of the sixth century BC, by an Aramaic script which, through the centuries to come, evolved into what is today known as the Jewish 'square' script, the standard printed form. From the second century BC on, graphically more or less different cursive systems further developed for casual handwriting. Two of these are still in use today: the modern cursive and a calligraphic development of the so-called Mashait cursive, the latter used today chiefly for printing the commentaries on the Bible and the Talmud of the eleventh-century Jewish scholar, Rashi (hence the name 'Rashi script').

Table 34.1 presents the consonantal letters of the major alternative scripts. Note that the letters *K*, *M*, *N*, *P* and *Ṣ* have special 'final' versions when they occur at the end of the word. These are parenthesised in the table. The names represent the Modern Hebrew pronunciation, as they are currently used. In the transcription column, the capital letter stands for the transliteration of the script, the letters after '~' show the Modern Hebrew pronunciation. These letters may serve as number symbols up to four hundred. They may be combined – thus *KZ* stands for 'twenty-seven', *RMḤ* for 'two hundred and forty-eight', etc.

Writing systems that transcribe words incompletely or inconsistently (English is an example of the latter) may be viewed as basically mnemonic devices rather than as truly efficient scripts. With the decline of Hebrew as a spoken tongue, the introduction of vowel symbols and other diacritics became necessary. In order not to alter the original sacred, consonantal texts, this was done by means of added symbols, dots or other reduced-size designs placed under, above and in some cases in the centre of the consonantal letters. These were always considered optional supplements, omissible at will. There were several such systems, chiefly the Babylonian and Tiberian vocalisations; the latter alone is now used. The introducers of these systems are called Masoretes, the 'carriers of tradition', who carried out their work between AD 600 and 1000.

In the Tiberian Masoretic system, for example, a dot over the top left corner of a letter indicates *ō*, and if a *W* had traditionally been used for the same sound, the dot is placed over the *W*, to distinguish it from *ū*, which has the dot in the middle. Dots in the middle of consonantal letters other than those marking laryngeals and, with some exceptions, *r* may mark gemination, doubling of the consonant. However, in the beginning

Table 34.1 The consonantal letters

Phoenician (=Old Hebrew)	Jewish Square (modern print)	Rashi	Cursive (modern)	Name	Transcription	Numerical Value
𐤀	א	ꜧ	k	alef	ʔ	1
𐤁	ב	פ	ꜿ	bet	B; b, ƀ~v	2
𐤂	ג	ג	ɗ	g'imel	G; g, g̱	3
𐤃	ד	ꞁ	ꜰ	d'alet	D; d, đ	4
𐤄	ה	ꜳ	ꜰ	he	H; h	5
𐤅	ו	ו	l	vav	W; w~v, u,o	6
𐤆	ז	ʄ	ƅ	z'ayin	Z; z	7
𐤇	ח	ꜰ	ꜳ	xet	Ḥ; ḥ~x	8
𐤈	ט	ꜱ	6	tet	Ṭ; ṭ~t	9
𐤉	י	ꞌ	ꞌ	yod	Y; y, i, e	10
𐤊	כ(ך)	כ (ך)	כ(ך)	kaf	K; k, ꝁ~x	20
𐤋	ל	ꞁ	ꞁ	l'amed	L; l	30
𐤌	מ(ם)	ם (ם)	N(ם)	mem	M; m	40
𐤍	נ(ן)	נ (ן)	J(l)	nun	N; n	50
𐤎	ס	פ	o	s'amex	S; s	60
𐤏	ע	פ	ꝡ	'ayin	ʕ	70
𐤐	פ(ף)	פ (ף)	ꝑ(ꝭ)	pe	P; p, ꝓ~f	80
𐤑	צ(ץ)	ꞁ (ץ)	3(ꝩ)	tsade	Ṣ; ṣ~c(= ts)	90
𐤒	ק	ꝗ	ꝓ	qof	Q; q~k	100
𐤓	ר	ꞁ	ꞁ	resh	R; r	200
𐤔	ש	ꞇ	e	shin	Š; š	300
𐤕	ת	ꜰ	ꞁ	tav	T; t~, ꞇ~t	400

of syllables, a dot in *B, G, D, K, P, T* (this is the traditional order of listing) means that they are to be pronounced as stops; absence of the dot points at the spirantised articulation *β* or *v*, etc. (see below). A dot in a final *h* indicates that it is to be pronounced and is not a mere dummy symbol, a tradition that has usually not been observed.

One diacritic symbol is used for a true phonemic distinction. Hebrew has separate letters for *Š* and *S*, but in some cases, the former is read [s] as well. To mark this, the *Š* symbol was supplemented with a dot in the right top corner for [š] and the left for [s]. This latter is usually transcribed *ś* and represents an original separate phoneme, a lateral fricative.

The vocalic notation was brilliantly constructed, yet it is not always perfectly adequate for all traditional pronunciations. A small T-shaped symbol underneath a consonant usually stands for a long *ā̊* but in some cases, in syllables that were originally closed, it may be a short *å* (< *u*), see the beginning of Section 4.1. Two vertically aligned dots underneath a letter, called 'shwa', may indicate lack of a vowel or, at the beginning of the word or after another shwa (and in some other cases), an ultrashort sound [ə]. After laryngeals, there are 'tainted shwas', ultrashort *ă, ɛ̆* and *å̆* (*ŏ*). At the end of a word, lack of vowel is indicated by the lack of any vowel symbol, although final shwa is written in some grammatical endings under -*T* (with a dot in the middle) and always in final -*K*.

The vowel symbol is supposed to be read after the consonantal letter to which it is attached, except in word-final *Ḥ, ʕ* and dotted *H* with an *A* underneath, where the vowel sounds first. This is called a 'furtive *a*', a euphonic development.

Table 34.2 illustrates the use of vowels and other diacritic symbols, traditionally called the 'pointing'.

Table 34.2 The Pointing

| A. | The dot in the consonant (*dagesh*) |

a. Spirantisation.

ב b, ב b; ג g, ג g; ד d, ד d̠; כ(ך) k, כ(ך) k̠; פ p, פ(ף) p̠; ת t, ת t̠

b. Gemination.

ב ...*bb*; ו ...*ww*; מ ...*mm*; ק ...*qq*...

| B. | The letter Š. |

שׁ š; שׂ ś

| C. | The vowels (combined with various consonants). |

Long		Short		Ultrashort	
	ט *ṭå̄*	ט *ṭa*		ֲ *'ă*	
לִי *lēy*	לֵ *lē*	לֶ *lɛ*		אֱ *ʔɛ̆*	
מוֹ *mōw*	ר *rō*	צ *ṣå*		ֳ *ḥå̆*	
תִּי *tīy*		ס *si*		ְ *zə, z*	
	נוּ *nuw*	נ *nu*			

As we have seen, the Biblical Hebrew script was not exclusively consonantal. The *mātrēs lectiōnis* indicated some of the vowels. The use of these was later extended. Already in Late Biblical Hebrew, we find *W* also for *ō* that does not come from **aw*. In Modern Hebrew, except for some very frequent words and common patterns (where a certain degree of convention has still been maintained), *W* may be used for any /u/ or /o/, and *Y* for any /i/.

In modern practice, consistent vowel marking is restricted to Biblical texts, poetry, dictionaries and children's books. Otherwise, only the consonantal script is used, with fuller application of *mātrēs lectiōnis* and with occasionally strategically placed vowel symbols to avoid potential ambiguities. It should be noted that the duality of 'obligatory' *W*'s and *Y*'s sanctified by tradition and 'optional' ones which may appear in unvocalised texts only is very confusing to the student of Modern Hebrew. Another serious problem, for native Israelis too, is that no consistent system has been worked out for the transcription of foreign words and names. Some conventions do exist, such as *G* with an apostrophe marking [ǰ], non-final *P* in word-final positions for final -*p*; yet this is insufficient, and many such words are often mispronounced.

It should be added that the texts of the Old Testament print cantillation marks (some above, some beneath the word), which note the melodic pattern to be used in chanting the texts in the synagogue service. Their exact position provides a clue to stress in Biblical Hebrew.

Table 34.3 reproduces part of verse 24 in chapter 13 of the book of Nehemiah. First the consonantal text is presented, then the same with full pointing.

3 The Periods of Hebrew

Hebrew may be historically divided into distinct periods on the basis of grammar and vocabulary.

Table 34.3 Part of Nehemiah 13.24

ואינם מכירים לדכר יהודית
Transliteration: W?YNM MKYRYM LDBR YHWDYT
וְאֵינָם מַכִּירִים לְדַבֵּר יְהוּדִית
Transliteration: wəʔēʸnˈåm makkīʸrˈīʸm lədabbˈēr yəhūʷdˈīʸt
Translation: 'and-they-do-not know [how]-/to/speak Judean'

3.1 Pre-Biblical Hebrew

Hebrew is a Canaanite language, closely related to Phoenician. It is even likely that its northern dialect barely differed from Phoenician. There exist Canaanite documents from the mid-twentieth century to the twelfth century BC, transcribed in Akkadian and Egyptian documents. It is hard to assess their exact relationship to the contemporary ancestor of Hebrew, but the two may be assumed to be identical in essence. Case endings and other archaic elements in phonology and morphology are found here. The most important source of these data are fourteenth-century BC letters found in Tell el-Amarna, Egypt.

3.2 Biblical Hebrew

This is the most important period, documented through the Old Testament (but note that substantial parts of the books of Daniel and Ezra are in Aramaic). This collection of texts spans over a millennium-long period (1200–200 BC). The literary dialect was based on southern (Judean) Hebrew, though the northern dialect of some authors does show through. It is wrong to think of Biblical Hebrew as a homogeneous dialect. It covers different places and periods.

This heterogeneity, in particular the coexistence of doublets (e.g. a dual tense system for the verb, see below), led some scholars to declare that Biblical Hebrew was a *Mischsprache*, a mixed language, representing the coalescence of the speech of Israelites arriving from Egypt and of the local Canaanites. Yet the doublets attested do not seem to be particularly exceptional in the history of standard dialects.

It is customary to speak of Early Biblical Hebrew (the Pentateuch, Joshua, Judges, Samuel, Kings, the prophetic books) and Late Biblical Hebrew (Chronicles, Song of Songs, Esther, etc.) but this is a simplification. The Song of Deborah (Judges 5) is considered to be the oldest text. In several books one finds traces of their having been compiled from different sources. Poetic texts such as the Psalms, the Song of Songs and poetic inserts elsewhere have their own grammatical and lexical features.

It should also be remembered that no matter how rich the material contained in the Hebrew Bible may be, no document of even that length can represent the full riches of a living language. We shall never know the true dimensions of Biblical Hebrew spoken at that time.

Biblical Hebrew ceased to be spoken at some unspecified time (the destruction of the First Temple in 586 BC may have been a major factor), yielding to Mishnaic Hebrew (see below) and Aramaic. The very last period of written Late Biblical Hebrew extends, however, into the Christian era, as represented by texts found in Qumran, known as the Dead Sea Scrolls.

One should thus keep in mind that what is described under the label 'Biblical Hebrew' is basically hybrid material: text in a consonantal script from between 1200 and 200 BC, while the pointing (vowels, indication of stress, gemination, spirantisation) comes from a much later date (after AD 600), when even the next stage of Hebrew, Mishnaic, had long ceased to be spoken. True, the pointing is based on authentic tradition, but certain distortions through the centuries were unavoidable.

3.3 Mishnaic Hebrew

This dialect represents the promotion into a written idiom of what was probably the spoken language of Judea during the period of Late Biblical Hebrew (sixth century BC) and on. It ceased to be spoken around AD 200, but survived as a literary language till about the fifth century AD. It is the language of the Mishnah, the central book of the Talmud (an encyclopedic collection of religious, legal and other texts), of some of the older portions of other Talmudic books and of parts of the Midrashim (legal and literary commentaries on the Bible).

3.4 Medieval Hebrew

This was never a spoken language, yet it is the carrier of a rich literary tradition. It was used by Jews scattered by now around the Mediterranean world, for poetry (both religious and secular), religious discussions, philosophy, correspondence, etc. The main spoken languages of Jews from that time on were varieties of Arabic, Spanish (later Judeo-Spanish, Ladino) and Judeo-German (Yiddish). The earliest layer of Medieval Hebrew is the language of the *Piyyut*, poetry written for liturgical use from the fifth to sixth centuries. After a period of laxity, the great religious leader of Babylon, Saadiah Gaon (892–942), heralded a new epoch in the use of Hebrew. This reached its culmination in the Hebrew poetry in Spain (1085–1145). The eleventh to fifteenth centuries saw a richness of translations into Hebrew, mainly from Arabic. The style developed by Jews of eastern France and western Germany, who later moved to eastern Europe, is known as Ashkenazic Hebrew, the written vehicle of speakers of Yiddish. The origin of the Ashkenazic pronunciation as known today is unclear; the earliest Ashkenazim did not have it.

The Medieval Hebrew period ended along with the Middle Ages, with the cessation of writing Hebrew poetry in Italy. In the interim period that followed, Hebrew writing was confined to religious documents.

3.5 Modern Hebrew

Even though Spanish and Italian Hebrew poetry did treat non-religious topics, it was the period of Enlightenment (Hebrew *Haskalah*, from 1781 on) that restored the use of Hebrew as a secular language. This led to important changes in style and vocabulary. Words denoting objects, persons, happenings of modern life were developed. Hebrew was becoming a European language. This development was concentrated in eastern Europe, with Warsaw and Odessa as the most important centres. The great writer Mendele Moikher Sforim (Sh. J. Abramowitz, 1835–1917) was perhaps the most important and most brilliant innovator. Hebrew began to be spoken regularly only with the establishment of Jewish settlements in Palestine, mainly from Russia. In this revolutionary development, Eliezer Ben-Yehuda (1858–1922) played the most important role as the initiator and leader of the movement. His first son, Itamar Ben-Avi, was the first native speaker of Modern Hebrew. Ben-Yehuda brought many innovations to the Hebrew language. The type of Hebrew developed for speech adopted the Sephardic pronunciation as uttered by an Ashkenazi. In 1922, Hebrew became one of the official languages of Palestine under the British Mandate. Hebrew literature, now transplanted to the Holy Land, experienced an impressive upsurge. With the creation of the State of Israel (1948), the status of Modern Hebrew as the national language became firmly established. Modern Hebrew has been to a great extent regulated by the Academy of the Hebrew Language. On the other hand, native speakers have become a majority in Israel, many of them children of native speakers themselves. In order to express themselves, they do not consult grammars and official decisions, but create their own style, their own language, based on the acquired material according to universal laws of linguistic evolution. This dialect, Spoken Israeli Hebrew, itself a multi-layered complex entity, has only recently been systematically described (see Coffin and Bolozky 2005), although its existence was earlier noted and its importance acknowledged. Israeli Hebrew has about five million speakers.

4 The Structure of Hebrew

In the following, emphasis will be placed on the culturally most important dialect, Biblical Hebrew. When warranted, indications will be given of parallel phenomena in later periods. Modern Hebrew data will be quoted below in phonemic transcription, between /oblique strokes/.

4.1 Phonology

There are many traditional schools of pronunciation for Hebrew. That of Biblical Hebrew is only a reconstruction. It is customary to divide the numerous traditions into two major trends: Sephardi(c) (Mediterranean) and Ashkenazi(c) (Central and Eastern European). The most striking differences between these are the pronunciation of $\bar{a}$ as Seph. a vs Ashk. o (but short $\mathring{a}$ is realised as o even in the Sephardic tradition) and t as Seph. t vs Ashk. s. To a declining extent $\hbar$ and Γ have been preserved in Sephardic only, vs Ashk. x and zero respectively.

For consonants, in the laryngeal domain, the Semitic sounds γ and Γ are represented by the single letter Γ, and x and $\hbar$ also by a single H in the Biblical Hebrew consonantal script. The emphatic consonants of Biblical Hebrew: t, s, q (or k) may have been pronounced glottalised (though there is no explicit proof of this). Today, there is no feature 'emphasis' and the three consonants are realised respectively as /t/, /c/ (= ts) and /k/. Thus, only the middle one remained a separate entity, the other two are pronounced the same way as original t and k.

Except for the laryngeals $?$, Γ, h, $\hbar$ and r (this one may have been at some time a uvular, since it belongs to this class), all consonants may be single or double (geminate) in Biblical Hebrew. Gemination disappeared from Modern Hebrew. Moreover, in the Masoretic tradition, the stops b, d, g, p, t, k were spirantised respectively into β, $\eth$, γ, f, θ, x in post-vocalic, non-geminate position, e.g. $bayi\theta$ 'house', $b\partial\beta ayi\theta$ 'in a house', vs $babbayi\theta$ 'in the house', $b\mathring{a}tt\bar{\imath}^ym$ 'houses'. As can be seen, alternations within the root have resulted from this conditioned spirantisation. Some incongruities in the system (such as 'houses' with a geminate after an apparently long vowel, *habbayθā̆h* '(to) home' with *θ* after a diphthong) make the phonemic status of both vocalic length and spirantisation rather unclear. Therefore, a non-committal transcription *b̄*, *d̄*, etc., rather than the independent symbols *β*, *ð*, etc., will be used below. Modern Hebrew has only the alternations /b/~/v/, /p/~/f/ and /k/~/x/.

The vowel system, as noted by the Masoretes, does have its problems. As just mentioned, the phonemicity of vowel length is debatable. This is why it is advisable to use the macron and not the modern symbol ꞉ to mark this questionable length. Yet it is clear that vocalic length was once indeed present in the Biblical Hebrew system and played an important role in it.

It seems that at some point in its history, Hebrew equalised the length of all full-vowelled syllables (other than /ə/). Already in Proto-Semitic, long vowels could occur in open syllables only. Now, all vowels in an open syllable became either long: **a > ā̊*, **i > ē*, **u > ō*, or ə. Short vowels were confined to closed syllables. However, word-final short vowels with grammatical functions survived for a while. The subsequent loss of these vowels, which made a CV̄CV# sequence into CV̄C#, did not occasion the shortening of V̄, even though the syllable became closed. This produced minimal pairs such as *zā̆kar* 'he remembered' (from **zakar*) vs *zā̆kā̆r* 'male' (from **zakur* + case ending).

The ultrashort vowel ə caused spirantisation of a subsequent non-emphatic stop. After laryngeals, it has the allophones: ultrashort *ă*, *ĕ* and *ŏ*, selected according to the context, mainly on a harmony principle. The vowel [ə] is called *shwa mobile* in contrast with *shwa quiescens*, i.e. lack of vowel, which is marked by the same diacritic symbol. From the written sign's point of view, the shwa is supposed to be pronounced (mobile) after the first consonant of a word, after a consonant cluster or a geminate and, in principle, after a long vowel; the shwa symbol stands for zero (quiescent) elsewhere. However, in some cases, a traditionally quiescent shwa does spirantise the subsequent stop (as it comes from an originally short vowel). This is called *shwa medium*.

Vocalic reductions producing shwas would occur when suffixes were added: *dā̆b̄ā̆r* 'thing, word', pl. *dəb̄ā̆rīʸm*; *dibbɛr* 'he spoke', pl. *dibbərū̆ʷ*.

Modern Hebrew gave up all length distinction and simplified the system. Shwa is pronounced only when otherwise an unpronounceable cluster would result.

Because of the tightly regulated syllable structure (only aggravated by some loopholes), it is impossible to decide which one(s) of the following features: spirantisation, vocalic length, gemination and shwa were phonemically relevant in Biblical Hebrew. By dropping length, Modern Hebrew unequivocally phonemicised spirantisation: BH *sā̆p̄ar* 'he counted' and MH *sā̆ppā̆r* 'barber' respectively became Modern Hebrew /safar/ and /sapar/.

Biblical Hebrew stress fell on one of the last two syllables of the word. In many cases it can be shown that final stress occurs when a word-final short open vowel had disappeared. Hence it was assumed that Proto-Hebrew had uniform penultimate stress. However, in other cases of final stress no such development can be posited, e.g. *ʔatt'ā̆ʰ* 'you (m. sg.)', *dibbər'ū̆ʷ* 'they (m.) spoke'. It is then possible that originally the placement of the stress was not conditioned, but may have been functionally relevant (see the discussion of the tense system below). In transcription, only penultimate stress is traditionally marked, not final stress.

A remarkable feature of Biblical Hebrew (like Classical Arabic) is the existence of 'pausal' forms. At the end of sentences, many words have special shapes, e.g. contextual/pausal:

(a) *šămərūᵂ/šăm'ắrūᵂ* 'they guarded';
(b) *k'ɛ̄lɛb/k'ắlɛb* 'dog', *b'ɛ̄gɛd/b'ắgɛd* 'clothing';
(c) *m'ayim/m'ắyim* 'water', *bắṭ'aḥtắ/bắṭ'ắḥtắ* 'you (m. sg.) trusted)';
(d) *yiṭhall'ēk/yiṭhall'ắk* 'he walks about';
(e) *wa-y-y'ắmåt/wa-y-yắm'ōṭ* 'he died'.

Though the pausal forms of (a) and (d) have archaic vowels, it would be wrong to view the pausal forms as simple survivals, especially in the domain of stress. They contain melodic signals of terminality, an artistic-expressive procedure. The basic principle was that stress, or rather the melismatic tune, fell on the last vowel of the word that was followed by a consonant. This refers to the period when pausal chanting was adopted. Thus, the penultimate vowel of (a) was saved from later reduction. The penultimate stress in (e) was brought to the end. In 'water' in (c), the *i* was not syllabic (**maym*). In (b), an epenthetic ε was added. With few exceptions, the melismatic syllable had to be long, thus original short vowels were lengthened. The retention of the original vowel in (d) needs clarification. Example (b) shows that we do not have here mere archaisms: 'dog' used indeed to be **kalb-*, and the *ắ* may be viewed as a survival; yet 'clothing' was **bigd-*, and the pausal *ắ* is only the result of a secondary lengthening of the ε.

4.2 Grammar

The Semitic root-and-pattern system (see Chapter 32, page 556) was complicated in Hebrew by the alternations introduced by spirantisation as imposed on root consonants according to position. Thus, the root *K-P-R* has, among others, the following manifestations: *kắpar* (MoH /kafar/) 'he denied', *yikpōr* (MoH /yixpor/) 'he will deny'; *kippɛr* (MoH /kiper/) 'he atoned', *yəkappēr* (MoH /yexaper/) 'he will atone'.

Inspired by their Arab colleagues, Hebrew grammarians adopted the practice of marking patterns by means of the 'dummy' root *P-ʕ-L* ('do, act' in real usage), e.g. *puʕʕal* means a form where the first root consonant is followed by an *u*, the second one is doubled and is followed by an *a*.

In the verbal system, seven derivational classes (*binyanim* 'structures') are to be distinguished:

(I)   *pắʕal* or *qal*, the basic form (with a special subclass where the non-past has the thematic vowel *a* instead of the usual *ō*);

(II)   *nipʕal* (marked by a prefix *n-*, assimilated to the first radical after a prefix), a passive of I if transitive, always an intransitive itself, occasionally inchoative;

(III)   *piʕʕēl* (with gemination of the middle radical), originally an iterative (for repeated actions), denominative and some other functions (often vaguely labelled 'intensive');

(IV)   *puʕʕal*, the passive of III;

(V)   *hipʕīʸl*, originally a causative;

(VI)   *håpʕal*, later *hupʕal*, the passive of V; and

(VII) *hiṭpaʕʕēl*, a reflexive or reciprocal, from Medieval Hebrew on, also a passive of III and with some other functions.

Note that the derivational 'meanings' are not always to be taken literally. From the transitive *binyanim* I, III and V, passive II, IV and VI may be freely formed, but a II verb does not necessarily come from a I. V may be the causative of I only when sanctioned by attestation in the sources; it is thus not productive. IV and VI have only restricted, mainly participial uses from Medieval Hebrew on. Some other derivational forms are occasionally found as archaisms or innovations.

In Biblical Hebrew the passive may have the syntax of an impersonal: *lōʔ yēʔā̆kēl ʔɛt bəśā̆rōʷ* (Exodus 21.28) 'not will-be-eaten acc. its-flesh' = 'its flesh will not be eaten', where an object prefix precedes what might have been expected to be subject of the passive (corresponding to the object of the corresponding active).

The weak-root classes are designated by means of two letters, the first of which indicates which radical is weak (using the *P-ʕ-L* system), the second specifying which weak consonant might disappear or be transformed in the conjugation. Thus *P:y* means that the first radical is a *y*. The main classes, beside regular (strong) roots, are *P:y* (with two subgroups), *P:n*, *P:ʔ*, *ʕ:w*, *ʕ:y*, *L:y* (often named *L:h* because the grapheme *H* is used here when there is no suffix), *L:ʔ* and *ʕ:ʕ* (verbs where the last two radicals are identical). For all these roots, the conjugation presents some special features in the various tenses and *binyanim*. When *ʕ* or *ḥ* is one of the radicals, changes occur in the vocalisation.

The tense system is among the most controversial and the most variable through the periods of Hebrew. The heterogeneity of Biblical Hebrew manifests itself the most strikingly precisely here.

It seems that the archaic system may be reduced to a dual opposition of two tenses (the traditional label 'aspect' for these is unjustified and rests on indefensible arguments): past and non-past (present and future in one, though the beginnings of a separate present already show), appearing in different guises in two main contexts: sentence-initial and non-initial. The jussive (the volitive mood, order, imperative, subjunctive) is homonymous with the non-past in most, but not all verb classes.

Like Semitic in general, Hebrew has a prefix conjugation and a suffix conjugation. In non-initial contexts (when a noun, a conjunction or an adverb opens the clause, in negation, etc.), the former is a non-past (present-future) and a jussive (imperative) and the latter a past. Note that occasionally, and almost always co-occurring with a coordinated suffixed form, the prefix form may stand for repeated, habitual actions in the past. This is a deviation from the straightforward pattern, yet it does not qualify for analysis as aspect. Sentence-initially, on the other hand, a prefix form preceded by *wa*+gemination of the next consonant (except when there is *yə-*) expresses the past and the suffix form preceded by *wə-*, with final stress in the first person singular and second person singular masculine (instead of penultimate) is non-past, actually very often a jussive because of the nature of the text. The following is a tabular representation of the four basic tense forms and the jussive, using two roots: *Q-W-M*, a *ʕ:w* root used here in the *pāʕal* for 'get up', and *D-B-R* in the *piʕʕēl* 'speak, talk', in the second person singular masculine, with the prefix *t-* or suffix *-tā̆*.

	Sentence-initial	Non-initial
Past	wa-t-tā̆qåm, wa-t-təđabbˈēr	qˈamtā̆, dibbˈartā̆
Nonpast	wə-ˈqamtˈā̆, wə-đibbartˈā̆	tå̄qˈūʷm, təđabbˈēr
Jussive	tå̄qˈōm, təđabbˈēr	

For *D-B-R* there is syncretism, only one type of prefix form, but the stress difference is found in the suffix forms. For *Q-W-M*, the non-initial non-past has a long *ū̄ʷ* (from an older **taqu:m-u* with an indicative ending), whereas the initial past and the jussive have a vowel with no *māter lectiōnis* in the same position (the differentiation *å/ō* is secondary). It is important to notice that this verb class exhibits a stress difference between the otherwise homonymous prefix past and the jussive. This suggests that the position of the stress must have been relevant in Proto-Hebrew (and in Proto-Semitic): **y'aqum* 'he got up'/**yaq'um* 'let him get up' (cf. **yaq'u:m-u* 'he gets up'), a distinction that must have disappeared in other verb classes.

This dual system may be explained by the assumption that in the literary dialect an archaic system became amalgamated with an innovative one. Then, the latter 'non-initial' system prevailed and became the only one in later periods of Hebrew (complemented by a new present tense). The 'initial' system has preserved the original decadent prefix-conjugated past, reinforcing it with an auxiliary of the new type: **haway(a)* 'was', later reduced to *wa-:-*, to avoid confusion with the new non-past that had become completely homophonous with it in most verb classes. As for the *wə-* + suffix form for non-past and jussive, this may have been more or less artificially created to make the system symmetrical. The fact that the two systems were distributed according to position in the sentence is not hard to explain. Proto-Hebrew must have had strict VSO order, whereas Biblical Hebrew shows gradual relaxation of this and the slow emergence of SVO (cf. the parallel phenomenon in Arabic). Thus, the old morphology was associated with the old word order and the new morphology with the new word order.

The opposite roles of prefix and suffix conjugations in the two contexts inspired the term 'converted tenses' for those preceded by *w-*, itself called 'waw conversive'. The term 'waw consecutive' is still very common, based on the contestable assumption that for its origin it is to be identified with the conjunction *wə* 'and' used as a link with what precedes, in a system where the verb is claimed to express aspect with relation to the preceding sentence, rather than tense. This is untenable. Secondarily, however, and independently of tense use, the conversive *waw* came indeed to be identified by the speakers of Biblical Hebrew as a conjunction, an understandable case of popular etymology, hence the creation of the *wə-* + suffix forms, and, more importantly, the use of the true conjunction *wə-* 'and' in the beginning of sentences, even texts (e.g. the beginning of Exodus vs the beginning of Deuteronomy), as a stylistic convention, before nouns, demonstratives, etc., as well.

After Late Biblical Hebrew the converted (*w*-marked) forms disappeared. Beginning already in Biblical Hebrew, the active participle gradually took over the expression of the present. The prefix forms were restricted to the function of jussive in Medieval Hebrew (which used a periphrastic expression for the future), but were revived also as a future in subsequent periods. 'Was' plus the active participle has been used as a habitual past from Medieval Hebrew on.

Since conjugation fully specifies the subject in the prefix and suffix conjugations, no subject pronoun is required in the first and second person. On the other hand, the active participle as a present form expresses in itself gender and number only, so that the co-occurrence of an explicit subject, noun or pronoun, is necessary. In Modern Hebrew, a third person pronoun is required in all tenses in the absence of a nominal subject. A third person plural masculine form without any pronoun or nominal subject is used as an impersonal: /hem amru/ 'they said', but /amru/ 'one said, it was said'. The first person distinguishes no gender.

Shown in the chart is the conjugation of the root *K-T-B* 'write' (*påʕal*) in Modern Hebrew. Note the alternation due to spirantisation /k/ ~ /x/. In verb-final position, only

/v/ may represent B. In literary usage, past pl. 2 m., f. /ktavt'em/, /ktavt'en/ and future pl. 2 = 3 f. /tixt'ovna/ are also attested. These continue the classical forms.

		Past		*Future*		
		Masculine	*Feminine*	*Masculine*	*Feminine*	
Sg.	1	kat'avti				ext'ov
	2	kat'avta	kat'avt	tixt'ov	tixtev'i	
	3	kat'av	katv'a	yixt'ov	tixt'ov	
Pl.	1	kat'avnu			nixt'ov	
	2	kat'avtem	kat'avten		tixtev'u	
	3	katv'u			yixtev'u	

	Present = Active Participle		*Passive Participle* ('written')	
	Masculine	Feminine	Masculine	Feminine
Sg.	kot'ev	kot'evet	kat'uv	ktuv'a
Pl.	kotv'im	kotv'ot	ktuv'im	ktuv'ot

Infinitive lixt'ov   *Verbal Noun* ktiv'a ('(the) writing')

In the nominal system, a distinction is made between a masculine and a feminine gender. The gender of objects is arbitrarily assigned. In the singular, feminine is most frequently marked by the ending -*ā̊ʰ* (< *-at*), but also by -V*t*. Some nouns are feminine without an external mark: most paired parts of the body (e.g. *ʕayin* 'eye') and a few more (*kikkā̊r* 'loaf'). Some nouns may have either gender (e.g. *š'ɛmɛš* 'sun', only feminine in Modern Hebrew). Beside the singular, there is a restricted dual and a plural. The dual ending -'*ayim* is used to express two units in a few nouns, mainly relating to time units (*šənā̊t'ayim* 'two years'); it marks the plural of paired elements, such as some body parts (*ʕē̊ʸn'ayim* 'two eyes' = 'eyes') and others (e.g. *mɛlqā̊ħ'ayim* 'tongs'). It cannot be freely used, most nouns accept the numeral 'two' only for the expression of double occurrence.

The masculine plural ending is -*ī̊ʸm* and feminine plural is -*ō̊(ʷ)t*. However, a restricted number of feminine nouns may have the apparently masculine plural ending (e.g. *šā̊nā̊ʰ* 'year', pl. *šā̊nī̊ʸm*) and, more frequently, some masculine nouns may have the feminine plural ending (e.g. *lūʷᵃħ* 'tablet', pl. *lūʷħōt*). Syntactically, however, the gender of a plural noun is always the same as in the singular (e.g. *šā̊nī̊ʸm rabbō̊ʷt* 'many years', where the quantifying adjective does carry the feminine plural ending). This morphologically incongruent plural marking may be a remnant of the old polarity system operative in the Semitic languages (see numerals below).

Nouns may change their internal vocalisation when they adopt the plural ending. An extreme and mysterious case is *b'ayit/bā̊ttī̊ʸm* 'house/houses'. The most systematic such change takes place in the case of the bisyllabic so-called 'segholate' nouns. These are characterised by a penultimate stress and a vowel ɛ (called *seghol*) in their last syllable, e.g. *m'ɛlɛk* 'king', *s'epɛr* 'book'. These originate in an old CVCC pattern *malk-* and *sipr-*, cf. still *malkā̊ʰ* for 'queen' in the feminine. The plural pattern of the segholates is CəCā̊C- – *məlā̊kī̊ʸm* 'kings', *məlā̊kō̊ʷt* 'queens', *səpā̊rī̊ʸm* 'books'. Though many scholars prefer to explain it as a phonetic reduction, this could very well be the survival of the old broken plural (see Chapter 32, page 555).

Nouns may also appear in the construct state, which means that they precede a genitival noun. Here the feminine ending -*ā̊ʰ* becomes -*at*, penultimate *ā̊* becomes ə, -*ayi-* is reduced to -*ē̊ʸ*-, the masculine plural has the ending -*ē̊ʸ* (borrowed from the dual) and some nouns do not change at all. Examples: *šənat* 'year of', *šənō̊ʷt* 'years of', *ʕē̊ʸn* 'eye of', *ʕēʸnēʸ* 'eyes of', *bēʸt* 'house of'; plurals of segholates: *mal(ə)kēʸ* 'kings of', *siprēʸ* 'books of', with the archaic singular vocalisation.

Hebrew has altogether three genitival constructions. The only one occurring in Biblical Hebrew consists of a possessum in the construct state followed by the possessor: *bēʸt hā̊-ʔīʸš* 'house + of the-man' ('the man's house'). Here the possessum is always understood to be definite and never takes the definite article, but adjectives referring to it do. Moreover, this construction may not be broken up by qualifiers. Adjectives follow the whole group, no matter which noun they refer to (only one of the nouns may be so qualified). Thus *bēʸt hā̊-ʔīʸš ha-g-gā̊dōʷl* 'house+of the-man the-big (m. sg.)' is ambiguously 'the great man's house' or 'the man's big house'. When the two nouns govern different agreements, ambiguity is dispelled: *mišpʼaḥat hā̊-ʔīʸš ha-g-gədōʷlā̊h* is only 'the man's big family', for feminine 'big' agrees with 'family', whereas *mišpʼaḥat hā̊-ʔīʸš ha-g-gā̊dōʷl* is clearly 'the great man's family'. There is no simple expression for 'the great man's big family' in Biblical Hebrew.

In the later stages of Hebrew the role of the above construction was reduced. In Modern Hebrew, it is basically a compounding device only, e.g. /bet xolim/ 'house + of sick-pl.' for 'hospital'. Here an article before the second noun definitises the whole expression: /bet ha-xolim/ 'the hospital'. Plurality is expressed on the first noun: /bate xolim/ 'hospitals' and /bate ha-xolim/ 'the hospitals'.

The other genitival constructions, introduced in Medieval Hebrew, use the genitive particle *šɛl* 'of', still in a possessum–possessor order, and no construct case: MoH /ha-bʼayit šel ha-iš/ 'the-house of the-man'. Here, an indefinite possessum may also occur. Alternatively, one may say /bet-o šel ha-iš/ 'house-his of the-man', where the possessum is always definite and its third person possessive pronominal ending agrees in number and gender with the possessor.

In Biblical Hebrew, pronominal possession is expressed by possessive endings. These are attached to a construct state-like form of the nouns, with archaic vocalisation for the segholates: *malk-īʸ* 'my king', *sipr-īʸ* 'my book', *bēʸt-īʸ* 'my house', *šənā̊t-īʸ* 'my year', etc. The plurality of the noun is expressed by a palatal element between the noun and the ending (which may be somewhat modified thereby): *ʕēʸn-īʸ* 'my eye', but *ʕēʸn-ay* 'my eyes', *ʕēʸn-ēk* 'your (f. sg.) eye', *ʕēʸn-ʼayik* 'your (f. sg.) eyes', *ʕēʸn-ōw* 'his eye', *ʕēʸn-ā̊ʸw* 'his eyes' (the last ʸ is traditionally silent) etc. In the feminine plural, the ending *-ōʷt* is retained: *šən-ōʷt-ay* 'my years'. In Modern Hebrew, a periphrastic construction is used for this with a conjugated form of *šɛl* /šel/ 'of', e.g. /ha-sʼefer šeli/ 'my book' ('the-book of + me'). Possessive endings are regularly used in a third kind of genitival construction (see above), occasionally in some kinship terms and other inalienable possessions (/šmi/ beside /ha-šem šeli/ for 'my name' and regularly, again, in idioms (/ma šlomxa/ 'how are you (m. sg.)?', lit. 'what (is) your+peace?'). Contrast /be-libi/ 'in my heart' used for 'inside me', 'in my thought' and /ba-lev šeli/ 'in my heart' in a physical sense.

Qualifying adjectives follow the noun and agree with it in gender, number and definiteness: *ha-m-məlā̊k-ōʷt ha-ṭ-ṭōʷḇ-ōʷt* 'the good queens' ('the-king-f.pl. the-good-f.pl.), in contradistinction to the predicative construction where no definiteness agreement is enforced: *ha-m-məlā̊k-ōʷt ṭōʷḇ-ōʷt* 'the queens are good'.

Adjectives may be derived from nouns by means of the ending *-īʸ*, a device very productive in Modern Hebrew: /sifruti/ 'literary' from /sifrut/ 'literature'. Adjectives may act as nouns as well.

Demonstratives follow the noun-adjective group: *ha-m-malk-ā̊h ha-ṭ-ṭōʷḇā̊h ha-z-zōʔt* 'this good queen'. Note the definite articles before all three words, omissible en bloc for stylistic variation. In predicative constructions the demonstrative is initial: *zōʔt malkā̆ʰ ṭōʷbā̆ʰ* 'this (is a) good queen'.

As examples have already shown, the definite article is a prefix *ha* + gemination of the next consonant.

The numeral 'one' is a regular adjective. From 'two' up, cardinal numerals precede the noun (in Biblical Hebrew they may occasionally follow as well). 'Two' appears in the construct case. From 'three' to 'ten' (and with some exceptions from 'eleven' to 'nineteen') the external gender mark of the numerals (the 'teen' part for the latter group) is the opposite of what one would expect: *ʔarbāʕ-ā̆ʰ bān-īʸm* 'four sons', where the numeral has the ending -*ā̆ʰ*, elsewhere a feminine, before a masculine noun, vs *ʔarbaʕ bān-ōʷt* 'four daughters', where the feminine numeral carries no ending. Traditional grammars sometimes adopt the misleading practice of labelling the numerals with -*ā̆ʰ* 'feminine' and stating that they co-occur with masculine nouns. This 'incongruence' is a residue of the old polarity system (see Chapter 31, page 549). Nouns appear in the plural after numerals, with few exceptions: 'year', 'day' and a few more have the singular after the round numerals from 'twenty', e.g. *ʔarbāʕīʸm šān-ā̆ʰ* 'forty years'.

Ordinal numerals, formed by means of the -*īʸ* ending for 'second' to 'tenth', are adjectives: *ha-y-yōʷm hā̆-rəbīʸʕīʸ* 'the fourth day'. From 'eleven' they are homonymous with the cardinal numbers, but exhibit the syntax of adjectives: *ha-y-yōʷmhā̆-ʔarbāʕīʸm* 'the fortieth day'.

The syntactic function of nouns in the sentence is expressed by means of prepositions. The subject carries no mark. The direct object has the preposition *ʔεt* when the object is definite. Contrast: *rā̆ʔ'īʸtīʸ ʔīʸš* 'I + saw (a) man/someone' and *rā̆ʔ'īʸtīʸ ʔεt hā̆ʔīʸš* 'I+saw acc. the+man'. Proper names as objects have *ʔεt* even without the definite article. On the other hand, nouns with possessive endings, though otherwise definite, receive no *ʔεt* in most cases in Biblical Hebrew. Three prepositions are written joined to the following word: *lə-* 'to', *bə-* 'in, with' (instrumental)' and *miC-* (with gemination of the next consonant, an alternative to *min*) 'from'. The rest (*ʕal* 'on', etc.) are separate words. They are conjugated by means of possessive endings of the singular type *l-īʸ* 'to-me' or the plural type *ʕāl-ay* 'on-me'. For pronominal object (accusative), the separate word *ʔō⁽ʷ⁾t-īʸ*, etc., for 'me' and so on had been available since the beginnings of Biblical Hebrew, but alternatively in Biblical Hebrew and in archaising style later, object suffix pronouns attached to the verb were also used, e.g. *rā̆ʔ'īʸtīʸ ʔōʷt-ōʷ* 'I+saw him' or *rəʔīʸtīʸw* with the pronominal suffix.

In the pronominal domain, three sets of pronouns are to be listed: independent subject or predicate pronouns, object pronoun suffixes and possessive pronoun suffixes. The latter are subdivided according to whether the preceding noun is singular or plural (see above). The object pronoun suffixes are homonymous with the singular possessive set, except in the first person singular, not considering the connective vowels (which are not specified in Table 34.4). No gender distinction exists for the first person.

For the indicative prefix-conjugated non-past, in those persons where no further suffix is used, the third person singular masculine/feminine object suffixes are -*nnūʷ*/-*nnā̆ʰ*. Thus, *yišmōr* 'he guards/will guard' (indic.) or 'let him guard' (jussive) is disambiguated: *yišmər'εnnūʷ* 'he guards/will guard him' vs *yišmər'ehūʷ* 'let him guard him'. These -*nn*- marked suffixes are not to be confused with the distributionally unlimited use of -*n*- between prefix-conjugated verbs and object suffixes, which are traces of the old 'energic' mood of the verb (for 'he *did* do; he did indeed'), the type *yišmər'enhūʷ* 'he does/will indeed guard him'.

Table 34.4 Personal Pronouns

		Independent Masculine	Feminine	Object ~ Sg. Poss. Masculine	Feminine	Pl. Poss. Masculine	Feminine
Sg.	1	Ɂănī̆ʸ=Ɂắnōkī̆ʸ		-nī̆ʸ (obj.)/ī̆ʸ (poss.)		-ay	
	2	Ɂattā̊ʰ	Ɂattᵊ	-kā̊	-ēk	-'ɛʸkā̊	-ayik
	3	hūʷɁ	hī̆ʸɁ	-ōʷ/-w/-hūʷ	-ā̊h/-hā̊	-ā̊ʸw	-'ɛʸhā̊
Pl.	1	Ɂăn'aḥnū̆ʷ		-'nū̆ʷ (unstressed)		-'ēʸnū̆ʷ	
	2	Ɂattɛm	Ɂatt'en(ā̊ʰ)	-kɛm	-kɛn	-ēʸkɛm	-ēʸkɛn
	3	h'em(mā̊ʰ)	h'ennā̊ʰ	-m	-n	-ēʸhɛm	-ēʸhɛn

The basic Biblical Hebrew word order is VSO with the converted form of the verb and 'verb-second' with a simple tense verb, where the first word is a topic. Medieval Hebrew is still basically VSO, but no more converted tenses are used. However, from Late Biblical Hebrew on, SVO has been becoming more and more common, and it is the basic order in Modern Hebrew. The adoption of the original active participle as a present tense encouraged the adoption of SVO.

Interrogative pronouns and the yes–no interrogative particle (Biblical Hebrew hă-, later haɁim) or the introduction of a question with an obvious answer ('isn't it the case that … ?') hălōɁ or hărēʸ are always sentence-initial. The negative lōɁ 'not' precedes the predicate. The rule that required that negation in the present tense should be effected by a pre-subject Ɂēʸn (originally the negation of yɛš 'there is') is widely disregarded in spoken Modern Hebrew. Contrast normative /eyn-i/ or /eyn'eni roce/ 'not-I want' and colloquial /ani lo roce/ 'I not want' for 'I don't want'.

Biblical Hebrew has no copula in the present. In later stages, a third person pronoun in agreement with the subject may stand for a present tense copula, obligatorily in Modern Hebrew if the predication is of some complexity: /g'ila hi ha-mora/ 'Gila is (= she) the-teacher' (definite predication). Hebrew has no verb 'to have'. Possessive predication is expressed by means of constructions like 'there is to': yɛš l-. An interesting development of colloquial Hebrew is that when the element possessed (the grammatical subject) is definite, it receives the accusative preposition /et/, as if it were the object of a transitive verb 'have': /yeš li et ha-b'ayit/ 'I have the house'.

Relative constructions follow the Semitic pattern (see page 558): ha-m-mắqōʷm Ɂắšɛr Ɂ attā̊ʰ ʕōʷmēđ ʕắlā̊ʸw 'the place that you (m. sg.) standing on+it' for 'the spot on which you are standing'. The invariable relative marker is Ɂắšɛr in Biblical Hebrew, originally a noun meaning 'place' with a functional change 'where' > 'that'. Medieval Hebrew uses the archaic particle šɛ-, which is also extended to many other subordinating functions. In Modern Hebrew /še-/ is the relative particle and the complementiser (Biblical Hebrew kī̆ʸ, cf. Biblical Hebrew Ɂå̆m'artī̆ʸ kī̆ʸ … , Modern Hebrew /am'arti še- … / 'I said that …'). In Modern Hebrew there is a tendency to bring forward the referential pronoun of the relative construction right after the relative pronoun: /ha-makom še-alav ata omed/ (see above).

Bibliography

Chomsky (1957) is a vividly written, scholarly but no longer up-to-date history of Hebrew, with special emphasis on its role among the Jews. Kutscher (1982), a posthumous publication, shows some unfortunate traces of being unfinished, yet is extremely rich in information on the history of the language and is characterised by a depth of scholarship.

For Biblical Hebrew, Gesenius (1910) is an indispensable classic; Blau (1976) is a rigorously scientific descriptive grammar, recommended to the student; Lambert (1972) is perhaps the linguistically most solid grammar. Segal (1927) is a clear descriptive grammar for all students of post-Biblical Hebrew. Coffin and Bolozky (2005) is an excellent grammar of Modern Hebrew.

Further recommended are the articles on 'Hebrew Language' and 'Pronunciations of Hebrew' in the *Encyclopaedia Judaica* (1972, vol. 13, pp. 1120–45 and vol. 16, pp. 1560–662); these are up-to-date presentations by C. Brovender, J. Blau, E.Y. Kutscher, E. Goldenberg, E. Eytan and S. Morag.

References

Blau, J. 1976. *A Grammar of Biblical Hebrew* (Otto Harrassowitz, Wiesbaden)

Chomsky, W. 1957. *Hebrew, the Eternal Language* (The Jewish Publication Society of America, Philadelphia)

Coffin, E.A. and Bolozky, S. 2005. *A Reference Grammar of Modern Hebrew* (Cambridge University Press, Cambridge)

Encyclopaedia Judaica. 1972 (Keter, Jerusalem)

Gesenius, W. 1910. *Gesenius' Hebrew Grammar, as Edited and Enlarged by the Late E. Kautsch*, 2nd English edn, ed. A.E. Cowley (Clarendon Press, Oxford)

Kutscher, E.Y. 1982. *A History of the Hebrew Language* (The Magnes Press, Jerusalem, E.J. Brill, Leiden)

Lambert, M. 1972. *Traité de grammaire hébraïque*, reprinted with additions (Gerstenberg, Hildesheim)

Segal, M.H. 1927. *A Grammar of Mishnaic Hebrew* (Clarendon Press, Oxford)

35

Amharic

Grover Hudson

1 History and Society

Amharic is the second most populous Semitic language, after Arabic, with some 20 million speakers (16 million of the 1994 Ethiopian census + expected growth rate to 2009). Amharic has long been the lingua franca of Ethiopia, and, despite recent movement toward local-language primary education, in most schools still the language of instruction in the early grades. (Since the late 1940s, English has been the language of secondary and higher education.) It is recognised in the 1994 constitution as the 'working language' of Ethiopian government.

Amharic is spoken as a second language by additional millions of Ethiopian urban dwellers, and Amharic readers certainly represent the large majority of the reported Ethiopian literacy rate of 42 per cent.

The internal grouping of Semitic languages is controversial, but three branches are usually mentioned: northeast, northwest and south. Northwest includes Arabic, Hebrew and Aramaic; northeast anciently known and long extinct Akkadian-Babylonian; and southern Semitic the ancient and modern languages native to South Arabia plus those of Ethiopia and Eritrea, of which there are some thirteen: Tigre and Tigrinya of Eritrea, with Tigrinya also spoken by some 3.5 million in Ethiopia; in Ethiopia are Amharic, Soddo (also known as Kistane), Mesqan, Chaha with several named dialects; Inor also with several named dialects, Argobba a language not quite mutually intelligible with Amharic, Harari (Adare), Silt'e with several named dialects, and Zay. Ethiopian Semitic Gafat has been extinct for some decades, and Ge'ez, for which there are epigraphic records dating from perhaps 2500 BP, survives as the liturgical language of the Ethiopian Orthodox Church. Ge'ez seems not to be the ancestor of any modern language.

The traditional home of Amharic is mountainous north-central Ethiopia, and Amharic dialects are recognised in the regions of Begemder, Gojjam, Menz-Wello and Shoa. These differ by features of pronunciation and grammatical morphology. The Ethiopian capital city Addis Ababa, Shoa, is the centre of Ethiopian political, economic and social life, and the Amharic variety of Addis Ababa has become recognised as prestigious.

There are Amharic manuscripts from the fourteenth century, and modern writings and publication in Amharic include poetry, newspapers, literary and news magazines, drama, novels, history, textbooks, etc. Amharic language magazines are published in Europe and the US to serve the now considerable Ethiopian expatriate populations there.

Amharic has borrowed words from Arabic, French, Italian, and now especially English, but these are not prominent. Ge'ez is favoured as a source for new word invention.

Because other anciently known Semitic languages notably Arabic, Aramaic, Hebrew, and Akkadian are all in the Middle East, and because there is evidence of South Arabian presence in northeast Africa from perhaps as early as 2500 BP, it is generally believed that Semitic languages were brought into northeast Africa in near historic time by migrations from South Arabia. However, because Semitic is only one of six branches in the family of Afroasiatic languages, and because Africa is home to the five non-Semitic groups Chadic (West Africa), Berber (North Africa), Egyptian (Egypt), Omotic (Ethiopia and eastern Sudan) and Cushitic (centred in Ethiopia), and because ancient Ethiopian Semitic culture and the modern languages have many features not descendant from those of South Arabia, it is also possible that Semitic origins are African and perhaps Ethiopian.

Ethiopian Semitic, Cushitic and Omotic languages have certainly coexisted in Ethiopia for at least two thousand years, and probably for this reason share numerous features of an Ethiopian language type characterised by phonological, morphological and syntactic features including glottalised ejective consonants, a special non-finite verb for verb sequences, verb idioms based on the verb 'say', and word-order characteristics of verb-final (SOV) languages. Many Semitic languages, indeed, are verb-initial (VSO) languages, including ancient Ethiopian Semitic Ge'ez, but Amharic and the other modern Ethiopian Semitic languages have some characteristics of both SOV and VSO types (notably VSO-type prepositions), which suggests that they have changed this aspect of their grammars under the influence of Cushitic and Omotic neighbours. Similarly, most Middle Eastern Semitic languages lack the Ethiopian areal feature of glottalised ejective consonants. In this case, however, the presence of glottalised ejectives in Chadic, South Arabian Semitic and some Arabic dialects suggests that in this characteristic Amharic and Ethiopian Semitic languages preserve the original Afroasiatic type.

2 Phonology

2.1 Consonants

Amharic has the thirty-one consonant phonemes of Table 35.1, where phonetic symbols have International Phonetic Association (IPA) values except that *y* = palatal glide *j*, *č* and *ǰ* = alveopalatal affricates *tʃ* and *ʤ*; *š* and *ž* = alveopalatal fricatives *ʃ* and *ʒ*; *ñ* = palatal nasal *ɲ*; and *r* is a tap and long *r* (*rr*) a trill.

The series of labialised 'velars' *kʷ*, *gʷ*, *kʷ'*, and *hʷ* (*hʷ* historically a velar < *xʷ*) might be considered sequences of consonant + *w* (which do arise in word-formation), but three facts suggest that these are best considered to be functionally unitary: (1) the consonant and *w* are never separated by vowels in word-formation processes as are root-consonant sequences; (2) they freely occur at the beginning of words where other

Table 35.1 Consonants

		Labial	Alveolar	Alveopalatal	Velar	Glottal
Stops	vls	*p*	*t*		*k, kʷ*	*ʔ*
	vd	*b*	*d*		*g, gʷ*	
	gl	*p'*	*t'*		*k', kʷ'*	
Affricates	vl			*č*		
	vd			*ǰ*		
	gl			*č'*		
Fricatives	vl	*f*	*s*	*š*		*h, hʷ*
	vd		*z*	*ž*		
	gl		*s'*			
Nasals		*m*	*n*	*ñ*		
Lateral			*l*			
Rhotic			*r*			
Glides		*w**		*y*		

Notes: vl = voiceless, vd=voiced; gl=glottalized.
* Has also velar articulation.

consonant sequences are absent or rare; and (3) they have special forms in the Amharic writing system.

Labials *p, p'* and *v* are rare: *p* and *p'* only in loanwords some of which like *ityopp'a* 'Ethiopia' < Greek are long established in the language, and the voiced labiodental fricative *v* is only in recent borrowings such as *volibol* 'volleyball'.

Consonant sequences are at most two; at the beginning of words these consist of C+r/l as in *gra* 'left' and *blen* 'pupil of eye', though these may also be considered *gɨra* and *bɨlen*. The glottal stop *ʔ* and labialised consonants do not occur at the end of syllables (or, thus, words), and the alveopalatal nasal *ñ* does not occur at the beginning of native words. The glottal stop may be considered an allophonic effect of syllable-initial vowels, as in [ʔ]*ityopp'ya* 'Ethiopia', *sə*[ʔ]*at* 'hour, clock/watch'. Glottalised ejective *s'* is replaced by *t'* in rural speech, and the voiced alveopalatals *ž* and *ǰ* are free or idiolectal variants. Voiceless released stops are slightly aspirated. The nongeminate voiced labial and velar stops *b* and *g* are spirants [β] and [ɣ] between vowels, as in *le*[β]*a* 'thief', *wa*[ɣ]*a* 'price'. The sequences *kʷ'ə* and *kʷ'ɨ* vary as *k'o* and *k'u*, respectively, as in *kʷ'əssələ~kʷ'ossələ* 'he was wounded', *kʷ'ɨt'ɨr~k'ut'ɨr* 'number'. The velar and labial stops tend to be labialised before round vowels, e.g. *bʷota* 'place', *kʷum* 'stop/stand!'. Between vowels the glides *w, y* are very lax (*haya* [haʸa] 'twenty'). In northern dialects except of Gondar there is palatalisation of obstruents as glide insertion before the front vowels *i* and *e*, which vowels may in this case be centralised, thus *bet* > *bʸɛt* 'house' and *hid* > *hʸɨd* 'go (Sg.2m.)!' In the Menz dialect velars *k* and *k'* are replaced by *č* and *č'* respectively before *i* and *e*.

Except for *h* and *ʔ*, consonants may be long between vowels and at the end of words. The long consonants are usually written here as sequences of like consonants, and the glottalised consonants as CC' not C'C. Grammatically significant length may be written C:, for example *t:* in *mət:a* 'he hit', to emphasise that length in this case is a function of the past conjugation and not a lexical characteristic of the verb 'hit'.

When followed by the suffix *-i* (instrumental, agentive, Sg.2f. subject) and *-e* of the Sg.1 conjunct, alveolar consonants except *r* are replaced by corresponding alveopalatals: *t > č, d >ǰ, s'* and *t' > č', s > š, z > ž* (optionally *ž >ǰ*), *n > ň*, and, except in the Menz dialect, *l > y*. For example, *tɨmət-i > tɨməč(i)* 'you (Sg.f.) hit', *hid-i > hiǰ(i)* 'Go (Sg.2f.)!', *yɨz-:e > yɨž:e* 'I holding'. The suffix *-i* may be absent with these replacements. (Sg.1 possessive *-e* does not have these palatalisations: *bet-e* 'my house'.)

2.2 Vowels

Amharic has the seven vowels of Table 35.2, in which phonetic symbols have International Phonetic Association values (much writing on Amharic has *ä* and *ə* respectively for *ə* and *ɨ*). Mid-front *e* has a variant *ε* after *h* as in *h[ε]də* 'he went'. Words begin and end in any of the vowels except that *ɨ* does not occur at the end of words except in the archaic question suffix *-nɨ*, nor *ə* at the beginning of words except in the interjection *ərə* 'Really?'

Table 35.2 Vowels

	Front	*Central*	*Back*
High	*i*	*ɨ*	*u*
Mid	*e*	*ə*	*o*
Low		*a*	

Non-low central vowels *ɨ* and *ə* are usually elided by adjacent vowels, and *ɨ* is elided by *ə*, for example *bə-anči > banči* 'by you (Sg.2f.)' and *bə-ɨrgit' > bərgit'* 'truly' (lit. 'in truth'). A sequence of like vowels is reduced to one: *asra-and > asrand* 'eleven', *yɨbəla-al > yɨbəlal* 'he eats'.

The high central vowel *ɨ* is usually considered to be inserted (epenthesised) to separate disallowed consonant sequences which frequently arise in word-formation, as in *y-wəsd-h > yɨwəsdɨh* 'he takes you (Sg.m.)'; most occurrences of this vowel may be considered to be epenthetic.

Sg.2f. and Pl.3 verb-subject suffixes *-i* and *-u* may be replaced by *y* and *w* respectively when followed by *a*: *tɨnəgri-alliš > tɨnəgryalliš* 'you (Sg.f.) tell', *nəggər-u-at > nəggərwat* 'they told her'; alternatively *y/w* may be inserted in these cases: *tɨnəgriyalliš*, *nəggəruwat*. Oppositely, the Sg.3m. and Pl.3 verb-subject prefix *y-* is replaced by *i* when it follows a consonant, as in *s-y-hed > sihed* 'when he goes'.

2.3 Stress

Stress is not prominent in Amharic. Suffixes except the plural suffix are unstressed, and, generally, stress is on a final closed syllable of a stem and otherwise next to last: *məskót* 'window', *mísa* 'lunch', *mísa-e* 'my lunch', *məskót-óčč* 'windows'. But stress is advanced to the vowel before a grammatically long consonant, as in *kábbədə* 'he broke', where the long consonant is a grammatical characteristic of the past tense; cf. *kəbbádə*, a male name, with next-to-last syllable stress.

3 Morphology

3.1 Pronouns

There are three pronoun sets (not including verb subject agreements), presented in Table 35.3: independent, object suffix and possessive suffix pronouns. Object pronouns are shown suffixed to the verb *nəggərə* 'he told' and the possessive pronouns suffixed to the noun *bet* 'house'. Gender and politeness are distinguished in the Sg.2 and Sg.3 forms. Polite forms are for elders and adult unfamiliars.

Independent Sg.2pol. *antu* is common only in Wello and Gondar. The four pronouns with *iss* each have alternate forms with *irs: irs-u, irs-wa, irs-wo* and *irs-aččəw*, reflecting the emphatic/reflexive origin of these as possessive forms of **irs* 'head' or **kirs* 'belly'. The Pl.2/3 independent forms reflect a plural morpheme *innə-* (as in *innə-təsfaye* 'those associated with Tesfaye') prefixed to the Sg.m. forms, respectively.

Pronouns are usually expressed by bound rather than independent forms, as verb subject, object and noun possessor. The verb subject pronouns are presented with discussion of verbs and conjugations, in Section 3.6 below.

The bound Sg.3m. object pronoun *-w* (Table 35.3) is replaced by *-t* after round vowels as in *nəggəru-t* 'they told him' and *nəgro-t* 'he, telling him'. The Sg.1, Sg.3m. and Pl.1 object suffixes have an initial vowel *ə* when they follow consonants other than alveopalatals; thus *nəggər-k-əňň* 'you (Sg.m.) told me' vs *nəggər-š-iňň* 'you (Sg.f.) told me', and *wisəd-əw* 'you (Sg.m.) take it/him!' vs *wisəǰ-iw* 'you (Sg.f.) take it/him!' The object and possessive Pl.2, Pl.3, and possessive Pl.1 suffixes include a plural morpheme *-ačč* probably cognate with the noun plural suffix *-očč*.

Two prepositions *-bb-* 'at, on' and *-ll-* 'to, for' are suffixed to verb stems and take object suffixes as their objects, except that of Sg.3m. is *-ət* (not *-əw*) for example *fərrədə-bb-əňň* 'he judged against me', *yifərd-ill-ət* 'he judges for him' (the *i* is epenthetic). (When not suffixed to verb stems, prepositions accept independent pronouns as their objects, as in *bəne* (< *bə-ine*) 'by/on me', *lanči* (< *lə-anči*) 'for you (Sg.f.)'.)

The bound Sg.3m. possessive pronoun *-u* 'his' is replaced by *-w* after vowels, for example *bək'lo-w* 'his mule'. The vowel *i* of Sg.2m. and Sg.2f. possessive suffixes is not epenthetic, as shown by the contrast of *bet-iš* 'your (Sg.f.) house' and *mot-š* 'you (Sg.f.) died', the latter with vowelless object *-š* and no epenthesis.

Table 35.3 Three pronoun sets

			Independent	*Verb object*	*Possessive*
Sg.	1		*ine*	*nəggərə-ňň*[*]	*bet-e*[**]
	2	m	*antə*	*nəggərə-h*	*bet-ih*
		f	*anči*	*nəggərə-š*	*bet-iš*
		pol	*isswo ~ antu*	*nəggərə-wo(t)*	*bet-wo*
	3	m	*issu*	*nəggərə-w*	*bet-u*
		f	*isswa ~ issʷa*	*nəggər-at*	*bet-wa*
		pol	*issaččəw*	(=Pl.3)	(=Pl.3)
Pl.	1		*iňňa*	*nəggərə-n*	*bet-aččin*
	2		*innantə*	*nəggər-aččihu*	*bet-aččihu*
	3		*innəssu*	*nəggər-aččəw*	*bet-aččəw*

Notes: * 'He told me'; ** 'my house'.

Reflexive-emphatic pronouns are formed as possessives of *ras* 'head', for example *ras-e* 'I myself', *ras-aččɨn* 'we ourselves' (*ɨne rase mətt'ahu* 'I myself came').

Interrogative pronouns include *man* 'who', *mɨn* 'what' (*mɨndɨr* in *mɨndɨr nəw* (> *mɨndɨnnəw*) 'What is it?'), *məče* 'when', and *yət* 'where'. These are suffixed by *-m* (*-ɨm* with epenthesis) to provide negative indefinite pronouns: *man-ɨm almətt'am* 'nobody came', *yət-ɨm alhedɨm* 'I won't go anywhere'. Other question words are *yətɨññaw* 'which', *sɨnt* 'how much', *ləmɨn* 'why' (lit. 'for what'), *ɨndə-mɨn* 'how' (*ɨndə* 'like'), and *ɨndet* 'how' (< *ɨndə-yət* 'like where').

3.2 Nouns

3.2.1 Gender

The gender of a noun is apparent in its choice of pronoun, agreement with the verb, demonstrative, and definite article suffix. There is no neuter, and the feminine class is mostly natural, except for a few inanimate nouns including the sun and moon, names of countries, and small animals such as cats and mice, perhaps reflecting a diminutive usage of the feminine. Many feminine human nouns end in an archaic and non-productive feminine *t*, including *ɨnnat* 'mother', *ɨhɨt* 'sister', *nigɨst* 'queen' (cf. *nigus* 'king'), and a few nouns have feminine suffix *-ɨt*, including *arogɨt* 'old woman' (*aroge* 'old') and *andɨt* 'a little one (f.)' (*and* 'one') (this also in the fem. definite article *-ɨt-u*).

3.2.2 Definiteness

Definite common nouns have suffixes *-u/-w* (*-w* after vowels) for masc. and *-wa* or less commonly *-itu* for fem. Masc. *-u* and *-wa* are identical to Sg.3m. possessives: *wɨša-w* 'the dog (m.)' (or 'his dog'), *dimmət-wa* 'the cat (f.)' (or 'her cat') or *dimmət-itu* 'the cat (f.)'. The definite suffix is mutually exclusive with the possessives. Nouns *səw* 'man' and *set* 'woman' have special definite-specific forms *səw-ɨyye-w* 'the man', *set-ɨyyo-wa* 'the woman'.

3.2.3 Indefinite Article

The numeral *and* 'one' functions as an indefinite-specific article, as in *and bet tək'att'ələ* 'a (certain) house burned down'. Repetition of *and* expresses plural indefinite 'some, various, a few': *andand bet tək'att'ələ* 'a few houses burned down.'

3.2.4 Plurality

The regular noun plural suffix is *-očč*: *bet-očč* 'houses', *səw-očč* 'people'. After nouns ending in *i* or *e*, *y* may be inserted: *gəbəre-yočč* 'farmers' (or reflecting *o* of the suffix, *gəbəre-wočč*), and *w* after *u* and *o*; *bək'lo-wočč* 'mules'. Suffix *o* may elide the noun-final vowel: *məkina-očč* > *məkinočč* 'cars', *bək'lo-očč* > *bək'ločč* 'mules'. There are some irregular plurals in *-at* and *-an*, probably Ge'ez or pseudo-Ge'ez formations, including *k'al-at* 'words' and *k'ɨddus-an* 'saints'. With plural quantifiers, the plural suffix may be absent: *bɨzu səw* 'many people', *hulət lɨj* 'two children'. Adjectives (see below) may also be pluralised. Other suffixes attach to the plural: *bet-očč-u* 'the houses', *bet-očč-aččɨn* 'our houses'.

3.2.5 Genitive

Possessive or genitive nouns and pronouns are prefixed by *yə-*: *yə-ssu bet* 'his house', *yə-kətəma lij* 'a town boy', *yə-bet k'ulf* 'lock of a house/house lock'. This prefix is absent following another prefix: *lə-ssu bet* 'for his house'. Familiar such relations may be expressed by simple juxtaposition, as in *təmari bet* 'school house'. This prefix also marks relative clauses (see below).

3.2.6 Definite object

Definite objects of verbs (also indefinites sometimes in older writing), are suffixed by *-n*: *bet-u-n wəddədə* 'he liked the house', *abbat-e-n ayyə-hu* 'I told my father'. Definite objects optionally and typically topicalised definite objects, which precede the sentence subject, are marked as 'resumptive' verb-object pronouns, as in *leba-w-n polis-očču yazzu-t* 'policemen caught the thief' (*-t* 'him').

3.2.7 Topicaliser

Nouns raised as topics, including those contrasted with others, are suffixed by *m*, as in *t'wat yohannis-im dəwwələ-ňň* 'in the morning YOHANNIS called me', and *yohannis-im yimət'al* 'As for Yohannis, he will come' or 'Yohannis will come too'. In questions an equivalent morpheme is *-ss*: *antə-ss?* 'What about you (Sg.m.)?' (This suffix is historically *mm*, but the length is now rarely heard. A cognate suffix has become obligatory on negative main verbs.)

3.2.8 Derived Nouns

There are a number of ways to derive nouns from verbs and other nouns. An instrument or location is formed on the verb infinitive by suffixing *-iya*: *mət'rəg-iya* 'broom' (*t'ərrəgə* 'he swept'), *məčərrəš-a* (< *məčərrəs-iya*) 'finish, conclusion' (*čərrəsə* 'he finished'). An agent of a verb is expressed by a special stem suffixed by *-i*; verbs with three or four root consonants have *a* after the next to last: *nəgari* 'teller' (root *ngr*), *tərg^wami* 'translator' (*trg^wm*); a derivation with a two-consonant root is *səmi* 'hearer' (root *sma*). Historical *y* or *w* appears in the agent of a two-consonant root whose basic form has *e < y* or *o < w*: *hiyaǰ(i)* 'goer' (*hedə* 'he went'), *k'əwami* 'stander' (*k'omə* 'he stood'). An agent based on a noun is formed on the noun suffixed by *-əňňa*: *k'əld-əňňa* 'joker' (*k'əld* 'joke'), *fərəs-əňňa* 'horseman' (*fərəs* 'horse'). (This suffix also forms ordinal from cardinal numerals; see below.) Nationality is expressed by a place-name and the suffix *-awi*: *ingliz-awi* 'English(man)'; also in *amət-awi* 'annually' (*amət* 'year'). An abstract noun of quality has the suffix *-nnət*: *set-innət* 'womanhood' (*set* 'woman'), *diha-nnət* 'poverty' (*diha* 'poor').

3.3 Adjectives

There are words whose usual function is as attribute to nouns including in comparisons, such as *tillik'* 'big, important' and *aroge* 'old (non-human)': *tillik' səw* 'big (important) person', *aroge bet* 'old house'. These may be nouns in fact (and only incipiently adjectives), understood as *tillik'* 'a big one', *aroge* 'an old one'; they take the definite article, definite object, and plural suffixes: *tillik'-u* 'the big one (m.)', *tillik'-očč* 'big ones', *k'onǰo-wa* 'the pretty one (f.)', *k'onǰo-wočč* 'pretty ones', *k'onǰo-wa-n məkina šət'ə* 'he sold the pretty car (f.).' As in the previous example, the definite suffix attaches to the adjective; but a possessive suffix attaches to the noun: *tillik'-u bet* 'the big house' vs *tillik' bet-u* 'his big house'. The plural suffix attaches to the noun: *k'onǰo məkin-očč* 'pretty cars' but optionally to the adjective: *k'onǰ-očč məkin-očč*. The quantifier *hullu* 'all' may follow its noun: *səw hullu* 'all the people'.

Adjectives may duplicate their middle consonant, which is followed or not by *a*, to form a plural of 'variousness', as in *tilillik' liǰočč* 'various big children' (*tillik'* 'big'), *rəǰajǰim wəttaddəročč* 'various tall soldiers' (*rəǰǰim* 'tall'). Like nouns these may be pluralised: *rəǰajǰim-očč naččəw* 'They are tall (ones)'.

An adjective meaning 'having particularly or excessively a quality of a noun' is the noun suffixed by *-am*: *hod-am* 'greedy, gluttonous' (*hod* 'stomach'), *məlk-am* 'attractive, nice' (*məlk* 'appearance'). An adjective of similar but intensified meaning has the suffix *-amma*: *firey-amma* 'fruitful' (*fire* 'fruit'), *t'en-amma* 'healthy' (*t'ena* 'health').

Comparison with an adjective is expressed by a prepositional phrase with *kə-* or *tə-* 'from' (*tə-* in northern dialects), as in *kə-ssu ine diha nəňň* 'I am poorer than he' (lit. 'from him I am poor'). Adjectives often have cognate verbs with which comparisons may also be expressed: *kə-ssu ine rəǰǰim nəňň* or *kə-ssu ine irəzzimalləhu* 'I am taller than he' (*rəzzəmə* 'he grew tall'). Comparisons may be reinforced by a fixed-form (lacking subject agreement) simple non-past verb such as *yilik'* (*lak'ə* 'he/it surpassed') or *yibəlt'* (*bəllət'ə* 'he/it exceeded'), as in:

haylu k-antə yibəlt' bət'am k'əčč'in nəw
haylu from-you.Sg.m. more very thin is.he
'Hailu is much thinner than you.'

A predicative superlative is a comparative in relation to *hullu* 'all': *kə-hullu innəssu diha naččəw* 'they are poorer than all'. Comparatives are discussed below in the section on syntax.

3.4 Demonstratives

See the demonstratives in Table 35.4; these distinguish singular and plural and near (proximal) and far (distal). Plural demonstratives consist of the plural prefix *innə-* plus locatives *izzih* 'here' and *izzya* 'there'. The demonstratives may be attributive as in *yih bet* 'this house' or pronominal as in *ya nəw* 'that's it'.

Table 35.4 Demonstratives

Singular	Near	m.	*yih*
		f.	*yi(hi)čč(i)*
	Far	m.	*ya*
		f.	*yačč(i)*
Plural	Near		*innə-zzih*
	Far		*innə-zzya*

3.5 Numerals

See cardinal numerals in Table 35.5. Ordinals are the cardinals suffixed by -əñña (a suffix which also forms noun agents): and-əñña 'first', haya hulət-əñña 'twenty-second'. In royal titles 'first' is k'ədam-awi (root k'əddəmə 'he preceded') and 'second' dagm-awi (dəggəmə 'he repeated'): k'ədamawi haylə sillasi 'Haile Sellasie I', dagmawi minilik 'Menelik II'.

Calendar years are expressed as in ši zət'əñ məto silsa sost (thousand nine hundred sixty-three) 'nineteen-sixty-three'.

Table 35.5 Cardinal Numbers

1	and	12	asra-hulət
2	hulət	20	haya
3	sost	30	səlasa
4	arat	40	arba
5	ammist	50	hamsa
6	siddist	60	silsa
7	səbat	70	səba
8	simmint	80	səmanya
9	zət'əñ	90	zət'əna
10	assir	100	məto
11	asr-and	1000	ši

3.6 Verbs

A verb is a stem plus (except in Sg.2m. imperative forms) a subject affix, and perhaps other affixes.

3.6.1 Roots and Stems

Semitic verbs are traditionally thought of as consonantal or largely consonantal roots completed as stems by a pattern of vowels and sometimes additional consonants. Amharic stems of representative verbs in the four main verb conjugations past, nonpast, imperative, and conjunct, and the infinitive, are exemplified in Table 35.6, where hyphens show the place of obligatory subject suffixes (of the past and conjunct conjugations) or prefixes (nonpast).

The 12 verbs are representative of the 12 most common types, which differ by the structure of their roots. Roots are minimal forms, thus material of the imperative column less vowels ə (supplied by verbal grammar) and (epenthetic) i. Some roots, the B-types, have long consonants shown as ':' and exemplified by the second verbs of the first three pairs in Table 35.6.

Consonant length of the historical next-to-last consonant is a characteristic of stems in the past, and in the nonpast of verbs of the types of -bar:ik, -məsək:ir, and -fənəd:a. The historical regularity was obscured by loss of the last or next-to-last consonant, usually leaving a vowel as reflex. In the column of the past these are the types of k'om, hed and sam which lost their next-to-last consonant, the types of bəl:a, lək:a, and fənəd:a which lost their last consonant, and the types of k'ər:ə and ləy:ə which lost a final consonant without leaving a vowel reflex. Verbs whose conjunct and infinitive stems are augmented by -t are those which lost the final consonant, for which the t substitutes. Infinitive stems of Table 35.6 are shown with the infinitive prefix mə-.

Table 35.6 Verb Stems of 12 Root Types

Type	Past	Nonpast	Imper.	Conjunct	Infinitive	Gloss
A	kəf:əl-	-kəfl	kifəl	kəfl-	mə-kfəl	'pay'
B	fəl:əg-	-fəl:ig	fəl:ig	fəl:ig-	mə-fəl:əg	'want'
A	k'ər:ə	-k'ər	k'ir	k'ər-t-	mə-k'rə-t	'remain'
B	ləy:ə	-ləy:	ləy:	ləy:-it-	mə-ləy:ə-t	'separate'
A	bəl:a	-bəla	bila	bəl-t-	mə-bla-t	'eat'
B	lək:a	-lək:a	lək:a	lək:-it-	mə-lək:a-t	'measure'
	k'om-	-k'om	k'um	k'um-	mə-k'om	'stand'
	hed-	-hed	hid	hid-	mə-hed	'go'
	sam-	-sim	sam	sim-	mə-sam	'kiss'
	bar:ək-	-bar:ik	bark	bark-	mə-barək	'bless'
	məsək:ər-	-məsək:ir	məskir	məskir-	mə-məskər	'testify'
	fənəd:a	-fənəd:a	fənda	fənd-it-	mə-fənda-t	'burst'

Table 35.7 Verb Stems with Initial *a*

Type	Past	Nonpast	Imper.	Conjunct	Infinitive	Gloss
A	al:əf-	-alf	iləf	alf-	m-aləf	'pass'
B	ad:ən-	-ad:in	ad:in	ad:in-	m-ad:ən	'hunt'
	ay:ə	-ay	iy	ay-t-	m-ayə-t	'see'
	am:a	-ama	ima	am-t-	m-ama-t	'slander'
	anək:əs-	-anək:is	ankis	ankis-	m-ankəs	'limp'

The 12 verb types have no meaning associations, but B-types tend to be transitive. The type of *bar:ək*, with *a* after the first consonant, is often termed 'C-type'. The first-row triconsonantal type of *kəf:əl* is the most numerous. In Shoan or Addis Ababa Amharic, the conjunct stems of biconsonantal verbs with a back-round vowel characteristic are *k'om* for *k'um* of the table and *hed* for *hid*.

Stems with initial *a*: some stems have initial *a*, the vowel reflex of a lost (pharyngeal or laryngeal) stem-initial consonant. Table 35.7 shows exemplary *a*-initial verbs corresponding to the types of rows 1–4 and 11 of Table 35.6.

So-called 'doubled verbs' have a repeated consonant in the pattern $C_1C_2C_2$ or $C_1C_2C_3C_3$. Table 35.8 shows exemplary stems of doubled verbs corresponding to the types of rows 1, 2 and 11 of Table 35.6. The doubled verb characteristic is shown in the table as repetition of a consonant, not to be confused with long consonants which characterise stems and shown with ':'.

3.6.2 Four Basic Conjugations

The past, nonpast, imperative, and conjunct conjugations are exemplified in Tables 35.9 and 35.10, by forms of the root *ngr* 'tell'.

In the past, Sg.1 suffix *-ku* and Sg.2.m. suffix *-k* have forms with *h* (from historical spirantisation of *k*) when the stem ends in a vowel (as so for five verb types in Table 35.6), for example *bəlla-hu* 'I ate', *k'ərrə-h* 'you (Sg.2.m.) remained'. But Sg.1 *-hu* may also appear after stem-final consonants: *kəffəl-hu* 'I paid', and in Amharic writing *-hu/-h* may be written even when *-ku/-k* is read.

Table 35.8 Stems of 'Doubled' Verbs

Type	Past	Nonpast	Imper.	Conjunct	Infinitive	Gloss
A	bər:ər-	-bərr	bərr	bərr-	mə-brər	'fly'
B	dəl:əl-	-dəl:il	dəl:il	dəl:il-	mə-dəl:əl	'cajole'
	dənəg:əg-	-dənəg:ig	dəngig	dənəg:ig-	mə-dəngəg	'decree'

Table 35.9 Past and Nonpast Conjugations

			Past	Nonpast minor verb	Nonpast main verb
Sg.	1		nəggər-ku	i-nəgr	i-nəgr-alləhu
	2	m.	nəggər-k	ti-nəgr	ti-nəgr-alləh
		f.	nəggər-š	ti-nəgr-i	ti-nəgr-i-alləš
		pol.	(=Pl.3)	(=Pl.3)	(=Pl.3)
	3	m.	nəggər-ə	yi-nəgr	yi-nəgr-al
		f.	nəggər-əčč	ti-nəgr	ti-nəgr-alləčč
		pol.	(=Pl.3)	(=Pl.3)	(=Pl.3)
Pl.	1		nəggər-(i)n	in(ni)-nəgr	in(ni)-nəgr-allən
	2		nəggər-aččihu	ti-nəgr-u	ti-nəgr-allaččihu
	3		nəggər-u	yi-nəgr-u	yi-nəgr-allu

Table 35.10 Jussive and Conjunct Conjugations

			Jussive	Minor verb conjunct	Main verb conjunct
Sg.	1		li-ngər	nəgir-:e	nəgir-:e-alləhu
	2	m.	ti-ngər	nəgr-əh	nəgr-əh-al
		f.	ti-ngər-i	nəgr-əš	nəgr-əš-al
		pol.	(=Pl.3)	(=Pl.3)	(=Pl.3)
	3	m.	yi-ngər	nəgr-o	nəgr-o-(w)al
		f.	ti-ngər	nəgr-a	nəgr-alləčč
		pol.	(=Pl.3)	(=Pl.3)	(=Pl.3)
Pl.	1		in(ni)-ngər	nəgr-ən	nəgr-ən-al
	2		ti-ngər-u	nəgr-aččihu	nəgr-aččihu-al
	3		yi-ngər-u	nəgr-əw	nəgr-əw-al

The vowel of Sg.1 *-ku/-hu* is voiceless when word-final, *nəggər-ku̥*, but is voiced if an object suffix follows: *nəggər-ku-t* 'I told him'. Pl.2 *-aččihu* reflects a plural suffix *-ačč* 'plural'. Stem-final vowels are absent with *-u* of Pl.3 (and equivalent polite forms), as in *bəll-u* 'they ate' (< *bəlla-u*); otherwise the usual vowel elisions apply: *k'ərrə-ə* > *k'ərrə* 'he remained', *ləkka-ə* > *ləkka* 'he measured'.

Verbs of stative and active meaning are interpreted differently in the past: stative verbs may be understood as present: *k'ərrə* 'he remained ~ he remains'; *səkkərə* 'he was/got drunk ~ he is drunk'; whereas actives are past.

Negative past has a prefix *al-* and, as a main verb, a suffix *-m(m)*: *k-al-nəggər-ku* 'if I don't tell' (minor verb with *k-* expressing 'if' and without *-m*), *al-nəggər-ni-m* 'we didn't tell' (main verb).

An object suffix pronoun follows the subject suffix and precedes *-m*: *nəggər-əčč-ih* 'she told you (Sg.m.)', *al-nəggər-ku-t-im* 'I didn't tell him'.

The nonpast conjugation has subject prefixes plus the Sg.2.f. suffix *-i* and Pl.3 (and polite form) *-u*; see Table 35.9, again exemplified by 'tell' (nonpast stem *-nəgr*). Nonpast subject prefix *t-* may be geminated when it follows an adverb-clause prefix such as *s-* 'when' (with which there is epenthesis): *s-t-nəgr-i > sɨt(tɨ)nəgri* 'when you (Sg.f.) tell'. Subject prefix *y-* after consonants is replaced by *i*: *s-y-hed > sihed* 'when he goes'. Stem-final alveolar consonants except *r* when followed by Sg.2f. suffix *-i* are replaced by alveopalatals as discussed in the above section on consonants.

Verbs of stative and active meaning are interpreted differently in the nonpast: active verbs in the nonpast may be understood as present or future: *yɨ-nəgr* 'he tells ~ will tell', whereas statives are only future: *yɨ-səkr* 'he will be (get) drunk' (or sometimes habitual present meaning).

Negative nonpasts have a prefix *a-* and, as main verbs, suffix *-m(m)*: *a-y-nəgr-im* 'he won't tell', *ba-n(nɨ)-nəgr* 'if we don't tell'. Negative nonpast Sg.1 prefix is *l-* instead of *ɨ-* of the affirmative: *a-l-hed-im* 'I won't go'. Subject prefix *t-* is usually lengthened after the negative prefix: *a-ttɨ-nəgɨr* 'she doesn't tell'.

The nonpast affirmative main verb (except when suffixed by *-nnu* 'and' in compound verbs) has auxiliary-verb suffixes historically forms of the verb of presence (*al-* + suffixes, see below). The final vowel of the Sg.1 auxiliary *-alləhu* is voiceless when word final, so this sounds like *alləw̥*. The Pl.2/3 suffix *-u* of the simple nonpast is absent upon suffixation of the plural auxiliary verb, unless Pl.3 (and polite-form) *-u* is followed by an object suffix, in which case the auxiliary verb is *-al* not *-allu*: for example *yɨ-nəgr-u-t-al* 'they tell him'.

As in the above example, an object pronoun precedes the suffixed auxiliary: *yɨ-nəgr-əččəw-al* 'he tells them/him.pol.', *ɨ-nəgr-ɨš-alləhu* 'I tell you.Sg.f.'.

The imperative(-jussive) conjugation is exemplified in Table 35.10, again with 'tell' (jussive stem *-ngər*). The jussive expresses a wish or polite command/request as in *yɨ-mt'a* 'let him come', *yɨ-ngər-ih* 'may (it be so that) he tell you.Sg.m.', with 1st and 3rd-person jussives typically understood as 'let V', for example *ɨnnɨ-hid* 'let us go'. The jussive is the imperative stem plus prefixes and suffixes of the nonpast except that instead of Sg.1 *ɨ-* the jussive has *l-* (as also in the negative nonpast).

The jussive is absent in minor clauses. Negative jussives like negative nonpasts are prefixed with *a-* and, as in the negative nonpast, 2nd-person negative jussives may have lengthening of subject prefix *t-*: *a-t(tɨ)-hid-u* 'don't go! (Pl.2)'.

Imperatives are 2nd-person jussive stems, respectively *nigər, nigər-i, nigər-u* (all having *ɨ*-epenthesis) 'tell! (Sg.m., Sg.f., Sg.pol./Pl.)'. Stem-final alveolar consonants of Sg.2f. have the usual palatalisations as in *wɨsəǰ(i)* 'take! (Sg.f.)' vs *wɨsəd*, Sg.m. The negative imperative is expressed by 2nd-person negative jussives prefixed by negative *a-*, in which 2nd-person subject prefix *t-* is usually lengthened: *a-ttɨ-ngər* 'don't tell! (Sg.m.)'.

The conjunct conjugation (sometimes termed 'gerundive' or 'converb') is exemplified in Table 35.10, as both minor and main verbs, again with forms of 'tell', stem *nəgr*. The minor-verb conjunct expresses all but the last of a sequence of states or events, the main verb being of any form, for example *kəfl-ən wətt'an* 'they paid and left' ('having paid, they left', with main verb in the past), *kəfl-ən ɨnnɨhedal_{ə}n* 'we will pay and go' ('having paid, we will go', main verb nonpast). Subjects of the conjunct and main verb need not be the same: *sərk'-o assər-u-t* 'he having robbed, they imprisoned him'.

The conjunct is a stem and subject suffixes. Conjunct stems are similar to but different from those of the nonpast (Table 35.6). A stem-final consonant is lengthened in Sg.1 necessitating epenthesis before the long consonant, e.g. *nəgɨr-:e-w wətt'ahu* 'I told him and left', which if alveolar other than *r* has the usual palatalisations, for example *wəsɨǰ-:e* 'I taking' (stem *wəsd*). Stem augment *t* is palatalised too: *mət'ɨč-:e* 'I coming' (stem *mət'-t*).

The conjunct lacks negative forms except in the Gojjam dialect, in which the negative conjunct like the past is prefixed by *al-* and suffixed by *-m*.

The main-verb conjunct like the main-verb nonpast combines with an auxiliary verb suffix based on the verb of presence to express a past event with still-present effects, like an English 'present perfect': *nəgr-o-al* 'he has told'. As in the nonpast, an object suffix precedes the auxiliary verb: *nəgr-o-ňň-al* 'he has told me'.

The infinitive is a deverbal noun, a stem prefixed by *mə-* as in *mə-ngər gɨdd nəw* 'to tell is a necessity', *mə-hed yɨwəddal* 'he likes to go'. Where purpose is expressed, the infinitive is prefixed by *lə-*: *lə-mə-hed yɨfəlligal* 'he wants to go'. In *a*-initial stems, *ə* of *mə-* is elided: *m-adər* 'to spend the night', *m-ayət* 'to see'. A negative infinitive is prefixed by *alə-*: *alə-mə-ngər* 'not to tell'. The infinitive may take the possessive pronoun suffixes (Table 35.3) as subject: *mə-ngər-wa* 'her telling', *mə-hed-aččɨn* 'our going'.

3.6.3 Other Conjugations

Verbs with other aspectual and modal meanings are constructed of one of the above as main verb plus an auxiliary verb. Some of these are: (1) a 'past perfect' for an event in the past prior to another, which is a minor-verb conjunct with auxiliary verb *nəbbər*: *ɨne s-ɨ-mət'a hed-o nəbbər* 'When I came, he had gone', *bəlt-ən nəbbər* 'we had eaten'; (2) for possibility or probability a minor-verb conjunct with nonpast *yɨ-hon-al* (*hon* 'become'): *k'ət'əro-w-n rəsɨč-:e yɨhonal* 'I might have (must have) forgotten the appointment' (*rəssa* 'he forgot'); (3) for 'imminence, an event about to happen', a minor verb nonpast prefixed by *l-* with a form of 'say' prefixed by *s-* 'when': *l-ɨ-hed s-ɨ-l* 'when he was about to go' (*ɨ-* of *s-ɨ* the postconsonantal form of the Sg.3m. *y-*, and *-l* the nonpast stem of 'say'); (4) for obligation an infinitive with the verb of presence (below) suffixed by *-bb-* and an object suffix: *məblat allə-bb-ɨňň* 'I have to eat', *məhed yəllə-bb-ɨš-ɨm* 'you (Sg.f.) don't have to go'; (5) for habitual or conditional past the simple nonpast with *nəbbər*: *yɨ-nəgɨr nəbbər* 'he used to tell'/'he would have told'; (6) for progressive aspect *ɨyyə-* prefixed to the past plus the copula (for which see below) in the nonpast and conjugated forms of *nəbbər* in the past: *ɨyyə-fəlləgə-w nəw* 'he is looking for it', *ɨzziya ɨyyə-sərr-ačč nəbbər-əčč* 'she was working there'.

3.6.4 The Copula

This is an irregular verb of being, with only the non-past forms seen in Table 35.11. The copula is a stem *n-* conjugated with object suffixes, except for alternative to Sg.3f. *n-at*, with an object suffix, *n-əčč* with the subject-suffix of the past. In fact *nəčč* is more common.

The negative nonpast copula is negative prefix *ay-*, the stem *dəllə* (*dollə* in Gojjam dialect), and suffixes of the regular past (Table 35.11). In the past, the *be*-verb is regular past forms of *nəbbər-*, for example *nəbbər-ku* 'I was', *nəbbər-k* 'you (Sg.m.) were', with regular negatives, *al-nəbbər-ku-m* 'I was not', etc. In the future, the *be*-verb is regular nonpast forms of *-hon* 'be/become', for example *ɨ-hon* 'I will be', *yɨ-hon* 'he will be'.

Table 35.11 Copula

			Affirmative	Negative
Sg.	1		nə-ññ	ay-dəllə-hu-m
	2	m.	nə-h	ay-dəllə-h-ɨm
		f.	nə-š	ay-dəllə-š-ɨm
		pol.	nə-wot	(=Pl.3)
	3	m.	nə-w	ay-dəllə-m
		f.	nə-čč ~ n-at	ay-dəllə-čč-ɨm
		pol.	(=Pl.3.)	(=Pl.3)
Pl.	1		nə-n	ay-dəllə-n-ɨm
	2		n-aččihu	ay-dəll-aččihu-m
	3		n-aččəw	ay-dəll-u-m

Table 35.12 Verb of Presence

			Affirmative	Negative
Sg.	1		allə-hu	yəllə-hu-m
	2	m.	allə-h	yəllə-h-ɨm
		f.	allə-š	yəllə-š-ɨm
		pol.	(−Pl.3)	(=Pl.3)
	3	m.	allə	yəllə-m
		f.	allə-čč	yəllə-čč-ɨm
		pol.	(=Pl.3)	(=Pl.3)
Pl.	1		allə-n	yəllə-n-ɨm
	2		all-aččɨhu	yəll-aččihu m
	3		all-u	yəll-u-m

3.6.5 Verb of Presence

There is an irregular verb for locative sentences and presentatives such as 'there is a _ ';
see Table 35.12. The stem is *allə* conjugated as a past although the meaning is present.
The negative nonpast verb of presence as a main verb has the stem *yəllə* with subject
suffixes of the past plus *-m*, as in *yəllə-hu-m* 'I am not present'. If there are locative
adverbs, the copula may replace the verb of presence: *ɨzzih nəw* ~ *ɨzzih allə* 'he/it is
here' (or 'here he/it is').

In the past the verb of presence and *be*-verb are nondistinct, for example *nəbbər-ku*
'I was (present)', *nəbbər-k* 'you (Sg.m.) were (present)'. The verb of presence in the
future employs the stem *nor* (< *nəbr*): *yɨ-nor-al* 'he/it will be' (which stem in the past
means 'reside, live': *ɨzzya nor-əčč* 'she lived there').

3.6.6 Possession

Possession is expressed by the verb of presence with object suffixes as possessor and
the verb stem ordinarily agreeing in gender and number with the thing(s) possessed:
məkina allə-ññ 'I have a car' (car is-to.me), *ɨhite bɨzu lɨjočč allu-at* 'My sister has many
children', *ɨhɨt alləčč-ɨw* 'he has a sister'. For possession in the past the stem is *nəbbər*
with the object suffixes: *bək'i gənzəb nəbbər-at* 'she had enough money'. Amharic has

other such 'impersonal' verbs, which take as their object the subject of their usual translation equivalent, including the verbs for being hungry and thirsty: *rabə-ňň* 'I am hungry' (it.hungers-me), *t'əmm-aččəw* 'they are thirsty' (it.thirsts-them).

3.6.7 Derived Verbs

Fully productive are two causatives with prefixes *a-* and *as-* and a passive-reflexive with prefix *t(ə)-*.

Causatives of intransitive verbs are typically formed with the prefix *a-*, for example *a-fəlla* 'he boiled (caused to boil)' (*fəlla* 'it boiled'); *y-a-wədk'* 'he makes fall' (*yɨ-wədk'* 'he falls'). Some transitives whose meanings involve benefit to the self including 'eat', 'drink' and 'dress' form causatives with *a-*: *a-bəlla* 'he caused to eat', *y-a-ləbs* 'he causes (others) to dress'. Both intransitive and transitive verbs having *a*-initial stems form causatives with *as-*, such as *as-amməna* 'he causes to believe'. Imperative-jussive and conjunct stems of *a*-causative stems of triconsonantal verbs differ from the basic stem as in *a-skɨr* 'cause to get drunk! (Sg.m.)' (cf. basic stem *sɨkər*), *a-skɨr-o* 'he, causing to get drunk' (cf. basic *səkr-o*). The imperative-jussive *a*-causative stem of verbs of the *samə* type (Table 35.6) also differs from the basic stem, as in *a-sɨm* 'cause to kiss (Sg.m.)!' (basic *sam* 'kiss (Sg.m.)!').

Causatives, or factitives, of transitive verbs are formed with the prefix *as-*, for example *as-gəddələ* 'he caused to kill', *y-as-fəllɨg* 'it is necessary' (lit. 'it causes to want/seek'). The *as*-causative of an intransitive is an 'indirect' causative perhaps with two agents, for example *as-mətt'a* 'he caused someone to bring (something)' (cf. *mətt'a* 'he came' with *a*-causative *a-mətt'a* 'he brought (caused to come)'). Both objects of the causative verb, if definite, are suffixed by the definite object suffix *-n*. *As*-causatives of A-type (non-geminating) stems are formed as B-types, having a long consonant; for example nonpast *as*-causative of A-type root *sbr* 'break' is *y-as-səb:ɨr*, with long *b*. The imperative-jussive *as*-causative stem of verbs of the *samə* type (Table 35.6) also differ from the basic stem, as in *as-lɨk-u* 'cause to send!' (cf. basic *lak* 'send!').

Passive-reflexive verbs are formed with the prefix *t(ə)-* and stem-changes, for example *tə-bəlla* 'it is eaten'. See passive-reflexive stems of the nonpast, imperative, and infinitive, some different from basic stems, in Table 35.13. Some of these derivatives express a reflexive, for example *t-att'əbə* 'he washed himself' (*att'əbə* 'he washed'), or the intransitive of a transitive, for example *tə-mələsə* 'he returned (vi)' (*mələsə* 'he returned (vt)').

Passive-reflexive nonpast and conjunct stems of A-type (non-geminating) verbs are formed as B-types, with a long consonant, for example, the nonpast *t*-passive of A-type root *kft* 'open' is *yɨ-k:əf:ət* 'it is opened', with long *f* of the B-type. In the nonpast the stem-initial consonant is long as the result of assimilation of the passive prefix *t*, thus *yɨ-k:əf:ət* < *yɨ-tkəf:ət*. Reflexive-passive *t-* of a nonpast, jussive, or infinitive of a verb with initial *a* is lengthened, as in *yɨ-tt-ammən* 'it is believed', *mə-tt-aləf* 'to be passed'.

A derived verb expressing reciprocity has the prefix *t(ə)-* and the vowel *a* after the first stem consonant: *tə-naggəru* 'they conversed (told to each other)' (*nəggərə* 'he told'), *tə-mattu* 'they hit each other' (*mətta* 'he hit'). This derivative may also express a habitual, as in *təballa* 'he habitually ate' (*bəlla* 'he ate'). The causative of this derivative is an adjutative ('help to V') as in *a-ffalləgə* 'he helped to seek' (*fəlləgə* 'he sought, wanted'), *a-wwalləd-əčč* 'she helped to give birth (as midwife)' (*wəlləd-əčč* 'she gave birth'), the stem-initial long consonant resulting from assimilation of *t-*.

Table 35.13 Reflexive-passive Stems of Verbs of the 12 Types

Nonpast	Imperative	Infinitive	Gloss
-k:əf:ət	tə-kəfət	mə-k:əfət	'be opened'
-f:əl:əg	tə-fələg	mə-f:ələg	'be sought'
-f:əǰ:	tə-fəǰ	mə-f:əǰə-t	'be consumed
-l:əy:	tə-ləy	mə-l:əyə-t	'be separated'
-b:əl:a	tə-bəla	mə-b:əla-t	'be eaten'
-l:ək:a	tə-ləka	mə-l:əka-t	'be measured'
-s:am	tə-sam	mə-s:am	'be kissed'
-š:om	tə-šom	mə-š:om	'be appointed'
-g:et'	tə-get'	mə-g:et'	'be adorned'
-b:ar:ək	tə-barək	mə-b:arək	'be blessed'
-m:əzəg:əb	tə-məzgəb	mə-m:əzgəb	'be recorded'
-z:ərəg:a	tə-zərga	mə-z:ərga-t	'be stretched'

Some verbs with *a*-initial basic stems take the compound prefix *as-t-* to form a causative of the passive: *as-t-awwək'ə* 'he notified, announced' (*awwək'ə* 'he knew'), *as-t-arrək'ə* 'he reconciled' (*t-arrək'u* 'they were reconciled').

A derived verb expressing repetition and attenuated action has reduplication of the historical next-to-last consonant preceded by stem-vowel *a*, for example *sasamə* 'he kissed repeatedly/a little' (*samə* 'he kissed'), *nəkakka* 'he repeatedly/barely touched' (*nəkka* 'he touched').

There are so-called 'defective verbs', which lack basic stems and occur only as a derivational type, for example, in the absence of verbs *dərrəgə* or *k'əmmət'ə* there are *a-dərrəgə* 'he did', *tə-dərrəgə* 'it was done', *as-k'əmmət'ə* 'he put, placed', and *tə-k'əmmət'ə* 'he was seated (seated himself)'. A non-productive prefix *n-* appears in a number of defective verbs, especially quadriconsonantal and reduplicatives, always with one of the prefixes *a-* or *t-*, for example *tə-n-bərəkkəkə* 'he knelt', *a-n-s'əbarrək'ə* 'it glittered'.

3.6.8 Denominal Verbs

Verbs may be derived from nouns, though not freely, by abstracting the consonants of the noun and assigning the resulting consonantal root to a verb type, often B-type, for example from *mərz* 'poison (n.)' *yɨ-mərrɨz* 'he poisons' (with long *r*), and from *č'amma* 'shoes' *tə-čamma* 'put on shoes'.

3.6.9 'Say-verbs'

A peculiarity of Ethiopian languages and especially Amharic is verbs consisting of an often seemingly ideophonic word with a final long consonant and a conjugated form of the verb 'say' (with forms *alə* 'he said' *yɨ-l* 'he says', *bəl* 'say!', *bɨl-o* 'he saying', *m-alə-t* 'to say'), for example *bɨkk' alə* 'he appeared', *k'učč' alə* 'he sat down', and *zɨmm alə* 'he was quiet'. Transitive verbs employ 'do' instead of 'say': *bɨkk' adərrəgə* 'he caused to appear', *lɨbb adɨrg* 'look out!' Two somewhat productive derivations of 'say' compound verbs are an attenuative exemplified by *wəddəkk' alə* 'he fell a little', and an intensive exemplified by *wɨdɨkk' alə* 'he fell hard', both derived from the root *wdk'* 'fall'.

4 Syntax

4.1 Basic Word Order

The verb is final in its clause with rare exception (cleft sentences, below), for example:

təmari-w t'ɨyyak'e t'əyyək'ə
student-the question asked.he
'the student asked a question'

Typically, the subject is first in its clause (SOV), as above, but when the verb object is definite and topicalised (or backgrounded) this usually precedes the subject, in which case the verb has a 'resumptive' object pronoun suffix, for example:

yɨh-ɨn wəmbər yohannɨs sərra-w
this-Obj chair Yohannes made.he-it
'Yohannes made this chair'

A clause-initial instrumental prepositional phrase is similarly resumptively expressed as a suffix on the verb.

bə-mət'rəgiya-w setɨyye-wa bet-u-n t'ərrəg-əčč-ɨbb-ət
with-broom-the woman-the house-the-Obj swept-she-with-it
'the woman swept the house with a broom'

Interrogative pronouns are not fronted but are preverbal: *yohannɨs mɨn nəggərə* 'What (*mɨn*) did Yohannis say?', *lɨǰočču ləmɨn yalək'sallu* 'Why (*ləmɨn*) do the children cry?'

4.2 Yes–No Questions

These may have rising intonation or less often sentence-final question words *ɨnde* 'really?', *wəy*, or the literary archaic verb suffix *-nɨ*; for example *aster tɨhedaləčč wəy*, *aster tɨhedaləčč ɨnde*, *aster tɨhedaləčč-ɨnɨ* 'Will Aster go?' A one-word 'reprise' question has the clause-final suffix *-ss*:

tɨhedallɨh (wəy) – awon. ančɨ-ss
'Will you (Sg.2m.) go? – Yes. And you (Sg.2f.)?'

4.3 Noun Phrases

The head noun is typically final in its phrase: *t'ɨru məls* 'a good answer', *y-abbate addis məkina* 'My father's new car'. In a few idioms borrowed from or modelled on Ge'ez, this order is reversed and *ə* is suffixed to the head noun: *betə məs'ahɨft* 'library' (lit. 'house-of books'), *betə məngɨst* 'palace' (lit. 'house-of government').

4.4 Prepositions

Frequent prepositions include *bə-* 'at, on', *ɨ-* 'at, in', *lə-* 'for', *kə-* 'from' (*tə-* in northern dialects), *sɨlə-* 'about', *ɨndə-* 'like' (the latter two may be written as separate words), and *wədə* 'to, towards' (always a separate word). Some positional relations are expressed with postpositional words historically nouns, including *lay* 'top', *wist'* 'interior', *fit* 'face' and *hʷala* 'back', for example *alga lay* 'on the bed', *hod wist'* 'in the belly'. Sometimes postpositions co-occur with prepositions, for example (*bə-*)*bet wist'* 'in the house', *kə-ssu bə-fit* 'in front of him', *kə-ne bə-hʷala* 'after/behind me'.

4.5 Coordination

Nouns are coordinated with *-nna* suffixed to the next-to-last: *bal-inna mist* 'husband and wife', *səw-inna set* 'man and woman'. Verbs may be coordinated with *-nna* if the verb suffixed by *-nna* is a past, minor-verb nonpast or imperative: *tənəssu-nna wətt'u* 'they got up and left', *yimət'a-nna yayal* 'he will come and see', *hid-inna iy* 'go (Sg.m.) and see!'

Alternatives are coordinated with *wəy* suffixed by *-m(m)* in statements (*-m(m)* the historical contrastive-topicalising suffix) and *-ss* in questions (*-ss* the contrast-question suffix): *izzih wəy-m izzya* 'here or there', *izzih wəy-ss izzya* 'here or there?' Alternatives may be simply juxtaposed: *məhon alə-məhon* 'to be or not to be'. Coordinated clauses are usually expressed by use of conjunct verbs, which need no conjunction, for example *bəltu t'ətt'u* 'he ate and drank', *t'wat wət'ičče mata dərrəsku* 'I left in the morning and arrived in the evening'. Contrast clauses are coordinated with *gin*, *nəgər gin*, or (somewhat literary) *daru gin* 'but': *mətt'ahu gin alhəllahum* 'I came but I didn't eat'.

4.6 Adjective (Relative) Clauses

These precede the noun they modify, and *yə-* (identical to the possessive prefix of nouns) is prefixed to the verb in the past and *yə-mm-* in the nonpast. In Gojjam dialect the prefix for nonpast verbs may be simply *m-* and in Menz and Wello dialects *imm-*, the latter also seen in old Amharic literature.

bə-sidamo yə-təgəňňə hawlt
in-Sidamo Rel-was.found.it statue
'a statue which was found in Sidamo'

silə-tege t'aytu yəmm-i-nəgir tarik
about-Empress Taitu Rel-it-tell history
'history which tells about Empress Taitu'

If the head noun of an adjective clause is object of a preposition 'on/at' (*bə-*) or 'for' (*lə-*), this appears as a pronoun suffixed to *-bb-* or *-ll-*, respectively, within the verb:

yih yə-tə-wəlləd-ku-bb-ət bet nəw
this Rel-Pas-born-I-in-it house is
'this is the house I was born in'

If the clause is object of a preposition, the verb of the clause may be prefixed by the preposition in which case the relative verb prefix *yə-* is absent: *silə-t'aytu bə-mm-i-nəgir məs'ihaf* 'in a book which tells about Taitu'. In the dialect of Gojjam and in old Amharic literature, the plural verb of an adjective clause may take the noun-plural suffix *-očč*, for example *yə-mətt'-očč səw-očč* 'people who came'.

611

For cleft sentences, also constructed with relative verbs, see below.

4.7 Noun Clauses

These may be formed on the verb in the nonpast, where the noun-clause and main-clause subjects are the same, with verb-prefix *l-*:

l-ɨwəsd-aččəw a-l-fəlləg-ɨm
that-I.take-them Neg-I-want-Neg
'I don't want to take them'

The same meaning may be expressed with an infinitive verb as follows:

ɨnnəssu-n lə-mə-wsəd a-l-fəllɨg-ɨm
them-Obj for-Inf-take Neg-I-want-Neg
'I don't want to take them'

A noun clause expressing purpose, whose subject may be different from the main-clause subject, employs the prefix *ɨnd-*:

ɨndɨ-n-mət'a yɨfəllɨg-allu
that-we-come want-Aux.they
'they want us to come'

A headless adjective clause functions as a noun clause (alternatively: these noun clauses may function as adjective clauses), for example:

yə-tə-gəññə-w sidamo wɨst' nə-w
Rel-Pas-found.it-the Sidamo in is-it
'what was (~where it was) found is in Sidamo'

yəmm-i-nəgr-ɨš wɨšət nə-w
Rel-he-tell-you.Sg.f. false is-it
'what he tells you (Sg.f.) is false'

Noun clauses functioning as objects of the verb are suffixed, on the verb of the clause, by the definite object suffix *-n*:

yə-s'af-k-əw-n anəbbəb-ku-t
Rel-wrote-you.Sg.m.-it-the read-I-it
'I read what you wrote'

So-called 'cleft' sentences expressing presuppositions and employing the nominalised relative clause are frequent in spoken and written Amharic. The following sentence presupposes 'someone ordered it'.

y-azzəz-u-t ɨssaččəw n-aččəw
Rel-ordered-he.pol-it he.pol is-he.pol
'it is he (pol.) who ordered it'

y-azzəz-u-t man n-aččəw
Rel-ordered-he.pol-it who is-he.pol
'who is it who ordered it?'

The latter clefted question may be as frequent as the simple question *man azzəzut* 'Who ordered it?'. The above sentence

yə-tə-gəňňə-w sidamo wɨst' nə-w
Rel-Pas-found.it-the Sidamo in is-it
'what was (~where it was) found is in Sidamo'

may be heard as equivalent to the simpler 'it was found in Sidamo'.

In such sentences an exception to verb-final order may occur, with the copular verb in medial position followed by the noun clause:

ɨssaččəw naččəw y-azzəz-u-t
he.pol is.he.pol Rel-ordered-he.pol-it
'it is he who ordered it' ('he's the one who ordered it')

(That is, instead of verb-final *y-azzəz-u-t ɨssaččəw naččəw.*) Such word order may be favoured for having the advantage for discourse of focusing, by moving forward (to the right), the presupposition.

4.8 Adverb Clauses

These have a complementising–subordinating prefix on the past or nonpast verb, having meanings like 'when', 'if', 'because', etc. A common time clause is expressed with the prefix *s-* 'when' (*t-* in northern dialects other than Gondar) and a common conditional clause with the prefix *b-* 'if', both with the nonpast verb, as follows:

təmari-w t'ɨyyak'e s-i-t'əyyɨk' astəmari-w a-y-məllɨs-ɨm
student-the question when-he-ask teacher-the Neg-he-answer-Neg
'when the student asks a question, the teacher doesn't answer'

b-i-zənb-ɨm a-n-hed-m
if-it-rain-Top Neg-we-go-Neg
'even if it rains we won't go'

'To be about to do' is expressed as direct speech in a time clause with *s-* and the verb 'say', for example *ɨwət'allɨhu s-i-l* 'when he was about to go out' (lit. 'when he said "I will go out"').

Some adverbial clauses are expressed by prepositional prefixes plus the past form of the verb, and with both a preposition and a postposition, for example, with *kə-* 'if', *ɨyyə-* 'while', *kə-* ... *ǰəmmɨro* 'since' (*ǰəmmɨr-o* a usually fixed Sg.3m. conjunct 'he beginning'), *bə-* ... *gize* 'when', *kə-* ... *bəhʷala* 'after' (*bə-hʷala* lit. 'at back'), *kə-* ... *bəfit* 'after' (*bə-fit* lit. 'at front'). An example of the latter is:

kə-zənnəbə bəfit bet gəbba-n
from-rained.it before house entered-we
'before it rained, we entered the house'

Three adverb clauses are expressed by prepositional prefixes which occur only with the past form of verbs or with the nonpast prefixed by *mm-* (the relative nonpast prefix less *yə-*); these are *ində-* 'like, as', *silə-* 'because' and *iskə-* 'until', as in *issu ind-alə* 'like he wrote' (with elision of *ə* of *ində-*), *issu silə-mm-i-s'if* 'because he writes', *iskə-mm-i-dərs* 'until he arrives'; *isk-* also constructs with the unprefixed nonpast: *isk-i-mət'a* 'until he comes'.

Comparative clauses may employ relative and causative conjunct forms of the verbs 'be less' and 'be more', for example relative verb *y-annəsə* 'which is less' and conjugated causative conjunct *a-bəlt'-* 'causing to be more'.

kə-ňňa y-annəsə innəssu sərr-u
from-we Rel-is.less.it they did-they
'they did less than us'

kə-ňňa isswa a-bəlt'-a tat'ənalləčč
from-us she Caus-be.more-she she.studies
'she studies more than us'

5 Writing

Amharic writing is a descendant of the ancient Ethiopic (Ge'ez) writing system known from about 2500 BP, and well attested in epigraphic records of the Aksumite Ethiopian kingdom. Like other ancient Semitic writing systems this is descendant of an adaptation of Egyptian hieroglyphic consonantal writing. Ethiopic was at first a consonantal writing system; vowels were not represented. In time Ethiopic underwent popular adaptation as graphs became less regular and angular, and eventually a practice of writing on parchment-paper arose. Perhaps as an influence of Greek writing, which was also known in Aksum and employed in inscriptions and coins of the kingdom, about 1600 BP Ethiopic began to be written from left-to-right, opposite that of most other Semitic writing systems, and, about the same time, vowels began to be represented, as additions or other modification of the consonantal graphs.

For example, the graph for *b* ቡ, descendant of the Egyptian hieroglyph of 'house' the first phone of which word is *b* in Semitic (Amharic *bet*, Arabic *bayt*), was modified as ቡ for *bu*, ቢ for *bi*, ቤ for *be*, etc. The original basic consonantal graph became the representation of the consonant plus the most frequent vowel, so ቡ is *bə* (originally *ba*, but *a* later became *ə*).

Upon the decline of Aksum after about 600 AD, Ethiopic writing disappeared in archaeology, to reappear around 1300 AD in manuscripts of Ethiopian Orthodox Christian religious literature and chronicles of kings. Shortly after this time a modified form of Ethiopic began to be used for writing Amharic. This required new graphs for the Amharic palatalised coronals *š*, *ž*, *č*, *č'* and *ň*, and a graph for spirantised *k*, or *x*, which weakened further as *h*. The Amharic writing system and its graphs are termed *fidel*.

Subsequently, Ethiopic was adapted to write Tigrinya (of Eritrea and northern Ethiopia), and recently Amharic writing has been adapted to write other Ethiopian languages including some which have different consonants and long vowels. Amharic writing today fulfils all the needs of modern literate society. The problems of Amharic typewriting including the large number of graphs and inappropriately small size of typescript have been alleviated or corrected with the use of computer mediated writing.

Table 35.14 presents the 31 Amharic consonants of Table 35.1. Because of mergers of formerly distinct sounds whose different graphs persist in the writing system, four consonants have more than one graph: *s* and *s'* and *ʔ* each have two, and *h* has four.

Table 35.14 Amharic Graphs in English Alphabetical Order

	ə	u	i	a	e	(i)	o
ʔ	አ*	ኡ	ኢ	አ	ኤ	እ	አ
	ዐ*	ዑ	ዒ	ዓ	ዔ	ዕ	ዖ
b	በ	ቡ	ቢ	ባ	ቤ	ብ	ቦ
č	ቸ	ቹ	ቺ	ቻ	ቼ	ች	ቾ
č'	ጨ	ጩ	ጪ	ጫ	ጬ	ጭ	ጮ
d	ደ	ዱ	ዲ	ዳ	ዴ	ድ	ዶ
f	ፈ	ፉ	ፊ	ፋ	ፌ	ፍ	ፎ
g	ገ	ጉ	ጊ	ጋ	ጌ	ግ	ጎ
gʷ	ጐ		ጒ	ጓ	ጔ	ጕ	
	ሀ*	ሁ	ሂ	ሃ	ሄ	ህ	ሆ
h	ሐ*	ሑ	ሒ	ሓ	ሔ	ሕ	ሖ
	ኸ*	ኹ	ኺ	ኻ	ኼ	ኽ	ኾ
	ኀ*	ኁ	ኂ	ኃ	ኄ	ኅ	ኆ
hʷ	ኈ		ኊ	ኋ	ኌ	ኍ	
j	ጀ	ጁ	ጂ	ጃ	ጄ	ጅ	ጆ
k	ከ	ኩ	ኪ	ካ	ኬ	ክ	ኮ
kʷ	ኰ		ኲ	ኳ	ኴ	ኵ	
k'	ቀ	ቁ	ቂ	ቃ	ቄ	ቅ	ቆ
kʷ'	ቈ		ቊ	ቋ	ቌ	ቍ	
l	ለ	ሉ	ሊ	ላ	ሌ	ል	ሎ
m	መ	ሙ	ሚ	ማ	ሜ	ም	ሞ
n	ነ	ኑ	ኒ	ና	ኔ	ን	ኖ
ň	ኘ	ኙ	ኚ	ኛ	ኜ	ኝ	ኞ
p	ፐ	ፑ	ፒ	ፓ	ፔ	ፕ	ፖ
p'	ጰ	ጱ	ጲ	ጳ	ጴ	ጵ	ጶ
r	ረ	ሩ	ሪ	ራ	ሬ	ር	ሮ
	ሰ	ሱ	ሲ	ሳ	ሴ	ስ	ሶ
s	ሠ	ሡ	ሢ	ሣ	ሤ	ሥ	ሦ
	ጸ	ጹ	ጺ	ጻ	ጼ	ጽ	ጾ
s'	ፀ	ፁ	ፂ	ፃ	ፄ	ፅ	ፆ
š	ሸ	ሹ	ሺ	ሻ	ሼ	ሽ	ሾ
t	ተ	ቱ	ቲ	ታ	ቴ	ት	ቶ
t'	ጠ	ጡ	ጢ	ጣ	ጤ	ጥ	ጦ
w	ወ	ዉ	ዊ	ዋ	ዌ	ው	ዎ
y	የ	ዩ	ዪ	ያ	ዬ	ይ	ዮ
z	ዘ	ዙ	ዚ	ዛ	ዜ	ዝ	ዞ
ž	ዠ	ዡ	ዢ	ዣ	ዤ	ዥ	ዦ

Note: * 1st-order vowel is *a* not *ə*.

Each of the resulting 37 graphs has seven shapes, one for each of the seven vowels of Table 35.2 (termed '1st-order', '2nd-order', etc.), except for the labiovelars which have only five. Because the pharyngeal and laryngeal consonants (which merged as *h* or *ʔ*) lowered a following vowel *ə* to *a*, the basic graphs of these have *a* where other consonants have *ə* (marked with asterisks in Table 35.14).

The 37 graphs (*fidel*) are read as simple syllables consisting of the consonant and a vowel, except for 6th-order graphs. Vowels are extensions and/or modifications of the 1st-order consonant graph, in four largely regular patterns seen in Table 35.15, which shows the consonants *t*, *b*, *t'* and *m* representative of 1-legged, 2-legged, 3-legged and legless graphs, respectively.

The parentheses around *i* of the 6th-form graphs – *t(i)*, *b(i)*, *t'(i)* and *m(i)* – show that these may be read with the vowel (the epenthetic vowel, with exceptions) or without it. Thus ልብ 'heart' with two 6th-order graphs is *libb*.

Although a graph is usually read as a syllable, Ethiopic is not a syllabic writing system (as is Japanese *kana* for example), because the vowels, although attached, are systematically recognisable apart from the consonants, just as in a so-called alphabetic system like English.

Similarities of graphs of Greek and Ethiopic writing (and Amharic, derived from Ethiopic) are owed to shared descent from Egyptian, for example Greek B and Ethiopic ቡ, Γ and ገ, Λ and ል, and Σ and ш. Direct influence of Greek is seen in comparison of the Ethiopic-Amharic and Greek numbers, in Table 35.16. Similarities of Greek and Ethiopic are particularly apparent for 2, 3, 9, 10, 80 and 100.

In two ways Ethiopic-Amharic writing fails to express the phonological contrasts of Amharic. Long and short consonants, which are contrastive between vowels and at the end of words, are written the same. Thus *alə* 'he said' and *allə* 'he is present' are both written አለ; and *bb* of ልብ *libb* 'heart' and *b* of ጅብ *jib* 'hyena' are both written ብ. The second failing has fewer but occasional manifestations: within a word before another consonant a 6th-order graph may be ambiguous between the consonant with and without *i*: thus *motiš* 'your (Sg.f.) death' and *motš* 'you (Sg.f) died' are both ሞትሽ.

Table 35.15 Four Patterns of Vowel Modification

1 leg	ተ	ቱ	ቲ	ታ	ቴ	ት	ቶ
	tə	*tu*	*ti*	*ta*	*te*	*t(i)*	*to*
2 legs	በ	ቡ	ቢ	ባ	ቤ	ብ	ቦ
	bə	*bu*	*bi*	*ba*	*be*	*b(i)*	*bo*
3 legs	ጠ	ጡ	ጢ	ጣ	ጤ	ጥ	ጦ
	t'	*t'u*	*t'i*	*t'a*	*t'e*	*t'(i)*	*t'o*
no legs	መ	ሙ	ሚ	ማ	ሜ	ም	ሞ
	mə	*mu*	*mi*	*ma*	*me*	*m(i)*	*mo*

Table 35.16 Ethiopic Numbers Compared to Greek

1	2	3	4	5	6	7	8	9	10
፩	፪	፫	፬	፭	፮	፯	፰	፱	፲
α	β	γ	δ	ε	σ	ζ	η	θ	ι
10	20	30	40	50	60	70	80	90	100
፲	፳	፴	፵	፶	፷	፸	፹	፺	፻
ι	κ	λ	m̈	n̈	ξ	ο	π	κ	ρ

Bibliography

The most thorough grammar of Amharic is Leslau (1995), although Dawkins (1969) is very efficient for getting the basics. The most thorough Amharic–English dictionary is Kane (1990), and the most thorough English–Amharic dictionary Leslau (1973). For learners a good bilingual dictionary is Leslau (1975). The most thorough textbook remains Leslau (1967), although Appleyard (1995) provides the best introduction for learners. Advanced students of Amharic language and society will find valuable the readings in Leslau and Kane (2001). An informative study of Amharic usage in Ethiopian schools and society is Meyer and Richter (2003).

References

Appleyard, D. 1995. *Colloquial Amharic* (Routledge, London)

Dawkins, C.H. 1969. *The Fundamentals of Amharic* (Sudan Interior Mission, Addis Ababa)

Kane, T. L. 1990. *Amharic–English Dictionary*, 2 vols (Harrassowitz, Wiesbaden)

Leslau, W. 1967. *Amharic Textbook* (Harrassowitz, Wiesbaden)

—— 1973. *English–Amharic Context Dictionary* (Harrassowitz, Wiesbaden)

—— 1975. *Concise Amharic Dictionary* (Harrassowitz, Wiesbaden)

—— 1995. *Reference Grammar of Amharic* (Harrassowitz, Wiesbaden)

Leslau, W., and Kane, T. 2001. *Amharic Cultural Reader* (Harrassowitz, Wiesbaden)

Meyer, R. and Richter, R. 2003. *Language Use in Ethiopia from a Network Perspective*. Schriften zur Afrikanistic Band 7 (Peter Lang, Frankfurt am Main)

36

Hausa and the Chadic Languages

Paul Newman

1 Chadic

The Chadic language family, which is a constituent part of the Afroasiatic phylum, contains some 140 languages spoken in the sub-Saharan region west, south and east of Lake Chad. The exact number of languages is not known since new languages continue to be discovered while other supposedly independent languages turn out to be mere dialects or terminological variants. The most important and best-known Chadic language is Hausa. Other Chadic languages are considerably smaller, ranging from a quarter of a million speakers to less than a thousand. Most of the languages at the lower end of the spectrum are now seriously endangered.

The languages in the family fall into three major branches plus a fourth independent branch. The West Chadic Branch, which includes Hausa, contains about 60 languages divided into seven groups. All of these languages are spoken in northern Nigeria. The Biu-Mandara (or Central) Branch contains over 45 languages, assigned to eleven groups, extending from the Gongola and Benue river basins in Nigeria to the Mandara Mountains in Cameroon. The East Chadic Branch contains about 25 languages belonging to six groups. These are scattered across central Chad in a southwest–northeast direction from the Cameroon border to the Sudan border. The Masa Branch consists of a single group of some half a dozen closely related languages spoken between the most southeasterly Biu-Mandara languages and the most southwesterly East Chadic languages. A comprehensive list of Chadic languages organised by branch and group is given in Table 36.1. Within each group, the languages are listed alphabetically rather than according to closeness of relationship. Names in parentheses indicate alternative nomenclature or dialect variants.

Although the relationship of Chadic (originally only Hausa) to other Afroasiatic languages was proposed some 150 years ago, it has gained general acceptance only within the last quarter of a century. The inclusion of Chadic within Afroasiatic is based on the presence of features such as the following: (a) a formative *t* indicating feminine, diminutive and singulative; (b) an *n/t/n* 'masculine/feminine/plural' agreement marking pattern in the deictic system; (c) an *m-* prefix forming agential, instrumental and locational nouns;

Table 36.1 The Chadic Language Family (Inventory and Classification)

I   West Chadic Branch
1 Hausa group: Gwandara, Hausa.
2 Bole group: Bele, Bole (Bolanci), Deno (Kubi), Galambu, Gera, Geruma, Kanakuru (Dera), Karekare, Kirfi, Kupto, Kwami, Maha, Ngamo, Pero, Piya (Wurkum), Tangale.
3 Angas group: Angas, Chip, Gerka (Yiwom), Goemai (Ankwe), Koenoem, Kofyar, Montol (Teel), Pyapun, Sura (Mupun), Tal.
4 Ron group: Fyer, Karfa, Kulere, Mundat, Ron (Bokkos, Daffo), Sha, Shagawu, Tambas.
5 Bade group: Bade, Duwai, Ngizim.
6 Warji group: Diri, Jimbin, Kariya, Mburku, Miya, Pa'a, Tsagu, Warji.
7 Zaar group: Barawa, Boghom, Dass, Dott, Geji, Guruntum, Guus (Sigidi), Jimi, Ju, Mangas, Polchi, Zaar (Sayanci), Zari (Zakshi), Zeem.

II Biu Mandara Branch
1 Tera group: Ga'anda, Hona, Jara, Tera (Pidlimdi, Yamaltu).
2 Bura group: Bura (Pabir), Chibak, Kilba, Margi, Putai (West Margi).
3 Higi group: Bana, Higi, Kapsiki.
4 Mandara group: Dghwede, Glavda, Guduf, Gvoko, Hdi (Hide), Lamang (Hitkala), Mandara (Wandala), Podoko.
5 Matakam group: Gisiga, Hurza-Vame, Mada, Matakam (Mafa), Mofu-Duvangar, Mofu-Gudur, Moloko, Muktele, Muyang, Uldeme, Zulgo.
6 Sukur group: Sukur.
7 Daba group: Buwal, Daba (Kola, Musgoi), Gawar, Hina.
8 Bata group: Bachama, Bata, Gude, Nzangi (Jeng).
9 Kotoko group: Buduma (Yedina), Kotoko, Logone.
10 Musgu group: Mbara, Musgu (Munjuk, Mulwi).
11 Gidar group: Gidar.

III East Chadic Branch
1 Somrai group: Gadang, Miltu, Mod, Ndam, Somrai (Sibine), Tumak.
2 Nancere group: Gabri (Tobanga), Kabalai, Lele, Nancere.
3 Kera group: Kera, Kwang (Modgel).
4 Dangla group: Bidiyo, Birgit, Dangla (Dangaléat), Jegu, Kujarge, Mawa, Migama (Jonkor of Abu Telfan), Mogum, Mubi, Toram.
5 Mokulu group: Mokulu (Jonkor of Guera).
6 Sokoro group: Barain, Saba, Sokoro.

IV Masa Branch
1 Masa group: Marba, Masa, Mesme, Musey, Zime (Lame, Peve).

(d) formation of noun plurals *inter alia* by a suffix *-n* and an infix *-a-*; (e) a common pronominal paradigm; (f) a pattern of suppletive imperatives with the verbs 'come' and 'go'; (g) shared gender specification of individual words; and (h) cognate items for basic vocabulary including 'body', 'die', 'drink', 'fire', 'know', 'name', 'water' and 'what'. Some scholars have suggested that Chadic is the most distant Afroasiatic family member (apart from Omotic), while others have suggested an especially close tie with Berber; but, so far, such proposals have been made essentially on impressionistic grounds.

Chadic languages belonging to separate groups appear quite different from one another, reflecting the great time depth within the family; nevertheless, they invariably can be identified as Chadic because of shared core features. In describing common Chadic characteristics, it should be kept in mind that these features are neither present nor found identically in all Chadic languages, nor are they necessarily reconstructable for Proto-Chadic.

All Chadic languages, as far as we are aware, are tonal. One finds simple two-tone systems (Margi), two tones plus downstep (Kanakuru), three tones (Tera) and three tones plus downstep (Ga'anda). Vowel systems range from two vowels, /ə/ and /a/ (as in Mandara), to seven vowels, /i e ɛ a ɔ o u/ plus distinctive vowel length (as in Dangla). Cross-height vowel harmony of the common West African type is rare in Chadic but it does occur, inexplicably, in Tangale. A typical Chadic feature is to have a different number of vowel contrasts depending on the position within a word. Old Hausa, for example, had two vowels initially, three plus vowel length medially and five vowels without a length contrast finally. Most Chadic languages have a set of glottalised consonants (usually laryngealised or implosive) in addition to the voiced and voiceless ones. Goemai and a few other languages in the same subgroup have the unusual feature of contrasting ejective and implosive consonants at the same position of articulation, e.g. /p'/ vs /ɓ/, /t'/ vs /ɗ/. While the glottal stop /ʔ/ occurs as a phoneme in many languages, it invariably represents a secondary historical development: it is not reconstructable for Proto-Chadic. Finally, one should note the widespread presence of lateral fricatives (/ɬ/ and /ɮ/) throughout the family. They have been lost in the East Chadic Branch and in some sub-branches of West Chadic, but elsewhere they are extremely common.

In the realm of morphosyntax, Chadic languages typically have pluractional verb stems (formerly called 'intensives') that indicate the plurality of action, i.e. action done a number of times, by a number of subjects or affecting a number of objects. These pluractional stems are formed by reduplication, gemination and/or by insertion of an internal -a-, e.g. Ga'anda ɓəl- 'kill', ɓəɓal- 'kill many'. In a few languages, the use of pluractional stems has become grammaticalised, resulting in ergative-type number agreement, i.e. obligatory use of pluractional stems with plural subjects of intransitive verbs and plural objects of transitive verbs, e.g. Kanakuru nà ɗòpè gámíníì 'I tied the rams'; (ɗope < *ɗoppe); gámíníì wù ɗòpò-wú 'the rams are tied'; cf. wù ɗòwè gámíì 'they tied the ram'; gámíì à ɗòwè-ní 'the ram is tied'. The Kanakuru examples illustrate another distinctive Chadic feature (but with scattered distribution), namely the so-called ICP ('Intransitive Copy Pronoun') construction. In various languages, all or some intransitive verbs optionally or obligatorily suffix a pronoun that copies the person and number of the subject. In Ngizim, for example, the use of the ICP is optional and adds an extra meaning of completeness to the verb phrase. In Kanakuru, on the other hand, the use of the ICP is obligatory with all intransitive verbs, but limited to certain tenses, e.g. kà pòrò-kó 'you went out', not *kà pòró; kíléi à tàɗè-ní 'the pot broke', cf. à tàɗè kíléi 'he broke the pot'. Note that ICPs in Chadic are different from reflexive pronouns in both form and function, the latter typically consisting of the noun for 'head' or 'body' plus a possessive pronoun and occurring syntactically as the direct object of a transitive verb.

Verbs in Chadic typically employ derivational extensions indicating action in, towards, down, up, away or totally or partially done. Sometimes the extensions are more grammatical in nature, indicating benefactive, perfective or transitivisation. In some languages, such as Tera, the extensions are separate particles; in some, such as Margi, they are semi-bound suffixes; in others, such as Hausa, they have become fused into the verb stem.

Grammatical gender in Chadic is a fairly straightforward phenomenon that goes back to Proto-Chadic (and more distantly to Proto-Afroasiatic as well). The many Chadic languages that do not now have gender have all lost it, this having happened independently a number of times at the level of language, group, subgroup and cluster. Languages that have gender invariably distinguish two genders (masculine and feminine) and in the singular only. Gender distinctions are absent in the plural. In the pronominal system, gender is typically marked in the second as well as the third person.

Regarding word order, Chadic languages are prepositional and place the possessor following the thing possessed. Many languages distinguish inalienable possession formed by simple juxtaposition from alienable possession, which makes use of a connecting particle, e.g. Tera ɓəmndə-ro 'your ear' vs kaskar ɓa-ro 'your sword'. Attributive adjectives usually follow the noun being modified and numerals invariably follow the noun. The most common order for verbal sentences is S(ubject)–V(erb)–O(bject), this almost certainly being the basic order in Proto-Chadic. SOV in Chadic is unattested. VSO does occur in a small number of Biu-Mandara languages spoken in the Nigerian–Cameroon border region; evidence suggests that this represents an areal innovation rather than being an archaic feature of the family.

2 Hausa

2.1 Introduction

Hausa is spoken as a mother tongue by some 25 to 30 million people representing the original Hausa population as well as by people of Fulani ancestry who established political control over Hausaland at the beginning of the nineteenth century. It is the majority language of much of northern Nigeria and of the Republic of Niger. Hausa speakers are also found in Togo and Ghana and in small colonies of settlers and traders in large towns in West Africa. In addition, there is a Hausa-speaking community in the Blue Nile area of Sudan, dating from the British take-over of northern Nigeria at the beginning of the twentieth century.

Hausa is also widely spoken as a second (or third) language in Nigeria and Niger, functioning as a lingua franca for commercial, informational and governmental purposes. Hausa is one of the three indigenous national languages recognised in the Nigerian constitution. Whereas secondary and higher education in northern Nigeria are generally in English, Hausa is commonly the de facto language of instruction in the primary schools. Hausa is now offered as a major degree subject in a number of Nigerian universities. There are many Hausa language newspapers and magazines, a thriving literature and extensive use of the language in radio and television. Hausa language broadcasting is provided not only within Nigeria and Niger, but also by international transmissions from Britain, the USA, Germany, Russia and China. With approximately 40 or so million first- and second-language speakers, Hausa ranks with Swahili as one of the two most important languages in sub-Saharan Africa.

Within the Chadic family, Hausa essentially constitutes a group by itself. Gwandara, the only other member of the group, is a historically relatively recent creolised offshoot of Hausa. The West Chadic groups most closely related to it are the Bole group and the Angas group. What sets Hausa apart from its sister (or cousin) languages is the richness of its vocabulary, due in large part to the enormous number of loanwords from other languages. Tuareg and Kanuri, for example, have contributed significantly to Hausa vocabulary; but the major influence by far has been Arabic (sometimes by way of one or the other of the just-mentioned languages). In certain semantic spheres, e.g. religion, government, law, warfare, horsemanship, literature and mathematics, Hausa is literally swamped with words of Arabic origin. In the past century, Hausa has absorbed a massive new wave of loanwords from English (in Nigeria) and French (in Niger). This influence continues unabated.

Compared with other large African languages, dialect variation within Hausa is relatively modest. Nevertheless, on the basis of systematic differences in pronunciation and grammar, it is possible to distinguish a Western dialect (or dialects) (e.g. Sokoto and Gobir) from an Eastern dialect (Kano and Zaria), with Katsina occupying an intermediate position. The dialect described here, which has become established as 'standard Hausa', is that of greater Kano, the largest and most important Hausa city.

2.2 Phonology

The phonemes of the standard dialect of Hausa are presented in Table 36.2. There are 32 consonants, 12 vowels (five basic vowels with corresponding long and short variants plus two diphthongs) and three tones (two basic tones plus a compound tone). The richness in the consonantal inventory is due to the presence of: (a) a set of glottalised consonants alongside the voiced and voiceless ones, e.g. /ɗ/ vs /t/ and /d/, and (b) palatalised and labialised consonants alongside simple ones, e.g. /ky/ and /kw/ vs /k/. In Table 36.2 (and in all examples given), the symbols *c* and *j* represent the affricates [ʧ] and [ʤ] respectively. The 'hooked' letters *ɓ* and *ɗ* represent laryngealised stops; *'y* is a laryngealised semi-vowel, historically derived from **dy*, whereas *ƙ, ƙy, ƙw* and *ts* are

Table 36.2 Phonemes of Hausa

Consonants

		lab.	cor.	pal.	vel.	lab. vel.	pal. vel.	laryn.
	vl		t	c	k	kw	ky	
	vd	b	d	(j)	g	gw	gy	
obst	gl	ɓ	ɗ	'y	ƙ	ƙw	ƙy	'
	vl	f, fy	s	sh				h
	vd		z	j				
	gl		ts					
		m	n					
			l					
son			r					
			r̃					
				y		w		

Vowels

Short			*Long*			*Diphthongs*	
i		u	ii		uu		
e	o		ee	oo			
a			aa			ai	au

Tones

High: á(a)   Low: à(a)   Falling: âa

ejectives. The standard pronunciation for the consonant written with the digraph *ts* is [s'] (an ejective sibilant), but there is individual and dialectal variation, including [tʃ'] and [ts']. The apostrophe /'/ by itself is used to represent the glottal stop phoneme.

The /f/ phoneme is variably pronounced as [f], [Φ] or [p]. Structurally, it fills the *p*-slot in the voiceless stop series. Before back vowels it is usually pronounced (and written) as /h/, e.g. *jèefí* 'throw', cf. *jéehóo* 'throw in this direction'. The nasals /n/ and /m/ are generally pronounced [ŋ] in final position, e.g. /nân/ 'here' [nâŋ]; /máalàm/ 'teacher' [máalàm] or [máalàŋ]. When immediately followed by a consonant, whether in the same word or across a word boundary, /n/ (always) and /m/ (usually) assimilate to the position of the abutting consonant, e.g. *sún bí* 'they followed' [súmbí]; *fàhímtàa* 'understand' [fàhíntàa]. Hausa has two distinct rhotics: a retroflex flap [ɽ] and an apical tap or roll [r]. The two sounds are not distinguished in Hausa orthography. In scholarly linguistic works, the tap/roll is sometimes indicated /r/ or /R/ or more often /r̃/, to set it apart from the flap, which is written as /r/, e.g. *ráanáa* 'sun', *fàrkáa* 'paramour', cf. *r̃iibàa* 'profit', *fár̃kàa* 'wake up'. All Hausa consonants can occur as geminates as well as singly, e.g. *cíllàa* 'shoot far', cf. *cílàa* 'pigeon'; *díddígèe* 'heel' (< *dígdígèe*), cf. plural *dìgàadìgái*. Although from a technical perspective the geminates need to be analysed at some level as unitary segments, for most purposes they can be viewed simply as two identical abutting consonants, i.e. *cíllàa* = /C₁íC₂.C₃àa/.

The five long vowels in Hausa have typical IPA 'Italian' values. In non-final position, short /i/, /a/ and /u/ are more lax and centralised. (Non-final short /e/ and /o/ have a marginal status in Hausa.) The contrast between long and short vowels is extremely important, both lexically and grammatically, e.g. *ɓáacèe* 'spoil', *ɓácèe* 'vanish'; *jíimàa* 'tanning', *jímàa* 'pass time'; *'ídòo* 'eye', *'ídó* 'in the eye'; *shàafée* 'wiping', *shàafé* 'wiped' (past participle); *táa* 'she (completive)', *tá* 'she (preterit)'. The two diphthongs /ai/ and /au/ are best treated as complex vocalic nuclei, although many Hausaists prefer to analyse them as /ay/ and /aw/. The former is generally pronounced [ei] or even [ee], tending to merge with long /ee/; the latter varies in the [ao], [au], [ou] range, normally remaining distinct from long /oo/.

Hausa has two basic tones: high, indicated *á(a)*, and low, indicated *à(a)*, e.g. *góoràa* 'bamboo', *gòoráa* 'large gourd', *màatáa* 'wife', *máatáa* 'wives', *kíráa* 'call', *kíràa* 'calling', *tá* 'she (preterit)', *tà* 'she (subjunctive)'. A sequence of high plus low on a single syllable is realised as a falling tone, e.g. *yâaráa* 'children' (= /yáàráa/), *mântáa* 'forget' (= /máǹtáa/). In many cases falling tones are the result of the grounding of a low tone belonging to a following morpheme, e.g. *kóomôowáa* 'returning' (= /kóomóòwáa/) comes from *kóomóo* 'return' plus `-wáa '-ing'. Falling tones, being tone sequences, only occur on heavy syllables, both CVV and CVC types. There is no rising tone corresponding to the fall. A low–high sequence on a single syllable is usually simplified to high, e.g. *tàusái* 'pity' < *tàusài* (< *tàusàyíi*); *ɗáukàa* 'take' < *ɗàúkàa*.

Hausa has three syllable types only: CV, which is light, and CVV (where VV can be a long vowel or a diphthong) and CVC, which are heavy, e.g. *súu.nán.sà* 'his name', *kú.jèe.râr̃* 'the chair', *'à.kwàa.tì* 'box'. While consonants may abut across syllable boundaries, e.g. *kás.kàa* 'tick', there are no consonant clusters within a syllable. Syllable weight is an extremely important variable in the language: it is crucial for metrical and tonal rules and plays a major role in morphological processes. Given the restriction on syllable types, it follows that long vowels cannot occur in closed syllables. Such overheavy syllables, which are created in intermediate structure by morphological formations, are eliminated phonologically by automatic reduction of the nucleus, e.g.

áikìi-n-sà → *'áikìnsà* 'his work' (lit. 'work-of-his'); *mâi-n gyàdǎa* → *mân gyàdǎa* 'groundnut oil'; **búuɗ-bùuděe* → *búbbùuděe* 'open many/often'; **fáaɗ mínì* (contracted from *fáaɗàa mínì*) → *fár̃ mínì* 'attack me'.

2.2.1 Orthography

Hausa makes use of two writing systems, one, called *bóokòo*, based on the Latin alphabet, the other, called *'àjàmí*, based on the Arabic writing system. The Latin system was introduced by the British in Nigeria at the beginning of the twentieth century. This western orthography is used in the schools, in the major Hausa newspapers and in most other modern books and magazines. The system as now established makes use of the symbols in Table 36.2 with the following differences. Glottal stop (') is not written in word-initial position. The phonemic distinction between the two Rs is ignored. Vowel length is not marked, nor is tone. An earlier attempt in Niger to mark vowel length by double letters was subsequently dropped, so that there is now a more or less uniform orthography in the former French and former British countries. On the whole the writing system is phonemic (even subphonemic in places) although some assimilatory changes are not noted in order to preserve morphological regularity. Thus one writes *sun bi* 'they followed', not *sum bi*, and *ribar nan* 'that profit', not *riban nan*.

The writing of Hausa in Arabic script (*'àjàmí*) dates from the beginning of the nineteenth century, possibly a little earlier. Although government policy since the beginning of this century has been to replace *'àjàmí* by *bóokòo*, it is still widely known and used. The *'àjàmí* script is learned in Koranic schools and is preferred over *bóokòo* not only by religious writers but also by many of the more popular traditional poets. After a long period of purposeful neglect, *'àjàmí* has begun to be used again in newspapers.

2.2.2 Morphophonemic processes

Hausa exhibits a tremendous amount of morphophonemic alternation, sometimes through active phonological rules, sometimes reflecting earlier historical changes. Depending on the phonological environment, the 'altered' segment may appear either in the basic form of a word or in a derived form. I shall here describe only some of the more general processes producing alternations.

(a) When followed by a front vowel, *t*, *s* and *z* palatalise to *c*, *sh* and *j*, respectively, e.g. *sáatàa* 'stealing', *sàacé* 'stolen'; *dùkùshíi* 'colt', pl. *dùkùsái*; *mijìi* 'husband/ male', pl. *mázáa* or *mázàajée*. The palatalisation rule does not apply automatically to recent loanwords, e.g. *tíitìi* 'street' (from English via Yoruba); *láfàzìi* 'pronunciation' (from Arabic). The voiced stop *d* also changes to *j* (with resulting neutralisation of the *d/z* contrast), but this change is not as regular as with the other alveolars, even in native words and constructions, e.g. *gídáa* 'house', pl. *gídàajée*; cf. *kádàa* 'crocodile', pl. *kádóodíi*; *kúdù* 'south', *bàkúdèe* 'southerner'. Palatalisation also affects velars, but it is not reflected in the orthography except in the case of the *w/y* alternation, e.g. *ɓàráawòo* 'thief', pl. *ɓàraayíi*.

(b) As indicated above, long vowels are automatically shortened in closed syllables. At normal speech tempos, resultant short *e* and *o* merge with short *a*, e.g. *dárée-n-nàn* → *dáránnàn* 'this night'; *kánóo-ncíi* → *kánáncíi* 'Kano dialect'. The original quality of the vowel often shows up as palatalisation or labialisation of the preceding consonant, e.g. *dàshée-n-sù* → *dàshánsù* 'their seedlings' (cf. *dásàa* 'transplant seedlings'); *gêefáa* → *gyâffáa* 'sides' (pl. of *géefèe*); *ƙóon-ƙòonáa* → *ƙwán-ƙòonáa* 'keep on burning'.

(c) In syllable-final position, obstruents historically underwent a series of lenition changes known as Klingenheben's Law (see Newman 2004). Velar and bilabial stops (the latter in Eastern dialects only and even there in incomplete fashion) weakened to *u* (with subsequent simplification of the diphthong *iu* to *uu*), e.g. *tálàkà* 'commoner', *táláucìi* 'poverty'; *búuzúu* 'Tuareg serf', pl. *búgàajée*; *júujíi* (< **júujíí*) 'rubbish heap', pl. *jíbàajée*. (Note that some of these synchronically irregular plurals are nowadays being replaced by more transparent forms such as *búuzàayée* and *júujàayée*.) The bilabial change also applied to *m*, but only when the abutting consonant was an alveolar sonorant, e.g. *'áurée* 'marriage', cf. *'ámáryáa* 'bride'.

(d) In syllable-final position, alveolar stops change to *r̃*, e.g. *fáɗäkár̃* 'wake up, enlighten', *fár̃kàa* 'wake up' (intransitive); *ɓátà* 'spoil', *ɓàr̃náa* 'destruction'; *káɗà* = *kâr̃* 'prohibitive marker'. This change both took place at a historically earlier period and is still operative synchronically. The rhotacism also applies to alveolar sibilants but only in the context of reduplication, e.g. *mázá* 'quickly', *mázámázá* = *már̃mázá* 'very quickly'; *tùmùs-músàa* → *tùmùr̃músàa* 'wallow in the dirt'.

(e) In reduplicative constructions, syllable final velars and labials form geminates with the following consonant rather than undergoing Klingenheben's Law, e.g. *zàaf-záafáa* → *zàzzáafáa* 'very hot' (not **zàuzáafáa*), *sáƙ-sàƙáa* → *sássàƙáa* 'carve'. Syllable-final alveolar obstruents also undergo gemination but usually as an alternative to rhotacism, e.g. *káɗ-kàɗäa* → *kákkàɗäa* or *kár̃kàɗäa* 'keep beating'.

2.3 Morphology

2.3.1 Pronominal System

The pronominal system distinguishes five categories in the singular (1, 2-masculine, 2-feminine, 3-masculine, 3-feminine) and four in the plural (1-pl., 2-pl., 3-pl. and the so-called '4-pl', which only occurs as an impersonal weak subject pronoun). There is no gender distinction in the plural. Variant pronoun sets, differing primarily in tone and vowel length, are shown in Table 36.3. Their use is determined by surface syntactic position and function.

The independent pronouns (set a) are used as absolute pronouns, e.g. *níi nèe* 'it's me'; as subjects of equational sentences, e.g. *kai yáaròo née* 'you're a boy'; as objects of the particle *dà* 'and/with', e.g. *sún zóo dà 'ítá* 'they came with her', *nii dà kée mún yàr̃dá* 'I and you (we) agree'; as direct objects when not immediately following the verb, e.g. *kàawóo mínì shíi* 'bring me it'; and as fronted, focused forms, e.g. *kée cèe múkà gáníi* 'you (fem.) were the one we saw', *súu nèe súkà tàfì* 'they were the ones who went'. The object pronouns (set b) are used as direct objects of verb 'grades' 1 and 4 (see Section 2.3.2 below for a discussion of the grade system), e.g. *náa kár̃àntáa sú* 'I read them'. Pronouns of the same form are also used as subjects of the verboid *zâa* 'be going', e.g. *zâa tá kàasúwáa* 'she's going to market', and of the negative particle *bâa*, e.g. *bâa shí dà táawùl* 'he doesn't have a towel' (lit. 'there-is-not him with towel').

The object clitics (set c) are used as direct objects of other verb grades, e.g. *náa tàmbàyée sù* 'I asked them', and as object of the common word *'àkwái* 'there is/are', e.g. *'àkwái sù dà yáwàa* 'there are many of them' (lit. 'there-are them with many'). The forms in set d are bound to the indirect object marker *má-* (with an assimilatory vowel), e.g. *másà, mínì, múkù* 'to him, to me, to you (pl.)'. The forms in set e are used with the gender-sensitive linkers *n(a)* (masculine and plural) and *ta/r̃* (fcmininc), c.g. *náakà* 'yours' (masculine or plural referent), *líttáafìnkà* 'your book', *táasù* 'theirs' (feminine referent), *móotàr̃sù* 'their car'. The first person is slightly irregular, e.g. *nàawá/tàawá* 'mine', *líttáafìináa* (-náa = ná + á) 'my book', *móotàatáa* (-táa = tá + á) 'my car'.

Hausa TAMs, which reflect tense, aspect, mood and aktionsart, or a combination thereof, are indicated by a marker attached in preverbal position to a weak subject pronoun. Some of the markers are clearly segmentable whereas others consist only of tone or vowel length modifications of the basic pronoun. In the case of the subjunctive, the marker is ∅. Thus it has become the convention in Hausa studies to treat the pronoun plus marker as a fused tense/aspect pronoun, also referred to as a person/aspect complex; see Table 36.4. Negative tense/aspect pronouns, which differ from the corresponding affirmative ones, are listed separately. Apart from the continuous, which uses a single negative marker *báa*, and the subjunctive, which uses a prohibitive particle *kádà*, verbal sentences are negated by means of a discontinuous morpheme *bà(a) ... bá*. The meanings of the tenses are roughly deducible from their labels and will not be

Table 36.3 Independent, Object and Possessive Pronouns

	a	b	c	d	e
1	níi	ní	-nì	-nì	-(w)á
2 m.	kái	ká	-kà	-kà	-kà
2 f.	kée	kí	-kì	-kì	-kì
3 m.	shíi	shí	-shì	-sà/shì	sà/shì
3 f.	'ítá	tá	-tà	-tà	-tà
1 pl.	múu	mú	-mù	-nà	-mù
2 pl.	kúu	kú	-kù	-kù	-kù
3 pl.	súu	sú	-sù	-sù	-sù

Note: a = independent; b = object pronoun; c = object clitic; d = indirect object; e = possessive

Table 36.4 Tense/Aspect Pronouns

	a	b	c	d	e	f	g	h	i	j
1	náa	ná	bàn...bá	zân	nâa	nákàn	'ìn	'ńnàa	nákè(e)	báanàa
2m.	káa	ká	bàkà...bá	záakà	kâa	kákàn	kà	kánàa	kákè(e)	báakàa
2f.	kín	kíkà	bàkì...bá	záakì	kyâa	kíkàn	kì	kínàa	kíkè(e)	báakyàa
3m.	yáa	yá	bài...bá	zâi	yâa	yákàn	yà	yánàa	yákè(e)	báayàa
3f.	táa	tá	bàtà...bá	záatà	tâa	tákàn	tà	tánàa	tákè(e)	báatàa
1pl.	mún	múkà	bàmù...bá	záamù	mâa	múkàn	mù	múnàa	múkè(e)	báamàa
2pl.	kún	kúkà	bàkù...bá	záakù	kwâa	kúkàn	kù	kúnàa	kúkè(e)	báakwàa
3pl.	sún	súkà	bàsù...bá	záasù	sâa	súkàn	sù	súnàa	súkè(e)	báasàa
4pl.	'án	'ákà	bà'à...bá	záa'à	'âa	'ákàn	'à	'ánàa	'ákè(e)	báa'àa

Notes: a = completive; b = preterit; c = neg completive; d = future; e = potential future; f = habitual; g = subjunctive; h = continuous; i = rel continuous; j = neg continuous.

discussed. A syntactic alternation involving the completive and the preterit and the two continuous TAMs is described in Section 2.4.

Except for the imperative, which is marked by low–high tone (sometimes plus a final vowel change), the verb itself is not conjugated, tense, person and number being shown by the tense/aspect pronoun, e.g. *náa záunàa* 'I sat'; *bà nâa záunàa bá* 'I don't intend to sit'; *záamù záunàa* 'we will sit'; *mù záunàa* 'let's sit'; *tákàn káamàa sú* 'she catches them'; *tánàa káamàa sú* 'she is catching them'; cf. *zàunáa* 'sit!'; *kàamáa sú* 'catch them!'

2.3.2 Verbal Morphology

Verbal morphology reflects the verb's 'grade' and its syntactic environment. The morphological distinctiveness in each category is defined in terms of the verb's final vowel (or -VC) and overall tone. The pattern for each grade, indicated for two- and three-syllable verbs, is presented in Table 36.5.

Grade 1 contains basic transitive verbs with underlying final -*a* as well as derived 'applicatives' (often required with indirect objects). Like the efferential (grade 5), grade 1 applicatives serve to transitivise intransitive verbs, e.g. *sún hákà ráamìi* 'they dug a hole' (basic); *kà fàdàa mánà gàskiyáa* 'you should tell us the truth' (applicative); *tánàa cíkà tùulúu* 'she is filling the pot' (applicative). Grade 2 contains basic transitive verbs with underlying final -*i* as well as derived verbs with a partitive sense, e.g. *hàkà fàdî gáskiyáa bá* 'you didn't tell the truth' (basic); *mù yànkí náamàa* 'let's cut off some meat' (partitive). Grade 3 is an exclusively intransitive grade containing verbs with underlying final -*a*, e.g. *fìtá* 'go out'; *cìká* 'be filled'. Grade 4 ('totality') indicates an action totally done or affecting all the objects, e.g. *rúwáa yáa zúbèe* 'the water all spilled out'; *záamù sáyè shìnkáafàa* 'we will buy up the rice'. When used with an indirect object, grade 4 often has a malefactive or deprivative sense. With many verbs, especially when used intransitively, Grade 4 is becoming a basic, semantically neutral form. Grade 5 ('efferential'), traditionally called 'causative' in early grammars, indicates action away from the speaker. It also serves to transitivise inherently intransitive verbs, e.g. *yáa 'áurár̃ dà 'yáa tásà* 'he married off his daughter'; *táa fítár̃* 'she took (it) out'. Note that Grade 5, whose suffix -*ar̃* derives historically from *-*as*, is the only grade that ends in a consonant. Grade 6 ('ventive') indicates movement in the direction of or for the benefit of the speaker, e.g. *kún sáyóo 'àsháanáa?* 'did you (pl.) buy (and bring) matches?'; *záatà fitóo* 'she will come out'. Grade 7 ('sustentative') indicates an agentless passive (or sometimes middle voice), action well done or the potentiality of

Table 36.5 The Hausa Grade System

	Form A		Form B		Form C	
Grade 1	-aa	H L (H)	-aa	H L (H)	-a	H L (L)
Grade 2	-aa	L H (L)	-ee	(L) L H	-i	(L) L H
Grade 3	-a	L H (L)	—			—
Grade 4	-ee	H L (H)	-ee	H L (H)	{ -e	H L (L) }
					{ -ee	H L (H) }
Grade 5	-ar̃	H H (H)	-shee	H H (H)		—
Grade 6	-oo	H H (H)	-oo	H H (H)	oo	H H (H)
Grade 7	-u	(L) L H	—			—

sustaining action, e.g. *náamàa yáa gàsú* 'the meat has been roasted'; *'àgóogó báayàa gyàarúwáa* 'the watch is not repairable'. Hausa has a small number of high-frequency monosyllabic verbs, e.g. *bí* 'follow', *cí* 'eat', *jáa* 'pull', *sháa* 'drink', *sóo* 'want'. These do not fit into grades 1, 2 or 3, but they do appear in the other grades (with slightly variant forms), e.g. *yáa shânyè rúwáa* 'he drank up the water' (gr. 4); *múkàn cíishée sù* 'we feed them' (gr. 5); *jàawóo nân* 'pull (it) here' (gr. 6); *hányàa tâa bìyú* 'the road will be passable' (gr. 7). Most scholars now incorporate these verbs into the grade system as grade ∅.

Cross-cutting the grades, verbs have three syntactically determined forms (omitting the pre-indirect object position, which poses special problems). Form B is used when the verb is immediately followed by a personal pronoun direct object. Form C is used when the verb is followed by any other direct object. Form A is used elsewhere, e.g.

táa tàimàkí Múusáa	'she helped Musa'	(gr. 2, C)
táa tàimàkée shì	'she helped him'	(gr. 2, B)
Múusáa nèe tá tàimákàa	'it was Musa she helped'	(gr. 2, A)
mún kářàntà jàříidàa	'we read the newspaper'	(gr. 1, C)
mún kářàntáa tá	'we read it'	(gr. 1, B)
wàccée kúkà kářàntáa?	'which did you (pl.) read?'	(gr. 1, A)

Grade 5 ('efferential') verbs do not have a C form since its semantic objects are expressed as oblique objects introduced by the particle *dà* (the same as or homophonous with the preposition *dà* 'with'), e.g. *yánàa kóoyář dà Háusá* 'he is teaching Hausa'. With object pronouns, one may use either the B form plus a pronominal clitic or the A form with the oblique object, e.g. *yáa cíishée tà = yáa cíyář dà 'ítá* 'he fed her'. Some verbs allow a short form variant without the suffix *-ář* before *dà*, e.g. *táa zúb dà rúwáa = táa zúbář dà rúwáa* 'she poured out the water'.

2.3.3 Verbal Nouns

While verbs as such are not inflected for tense, in the continuous tenses they are subject to replacement by verbal-nominal forms, of which there are three general classes: (1) weak verbal nouns (`-wáa* forms), (2) inflectional verbal nouns, (3) base-derived verbal nouns. (1) When no object is expressed, verbs of grades 1, 4, 5, 6 and 7 use a present participial-like stem formed with the suffix `-wáa, (i.e. *wáa* preceded by a floating low tone), e.g. *tánàa rúfèewáa* 'she is closing (it)', cf. *tánàa rúfè táagàa* 'she is closing the window'; *báasàa kóomôowáa* 'they are not returning', cf. *bàsù kóomóo bá* 'they didn't return'; *báasàa gyàarúwáa* 'they are not repairable'. (2) Grades 2 and 3 form verbal nouns by means of a suffix *-aa* or by vowel length, e.g. *Múusáa nèe yákèe fìtáa* 'It's Musa who is going out', cf. *Múusáa nèe yá fìtá* 'It's Musa who went out'. Grade ∅ verbs form verbal nouns by vowel length (which operates vacuously if the final vowel is already long) plus low tone, e.g. *yánàa sôo* 'he wants (it)'. If these verbal nouns are followed by an object, they take a connecting linker (*-n* or *-ř*) and the 'object' pronoun is represented by a possessive form, e.g. *múnàa cîn náamàa* 'we are eating meat', cf. *mún cí náamàa* 'we ate meat'; *tánàa tàmbáyàřsà* 'she is asking him', cf. *táa tàmbàyée shì* 'she asked him'. (3) Many verbs have lexically related verbal nouns that are used instead of or as an optional alternative to verbs or other verbal nouns. Like inflectional verbal nouns, these forms require a linker before expressed objects. The shape of base-derived verbal nouns is lexically specific and cannot be predicted from the form of the related verb. The following are some of the more common formation patterns:

(a) *-ii* H L: *gínìi* 'building'; *dínkìi* 'sewing'
(b) *-ee* L H: *sàyée* 'buying'; *bìncìkée* 'investigating'
(c) *-aa* H H: *gyáaráa* 'repairing'; *néemáa* 'seeking'
(d) *-oo* (variable): *cíizòo* 'biting'; *kòoyóo* 'learning'
(e) Ablaut H L: *jíimàa* 'tanning' (cf. *jéemàa* 'tan'); *súukàa* 'piercing' (cf. *sòokáa* 'pierce').

Finally, before leaving verbal morphology, two regular deverbal constructions should be mentioned. Adverbs of state are formed from verb stems by means of a suffix *-e* (with short vowel) and an L H tone pattern, e.g. *zàuné* 'seated', *dàfé* 'cooked', *wàřwàatsé* 'scattered'. Past participial adjectives are formed from verbs by reduplicating the stem-final consonant in geminate form and adding a suffix *-ee* (masculine), *-iyaa* (feminine), with L H H tone, or *-uu* (plural), with L L H tone, e.g. *dàfáffée* (m.), *dàfáffíyáa* (f.), *dàfáffúu* (pl.) 'cooked', *gàagàrárrée*, *gàagàrárríyáa*, *gàagàràrrúu* 'obstinate, rebellious'.

2.3.4 Nominal Morphology

The major parameters in nominal morphology are gender and number. Hausa has two genders, masculine and feminine, morphologically and grammatically distinguished in the singular only. Masculine words are generally unmarked, ending in consonants and in all five vowels. e.g. *téebùř* 'table', *kíifìi* 'fish', *zóobèe* 'ring', *bàkáa* 'bow', *nóonòo* 'breast', *tùulúu* 'pot'. With few exceptions, e.g. *màcè* 'woman', feminine words end in *-aa*, *-(i)yaa* or *-(u)waa*, e.g. *kúuráa* 'hyena', *múndúwáa* 'anklet', *kíbíyàa* 'arrow', *kàazáa* 'hen', *túbúryáa* 'pestle'. Adjectives are inflected for gender and number, the feminine being formed from the masculine by the addition of *-aa* (with automatic glide insertion where required), and the plural employing one of the normal nominal formations, e.g. *fáríi* (m.), *fáráa* (f.), *fáràarée* (pl.) 'white'; *shúudìi*, *shúudìyáa*, *shûddáa* 'blue'; *dóogóo*, *dóogúwáa*, *dóogwàayée* 'tall'; *sàatáccée*, *sàatácciyáa*, *sàatàttúu* 'stolen'.

At the derivational level, many feminine counterparts to masculine humans and animals make use of a suffix *-n(i)yaa*, e.g. *yáaròo*, *yáarínyàa* 'boy, girl'; *màkáahòo*, *màkáuniyáa* 'blind man, woman', *bírìi*, *bírínyàa* 'monkey m./f.' Other male/female pairs use the inflectional *-aa* suffix, e.g. *jàakíi*, *jàakáa* 'donkey m./f.'; *kàrée*, *kàryáa* 'dog, bitch'.

Nominal plurals represent one of the most complex areas of Hausa morphology. On the surface there are some forty different plural formations making use of infixes, suffixes, reduplication, etc. If, however, one focuses on tone and final vowel, the various plurals can be grouped into a manageable number of basic patterns, see Table 36.6. Although the plural of any given word is not totally predictable, there are correlations and restrictions that hold. For example, almost all singular words that have type (2) plurals have H H tone – but not all H H singulars have type (2) plurals – whereas type (3) plurals are limited to H L singulars. Within type (2), the variant manifestations of the plural are determined by canonical syllabic structure. If the singular has a light first syllable, it takes a reduplicated plural; if it has an initial open heavy syllable, it takes a glide-containing suffix; if it has an initial closed syllable, it takes an infixing plural. Since there is no one-to-one fit between singulars and plurals, it is not surprising that

Table 36.6 Common Plural Patterns

Type	Plural	Singular	Gloss
(1) ooCii	gúnóoníi	gúnàa	'melon'
All H	tsáróokíi	tsárkìyáa	'bowstring'
	túmáakíi	túmkìyáa	'sheep'
(2) aa...ee	fágàagée	fágée	'field'
H L H	zóomàayée	zóomóo	'hare'
	kásàakée	káskóo	'bowl'
(3) aa...aa	sířàadáa	sířdìi	'saddle'
H L H	sâssáa	sáashèe	'section'
	yâaráa	yáaròo	'boy'
(4) uKaa	rìigúnàa	rìigáa	'gown'
H H L	cíkúnkúnàa	cíkìi	'belly'
[K = n, k, w or C$_{final}$]	gáařúkàa	gàařúu	'wall'
	yáazúuzúkàa	yáajìi	'spice'
	gárúurúwàa	gàríi	'town'
	cóokúlàa	cóokàlíi	'spoon'
(5) Kii/Kuu	wàtànníi	wátàa	'moon, month'
L L H	gòonàkíi	góonáa	'farm'
	ràanàikúu	ráanáa	'sun, day'
(6) ee...aKii	gářèemáníi	gàřmáa	'plough'
H L H H	gáawàwwákíi	gáawáa	'corpse'
	márèemáríi	mármáráa	'laterite'
(7) ii/uu	bàrèeyíi	bàréewáa	'gazelle'
L L H	jèemàagúu	jéemáagèe	'bat'
	màgàngànúu	màgánàa	'speech'
(8) ai	kùnkùrái	kùnkúrúu	'tortoise'
L L H	dùbbái	dúbúu	'thousand'
	fikàafikái	fìffìkèe	'wing'
(9) Final vowel change	yáatsúu	yáatsàa	'finger'
...H	máasúu	máashìi	'spear'
	'ářnáa	'ářnèe	'pagan'
	mázáa	míjìi	'husband, male'
	bírái	bírìi	'monkey'
	cínái	cínyàa	'thigh'
	kàajíi	kàazáa	'hen'
	bàaƙíi	bàaƙóo	'stranger'

many words allow more than one plural, e.g. *léeɓèe* 'lip', pl. *lâɓɓáa* or *léeɓúnàa*; *ɓéeřáa* 'rat', pl. *ɓéeřàayée* or *ɓéeřàřřákii*. An ongoing process in Hausa is the treatment of historically original plurals as singulars, with the subsequent formation of new plurals. In some cases the original singular form has to be postulated; in others, it still exists as a dialect variant, e.g. *dúmáa* 'gourd' (orig. pl. of *dúmèe*), pl. *dúmàamée*; *háƙóoríi* 'tooth' (orig. pl. of **háƙrèe* still found as *háurèe*), pl. *háƙòoráa*; *gídáa* 'home' (orig. pl. of *gíjìi*), pl. *gídàajée*.

Hausa has a number of productive and semi-productive nominal derivational constructions, some using prefixes, others using suffixes, some using both.

(a) Ethnonymics, indicating a person's geographical or ethnic origin, social position or, less often, occupation are formed with a prefix *ba-* in the singular and a suppletive suffix -*aawaa* in the plural, e.g. *bàháushèe, bàháushìyáa, hàusàawáa* 'Hausa man, woman, people'.

(b) Agentials are formed from verbs using a prefix *ma-*, a widespread Afroasiatic formative, e.g. *mánòomíi, mánóomìyáa, mánòomáa* 'farmer (m./f./pl.)'.

(c) Instrumentals use the same *ma-* prefix as agentials, but with a different tone pattern and different plural formation, e.g. *mábúuɗíi, màbùuɗái* 'opener (m./pl.)'.

(d) Locationals use the same *ma-* prefix, but are usually feminine and end in -*aa*, e.g. *má'áikátáa, mà'àikàtái* 'work-place (f./pl.)'.

(e) Language names take a suffix -*(n)cii* and an all H tone pattern, e.g. *láařábcíi* 'Arabic', *kánáncíi* 'Kano dialect' (but not **háusáncíi*, the language name being *háusá*).

(f) Abstract nouns make use of an array of related -*(n)taa* and -*(n)cii* suffixes with varying tones, e.g. *bàutáa* 'slavery', *gájártàa* 'shortness', *gùrgùntáa* 'lameness', *gwàníntàa* 'expertise', *fátáucìi* 'commerce', *súusáncìi* 'foolishness'. Another suffix -*(n)tákàa* is sometimes used instead of or in addition to the above, e.g. *shèegàntákàa* 'rascality', *jàařùntákàa* = *jáarúntàa* 'bravery', but *mùtùntákàa* 'human nature' ≠ *mútúncìi* 'humaneness, decency'.

(g) Mutuality or reciprocity is indicated by a suffix -*áyyàa* and/or -*éenìyáa*, e.g. *'àuràtáyyàa* 'intermarriage', *bùgáyyàa* = *bùgággéenìyáa* 'hitting one another', *yàřjéejéenìyáa* 'mutual consent'.

2.4 Syntax

2.4.1 The Noun Phrase

The key to the Hausa noun phrase is the 'NP–of NP' construction, e.g. *kàaká-n yáaròo* 'the boy's grandfather' (lit. 'grandfather-of boy'); *móotà-ř-kù* 'your car' (lit. 'car-of you (pl.)'); *móotóocí-n sárkíi* 'the chief's cars' (lit. 'cars-of chief'). The 'linker', as it is called by Hausaists, has two forms: -*n* (a contraction of *na*) and *ř* (a contraction and modification of *ta*). The former is used if the first noun is masculine or plural or ends in a vowel other than -*a*; the latter is used if the first noun is feminine singular *and* ends in -*a*. In all cases, the gender of the second nominal is irrelevant. Constructions with the linker have a wide variety of uses, as can be seen from the following typical examples: *bángón ɗáakìi* 'wall of the room', *gàbán mákářántáa* 'in front of the school', *ɗáyářsù* 'one of them', *'yáa'yán 'ìtàacée* 'fruit' (lit. 'offspring of tree'), *jírgín sámà* 'aeroplane' (lit. 'vehicle of sky'), *'úwář rìigáa* 'body (lit. 'mother') of a robe'. The linker also serves to connect a noun and a following demonstrative, e.g. *jàakín nàn* 'this (here) donkey', *túnkìyâř nán* 'this (previously referred to) sheep', *dàwàakán càn* 'those horses', and, as mentioned earlier, to connect verbal nouns with their semantic objects.

There are a number of ways of expressing what in English are translated as adjectival modifiers. One means is to use 'true adjectives' before the modified noun in a linking construction, e.g. *fárí-n zánèe* 'white cloth', *fárá-ř rìigáa* 'white robe', *fàsàssú-n kwálàabée* 'broken bottles'. Alternatively (under poorly understood conditions) the adjective can occur to the right of the noun without the use of the linker, e.g. *zánèe fáríi, rìigáa fáráa, kwálàabée fàsàssúu*. Attributive cardinal numerals only occur in this post-nominal position, e.g. *jàakíi ɗáyá* 'one donkey', *máatáa 'úkù* 'three women', *máyàaƙáa dúbúu* 'a thousand warriors' (cf. *dúbú-n máyàaƙáa* 'thousands of warriors'). Ordinals also occur to the right of the noun, but make use of a linker (usually non-contracted), e.g.

ƙár̃nìi ná 'àshìr̃ín 'twentieth century', *'àláamàa tá bíyú* 'the second sign'. Modifiers are also commonly expressed by use of *mài/màasú* 'owner, possessor of (sg./pl)' plus an abstract qualitative nominal, e.g. *ríijìyáa mài zúrfíi* 'a deep well' (cf. *zúrfìntà* 'its depth'), *léebùr̃óor̃ìi màasú ƙárfíi* 'strong labourers'. This construction has a negative counterpart using *màr̃àr̃/màr̃àsáa*, e.g. *ríijìyáa màr̃àr̃ zúrfíi* 'a not deep well', *léebùr̃óor̃ìi màr̃àsáa ƙárfíi* 'not strong labourers'.

Hausa lacks an exact equivalent of the English definite and indefinite articles. The bare noun *yáaròo* could mean 'a boy' or 'the boy' depending on the context. To specifically indicate that a word has been previously referred to or is the thing in question, there is a suffix identical in segmental shape to the linker but with inherent low tone: *`-n* (m./pl.), *`-r̃* (f.), e.g. *yáaròn* 'the boy in question', *túnkìyár̃* 'the sheep in question', *mútàanên* 'the men referred to'. To indicate particularised indefiniteness, Hausa uses the words *wání*, *wátá*, *wású* (= *wáɗànsú*) 'some (m./f./pl.)', e.g. *wání yáaròo yánàa kúukáa* 'a/some boy is crying'; *wású bàaƙíi súnàa jírànkà* 'some strangers are waiting for you'.

2.4.2 The Sentence

Hausa has four main sentence types, which can be labelled (a) verbal, (b) tensed nonverbal, (c) existential, and (d) equational.

(a) Verbal sentences have the core structure subject, tense/aspect pronoun, verb, indirect object, direct object or locative goal, instrumental, e.g. *yáaròo yánàa gáyàa másà làabáar̃ìi* 'the boy (he) is telling him the news'; *máháukácìyáa táa káshèe shí dà wúƙáa* 'the crazy woman (she) killed him with a knife', *wàkìilái záasù kóomàa ƙásár̃sù* 'the representatives will return to their countries'. Conditionals, temporals and other complement phrases and clauses occur both before and after the core, e.g. *'ín káa yàr̃dá záamù záunàa nân sái táa zóo* 'if you agree we will sit here until she comes'. In sentences without overt subjects, the tense/aspect pronoun translates as the subject, but syntactically it should not be thought of as such. Thus the sentence *yáa húutàa* 'he rested' has the structure $\emptyset_{subj}$ *yáa húutàa* parallel to the sentence *yáaròo yáa húutàa* 'the boy rested'. The TAMs with the segmentally full markers *nàa*, *kèe* and *kàn* do not require the third person pronominal element if an overt subject is present, e.g. *mútàanée (sú)nàa bínsà* 'the men are following him', *dón mèe yáarínyàa (tá)kèe kúukáa?* 'why is the girl crying?'

The normal position for the indirect object is immediately following the verb and before the direct object. Indirect object pronouns are formed with *má-*; indirect object nouns make use of a prepositional element *wà* or *mà*, e.g. *tóocìlàn táa mácèe mánà* 'the flashlight died on us', *kádà kà káawóo wà ɗàanáa bíndígàa* 'don't bring my son a gun'. A long and complex indirect object is likely to be expressed as a prepositional phrase occurring after the direct object. The preposition used in this case is *gà*, etymologically probably the same as *wà*, e.g. *náa núunà tákàr̃dáa gà mùtúmìn dà ná gàmú dà shíi 'à ƙóofàa* 'I showed the letter to the man I met (lit. 'man that I met with him') at the door'. Compare the normal *náa núunàa wà mùtúmìn tákàr̃dáa* 'I showed the man the letter'.

Focused elements are fronted, as is the case with most question words. One consequence (shared with relativisation) is the obligatory substitution of the preterit and rel-continuous for the corresponding completive and continuous TAMs, e.g. *mèe súkà sàyáa?* 'what did they buy?', cf. *sún sàyí kíifíi* 'they bought fish'; *wàa yákèe kíɗàa?*

'who is drumming?' cf. *Múusáa yánàa kídầa* 'Musa is drumming'; *'ítá cèe ná gáyàa wà* 'it was she I told', cf. *náa gáyàa mátà* 'I told her'. Another consequence is the use of resumptive pronouns to fill the place of fronted instrumentals and (optionally) indirect objects, e.g. *mèe záamù dầurè ɓàráawòo dà shíi?* 'what will we tie up the thief with (it)?'; *Hàdíizà múkèe kóoyàa mátà (= kóoyàa wà) túuřáncii* 'it's Hadiza we're teaching (to her) English'.

(b) Tensed nonverbal sentences make use of the continuous tense/aspect pronouns and a non-verbal predicate, of which there are three major types: locative, 'have' and stative, e.g. *múnàa nân* 'we're here'; *Wùdíl báatàa néesà dà Kánòo* 'Wudil is not far from Kano'; *súnàa dà móotàa mài kyâu* 'they have (lit. 'are with') a good car', *kwáalín nàn yánàa dà náuyíi* 'this carton is heavy' (lit. 'is with heaviness'); *'àbíncí yánàa dầfé* 'the food is cooked' (< *dáfầa* 'cook'); *tún jiyà súnàa zàuné 'à kóofầř gídánkà* 'since yesterday they have been sitting at the door of your house' (< *záunàa* 'sit'); *múnàa sàné dà shíi* 'we are aware of it' (< *sánìi* 'know'). As in the case of verbal sentences, fronting of a questioned or focused element in these sentence types triggers the use of rel-continuous tense/aspect pronouns, e.g. *'ìnáa súkè yànzú?* 'where are they now?'; *mèe kákè dà shíi?* 'what do you have?' (lit. 'what are you with it'); *tùulúu 'à cìké yákè* 'the pot is *filled*' (lit. 'the pot filled it is'). (Note that the form of the rel-continuous differs slightly here in having a short final vowel.)

As a general rule, Hausa is a language with fairly fixed word order. Changes from normal order occur for specific grammatical or pragmatic purposes such as when questioned or focused elements are fronted. Hausa does not deviate from normal word order in yes–no questions. These are indicated simply by a question tag (such as *kóo* 'or' or *fà* 'what about?') or by question intonation (consisting in part of an old question morpheme now reflected only as vowel length often with low tone), e.g. *Múusáa zâi yàřdá kóo?* 'Musa will agree, right?'; *bàakíi sún fitâa?* 'did the guests go out?' (*fitâa* = *fitá* + `:), cf. *bàakíi sún fitá* 'the guests went out'.

(c) Existential sentences, which are high frequency in the language, are formed with the word *'àkwái* 'there is/there are' and the negative counterpart *bâa* (or *báabù*) 'there's not', e.g. *'àkwái 'àbíncí mài dáadíi* 'there is delicious food'; *bâa 'isásshén kúdíi* 'there is not enough money'.

(d) Equational sentences have the structure (NP) NP *nee/cee* (with polar tone), where *nee* has masculine and plural agreement and *cee* (< **tee*) has feminine agreement, e.g. *shíi sóojà née* 'he is a soldier', *móotầř nân sáabúwáa cèe* 'this car is new'. These sentences are negated by sandwiching the second noun phrase between *bàa ... bá*, e.g. *shíi bàa sóojà bá nèe* 'he is not a soldier', *móotầř nân bàa sáabúwáa bá cèe* 'this car is not new'. If the first noun phrase is missing, one has an identificational sentence comparable to English 'it's a ...', e.g. *kàrée nèe* 'it's a dog'; *bàa tàawá bá cèe* 'it's not mine'. Equational sentences are not marked for tense; thus the preceding sentence could equally mean 'it wasn't mine'.

Bibliography

Newman (1977), which builds on Newman and Ma (1966), is the standard work on Chadic classification and on the reconstruction of Proto-Chadic, whereas Newman (1980) provides the basis for the membership of Chadic within the Afroasiatic phylum. Three solid reference grammars of Hausa are Wolff (1993), Newman (2000) and Jaggar (2001). The classic grammar of Abraham (1959), which dates back to 1940, is still worth consulting. Parsons (1981) is an invaluable collection of papers and lecture notes by the leading Hausaist of his time. A translation of Klingenheben's Law with commentary is provided in Newman (2004). Abraham (1962) and Bargery (1934) are outstanding comprehensive Hausa–English dictionaries. The English–Hausa dictionary of R.M. Newman (1990) contains a wealth of illustrative examples, all accurately marked for tone and vowel length. A Hausa–English counterpart to this dictionary is now available (Newman 2007). A convenient pocket dictionary is Awde (1996). For a fully comprehensive bibliography of works on Chadic and Hausa up to the time of its publication, see Newman (1996).

References

Abraham, R.C. 1959. *The Language of the Hausa People* (University of London Press, London)
—— 1962. *Dictionary of the Hausa Language*, 2nd edn (University of London Press, London)
Awde, N. 1996. *Hausa–English English–Hausa Dictionary* (Hippocrene Books, New York)
Bargery, G.P. 1934. *A Hausa–English Dictionary and English–Hausa Vocabulary* (Oxford University Press, London; reprint with supplement and new introduction by A.N. Skinner, Ahmadu Bello University Press, Zaria, 1993)
Jaggar, P.J. 2001. *Hausa*. London Oriental and African Language Library, 7 (John Benjamins, Amsterdam)
Newman, P. 1977. *Chadic Classification and Reconstructions* (Undena, Malibu, Calif.)
—— 1980. *The Classification of Chadic within Afroasiatic* (Universitaire Pers, Leiden)
—— 1996. *Hausa and the Chadic Language Family: A Bibliography* (African Linguistic Bibliographies, 6). (Rüdiger Köppe Verlag, Cologne)
—— 2000. *The Hausa Language: An Encyclopedic Reference Grammar* (Yale University Press, New Haven)
—— 2004. *Klingenheben's Law in Hausa*. Chadic Linguistics, 2 (Rüdiger Köppe Verlag, Cologne)
—— 2007. *A Hausa–English Dictionary* (Yale University Press, New Haven)
Newman, P. and Ma, R. 1966. 'Comparative Chadic: Phonology and Lexicon', *Journal of African Languages*, vol. 5, pp. 218–51.
Newman, R.M. 1990. *An English–Hausa Dictionary* (Yale University Press, New Haven)
Parsons, F.W. 1981. *Writings on Hausa Grammar*, ed. G. Furniss, 2 vols (School of Oriental and African Studies, London)
Wolff, Ekkehard. 1993. *Referenzgrammatik des Hausa*. Hamburger Beiträge zur Afrikanistik, 2 (Lit, Münster and Hamburg)

37

Tamil and the Dravidian languages

Sanford B. Steever

1 The Dravidian Languages

The Dravidian language family, the world's fourth largest, consists of twenty-five languages spread over the South Asian subcontinent. It has four branches: South Dravidian with Tamil, Malayāḷam, Iruḷa, Koḍagu, Kota, Toda, Badaga, Kannaḍa and Tulu; South-Central Dravidian with Telugu, Savara, Goṇḍi, Koṇḍa, Pengo, Manḍa, Kūi and Kūvi; Central Dravidian with Kolami, Naiki, Parji, Ollari and Gadaba; and North Dravidian with Kūṟux, Malto and Brahui. Reports of other languages have appeared, but without adequate grammars we cannot determine whether these are new independent languages or simply dialects of ones already known. Indu and Āwē have been reported in South-Central Dravidian; Kuruba, Yerava, Yerukula, Kaikuḍi, Korava, Koraga, Bellari and Burgundi in South Dravidian. Certain dialects of Goṇḍi and Kūṟux may prove under closer inspection to be independent languages. The Dravidian languages are spoken by approximately 220,000,000 people.

Though concentrated in South India (see Map 37.1), the Dravidian languages are also found in Maharashtra, Madhya Pradesh, Orissa, West Bengal and Bihar; and, outside India, in Sri Lanka, Pakistan, Nepal and the Maldives. The Dravidian languages share the South Asian subcontinent with three other language families: the Indo-Aryan branch of Indo-European, the Munda branch of Austro-Asiatic and Sino-Tibetan. Commerce and colonisation have carried some Dravidian languages, particularly Tamil, beyond South Asia to Burma, Indonesia, Malaysia, Fiji, Madagascar, Mauritius, Guyana, Martinique and Trinidad.

The Eighth Schedule of the Indian Constitution (1951) mandates the creation of states along linguistic lines, and accords official status to four Dravidian languages: Tamil in Tamil Nadu, Malayāḷam in Kerala, Kannaḍa in Karnataka and Telugu in Andhra Pradesh. These four have long histories, recorded in epigraphy and native literatures: Tamil dates from the second century BC; Kannaḍa from the fourth century AD; Telugu from the seventh century AD; and Malayāḷam from the tenth century AD.

Starting with Caldwell's (1875) *Comparative Grammar of the Dravidian Languages*, linguists have reconstructed a fragment of Proto-Dravidian. This fragment incorporates

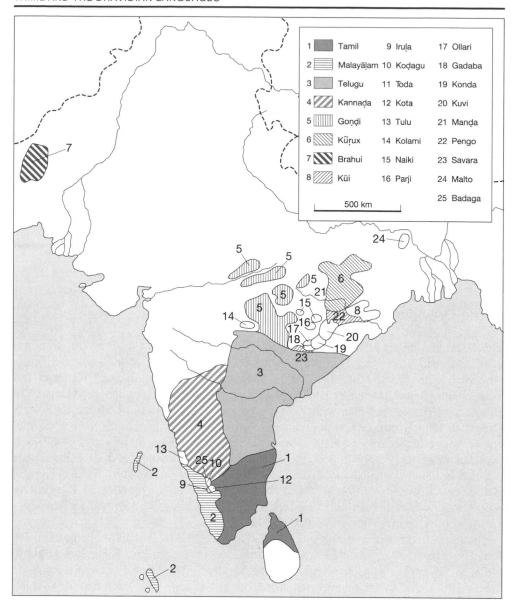

Map 37.1 The Dravidian Languages.

those features the Dravidian languages have in common and may be said to typify what is 'Dravidian' in a language. Proto-Dravidian has ten vowels, five short and five long: *a, ā, i, ī, u, ū, e, ē, o, ō*. It has sixteen consonants, including an unusual system of stops contrasting in six points of articulation: labial, dental, alveolar, retroflex, palatal and velar, viz. *p, t, R, ṭ, c, k*. Four nasals, *m, n, ṇ, ñ*; four resonants, *l, ḷ, r, ẓ*; and two glides, *v, y*, complete the inventory of consonants. Alveolars, retroflexes and resonants do not occur word-initially. Caldwell's Law describes the allophony of stops: they are voiceless when they occur initially or geminated, but voiced when they occur intervocalically or after nasals. Several metrical rules govern the composition of syllables, e.g. $(C_1)\breve{V}C_2$ alternates with $(C_1)\breve{V}C_2C_3$ as in the two stems of the verb 'see', *$k\bar{a}\underline{n}$- vs *$ka\underline{n}\underline{t}$-. Though bisyllabic roots are occasionally indicated, reconstructed lexical roots are by and large monosyllabic. While any of the five vowel qualities may appear in a root, only *a*, *i*, *u* may appear in a derivative suffix.

Dravidian morphology is transparent, agglutinating and exclusively suffixal. The order of elements in a word is: lexical root, derivational suffix, inflectional suffix. Proto-Dravidian has two parts of speech: noun and verb, both of which appear in simple and compound forms. Nouns inflect for case, person, number and gender. Proto-Dravidian has eight cases: nominative, accusative, sociative, dative, genitive, instrumental, locative and ablative. These eight are supplemented by postpositions, derived from independent nouns or non-finite verbs. Predicate nominals can be inflected to agree with their subjects, e.g. in Ancient Tamil -*ōm* marks the first person plural in *nām nāṭṭ-ōm* 'we[1] (are) countrymen[2]'. Proto-Dravidian has two numbers: singular and plural. Proto-Dravidian gender distinguishes animate and inanimate nouns on the basis of the natural gender of the referent, not 'grammatical' or conventional gender. Animate nouns may further be classified as honorific, masculine or feminine. A noun's animacy helps determine other of its grammatical features: animates take the locative case marker *-iṭam*, inanimates *-il*; most animates have the plural marker *-ir*, inanimates *-kaḷ*; the accusative case marker *-ay* is obligatory for animates, but optional for inanimates. The very extensive system of compound nouns can be illustrated by the set of deictic pronouns, which contrast in four degrees: *ivan* 'this man', *uvan* 'that man nearby', *avan* 'that man yonder', *evan* 'which, any man'. These are compound nouns, e.g. *avan* 'that man yonder' consists of the nouns *a-* 'that (one) yonder' and *-(v)an* 'man'. Complex compound nouns are often translated into English as a sequence of numeral, adjective and noun; but the internal structure of these Dravidian expressions is that of a compound noun.

Proto-Dravidian verbs are those forms that inflect for verbal categories such as tense and mood. There are two tenses, past and non-past, and two moods, modal and indicative. From a formal viewpoint verbs are finite or non-finite. Finite verbs inflect for tense and subject–verb agreement. These inflections are overt, or, in the imperative and optative, covert. Proto-Dravidian has a constraint that limits the number of finite verbs in a sentence to a maximum of one: that lone verb stands at the extreme end of the sentence and commands all other verbs within. In effect, it brings the sentence to a close. All remaining verbs in the sentence must be non-finite. The first major set of non-finite verbs is defined as those which combine with a following verb, with or without other grammatical material coming between the two. In this set we find the infinitive, conjunctive participle and conditional. The second major set comprises all those non-finite verbs that combine with a following noun to form relative clauses and similar structures. Dravidian languages rely on a rich system of compound verbs to extend the somewhat limited set of simple verb forms. Lexical compound verbs supplement the lexicon by providing a complex morphosyntactic vehicle for combinations of lexical meanings which are not encoded in any single lexeme of the language. For example, the Tamil lexical compound *koṇṭu vara* 'bring' consists of the conjunctive participle of *koḷḷa* 'hold' and an inflected form of *vara* 'come'. Auxiliary compound verbs, on the other hand, provide morphosyntactic vehicles for those verbal categories which are not encoded in any simple verb form of the language, e.g. perfect tense, benefactive voice. In this colloquial Kannaḍa example the auxiliary verb *iru* 'be' conveys the perfect tense: *nān band(u) iddīni* 'I[1] have[3] come[2]'.

637

The basic word order in the Proto-Dravidian sentence is subject–object–verb (SOV). In Dravidian, as in other rigid SOV languages, genitives precede the nouns they modify, main verbs precede auxiliaries and complements precede their matrix clauses. Though explicit nominal morphology allows some freedom of variation in word order, verbs stay at the end of their clauses. Simple sentences consist of a subject and predicate. The subject is a noun phrase inflected for the nominative or, in certain predictable cases, the dative case; the predicate may be a verb or predicate nominal. Section 2.4 on Tamil syntax below addresses the issue of complex sentences in Dravidian, in particular how finite verbs and predicate nominals can be embedded.

Subsequent developments have naturally altered this picture. For example, metathesis in South-Central Dravidian permits alveolars, retroflexes and resonants to appear initially, e.g. Telugu *lē-* 'young (one)' from **iḷay* 'id.' The influx of Indo-Aryan loanwords has introduced both initial voiced stops and the distinction between aspirated and non-aspirated stops in some languages, e.g. Malayāḷam, Kūṟux. The contrast between the dative and accusative cases has been neutralised in Pengo animate nouns in favour of what historically was the dative. When the joints of auxiliary compound verbs fuse, new conjugations arise, e.g. the Medieval Tamil present tense, the Kūi objective conjugation, the Pengo present perfect tense. The syntactic influence of neighbouring Indo-Aryan languages has reversed the order of complement and matrix in North Dravidian. Thus, Malto *ā loker ṭuṇḍnar tan laboh ote* 'those, people₂ saw₃ that₄ (it) was₆ heavy₅' contrasts with the common Dravidian order in Tamil *kaNamāka irukkiRatu eNRu avarkaḷ pārttārkaḷ* 'they₄ saw₅ that₃ (it) is₂ heavy!' Despite a certain measure of change in phonology and lexicon, Proto-Dravidian morphology and syntax has persisted remarkably well in South, South-Central and Central Dravidian.

2 Tamil

2.1 Historical Background

Tamil (*tamiẕ*) belongs to the South Dravidian branch of the Dravidian family: like other members of this branch it lost Proto-Dravidian **c-*, e.g. *il* 'not be' from **cil-*, *īy-* 'give' from **cīy-*, *āRu* 'six' from **cāRu*; and it replaced the Proto-Dravidian copula **maN* 'be located' with *iru* 'be located'. It has been spoken in southern India and northeastern Sri Lanka from prehistoric times. The earliest records of Tamil, lithic inscriptions in a variety of Aśokan Brāhmī script, date from 200 BC. Alongside these inscriptions stands a vast and varied literature, preserved on palm-leaf manuscripts and by rote memory, covering two thousand years. Within this literary corpus is an indigenous grammatical tradition, separate from the Sanskrit grammarians: its two outstanding texts are *tolkā ppiyam* (c. 200 BC) and *naNNūl* (c. AD 1000). There are three distinct stages of Tamil revealed in these records: Ancient Tamil, 200 BC to AD 700; Medieval Tamil, AD 700 to 1500; and Modern Tamil, AD 1500 to the present.

Ancient Tamil has just two tenses, past and non-past; Medieval and Modern Tamil have three, past, present and future. Ancient Tamil has many subject–verb agreement markers for each member of the paradigm, e.g. the first person singular is signalled by *-ēN, -eN, -aN, -al, -ku, -ṭu, -tu.* But Medieval Tamil retains only the first three, while Modern Tamil keeps only the first. In Ancient and Medieval Tamil, as opposed to their modern successor, predicate nominals can be inflected for subject–verb agreement, so that *-ai* marks the second person singular in *nī nāṭṭ-ai* 'you₁ (are a) countryman₂' while *-ēN* marks the first person singular in *nāN pāvi-(y)ēN* 'I₁ (am a) sinner₂'. In Medieval Tamil the set of verbal bases was open and accommodated many Sanskritic loanwords, e.g. Tamil *aNupavikka* 'to experience', derived from Sanskrit *anubhava* 'experience', but it is closed in Modern Tamil.

Between AD 800 and 1000 the western dialects of Tamil, geographically separated from the eastern by the Western Ghats, broke off and developed into Malayāḷam. Malayāḷam lost its rules of subject–verb agreement while Tamil maintained them, and it welcomed into its lexicon a great number of Sanskrit loanwords. The Iruḷa language, spoken in the hilly spurs of the Nilgiris between Kerala and Tamil Nadu, is also closely related to Tamil.

During the past two thousand years, Tamil dialects have evolved along three dimensions: geography, caste-based society and diglossia. Today there are six regional dialects: (1) Sri Lanka; (2) Northern, spoken in the Chingleput, North Arcot and South Arcot districts; (3) Western, spoken in the Coimbatore, Salem and Dharmapuri districts; (4) Central, spoken in the Tirichirapalli, Tanjore and Madurai districts; (5) Eastern, spoken in the Putukottai and Ramanathapuram districts; and (6) Southern, spoken in the Nagercoil and Tirunelveli districts. Sri Lankan Tamil seems to be the most conservative: it preserves the four-way deictic contrast lost in the continental dialects during the Medieval period, e.g. *ivaN* 'this man', *uvaN* 'that man nearby', *avaN* 'that man yonder', *evaN* 'which, any man'. It still resists the use of initial voiced stops so that continental Tamil *dōcai* 'rice pancake' becomes *tōcai* 'id.' in Sri Lankan Tamil. Throughout its history, but most notably during the Chola Empire, AD 850 to 1250, Tamil travelled beyond South Asia to kingdoms in Burma, Cambodia, Sri Vijāya and Indonesia. During the British Raj of the nineteenth century, it was carried to South Africa, British Guiana and other parts of the British Empire.

The social dialects of Tamil particularly accentuate the distinction between brahmin and non-brahmin castes. Among brahmins the word for 'house' is *ām*, among non-brahmins *vīṭu*; among brahmins the polite imperative of *vara* 'come' is *vāṅkō*, among non-brahmins *vāṅka*. For 'drinking water' Vaisnavite brahmins say *tīrttam*, Saivite brahmins *jalam* and non-brahmins *taṇṇīr*. Even finer gradations of caste dialects can be found in kinship terminology and proper names.

Finally, Tamil dialects show diglossic variation in which a 'high' formal variety (*centamiz*) contrasts with a 'low' informal variety (*koṭuntamiz*). The difference between these two corresponds only roughly to the difference between written and spoken Tamil. The high variety is used in most writing, radio and television broadcasts, political oratory and public lectures. While the low variety is used in virtually all face-to-face communication, it also appears in the cinema, some political oratory and some modern fiction. In Akilan's novel *ciNēkiti* 'The Girl-Friend' (1951), both dialogue and narration are in the high variety; in Janakiraman's *ammā vantāḷ* 'Here Comes Mother' (1966) the former is in low, the latter in high Tamil; and in Jeyakantan's *cila nēraṅkaḷil cila maNitarkaḷ* 'Certain Men at Certain Moments' (1970) both are in low Tamil. In high Tamil the animate and inanimate locative case markers are *-iṭam* and *-il*, respectively; but in low Tamil they are *-kiṭṭa* and *-le*. The polite imperative of *vara* 'come' is *vāruṅkaḷ* in high Tamil, but *vāṅka* or *vāṅkō* in low. The word for 'much' or 'very' is *mika* in high Tamil, but *rompa* in low (both come from the infinitives of verbs that mean 'exceed' or 'fill'). Palatalisation of *-nt-* and *-tt-* following *i*, *ī* or *ai* is common in low Tamil, but not in high, e.g. low *aṭiccu* 'beating' corresponds to high *aṭittu* 'id.' All

639

speakers of Tamil, even illiterates, have recourse to both varieties and, according to the situation, must navigate between the phonological, lexical and grammatical differences that distinguish them.

The Pure Tamil Movement (*taNit tamiz iyakkam*) of the 1900s, a cultural branch of the politically oriented Dravidian Movement, attempted to purge Tamil of its foreign elements, especially its Sanskritic vocabulary. The first part of the legacy of this movement is the intense loyalty that Tamils feel for their language; the second is that the scientific and bureaucratic gobbledygook is ultra-Tamil, not Sanskrit as in other Indic languages. At the turn of the century, the brahmin dialect of Madras City (Chennai) seemed destined to become the standard dialect of Modern Tamil. Today, however, it is the high non-brahmin dialect of the Central dialect, including the cities of Tanjore, Tirichirapalli and Madurai, that is emerging as the standard dialect. This chapter describes modern standard Tamil, which is based upon and shares features of both the written language and the standard spoken Central dialect.

Tamil is recognised as one of India's fourteen national languages in the Eighth Schedule of the Indian Constitution (1951). The Tamil Nadu Official Language Act of 1956 establishes Tamil as the first official language of Tamil Nadu and English as the second. In Sri Lanka, Tamil shares with Sinhalese the title of official language. Today, Tamil is spoken by over sixty million in India, three million in Sri Lanka, and one million elsewhere.

2.2 Phonology and Orthography

The lack of an adequate phonology of modern standard Tamil has led linguists to adopt the following strategy. A transcription of written Tamil is taken as the underlying phonological representation, which is simultaneously the output of the syntactic rules and the input to the phonological rules. The corresponding spoken form is taken as the surface representation, the output of the phonological rules. Hence, the rules that convert the one into the other are held to constitute the substance of Tamil phonology. In effect, these rules enable one to read a passage of written Tamil and pronounce it in spoken Tamil. While this strategy undoubtedly fails to address some facets of modern standard Tamil phonology, it does in the long run provide a good general picture of the phonological structure. The reason for this success can be traced directly to the transparent, agglutinating morphology of modern standard Tamil, which inhibits the growth of complicated phonological alternations.

The inventory of systematic phonemes in modern standard Tamil has a 'low' native core and a 'high' borrowed periphery. Though both are used by educated speakers, the periphery is often assimilated to the core in informal settings and in rapid, unguarded speech. Both appear in Table 37.1, where parentheses enclose the sounds of the periphery. The two nasals enclosed in square brackets are graphemically but not phonemically distinct from /n/.

The core contains twelve vowels and sixteen consonants. It has five short vowels, *a, i, u, e, o*; five long vowels, *ā, ī, ū, ē, ō*; and two diphthongs, *ai, au*, each with the length of a short vowel. Included among the consonants are six stops, *p, t, R, ṭ, c, k*; four nasals, *m, n, ṇ, ñ*; two laterals, *l, ḷ*; two glides, *v, y*; one tap, *r*; and one approximant, *ẓ*. Subscript dots indicate retroflection, one of the more salient features of Tamil phonology. The sounds that appear word-initially are: all vowels, *p, t, ṭ, c, k, m, n, ṇ, ñ, l, r, y, v* (*ṭ* and *ṇ* occur in onomatopoeia, *l* and *r* often take a prosthetic *i*). The sounds that appear word-finally are all vowels except *e*, and *m, n, ṇ, l, ḷ r, ẓ, y* (a half-short,

Table 37.1 The Sounds of Modern Standard Tamil

	Stop vls.	vd.	Fricative	Sibilant	Nasal	Lateral	Tap	Approximant	Glide
Labial	p	(b)	(f)		m				v
Dental	t	(d)			n	l	r		
Alveolar	R				[N]				
Retroflex	ṭ	(ḍ)		(ṣ)	ṇ	ḷ		ẓ	
Palatal	c	(j)		(ś)	ñ				y
Velar	k	(g)			[ṅ]				(h)

		Front	Central	Back
High	long	ī		ū
	short	i		u
Mid	long	ē		ō
	short	e	(ə)	o
Low	long	(æ̆)	ā	(ɔ)
	short		a	
Diphthong		ai		au

Notes: (X), X is part of the peripheral phonology of Tamil. [X], X is graphemically, but not phonemically distinct.

high, back unrounded enunciative vowel often follows the consonants). In the following, words in italics represent a transliteration of the orthography; slashes enclose the phonemic analysis and square brackets the modern standard Tamil pronunciation.

Stops are voiced intervocalically and following nasals, e.g. /atu/ 'it' [aδu]; /anke/ 'there' [aṅgē], but voiceless elsewhere, viz. initially, doubled or in other clusters. Intervocalic stops also undergo spirantisation so that /VkV/ becomes [VɣV] /VtV/ becomes [VδV] and /VcV/ becomes [VjˆV]. Moreover, the ɣ-allophone of /k/ becomes [h]; the jˆ-allophone of /c/, [s]. Initial /c/ is often pronounced as *s* in the speech of many educated speakers. Nasalisation converts a sequence of vowel and word-final nasal into a nasalised vowel, e.g. /maram/ 'tree' becomes [marã], but when the interrogative clitic is added to form *maram-ā* 'a tree?', nasalisation is blocked. Glide insertion transforms initial *ĕ-* and *ŏ-* into *yĕ-* and *vŏ-*, respectively. Palatalisation converts *-tt-* and *-nt-* into *-cc-* and *-ñc-*, respectively, when they follow *i*, *ī* or *ai*, e.g. /cirittēN/ 'I smiled' becomes [siricc̃e]. Cluster simplification eliminates triliteral consonant clusters either by the epenthesis of a vowel, e.g. Sanskrit *tattva* 'truth, reality' becomes Tamil *tattuvam*, or by the deletion of a consonant, e.g. /tīrttēN/ 'I finished' becomes [tītt̃e] (palatalisation precedes cluster simplification so [tīcc̃e] does not occur).

Vowel lowering lowers the high vowels *i* and *u* to *e* and *o*, respectively, when followed by no more than one consonant and the vowel *ă* or *ai*, e.g. /vilai/ 'price' becomes [velai]; /utavi/ 'help', [oδavi]. The diphthongs *ai* and *au* undergo a number of changes. Non-initial *ai* becomes *e* so that /vilai/ 'price' becomes [velai], then [vele]; initial *ai* may be preserved, e.g. *vaikai* 'Vaigai River'; or become *a*, e.g. /aintu/ 'five' becomes [aiñcu] by palatalisation, then [añcu]. *ai* and *au* are often reanalysed as *a+y* and *a+v*, respectively, so that /paiyaN/ 'boy' becomes [payyã], while English 'town' becomes [ṭavuṇ]. Occasionally, the front high and mid vowels, *ī* and *ĕ*, are transformed into their back counterparts, *ŭ* and *ŏ*, when they appear between a labial and a retroflex consonant, e.g. /vīṭu/ 'house' becomes [vūḍu]. While some brahmin dialects of Tanjore

641

still pronounce *z̤* as a voiced retroflex approximant, most dialects merge it with *ḷ*, e.g. /maz̤ai/ 'rain' becomes [maḷe]. *N* is pronounced as *n*; *R* as *r*, except in the Southern dialect where it is a trill as opposed to the flap *r*. The cluster *NR* is pronounced as *ndr* and, ultimately, *nn*, e.g. /eNRu/ 'saying' becomes [endru], then [ennu]; the cluster *RR* is pronounced as *ttr*, then *tt*, e.g. /viRReN/ 'I sold' becomes [vittrẽ], then [vittẽ].

The peripheral sounds of modern standard Tamil include nine consonants, *b, d, ḍ, j, g, f, ṣ, s, h*, and three vowels, *ə, æ, ɔ*. In pronunciation, these sounds undergo rules that assimilate them to the nearest corresponding sounds of the phonological core. /f/ in /faiyal/ 'file' becomes *p* in *paiyal*. Voiced stops contrast with voiceless stops only in initial position because in non-initial position they are interpreted as the voiced allophones of the core's voiceless stop phonemes, so that Sanskrit *agrahāra* 'brahmin settlement' is phonemicised in modern standard Tamil as /akkirakāram/, where both Sanskrit *g* and *h* are treated as allophones of /k/. Initial voiced stops are usually devoiced in rapid speech so that both /bāvam/ 'facial expression' and /pāvam/ 'sin' are pronounced as [pāvã]. Sibilants tend to assimilate to /c/. The vowels *ə, æ* and *ɔ* assimilate to *a, ē* and *ā*, respectively. English loanwords have complicated the set of consonant clusters in modern standard Tamil: 'agent' is borrowed as *ēyjeṇṭṭu* with a cluster of nasal and voiceless stops, one which Tamil grammar traditionally prohibits.

Stress in modern standard Tamil is not distinctive and is fixed on the first syllable of every word. The syllabic structure of words is based on quantitative units known as *morae* (*acai* in traditional Tamil grammar). Handbooks of Tamil discuss other issues of segmental and suprasegmental phonology in greater detail.

Tamil is written in a syllabic script which historically derives from a version of Aśōkan Brāhmī script (see Table 37.2). Each vowel has two forms in this syllabary: an independent symbol to represent it at the beginning of a word and an auxiliary symbol, which combines with consonant symbols, to represent it elsewhere. In initial position, *ā* is represented by ஆ; but elsewhere by ா, as in கா *kā*, தா *tā* and பா *pā*. In initial position, *i* is represented by இ, but ி elsewhere, as in கி *ki*, தி *ti*, and பி *pi*. Each consonant is represented by a basic symbol which has the inherent vowel *a* in the order *Ca*, so that க is read as *ka*; த as *ta*; and ப as *pa*. When any auxiliary symbol is added to the consonant symbol, the inherent vowel *a* is suppressed, e.g. the symbols க *ka* and இ *i* combine to form the symbol கி, which is read as *ki*, not **kai*. The addition of a dot, called *puḷḷi*, above the consonant symbol removes the inherent vowel altogether, so that க் represents *k*; த், *t*; and ப், *p*. The use of *puḷḷi* is instrumental in the correct representation of consonant clusters: இப்ப represents *ippa* 'now', not **ipapa*. The top row in Table 37.2 presents the independent vowel symbols; the leftmost column, the basic consonant symbols modified by *puḷḷi*; and the column second from the left, the basic consonant symbol with the inherent vowel *a*. The remaining cells present the graphemic representation of the combination of basic consonant symbol and auxiliary vowel symbol.

Modern standard Tamil has a graphemic convention whereby initial stop consonants are doubled when preceded by certain forms such as the dative case marker, the accusative case marker and the demonstrative adjectives, e.g. /inta pāvam/ 'this sin' is written as *intap pāvam*. Doubling does not take place when the initial stop is voiced, e.g. /inta bāvam/ 'this facial expression' is written as *inta pāvam* (since *inta pāvam* is treated as a compound, *p* is treated as intervocalic and, therefore, voiced). The Tamil alphabetic order is *a, ā, i, ī, u, ū, e, ē, ai, o, ō, au, k, ṅ, c, ñ, ṭ, ṇ, t, n, p, m, y, r, l, v, z̤, ḷ, R, N*. Six additional symbols may be used to represent letters in Sanskrit loans: *j, ś, ṣ, s,*

642

Table 37.2 The Tamil Syllabary

	a	ā	i	ī	u	ū	e	ē	ai	o	ō	au
	அ	ஆ	இ	ஈ	உ	ஊ	எ	ஏ	ஐ	ஒ	ஓ	ஔ
k	ka	kā	ki	kī	ku	kū	ke	kē	kai	ko	kō	kau
ṅ	ṅa	ṅā	ṅi	ṅī	ṅu	ṅū	ṅe	ṅē	ṅai	ṅo	ṅō	ṅau
c	ca	cā	ci	cī	cu	cū	ce	cē	cai	co	cō	cau
ñ	ña	ñā	ñi	ñī	ñu	ñū	ñe	ñē	ñai	ño	ñō	ñau
ḍ	ḍa	ḍā	ḍi	ḍī	ḍu	ḍū	ḍe	ḍē	ḍai	ḍo	ḍō	ḍau
ṇ	ṇa	ṇā	ṇi	ṇī	ṇu	ṇū	ṇe	ṇē	ṇai	ṇo	ṇō	ṇau
t	ta	tā	ti	tī	tu	tū	te	tē	tai	to	tō	tau
n	na	nā	ni	nī	nu	nū	ne	nē	nai	no	nō	nau
p	pa	pā	pi	pī	pu	pū	pe	pē	pai	po	pō	pau
m	ma	mā	mi	mī	mu	mū	me	mē	mai	mo	mō	mau
y	ya	yā	yi	yī	yu	yū	ye	yē	yai	yo	yō	yau
r	ra	rā	ri	rī	ru	rū	re	rē	rai	ro	rō	rau
l	la	lā	li	lī	lu	lū	le	lē	lai	lo	lō	lau
v	va	vā	vi	vī	vu	vū	ve	vē	vai	vo	vō	vau
z	za	zā	zi	zī	zu	zū	ze	zē	zai	zo	zō	zau
ḷ	ḷa	ḷā	ḷi	ḷī	ḷu	ḷū	ḷe	ḷē	ḷai	ḷo	ḷō	ḷau
R	Ra	Rā	Ri	Rī	Ru	Rū	Re	Rē	Rai	Ro	Rō	Rau
N	Na	Nā	Ni	Nī	Nu	Nū	Ne	Nē	Nai	No	Nō	Nau

Source: Adapted from Pope 1979.

h, ṣ. But these symbols may be replaced by others, e.g. *kṣ* by *ṭc.* The Tamil syllabary is adequate to represent the core phonology of modern standard Tamil.

2.3 Morphology and Parts of Speech

Although some grammars of Tamil list as many as ten parts of speech, all of them can be resolved into one of two formal categories: noun and verb. These two are distinguished by the grammatical categories for which they are inflected. (The so-called indeclinables, including interjections, seem to be variously nouns or verbs.) The morphology is agglutinating and exclusively suffixal: the inflections are marked by suffixes joined to the lexical base, which may or may not be extended by a derivational suffix. Nouns and verbs both appear in simple and compound forms.

Nouns are inflected for person, case, number and gender. This class includes common nouns, proper names, numerals, pronouns and some so-called adjectives. There are two numbers: singular and plural. Tamil gender is based on the natural gender of a noun's referent, not on conventionally ascribed grammatical gender. There are two basic genders: 'rational' (*uyartiṇai*) and 'irrational' (*ahRiṇai*) corresponding roughly to human and non-human. Rational nouns are further classified as honorific, masculine and feminine. Nouns referring to deities and men are classified as rational; in some dialects women are classified as rational, in others as irrational. (Children and animals are normally classified as irrational.) In some cases, conventionally rational nouns are treated as irrational, e.g. when a proper name is given to an animal. By the same token, conventionally irrational nouns are treated as rational when used as epithets for men. In *ramu eṅkē? antak kaẓutai eṅkēyō pōy irukkiRāN* 'where₂ (is) Ramu₁? That₃ ass₄ has₇ gone₆ (off) somewhere₅' *kaẓutai* 'ass' is treated as a rational noun for the purposes of subject–verb agreement. A noun's gender determines other of its grammatical properties such as the choice between the animate locative case marker *-iṭam* and the inanimate *-il.*

Modern standard Tamil has eight cases: nominative, accusative, dative, sociative, genitive, instrumental, locative, ablative. There is just one declension: once the nominative singular, nominative plural and oblique stem are known, all the other forms can be predicted. Moreover, the nominative plural and oblique stem can generally be predicted from the gender and phonological shape of the nominative singular. The chart given here presents the declension of four nouns: *maNitaN* 'man', *maram* 'tree', *āRu* 'river' and *pū* 'flower'. In addition to eight cases, modern standard Tamil has postpositions, derived from independent nouns or non-finite verbs. The postposition *pārttu* 'towards', which governs the accusative case, e.g. *avaNaip pārttu* 'towards him', comes from the adverbial participle *pārttu* 'looking at'.

The Declension of Four selected Tamil Noums I

Singular	maNitaN 'man'	maram 'tree'	āRu 'river'	pū 'flower'
Oblique Stem	maNitaN-	maratt-	āRR-	pū(v)-
Nominative	maNitaN	maram	āRu	pū
Accusative	maNitaN-ai	maratt-ai	āRR-ai	pūv-ai
Dative	maNitaN-ukku	maratt-ukku	āRR-ukku	pūv-ukku
Sociative	maNitaN-ōṭu	maratt-ōṭu	āRR-ōṭu	pūv-ōṭu
Genitive	maNitaN-uṭaiya	maratt-uṭaiya	āRR-uṭaiya	pūv-uṭaiya
Instrumental	maNitaN-āl	maratt-āl	āRR-āl	pūv-āl
Locative	maNitaN-iṭam	maratt-il	āRR-il	pūv-il
Ablative	maNitaN-iṭamiruntu	maratt-iliruntu	āRR-iliruntu	pūv-iliruntu

The Declension of Four selected Tamil Nouns II

Plural	maNitarkaḷ	maraṅkaḷ	āRukaḷ	pūkkaḷ
Nominative	maNitarkaḷ	maraṅkaḷ	āRukaḷ	pūkkaḷ
Accusative	maNitarkaḷ-ai	maraṅkaḷ-ai	āRukaḷ-ai	pūkkaḷ-ai
Dative	maNitarkaḷ-ukku	maraṅkaḷ-ukku	āRukaḷ-ukku	pūkkaḷ-ukku
Sociative	maNitarkaḷ-ōṭu	maraṅkaḷ-ōṭu	āRukaḷ-ōṭu	pūkkaḷ-ōṭu
Genitive	maNitarkaḷ-uṭaiya	maraṅkaḷ-uṭaiya	āRukaḷ-uṭaiya	pūkkaḷ-uṭaiya
Instrumental	maNitarkaḷ-āl	maraṅkaḷ-āl	āRukaḷ-āl	pūkkaḷ-āl
Locative	maNitarkaḷ-iṭam	maraṅkaḷ-il	āRukaḷ-il	pūkkaḷ-il
Ablative	maNitarkaḷ-iṭamiruntu	maraṅkaḷ-iliruntu	āRukaḷ-iliruntu	pūkkaḷ-iliruntu

Modern standard Tamil has no formal class of articles: other grammatical devices assume their function. The numeral *oru* 'one' often functions as an indefinite article; so, by way of contrast, its absence with a rational noun conveys the meaning of a definite article, e.g. *oru maNitaN* 'a man' but ∅ *maNitaN* 'the man'. Irrational direct objects are interpreted as indefinite when inflected for the nominative case, but definite when inflected for the accusative, e.g. *nāN maram pārttēN* 'I$_1$ saw$_3$ a tree$_2$', but *nāN marattaip pārttēN* 'I$_1$ saw$_3$ the tree$_2$'.

A small but significant subset is marked for first or second person. These are the personal pronouns: *nāN* 'I' (obl. *eN(N)-*); *nām* 'we and you' (obl. *nam-*); *nāṅkaḷ* 'we but not you' (obl. *eṅkaḷ-*); *nī* 'thou' (obl. *uN(N)-*); *nīṅkaḷ* 'you' (obl. *uṅkaḷ-*). There are two third person anaphoric pronouns, called reflexives, *tāN* 'self' (obl. *taN(N)-*); and *tā ṅkaḷ* 'selves' (obl. *taṅkaḷ*); the antecedent must be a subject, of either the same or a superordinate clause. Modern standard Tamil has deictic pronouns which are formally compound nouns. *avaN* 'that man' consists of *a-* 'that (one)' and *-(v)aN* 'man'. Continental Tamil makes three deictic distinctions, e.g. *ivaN* 'this man', *avaN* 'that man', *evaN* 'which, any man', as opposed to Sri Lanka Tamil which preserves the older Dravidian system with four. Distal pronouns, marked by *a-*, are less marked than the proximate, marked by *i-*: they appear in contexts of neutralisation and translate English, 'he', 'she', 'it', 'they', etc.

In Ancient and Medieval, but not modern standard Tamil, nouns, often predicate nominals, were inflected for person, e.g. *-ai* marks second person singular in *nī nāṭṭ-ai* 'you$_1$ (are a) countryman$_2$'. In Medieval Tamil such nouns could also be inflected for case: in *tēvar-īr-aip pukaẓntu* 'praising$_2$ you (who are a) god$_1$' the accusative case marker *-ai* is suffixed to the second person marker *-īr* which in turn is suffixed to the noun *tēvar* 'god'.

Compound nouns are very common. The nouns *maram* 'tree' (obl. *maratt-*), *aṭi* 'base' and *niẓal* 'shadow' combine to form the compound *maratt-aṭi-niẓal* 'shadow at the base of the tree'. Coordinate compounds in which each part refers to a separate entity are also common, e.g. *vīratīracākacaṅkaḷ* 'courage, bravery and valour' consists of *vīram* 'courage', *tīram* 'bravery', *cākacam* 'valour' and the plural suffix *-kaḷ*. Such *dvandvā* compounds contrast with English compounds such as *secretary–treasurer* which refers to a single individual. Some of the so-called adjectives of modern standard Tamil are bound nouns which must occur in compound nouns, but not as their head, e.g. both *nalla nāḷ* 'good$_1$ day$_2$' and *nalla-(v)aN* 'good man' imply a noun *nal* 'goodness' which never occurs by itself. So pervasive are compound nouns that even the Sanskrit privative prefix *a-*, *ava-* 'not, without' has been reanalysed in Tamil as a noun in a compound. Tamil borrowed hundreds of pairs of Sanskrit nouns, one without the privative prefix and one with it, e.g. *mati* 'respect', *ava-mati* 'disrespect'. *ava-mati* is treated like the compound *maratt-aṭi* 'tree-base': the second element is identified with the independent noun *mati* 'respect', while the first element *ava-* is treated as the oblique form of an independent noun *avam* 'void, nothingness, absence'. This reanalysis preserves the strictly suffixal nature of modern standard Tamil morphology.

Verbs are inflected for verbal categories, participating notably in the oppositions of mood and tense. Formally, a verb consists of a verb base and grammatical formative. The base itself consists of a stem and, optionally, two suffixes, one for voice and one for causative. The stem lexically identifies the verb. Sixty per cent of modern standard Tamil verbs participate in the opposition of affective versus effective voice. An affective verb is one the subject of which undergoes the action named by the stem; an effective verb is one the subject of which directs the action named by the stem. The category of effectivity differs from both transitivity and causation. Affective *vilaka* 'separate' and effective *vilakka* 'separate' minimally contrast since both are transitive: *vaṇṭi pātai-(y)ai vilakiNatu* '(the) cart$_1$ left$_3$ (the) path$_2$' vs *avaN vaṇṭi-(y)ai (pātai-(y)iliruntu) vilakkiNāN* 'he$_1$ drove$_4$ (lit. separated) the cart$_2$ (off the path)$_3$'. Though very productive in Medieval Tamil, the causative suffix *-vi, -ppi*, which conveys causation, is lexically restricted in modern standard Tamil, having given way to periphrastic causative constructions.

All modern standard Tamil verb forms are inflected for mood, the verbal category which characterises the ontological status of the narrated event either as unreal, possible, potential (modal) or as real, actual (indicative). Mood is implicitly marked in the grammatical formative following the verb base: the past tense, present tense and adverbial participle are indicative; the rest are modal. Modern standard Tamil has three simple tenses, past, present and future, as well as several periphrastic tenses like the perfect series. Some deverbal nouns, such as *pirivu* 'separation' derived from *piriya* 'separate', mark neither tense nor mood.

Modern standard Tamil verbs are finite or non-finite. Finite verbs are inflected for tense and subject–verb agreement, overtly or, in the imperative and optative, covertly. A verb's finiteness has a direct bearing on modern standard Tamil syntax: there can be only one finite verb per sentence. All remaining verbs must be non-finite and belong to one of three classes.

One class of non-finite verbs consists of relative participles, called *peyareccam* '(verbs) deficient in a noun', which are instrumental in the formation of relative clauses and similar structures. They are verb forms marked for tense which combine with a following noun: in the following examples the relative participle *vanta* 'which came' links the preceding clause to the following nouns, e.g. *nēRRu vanta oru mantiri* 'a$_3$ minister$_4$ (who) came$_2$ yesterday$_1$', *mantiri nēRRu vanta ceyti* '(the) news$_4$ (that) (the) minister$_1$ came$_3$ yesterday$_2$'. The second class of non-finite verbs, called *viNaiyeccam* '(verbs) deficient in a verb', includes the infinitive, adverbial participle, conditional, negative verbal participle and negative conditional. All are verb forms that combine with a following verb, with or without other lexical material coming between the two verbs. Given the restriction on finite verbs, these forms are crucial in the formation of complex sentences. The infinitive and adverbial participle are instrumental in the formation of compound verbs, as well. The third class of non-finite verbs includes all verbal nouns, called *viNaippeyar* 'verbal nouns', forms derived from verbs but capable of having nominal inflections. Some retain their verbal characteristics better than others: in the chart showing the conjugation of *piriya* 'separate', *piri-nt-atu* 'separation' takes a nominative subject while *pirivu* 'separation' takes a genitive. Consult the chart

646

for the simple verb forms of Tamil, using *piriya* 'separate' as an example. Modern standard Tamil has seven morphophonemically distinct conjugations, details of which can be found in most grammars.

The Conjugation of *piriya* 'separate'

Finitive verb Forms

	Past	Present	Future	Future Negative
1 sg.	piri-nt-ēN	piri-kiR-ēN	piri-v-ēN	piriya māṭṭ-ēN
2 sg.	piri-nt-āy	piri-kiR-āy	piri-v-āy	piriya māṭṭ-āy
3 sg. hon.	piri-nt-ār	piri-kiR-ār	piri-v-ār	piriya māṭṭ-ār
3 sg. m.	piri-nt-āN	piri-kiR-āN	piri-v-āN	piriya māṭṭ-āN
3 sg. f.	piri-nt-āḷ	piri-kiR-āḷ	piri-v-āḷ	piriya māṭṭ-āḷ
3 sg. irr.	piri-nt-atu	piri-kiR-atu	piri-(y)-um	piri-(y)ātu
1 pl.	piri-nt-ōm	piri-kiR-ōm	piri-v-ōm	piriya māṭṭ-ōm
2 pl.	piri-nt-īrkaḷ	piri-kiR-īrkaḷ	piri-v-īrkaḷ	piriya māṭṭ-īrkaḷ
3 pl. rat.	piri-nt-ārkaḷ	piri-kiR-ārkaḷ	piri-v-ārkaḷ	piriya māṭṭ-ārkaḷ
3 pl. irr.	piri-nt-aNa	piri-kiNR-aNa	piri-(y)um	piri-(y)ātu

Non-Future Negative   *piriya (v)illai* for all persons, numbers and genders

	Imperative	Negative Imperative	Optative
Sg.	piri	piri-(y)ātē	
Pl., hon.	piri-(y)uṅkaḷ	piri-(y)ātīrkaḷ	piri-ka

Non-finite Verb Forms

	Past	Present	Future	Negative
Rel. part.	piri-nt-a	piri-kiR-a	piri-(y)um	piri-(y)āta
V. n.	piri-nt-atu	piri-kiR-atu	piri-v-atu	piri-(y)ātatu
Adv. part.:	piri-ntu	infin.: piri-(y)a	neg. v. part.: piri-(y)āmal	
Cond.:	piri-ntāl	neg. cond.: piri-(y)āviṭṭāl		
De-v. n.:	piri-tal, piri-kai, piri-vu.			

Modern standard Tamil has two kinds of compound verb: lexical and auxiliary. Lexical compound verbs are complex morphosyntactic vehicles, made up of two or more simple verbs, that encode those lexical meanings which are not encoded in any single lexeme. *aruka vara* 'approach' consists of the infinitive *aruka* 'near' and an inflected form of *vara* 'come'; *kūrntu kavaNikka* 'peer' consists of the adverbial participle *kūrntu* 'sharpening (i.e. sharply)' and an inflected form of *kavaNikka* 'notice'. By contrast, auxiliary compound verbs are complex morphosyntactic vehicles, made up of two or more simple verbs, that encode those verbal categories which are not encoded in any simple verb form, such as the perfect tense or the causative. *varac ceyya* 'make₂ X come₁' consists of the modal auxiliary *ceyya* 'make, do' and the infinitive of the main verb *vara* 'come'; *vantu irukka* 'X has₂ come₁' consists of the indicative auxiliary *irukka* 'be' and the adverbial participle of the main verb *vara* 'come'. The two kinds of compound verbs have different grammatical properties: for example, additional lexical material can separate the components of a lexical compound, but not those of an auxiliary compound, e.g. *kūrntu avaḷaik kavaNikka* 'peer₁₊₃ (at) her₂', but **vantu vīṭṭukku irukka* 'X has₃ to the house₂ come₁'.

Modern standard Tamil has about fifty auxiliary verbs, half modal and half indicative. It lacks simple adverbs like English *not* and instead uses modal auxiliary verbs to express negation: in *vara māṭṭāN* '(he) won't₂ come₁' the auxiliary verb *māṭṭa* 'not' signals the future negative of *vara* 'come'. Ancient and Medieval Tamil had a synthetic negative conjugation, remnants of which survive in the third person irrational forms of the future tense.

Modern standard Tamil also compensates for the lack of basic adverbs by a very productive set of noun + verb compounds whose second member is the infinitive *āka* 'become' and which function adverbially. *cikkiramāka* 'quickly, urgently' consists of the noun *cikkiram* 'urgency' and *āka* 'become'.

2.4 A Skeleton Account of Simple and Complex Sentences in Modern Standard Tamil

Simple sentences in modern standard Tamil consist of a subject and a predicate. The subject is a nominal which is inflected for the nominative or, in certain cases, the dative case. The predicate is either a finite verb or a predicate nominal which appears without a copula. From the various combinations of subject and predicate, four basic sentence types emerge: (1) nominative subject and predicate nominal, e.g. *avaN oru maNitaN* 'he₁ (is) a₂ man₃'; (2) nominative subject and finite verb, e.g. *avaN vantāN* 'he₁ came₂'; (3) dative subject and predicate nominal, e.g. *avaNukku oru makaN* 'he₁ (has) a₂ son₃' (lit. 'to him (is) a son'); and (4) dative subject and finite verb, *anaNukkut tōcai piṭikkum* 'he₁ likes₃ dosais₂ (South Indian Crêpes)'.

While dative subjects do not trigger subject–verb agreement, unlike other datives they possess such subject-like properties as the ability to be the antecedent of a reflexive pronoun. Dative subjects typically combine with stative predicates, favouring particularly those that denote a mental or emotional state, e.g. *ataip paRRi avaNukku cantē kam* 'he₃ (has) doubts₄ about₂ that₁', *avaNukkuk kōpam pukaintatu* 'he₁ smoked₃ with anger₂'. Nominative subjects do trigger subject–verb agreement. Verbs agree with their subjects in person, number and, in the third person, gender.

The four basic sentence types function as templates through which other syntactic structures are fitted. Modern standard Tamil has a rule of clefting, which postposes a nominal phrase to the right of the clause-final verb. Simultaneously, the verb becomes a verbal noun inflected for the nominative case and the oblique case marking on the postposed noun, if any, is optionally deleted. Clefting thus transforms *nāN maturai-(y)il piRaniēN* 'I₁ was born₃ in Madurai₂' into *nāN piRantatu maturai* 'Madurai₃ (is where) I₁ was born₂', i.e. 'it is Madurai where I was born'. Observe how the output of clefting conforms to the first basic sentence type above, where a nominative subject, here the verbal noun *piRantatu*, and a predicate nominal, here *maturai*, combine to form a simple sentence.

The basic word order of modern standard Tamil is SOV. As in other rigid SOV languages, genitives precede the nouns they modify, main verbs precede their auxiliaries and complement clauses precede main clauses. Despite the use of cases and postpositions to mark the grammatical relations of noun phrases, modern standard Tamil word order is not entirely free. Although variations do exist, the verb in a simple sentence must remain at the extreme right end of the clause. The unmarked order of *avaN nēRRu avaḷaip pārttāN* 'he₁ saw₄ her₃ yesterday₂' can be varied as follows: *avaḷai avaN nē RRu pārttāN; nēRRu avaN avaḷaip pārttāN; avaN avaḷai nēRRu pārttāN*. No semantic difference accompanies these variations, but the verb remains fixed at the end of the clause. A subject may in rhetorically marked contexts be postposed rightwards over a finite verb, typically when its referent is the hero in a narrative whom the speaker wishes to make prominent, e.g. *cītaiyaip pārttāN rāmaN* 'Rama₃ saw₂ Sita₁'.

The structure of complex sentences is a particularly fascinating part of modern standard Tamil syntax. Recall that modern standard Tamil preserves the Proto-Dravidian constraint limiting the number of finite verbs in a sentence to a maximum of one. This necessitates the use of non-finite verbs such as the infinitive, adverbial participle or relative participle in the construction of complex sentences, be they coordinate or subordinate. In *maẓai peytu kuḷam niRaintatu* 'rain$_1$ fell$_2$, (and) the reservoir$_3$ filled$_4$', the adverbial participle *peytu* 'raining' joins two clauses to form a coordinate sentence. By contrast, in *avaḷ nāN colli kēṭka villai* 'she$_1$ didn't$_5$ listen$_4$ (to what) I$_2$ said$_3$', the adverbial participle *colli* 'saying' joins a subordinate clause to its main clause. In *makaN pōka makaḷ vantāḷ* '(as) the son$_1$, went$_2$, the daughter$_3$ came$_4$', the infinitive *pōka* 'go' conjoins two clauses in a coordinate sentence; but in *nāN avaNai varac coNNēN* 'I$_1$ told$_4$ him$_2$ to come$_3$', the infinitive *vara* 'come' joins the subordinate clause to the main clause. In *avaN vantāl avaN-iṭam nāN pēcuvēN* 'if$_2$ he$_1$ comes$_2$, I$_4$ will speak$_5$ with him$_3$', the conditional verb *vantāl* 'if X comes' simultaneously marks the protasis of a conditional sentence and joins it to the apodosis. In all these sentences the single finite verb appears at the extreme right end of the sentence, in the main clause. Non-finite verbs are still used in complex sentences even when the rightmost predicate is a predicate nominal, as in *kavalaippaṭṭu uṅkaḷukku eNNa payaN?* 'what$_3$ use$_4$ (is it) for you$_2$ to worry$_1$?'; the adverbial participle *kavalaippaṭṭu* 'worrying' links two clauses.

Relative participles also serve to build complex sentences. In *nēRRu vanta oru mantiri* 'a$_3$ minister$_4$ (who) came$_2$ yesterday$_1$', the relative participle *vanta* 'which came' joins a relative clause to the head noun *mantiri* 'minister'. Relative participles appear in factive complements, as well: in *mantiri nēRRu vanta ceyti* '(the) news$_4$ (that) the minister$_1$ came$_3$ yesterday$_2$', the relative participle *vanta* 'which came' joins the factive complement to the head noun *ceyti* 'news'.

Despite the ingenuity and dexterity with which non-finite verbs are used to create complex sentences, the restriction against more than one finite verb per sentence raises serious questions. First, how does one represent direct discourse, which requires the preservation of finite verbs in quoted material? Second, how does one embed sentences with predicate nominals? Neither task can be accomplished by recourse to non-finite verbs. Instead, modern standard Tamil employs two special verbs to solve these and other related syntactic problems: *āka* 'become' and *eNa* 'say'. These verbs take as their direct objects expressions of any category and any complexity, without requiring any morphological change in those expressions (such as requiring the accusative case or a non-finite verb form). They can combine with single words, phrases or entire sentences without disturbing the form of these operands. As verbs, they may subsequently be inflected for non-finite verb morphology and, as described above, function in the construction of complex sentences, bringing their objects with them. The sentence *avaNukku oru makaN* 'he$_1$ (has) a$_2$ son$_3$' can be embedded under the verb of propositional attitude *niNaikka* 'think' using the adverbial participle *eNRu* 'saying' to link the two: *avaNukku oru makaN eNRu nāN niNaikkiRēN* 'I$_5$ think$_6$ that$_4$ (lit. saying) he$_1$ (has) a$_2$ son$_3$'. The conditional form *āNāl* 'if becomes' allows finite verbs to appear in the protasis of conditional sentences: *avaN varuvāN āNāl nāN avaNiṭam pēcuvēN* 'if$_3$ he$_1$ will come$_2$, I$_4$ will speak$_6$ with him$_5$'. These verbs also help to represent direct discourse: in *nāN varuvēN eNRu avaN coNNāN.* 'he$_4$ said$_5$, "I$_1$ will come$_2$"', the adverbial participle *eNRu* 'saying' embeds the direct quotation beneath the verb of quotation *colla* 'tell, say'. To make adverbial expressions, *āka* 'become' embeds individual nouns, while *eNa* 'say' embeds onomatopoeic expressions.

Modern standard Tamil uses the particles *-ē* 'even, and' and *-ō* 'or, whether' to subordinate finite verbs in complex sentences, as well. In *avaN vantāN-ō eNakku cantēkam* 'I$_3$ (have) doubts$_4$ whether (= -ō) he$_1$ came$_2$', the clitic *-ō* subordinates one clause to another. In *nēRRu vantān-ē nāN avaNaic cantittēN* 'I₃ met₅ him₄ (who) came₂ yesterday₁', the clitic *-ē* serves to join the two parts of a correlative relative clause, both of which have finite verbs, i.e. *vantāN* 'he came', *cantittēN* 'I met'.

The constraint against multiple finite verbs in a sentence must be revised in light of these other devices used to construct complex sentences. The number of finite verbs per sentence is limited to a maximum of $n+1$, where n equals the number of occurrences of *āka* 'become', *eNa* 'say', *-ē* 'even, and' and *-ō* 'or, whether' that function as complementisers.

This short sketch of Tamil syntax will show, I hope, how much modern standard Tamil syntax relies upon the morphological and lexical resources of the language. The cases of nouns, the distinction between finite and non-finite verbs and the lexemes *āka* 'become' and *eNa* 'say' are indispensable elements of the Tamil sentence.

2.5 The Grammar of Affective Language in Modern Standard Tamil

Like many languages of the world, modern standard Tamil provides its speakers with a variety of grammatical devices which are conventionally used to express the speaker's affective or emotional state. Three such stylistic devices are discussed to give the reader an idea of the rhetorical possibilities of the language.

Onomatopoeic words (*olikuRippu*) are so numerous in modern standard Tamil that they fill an entire dictionary. Such words generally represent a sound and are syntactically joined to a sentence by means of the verb *eNa* 'say', e.g. *kācu ṇaṅ eNRu kīzē vizuntatu* '(the) coin₁ fell₅ down₄ with₃ (lit. saying) a clang₂', *pustakam top(pu) eNRu kīzē vizuntatu* '(the) book₁ fell₅ down₄ with₃ (lit. saying) a thud₂'. Many occur reduplicated, e.g. *muṇumuṇu* 'murmur, mutter', *toṇutoṇu* 'sound of beating drums'. Often they acquire an extended meaning so that *toṇutoṇu* comes to mean 'bitching, complaining', while *kuRukuRu* 'scratching, throbbing pulse' comes to mean 'guilt', e.g. *avaN maNacu kuRukuRu eNRu mayaṅkiNatu* 'his₁ mind₂ was confused₅ with₄ (lit. saying) guilt₃'. Some onomatopoeic stems, but by no means all, can themselves be inflected as verbs, e.g. *avaN ōyāmal toṇutoṇukkiRāN* 'bitches₃ ceaselessly₂'. The phonological shapes of these words often depart from what the phonotactic rules of modern standard Tamil allow: *ṇaṅ* 'clang' has an initial retroflex and a final velar nasal. But despite that and despite the jaunty air they impart to a sentence, they are still an integral part of modern standard Tamil and cannot be dismissed as quaint and ephemeral slang. Such forms loosely correspond to English onomatopoeic expressions with the prefix *ka-* or *ker-*, e.g. *the bomb went ka-boom, the boy fell ker-splash into the lily pond.*

Like other Dravidian languages, modern standard Tamil has a verbal category called attitude, which characterises the speaker's subjective evaluation of the narrated event. It is grammatically encoded in a subset of the indicative auxiliary verbs. For the most part, these auxiliaries convey the speaker's pejorative opinion of the narrated event and its participants. The auxiliary *tolaiya* 'get lost', which combines with the adverbial participle of the main verb, expresses the speaker's antipathy towards the narrated event, e.g. *avaN vantu tolaintāN* 'he₁ came₂, damn it₃'. The auxiliary *oziya* 'purge' expresses the speaker's relief that an unpleasant event has ended, combining aspect and attitude, e.g. *tiruṭaN pōy ozintāN* '(the) thief₁ left₂, whew₃ (am I glad)!' In *kaṇṇāṭi uṭaintu pōyiRRu* '(the) mirror₁ got₃ broken₂', the auxiliary *pōka* 'go' conveys the speaker's opinion that the event named by the main verb, *uṭaiya* 'break', culminated in an undesirable result. Modern standard Tamil has at least twelve such attitudinal auxiliaries which behave in all respects like other indicative auxiliary verbs, as opposed to modal auxiliaries and lexical compound verbs. Their stylistic impact on a sentence can be compared with the use of *up*, *get* and *go* in the following three English examples: *she upped and left him*; *he got himself beaten up*; *the thief went and charged a colour TV on my credit card*. Once again we see how compound verbs compensate for the lack of simple adverbs in modern standard Tamil, here ones that express the speaker's affective state of mind.

Modern standard Tamil has a series of compound words generated through reduplication, e.g. *avaN* 'that man' is reduplicated as *avaNavaN* 'each man, every man' while *vantu* 'coming' is reduplicated as *vantu vantu* 'coming time and again'. As these examples show, reduplicated compounds have a distributive and universal sense. However, modern standard Tamil has a special subset of reduplicated compounds in which the second member of the compound does not exactly duplicate the first. These are called echo-compounds: the second member, the echo-word, partially duplicates the first, the echoed word. The echo-word is the same as the echoed word except that it substitutes *ki-* or *kī-* for the first syllable of the echoed word, depending on whether it is short or long. Thus, from *viyāparam* 'business' we can form the echo compound *viyāparam-kiyāparam* 'business and such', from *māṭu* 'cattle', *māṭu-kīṭu* 'cattle and such'. However, words which begin with *ki-* or *kī-* cannot themselves be echoed this way: from *kiNaRu* 'well' we cannot form the echo-compound **kiNaRu-kiNaRu* 'wells and such' even though vowel lowering would convert the echoed word, but not the echo-word, into *keNaRu* (echo-compounds can be formed from words whose initial syllable is underlying *ke-* or *kē-*). In such cases, an alternative echo-word with initial *hi-* or *hī-* may be formed, e.g. from *kiḷi* 'parrot' we can form *kiḷi-hiḷi* 'parrots and such'. But since initial *h-* belongs to the phonological periphery, many speakers prefer to form no echo-compound at all rather than to create an echo-word with initial *h-*. Verbs may be echoed as well as nouns (but not pronouns): in *pāttirattai uṭaittāy kiṭaittāy eNRāl uNNai cummāka viṭa māṭṭēN* 'if₄ (you) broke₂ (the) pots₁ or did-any-such-thing₃, (I) won't₈ let₇ you₅ alone₆', the echo-compound *uṭaittāy-kiṭaittāy* 'break or do some such thing' is based on the finite verb *uṭaittāy* 'you broke'.

Echo-compounds occur in rhetorically marked settings: in grammatical terms this includes modal verb forms such as the future tense and conditional, as well as negative and interrogative contexts, but not indicative forms, e.g. *māṭu kīṭu varum* 'Cows₁ and such₂ will come₃', but **?māṭu kīṭu vantatu* 'Cows₁ and such₂ came₃'. Echo-compounds have two facets of meaning. First, like other reduplicated compounds, they have a distributive meaning so that the compound conveys the idea, 'entities or actions, of which the echoed word refers to a random example from a general range'. According to context, *māṭu-kīṭu* 'cows and such' could refer to a group of domestic animals, the components of a dowry, etc. Second, echo-compounds conventionally carry a pejorative nuance to the effect that the speaker neither likes nor cares enough about the entity or action to specify it any further. And, in this respect, modern standard Tamil echo-compounds resemble those in Yiddish English where the echo-word is made with the prefix *shm-*, e.g. *fancy-shmancy*, *cordiality-shmordiality*, *Oedipus-Shmoedipus*, *at least he loves his mother!*

There are also echo-compounds in modern standard Tamil in which the shape of the echo-word is not predictable and is idiomatically associated with the echoed word, e.g. from *koñcam* 'little' comes the echo-compound *koñcam-nañcam* 'itsy-bitsy'. Most South, South-Central and Central Dravidian languages have both kinds of echo-compound, but as we pass from Central Dravidian into North Dravidian, the second kind comes to predominate.

These and similar grammatical devices, such as the affective lengthening of vowels, exist in other Dravidian languages. The fact that they conventionally encode the speaker's affective state is no reason to consider them anything less than an integral part of the language and its grammar. Since they can reveal as much about the phonological, morphological and syntactic structure of a language as other, more prosaic rules and constructions, they deserve greater recognition in grammatical theory than they have hitherto received.

Bibliography

For general surveys, reference may be made to Steever (1998) and Krishnamurti (2003). Caldwell (1875) is the starting point of modern comparative Dravidian studies. Zvelebil (1970) is an excellent analysis and summary of phonological reconstruction in Dravidian. Bloch (1946) is the standard study of Dravidian comparative grammar, while Andronov (1970) is a good overview of Dravidian morphology. Emeneau (1967) shows, as does Bloch (1946), how much the non-literary languages can reveal about comparative Dravidian. Steever (1981) contains a number of essays concentrating on the analysis of some pressing morphological and syntactic problems in the Dravidian languages. Krishnamurti (2001) collects articles by one of the major figures in the field.

For Tamil, Arden (1942) is a thorough grammar of modern literary Tamil, beginning with a helpful skeleton grammar, later amplified, while Lehmann (1993) provides a more modern account. Andronov (1969) is a comprehensive grammar, concentrating on morphology. Pope (1979) is a teaching grammar providing an introduction to modern literary Tamil. For the spoken variety of Tamil, Schiffman (1979) is a fine sketch, while Asher (1983) is a detailed grammar following the framework of the Lingua Descriptive Studies series (now Routledge Descriptive Grammars). Paramasivam (1983) is an excellent introduction to the linguistic structure of modern Tamil; an English translation is in preparation.

References

Andronov, M.S. 1969. *A Standard Grammar of Modern and Classical Tamil* (New Century Book House, Madras)
—— 1970. *Dravidian Languages* (Nauka, Moscow)
Arden, A.H. 1942. *A Progressive Grammar of the Tamil Language* (Christian Literature Society, Madras)
Asher, R. 1983. *Tamil* (North-Holland, Amsterdam; now distributed by Routledge, London)
Bloch, J. 1946. *Structure grammaticale des langues dravidiennes* (Adrien-Maisonneuve, Paris)
Caldwell, R. 1875. *A Comparative Grammar of the Dravidian or South-Indian Family of Languages*, 2nd edn (University of Madras, Madras)
Emeneau, M.B. 1967. *Collected Papers: Dravidian Linguistics, Ethnology, and Folktales* (Annamalai University Press, Annamalainagar)
Krishnamurti, B. 2001. *Comparative Dravidian Linguistics: Current Perspectives* (Oxford University Press, Oxford)
—— 2003. *The Dravidian Languages* (Cambridge University Press, Cambridge)
Lehmann, T. 1993. *A Grammar of Modern Tamil* (Institute of Linguistics and Culture, Pondicherry)
Paramasivam, K. 1983. *Ikkālat tamiẓ marapu* (Annam, Sivagangai)
Pope, G.U. 1979. *A Handbook of the Tamil Language* (Asian Educational Services, New Delhi)
Schiffman, H. 1979. *A Grammar of Spoken Tamil* (Christian Literature Society, Madras)
Steever, S.B. 1981. *Selected Papers on Tamil and Dravidian Linguistics* (Muttu Patippakam, Madurai)
—— 1998. *The Dravidian Languages* (Routledge, London)
Zvelebil, K. 1970. *Comparative Dravidian Phonology* (Mouton, The Hague)

38

Tai languages

David Strecker

Tai is the most widespread and best known subgroup of the Kadai or Kam-Tai family. Map 38.1 shows the distribution of the Kadai languages and Map 38.2 shows, in an approximate and oversimplified way, the distribution of the Tai languages (the actual linguistic geography of Tai is very complex, with much overlapping and interpenetration of languages). The Tai group comprises the following branches:

- Southwestern, including Ahom (extinct), Khamti, Tai Nuea (Chinese Shan, Dehong Dai), Tai Long (Shan), Khuen, Tai Lue (Xishuangbanna Dai), Kam Muang (Tai Yuan, Northern Thai), Thai (Siamese, Central Thai), Southern Thai, Lao (Lao dialects in Thailand are also called 'Northeastern Thai'), White Tai, Tai Dam (Black Tai), Red Tai and several other languages which could not be shown in Map 38.2 for lack of space.
- Central, an extraordinarily diverse group of dialects known by such names as Tay, Nung and Tho.
- Northern, including the languages officially known in China as Bouyei (Buyi) and Zhuang (these actually appear to constitute a dialect continuum, and the name *Zhuang* is also, confusingly, applied to certain Central dialects) and the Yay language in Vietnam.
- Saek, generally treated as a Northern Tai language, but showing certain phonological peculiarities that set it apart from all other Tai languages, including Northern.

The total number of native speakers of Tai languages is probably somewhere in the neighbourhood of 80 million. The largest number of speakers live in Thailand, perhaps somewhere in the neighbourhood of 45 million or more (including speakers both of Thai and of other Tai languages) and the next largest number live in China, about 25 million. Smaller numbers of Tai speakers live in the other countries shown in Map 38.2. To this we should add maybe a million or more Tai speakers living in the USA, France and other Western countries, including both many refugees from the Indochinese War and many who emigrated under peaceful circumstances.

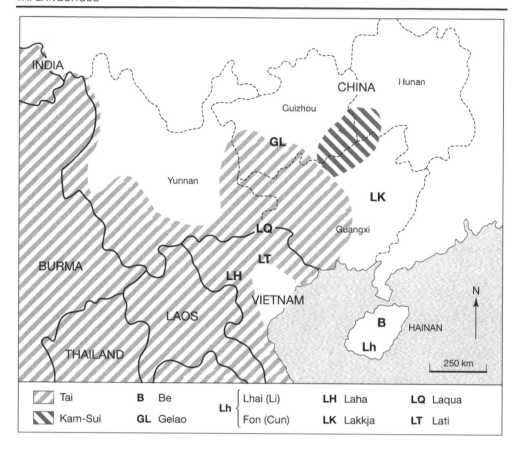

Map 38.1 The Kadai Language Family.

The name *Tai* or *Thai* is the name by which speakers of many, though not all, South-western and Central Tai languages call themselves. In accordance with regular rules of sound correspondence, the name is pronounced with either an unaspirated or an aspirated *t*, depending on the particular language. Earlier writers on comparative Tai usually called the family *Thai*, but most Tai specialists nowadays call it *Tai*. The form *Thai* nowadays usually refers to one particular Tai language, the national language of Thailand. Some writers, notably A.-G. Haudricourt, restrict the term *Tai* to the Southwestern and Central branches of Tai, but I will follow the usage of F.-K. Li, W. Gedney and others and use *Tai* for the whole group, including the Northern branch.

In phonology and syntax the Tai languages differ from one another about as much as do the Romance languages. The same applies to much of their basic lexicon; for more abstract and technical vocabulary the languages of Vietnam, Guangxi and Guizhou tend to borrow from Chinese whereas those further to the west tend to borrow from Sanskrit and Pali. There is also surprising diversity in grammatical morphemes (e.g. prepositions and aspect and mood particles) and in certain common words such as 'to speak' and 'delicious', which contributes greatly to mutual unintelligibility among Tai languages that in most respects are very close. Certain words serve to identify the different branches of the Tai family. For example *kuk* or *kuuk* is a characteristic Northern Tai word

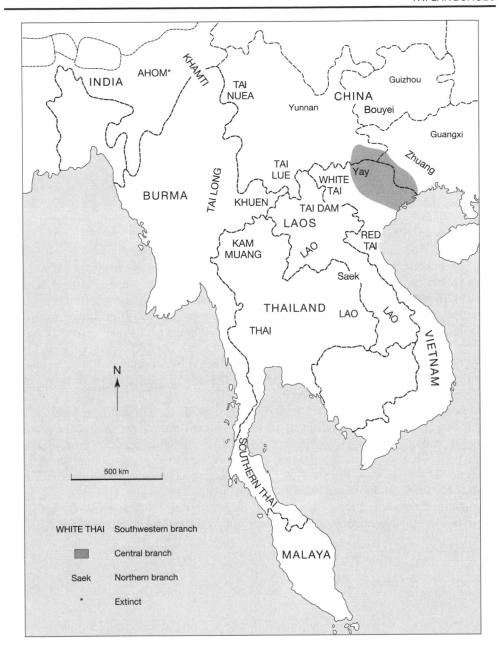

Map 38.2 Approximate General Location of Some Tai Languages.

for 'tiger'; Southwestern and Central Tai use a different word, represented by Thai *sǐa* and its cognates.

In Tai languages, as in many other South-East Asian languages, most words are monosyllabic. All the exceptions to this rule in Tai languages seem to be either loan-words or reduced compounds, such as Kam Muang *pàtŭu* 'door', probably from **pàak tŭu* 'mouth of the door'. All Proto-Tai words that have been reconstructed with any

655

certainty are monosyllabic. On the basis of internal reconstruction some Tai comparativists have derived certain Proto-Tai monosyllables from pre-Tai bisyllabic forms, but this proposal is controversial.

The Proto-Tai syllable had four parts: initial, vowel, final consonant and tone. For example, Proto-Tai *$thraam^A$, 'two or more persons carry', had the initial *thr-, the vowel *-aa-, the final consonant *-m and the tone symbolised by superscript A. The Proto-Tai initial system comprised a rich inventory of consonants and clusters. The vowel system comprised both monophthongs and diphthongs, but despite considerable research on the subject, it is still not at all certain just how many different vowel nuclei Proto-Tai had. The final consonant system was very simple: *-p, *-t, *-k, *-m, *-n, *-$ŋ$ and *-l. There were also syllables with no final consonant, e.g. *haa^C 'five'. Some writers add three semi-vowels to the final consonant inventory, as in *pay^A 'to go', *$ʔbay^A$ 'leaf', *$ʔbaw^A$ 'light in weight'. Others prefer to write these as parts of diphthongs: *pai^A, *$ʔbai^A$ *$ʔbau^A$. This is merely a notational difference.

Proto-Tai had three tones on syllables ending in a vowel, semi-vowel, nasal or lateral. Their phonetic values have not been determined, and it is customary to refer to them simply as A, B and C. (A few Tai comparativists use 0, 1 and 2 instead of A, B and C.) Stop-final syllables had no tonal contrasts but since tonal contrasts on stop-final syllables did develop in the modern languages it is convenient to designate stop-final syllables as a fourth tonal category, tone D. More often than not, tonal correspondences among Tai languages are very regular and easy to work out. When working on a new language or dialect, Tai comparativists generally begin by working out the tonal correspondences and then use tone as a check on the accuracy of their work when they move on to the vowels and consonants.

Although comparative Tai is a well-developed field, the comparative study of the Kadai family as a whole is still in its infancy, so that little can be said at the moment about phonological changes which separate Tai from the other branches of Kadai. One thing which has been discussed in the literature has to do with initial nasals. For example, Sui, which is one of the Kam-Sui languages, has no fewer than three different kinds of syllable-initial nasals: voiceless, preglottalised and voiced. In Proto-Tai the preglottalised nasals fell together with the voiceless nasals, so that Proto-Tai had only two types of syllable-initial nasals, voiceless and voiced, for example:

	Sui	Proto-Tai
'dog'	m̥a¹	*m̥aa^A
'mark'	ʔme¹	*m̥aay^A
'yam'	man²	*man^A

We may now move on to changes specifically within the Tai group. In the development from Proto-Tai to the modern Tai languages, one change which occurs in all languages is the Great Tone Split. What happened was that in each Tai language, tones developed different allotones conditioned by the manner of articulation of the initial consonant of the syllable. Then certain consonants fell together so that these originally allophonic tonal distinctions became contrastive, as for example in the words for 'face' and 'mother's younger sibling' in Thai:

	Proto-Tai	Thai
'face'	*ŋaa^C	nâa (falling tone)
'mother's younger sibling'	*naa^C	náa (high tone)

Notice that in Proto-Tai, 'face' and 'mother's younger sibling' had the same tone but different initials whereas in modern Thai they have the same initial but different tones. Thus the overall effect of the Great Tone Split has been to cause modern Tai languages to have fewer initials and more tones than Proto-Tai did. The Great Tone Split was a South-East Asian areal change, affecting not only Tai but also most other Kadai languages, most Hmong-Mien languages, Chinese, many Tibeto-Burman languages, Vietnamese and so forth. Some Southwestern Tai languages are written in orthographies that were developed before the Great Tone Split took place, so that in Thai, for example, 'face' and 'mother's younger sibling' are spelled หน้า {hňaa} and น้า {ňaa} respectively, with the same tonal diacritic, ˇ, but different initials: {hn} versus {n}.

The major phonological differences among the different branches of the Tai family include:

(1) differences in tone reflecting an earlier difference between a voiced initial in one group of dialects versus a voiceless initial in others,
(2) differences in vowels.

The examples in the chart given here illustrate the tonal differences.

	Thai (SW)	Longzhou (Central)	Yay (Northern)	Proto-Tai
'to plough'	thăy (rising)	thay¹ (mid level)	say¹ (mid-low level)	*thlayᴬ
'to reach, arrive'	thĭŋ (rising)	thɔŋ¹ (mid level)	taŋ⁴ (high rising falling)	—
'to smear, paint'	thaa (mid)	taa² (mid falling)	taa⁴ (high rising-falling)	*daaᴬ

All three words appear to have had tone A in Proto-Tai. After voiceless aspirated stops, tone A became Thai rising tone, Longzhou mid level tone and Yay mid-low level tone, as in 'to plough'. After voiced stops it became Thai mid, Longzhou mid falling and Yay high rising-falling, as in 'to smear'. The problem is determining the initial of 'to reach': in Southwestern and Central Tai this word has the tone which developed after voiceless aspirated stops, as if from Proto-Tai *thĭŋᴬ, whereas in Northern Tai it has the tone which developed after voiced stops, as if from Proto-Tai *dĭŋᴬ. One possibility is that the Proto-Tai form was *dɦĭŋᴬ, with a murmured stop which subsequently fell together with *d in the Northern branch but with *th in Southwestern and Central.

The problem with vowels is analogous to the problem with tones. Consider the examples 'year', 'fire' and 'to plough' in the chart.

	Thai (SW)	Longzhou (Central)	Yay (Northen)	Proto-tai
'year'	pii	pii¹	pi¹	*piiᴬ
'fire'	fay	fay²	fi⁴	—
'to plough'	thăy	thay¹	say¹	*thlayᴬ

It is reasonably certain that 'year' had Proto-Tai *ii and that 'to plough' had Proto-Tai *ay, but what about 'fire'? In Southwestern and Central Tai 'fire' regularly rhymes with 'to plough', whereas in Northern Tai it regularly rhymes with 'year'. Some Tai comparativists have proposed a special diphthong in 'fire' and other words showing the same pattern. This diphthong subsequently merged with *ay in Southwestern and Central Tai and with *ii in Northern Tai. Others have suggested that such words as 'fire' were originally bisyllabic. Thus 'fire' might have been something like Proto-Tai *$avii^A$. In Northern Tai the weak pretonic syllable a was simply lost, giving *vii^A, whereas in Southwestern and Central Tai it interacted with the vowel of the tonic syllable, giving *vay^A. Both suggestions are plausible but difficult to prove. The reconstruction of Proto-Tai vowels is perhaps the most controversial and vexing area in comparative Tai.

Since the Tai languages are uninflected, Tai comparativists have not been able to draw upon comparative morphology in the way that Indo-Europeanists have. This has not been a handicap, since the purely phonological comparisons have been extremely fruitful. Almost no research has been done on comparative Tai syntax. One difference which has been noted involves the order of noun, numeral and classifier. In Tai languages of Vietnam, Guangxi and Guizhou the order is usually numeral + classifier + noun, e.g. Tai Dam:

sɔŋ[1]	fɨn[1]	faa[3]
two	(classifier)	clothes

'two pieces of clothes'

It is possible that this is a result of the influence of Chinese, which has the same order. In languages further to the west the order is usually noun + numeral + classifier, e.g. Thai:

phâa	sɔ̌ɔŋ	phɨɨn
cloth	two	(classifier)

'two pieces of cloth'

Almost all Tai languages have subject–verb–object word order, but in Khamti and other Tai languages of northeastern India the order is subject–object–verb, possibly as a result of influence from Tibeto-Burman or Indo-Aryan languages.

Finally, I will say a few words about Tai writing systems. Some Tai languages are not written. Speakers of Saek, for example, are literate in Thai or Lao but do not write their own language. But a good many Tai languages do have written forms. Central Tai languages, and Northern Tai languages in Guangxi and Guizhou, are generally written with Chinese characters. The details are complex: some characters represent a Tai word similar in *meaning* to the Chinese word, others represent a Tai word similar in *sound* to the Chinese word and in still other cases Tai-speakers have coined new characters which are not used in Chinese. Southwestern Tai languages are generally written in alphabetic scripts derived from those of India, usually not directly from Indian scripts but rather via other South-East Asian scripts such as that of Cambodian. A great many such Tai alphabets exist; they are often quite different from one another superficially, but systematic study reveals similar patterns in, for example, the representation of vowels and diphthongs and similarities in the shapes of many letters.

Bibliography

The standard handbook is Li (1977). For the relationship of Tai to Kam-Sui, reference may be made to Li (1965). Tai phonology is treated in Harris and Noss (1972) and Haudricourt (1972). Three valuable collections of articles are Harris and Chamberlain (1975), Gething et al. (1976) and Gedney (1989). For more recent statements, see Edmondson and Solnit (1988, 1997). Enfield (2007) provides a detailed grammatical description of Lao. Diller et al. (2008) appeared just as this volume was going to press.

References

Diller, A.N.V., Edmondson, J.A. and Luo, Yongxian (eds) 2008. *The Tai-Kadai Languages* (Routledge, London)

Edmondson, J.A. and Solnit, D.B. (eds) 1988. *Comparative Kadai: Linguistic Studies Beyond Tai* (Summer Institute of Linguistics and Arlington, University of Texas at Arlington, Dallas)

—— (eds) 1997. *Comparative Kadai: The Tai Branch* (Summer Institute of Linguistics and Arlington, University of Texas at Arlington, Dallas)

Enfield, N.C. 2007. *A Grammar of Lao* (Mouton de Gruyter, Berlin)

Gedney, W.J. 1989. *Selected Papers on Comparative Tai Studies*, ed. R.J. Bickner, J. Hartmann, T.J. Hudak and P. Peyasantiwong (University of Michigan Centers for South and Southeast Asian Studies, Ann Arbor)

Gething, T.W., Harris, J.G. and Kullavanijaya, P. (eds) 1976. *Tai Linguistics in Honor of Fang-Kuei Li* (Chulalongkorn University Press, Bangkok)

Harris, J.G. and Chamberlain, J.R. (eds) 1975. *Studies in Tai Linguistics in Honor of William J. Gedney* (Central Institute of English Language, Bangkok)

Harris, J.G. and Noss, R.B. (eds) 1972. *Tai Phonetics and Phonology* (Central Institute of English Language, Bangkok)

Haudricourt, A.G. 1972. *Problèmes de phonologie diachronique* (Société pour l'Étude des Langues Africaines, Paris)

Li, F.-K. 1965. 'The Tai and Kam-Sui Languages', *Lingua*, vol. 14, pp. 148–79

—— 1977. *A Handbook of Comparative Tai* (University Press of Hawaii, Honolulu)

39

Thai

Thomas John Hudak

1 Historical Background

Thai (Siamese, Central Thai) belongs to the Tai language family, a subgroup of the Kadai or Kam-Tai family. A number of linguists now regard Kam-Tai, along with Austronesian, as a branch of Austro-Tai, although this hypothesis remains controversial. All members of the Tai family derive from a single proto-parent designated as Proto-Tai. Linguistic research has shown the area near the border of northern Vietnam and southeastern China as the probable place of origin for the Tai languages. Today the Tai family includes languages spoken in Assam, northern Burma, all of Thailand including the peninsula, Laos, northern Vietnam and the Chinese provinces of Yunnan, Guizhou (Kweichow) and Guangxi (Kwangsi). Linguists, notably Fang Kuei Li, divide these languages into a Northern, a Central and a Southwestern branch. Others, in particular William J. Gedney and A.-G. Haudricourt, view the Central and Southwestern branch as a single group. In the tripartite division, Thai falls into the Southwestern branch.

Sukhothai, established in central Thailand in the early and mid-thirteenth century, represents the first major kingdom of the Thai. Current theories state that the language spoken in Sukhothai resembled Proto-Tai in tonal structure. This early system consisted of three tones on syllables ending in a long vowel, a semi-vowel or a nasal (*kham pen* 'live syllable' in traditional Thai grammatical terms). On syllables ending in *p*, *t*, *k* or in a glottal stop after a short vowel a fourth tone existed, although these syllables showed no tonal differentiation at all (*kham taay* 'dead syllable' in traditional Thai grammatical terms). While the presence of some type of suprasegmental contrasts is considered conclusive at this early stage of the language, the phonetic nature of these contrasts still remains a matter of speculation. This system prevailed at the time of the creation of the writing system by King Ramkhamhaeng (1275–1317) in the latter part of the thirteenth century.

In 1350 the centre of power shifted from Sukhothai to Ayutthaya. Recent theories, which will not be discussed here for lack of space, claim that the Sukhothai and Ayutthaya dialects underwent different sound changes. These theories, furthermore, claim that Southern Thai evolved from the Sukhothai dialect and Central Thai or Thai from the Ayutthaya dialect (see Brown 1965). The generally accepted theory, however, holds that Thai descended from the Sukhothai dialect with the following sound changes.

The first of the changes, the sound changes known as the tonal splits, affected all of the languages in the Tai family (see Chapter 38). Because of the splits, sound systems with three contrasting tones, for example, became systems typically with six tones, two different tones from each of the three earlier tones. In some dialects, however, special characteristics of the dialect created more or fewer tones. Thai, for example, now has five tones. In brief, these shifts resulted when the phonetic nature of the initial consonant of each syllable conditioned an allophonic pitch difference. Subsequent changes in the initial consonant, then, caused these allophonic non-contrastive pitches to become contrastive (see Section 2 for details of the early tones and the tone split in Thai). Linguists frequently set a date as early as AD 1000 for these sound changes. For the Thai spoken in Ayutthaya, however, the splits seem to have occurred much later.

Several factors suggest a later date for the splits in Thai. First, late thirteenth-century and early fourteenth-century Ayutthayan poetic compositions appear in the three-tone language. Second, Khmer loanwords, which probably entered the language after the Thai conquest of Angkor in 1431, also predate the split. In addition, seventeenth-century descriptions of the Thai alphabet demonstrate that the consonant changes involved with the tonal splits had already taken place by that date. Citing this evidence, Gedney proposes a date some time between the mid-fifteenth and the mid-seventeeth centuries for the tone splits in Thai.

The Ayutthaya period (1350–1767) also saw large numbers of Sanskrit and Pali words borrowed, although this phenomenon was not strictly limited to this period. These Indic loanwords comprise a large portion of the technical vocabularies for science, government, education, religion and literature. Gedney (1947: 1) states that these loanwords are as common in spoken Thai as Latin and Greek forms are in spoken English. Sanskrit and, to a much lesser extent, Pali assume the same cultural importance for Thai as Latin does for English. Many of these loanwords exist in both a short and a long form. The shorter form represents the usual Thai pronunciation: *rát* 'state', *thêep* 'god'. The longer alternant usually, but not always, functions as a combining form: *rátthàbaan* 'government' (latter constituent *baan* 'protector, protection'); *thêepphábùt* 'angel' (latter constituent *bùt* 'son'). Most of these compounds seem to have been formed in modern Thai since they do not appear in either Sanskrit or Pali.

During the Ayutthaya period, Thai began to acquire other characteristics that have led the Thai to regard their language as highly complex and stratified, difficult to acquire even for the very educated. In part, this impression grew because of the Indic loanwords. But far more central to the creation of this image was the proliferation of titles, ranks, pronouns, royal vocabulary and royal kin terminology that reflected the growing stratification and complexity of the society. Although much of the complexity applied only to the court, Thai speakers nevertheless interpreted these changes as changes in their own language.

Many of these new terms had their origin in Sanskrit and Pali. Still others came from Khmer. Khmer institutions had always had an influence on the Thai court and this influence increased when the Thai imported Khmer intelligentsia into Thailand after the fall of Angkor. Royal titles provide a good example of this increasing complexity. Originally, during the Sukhothai period, the Khmer title *khŭn* referred to the king. By the Ayutthaya period, this title applied only to officials and the king had acquired far more elaborate ones. Other changes affected the titles for the king's offspring. Newly created titles included those for children by a royal queen, for children by a non-royal queen and for grandchildren. In the nineteenth century titles for great-grandchildren and great-great-grandchildren were also added.

Royalty who assisted the king in the performance of his duties received another set of titles, the *krom* titles, another Khmer institution. Introduced in the seventeenth century, these titles probably first indicated private administrative units, then ministries and finally departments within the ministries. Non-royalty working in the expanding civil service received a different set of titles, also from the Khmer.

This terminology and the emphasis upon its correct use began to be standardised during the reign of King Mongkut (1851–68). Valuing adherence to ancient patterns that produced a 'correctness' in the language, Mongkut issued decrees and proclamations that formalised place names and titles. In addition to these terms, he directed his attention to function words such as prepositions and adverbs. In a letter to Norodom of Cambodia, he listed the rules for correct pronoun usage. Both King Chulalongkorn (1868–1910) and King Vajiravudh (1910–26) added to the regulating of this system. Among other things, Chulalongkorn wrote a lengthy essay explaining the Thai system of royal titles in his reign and Vajiravudh created titles for the ministries and regulated titles for women. In 1932, the revolution abandoned the nobility and granting of titles, other than to the royal offspring. The Thai perceptions of their language, however, were not altered, and Thai is still regarded as a highly complex and difficult language.

In Thailand, Thai serves as the official national language. It is the language taught and used in the schools, the one used by the media and the one used for all government affairs. According to the estimate for mid-2007, 65 million people live in Thailand. An estimated 80 per cent of this total or about 52,000,000 people speak Thai. Outside of Bangkok and the central plains, other dialects and languages of the Tai family coexist with the standard: Northern Thai (Kam Muang or Yuan) in the north, Southern Thai in the south and Lao or Northeastern Thai in the north-east. Still other Tai languages such as Lue, Phuthai and Phuan are spoken as small speech islands in various parts of the country. In addition, Thailand has many minority groups who speak languages that do not belong to the Tai family.

2 Phonology

Spoken Thai divides into clearly marked syllables bounded on either side by juncture. Each syllable consists of a vocalic nucleus and a tone. In addition, an initial consonant, a final consonant or an initial and final consonant may or may not occur. Possible syllable shapes include V, VV, VC, VVC, CV, CVV, CCV, CCVV, CVC, CVVC, CCVC and CCVVC, where VV represents a long vowel.

2.1 Consonants

Table 39.1 lists the twenty segmental consonant phonemes in Thai.

All twenty consonants may appear in initial position. Permitted initial consonant clusters include labials – *pr, pl, phr, phl*; alveolars – *tr, thr*; and velars – *kr, kl, kw, khr, khl, khw*. Only *p, t, k, m, n, ŋ, w, y* occur in final position. No consonant clusters exist in final position.

Table 39.1 Thai Consonants

	Bilabial	Labio-dental	Alveolar	Palatal	Velar	Glottal
Stops						
Vls. unaspirated	p		t	c	k	
Vls. aspirated	ph		th	ch	kh	
Voiced	b		d			
Fricatives		f	s			h
Sonorants						
Nasals	m		n		ŋ	
Lateral			l			
Trill/Tap			r			
Semi-vowels	w			y		

At this point, some elaboration will help to clarify the status of the glottal stop in this description and the general status of /l/ and /r/ in Thai. Because of its predictability, the glottal stop is not listed as a separate phoneme. It appears initially before a vowel that lacks a syllable-initial consonant or consonant cluster: *ʔaahǎan* 'food'. Finally, it appears with the cessation of a short vowel nucleus followed by no final consonant: *tóʔ* 'table'. Internally, in words of more than one syllable, the glottal stop is frequently omitted, particularly at rapid, conversational speed: *pràʔwàt* → *pràwàt* 'history'.

The phonemic status of /l/ and /r/ in Thai appears to be in a state of flux; however, all phonemic descriptions of Thai still list the two sounds as separate phonemes. The writing system, moreover, has separate symbols for each of them. Most Thai, especially the educated, claim to distinguish between the two. This seems to be the case for slow and highly conscious speech. In fast speech, however, /r/ freely alternates with /l/, although certain forms occur more often with /l/ than with /r/. Many speakers regard these alternating forms as indicative of 'less correct' or 'substandard' speech. Linguistic hypotheses suggest that this lack of stable contrast may signal a sound change in process.

2.2 Vowels

Table 39.2 lists the nine vowel phonemes.

Each vowel may occur phonemically short or long. When long, the nuclei may be interpreted as two instances of the corresponding short vowel: *ii, ɨɨ, uu, ee, əə, oo, εε, aa, ɔɔ*. Phonetically, the long vowels average in duration about twice as long as the short vowels. All 18 vocalic nuclei may occur alone, with an initial consonant, with a final consonant or with an initial and final consonant.

Table 39.2 Thai Vowels

	Front	Back unrounded	Back rounded
High	i	ɨ	u
Mid	e	ə	o
Low	ε	a	ɔ

2.3 Diphthongs

Each of the three short and long high vowels may be followed by a centring off-glide *a*. The rare short combinations occupy about as much time as the single short vowels and the long combinations about as much time as the long vowels.

Transcriptions of these diphthongs differ. Some studies make no distinction between the long and the short. Others transcribe the short diphthongs as *ia, ɨa, ua* and the long as *iia, ɨɨa, uua*. Still another interprets the short combination as a single short vowel plus *ə*. Because of the relative rarity of the short diphthongs, this description designates both the short and long forms as a sequence of VV.

Gedney notes (1947: 14, 20, 21) that for the short diphthongs only *p, t, c, k, ph, th, ch, kh* seem to appear as initials and only *p, t, k* as finals. The long diphthongs seem to have no restrictions on the permitted initials and finals.

2.4 Tones

Each syllable in Thai carries one of five phonemic tones. These tones, with the symbols used in this transcription placed over the first vowel, include: a mid tone (unmarked, *khaa* 'to be lodged in'); a low tone (*khàa* 'a kind of aromatic root'); a falling tone (*khâa* 'servant, slave'); a high tone (*kháa* 'to do business in'); and a rising tone (*khǎa* 'leg'). Tones in Thai may be described in terms of pitch contour, pitch height and glottalised or non-glottalised voice quality (Table 39.3).

Based on tonal occurrences, syllables can be divided into three types:

(1) Syllables ending in a long vowel, a semi-vowel or a nasal. All five tones occur on these syllables (see above examples).
(2) Syllables ending with a short vowel and a stop or no final. These syllables have either a low or high tone: *phèt* 'to be peppery, spicy'; *ké* 'sheep'; *rák* 'to love'. Occasionally a falling tone occurs: *kɔ̂* 'then, consequently'. The mid and rising tones do not occur on syllables with this structure.
(3) Syllables with a long vowel followed by a stop. These syllables usually have low and falling tones: *pàak* 'mouth', *châat* 'nation'. Occasionally a high tone appears: *nóot* 'note'; *khwɔ́ɔt* 'quart' (both English borrowings). Mid and rising tones never occur on syllables with this structure.

In addition to these five tones, some linguists analyse a variant of the high tone as a sixth tone. Occurring in emphatic exclamations, this tone, higher in pitch and longer than the normal high tone, may replace any one of the five tones: *dīidii* 'very good' (see Section 4, pages 668–669).

Table 39.3 Tones in Thai

Tone	Pitch contour	Pitch height	Voice quality
Mid	Level	Medium	Non-glottalised
Low	Level	Low	Non-glottalised
Falling	Falling	High to low	Glottalised
High	Level	High	Glottalised
Rising	Rising	Low to high	Non-glottalised

The historical development of the Thai tonal system has long been of great interest. Early Thai (pre-fifteenth century) had a system of three tones, A, B, C, on syllables ending in a long vowel, a semi-vowel or a nasal. Syllables with no tone mark had the A tone. Syllables with the *máy èek* (') tone mark had the B tone and those with the *máy thoo* (ˇ) tone mark had the C tone. Checked syllables, i.e. those terminating in *p*, *t*, *k* or in a glottal after a short vowel, had a fourth tone D, although these syllables actually showed no tonal differentiation at all. It should be noted that these designated tones and tone markers reveal nothing about the phonetic nature of the ancient tones. Although various theories about the tonal phonetics have been offered, the question remains controversial.

Probably between the fifteenth and seventeenth centuries, the tones in each of the categories split, conditioned by the phonetic nature of the initial consonant of each syllable. In some cases, the presence or absence of friction or aspiration caused the split. In others, the conditioning factor was the presence or absence of voicing. For the checked syllables, both the phonetic nature of the initial and the quantity of the nuclear vowel conditioned the split. Table 39.4 summarises these splits.

Table 39.4 Tone Splits in Thai

Initials at time of split / Tones at time of split	A	B (ˈ)	C (ˇ)	D Short vowel nucleus	D Long vowel nucleus
Voiceless friction: h, ph, hm, etc.	Rising tone	Low tone	Falling tone	Low tone	Low tone
Voiceless unaspirated and glottal	Mid tone				
Voiced		Falling tone	High tone	High tone	Falling tone

Note: This chart does not account for words with *máy trii* (ˇ) or *máy càttàwaa* (+) tone marks. Words with these tones must have resulted from other changes in the language after the tone splits. Borrowings from other dialects or languages represent other possible sources for these words. The tone marks were created after the words entered the language.

Following the split, some initial consonants also changed, for example voiced consonants to voiceless ones:

*gaa^B → gâa → khâa 'fee, cost'

Originally, both in sound and in spelling, the initial consonant and tone distinguished *gaa^B* from *khaa^C* 'slave, servant'. However as a consequence of the tone split and subsequent changes *gaa^B* changed to *khâa* while *khaa^C* changed to *khâa*. Thus the two forms came to be pronounced exactly alike, but spelled differently. Much of the complication of the spelling system results from these types of sound changes.

2.5 Stress

The question of stress in Thai remains a much debated issue with no consensus whether stress is conditioned by rhythm or rhythm by stress or whether both are phonemic. Most studies agree, however, that the syllable in final position has the greatest prominence or stress. In disyllabic and polysyllabic words, the remaining vowels are reduced, although the reduced vowel may not be as short as a phonemically short vowel. Tone neutralisation may also occur with the vowel reduction.

3 Writing System

The Thai writing system uses as a base an Indic alphabet originally designed to represent the sounds of Sanskrit. King Ramkhamhaeng (1275–1317) of Sukhothai generally receives credit for creating the new alphabet some time prior to AD 1283, the date of the earliest extant inscription written in the alphabet. Borrowing the alphabet then in use by the Khmers, Ramkhamhaeng kept the symbols for the Sanskrit sounds not found in Thai and used them in Indic loanwords to reflect the origin of their pronunciation. For Thai sounds not accommodated by the alphabet, he created new symbols, including those for tones. Because of the redesigning of the symbols to fit Khmer first and then to fit Thai, the eventual system created by Ramkhamhaeng had little resemblance to the Sanskrit originals.

The two types of symbols in the alphabet resulted in a system characterised by several symbols for the same sound. The division of the consonants into three groups (high, mid, low) to indicate tone in spelling further complicated the system. High class consonants represent the original voiceless aspirated sounds, the mid class represent the original voiceless non-aspirated and the preglottalised voiced sounds and the low class represent the original voiced sounds.

Table 39.5 lists the 44 consonants in their alphabetic arrangement and in their consonant classes. To read the chart, proceed from left to right until the solid line, then move to the next line. At the completion of the first section (ม), move up to the beginning of the

Table 39.5 Consonants

Mid	Mid	High	High	Low	Low	Low	Low	Low	High	
ก	ข	ฃ	ค	ฅ	ฆ	ง				*High* ห
k	kh	kh	kh	kh	kh	ŋ				h
จ	ฉ			ช	ซ	ฌ	ญ	ย	ศ	*Low* ฬ
c	ch			ch	s	ch	y	y	s	l
ฎ	ฏ	ฐ		ฑ		ฒ	ณ	ร	ษ	*Mid* อ
d	t	th		th		th	n	r	s	?
ด	ต	ถ		ท		ธ	น	ล	ส	*Low* ฮ
d	t	th		th		th	n	l	s	h
บ	ป	ผ	ฝ	พ	ฟ	ภ	ม	ว		
b	p	ph	f	ph	f	ph	m	w		

Source: Adapted from Brown vol. 3, 1967: 212.

next section ย and continue as before. Table 39.6 lists the symbols for the 18 vowels and the six diphthongs. A ก indicates an initial consonant and a น a non-specific final.

Table 39.6 Vowels

	Long			Short					
	With final		Without final	With final				Without final	
	y	Other		y	w	m	Other		
a		กา		ไก	ใก	เกา	กำ	อัน	กะ	ก
ə	เกย	เกิน	เกอ						เกอะ
e		เก				เก็น			เกะ
o		โก				กน			โกะ
ua	กวน		กัว			*			กัวะ
ia		เกีย				*			เกียะ
ɨa		เกือ				*			เกือะ
ɛ		แก				แก็น			แกะ
ɔ		กอ				กอน			แกาะ
ɨ	กีย		กือ			กี			
i		กี				กี			
u		กู				กุ			

Source: Adapted from Brown vol. 3, 1967: 212

Note: * This chart does not include the symbols for the rare short diphthongs plus final consonant.

Table 39.7 shows the five tones as they appear on each of the syllable types in each of the three consonant groups.

4 Morphology

Thai has no inflections for case, gender, tense or number. Affixing, compounding and reduplicating represent the major derivational processes.

4.1 Affixing

Derivatives may be formed with a few prefixes and suffixes. The more common affixes include:

(1) *kaan-* 'the act of, affairs of, matter of' forms abstract nouns from verbs and some nouns: e.g. *lên-* 'to play', *kaanlên* 'playing'; *mɨaŋ* 'city', *kaanmɨaŋ* 'politics'.
(2) *khwaam-* 'the condition of' forms abstract nouns that express a quality or state: e.g. *rúusɨk* 'to feel'; *khwaamrúusɨk* 'feeling'.
(3) *khîi-* 'characterised by': e.g. *bòn* 'to complain'; *khîibòn* 'given to complaining'.
(4) *khrɨaŋ-* 'a collection, equipment': e.g. *khian* 'to write'; *khrɨaŋkhian* 'stationery'.
(5) *nâa-* 'worthy of': e.g. *rák* 'to love'; *nâarák* 'cute, lovable'.
(6) *nák-* 'expert, authority': e.g. *rian* 'to study'; *nákrian* 'student'.
(7) *-sàat* 'branch, field of knowledge': e.g. *daaraa* 'star'; *daaraasàat* 'astronomy'.

Table 39.7 Syllable Types, Consonant Classes and Their Respective Tones

Syllables with final long vowel, m, n, ŋ, w,y

Consonant class \ Tone mark	No mark	Low tone mark '	Falling tone mark ˇ	High tone mark ꞈ	Rising tone mark +
High	Rising tone				
		Low tone	Falling tone		
Mid				Low Tone	Rising tone
	Mid tone				
Low		Falling tone	High tone		

Syllables ending with final p, t, k or syllables ending with short vowel and no final

Consonant class	Short vowel*	Long vowel**
High		
Mid	Low tone	
Low	High tone	Falling tone

Source: Adapted from Brown vol. 3, 1967: 213

Notes: * In rare instances, a falling tone will appear on a syllable with a short vowel ending in a *p*, *t* or *k*.
** In rare instances, a high tone will appear on a syllable with a long vowel ending in *p*, *t* or *k*.

4.2 Compounding

Compounds in Thai are endocentric constructions in which the first constituent generally determines the syntactic word class. Compounds may be coordinate or attributive. Coordinate nouns include *phɔɔmɛ̂ɛ* 'parents' (*phɔɔ* 'father' + *mɛ̂ɛ* 'mother'); *phîinɔ́ɔŋ* 'brothers and sisters' (*phîi* 'older sibling' + *nɔ́ɔŋ* 'younger sibling'). Coordinate verbs include *hŭŋtôm* 'to cook' (*hŭŋ* 'to cook rice' + *tôm* 'to boil food'); *ráprúu* 'to acknowledge, take responsibility' (*ráp* 'to take, accept' + *rúu* 'to know'). Attributive compounds include *námkhɛ̌ŋ* 'ice' (*nám* 'water' + *khɛ̌ŋ* 'to be hard'); *rótfay* 'train' (*rót* 'vehicle, car' + *fay* 'fire').

4.3 Reduplication

Three general types of reduplication occur in Thai: reduplication of a base form with no changes, ablauting reduplication and reduplication with an accompanying change in tone.

Reduplication of the base conveys several different meanings: softens the base, *dii* 'good' → *diidii* 'rather good'; indicates plurality, *dèk* 'child' → *dèkdèk* 'children'; forms imitatives, *khέk* 'to knock' → *khέkkhέk* 'rapping sound'; intensifies meaning, *ciŋ* 'to be true' → *ciŋciŋ* 'really'.

Examples of ablauting reduplication include: (1) the alternation of a back vowel with its corresponding front vowel, *yûŋ* 'to be confused' → *yûŋyîŋ; soosee* 'to stagger'; and

(2) the alternation of any vowel with *a*, *chaŋ* 'to hate' → *chiŋchaŋ* 'to hate, detest, loathe'.

Reduplication with an accompanying change in tone generally signifies emphasis in speech. Used more often by women than men, the intensified form consists of the base word with any of the five tones preceded by the reduplication which carries a high tone higher in pitch and longer than the normal high tone: *dii* 'good' → *dīidii* 'really good'.

4.4 Elaborate Expressions

Elaborate expressions, a common South-East Asian areal feature, represent a special type of compounding achieved through the reduplication of part of a compound and the addition of a new part. Usually the expression consists of four syllables, with the repeated elements the first and third syllable or the second and fourth.

tɨɨn	taa	tɨɨn	cay
to wake	eye	to wake	heart

'to be full of wonder and excitement'

Frequently rhyme occurs as part of the expression, in which case the second and third syllables rhyme.

hùu	pàa	taa	thɨan
ear	forest	eye	forest

'to be ignorant of what is going on'

The new syllable may be added solely for rhyme and/or it may have some semantic relationship to the original part.

For the Thai, the ability to use elaborate expressions is an essential quality of speaking well and fluently (*phayrɔ́*). Attempts to classify the expressions according to the structure and semantics of the components have largely been unsuccessful.

5 Syntax

Subject–verb–object, in that order, constitutes the most favoured word order in Thai:

khǎw	sɨ́ɨ	aahǎan
he	buy	food

'He buys food.'

Both subject and object may be filled with: (1) a noun phrase consisting of a noun, a pronoun, a demonstrative pronoun or an interrogative-indefinite pronoun; or (2) a noun phrase consisting of noun + attribute in which case the head noun always precedes the attribute. Noun + attribute constructions may be simple or complex. Predicates may be nominal or verbal, simple or complex.

5.1 Noun Phrases

5.1.1 Nouns

Nouns form one of the largest classes of words in the vocabulary, the other being the verbs. Single nouns may occupy the subject or object position (see above example). Typically nouns occur as the head of noun expressions (see noun + attribute).

5.1.2 Pronouns

Like many other South-East Asian languages, Thai exhibits a complex pronoun system. The choice of pronoun used in any one situation depends upon factors such as sex, age, social position and the attitude of the speaker towards the addressee. In those contexts in which the referent is understood, the pronoun is frequently omitted. Common first and second person singular pronouns include those given in Table 39.8.

Table 39.8 First and Second Person Singular Pronouns

Situation		First Person	Second Person
1	Polite conversation with strangers and acquaintances	phǒm (used by male) dìchǎn (used by female)	khun
2	Speaking to a superior, showing deference	phǒm (used by male) dìchǎn (used by female)	thân
3	Informal conversation with close friends and family	chǎn	thəə
4	Conversation between intimates of the same sex	kan	kɛɛ
5	Adult to a child	chǎn or kinship term	nǔu or kinship term
6	Child to adult	nǔu	kinship term
7	Child to older sibling	nǔu	phîi

Fewer choices exist for third person singular pronouns. In general, *man* is used for inferiors, for non-humans and for expressing anger. *khǎw* is the general polite form and *thân* the form for superiors. Additional forms not discussed here are employed for royalty.

raw, which may be inclusive or exclusive, expresses first person plural. It may also be used to mean 'I' when addressing inferiors or oneself.

Second and third person plural forms are generally expressed by the singular forms.

Kinship terms and other nouns referring to relationships may also be used as pronouns. For example, *mɛ̂ɛ* 'mother' may mean 'you, she' when speaking to or about one's mother or 'I, mother' when the mother speaks to her child. Other terms following this pattern include *phɔ̂ɔ* 'father', *lûuk* 'child', *phîi* 'older sibling', *nɔ́ɔŋ* 'younger sibling', *phɨ̂an* 'friend'.

5.1.3 Demonstrative Pronouns

Demonstrative pronouns may occupy positions available to nouns, although they never occur with attributes. These pronouns include *nîi* 'this one', *nân* 'that one', and *nôon* 'that one over there'.

nîi	sŭay	mâak
this one	beautiful	much, many

'This one is very beautiful.'

For some speakers, the demonstrative adjectives, *níi* 'this', *nán* 'that', *nóon* 'that over there', also function as demonstrative pronouns.

5.1.4 Interrogative–indefinite Pronouns

In Thai, the interrogatives and indefinite pronouns have the same form. Occurring in the same positions as nouns, these words make a question or an indefinite statement:

khray	rian	phaasăa	thay
who	study	language	Thai

'Who's studying Thai?

mây	mii	khray	rian	phaasăa	thay
negative	have	anyone	study	language	Thai

'No one's studying Thai.'

Besides *khray* 'who?, anyone', this group includes *àray* 'what?, anything', *năy* 'which?', *thîi năy* 'where?, anywhere', *day* 'which?, what?, any'.

5.1.5 Noun + Attribute: Simple

Simple attributes consist of single constituents. These constituents may be another noun, a pronoun, a demonstrative adjective or a verb. A noun following the head noun may function as the possessor and the head noun the possessed: *nâŋsŭ dèk* ('book child') 'child's book'. A complex noun phrase with the preposition *khŏɔŋ* 'of' frequently replaces this construction: *nâŋsŭ khŏɔŋ dèk* 'child's book'. *dèk* may also modify the head noun in which case the expression means 'a book for children'. When a pronoun, the attribute functions as a possessive adjective: *mêe phŏm* ('mother I') 'my mother'. The three demonstrative adjectives, *níi* 'this, these', *nán* 'that, those', and *nóon* 'that, those over there', may also fill the attribute position.

Words considered to be adjectives in English (*sŭay* 'beautiful', *dii* 'good', *yaaw* 'long') may function as nominal attributes, verbal attributes or as predicates. Because these words behave syntactically as verbs without a copula, they are treated here as verbs. Thus, *bâan sŭay* may be translated as 'the house is beautiful' or 'a beautiful house'.

5.1.6 Noun + Attribute: Complex

Complex attributes consist of more than one constituent. The use of classifiers, one of the most characteristic features of Thai syntax, serves to illustrate a typical complex attribute. With quantifiers, classifiers are obligatory, and the usual word order is noun + quantifier + classifier:

dèk	săam	khon
child	three	classifier

'three children'

This regular order changes in two situations. First, when the numeral 'one' is used, the numeral and classifier rearrange to indicate an indefinite meaning: *dèk khon nɨ̀ŋ* 'a child'. To specify the number of objects, the original order remains: *dèk nɨ̀ŋ khon* 'one child'. Second, with the verb *hây* 'to give' and an indirect object, the word order following *hây* becomes thing given, person given to, and amount given:

khruu   hây   sàmùt   nákrian   săam   lêm
teacher give   notebook student   three   classifier
'The teacher gave the student three notebooks.'

In each noun + classifier construction, the head noun determines the choice of classifier. Examples include *khon* for human beings, *tua* for animals, tables, chairs, clothes, *lêm* for books, carts, sharp pointed instruments and *muan* for cigars and cigarettes. Although unsuccessful, various attempts have been made to link the nouns semantically with their respective classifiers. When referring to a group, more general classifiers such as *fŭuŋ* 'flock, herd' may be used.

Expanding the attribute forms more complex noun phrases:

Noun	*Attribute*	
dèk	săam khon	'three boys'
dèk	lɔɔ săam khon	'three handsome boys'
dèk	lɔɔ săam khon níi	'these three handsome boys'

In more precise and particularised speech, a classifier is used between the noun and the following verbal attribute or demonstrative adjective: *dèk khon lɔɔ* 'the handsome boy'; *dèk khon níi* 'this very boy'; *dèk khon lɔɔ săam khon níi* 'these three handsome boys'.

5.2 Predicates

Normal word order places the predicate immediately after the subject. Thai verbs have no inflection for tense or number. Context, added time expressions or preverbs generally specify the tense:

khăw   àan   nâŋsɨɨ   dĭawníi
he   read   book   now
'He is reading a book now.'

mây 'not' negates the verb:

khăw   mây   àan   nâŋsɨɨ   dĭawníi
'He isn't reading a book now.'

Predicates may be nominal or verbal, simple or complex.

5.2.1 Nominal Predicate

In predicates of this type, no verb appears, only a noun phrase.

nîi	rooŋrian	phŏm
this one	school	I

'This is my school.'

Far more frequent are verbal predicates.

5.2.2 Verbal Predicate: Simple

Main verbs, the semantics of which roughly correspond to English verbs, form the nucleus of simple predicates.

5.2.3 Verbal Predicate: Complex

Complex verbal predicates consist of a collocation of verbs generally referred to as serial verbs. In complex collocations, the meaning of the main verb is modified by two classes of secondary verbs, one which precedes the main verb and one which follows. The first class of secondary verbs, those that precede the main verb and follow the subject, often translate as English modals or adverbs:

khăw	tôŋ	klàp	bâan
he	must	return	home

'He must return home.'

khăw	yaŋ	rian	wíchaa	nán
he	still	study	subject	that

'He's still studying that subject.'

Other examples of these verbs include *cà* 'shall, will', *mây* 'not', *khuan* 'should, ought to', *khəəy* 'ever, to have experienced', *àat* 'capable of', *yàak* 'to want to, wish for'. Verbs in this class may occur together, in which case their order is fixed.

phŏm	mây	yàak	cà	rian	wíchaa	nán
I	not	want to	will	study	subject	that

'I don't want to study that subject.'

The preverb *dây* frequently indicates the past tense: *mây dây pay* 'did not go'.

The second class of secondary verbs follows both transitive and intransitive main verbs.

khăw	yók	nâatàaŋ	khîn	
he	raise	window	up	(transitive)

'He raised the window up.'

dɨŋ	tàbuu	ɔ̀ɔk	
pull	nail	out	(transitive)

'Pull the nail out'

khăw	nâŋ	loŋ	
he	sit	down	(intransitive)

'He sat down'

As a class, these verbs have a general meaning of having successfully completed the action begun by the main verb. Other representative examples of this large class include *dây* 'to be able', *pen* 'to know how to, to do from habit', *wǎy* 'to be physically capable of', *pay* 'action away from the speaker', *maa* 'action toward the speaker', *lέεw* 'completed action', *yùu* 'ongoing action'. Many of the secondary verbs may also function as main verbs. As a main verb, *khûn* in the above example, means 'to rise, grow, board, climb'.

Frequently, the collocation may consist of all three types of verbs:

khun	cà	thon	yùu	kàp	chaawbâan	wǎy	rǐi
you	will	endure	live	with	villagers	to be physically capable of	question particle

'Can you stand living with villagers?'

5.2.4 Particles

Thai has a large class of particles that end an utterance. These particles can be divided into three broad groups: question particles, polite particles and mood particles.

Question particles form questions that require a yes–no answer. These questions result when the particle is placed at the end of a statement. Two main particles, alone and in combinations with other words, occur: *máy* and *rǐi*.

(a) khun cà pay hǎa phîan máy
you will go see friend Q-particle
'Are you going to see a friend?'

In this situation, the speaker has no particular expectation as to what the answer will be.

(b) khun cà pay hǎa phîan rǐi
'Are you going to see a friend?'

With *rǐi* the speaker has reason to believe his assumption is correct, and the addressee will confirm it.

(c) khun càpay hǎa phîan rǐi plàaw
Are you going to see a friend or not?'

This question is similar to the first question, with no particular expectation for an answer. Literally, *plàaw* means 'to be empty'. In a question, it means 'or not so'.

(d) khun cà pay hǎa phîan chây máy
'You're going to see a friend, aren't you?'

With *chây máy* 'isn't that so', the speaker is quite certain of his statement and expects agreement. This particle is similar to English tag questions.

Polite particles show respect or deference towards the addressee. Marked for gender, these particles include: *khâ* – marks statements by women; *khá* – marks questions by women; *khráp* – marks statements and questions by men.

Mood particles form the third general group of particles. These particles signal the attitude or emotion of the speaker towards the situation at the time of speaking. Representative examples include *nâ* – indicates urging, persuading; *rɔ̀ɔk* – used with negative statements, usually makes a statement milder or corrects a misapprehension; *ləəy* – encourages the addressee to do something; *sí* – softens requests or commands.

All of these particles may be used in clusters, in which case their order is fixed.

5.3 Complements

Three examples serve to illustrate complements in Thai.

5.3.1 Relative Clauses

The word *thîi* introduces relative clauses. In literary contexts, *sɨŋ* replaces *thîi*, although the exact distribution of these two relative pronouns remains unclear.

dèk	thîi	rian	phaasăa	thay	maa	lɛ́ɛw
child	relative pronoun	study	language	Thai	come	already

The child who is studying Thai has come already.'

5.3.2 Causatives

The verb *hây* 'to give' forms causatives with the result following *hây*.

phǒm	cà	àthíbaay	hây	khun	khâwcay
I	will	explain	make, give	you	understand

'I'll explain so you understand.'

5.3.3 Comparative–superlative

kwàa 'more' and *thîisùt* 'most' inserted after the verb form the comparative, (a), and the superlative, (b):

(a)	năŋsɨɨ	níi	yâak	kwàa	năŋsɨɨ	nán
	book	this	hard	more	book	that

'This book is harder than that one.'

(b)	năŋsɨɨ	níi	yâak	thîisùt
	book	this	hard	most

'This book is the hardest.'

Bibliography

Brown (1965) presents a theory of sound change in Thai dialects; this is a difficult, but worthwhile work. There are now several good recent reference grammars in English, ranging from the brief Smyth (2002) to the extensive Iwasaki and Ingkaphirom (2005) and Higbie and Thinsan (2003), the last grounded in the spoken language; Brown (1967–79) is a standard course book in spoken Thai, including separate volumes for reading (1979) and writing (1979). On individual problems, Cooke (1968) is probably the most comprehensive examination of pronouns in Thai available; Haas (1942) is a basic work on classifiers. Warotamasikkhadit (1972) is a generative approach to Thai syntax. Gedney (1961) is a discussion of royal vocabulary.

References

Brown, J.M. 1965. *From Ancient Thai to Modern Dialects* (Social Science Association Press of Thailand, Bangkok)

—— 1967–79. *AUA Center Thai Course*, 5 vols (AUA Language Center, Bangkok)

Cooke, J.R. 1968. *Pronominal Reference in Thai, Burmese, and Vietnamese* (University of California Press, Berkeley)

Gedney, W.J. 1947. 'Indic Loanwords in Spoken Thai' (PhD dissertation, Yale University)

—— 1961. *Special Vocabularies in Thai*. Georgetown University Institute of Languages Monograph Series on Languages and Linguistics, Vol. 14 (Georgetown University, Washington DC), pp. 109–14.

Haas, M.R. 1942. 'The Use of Numeral Classifiers in Thai', *Language*, vol. 18, pp. 201–5

Higbie, J. and Thinsan, S. 2003. *Thai Reference Grammar: The Structure of Spoken Thai* (Orchid Press, Bangkok)

Iwasaki, S. and Ingkaphirom, P. 2005. *A Reference Grammar of Thai* (Cambridge University Press, Cambridge)

Smyth, D. 2002. *Thai: An Essential Grammar* (Routledge, London)

Warotamasikkhadit, U. 1972. *Thai Syntax* (Mouton, The Hague)

40

Vietnamese

Đình-Hoà Nguyễn

1 Background

The language described here, known to its native speakers as *tiếng Việt-nam* or simply *tiếng Việt* (literary appellations: *Việt-văn* or *Việt-ngữ*) is used in daily communication over the whole territory of Vietnam, formerly known as Annam (whence the older name for the language, Annamese or Annamite). It is the mother tongue of the ethnic majority called *người Việt* or *người Kinh* – some 66 million inhabitants who live in the delta lowlands of Vietnam, plus over one million overseas Vietnamese, in France, the USA, Canada, Australia, etc. Other ethnic groups (Chinese, Cambodians, Indians and the highlanders called 'Montagnards') know Vietnamese and can use it in their contacts with the Vietnamese.

Although Chinese characters were used in literary texts, in which Chinese loanwords also abound (on account of ten centuries of Chinese political domination), Vietnamese is not at all genetically related to Chinese. It belongs rather to the Mon–Khmer stock, within the Austro-Asiatic family, which comprises several major language groups spoken in a wide area running from Chota Nagpur eastward to Indochina.

In comparing Vietnamese and Mường, a language spoken in the highlands of northern and central Vietnam and considered an archaic form of Vietnamese, the French scholar Jean Przyluski maintained that ancient Vietnamese was at least closely related to the Mon–Khmer group of languages, which have no tones but several prefixes and infixes. Another French linguist, Henri Maspéro, was more inclined to include Vietnamese in the Tai family, whose members are all tonal languages. According to Maspéro, modern Vietnamese seems to result from a mixture of many elements, precisely because it has been successively, at different times in its history, at the northern limit of the Mon–Khmer languages, the eastern limit of the Tai languages and the southern boundary of Chinese. More recently, however, the French botanist–linguist A.-G. Haudricourt pointed out the origin of Vietnamese tones, arguing lucidly in his 1954 article that Vietnamese, a member of the Mon–Khmer phylum, had, as a non-tonal language at the beginning of the Christian era, developed three tones by the sixth century, and that by the twelfth century it had acquired all six tones which characterise it today. This explanation of Vietnamese tonogenesis has thus helped us to point conclusively to the true genetic relationship of Vietnamese: its kinship to Mường, the sister language, with which it forms the Vietnamese–Mường group within the Mon–Khmer phylum.

Up to the late nineteenth century, traditional Vietnamese society comprised the four classes of scholars, farmers, craftsmen and merchants. The French colonial administration, which lasted until 1945, created a small bourgeoisie of functionaries, merchants, physicians, lawyers, importers and exporters, etc., within and around the major urban centres. The language of the class of rural workers retains dialect peculiarities, in both grammar and vocabulary, whereas the language of the city dwellers accepts a large number of loanwords from Chinese and from French, the latter having been the official language for more than eighty years. Since 1945, Vietnamese has replaced French as the medium of instruction in all schools of the land.

The history of Vietnamese has been sketched by Maspéro as follows:

(1) Pre-Vietnamese, common to Vietnamese and Mường before their separation;
(2) Proto-Vietnamese, before the formation of Sino-Vietnamese;
(3) Archaic Vietnamese, characterised by the individualisation of Sino-Vietnamese (towards the tenth century);
(4) Ancient Vietnamese, represented by the Chinese–Vietnamese glossary *Hua-yi Yi-yu* (sixteenth century);
(5) Middle Vietnamese of the Vietnamese–Portuguese–Latin dictionary of Alexandre de Rhodes (seventeenth century); and
(6) Modern Vietnamese, beginning in the nineteenth century.

There are three distinct writing systems: (1) Chinese characters, referred to as *chữ nho* 'scholars' script' or *chữ hán* 'Han script'; (2) the demotic characters called *chữ nôm* (from *nam* 'south') 'southern script'; and finally (3) the Roman script called *chữ quốc-ngữ* 'national script'.

Written Chinese characters, shared by Japanese and Korean, the other two Asian cultures that were also under Chinese influence, for a long time served as the medium of education and official communication, at least among the educated classes of scholars and officials. Indeed, from the early days of Chinese rule (111 BC–AD 939) the Chinese rulers taught the natives not only Chinese calligraphy, but also the texts of Chinese history, philosophy and literature.

The so-called Sino-Vietnamese pronunciation is based on the pronunciation of Ancient Chinese, learned first through the spoken language of the rulers, then later through the scholarly writings of Chinese philosophers and poets. The latter constituted the curriculum of an educational system sanctioned by gruelling literary examinations which were designed to recruit a local scholar-gentry class, thus denying education to the vast majority of illiterate peasants.

While continuing to use Chinese to compose regulated verse as well as prose pieces, some of which were real gems of Vietnamese literature in classical *wen-yen*, Buddhist monks and Confucian scholars, starting in the thirteenth century, proudly used their own language for eight-line stanzas or long narratives in native verse blockprinted in the 'southern characters'. The *chữ nôm* system, whose invention definitely dated from the days when Sino-Vietnamese, or the pronunciation of Chinese graphs *à la vietnamienne*, had been stabilised (i.e. around the eleventh century), was already widely used under the Trần dynasty. Samples of these characters, often undecipherable to the Chinese, have been found on temple bells, on stone inscriptions and in Buddhist-inspired poems and rhymed prose pieces. A fairly extensive number of *nôm* characters appeared in Nguyễn Trãi's *Quốc-âm Thi-tập* (Collected Poems in the National Language), as the seventh volume in the posthumous works of this scholar–poet–strategist involved in the anti-Ming campaign by his emperor Lê Lợi. The 254 charming poems, long thought lost, yield the earliest evidence of Vietnamese phonology, since many characters, roughly including a semantic element and a phonetic element, shed light on fifteenth-century Vietnamese pronunciation, some features of which were later corroborated in the *Dictionarium Annamiticum-Lusitanum-et-Latinum* and *A Catechism for Eight Days* authored by the gifted Jesuit missionary Alexandre de Rhodes and published in Rome in 1651. (See Table 40.1.)

Vietnam owes its Roman script to Catholic missionaries, who at first needed some transcription to help them learn the language of their new converts to Christianity, and some of whom succeeded in learning the tonal language well enough to preach in it in the middle of the seventeenth century. The French colonialists saw in this Romanisation an effective tool for the assimilation of their subjects, who, they thought, would through the intermediary transliteration of Vietnamese in Latin letters make a smooth transition to the process of learning the language of the *métropole. Quốc-ngữ* proved to be indeed

Table 40.1 Some Examples of Chữ Nôm

Chữ nôm	Modern Vietnamese	Gloss	Comments
才	tài	talent	Chinese character for Sino-vietnamese *tài* 'talent'.
符	bùa	written charm	Chinese character for Sino-Vietnamese *phù* 'charm'; the reading *bùa* is earlier than the learned *phù*.
𡞕	làm	do, make	part of the Chinese character for Sino-Vietnamese *vi* 'act': 爲
没	một	one	Cf. the homonymous Sino-Vietnamese *một* 'die', for which this is the Chinese character.
別	biết	know	Cf. the nearly homonymous Sino-Vietnamese *biệt* 'separate', for which this is the Chinese character.
買‹	mới	new	Cf. the nearly homonymous Sino-Vietnamese *mãi* 'buy'; the chữ nôm is the Chinese character for this Sino-Vietnamese syllable with the addition of diacritic: ‹.
巴頼	trái	fruit	A compound of the two Chinese characters, with Sino-Vietnamese readings *ba* and *lại*, respectively, to give a pronunciation with initial *bl-*, as recorded in the 1651 dictionary: 巴頼
𡗶	trời	sky	A semantic compound, using the Chinese characters for, respectively, 'sky' and 'high': 天 上
找	quơ	reach for	A combination of, respectively, the Chinese character for 'hand' (semantic component) and the character with the Sino-Vietnamese reading *qua* (phonetic component): 扌 戈
𦻧	cỏ	grass	A combination of, respectively, the Chinese character for 'grass' (semantic component) and the character with the Sino-Vietnamese reading *cổ*: 草 古

an adequate system of writing, enabling Vietnamese speakers to learn how to read and write their own language in the space of several weeks. Not only did the novel script assist in the literacy campaign, it also helped the spread of education and the dissemination of knowledge, including information about political and social revolutionary movements in Europe and elsewhere in Asia. Nowadays, *quốc-ngữ* often called *chữ phổ-thông*, 'standard script', serves as the medium of instruction at all three levels of education and has been successfully groomed as the official orthography; both before and after reunification in 1976, conferences and seminars have been held to discuss its inconsistencies and to recommend spelling reforms, to be carried out gradually in the future.

Maspéro divided Vietnamese dialects into two main groups: the Upper Annam group, which comprises many local dialects found in villages from the north of Nghệ-an Province to the south of Thừa-thiên Province, and the Tonkin–Cochinchina dialect which covers the remainder.

Phonological structure diverges from the dialect of Hanoi (Hà-Nội), for a long time the political and cultural capital of the Empire of Annam, as one moves towards the south. The second vowel of the three diphthongs *iê*, *uô* and *ươ* for example, tends towards *â* in the groups written *iêc* [iʌk], *iêng* [iʌŋ], *uôc* [uʌk] and *uông* [uʌŋ]. The Vinh dialect, which should belong to the Upper Annam group, has three retroflexes: affricate *tr* [tʂ], voiceless fricative *s* [ʂ] and voiced fricative *r* [ʐ]. The Huế dialect, considered archaic and difficult, has only five tones, with the hỏi and ngã tones pronounced in the same way with a long rising contour. The initial *z-* is replaced by a semi-vowel *y-*, and the palatal finals *-ch* and *-nh* are replaced by *-t* and *-n*.

In the dialect of Saigon (Sài-Gòn, now renamed Ho Chi Minh City) the phonemes generally are not arranged as shown in the orthography. However, the consonants of the Saigon dialect present the distinction between ordinary and retroflex initials. Also, the groups *iêp*, *iêm*, *uôm*, *ươp* and *ươm* are pronounced *ip*, *im*, *um*, *up* and *um* respectively.

Most dialects form part of a continuum from north to south, each of them different to some extent from the neighbouring dialect on either side. Such major urban centres as Hanoi, Hue and Saigon represent rather special dialects marked by the influence of educated speakers and of more frequent contacts with the other regions.

The language described below is typified by the Hanoi dialect, which has served as the basis for the elaboration of the literary language. The spoken style keeps its natural charm in each locality although efforts have been made from the elementary grades up to nationwide conferences and meetings 'to preserve the purity and the clarity' of the standard language, whether spoken or written. The spoken tongue is used for all oral communications except public speeches, whereas the written medium, which one can qualify as literary style, is uniformly used in the press and over the radio and television.

While noting the inconsistencies of the Roman script, French administrators tried several times to recommend spelling reforms. However, efforts at standardisation, begun as early as 1945, started to move ahead only in 1954, when the governments in both zones established spelling norms, a task now facilitated by the spread of literacy to thousands of peasants and workers between 1954 and 1975. There is a very clear tendency to standardise the transliterations of place names and personal names from foreign languages, as well as the transliteration and/or translation of technical terms more and more required by progress in Vietnamese science and technology. Committees responsible for terminological work, i.e. the invention, elaboration and codification of terms in exact sciences as well as in human and social sciences, have contributed considerably to the enrichment of the national lexicon.

Members of the generations that grew up under French rule are bilingual, but later on have added English. The generation of 1945, for whom French ceased to be the medium of instruction, speaks Vietnamese and English. Because of the influence of socialist countries, Chinese, i.e. Mandarin, and Russian have become familiar to classes of professors, researchers, cadres and students exposed to various currents of Marxist thought, chiefly in the northern half of the country. In the south, English gained the upper hand over French as a foreign language taught in schools, while French remained and will remain the official language in diplomatic and political contacts. Chinese characters continue to be taught as a classical language needed for studies in Eastern humanities.

2 Phonology and Orthography

The *quốc-ngữ* writing system has the advantage of being close to a phonemic script, to which Portuguese, French and Italian, undoubtedly assisted by Vietnamese priests, contributed. It is fairly consistent, and in what follows Vietnamese orthography is used to represent the phonology, with comments on the few areas of discrepancy.

A syllable has a vocalic nucleus, with a single vowel or two vowels, optionally preceded by an initial consonant and/or followed by a final consonant; this final consonant can only be a voiceless stop or a nasal. There may be an intercalary semi-vowel /w/ (spelled *o* before *a*, *ă*, *e*, otherwise *u*). These possibilities can be summarised by the formula (C_1) *(w)* V_1 (V_2) (C_2). The syllable carries an obligatory toneme.

The vowels are presented in Table 40.2.

Table 40.2 Vietnamese Vowels

Front	Central	Back	
		Unrounded	Rounded
i, y		ư	u
ê		ơ	ô
e	ă	â	o
a			

There are some discrepancies between the phonology and orthography of vowels:

(1) the letters *i* and *y* are purely orthographic variants representing the phoneme /i/, while *o* and *u* are orthographic variants in representing intercalary /w/ or V_2 (but not V_1).

(2) The orthography does not represent the predictable V_2 after a high or high mid vowel not followed by some other V_2, i.e. we find [iị] in *đi* 'go', [êị] in *đê* 'dike', [ưự] in *đứ đừ* 'exhausted', [ơự] in *tơ* 'silk', [uụ] in *mù* 'blind', and [oụ] in *đổ* 'pour'.

(3) Phonemically, there are only four possible V_2s: *i, u, ư, â*, though there are phonetic and orthographic complications in addition to those already noted:

(a) /â/ as V_2 is written *a* in open syllables (e.g. *mía* 'sugar cane', *mưa* 'to rain', *mua* 'buy'), but in closed syllables the orthographic representation depends on the V$_1$: *iê, ươ, uô*, and the pronunciation is with *â* before *ng* (e.g. *miếng* 'morsel', *mương* 'canal', *muống* 'bindweed'), but *ê, ơ* or *ô* (depending on the V$_1$) before *n* (e.g. *miền* 'region', *vườn* 'garden', *muôn* 'ten thousand');

(b) the spellings *uc, ung, oc, ong, ôc, ông* represent [uᵘkᵖ], [uᵘngᵐ], [ăᵘkᵖ], [ăᵘngᵐ], [âᵘkᵖ], [âᵘngᵐ] respectively, with final labio-velar coarticulation, as in *cúc* 'chrysanthemum', *cốc* 'glass', *cọc* 'stake', *cung* 'arc', *công* 'effort', *cong* 'curve';

(c) syllable-final *ch* and *nh* are orthographic representations of [ik] and [ing] respectively, e.g. *anh* [ăing] 'elder brother'.

(4) /ă/ is spelled *a* before *ch, nh, u* and *y*, e.g. *bạch* 'white', *tranh* 'picture', *tàu* 'ship', *vay* 'borrow' (/a/ does not occur before *ch* and *nh*, while /ai/ is written *ai*, e.g. *vai* 'shoulder' and /au/ is written *ao*, e.g. *cao* 'high').

(5) /â/ is spelled *ê* before *ch* and *nh*, e.g. *bênh* 'protect'.

The six tonemes that affect the vocalic nucleus of each syllable are noted by means of diacritics as in Table 40.3; when C$_2$ is a final stop, only tones 2 and 6 are possible.

Table 40.3 Vietnamese Tones

Name		Symbol	Pitch-level	Contour	Other features
1	bằng/ngang	(no mark)	high mid	drawn out, falling	
2	sắc	/´/	high	rising	tense
3	huyền	/`/	low	drawn out	lax
4	hỏi	/ˀ/	mid low	dipping-rising	tense
5	ngã	/˜/	high	rising	glottalised
6	nặng	/./	low	falling	glottalised or tense

The consonant inventory is given in Table 40.4. Syllable-finally, the voiceless stops are unexploded. The voiced stops *b, đ* are preglottalised and often implosive; note that *b*, occurring only syllable-initially, is in fact in complementary distribution with *p*, which occurs only syllable-finally. Word-final *k, ng* after *u* have labio-velar articulation (see the examples for point (3b) under vowels). /g/ is a voiced stop after a syllable ending in *ng*, otherwise a voiced fricative, e.g. *gác* 'upper floor' (fricative), but *thang gác* 'staircase' (stop). Word-finally, *ch* is pronounced /ik/ and *nh* is pronounced [ing], as already noted in the discussion of vowels.

Table 40.4 Vietnamese Consonants

	Labial	Labio-dental	Alveolar	Retroflex	Palatal	Velar	Laryngeal
Voiceless stop	p		t	tr	ch	c	
Aspirated stop			th				
Voiced stop	b		đ				
Voiceless fricative		ph	x	s		kh	h
Voiced fricative		v	d	r	gi	g	
Nasal	m		n		nh	ng	
Lateral			l				

The voiceless velar plosive is spelled *q* before /w/ (i.e. *qu*), *k* before *i/y*, *e*, *ê* and *c* elsewhere. Following the Italian convention, /g/ is spelled *gh* (and /ng/ *ngh*) before *i*, *e*, *ê*. The voiced palatal fricative is spelled *g* before *i* (and *iê*), e.g. *gì* 'what', but *gi* elsewhere, e.g. *giời* 'sky'.

In the Hanoi dialect, *tr* merges in pronunciation with *ch* (palatal), *s* with *x* (alveolar), while all three of *d*, *gi*, *r* merge as a voiced alveolar fricative.

3 Syntax

The noun phrase consists of a head noun, which may be followed by other words (noun, pronoun, place-noun, numeral, classifier, verb, demonstrative or even a relative clause). Examples of different constituents following the head noun follow:

(1) Noun–noun: no function word occurs between the head noun and the second noun; this construction can express (a) measure: *tạ gạo* 'quintal$_1$ of rice$_2$', *lít nước* 'litre$_1$ of water$_2$', *bát cơm* 'bowl$_1$ of rice$_2$', *cốc nước* 'glass$_1$ of water$_2$'; (b) space: *bao thuốc lá* 'pack$_1$ of cigarettes$_{2-3}$', *phòng khách* 'guest$_2$ room$_1$', *chuồng lợn* 'pig$_2$ sty$_1$'; (c) groups: *đàn bò* 'herd$_1$ of cows$_2$', *đoàn sinh-viên* 'group$_1$ of students$_2$', *nải chuối* 'hand$_1$ of bananas$_2$'; (d) images: *tóc mây* 'soft hair' (lit. 'hair cloud'), *cổ cò* 'crane$_2$ neck$_1$', *ngón tay búp măng* 'tapered fingers' (lit. 'bamboo$_4$ shoot$_3$ finger$_{1-2}$'), *tóc rễ tre* 'hair$_1$ stiff as bamboo$_3$ roots$_2$'; (e) characteristics: *gà mẹ* 'mother$_2$ hen$_1$', *máy bay cánh quạt* 'propeller$_{3-4}$-driven aeroplane$_{1-2}$'; (f) identity: *làng Khê-hồi* 'the village$_1$ of Khe-hoi$_2$', *sông Hương* 'the Perfume$_2$ River$_1$', *tuổi Hợi* 'the sign$_1$ of the Pig$_2$'.

(2) Noun–preposition–noun: *vấn-đề của tôi* 'my$_3$ problem$_1$' (note that the second noun may be replaced by a pronoun), *kỳ thi ở Huế* 'the examination$_{1-2}$ in$_3$ Hue$_4$', *cấu-trúc về chi-tiết* 'detailed$_3$ structure$_1$', *bổn-phận đối với cha mẹ* 'duty$_1$ towards$_{2-3}$ one's parents$_{4-5}$'. The preposition may be absent when the idea of kinship, ownership, origin or utility is obvious: *nhà mày* 'your$_2$ house$_1$', *cha (của) Nguyễn Trãi* 'Nguyen$_3$ Trai's$_4$ father$_1$', *nhà (bằng) gạch* 'brick$_3$ house$_1$', *vải (ở) Tó* 'lychees$_1$ from$_2$ To$_3$', *sách (cho) lớp tám* 'textbook$_1$ for$_2$ the eighth$_4$ grade$_3$'.

(3) Noun–place–noun: *nhà trên* 'main$_2$ building$_1$', *nhà dưới* 'annex$_2$ building$_1$', *ngón giữa* 'middle$_2$ finger$_1$'.

(4) Noun–numeral: *hàng sáu* 'row$_2$ six$_1$, six abreast', *lớp nhất* 'upper$_2$ grade$_1$', *tháng ba* 'March' (lit. 'month three'). In cardinal numeral constructions, however, a classifier must be used with the numeral; the usual order is numeral–classifier–noun, though noun–numeral–classifier is also possible: *hai cây nến* 'two$_1$ candles$_3$', *ba quyển sách* 'three$_1$ books$_3$', *bốn tờ giấy* 'four$_1$ sheets$_2$ of paper$_3$', *vài chú tiều* 'a few$_1$ woodcutters$_3$', or *tiều vài chú*. Nouns denoting concrete time units do not require a classifier, e.g. *hai năm* 'two years', *ba tuần* 'three weeks'. The choice of classifier is dependent on such features as the animateness, humanness (and social position for humans), and shape (for inanimates) of the noun; e.g. *cây* is used for stick-shaped objects, *quyển* for scrolls and volumes, *tấm* for sheet-like objects, *con* for animals, and *cái* for miscellaneous inanimates.

(5) Noun–verb/adjective (in Vietnamese, there is little reason for setting up distinct classes of verb and adjective – see Section 4): *thịt kho* 'meat$_1$ stewed in fish

sauce$_2$', *thịt nướng* 'broiled$_2$ meat$_1$', *thịt sống* 'raw$_2$ meat$_1$', *đường về* 'the way$_1$ back$_2$', *con người khổ sở* 'miserable$_{3-4}$ person$_{1-2}$'.

(6) Noun–demonstrative: *cô này* 'this$_2$ young lady$_1$', *ông nọ* 'the other$_2$ gentleman$_1$', *bà kia* 'the other$_2$ lady$_1$'. In such phrases with a demonstrative, a classifier is often used, the order then being classifier–noun–demonstrative: *cái bàn này* 'this$_3$ table$_2$', *con bò ấy* 'that$_3$ cow$_2$'.

(7) Noun–relative clause: *ngôi nhà mà chú tôi vừa tậu năm ngoái* 'the house$_{1-2}$ that$_3$ my$_5$ uncle$_4$ just$_6$ bought$_7$ last$_9$ year$_8$', *voi làm ở Việt-nam* 'the (ceramic) elephants$_1$ made$_2$ in$_3$ Vietnam$_4$'.

The verb phrase consists of a head verb followed by one or two noun phrases, a place-noun, a numeral, another verb, or an adjective (i.e. a stative verb). Likewise, when the head verb is stative ('adjectival'), several different configurations are possible:

(1) Verb–noun (direct object): *xây nhà* 'build$_1$ a house$_2$', *yêu nước* 'love$_1$ one's country$_2$', *ăn đũa* 'eat$_1$ with chopsticks$_2$', *cúi đầu* 'bow$_1$ one's head$_2$', *hết tiền* 'lack$_1$ money$_2$', *nghỉ hè* 'take a summer vacation' (lit. 'rest summer'), *trở nên người hữu-dụng* 'become$_{1-2}$ a useful$_4$ person$_3$'.

(2) Verb–noun–noun (the basic order is for direct object to precede indirect object, but the direct object may also follow if it consists of more than one syllable): *gửi tiền cho bố* 'send$_1$ money$_2$ to$_3$ his father$_4$', *gửi cho bố nhiều tiền* 'send$_1$ his father$_3$ a lot$_4$ of money$_5$', *lấy của ông Giáp hai bộ quần áo* 'steal$_1$ two$_5$ suits$_{6-7}$ from$_2$ Mr$_3$ Giap$_4$', *thọc tay vào túi* 'thrust$_1$ his hand$_2$ into$_3$ his pocket$_4$'.

(3) Verb–noun–verb: *mời sinh-viên ăn tiệc* 'invite$_1$ the students$_2$ to eat$_3$ dinner$_4$', *dạy tôi chữ Hán* 'teach$_1$ me$_2$ Chinese$_4$ characters$_3$'.

(4) Verb–place–noun: *ngồi trên* 'sit$_1$ at a higher position$_2$'.

(5) Verb–numeral: *về nhất* 'finish$_1$ first$_2$', *lên tám* 'be eight years old' (lit. 'reach eight').

(6) Verb–verb(–verb): *lo thi* 'worry about examinations' (lit. 'worry take-examination'), *liều chết* 'risk death' (lit. 'risk die'), *đi học* 'go to school' (lit. 'go study'), *ngủ ngồi* 'fall asleep in one's chair' (lit. 'sleep sit'), *chôn sống* 'bury alive' (lit. 'bury live'), *ngủ dậy* 'wake up, get up' (lit. 'sleep wake'), *đi học về* 'come back from school' (lit. 'go study return').

(7) Verb–adjective (there is no separate class of adverbs of manner): *ăn nhanh* 'eat$_1$ fast$_2$', *bôi bẩn* 'smear' (lit. 'spread dirty'), *đối-đãi tử-tế* 'treat$_1$ nicely$_2$'.

(8) Adjective–noun: *mù mắt* 'blind$_1$ in the eyes$_2$', *mỏi tay* 'tired$_1$ in the arms$_2$', *đông người* 'crowded$_1$ with people$_2$', *giống bố* 'resemble$_1$ one's father$_2$', *thạo tiếng Nhật* 'good$_1$ at Japanese$_3$ language$_2$'.

(9) Adjective–verb: *khó nói* 'difficult$_1$ to say$_2$'.

(10) Adjective–adjective: *mừng thầm* 'inwardly$_2$ happy$_1$'.

A normal message consists of two parts, the subject and the predicate; these two parts are separated by a pause, e.g. *ông ấy/đến rồi* 'he$_{1-2}$ has already$_4$ arrived$_3$', *bà ấy/là người Hành-thiện* 'she$_{1-2}$ is$_3$ a native$_4$ of Hanh-thien$_5$'. However, the subject can be ellipted, i.e. one can say simply *đến rồi là người Hành-thiện*.

In addition to the subject and predicate, a sentence may optionally contain supplementary terms; these other phrases manifest complements of time, location, cause, goal, condition, concession, etc.: *đêm qua ra đứng bờ ao* 'last$_2$ night$_1$ I went$_3$ to stand$_4$ on the edge$_5$ of the pond$_6$', *ở Việt-nam chúng tôi học theo lục-cá-nguyệt* 'in$_1$ Vietnam$_2$, we$_{3-4}$ study$_5$ following$_6$ the semester$_7$ system', *tại vợ nó nó mới chết* 'because of$_1$ his$_3$ wife$_2$, he$_4$ died$_6$', *vì tổ-quốc chúng ta phải hi-sinh tất cả* 'we$_{3-4}$ must$_5$ sacrifice$_6$ everything$_{7-8}$ for$_1$ the fatherland$_2$', *nếu anh bậ thì tôi sẽ đi một mình* 'if$_1$ you$_2$ are busy$_3$, then$_4$ I$_5$ will$_6$ go$_7$ by myself$_{8-9}$', *tuy nghèo, nhưng anh thích giúp bạn* 'though$_1$ poor$_2$, yet$_3$ he$_4$ likes$_5$ to help$_6$ his friends$_7$'.

Word order is important, especially given the virtual absence of other overt indicators of grammatical relations, for instance the subject normally precedes its verb while the direct object normally follows. The adverbial of time *bao giờ* or *khi nào* 'when' is placed at the beginning of the sentence to indicate future time reference and at the end to indicate past time reference, e.g. *khi nào cô thư-ký đến?* 'when$_{1-2}$ will the secretary$_{3-4}$ arrive$_5$?', *cô thư-ký đến khi nào?* 'when did the secretary arrive?'

A noun phrase can be highlighted by placing it at the beginning of the sentence: it then announces a topic ('as for ...'), and we have a specific reference to a certain person, a certain thing, a certain concept, an exact location, a given time, a precise quantity or a determined manner, e.g. *chúng tôi thì chúng tôi học theo lục-cá-nguyệt* 'as for us, we follow the semester system', *nước mắm anh ấy ăn được* 'fish$_2$ sauce$_1$ he$_{3-4}$ can$_6$ eat$_5$'. In the first example, the subject is repeated as topic with the particle *thì*; in the second, the direct object is simply preposed (cf. *anh ấy ăn được nước mắm* 'he can eat fish sauce'). With the particle *cũng* 'even', such preposing can indicate the extent of the scope of the particle: compare *ông ấy mời mời sinh-viên ăn cơm* 'he invites the students to eat dinner', with *sinh-viên, ông ấy cũng mời ăn cơm* 'he invites even the students to eat dinner' and *ăn cơm, ông ấy cũng mời sinh-viên* 'he invites the students even to eat dinner'. Other examples of topicalisation are *ông ấy tên là Bảng* 'he is named Bang' (lit. 'he$_{1-2}$ name$_3$ is$_4$ Bang$_5$') (cf. *tên ông ấy là Bảng* 'his$_{2-3}$ name$_1$ is$_4$ Bang$_5$'), *bà cụ mắt kém* 'the old lady has poor eyesight' (cf. *mắt bà cụ kém* 'the old$_3$ lady's$_2$ eyes$_1$ are weak$_4$').

A number of verbs denoting existence, appearance or disappearance may have the object whose existence, etc., is expressed either before or after the verb; in the latter case, the verb may be preceded by a noun phrase expressing the experiencer of the existence, etc., e.g. *đê vỡ* 'the dike$_1$ broke$_2$' or *vỡ đê; tiền mất, tật mang* 'the money$_1$ has gone$_2$, the sickness$_3$ remains$_4$', *(tôi) mất tiền* 'I lost some money'. In such sentences, the noun phrase before the verb is best analysed as a topic.

Passive sentences are found in Vietnamese, e.g. the active *Tám yêu Hiền* 'Tam$_1$ loves$_2$ Hien$_3$' may also appear as *Hiền được Tám yêu* 'Hien is loved by Tam'. However, such passives are best analysed as a subordinate clause *Tám yêu (Hiền)*, dependent on the main verb *được* 'get, enjoy'. If, instead of obtaining a happy result, the party involved suffers from a disadvantage or unpleasant experience, then the main verb *bị* 'suffer' will be used, e.g. *Liên bị Tám ghét* 'Lien is hated by Tam' (cf. *Tám ghét Liên* 'Tam$_1$ hates$_2$ Lien$_3$'). Such passives are not to be confused with instances of topicalisation discussed above, even though the latter are sometimes translatable into English as passives (e.g. *cơm thổi rồi* as 'the rice$_1$ has already$_3$ been cooked$_2$', but cf. *cơm, mẹ thổi rồi* 'the rice$_1$, mother$_2$ has already$_4$ cooked$_3$').

Negation is expressed by means of the negative marker *không*, which literally means 'null, not to be, not to exist', and whose emphatic equivalents are *chẳng* and *chả*, e.g. *ông ấy không/chẳng/chả đến* 'he$_{1-2}$ is not$_3$ coming$_4$'. Either *chưa* or *chửa* means 'not yet', e.g. *ông ấy chưa/chửa đến* 'he hasn't arrived yet'. Before the copula *là*, negation is expressed by *không phải* literally '(it) is not correct (that) it is ...', e.g. *bà ấy không phải là người Hành-thiện* 'she's not a native of Hanh-thien'. Stronger denial may be achieved by means of an interrogative pronoun used as an indefinite pronoun (see page 687), e.g.

ông ấy có đến đâu! (lit. 'he$_{1-2}$ indeed$_3$ arrive$_4$ where$_5$'), *ông ấy đâu có đến!* 'no, he did not show up!', or even *ông ấy không đến đâu!* 'he's not coming, I tell you!', *bà ấy có phải là người Hành-thiện đâu!* or *bà ấy đâu có phải là người Hành-thiện!* 'she's not at all a native of Hanh-thien!'

Interrogative sentences have three basic structures. The first is used for alternative questions, i.e. the interlocutor has to choose between two terms separated by the conjunction *hay* 'or', e.g. *cô ấy đi hay ông đi?* 'is she$_{1-2}$ going$_3$ or$_4$ are you$_5$ going$_6$?', *nó đi học hay không đi học?* 'is he$_1$ going$_2$ to school$_3$ or$_4$ isn't$_5$ he going$_6$ to school$_7$?'. With the latter example, where the choice is between affirmative and negative alternants, the second clause may be reduced right down to the particle *không*, i.e. *nó có đi học hay không đi học?*, *nó có đi học hay không?*, *no có đi học không?*, *no đi học không?* In such examples where the predicate is nominal, the confirmative particle *có* is obligatory in the first clause: *bà ấy có phải là người Hành-thiện không?* 'is she a native of Hanh-thien?' When the question is about the realisation of an action or process ('yet'), the group *có không* is replaced by *đã chưa* e.g. *ông ấy (đã) đến chưa?* 'has he$_{1-2}$ arrived$_4$ yet$_{3-5}$?', cf. the fuller version *ông ấy đã đến hay chưa (đến)?* Such questions (lacking an interrogative pronoun) normally have sostenuto intonation, in which the pitch level of each toneme is somewhat higher than in a normal sentence, rather than the more normal diminuendo intonation (in, for instance, statements), in which the intensity gradually diminishes from the beginning of the syllable.

The basic answers to such questions are *có* 'yes' and *không* 'no', e.g. *có, no có đi học* 'yes, he is going to school', *không, no không đi học* 'nó, he isn't going to school'. But different answers are required with a nominal predicate: *phải, bà ấy là người Hành-thiện* 'yes, she is a native of Hanh-thien', *không phải, bà ấy không phải là người Hành-thiện* 'no, she isn't a native of Hanh-thien', and with 'yet' questions: *rồi, ông ấy đến rồi* 'yes, he has already arrived', *chưa, ông ấy chưa đến* 'no, he hasn't arrived yet'.

The second type of interrogative structure is the content question (*wh*-question), with an interrogative substantive: *ai?* 'who?', *gì?* 'what?', *nào?* 'which?', *đâu?* 'where?', *bao giờ?* 'when?', *bao nhiêu?* 'how much?', *bao lâu?* 'how long?', *sao?* 'why?' The interrogative substantive normally occurs in the same position in the sentence as would an equivalent ordinary noun phrase, as can be seen in the following question and answer pairs: *ai đến? ông Nam đến?* 'who$_1$ has arrived$_2$? Mr$_3$ Nam$_4$ has arrived$_5$'; *nó bảo ai? nó bảo tôi* 'who$_3$ did he$_1$ tell$_2$? he$_4$ told$_5$ me$_6$'; *người nào đi với anh? ông Nam đi với tôi* 'which$_2$ person$_1$ is going$_3$ with$_4$ you$_5$? Mr$_6$ Nam$_7$ is going$_8$ with$_9$ me$_{10}$'; *anh đi với người nào? tôi đi với sinh-viên* 'which$_5$ people$_4$ are you$_1$ going$_2$ with$_3$? I'm$_6$ going$_7$ with$_8$ the students$_9$'; *nó ăn gì? nó ăn cá* 'what$_3$ does he$_1$ eat$_2$? he$_4$ eats$_5$ fish$_6$'; *ông ấy ở đâu? ông ấy ở Cần-thơ* 'where$_4$ does he$_{1-2}$ live$_3$? he$_{5-6}$ lives in$_7$ Can-tho$_8$'. Content questions usually have crescendo intonation, with the main stress on the interrogative substantive. Incidentally, these same interrogative substantives can also have the function of indefinite pronouns, e.g. *không ai nói* 'no one spoke' (lit. 'not who spoke'); especially in women's speech, they can even have negative indefinite function, provided the interrogative substantive receives very heavy stress, e.g. *ai nói*, with very heavy stress on *ai*, 'no one spoke'.

The confirmation-seeking tag is *phải không*, often reduced to *phỏng*, e.g. *không ăn, phải không? không ăn phỏng?* 'you're not$_1$ eating$_2$, are you?' A number of final particles serve to mark various nuances of interrogation. Thus *a, à* and *ư* are used to express astonishment or to seek confirmation of what is supposed or has been discovered, e.g. *anh chịu à?* 'you$_1$ gave up$_2$? I'm surprised!', *ông không mệt à?* 'aren't$_2$

you$_1$ tired$_3$?'. In the sentence *sao con lại làm thế hử?* 'how$_1$ did you$_2$ dare$_3$ do$_4$ that$_5$ my dear?', the particle *hử* expresses a mild reproach while pressing the culprit for a reply. The particle *nhỉ* is used to elicit the confirmation of something just noticed, e.g. *ông Chân có cái nhà to nhỉ?* 'Mr$_1$ Chan$_2$ has$_3$ a big$_6$ house$_{4-5}$, hasn't he?' The dubitative sentence, which expresses doubt or uncertainty, contains the particle *chăng: trời sắp sửa mưa chăng?* 'could it be that it's going to rain?' (lit. 'sky about-to rain'), *có lẽ họ không đến chăng* 'maybe$_{1-2}$ they$_3$ are not$_4$ coming$_5$'.

Other particles occur at the end of a sentence to lend more movement or force to it: in order to show politeness, the particle *a* is used in a social context where the speaker assumes an inferior attitude, expected of children, students, domestic help, etc., e.g. *mời Bố xơi cơm ạ* 'please$_1$ eat$_3$ the meal$_4$, Daddy$_2$', *thưa Thầy, hôm nay thứ năm ạ* 'Teacher$_1$, today$_{2-3}$ is Thursday$_{4-5}$', *ông đưa tiền cho tôi rồi ạ* 'you$_1$ already$_6$ handed$_2$ the money$_3$ to$_4$ me$_5$, sir'.

In order to remind someone of something, the final particle *nghe* or *nhé* is used, e.g. *em đứng đây chờ anh nhé!* 'you$_1$ stand$_2$ wait for$_4$ me$_5$ here$_3$, OK?'

The particle *chứ* is used to seek confirmation, e.g. *ông uống cà-phê rồi chứ* 'you$_1$ already$_4$ had$_2$ your coffee$_3$, I presume', *ông uống cà-phê chứ* 'you will have some coffee, won't you?'

Exhortation is expressed by means of *đi* which marks the imperative or injunctive, e.g. *anh đi ăn đi* '(you$_1$) go$_2$ and eat$_3$!', *chúng ta đi ăn đi* 'let us$_{1-2}$ go$_3$ and eat$_4$!', *lấy vợ đi chứ* 'get married$_{1-2}$! what are you waiting for?'

The particle *mà*, occurring at the end of a statement, connotes insistence: *tôi biết mà* 'I$_1$ know$_2$ it all', *tôi không biết mà* 'I told you I$_1$ didn't$_2$ know$_3$ it at all!'

In addition to the injunctive particle *đi* which indicates a mild order, a curt intonation makes a statement into a command, e.g. *đứng lại* 'halt!', *im* 'quiet! shut up!', *nín!* 'shut up! stop crying!', *thôi!* 'enough!' When inviting or exhorting someone to do something, one uses the particle *hãy* placed before the verb, with or without an expressed subject: *anh hãy ngồi đây* '(you$_1$) sit$_3$ here$_4$', *hãy ăn cơm đi đã* 'go$_4$ ahead and eat$_{2\ 3}$ first$_5$'. To express prohibition or dissuasion, the particle *đừng* or *chớ* put before the verb of action: *anh đừng hút thuốc lá nữa* '(you$_1$) don't$_2$ smoke$_3$ cigarettes$_{4-5}$ any more$_6$', *chớ nói nhảm* 'don't$_1$ talk$_2$ nonsense$_3$'.

A complex sentence may contain as many clauses as there are action verbs or stative verbs, and under this general heading we may examine both subordination and coordination. The main kinds of subordinate clauses are noun clauses, relative clauses and adverbial clauses.

A noun clause, always placed after the main clause, functions as object of the main clause. It is linked to the main clause either directly, or through the intermediary of the particles *rằng* or *là* 'that', e.g. *đừng cho nó biết (là) tôi trượt* 'don't$_1$ let$_2$ him$_3$ know$_4$ (that$_5$) I$_6$ flunked$_7$', *tôi hi-vọng (rằng) họ sẽ giúp tôi* 'I$_1$ hope$_2$ (that$_3$) they$_4$ will$_5$ help$_6$ me$_7$'.

A relative clause functions as an attribute modifying a noun phrase in the main clause, and is often, though optionally, introduced by the particle *mà*, e.g. *quyển sách (mà) tôi nói hôm nọ bị mất rồi* 'the book$_{1-2}$ (that$_3$) I$_4$ told$_5$ you about the other$_7$ day$_6$ has already$_{10}$ been$_8$ lost$_9$', where the relative clause *(mà) tôi nói hôm nọ* helps specify which book is being spoken of; in *thím tôi đã bán ngôi nhà (mà) chú tôi vừa tậu năm ngoái* 'my$_2$ aunt$_1$ has already$_3$ sold$_4$ the houses$_{5-6}$ (that$_7$) my$_9$ uncle$_8$ just$_{10}$ bought$_{11}$ last$_{13}$ year$_{12}$', the clause *(mà) chú tôi vừa tậu năm ngoái* describes further the house that is being discussed. Relative clauses follow their antecedent.

Adverbial clauses serve the same functions as adverbs in the main clause, and express such ideas as purpose, cause, condition, concession, etc. Adverbial clauses are introduced by conjunctions, such as *để (cho)* 'so that', *bởi vì* 'because', *nếu* 'if, *giá* 'suppose', *dù* 'though'. Examples follow; note that the adverbial clause may either precede or follow the main clause: *tôi xin nói để quí-vị biết* 'I$_1$ beg$_2$ to speak up$_3$ so that$_4$ you$_5$ may know$_6$', *vì anh ấy không có tiền cho nên chúng tôi cho miễn học-phí* 'because$_1$ he$_{2-3}$ has$_5$ no$_4$ money$_6$, so$_{7-8}$ we$_{9-10}$ gave$_{11}$ him a tuition$_{13}$ waiver$_{12}$', *nếu tôi có tiền, tôi đã mua quyển sách ấy* 'if$_1$ I$_2$ had had$_3$ money$_4$, I$_5$ would already$_6$ have bought$_7$ that$_{10}$ book$_{8-9}$', *giá anh nghe tôi thì việc đó không hỏng* 'suppose$_1$ you$_2$ had listened$_3$ to me$_4$, then$_5$ that$_7$ thing$_6$ would not$_8$ have failed$_9$', *dù phải khó nhọc, nhưng/song họ không nản* 'although$_1$ it was indeed$_2$ tough going$_{3-4}$, yet$_5$ they$_6$ did not$_7$ get discouraged$_8$'.

As for coordination, several independent clauses may either be juxtaposed without any connective, or may be conjoined by means of such conjunctions as *và* 'and', *mà* 'but, yet', *nhưng* 'however', *song* 'nevertheless', e.g. *tôi rửa mặt, chải đầu, đánh răng, ăn sáng* 'I$_1$ washed$_2$ my face$_3$, combed$_4$ my hair$_5$, brushed$_6$ my teeth$_7$ and ate$_8$ breakfast$_9$', *tôi cho hắn vay tiền và giúp hắn tìm con* 'I$_1$ lent$_{2-4}$ him$_3$ money$_5$ and$_6$ helped$_7$ him$_8$ find$_9$ his child$_{10}$', *ông dùng cơm hay dùng bánh mì ạ* 'would you$_1$ like to eat$_2$ rice$_3$ or$_4$ eat$_5$ bread$_{6-7}$?', *no bụng mà vẫn con đoi* 'his belly$_2$ is full$_1$, yet$_3$ he's still$_4$ hungry$_5$ in his eyes$_{6-7}$', *cái bút này rẻ nhưng tốt* 'this$_3$ pen$_{1-2}$ is cheap$_4$, but$_5$ good$_6$'.

4 Word Classes and Grammatical Categories

In the absence of purely morphological criteria, lexico-syntactic criteria are used to distinguish word classes, i.e. the environment of a word and its possible combinations in the spoken chain are examined together with its meaning(s).

A large number of nouns can be identified by means of such prefixed elements as *cái* 'thing, object', *sự* 'fact', *việc* 'action', *niềm* 'sentiment', *chủ-nghĩa* 'ideology, -ism'. The classifier *cái* serves to create a noun from an adjective (*cái đẹp* 'beauty') or from a verb (*cái tát* 'a slap'). Likewise, with the classifier *cuộc* 'action, process, game' one can construct such nouns as *cuộc đình-công* 'a strike (industrial)' (from the verb *đình-công* 'be on strike'), *cuộc vui* 'party' (from the adjective *vui* 'merry, fun').

In the southern dialect, such kinship terms as *ông* 'grandfather', *bà* 'grandmother', *cô* 'paternal aunt', *anh* 'elder brother', *chị* 'elder sister' followed by the demonstrative *ấy* 'that' take the dipping-rising *hỏi* tone to function as third person pronouns, e.g. *ổng* 'he', *bả* 'she', *cổ* 'she', *ảnh* 'he', *chỉ* 'she'. The words indicating a given point or position in space or time also display this morphophonemic trait, e.g. *trong ấy* becomes *trỏng* 'in there', *ngoài ấy* becomes *ngoải* 'out there', *trên ấy* becomes *trển* 'up there'. The words designating portions of space have other characteristics of the noun class. This is why it is preferable to put them among nouns instead of considering them prepositions. Predicatives consist of verbs and adjectives. The latter, which are actually stative verbs, or verbs of quality, can be preceded by *rất* 'very', *khá* 'rather' but cannot occur with the exhortative particle *hãy!*: contrast *hãy chăm-chỉ học-hành* 'study$_3$ hard$_2$!' with **hãy đúng!* 'be accurate!'. Moreover, only verbs of action can be followed by a verb of direction ('coverb') (*ra* 'exit', *vào* 'enter', *lên* 'ascend', *xuống* 'descend'), or be used in the frame … *đi* … *lại* to mark repetition of an action, e.g. *chạy ra* 'run out(side)', *chạy xuống* 'run down', *chạy đi chạy lại* 'run back and forth' (but not with *mặn*, 'salty', **mặn ra*, **mặn xuống*, **mặn đi mặn lại*).

A noun, often defined as a word which denotes a being or thing, can function as predicate only if it is preceded by the copula *là* or its negative *không phải là*. It cannot follow the injunctive particle *hãy* or the prohibitive particles *đừng, chớ*. It can constitute a nominal phrase when it is combined with a numeral or plural particle (*những, các*) and a classifier, or with a demonstrative (*này* 'this', *ấy* 'that'). Likewise, certain particles can be used to establish the class of verbs, which can be preceded by aspect markers such as *sẽ* 'future', *đã* 'completion', *đều* 'togetherness'. On the other hand, by considering the position of a word in a syntactic group within a sentence, we can confirm its word class: in the noun phrase *khó-khăn của người công-chức* 'the difficulties₁ of₂ an official₃₋₄', the possessive element *của người công-chức* helps us to establish the noun status of *khó-khăn* even when it does not follow a classifier like *nỗi* or a pluraliser like *những*.

Such tests suggest that lexical items in Vietnamese fall into eight broad classes, as follows: nouns, verbs, quantifiers, substitutes, particles, connectors, modals, interjections. The first four classes consist of 'full (content) words', whereas the remaining four represent 'empty (function) words'.

The language does not have paradigms in the classical sense. There are, however, categories, some of which are non-existent in Indo-European languages. Within the class of nouns, it is necessary to mention, besides number, the various features that determine the choice of classifier (see page 683), such as animateness, humanness, shape and social status. Verbs, or more generally predicatives, manifest such categories as tense, result, direction, voice, intensity, orientation. Thus, in addition to the simple sentence *ông ấy đi* one can specify time reference by means of particles: *ông ấy sẽ đi* 'he will go', *ông ấy sắp đi* 'he is about to go', *ông ấy đã đi rồi* 'he has already gone', *ông ấy vừa/mới đi* 'he has just gone', *ông ấy đang đi* 'he is on his way'. Other categories are illustrated by the following: *tìm thấy* 'find' (lit. 'search find'), *chịu được* 'endure' (lit. 'endure gain'), *bỏ đi* 'abandon' (lit. 'drop go'), *đóng vào* 'close' (lit. 'close enter'), *nhận ra* 'recognise' (lit. 'notice') *phải phạt* 'be punished' (lit. 'suffer punish'), *bị thua* 'be defeated' (lit. 'undergo lose'), *được thưởng* 'be rewarded' (lit. 'gain reward'). Intensity is expressed by repeating the verb, with main stress on the first occurrence, e.g. *'đau đau đau là!* 'oh how it hurts!'

In the family, kinship terms are used in place of personal pronouns, e.g. *bố cho con tiền ạ!* 'please give me some money, Dad' (lit. 'father give child money please'), *bố không muốn cho con tiền* 'I (lit. 'father') don't want to give you (lit. 'child') money'. Each individual must use appropriate terms of address and reference which place him where he belongs in the clan, and the terms are dictated by the relationship shown in a very precise nomenclature. The term *ông* 'grandfather' is used in formal conversation with a stranger one meets for the first time. The correct first person pronoun is *tôi* 'servant'. Between friends, the term *anh* 'elder brother' is applied to the hearer. Some arrogant pronouns (*tao* 'I', *mày* 'you', etc.) are used only in a familiar or vulgar context. Normally, etiquette recommends an attitude of humility before others, who are addressed in honorific terms (e.g. *cụ* 'greatgrandfather', *ngài* 'your excellency', *thày* 'master'), which show respect for the hearer's age, knowledge and social rank.

5 Lexicon

Although the great majority of words have only one syllable (e.g. *nhà* 'house', *có* 'have', *ma* 'ghost', *ăn* 'eat', *cơm* 'rice', *ngon* 'delicious'), one cannot help noticing in modern Vietnamese numerous forms that have two or more syllables. These disyllabic or polysyllabic forms are either native compounds or compounds borrowed from Chinese.

Reduplication, a very frequent derivational process, can be total or partial: *ba-ba* 'river turtle', *chuồn-chuồn* 'dragonfly', *cào-cào* 'grasshopper', *đa-đa* 'partridge', *tùng-tùng* (representation of the sound of a drum); *châu-chấu* 'grasshopper', *đom-đóm* 'firebug', *đu-đủ* 'pawpaw, papaya', *đo-đỏ* 'reddish', *trăng-trắng* 'whitish' (note the tonal modifications in this group and the next); *ngấm-ngầm* 'secret(ly)' (cf. *ngầm*), *ngoan-ngoãn* 'well behaved' (cf. *ngoan*); *mạnh-mẽ* 'strong(ly)' (cf. *mạnh*), *xấu-xa* 'hideously' (cf. *xấu*), *nhẹ-nhàng* 'gently' (cf. *nhẹ*), *sẵn-sàng* 'all ready' (cf. *sẵn*) *tỉ-mỉ* 'meticulous', *lang-thang* 'wander', *bồi-hồi* 'anxious, nervous', *lẩm-bẩm* 'mumble'; *học-hiệc* 'to study and the like' (cf. *học*), *xe-xiếc* 'cars and the like' (cf. *xe*); *lơ-tơ-mơ* 'vague, obscure', *sạch-sành-sanh* 'completely (empty)'; *líu-lo líu-lường* 'twitter, jabber', *đủng-đa đủng-đỉnh* 'slowly taking one's time'.

Composition consists in combining two or more lexical bases. Sometimes, the relation among the components is one of coordination, e.g. *nhà cửa* 'house, home' (lit. 'house door'), *bàn ghế* 'furniture' (lit. 'table chair'), *giàu sang* 'rich₁ and noble₂', *ăn uống* 'eating₁ and drinking₂', *được thua* 'win₁ or lose₂', *bờcõi* 'limits, border' (lit. 'edge region'), *đường* 'roads' (lit. 'road street'). In other instances there is a relation of dependency between the two components, e.g. *nước mắt* 'tears' (lit. 'water eye'), *bánh ngọt* 'cake' (lit. 'pastry sweet'), *tháng hai* 'February' (lit. 'month two'), *nhà tấm* 'bathroom' (lit. 'house bathe'), *tàu bò* 'tank' (lit. 'ship crawl'), *đỏ ối* 'scarlet' (lit. 'red dark-red'), *đánh mất* 'lose' (lit. 'hit lose'); *trắng nõn* 'pure white (of skin)' (lit. 'white bud'); *bao-giờ* 'when' (lit. 'what time'), *bây-giờ* 'now' (lit. 'this time'), *bấy-giờ* 'then' (lit. 'that time'). A special case of this dependent relationship is complementation, as in *vâng lời* 'obey' (lit. 'obey words'), *qua đời* 'pass away' (lit. 'pass life'), *khó tính* 'difficult to please' (lit. 'difficult character'); *buồn ngủ* 'sleepy' (lit. 'desire sleep'), *dễ bảo* 'docile' (lit. 'easy tell'). The numerals, which are based on the decimal system, combine dependence and coordination, e.g. *bốn mươi chín* 'forty-nine', literally 'four ten nine', i.e. (4×10) + 9.

Within native Vietnamese compounds, the usual order is modified–modifier. Among the numerous Chinese loans, this order applies in cases of complementation (e.g. verb–object), such as *thu-ngân* 'cashier' (lit. 'collect money'), *vệ-sinh* 'hygiene, sanitary' (lit. 'guard life'), but the order is modifier–modified if the head component is a noun, e.g. *giáo-sư* 'teacher' (lit. 'teach master'), *đại-học* 'university' (lit. 'great study'), *ngữ-pháp* 'grammar' (lit. 'language rules'), *Pháp-ngữ* 'French language', *quan-sát-viên* 'observer' (lit. 'observe person'). This parallels the fact that modifiers normally follow the head noun in noun phrases in Vietnamese, but precede in Chinese.

One can even speak of prefixes and suffixes in the Sino-Vietnamese compounds, such as *bất-* (e.g. *bất-hợp-pháp* 'illegal'), *vô-* (e.g. *vô-ích* 'useless'), *khả* (e.g. *khả-ố* 'loathsome'), *phản-* (e.g. *phản-cách-mạng* 'counter-revolutionary'), *thân-* (e.g. *thân-chính-phủ* 'pro-government'), *đệ* (ordinal prefix, e.g. *đệ-nhất* 'first'); *-giả* (e.g. *tác-giả* 'author'), *-gia* (e.g. *khoa-học-gia* 'scientist'), *-sư* (e.g. *kiến-trúc-sư* 'architect'), *-sĩ* (e.g. *văn-sĩ* 'writer'), *-viên* (e.g. *đoàn-viên* 'member (of group)'), *-hoá* (e.g. *âu-hoá* 'Europeanise'), *-trưởng* (e.g. *viện-trưởng* 'rector').

Descriptive forms have been created to denote articles of merchandise imported from abroad, e.g. *cái bật lửa* 'cigarette lighter' (lit. 'thing switch fire'), *cái gạt tàn thuốc là* 'ash tray' (lit. 'thing shake-off ash drug leaf'), *máy thu thanh* 'radio receiver' (lit. 'machine gather sound'), *máy quay phim* 'movie camera' (lit. 'machine turn film'), *máy bay cánh cụp cánh xòe* 'F-111' (lit. 'machine fly wing close wing spread'), *tầu há mồm* 'landing craft' (lit. 'ship open mouth').

The Chinese lexical fund being predominant in literary and scholarly language, an educated speaker often has access to two synonymous terms, a native one used in daily parlance and the other, of Chinese origin, reserved for written texts. For instance, 'train' is either *xe lửa* (lit. 'vehicle fire') or *hoả-xa* and 'aeroplane' is either *máy bay* (lit. 'machine fly') or *phi-cơ*. Some advocates of standardisation have advocated the exclusive use of native words in place of Sino-Vietnamese loanwords, e.g. *máy bay lên thẳng* (lit. 'machine fly ascend straight') instead of *máy bay trực-thăng* 'helicopter', *Tòa Nhà Trắng* (lit. 'building house white') instead of *Tòa Bạch-ốc* 'White House', *Lầu Năm Góc* (lit. 'palace five angle') instead of *Ngũ-giác-đài* 'Pentagon', *vùng trời* (lit. 'area sky') instead of *không-phận* 'airspace'.

The use of abbreviations to replace entire appellations of administrative units or publications is very widespread, but each syllable (rather than each word) is represented by its initial, e.g. *TCPV* for *Tối-cao Pháp-viện* 'Supreme$_1$ Court$_2$', *DHVK* for *Đại-học Văn-khoa* 'Faculty$_1$ of Letters$_2$', *TCVH* for *Tạp-chí Văn-học* 'Review$_1$ of Literature$_2$'. This practice is, however, limited to the written language, and administrative titles are sometimes very long, e.g. *TGD-TTHBDHV* for *Tổng-giám-đốc Trung, Tiểu-học và Bình-dân Học-vụ* 'Director-General$_1$ of Secondary$_2$, Primary$_3$ and$_4$ Popular$_5$ Education$_6$'.

Since Vietnamese was strongly influenced by Chinese during the ten centuries of Chinese rule, the number of words of Chinese origin is inevitably very large: simple words, disyllables, as well as whole expressions make up the majority of lexical items in any written text of a technical nature. However, this invasion is limited to the large body of content words, while grammatical morphemes ('function words') retain their native identity. 'Suffixes' borrowed from Chinese are sometimes abused, and people say things like *cửa hàng trưởng* for 'store$_{1-2}$ manager$_3$', *đại-khái chủ-nghĩa* 'doctrine$_2$ of approximation$_1$'. A recent convention distinguishes the noun *chủ-nghĩa xã-hội* 'socialism' (lit. 'doctrine society/socialist') from the adjective *xã-hội-chủ-nghĩa* 'socialist'.

Loans from French are relatively less numerous: *ga* 'station', *cà-phê* 'coffee', *xà-phòng* 'soap', *cao-su* 'rubber', *bồ-tạt* 'potash', *xi-măng* 'cement', *bơm* 'pump', *xúc-xích* 'sausage', etc. The spoken language under certain circumstances tolerates such forms, with French bound morphemes, as: *qua-loa-rơ-măng* 'just so and so, not thoroughly' (cf. *qua-loa* 'rough, summary' and the French adverbial suffix *-ment*), *bét-đem* 'the bottom one' (cf. *bét* 'last' and the French ordinal suffix *-ième*), *inchêable* 'impeccable' (with the French negative prefix *in-*, Vietnamese *chê* 'denigrate', and the French adjectival suffix *-able*)!

Bibliography

Nguyễn Đình-Hoà (1997) provides a detailed overview of the language. For the social background to Vietnamese, reference may be made to Nguyễn Đình-Hoà (1980). For the genetic classification, see Haudricourt (1953, 1954); more specific historical topics are covered by Maspéro (1912) and Gregerson (1969), while Nguyễn Đình-Hoà (1982–4) is the state-of-the-art discussion of *chữ nôm*.

In the absence of a single comprehensive and authoritative grammar of Vietnamese, the reader will need to refer to a range of sources, such as Cadière (1958), Emeneau (1951), Lê (1960), Nguyễn Đăng Liêm (1969), Thompson (1965), Trần et al. (1943) and Trương (1970). For special topics, Honey (1959) may be consulted for word classes, and Nguyễn Đình-Hoà (1972a, 1972b, 1979) for various facets of the verb.

A useful collection of articles is Nguyễn Khắc Viện et al. (1976).

References

Cadière, L.M. 1958. *Syntaxe de la langue vietnamienne* (= Publications de l'École Française d'Extrême-Orient, vol. XLII) (École Française d'Extrême-Orient, Paris)

Emeneau, M.B. 1951. *Studies in Vietnamese (Annamese) Grammar* (University of California Press, Berkeley and Los Angeles)

Gregerson, K.J. 1969. 'A Study of Middle Vietnamese Phonology', *Bulletin de la Société des Études Indochinoises*, vol. 44, no. 2, pp. 131–93

Haudricourt, A.-G. 1953. 'La place du vietnamien dans les langues austroasiatiques', *Bulletin de la Société Linguistique de Paris*, vol. 49, pp. 122–8

—— 1954. 'De l'origine des tons en vietnamien', *Journal Asiatique*, vol. 242, pp. 69–82

Honey, P.J. 1959. 'Word Classes in Vietnamese', *Bulletin of the School of Oriental and African Studies*, vol. 18, pp. 534–44

Lê Văn Lý. 1960. *Le Parler vietnamien: sa structure phonologique et morphologique functionnelle: esquisse d'une grammaire vietnamienne*, revised edn (Publications de l'Institut des Recherches Historiques, Saigon)

Maspéro, H. 1912. 'Études sur la phonétique historique de la langue annamite: les initiales', *Bulletin de l'École Française d'Extrême-Orient*, vol. 12, pp. 1–127

Nguyễn Đăng Liêm. 1969. *Vietnamese Grammar: A Combined Tagmemic and Transformational Approach: A Contrastive Analysis of English and Vietnamese*, vol. 2 (Research School of Pacific Studies, Canberra)

Nguyễn Đình-Hoà. 1972a. 'Passivization in Vietnamese', in L. Bernot and J.M.C. Thomas (eds) *Langues et techniques, nature et société* (Klincksieck, Paris), pp. 179–87

—— 1972b. 'Vietnamese Categories of Result, Direction and Orientation', in M.E. Smith (ed.) *Studies in Linguistics: Essays in Honor of George L. Trager* (Mouton, The Hague), pp. 395–412

—— 1979. *201 Vietnamese Verbs* (Barron's Educational Series, Woodbury, NY)

—— 1980. *Language in Vietnamese Society* (Asia Books, Carbondale, IL)

—— 1982–4. 'Studies in Nôm Characters: The State of the Art'. *Vietnam Culture Journal*, vol. 1, no. 1, pp. 25–36; vol. 2, nos 1–2 and vol. 3, no. 1, pp. 107–13

—— 1997. *Vietnamese* (John Benjamins, Amsterdam)

Nguyễn Khắc Viện, et al. 1976. *Linguistic Essays* (Xunhasaba, Hanoi)

Thompson, L.C. 1965. *A Vietnamese Grammar* (University of Washington Press, Seattle)

Trần Trọng Kim, Phạm Duy Khiêm and Bùi Kỷ. 1943. *Grammaire annamite*, 2nd edn (Lê Thăng, Hanoi)

Trương Văn Chình. 1970. *Structure de la langue vietnamienne* (Librairie Orientaliste Paul Geuthner, Paris)

41

Sino-Tibetan Languages

Scott DeLancey

1 Introduction

The Sino-Tibetan family consists of two branches: Sinitic, consisting of the Chinese languages and possibly the aberrant Bai or Minjia language of Yunnan (although Bai may also be a heavily Sinicised Tibeto-Burman language), and Tibeto-Burman, which includes several hundred languages spoken from the Tibetan plateau in the north to the Malay peninsula in the south and from northern Pakistan in the west to northeastern Vietnam in the east. Earlier classification schemes included Miao-Yao, Tai and Vietnamese in the Sino-Tibetan family on the basis of their remarkable typological resemblance to Chinese, but it is now clear that the structural resemblances and shared vocabulary among these languages are areal features rather than shared inheritance from a common ancestor.

Comparative Tibeto-Burman is a relatively unexplored field and there is not yet a complete and reliable schema for the genetic relationships among the various sub-branches of the family. (Indeed, we cannot say for certain how many Tibeto-Burman languages there are or even whether there may not still be a few – possibly in western Nepal, very probably in northern Burma and southeastern Tibet – that are yet to be discovered.) With the exception of the problematic Rung group, there is general agreement that the groupings listed below constitute genetic units at some level. (Note that many languages are known in the literature by several names, usually including one or more Chinese, Burmese or Indic ethnonyms which sometimes label groups speaking rather diverse languages. A very useful list of language names is given in Hale (1982).)

Bodish: includes Tibetan; Kanauri, Bunan and other poorly documented languages of the Himalayan frontier of India; Gurung, Tamang, Thakali; probably Newari, the old state language of Nepal; and some (but not all) other Tibeto-Burman languages of Nepal.

East Himalayan: includes the Kiranti/Rai (Limbu, Thulung, Bahing, Vayu, etc.) languages and probably some others in eastern Nepal. Most closely related to Bodish.

Bodo-Garo: includes Bodo (Boro), Garo and a number of other languages spoken in Assam.

Konyak: a group of languages (Nocte, Chang, Wancho, etc.) spoken by tribal peoples in Arunachal Pradesh in India and probably adjacent areas of Burma. The Indian ethnonym 'Naga' is applied to these groups as well as to those speaking 'Naga' languages (see below). The Konyak 'Naga' languages are probably most closely related to the Bodo-Garo group.

Naga: languages (Angami, Sema, Rengma, Lotha, etc.) spoken by tribal peoples in Arunachal Pradesh and adjacent areas of Burma. These 'Naga proper' languages are most closely related to the Kuki–Chin and Mikir–Meithei groups.

Kuki-Chin: called Kuki in India, Chin in Burma; includes Lushai, Lakher and numerous other languages in western Burma and easternmost India and Bangladesh.

Mikir-Meithei: two languages of Manipur and Assam states in India; closely related to Naga and Kuki-Chin.

Abor-Miri-Dafla: a group of little-known languages of Arunachal Pradesh and adjacent areas of Tibet. Reliable documentation, which is only now beginning to become available, may permit the assignment of some or all of these languages to other groups.

Kachinic: includes at least the conservative and historically important Jinghpo (Jinghpaw, Chinghpo, often erroneously called 'Kachin', a Burmese ethnonym which refers to speakers of the Burmish Lawng and Zaiwa languages as well as of Jinghpo) dialects of Yunnan, Assam and northern Burma and perhaps the inadequately documented Luish languages.

Lolo-Burmese: the Burmish sub-branch includes Burmese and a few minor languages of Yunnan and northern Burma (notably Lawng or Maru and Zaiwa or Atsi). The Loloish languages are spoken by hill tribes in northern Burma and Thailand, Laos, Yunnan and Vietnam. Important members of Loloish include Yi (Lolo), Lahu, Lisu and Hani (Akha). The Naxi or Moso language of Yunnan is generally considered to be closely linked to Lolo-Burmese and by some scholars to fit in or near the Loloish sub-branch.

Rung: a cover term for several morphologically conservative languages of western China and northern Burma, including the Nung languages (Rawang and Trung), Gyarong, the Qiang languages (Qiang and Primi) and the extinct Tangut. (This corresponds roughly to a grouping called 'Sifan' in early work on Tibeto-Burman.) The relationships of these languages to one another and to the rest of the family are controversial; Nung and Qiang–Tangut show evidence of close relationship to Naxi and Lolo-Burmese, while Nung shows lexical links to Jinghpo, and Gyarong to Tibetan (although this is apparently a result of borrowing) and Kamarupan.

Karen: several closely related dialects spoken in eastern Burma and adjacent parts of Thailand. Karen is typologically quite divergent from the rest of the family, manifesting fairly consistent SVO syntactic patterns where other Tibeto-Burman languages are resolutely SOV. Largely on this basis there remains some doubt as to whether Karen represents another branch of Tibeto-Burman, coordinate with the others, or one branch of a higher-order Tibeto-Karen family, the other branch of which is Tibeto-Burman. Currently opinion in the field is inclining towards the first alternative, but the problem is not yet settled.

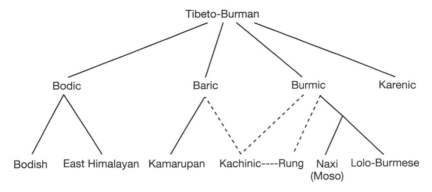

Figure 41.1 Higher-order Groupings within Tibeto-Burman.
Note: Dotted lines represent uncertain or controversial relationships.

The higher-order grouping of the Tibeto-Burman languages is problematic. The system proposed by Shafer (1966–73) and some tentative suggestions by Benedict (1972) are generally accepted as credible working hypotheses; although several other classification schemes have been proposed, none can be considered reliable. The best-known classifications are summarised and compared in Hale (1982); for a recent statement, see Thurgood (2003). Rather than repeat these readily available schemes here I have represented in Figures 41.1 and 41.2 a classification which incorporates several hypotheses being considered in current published and unpublished work by a number of scholars; this should not be taken as necessarily more correct than earlier suggestions of Shafer and Benedict.

The best-known Tibeto-Burman languages are Tibetan and Burmese, the two which have the longest and most extensive literary traditions. Both have a primarily Buddhistic literature written in an Indic script; the Tibetan script dates to the seventh century. The earliest attestations of Burmese are in twelfth-century inscriptions; the earliest Tibetan writings extant were discovered in the caves at Tun-huang and date from the ninth century.

The vast majority of Tibeto-Burman languages are (or were until this century) non-literate, but a few have writing systems of one sort or another. In the sphere of Indian influence, Newari (spoken in Nepal), Lepcha (in Sikkim) and Meithei or Manipuri (Manipur State, India) have independently developed Devanāgarī-based alphabets (although the Lepcha, in particular, is scarcely recognisable as Indic at first glance), in which there exist historical and religious texts which have yet to be investigated linguistically. Apparently all three systems are now considered obsolete and these languages, like others in Nepal and India, are now written in Hindi or Nepali script.

Within the Chinese sphere we find two extremely interesting indigenous writing systems. The better-known is that of Tangut or Xixia, the apparently extinct language used in the Tangut kingdom which existed in the north-west of China until 1227. The Tangut script consists of characters reminiscent of and obviously modelled after Chinese, but nevertheless quite distinct. Tangut and its script have been intensively studied in recent decades by scholars in Japan and the Soviet Union. The other system is a basically pictographic script, with a few syllabic phonetic elements, used by priests among the Naxi (Nakhi) or Moso of Yunnan; a very similar system was used among the neighbouring Yi (Lolo). It is generally assumed that the original stimulus for the development of this system was a vague acquaintance with Chinese writing, although there are few recognisably Chinese elements in the system.

695

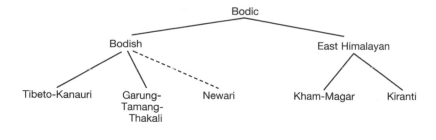

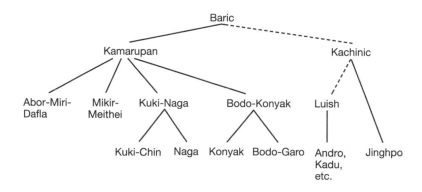

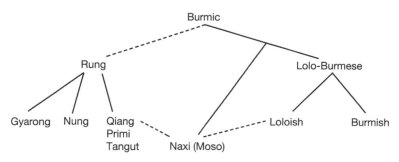

Figure 41.2 Middle-level Relationships within Tibeto-Burman.

2 Comparative Sino-Tibetan Phonology

Our current understanding of Proto-Tibeto-Burman phonology is still uncertain, although considerable progress has been made in the reconstruction of a few sub-branches, in particular Lolo-Burmese. However, the segmental inventory given in Table 41.1 is generally accepted by most researchers. Proto-Tibeto-Burman is reconstructed as having two series of stops (the third series found in written Tibetan, Burmese, Jinghpo and several other languages can be shown to be secondary innovations which occurred independently in various languages, usually conditioned by the loss of earlier prefixes) and one of nasals (again, many languages have both voiced and voiceless resonants, but the voiceless series reflect an earlier voiceless prefix, most commonly *s-).

696

Table 41.1 The Consonants of Proto-Tibeto-Burman

p	t	k
b	d	g
m	n	ŋ
	s	
	z	
	l	r
w		y

Proto-Tibeto-Burman certainly had no more than five phonemic vowels, and there remains some question about the Proto-Tibeto-Burman status of the mid vowels.

The relationship of this (or any alternative) Proto-Tibeto-Burman system to that of Proto-Sino-Tibetan is rather difficult to assess, given the considerable uncertainty which remains with respect to the phonological reconstruction of Early Chinese. However, recent work in that area (in particular by F.-K. Li and by N. Bodman and W. Baxter, as well as some less widely accepted proposals by E.G. Pulleyblank and A. Schuessler) present a picture which is much closer to that reconstructed for Proto-Tibeto-Burman than was the earlier and still widely cited system of B. Karlgren.

Historical developments in the Sino-Tibetan sound systems are best described in terms of syllable structure. Like modern East Asian languages, Proto-Tibeto-Burman and Proto-Chinese permitted only a subset of the consonant inventory to occur in syllable-final position; these included one series of stops (presumably voiceless), the nasals, *s, *r, *l, *w and *y. This inventory is greatly reduced in most attested languages; Tibetan orthography preserves all but the semi-vowels, but most languages preserve only the stops and nasals. Modern Central Tibetan allows only /p/ and /m/ in final position, while some Chinese, Loloish and Naga languages have no syllable-final consonants at all. The depletion of the inventory of final consonants typically correlates with a con-comitant increase in the number of vowel and tone distinctions in the syllable nucleus.

In syllable-initial position clusters of obstruent or nasal plus medial *y, *w, *r and *l occurred. These are preserved in part in Tibetan and Burmese orthography and some modern languages, but in general they have simplified, typically with *Cl- merging with *Cy- or *Cr-, *Cy- giving either simple *C- or a new palatal series and *Cr- simpli-fying, merging with *Cy- (as in Burmese), or giving a new retroflex series (as in Central Tibetan). In addition, Benedict and most other scholars reconstruct at least some of the famous Tibetan initial clusters for Proto-Tibeto-Burman. These are probably all ety-mologically bimorphemic, but it is likely that fossilised, synchronically unanalysable clusters existed in Proto-Tibeto-Burman, if not Proto-Sino-Tibetan. It is, however, extre-mely common to find the same etymon occurring in different languages with different prefixes, as for example Written Tibetan *rna*, Balti Tibetan *sna*, Tangkhul *khana* < *g-na 'ear', or Balti Tibetan *gwa*, Written Burmese *swa* 'go'. Some such cases may represent lexical alternants at the Proto-Tibeto-Burman level, but others reflect independent sec-ondary compounding in the daughter languages. For example, Balti *gwa* and Burmese *swa* represent independently developed compounds of a Proto-Sino-Tibetan root *wa 'go' with other motion verbs *ga and *sa.

The historical status of tone in Tibeto-Burman and Sino-Tibetan remains a topic of some controversy. Probably a majority of Tibeto-Burman languages have phonemic tone and/or voice register distinctions, as do Chinese and the unrelated Tai, Miao–Yao and

Vietnamese languages. In the earliest days of Sino-Tibetan studies, lexical tone was considered a diagnostic Sino-Tibetan feature, an assumption which played a major role in the erroneous assignment of Tai and Vietnamese to the Sino-Tibetan family. It is now clear that the strikingly parallel tone systems of these languages and Chinese represent an areal feature which had diffused across genetic lines; however, the original source of the feature remains unclear.

There is now considerable evidence to suggest that the various tone systems within Sino-Tibetan may not be directly cognate, i.e. that tone systems have developed independently in various branches of the family. Research on the origin of tone systems has demonstrated that phonemic tone can develop in the course of the loss of distinctions between syllable-initial and/or -final consonants. Typically the loss of a voicing contrast in initial consonants results in a phonemic high/low tone distinction, with earlier voiced initial syllables developing low tone and voiceless initial syllables developing high tone, while the depletion of the inventory of possible syllable-final consonants results in a distinction between open syllables and those ending in a glottal stop or constriction, with the latter eventually giving rise to rising or falling tones. Such is the origin, for example, of the secondarily developed tone systems found in the Central Tibetan dialects. Several scholars have presented evidence suggesting that the tones of Chinese may have originated in this way at a date considerably later than the separation of the Chinese and the Tibeto-Burman branches of Sino-Tibetan.

If the tone systems of the Sino-Tibetan languages represent parallel independent developments rather than common inheritance, this would explain the existence of numerous non-tonal Tibeto-Burman languages and the considerable difficulty which has been encountered in attempts to find correspondences among the tones of the various tonal Tibeto-Burman languages. Within major branches tone correspondences can sometimes be found; for example, the tones of the Lolo-Burmese languages correspond regularly and it is clear that a tone system can be reconstructed for Proto-Lolo-Burmese. However, when this system is compared with the tone system of other tone languages such as Jinghpo or Tamang, it frequently turns out that otherwise clearly cognate items do not correspond in tone class, suggesting that the tone systems developed after the separation of the languages being compared.

Nevertheless, the hypothesis of the secondary origin of Sino-Tibetan tone systems is not yet universally accepted. Benedict, in particular, has called attention to some regular correspondences which can be found between the tone classes of cognate morphemes in Chinese and certain Tibeto-Burman languages, particularly Burmese and Karen, on the basis of which he reconstructs a two-tone system for Proto-Sino-Tibetan. This hypothesis entails the wholesale loss of tone in many Tibeto-Burman languages, particularly in the Himalayan branch, subsequently followed by their re-emergence in Central Tibetan and a few other Himalayan languages; this consequence has resulted in considerable resistance in the field to Benedict's proposal.

3 Tibeto-Burman Typology and Reconstruction: Morphology and Syntax

With the exception of Karen, all of the Tibeto-Burman languages are postpositional SOV languages with predominantly agglutinative morphology (Burmese, described in a separate chapter in this volume, is in most respects typical) and this must also have been true of Proto-Sino-Tibetan. Several languages retain traces of older inflectional alternations in the verb, and a few show innovative case alternations in pronouns. A number of case marking typologies occur in the family, including consistently ergative marking (Gurung), aspectually split ergative or active/stative patterns (Newari and various Tibetan dialects), split ergative marking in which third person transitive subjects take ergative case while first and second persons do not (Kiranti, Gyarong) and variations on a more-or-less nominative–accusative topic marking scheme (most Lolo-Burmese languages; see Chapter 43). A detailed examination of an example of this last type can be found in Hope (1974).

Current comparative work on Tibeto-Burman morphological structure presents a picture quite different from what has historically been assumed about Tibeto-Burman languages. Proto-Tibeto-Burman is now reconstructed with a split-ergative case marking and verb agreement system of the sort exemplified by the following Gyarong examples, in which third person but not first and second person transitive subjects are case marked (in the modern languages which retain this system the ergative marker is often identical to the instrumental and/or ablative postposition), while the verb shows pronominal concord with any first or second person argument, regardless of its grammatical role:

ŋa   mə   nasŋo-ŋ
I   s/he   scold-1 sg.
'I scold him/her.'

ŋə-njɔ   mə   nasŋo-č
I-du.   he   scold-1 du.
'We two scold him/her.'

ŋə-ñiɛ   mə   nasŋo-i
I-pl.   s/he   scold-1 pl.
'We (pl.) scold him/her.'

mə-kə   ŋa   u-nasŋo-ŋ
s/he-crg.   I   dir.-scold-1 sg.
'S/he scolds me.'

mə-ñiɛ-kə   ŋa   u-nasŋo-ŋ
he-du.-erg. I   dir.-scold.-1 sg.
'They two scold me.'

mə-kə   ŋə-njɔ   u-nasŋo-č
he-erg. I-du   dir.-scold-1 du.
'S/he scolds us two.'

Note the ergative postposition -kə marking third but not first person subjects and the fact that both person and number agreement are always with the first person participant, whether it is subject or object.

Both the pronominal and the verb agreement systems probably distinguished dual as well as singular and plural number, as well as an inclusive/exclusive distinction. In a number of modern languages (e.g. Gyarong, Chepang, Nocte) the verb also marks in transitive clauses whether the subject is higher or lower than the object on a 1st > 2nd > 3rd or 1st = 2nd > 3rd person hierarchy, and this 'direct/inverse' marking system is probably also to be reconstructed for the Proto-Tibeto-Burman verb. While no modern language preserves this reconstructed system in its entirety, most of these categories are retained at least vestigially in a large number of languages which represent nearly every major division of the family. (The most conservative morphology is found in the East Himalayan, Rung and Jinghpo languages.) Probably the closest attested system to the Proto-Tibeto-Burman system is that of Gyarong, spoken in Sichuan; the example sentences above and the paradigms in Tables 41.2 and 41.3 (from the work of Jin Peng) exemplify the system.

The *-ŋ* and *-n* suffixes reflect the Proto-Sino-Tibetan pronouns **ŋa* and **na(ŋ)*, while the dual and plural suffixes *-č* and *-i* are probably reconstructible for Proto-Tibeto-Burman, although their exact form is uncertain. Both series of prefixes are almost certainly reconstructible for Proto-Tibeto-Burman. The *u-* and *a-* are direct/inverse markers; the *tə/kə-* series may also have been part of the direct/inverse system, although their original function is quite unclear. Reflexes of one or the other occur in a great many modern languages as second person agreement indices and in Gyarong one or the other occurs in all and only those verbs with a second person participant, but in the Nung and some other languages a member of the series also occurs on transitive verbs with third person subject and first person object.

Early work on comparative Tibeto-Burman assumed that, since this verbal morphology is not found in Tibetan or Burmese, it must be a secondary innovation in those languages which manifest it; hence all such languages were lumped together in a putatively genetic group of 'pronominalised' languages. Recent research has shown,

Table 41.2 Intransitive Agreement Affixes in Gyarong (Suomo Dialect)

	Sg.	*Du.*	*Pl.*
1st person	V-ŋ	V-č	V-i
2nd person	tə-V-n	tə-V-n-č	tə-V-ñ
3rd person		∅	

Note: V indicates position of the verb stem.

Table 41.3 Transitive Verb Affixes in Gyarong (Suomo Dialect)

Object		*1st person*			*2nd person*			*3rd person*
		Sg.	Du.	Pl.	Sg.	Du.	Pl.	
Subject 1st	Sg. Du. Pl.				tə-a-V-n	tə-a-V-n-č	tə-a-V-ñ	V-ŋ V-č V-i
2nd	Sg. Du. Pl.	kə-u-V-ŋ	kə-u-V-č	kə-u-V-i				tə-V tə-V-n-č tə-V-ñ
3rd		u-V-ŋ	u-V-č	u-V-i	tə-u-V-n	tə-u-V-n-č	tə-u-V-ñ	V-u u-V

however, that while the system is apparently completely extinct in Lolo-Burmese, Bodo-Garo and Tibetan proper, it is found in near relatives of each of these and is attested in all other major Tibeto-Burman subgroups except for Karen with a consistency that makes it clear that some version of it must have been a Proto-Tibeto-Burman feature. A good description of a language of this type is Caughley (1982), which also summarises much of the available data on verb paradigms in other Tibeto-Burman languages.

Several other verbal affixes can be reconstructed for Proto-Tibeto-Burman and probably Proto-Sino-Tibetan, although the original functions of most of them remain unclear. A causative *s- prefix is clearly reconstructible for Proto-Sino-Tibetan and an intransitivising *m- definitely for Proto-Tibeto-Burman and probably for Proto-Sino-Tibetan. An *-s suffix is also reconstructed for Proto-Sino-Tibetan; there is good evidence for both perfectivising and nominalising functions for such a suffix and it is possible that these functions reflect two different etyma. There is also phonological evidence for a dental stop suffix with similar functions, which may originally have been a conditioned allomorph of *-s. We also find evidence (particularly from the complex verbal system of Classical Tibetan) for prefixed *g- (or *kV-) and *l- and/or *r- (or *lV-, *rV-) of Proto-Tibeto-Burman provenience, but their original function is not yet recoverable.

There is evidence for a considerable amount of derivational morphology in Tibeto-Burman and Sino-Tibetan, most of which originated in compounding processes. Most if not all of the modern Sino-Tibetan languages and certainly all reconstructible ancestral stages have very productive compounding processes which create bimorphemic two-syllable nouns (and sometimes verbs). In the Tibeto-Burman languages these tend diachronically to reduce one syllable (generally the first), thus eventually creating what appears synchronically and etymologically to be a derivational prefix. The process is illustrated by the following forms from the Yunnan dialect of Jinghpo (for which example I am indebted to L. Diehl): the word *lam* 'road, path' occurs both free and in compounds such as *lamsun* 'narrow path', *lamshe* 'side road', *lamtaʔ* 'level path (along a mountainside)'. But each of these also occurs in one or more reduced forms, e.g. *lamsun~masun~nsun, lamshe~mashe, lamtaʔ~ntaʔ*; thus there is an identifiable set of forms in which there appears to be a prefix *ma-* or *n-* meaning 'road, path'. The prevalence of this pattern of development has considerably slowed progress in lexical comparison and phonological reconstruction both for Tibeto-Burman and between Tibeto-Burman and Chinese, since these secondary prefixes typically disappear, but before doing so can affect the phonological development of the root initial consonant, thus leaving perturbations in the pattern of regular sound correspondences between attested languages.

Bibliography

Benedict (1972), actually written in the 1940s and out of date in some respects, is still the closest the field has come to a handbook of comparative Sino-Tibetan. Matisoff (2003) is the first publication of a projected series on comparative Sino-Tibetan; reference can also be made to the website of his Sino-Tibetan Etymological Dictionary and Thesaurus (STEDT) project: http://stedt.berkeley.edu/index.html. Thurgood and LaPolla (2003) is the most recent detailed overview of the family, including sketch descriptions of individual languages. The extent to which subgrouping of Sino-Tibetan continues to generate controversy can be seen, for instance, in the interchange between van Driem (1997) and Matisoff (2003).

Bibliographical sources are Shafer (1957–63) and Hale (1982), which latter updates Shafer's bibliography to the mid-1970s and includes a valuable synopsis of the various classification schemes for the family, which with the extensive language index makes it possible to deal with the considerable nomenclatural confusion in the field. Wolfenden (1929) is the classic survey of Tibeto-Burman morphology, outdated but not yet supplanted. Matisoff (1978) provides an excellent introduction to the problems of Sino-Tibetan lexical comparison.

The following grammars will give an impression of some of the range of variation found within Tibeto-Burman: Caughley (1982) is a detailed presentation of the verbal system of a conservative 'pronominalised' language and includes a synopsis of verb paradigms from other morphologically conservative languages; Hope (1974) is a detailed presentation of clause organisation in a language which has completely lost the Proto-Tibeto-Burman morphological system; Matisoff (1973) is the most complete grammatical description in existence of any Tibeto-Burman language.

References

Benedict, P.K. 1972. *Sino-Tibetan: A Conspectus* (Cambridge University Press, Cambridge)

Caughley, R. 1982. *The Syntax and Morphology of the Verb in Chepang* (Research School of Pacific Studies, Australian National University, Canberra)

Hale, A. 1982. *Research on Tibeto-Burman Languages* (Mouton, The Hague)

Hope, E. 1974. *The Deep Syntax of Lisu Sentences* (Research School of Pacific Studies, Australian National University, Canberra)

Matisoff, J. 1973. *The Grammar of Lahu* (University of California Press, Berkeley)

—— 1978. *Variational Semantics in Tibeto-Burman: The 'Organic' Approach to Linguistic Comparison* (ISHI Press, Philadelphia)

—— 2000. 'On "Sino-Bodic" and Other Symptoms of Neosubgroupitis', *Bulletin of the School of Oriental and African Studies*, vol. 63, pp. 356–69

—— 2003. *Handbook of Proto-Tibeto-Burman: System and Philosophy of Sino-Tibetan Reconstruction* (University of California Press, Berkeley)

Shafer, R. 1957–63. *Bibliography of Sino-Tibetan Languages*, two parts (Otto Harrassowitz, Wiesbaden)

Thurgood, G. 2003. 'A subgrouping of the Sino-Tibetan languages: between language contact, change, and inheritance'. In Thurgood and LaPolla, pp. 1–21.

Thurgood, G. and LaPolla, R.J. 2003. *The Sino-Tibetan Languages* (Routledge, London)

van Driem, G. 1997. 'Sino-Bodic', *Bulletin of the School of Oriental and African Studies*, vol. 60, pp. 455–88

Wolfenden, S. 1929. *Outlines of Tibeto-Burman Linguistic Morphology* (Royal Asiatic Society, London)

42

Chinese

Charles N. Li and Sandra A. Thompson

1 Introduction: The Five Major Dialect Groups of Chinese

It is estimated that well over 1,000,000,000 people, approximately one-fifth of the earth's population, are speakers of some form of Chinese. Genetically, Chinese is an independent branch of the Sino-Tibetan family of languages (see Chapter 41). Within the Chinese branch, there are a number of dialects, which can be classified into a minimum of five groups on the basis of their structural affinities.

Mandarin. This is the major dialect group in China, both in terms of political importance and in terms of number of speakers. The native speakers of this dialect group represent approximately 70 per cent of the total Chinese population. They occupy the North China plain, the middle Yángzǐ plain, the Huái plain, the north-east plain, the Sìchuān basin and most of Guǎngxī, Guèizhōu and Yúnnán provinces. The term 'Mandarin' is an English translation of the old Běijīng expression *guān-huà* 'official language', which was for many centuries the dialect of Běijīng. In modern China, Běijīng dialect was accepted as a standard for the official language in the early part of this century. Since the 1950s, because of political and geographical boundaries, the official language of China, called *pǔtōnghuà* 'common speech', and the official language of Táiwān, called *guóyǔ* 'national language', have differed from each other slightly in both vocabulary and grammar, although both are based on the Běijīng dialect. One of the four official languages of Singapore, *huáyǔ*, is also based on the Běijīng dialect. Again, it is somewhat different from both *pǔtōnghuà* and *guóyǔ*. The other basis for considering Mandarin as the 'major' Chinese dialect group is that, in terms of both vocabulary and structure, the modern written language is closer to Mandarin than to any of the other dialects.

Wú. The Wú dialects are spoken around the lower Yángzǐ River and its tributaries: the provinces of Jiāngsū, Zhèjiāng and Ānhuī, which include the major urban centres of Shànghǎi, Sūzhōu and Wēnzhōu.

Mǐn. These dialects are spoken by people living in Táiwān and Fújiàn provinces and Hǎinán Island in the Gulf of Tonkin. In English, these dialects are sometimes referred

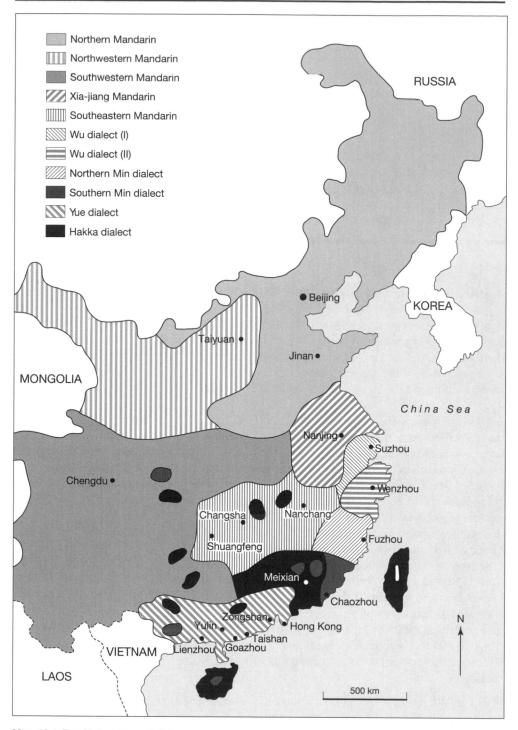

Map 42.1 The Dialect Map of China.

to as 'Fukkianese', 'Hokkianese', 'Amoy' and 'Taiwanese'. Most of the people of Táiwān are descendants of Mǐn speakers who emigrated from the coastal regions of Fújiàn province. For this reason, 85 per cent of the people in Táiwān still speak a Mǐn dialect as their native language. For the same reason, most of the speakers of Chinese in Singapore are also native speakers of a Mǐn dialect.

Yuè. The Yuè dialects are spoken primarily in the province of Guǎngdōng. Yuè dialects, including the well-known Cantonese, the language of Guǎngzhōu (Canton), are spoken in many parts of the Chinese diaspora, particularly Hong Kong and overseas Chinese settlements such as the Chinatowns in the United States, Europe and South-East Asia. For this reason, many of the English words borrowed from Chinese have their origins in Cantonese, such as *kumquat* from Cantonese [kamkwat] and *chop suey* from Cantonese [tsap sui].

Hakka. The Hakka dialects are the least well known outside of China, because few of the Hakka people have emigrated from China. Most of the Hakka are scattered throughout south-eastern China in Guǎngxī province and throughout the Mǐn and Yuè regions, as small, tightly knit agricultural communities. Historically, the Hakka people were northerners who moved south during several waves of migration. Their name Hakka means 'guest', indicating their immigrant status in the southern areas to which they moved.

We have chosen to use the term 'dialect' for these five major groups of languages, even though the differences among them, in terms of both vocabulary and structure, are sufficient to cause mutual unintelligibility. There are two reasons for this choice. First, genetically related languages of one nation are typically considered 'dialects'. Second, China has always had a uniform written language which is logographic. People who cannot understand each other's speech can still read the same written language provided that they are educated. This tends to reinforce the idea of 'dialects' as opposed to separate languages.

We adopt this usage of dialect, even though it is based on political and social considerations rather than linguistic ones. In Section 5, we will discuss the written language, but first we will describe some of the structural properties common to Chinese dialects.

2 Phonology

All Chinese dialects, with rare exceptions, share two easily perceptible phonological properties: they are all tone languages, and they have a very highly constrained syllable structure. We will talk about each of these properties in turn.

2.1 Tone

When we speak of a tone language, we mean a language in which every stressed syllable has a significant contrastive pitch. This pitch may be level or contour, but it is an integral part of the pronunciation of the syllable and it serves to distinguish one syllable from another. Běijīng Mandarin serves as a good example, since it has one of the simplest tone systems of the Chinese dialects. As shown in Table 42.1, it has four basic tones.

Table 42.1 Běijīng Mandarin Tones

Tone 1:	high level	⌐	55
Tone 2:	high rising	⌐	35
Tone 3:	dipping/falling	⅃	214
Tone 4:	high falling	⅁	51

The symbols in the column second from the right are known as tone letters. They provide a simplified time-pitch graph of the voice, where the vertical line on the right serves as a reference line for pitch height. The numbers at the right represent the pitch of the tone according to a scale of five levels, with 1 being the lowest and 5 the highest. Thus, tone 1 is a high level tone pronounced at the same high pitch (level 5) for its duration, while tone 4 is a falling tone which starts with the high pitch at level 5 and ends with the low pitch at level 1.

If we take the syllable [i] in Běijīng Mandarin with each of the four tones, we have four different words, as is shown in Table 42.2.

Table 42.2 Four Words in Běijīng Mandarin

$[i]^{55}$	⌐	'cloth'
$[i]^{35}$	⌐	'to suspect'
$[i]^{214}$	⅃	'chair'
$[i]^{51}$	⅁	'meaning'

The Romanisation system officially adopted by the government in Běijīng, called Pīnyīn, represents the tones by means of diacritic marks above the nuclear vowel of the word. The diacritic mark for the high level tone is /ˉ/, for the rising tone, /´/, for the curve tone, /ˇ/, and for the falling tone /`/. For example, the four words of Table 42.2 written in Pīnyīn are: yī 'cloth', yí 'to suspect', yǐ 'chair', yì 'meaning'.

Tonal variation accounts for the most common differences among the dialects of China. It is often true that the dialects in two villages, just a few miles apart, have different tone systems. As we have stated, Běijīng Mandarin has one of the simplest tone systems of all dialects: it has the second smallest number of tones (only four) and the rules governing the behaviour of the tones are relatively simple. In contrast, Cantonese has nine tones, six of regular length, and three for so-called 'short' syllables, as shown in Table 42.3 (the short syllables are those with short vowels which end in *p*, *t* or *k*). (Tone 1 has a free variant 53.)

Table 42.3 The Tones of Cantonese

(1)	55	(4)	21	(7)	5
(2)	35	(5)	23	(8)	3
(3)	33	(6)	22	(9)	2

In many dialects, the complexity of the tone system may be manifested not only in the number of tones, but also in the phenomenon of 'tone sandhi', that is, a change of tones when two or more syllables are pronounced together. The most complicated tone sandhi phenomena can be found in the Wú and Mǐn dialects. For example, in Cháozhōu, a southern Mǐn dialect, there are eight tones for syllables in isolation, including two short tones belonging to syllables with final stops. When a syllable is followed by another syllable, however, tone sandhi occurs: that is, each 'isolation tone' changes to a different tone, called a 'combination tone'. Table 42.4 shows the Cháozhōu isolation tones and their corresponding combination tones.

Table 42.4 Cháozhōu Tones

Isolation tones	5 ˥	2 ˨	33 ˧	11 ˩	35 ˩˥	53 ˥˧	213 ˨˩˧	55 ˥˥
Combination tones	3 ˧	5 ˥	33 ˧	11 ˩	31 ˧˩	35 ˩˥	53 ˥˧	13 ˩˧

This means that for each monosyllabic word, speakers of the Cháozhōu dialect learn its isolation tone, the tone it has when it stands by itself, and the rules converting the isolation tone to the combination tone, the tone it has when it is followed by another syllable.

Let us look at an example of how tone sandhi works in Cháozhōu. In Table 42.4 we can see that the high short tone in the first column becomes a mid short tone in combination. Thus, if we take the word for 'one' in isolation, we have

[tsɔk] ˥ 5 'one'

but if we put it in front of the syllables meaning 'meal', it changes to

[tsek] ˧ 3

like this:

[tsek] ˧ 3 [tuɯŋ] ˥˧ 53 [puŋ] ˩ 11 'one meal'

A glance at Table 42.4 will reveal that the isolation tone of the second syllable [tuɯŋ], which is a 'classifier' (see pages 713–714), is ˨˩˧ 213.

2.2 Syllable Structure in Chinese

The syllable structure of all the Chinese dialects is relatively simple compared with that of, say, English: no dialect, for example, allows consonant clusters and all dialects allow only a restricted set of consonants in syllable-final position. As with tone, Běijīng Mandarin has a relatively simple syllable structure:

(C) (V)V($\substack{V \\ N}$)

Every syllable has a nuclear vowel, which may occur with another vowel to form a diphthong or with two other vowels to form a triphthong. Initial and final consonants are optional and the only final consonants which are permitted are nasals (specifically, [n] and [ŋ]).

To take an example which differs from Mandarin, in Cantonese, a syllable may have a diphthong, but not a triphthong. Also, a Cantonese syllable may have an unreleased stop ([p], [t], [k]) or a nasal ([m], [n], [ŋ]) in the final position. The Cantonese syllable structure may be represented by the following schema:

(C)(V)V(C)

3 Morphology

Morphology concerns the internal structure of words. When a Chinese dialect is compared to a Slavonic or Romance language, for instance, one of the most obvious features to emerge is the relative simplicity of its word structure. Most Chinese words are made up of just one or two morphemes. In particular, Chinese dialects have few inflectional morphemes. Thus, while many languages, including those in the Indo-European, Semitic, Bantu, Altaic and Tibeto-Burman families, typically have inflectional morphemes indicating categories such as tense/aspect and number/person of the subject or object for verbs or categories such as gender and case for nouns, no such inflectional categories exist for Chinese dialects.

The type of morphological device found in Chinese dialects tends to involve compounds and derivational morphemes rather than inflectional ones. This type of morphological device is especially common in modern Mandarin. Because of this, the traditional characterisation of Mandarin as 'monosyllabic' is no longer accurate. A 'monosyllabic' language would be one in which each word consisted of just one syllable. While no language could be expected to be totally monosyllabic, this characterisation is certainly more applicable to the Yuè and Mǐn dialect groups than it is to Mandarin. According to one popular dictionary, roughly two-thirds of the basic everyday Běijīng Mandarin vocabulary consists of polysyllabic words. Table 42.5 provides a sample of disyllabic words in Běijīng Mandarin whose counterparts in Guǎngzhōu (Yuè) and Shàntóu (Mǐn) are monosyllabic.

There is a historical explanation for the fact that Mandarin has the highest proportion of polysyllabic words of all the Chinese dialects. The ancestral language of the modern Chinese dialects was monosyllabic. Because of phonological changes that have taken place, more extensively in Mandarin than in the southern dialects, many formerly distinct syllables in Mandarin have become homophonous. Thus, where Guǎngzhōu, for example, still has a contrastive distinction between syllable-final [m] and [n] as shown in the words: [kɐm] 'gold' and [tɐn] 'tael', Běijīng Mandarin no longer retains that contrastive distinction. The Běijīng counterpart of the two distinct Guǎngzhōu syllables is just the one syllable, [tɕīn]. If the Běijīng word for 'gold' (as listed in Table 42.5) hadn't become the disyllabic form [tɕīn-tsɪ], the two Běijīng words for 'gold' and 'tael' would have been homophonous in the form [tɕīn]. The threat of too many homophonous words has forced the language to increase dramatically the proportion of polysyllabic

Table 42.5 Mandarin Polysyllables

	Běijīng Mandarin	Guǎngzhōu (Yuè)	Shàntóu (Mǐn)
'gold'	[tɕin-tsɪ]	[kɐm]	[kim]
'pond'	[tʂʰɪ-tsɪ]/[tʂʰɪ-tʰaŋ]	[tʰɔŋ]	[ti]
'ant'	[ma-i]	[ŋɐi]	[hia]
'tail'	[uei-paɭ]/[i-pa]	[mei]	[bue]
'clothing'	[i-ʂaŋ]	[sam]	[sã]
Negative existential verb	[mei-iou]	[mou]	[bo]
'good-looking'	[xau-kʰan]	[lɛŋ]	[ŋia]
'to know'	[tʂɪ-tau]	[tɕi]	[tsai]
'contemptible'	[tʰau-iɛn]	[tsɐŋ]	[lou]

words, principally by means of compounding or adding on a derivational suffix. As an example of the latter, the second syllable of the disyllabic Běijīng word, [tɕīn-tsɹ] 'gold', was formerly a diminutive suffix. It has lost its diminutive meaning in the word [tɕīn-tsɹ] and is now merely a part of the word for 'gold'. Let us also look at an example of a disyllabic Běijīng word obtained through compounding: [tʰău-ièn] 'contemptible'. This is a compound historically derived from two monosyllabic words, [tʰău] 'to beg' and [ièn] 'contempt'. The Guǎngzhōu and the Shàntóu words for 'contemptible' remain monosyllabic, as shown in Table 42.5.

3.1 Compounds

3.1.1 Resultative Verb Compound

One important type of verb compound is known as the 'resultative verb compound', where the second part of the compound signals some result of the action or process conveyed by the first part. Here are some examples from Běijīng Mandarin:[1] dǎ-pò 'hit-broken = hit (it) with the result that it is broken', mà-kū 'scold-cry = scold (someone) with the result that s/he cries'. The following sentences illustrate the use of these two sample resultative verb compounds.

wǒ	bǎ	píngzi	dǎ-pò	le
I	*ba*	bottle	hit-broken	crs.

'I broke the bottle.'

tā	bǎ	wǒ	mà-kū	le
s/he	*ba*	I	scold-cry	crs.

'S/he scolded me so much that I cried.'

One characteristic of all resultative verb compounds is that they may occur in what is known as the 'potential' form, which involves the insertion of -de- or -bu- between the two parts of the compound. The insertion of -de- has the effect of giving the compound an affirmative potential meaning, i.e. 'can', while the insertion of -bu- gives the compound the negative potential meaning 'cannot'. Consider one of the examples above, dǎ-pò 'hit-break'. Its two potential forms would be:

dǎ-de	-pò	dǎ-bu	-pò
hit-can	-broken	hit-cannot	-broken

Here they are used in sentences:

tā	*dǎ*	*-de*	*-pò*	nèi	-ge	píngzi
s/he	hit	-can	-broken	-that	-cl.	bottle

'S/he can break that bottle'.

tā	*dǎ*	*-bu*	*-pò*	nèi	-ge	píngzi
s/he	hit	-cannot	-broken	that	-cl.	bottle

'S/he cannot break that bottle.'

709

Another type is the directional resultative verb construction. The first verb in a directional resultative verb construction implies movement and the second, which may itself be a compound, signals the direction in which the person or thing moves as a result. Here is an example and a sample sentence in which it occurs:

pǎo-húi   -lái
run-return -come
'run back'

tā   *pǎo-húi*   *-lái*   le
s/he   run-return   -come   crs.
'S/he ran back.'

3.1.2 Parallel Verb Compounds

The two verbs that constitute a parallel verb compound are either synonymous, nearly synonymous or similar in meaning. Here are some examples:

pí-fá	'tired-tired = tired'	jiàn-zhú	'build-build = build'
fáng-shŏu	'defend-defend = defend'	bāng-zhù	'help-help = help'
fàng-qì	'loosen-abandon = to give up'	piāo-liú	'drift-flow = drift'

3.1.3 Nominal Compounds

As in English, Chinese has a wide range of nominal compound types. Here are a few examples, illustrating the different semantic relations between the nominal components of the compound.

(i) N_2 is made of N_1
      máo-yī   'wool-clothing = sweater'
      tiĕ-hézi   'iron-box = iron box'

(ii) N_2 is a container of N_1
      fàn-wăn   'rice-bowl = rice bowl'
      shŭi-píngzi 'water-bottle = water bottle'

(iii) N_1 and N_2 are parallel
      fù-mŭ   'father-mother = parents'
      guó-jiā   'country-home = country'

(iv) N_2 denotes a product of N_1
      jī-dàn   'chicken-egg = egg'
      mĕiguó-huò   'America-product = American product'

(v) N_2 denotes a malady of N_1
      xīngzàng-bìng 'heart-disease = heart disease'
      fèi-yán   'lung-inflammation = inflammation of the lung'

(vi) N₂ is used for N₁
      qiāng-dàn   'gun-bullet = bullet'
      xié-yóu   'shoe-oil = shoe polish'

(vii) N₁ denotes the location of N₂
      tián-shǔ 'field-mouse = field mouse'
      tái-bù   'table-cloth = tablecloth'

3.1.4 Noun–Verb Compounds

The Chinese dialects also have several types of compounds consisting of a noun and a verb. One type might be called the 'subject–predicate' compound, where the first element historically has a 'subject' relationship to the second element. Here are two examples with sentences illustrating their usage:

dǎn-dà   'gall-big = brave'

tā	hěn	*dǎn-dà*
s/he	very	brave

'S/he is very brave.'

mìng-kǔ 'life-bitter = ill-fated'

wǒ	hěn	*mìng-kǔ*
I	very	ill-fated

'I have a hard life.'

Another type of noun–verb compound is one in which the second element historically bears a 'direct object' relationship to the first element. Here are two examples with sentences illustrating their usage:

xíng-lǐ   'perform-salutation = salute'

wǒ	gěi	tā	*xing-lǐ*
I	to	s/he	salute

'I saluted him/her'.

zhěn-tóu   'rest-head = pillow'

wǒ	yǒu	liǎng	-ge	*zhě-tóu*
I	have	two	cl.	pillow

'I have two pillows.'

3.2 Reduplication

As a morphological process, 'reduplication' means that a morpheme is repeated so that the original morpheme together with its repetition form a new word. One way in which reduplication is used in Chinese is to indicate that an action is being done 'a little bit'. Here is an example:

shuō-shuo   'speak-speak = speak a little'

nǐ	*shuō-shuo*	nei	-jiàn shì
you	speak a little	that	-cl. matter

'Speak a little about that matter!'

Adjectives can also be reduplicated, the semantic effect of which is to intensify their meaning. For example: *hóng* 'red', *hóng-hóng* 'vividly red'.

    Manner adverbs can be formed from reduplicated adjectives. For example, *màn* 'slow' is an adjective but *màn-màn-de* 'slowly' is an adverb formed by reduplicating the adjective *màn* and adding on the particle *-de*. The following sentence illustrates the usage of the adverb, *màn-màn-de* 'slowly':

tā	*màn-màn-de*	pǎo
s/he	slowly	run

'S/he runs slowly.'

3.3 Affixation

Affixation is the morphological process whereby a bound morpheme is added to another morpheme to form a larger unit. Compared to Indo-European languages, Chinese has few affixation processes and most of them are not inflectional, but derivational.

3.3.1 Prefixes

There are very few prefixes in Chinese. *Kě-* is an example of a prefix which can be added to verbs to form adjectives; its meaning can be described as '-able', as shown in the following examples:

kě-ài	'lovable'	ài	'to love'
kě-xiào	'laughable'	xiào	'to laugh'
kě-kào	'dependable'	kào	'to depend'

Another prefix is *dì-*, which is added to numerals to form ordinals, as in:

dì-liù   'sixth'   liù   'six'

3.3.2 Suffixes

There are several categories of suffixes which are very important in Chinese grammar. Foremost among them is the category of verb suffixes serving as aspect markers. Aspect markers vary from dialect to dialect. Here, we will cite two examples from Běijīng Mandarin.

712

'Aspect' refers to how a situation is viewed with respect to its internal make-up. To take an example, let us first look at an English sentence:

Cheryl *was watching TV* when *I spilled the tea*.

In this English sentence, the first verb phrase, *was watching TV*, differs significantly from the second verb phrase, *spilled the tea*, because the two phrases reflect different ways in which the two situations are viewed. The second verb phrase presents the totality of the situation referred to without reference to its internal make-up: the entire situation is viewed as a single unanalysable whole. When a language has a special verb form to indicate the viewing of an event in its entirety, we say that that form signals the 'perfective' aspect. In Běijīng Mandarin, the suffix *-le* is used for the perfective aspect.

The first verb phrase, *was watching TV*, does not present the situation of Cheryl's watching TV in its entirety. Instead, it makes explicit reference to the internal make-up of 'TV watching', presenting it as ongoing, referring neither to its beginning nor its end, but to its duration. Verbal markers signalling this ongoing/durative aspect can be called 'durative' aspect markers. In Běijīng Mandarin, the durative suffix is *-zhe*, whose occurrence is restricted to certain semantic types of verbs.

Here are some examples of the perfective and the durative suffixes in Běijīng Mandarin:

tā	bǎ	chēzi	mài	-le
s/he	*ba*	car	sell	-perf.

'S/he sold the car'.

wǒ	chī-le	sān	-wǎn	fàn
I	eat-perf.	three	-bowl	rice

'I ate three bowls of rice.'

tā	chuān	-zhe	yī	-shuāng	xīn	xiézi
s/he	wear	-dur.	one	-pair	new	shoe

'S/he is wearing a pair of new shoes.'

qiáng	-shàng	guà	-zhe	yī	-fu	huà
wall	-on	hang	-dur.	one	-cl.	painting

'There is a painting hanging on the wall.'

Another important category of suffixes is classifiers. A classifier is a morpheme co-occurring with a noun which is individuated or specified in the discourse, that is, a noun which occurs with a numeral, a quantifier or a demonstrative. Classifiers do not occur with a noun which is non-referential or non-specific. When a noun is individuated, quantified or specified, the classifier occurs as a suffix of the numeral, the quantifier or the demonstrative. Other than the general classifier *-ge* which can occur with most nouns, a noun in Chinese can in general occur with only one classifier and the speaker must learn which classifier goes with which noun. For example, the Běijīng classifier for books is *-běn*, so that 'that book' is:

nèi-*běn*	shū
that-cl.	book

The classifier for snakes is *-tiáo*, so that 'four snakes' is:

sì-*tiáo*   shé
four-cl.   snake

Here are a few other classifiers:

-zhāng   for tables, maps, papers, etc.
-jiàn   for garments such as shirts, coats, sweaters, and events, news, etc.
-lì   for pearls, marbles, grains of sand, wheat, rice, corn or millet, etc.

Earlier we pointed out that classifiers are not used when a noun is non-referential or non-specific. The following sentence contains an example of a non-referential noun, *diànyǐng* 'movie':

wǒ   bu   cháng   kàn   diànyǐng
I   not   often   see   movie
'I don't see movies often.'

A third important category of suffixes in Chinese is that of locative suffixes. These occur with nouns – often marked with a preposition – to specify location with respect to the referent of the noun. Here are some examples:

tā   zài   chuáng   *-shàng*
s/he   at   bed   -on
'S/he is on the bed.'

tā   cóng   fángzi-li   pǎo-chū-lái   le
s/he   from   house-in   run-exit-come   crs.
'S/he came running out from the house.'

Besides the three categories of grammatical suffixes mentioned above, there are the genitive morpheme *-de* and the manner adverbial marker, which also has the form *-de*. Both the genitive morpheme and the adverbial marker occur as suffixes. Examples follow:

wǒ   *-de*   qìchē
I   -gen.   car
'my car'

màn-man-*de*   zǒu
slowly   walk
'Walk slowly!'

Finally we will cite two derivational suffixes. Productive derivational suffixes are not numerous in Chinese, and they do not occupy a very important position in Chinese grammar. One example of a derivational suffix is *-xué* '-ology', as in:

dòngwù-xué	'animal-ology = zoology'
zhíwù-xué	'plant-ology = botany'
shéhuì-xué	'society-ology = sociology'
lìshǐ-xué	'history-ology = history'

Another example of a derivational suffix is *-jiā* '-ist', as in:

lìshǐxué-jiā	'history-ist = historian'
lǐlùn-jiā	'theory-ist = theorist'
xiǎoshuō-jiā	'novel-ist = novelist
dòngwuxué-jiā	'zoology-ist = zoologist'

4 Syntax

4.1 Chinese as an Isolating Language

One of the first things a person familiar with Indo-European languages notices about Chinese is its lack of grammatical inflections. Although there is a morphological category of aspect in Chinese (as discussed above in Section 3.3), most words in Chinese have one immutable form, which does not change according to number, case, gender, tense, mood or any of the other inflectional categories familiar from other languages. Languages with very little grammatical inflectional morphology are known as 'isolating' languages. What are some of the concomitant factors of the isolating character of Chinese?

First, there is no case morphology signalling differences between grammatical relations such as subject, direct object or indirect object, nor is there any 'agreement' or cross-indexing on the verb to indicate what is subject and what is object. In Chinese, in fact, there are few grammatical reasons for postulating grammatical relations, although there are, of course, ways of distinguishing who did what to whom, just as there are in all languages. One way to tell who did what to whom is by word order: ordinarily, the noun phrase before the verb is the agent or the experiencer and the noun phrase after the verb is the patient or affected participant, much as in English. Furthermore, in natural discourse, it is usually clear who is the agent and who or what is the patient without any special marking.

A corollary to this de-emphasis of grammatical relations is the fact that Chinese discourse makes extensive use of 'topic-comment' constructions, as shown in the following examples (with italics indicating the topic):

zhèi-ge	*dìfang*	zhòng	màizi	hǎo
this-cl.	place	plant	wheat	good

'At this place, it is good to plant wheat.'

jiāzhōu	qìhou	hǎo
California	climate	good

'California, its climate is good.'

A second factor in the lack of grammatical inflectional morphology is that gender, plurality and tense are either indicated by lexical choice or not indicated at all.

715

A third factor is the absence of overt markers signalling the relationship of the verbs in the 'serial verb construction'. For instance, consider the following example:

wǒ	jiào	tā	mǎi	júzī	chī
I	tell	s/he	buy	orange	eat

'I told him/her to buy oranges to eat.'

Notice that the English translation of this sentence contains the morpheme *to*, which signals that *buy* and *eat* are subordinate verbs with unspecified future tense. The Běijīng Mandarin version has no such overt signal; the relationship between the verbs must be inferred from their meanings and from the discourse context in which the combination occurs. In Chinese, there are many different types of such inferred relationships. Here are a few examples where the English translations indicate the various relationships.

wǒ	yǒu	yí	-ge	píngguǒ	hěn		hǎo	chī
I	have	one	-cl.	apple	very		good	eat

'I have an apple which is very delicious.'

tā	tǎng	zài	chuáng-shang	kàn	shū	
s/he	lie	at	bed	-on	see	book

'S/he lay in bed reading.'

tā	qù	zhōngguó	xué	zhōngguó	huà
s/he	go	China	learn	China	painting

'S/he went to China to learn Chinese painting.'

Finally, sentences containing coverbs may be viewed as a type of serial verb construction. The class of coverbs contains words that are partly like verbs and partly like prepositions. They have this mixed status because most of them used to be verbs at earlier stages of the language and many of them still have the properties of verbs and can be used as verbs that have similar meaning. Consider, for example, the following sentences:

tā	zài	jiā	-li	gōngzuò
s/he	at	home	-in	work

'S/he works at home.'

tā	dào	Běijīng	qù-le
s/he	arrive	Běijīng	go-perf.

'S/he went to Běijīng.'

Zài and *dào* are coverbs. Both may serve as verbs, as in the following:

nǐ	zài	nǎr?
you	at	were

'Where are you?'

wǒmen	dào	-le	Běijīng	le
we	arrive	-perf.	Běijīng	crs.

'We have arrived in Běijīng.'

The Chinese coverb phrase consisting of a coverb and a noun is equivalent to the English prepositional phrase. In English a preposition is normally distinct from a verb. In Chinese, however, the separation of a coverb and a verb is much less clear-cut, and sentences containing coverbs such as those above can be viewed as a type of serial verb construction.

4.2 'Adjectives'

Strictly speaking, there is no class of words in Chinese that we can call 'adjective'. That is, while there are certainly words which denote qualities or properties of entities, from a grammatical point of view it is difficult to distinguish 'adjectives' from 'verbs'. There are at least three ways in which 'adjectives' can be seen to behave like verbs.

First, in Chinese, words denoting qualities and properties do not occur with a copula as they do in Indo-European languages. For example, the English and Běijīng Mandarin versions of a sentence such as *Molly is very intelligent* differ with respect to the presence or absence of the copular verb.

mǎlì	hěn	cōngming
Molly	very	intelligent

'Molly is very intelligent.'

Thus, in English, adjectives have the distinguishing characteristic of occurring with a copula when they are used predicatively. In Chinese, on the other hand, such words appear without any copula, just as verbs do.

Second, quality and property words in Chinese are negated by the same particle *bù* as are verbs:

tā	*bù*	kāixīn
s/he	not	happy

'S/he is not happy.'

tā	*bù*	chī	ròu
s/he	not	eat	meat

'S/he does not eat meat.'

Third, when an 'adjective' modifies a noun, it occurs with the same nominalising particle *de* as verb phrases do:

kāixīn	*-de*	rén
Happy	noms.	person

'people who are happy'

chī	*ròu*	*de*	rén
Eat	meat	noms.	person

'people who eat meat'

For these reasons, it is sensible to consider quality and property words in Chinese simply as a subclass of verbs, one which we might call 'adjectival verbs'.

4.3 Questions

4.3.1 Question-word Questions

Question-word questions are formed in Chinese by the use of question words whose position is the same as non-question words having the same function. For example, consider the positions of *shéi?* 'who?' and *shénme?* 'what?' in the following examples:

tā	zhǎo	*shéi?*
s/he	look-for	who

'Who is s/he looking for?'

shéi	zhǎo	tā?
Who	look-for	s/he

'Who is looking for him/her?'

nǐ	shuō	*shénme?*
You	say	what

'What are you saying?'

shénme	guì?
What	expensive

'What is expensive?'

Similarly, *nǎlǐ?* 'where?' can occur wherever a locative noun phrase can occur:

tā	zài	*nǎlǐ*	yóuyǒng?
s/he	at	where	swim

'Where does s/he swim?'

As would be expected, question words which modify nouns occur before the noun, the position in which ordinary noun modifiers are found. The following sentence illustrates the prenominal position of *duōshǎo?* 'how many?':

nǐ	mǎi-le	*duōshǎo*	rìlì?
You	buy-perf.	how many	calendar

'How many calendars did you buy?'

4.3.2 Yes–No Questions

Chinese has several processes for forming 'yes–no' questions. First, such a question can be signalled by intonation: a rising intonation with a declarative clause has an interrogative force, as in most languages.

Another way to signal yes–no questions is to use a question particle at the end of the sentence. In Běijīng Mandarin the particles *ma* and *ne* are used for this purpose, as in:

nǐ	xǐhuan	Xiān	*ma?*
You	like	Xiān	Q

'Do you like Xiān?'

nǐ	jiějie	shì	gōngchéngshī,nǐ	mèimei	*ne*?
you	elder-sister	be	engineer	you	younger-sister	Q

'Your elder sister is an engineer – what about your younger sister?'

Chinese also has another way of forming yes–no questions: an affirmative and a negative version of the same proposition can be combined to make what is known as an 'A–not-A' question. Here are some examples from Běijīng Mandarin:

nǐ	*xǐhuan*	*-bu*	*-xǐhuan*	tā?
You	like	-not	-like	s/he?

'Do you like him/her?'

tǎ	*chī-bu*	*-chī*	píngguǒ?
s/he	eat-not	-eat	apple

'Does s/he eat apples?'

5 The Writing System

The Chinese writing system is called a logographic or character system, because each symbol is a character/logograph. There are five processes by which the characters are created. We will briefly discuss those five processes in the following.

5.1 Pictographs

Writing in China began over 4,000 years ago with drawings of natural objects. The pictures were gradually simplified and formalised, giving rise to pictorial characters, called pictographs. See Table 42.6.

Table 42.6 Pictographs in Chinese Writing

Old form	Modern form		Meaning
ᛁᛁ	林	/lín/	'forest'
⦗⦗⦗	川	/chuān/	'river'
⊙	日	/rì/	'sun'

5.2 Ideographs

Ideographs are characters derived from diagrams symbolising ideas or abstract notions. For example, the diagrams ⌐ and ⌐ were created to symbolise the notions 'above' and 'below'. Today the characters denoting 'above' and 'below' have become 上 /shàng/ and 下 /xià/ respectively.

5.3 Compound Ideographs

A compound ideograph is a character whose meaning is in some way represented by the combination of the meanings of its parts. For example, the character 畾 /tā/, meaning

719

'loquacious', is formed by combining the character 言 /yán/ 'speak' three times; and the character 明 /míng/ 'bright' is a compound of the character 日 /rì/ 'sun' and the character 月 /yuè/ 'moon', because the sun and the moon are the natural sources of light.

5.4 Loan Characters

Loan characters result from borrowing a character for a word whose pronunciation is the same as that of another word represented by that character. For example, in an earlier stage of the Chinese language, the character 易 /yì/ denoting 'scorpion' was borrowed to stand for the word meaning 'easy' because 'easy' and 'scorpion' had the same pronunciation. In modern Chinese, a new character has been created for the word 'scorpion' and the character, 易 /yì/, denotes 'easy'.

5.5 Phonetic Compounds

A phonetic compound is the combination of two characters, one representing a semantic feature of the word, the other representing the phonetic, i.e. the pronunciation of the word. Consider the character, 鈾 /yóu/ 'uranium', for example. The character is composed of the two characters, 金 /jīn/ and 由 /yóu/. The first, 金 /jīn/, has the meaning 'metal', signifying the metallic nature of uranium. The second character, 由, /yóu/, has a pronunciation which approximates the first syllable of the English word *uranium*, because when the new chemical element, uranium, was discovered, it was decided that the Chinese character should approximate the sound of the first syllable of the English word, *uranium*. Over 90 per cent of all modern Chinese characters are phonetic compounds and the process of forming phonetic compounds remains the standard method for creating new characters.

5.6 Simplification of the Writing System

The movement to simplify the Chinese writing system originated in the 1890s. However, it did not crystallise into an official policy enforced by the government throughout the country until the 1950s. The strategy of simplification involves a reduction in the number of strokes of commonly used characters. This reduction is achieved by eliminating parts of a character, condensing several strokes into one and replacing a complex character or parts of a complex character with a simpler one. Some examples are provided in Table 42.7:

Table 42.7 Simplified Characters

Meaning	Original version	Simplified version	Pronunciation (Pīnyīn)
'to bid farewell'	辭	辞	cí
'to cross'	過	过	guò
'should'	應	应	yīng
'solid'	實	实	shí
'door'	門	门	mén
'strong'	鞏	巩	gǒng

Acknowledgement

During the preparation of this paper, Charles N. Li was partially supported by National Science Foundation Grant #BNS 83 08220.

Appendix

The Pīnyīn symbols and their corresponding IPA values

| A. Consonants | |
Pīnyīn symbol	IPA
b	p
p	pʰ
m	m
f	f
d	t
t	tʰ
n	n
l	l
z	ts
c	tsʰ
zh	tʂ
ch	tʂʰ
sh	ʂ
r	ʐ
j	tɕ
q	tɕʰ
x	ɕ
g	k
k	kʰ
h	x
ng	ŋ
w	w
y	j

B. Vowels

Pīnyīn symbol	IPA	Context
a ⟶	{ [ɛ] [a]	/ i___n
o ⟶	{ [o] [u]	/ { u___ / C___# } / { a___ / ___ng }

continued on next page

721

continued

B. Vowels

Pīnyīn symbol	IPA	Context
e	[ə]	/ ___N
	[ɛ]	/ { i / ü— }
	[i]	/ ___ i
	[ɣ]	
i	[ɿ]	/ { zh / ch / sh / r } -
	[ʮ]	/ { z / c / s } -
	[i]	
u	[y]	/y___
	[u]	
ü	[y]	
er	[ɚ]	

Note

1 Most of the examples given from here on will be from Běijīng Mandarin, which has an accepted Romanisation (Pīnyīn) familiar to some readers, rather than from other dialects for which we would have to use a phonetic notation. A table of Pīnyīn symbols and their corresponding IPA values is provided in the Appendix.

Bibliography

Newnham (1971) is a popular introduction to the Chinese language, while Norman (1988) is a thorough introduction to the synchrony and diachrony of Chinese. Alleton (1973) is an introductory sketch of Chinese grammar. More thorough reference grammars are Chao (1968), a rich source of insightful observations and data, and Li and Thompson (1981), a major description of the syntactic and morphological structures of Chinese from the viewpoint of the communicative function of language. Rygaloff (1973) contains some interesting descriptive observations on Chinese grammar, while Henne et al. (1977) is pedagogical. For non-Mandarin varieties, Matthews and Yip (1994) provide a particularly detailed account of Cantonese grammar.

For sociolinguistics, Dil (1976) is a collection of articles on Chinese dialects, the Chinese writing system and issues on language and society by Y.-R. Chao; all are informative and comprehensible. DeFrancis (1967) is an informative article describing in detail the history of and governmental policies concerning the Chinese writing system. For Chinese dialects, Egerod (1967) is an important and valuable survey of the dialects themselves as well as of research into them. Hashimoto (1973) is a modern description of the Hakka dialect with a strong tilt towards historical phonology. Li (1983) offers a glimpse of the complex language-contact situation in western China.

Karlgren (1923) is an introduction to Chinese from the viewpoint of historical phonology. Yang (1974) is a useful source book for research, especially in the area of historical phonology.

References

Alleton, V. 1973. *Grammaire du chinois* (Presses Universitaires de France, Paris)

Chao, Y.-R. 1968. *A Grammar of Spoken Chinese* (University of California Press, Berkeley and Los Angeles)

DeFrancis, J. 1967. 'Language and Script Reform', in T. Sebeok (ed.) *Current Trends in Linguistics*, vol. 2, *Linguistics in East Asia and South East Asia* (Mouton, The Hague)

Dil, A.S. (ed.) 1976. *Aspects of Chinese Sociolinguistics: Essays by Yuen Ren Chao* (Stanford University Press, Stanford)

Egerod, S. 1967. 'Dialectology', in T. Sebeok (ed.) *Current Trends in Linguistics*, vol. 2, *Linguistics in East Asia and South East Asia* (Mouton, The Hague)

Forrest, R.A.D. 1965. *The Chinese Language* (Faber and Faber, London)

Hashimoto, M.J. 1973. *The Hakka Dialect: A Linguistic Study of its Phonology, Syntax and Lexicon* (Cambridge University Press, Cambridge)

Henne, H., Rongen, O.B. and Hansen, L.J. 1977. *A Handbook on Chinese Language Structure* (Universitetsforlaget, Oslo)

Karlgren, B. 1923. *Sound and Symbol in Chinese* (Oxford University Press, London)

Li, C.N. 1983. 'Language in Contact in Western China', *Journal of East Asian Languages*, vol. 1, pp. 31–54

Li, C.N. and Thompson, S. 1981. *Mandarin Chinese: A Functional Reference Grammar* (University of California Press, Berkeley and Los Angeles)

Matthews, S. and Yip, V. 1994. *Cantonese: A Comprehensive Grammar* (Routledge, London)

Newnham, R. 1971. *About Chinese* (Penguin Books, Harmondsworth)

Norman, J. 1988. *Chinese* (Cambridge University Press, Cambridge)

Rygaloff, A. 1973. *Grammaire élémentaire du chinois* (Presses Universitaires de France, Paris)

Yang, P.F.-M. 1974. *Chinese Linguistics: A Selected and Classified Bibliography* (The Chinese University, Hong Kong)

43

Burmese

Julian K. Wheatley

1 Historical Background

Burmese is the national language of Burma or Myanmar. (Since 1989, the official name of the country has been the Union of Myanmar, and that of the language, Myanmar; in English, the language, at least, is still usually called Burmese.) The nation is situated between the Tibetan plateau and the Malay peninsula, sharing borders with Bangladesh and India to the west, with China to the north-east, with Laos to the east and with Thailand to the south-east. Burmese belongs to the Burmish sub-branch of the Lolo-Burmese (or Burmese-Lolo) branch of the Tibeto-Burman family, and is one of the two languages in that family with an extensive written history (the other being Tibetan).

Standard Burmese has evolved from a 'central' dialect spoken by the Burman population of the lower valleys of the Irrawaddy and Chindwin rivers. Although it is now spoken over a large part of the country, regional variation within the standard remains relatively minor; apart from a few localisms, the speech of Mandalay in Upper Burma, for example, is indistinguishable from that of Rangoon, 400 miles to the south. However, a number of regional dialects, showing profound differences in pronunciation and vocabulary, are found in peripheral regions. The best known of these are Arakanese in the south-west, Tavoyan in the south-east and Intha in the east. Despite being heavily influenced in formal registers by the national language, the dialects preserve many features attested in the modern orthography but lost in standard speech.

Burma is a multi-national state. About two-thirds of its population are Burmans. The other third is made up of a variety of ethnic groups, including other Tibeto-Burman-speaking peoples such as the Chin, Naga and Karen, Mon–Khmer peoples such as the Mon and Padaung, the Shan, whose language is closely related to Thai, and Chinese and Indians, who live mostly in the towns. Most of the population of the country, provisionally put at about 47 million (CIA, 2006), speaks Burmese as either a first or second language.

Linguistic evidence suggests that the ancestor of the Burmese language spread south and southwestwards, diverging from the closely related Loloish group of languages whose heartland is now in southwest China. In doing so, it passed from the margins of the Chinese cultural sphere to a region profoundly influenced by Indian tradition, and by the time the Burmese emerge on the historical scene, they have already begun to take on the religious and political features of the Indianised kingdoms that flourished in what is now the heart of Burma.

In the dry zone of central Burma, Burmese speaking people would have encountered the literate, urbanised culture of the Pyu, whose language is known only from a few inscriptions, but is thought to be Tibeto-Burman, if not Lolo-Burmese. These linguistic cousins of the Burmese, once dominant in the Irrawaddy basin, gradually lost political power, possibly as a consequence of wars with Nan Chao, a kingdom that flourished in southwest China at that time. By the middle of the ninth century, the Burmese had founded a kingdom at Pagan that eventually absorbed the remnants of the Pyu and came to dominate most of what is now modern Burma. The Burmese were also in close contact with another literate, urbanised culture, the Mon, who spoke a Mon-Khmer language of the same name. The Mon retained considerable political power in Lower Burma, at least, until the middle of the eighteenth century, when the last Mon kingdom was defeated by the Burmese. (To commemorate the end of that war, the town of Dagon in Lower Burma was renamed Yangon — Rangoon in English, meaning 'fighting is over'.) Mon continues to be spoken, mostly as a second language, in parts of Lower Burma and Thailand.

Until recently, the earliest reliable written specimen of Burmese was generally considered to be the Rajakumar (or Myazedi) inscription, dated to 1111 or 1112 AD, which records the offering of a gold Buddha image in four languages, Pyu, Pali, Burmese and Mon. The Pali, Burmese and Mon faces are all written in the same script – the Burmese-Mon script – based ultimately on a south Indian model; the script of the Pyu face, however, is slightly different from the other three in both its form and its features. Because of the near identity of the Mon and Burmese scripts, because Mon inscriptions in central Burma were thought to antedate Burmese, and because the Mon were associated, historically, with earlier coastal cultures known to have been disseminators of Indian tradition, the Mon have usually been regarded as the source of Burmese writing, as well as the inspiration for features of their early art, architecture, religion and government. However, Aung-Thwin (2005: 183 and passim) reveals specimens of Burmese writing from the eleventh century that may significantly pre-date the earliest Mon inscriptions; he also undermines the case for contemporary Mon hegemony in Lower Burma. Instead, he argues for the Pyu as the main substrate (or amalgam) in early Burmese culture, and Pyu writing as the model for Burmese writing, with the latter ultimately being adapted to write Mon rather than the other way round.

While there are probably enough Pyu inscriptions to make a case for or against its script being the progenitor of the Burmese writing system, there is unlikely to be sufficient linguistic evidence for an early nexus between Pyu and Burmese over and beyond the putative common origin in Tibeto-Burman. Mon, however, being much better attested and having a distinctive lexical stock, has left traces on Burmese in the form of loanwords having to do with the natural and man-made environment as well as some Indic loanwords showing the effects of transmission by way of Mon. In addition, it has been suggested that the iambic word structure of minor syllable followed by major, found in Burmese, but otherwise associated with Mon-Khmer languages rather than Tibeto-Burman, may have developed by way of contact with Mon.

Beginning in the thirteenth century, Tai migrations down the major river valleys of the Southeast Asian mainland also brought Tai speaking peoples, particularly the Shan (close kin of the Thai), into contact, and occasionally, friction, with Burmese. Still later, the Burmese incursions to the east brought them into Thai territory. Twice they conquered the Thai capital of Ayuttaya (once in the mid-sixteenth century, then again in the mid-eighteenth), and Burmese secular drama owes its beginnings to Thai influence following the last of these invasions. But Thai and Shan influence on the Burmese language seems to be limited to a few loanwords for cultural objects (including *hkauʔhswὲ*, the name of a popular Burmese noodle dish that is borrowed from Shan).

The first notable European presence in Burma was that of the Portuguese in the sixteenth century, followed in the next by small numbers of British, Dutch and French. The nineteenth century brought Burma into conflict with the British in India, who eventually annexed the country in three stages between 1826 and 1886; from 1886 until 1937, it was administered as a province of British India. Independence was restored in 1948.

British rule introduced a large number of words of English origin into Burmese. Many of these were later replaced by Burmese or Indic forms, but large numbers remain and new ones continue to appear, particularly in the fields of science, technology, business and politics. Loanwords tend to be fully adapted to Burmese segmental phonology, but in many cases they remain identifiable by their polysyllabic morphemes and their resistance to internal sandhi processes.

Rather than adapting English or other foreign phonetic material, the Burmese often form neologisms from their own lexical stock or from the highly esteemed classical languages of India, which are to Burmese (and many South-East Asian languages) what Latin and Greek are to European languages. Thus the word for 'spaceship', *ʔa+ka +θáyin* (plusses represent phonological boundaries: see pages 729–730) is composed of *ʔa+ka+θá,* a learned term meaning 'space, expanse', originally from Pali ĀKĀSA (transliterations are capitalised) and *yin,* spelled YĀÑ, derived from Pali YĀNA 'vehicle'. *Yin* also appears with *yəhaʔ* 'a reel', originally from Hindi, in the word for 'helicopter', *yəhaʔyin,* a compound coexisting with the English loan, *hɛli+kɔ́+pəta.* Similar competition between a native formation and a loanword is seen in the two words for 'television', the transparent *yoʔmyin+θancà,* 'image-see sound-hear', and the opaque *tɛlibìhyìn.*

Pali has been one of the main sources of new lexical material throughout the attested history of Burmese, with the result that the Burmese lexicon has come to have a two-tiered structure not unlike that of English, with its learned Romance and classical elements side by side with older and more colloquial Germanic forms. In Burmese the most common locutions, including grammatical words and formatives, nouns referring to basic cultural material and almost all verbs, tend to be composed of monosyllabic morphemes of Tibeto-Burman stock. Learned or specialised words (many of which must have entered the spoken language by way of the 'literary' language) often contain Pali material, frequently compounded with native stock. Pali is phonotactically quite compatible with Burmese, having neither initial clusters nor (word-)final consonants. Its morphemes are generally not monosyllabic, however. Disyllabic Pali words ending in a short A are usually rendered as a single syllable in Burmese, e.g.: *kan,* spelled KAM, 'fortune, deeds', from Pali KAMMA; *yoʔ,* spelled RUP, 'image', from Pali RŪPA. But otherwise, Pali loans (like those from English) are set off by the length of their morphemes: cf. *taya* 'constellation (of stars)', from Pali TĀRĀ, versus *cɛ* 'star', a Tibeto-Burman root; *htaná,* spelled ṬHĀNA 'place, department (in a university, etc.)', from Pali ṬHĀNA, versus *neya* 'place', a compound of the native morphemes *ne* 'to live, be at' and *(ʔə)ya* 'place, thing'.

It is not uncommon to find two versions of a Pali word in Burmese, one closer to the Pali prototype than the other, e.g.: *man* and *maná*, both 'pride, arrogance' and both from Pali MĀNA, which occur together in the pleonastic expression *man maná hyí-* 'to be haughty, arrogant'.

Often a Pali prototype will be represented in a number of South-East Asian languages, providing a pan-South-East Asian technical lexicon comparable to the 'international' scientific vocabulary based on Latin and Greek: cf. Burmese *seʔ*, Mon *cɒt*, Khmer *cyt*, Thai *cìt*, all from Pali CITTA 'mind'.

Despite inconsistent spelling and a restricted subject matter, the early inscriptional records probably render the spoken language of the time – Old Burmese – fairly directly. The inscriptional orthography, which can be interpreted in terms of Indic sound values, reveals a language phonetically very different from the modern spoken standard. It also shows major differences in lexical content, particularly among grammatical words and suffixes. But the grammatical categories and the order of words have remained relatively stable over the intervening 900 years.

The orthography underwent a number of changes after the inscriptional period, apparently reflecting a redistribution of certain vowels and a reduction in the number of medial consonants (see pages 732 733). By the end of the sixteenth century the orthography had assumed more or less its modern form, though there have been modifications in the spelling of individual words since. Pronunciation continued to change, though, so there is now a wide gap between the spoken and literal values of the script, e.g.: *ceʔ* 'chicken' is spelled KRAK; *-θɛ*, an agentive suffix, is spelled -SAÑ.

The modern orthography (sometimes called 'Written Burmese') is often taken as the reflection of an intermediate stage in the history of the language, i.e. Middle Burmese. The construct is a useful one, though the precise nature of the relationship still needs to be worked out.

Along with the orthography, some grammatical and lexical forms from earlier stages of Burmese live on in the language used for literature and most written communication, Literary Burmese. Particularly in this century, differences between literary and spoken styles have tended to diminish, so that nowadays, although other 'classical' elements may still appear in Literary Burmese, the only feature consistently distinguishing the two is the choice of the textually frequent post-nominal and post-verbal particles and other grammatical words. Literary Burmese retains a set of archaic grammatical morphemes, some reflecting earlier versions of their spoken equivalents, others reflecting forms that have been replaced in the spoken language. For example, instead of the locative postposition *-hma* 'in, at', Literary Burmese uses -NHUIK (read *-hnaiʔ*) or -TWAṄ (read *-twin*); instead of the interrogative particles *-là* and *-lè*, it has -LO (read *-lɔ̀*) and -NAÑ (read *-nì*), respectively; instead of the possessive marker *-yɛ́* (-RAIʔ), it has -ʔI (read *-ʔì*).

Not all the literary particles are functionally homologous with spoken forms. Whereas the spoken language makes use of a single postposition, *-ko* (-KUI), to mark both objects and goals of motion, the literary language makes use of three: -KUI 'object', -ʔĀ: (read *-ʔà*) '(usually) second or indirect object', and -SUIʔ (read *-θó*) 'goal of motion'.

It is possible to write Burmese as it is spoken, i.e. using the standard orthography with the syntax and lexicon of the spoken language. Indeed, in the 1960s an association of writers based in Mandalay advocated the development of such a 'colloquially based' literary style. Despite the appearance of a number of works in the new style, it was not generally adopted. This was partly because it lacked official sanction, but also because no style evolved which could convey the seriousness of purpose connoted by formal Literary Burmese.

Particularly in the older and more classical styles of Literary Burmese, the influence of Pali grammatical structures can also be seen; for until the nineteenth century, prose writing was mostly translations, adaptations and studies of Pali texts. The extreme case is that of the 'nissaya' texts, which have a history dating from the inscriptional period to the present day (cf. Okell 1965). In these, Burmese forms are inserted after each word or phrase of a Pali text; in many cases the Pali is omitted, resulting in a Burmese 'calque' on the original – Burmese words with Pali grammar. The interesting point is that in addition to mirroring Pali syntax, the nissaya authors developed conventions for representing Pali inflectional categories in Burmese, an uninflected language. For example, the Pali past participle, a category quite alien to Burmese, was represented periphrastically by placing the 'auxiliary' ?AP 'be right, proper' after the verb: KHYAK ?AP SO CHWAM: 'the food that was cooked, the cooked food'. In the spoken Burmese equivalent no auxiliary is required.

Not surprisingly, given the exalted position of Pali studies in Burmese culture, nissaya forms spread to other kinds of prose, so that Pali can be considered a significant substratum in many styles of Literary Burmese.

2 Phonology

In presenting the inventory of phonological oppositions in Burmese, it is necessary to distinguish between full, or 'major', syllables and reduced, or 'minor', ones. In reduced syllables the functional load is borne by the initial; no medial or final consonants are possible, and there are no tonal contrasts; the vowel is mid central and lax. Minor syllables occur singly or, occasionally, in pairs, always bound to a following major syllable. They can often be related to full syllables, if not synchronically, then historically: the first syllable of *səpwὲ* 'table' is shown from the spelling to derive from *sà* 'to eat'; the word arose as a compound of 'eat' and 'communal event'.

In major syllables, phonological oppositions are concentrated at two points, the initial and the vowel. There are two possible medial consonants, only one final consonant and four tonal contrasts, one of which is partially realised as final consonantism. The inventory of phonological oppositions can be discussed in terms of five syntagmatic positions: initial (C_i), medial (C_m), vowel (V), final (C_f) and tone (T). Of these, C_i, V and T are always present (though the glottal initial is represented by 'zero' in some transcriptions).

Table 43.1 lists 34 possible C_i, of which three are marginal: *r-* is found mostly in loanwords from Pali or other languages; *hw-* or ð are very rare. In the table, C_i are arranged in three series, labelled 'aspirate', 'plain' and 'voiced'. The aspirates consist of aspirated stops and fricatives and voiceless nasals and resonants; the plain, of voiceless unaspirated stops and fricatives and voiced nasals and resonants; the voiced of voiced stops and fricatives only. The basis of this classification is morphological. First of all, while the plain and aspirate series may appear in absolute initial position (i.e. after pause) in both major word classes, the voiced series is restricted in that position mainly to nouns. The fact that such nouns can often be matched to verbs with plain or aspirate initials (e.g. *bí* 'a comb', *hpí* 'to comb') suggests that deverbative prefixes or other syllables are responsible for the voiced initials; assimilatory processes such as voicing are characteristic of word-internal positions in Burmese (see page 730). The incidence of nouns with C_i in the voiced series has been enlarged by loanwords, but the functional yield of the voiced series remains relatively low.

The aspirate series of C_i is not restricted to a particular class of words like the voiced, but it is associated with one member of derivationally related pairs of verbs such as the following: *pyɛʔ* 'be ruined', *hpyɛʔ* 'destroy'; *myín* 'be high', *hmyín* 'raise, make higher'. In these, the stative or intransitive member has a plain C_i, the causative or transitive, an aspirate. The alternation is represented by over 100 pairs of verbs, but it is not productive. The aspirates in these verbs record the effects of a sibilant causativising prefix, reconstructed at the Proto-Tibeto-Burman level as **s-* (see page 701). The original value of this prefix is reflected in 'irregular' pairs such as *ʔeʔ* 'sleep', *θeʔ* 'put to sleep' (the latter spelled SIP). The process has contributed to the incidence of the typologically rare voiceless nasals (*hm-, hn-, hɲ, hŋ-*). As in many of the modern transcriptions of Burmese, the members of the aspirate series are consistently transcribed with a prescript 'h'; *hl-* and *hw-*, the latter found mostly in onomatopoeic words, are voiceless; *hy-* is actually a sibilant, [ʃ] or [ɕ], in pairs such as *yɔ́* as 'be reduced, be slack', *hyɔ́* [ʃɔ́] 'reduce, slacken'.

The medials are -*y*- and -*w*-. The second co-occurs with most C_i, but the first is only found with labials and the lateral.

In terms of our transcription there are two C_fs, -*n* and -*ʔ*, but in phonological terms -*ʔ* can be regarded as a fourth tone; it precludes the possibility of any of the other tones and, though it almost always has some segmental realisation, it is also associated with a very short, high and even pitch contour. The reasons for transcribing it as though it were a C_f are partly historical: -*ʔ* derives from an earlier set of final oral stops and is symbolised in the writing system as such.

To discuss the realisation of -*n* and -*ʔ*, it is necessary to begin with the topic of sandhi. The shape of a syllable in Burmese varies according to the degree of syllable juncture. At least two degrees of juncture need to be recognised: open, representing

Table 43.1 Burmese Phonological Oppositions

		Stops and affricates				*Fricatives*	*Nasals*				*Resonant*			
C_i	Aspirate	hp	ht	hc	hk	hs	hm	hn	hɲ	hŋ	hl	hy	hw	h
	Plain	p	t	c	k	s θ	m	n	ɲ	ŋ	l	y	w r	ʔ
	Voiced	b	d	j	g	z ð								

V	Syllable type							
	Open	(-∅)	i	e	ɛ	a	ɔ		o	u
	Closed	(-n)	ɪ	eɪ		a		aɪ	au	ou ʊ
		(-ʔ)	ɪ	eɪ	ɛ	a		aɪ	au	ou ʊ

Transcribed as:		i	e	ɛ	a	ɔ	ai	au	o	u

C_m -*y*-,   -*w*- C_f -*n*,   (-*ʔ*)

T   ´ (creaky),   ∅ (low),   ` (high),   -ʔ (checked)

minimal assimilation between syllables, and close, representing maximal. The distinction is realised mainly in terms of the duration, tonal contour and C_f-articulation of the first syllable and the manner of the C_i of the second. Phonetic values vary with tempo but can be generalised as follows: successive major syllables linked in *open* juncture preserve citation values of all variables; for the C_fs -*n* and -*ʔ*, these are nasalisation of the preceding vowel (*θòn*, [θ̀ðũ]) and (along with pitch and other features) final glottal stop (*hyiʔ*), [çɪʔ] respectively. In successive major syllables in *close* juncture, the first is shortened and has a truncated pitch contour, while the C_f of the first and the C_i of the second undergo varying degrees of mutual assimilation, the final tending to adopt the *position* of articulation of the following initial, the initial tending to adopt the *manner* of articulation of the preceding final, e.g.: *lè-hkàn* 'four rooms' is realised [lègã̂], with perseverative voicing on the internal velar stop; *θòn-hkàn* 'three rooms' is realised [θ̀ðũŋgã̂] with the same voicing but, additionally, anticipation of the velar stop by the nasal final; while *hyiʔ-hkàn* 'eight rooms' is realised [ʃɪkkʰã̂], the aspirate remaining after the checked final, the final taking on the position of the following stop. In this last case, the phonetic final segment associated with -*ʔ* may disappear, leaving only pitch, duration and, in some cases, allophonic vowel quality, to signal the checked tone ([ʃɪkʰã̂]). In the first two cases – those involving smooth (-∅, -*n*) syllables – these phonological processes result in the neutralisation of manner distinctions for some C_i in favour of the voiced, e.g.: *hk-*, *k-* and *g-* are all realised [g-].

Sandhi affects combinations of minor and major syllables slightly differently, with interesting results. When the first syllable of two is a minor one, the voicing process does not extend to the aspirates: in *sәpwὲ* 'table', internal -*p*- is voiced, but in *tәhkàn* 'one room', the internal -*hk*- remains aspirated. In addition, the initial of a minor syllable often harmonises with the voicing of the following consonant: *sәpwὲ* is most often pronounced [zәbwὲ] with voicing throughout; but *tәhkàn* is realised [tәkʰã̂] with both stops voiceless. This sporadic process of consonant harmony reduces even further the number of initial oppositions available for minor syllables.

Close juncture is characteristic of certain grammatical environments, e.g.: noun – classifier, illustrated above, and noun – adjectival verb: (*ʔen-θiʔ* 'new-house', is pronounced [ʔẽ̀ĩnðɪʔ]). Most particles are also attached to preceding syllables in close juncture: *θwà–hpó* 'in order to go', is pronounced [θwàbó]. But within compounds the degree of juncture between syllables is unpredictable; the constituents of disyllabic compound nouns (other than recent loanwords) tend to be closely linked, but compound verbs vary, some with open, some with close juncture.

In our transcription, syllabic boundaries are shown as follows: open juncture is represented by a space between syllables and open juncture within a compound by a plus. *hkwὲ+hkwa* 'to separate, leave' is pronounced [kʰwὲkʰwa]. Close juncture within a compound is indicated by lack of a space between the syllables (*hkúhkan* 'to resist' is pronounced [kʰúgã̂]), while close juncture between phrasal constituents is marked with a hyphen (as in the examples of the previous paragraph).

Moving on to the vowels, we find that the number of vocalic contrasts varies according to the type of syllable (see Table 43.1): in smooth syllables (-∅, -*n*), there are seven contrasts, in checked (-*ʔ*), eight. In phonetic terms, however, the line of cleavage is not between smooth and checked but between open and closed: vowels in closed syllables (-*n*, -*ʔ*) tend to be noticeably centralised or diphthongised compared to those in open syllables. For purposes of transcription it is of course possible to identify certain elements of the different systems, as in the chart. And it would be possible to reduce the number of symbols even further by identifying the ɔ of open syllables with either the *ai* or *au* of closed. Historically (and in the writing system) ɔ is connected with *au* (and *o* with *ai*). Such an analysis is not motivated synchronically, nor does it have much practical value, so, like most of the transcriptions in use, we indicate nine vowels (plus the ə of reduced syllables).

Four tonal distinctions can be recognised, the 'creaky', the 'low' (or 'level'), the 'high' (or 'heavy') and the 'checked', the last symbolised by -ʔ. Tone in Burmese has a complex realisation of which pitch is only one feature. In the case of the checked tone, segmental features of vowel quality and final consonantism as well as suprasegmental features of pitch and duration are involved. The relative presence of these features varies with context. It has been observed, for example, that in disyllabic words such as *zaʔpwὲ* '(a) play', the pitch of the checked tone (high, in citation) may range from high to low. The same kind of variation is characteristic of creaky tone as well.

In citation form, the three tones that appear in smooth syllables have the following features: the 'creaky', (transcribed ´): tense or creaky phonation (sometimes with final lax glottal stop), medium duration, high intensity and high, often slightly falling pitch; the 'low' (unmarked): normal phonation, medium duration, low intensity and low, often slightly rising pitch; the 'high' (transcribed `): sometimes slightly breathy, relatively long, high intensity and high pitch, often with a fall before a pause.

In citation form, the creaky tone is much less common than the others, a fact accounted for by its relatively late development from affixal elements. The balance is partially restored, however, by the incidence of morphologically conditioned creaky tone (see pages 735–736).

3 The Writing System

The Burmese–Mon script is derived ultimately from a south Indian antecedent, but shaped by a number of intermediaries. With some adjustments, the same script was later adapted to the writing of Shan and, in colonial times, also to some Karen dialects. The script preserves the main features of its Indian prototype, and retains signs for non-Burmese sounds, such as the Indic retroflex and voiced aspirated series, so that Indic loanwords can be reproduced in Burmese with their original spelling.

The script is alphabetic in principle, with letters representing phonemes, though the sound values of many of these letters have changed considerably since it was first introduced. A few very common literary Burmese grammatical morphemes are represented by logograms – word signs – but these originated as abbreviations of phonographic combinations. Like all Indic scripts, the Burmese differs from European alphabetic scripts in two important respects. First, neither the sequence in which the letters appear nor the order in which they are written reflects the temporal order of phonemes. Vowel signs appear before, after, above or below C_I signs. (Abbreviations such as C_I with capitalised subscripts refer to positions in the written syllable.) Second, a plain consonant sign without any explicit vowel sign represents the vowel A.

Table 43.2 shows the consonant signs together with a Romanised transliteration based on original Indic values and a transcription of their regular modern pronunciation. The transliteration is a capitalised and otherwise slightly modified version of the widely used Duroiselle system (see Okell 1971). Many of the differences between the transliteration and the transcription reflect changes in the spoken language since the writing system was introduced. Some of these are discussed below.

Table 43.2 The Burmese Writing System: Consonants

		Transliteration i	ii	iii	iv	v	Transcription i	ii	iii	iv	v
C_I	I	K	KH	G	GH	Ṅ	k	hk	g	g	ŋ
	II	C	CH	J	JH	Ñ	s	hs	z	z	ɲ
	III	T	TH	D	DH	N	t	ht	d	d	n
	IV	T	TH	D	DH	N	t	ht	d	d	n
	V	P	PH	B	BH	M	p	hp	b	b	m
	VI	Y	R	L	W	S	y	y	l	w	θ
	VII	H	Ḷ	?			h	l	?		

C_M

-Y-	-R-	-W-	-H-
-y-	-y-	-w-	h-

The 33 consonant signs are given in the traditional Burmese (and Indian) order. Almost all the consonant signs can appear initially, but only the plain series (K, C, T, P), their nasal counterparts (Ṅ, Ñ, N, M) and Y occur finally in native words. The boxed row (III) representing the Indian retroflex series, is pronounced like the dental series shown below it. The boxed columns (iii, iv), representing the Indian voiced and voiced aspirated series, are usually pronounced alike. Note that the *spoken* voiced series, discussed earlier, is often written with the plain or aspirate voiceless consonant signs.

There are four medial consonant signs: Y, R, W, H. The last is subscribed to nasal and resonant C_Is to indicate the aspirates of those series, e.g.: LHA, *hlá* 'beautiful'. In Old Burmese writing, a medial -L- was also found (see below).

The writing system reflects a number of consonantal changes. The development of C_Fs will be discussed separately below. As initials, some consonants have undergone phonetic changes, but distinctions have generally been preserved. Row II in Table 43.2 shows a shift from palatal affricate to dental sibilant. From the representation of Burmese words in certain Portuguese and English records of the eighteenth and nineteenth centuries, the Burmese scholar Pe Maung Tin ('Phonetics in a Passport', *Journal of the Burma Research Society*, vol. 12 (1922), pp. 129–31) concluded that this change and the shift from $s > \theta$ (VI, v) began in the late eighteenth century and were followed by the palatalisation of velar stops before medial -*y*- (written -Y- and -R-). The three shifts form a 'drag chain', the first clearing the way for the second, the second for the third ($s > \theta$, $c > s$, $ky > c$, etc.). Two typologically rare consonants arose as a result of these developments: θ, pronounced [t^θ] and *hs*-, an aspirated sibilant ($< c^h$). The functional yield of the latter is very low.

Contrasts among medial consonants have been reduced from four in Old Burmese to three in Middle Burmese (reflected in the standard orthography), to two in the modern spoken language. The medial -*l*- attested by the inscriptions merged with either -*y*- or -*r*-, according to whether the initial consonant was velar or labial, respectively, i.e.: OBs. *kl*- > MBs. *ky*-, OBs. *pl*- > MBs. *pr*-. MBs. *r* then merged with y in all positions, initial as well as medial (so that 'Rangoon', for example, is now transcribed as *Yankon*). Some of the dialects attest to the earlier stages. In Tavoyan, the medial -*l*- of Old Burmese usually survives as such, while earlier -*r*- and -*y*- merge as -*y*-: cf. standard *cá* 'to fall', spelled KYA in the orthography and KLA in the inscriptions, pronounced *klá* in Tavoyan. In Arakanese, on the other hand, earlier *-l-* is distributed between *-r-* and *-y-* with the latter two remaining distinct, e.g. standard *cɛʔ* 'chicken', spelled KRAK, is *kraʔ* in Arakanese, the *-r-* realised as a retroflex continuant.

Whether we are dealing with the script or the spoken language, vowel, final consonant and tone are conveniently treated as a unit, the 'rhyme'. Table 43.3 shows the main (or 'regular') rhymes of Burmese, arranged according to written vowels. (To save space, tonal markings are only indicated where they are incorporated in a vowel sign.) Comparing the transliteration with the transcription reveals both a large reduction in the number of C_Fs and a major restructuring of the vowel system.

Consonant signs are marked as final by the superscript hook, or 'killer' stroke. The orthography shows four positions of final oral and nasal stops, and -Y, which – in native words – represents only the rhyme *-ɛ*. ('Little Ñ', the second of the two signs for Ñ, is a modern variant of the first, used to signal the pronunciation *-in* over the otherwise unpredictable alternatives, *-i, e* and *ɛ*.) From the table, it can be seen that many combinations of written final and vowel do not occur. Finals -C and -Ñ, for instance, occur only with the 'intrinsic' vowel A. Comparative evidence shows that the 'extra' A-rhymes derive from earlier *-ik* and *-iŋ*, respectively, the 'missing' velar rhymes of the high front series (row II). Palatal finals are rare in Tibeto-Burman languages, but common in Mon–Khmer; it is likely that the appearance of these finals in Burmese is another result of Mon influence.

Neither the distributional evidence nor the comparative evidence is clear enough to explain the other gaps in the system of orthographic rhymes.

All positions of final stops have been reduced to just one in the modern language, represented by *-ʔ* for oral stops, *-n* for nasal. The association of high pitch with the former can probably be attributed to the well-documented pitch-raising effects of final tense glottal stop. This glottal stop is quite different from the lax glottal stop that sometimes appears in creaky-toned syllables, which would be expected to depress pitch.

From Table 43.3, vowels can be seen to have split according to the type of syllable they were in, open or closed; thus written I is read *i* or *e*, written U, *u* or *o*, written UI, *o* or *ai*, written O, *ɔ* or *au*, with the first, higher vowel quality found in reflexes of open syllables. (Written UI and O are both digraphs in the script, but only the first is transliterated according to its parts, U + I; the symbol appears in Mon as well, where it represents a mid front rounded vowel.) Written A attests to a three-way split of *a* into *a, i* and *ɛ*, conditioned by the final. To an extent, these developments, coupled with the reduction in the number of final consonants, filled the gaps in the pattern of (written) rhymes, so that the only asymmetries in the modern system are the missing nasal rhyme, *-ɛn*, and the uncertain relationship between open *ɔ* and closed *ai* and *au*, discussed above (see Table 43.1).

Table 43.3 also shows the relationship between V- and C_F-signs and the representation of tones in Burmese. Since Indian languages lacked tone, there were no ready made symbols for representing the Burmese tones. However, the Indic script did have distinct graphs to represent long and short versions of the corner vowels, *a, i* and *u*. In the new script, these were apparently matched to phonetic differences in vowel length associated with syllable type and tone. The Indic short vowel symbols were assigned to Burmese creaky toned and closed syllables, while the long vowel symbols were used for (non-creaky) open syllables. So in Table 43.3, the three 'corner' vowels (II, V) have two written forms; in Indian terms – also the basis of our transliteration – the first is short, the second (with the additional stroke) long ($\bar{V}$). The first indicates a creaky-toned

Table 43.3 The Burmese Writing System: Regular Rhymes

	Open	Closed					Open	Closed					
					IT e?	IP e?		WAṄ (win) X	WAN un	WAM un	WAK (we?) X	WAT u?	WAP u?
I	ḭ / ì	X					ḭ / ü						
II	I / Ī i, Ī i	IN en	IM en	X	IT e?	IP e?	U ṵ, Ū u	UN on	UM on	X	X	UT o?	UP o?
III	E e, -ɛ̀						UI o, 6-ɔ, 6-ɔ	UIṄ ain	UIK ai?	X	6-ɔc X	X	
IV	AI ɛ̰, AY ɛ			-ð/ᷛ			O ɔ̰, OW ɔ	OṄ aun	OK au?	-ᷛ			X
V	A à, Ā a			AṄ in	AÑ i, (e, ɛ)/in		AN an, AÑ an	AK ɛ?	AC i?	AT a?	AP a?	AM an	AN an

Note: Tones not incorporated in a vowel sign are written as follows: -. (originally -ɜ) for creaky; -: ('visarga') for *high*; unmarked for *low*.

syllable, the second a low-toned syllable. With all other finals, creaky tone was indicated by the sign for glottal onset, reduced to just a dot in the modern orthography (but, for clarity, still transcribed as ʔ herein: UIʔ = *ó*).

There was, apparently, no clear analogue in the Indian prototype to the opposition between high and low tones and for some six centuries the two were not consistently distinguished in the orthography. In the modern script, the lower-mid vowel signs (IV) are intrinsically high-toned, with additional strokes ('killed-Y' in one case, the killer alone – originally a superscript killed-W – in the other) changing them to low. Elsewhere, high tone is indicated by two post-scriptal dots ('visarga'): UI: = *ò*. The modern use of visarga (which represents final *-h* in Old Mon) to signal the high tone was occasionally anticipated in the earliest inscriptions, which suggests that breathiness has long been a feature of that tone.

Except in those cases in which the vowel sign is intrinsically creaky or high, the low tone is unmarked: UI = *o*. The checked tone is symbolised by the presence of a final oral stop.

One of the characteristics of Indic alphabets is that vowels are written with special signs when they are in syllable-initial position. Such 'initial-vowel symbols' exist for all but three of the Burmese vowels (Table 43.4). Nowadays, they are found only in a small number of words – most of them loanwords. In the modern orthography, 'initial' vowels – actually vowels with glottal onset – are generally written with a combination of the vowel support sign (which represents *ʔ-*) and ordinary vowel signs.

A few other signs also appear in the script; for these and other irregularities, the reader is referred to Roop (1972) and Wheatley (1996).

4 Morphology

Morphology in Burmese is primarily derivational morphology and compounding; there is little to discuss under the heading of 'inflection'. Grammatical functions that might be realised as inflections in other languages are mostly carried out by word order or by grammatical particles. There is, however, one phenomenon that can be considered inflectional, and that is the 'induced creaky tone' (Okell's term). Under certain conditions,

Table 43.4 The Burmanese Writing System: Additional Symbols

Initial vowel signs									
	ဣ	ဤ				ʔí	ʔi		
	ဥ	ဦ	ဦး			ʔú	ʔu	ʔù	
		ဧ	(ဧ)				ʔe	ʔè	
		ဪ	ဩ				ʔɔ	ʔɔ̀	
Numerals									
၁ 1	၂ 2	၃ 3	၄ 4	၅ 5	၆ 6	၇ 7	၈ 8	၉ 9	၀ 0

words with otherwise low tones and sometimes those with high shift to the creaky tone. This shift has a number of apparently disparate functions (cf. Allott 1967). Some of them seem to exploit the sound symbolism of the features of creaky phonation and high intensity: with sentence-final 'appellatives' (kin terms, titles, etc., that pick out the audience and convey information about social distance) the induced creaky tone suggests abruptness and urgency. It also appears with the first occurrence of certain repeated words, e.g. *ʔinmətan* 'very', but *ʔinmətán ʔinmətan* 'very, very'.

At other times, the induced creaky tone has a specific grammatical function. Usually only with pronouns and nouns of personal reference, it may signal 'possession' or 'attribution': *θu* 'he, she', *θú ʔəmyò+θəmì* 'his wife'. In such cases, the creaky tone looks like an allomorph of the creaky-toned possessive particle, *-yɛ́* (*-kɛ́* after checked syllables); but although the two often alternate, they may also co-occur, so their relationship is now only historical.

The induced creaky tone also tends to appear – again, mainly with personal referents – before the locative postposition, *-hma* 'in, at', and the 'accusative' postposition, *-ko* 'object, goal, extent'. With objects in particular, *-ko* is often omitted, leaving the creaky tone to mark the grammatical role: *θú(-ko) mè-laiʔ-pa* 'ask him!'.

Apart from the regular but non-productive patterns involving aspiration and voicing illustrated earlier, almost all derivational morphology in Burmese involves prefixation of a minor syllable, partial or complete reduplication or a combination of the two. Derivational processes generally act on verbs, turning them into nouns or noun-like expressions that can often function as either nominals or adverbials. Verbs themselves are very rarely derived (just as they are very rarely borrowed). The verbal inventory is expanded through compounding or through the lexicalisation of verb + complement constructions, e.g. *ʔəyè cì-* 'affair-be big = be important'; the latter retain most of the syntactic properties of phrases. In contrast to verbs, adverbials are almost always derived.

The general function of the productive derivational processes in Burmese is to subordinate verbs. Complete reduplication of stative verbs (with close juncture distinguishing them from iterative repetition) forms manner adverbials: *ca* 'be long (time)', *caca* 'for (some) time'; *θehca* 'be sure, exact', *θeθe+hcahca* 'exactly, definitely'. Prefixation of action verbs by the nominalising prefix *ʔə-* creates action nominals: *kaiʔ* 'to bite', but *ʔəkaiʔ hkan-yá-* 'biting-suffer-get = get bitten' (a 'passive of adversity', see page 739); *hcɛʔ* 'to cook', but *ʔəhcɛʔ θin-* 'cooking-learn = learn to cook'. The same process forms adverbials: *myan* 'be fast', but *ʔəmyan θwà-* 'go in haste, go quickly'; or, with a different prefix, *ʔəyè+təcì* 'urgently', from the syntactic compound meaning 'be important', mentioned at the end of the last paragraph. Whether reduplicated or prefixed, the verbs may retain nominal complements: *təlá caca nei-* 'one-month-long-stay = to stay for a month'; *hcin (ʔə)kaiʔ hkan-yá-* 'get bitten by a mosquito'. In the latter type, the prefix is often deleted and the verbal noun appears in close juncture with the preceding complement as a kind of nonce compound.

Prefixation, but not complete reduplication, is also attested in lexicalised form, e.g. *əhkwá* 'fork (of a tree)', from the verb *hkwá* 'to fork in two'. In cases involving a prefixed verb and a complement, the lexicalised version becomes a syntactic compound, e.g. *htəmìnhcɛʔ* 'a cook', derived from the deverbal *ʔəhcɛʔ* with the generic object, *htəmin* 'rice, food'. In principle, derived forms such as these can be interpreted literally or idiomatically; *htəminhcɛʔ* could also be an action nominal with the meaning of 'cooking'.

Other kinds of compounding are well utilised in Burmese as a means of deriving nouns and verbs. Nominal patterns are more varied and several are recursive; compound verbs are usually composed of pairs of verbs. Compounding is a favourite way of coining new technical vocabulary, e.g. *kon+tin+kon+hcá+maùn,* lit. 'an arm (that) loads (and) unloads goods', i.e. 'a crane'; *mainhnòn+pyá+dain-hkwɛʔ* 'a dial (that) shows mile-rate', i.e. 'a speedometer'. *Mainhnòn* and *dainhkwɛʔ* are themselves compounds that combine loanwords from English (*main* from 'mile', *dain* from 'dial') with words from Burmese, a practice that is quite common.

Burmese vocabulary also attests to a variety of processes that straddle the line between derivation and compounding. They apparently satisfy an urge, most noticeable in formal and literary styles, to add weight and colour to the monosyllabic root. Nouns and verbs often have pleonastic versions formed by the addition of a near synonym: *yè* and *yè+θà,* both 'write', the latter containing the verb *θà* 'inscribe'; *cí* and *cí+hyú* both 'look at', with *hyú,* a less common verb than *cí,* meaning 'to behold'. The enlarged version may be phonologically as well as semantically matched: *po* and *pomo,* both meaning 'more', the latter with the rhyming and nearly synonymous *mo.* Or it may be phonologically matched but semantically empty: *hkɔ* and *hkɔwɔ* 'call', the latter containing the otherwise meaningless rhyming syllable *-wɔ; ɲi* and *ɲiɲa* 'be even', with the meaningless 'chiming' syllable *-ɲa.* In the 'elaborate' adverbial *wòdò+wàdà* 'blurred, unclear', rhyme and chime are intermeshed.

The pattern of four rhythmically or euphonically balanced syllables is prolific. Elaborate nouns are frequently formed by the addition of *ʔə* to both parts of a compound verb: *hnáun+hyɛʔ* 'annoy', *ʔəhnáun+ʔəhyɛʔ* 'annoyance'. Elaborate adverbs may contain any of a variety of minor syllables: *bəyòn+bəyìn* 'tumultuously'; *kəbyàun +kəbyan* 'in an illogical, backwards way'; *təsì+təlòn* 'in unity'. As these examples show, the language has vast resources for expressing fine nuances through the adverbial position. Many adverbials are onomatopoeic or ideophonic, e.g. the pattern *tə-* plus reduplication, as in *təzizi* 'buzzing with noise'; or the pattern of an imitative syllable plus the suffix *-hkənɛ̀* the latter associated with sudden movement: *hyuʔhkənɛ̀* 'whoosh'; *htwihkənɛ̀* 'ptui' (spitting sound, expressing disgust).

5 Syntax

In Burmese the verb and its modifiers occupy the final position in the clause, with nominals and other complements 'freely' ordered before it. There is neither agreement between constituents nor concord within them. The grammatical apparatus consists mainly of postpositional particles – many of them deriving from nouns or verbs – whose relative ordering, though often fixed, tends to accord with their semantic scope: *yu-la-se-hcin-tɛ* 'carry-come-cause-want-realis = (he) wanted to make (him) bring (it)'; *cènaun hsəya-ká-lɛ́-hpɛ́ (cènaun tì-tɛ)* 'gong-master-contrastive subject-additive-restrictive = and the gong-master, for his part, just (plays the gong)'. The only obligatory grammatical categories involve the verb; with some exceptions, final verb phrases are followed by one of a small set of functionally disparate particles that signal, simultaneously, features of polarity and mood, or polarity, mood and aspect. Thus, *-tɛ, -mɛ* and *-pi* carry, in addition to the meanings 'positive' and 'non-imperative', the aspectual distinctions of realis, irrealis and punctative, respectively. The punctative expresses the realisation of a state (*tɔ-pi* '(that)'s enough') or the initiation of an action (*sà-pi* '(I)'m eating (now)'), different manifestations of the notion 'change of state'. Grammatical categories of voice, tense and definiteness are not found at all. Nor is 'number' truly grammaticalised.

Though there are suffixes associated with plurality, they do not co-occur with number-classifier expressions. In fact, they reveal themselves to be 'collectives' rather than plural markers. The suffix *tó* that seems to mark number in pronouns (*θu* 'he; she', *θu-tó* 'they; them'), has collective meaning when combined with nouns: *Ko Nandá-tó* 'Ko Nanda and his family'. Similarly *te* (or more formally, *twe*), a plural suffix for countable nouns (*lu-te* 'people') signifies 'a large amount of' with mass nouns: *sɛʔku-te-nɛ̀* 'paper PLUR with = with a lot of paper'.

The verbal phrase itself, as we saw in the earlier example, often consists of a string of verbs, verb-like morphemes and particles. These exhibit a variety of syntactic and semantic properties. In the phrase *htɛ̀ θwà* 'put in-go = to take (it) in (it)', two verbs combine in open juncture and retain their lexical meanings; in *htɛ̀ pè*, 'put (something) in for (someone)', open juncture is still usual, but the second morpheme, *pè,* has its benefactive meaning of 'for the sake of' rather than its literal meaning of 'give'; in *htɛ̀-laiʔ* 'just put (it) in', *htɛ̀* is followed in close juncture by a morpheme whose lexical meaning is 'to follow' but which, as a verbal modifier, signals an 'increase in transitivity', and is often translated as 'effective or abrupt action'. The functions of the verbal modifiers are surprisingly diverse: *-hya,* the 'commiserating' particle (with no verbal prototype) conveys 'pity or compassion, usually towards a third person': *la-yá-pyan-hya-tɛ* 'come-had to-again-pity-realis = [she] had to come back, unfortunately'. The directional particle, *-hkɛ̀* (again, with no obvious lexical prototype), signifies 'displacement in space or time', as in *Pagan myó-ká wɛ-hkɛ̀-tɛ* 'Pagan-town-from-buy-there-realis = (we) bought (it) back in Pagan'.

Within the noun phrase, the order of constituents is primarily modifier before modified, with the main exception being stative verb modifiers which follow their head nouns either in close juncture or with the nominalising prefix *ʔə-*. Demonstratives precede their head: *di mìpon* 'this/these lantern(s)'. So do genitive phrases and other nominal modifiers: *ʔəpyó ʔen* 'the young woman's house' (with induced creaky tone on *ʔəpyo* marking possession). So, too, do most relative clauses: *baθasəkà léla-tɛ̀ lu-te* 'language-study-realis (with induced creaky tone showing subordination)-person-plural = people that study language'. Unlike English, the original semantic role of the relativised noun is not indicated: *θu gàun səpwɛ̀-nɛ̀ taiʔ mí-te* 'he-head-table-with-hit-inadvertently-realis = he hit (his) head on the table', but *θu gàun taiʔ-mí-tɛ̀ səpwɛ̀* 'the table that he hit (his) head (on)'.

Burmese, like many of the languages spoken on the mainland of South-East Asia, requires classifiers (or 'measures') for the quantification of what in English would be called count nouns. Numeral and classifier follow the quantified noun in an appositional relationship: *θwà lè-hcàun* 'tooth-four-peg = four teeth'; *θəhcìn lè-poʔ* 'song-four-stanza = four songs'. Some nouns can be self-classifying: *ʔen lè-ʔen* 'four houses'. Classifiers often reflect the shape or some other salient feature of a nominal referent. In many cases, nouns may be classified in several ways, according to the particular aspect of an object the speaker chooses to emphasise; in the case of animate nouns the choice usually reflects status: *lu təyauʔ* 'one (ordinary) person', *lu təʔù* 'one (esteemed) person'. But probably as a result of material and cultural change, the semantic or conceptual basis of classification in Burmese is now often obscure, so possible classifiers must be listed with nouns in the dictionary as lexical facts.

Although certain orders of clause elements are much more common than others – agent–beneficiary–patient, for example – order of elements before the verb is, in principle, free. As a result, a sentence such as *Maun Hlá Maun Ŋɛ yaiʔ-tɛ* is ambiguous, each nominal capable of being interpreted as agent or patient: 'Maung Hla struck Maung

Nge' or 'Maung Hla was struck by Maung Nge'. Where context is insufficient to ensure the intended interpretation, semantic relations can be marked by postpositional particles. In this case, the agent can be signalled by *-ká*, the patient by *-ko: Maun Hlá-ko Maun Ŋɛ-ká yaiʔ-tɛ* 'Maung Hla was struck by Maung Nge'. These, like many of the other postpositional particles, have several different senses. With locations they mark 'source' and 'goal', respectively: *Yankon-ká Mandəlè-ko θwà-tɛ* 'S(he) went from Rangoon to Mandalay'. Other functions of *-ko*, such as the marking of beneficiary and extent or degree can be subsumed under the notion of 'goal'. But *-ká* has one other very common function that is not obviously related to the notion of source: where *-ká* does not serve a disambiguating function – in intransitive clauses, for example – it signals 'contrastive topic'; *di-ká təcaʔ, da-ká caʔ-hkwè* 'this-ká (costs) one kyat, that-ká, one and a half'. *-ká* in this sense may appear with nominals already marked for semantic roles: *ʔəhtè-htè-hma-ká* 'inside-in-at-ká', as in **'inside** it's crowded (but outside it's not').

The last example illustrates the origin of many of the more specific relational markers. *ʔəhtè* is a noun meaning 'the inside', which can function as head to a genitive phrase with the meaning 'the inside of': *yehkwɛʔ ʔəhtè* 'the inside of the cup'. Without its prefix, and closely bound to the preceding syllable, the morpheme occurs in locative phrases that may be explicitly marked as such by the particle *-hma*: *yehkwɛʔ-htè-hma* 'in the cup'.

Although word order is 'free' in the sense that it does not indicate the grammatical or semantic roles of constituents, it is not without significance. It is conditioned by the pragmatic notions of topic, which establishes a point of departure from previous discourse or from context, and 'comment', which contains the communicative focus of the utterance. It is this pragmatic organisation that leads us to translate the sentence *Maun Hlá-ko Maun Ŋɛ ká yaiʔ-tɛ* with the English passive, i.e. 'Maung Hla was struck by Maung Nge', rather than the active 'Maung Nge struck Maung Hla'. For, by mentioning Maung Hla first, we take the patient's point of view, just as we do when using the passive in English. But unlike the English, topicalising the patient changes neither the grammatical relations of the nominals (the agent is not demoted) nor the valence of the verb (which keeps the same form), so the term 'passive' does not apply. The closest Burmese gets to a passive construction is a 'passive of adversity', which, as the name suggests, is associated primarily with events that affect a person (or patient) unpleasantly. Thus the unlikely perspective of the sentence, *kà θú-ko taiʔ-tɛ* 'car-he-obj.-hit-realis = the car hit him', can be reversed by making *taiʔ* a nominal complement of a verb phrase containing the verbs *hkan* 'suffer; endure', and *yá* 'get, manage to': *θu kàtaiʔ hkan-yá-tɛ* 'he-car-hitting-suffer-get-realis = he got hit by a car'. But this construction is not nearly as frequent as the passive is in English.

A topic, once established, may remain activated over several sentences. Its pragmatic role, in other words, may be 'given'. English typically leaves a pronominal trace in such cases; Burmese generally does not. Nominals, topical or otherwise, whose reference can be recovered from previous discourse or context can be omitted, a process sometimes known as 'zero-pronominalisation'; *pyin pè-mɛ* 'fix-(give)-irrealis = (I)'ll fix (it) for (you)'. Such sentences are grammatically complete like their English counterparts. Pronouns, which almost always have human referents in Burmese, are used either as a hedge against misinterpretation or as a means of making the relative status of the participants explicit.

The primacy of the topic–comment organisation of the sentence in Burmese is also illustrated by sentences of the following type: *di hkəlè θwà cò-θwà-tɛ* 'this-child-teeth-break (intransitive)-(go)-realis = this child has broken (his) teeth'. The verb is intransitive (its corresponding transitive is aspirated) and the two noun phrases are not in a possessive relationship but are clausal constituents; a more literal translation would read 'the child, teeth have been broken'. In such cases, the first topic, *hkəlè*, is a locus for the second topic, *θwà*, and only the second is matched to the selectional requirements of the verb.

Bibliography

Okell (1969) is the most thorough and useful grammatical description of Burmese; Part 1 is a structural analysis, Part 2 a conspectus of grammatical morphemes. For those who can read the examples in Burmese script, Okell and Allott (2001) expands coverage of the colloquial forms given in Part 2 of Okell (1969) and includes literary forms as well. Allott (1985) is an important sociolinguistic study. Watkins (2005) is a recent collection of articles on grammatical and other issues. Aung-Thwin (2005), particularly Chapters 7 and 8, questions critical assumptions about the early influences on the Burmese language.

For the writing system, reference may be made to Roop (1972), a programmed course, and Wheatley (1996), a short description. Okell (1971) deals with issues of transliteration and transcription of Burmese, and includes descriptions of the most important systems of Romanisation.

References

Allott, A. 1967. 'Grammatical Tone in Modern Spoken Burmese', *Wissenschaftliche Zeitschrift der Karl-Marx Universität Leipzig, Gesellschafts- und Sprachwissen schaftliche Reihe*, vol. 16, pp. 157–62
—— 1985. 'Language Policy and Language Planning in Burma', in D. Bradley (ed.) *Papers in South-East Asian Linguistics*, No. 9, *Language Planning and Sociolinguistics in South-East Asia*, pp. 131–54; *Pacific Linguistics* A-67
Aung-Thwin, Michael. 2005. *The Mists of Rāmañña: The Legend That Was Lower Burma* (University of Hawai'i Press, Honolulu)
Bernot, D. 1963. 'Esquisse d'une description phonologique du birman', *Bulletin de la Société Linguistique de Paris*, vol. 58, pp. 164–224
—— 1980. *Le Prédicat en birman parlé* (Centre Nationale de la Recherche Scientifique, Paris)
Judson, Rev. A. 1888. *A Grammar of the Burmese Language* (Baptist Board of Publications, Rangoon)
Okell, J. 1965. 'Nissaya Burmese: A Case of Systematic Adaptation to a Foreign Grammar and Syntax', *Lingua*, vol. 15, pp. 186–227
—— 1969. *A Reference Grammar of Colloquial Burmese*, 2 vols (Oxford University Press, London)
—— 1971. *A Guide to the Romanization of Burmese* (Luzac, London)
Okell, John and Allott, Anna. 2001. *Burmese/Myanmar Dictionary of Grammatical Forms* (Curzon Press, Richmond, Surrey)
Roop, D.H. 1972. *An Introduction to the Burmese Writing System* (Yale University Press, New Haven)
Watkins, Justin (ed.) 2005. *Studies in Burmese Linguistics*. Pacific Linguistics 570 (Australian National University, Canberra, Australia)
Wheatley, Julian K. 2009 [1996] 'Burmese Writing', in Peter T. Daniels and William Bright (eds) *The World's Writing Systems* (Oxford University Press, Oxford)

44

Japanese

Masayoshi Shibatani

1 Introduction

Japanese is spoken by virtually the entire population of Japan – some 127 million people as of July 2006. In terms of the number of native speakers, it is thus comparable to German and ranks sixth among the languages of the world. Yet, despite its status as a world's major language and its long literary history, Japanese is surrounded by numerous myths, some of which are perpetuated by Japanese and non-Japanese alike. There are a number of factors which contribute to these myths, e.g. the uncertainty of the genetic relationship of Japanese to other languages, its complex writing system and the relatively small number of non-Japanese (especially Westerners) who speak it.

One of the persistent myths held by the Japanese concerning their language is that it is somehow unique. This myth derives mainly from the superficial comparison between Japanese and closely related Indo-European languages such as English, German and French and the obvious disparities which such work reveals. Another persistent myth is that Japanese, compared to Western languages, notably French, is illogical and/or vague. This belief, remarkable as it may be, is most conspicuously professed by certain Japanese intellectuals well versed in European languages and philosophy. Their conviction is undoubtedly a reflection of the inferiority complex on the part of Japanese intellectuals toward Western civilisation. After all, Japan's modernisation effort started only after the Meiji Restoration (1867). Prior to this, Japan had maintained a feudalistic society and a closed-door policy to the rest of the world for nearly 250 years.

However understandable the historical or cultural causes may be, widespread characterisation of Japanese as a unique and illogical language grossly misrepresents the true nature of the language. In fact, in terms of grammatical structure, Japanese is a rather 'ordinary' human language. Its basic word order – subject–object–verb – is widespread among the world's languages. Also other characteristics associated with an SOV language are consistently exhibited in Japanese (see Section 5). In the realm of phonology too, it is a commonplace language, with five hardly exotic vowels, a rather simple set of consonants and the basic CV syllable structure (see Section 4).

As for the claim that Japanese is illogical or vague, one can argue that Japanese is in fact structurally superior to Western languages in that the language makes a clear structural distinction between two types of judgement known as thetic judgement and categorical judgement. The English expression *The sky is blue*, for example, would be rendered either as *Sora-ga aoi* (sky-NOM blue) or *Sora-wa aoi* (sky-TOP blue) depending on the type of judgement one is making (see Section 6). While the notion of uniqueness as applied to the entire domain of a given language is dubious, especially in the case of Japanese as pointed out above, each language does possess certain features that are unique or salient in comparison to other languages. For Japanese, these include honorifics, certain grammatical particles, some of which are distinct for male and female speakers, and the writing system. In this chapter, I shall attempt to include in the discussion those aspects of Japanese that constitute a notable feature of this language which I believe is not shared by many other languages and which makes learning Japanese difficult for many foreigners.

2 Historical Setting

Like Korean, its geographical neighbour, Japanese has long been the target of attempts to establish a genetic relationship between it and other languages and language families. Hypotheses have been presented assigning Japanese to virtually all major language families: Altaic, Austronesian, Sino-Tibetan, Indo-European and Dravidian. The most persuasive is the Altaic theory, but even here evidence is hardly as firm as that which relates the languages of the Indo-European family, as can be seen in ongoing speculations among both scholars and linguistic amateurs.

With regard to individual languages, Ryūkyūan, Ainu and Korean have been the strongest candidates proposed as possible sister languages. Among these, the Japanese–Ryūkyūan connection has been firmly established. Ryūkyūan, spoken in Okinawa, is, in fact, now considered to be a dialect of Japanese. A Japanese–Ainu relationship has been hypothesised, but evidence is scanty. On the other hand, the Japanese–Korean hypothesis stands on firmer ground and perhaps it is safe to assume that they are related, though remotely.

The earliest written records of the Japanese language date back to the eighth century. The oldest among them, the *Kojiki* ('Record of Ancient Matters') (AD 712) is written in Chinese characters. The preface to this work is written in Chinese syntax as well. What was done is that the characters whose meanings were equivalent to Japanese expressions were arranged according to Chinese syntax. Thus, the document is not readily intelligible to those who do not know how the Chinese ordering of elements corresponds to the Japanese ordering, since Chinese word order is similar to English, e.g. *Mary likes fish*, as opposed to the Japanese order of *Mary fish likes*. Furthermore, it is not clear how such characters were read; they may have been read purely in the Chinese style in imitation of the Chinese pronunciation of the characters used or they may have been read in a Japanese way, i.e. by uttering those Japanese words corresponding in meaning to the written Chinese characters and inverting the order of elements so as to follow the Japanese syntax. Perhaps both methods were used. This means that a character such as 山 'mountain' was read both as *san*, the Chinese reading, and as *yama*, the semantically equivalent Japanese word for the character. This practice of reading Chinese characters both in the Chinese way and in terms of the semantically equivalent Japanese words persists even today.

By the time the *Manyōshū* ('Collection of a Myriad Leaves'), an anthology of Japanese verse, was completed (AD 759), the Japanese had learned to use Chinese characters as phonetic symbols. Thus, the Japanese word *yama* 'mountain' could be written phonetically by using a character with the sound *ya* (e.g. 夜 'evening') and another with the sound *ma* (e.g. 麻 hemp'), as 夜麻. In other words, what stands for 'mountain' could be written in two ways. One used the Chinese word 山 as discussed above. The other way was to choose Chinese characters read as *ya* and *ma*. It is this latter phonetic way of writing which gave rise to the two uniquely Japanese syllabary writings known as *kana*.

Since things Chinese were regarded as culturally superior to their native equivalents, the Chinese manner was a formal way of writing. The phonetic representation of Japanese was considered only 'temporary' or mnemonic in nature. Thus, the phonetic writing was called *karina* 'temporary letters' while the Chinese way of writing was called *mana* 'true letters'.

Present-day *karina* (now pronounced as *kana*) have developed as simplified Chinese characters used phonetically. There are two kinds of *kana*. The original *kana* were used as mnemonic symbols in reading characters and were written alongside them; hence they are called *kata-kana* 'side *kana*'. *Hira-gana* 'plain *kana*' have developed by simplifying the grass style (i.e. cursive) writing of characters. These two *kana* syllabaries are set out in Table 44.1.

Katakana were originally used in combination with Chinese characters. *Hiragana*, on the other hand, were mainly used by women and were not mixed with characters. The contemporary practice is to use Chinese characters, called *kanji*, for content words, and *hiragana* for grammatical function words such as particles and inflectional endings. *Katakana* is used to write foreign loanwords, telegrams and in certain onomatopoeic expressions.

In addition, there is *rōmaji*, which is another phonetic writing system using the Roman alphabet. *Rōmaji* is mainly employed in writing station names as an aid for foreigners, in signing documents written in Western languages and in writing foreign acronyms (e.g. *ILO*, *IMF*). It is also used in advertising. Thus the word for 'mountain' can be written as 山 in *kanji*, as ヤマ in *katakana*, as やま in *hiragana* and as *yama* in *rō maji*. Sometimes all these four ways of writing can be found in one sentence; e.g. the sentence *Hanako is an OL* (< *office lady* i.e. 'office girl') *working in that building* can be written as below:

花子	は	あの	ビル	で	働いている	OL	です。
Hanako	wa	ano	biru	de	hataraite-iru	ooeru	desu.
	top.	that	building	at	work-ing	OL	cop.

The traditional way of writing is to write vertically, lines progressing from right to left. Today both vertical writing and horizontal writing, as illustrated above, are practised.

As may be surmised from the above discussion, learning how to write Japanese involves considerable effort. Japanese children must master all four ways of writing by

Table 44.1 Japanese *Kana* Syllabaries

Hiragana

A	KA	SA	TA	NA	HA	MA	YA	RA	WA	
あ	か	さ	た	な	は	ま	や	ら	わ	
I	KI	SI	TI	NI	HI	MI		RI		
い	き	し	ち	に	ひ	み		り		
U	KU	SU	TU	NU	HU	MU	YU	RU		
う	く	す	つ	ぬ	ふ	む	ゆ	る		
E	KE	SE	TE	NE	HE	ME		RE		
え	け	せ	て	ね	へ	め		れ		
O	KO	SO	TO	NO	HO	MO	YO	RO	WO	N
お	こ	そ	と	の	ほ	も	よ	ろ	を	ん

Katakana

A	KA	SA	TA	NA	HA	MA	YA	RA	WA	
ア	カ	サ	タ	ナ	ハ	マ	ヤ	ラ	ワ	
I	KI	SI	TI	NI	HI	MI		RI		
イ	キ	シ	チ	ニ	ヒ	ミ		リ		
U	KU	SU	TU	NU	HU	MU	YU	RU		
ウ	ク	ス	ツ	ヌ	フ	ム	ユ	ル		
E	KE	SE	TE	NE	HE	ME		RE		
エ	ケ	セ	テ	ネ	ヘ	メ		レ		
O	KO	SO	TO	NO	HO	MO	YO	RO	WO	N
オ	コ	ソ	ト	ノ	ホ	モ	ヨ	ロ	ヲ	ン

Note: Voicing oppositions, where applicable, are indicated by the diacritical dots on the upper right hand corner of each *kana*; e.g. *gi* ぎ as opposed to *ki* き.

the time they complete nine years of Japan's compulsory education. Of these, the most difficult is the Chinese system. For each *kanji*, at least two ways of reading must be learned: one the *on-yomi*, the Sino-Japanese reading, and the other the *kun-yomi*, the Japanese reading. For the character 山 'mountain', *san* is the Sino-Japanese reading and *yama* the Japanese. Normally, the Sino-Japanese reading is employed in compounds consisting of two or more Chinese characters, while in isolation the Japanese reading is adopted.

An additional complication is the multiplicity of Sino-Japanese readings. This is due to the fact that Chinese characters, or rather their pronunciations, were borrowed from different parts of China as well as at different times. Thus, dialectal differences in pronunciation also had to be learned by the Japanese. One of the two major sources of borrowing was the Wu area of China during the Six Dynasties period. The reading reflecting this dialect is called *go'on*. The other reading called *kan'on* reflects a newer dialect of *Chang-an*, which is believed to be the standard language of the Tang period. The character 米 for 'rice' is pronounced *mai* in *go'on*, *bei* in *kan'on* and *kome* and *yone* in the Japanese reading. Unlike the *on-yomi* versus *kun-yomi*, there is no systematic rule for determining whether a given character is to be read in *kan'on* or in *go'on*; each expression must be learned as to which way it is read. The character 米 for 'rice', for example, will be read in *go'on* in a form like 外米 *gai mai* 'imported rice', but in *kan'on* in a form like 米国 *bei koku* 'America'. That is, the *go'on/kan'on* distinction is purely historical and speakers of Japanese must simply live with the fact that in addition to the Japanese way of reading, most *kanji* have two or more Chinese ways of reading them and that the same *kanji* is likely to be pronounced differently depending on the expression in which it is used.

Because of this kind of complexity caused by retaining all these writing methods, there have been movements for abolishing Chinese characters in favour of *kana* writing and even movements for completely Romanising the Japanese language. All these, however, have so far failed and it is safe to say that Chinese characters are here to stay. What has been done instead of abolishing Chinese characters altogether is to limit the number of commonly used characters. In 1946, the Japanese government issued a list of 1,850 characters for this purpose. The list was revised in 1981, and the new list, called *Jōyō Kanji Hyō* ('List of Characters for Daily Use'), contains 1,945 characters recommended for daily use. This is now regarded as the basic list of Chinese characters to be learned during elementary and intermediate education. Also, most newspapers try to limit the use of characters to these 1,945 characters; when those outside the list are used, the reading in *hiragana* accompanies them. An interesting new phenomenon due to the efficient word-processing programs available on the computer is the use of more complex characters, which one would avoid if he or she were to handwrite them.

Japan, a mountainous country with many islands, has a setting ideal for fostering language diversification; and, indeed, Japanese is rich in dialectal variation. Many dialects are mutually unintelligible. For example, speakers of the Kagoshima dialect of the southern island of Kyūshū would not be understood by the majority of the speakers on the main island of Honshū. Likewise, northern dialect speakers of Aomori and Akita would not be understood by the people of metropolitan Tokyo or by anyone from western Japan. Communication among people of different dialects has been made possible through the spread of the so-called *kyootuu-go* 'common language', which consists essentially of versions of local dialects modified according to the 'ideal' form called *hyoozyun-go* 'standard language', which in turn is based on the dialect of the capital Tokyo.

Hyoozyun-go is used in broadcasting, and it is this form of Japanese which elementary education aims at in teaching children. The following description is based on this dialect, sometimes referred to as the standard dialect.

3 Lexicon

The fact that Japan has never been invaded by a foreign force or colonised by a foreign interest causes surprise when one examines the Japanese lexicon, for it shows a characteristic of those languages whose lands have been under foreign control at one time or another. Namely, Japanese vocabulary abounds in foreign words. In this regard, Japanese is similar to Turkish, which has borrowed a large number of Arabic and Persian words without ever being ruled by Arabs or Persians, and contrasts with English and others that have incorporated a large quantity of words from invaders' languages.

In addition to the abundance of foreign words, the Japanese lexicon is characterised by the presence of a large number of onomatopoeic words. This section, still in the spirit of presenting an overall picture of Japanese, surveys these two characteristic aspects of the Japanese lexicon.

Japanese has borrowed words from neighbouring languages such as Ainu and Korean, but by far the most numerous are Chinese loanwords. Traditionally, the Japanese lexicon is characterised in terms of three strata. The terms *wago* 'Japanese words' and

Yamato-kotoba 'Yamato (Japanese) words' refer to the stratum of the native vocabulary and *kango* 'Chinese words' refers to loanwords of Chinese origin (hereafter called Sino-Japanese words). All other loanwords from European languages are designated by the term *gairaigo* 'foreign words' (lit. 'foreign coming words'). The relative proportions of these loanwords in the *Genkai* dictionary (1859) were: Sino-Japanese words 60 per cent, foreign words 1.4 per cent, the rest being native words. Although the proportion of foreign words has been steadily increasing (see below), that of the Sino-Japanese words remains fairly constant.

The effect of loanwords on the Japanese language is not insignificant. In particular, the effects of Sino-Japanese borrowing have been felt in all aspects of the Japanese language, including syntax. Restricting our discussion to the domain of the lexicon, however, Sino-Japanese and foreign loanwords have resulted in a large number of synonymous expressions. This demonstrates that Japanese has borrowed even those words whose equivalents already existed in the language. This may appear at first to be unmotivated and uneconomical. However, synonymous words are often associated with different shades of meaning and stylistic values, thereby enriching the Japanese vocabulary and allowing for a greater range of expression. For example, some interesting observations can be made with regard to the following sets of synonymous triplets:

Gloss	'inn'	'idea'	'acrobat'	'detour'	'cancellation'
Native	yadoya	omoituki	karuwaza	mawarimiti	torikesi
S-J	ryokan	tyakusoo	kyokugei	ukairo	kaiyaku
Foreign	hoteru	aidea	akurobatto	baipasu	kyanseru

In general, the native words have broader meanings than their loan counterparts. For example, *torikesi* can be applied to various kinds of cancellation-type acts, even in taking back one's words. The Sino-Japanese word *kaiyaku* is normally used with reference to the cancellation of contracts and other formal transactions. The foreign word *kyanseru*, on the other hand, is used for the cancellation of appointments or ticket reservations, etc. The Sino-Japanese words, which generally convey a more formal impression, tend to be used with reference to higher-quality objects than do the native equivalents. On the other hand, the foreign words have a modern and stylish flavour.

Though various factors can be pointed out to account for the ready acceptance of loanwords in Japanese, the main linguistic reasons have to do with the lack of nominal inflections and the presence of a syllabic writing system. Since Japanese does not mark gender, person or number in nouns and since cases are indicated by separate particles, a loanword can simply be inserted into any position where a native nominal might appear with no morphological readjustment. For the borrowing of verbal expressions, Japanese utilises the verb *suru*, which has the very general meaning 'do'. This useful verb can attach to the nominal forms of loanwords to create verbal expressions; e.g. the Sino-Japanese word *hukusya* 'copy' yields *hukusya-suru* 'to copy' and the English loan *kopii* 'copy' yields *kopii-suru* 'to copy'.

The proportion and the status of the Sino-Japanese words in Japanese are strikingly similar to those of the Latinate words in English. The proportion of Latinate words in English vocabulary is estimated to be around 55 per cent, while that of Germanic (Anglo-Saxon) words and of other foreign loans are 35 per cent and 10 per cent, respectively. Furthermore, the status of the Sino-Japanese words in Japanese is quite similar to that of Latinate words in English. As they tend to express abstract concepts, Sino-Japanese words make up the great majority of learned vocabulary items.

Loanwords other than those belonging to the stratum of Sino-Japanese words are called *gairaigo*. The first Japanese contacts with the western world came about in the middle of the sixteenth century, when a drifting Portuguese merchant ship reached the island of Tanegashima off Kyūshū. The Portuguese were followed by the Spaniards and Dutch. Thus, most of the earliest foreign words were from Portuguese, Spanish and especially Dutch. Towards the latter part of the nineteenth century, English replaced Dutch as the language of foreign studies; and presently, roughly 80 per cent of the foreign vocabulary of Japanese are words of English origin.

English terms were first translated into Japanese semantically using Chinese characters, which resulted in a large number of *kango* 'Chinese words' coined in Japan. This was in keeping with the traditional practice of assigning semantically appropriate Chinese characters to foreign loanwords. In order to represent the original sounds, a *katakana* rendering of the original pronunciation accompanied the translated word. Thus, in the initial phase of loan translation, there were, for each word, both character and *katakana* representations, the former representing the meaning and the latter the sound. These foreign words then had two paths open to them: some retained the character rendering and began to be pronounced according to the readings of the characters, while others preserved the *katakana* rendering. A good number of words took both paths, resulting in the formation of many doublets – the *kango* version and the foreign (phonetic) version; e.g. *kentiku:hirudingu* 'building', *sikihu:siitu* 'sheet', *tetyoo:nooto* 'notebook', and more recently *densikeisanki:konpyuutaa* 'computer'.

Contemporary practice is to borrow by directly representing just the sounds using *katakana*. But when foreign loanwords are rendered in *katakana*, the original pronunciation is most often grossly altered. Since all the *katakana* except ン end in a vowel, consonant clusters and a final consonant of a loanword are altered into sequences consisting of a consonant and a vowel. Thus, a one-syllable word like *strike* becomes the five-mora word *sutoraiku* (see Section 4). As a consequence, many Japanese words of English origin are totally incomprehensible to the ears of the native English speaker, much to the chagrin of the Japanese.

In addition to the phonological process, there are three other factors which annoy non-Japanese when encountering Japanised borrowings from their native tongues. They are: (1) change in semantics, e.g. *sutoobu (< stove)* exclusively designates a room heater; (2) Japanese coinages, e.g. *bakku miraa* (< *back+mirror*) for the rear-view mirror of an automobile; and (3) change in form due to simplification, *pan-suto (< panty stockings)* 'panty hose, tights'.

Foreign words are conspicuous not only in number (they abound in commercial messages and inundate Japanese daily life), but also in form, as they are written in *katakana*. The ubiquity and conspicuousness of foreign words in contemporary Japan as well as the fact that they are often used without precise understanding of their original meanings alarm language purists. Occasional public outcries are heard and opinions for curbing the use of foreign words are voiced. However, such purists are fighting a losing battle and, to their dismay, foreign words are gaining a firm footing in the Japanese language.

Foreign loanwords, like slang expressions, are quickly adopted and then abandoned. Only those that are firmly entrenched in the language can be found in dictionaries. The proportion of foreign loanwords in dictionaries is, however, steadily increasing. The ratio of the foreign words in the *Genkai*, published in 1859, was only 1.4 per cent. The rate increased to 3.5 per cent in the *Reikai Kokugojiten* published in 1956. The 1972 version of *Shin Meikai Kokugojiten* has *gairaigo* comprising 7.8 per cent of its entries. It is predicted that foreign words would claim at least a 10 per cent share of the entries in a dictionary compiled today.

Onomatopoeic and other sound symbolic words form another conspicuous group of words in the Japanese lexicon. In a narrow sense, onomatopoeia refers to those conventionalised mimetic expressions of natural sounds. These words are called *giongo* 'phonomimes' in Japanese; e.g. *wan-wan* 'bow-wow', *gata-gata* '(clattering noise)'. In addition to phonomimes, the Japanese lexicon has two other classes of sound symbolic or synaesthetic expressions. They are *gitaigo* 'phenomimes' and *gisyoogo* 'psychomimes'. Phenomimes 'depict' states, conditions or manners of the external world (e.g. *yoboyobo* 'wobbly', *kossori* 'stealthily'), while psychomimes symbolise mental conditions or states (e.g. *ziin* 'poignantly', *tikutiku* 'stingingly'). In the following discussion, all these classes of sound symbolic words will be collectively referred to as onomatopoeic words.

In comparison to English, many Japanese verbs have very general meanings. *Naku*, for example, covers all manners of crying that are expressed in specific English verbs such as *weep* and *sob*. Similarly, *warau* is a general term for laughing. This lack of specificness of the verb meaning is compensated by the presence of onomatopoeic words. Indeed, one may argue that the differences between *weep* and *sob* and between *chuckle* and *smile*, etc. are more expressive in Japanese. Some examples follow: 'cry' *waa-waa naku*, 'weep' *meso-meso naku*, 'sob' *kusun-kusun naku*, 'blubber' *oi-oi naku*, 'whimper' *siku-siku naku*, 'howl' *wan-wan naku*, 'pule' *hii-hii naku*, 'mewl' *een-een to naku*; 'laugh' *ha-ha-ha to warau*, 'smile' *niko-niko to warau*, 'chuckle' *kutu-kutu to warau*, 'haw-haw' *wa-ha-ha to warau*, 'giggle' *gera-gera to warau*, 'snigger' *nita-nita warau*, 'simper' *ohoho to warau*, 'grin' *nikori to warau*, 'titter' *kusu-kusu warau*.

Sound qualities and synaesthetic effects are correlated to a certain extent, especially with regard to the voicing opposition and differences in vowel quality. In reference to the voicing opposition, the voiced versions relate to heavier or louder sounds or stronger, bigger, rougher actions or states and the voiceless versions to lighter or softer sounds or crisper or more delicate actions or states.

Differences in vowel quality also correlate with differences in the texture of observed phenomena. High or closed vowels are associated with higher or softer sounds or activities involving smaller objects, with low vowels correlating with the opposite phenomena. The front–back opposition is similarly correlated with loudness and size, as is the high–low opposition. Thus, *kiin* is a shrill metallic sound, while *kaan* is the sound of a fairly large bell and *goon* the sound of a heavy bell of a Buddhist temple. *Boro-boro* symbolises the vertical dropping of relatively small objects such as teardrops, as opposed to *bara-bara*, which depicts the dropping of objects by scattering them. A small whistle sounds *pippii* and a steam whistle goes *poppoo*. A goat bleats *mee*, and a cow lows *moo*. *Gero-gero* is the way a frog croaks, but *goro-goro* is the rumbling of thunder.

Onomatopoeic expressions permeate Japanese life. They occur in animated speech and abound in literary works to the chagrin of the translators of Japanese literature. In baby-talk, many animals are referred to by the words that mimic their cries; *buu-buu* 'pig', *wan-wan* 'dog', *nyan-nyan* 'cat', *moo-moo* 'cow'. Indeed, names of many noise-making insects and certain objects are derived by a similar process; *kakkoo* 'cuckoo', *kirigirisu* '(a type of grasshopper)', *gatya-gatya* '(a noise-making cricket)'. There are said to be more than thirty kinds of cicadas in Japan and many of them are named after the noises they make: *tuku-tuku-boosi*, *kana-kana*, *min-min-zemi*, *tii-tii-zemi*, etc. A hammer is sometimes called *tonkati* and a favourite pastime of the Japanese is *patinko* 'pinball game', which is sometimes referred to by the more expressive form *tinzyara*, mimicking the noise of the *patinko* parlour.

4 Phonology

Although different phonemic interpretations are possible, perhaps the most orthodox inventories of Japanese segmental phonemes are those set out in Table 44.2.

Table 44.2 Segmental Phonemes of Japanese

Vowels			i		u			
			e		o			
				a				
Consonants								
		p	t			k		
		b	d			g		
			s				h	
			z					
				r				
		m	n					
		w		j		N	Q	

The basic vowel phonemes of the standard dialect are rather straightforward. However, a great deal of dialectal variation in the vocalic system is observed. Dialectal systems range from a three-vowel system (/i/, /u/, /a/) in the Yonaguni dialect of Okinawa to an eight-vowel system in the Nagoya dialect, which, in addition to the five vowels of the standard dialect, possesses the central vowels /ü/ and /ö/, as well as the low front vowel /æ/. Despite these variations, it is generally believed that the basic vowels of the Japanese language are those five vowels set out in Table 44.2, which are observed in the major dialects of Tōkyō, Kyōto, Ōsaka, etc., and that the other dialectal systems have evolved from the five-vowel system.

In the standard dialect, there are two characteristics concerning vowels. One is the articulation of /u/; it is unrounded [ɯ]. The other is the devoicing of high vowels /u/ and /i/ in a voiceless environment; [kɯtsɯ] 'shoe', [haʃi] 'chopstick', [sɯsɯki] 'eulalia'. Specifying the notion of voiceless environment precisely is not easy, but the following factors have been identified so far: (1) /i/ and /u/ will only devoice if not contiguous to a voiced sound; (2) the high vowels do not devoice when they are initial even followed by a voiceless sound; and (3) accented high vowels do not devoice even if flanked by voiceless consonants. The phenomenon also depends on speech tempo; in slow, deliberate speech, devoicing is less frequent.

Among the consonants, notable phenomena are two pervasive allophonic rules: the palatalisation and affrication of dental consonants. The former involves /s/, /z/, /t/ and /d/ and the latter /t/, /d/ and /z/.

In the non-Sino-Japanese vocabulary of the Japanese lexicon (cf. Section 3), the dental consonants and their palatalised or affricated versions are in complementary distribution:

/s/:	[ʃ]	before *i*
	[s]	elsewhere
/z/:	[dʒ]	before *i*
	[dz]	before *u*
	[z]	elsewhere
/t/:	[tʃ]	before *i*
	[ds]	before *u*
	[t]	elsewhere
/d/:	[dʒ]	before *i*
	[dz]	before *u*
	[d]	elsewhere

In the Sino-Japanese vocabulary, there is a contrast between the dentals and their palatalised versions; e.g. [sa] 'difference': [ʃa] 'diagonal', but these are generally analysed as /sa/ and /sya/, the latter of which undergoes the palatalisation process just like the /si/ sequence seen above. (Except for proper nouns, which are transliterated in *rōmaji*, the Japanese expressions in this text are transliterated according to the phonemic representation; thus what is transliterated as *si*, *ti*, *tu*, etc., should be read with appropriate palatalisation and affrication as [ʃi], [tʃi], [tsɯ], etc., according to the above distributional pattern.)

The palatalisation and the affrication described here are very pervasive and cause morphophonemic alternations. Thus, when verb stems that end in a dental consonant are affixed with suffixes beginning in a high vowel, palatalisation or affrication occurs. Observe the alternations: [kas-ɯ] 'lend-pres.': [kas-anai] 'lend-neg.': [kas-e] 'lend-imper.': [kaʃ-imas-ɯ] 'lend-polite-pres.', [kats-ɯ] 'win-pres.': [kat-anai] 'win-neg.': [kat-e] 'win-imper.': [katʃ-imas-ɯ] 'win-polite-pres.'.

The same rules apply to loanwords; e.g. [ʃiidzɯm] *season*, [tʃiimɯ] *team*, [tsɯaa] *tour*. Many younger speakers have begun to pronounce forms such as *party* and other recent loans with [t]. On the other hand, the pronunciation of [s] before [i] appears to be more difficult, so that words such as *seat* and *system* are almost invariably pronounced with [ʃi].

Other pervasive phonological rules are seen in verb inflection, which involves affixation of various suffixes. The most important consideration here is the distinction between verb stems ending in a consonant (C-stems) and those ending in a vowel (V-stems), for this distinction largely determines the shape of the suffixes. The clearest such case is the choice of an imperative suffix: C-stems take -*e* and V-stems -*ro*; *kak-e* 'write-imper.', *mi-ro* 'look-imper.'

In other situations, phonological rules intervene to resolve consonant clusters and vowel clusters resulting from the joining of C-stems and consonant-initial suffixes (C-suffixes) and of V-stems and vowel-initial suffixes (V-suffixes). In the former case, the suffix-initial consonants are elided and in the latter, the suffix-initial vowels are elided. For example, the initial consonant of the present tense suffix /-ru/ is elided after a C-stem verb like /kak-/ 'to write', while it is retained after a V-stem verb like /mi-/ 'to see', as seen in the contrast, *kak-u:mi-ru*. As an example of a suffix with an initial vowel, take the negative /-anai/. With /kak-/, it retains the initial vowel, while it is lost after /mi-/: *kak-anai:mi-nai.* The other inflectional categories are exemplified in the chart of verb inflection.

Japanese Verb Inflection

	C-stem	V-stem	
	'to cut'	'to wear (clothes)'	
Imperative	kir-e	ki-ro	
Present	kir-u	ki-ru	
Past	kit-ta	ki-ta	
Participial/Provisional	kit-te/kir-eba	ki-te/ki-reba	C-suffixes
Tentative	kir-oo	ki-yoo	
Passive	kir-are-ru	ki-rare-ru*	
Causative	kir-ase-ru	ki-sase-ru	
Negative	kir-ana-i	ki-na-i**	
Polite	kir-imas-u	ki-mas-u	V-suffixes
Desiderative	kir-ita-i	ki-ta-i	
Infinitive	kir-i	ki	

The basic syllable structure of Japanese is CV and this canonical pattern is also imposed on loanwords. A consonant cluster and a syllable-final consonant will be made into a CV sequence by inserting [ɯ] (or [o] after a dental stop; remember that [tɯ] or [dɯ] do not occur phonetically in Japanese). Thus, a word like *strike* will be turned into [sɯtoraikɯ]. As this word indicates, a vowel by itself forms a syllable – or more precisely a mora (see below) – and sequences of vowels occur. This is one deviation from the basic CV pattern. The other deviation has to do with two types of consonants that may close a syllable. They are non-nasal consonants followed by homorganic consonants of the following syllable and a nasal that closes a syllable; e.g. [jappari] 'as expected', [jatto] 'finally', [jɯkkɯri] 'slowly', [hontoo] 'truly', [hampa] 'haphazard', [koŋgari] 'crisply', [hoN] 'book'.

Since the phonetic values of all these syllable-final consonants, except the word-final nasal in [hoN] and other such words, are entirely predictable from the nature of the following consonants, they are assigned to two archiphonemes: /Q/ for the non-nasal consonants and /N/ for the nasal consonants. When /N/ occurs word-finally it assumes the value of the uvular nasal [N] or simply nasalisation of the vowel identical to the preceding vowel. Thus, /hoN/ 'book' will be [hoN] or [hoõ]. (Words such as *pen* and *spoon*, which end in [n], are borrowed with the [N] replacing the final nasal, as [peN] and [sɯpɯɯN], respectively.)

The syllable-final consonants constitute one rhythmic unit, much like the syllabic [n̩] and [l̩] in English. This leads us to a discussion of an important phonological unit of Japanese, namely the *mora*. In Japanese phonology, a distinction needs to be made between the suprasegmental units syllable and mora. A form such as *sinbun* 'newspaper' consists of two syllables *sin* and *bun*, but a Japanese speaker further subdivides the form into four units *si, n, bu* and *n*, which correspond to the four letters of *kana* in writing the word. A mora in Japanese is a unit which can be represented by one letter of *kana* and which functions as a rhythmic unit in the composition of Japanese *waka* and *haiku*, the Japanese traditional poems. Thus, in poetic compositions, *sinbun* is counted as having four, rather than two, rhythmic units, and would be equivalent in length to *hatimaki* 'headband'.

While ordinary syllables include a vowel, morae need not. In addition to the moraic nasal seen in *sinbun* above, there are consonantal morae. These occur as the first element in geminate consonants discussed above, e.g. *hakkiri* 'clearly', *yappari* 'as expected', *tatta* 'stood up'. Although these geminate consonants have different phonetic values, the first segments, which constitute morae, are written in *hiragana* with a small つ ([tsɯ]). *Hakkiri* is written with four letters and counted as having four morae – *ha-k-ki-ri*. If a native speaker is asked to pronounce this word slowly marking off each mora unit, he would pronounce it according to the way it is written in *hiragana*, namely as *ha-tu-ki-ri*.

Long vowels, written with two of the same *kana* or with one *kana* followed by a bar indicating length, also count as two morae: e.g. *ookii* 'big' is a two-syllable (*oo-kii*), four-mora (*o-o-ki-i*) word.

Both morae and syllables play an important role in the Japanese accentual system. For one thing, pitch change occurs at the mora level. The one-syllable word *kan* 'completion', for example, has a pitch drop after the first mora as $\overline{kan}$. This contrasts with another *kan* 'sense', which has the pitch configuration $\underline{ka\overline{n}}$. Moreover, in the standard dialect the initial low pitch can be only one mora in length. Thus, if the first syllable contains two morae, as in *ooi* 'many' or *hantai* 'opposite', only the first mora will have the low pitch: $\underline{o}\overline{oi}$, $\underline{ha}\overline{ntai}$. If the initial syllable has just one mora, it of course will have the low pitch (unless it is accented); $\underline{ha}\overline{tumei}$ 'invention'. (Forms beginning with high pitch can also have high pitch but only for one mora, the second mora and the rest being low pitched.)

The concept of syllable also plays a role in Japanese accentuation. In the standard dialect, it is the syllabic unit which carries accent or the mark of pitch fall. This is seen from the fact that two-mora syllables always have the accent on the first mora. That is, while there are forms like *ko'orogi* 'cricket', which is realised as $\overline{koorogi}$, there is no form like *koo'rogi*, with an accent on the second mora of the first syllable, which would be pronounced as $\overline{koorogi}$. This does not mean that there is no form with a high-pitched second mora. Such forms occur in two situations. One case occurs when the word contains no accent, e.g. $\underline{ko}\overline{oru}$ 'to freeze'. The other case is when the second mora is an independent syllable and carries the accent as in *koga'isya* ($\overline{kogaisya}$) 'subsidiary company'. The same applies with other types of mora. There are forms like *ga'nko* 'stubborn', but none like *gan'ko*, with an accent on the second mora of the first syllable. If a mora were an accentual unit, there should be no reason for such a restriction. Thus, Japanese accentuation rules must refer to both moraic and syllabic units.

Incidentally, not all Japanese dialects have both syllabic and moraic units. Certain dialects in the northern Tōhoku region and the southern Kyūshū region do not count forms like *matti* 'match' and *honya* 'book-store' as having three rhythmic units. Rather they are separated into only two units, *mat-ti* and *hon-ya*. A syllable with a long vowel is also counted as one unit in these dialects. Furthermore, in these dialects the syllable is also the unit of pitch assignment.

Since these dialects which recognise only syllabic units occur in the peripheral areas of northern and southern Japan, the Japanese dialectologist Takesi Sibata hypothesises that Japanese was once a syllable language from which the more contemporary mora dialects have developed.

As the preceding discussion indicates, Japanese accentuation involves pitch differences. If a textbook definition were to be applied to Japanese, most Japanese dialects would be called tone languages. In the Kyōto dialect, for example, the segmental form *hasi* has three pitch patterns each associated with a distinct meaning: *hasi* with H(igh) H(igh) is 'edge', *hasi* with L(ow) H is 'chopsticks', and *hasi* with HL is 'bridge'. In certain dialects not only the level tones H and L, but also a contour tone H–L is observed. Again, in Kyōto, *saru* 'monkey' is L H–L; that is, the second mora *ru* begins high and falls to low.

However, the Japanese accentual system is characteristically distinct from the archetypal tone languages of the Chinese type. In this type of language, it is necessary to specify the tone for each syllable. If a word or phrase has two or more syllables, each syllable needs to have a tone specified for it; there is no way of predicting the tone of each syllable of a word or phrase from something else. This is not the case for Japanese. In the majority of Japanese dialects, given diacritic accent markers and a set of rules, the pitch of each syllable of a phrase can be predicted, thereby making the specification of the pitch for each individual syllable unnecessary. In other words, the phonemic nature of the Japanese accentuation is reducible to the abstract accent marker that indicates the location of pitch fall.

Rules that predict actual pitch shapes differ slightly from one dialect to another, but in the standard dialect, the following three ordered rules assign correct pitches (indicated in parentheses) to phonemic representations of such words as /sakura/ (LHH) 'cherry', /za'kuro/ (HLL) 'pomegranate', /koko'ro/ (LHL) 'heart', as well as to those of phrases like /sakura ga/ (LHH H) 'cherry nom.', /miyako' ga/ (LHH L) 'capital nom.', etc.:

(a) Assign high pitch to all morae.
(b) Assign low pitch to all morae following the accent.
(c) Assign low pitch to the first mora if the second is high pitched.

In the standard dialect, one only needs to know the location of pitch fall in predicting the phonetic pitch shape. However, in other dialects additional information may be called for. In some dialects (e.g. Kyōto, Ōsaka) more than the location of pitch change needs be specified in order to assign the pitch contour to a word; specifically, whether a word begins with high pitch or with low pitch must be indicated. The standard dialect has predominant high pitch, as can be noticed from the first of the rules given above, but some dialects (e.g. Kagoshima) have a system with predominant low pitch, in which pitch changes all entail the raising of pitch. Finally, some dialects (e.g. Miyakonojō) have just one accentual pattern, which perforce makes the system non-phonemic.

5 Syntax

The basic word order in Japanese is subject, (indirect object) direct object, verb; e.g.

(a) Taroo ga   Hanako ni   sono hon   o   yatta.
           nom.   dat. that book acc. gave
     'Taro gave that book to Hanako.'

However, emphatic fronting may move a non-subject element to sentence-initial position and therefore variously reordered sentences are possible – an important consideration being that the verb always remains in final position. But there seems to be a restriction: when more than one element is fronted, the resulting sentences are not so

753

well formed as the ones that involve the movement of one element. Thus, the above sentence has the following well-formed and less well-formed variations:

(b) Hanako ni Taroo ga sono hon o yatta (fronting of the indirect object).
(c) Sono hon o Taroo ga Hanako ni yatta (fronting of the direct object).
(d) ?Hanako ni sono hon o Taroo ga yatta (fronting of both indirect and direct object).
(e) ?Sono hon o Hanako ni Taroo ga yatta (fronting of both indirect and direct object).
(f) Taroo ga sono hon o Hanako ni yatta (reversing the order of indirect and direct object).

Related to the basic SOV word order are the following characteristics that are shared by a large number of other SOV languages:

(a) Nominal relations are expressed by postpositional (as opposed to prepositional) particles. (See the above examples.)
(b) The demonstrative, numeral (plus classifier) and descriptive adjective precede the noun in that order; e.g. *sono san-nin no ookii kodomo* (that three person of big child) 'those three big children'. (In this kind of combination, the numeral and adjective expressions may be in reverse order.)
(c) The genitive noun precedes the possessed noun; e.g. *Taroo no hon* (Taro of book) 'Taro's book'.
(d) The relative clause precedes the noun modified; e.g. *[Taroo ga katta] hon* ([Taroo nom. bought] book) 'the book which Taro bought'.
(e) The proper noun precedes the common noun; e.g. *Taroo ozisan* (Taro uncle) 'Uncle Taro'.
(f) The adverb precedes the verb; e.g. *hayaku hasiru* (quickly run) 'run quickly'.
(g) Auxiliaries follow the main verb; e.g. *ik-itai* (go-want) 'want to go', *ik-eru* (go can) 'can go'.
(h) The comparative expression takes the order standard-marker of comparison-adjective; e.g. *Taroo yori kasikoi* (Taroo-than-smart) 'smarter than Taro'.
(i) Questions are formed by the addition of the sentence-final particle *ka*; e.g. *Taroo ga kita* 'Taro came' → *Taroo ga kita ka* 'did Taro come?' Also, unlike English, there is no movement of a *wh-* element in a *wh-* question. Thus, the question word *nani* 'what' remains in object position in the question: *Taroo wa nani o katta ka* (Taroo top. what acc. bought Q) 'What did Taro buy?'

The basic Japanese sentence type exhibits the nominative–accusative case marking pattern, whereby the subjects of both transitive and intransitive sentences are marked by the particle *ga* and the object of a transitive sentence with a distinct particle, *o*. There are, however, three noteworthy deviations from this basic pattern. They are illustrated below along with the basic pattern.

(a) Taroo   ga   kita.
              nom.   came
     'Taro came.'

(b) Taroo   ga   hebi   o   korosita.
              nom.   snake   acc.   killed
     'Taro killed the snake.'

(c) Taroo   ga   Hanako   ni   atta.
         nom.   dat.   met
   'Taro met Hanako.'

(d) Taroo   ni   eigo   ga   wakaru.
         dat.   English nom. understand
   'Taro understands English

(e) Taroo   ga   Hanako   ga   suki   da.
         nom.   nom. like   copula
   'Taro likes Hanako.'

While English consistently exhibits the basic transitive sentence pattern for all these expressions, it is rather exceptional in this regard. Many other languages belonging to different language families show similar deviations along the lines of Japanese. The nominative–dative pattern of (c) is seen in German with verbs like *helfen* 'help' and *danken* 'thank'. The dative–nominative pattern seen in (d) is also very frequently seen in Indo-European languages as well; e.g. Spanish *me gusta la cerveza* 'I like beer', Russian *mne nravitsja kniga* 'I like a book'. In Japanese, predicates like *aru* 'have', *dekiru* 'can do' and *hituyoo da* 'necessary' govern the dative–nominative pattern.

Less frequently seen is the nominative–nominative pattern in (e). As the above examples from Spanish and Russian indicate, the predicate 'like' is normally subsumed under the dative–nominative pattern in those languages that exhibit this pattern. Japanese has a distinct nominative–nominative pattern for predicates such as *suki da* 'like', *zyoozu da* 'good at', *hosii* 'want', etc. Another language that has this pattern regularly with predicates similar to those given here is Korean.

Japanese, being an agglutinative language, expresses various grammatical categories by means of affixes. Voice and tense, for example, are indicated by verbal suffixes, as in the following example.

(a) Taroo   ga   hahaoya   ni   itiba   ni   ika-se-rare-ta.
   Taro   nom. mother   dat. market all. go-causative-passive-past
   'Taro was made to go to the market by Mother.'

Two other means of expressing grammatical categories are compounding and gerundive (or converbal) verbal complex. In many of these forms, the etymological origins of the grammatical forms are still transparent, as in the following examples.

(b) Taroo   ga   hanas-i-hazime-ta/hanas-i-tuzuke-ta.
   Taro   nom. speak-infinitive-begin-past/speak-infinitive-continue-past
   'Taro started/continued to speak.'

(c) Taroo   ga   hanas-i-te i-ru.
   Taro   nom. speak-infinitive-gerundive be/exist-present
   'Taro is speaking.'

Just as in many other languages, many important syntactic phenomena centre around the subject noun phrase. We will discuss some of them, but since they can be best treated in comparison to the topic noun phrase, we shall now turn to discourse-related phenomena.

6 Discourse Phenomena

One of the most important aspects of Japanese grammar has to do with the construction involving the particle *wa*. This particle, generally regarded as a topic marker, attaches to various nominals and adverbials, as seen below, and those constructions with a *wa*-marked constituent are called the topic construction.

(a) Taroo ga   Hanako ni   sono   hon   o   nitiyoobi ni   watasita.
         nom.   dat.   that   book   acc.   Sunday   on   gave
      'Taro gave that book to Hanako on Sunday.'

(b) Taroo wa Hanako ni sono hon o nitiyoobi ni watasita.
      (Topicalisation of the subject)

(c) Hanako ni wa Taroo ga sono hon o nitiyoobi ni watasita.
      (Topicalisation of the indirect object)

(d) Sono hon wa Taroo ga Hanako ni nitiyoobi ni watasita.
      (Topicalisation of the direct object)

(e) Nitiyoobi ni wa Taroo ga sono hon o Hanako ni watasita.
      (Topicalisation of the adverbial)

As seen above, the nominative particle *ga* as well as the accusative *o* drop when *wa* is attached, while other particles tend to be retained (see the dative *ni* in (c), for example).
    It is also possible to have two or more *wa*-attached constituents, as in the following example:

(f) Nitiyoobi ni wa, Taroo wa Hanako ni sono hon o watasita.
      (Topicalisation of the adverbial and the subject)

In the above examples, the topic has been 'extracted' from clause-internal position. While these are typical topic constructions, there are others whose topics cannot be related to a non-topic structure, i.e. the comment is itself a complete clause structure. For example:

(a) Sakana wa   tai   ga   ii.
      fish   top.   red snapper   nom.   good
      'As for fish, red snappers are good.'

(b) Huro   wa   kimoti   ga   ii.
      bath   top.   feeling   nom.   good
      'As for the bath, it feels good.'

Japanese grammars, whether published in Japanese or English, allocate a fair number of pages to explicate the difference between topic and non-topic sentences. Traditional

Japanese grammars distinguish two types of sentences in explaining the relevant difference. Depictive sentences describe a state of affairs unfolding itself right before
one's eyes. No topic constructions would be used in this type of sentence. Thus, when
one looks up the sky and finds it blue, he would utter (a) below.

(a) Sora   ga   aoi.
    sky   nom.   blue
    'The sky is blue.'

(b) Sora   wa   aoi.
    sky   top.   blue
    'The sky is blue.'

Topic sentence (b) above is used when one is making a categorical judgement about the
sky, namely asserting its generic property. While sentence (a) cannot be uttered when
the sky is cloudy, (b) can be. In English the distinction between these two types of
sentence is made by intonation contour. (a) would be uttered with a high pitch on 'the
sky', while (b) would require a low pitch on 'the sky' and a high pitch on 'blue'. The
relevant distinction here in terms of 'depictive sentences' and 'judgement sentences' is
somewhat misleading since depictive sentences also express the speaker's judgements
concerning his recognition of the state of affairs in question and its participants. The
distinction in terms of 'thetic judgement' and 'categorical judgement' is gaining wide
acceptance among linguists describing the two types of judgement made by non-topic
sentences and topic sentences (see Kuroda 1973).

Because the type of judgement the speaker makes can vary depending on the context,
there is a certain degree of freedom as to the use and non-use of the topic construction
depending on whether the narration involves making judgement or not. For example, in
the following narrative, there is no topic construction involved:

(a) Hitori no   kodomo   ga   aruite   kita.
    one   of   child   nom.   walking   came
    'A child came walking.'

(b) Soko   e   inu   ga   hasitte   kita.
    there   at   dog   nom.   running   came
    'There came a dog running.'

(c) Sosite   sono   inu   ga   kodomo   ni   kamituita.
    and then   that   dog   nom.   child   to   bit
    'And then, the dog bit the child.'

In the popular discourse-based account, *wa* is attached to an entity referring to old
information. *Inu* 'dog' in sentence (c) is expected to be marked *wa*, for it has been
previously introduced into the discourse and is hence old information. But the sentences (a)-(c) constitute a perfectly well-formed chunk of a narrative. Of course, the *inu*
in question can be topicalised, as below, but then there is a slight difference between
the two versions of the narrative.

(c') Sosite   sono   inu   wa   kodomo   ni   kamituita.
    and then   that   dog   top.   child   to   bit
    'And then, the dog, it bit the child.'

The difference is this: in the (a)–(c) version, each event is described as if witnessed afresh. To seek analogy in cinema, the (a)–(c) version involves three scenes in succession. In the (a)–(c') version, on the other hand, the first two sentences describe two successive events, presented as two discrete scenes, but the (c') sentence does not constitute a different scene; it rather dwells on the scene introduced by the (b) sentence by detailing on the dog introduced there. In uttering (c'), the speaker is not simply saying what has happened next; rather, he is elaborating on the scene described by (b) by talking more about the dog, i.e. telling us what can be said about the dog that came running.

The discussion of the topic construction along these lines accounts naturally for a number of facts. The restriction that only what is identifiable (i.e. old information or given) can be topicalised follows naturally from the notion of making a categorical judgement; one would not make such judgement about something which is not part of the hearer's presumed knowledge. Also, the fact that subordinate clauses do not admit the topic construction is understandable in view of the fact that subordinate clauses normally describe background events and, as seen above, simple descriptions of events are done in non-topic sentences.

In the tradition of Japanese grammar, the notions of topic and subject are often confused, for, as seen above, they are not clearly separated in languages like English. However, the topic has a status distinct from that of the grammatical subject. That is, the Japanese topic does not participate in many of the syntactic processes that the subject does. The only exception is the topic that also bears the subject relation such as the *sono inu wa* (that dog top.) in (c') above. We will show this in terms of two grammatical phenomena in which the subject figures importantly, namely reflexivisation and subject honorification.

In Japanese, there is a general constraint that the antecedent of the reflexive form *zibun* 'self' must be the subject at some stage of derivation. Thus, in the following sentence, the reflexive form is coreferential only with the subject Taro.

(a) Taroo   ga   Hanako   ni   zibun   no   hon   o   watasita.
    nom.   dat.   self   of   book   acc.   handed
    'Taro handed his own book to Hanako.'

Taroo in (a) functions like a subject even if it is topicalised, but that the subject function is not the property of the topic is seen from the fact that when non-subjects are topicalised, they exhibit no subject properties. In other words, the topicalisation of the indirect object *Hanako* of (a) confers no subject properties on it, as the following sentence cannot be understood to mean that Hanako and *zibun* are coreferential.

(b) Hanako ni wa Taroo ga zibun no hon o watasita.
    'As for Hanako, Taro handed his own book.'

Just as the term 'subject honorification' indicates, there is an honorific phenomenon that is 'triggered' when the subject refers to someone worthy of the speaker's respect.

The process essentially involves attaching the prefix *o* to the infinitive form of the verb and then extending the sentence with the verbal form *naru* 'become'. This converts a plain sentence like (a) below into an honorific form as in (b).

(a) Sensei   ga   waratta.
     teacher   nom.   laughed
     'The teacher laughed.'

(b) Sensei ga o-warai-ni natta.
     lit. 'The teacher became to be laughing.'

Again, the subject-based topic can trigger subject honorification and the conversion of the *sensei ga* in (b) above into *sensei wa* results in a good sentence. But, the topic 'deriving' from non-subjects cannot trigger this process and (b) below is inappropriate; it expresses deference towards the speaker himself.

(a) Boku   ga   sensei   o   tasuketa.
     I   nom. teacher   acc.   helped
     'I helped the teacher.'

(b) Sensei   wa   boku ga   o-tasuke-ni   natta.
     teacher   top. I   nom.   helped   (honorific)
     'As for the teacher, I helped him.'

What is called for in a situation like (a)–(b) above is the other honorification process, called 'object honorification', which expresses the speaker's deference towards the referent of a non-subject nominal.

(c) Boku   ga   sensei   o   o-tasuke   sita.
     I   nom. teacher   acc.   helping   did
     lit. 'I did the helping of the teacher.'

(d) Sensei wa boku ga o-tasuke sita.
     lit. 'As for the teacher, I did helping of him.'

The topic and the subject also show an important difference with respect to the scope of discourse domain. Although both subject and topic can function as a reference for a gapped element, the topic has a far larger scope in this function. In an English coordinate expression such as the following, the gap, indicated by ∅, in the second clause is understood to be identical with the subject of the first clause.

(a) John came and ∅ took off his coat.

When the first clause is a subordinate clause, gapping of the subject of the main clause is not permitted; thus the following are not well formed.

(b) *When John came, ∅ took off his coat.
(c) *As soon as John came, ∅ took off his coat.

In Japanese, all of the above sentences are grammatical, for it allows elliptical expressions for a situation where English typically has pronominal expressions. However, note that the coordinate and subordinate clauses are in this respect grammatically distinct. In the case of coordination, as exemplified in (a) below, the gapped subject of the second clause must be interpreted as identical with the subject of the first clause. But in the case of subordination, as exemplified in (b)–(c) below, the gapped subjects of the main clause must be interpreted as different from the subject of the subordinate clause.

(a) Taroo ga ki-te, suguni Ø uwagi o nuida.
          nom. came immediately coat acc. took off
    'Taro$_i$ came, and immediately Ø$_j$ took off the coat.'

(b) Taroo ga kuru-to, suguni Ø uwagi o nuida.
          come-when
    'When Taro$_i$ came, immediately Ø$_j$ took off the coat.'

(c) Taroo ga kuru-ya inaya, suguni Ø uwagi o nuida.
          come-as soon as
    'As soon as Taro$_i$ came, immediately Ø$_j$ took off the coat.'

In the above examples, the subject of the first coordinate clause and the subject of the subordinate clauses are retained. The same situation obtains even in the reverse expressions, where the subject of the second coordinate clause and that of the main clause are retained.

(a) Ø kite, suguni Taroo ga uwagi o nuida.
    'Ø$_i$ came, and immediately Taro$_j$ took off the coat.'

(b) Ø kuruto, suguni Taroo ga uwagi o nuida.
    'When Ø$_i$ came, immediately Taro$_j$ took off the coat.'

(c) Ø kuru-ya ina ya, suguni Taroo ga uwagi o nuida.
    'As soon as Ø$_i$ came, immediately Taro$_j$ took off the coat.'

However, when the topic form is used, the restriction on (b)–(c) does not obtain and the topic can function in reference to both the subject of the subordinate clause and that of the main clause.

(b') Taroo wa, kuru-to, suguni uwagi o nuida.
          top. come-when immediately coat acc. took off
    'As for Taro$_i$, Ø$_i$ immediately took off the coat when Ø$_i$ came.'

(c') Taroo wa, kuru-ya inaya, suguni uwagi o nuida.
    'As for Taro$_i$, Ø$_i$ took off the coat as soon as Ø$_i$ came.'

As the comma after the topic in (b')–(c') above indicates, the structure of these differs from that underlying the non-topic sentences (b)–(c). That is, while the non-topic subordinate structure is like (a) below, the topic version is like (b):

(a) [Taroo ga kuru]-to suguni ∅ uwagi o nuida
(b) Taroo wa [∅ kuru]-to suguni ∅ uwagi o nuida

While the (b) structure above is the normal pattern, the topic can be retained in the subject position of the main clause, but still the topic functions as a reference for the gapped subject of the subordinate clause; e.g.

(c) [∅ kuru]-to suguni Taroo wa uwagi o nuida

In other words, the topic has the scope over the entire sentence with the role of a reference for the gapped subject of both the subordinate and the main clause. The subject of the subordinate clause or of the main clause, on the other hand, has no such wide scope of reference.

7 Contextual Dependency

Compared to English, Japanese utterances are more context-dependent. This can be seen in assessing the appropriateness of the following two 'equivalent' expressions.

(a) I'd see him.

(b) Atasi kare ni au wa.
    I he dat. meet

Aside from semantic and discourse factors that preclude the possibility of (a), it is rather difficult to find a context in which the English sentence (a) is inappropriate. However, this is not the case for (b); there are a number of contextual factors that must be satisfied in order for the sentence to be an appropriate utterance. First, the sex of the speaker must be considered. Only a female speaker can utter this sentence. The first person pronoun *atasi* is a form exclusively used by a female speaker. And the sentence-final particle *wa*, which has the effect of softening the assertion, is also from the repertory of the particles for female speakers. If a comparable expression were to be uttered by a male speaker, it would be something like the following, where the pronoun for a male *boku* and a sex-neutral particle, *yo*, are used:

(c) Boku kare ni au yo.

Second, the (b) sentence is only appropriate when uttered in a very informal setting. The sentence-final particle like *wa* would not be used in a formal setting and the first person pronoun *atasi* is a rather vulgar or coquettish form. Related to this is the status of the addressee. If the addressee is someone superior to the speaker, the addressee honorific ending *-imasu* needs to be employed. Thus, a more appropriate form for a little more formal setting would require the dropping of the sentence-final particle *wa*, the replacement of the pronoun *atasi* by the more formal form *watakusi* and the adjustment of the verbal ending. In other words, (b) would be replaced by the following expression on a little more formal occasion.

(b') Watakusi kare ni a-imasu.

The sentence (b') can still be inappropriate depending on the person being referred to by the third person pronoun *kare* 'he'. If the person referred to is someone to whom the speaker is obliged to be deferential, then it is not quite appropriate to refer to him as *kare*; such a person is better referred to by *sono kata* 'that person' (lit. 'that direction'). Referring to the person by *sono kata* requires the use of the object honorific form of the verb, *o-ai suru* (see Section 5). Should one want to make the utterance even more polite, the suppletive form of 'to see/meet' *o-me ni kakaru* would be used. These modifications yield the following forms:

(b") Watakusi sono kata ni o-ai s-imasu.
(b''') Watakusi sono kata ni o-me ni kakar-imasu.

One can still go on elaborating the sentence, but the point should be clear. Japanese has different sets of personal pronouns for male and female speakers and for appropriate levels of politeness. Some of the sentence-final particles, which are used in moderating or strengthening the assertion one way or another, also differ for men and women. Thus, an adequate command of Japanese means both grammatical and sociolinguistic knowledge of the appropriate forms of subject or object honorific address. (Notice that at the elevated level of speech, speech style distinctions according to sex tend to be neutralised; thus, a form such as (b''') above can be used by both male and female speakers.)

All these considerations mean that there are many synonyms that are differently used in reference to the speaker's sex, the addressee, as well as the referents of the nominals within a sentence. Addressee honorification and subject and object honorification are in general regular, but there are sufficient suppletive forms that are used regularly and so need to be learned separately. Thus, while speech levels are observed in other languages including English, Japanese has a highly grammaticalised system, which entails many synonymous expressions which must be used appropriately according to the context.

We have seen that numerous synonyms have also been created through borrowing from Chinese and other foreign languages. In addition, one must contend with four kinds of writing systems. It is this multiplicity of coding possibilities which constitutes one unique aspect of Japanese and it is the multitude of synonymous expressions and the complexity of the contextual factors determining the appropriate choice that make the learning of Japanese very difficult for non-Japanese.

Bibliography

Miller (1967) is a comprehensible general account of Japanese with emphasis on the historical development; Miller (1971) presents documentation of the hypothesis relating Japanese to the Altaic family. Sansom (1928) is an excellent account of the grammar of Old Japanese, with a detailed discussion of the development of the writing system.

Martin (1975) is the most comprehensible account of the grammar of modern Japanese written in English, with numerous examples taken from actual published materials. Martin (1987) is a historical study of Japanese complementing his synchronic opus magnum of (1975).

Alfonso (1966) is a useful introduction to the structure of Japanese, while Kuno (1973) is particularly useful on particles and the topic construction. Hinds (1986) is written in a format convenient for looking up specific constructions and phenomena for contrastive and comparative studies. It is also unique among the available reference works for its inclusion of a large amount of actual conversational data. For phonology, McCawley (1968) is a generative treatment, including a useful survey of the accentual systems of Japanese dialects. Shibatani (1976) is a collection of papers dealing with selected topics in Japanese syntax within the framework of generative grammar. Shibatani (1982), another collection of papers, includes papers dealing with Japanese dialectology and sociolinguistics.

Kuroda (1992) contains author's important but technical papers on various aspects of Japanese syntax and semantics. Shibatani (1990) is a major survey of Japanese and the Ainu language. Iwasaki (2002) is a concise introduction to the main aspects of Japanese grammar.

References

Alfonso, A. 1966. *Japanese Language Patterns*, 2 vols (Sophia University Press, Tokyo)

Hinds, J. 1986. *Japanese* (Croom Helm Descriptive Grammars; Croom Helm, London)

Iwasaki, S. 2002. *Japanese* (John Benjamins, Amsterdam)

Kuno, S. 1973. *The Structure of the Japanese Language* (MIT Press, Cambridge, MA)

Kuroda, S.-Y. 1973. 'The Categorical and the Thetic Judgment; Evidence from Japanese', *Foundations of Language*, vol. 9, no. 2, pp. 153–85

—— 1992. *Japanese Syntax and Semantics: Collected Papers* (Kluwer Academic, Dordrecht)

McCawley, J.D. 1968. *The Phonological Component of the Grammar of Japanese* (Mouton, The Hague)

Martin, S.E. 1975. *A Reference Grammar of Japanese* (Yale University Press, New Haven)

—— 1987. *The Japanese Language through Time* (Yale University Press, New Haven)

Miller, R.A. 1967. *The Japanese Language* (University of Chicago Press, Chicago)

—— 1971. *Japanese and the Other Altaic Languages* (University of Chicago Press, Chicago)

Sansom, G. 1928. *An Historical Grammar of Japanese* (Oxford University Press, Oxford)

Shibatani, M. (ed.) 1976. *Japanese Generative Grammar* (Academic Press, New York)

——(ed.) 1982. *Studies in Japanese Linguistics* (= *Lingua*, vol. 57, nos 2–4) (North-Holland, Amsterdam)

—— 1990. *The Languages of Japan* (Cambridge University Press, Cambridge)

45

Korean

Nam-Kil Kim

1 Historical Background

For a long time scholars have tried to associate the Korean language to one of the major language families but have not been successful in this venture. There have been many theories proposed on the origin of Korean. Based on the views as to where the Korean language first originated, two prominent views, which are called the Southern theory and the Northern theory, have been advocated by some scholars. According to the Southern theory, the Korean people and language originated in the south, namely the South Pacific region. There are two versions of this theory. One is that the Korean language is related to the Dravidian languages of India. This view is not taken seriously by contemporary linguists, but it was strongly advocated by the American scholar Homer B. Hulbert in the early twentieth century. His argument was based on the syntactic similarities of Korean and the Dravidian languages. For instance, both languages have the same syntactic characteristics: the word order subject–object–verb, postpositions instead of prepositions, no relative pronouns, modifiers in front of the head noun, copula and existential as two distinct grammatical parts of speech, etc.

The other version of the Southern theory is the view that Korean may be related to the Austronesian languages. There are some linguistic as well as anthropological and archaeological findings which may support this view. The linguistic features of Korean which are shared by some Polynesian languages include the phonological structure of open syllables, the honorific system, numerals and the names of various body parts. The anthropological and archaeological elements shared by Koreans and the people in other regions of the South Pacific are rice cultivation, tattooing, a matrilineal family system, the myth of an egg as the birthplace of royalty and other recent discoveries in Palaeolithic or preceramic cultures. Although this Southern theory has been brought to the attention of many linguists, it is not accepted as convincing by linguists.

The Northern theory is the view that Korean is related to the Altaic family. Although this view is not wholly accepted by the linguistic community, the majority of Korean linguists and some western scholars seem inclined towards believing this view. The major language branches which belong to the Altaic family are Turkic, Mongolian and Tungusic. The area in which the Altaic languages are spoken runs from the Balkans to the Kamchatka peninsula in the North Pacific. The Northern theory stipulates that the Tungusic branch of Altaic tribesmen migrated towards the south and reached the Korean peninsula. The Tungusic languages would include two major languages: Korean and Manchu. The view that Korean is a branch of the Altaic family is supported by anthro-archaeological evidence such as comb ceramics (pottery with comb-surface design), bronze-ware, dolmens, menhirs and shamanism. All these findings are similar to those found in Central Asia, Siberia and northern Manchuria. Korean is similar to the Altaic languages with respect to the absence of grammatical elements such as number, genders, articles, fusional morphology, voice, relative pronouns and conjunctions. Vowel harmony and agglutination are also found in Korean as well as in the Altaic languages. Comparing the two theories, it is apparent that the Northern influence in the Korean language is more dominant than the Southern.

It has been discovered in recent archaeological excavations that the early race called Palaeosiberians lived in the Korean peninsula and Manchuria before the Altaic race migrated to these areas. The Palaeosiberians, who include the Chukchi, Koryaks, Kamchadals, Ainu, Eskimos, etc., were either driven away to the farther north by the newly arrived race or assimilated by the conquerors when they came to the Korean peninsula. It is believed that the migration of the new race towards the Korean peninsula took place around 4000 BC. Nothing is known about the languages of the earliest settlers. After migration, some ancient Koreans settled down in the regions of Manchuria and northern Korea while others moved farther to the south. Many small tribal states were established in the general region of Manchuria and the Korean peninsula from the first century BC to the first century AD. The ancient Korean language is divided into two dialects: the Puyŏ language and the Han language. The Puyŏ language was spoken by the people of tribal states such as Puyŏ, Kokuryŏ, Okchŏ and Yemaek in Manchuria and northern Korea. The Han language was spoken by the people of the three Han tribal states of Mahan, Chinhan and Byŏnhan which were created in southern Korea.

Around the fourth century AD the small tribal states were vanquished and three kingdoms with strong central governments appeared in Manchuria and the Korean peninsula. Of these three kingdoms, the biggest kingdom, Kokuryŏ, occupied the territory of Manchuria and the northern portion of the Korean peninsula. The other two kingdoms, Paekche and Silla, established states in the southwestern and the southeastern regions of the Korean peninsula respectively. It is believed that the Kokuryŏ people spoke the Puyŏ language and the Silla people spoke the Han language; however, it is not certain what language the Paekche people spoke because the ruling class of the Paekche kingdom consisted of Puyŏ tribesmen who spoke the Puyŏ language. When the Korean peninsula was unified by Silla in the seventh century, the Han language became the dominant dialect paving the way for the emergence of a homogeneous language. The Han language finally became the sole Korean language through the two succeeding dynasties of Koryŏ (936–1392) and Chosŏn (1392–1910).

Since Silla's unification of the Korean peninsula in the seventh century, it appears that the language spoken in the capital has been the standard dialect. Thus, the Silla capital, Kyŏngju, dialect was the standard dialect during the unified Silla period from the seventh century to the tenth century. When Silla was succeeded by Koryŏ in the tenth century, the capital was moved from Kyŏngju, which was located in the southeastern region of the Korean peninsula, to Kaegyŏng in the central region of Korea and subsequently the dialect spoken in this new capital became the standard language in Koryŏ from the tenth century to the end of the fourteenth century. When the Yi (or Chosŏn) Dynasty succeeded Koryŏ at the end of the fourteenth century, the capital was established at Seoul, the present capital of South Korea, and the language spoken in this area became the standard dialect and has continued as a standard dialect to the present time. Thus, it is obvious that the formation of the standard dialect has been dominated by political decisions. We can find this even in the twentieth century. There are officially two standard dialects existing in Korea; one is the Seoul dialect in South Korea and the other the Pʰyŏng'yang dialect in North Korea. Each government has established prescriptive criteria for its own standard dialect and made separate policies on language.

Though the dialect distinction of one region from the other is not drastic owing to the relatively small size of the Korean peninsula, each region has its own characteristic dialects. For instance, in the Hamgyŏng dialect of northern Korea the final p of verb bases ending in p is pronounced as [b] before suffixed morphemes starting in a vowel, while in the standard Seoul dialect this final p is pronounced as [w] before a vowel; $təp$- 'hot' is pronounced [təbə] in the Hamgyŏng dialect but [təwə] in the standard dialect. As another example, in the standard dialect palatalisation is normal but in the Pʰyŏng'yang dialect palatalisation does not take place: $katʰi$ 'together' is pronounced as [kacʰi] in the standard dialect but as [katʰi] in the Pʰyŏng'yang dialect. Historically, both Hamgyŏng and Pʰyŏng'yang dialects reflect archaic forms. That is, in the nineteenth-century Yi Dynasty language the words $təp$- and $katʰi$ were pronounced as they are pronounced in the Hamyŏng and Pʰyŏng'yang dialects; and the pronunciation of these words in the standard dialect reflects this historical change.

The Korean language spoken before the fifteenth century is not well known because there are not many records or documents revealing how the language was used before the fifteenth century. It was in the fifteenth century that the alphabetic script (Han'gŭl) for writing Korean was invented by King Sejong. Before the Korean script was invented, only Chinese characters were used for the purpose of writing. But Chinese characters could not depict the living language spoken by Korean people, since Chinese characters were meaning-based and the grammar of classical Chinese did not have any connection with Korean grammar. Even after the Korean script was invented, Chinese characters were continuously used as the main means of writing until the twentieth century. In traditional Korean society, the learning and study of Chinese characters and classical Chinese were entirely monopolised by a small class of elite aristocrats. For average commoners, the time-consuming learning of Chinese characters was not only a luxury but also useless, because they were busy making a living and knowledge of Chinese characters did not help in improving their lives.

The use of Chinese characters imported a massive quantity of loanwords into the Korean lexicon. More than half of Korean words are Chinese-originated loanwords. Although Chinese loanwords and Korean-originated words have always coexisted, the Chinese loanwords came to dominate the original Korean words and subsequently many native Korean words completely vanished from use. A movement by people who wanted to restore native culture at the end of the nineteenth century tried to stimulate mass interest in the study of the Korean language. When the government proclaimed that the official governmental documents would be written both in Korean script and in Chinese characters, the first newspapers and magazines were published in Korean script and the use of the Korean alphabet expanded. In the early twentieth century, more systematic studies on the Korean language were started and a few scholars published Korean grammar books. However, the active study of Korean grammar was discontinued owing to the Japanese colonial policy suppressing the study of Korean.

The study of the Korean language resumed after the end of World War II, but Korea was divided into two countries by the Big Powers. The language policies proposed and implemented by the two governments in the South and the North were different from each other. While both the Korean alphabet and Chinese characters were used in the South, only the Korean alphabet was used in the North. In the North the policy on the use of Chinese characters has been firm: that is, no instruction in Chinese characters has been given to students and Chinese characters are not used in newspapers, magazines or books. This policy has never been changed in the North. Contrary to this, in the South the policy on the instruction of Chinese characters has been inconsistent; whenever a new regime has come to power, both proponents and opponents of the use of Chinese characters have tried to persuade the government to adopt their views. Though the instruction of Chinese characters was abolished a couple of times by the government in the past, this abolition never lasted more than a few years. At the present time in the South, the government has adopted a policy to teach 1,800 basic Chinese characters to students, but each school decides whether Chinese characters are taught in their schools.

The South and the North also have different policies on the so-called 'purification' of Korean. The purification of Korean means the sole use of native Korean words in everyday life by discontinuing the use of foreign-originated words. The main targets of this campaign are Sino-Korean words. In the North, the government has been actively involved in this campaign, mobilising newspapers and magazines to spread the newly translated or discovered pure Korean words to a wide audience of readers. In the South, some interested scholars and language study organisations have tried to advocate the purification of Korean through the media and academic journals, but the government has never officially participated in this kind of movement. It will be interesting to see what course each of the two governments will take in future with respect to language policy.

2 Phonology

The sound system of Korean consists of 21 consonants and ten vowels. The vowels can be classified by the three positions formed by the vocal organs. The first is the height of the tongue, the second is the front or the back of the tongue and the third is the shape of the lips. The vowel systems of Korean can be represented as in Table 45.1.

The vowels /ü/ and /ö/ have free variants [wi] and [we] respectively; thus, /kü/ 'ear' is pronounced either [kü] or [kwi] and /kömul/ 'strange creature' is pronounced either

Table 45.1 Korean Vowels

	Front Unrounded	Rounded	Back Unrounded	Rounded
High	i	ü	ŭ	u
Mid	e	ö	ə	o
Low	æ		a	

[kömul] or [kwemul]. The vowel *ŭ* is always pronounced [u] after labial sounds; *sŭlpʰŭta* is pronounced as [sŭlpʰuda] and *kamŭm* 'draught' is pronounced as [kamum].

Korean has a large number of morphophonemic alternations. As major examples of Korean morphophonemic processes involving vowels, we can name the following kinds: vowel harmony, glide formation, vowel contraction and vowel deletion. When non-finite endings starting with ə are attached to verbal bases, the initial *a* of the ending is changed to *a* after *a* and *o* as in *nok-əsə* 'melting' → [nokasə], and *mac-əsə* 'be hit' → [macasə]; elsewhere ə is not changed as in *mək-əsə* 'eat' → [məkəsə], *kipʰəsə* 'deep' → [kipʰəsə], *kæ-əsə* 'clear' → [kæəsə] and so on.

The vowels *o*, *i* and *a* undergo vowel contraction with the vowel *i* when the vowels in verbal bases and other morphemes such as the causative and passive are combined with each other. Korean has the following kinds of vowel contraction; *o+i* → *ö: po-i-ta* 'be seen' → [pöta]; *ə+i* → *e: sə-iu-ta* 'raise' → [seuta]; *a+i* → *æ: ca-iu-ta* 'make sleep' → [cæuta]; *u+i* → *ü: pak'u-i-ta* 'be changed' → [pak'üta].

The front vowel *i* and the back vowels *u* and *o* of verbal bases undergo glide formation when they are immediately connected to ə or *a* of suffixes such as -ə and -əsə; *i* becomes *y* and *u* and *o* become *w*: *ki-əsə* 'crawl' → [kyəsə], *tu-əsə* 'leave' → [twəsə] and *po-asə* 'see' → [pwasə]. As examples of vowel deletion, Korean has two kinds. *ŭ*-deletion and ə-deletion. When verbal bases ending in the vowel *ŭ* are attached to an ending starting with the vowel ə, the vowel *ŭ* is deleted: *s'ŭ-ə* 'write' → [s'ə] and *k'ŭ-əsə* 'extinguish' → [k'əsə].

Finally, ə-deletion occurs when endings starting with the vowel ə are combined with verbal bases ending with the vowels *e*, *æ*, ə and *a*; thus we have the following examples: *se-əs'ta* 'counted' → [ses'ta], *kæ-əsə* 'clear' → [kæsə], *sə-ə* 'stand' → [sə] and *ka-əto* 'even if he goes' → [kato]. Interestingly, the vowels which force ə-deletion are those vowels which do not undergo either glide formation or *ŭ*-deletion, i.e. *i*, *u* and *o* undergo glide formation; *ü* and *ö* have free variant forms [wi] and [we] respectively as in *tü-əs'-ta* 'jumped' → [twiəs'ta] and *k'ö-əs'ta* 'lured' → [kweəs'ta]; *ŭ* is deleted before ə as in *s'ŭ-əs'ta* 'wrote' → [s'əs'ta]. From the above discussion of glide formation and vowel deletion, we can see that all the vowels in the Korean vowel system participate in phonological processes without exception when verbal bases are combined with suffixes starting in ə.

Of the 21 consonants, there are nine stops, three affricates, three fricatives, three nasals, one liquid and two semi-vowels. The Korean consonants can be illustrated as in Table 45.2.

Let us now briefly describe the sound of Korean obstruents (stops, affricates and fricatives). The Korean laxed obstruents are weaker than English voiceless obstruents with respect to the degree of voicelessness. This seems to be due to the fact that Korean obstruents have two other stronger voiceless consonants, the tensed and the aspirated. The laxed obstruents are produced without voice and without aspiration and glottal tension. However, the laxed stops and affricates /p,t,k,c/ are pronounced as the voiced obstruents [b,d,g,j] when they occur between two voiced sounds. Even if some voiceless obstruents have voiced allophones, Korean speakers are not aware of this change. For instance, the word /aka/ 'baby' is pronounced [aga] because /k/ occurs between two vowels, which are voiced sounds.

The Korean aspirated obstruents are produced with stronger aspiration than English aspirated sounds. The Korean tensed obstruents are one of the most peculiar sounds among Korean consonants. The tensed obstruents are produced with glottal tension, but these sounds are not glottal sounds or ejectives. For instance, the Korean /t'/ is phonetically

Table 45.2 Korean Consonants

	Manner	Point	Labial	Dental	Palatal	Velar	Glottal
Stops	voiceless	laxed	p	t		k	
		aspirated	p^h	t^h		k^h	
		tensed	p'	t'		k'	
Affricates	voiceless	laxed			c		
		aspirated			c^h		
		tensed			c'		
Fricatives	voiceless	laxed		s			h
		tensed		s'			
Nasals	voiced		m	n		ŋ	
Liquid	voiced			l			
Semi-vowels			w	y			

similar to the sound [t'] in English which is pronounced after [s] in the word *stop* [stap]; however, the Korean tensed obstruent must be pronounced with more glottal tension.

Liquids and semi-vowels need some explanation. The Korean liquid /l/ has two variants; one is the lateral [l] and the other the flap [r]. The liquid /l/ is pronounced as the lateral [l] in word-final position and in front of another consonant as in *tal* [tal] 'moon' and *salku* [salgu] 'apricot', and as the flap [r] in word-initial position and between two vowels as in *tali* [tari] 'leg'. The Korean semi-vowels, /w/ and /y/, occur only as on-glides, never as off-glides as in *waŋ* 'king' and *yaŋ* 'sheep'.

In the above, the general qualities of Korean consonants were briefly described. Let us now discuss some of the phonological processes affecting Korean consonants. In pronunciation, consonants are always unreleased in word-final position and before another obstruent. Because of this, consonants belonging to a given phonetic group are pronounced identically in word-final position and before other obstruents. For instance, the labial stops /p/, /p^h/ and /p'/ are all neutralised into /p/ in word-final position; in the same manner, the velar stops /k/, /k^h/ and /k'/ are neutralised to /k/. The largest group of consonants comprises the dental and palatal obstruents, which are pronounced /t/: /t/, /t^h/, /t'/, /c/, /c^h/, /c'/, /s/ and /s'/. When examining consonant clusters, it is found that only single consonants occur in both initial and final position of words. Consonant clusters occur only in medial position in words and only clusters of two consonants are permitted to occur there. Some words have final two-consonant clusters in their base forms, but only one consonant is pronounced and the other consonant is deleted; for instance, the word /talk/ 'chicken' has the *lk* cluster in its base, but it is pronounced [tak], losing *l* when it is pronounced alone. However, the cluster *lk* occurs in inter-vocalic positions: /talk/+/i/ → [talki]. When the final cluster occurs before a consonant, again one consonant must be deleted as in word-final position to obey the two consonant constraint; e.g. /talk/ 'chicken' + /tali/ 'leg' [taktali] 'chicken leg'.

One of the most interesting characteristics of Korean phonology is its rich consonant assimilation. Korean consonant assimilation comprises nasalisation, labialisation, dentalisation, velarisation, palatalisation and liquid assimilation. Of these, nasalisation is the most productive; for instance, the stops *k*, *t* and *p* (including the neutralised stops) become *ŋ*, *n* and *m* respectively before nasals: /kukmul/ 'soup' → [kuŋmul], /patnŭnta/

'receive' → [pannŭnda], and /capnŭnta/ 'catch' → [camnŭnda]. As another example of nasalisation, the liquid *l* becomes *n* after the nasals *m* and *ŋ* and the stops *k*, *t*, *p*: e.g. /kamlo/ 'sweet' → [kamno], /pækli/ 'one hundred *li*' → [pækni], /matlyaŋpan/ 'the head of the family' → [matnyaŋpan] and /aplyək/ 'press' → [apnyək]. Interestingly, in the last three examples, the stop sounds which caused *l* to nasalise assimilate to the following new nasals and become nasals themselves: [pækni] → [pæŋni], [matnyaŋban] → [mannyaŋban] and [apnyək] → [amnyək]; thus these three examples undergo two nasalisation processes.

The consonant *h* behaves interestingly in medial positions; when *h* occurs in intervocalic position, it is deleted: /cohŭn/ 'good' → [coŭn]; and when *h* occurs before laxed stops and affricates, metathesis takes place as in the following example: /hayah-ta/ 'white' → [hayatha] → [hayatʰa]. As another example of consonant deletion, we can name *l*-deletion: when the consonant *l* occurs in the initial position, it is deleted: /lyaŋpan/ 'aristocrat' → [yaŋban]. However, *l*-deletion in the initial position is not absolute, because *l* is changed to *n* in the same position depending on the following vowels, as in /lokuk/ 'Russia' → [noguk]. Thus, the right way of explaining the *l* phenomena would be to say that the consonant *l* does not occur in initial position.

Thus far, we have seen the Korean phonemic system and some of its phonological processes. In the remaining portion of this section, the Korean writing system will be briefly presented.

As can be seen from Table 45.3, the Korean alphabet, which is called *Han'gŭl*, consists of 40 letters: 10 pure vowels, 11 compound vowels, 14 basic consonants and 5 double consonants. The Korean writing system is based on the 'one letter per phoneme' principle. However, comparing the number of phonemes with the number of letters, it is found that the writing system has nine more letters. This is because the diphthongs are also represented by their own letters. Thus, the semi-vowels *y* and *w* do not have their own independent letters. They are always represented together with other vowels occurring with them. For instance, the letter ㅑ is a combination of *y* and *a*, and the letter ㅘ is a combination of *w* and *a*.

As a general rule, in writing, Korean letters are formed with strokes from top to bottom and from left to right. The letters forming a syllable have a sequence of CV(C)(C) and they are arranged as a rebus: e.g. *ka* 'go' → 가; *kak* 'each' 각; *talk* 'chicken' 닭. One interesting thing about the Korean writing system is that a vowel cannot be written alone; for instance, *a* cannot be written as ㅏ and *u* cannot be written as ㅜ. In the Korean writing system, the absence of a consonant is represented by a ∅ consonant, which is shown by the symbol ㅇ and written to the left or top of the vowel. Thus, *a* is written as 아 and *u* is written as 우. For instance, the word *au* 'brother' which consists of the two vowels *a* and *u*, is written as 아우.

3 Morphology

Korean words can be divided into two classes: inflected and uninflected. The uninflected words are nouns, particles, adverbs and interjections. Inflected words are classed as action verbs, descriptive verbs, copula and existential. The distinction between action and descriptive verbs can be shown by the way in which paradigmatic forms such as propositive and processive are combined with verbal forms. For instance, a descriptive verb lacks propositive and processive forms. Thus, whereas the action verb

Table 45.3 Korean Alphabet

Letter	Transcription	Letter	Transcription
Pure vowels:			
ㅣ	/i/	ㅡ	/ü/
ㅔ	/e/	ㅓ	/ə/
ㅐ	/æ/	ㅏ	/a/
ㅟ	/ü/	ㅜ	/u/
ㅚ	/ö/	ㅗ	/o/
Compound consonants:			
ㅑ	/ya/	ㅘ	/wa/
ㅒ	/yæ/	ㅙ	/wæ/
ㅕ	/yə/	ㅝ	/wə/
ㅖ	/ye/	ㅞ	/we/
ㅛ	/yo/	ㅢ	/ŭi/
ㅠ	/yu/		
Consonants:			
ㄱ	/k/	ㅇ	/ŋ/
ㄴ	/n/	ㅈ	/c/
ㄷ	/t/	ㅊ	/cʰ/
ㄹ	/l/	ㅋ	/kʰ/
ㅁ	/m/	ㅌ	/tʰ/
ㅂ	/p/	ㅍ	/pʰ/
ㅅ	/s/	ㅎ	/h/
Double consonants:			
ㄲ	/k'/	ㅆ	/s'/
ㄸ	/t'/	ㅉ	/c'/
ㅃ	/p'/		

plus the propositive *ca* or the processive *nŭn* is grammatical, the combinations of descriptive verbs with the same endings are not: *mək-ca* 'let's eat' and *mək-nŭn-ta* 'is eating' but *alŭmtap-ca 'let's be beautiful' and *alŭmtap-nŭn-ta 'is being beautiful'. While the copula behaves like a descriptive verb, the existential behaves like an action verb with respect to conjugation; thus, *i-ca 'let's be' and *i-n-ta 'is being' are ungrammatical but *is'-ca* 'let's stay' and *is'-nŭn-ta* 'is staying' are grammatical.

As predictable from the above discussion, each inflected form consists of a base plus an ending. Bases and endings can be classed into groups according to the ways in which alternant shapes of bases are combined with endings. There are two kinds of ending: one-shape endings such as *-ko*, *-ta*, *-ci* and *-kes'* and two-shape endings such as *-sŭpnita/-ŭpnita*, *-ŭna/-na* and *-ŭn/-n*. Two-shape endings are phonologically conditioned alternants; thus, for instance, the formal form *-sŭpnita* occurs only with base forms ending in a consonant, but the alternant form of the formal form *-pnita* occurs only with base forms ending in a vowel. Based on these classes of endings, verb bases can be divided into two groups: consonant bases (i.e. bases ending in a consonant) and vowel bases (i.e. bases ending in a vowel). There are, however, some classes of bases whose final sounds are changed when attached to endings. Thus, in addition to regular bases which do not alter when combined with the ending, there are about five classes of consonant bases which alter with the ending: bases ending in *t*, bases ending in *w*, bases ending in *h*, bases ending in sonorants and *s*-dropping bases. Vowel bases have three classes in addition to the regular vowel bases: *l*-extending vowel bases, *l*-doubling bases and *l*-inserting vowel bases.

In order to see how the base form is changed when it is attached to the endings, the partial conjugation of regular and irregular bases ending in *t* is illustrated:

	Irregular	*Regular*
Base	/mut-/ 'ask'	/tat-/ 'close'
Gerund	[muk-ko]	[tak-ko]
Suspective	[muc-ci]	[tac-ci]
Formal Statement	[mus-sŭmnita]	[tas-sŭmnita]
Infinitive	[mul-ə]	[tat-ə]
Adversative	[mul-ŭna]	[tat-ŭna]

When comparing the two base forms, *mut* 'ask' and *tat* 'close', ending in *t*, it is found that both forms undergo morphophonemic changes when combined with endings starting with a consonant. These morphophonemic changes are phonologically conditioned; *t* is changed to *k* before *k*; *t* is changed to *s* before *s* and so on. However, *t* is changed to *l* before vowels only in the base *mut*, but not in the base *tat*.

Below, the partial conjugation of an *l*-inserting vowel base is illustrated together with the conjugation of an ordinary vowel base.

	Irregular	*Regular*
Base	/pʰulŭ-/ 'be blue'	/t'alŭ-/ 'obey'
Gerund	[pʰulŭ-ko]	[t'alŭ-ko]
Suspective	[pʰulŭ-ci]	[t'alŭ-ci]
Formal Statement	[pʰulŭ-mnita]	[t'alŭ-mnita]
Infinitive	[pʰulŭl-ə]	[t'al-ə]
Adversative	[pʰulŭl-ŭna]	[t'al-ŭna]

In regular vowel bases such as *t'alŭ-*, the final vowel is deleted when attached to the endings starting with a vowel, as shown in the conjugation of the infinitive and the adversative. However, in the case of irregular vowel bases such as *pʰulŭ-*, *l* is inserted before the same endings.

The number of endings which can be attached to the base is said to be over 400. In finite verb forms, there are seven sequence positions where different endings can occur: honorific, tense, aspect, modal, formal, aspect and mood. The honorific marker (*ŭ*)*si* is attached to the base to show the speaker's intention or behaviour honouring the social status of the subject of the sentence. Tense has marked and unmarked forms; the marked form is past and the unmarked form present. The past marker (*ə*)*s'* has the meaning of a definite, completed action or state.

With respect to an event that has occurred in the past, there are two constructions, (*ə*)*s'-əs'* and *tə*, which refer to the past event expressing the meaning of modality: experiential-contrastive and perceptual evidential respectively. The experiential-contrastive (*ə*)*s'-əs'*, which has the same form as the past tense marker and only occurs after the past tense, has been called 'the double past'. The two sentences, *John i hakkyo e ka-s'-ta* and *John i hakkyo e ka-s'-əs'-ta*, are usually translated in the same way as 'John went to school'. However, this does not mean that they have the same meaning. To translate them more precisely, the first sentence merely indicates the fact that the subject has gone to school and is there now. But the second sentence has the meaning that the subject has had the experience of being in school or that he had been in school before but has come back to the place where he is now. Thus, the two sentences have quite different meanings. Only the second sentence has a modal meaning of experiential-contrastive.

The perceptual evidential *tə* indicates that the speaker perceived something in the past and reports it in the present situation. The sentence *John i cip e ka-tə-la* has roughly the meaning 'I observed that John was going home and now I report to you what I observed'.

The modal *kes'* has the meaning indicating the speaker's volition or supposition and is used both for a definite future and a probable present or past. When the modal *kes'* is attached to a verb whose subject is first person, the sentence only has the volitional meaning and is used only with reference to the future: *næ ka næil ka-kes'-ta* 'I will go tomorrow' but **næ ka næil ka-s'-kes'-ta*. When the modal *kes'* occurs in a sentence whose subject is second or third person, the sentence has only the suppositional meaning and is used for both a definite future and a probable present or past: *Mary ka næil ka-kes'-ta* 'I suppose that Mary will go tomorrow' and *Mary ka əce ka-s'-kes'-ta* 'I suppose that Mary left yesterday'.

The formal form *sŭpni/pni* is used for the speaker to express politeness or respect to the hearer: *onŭl təp-sŭpni-ta* 'it is hot today' and *onŭl təp-ta* 'it is hot today'. The only difference between the two sentences is the presence or absence of the polite form *sŭpni* in the verbal form. The first sentence could be used for addressing those whose social status is superior to the speaker's but the second sentence would be used for addressing one who is inferior or equal to the speaker in social status (here, social status includes social position, age, sex, job, etc.).

Among a large number of mood morphemes, the most typical moods are declarative, interrogative, imperative and propositive. In Korean, sentence types such as declarative, interrogative, imperative and propositive sentences are identified by the mood morphemes: *ta*, *k'a*, *la* and *ca*. These mood morphemes occur in the final position of finite verbal forms, e.g. declarative: *ka-pni-ta* 'he is going'; interrogative: *ka-pni-k'a* 'is he going?'; imperative: *ka-la* 'go'; propositive: *ka-ca* 'let's go'.

One of the outstanding characteristics in mood-ending morphemes such as *kun*, *ne*, *nun-te* and *ci* is that the various modality meanings are expressed by these morphemes. Modality is concerned with the speaker's attitude or opinion towards the content of the sentence expressed or the situation that the sentence describes. In the following two sentences: *pi ka o-nŭn-kun* 'it's raining' and *pi ka o-ne*, both *kun* and *ne* express the speaker's surprising attitude towards what he is currently observing, but *ne* expresses the additional meaning that what he observed is unexpected or contrary to what he expected. In the sentence *pi ka o-nun-te*, *te* expresses the same modal meaning as *kun* and *ne* do, but it implies the additional meaning that the speaker or the hearer has to do something for the event expressed by the uttered sentence. The ending *ci* expresses the meaning soliciting the hearer's consent or agreement in the following sentence: *pi ka o-ci* 'it's raining, isn't it'.

Thus far, we have seen suffixes occurring at the position of verbal endings, namely, finite verbal forms. However, there are three suffixes *nun*, *(ŭ)n* and *(ŭ)l* which occur at non-finite verbal forms and refer to the present, past and future respectively. These suffixes function to modify the following nouns in adnominal (or relative) clauses: *ka-nŭn salam* 'the person who is going', *ka-n salam* 'the person who went' and *ka-l salam* 'the person who will go'.

Among the three suffixes *nun*, *(ŭ)n* and *(ŭ)l*, the suffix *(ŭ)l* is the most interesting because it forms many periphrastic constructions with different grammatical elements such as dependent nouns, verbs, sentential endings and conjunctives. The newly formed periphrastic constructions function as modals expressing many different modal meanings including possibility, probability, counter-factuality, volition, admonition, fear, future and hypothetical concession. The following are just two examples of these modal constructions expressing epistemic possibility and ability: *John i hankuk e ka-l ci mol-ŭn-ta* 'John may go to Korea' and *John i i il ŭl ha-l su is'-ta* 'John can do this work'. In the first sentence, the modal construction consists of the suffix *l*, the complementiser *ci*, and the verb *molŭ* 'not to know', while in the second sentence, the modal construction consists of the suffix *l*, the dependent noun *su*, and the verb *is'* 'to exist'.

Passive and causative verbal forms can be derived by adding suffixes to bases. There are several passive and causative suffixes such as *i*, *hi* and *li* which have common shapes. Generally, causative suffixes can be divided into three groups according to the vowel in the suffix: *i*-theme causatives, *u*-theme causatives and *æ*-theme causatives. Passive suffixes can be grouped with the *i*-theme causative because their theme vowel is only *i*. Because both causative and passive suffixes have identical shapes, homonymous causative and passive verbal forms are frequently produced from the same base: *k'ak'-i* 'cause to cut' and *k'ak'-i* 'be cut' from the base *k'ak'* 'cut'; *anc-hi* 'seat' and *anc-hi* 'be seated' from *anc* 'sit'. Besides the causative morphemes -*i*- and -*hi*-, there are -*ki*-, *uk^hi*-, -*ik^h*-, -*li*-, -*liu*- and -*iu*- morphemes in *i*-theme causatives.

In addition to lexical causatives and passives which are derived from the combination of verb bases with the causative or passive suffixes, Korean has periphrastic causatives and passives. The periphrastic causative is formed by the combination of verb base with the adverbial ending -*ke* followed by the verb *ha* 'do', e.g. *ip-ke-ha-n-ta* 'make (someone) put on'. Some verbs take both lexical and periphrastic causatives, but some other verbs take only periphrastic causatives. Comparing the two types of causative, periphrastic causatives are more productive than lexical causatives in Korean.

In Korean, passives are not so commonly used as in some other languages, such as English or Japanese. There are many transitive verbs which do not undergo passivisation; for instance, the verb *cu* 'give' does not undergo either lexical or periphrastic passivisation. Thus, the number of transitive verbs which undergo passive formation with the passive suffix is limited to a certain group of verbs. There are two kinds of verbs which undergo periphrastic passivisation: one is a group of verbs which take an inchoative verb *ci* and the other a group of verbs which take an inchoative verb *tö* in their passive formation. The passive of the first group is formed by adding the infinitive ending *ə* to the base followed by the inchoative verb *ci*: *pusu-ə ci-ta* 'be broken'. All the transitive verbs which take the inchoative verb *tö* in passive formation are derived from Chinese-originated loan verbs plus the verbaliser *ha*. In the passive formation of these verbs, the verbaliser *ha* is changed to the inchoative verb *tö*; thus, the passive of *sæŋkakha-ta* 'think' is *sæŋkaktö-ta* 'be thought'.

Finally, there are a great number of nouns which are derived from verbs by adding the nominalising morphemes to verbal bases. There are three nominalisers *ki*, *ŭm/m* and *i* which can be added to the base. As examples of derived nouns, we have the following: *ki*-derived nouns: *talliki* 'running', *næki* 'bet', *c^haki* 'kicking' and *poki* 'example'; *ŭm/m*-derived nouns: *əlŭm* 'ice', *cam* 'sleep', *k'um* 'dream' and *chum* 'dance'; *i*-derived nouns: *kəli* 'hanger', *noli* 'game', *kili* 'length' and *nəlpi* 'width'. Though there is no general rule deciding which nominaliser is attached to which base, more nouns are derived from verbal bases by adding the nominalisers *ŭm/m* and *i* than the nominaliser *ki*.

4 Syntax

In this brief sketch of Korean syntax, the discussion will concentrate on representative examples which make Korean different from many Indo-European languages, especially English. One of the most frequently cited features of Korean syntax is the word order. Korean is a SOV language, meaning that the basic word order of transitive sentences is subject–object–verb. Korean has a relatively free word order compared to English; here, the phrase 'relatively free' means that Korean is not a completely free word order language. The Korean language obeys a strict grammatical constraint requiring that the sentence end with a verb. As long as the sentence obeys this constraint, a permutation of the major constituents in a sentence is permissible; thus, the sentence *John i Mary eke cʰæk ŭl cu-əs'-ta* 'John gave a book to Mary' can also be said in the following ways: *John i cʰæk ŭl Mary eke cu-əs'-ta*; *Mary eke John i cʰæk ŭl cu-əs'-ta*; *cʰæk ŭl John i Mary eke cu-əs'-ta'*; *cʰæk ŭl Mary eke John i cu-əs'-ta*. However, the following sentences are ungrammatical: **John i Mary eke cu-əs'-ta cʰæk ŭl*; **John i cu-əs'-ta cʰæk ŭl Mary eke*. The ungrammaticality of the last two sentences is due to the violation of the verb-final constraint.

In the above examples of Korean sentences, the grammatical elements *i*, *eke* and *ŭl* are postpositional particles corresponding to the cases nominative, dative and accusative. There are other kinds of postpositional particles such as *e* 'to/at', *esə* 'at/in', *to* 'also', *nŭn* 'topic', *putʰə* 'from' and *k'aci* 'to/till'. All these particles must occur after nouns, but some of them can occur after other particles; *ice putʰə to ha-l-su is'-ta* 'we can do it from now, too'; *uli tosəkwan e nŭn cʰæk i manh-ta* 'in our library, there are many books'.

Comparing the Korean example with its English translation, it is found that *cʰæk* 'book' in Korean does not have any number marker, singular or plural, whereas *books* in the English translation has a plural marker *s*. This does not mean that Korean does not have a plural marker. In Korean, the plural marker attachment is not so obligatory as in English. Especially in cases where quantifiers or numerals appear in sentences as in the above example, the plural marker is usually not attached to the noun. Another characteristic of number in Korean is that the plural marker can be attached to adverbs, e.g. *p'alli-tŭl il ŭl ha-n-ta* 'they do work fast'. In the example, the plural marker *tŭl* is attached to the adverb *p'alli* 'fast'. Usually, in this kind of sentence, the subject is deleted, but it is understood that the subject of the sentence is plural instead of singular owing to the presence of the plural marker on the adverb.

When nouns occur with numerals, classifiers are attached to numerals almost obligatorily. Korean has a rich system of classifiers. Each classifier is related to a class of nouns. In other words, a certain classifier occurs only with a certain class of nouns, e.g. *cʰæk han-kwən* 'one volume of a book'; *mækcu tu-pyəŋ* 'two bottles of beer'; *namu han-kŭlu* 'one tree'; *coŋi han-caŋ* 'one piece of paper'. Another interesting thing with respect to numerals is that there is an alternative word order. Thus, the sequence of numeral + classifier, which occurs after nouns in the above examples, can also occur before nouns. When this floating takes place, the genitive particle *ŭi* is inserted between numeral + classifier and the noun: *han-kwən ŭi cʰæk* 'one volume of a book'; *tu-pyəŋ ŭi mækcu* 'two bottles of beer'; *han-kŭlu ŭi namu* 'one tree'; *han-caŋ ŭi coŋi* 'one piece of paper'.

As may have been noticed in some of the examples, deletion of subjects is allowable as long as subjects are recoverable from linguistic or non-linguistic context. Deletion of the first person and second person in Korean is especially free, as in *cʰæk ul sa tŭli-kes'-ŭpni-ta* 'I will buy you a book'; *ɔnce t'ɔna-seyo?* 'When do you leave?' In the first sentence, the first person subject is deleted and in the second, the second person subject is deleted because these subjects are recoverable in a discourse context. Although deletion of the third person subject is not so common as deletion of first and second person subjects, it is also possible: *Mary ka cip e kass-ŭlt'æ Ø upʰyɔnpætalpu lŭl manna-s'-ta* 'When Mary went home, she met the mailman'. The Ø indicates the position where the third person subject is deleted. In the last example, we discover another difference between Korean and English. In the English translation of the last Korean example, the noun *mailman* is preceded by the definite article *the*. This same noun could be preceded by the indefinite article *a*. This means that English has distinct definite and indefinite articles. But Korean does not have articles indicating definiteness or indefiniteness. Although definiteness is indicated by demonstratives in some cases, the distinction between definite and indefinite, in general, is not made in Korean.

Modifiers such as demonstratives, genitives, adjectives and relative clauses precede head nouns in Korean, e.g. *i cʰæk ŭn cæmiis'ta* 'this book is interesting'; **John ŭi** *apɔci nŭn ŭisa-ta* 'John's father is a doctor'; **yep'ŭn** *k'ocʰi is'-ta* 'there is a pretty flower'; **hakkyo e ka-ko is'-nŭn** *haksæŋ ŭn na ŭi chinku-ta* 'the student who is going to school is my friend'. All constituents in bold print are located to the left of the head noun. These modifying constituents make Korean a left-branching language. The notion of left-branching becomes clear in the following sentence containing three relative clauses [[[[*næ ka a-nŭn*] *haksæŋ i tani-nŭn*] *hakkyo ka is'-nŭn*] *tosi nŭn kʰŭ-ta*] '[the city [where the school is [where my friend goes [who I know is big]]]]'. One of the characteristics of the relative clause in Korean is that it lacks relative pronouns. Demonstratives can also be classified as one class of modifiers. Korean demonstratives have two distinct characteristics which differ from English demonstratives. First, Korean demonstratives cannot occur independently, i.e. they must occur with nouns. The second difference is that Korean demonstratives have a triple system, unlike that of English. In addition to the demonstratives 'this' and 'that', Korean has a demonstrative which has the meaning 'that over there': *i* 'this', *kŭ* 'that' and *cɔ* 'that over there'. The same triple system is found in demonstrative locative nouns, e.g. *yɔki* 'here', *kɔki* 'there' and *cɔki* 'yonder'.

Korean predicates do not agree in number, person or gender with their subjects. However, predicates show agreement with honorificness and politeness in different styles of speech. Three main levels of speech are distinguished with respect to politeness: plain, polite and deferential. Many other speech levels can also be represented among these three basic speech levels by different endings. The three main speech levels of declarative sentences have the following ending forms: plain: *ta*; polite: *yo*; deferential: *(sŭ)pnita*. Thus, when the speaker expresses his politeness towards the hearer, either the polite or the deferential speech level is used, e.g. *sɔnsæŋnim i cip e ka-yo* 'the teacher is going home'; *sɔnsæŋnim i cip e ka-pnita*. In contrast to this, when the speaker does not express any particular politeness towards the hearer, the plain speech level is used; e.g. *sɔnsæŋnim i cip e ka-n-ta*.

If the speaker wants to express his respect towards the referent of the subject, the honorific marker *si* is inserted between verbal bases and endings: e.g. *sɔnsæŋnim i cip e ka-si-ɔyo*; *sɔnsæŋnim i cip e ka-si-pnita*; *sɔnsæŋnim i cip e ka-si-n-ta*. In the last example, the insertion of the honorific marker *si* is possible in the predicate of a sentence ending in the plain speech level, since the honorificness is expressed to the subject, but not to the hearer. In the above example, if the subject is a student instead of a teacher, then unacceptable sentences are produced: *haksæŋ i hakkyo e ka-si-əyo; *haksæŋ i hakkyo e ka-si-pnita; *haksæŋ i hakkyo e ka-si-nta. The ungrammaticality of the last examples is due to the violation of agreement between the subject and the predicate with respect to honorificness. In other words, the subject haksæŋ 'student' cannot occur with the predicate containing the honorific marker si, because haksæŋ belongs to the class of nouns which cannot be referred to with the honorific marker si.

Let us now turn to negation. Korean has three different negative morphemes: an, ma and mos. The morpheme an occurs in declarative and interrogative sentences and the morpheme ma occurs in propositive and imperative sentences, e.g. declarative: cip e an ka-n-ta 'I do not go home'; interrogative: cip e an ka-ni 'don't you go home?'; propositive: cip e ka-ci mal-ca 'let's not go home'; imperative: cip e ka-ci ma-la 'don't go home'. The remaining negative morpheme mos has the meaning 'cannot', e.g. cip e mos ka-n-ta 'I cannot go home'. There are three types of negation in Korean. In the first type, the negative morphemes an and mos occur immediately before the main verb, as in the declarative and interrogative, as in the last example. The other two types involve more complicated operations. In the second type, the negative behaves like the main predicate and the complementiser ci is incorporated, as in the propositive and imperative. The third type of negation involves the main predicate ha 'do' in addition to ci complementation; cip e ka-ci ani ha-n-ta 'I don't go home'; cip e ka-ci mos ha-n-ta 'I cannot go home'. From these three types of negation, we can observe different occurrences of negative morphemes. That is, while the negative morpheme an appears in all three types of negation, the morpheme mos appears in the first and third types of negation. The remaining negative morpheme ma appears only in the second type of negation.

As a final example of Korean syntactic characteristics, Korean sentential complements will be briefly discussed. Sentential complements are marked with the nominalisers kəs, ki, ŭm and ci and with the complementiser ko. Several differences exist between nominalisers and complementisers: first, case particles occur after nominalisers but cannot occur after complementisers: e.g. in the sentence na nŭn i cʰæk i cæmiis'-nŭn kəs ŭl a-n-ta 'I know that this book is interesting', the accusative particle ŭl occurs right after the nominaliser kəs, but in the sentence *na nŭn i cʰæk i cæmiis'ta ko lŭl sæŋkakha-n-ta 'I think that this book is interesting', the variant accusative particle lŭl cannot occur after the complementiser ko. Second, while the nominaliser is preceded by non-finite modifier forms -nŭn- and -n/ŭn-, the complementiser is preceded by the finite verbal ending form -ta. Third, the nominaliser occurs in both the subject and object positions, but the complementiser occurs only in object position. Sentential complements containing the nominaliser have different syntactic behaviour from sentential complements containing the complementiser. Sentential complements containing the nominaliser behave like regular noun phrases. Thus, whereas sentential complements with the nominaliser undergo syntactic processes such as topicalisation, pseudo-cleft formation, passivisation, noun phrase deletion and pronominalisation, sentential complements with the complementiser do not undergo the same syntactic processes. Of the above nominalisers and complementisers, ci is used as a question nominaliser and ko is used as quotative complementiser: na nŭn John i ənce o-nŭn ci molŭ-n-ta 'I do not know when John will come'; na nŭn John i næil o-n-ta ko malha-yəs'-ta 'I said that John would come tomorrow'.

Sentential complements containing ki can be differentiated from sentential complements containing ŭm/m by syntactic and semantic characteristics. In the majority of cases, ŭm/m is used for factive complements (i.e. complements whose truth is presupposed), but *ki* is used for non-factive complements. A given predicate will take only one of these two nominalisers, e.g. *na nŭn John i cip e ka-l-kəs ŭl wənha-n-ta* 'I want John to go home'; **na nŭn John i cip e ka m ŭl wənha-n~ta*; *na nŭn John i cip e ka m ŭl al-as'-ta* 'I knew that John was going home'; **na nŭn John i cip e ka ki lŭl al-as'-ta*. The examples show that the non-factive predicate *wənha* 'want' occurs only with *ki* and the factive predicate *al* 'know' occurs with *ŭm/m*. The nominaliser *kəs* occurs with both factive and non-factive complements: *na nŭn John i cip e ka-nŭn kəs ŭl wənha-n-ta* 'I want John to go home'; *na nŭn John i cip e ka-nŭn kəs ŭl al-as'-ta* 'I knew that John was going home'.

Bibliography

For a detailed general overview of Korean, reference may be made to Sohn (1999). For discussion of the origins and history of Korean, reference may be made to Chin Wu Kim (1974) and Ki-Moon Lee (1967), the latter also available in a German translation. Ho (1965), a monograph treatment of Korean phonology, is available only in Korean, but two studies are available in English: Martin (1954), a classic treatment of Korean morphophonemics, and B.K. Lee (1977), from the generative viewpoint. Among descriptive grammars, Choi (1954) is available only in Korean, while in English there is the monumental Martin (1992) and, in the Routledge Descriptive Grammars series, Sohn (1994); the pedagogical texts by Martin (1969) and Lukoff (1982) are also useful sources of general information on Korean grammar. Nam-Kil Kim (1984) is a study of Korean sentence complementation from a generative viewpoint.

References

Choi, Hyon Bae. 1954. *Uli Malbon* (Jŏngŭmsa, Seoul)

Ho, Woong. 1965. *Kukŏ Umunhak* (Jŏngŭmsa, Seoul)

Kim, Chin-Wu. 1974. *The Making of the Korean Language* (Center for Korean Studies, University of Hawaii, Honolulu)

Kim, Nam-Kil. 1984. *The Grammar of Korean Complementation* (Center for Korean Studies, University of Hawaii, Honolulu)

Lee, B.K. 1977. *Korean Generative Phonology* (Iljisa, Seoul)

Lee, Ki-Moon. 1967. 'Hankukŏ Hyŏngsŏngsa', in *Hankuk Munhwasa Taekye*, vol. 5 (Korea University Press, Seoul; also available in German translation, *Geschichte der koreanischen Sprache*, translated by B. Lewin, Dr Ludwig Reichert Verlag, Wiesbaden, 1977)

Lukoff, F. 1982. *An Introductory Course in Korean* (Yonsei University Press, Seoul)

Martin, S. 1954. *Korean Morphophonemics* (Linguistic Society of America, Baltimore)

—— 1969. *Beginning Korean* (Yale University Press, New Haven)

—— 1992. *A Reference Grammar of Korean* (Tuttle, Rutland and Tokyo)

Sohn, Ho-Min. 1994. *Korean* (Routledge, London)

—— 1999. *The Korean Language* (Cambridge University Press, Cambridge)

46

Austronesian Languages

Ross Clark

1 Membership, Distribution and Status

The name 'Austronesian' was coined in 1899 by P.W. Schmidt, combining two existing formatives, *Austro-* (Latin *auster* 'south') and *-nesian* (Greek *nesos* 'island'). Austronesian languages are in fact spoken primarily on islands rather than continental areas, and have a slight southern bias, though they are to be found on both sides of the Equator. The number of languages in the family is estimated at about a thousand. The core of 'Austronesia' includes Madagascar, Indonesia, the Philippines, Taiwan and the Pacific island groups of Melanesia, Micronesia and Polynesia. Apart from recent intrusions, the only non-Austronesian languages in this domain are found on the island of New Guinea (where Austronesian speakers are confined to coastal areas) and some islands near it, including Timor and Halmahera to the west and New Britain and Bougainville to the east.

Austronesia can be divided geographically at about 130 degrees east longitude, a line running just west of the Caroline Islands and New Guinea. The more than 600 languages spoken west of this line have a total of over 350 million speakers. Among these, Javanese has by far the largest number of speakers (at least 75 million), and also the longest written tradition (inscriptions dating from the early ninth century AD), embodying an important literature. Malay, with far fewer native speakers, has nevertheless achieved wider currency, as the lingua franca of the Malay Archipelago for several centuries, and now serves as a national language of Indonesia, Malaysia and Brunei. Other languages of regional importance in this area include Acehnese, Batak and Minangkabau of Sumatra, Sundanese of western Java, Madurese, Balinese and Sasak on islands east of Java, Iban and Ngadju of Borneo and Macassarese and Buginese of Sulawesi.

More than a hundred Austronesian languages are spoken in the Philippines. The national language (Pilipino) is based on Tagalog, which has 15 million native speakers in southwestern Luzon. Other important languages include Ilokano and Bikol, also of Luzon, and Cebuano and Hiligaynon (Ilongo) of the central islands.

The indigenous people of Taiwan (Formosa) spoke Austronesian languages, but large-scale Chinese settlement since the seventeenth century has made them a small minority of its population, living mainly in the mountainous interior and along the east coast, and subject to cultural and linguistic assimilation to the Chinese. About twenty Formosan languages have been recorded, of which half are now extinct or moribund, the remainder having perhaps 350,000 speakers in all.

The Austronesian presence on the Asian continent is confined to Malay (on the Malay Peninsula) and the Chamic languages. There are about ten Chamic languages, spoken by ethnic minorities in southern Vietnam and Cambodia, numbering about a million speakers all together. Another Chamic language, Tsat, is spoken by a few thousand people on Hainan Island in southern China.

The people of the Malagasy Republic, the far western outpost of Austronesia, speak a group of dialects diverse enough to be considered several different languages, though they are all conventionally referred to as Malagasy. Merina, spoken by about a quarter of the population, is the national standard.

The most striking contrast between the western and eastern regions of Austronesia is in the scale of the speech communities. There are over 400 languages in the eastern region, but the total number of speakers is fewer than 4 million – a figure exceeded by several individual languages of Indonesia and the Philippines. In Melanesia, one of the world's major foci of linguistic diversity, a typical language has only a few thousand or even a few hundred speakers. Among the larger Austronesian language communities in Melanesia are Tolai (60,000) at the eastern end of New Britain and Motu (15,000) on the south coast of New Guinea. Both these languages have acquired greater importance as a result of close contacts with European colonial administration, Tolai being spoken around the old German capital of Rabaul and Motu in the vicinity of Port Moresby, now the capital of Papua New Guinea. A simplified form of Motu (earlier called 'Police Motu' and now 'Hiri Motu') serves as lingua franca in much of the southern half of the country and has been recognised as one of the official languages of the National Parliament – the only Melanesian language to achieve such an official status. Other languages in Melanesia, while not necessarily having large numbers of speakers, have achieved regional importance through missionary use. Examples are Yabem and Gedaged on the north coast of New Guinea, Roviana in the western Solomon Islands and Mota in Vanuatu. The last, while spoken originally by only a few hundred people on one tiny island in the Banks group, has been widely used by Anglicans in both northern Vanuatu and the southeast Solomons.

While the typical pattern in Melanesia is one or more languages per island, in Fiji, Polynesia and Micronesia languages frequently extend over several neighbouring islands and correspondingly larger speech communities are common. Samoan (370,000 speakers), Tongan (100,000) and Fijian (330,000) are national languages of independent states. Other Polynesian languages in wide use are Tahitian (120,000), a lingua franca throughout French Polynesia; and Rarotongan or Cook Islands Maori (40,000). Several Polynesian languages are now also spoken by sizable emigrant communities in New Zealand, the United States and elsewhere.

Hawaii and New Zealand have had a linguistic history very different from that of the rest of Polynesia. Until the end of the eighteenth century both were populated entirely by Polynesians, but over the following hundred years massive intrusion by Europeans (and also Asians in the case of Hawaii) reduced the indigenous population to a relatively powerless minority, whose language was largely excluded from public life and actively suppressed in the schools. In the twentieth century, the erosion of Polynesian-speaking rural communities by migration to the cities and the spread of English-language mass communications have accelerated the decline. There are now fewer than a thousand native speakers of Hawaiian. New Zealand Maori, with more than 20,000 native speakers, seems in less immediate danger. But in both places the native-speaker population is aging, and very few communities use the language as an everyday medium. Nevertheless, increased formal teaching of both languages (from pre-school immersion to university level) has produced a significant number of second-language speakers with varying degrees of skill, and progress has been made in public use and official recognition. Both languages continue to have an important role as vehicles for the arts of oratory and poetry, and as symbols of Polynesian identity in their respective countries.

The small and scattered islands of Micronesia have about a dozen languages among them. Some of these are spread over wide areas, such as Chuukic dialect chain occupying much of the western Caroline Islands, with about 60,000 speakers; Chamorro, spoken on Guam and the Marianas Islands to the north (75,000); and the languages of the Marshall Islands (45,000) and Kiribati (70,000). Others, such as the languages of Belau (Palau), Yap, Ponape, Kosrae (Kusaie), Nauru and the Polynesian atolls Nukuoro and Kapingamarangi, are restricted to single islands or compact groups.

2 Comparative Austronesian

The connection between Malagasy and Malay was recognised by Dutch writers in the early seventeenth century. At about the same time the Dutch traders Lemaire and Schouten were collecting the first Polynesian word lists. Though there is no explicit comment, the inclusion of Malay words in these accounts indicate that at least some of the crew were familiar with Malay, and resemblances such as the following can hardly have escaped their notice:

	Malay	*Futuna (Polynesian)*
'two'	dua	lua
'five; hand'	lima	lima
'eye'	mata	mata
'car'	telinga	talinga
'liver'	hati	'ate
'stone'	batu	fatu
'fish'	ikan	ika
'yam'	ubi	'ufi
'taro'	talas	talo

The major languages of Indonesia and the Philippines were readily seen to belong to the same family, as were Tongan, Hawaiian, Maori and other Polynesian languages that became known to Europeans during the eighteenth century. Many Melanesian and Micronesian languages, however, had undergone such extensive phonological and lexical changes that their Austronesian origins were much less apparent, and it was not until the early twentieth century that the full extent of the family was understood.

The German scholar Otto Dempwolff, in the 1920s and 1930s, laid the foundations of comparative Austronesian linguistics. He demonstrated the regular sound correspondences among many of the better-known languages and reconstructed a large number of words of the ancestral language, Proto-Austronesian. Dempwolff also made an important advance in subgrouping (the establishment of the successive stages of differentiation from the ancestral language to the present diversity) by showing that almost all the languages of eastern Austronesia form a single subgroup. Earlier classifications had followed the geographical division into Indonesia, Melanesia, Micronesia and Polynesia and had been strongly influenced by the cultural and racial differences among Austronesian speakers. Dempwolff's group (now known as Oceanic) comprises all the languages of the eastern region with the exception of Palauan and Chamorro in Micronesia (which appear to have their closest connections in the Philippine area) and the languages of the western end of New Guinea, which group with Halmahera in eastern Indonesia.

Research since Dempwolff's time has greatly increased the amount of descriptive information on Austronesian languages from all areas. An issue of particular importance in comparative work has been the position of the Formosan languages, which Dempwolff did not treat for want of adequate data. Since the 1970s, R. Blust has argued for a subgrouping (Figure 46.1) in which the primary division of Austronesian is into several Formosan groups (originally three, later as many as nine) and a single non-Formosan group, for which Blust has proposed the term Malayo-Polynesian (formerly used as a synonym for Austronesian). Malayo-Polynesian in turn is divided into four subgroups, related as shown in the diagram. Central Malayo-Polynesian consists of about fifty languages of the Lesser Sunda Islands and the Moluccas, while South Halmahera–West New Guinea includes about forty-five languages, extending as far east as Cenderawasih Bay. This leaves two very large groups: Oceanic, as defined above, and Western Malayo-Polynesian, which comprises all the remaining languages of western Austronesia, along with Chamorro and Palauan. Since these two groups between them account for at least 80 per cent of Austronesian languages, including all the well-known ones, the earlier view of Austronesian as divided into an 'eastern' and a 'western' group now appears as a reasonable simplification.

Subgrouping of Austronesian remains a subject of argument at many points. There are dissenters from the primacy of Formosan, as shown above. While the unity of Oceanic is undisputed, it is unclear whether 'Western Malayo-Polynesian' is more than a residual category. Thirty or so local groupings can be defined, usually geographically coherent and ranging in size from a single language to several dozen. But what the intermediate units of classification are – or indeed whether there are any – is still unclear. Ross (1988) proposes a subgrouping of Oceanic with a primary division between the Admiralty Islands and the rest, followed by an East–West differentiation; but units within this schema are often defined by overlapping isoglosses rather than clear splits.

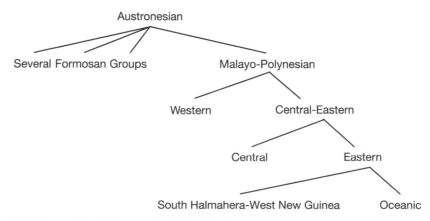

Figure 46.1 Subgrouping of Austronesian (after Blust).

A great deal of the comparative research on Austronesian languages has been inspired by curiosity as to the origins and migrations of the far-flung Austronesian-speaking peoples. The subgrouping just outlined has certain implications for these questions of prehistory. First, it supports the generally assumed progression of Austronesian speakers from somewhere in the southeast Asian islands, eastward by stages further and further into the Pacific. The view, popular with many nineteenth-century theorists, that particular areas of Oceania were peopled by long-distance migrations from particular islands in Indonesia, finds no support in the linguistic evidence.

Language relationships also shed some light on the remoter fringes of the Austronesian family. In the 1950s, O.C. Dahl showed that the closest relative of Malagasy was the Ma'anyan language of southeast Borneo. This gives a fairly precise homeland for the Austronesian traders who first settled Madagascar, apparently early in the Christian era.

At the other end of Austronesia, the migrations of the Polynesians have been a tempting subject for both science and fantasy. Linguistically, Polynesian is a clearly defined subgroup consisting of about twenty languages in the triangle defined by Hawaii, New Zealand and Easter Island, plus a further fifteen small enclaves in Melanesia and Micronesia. These latter 'outliers' have been shown to be most closely related to Samoan and its near neighbours in western Polynesia, from which they apparently dispersed westward over a long period of time. The close relatedness of all Polynesian languages suggests a fairly recent dispersal and this is consistent with archaeological evidence of the break-up of the original community in western Polynesia by about 500 BC and eventual settlement of the furthest islands of Polynesia by AD 1000.

The external relations of Polynesian also provide some clues as to the further origins of its speakers. Polynesian's closest relatives are Fijian and Rotuman, with which it makes up the Central Pacific group. Central Pacific, in turn, is related to languages of Vanuatu, the southeast Solomon Islands and Micronesia in a 'Central/Eastern Oceanic' subgroup. Once again the linguistic relationships suggest a progression by short moves rather than sudden trans-oceanic migrations.

A different approach to prehistory through language is via the study of the content of reconstructed vocabulary. In some cases this only confirms what has been generally assumed about the early Austronesians: for example, that they cultivated crops such as taro and yams and were familiar with sailing outrigger canoes. Recent work by Blust, however, has advanced more controversial hypotheses about material culture (rice cultivation, metal-working) and has combined linguistic with ethnographic data to reconstruct aspects of the social structure of the Proto-Austronesian community.

Is Austronesian related to any other language family? Certainly suggestions have not been wanting, but proposed links with Japanese or Indo-European have not been supported by any significant evidence. Hypotheses of a connection with Daic (Tai–Kadai), with Austroasiatic, and with Sino-Tibetan have all been investigated by serious scholars in recent years, but none has reached the point of being considered proven.

3 Structural Characteristics

Any generalisation about a large and diverse language family must be taken with caution, but certain structural features are sufficiently widespread to be considered typically Austronesian. These are shared by at least the more conservative languages in all regions, and were probably features of Proto-Austronesian.

The phonemic systems of Austronesian languages range from average complexity to extreme simplicity. Hawaiian, with just thirteen phonemes (*p, k, ?, h, m, n, l, w, i, e, a, o, u*), was long considered the world's simplest, but it now appears that non-Austronesian Rotokas of Bougainville (North Solomons Province, Papua New Guinea) has only eleven. Austronesian languages commonly allow only a restricted range of consonant clusters. Nasal + stop is the most widespread type, though in many Oceanic languages such phonetic sequences are treated as single prenasalised consonants. Final consonants were present in Proto-Austronesian, but have been categorically lost in many of the Oceanic languages. Lexical morphemes are typically bisyllabic.

Morphological complexity is likewise average to low. Nouns are suffixed for pronominal possessor in almost all Austronesian languages, though in Oceanic languages this is restricted to one category of possession. (See the description of Fijian below.) Verbs are prefixed, infixed or suffixed to indicate transitivity, voice and focus and to produce nominalised forms. Reduplication is extensively used to mark such grammatical categories as number and aspect. A distinct pronoun category for reference to both speaker and hearer (so-called 'first person inclusive') is virtually universal in Austronesian.

Word order in Austronesian is predominantly verb-initial or verb-second and prepositional. (A number of languages in the New Guinea area have become verb-final and postpositional under the influence of neighbouring non-Austronesian languages.) Articles, which often distinguish a 'proper' from a 'common' class of nouns, precede the noun; adjectives and relative clauses follow. The multi-voice 'focus' type of case marking most often associated with Philippine languages, but also found in Formosan languages, may have been a feature of Proto-Austronesian, but survives only in simplified form elsewhere.

Since three representative Western Malayo-Polynesian languages (Malay, Javanese and Tagalog) are described elsewhere in this volume, I will conclude this chapter with a brief sketch of some features of a typical Oceanic language, Fijian.

The dialects of Fiji, like those of Madagascar, are sufficiently diverse to be considered at least two, if not several, distinct languages. Standard Fijian, the national language, is based on the speech of the southeastern corner of the island of Viti Levu. This area has long been politically powerful and it is likely that its dialect was widely understood even before it was selected as a standard by Protestant missionaries in the 1840s. The examples given here are in the formal type of standard Fijian described in the grammars, which differs in some ways from colloquial usage.

Fijian has the following consonants (given in Fijian orthography, with unexpected phonetic values shown in square brackets):

Voiceless stops: t, k
Voiced (prenasalised) stops: b [^{m}b], d [^{n}d], q [^{ŋ}g]
Fricatives: v [β], s, c [ð]
Nasals: m, n, g [ŋ]
Liquids: l, r, dr [^{n}ɼ]
Semi-vowels: w, y

The vowels are *i, e, a, o* and *u*, all of which may be either long or short. Vowel length is not normally indicated in writing Fijian, but here it will be shown by doubling the vowel letter. This treatment makes it possible to state the position of the main word stress very simply: it falls on the second-last vowel of the word.

Fijian nouns can be divided into common and proper. Common nouns are preceded by the article *na* (*na vale* 'the house'). Proper nouns, which include names of persons and places as well as personal pronouns, are preceded by the article *ko* (*ko Viti* 'Fiji', *ko ira* 'they'). Certain expressions referring to persons, however, though they involve common nouns, may optionally be preceded by *ko*, sometimes with *na* following: *na ganequ* or *ko na ganequ* 'my sister'. This choice provides for subtle distinctions of intimacy and respect.

The Fijian personal pronouns express four categories of number and four of person. In standard Fijian the independent pronoun forms are as follows:

	Singular	Dual	Paucal	Plural
First Person ('exclusive')	au	keirau	keitou	keimami
Inclusive	—	kedaru	kedatou	keda
Second Person	iko	kemudrau	kemudou	kemunii
Third Person	koya	rau	iratou	ira

The paucal category refers to a small number, greater than two. (These pronouns are misleadingly termed 'trial' in Fijian grammars.) As explained above, the inclusive category is used when both speaker and hearer are included, whereas first person and second person definitely exclude the other. Thus *kedatou* could be paraphrased 'a small group of people including both you and me', and *keimami* as 'a large group of people including me but not including you'. It will be seen from the definitions that the inclusive singular form is missing because such a combination is logically self-contradictory.

Like most Oceanic languages, Fijian distinguishes more than one relation within what is broadly called 'possession'. In standard Fijian there are four possessive categories. Familiar (inalienable) possession includes the relation between whole and part, including parts of the body, and most kin relations. With a pronominal possessor, familiar possession is indicated by suffixing the possessor directly to the noun: *na yava-qu* 'my leg', *na tama-na* 'her father'. In each of the other three possessive categories, the possessor is suffixed not to the noun but to a distinctive possessive base which precedes it. Edible and drinkable possession, not surprisingly, include the relation of a possessor to something which is eaten or drunk: *na ke-mu dalo* 'your taro', *na me-dra tii* 'their tea'. Eating and drinking are of course culturally defined, so that tobacco counts as edible, whereas various watery foods such as oysters, oranges and sugar cane are drinkable. The edible category also includes certain intrinsic properties and relations of association: *na ke-na balavu* 'its length, his height', *na ke-na tuuraga* 'its (e.g. a village's) chief'. (This appears to be the result of the merger of two historically distinct categories, rather than any conceptual association of such relations with eating.) The fourth category, *neutral*, includes relations not covered by the three more specific types: *na no-qu vale* 'my house', *na no-mu cakacaka* 'your work'.

Certain nouns tend to occur typically with certain possessive types because of their typical relation to possessors in the real world. And there are certain cases of apparently arbitrary assignment: *na yate-na* 'his liver', but *na no-na ivi* 'his kidneys'. Nevertheless, the system cannot be explained as a simple classification of nouns. There are numerous examples of the same noun in two different possessive relations, with the appropriate difference of meaning: *na no-qu yaqona* 'my kava (which I grow or sell)', *na me-qu yaqona* 'my kava (which I drink)'; *na no-na itukutuku* 'her story, the story she tells', *na ke-na itukutuku* 'her story, the story about her'.

The essential elements of the Fijian verb phrase are the verb itself and a preposed pronoun: *daru lako* (incl.-du. go) 'let's go', *e levu* (3-sg. big) 'it's big'. Most verb phrases

787

also include one or more particles preceding or following the verb, which mark such categories as tense, aspect, modality, direction and emphasis: *keimami aa lako tale gaa mai* (1-pl. past go also just hither) 'we also came'; *era dui kanakana tiko* (3-pl. separately eat imperfective) 'they are eating each by himself'.

Transitivity is a highly developed lexical–semantic category in Fijian. A plain verb stem is normally intransitive and can be made transitive by the addition of a suffix: *lutu* 'fall', *lutu-ka* 'fall on (something)'; *gunu* 'drink', *gunu-va* 'drink (something)'; *boko* 'go out (of a fire, etc.)', *boko-ca* 'extinguish (something)'. As the examples show, the subject of the intransitive verb may correspond to the subject of the transitive (as with *lutu* and *gunu*) or to the object (as with *boko*).

The transitive suffixes just illustrated are all of the form *-Ca*, where C is a consonant (or zero). Which consonant is used must in general be learned as a property of a particular verb, though there is some correlation with verbal semantics. There are also transitive suffixes of the form *-Caka*, and many verbs may occur with either type of suffix. In such cases, the two transitive forms generally differ as to which additional participant in the action is treated as the object of the verb. Thus: *vana* 'shoot', *vana-a* 'shoot, shoot at (a person, a target, etc.)', *vana-taka* 'shoot with (a gun, a bow, etc.)'; *masu* 'pray', *masu-ta* 'pray to', *masu-laka* 'pray for'.

When the verb phrase is accompanied by a full noun phrase subject or object, the normal order is verb phrase–object–subject:

era	aa	rai-ca	na	yalewa	na	gone
3pl.	past	see-tr.	the	woman	the	child

'The children saw the woman.'

In this sentence the word order identifies *na yalewa* as object and *na gone* as subject. Note also that *na gone* is specified as plural not by marking on the noun phrase itself, but by its coreference with the subject pronoun *era* in the verb phrase.

When the object is proper (in the sense defined above), it occurs within the verb phrase, immediately following the verb, the proper article *ko* is dropped and the final vowel of the transitive suffix changes from *a* to *i*:

era	aa	rai-ci	Viti	kece	gaa	na	gone
3pl.	past	see-tr.	Fiji	all	just	the	child

'The children all saw Fiji.'

A non-singular human object requires a coreferent object pronoun in this position, which provides another possibility for number marking:

era	aa	rai-ci	rau	na	yalewa	na	gone
3pl.	past	see-tr.	3 du.	the	woman	the	child

'The children saw the two women.'

The transitive suffix in *-i* also appears in reciprocal and passive constructions:

era	vei-rai-ci	na	gone
3pl.	recip.-see-tr.	the	child

'The children look at each other'.

e	aa	rai-ci	ko	Viti
3sg.	past	see-tr.	art.	Fiji

'Fiji was seen.'

Note that in the last example the appearance of *ko* indicates that 'Fiji' is subject and not object.

It will be seen that -C*i* is the more general form of the transitive suffix and that -C*a* occurs only with third person objects which are either singular or non-human. If we take -C*a* to be a reduced form of -C*i-a*, where -*a* is a third person singular/non-human object pronoun, we see that the general rule is that all external object noun phrases must be accompanied by a coreferent object pronoun. This analysis is confirmed by the majority of Fijian dialects and other Oceanic languages.

Finally, Fijian has one verb–object structure where transitive marking does not appear. A generic or non-specific object immediately follows the verb, without suffix or article:

erau	rai	vale	tiko	na	yalewa
3du.	see	house	imperf.	the	woman

'The two women are looking at houses.'

Bibliography

The two volumes by Lynch et al. (2002) and Adelaar and Himmelmann (2005) together cover the entire Austronesian family, with survey articles on various topics and substantial descriptions of selected languages. Tryon (1995) also has survey articles, briefer sketches and a very large synonym-vocabulary of some eighty languages. For the geographical distribution of Austronesian languages, Wurm and Hattori (1981–4) is an indispensable work, covering all of Austronesia and several neighbouring families; in addition to excellent maps there is much information on subgrouping and numbers of speakers, as well as references to more detailed studies.

For comparative phonology, Dempwolff (1934–8) is still the fundamental work on comparative Austronesian. Blust's most recent statement on high-level subgrouping can be found in Blust (1999). Linguistic evidence concerning early Austronesian culture history is presented in Blust (1976, 1980). Ross (1988) is a landmark work on the subgrouping of Oceanic.

Grammars of Fijian include Churchward (1941), a concise but perceptive missionary grammar, and Milner (1972), ostensibly pedagogical but usable as reference; however, Schütz (1986) is the most comprehensive and systematic description to date, covering not only grammar and phonology but also the history of the study of the language, the development of the writing system, etc. Dixon (1988) is a detailed description of a non-standard Fijian dialect. Geraghty (1983) is the definitive study of Fijian linguistic diversity and its historical origins.

References

Adelaar, A. and Himmelmann, N.P. (eds) 2005. *The Austronesian Languages of Asia and Madagascar* (Routledge, London)

Blust, R. 1976. 'Austronesian Culture History: Some Linguistic Inferences and Their Relations to the Archaeological Record', *World Archaeology*, vol. 8, pp. 19–43

—— 1980. 'Early Austronesian Social Organization: The Evidence of Language', *Current Anthropology*, vol. 21, pp. 205–47

—— 1999. 'Subgrouping, Circularity and Extinction: Some Issues in Austronesian Comparative Linguistics', in E. Zeitoun and P.J.-K. Li (eds) *Selected Papers from the Eighth International Conference on Austronesian Linguistics* (Academia Sinica, Taipei), pp. 31–94

Churchward, C.M. 1941. *A New Fijian Grammar* (reprinted by Government Press, Suva, 1973)

Dempwolff, O. 1934–8. *Vergleichende Lautlehre des austronesischen Wortschatzes*, 3 vols (Dietrich Reimer, Berlin)

Dixon, R.M.W. 1988. *A Grammar of Boumaa Fijian* (University of Chicago Press, Chicago)

Geraghty, P.A. 1983. *The History of the Fijian Languages* (University Press of Hawaii, Honolulu)

Lynch, J., Ross, M. and Crowley, T. 2002. *The Oceanic Languages* (Routledge, London)

Milner, G.B. 1972. *Fijian Grammar*, 3rd edn (Government Press, Suva)

Ross, M. 1988. *Proto Oceanic and the Austronesian Languages of Western Melanesia* (Pacific Linguistics, Canberra)

Schütz, A.J. 1986. *The Fijian Language* (University Press of Hawai'i, Honolulu)

Tryon, D.T. (ed.) 1995. *Comparative Austronesian Dictionary* (Mouton, Berlin)

Wurm, S.A. and Hattori, S. (eds) 1981–4. *Language Atlas of the Pacific Area*, 2 parts (Australian Academy of the Humanities, Canberra)

47

Malay-Indonesian[1]

Uri Tadmor

1 Introduction

Malay-Indonesian is an Austronesian language spoken in many diverse forms throughout Southeast Asia. The indigenous name of the language is *Bahasa Melayu* (literally, 'the Malay language'), but the standard variety used in Indonesia (along with some regional colloquial varieties) is called *Bahasa Indonesia* ('the Indonesian language'). Similar forms of standard Malay-Indonesian serve as the national languages of Indonesia, Malaysia, Brunei and Singapore;[2] the latter three are particularly close to each other. This chapter, unless otherwise noted, will be dealing with the most widely used variety, standard Indonesian, which will be referred to simply as 'Indonesian'. Standard Malay as used in Malaysia will be referred to as 'Malaysian'.

With over 250 million speakers, Malay-Indonesian is the most widely spoken language in Southeast Asia. Most speakers, however, do not acquire it as their first language. The number of native speakers is difficult to estimate; perhaps 20 per cent of the current total number of speakers acquired a colloquial variety of Malay-Indonesian as their first language. This figure is rapidly increasing, as more and more people in Indonesia, Malaysia and Brunei shift from their ancestral home languages to Malay-Indonesian. As will be explained below, colloquial varieties of Malay-Indonesian exhibit a great diversity, and most are quite different from the standard variety discussed in this chapter.

Malay-Indonesian is a member of the Malayic subgroup of Western Malayo-Polynesian, a branch of the Austronesian language family. While there is wide agreement about the existence of the Malayic subgroup (and within it of Malay-Indonesian as a separate language), linguists have not been able to agree on its classification, either external or internal. Malayic used to be classified together with Javanese, Sundanese, Madurese, Acehnese and Lampung in a putative 'Malayo-Javanic' branch, but strong doubts have been cast on the validity of this classification. It is now clear that Malayic is more closely related to the Chamic languages, spoken in Cambodia, Vietnam and Hainan Island (southern China), than to any of the above languages. Recent research indicates that Malayo-Chamic languages are in turn most closely related to Bali–Sasak–Sumbawan, a group of languages spoken on several islands east of Java. One factor hindering the external

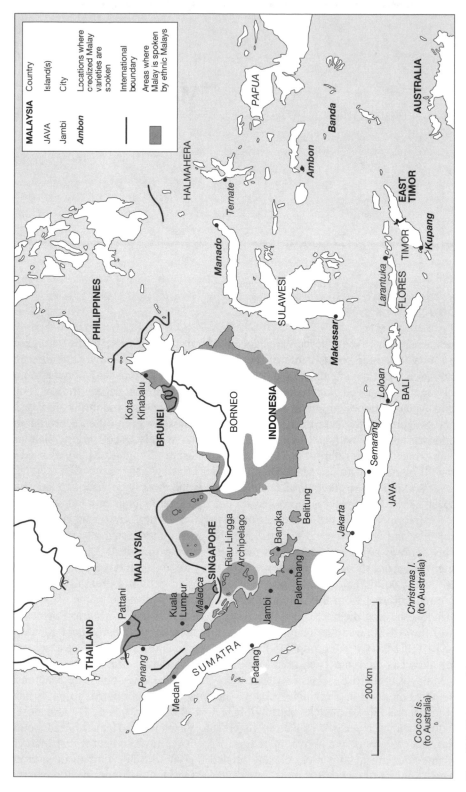

Map 47.1 Malay-speaking areas.

classification of Malayic is that many languages in the region have borrowed heavily from Malay-Indonesian, which has served as a regional lingua franca for many centuries. Similarly, no linguistic criteria have been established for distinguishing between Malayic languages and dialects of Malay-Indonesian, and there are no widely accepted subgrouping theories for either. Many scholars in the field have therefore preferred using the neutral term 'isolect' to refer to any Malayic speech form which has a name of its own and is regarded by its speakers as distinct from other varieties. This practice will be followed in this chapter.

Malayic isolects vary greatly, and many of them are not mutually intelligible. They fall into several broad categories. Some, like Riau Malay (spoken in the Riau-Lingga archipelago in Indonesia) or Kedah Malay (spoken in the Malaysian state of Kedah), are thought to be direct descendants of Proto Malayic, a hypothetical language reconstructed on the basis of modern isolects. Other isolects, however, have had a more complex history, and owe their emergence to language contact and language shift. For example Betawi, the language of the indigenous ethnic group of Jakarta, is based on Malay, but has incorporated lexical and grammatical elements from Balinese, Javanese, Sundanese, Portuguese Creole and Chinese languages, which were spoken by the ancestors of today's speakers. Some isolects have developed from pidginised forms of Malay, collectively known as Bazaar Malay, which originally served only for inter-ethnic communication, not as a first language. Baba Malay, spoken by acculturated Chinese communities in Malacca, Penang and Singapore, is thought to have developed from Bazaar Malay, which gradually became the speakers' first language. Most Malayic isolects spoken in eastern Indonesia have probably also developed from early pidginised forms of Malay. This complex situation has contributed to the difficulty of classifying Malayic isolects.

Colloquial varieties of Malay-Indonesian differ greatly from each other and, as already mentioned, also from the standard language. These differences may involve any aspect: pronunciation, word formation, syntax, lexicon, semantics and pragmatics. It will of course be impossible to describe all these diverse varieties within this chapter. Therefore, as mentioned above, the description will involve mainly one variety, standard Indonesian. However, it should always be kept in mind that this is just one of a very large number of diverse varieties.

2 History

The cradle of Malay language and civilisation was in south-central Sumatra. Many scholars believe, however, that Proto Malayic was spoken in western Borneo. The original place name Malayu (= Malay) has been identified with the former Malay kingdom of Jambi in central Sumatra. The Chinese monk Yiqing (I Ching), who visited the area in the seventh century, reported about a place called 'Mo-lo-yu'; later Javanese inscriptions and manuscripts also refer to the area of Jambi as 'Malayu'. The *Sejarah Melayu* ('Malay Annals'), the canonical work of classical Malay literature, traces Malay origins to Palembang, a city south of Jambi, which historians and archaeologists identify with the centre of the ancient maritime empire of Srivijaya.

The earliest direct evidence of Malay comes from a handful of seventh-century inscriptions found in southern Sumatra and on the nearby island of Bangka, and associated with Srivijaya. Not all scholars agree that the language of these inscriptions is the direct ancestor of modern Malay-Indonesian, but it is commonly referred to as Old

Malay. The inscriptions were written in a formal language which borrowed heavily from Sanskrit (and indeed they contain entire passages in Sanskrit); there is no direct evidence about the language ordinary people spoke in their daily lives. Old Malay inscriptions dating from the eighth–ninth centuries have also been found in areas where Malay was not indigenous, like Java and the Philippines, showing the early spread of Malay in the region.

The use of (Old) Malay as a literary language in Java and in the Philippines did not survive long. However, in Sumatra it has continued uninterrupted until today. Even among ethnic groups who speak non-Malayic languages, like Rejang and Lampung, Malay (written in an Indian-derived script) has continued to serve as the major literary language. The oldest extant Malay manuscript is a recently rediscovered fourteenth-century work originating from southwestern Sumatra. Some letters and longer works from the sixteenth century are preserved in collections in the West, and from the seventeenth century onwards surviving Malay manuscripts become numerous. The contents of these works are varied, and range from legends, chronicles and religious treatises to legal documents and personal letters. The language of these manuscripts, while showing some variation across time, space and style, is nevertheless remarkably uniform, and has been termed Classical Malay.

Modern standard Malay-Indonesian developed in the nineteenth century as a continuation of Classical Malay, aided by the efforts of local and Western scholars. The great Malay scholar Raja Ali Haji (c.1809–70) composed a grammar and a dictionary of standard Malay. Later, the Dutch scholar C.A. van Ophuysen (1854–1917) formalised the grammar for use at schools throughout the Dutch Indies. In 1928, a congress of nationalist students declared Malay – under the name *Bahasa Indonesia* – to be the national language of the Indonesian people. (The text of this declaration is appended to this chapter.) During the Japanese occupation (1942–5), the modernisation of Malay-Indonesian was accelerated, as it was widely used in the administrative and educational systems and in the mass media. Indonesia declared its independence in 1945, whereby Indonesian became the sole official language of the new republic. When Malaysia, Singapore and Brunei followed suit, similar forms of standard Malay-Indonesian became their national languages as well. In 1972 the spelling of Malay-Indonesian was reformed and harmonised, and a joint council (known by its acronym MABBIM) has been coordinating language-planning activities in these countries ever since.

Throughout its history, Malay-Indonesian has been in contact with, and influenced by, various languages. These are briefly discussed in the last section of this chapter.

3 Writing and Orthography

The writing system used in the earliest Old Malay inscriptions (dating back to the seventh century) was based on the Pallava script of southern India. The earliest extant Malay manuscript, written about seven centuries later, was written on bark paper in a script similar to the Kawi script (used for Old Javanese). Various Indian-derived scripts are still used in Sumatra for writing local languages and occasionally Malay as well. However, Classical Malay was mainly written in an Arabic-based script called *Jawi*, which developed after the Islamisation of the Malays. The earliest example of *Jawi* is the Trengganu inscription of 1303; the earliest *Jawi* manuscripts are two letters written by the sultan of Ternate (in the east of modern Indonesia) to the king of Portugal in 1521 and 1522. The oldest example of Romanised Malay comes from a word list prepared by the Italian explorer Pigafetta in 1521. Pigafetta was not attempting to devise an alphabet for writing Malay, but simply to record Malay words in the writing system he knew. More systematic attempts to write Malay in Latin characters were made in the seventeenth century, and for several centuries Romanised Malay (known as *Rumi*) existed side by side with *Jawi*.[3] *Rumi* was used mostly by Europeans, for example for bible translations and in schools, while *Jawi* was used mostly by indigenous writers. Towards the end of the nineteenth century, *Rumi* spelling was standardised by the British for use in their possessions in the Malay Peninsula and North Borneo, while a different standard was established by the Dutch for use in the Netherlands Indies. As already mentioned, in 1972 the orthography was reformed, and the two standards were harmonised by mutual agreement. Today *Jawi* is rarely used in Indonesia, and is rapidly disappearing from daily life in Malaysia as well, although it still has a relatively strong position among ethnic Malays in southern Thailand.

4 Phonology

Modern Malay Indonesian consonants which occur in inherited vocabulary are summarised in Table 47.1. Internal reconstruction of Proto Malayic reveals that *w* and *y* never contrasted with *u* and *i*, so their status was not phonemic. They phonemicised later through a combination of external factors (basically borrowing) as well as internal factors. The same can be said for the glottal stop. The language also has some loan consonant phonemes, which are discussed below.

Loan consonants were introduced together with the large influx of loanwords from Arabic and later from Dutch. They include *f*, *sy* (usually realised as [ç] in Indonesian), *z* and *x*, which only occur in loanwords, e.g. *huruf* 'letter [of the alphabet]' (< Arabic *ḥurūf*), *syair* 'poem' (< Arabic *šaʕīr*), *famili* 'relatives' (< Dutch *familie*), *izin* 'permission' (< Arabic *iḍn*), *akhir* [axir] 'last' (Arabic *āḫir*). The use of these loan phonemes is not consistent: *f* is frequently realised as [p]; *z* as [s] or [j]; and *x* as [k], [h] or [kh].[4]

Table 47.1 Consonant Phonemes in Inherited Malay-Indonesian Vocabulary

	Bilabial	Dental/Alveolar	Palatal	Velar	Glottal
Voiced stops	b	d	ɟ	g	
Voiceless stops	p	t	c	k	ʔ
Nasals	m	n	ɲ	ŋ	
Liquids		l r			
Fricatives		s			h
Glides	w		y		

Table 47.2 Vowel Phonemes in Inherited Malay-Indonesian Vocabulary

	Front	Central	Back
High	i		u
Mid	e	ə	o
Low		a	

Vowels which occur in inherited Malay vocabulary are listed in Table 47.2. The vowel system has also been affected by language contact; the phonemicisation of the mid vowels (*e*, *ə*, *o*) is the product of a combination of internal and external factors.

An examination of inherited Malay morphemes in Indonesian reveals a relatively simple syllable structure. The syllable consisted minimally of a single vocalic nucleus, optionally preceded and/or followed by a single consonant. The resulting syllable structure is (C)V(C). There are thus four possible syllable shapes in inherited Malay-Indonesian vocabulary: V, CV, VC and CVC. Examples for each of the possible syllable shapes are given in Table 47.3.

Table 47.3 Syllable Shapes in Inherited Malay Morphemes

Syllable shape	Initial syllable	Final syllable
V	*i*.kan 'fish'	ba.*u* 'smell'
CV	*ba*.tu 'stone'	a.*pa* 'what'
VC	*um*.pan 'bait'	ma.*in* 'play'
CVC	*han*.tu 'ghost'	da.*pat* 'get'

There is a preference for consonant-initial syllables, which are much more common than onsetless syllables. However, there does not seem to be a statistically significant preference for either open or closed syllables.

Mostly through the influx of a large number of loanwords, the syllable structure of modern Indonesian has undergone radical restructuring. The number of possible consonants in the onset and coda has increased from just one consonant to three, for example in the Indonesian words *struk* 'cash-register receipt' and *korps* 'corps', both borrowed from Dutch. The syllable structure of modern Indonesian is therefore (C)(C)(C)V(C)(C)(C).

Voiced stops do not occur in final position; thus the loanwords *jawab* 'answer' (< Arabic), *masjid* 'mosque' (< Arabic) and *zig-zag* (< English) are realised [jawap], [masjit] and [siksak], respectively. Palatals do not occur in final position in inherited vocabulary, but do occur marginally in loanwords such as *bridge* [bric] (the card game), *peach* [pic] (the colour) and *Mikraj* [miʔrac] (a Muslim holiday). The combination *si* is often realised as [ç] if immediately followed by another vowel. Thus the initial syllables of *syair* 'poem' and *siapa* 'who' can be pronounced identically as [ça]: [çaʔir], [çapa]. In Malaysian (but not in Indonesian) final *k* in inherited vocabulary is realised as a glottal stop.

Relatively complex morphophonemic alternation rules affect the junctures between some affixes and roots which follow them. These affixes are the prefixes *meng-* (which marks active verbs) and *peng-* (which derives agents; it is also present in the circumfix *peng-an* which derives verbal nouns). Generally speaking, the velar nasal *ng-* in the affix assimilates to place of articulation of the root-initial consonant, and in some cases this initial consonant deletes. These rules can be summarised as follows.

■ If *ng-* is followed by a root-initial voiced oral stop, it assimilates to it: *meng +bawa* → *membawa* 'to bring', *meng+dapat* → *mendapat* 'to get', *meng +ganggu* → *mengganggu* 'to disturb'.

■ If *ng-* is followed by a root-initial voiceless oral stop, it assimilates to it, and the consonant which conditions the assimilation then deletes: *meng+pilih* → *memilih* 'to choose', *meng+tulis* → *menulis* 'to write', *meng+kirim* → *mengirim* 'to send'.

■ If *ng-* is followed by a sonorant, it deletes, preventing the creation of an unphonotactic cluster or geminate: *meng+masuk+i* → *memasuki*[5] 'to enter', *meng +naik+i* → *menaiki* 'to ascend (something)', *meng+nyanyi* → *menyanyi* 'to sing', *meng+nganga* → *menganga* 'to open wide', *meng+lihat* → *melihat* 'to see', *meng+rayap* → *merayap* 'to creep', *meng+wakil+i* → *mewakili* 'to represent', *meng+yakin+i* → *meyakini* 'to convince'.

■ Roots which begin with *s-*, *sy-*, *c-* and *j-* behave more idiosyncratically. A root-initial *s-* triggers a change in the preceding *-ng-*, which becomes *ny* before the *s-* deletes: *séwa* → *menyéwa* 'to rent'. This probably indicates that when the assimilation rule first applied, *s* was a palatalised consonant; it is still palatalised in some modern dialects.[6] The palatals *c-* and *j-* cause the preceding *ng-* to become the alveolo-dental *n-* instead of the expected palatal nasal *ny-*: *meng+cuci* → *mencuci* 'to wash', *meng+jemput* → *menjemput* 'to pick up'.[7] Roots which begin with the loan phoneme *sy* ([ç]) are inconsistent; some behave like *s*-initial roots (*peng+syair* → *penyair* 'poet') while others behave like *c*-initial roots (*meng+syukur+i* → *mensyukuri* 'to thank God [for something]'). (The reason *ng-* changes to *n* rather than to the expected *ny* before palatal-initial bases is that, as mentioned above, Malay-Indonesian phonotactics preclude the occurrence of palatals – and especially the palatal nasal – in final position.)

■ Root initial *f-* and *z-*, both loan phonemes, trigger the expected assimilation of *ng-*: *meng+fokus* → *memfokus* 'to focus', *meng+zalim+i* → *menzalimi* 'to treat cruelly'.

No changes affect *ng*-final prefixes if the following root begins with a vowel, the glottal fricative *h* or the velar fricative *kh*: *meng+ukur* → *mengukur* 'to measure', *meng+hafal* → *menghafal* 'to memorise', *meng+khianat+i* → *mengkhianati* 'to betray'.

These morphophonemic alternations basically involve two processes: nasal assimilation and the deletion of certain consonants.[8] Neither process is required by the phonotactics of modern Indonesian. Thus one finds (in loanwords) unassimilated nasals preceding oral stops, as in *tanpa* 'without' (< Javanese), *angpao* 'gift envelope' (< Hokkien) and *anbia* 'prophets' (< Arabic). And root-initial voiceless stops sometimes fail to delete, not only with borrowed roots such as in *meng+taat+i* → *mentaati* 'to obey' (< Arabic) and *meng+kopi* → *mengkopi* 'to make a copy' (< English) but also with inherited roots such as in *meng+punya+i* → *mempunyai* 'to have, own' and *meng+kilap* → *mengkilap* 'to shine'.

5 Morphology

The principal morphological processes in Malay-Indonesian are affixation, compounding and reduplication. Affixes play a very important role in the standard language, although a significantly smaller one in most colloquial varieties. There are three types of affixes: prefixes, suffixes and circumfixes (simulfixes), the latter consisting of morphs attached simultaneously to the beginning and end of a base. In addition there are traces of infixation, although infixes have never been productive in Malayic. Most affixes also interact with reduplication to produce complex, discontinuous grammatical morphemes. The principal productive affixes are listed in Table 47.4.

Table 47.4 Affixes in Malay-Indonesian

Form	Main meaning or function	Examples	Base
meng-	Active	*meng-ambil* 'to take'	*ambil* 'take'
di-	Passive	*di-ambil* 'to be taken'	*ambil* 'take'
ber-	Intransitive	*ber-baring* 'to lie down'	*baring* 'lie down'
ter$_1$-	Adversative passive	*ter-telan* 'to get swallowed (accidentally)'	*telan* 'swallow'
ter$_2$-	State/potentiality	*ter-buat* 'made (of)'	*buat* 'make'
		ter-lihat 'visible'	*lihat* 'see'
ter$_3$-	Superlative	*ter-besar* 'biggest'	*besar* 'big'
per-	Causative	*per-besar* 'enlarge'	*besar* 'big'
pe-	Agent of *ber*-verb	*pe-tani* 'farmer'	*ber-tani* 'to farm'
peng-	Agent of *meng*-verb	*peng-ambil* 'taker'	*meng-ambil* 'to take'
ke-	Ordinal numeral	*ke-dua* 'second'	*dua* 'two'
-an	Recipient or result of action	*makan-an* 'food'	*makan* 'eat'
		tulis-an 'writing'	*tulis* 'write'
-i	Transitive	*datang-i* 'approach'	*datang* 'come'
-kan	Applicative (e.g. causative, benefactive)	*datang-kan* 'bring'	*datang* 'come'
		buat-kan 'make [something for someone]'	*buat* 'make'
ke-an$_1$	Abstract noun	*ke-baik-an* 'kindness'	*baik* 'good, kind'
ke-an$_2$	Unintentional event	*ke-hujan-an* 'to get caught in the rain'	*hujan* 'rain'
per-an$_1$	Collective noun	*perikanan* 'fishery'	*ikan* 'fish'
per-an$_2$	Verbal noun (for *ber*-verbs)	*per-temu-an* 'meeting'	*ber-temu* 'to meet'
peng-an	Verbal noun (for *meng*-verbs)	*peng-ambil-an* '(the) taking'	*meng-ambil* 'to take'
se-nya*	Adverb	*se-benar-nya* 'actually'	*benar* 'true'

Note:
* Historically made up of the clitics *se-* 'as' and *-nya* 'determiner', but synchronically functions as an affix.

Affixed words can serve as the base for further affixation, as in the forms *mem-ber-laku-kan* 'to enforce' (< *ber-laku* 'to be in force'), *di-per-besar* 'to be enlarged' (< *per-besar* 'enlarge') and *ke-ter-lambat-an* 'tardiness' (< *ter-lambat* 'late'). While the first example is lexicalised, the latter two are fully productive: any *ter*-adjective can undergo affixation with *ke-an*, and any *per*-verb can be prefixed with *di-*.

Compounding is also a common morphological process in Indonesian. The criteria for determining whether a group of morphemes constitute a compound or a phrase are mostly semantic and syntactic, rather than phonological. A sequence of two words can be said to be a compound if its compositional semantics is unpredictable yet it is used consistently. For example, *kamar kecil* means 'a small room' when used as a phrase, but as a compound it means 'toilet', a meaning that cannot be predicted based on the meaning of its constituents alone. Compounds function as a single lexical unit; their constituents cannot be separated from each other by any process, such as relativisation.

Thus, *kamar yang kecil* (*yang* is a relativiser) would only have the phrasal reading of 'a small room', not 'toilet'. Sometimes the criterion is word order, e.g. *rambut panjang* 'long hair' vs *panjang rambut* 'long-haired'. The claim that *panjang rambut* is a compound that means 'long-haired' rather than a phrase that means 'long hair' is supported by the grammaticality of sentences such as *Tuti punya rambut panjang* 'Tuti has long hair' versus the ungrammaticality of sentences like **Tuti punya panjang rambut* (which would literally mean 'Tuti has long-haired'). Lack of affixation can also indicate compounding, e.g. *jual-beli* 'trade' (lit. 'sell buy'; 'to sell and to buy' would be *menjual dan membeli*). Compounds may undergo affixation as a single unit, as in *menandatangani* 'to sign' (from the compound base *tanda tangan* 'signature', lit. 'sign hand') and *memperjualbelikan* 'to trade [in]' (from the base *jual-beli* 'trade', lit. 'sell buy').

The third major morphological process in Indonesian is reduplication. A distinction should be made between lexical reduplication (where the word only occurs in a reduplicated form) and morphological reduplication (where the reduplicated form is derived from an existing base by a regular process). An example of lexical reduplication is found in the word *kupu-kupu* 'butterfly'. This word only occurs in its reduplicated form; the putative base **kupu* does not occur by itself, and has no meaning. One the other hand, *jalan-jalan* 'to go for a walk' is transparently derived from the base *jalan* 'walk'. Of the two types of reduplication, only morphological reduplication constitutes a derivational process.

Reduplication fills a large number of functions in Malay-Indonesian, only some of which can be mentioned here. One of the most important ones is forming collectives, as in *anak-anak* '(a group of) children' (from *anak* 'child'). An adjective can also be reduplicated to indicate that it modifies a collective noun: *anak rajin-rajin* '(a group of) hard-working children'.

Another function of reduplication is to indicate resemblance. Reduplicated nouns (sometimes with the addition of the suffix *-an*) denote things that appear similar to the referent of the simple base but are actually quite different, e.g. *langit-langit* 'palate' < *langit* 'sky', *rumah-rumahan* 'dollhouse' < *rumah* 'house'. In verbs, the process creates atelic verbs whose action is performed with no objective in mind or purely for enjoyment: *minum-minum* 'to have a drink (for enjoyment)' < *minum* 'drink (to quench one's thirst)'; *baca-baca* 'to glance, read here and there' < *baca* 'read (in order to gain knowledge)'. Reduplication combined with the circumfix *ke-an* creates adjectives whose meaning involves resemblance to that of the simple, unreduplicated form, e.g. *kebarat-baratan* 'Western-like, Westernised' < *barat* 'west', *kemérah-mérahan* 'red-like, reddish' < *mérah* 'red'.

In addition to full reduplication, where the entire base is reduplicated, Malay-Indonesian used to have a process of partial reduplication, which reduplicated just the onset and nucleus (initial consonant + vowel) of the initial syllable. The vowel of the initial syllable was then reduced to schwa by a regular phonological process.[9] While no longer productive in modern standard Indonesian, partial reduplication is still exhibited in numerous older words, such as *lelaki* 'man, male' < *laki* 'husband' and *tetangga* 'neighbour' < *tangga* 'ladder' (i.e. not 'the person next door' but rather 'the person next ladder', reflecting traditional Malay architecture). There are also more complex types of reduplication which involve some mutation of the reduplicant, such as *bolak-balik* 'back and forth' < *balik* 'to go back' and *sayur-mayur* '(various) vegetables' < *sayur* 'vegetable'.

In addition to these major morphological processes, abbreviations are also very common in Indonesian. These include clipped words, which combine syllables of words that make up a larger syntactic unit, e.g. *balita* 'infant' from **bawah lima tahun** 'under five years'; initialisms, formed from the names of the initial letters of two or more words, e.g. *DPR* [depeʔer] 'the Indonesian parliament' from **Déwan Perwakilan Rakyat** 'People's Representative Assembly'; acronyms, formed from initial letters but pronounced as a single word, e.g. *ASI* [ʔasi] 'mother's milk', from *Air Susu Ibu* 'mother's breast liquid'; and truncated forms, where a word is reduced by deleting some of its phonological material, e.g. *Pak* 'Sir, epithet that precedes names of adult males' from *bapak* 'father'.

6 Syntax

6.1 Word Classes

Although they may use different terms, practically all scholars agree that content words are distinguished syntactically from function words in Malay-Indonesian. Many also recognise the existence of categories such as nouns, verbs, adjectives, prepositions and a few minor categories, and this approach is taken up in this chapter. An alternative is to analyse the roots of content words as not belonging to any particular word class, with syntactic categories assigned by affixes. This analysis, however, would require positing zero derivation for a large number of nouns and adjectives.

6.2 Nouns and Noun Phrases

Although there are various noun-forming affixes, most nouns are not overtly marked as such. In noun phrases, modifiers such as demonstratives, adjectives and attributive nouns usually follow the head:

(1a)		(1b)		(1c)	
rumah	*ini*	*rumah*	*besar*	*rumah*	*batu*
house	dem. prox.	house	big	house	stone
'this house'		'a/the big house'		'a/the stone house'	

The unmarked position of quantifiers is before the noun:

(2a)		(2b)		(2c)	
satu	*rumah*	*banyak*	*rumah*	*semua*	*rumah*
one	house	many	house	all	house
'one house'		'many houses'		'all houses'	

However, the quantifier may occur after the noun in some more marked constructions.

Possession is indicated by simple juxtaposition of the nouns, with the possessor following the possessed:

(3a)		(3b)		(3c)	
rumah	*guru*	*rumah*	*saya*	*rumah*	*Tuti*
house	teacher	house	1sg.	house	Tuti
'a/the teacher's house'		'my house'		'Tuti's house'	

Other types of possessive constructions also occur, but their use in the standard language is limited.

6.3 Numerals and Classifiers

The cardinal numbers from one to ten are *satu* '1'; (clitic form: *se-*), *dua* '2', *tiga* '3', *empat* '4', *lima* '5', *enam* '6', *tujuh* '7', *delapan* '8', *sembilan* '9', *sepuluh* '10' (from *se-* 'one' + *puluh* 'ten'). Numbers between 11 and 19 are formed with the element *belas* '-teen': *sebelas* '11', *dua belas* '12', etc. Tens are formed by adding *puluh* 'ten': *dua puluh* '20', *tiga puluh* '30', etc. Larger numbers are formed by juxtaposition in descending order, with no conjunction:

(4) *seribu*   *sembilan*   *ratus*   *empat*   *puluh*   *lima*
     one-thousand   nine   hundred   four   ten   five
     '1945'

Ordinal numbers are formed with the suffix *ke-*: *kedua* 'second', *kelima* 'fifth', *kesebelas* 'eleventh', *kedua puluh tujuh* 'twenty-seventh'. The common word for 'first' is *pertama*, a loanword from Sanskrit. The expected form *kesatu* also exists but is rarely used.

Several numeral classifiers exist, but their use is not obligatory, and most also occur as nouns. Only three classifiers are in common use: *orang* (literally 'person') for humans, *ékor* (literally 'tail') for animals, and *buah* (literally 'fruit') for inanimate objects and entities. When both a numeral and a classifier are used, the usual order is numeral–classifier–noun:

(5a)   (5b)   (5c)
dua orang   *guru*   *tiga*   *ékor*   *kucing*   *lima*   *buah*   *rumah*
two person   teacher   three   tail   cat   five   fruit   house
'two teachers'   'three cats'   'five houses'

The order noun–numeral–classifier also occurs, especially in lists.

6.4 Adjectives and Adjective Phrases

Some authorities classify adjectives together with verbs, because they fill similar syntactic positions. They may also occur with phonetically identical affixes, but the meaning of each affix varies in unpredictable ways according to whether the base is a verb or an adjective. Thus, when added to adjectives, the prefix *ter-* derives superlatives (*besar* 'big', *terbesar* 'biggest'), but when added to verbs it produces adversative, potential or stative forms which bear no clear semantic or functional relation to superlatives. Moreover, not all affixes which occur with verbs also occur with adjectives. For example, the prefix *di-* forms the passive from verbal bases, but does not occur with adjectives, not even transitive adjectives.

Adjectives (again unlike verbs) may be modified by an adverb of degree, such as *sangat* 'very', *sekali* 'very', *agak* 'fairly, quite' and *kurang* 'insufficiently'. Most such adverbs occur before the adjective: *sangat besar* 'very large', *agak besar* 'fairly large', *kurang besar* 'not large enough'. However, a few occur after the adjective, such as *sekali*: *besar sekali* 'very large'.

There are two equative constructions. The simpler one is created by preposing the clitic *se-* 'as' to the adjective, and placing it between the two compared entities:

(6) *Budi   sangat   tinggi;   dia   setinggi   Tuti.*
     Budi   very   tall   3sg.   as-tall   Tuti
     'Budi is very tall; he is as tall as Tuti.'

Alternatively, the adjective is preceded by *sama* 'same, equal' and followed by the 3rd-person enclitic pronoun *-nya*:

(7) *Budi   sama   tingginya   dengan   Tuti.*
     Budi   same   tall-3   with   Tuti
     'Budi is as tall as Tuti.'
     (lit. '(As for) Budi, his tallness is the same as Tuti's'.)

The comparative is formed by placing the word *lebih* 'more' before the adjective and *daripada* '(rather) than' after it. (The preposition *dari* 'from' can be used instead of *daripada*, but this is considered informal.)

(8) *Budi   lebih   tinggi   daripada/dari   Tuti.*
     Budi   more   tall   than/from   Tuti
     'Budi is taller than Tuti.'

The superlative can be formed in two ways. In formal Indonesian, an adjective may be prefixed by *ter-*: *baik* 'good', *terbaik* 'best'; *besar* 'big', *terbesar* 'biggest' (Example 9). The alternative construction, used in formal as well as colloquial Indonesian, is formed by placing the word *paling* 'most' before the adjective: *paling baik* 'best', *paling besar* 'biggest' (Example 10).

(9) *Tuti   dan   Budi   mémang   tinggi,   tetapi   Edi   yang   **ter**tinggi.*
     Tuti   and   Budi   indeed   tall   but   Edi   rel.   sup.-tall
     'Tuti and Budi are tall, but Edi is the tallest.'

(10) *Tuti   dan   Budi   mémang   tinggi,   tetapi   Edi   yang   **paling**   tinggi.*
     Tuti   and   Budi   indeed   tall   but   Edi   rel.   most   tall
     'Tuti and Budi are tall, but Edi is the tallest.'

6.5 *Prepositions and Prepositional Phrases*

The basic prepositions of Malay-Indonesian are *di* 'in, at', *ke* 'to' and *dari* 'from':

(11) *Setelah   makan   **di**   hotel,   Budi   berangkat   **dari**   Jakarta   **ke**   Solo.*
     after   eat   at   hotel   Budi   depart   from   Jakarta   to   Solo
     'Having dined at his hotel, Budi left Jakarta for Solo.'

Some other prepositions that express spatial relations are *atas* 'above, over', *bawah* 'below, under', *sebelah* 'next to', *keliling* 'around', *belakang* 'behind' and *depan* 'in front of'. In formal Indonesian these prepositions are often preceded by *di* 'at', betraying their nominal origin. Other prepositions include *untuk* 'for', *dengan* 'with' and *tanpa* 'without'.

6.6 Verbs and Verb Phrases

In standard Malay-Indonesian most verb forms must be preceded by a verbal prefix, such as *meng-* 'active', *di-* 'passive' and *ber-* 'intransitive'. Thus the root *isi* 'fill/contents' serves as the base for *mengisi* 'to fill', *diisi* 'to be filled' and *berisi* 'to have contents or a filling'. Exceptions include imperatives, object voice verbs (see below) and a small set of intransitive verbs that do not take prefixes (unless also suffixed), such as *datang* 'come', *pergi* 'go' and *tidur* 'sleep'.

Active forms of transitive verbs in declarative sentences are usually marked with the prefix *meng-* (Example 12) and passive forms with the prefix *di-* (13). The agent of a passive verb is optionally marked with *oleh* 'by' (14).

(12) *Budi   membaca   buku   itu.*
     Budi   act.-read   book   dem. dist.
     'Budi   reads that book.'

(13) *Buku   itu   dibaca   Budi.*
     book   that   pass.-read   Budi
     'That book is read by Budi.'

(14) *Buku itu   dibaca   (oleh)   Budi.*
     book   that   pass.-read   by   Budi
     'That book is read by Budi.'

Expression of the agent is not obligatory; in fact, most passive sentences in Indonesian, like the following example, are agentless:

(15) *Buku itu   dibaca.*
     book   that   pass.-read
     'That book is read.'

When the object occurs before the verb, use of the passive is obligatory. Passive verb forms are very frequent in Indonesian because of a preference for focusing on (and fronting) the object.

Passive *di-* forms are used only when the agent is not expressed or when it is a third person. When the agent is a first person (16) or second person (17), object voice is used. In this construction, which Indonesians call *pasif semu* 'pseudo-passive', the bare root form of the verb is immediately preceded by the agent:

(16) *Buku itu   saya   baca.*
     book   dem. dist.   1sg.   read
     'I read that book.'

(17) *Buku itu   kamu baca.*
     book   dem. dist.   2   read
     'You read that book.'

Object voice can also be used with 3rd-person agents, as an alternative to passive constructions with *di-*:

(18) *Buku   itu   dia   baca.*
      book   dem. dist.   3sg.   read
      'He/she read that book.'

The agent and the verb in object voice constructions cannot be separated from each other; no element (such as a negator or an aspect marker) can come between them. Although the *di-* passive and object voice appear in near complementary distribution, the two constructions have very different properties. As we saw above, in the *di-* passive the agent is optional, and is clearly an adjunct when it occurs. In contrast, in the object voice construction the agent is obligatory, and has been shown to share subject properties with the passive subject (the patient).

A few other passive-like constructions can also be formed with the prefix *ter-* (19), the circumfix *ke-an* (20), and the auxiliary verb *kena* (21). All three indicate that the action denoted by the verb is unintentional. Examples are given below.

(19) *Kaki Budi   terinjak.*
      foot   Budi   unint.-step
      'Someone stepped on Budi's foot.'

(20) *Karena   macét   saya   kemalaman.*
      because   jam   1sg.   unint.-night-circ..
      'Because of the traffic jam I came home late at night.'

(21) *Kuenya   ketinggalan   di   luar   lalu   kena   hujan.*
      cake-3sg.   unint.-leave-circ.   at   out   then   unint.   rain
      'The cake got left outside and then got rained on.'

6.7 Auxiliary Verbs

Auxiliary verbs occur before the main verb, and denote concepts such as ability and possibility. When they co-occur with a negator, the order is negator–auxiliary–main verb:

(22) *Budi   tidak   boleh   makan   babi   tapi   boleh   makan   sapi.*
      Budi   neg.   may   eat   pig   but   may   eat   cow
      'Budi may not eat pork, but he may eat beef.'

In addition to *boleh* 'may, might', some other common auxiliary verbs include *bisa* 'can', *dapat* 'can', *mampu* 'able to', *suka* 'like to', *sempat* 'have occasion to', *harus* 'must' and *perlu* 'need'.

6.8 Adverbials

Adverbs of manner can be formed in several ways. Often, an unmodified adjective functions as an adverb:

(23) *Budi   berjalan   cepat   sedangkan   Tuti   berjalan   lambat.*
      Budi   act.-walk   quick   while   Tuti   intr.-walk   slow
      'Budi walks quickly whereas Tuti walks slowly.'

The adjective can be reduplicated, which reinforces its 'adverbiality'; for some speakers, this also adds intensity:

(24) *Budi   berjalan   cepat-cepat   sedangkan   Tuti   berjalan   pelan-pelan.*
     Budi   intr.-walk red.-quick   while   Tuti   intr.-walk red.-slow
     'Budi walks (very) quickly whereas Tuti walks (very) slowly.'

The adjective (either in its simple form or in a reduplicated form) may also be preceded by *dengan* 'with' to form an adverbial, e.g. *dengan cepat ~ dengan cepat-cepat* 'quickly'.

The choice of which pattern of adverbial formation is used has to do more with idiomaticity than with grammaticality; note that in the examples above, two different words for 'slow' are used, depending on the particular pattern chosen.

Some adverbials, usually of a more abstract nature, are formed with *secara* 'in a manner', e.g. *secara teoretis* 'theoretically', *secara logis* 'logically'. Yet others use the suffix *-nya*, as in *pokoknya* 'basically', sometimes preceded by the preposition *pada* (e.g. *pada umumnya* 'generally') or the clitic *se-* (e.g. *sebenarnya* 'actually'). This latter pattern, when used with adjectives (optionally reduplicated), also has the sense of 'as x as possible', e.g. *secepatnya ~ secepat-cepatnya* 'as quickly as possible, as soon as possible'.

6.9 Predication

Any type of phrase can serve as predicate, including a noun phrase (25), a verb phrase (26), an adjective phrase (27) or a prepositional phrase (28).

(25) *Budi   orang   Indonesia.*
     Budi   person   Indonesia
     'Budi is an Indonesian.'

(26) *Tuti   makan   pisang.*
     Tuti   eat   banana
     'Tuti is eating bananas.'

(27) *Budi   tinggi   sekali.*
     Budi   tall   very
     'Budi is very tall.'

(28) *Budi   di   rumah.*
     Budi   at   house
     'Budi is home.'

Sentences with a nominal predicate can optionally use the copula *adalah*:

(29) *Budi   adalah   orang   Indonesia.*
     Budi   cop.   person   Indonesia
     'Budi is an Indonesian.'

805

6.10 Negation

Generally speaking, noun phrases are negated by *bukan* (30), while other phrases are negated by *tidak* (31).

(30) *Budi   tidak   tahu   bahwa   Tuti   bukan   orang Amérika.*
    Budi   neg.   know   comp.   Tuti   neg.   person America
    'Budi didn't know that Tuti wasn't American.'

(31) *Tuti   tidak   senang   karena   Budi   tidak   di rumah.*
    Tuti   neg.   happy   because   Budi   neg.   at house
    'Tuti wasn't happy because Budi wasn't home.'

Bukan can also negate words and syntagms other than noun phrases, including entire sentences, but then it has the meaning 'it is not the case that ...':

(32) *Budi   bukan   tidak   mau   datang,   tapi   mémang   tidak   bisa   datang.*
    Budi   neg.   neg.   want   come   but   indeed   neg.   can   come
    'It's not that Budi doesn't want to come, he really can't come.'

A negative imperative is expressed by *jangan*:

(33) *Jangan   makan!*
    neg.   eat
    'Don't eat!'

Other negators include *belum* 'not yet', *tidak lagi* 'not any more' and *tidak usah* 'not necessary', corresponding to *sudah* 'already', *masih* 'still' and *harus* 'necessary', respectively.

6.11 Time and Aspect Marking within Predicates

Tense is not obligatorily expressed in Malay-Indonesian. Often the time of the event must be inferred from the linguistic or non-linguistic context. It can also be expressed by optional temporal markers, such as the past marker *telah* (34) and the future marker *akan* (35):

(34) *Budi telah makan.*   (35) *Budi akan makan.*
    Budi past. eat   Budi fut. eat
    'Budi ate.'   'Budi will eat.'

Although the particles *sedang* and *sudah* are often said to mark present and past actions respectively, they are actually aspect markers: *sudah* marks an action as having been completed (perfective), while *sedang* indicates that it has not been completed (imperfective).[10] Thus in (35), *sudah* is used to mark an action that will take place in the future, while in (36) *sedang* marks an action that took place in the past:

(35) *Besok   Tuti pasti   sudah   selesai.*
    tomorrow Tuti certain perf. finish
    'Tuti will certainly have finished by tomorrow.'

806

(36) *Waktu Budi datang, Tuti sedang makan.*
time Budi come Tuti imperf. eat
'When Budi came, Tuti was eating.'

6.12 Relativisation

Relative clauses are formed with the relativiser *yang* followed by a phrase. Sometimes this phrase adds information about a head noun phrase (37), but just as often it occurs headless (38, 39). This distributional pattern is quite different from that of many other languages, in which headless relative clauses are rare or non-existent.

(37) *Wanita yang makan pisang itu* *Tuti.*
woman rel. eat banana dem. dist. Tuti
'That woman (who is) eating a banana is Tuti.'

(38) *Yang makan pisang itu* *Tuti*
rel. eat banana dem. dist. Tuti
'The one (who is) eating a banana is Tuti.'

(39) *Yang tidak berkepentingan* *dilarang* *masuk.*
rel. neg. intr.-abstr.-important-circ. pass.-prohibit enter
'Whoever has no official business is prohibited from entering.' (Door sign)
(= 'No entry unless on duty.')

In formal Malay-Indonesian the predicate of the relative clause must be a verb phrase, adjective phrase or prepositional phrase. Colloquially, however, the predicate may also be a noun phrase (40). This usage is becoming acceptable in the standard language as well.

(40) *Coca Colanya mau yang kaléng atau yang botol?*
Coca-Cola-det. want rel. can or rel. bottle?
'Would you like your coke in a can or in a bottle?'

In formal Malay-Indonesian, only the subject of a transitive verb can be relativised. Thus, (41) is a grammatical sentence, but not (42).

(41) *Anak-anak yang sudah membaca buku itu* *boleh pulang.*
red-child rcl. perf. act.-read book dem. dist. may go.home
'The children who have already read the book can go home.'

(42) **Buku yang anak-anak sudah membaca itu* *menarik.*
book rel. red-child perf. act.-read dem. dist. act.-pull
'The book that was read by the children is interesting.'

However, in less formal Malay-Indonesian speakers accept sentences such as (43):

(43) *Buku yang anak-anak sudah baca itu* *menarik.*
book rel. person perf. read dem. dist. act.-pull
'The book that was read by the children is interesting.'

Locative relative clauses are a relatively recent development, due to the influence of Dutch and English. Instead of *yang*, such clauses use a locative interrogative (usually *di mana* 'where') as a relativiser:

(44) *Tuti   pulang   ke   hotel   di mana   dia   menginap.*
　　　Tuti　 go.back to   hotel   at which 3sg. act.-stay.overnight
　　　'Tuti went back to the hotel where she was staying.'

Some speakers view this construction as too 'foreign-sounding', and prefer using *tempat* 'place' instead of an interrogative (45). However, this does not make this construction more 'Indonesian', as it has no precedent in previous stages of the language.

(45) *Jalan   tempat   Budi   melihat   Tuti   adalah   Jalan   Sudirman.*
　　　street place   Budi   act.-see Tuti   cop.   street Sudirman
　　　'The street where Budi saw Tuti is Sudirman Street.'

6.13 Questions

Yes–no questions can be formed simply by using a specific intonation contour. Thus the structure of the following two sentences is identical, even though (46) is statement and (47) is a question:

(46) *Budi   sudah   makan.*
　　　Budi　 perf.　 eat
　　　'Budi has already eaten.'

(47) *Budi   sudah   makan?*
　　　Budi　 perf.　 eat
　　　'Has Budi eaten yet?'

In formal Indonesian, the particle *apakah* (historically derived from *apa* 'what' and the interrogative clitic *-kah*, see below) can be placed at the beginning of a sentence to indicate that it is a yes–no question:[11]

(48) *Apakah   Budi   sudah   makan?*
　　　YNQ　　　Budi　 perf.　 eat
　　　'Has Budi eaten yet?'

Information questions are formed with interrogative pronouns. These include *apa* 'what?', *siapa* 'who?', *mana* 'which?', *kapan* 'when?', *bagaimana* 'how?', *mengapa* 'why?' and *berapa* 'how much/many?' Locative interrogatives are formed with a preposition followed by *mana* 'which?': *di mana* 'where?', *ke mana* 'to where, whither?', *dari mana* 'from where, whence?'

Some interrogatives undergo movement, while others may be left *in situ*. *Mengapa* 'why' and *bagaimana* 'how' are usually fronted:

(49a) *Tuti makan karena lapar.*
　　　 Tuti eat   because hungry
　　　 'Tuti ate because she was hungry.'

(49b) *?Tuti makan mengapa?*
Tuti   eat   why
'Why did Tuti eat?'

(49c) ✔ *Mengapa Tuti makan?*
why   Tuti eat
'Why did Tuti eat?'

(50a) *Budi makan pakai séndok.*
Budi eat   use   spoon.
'Budi eats with a spoon.'

(50b) *?Budi makan bagaimana?*
Budi eat   how
'How does Budi eat?'

(50c) ✔ *Bagaimana Budi makan?*
how   Budi eat
'How does Budi eat?'

Kapan 'when?' and locative interrogatives (*di mana* 'where?', *ke mana* 'whither?', *dari mana* 'whence?') can occur either *in situ* or fronted:

(51a) *Tuti datang tadi.*
Tuti come   earlier
Tuti came earlier.

(51b) ✔ *Tuti datang kapan?*
Tuti come   when
'When did Tuti come?

(51c) ✔ *Kapan Tuti datang?*
when   Tuti come
'When did Tuti come?'

(52a) *Budi di rumah.*
Budi at house
'Budi is home.'

(52b) ✔ *Di mana Budi?*
at   which Budi
'Where is Budi?'

(52c) ✔ *Budi di mana?*
Budi at which
'Where is Budi?'

Object *apa* 'what?' and *siapa* 'who?' may be left *in situ*:

(53a) *Tuti makan pisang.*
Tuti eat   banana
'Tuti is eating bananas.'

(53b) *Tuti makan apa?*
Tuti eat   what
'What is Tuti eating?'

(54a) *Budi melihat Tuti.*
Budi act.-see Tuti
'Budi sees Tuti.'

(54b) *Budi melihat siapa?*
Budi act.-see who
'Who does Budi see?'

Both subject and object *apa* and *siapa* may occur in initial position. However, a cleft sentence must then be used. It is created by inserting *yang* in front of the verb phrase, thus converting it into a headless relative clause, and turning the subject (the interrogative) into the predicate.

(55a) *Gempa   bumi mengguncang pulau Bali.*
earthquake earth act.-shake   island Bali
'An earthquake shook the island of Bali.'

(55b) *Apa   mengguncang   Bali?
      what   act.-shake   Bali
      'What shook Bali?'

(55c) ✔ Apa   yang   mengguncang   Bali?
        what   rel.   act.-shake   Bali
        'What shook Bali?

(55d) *Apa   diguncang   gempa?
      what   pass.-shake   quake
      'What was shaken by the quake?'

(55e) ✔ Apa   yang   diguncang   gempa?
        what   rel.   pass.-shake   quake
        'What was shaken by the quake?'

(56a) Budi   melihat   Tuti.
       Budi   act.-see   Tuti
       'Budi sees Tuti.'

(56b) *Siapa   melihat   Tuti?
      who   act.-see   Tuti
      'Who sees Tuti?'

(56c) ✔ Siapa   yang   melihat   Tuti?
        who   rel.   act.-see   Tuti
        'Who sees Tuti?'

(56d) *Siapa   dilihat   Budi?
      who   pass.-see   Budi
      'Who was seen by Budi?'

(56e) ✔ Siapa   yang   dilihat   Budi?
        who   rel.   pass.-see   Budi
        'Who was seen by Budi?'

In formal Indonesian, questions are also formed with the interrogative clitic *-kah*. It is attached to the interrogative (57) or in questions without an interrogative, to the predicate (58). If the predicate contains an auxiliary verb, *-kah* is attached to it (59).

(57) Ke   manakah   Tuti   pergi?
      to   which-inter.   Tuti   go
      'Where did Tuti go?'

(58) Besarkah   rumah   Budi?
      big-inter.   house   Budi
      'Is Budi's house big?'

(59) Bisakah   Budi   datang?
      can-inter.   Budi   come
      'Can Budi come?'

6.14 Imperatives

Like questions, imperative sentences can be formed by using a special intonation contour. The active prefix *meng-* (see above), obligatory for many verbs in declarative sentences, is generally dropped in imperative sentences.[12] Optionally, the clitic *-lah* is attached to the verb.

(60) Kamu membaca buku itu.
      2   act.-read book dem. dist.
      'You are reading that book.'

(61) Baca(lah)   buku itu!
     read-imper. book dem. dist.
     'Read that book!'

Negative imperatives are formed with the negator *jangan*:

(62) *Jangan datang!*
      neg.   come
      'Don't come!

Passive imperatives are perceived as less emphatic (and thus more polite) than active imperatives. They are thus often used in invitations and requests.

(63) *Dimakan(lah)!*
      pass.-eat-imper.
      '(Please) eat it!', '(Please) have some!' (lit. 'Let it be eaten!')

6.15 Coordination

Words, phrases and clauses may be linked by conjunctions. The most common conjunctions linking words and phrases are *dan* 'and' (64), *atau* 'or' (65) and *tapi/tetapi* 'but' (66):

(64) *Tuti dan Budi makan pisang.*
      Tuti and Budi eat   banana
      'Tuti and Budi are eating bananas.'

(65) *Mau makan jeruk   manis atau asam?*
      want eat   orange sweet or   sour
      'Would you like to eat a sweet orange or a sour orange?'

(66) *Buah jeruk   asam tapi enak.*
      fruit orange sour but   delicious
      'Oranges are sour but delicious.'

In addition to these, clauses may be linked by a wider range of conjunctions, including *sedangkan* 'while' and *lalu* 'then'.

(67) *Tuti   makan pisang, sedangkan Budi makan jeruk.*
      Tuti eat banana while   Budi   eat   orange
      'Tuti is eating bananas, while Budi is eating oranges.'

If the subject of a clause is identical to that of a preceding clause, it is often omitted; the verb may be omitted as well:

(68) *Budi makan pisang lalu jeruk.*
      Budi eat   banana then orange
      'Budi ate bananas and then oranges.'

6.16 Subordination

An independent clause can be joined to a dependent clause to form complex sentences, with a subordinator preceding the dependent clause.

811

(69) *Tuti makan pisang karena lapar.* (Reason)
    Tuti eat   banana because hungry
    'Tuti ate a banana because she was hungry.'

(70) *Budi makan pisang supaya tidak lapar.* (Purpose)
    Budi eat   banana in.order.to neg. hungry
    'Budi ate a banana so that he wouldn't be hungry.'

(71) *Tuti makan pisang walaupun belum lapar.* (Concession)
    Tuti eat   banana although not.yet hungry
    'Tuti ate a banana, even though she wasn't hungry yet.'

(72) *Budi makan pisang kalau dia lapar.* (Condition)
    Budi eat   banana if   3sg. hungry
    'If Budi is hungry, he eats bananas.'

The order of the clauses can be freely reversed:

(73) *Karena lapar,   Tuti makan pisang.*
    because hungry Tuti eat   banana
    'Tuti ate a banana because she was hungry.'

7 Deixis

7.1 Person deixis

Pronoun use in Malay-Indonesian is a complex matter. When choosing a pronoun, the speaker may take several factors into consideration: style, formality, the kind of relationship between the speaker and the referent of the pronoun, the age of the referent vis-à-vis the speaker's, and even the ethnicity of the referent. The basic pronouns of Indonesian are summarised in Table 47.5.

The historical first person pronouns, *aku* and *kami*, are still widely used in formal and literary Indonesian. *Aku* is also used informally when addressing equals and inferiors. In formal Indonesian *kita* is used as a combined first + second person pronoun

Table 47.5 Major Pronouns of Malay-Indonesian

Person	*Number*	
	Singular	*Plural*
1st person	*aku* (literary, informal)	*kami* (formal)
	saya (general)	*kita* (informal)
1st + 2nd person	—	*kita* (formal)
2nd person	*engkau/kau* (literary)	*engkau/kau* (literary)
	kamu (informal)	*kamu* (informal)
	anda (formal)	*kalian* (semi-formal)
3rd person	*ia* (formal)	*meréka* (general)
	dia (general)	

('you and I/we'), but informally it is used as a simple first person plural pronoun, which may or may not include the addressee(s), much like English 'we'.

The historical singular second person pronoun, *engkau/kau*, is now used only in literary and poetic styles, and sometimes occurs with a plural meaning. The historical plural second person pronoun, *kamu*, has undergone a universally common pattern of change, by first expanding its meaning to include honorific second person singular, and then being gradually bleached of its honorific contents, until it became a simple pronoun unmarked for number. This meant that there was no longer a formal second person pronoun, and a wide range of substitutes came to be used instead, such as kinship terms, titles and personal names preceded by epithets. The most widely used formal pronoun substitutes are *bapak* 'father' and *ibu* 'mother'. In the 1950s a new pronoun, *anda*, was artificially introduced to fill the function of a formal second person pronoun.[13] However, it did not become popular in everyday speech, because it was perceived as distant and impersonal. It is now used mostly in advertisements, signs and product markings.

The common third person singular pronoun, *dia*, was originally used only in object position, as the counterpart of the subject pronoun *ia*. However, *dia* is now used in both subject and object positions, and *ia* is used only in formal or literary styles.

As already mentioned, in many situations Indonesians prefer to use kinship terms, epithets, personal names or a combination of these, rather than using a pronoun. There can be various reasons for wishing to avoid using pronouns, and this also affects self-reference. For example, a man called Budi addressing a woman called Tuti might produce any of the following sentences, all with the same meaning, depending on the particular situation: 'Let me go with you', 'Let Father go with Tuti', 'Let Budi go with Tuti', 'Let Budi go with Mother', 'Let Budi go with Doctor', 'Let Budi go with Doctor Tuti', or any of a practically unlimited range of other choices, based on the particular context and situation where the sentence is said.

7.2 Time Deixis

As mentioned above, while tense is not obligatory in Malay-Indonesian, it can be expressed by optional temporal markers such as *telah* and *akan*, which indicate past and future events, respectively. *Sekarang* 'now' marks the present; *tadi* 'earlier' and *nanti* 'later' are commonly used to indicate the relative time of events.

(74) *Budi*   *tadi*   *memberitahu*   *bahwa*   *dia*   *tidak*   *bisa*   *ikut*   *nanti.*
     Budi   earlier   act.-inform   comp.   3sg.   neg.   can   join   later
     'Budi informed us (earlier) that he won't be able to attend (later)'.

'Today' is expressed by *hari ini*, literally 'this day', 'yesterday' by *kemarin*, and 'tomorrow' by *besok*.

7.3 Place Deixis

The proximal demonstrative *ini* 'this' and the distal demonstrative *itu* 'that' indicate the location of entities with relation to the speaker: *rumah ini* 'this house (near the speaker)', *rumah itu* 'that house (away from the speaker)'. They are also used as topic markers. Usually *ini* 'this' is used if the referent is present, while *itu* 'that' is used if the referent is absent. Thus in (75) Budi may be the speaker, the addressee or a third person taking part in the conversation, while in (76) Budi is not among those present:

(75) *Budi ini   orang Indonesia.*
    Budi dem. prox. person Indonesia
    'I'm Indonesian.'/'You're Indonesian.'/'Budi is Indonesian.'

(It is necessary to know the context in which the sentence was said in order to ascertain which of the possible readings is the right one.)

(76) *Budi itu   orang Indonesia.*
    Budi dem. dist. person Indonesia
    'Budi is Indonesian.'

Adverbs which mark relative locations are *sini* 'here', *situ* 'there (usually within sight/ earshot)' and *sana* 'there (usually out of sight/earshot)'. *Sini* and *sana* are also used as imperatives: *Sini!* 'Come here!', *Sana!* 'Go away!.

8 Foreign Influence on Malay-Indonesian[14]

Since prehistoric times, Malay-Indonesian has been in contact with various languages. The earliest foreign language known to have had significant influence on Malay-Indonesian was Sanskrit. The oldest Malay inscriptions (seventh century AD) alternate between Malay and Sanskrit, and even the Malay sections contain many Sanskrit loanwords. Sanskrit continued to be used in the Malay-speaking world for centuries as a liturgical language (for both Hinduism and Buddhism). Newer Indic languages such as Hindi-Urdu as well as Dravidian languages were also in contact with Malay-Indonesian, and have left traces in the form of numerous loanwords.

Chinese pilgrims and traders have been visiting Indonesia for well over a thousand years, and Chinese communities have also existed throughout the archipelago for many centuries. Various southern Chinese languages are spoken in Indonesia, and have influenced colloquial varieties of Indonesian, although in the standard language their influence has been limited and purely lexical.

Traders from the Near East first arrived in Indonesia during the second half of the first millennium AD. Eventually the Arabic and Persian languages were to have a strong impact on Malay-Indonesian. However, this did not take place until several centuries later, when local inhabitants began converting to Islam. The influence of Arabic has been especially strong, in the form of a great many loanwords, most of which did not enter the language from spoken Arabic, but rather through Arabic literature as well as Persian literature (where Arabic loanwords abound). Because many religious and other texts were translated into Malay-Indonesian from Arabic, sometimes quite literally, Arabic also had some grammatical influence on the language.

The earliest Europeans with a substantial presence in Indonesia were the Portuguese, who first arrived in the first half of the sixteenth century. There are numerous Portuguese loanwords in Indonesian, many of them originating from creolised varieties rather than from metropolitan Portuguese. Some colloquial varieties of Malay-Indonesian were impacted grammatically as well, but the grammar of the standard language was not affected.

The next Europeans on the scene were the Dutch, who sent their first expedition in 1595, and eventually came to control all of present-day Indonesia until the mid-twentieth century. The use of Dutch in Indonesia was rather limited and only a tiny fraction of the population ever gained any fluency in the language. Nevertheless, since the few Indonesians who spoke Dutch belonged to the influential elite, Dutch had a strong impact on the Indonesian lexicon, and some impact on its grammar as well.

Following independence, English quickly replaced Dutch as the most widely studied foreign language. Although English instruction in Indonesian schools has not been very successful, members of the educated elite generally have a good knowledge of English. Code switching between English and Indonesian has become the hallmark of foreign-educated Indonesians and even some locally educated ones. English is also heard daily on television and in cinemas, so most Indonesians have at least some exposure to it.

In addition to coming in contact with foreign languages, Malay-Indonesian has been in contact with hundreds of local languages, principally via its role as a lingua franca throughout the archipelago. The most influential of these local languages overall was Javanese, which has existed in a state of quasi-symbiosis with Malay-Indonesian for well over a millennium. Today, native speakers of Javanese form the largest group of speakers of Indonesian. Another language that has had some influence on Standard Indonesian is Minangkabau, a Malayic language of western Sumatra. Many Indonesian authors and educators, especially those active in the early formative years of modern standard Indonesian, were native speakers of Minangkabau. Balinese and Sundanese have had a strong impact on the Jakarta dialect, and through it on the standard language as well. Because of the similarity among them, it is often difficult to tell whether a particular word or feature has been borrowed from Javanese, Balinese or Sundanese. However, borrowings from Old Javanese are often distinguishable by their distribution, as they are present in Classical Malay literature and in areas which have been minimally influenced by modern Indonesian languages, such as the Malay peninsula.

It is important to note that many borrowed features (lexical as well as grammatical), especially the oldest and best-integrated ones, entered the language not via widespread bilingualism, but rather through written literary languages used by small minorities. Such changes affected the language of the elite first, and slowly spread to the general community. Examples of some common loanwords are provided in Appendix 1.

Appendix 1: Some Loanwords in Indonesian

A large part of the vocabulary of modern Indonesian has been borrowed from other languages. A recent study (Tadmor forthcoming) suggests that about a third of the vocabulary of Indonesian is borrowed, not including words derived from borrowed bases. Some common loanwords are listed below by source language.

Sanskrit: *suami* 'husband', *istri* 'wife', *kepala* 'head', *muka* 'face', *kunci* 'key', *gula* 'sugar', *kerja* 'work', *cuci* 'wash', *pertama* 'first', *semua* 'all'.

Arabic: *badan* 'body', *dunia* 'world', *nafas* 'breathe', *lahir* 'born', *kuat* 'strong', *séhat* 'healthy', *kursi* 'chair', *waktu* 'time', *pikir* 'think', *perlu* 'need'.

Chinese (Hokkien): *cat* 'paint', *toko* 'store', *hoki* 'lucky', *téko* 'teapot', *mi* 'noodles', *kécap* 'soy sauce', *giwang* 'earrings'.

Persian: *kawin* 'marry', *domba* 'sheep', *anggur* 'grapes, wine', *pinggan* 'dish', *gandum* 'wheat', *saudagar* 'merchant'.

Portuguese and Portuguese Creole: *garpu* 'fork', *kéju* 'cheese', *sepatu* 'shoes', *jendéla* 'window', *méja* 'table', *roda* 'wheel', *bola* 'ball', *minggu* 'week', *dansa* 'dance', *séka* 'wipe'.

Dutch: *kelinci* 'rabbit', *open* 'oven', *sup* 'soup', *handuk* 'towel', *kamar* 'room', *mobil* 'car', *gelas* 'glass', *duit* 'money', *koran* 'newspaper'.

English: *koin* 'coin', *bolpoin* 'pen', *strés* 'stress', *tivi* 'television', *tikét* 'ticket', *pink* 'pink', *gaun* 'formal dress', *komputer* 'computer', *notes* 'notepad', *flu* 'flu'.

Appendix 2: Sample Text

This short text consists of the Youth Pledge (*Sumpah Pemuda*), adopted on 28 October 1928 by the Second Pan-Indonesian Youth Congress. It constitutes the first official designation of Malay, under the name *Bahasa Indonesia* ('the Indonesian language'), as the national language of the Indonesian people.

Pertama: Kami, putra dan putri Indonesia, mengaku
first   1pl.   son and daughter Indonesia act.-claim
First: We, the sons and daughters of Indonesia, assert that

bertumpah-darah yang satu, Tanah Indonesia.
intr.-spill-blood rel. one land Indonesia
we have one homeland, the Land of Indonesia.

Kedua: Kami, putra dan putri Indonesia, mengaku
second 1pl. son and daughter Indonesia act.-claim
Second: We, the sons and daughters of Indonesia, assert that

berbangsa yang satu, Bangsa Indonesia.
intr.-nation rel. one nation Indonesia
we belong to one nation, the Indonesian Nation.

Ketiga: Kami, putra dan putri Indonesia, menjunjung
third 1pl. son and daughter Indonesia act.-carry.on.head
Third: We, the sons and daughters of Indonesia, uphold

bahasa persatuan, Bahasa Indonesia.
language NMLZ-one-circ. language Indonesia
the language of unity, Indonesian.

Notes

1 This chapter is dedicated to the memory of Jack Prentice, who wrote the chapter 'Malay (Indonesian and Malaysian)' for the first edition of this book. I am indebted to Peter Cole and David Gil for their helpful comments on an earlier draft of this chapter. Responsibility for its contents remains entirely with the author.

2 Singapore has four official languages – Mandarin, English, Malay and Tamil – but only Malay is designated as the 'national' language. Practically, however, only English and Mandarin are widely used, and the actual status of Malay is rather marginal.

3 The terms *Jawi* and *Rumi* are used mostly in Malaysia; Indonesians call Malay-Indonesian written in Arabic letters *Arab gundul* (in fact this term properly refers to Arabic written without vowel signs) or *Pégon* (although this more precisely means Javanese written in Arabic characters). Indonesian does not have a special term for Romanised Malay-Indonesian, as this has long been the norm.

4 Some authorities claim that *v* is a loan phoneme in Indonesian, although it does not in fact occur. Orthographic *v* is realised as [f] or as [p].

5 This form and some following examples contain the transitivising suffix *-i*.

6 Indeed, *s* is often palatalised in languages which do not have two separate phonemes for *s* and *ʃ*.

7 It should be noted that in some dialects whose syllabification rules are different from those of standard Malay-Indonesian one does encounter the expected *ny-*. Moreover, in some dialects a root-initial *c-* deletes following the assimilation, as one would expect of a voiceless stop.

8 The historical explanation is more complex, but cannot be discussed within the limits of this chapter.

9 It is also possible to analyse this process as the reduplication of the initial consonant with a phonetically inserted vowel between the resulting initial two consonants.

10 It is also possible to interpret *sedang* as a progressive marker.

11 Colloquially, *apa* 'what' (without *-kah*) may also be used as a yes–no question marker, but this mostly occurs in Indonesian spoken by native speakers of Javanese, and is patterned after a similar construction in that language.

12 *Meng-* is retained in a small number of denominal verbs.

13 Legend has it that this was done under the influence of socialism (which was officially sanctioned by the Soekarno regime) in order to produce a neutral, non-honorific pronoun. However, it is derived from the Malay honorific suffix *-(a)nda*, and was in fact intended to be respectful rather than egalitarian.

14 This section is based on Tadmor 2007.

Bibliography

The most comprehensive work on historical Malayic to date is Adelaar (1992), but this is a highly technical work meant for linguists. Collins (1998) offers a very accessible – and colourful – concise history of Malay. Sneddon (2003) is a good introduction to the history of Indonesian. The standard reference grammar of Indonesian in English is Sneddon (1996); for modern Malaysian, Safiah Karim (1995) is the most comprehensive, although Winstedt (1927) (based mostly on Classical Malay) is still useful. A good student's grammar which covers both Malaysian and Indonesian is Mintz (2002).

The standard English–Indonesian dictionary for decades has been Echols and Shadily (1975). Its Indonesian–English counterpart was likewise the standard work of its type for many years, especially in its greatly expanded third edition (Echols and Shadily, 1989). It has now been eclipsed by the even more comprehensive Stevens and Schmidgall-Tellings (2004). The most authoritative dictionary of (Malaysian) Malay–English dictionary is still Wilkinson (1959). This dictionary includes many dialectal and Indonesian entries, but is very dated, having been compiled before World War II. The most comprehensive English–Malaysian dictionary by far is Johns and Prentice (1992).

References

Adelaar, K. Alexander. 1992. *Proto Malayic: The Reconstruction of its Phonology and Parts of its Lexicon and Morphology*. Pacific Linguistics C–119 (Australian National University, Sydney)

Collins, James T. 1998. *Malay, World Language*, 2nd edn (Dewan Bahasa dan Pustaka, Kuala Lumpur)

Echols, John M. and Shadily, Hassan. 1975. *An English–Indonesian Dictionary* (Cornell University Press, Ithaca)

—— 1989. *An Indonesian–English Dictionary*, 3rd edn, revised and edited by John U. Wolff and James T. Collins in cooperation with Hassan Shadily (Cornell University Press, Ithaca)

Johns, A.H. and Prentice, D.J. (eds in chief) 1992. *An English–Malay Dictionary* (Dewan Bahasa dan Pustaka, Kuala Lumpur)

Mintz, Malcolm W. 2002. *An Indonesian and Malay Grammar for Students* (Malay Texts and Resources, Perth)

Safiah Karim, Nik. 1995. *Malay Grammar for Academics and Professionals* (Dewan Bahasa dan Pustaka, Kuala Lumpur)

Sneddon, James Neil. 1996. *Indonesian Reference Grammar* (Allen and Unwin, St Leonards, NSW)

—— 2003. *The Indonesian Language: Its History and Role in Modern Society* (UNSW Press, Sydney)

—— 2006. *Colloquial Jakartan Indonesian*. Pacific Linguistics 581 (Australian National University, Canberra)

Stevens, Alan M. and Schmidgall-Tellings, A. (eds) 2004. *A Comprehensive Indonesian–English Dictionary* (Ohio University Press, Athens, OH)

Tadmor, Uri. 2007. 'Grammatical Borrowing in Indonesian', in Yaron Matras and Jeanette Sakel (eds) *Grammatical Borrowing in Cross-linguistic Perspective* (Mouton de Gruyter, Berlin), pp. 301–28

—— forthcoming. 'Loanwords in Indonesian', in Martin Haspelmath and Uri Tadmor (eds) *Lexical Borrowing in Cross-linguistic Perspective* (Mouton de Gruyter, Berlin)

Wilkinson, R.J. 1959. *A Malay–English Dictionary (Romanised)* (Macmillan, London)

Winstedt, R.O. 1927. *Malay Grammar* (Clarendon Press, Oxford)

48

Javanese

Michael P. Oakes

1 Introduction

Javanese is one of the Austronesian languages, belonging to the Western Malayo-Polynesian subgroup and the Sundic family. In keeping with the other members of the subgroup, most Javanese root words consist of two syllables, and from these grammatical variants are derived by means of affixes, as described in Section 4. Austronesian languages use reduplication of words to indicate the plural and other grammatical concepts, and the use of reduplication in Javanese will be discussed in Section 5. The Austronesian languages in general exhibit a high ratio of vowels to consonants. Other Sundic languages are Sundanese, Tenggerese, Osing, Madurese and Balinese, which are all spoken on or near the island of Java. Nothofer, reported in Purwo (1993: 245), estimates that Javanese is about 37 per cent cognate with Madurese, and about 33 per cent cognate with Sundanese. An ancestor language for Javanese, Proto-Malayo-Javanic, has been reconstructed by Nothofer (1975).

Javanese does not have the status of an official language in Indonesia (although it does have the status of a regional language), but has by far the largest number of native speakers of any Austronesian language. Javanese is spoken by about 90 million people, representing 40 per cent of the people of Indonesia, making it the twelfth most widely spoken language in the world (Weber 1997). It is taught in schools, and represented in the mass media (NVTC 2007), but may be losing in influence to the national language, Bahasa Indonesia. Java is the most populous island in Indonesia, and about two-thirds of the people on the island speak Javanese. Javanese is spoken mainly in central and eastern Java. It is also spoken in a thin strip along the north coast of west Java except for the area around Jakarta, where a form of Malay is spoken.

There are three dialects of Javanese which are 'more or less' mutually intelligible (NVTC 2007). The regional dialect of Solo and Yogyakarta, the historical centres of Javanese culture, is called Kejawen, and is considered the standard form of Javanese. East Javanese is spoken in Surabaya, Malang and Pasuran (Gordon 2005). West Javanese is spoken in Banten, Cirebon and Tegal; Cirebonan is much influenced by Sundanese. The Banyumasan dialect (Logat Banyumasan, spoken in Purwokerto) is the oldest Javanese dialect, where a number of Sanskrit words such as *rika* (you) are still used. Consonants are more stressed, such as a final *k* being read almost like a *g*. It has a number of unique particles, such as *baén* or *baé* (only) (Sayoga 2004). The largest group of Javanese speakers outside Java live in Malaysia, where there are about 300,000 speakers.

The history of Javanese literature starts with an inscribed stone found in the area of Sukabumi, East Java. This stone, referred to as 'Prasasti Sukabumi', is dated the equivalent of 25 March 804, and refers to the construction of a dam. It is the oldest text written entirely in Javanese, but is in fact a copy of a now-lost original written 120 years earlier. Old, incomplete, poems called kakawin have also been found engraved on stone. The Javanese 'Ramayana', thought to have been written in 856, is considered the principal, earliest, longest and most beautifully written kakawin of the Hindu-Java period (Wikipedia, Malay Wikipedia).

2 Speech Levels

An important characteristic of Javanese is the speech decorum of the language, where different levels or stylemes of speech are used depending on the relative social status of the two speakers. This system has been in existence since the sixteenth century, and may be a legacy of the feudal system left behind by the old Hindu court tradition. However, some authors believe that the speech levels developed during the time of the Martaram empire of Central Java (Moedjanto 1985, reported in Purwo 1993: 260). The speech levels are not different languages, but different manners of speaking which vary according to the relationship between the speaker and the addressee. Each level within the language has its own characteristic set of vocabulary.

The three main levels of modern Javanese are krama, madya and ngoko – high, middle and low – of which krama and ngoko are most commonly used. Someone of high status speaking to someone of low status will use ngoko, while the other will use the (more formal) krama. The basic level ngoko is used between friends and equals. Ngoko is the ngoko form of 'I', while krama means 'marriage'. The madya level consists of krama containing certain words shortened and with ngoko-style affixes. It is often used among strangers. There are also a few hundred modesty words called krama inggil, where inggil means 'high'. These words can be mixed into either ngoko or krama as required. There are two types of krama inggil: one is 'honorific', words used when one either speaks about the person, actions or possessions of someone to whom respect is due, or speaks to that person. The other is deferential, where the verbs 'accompany', 'request', 'offer' and 'inform' take inggil forms when used of oneself in relation to the respected person. Examples of the use of different levels of Javanese speech are given by Robson (1992: 16–17).

- Ngoko (girl to her younger sister): *Aku wis mangan segane* (I have eaten the rice).
- Krama (girl to her uncle): *Kula sampun nedha sekulipun* (I have eaten the rice).
- Krama with krama inggil (girl to her uncle about her father): *Bapak sampun dhahar sekulipun* (Father has eaten the rice).
- Ngoko with krama inggil (girl to her sister about her father): *Bapak wis dhahar segane* (Father has eaten the rice).
- Madya (the old servant to the girl): *Kula mpun nedha sekule* (I have eaten the rice).

Another form, basongan, is only used in the kratons (Sultan's palaces) of Jogjakarta and Solo. The language of religion is called Jawa Halus (Refined Javanese); many words are based on Sanskrit or Kawi, but a diminishing number of people are able to use that form of the language. The number of levels may vary according to regional dialect, and between urban and rural areas (Geertz 1960). A sample of words which differ at four different levels found in Nugroho's (1995) dictionary is shown in Table 48.1.

Table 48.1 Words which Differ at Four Different Levels

English	Ngoko	Madya	Krama	Krama Inggil
Allow	Kareben	Kajenge	Kajengipun	Kersanipun
Obedient	Gugu	Dharatur	Gega	Ngestokaken dhawun
Speak	Celathu	Canten	Wicanten	Ngendika
Wear	Enggo	Ngge	Engge	Agem

For some words, this dictionary subdivides krama into 'standard (krama)' and 'substandard (krama andhap)' forms, e.g. *adhi* and *rayi* respectively for 'little brother', and *benjing* and *benjang* for 'tomorrow'. As a rough guide to the relative frequencies of ngoko, madya and krama words, I looked at the first 500 headwords in Nugroho's dictionary, for which ngoko forms were given for all 500. Krama 'standard' terms were given for 463 of the headwords, and 'substandard' terms for 87. Another 122 of the concepts had terms in krama inggil, and only 21 of them had equivalents in madya. Ühlenbeck (1978: 282) estimates that there are about 2,000 ngoko–krama pairs or 'oppositions', covering 10 to 20 per cent of the total morpheme stock. The Malay Wikipedia also distinguishes three levels of ngoko: ngoko kasar (rough), ngoko alus (refined) and 'ngoko meninggikan diri sendiri' (raising oneself). The related languages of Madurese, Sundanese and Balinese also have krama forms, probably as a result of borrowings from Javanese. In terms of its krama vocabulary, Balinese has the closest correspondence with Javanese. The phenomenon of 'level reversal' also exists, where a ngoko variant in one language is a higher level variant in another language. For example, *suku* is the Javanese krama word for 'foot' or 'leg', while *suko* is the ngoko variant with the same meaning in Madurese (Purwo 1993: 260). Uhlenbeck (1978: 288) distinguishes a number of patterns relating ngoko words with their krama equivalents. Many words form 'unique pairs', which are phonetically unrelated, such as *panah* (bow) and its krama form *jemparing*. Other pairs follow each other closely, as in the ngoko: krama pairs *tali:tangsul*, *bali:wangsul*, *kuwali:kuwangsul* and *kendhali:kendhangsul*. Even some loan words can generate krama forms by analogy, such as *patikelir* (private person) which comes from the Dutch *partikulier*. Following the pair *pati:pejah* (die), the krama form of *patikelir* is *pejahkelir*. In this chapter, ngoko forms are used throughout unless otherwise stated.

3 Phonology

The Javanese vowels are *a*, *e*, *i*, *o* and *u*, and there are open (long) and closed (short) forms of each. There is also a variant of the open *a* when it is the final syllable, pronounced halfway between *o* and *a*, and a neutral (pepet) *e*, as in the English word *open*. Following Robson (1992: 6–7), this chapter will distinguish the full length *e* from the pepet *e*, by marking it with an accent, *é* or *è*, according to whether it is found in an open syllable such as *ké* in *kéré* (beggar) or a closed one such as *nèn* in *Senèn* (Monday). *é* is pronounced as in *fiancé*, while *è* is pronounced as in the English *den*.

The Javanese consonants may be laid out as shown in Table 48.2 (Robson 1992: 10). The unvoiced stops are almost totally unaspirated, as is the case when they occur at the end of words in Malay. A piece of paper held in front of the lips should not move when

Table 48.2 The Javanese Consonants

	Unvoiced	Voiced	Nasal
Labial	p	b	m
Dental	t	d	n
Retroflex	th	dh	
Palatal	c	j	ny
Velar	k	g	ng
Liquids		r	l
Semivowels		y	w
Sibilant		s	
Aspirant		h	

the voiced stops are articulated. In Javanese, the consonants *b*, *d* and *g* are also pronounced as unvoiced (*p*, *t* or *k* respectively) when they are found at the end of a word. The English *d* and *t* are somewhere in between the Javanese dental and retroflex forms. The dental forms require pressing the tongue on the back of the front teeth, while the retroflex forms are so called because the tongue is bent back and pressed on the back of the upper gum. *c* is similar to 'ch' in English, and *ng*, which can appear at the front of a word, is always pronounced as in 'singer' rather than 'finger' (Robson 1992: 11).

Root words are typically disyllables of the form (C1) V1 (C2) V2 (C3), where (C1), (C2) and (C3) are optional consonant clusters. The most common sequences are CVCVC followed by CVCCVC. Allowable consonant clusters include *mb*, *nd*, *ndh*, *nj* and *nng*, which can all occur in the initial position. There is a light stress on the second-last syllable, or the final syllable when the second-last syllable contains a neutral *e*. This light stress does not occur when a suffix is added.

4 Affixes

Grammatical variants of a root word may be composed by affixation, reduplication or combination. Affixes, which may be prefixes, suffixes or infixes, are more common in Javanese and Tagalog than in Malay. Affixes may result in the production of either a noun or a verb. Sometimes the surface forms of affixes that result in the formation of a noun are identical with those which result in the formation of a verb. Adjectives can take affixes, e.g. *cukup* (enough) + *-an* = *cukupan* (more or less enough), *dhuwur* (high) + *ke-an* = *kedhuwuren* (too high). Adjectives can also be formed from nouns with affixes, e.g. *jamur* (fungus) + *-an* = *jamuren* (mouldy). In the remainder of this section, we will consider the great variety of ways that affixes can transform nouns and verbs in Javanese.

4.1 Nouns

As is typical in Malayo-Polynesian languages, nouns do not change according to gender or case. They do not change either with definite number, as in *wong* (person), *wong telu* (three people, where the numeral follows the noun). However, indefinite number can be expressed by reduplication of the noun, as described in Section 5. Nouns may be in the form of a root word without affixes, such as *omah* (house), *dalan* (road) and *manuk* (bird). Only those affixed forms which are relatively common will be discussed here. Abstract nouns can be formed with the prefix *ka-* and the suffix *-an* added to root words. These root words may be verbs, as in *ana* (to be) yielding *kaanaan* (state or condition) nouns, as in *lurah* (village headman) giving *kalurahan* (area controlled by the headman), or adjectives, where *rosa* (strong) becomes *karosaan* (strength). The prefix *pa-* can be added to any active nasalised verb (see Section 4.2) as in *njaluk* (to ask) and *panjaluk* (request). The prefix *pa-* and the suffix *-an* can be added to both nouns and verbs to yield a noun of place, as in *kubur* (grave), *pakuburan* (cemetery), *désa* (village), *padésan* (countryside), *turu* (to sleep), *paturon* (bed). A small number of common words are made with the prefix *pi-*, and are considered as being more digni-fied or archaic than their unaffixed variants, such as *karep* (wish), *pikarep* (a wish). The suffix *-an* produces various types of meaning. This can be locative, as in *tegal* (non-irrigated field) and *tegalan* (area of non-irrigated fields), *gemblak* (a brass-smith) and *gemblakan* (the brass-smith's workshop). The meaning of imitation or miniature can be rendered by adding *-an*, as in *jaran* (horse) and *jaranan* (hobby-horse), *bajing* (squirrel) and *bajingan* (petty thief). The suffix may denote a ceremony, as in selapan (35-day calendar cycle, see Section 10), and *selapanan* (ceremony to celebrate the first 35-day cycle after birth). A large number of verbs can take *-an* to produce nouns describing the result of their action, such as *nandur* (to plant), *tanduran* (a crop), *nggagas* (to think over), *gagasan* (idea). We can also use *-an* to indicate the instrument by which a verb is carried out, e.g. *mikul* (to carry on a pole over the shoulder), *pikulan* (carrying pole which goes over the shoulder), *timbang* (to weigh), *timbangan* (weighing balance). Other suffixes can occur with reduplicated forms of the noun, as described in Section 5 (Robson 1992: 20–32).

4.2 Verbs

Robson (1992) feels that the verb is the most complicated aspect of Javanese grammar. Verbs may be transitive, taking both subject and object, or intransitive, taking a subject only. Transitive verbs can take either the active or the passive voice. Intransitive verbs often occur as unaffixed root words, such as *lunga* (to go), *weruh* (to know) and *teka* (to come). Other verbs can be made by adding affixes to the root-word verbs. Some root-word verbs have a dual role as noun or verb, such as *jeneng* (a name, to be called), *kembang* (a flower, to bloom) and *crita* (a story, to tell). Many verbs can be formed by partial or complete doubling of a root-word, as described in Section 5. A group of intransitive verbs still retains a form of the historical infix *-um-*, which is still widely used in Tagalog verbs, such as (in Javanese) *mlebu* (go in, from *lebu*, entry), *mlaku* (to walk, from *laku*, walking or gait), *muni* (to sound, call or say, from *uni*, a sound or call). Most transitive verbs and some intransitive ones have nasa-lised forms. The rules for the nasalisation of root words are given in Table 48.3. Exceptions are *cocog* → *nocogi* (agree with), *susu* → *nusoni* (suckle), where the second

Table 48.3 Formation of Nasalised Forms of Javanese Verbs

Un-nasalised initial sequence	Nasalised initial sequence
p-	m-
b-	mb-
t-	n-
d-	nd-
th-	n-
dh-	ndh-
c-	ny-
j-	nj-
k-	ng-
g-	ngg-
r-	ngr-
l-	ngl-
s-	ny-
w-	m- or ngw-
n-, m-, ng- (already begins with a nasal)	no change
vowel	ng + vowel-

consonant c or s is the same as the initial consonant, and when the root is a monosyllable, such as *tik* (to type), the pepet *e* comes before it in the nasalised form, in this case (*ngetik*).

Nasalised intransitive verbs include *ngiwa* (to move to the left, from *kiwa*, left); *ndhalang* (to act as a wayang-kulit puppeteer, from *dhalang*, wayang kulit puppeteer); *nglenga* (glisten like oil, from *lenga*, oil); *mbécak* (ride in a trishaw, from *bécak*, trishaw). Nasalised transitive verbs can occur with the suffixes *-i* or *-ake*, or with no suffix. In some respects the suffix *-i* can correspond to a preposition in English. For example, *lungguh* (to sit) becomes *nglungguhi* (to sit on), *mundur* (to go backwards) becomes *munduri* (to withdraw from). Sometimes the *-i* form is more specific in meaning than its corresponding unsuffixed form, where for example *padha* (to be the same) becomes *madhani* (to equal or match); *nemu* (to find) becomes *nemoni* (to go and see a particular person). Transitive verbs with the sense of providing someone with something can be made by the addition of *-i* to the relevant noun: examples are *tamba* (medicine) becomes *nambani* (to treat with a medicine); *warah* (knowledge or science) becomes *marahi* (to instruct). Adjectives and verbs can take the *-i* suffix to form verbs of causation, such as *resik* (clean) produces *ngresiki* (to make clean) and *kebak* (full) making *ngebaki* (to fill up). The *-i* form can also indicate plurality or repetition of the subject or object, as in *mangan* (to eat) giving *mangani* (to eat many things or eat again and again). Some intransitive verbs can take *-i,* such as *bocah* (child) can make *mbocahi* (to act childishly), and *wédok* (female) giving *médoki* (to be effeminate).

Verbs created with the suffix *-aké* are always transitive. To add the suffix *-ake* to a root word ending in a consonant, e.g. *dadi* (to become) produces *ndadèkaké* (to make or appoint). Glottal stops are inserted after terminal vowels, and in place of terminal *-n,* so *takon* (ask) becomes *nakokaké*, and *tata* (order, structure) becomes *natakaké* (to put in order). Both *-i* and *-ake* forms can produce a causative meaning, but there is a subtle distinction: *dawa* (long) gives both *ndawakaké* (to lengthen) and *ndawani* (to make longer than something else). Sometimes the *-ake* form implies that the causation is not intended, as in *tugel* (snapped in two) making *nugelaké* (to break or snap something accidentally). It can also be used to mean consider to have the property of the root word, as in the pair *mokal* (impossible), *mokalaké* (to regard as impossible). Another role played by the *-i* and *-aké* suffixes is to distinguish the direct and indirect object: compare *wèneh* (to give) with *mènehi*, to give (something) to someone, and *menèhaké*, give something to (someone). Although the *-i* and *-aké* suffixes are very productive, not all verbs can take them. Four common transitive verbs do not take nasalised forms: *éntuk* (to get), *gawé* (to make or to cause), *tuku* (to buy) and *duwé* (to have or to possess).

The passive voice is more commonly used in Javanese than in English, and Robson (1992: 87–91) lists four forms of the passive. The first passive takes different prefixes for the first, second and third person. Using the verb *njupuk* (to take), we can form *dakjupuk* (taken by me), *kojupuk* (taken by you) and *dijupuk* (taken). The third person *di-* form does not specify who did the taking, so if necessary this must be specified in addition, e.g. *dijupuk kancaku* (taken by my friend). The passive prefix *di-* can also be added to verbs with *-i* and *-aké*, with no change in the suffix. The more formal second passive corresponding to the prefix *di-* adds instead the prefix *ka-*, and if the verb has the suffix *-i*, this is changed to *-an* (e.g. *nglakoni*, to carry out, *kalakon*, carried out). The third passive is an archaic form, used more in poetry than in conversation, and also corresponds to the third person *di-* forms. If the root begins with a consonant, as in *gawé* (make), the third passive inserts *-in* immediately after the initial consonant to give *ginawé* (made). If the root begins with a vowel, as for *utus* (to send), the prefix *-ing* yields the third passive *ingutus* (sent). The fourth passive, indicated by the prefix *ke-* (simply *k* before *r* or *l*, and *ku* before *w*) shows that the action is accidental, as in *payungé kegawa kancaku* (my friend accidentally took the umbrella). Note the change in word order required by the passive, compared with the active *kancaku kegawa payungé*. The passive voice cannot be used in conjunction with nasalised forms.

Other forms of the verb are formed simply by the addition of the particles *dak* and *ya*. *Dak* is used with the first person singular to emphasise that *I* will do it (as in 'Let me …'). For example, *aku dak turu* is 'I'll have a sleep'. The imperative is formed with *ya*, and more politely with the passive voice, as in *lawangé ditutup, ya* (close the door, will you) (Robson 1992).

5 Reduplication

A notable feature of Austronesian languages is that of word reduplication, where the reduplicated form of a word, although related to the single root word, may have a number of other connotations, such as plurality, repetition or vagueness. Suharto (1982) lists six syntactic forms of word reduplication. First, whole words can be reduplicated without any phonological change, as in *mangan* (eat) and *mangan-mangan* (eat informally with other people). There can also be partial doubling, producing a noun from an adjective, as in *lara* (sick) and *lelara* (sickness), or *peteng* (dark) and *pepeteng* (darkness). The reduplicated fragment is a prefix consisting of the first phoneme of the root word followed by *pepet e*. A combination of partial doubling and the prefix *-an* yields such pairs as *tembung* (word) and *tetembungan* (wording, expression). Duplication can involve whole word repetition of a verb with a phonological change, as in *bali* (return) and *bola-bali* (to and fro); *mubeng* (go around) and *mubang-mubeng* (beat around the bush). In lexical doubling, the root words are already doubled, since the single form does not exist. For example *ali-ali* means ring, while *ali* does not exist. In morphological doubling, a completely new meaning is formed in contrast to the non-doubled one. Ühlenbeck (1953) gives examples where the duplicated form is not exactly a repletion of the unduplicated form, such as *puji* (praise) making *pujeq-pujeqna* (pray for me, keep your fingers crossed for me).

Robson (1992) lists a number of semantic categories which result from reduplication. One is to do something at leisure, as in *mlaku* (walk) and *mlaku-mlaku* (go for a stroll). Reduplication can imply repetition, as in *njerit* (shout) and *jerit-jerit* (shout repeatedly). Interrogative pronouns can be given indefinite meaning, as in *sapa* (who) and *sapa-sapa* or *sapaa* (anyone). Mild exasperation can be expressed through reduplication, as in *mentah-mentah iya dipangan* (even though it's unripe he still eats it). Repetition expresses general plurality of nouns, as in *wet-wet* (trees), or plurality with diversity for both adjectives and nouns, as in *gedhong dhuwur-dhuwur* (highish buildings). Other uses are to express doing something together, e.g. *omong-omongan* (to chat together), and to compete in, e.g. *gelis-gelisan* (to see who is fastest at running).

6 Pronouns

The Javanese personal pronouns are shown in Table 48.4.

Table 48.4 The Javanese Personal Pronouns

English	Ngoko	Madya	Krama	Krama Inggil
I	Aku	——	Kula	Dalem
You	Kowé	Samang	Sampéyan	Panjenengan
He, She	Dhèweké	—	Piyambakipun	Panjenengané, panjenenganipun

For *we*, ngoko uses *awaké dhéwé*, while both ngoko and krama can use the Indonesian loanword *kita*. The second and third person pronouns are rarely used, and are generally replaced by kinship terms, titles or proper names. For example, a woman may be addressed as *Bu* (literally, *mother*) or a young man as *Mas* (elder brother). A pronoun may be omitted altogether if the referent's identity is understood. The ngoko forms of possessive pronouns are produced by the suffixes *-ku*, *-mu* and *é/né* for the first, second and third person respectively. For example, *kembang* (flower) gives *kembangku* (my flower), *omah* (house) gives *omahmu* (your house). A word ending with a consonant usually adds *-é* to denote 'his/her', while words ending in vowels take the suffix *-né*. Two nouns in a relation of possession are linked using *-ing or -ning*. In the krama form, the noun or pronoun indicating the possessor is written immediately after the word indicating the object possessed, as in *serat kula* (my letter). The suffixes *-ipun* and *-nipun* correspond to the ngoko *-é* and *né* respectively, as in *sabinipun* (his irrigated field) and *méndanipun* (his goat) (Robson 1992: 33–42).

7 Tense and Aspect

Verbs are not inflected to denote tenses, but instead auxiliary words are used as aspect markers preceding the verb. The list given by Robson (1992: 65) is given in Table 48.5. Some auxiliaries can stand alone to make a fully syntactic sentence: *aja!* (don't!), *durung* (no, not yet), *isih* (yes, still), *ora* (I don't or No it isn't) or *wis* (Yes I have, or Yes it is). Two or more auxiliaries can be used together, as in *isih ora* (still not). Auxiliaries can be used with adjectives as well as nouns, as in *Aja nakal* (don't be naughty), *isih mentah* (still unripe).

Table 48.5 Aspect Markers in Javanese

Ngoko	Krama	Meaning
Aja	Sampun	Don't
Arep, bakal	Badhé	Will
Durung	Dèrèng	Not yet
Isih	Taksih	Still
Lagi	Saweg	In the process of doing
Mèh	—	Almost
Meksa		Even so, still
Ora	Mboten	Not
Padha	Sami	Also; indicates the plurality of the subject performing the action
Sok	—	On occasion, ever
Tansah		Always, constantly
Wis	Sampun	Already

8 Syntax

The normal word order within the modern Javanese sentence is subject–verb–object (SVO). There is no copulative verb, e.g. *klambiku reged* (my shirt is dirty). No changes are found in nouns or verbs for number, case or gender. A definite noun can be made from a simple word verb or noun by the addition of *-é* if it ends in a consonant, or *-né* if it ends with a vowel. Examples are *jaran* (horse), *jarané* (the horse), *sapi* (bull), *sapiné* (the bull), *tuku* (buy), *tukuné* (the purchase). An adjective follows the noun it qualifies, as in *anyar* (new) with *kreteg* (bridge) giving *kreteg anyar* (new bridge).

In Javanese, the most extensive progressive nominal group encountered by Ühlenbeck (1965) consists of seven elements, for example in the group *bocah* (subject, boy) *cilik* (adjective, small) *wolu* (numeral, eight) *iku* (demonstrative pronoun DP, those) *kabèh* (all) *mau* (previously mentioned) *waé* (only), with the overall meaning 'only all those eight boys previously mentioned'. Simpler constructions can be made by omitting some of these words, but the order subject–adjective–numeral–DP–*kabèh*–*mau*–*waé* must be maintained. Thus the sequences *bocah waé* (only boys) or *bocah wolu kabèh waé* (only all eight boys) are allowed, but not **bocah wolu cilik iku*. However, there is some flexibility in the allowable positions of *kabèh*.

Progressive structures consisting only of pronouns can have up to three constituents, and word order is determined by the types of pronouns used. For example, if a personal pronoun occurs in the first position, the neutral demonstrative occupies the final position, e.g. *aku* (I) *kéné* (here) *iki* (this), *kowé* (you) *kono* (there), *iku* (that). Only the following three sequences of two pronouns modifying a noun are allowed: (a) locative DP–neutral DP, as in *bocah kono iku* (those boys there); (b) modal DP–neutral DP, as in *prekara mengkono iku* (such a question); and (c) quantitative DP–neutral DP, as in *dhuwit semono iku* (so much money) (Uhlenbeck 1965).

9 Javanese Numerals

The cardinal numbers in Javanese, shown in Table 48.6 (Robson 1992: 75–6) are fairly irregular, and exist in both ngoko and krama forms. Note the special terms for 25, 50 and 60. In Javanese, the numeral follows the noun it refers to, e.g. *jeruk lima* (five oranges). For expressing measures, the numbers 1 to 9 take the forms found in the terms for units of ten in the cardinal numbers, e.g. *rong puluh* (20), *rong kilo* (two kilos). The ordinal numbers are formed by placing the word *ping* before the cardinal number, the first five being *ping sapisan* (first or once), *ping pindho* (second or twice), *ping telu* (third or thrice), *ping pat* (fourth or four times) and *ping lima* (fifth or five times). Note the terms for first and second are irregular. The numerals can be used to derive other kinds of words, e.g. *telu* (three), *telu-telu* (in threes, three each); *loro* (two), *loro-loroné* (both), *telung atus* (300), *telung atusan* (about 300).

10 Javanese Names

Forms of the definite article precede Javanese names, the so-called personal articles *si* in ngoko and *pun* in krama. Proper names do not take suffixes. With a few exceptions, names are either masculine or feminine. Some names are reserved for low social class, while others are not associated with class. Masculine names are also either *nama alit* (little names), traditionally given by the father at the *slametan pasaran* name-giving ceremony which takes place five days after birth, or *nama sepuh* (adult names) selected by the adult man himself. A *nama sepuh* is chosen to replace the *nama alit* at a key juncture in the man's life, such as his wedding, upon taking a new job or after recovery from a serious illness. Upon marriage women also discard their birth names, taking instead the title *mboq* (mother), followed by the husband's *nama sepuh*, possibly abbreviated. Some names are merely morphologically Javanese, while others (described as 'motivated' by Ühlenbeck (1969)) have meanings in the Javanese lexicon. The unmotivated female lower-class names often take the vowel pattern *a-i-pepet e*, and end in *-em* or *-en*, as in *Ardinem, Waginem, Jaminten*. The corresponding masculine names often take the vowel pattern *a-i-a* and end in *-an* or *-in*, such as *Ardiman, Jandiman* and *Sukiman*. The lower-class motivated names are often taken from the Javanese calendar for boys, although *Legi* in the market week (see Section 11) is reserved for girls, and *Paing* can be taken by either gender. They may also be the names of tools, such as *Ganden* (mallet) or *Palu* (hammer) for boys, or *Tumbu, Kendil* or *Genting* for girls (these three names are types of baskets or pots). These names may describe personal qualities, usually but not always favourable: examples are *Onjo* (excellent), *Susah* (sorrowful) for girls, *Lantip* (clever, shrewd) or *Sabar* (patient) for boys. Also in this category are names of animals and plants, such as *Kampret* (bat), *Bajing* (squirrel) and *Jaran* (horse) for boys, and *Cebong* (tadpole) and *Atat* (parrot) for girls. Feminine

Table 48.6 Cardinal Numbers in Javanese

	Ngoko	*Krama*
1	Siji	Satunggal
2	Loro	Kalih
3	Telu	Tiga
4	Papat	Sakawan
5	Lima	Gangsal
6	Nem	
7	Pitu	
8	Wolu	
9	Sanga	
10	Sapuluh	Sadasa
11	Sawelas	
12	Rolas	Kalih-welas
13	Telu-las	Tiga-welas
14	Pat-belas	Kawan-welas
15	Lima-las	Gangsal-welas
16	Nem-belas	
17	Pitu-las	
18	Wolu-las	
19	Sanga-las	
20	Rong puluh	Kalih dasa
21	Salikur	
22	Ro-likur	Kalih-likur
23	Telu-likur	Tiga-likur
24	Pat-likur	Kawan-likur
25	Salawé	Salangkang
26	Nem-likur	
27	Pitu-likur	
28	Wolu-likur	
29	Sanga-likur	
30	Telung puluh	Tigang dasa
31	Telung puluh siji	Tigang dasa satunggal
40	Patang puluh	Kawan dasa
50	Sèket	
51	Sèket siji	Sèket satunggal
60	Sawidak	
62	Sawidak loro	Sawidak kalih
70	Pitung puluh	Pitung dasa
75	Pitung puluh lima	Pitung dasa gangsal
80	Wolung puluh	Wolung dasa
90	Sangang puluh	Sangang dasa
100	Satus	
105	Satus lima	Satus gangsal
200	Rong atus	Kalih atus
1,000	Sèwu	
2,000	Rong èwu	Kalih ewu
10,000	Saleksa	
100,000	Sakethi	
1,000,000	Sayuta	

names and *nama atit*, when unmotivated and not associated with social class often end in *-ah*, and tend to take either *-n-* or *-y-* as an intervocalic consonant, such as *Jakinah* or *Jatinah*. Another group all end in *-i*, with *a* as the penultimate vowel, as in *Maryati*, *Sukarti*. This group can often generate masculine names by replacing the terminal *-i* with *-a*, yielding feminine–masculine pairs such as *Sugianti* and *Sugianta*, *Sumarni* and *Sumarna*. The motivated names not associated with social class include the names of important figures in the *wayang kulit* stories, such as *Wibisana*, or *Indrajit*, but not *Arjuna* or *Rama*. In contrast, lower-class names might be the names of lesser characters in these plays. Classless names may be personality traits, such as *Seneng* (splendour) or *Puji* (praise) for girls, *Mulya* (exalted) or *Waskata* (wise) for boys. The classless *nama sepuh* nearly always consist of two components, usually verbs or nouns of Sanskrit origin, e.g. *Wangsa-guna*, *Karta-Semita*. Lower-class variants can be generated from these by processes such as abbreviation and simplification of consonant clusters, as in *Singa-Semita* making *Sasmita* and in turn *Semita*. Some Sanskrit elements are exclusive to classless names, such as *kusuma*, *wijaya* and *surya* (Ühlenbeck 1969).

11 The Javanese Calendar

The days in the international seven-day week, which in Java begin at sunset, are derived from Arabic, i.e. *Ngahad* (Sunday, alternatively the Indonesian *minggu*), *Senin* (Monday), *Selasa* (Tuesday), *Rebo* (Wednesday), *Kemis* (Thursday), *Jumat/Jumuwat* (Friday) and *Setu* (Saturday). These names exist alongside the older *Redité*, *Soma*, *Anggara*, *Buda*, *Respati*, *Sukra* and *Tumpak/Saniscara*. The seven-day week is the most widely used in commerce and modern life generally, but apart from this seven-day week, Java also has an ancient five-day market week (*Pasaran*): *Pon*, *Wagé*, *Kliwon*, *Legi* and *Paing*. Dates such as birthdays can be specified on a 35-day cycle (*selapan dina*) by the pairing of the days from the seven-day and five-day weeks, such as *Senin Pon*. *Jumat Kliwon* is said to be inauspicious. This superimposition of the five-day and seven-day weeks is called *Wetonan* (Coincidence). The Javanese have three sets of months: the 12 months of the Western solar year, the 13 Islamic lunar months which add up to a year of 354 or 355 days, and a set of months called *Pranata Mangsa*, of irregular length, which were used as agricultural seasons. The first day of the lunar month of *Sura* is the first day of the Javanese year (*taun Jawa*), and eight such years form a *windu*. Finally, there is a cycle of four *windu*: *Adi*, *Kunthara*, *Sengara* and *Sancaya* (Robson 1992: 145–6; Arcinega 2005).

12 Javanese Writing Systems

Traditional Javanese script (Kawi) is based on the Pallava script of South India. The earliest inscription, which originates from the town of Malang, was written in Sanskrit and dated 760. The earliest text written in Old Javanese is the Sukabumi inscription (see Section 1). Kawi evolved into 'later Kawi', used in the Majapahit period (1250–1450 AD). From the fourteenth century, after the arrival of Islam, there was limited use of Arabic script called *pégon* or *gundil*. By the seventeenth century, the Javanese alphabet, also known as *tjarakan* or *carakan*, had developed into its current form. During the Japanese occupation of Indonesia between 1942 and 1945, the Javanese alphabet was prohibited (Omniglot). The period of Dutch colonisation did not greatly influence Javanese writing until early in the twentieth century, when Roman scripts came into fashion. *Kawi* scripts, although by now largely supplanted by Roman scripts, are still used by scholars and *wayang kulit* puppeteers (Phlong).

Notable features of Javanese script, given by Omniglot, are first that it is a syllabic alphabet, where each consonant is followed by the vowel *a*, unless specified otherwise by a system of diacritics which appear above, below, in front of or after the main letter. There are a number of special consonants called *aksara murda* or *aksara gedhe* (great letters) which are used for honorific purposes, such as to write the names of respected people or towns. The corresponding vowels are called *aksara swara* (voice letters). The order of the consonants in the Javanese alphabet makes the saying '*hana caraka, data sawala padha jayanya, maga bathanga*' meaning 'there were (two) envoys, they had a difference of opinion, they were equal in strength, both of them died'. The alphabet, in this order, is given below:

ꦲꦤ ꦕꦫꦏ ꦢꦠ ꦱꦮꦭ ꦥꦝ ꦗꦪꦚ ꦩꦒ ꦧꦛꦔ

Each consonant has two forms: the *aksara* form is used at the beginning of the syllable, while the *pasangan* form, which usually appears below the *aksara* form, is used for the second consonant of a consonant cluster and mutes the vowel of the aksara. The full set of *pasangan* characters shown in conjunction with their corresponding *carakan* is:

ꦲ꧀ꦲ ꦤ꧀ꦤ ꦕ꧀ꦕ ꦫ꧀ꦫ ꦏ꧀ꦏ ꦢ꧀ꦢ ꦠ꧀ꦠ ꦱ꧀ꦱ ꦮ꧀ꦮ ꦭ꧀ꦭ ꦥ꧀ꦥ ꦝ꧀ꦝ ꦗ꧀ꦗ ꦪ꧀ꦪ ꦚ꧀ꦚ ꦩ꧀ꦩ ꦒ꧀ꦒ ꦧ꧀ꦧ ꦛ꧀ꦛ ꦔ꧀ꦔ

The *aksara murda* and *aksara swara* are as follows:

ꦟ (Na), ꦑ (Ka), ꦡ (Ta), ꦯ (Sa), ꦦ (Pa), ꦘ (Nya), ꦓ (Ga), ꦨ (Ba);
ꦄ (A), ꦆ (I), ꦈ (U), ꦌ (E), ꦎ (O).

The *aksara murda* have corresponding *pasangan* forms, not shown here.

The digits (*Angka* or *Wilangan*) from 0 to 9 are as follows: ꧐ (0), ꧑ (1), ꧒ (2), ꧓ (3), ꧔ (4), ꧕ (5), ꧖ (6), ꧗ (7), ꧘ (8), ꧙ (9). A number of punctuation symbols exist, such as *pada lungsi* ꧉ (full stop), *pada lingsa* ꧈ (comma), *pada guru* ꧋꧐꧋ (start of a letter or story), *pada pancak* ꧉꧐꧉ (end of a letter or story). There is also a small set of characters called *aksara rekan* which represent sounds in words derived from foreign languages, particularly Arabic: ꦏ꦳ (kh), ꦥ꦳ (f), ꦢ꦳ (dz), ꦒ꦳ (gh), ꦗ꦳ (z). The 'Hanacaraka' Javanese font, developed by Teguh Budi Sayoga, was used to reproduce all the Javanese script used in this article. It may be downloaded free of charge from http://hanacaraka.fateback.com, along with a tutorial on how to write with the Javanaese alphabet.

As an example of Javanese writing, ꦕꦤ꧀ꦝꦶꦧꦺꦴꦫꦺꦴꦧꦸꦢꦸꦂ reads Candhi Borobudur, the name of the famous Buddhist temple just outside Yogyakarta. It contains the *aksara carakan* ꦕ (ca) followed by ꦤ (na). The *a* of *na* is muted by the *aksara pasangan dh* written beneath: thus the sequence ꦕꦤ꧀ꦝ is pronounced (*candh*). The following *i* sound is produced by the diacritic (*sandangan*) written above, so ꦕꦤ꧀ꦝꦶ is *candhi*. The *aksara carakan* ꦧ (ba) has its vowel changed to *o* by a combination of the preceding and following characters: ꦧꦺꦴ. Similarly, ꦫ (ra) becomes ꦫꦺꦴ (ro). ꦧ (ba) then becomes ꦧꦸ (bu) as a result of the '*suku*' beneath. In the same way, ꦢ (da) becomes ꦢꦸ (du). The final *r* is denoted by a final consonant diacritic (layar) above, so ꦢꦸꦂ represents *dur*.

References

Arcinega, Matthew. 2005. *The Javanese Calendar*, http://xentana.com/java/calendar.htm

Geertz, C. 1960. *The Religion of Java* (Free Press, New York)

Gordon, Raymond G. Jr (ed.) 2005. *Ethnologue: Languages of the World*, 15th edn (SIL International, Dallas, TX). Online version: http://www.ethnologue.com/

Nothofer, B. 1975. *The Reconstruction of Proto-Malayo-Javanic* (Martinus Nijhoff, The Hague)

Nugroho, K. (1995) *Kamus Indonesia-Jawa* (CV Buana Raya, Solo)

NVTC (National Virtual Translation Centre) 2007. *Javanese*, Languages of the World, http://www.nvtc.gov/lotw/months/june/Javanese.html

Omniglot. *Javanese Alphabet*, http://www.omniglot.com/writing/javanese.htm

Phlong, Pisith. *About Javanese*, South Asia Digital Library, http://sea.lib.niu.edu/lang.java.html

Pigeaud, Theodore G. 1967. *Literature of Java: Catalogue Raisonne of Javanese Manuscripts in the Library of the University of Leiden*, Volume 1 (Leiden University Press, Leiden)

Purwo, Bambang Kaswanti. 1993. 'Factors Influencing Comparison of Sundanese, Javanese, Madurese and Balinese', in Ger P. Reesnik (ed.) *Topics in Descriptive Austronesian Linguistics*, Semaian 11 (Vakgroep Talen en Culturen van Zuidoost-Azië en Oceanië, Rijksuniversiteit te Leiden, Leiden), pp. 245–91

Robson, Stuart. 1992. *Javanese Grammar for Students*. Monash Papers on South East Asia 26 (Monash University, Clayton, Victoria, Australia)

Sayoga, Teguh Budi. 2004. *The Official Site of Aksara Jawa*, http://hanacaraka.fateback.com

Suharno, Ignatius. 1982. *A Descriptive Study of Javanese*. Pacific Linguistics, Series D, no. 45 (Research School of Pacific Studies, Canberra, Australia)

Uhlenbeck, E.M. 1953. 'Word Duplication in Javanese', *Bidragen tot de Taal-, Land-en Volkenkunde (BKI)*, Vol. 109, pp. 52–61

—— 1965. 'Some Preliminary Remarks on Javanese Syntax', *Lingua*, Vol. 15, pp. 53–70

—— 1969. 'Systematic Features of Javanese Personal Names', *Word*, Vol. 25, No. 3, pp. 321–35

—— 1978. *Studies in Javanese Morphology*. Translation Series 19 Koninklijk Instituut voor Taal-, Land-en Volkenkunde (Martinus Nijhoff, The Hague)

Wikipedia, Malay edition, *Sastera Jawa*, http://ms.wikipedia.org/wiki/Sastra_Jawa

Wikipedia, *Old Javanese Language*, http://en.wikipedia.org/wiki/Old_Javanese_language

All websites were accessed on 5 November 2007.

49

Tagalog

Paul Schachter

Revised by Lawrence A. Reid

1 Historical Background

Tagalog is a member of the Central Philippine subgroup of Philippine languages, forming part of the Western-Malayo-Polynesian set of Austronesian languages. It belongs in a subgroup with Bikol, Bisayan and Mansakan languages and was originally probably native to the eastern Visayas or northeast Mindanao in the Central Philippines (Zorc 1993). By the time the Spanish arrived in the Philippines (1521), Tagalog speakers had migrated north into the southern part of the island of Luzon in the Philippines, with Tagalog becoming the major language spoken in Manila and surrounding provinces; it has in recent years spread as a second language over virtually the entire Philippine archipelago. Thus, while only about a quarter of the population of the Philippines were Tagalog-speaking in 1940, in 1970 approximately half of the population were, and today it is estimated that well over 90 per cent of the 80 million total population of the Philippines is either a first- or second-language speaker of the language.

Tagalog was selected in 1937 as the national language of the Philippines, and was established as such in the 1987 Constitution of the country. Under the name of Filipino, Tagalog is now taught in schools throughout the Philippines. The spread of the language has also been favoured by urbanisation – Tagalog is native to the largest city of the Philippines, Manila, and it is used as a lingua franca in many cities with mixed populations – as well as by its prominence in the mass media.

The dialect of Tagalog which is considered standard and which underlies Filipino is the educated dialect of Manila. Other important regional dialects are those of Bataan, Batangas, Bulacan, Tanay-Paete and Tayabas. The lexicon of educated Manila Tagalog contains many borrowings from Spanish and English, the former reflecting over three centuries of colonial domination of the Philippines by Spain, the latter reflecting the period of American hegemony (1898–1946), as well as the current status of English as one of the languages (along with Filipino) of higher education in the Philippines and a lingua franca second in importance only to Filipino itself. Spanish and English have also had some impact on the phonology of Tagalog (see Section 2, below), but little if any on the syntax and morphology. (See Section 4, however, for some instances of borrowed Spanish gender distinctions.)

2 Phonology and Orthography

Tagalog phonology has been significantly affected by the incorporation into the language of many loanwords from Spanish, English and other languages. One effect of this incorporation has been an expansion of the phonemic inventory of the language, an expansion that has influenced both the vowel and the consonant systems.

Contemporary Tagalog has the five vowel phonemes shown in Table 49.1.

Table 49.1 Tagalog Vowel Phonemes

	Front	Central	Back
High	i		u
Mid	e		o
Low		a	

This five-vowel system no doubt developed out of a three-vowel system in which [i] and [e] were allophones of a single phoneme and [u] and [o] were allophones of another. Contrasts between /i/ and /e/ and between /u/ and /o/ are, however, well established in contemporary Tagalog, not only in borrowed vocabulary (*misa* /mi:sa/ 'mass' vs *mesa* /me:sa/ 'table', *bus* /bu:s/ 'bus' vs *bos* /bo:s/ 'boss') but, albeit less commonly, in native vocabulary as well (*iwan* /ʔi:wan/ 'leave' vs *aywan* /ʔe:wan/ 'not known', *babuy* /ba:buy/ 'pig-like person' vs *baboy* /ba:boy/ 'pig'). Vowel length in non-word-final syllables is phonemic, as the following examples illustrate: *aso* /ʔa:so/ 'dog', *aso* /ʔaso/ 'smoke', *maglalakbay* /magla:lakbay/ 'will travel', *maglalakbay* /maglalakbay/ 'travel a lot'. In word-final syllables of native words, vowel length is not phonemic: the general rule is that phrase-final syllables are long, non-phrase-final syllables short. Thus *sibat* /sibat/ 'spear' is pronounced [siba:t] phrase-finally, but not in *sibat ba?* /sibat ba/ [sibat ba:] 'is it a spear?' Word-final syllables of non-native words may, however, show phonemic length. For example, borrowed monosyllabic names have a long vowel in any context: e.g. *Si Bob ba?* /si ba:b ba/ [si ba:b ba:] 'Is it Bob?'

There are sixteen consonant phonemes that occur in native words. These are displayed in Table 49.2. Probably [d] and [r] were once allophones of a single phoneme, as is evidenced by a good deal of free or morphophonemically conditioned alternation between them (e.g. *daw* /daw/ ~ *raw* /raw/ 'they say', *dalita* /dalitaʔ/ 'poverty' vs *maralita* /mara:litaʔ/ 'poor'). There is no doubt, however, that they now contrast, not only in loanwords (*dos* /do:s/ 'two' vs *Rose* /ro:s/ 'Rose') but in native words as well (*maramdamin* /maramdamin/ 'sensitive' vs *madamdamin* /madamda:min/ 'moving').

In addition to the consonant phonemes found in native Tagalog words, shown in Table 49.2, there are several others that only occur in loanwords but are commonly heard in the speech of many Tagalog speakers, especially those with higher education in English. These include the labio-dental fricatives /f/ and /v/ and the alveolar affricates

Table 49.2 Tagalog Consonant Phonemes

	Labial	Dental	Alveolar	Palatal	Velar	Glottal
Voiceless stop	p	t			k	ʔ
Voiced stop	b	d			g	
Nasal	m	n			ŋ	
Fricative			s			h
Lateral			l			
Tap or trill			r			
Glide	w			y		

/ʧ/ and /ʤ/ (typically represented as *ts* and *dy* respectively), e.g. *Flora* /floːra/ 'Flora', *Victor* /viːktor/ 'Victor', *tsuper* /ʧuːper/ 'driver of a motor vehicle', *kotse* /koːʧe/ 'car' and *dyip* /ʤiːp/ 'jeep', although their status as fully adopted phonemes in the language is questionable (French 1988: 56).

In native words tautosyllabic consonant clusters are restricted to syllable-initial clusters in which the second consonant is a glide: e.g. *diyan* /dyan/ 'there', *buwan* /bwan/ 'month'. In loanwords syllable-initial clusters whose second consonant is /l/ or /r/ are also common, e.g. *plato* /plaːto/ 'plate', *grado* /graːdo/ 'grade'; and various syllable-final clusters are found in borrowings from English, e.g. *homework* /hoːmwoːrk/, *dimples* /diːmpols/, *bridge* /briːds/.

The most common syllable patterns are CV and CVC, in both final and non-final syllables, and CV:, in non-final syllables only. When a CVC syllable occurs as the initial syllable of disyllabic word, a very wide range of medial CC clusters is attested. Word-internal geminate clusters do not, however, occur.

Stress is closely tied to vowel length, with some analysts considering stress as primary, while others consider vowel length to be primary. Syllables with phonemically long vowels are always stressed. Syllables with vowels that are not phonemically long but are phonetically long as a result of their occurrence in phrase-final position are also stressed if there are no phonemically long vowels in the phrase-final word. Thus the final syllable of *magaling* /magaliŋ/ [magaliːŋ] 'excellent' is stressed in citation, but in *magaling na* /magaliŋ na/ [magaliŋ naː] 'it's excellent now', the stress falls on *na* instead. Unstressed vowels are not reduced and the language is syllable-timed rather than stress-timed.

A significant morphophonemic alternation that occurs across word boundaries includes the replacement of word-final glottal stop /ʔ/ by vowel length in non-phrase-final position, e.g. *maputi* /maputiʔ/ 'white', *maputi nga* /maputiː ŋaʔ/ 'it's really white', *maputi nga po* /maputiː ŋaː poʔ/ 'it's really white, sir/madam'. Significant morphophonemic alternations *within* the word include a 'rightward' shift of vowel length – and hence of stress – before the verbal suffixes *-an* and *-in*, e.g. *tasa* /taːsa/ 'assessment' + *-an* → *tasahan* /tasaːhan/ 'to assess s.t.', *pala* /paːla/ 'shovel' + *-in* → *palahin* /palaːhin/ 'to shovel s.t.', insertion of /h/ between a vowel final word and the verbal suffixes *-an* and *-in* (as in the previous examples), and a set of assimilations involving prefixes that end in nasals, such as the verbal prefix /maN-/ (where /N/ represents an unspecified nasal consonant): e.g. /maN-/+/p/ → /mam-/, /maN-/+/t/ → /man-/, /maN-/+/k/ → /maŋ-/, as in *mamili* (/maN-/+/piːliʔ/ → /mamiːliʔ/) 'choose', *manakot* (/maN-/+/taːkot/ → /manaːkot/) 'frighten', *mangailangan* (/maN-/+kaʔilaŋan/ → /maŋaʔilaŋan/) 'need'.

Tagalog is not a tone language. It does, however, have a complex intonational system. As in English, intonation may be used to distinguish pragmatically different sentence types (e.g. requests for information vs requests for repetition), to express speaker attitudes (e.g. cordiality), to indicate contrast or emphasis, etc.

Prior to the Spanish colonisation of the Philippines, a syllabary, probably ultimately of Indian origin, had been used for writing Tagalog, but under the Spanish this was supplanted by a version of the Roman alphabet. Nowadays Tagalog uses the same 26 letters that are used for writing English, although the seven letters *c, f, j, q, v, x* and *z* are used chiefly in proper names of foreign origin and in certain other borrowings from English or Spanish. These seven letters are not included in the conventional Tagalog alphabet, or *abakada*, which consists of 20 letters (including the digraph *ng*, used for /ŋ/), in the following order: *a b k d e g h i l m n ng o p r s t u w y*. The writing system does not indicate vowel length (or stress), and does not mark /ʔ/ except as a hyphen between consonant final prefixes and words that begin with a glottal stop that would otherwise be written as vowel-initial, for example *mag-iigi* /magʔiːʔiːgi/ 'to adjust'. Thus words that differ from one another only in vowel length (see examples above) or only in that one ends in a vowel and the other in /ʔ/ (e.g. *bata* /baːta/ 'bathrobe' and *bata* /baːtaʔ/ 'child') are spelled identically. There is also some inconsistency – as well as some debate – with regard to the spelling of loanwords, e.g. *molecule* vs *molikyul*. And there are two very common words, the case-marking form /naŋ/ and the plural form /maŋa/, whose conventional spellings, respectively *ng* and *mga*, are non-phonemic. With these and a few other exceptions, however, there is a fairly good match between spelling and pronunciation.

3 Syntax

The syntax of Tagalog and other Philippine languages has been the subject of an ongoing debate among syntacticians in recent years, as a clearer understanding of the nature of the relationships between the different constructions in the language have become clearer, and the goals of linguistic theory and description have changed. The first grammars by Spanish linguists and missionaries in the sixteenth and seventeenth centuries described the language in traditional Latin grammar terminology, but following the structuralist analyses of Bloomfield in the early part of the twentieth century, a model was established that typically described the language as containing a 'focus' system thought to be unique among the world's languages, in which the semantic role of one of the arguments, actor, experiencer, goal, instrument, location, beneficiary, etc., could be marked with an affix on the verb, thus 'focusing' that participant and creating a paradigm of structural types, one of which was active (or 'actor focus') and the others passive (goal passive or 'object focus', instrument passive or 'instrument focus', and so on). The 'focused' argument has been variously labelled as topic, subject, trigger and pivot.

Various problems with the 'focus' model, including the fact that the so-called 'passive' constructions do not function as typical passives, but are the unmarked way to express any structure containing a definite patient, have resulted in a number of different approaches that are more consistent with modern linguistic theory. These approaches fall into two main categories, those that consider Tagalog (or some other Philippine language) to be an ergative or a split-ergative language, and those that consider it to have either an 'active', 'fluid', 'hybrid' or 'symmetrical' voice system. To date, the ergative analysis is the most common among studies written in a wide range of theoretical frameworks, including Relational Grammar, Role and Reference Grammar,

Categorial Grammar, Lexicase, Localist frameworks, Dixon's Basic Linguistic Theory, Government and Binding, and Minimalist frameworks, as well as general typological approaches, and will be the approach followed in the following description.

Tagalog is a predicate-initial language. That is, in the most common and basic type of clause, words or phrases that express predicates precede words or phrases that express arguments. Predicates belong to one of two classes: verbal and non-verbal. The structures of basic clauses containing these two types of predicates are discussed in turn below.

Clauses with verbal predicates consist of a verb followed by one or more arguments (noun phrases, pronouns, etc.). These arguments do not in general occur in a fixed order, although the 'focused noun phrase', referred to hereafter as the grammatical subject (or absolutive noun phrase), commonly occurs last, and word order is not used in distinguishing the roles that are assigned to the various arguments, e.g. in distinguishing an actor argument (see below) from a patient argument. Instead these roles are indicated by the form of the verb and/or the form of the argument expressions themselves.

The verb typically contains an affix – which may be a prefix, an infix or a suffix – that indicates the semantic role of the grammatical subject. This phrase has the same form, whatever the semantic role of its referent. The semantic roles of any *other* arguments in the clause, however, are indicated by the forms of the noun phrases themselves: for example, an argument that expresses the actor of a transitive clause (that is, the ergative noun phrase) is introduced by *ng* /naŋ/ if it is a common noun, or by *ni* if it is a personal name.

As an ergative language, the case-marking of the actor or experiencer of an intransitive sentence (indicated in Examples 1a–b as S) is identical to that of the most patient-like argument of a transitive sentence (indicated in Examples 2a–d as P). In these sentences the specifiers of the S and the P phrases are shown in bold font. The agent of a transitive sentence (indicated as A) carries ergative case-marking. Examples 2b–d are also transitive sentences, having the same structural features as 2a, except that the semantic role of the absolutive is different, location in 2b, beneficiary in 2c, and instrument in 2d, each marked by a different form of the transitive verb. Of each of the square-bracketed noun phrases in the examples, only those marked as S, A and P are core noun phrases, implied by the verbal semantics, others phrases are adjuncts and optional. (All of the verbs in these examples contain a reduplicating imperfective aspect prefix CV:-, thus *aalis* /ʔaːʔalis/; other affixes, shown in bold font, either mark the semantic role of the absolutive phrase, or carry other aspectual meanings whose functions will be explained in Section 4).

1 Intransitive

 a *Aalis* [**ang** *tindero*]_{abs.} [*sa Lunes.*]_{loc.}
  will.leave S storekeeper Monday
  'The storekeeper will leave on Monday.'

 b **Magluluto** [**ang** *tindero*]_{abs.} [*para sa babae.*]_{ben.}
  will.cook S storekeeper   woman
  'The storekeeper will cook for the woman.'

2 Transitive

 a *Aalis**in*** [*ng tindero*]_{erg.} [**ang** *bigas*]_{abs.} [*sa sako.*]_{loc.}
  will.take.out A storekeeper P rice   sack
  'A/The storekeeper will take the rice out of the sack.'

b *Aalisan*   [*ng   tindero*]_{erg.} [*ng   bigas*]_{obl.} [***ang*   *sako.*]_{abs.}
   will.take.out.of   A   storekeeper   rice   P   sack
   'A/The storekeeper will take some rice out of the sack.'

c ***Ipag****aalis*   [*ng   tindero*]_{erg.} [*ng   bigas*]_{obl.} [***ang*   *babae.*]_{abs.}
   will.take.out.for A   storekeeper   rice   P   woman
   'A/The storekeeper will take out some rice for the woman.'

d ***Ipang****aalis* [*ng   tindero*]_{erg.} [*ng   bigas*]_{obl.} [***ang*   *sandok.*]_{abs.}
   will.take.out.with A   storekeeper   rice   P   ladle
   'A/The storekeeper will take out some rice with the ladle.'

The literal translations of the verbs in Examples 2b–d reflect an analysis that treats these structures as applicatives. Thus the verb in 2b is a 'locative-effect' verb, that in 2c is a 'beneficiary-effect' verb, while that in 2c is an 'instrumental-effect' verb. Example 2a is considered to be a simple transitive sentence.

The phrases marked as absolutive in the above examples are all introduced by the specifier *ang* that marks the following noun as a definite common noun. They are introduced by *si* if the following noun is a personal name. These forms do not themselves mark the case of the noun phrase, as phrases marked in this way can also occur with functions other than the grammatical subject of a sentence, such as nominal predicates or fronted topics. Absolutive phrases, however, can be substituted with one from the set of unmarked pronouns (see below), one of which (second person singular *ka*) unambiguously marks the phrase as the grammatical subject. Absolutive phrases typically have definite reference, whether or not they contain a demonstrative, relative clause or other means to mark definiteness. In many analyses of Tagalog, the absolutive phrase is labelled nominative, highlighting the generalisation that the syntactic properties of the phrase are almost identical in both accusative and ergative languages.

Ergative noun phrases expressing the agent of a transitive sentence are introduced by the common noun marker *ng* (/naŋ/) or by the personal noun marker *ni*, and can be substituted with one from a set of pronouns which also function as possessive pronouns, making such phrases formally identical to post-nominal possessive phrases. In many descriptions they are therefore referred to as having genitive case-marking. Ergative common noun phrases are unmarked as to definiteness, and may therefore be interpreted as either definite or indefinite, unless they contain a demonstrative or other means to mark definiteness or specificity.

The preposition *sa* (in Examples 1a and 2a) introduces a locative noun phrase expressing either temporal or common noun spatial locations, and in combination with *para* (Example 1b) marks benefactive phrases. The equivalent personal noun marker in such phrases is *kay*.

The oblique noun phrases in the above examples are also introduced by the common noun marker *ng* (/naŋ/), and in many descriptions are referred to also as genitive. They are however distinct from ergative (or genitive) noun phrases in several respects. An oblique noun phrase can only be interpreted as indefinite and cannot be substituted with either a personal noun or a pronoun. In transitive constructions of the sort illustrated above oblique noun phrases are optional.

There is one other construction in which an oblique noun phrase occurs, but as an obligatory noun phrase implied by the verb, and expressing an indefinite theme. This is analysed here as a dyadic intransitive construction. This construction is illustrated in 3 below, in which the oblique phrase is labelled E for 'extended', following the Dixon–Aikhenvald terms used in their Basic Linguistic Theory. Like the oblique adjuncts marked by *ng* in transitive sentences, this phrase is obligatorily indefinite and cannot be substituted with a personal noun or pronoun. This structure has been variously labelled as pseudo-transitive, or as anti-passive, and its analysis is the source of much controversy in the literature. For linguists who consider the semantic transitivity of this structure as primary, the phrase marked here as oblique is analysed as accusative, making Tagalog a split-ergative language. For linguists who consider that the forms of the verbal prefixes in these structures, matching as they do the affixation on monadic intransitive verbs (compare 3a with 1a, and 3b with 1b), but not the affixation of unambiguously transitive constructions, the structures are syntactically intransitive. Some contend that since this phrase is a core argument, Tagalog should be considered to have a symmetrical voice system.

3   Dyadic intransitive

a   *Gagawa*   [*ng*   *kubo*]$_{\text{obl.}}$ [*ang*   *tindero.*]$_{\text{abs.}}$
     will.make   E   hut   S   storekeeper
     'The storekeeper will make a hut.'

b   *Mag-aalis*   [*ng*   *bigas*]$_{\text{obl.}}$ [*ang*   *tindero.*]$_{\text{abs}}$
     will.take.out E   rice   S   storekeeper
     'The storekeeper will take out some rice.'

The distinction between each of the structures illustrated above has often been characterised as 'voice' so that Examples 3a–b are 'actor voice', 2a 'patient voice', 2b 'locative voice', 2c 'beneficiary voice' and 2d 'instrumental' or 'conveyance voice'. The four transitive voice types have also been labelled as 'undergoer voice', because of their structural similarities.

Some linguists have also argued that the so-called locative, beneficiary and instrumental voices are derived applicative constructions.

As noted previously, the order of post-verbal arguments is generally free. Thus in addition to the orderings shown above, any other ordering of the arguments in the examples would also be grammatical (although some would be unusual). There is, however, a general preference for the actor as the first argument in a transitive clause and for either the actor or the oblique patient as the first argument in an extended intransitive clause.

There is also one set of nominal expressions whose order in relation to other nominal expressions and to one another is not free. These are the absolutive and ergative personal pronouns, which are *enclitics*: i.e. they occur in a fixed position immediately after the clause-initial constituent. If there are two enclitic pronouns in the same clause, they observe the rule that monosyllabic pronouns precede disyllabic pronouns. Thus in the following sentence the order of all the words is fixed:

Nakita   *mo*   *siya*   *kahapon.*
saw   erg.2.sg.   abs.3.sg.   yesterday
'You saw him yesterday.'

This contrasts with the variable ordering observable in the following sentences, which show that argument expressions are freely ordered in relation not only to one another but also to adverbs such as *kahapon* 'yesterday':

Nakita ni *Juan* si *Maria kahapon.*
saw   erg. Juan abs.   Maria yesterday
Nakita ni Juan kahapon si Maria.
Nakita si Maria ni Juan kahapon.
Nakita si Maria kahapon ni Juan.
Nakita kahapon ni Juan si Maria.
Nakita kahapon si Maria ni Juan.
'Juan saw Maria yesterday.'

In addition to enclitic pronouns, Tagalog also has a set of enclitic *adverbial particles* that occur in a fixed position in relation to other sentence elements. Note, for example, the position of the interrogative *ba* in the following sentence:

Nakita *mo* *ba* *siya* *kahapon?*
saw   erg.2.sg. Q   abs.3.sg.   yesterday
'Did you see him yesterday?'

Clauses with non-verbal predicates are in many cases translated into English by sentences with the main verb *be*, which has no Tagalog counterpart. These clauses consist of a predicate expression followed by an absolutive noun phrase. The predicate expression may be a noun, an adjective or a prepositional phrase. Some examples are:

Abogado *ang* *bunso.*
be.lawyer   spcf.   youngest.child
'The youngest child is a lawyer.'

Hinog *ang* *mga* *mangga.*
be.ripe   spcf.   pl.   mango
'The mangos are ripe'

Nasa *kusina* *si* *Nene.*
be.in   kitchen   spcf.pers.   Nene
'Nene is in the kitchen.'

A construction consisting of a non-verbal phrasal predicate having an existential word immediately followed by an unmarked noun and an absolutive phrase is also used to express possession, as in:

[*May* trak]pred. *si* *Ben.*
exist   truck   spcf.pers.   Ben
'Ben has a truck.'

The same type of non-verbal predicate is also used to express existence. In this case, however, the predicate is not followed by an absolutive phrase, but is instead typically followed by a locative adverb, e.g.

[*May* *trak*]pred. *doon.*
exist   truck   there
'There's a truck over there.'

Although Tagalog is basically predicate-initial, there are certain fairly common constructions in which some other constituent precedes the predicate. In one such construction, the sentence-initial constituent – which may be the absolutive argument, an adverbial expression or one of certain other types of arguments – is immediately followed by the form *ay* without any change in the denotation of the construction.

Ang	*sulat*	*ay*	*tinanggap*	*ko*	*kahapon.*
spcf.	letter		received	gen.1.sg.	yesterday

'I received the letter yesterday.'

Saanman	*ay*	*makakaabot*	*ang*	*koreyo.*
to.any.place		can.reach	spcf.	mail

'The mail can reach any place.'

Ay constructions are more common in writing and in formal speech than they are in ordinary conversation. It has been suggested that in narratives the referent of the constituent preceding *ay* is often one that has been referred to at some earlier point and that *ay* is typically used to reintroduce such a referent.

In other types of non-predicate-initial constructions, the pre-predicate constituent may have a special discourse function, such as contrast or emphasis. When the fronted constituent is contrastive, it is typically expressed with a falling intonation and is followed by a pause (indicated in the examples with a comma). When a constituent is fronted for emphasis, there is no special intonation or pause. Some examples are:

Bukas,	*magpapahinga*	*ako.*	*Ngayon,*	*dapat*	*akong*		*magtrabaho.*
tomorrow	will.rest	abs.1.sg	today	must	abs.1.sg. =	lig.	at-work

'Tomorrow, I'll rest. Today, I've got to work.'

Bukas,	*aalis*	*si*	*Pedro.*
tomorrow	will.leave	spcf.pers.	Pedro

'It's tomorrow that Pedro is leaving (not today).'

Sa	*kantong*	*ito*	*umaalis*	*ang*	*bus.*
from	corner = lig.	this	leaves	spcf.	bus

'This is the corner the bus leaves from.'

Just as the ordering of clause constituents shows considerable variability, so does the ordering of constituents of noun phrases. Although certain modifiers, such as numbers and other quantifiers, regularly precede the head noun and others, such as possessive noun phrases, regularly follow it, there are also several types of modifiers that may either precede or follow the head noun, e.g. demonstratives, adjectival verbs and possessive pronouns.

A demonstrative or an adjectival verb, whether it precedes or follows the noun, is linked to it by a *ligature*. The ligature has two morphophonemically conditioned alternants: if the citation form of the preceding word ends in a vowel, /ʔ/ or /n/, the ligature takes the form of /ŋ/ (*ng*) replacing the final consonant; in all other cases, the ligature takes the form /na/ (*na*). (Ligatures also occur in certain other constructions, such as constructions involving auxiliary verbs like *dapat* 'must'.) For example, when the demonstrative *ito* 'this' precedes the ligature, the /ŋ/ form occurs and when the noun *galang* /galaŋ/ 'bracelet' precedes, the /na/ form occurs: thus *itong galang* /itoŋ galaŋ/, *galang na ito* /galaŋ na itoh/ 'this bracelet'. Similarly, the noun *bata* /ba:taʔ/ 'child' and the adjective *gutom* /gutom/ 'hungry' respectively require the /ŋ/ and /na/ forms of the ligature in *batang gutom* /ba:taŋ gutom/ 'hungry child' and *gutom na bata* /gutom na ba:taʔ/.

Although a demonstrative and the noun it modifies may occur in either order, the alternative orderings are generally not in free variation, but are, rather, conditioned by discourse factors. The constituent that comes second typically represents the more salient information and may, for example, be contrastive. Thus:

Mahal	*itong*	*galang.*	*(Pero*	*mura*	*itong*	*singsing.)*
be.expensive	this = lig.	bracelet	but	cheap	this = lig.	ring

'This bracelet is expensive. (But this ring is cheap.)'

Mahal	ang	galang	*na ito.*	*(Pero*	*mura*	ang	galang	*na*	*iyan.)*
be.expensive	spcf.	bracelet	lig. this	but	cheap	spcf.	bracelet	lig.	that

'This bracelet is expensive. (But that bracelet is cheap.)'

(As the first example illustrates, when the grammatical subject begins with a demonstrative, no specifying form is used.) The alternative orderings of adjectival verbs and the nouns they modify, on the other hand, often do appear to be a matter of free variation. Some analysts, however, contend that the initial form in such constructions is the syntactic head, and the form that follows the ligature is a relative clause with a predicate nominal as its head, i.e. 'this one which is a bracelet' vs 'the bracelet which is this one'; see the discussion on relative clauses below.

Possessive pronouns, as noted, may also either precede or follow the noun, but in this case a difference in form is associated with the difference in order. When the possessive pronoun precedes, it takes the locative form and is obligatorily linked to the following noun by a ligature. When the possessive pronoun follows, it takes a form that has been called the genitive form and there is no ligature. For example, 'my house' may be expressed as either *aking bahay* (the locative first person singular pronoun *akin* + ligature + *bahay* 'house', i.e. 'mine which is a house') or *bahay ko* (*bahay* + the genitive first person singular pronoun *ko*). The orderings are both very common and there is no obvious difference in usage between them.

Yes–no questions in Tagalog are characterised by rising intonation, as opposed to the characteristic falling intonation of statements. A yes–no question may be distinguished from the corresponding statement by intonation alone or it may, in addition, be marked by the enclitic interrogative form *ba*. This word also occurs optionally in question-word questions. The latter, however, have their own distinctive intonation patterns, which differ from those of both yes–no questions and statements. (The most common intonation patterns for both question-word questions and statements are falling patterns, but the patterns differ in detail: the question-word questions start with high pitch and fall steadily throughout; the statements start with mid pitch, rise to high pitch on the last stressed syllable and then fall.)

The questioned constituent normally comes first in a question-word question. If this constituent is an adverbial argument or a locative argument, any clitic pronouns and/or adverbs contained in the clause attach to it, as with other fronted constituents, e.g.

Kailan   mo   (ba)   siya   nakita?
when   gen.2.sg.   Q   abs.3.sg.   saw
'When did you see him?'

Sa   aling   parti   ka   (ba)   pumunta?
loc.   which = lig.   party   abs.2.sg.   Q   went
'Which party did you go to?'

If the questioned constituent is an absolutive noun phrase, a wh-cleft construction is used, the question word itself forming the predicate, and the rest of the clause expressed as an absolutive construction introduced by one of the specifiers that introduce such phrases, such as *ang*. Some examples are:

Ano   (ba)   ang   ginawa   mo   kahapon?
what   Q   spcf.   did   gen.2.sg   yesterday
'What did you do yesterday?' Lit. 'What is it that you did yesterday?'

Sino   (ba)   ang   gumawa   ng   sapatos   na   iyon?
who   Q   spcf.   made   obl.   shoes   lig.   that
'Who made those shoes?' Lit. 'Who is it that made those shoes?'

If the questioned constituent is a genitive noun phrase, a wh-in situ construction is used, a genitively marked question word appearing in the body of the clause, following the predicate, such as:

Ninakaw   nino   ang   kotse   mo?
stole   gen.who   spcf.   car   gen.2.sg
'Who stole your car?' (Kroeger 1993: 212)

Imperative sentences of the most common type have a falling intonation pattern like that of question-word questions. Syntactically they are just like statements with verbal predicates and second-person actors (which are either absolutive, if the patient is indefinite, or genitive, if the patient is definite), except that the verb is in the infinitive form, rather than one of the finite forms that are found in statements. Some examples are:

Mag-alis   ka   ng   bigas   sa   sako!
take.out   abs.2.sg.   obl.   rice   loc.   sack
'Take some rice out of a/the sack.'

Basahin   mo   nga   ang   librong   ito!
read   gen.2.sg   please   spcf.   book = lig.   this
'Please read this book.'

(*Nga* 'please' in the last example is an enclitic adverbial particle.)

Hortative sentences are identical to imperatives, except that the actor is a first person plural inclusive pronoun (see Section 4). For example:

Mag-alis   tayo   ng   bigas   sa   sako.
take.out   abs.1.incl.pl.   obl.   rice   loc.   sack
'Let's take some rice out of a/the sack.'

Basahin   nga   natin   ang   librong   ito.
read   please   gen.1.incl.pl.   spcf.   book = lig.   this
'Please let's read this book.'

Tagalog has distinct ways of negating imperative/hortative clauses, existential/posses-sive clauses and clauses of other types. Imperatives and hortatives are negated with the clause-initial prohibitive form *huwag*, which is immediately followed by any enclitic pronouns and adverbs, then by a ligature and then by the verb. Examples are:

Huwag   kang   mag-alis   ng   bigas   sa   sako!
proh.   abs.2.sg. = lig.   take.out   obl.   rice   loc.   sack
'Don't take any rice out of a/the sack!'

Huwag nga   nating   basahin ang   librong   ito.
proh.   please gen.1.incl.pl. = lig.   read   spcf. book = lig.   this
'Please, let's not read this book.'

Existential and possessive clauses are negated with the clause-initial negative existential form *wala*. *Wala* replaces the affirmative existential form *may(roon)*, and is followed by a ligature. Any enclitics in the clause come between *wala* and the ligature. Examples are:

Wala   akong   pera.
neg.exist   abs.1.sg. = lig.   money
'I don't have any money.'

Walang   bahay   doon.
neg.exist = lig.   house   there
'There isn't a house there.'

Clauses of other types are negated with the clause-initial negative form *hindi*. Again, any enclitics immediately follow the negative form. *Hindi* is not, however, followed by a ligature.

Hindi   ko   nakita   si   Rosa.
neg.   gen.1.sg.   saw   spcf.pers.   Rosa
'I didn't see Rosa.'

Hindi   mayaman   si   Rosa.
neg.   rich   spcf.pers.   Rosa
'Rosa isn't rich.'

It should be noted that there are certain subject-like properties that are associated not with the absolutive noun phrase but, rather, with the actor. For example, as we have already seen, the actor, whether or not it also happens to be the grammatical subject, always represents the addressee of an imperative sentence. It is also the actor that controls the reference of a reflexive (expressed by a possessive pronoun and the nominal *sarili* 'self'), as illustrated by the following sentences:

Mag-aalaala	*ang*	*lolo*		*sa*	*kaniyang*	*sarili.*
worry.about	spcf.	grandfather		loc	poss. = lig.	self

'Grandfather will worry about himself.'

Aalalahanin	*ng*	*lolo*	*ang*	*kaniyang*	*sarili.*
worry.about	gen.	grandfather	spcf.	poss. = lig.	self

'Grandfather will worry about himself.'

Since the first of these sentences has an intransitive verb, the actor, which is the reflexive controller, happens to be the grammatical subject as well. The second sentence, however, has a transitive verb and here we can see clearly that the reflexive controller is the actor and *not* the grammatical subject, since in this case it is the subject itself that is reflexivised.

On the other hand, there *are* certain subject-like properties that are associated with the absolutive noun phrase. One such property is relativisability. Only absolutive arguments (and certain constituents of such arguments) may be relativised in Tagalog. Thus if one wishes to relativise an actor, an intransitive clause must be used; if one wishes to relativise a patient, a transitive clause must be used; etc. The following examples illustrate this. (As the examples show, relativisation in Tagalog involves the deletion of the relativised argument from the relative clause. The head of the relative clause and the clause itself may occur in either order, but head-first is the more common ordering. A ligature occurs between the head and the relative clause.)

Iyon	*ang*	*babaeng*	*magluluto*	*ng*	*isda.*
that	spcf.	woman = lig.	will.cook	obl.	fish

'That's the woman who will cook some fish.'

Iyon	*ang*	*isdang*	*iluluto*	*ng*	*babae.*
that	spcf.	fish = lig.	will.cook	gen.	woman

'That's the fish that a/the woman will cook.'

In the first sentence the actor is relativised, so the verb in the relative clause must be intransitive; in the second sentence the patient is relativised, so the verb in the relative clause must be transitive. Similarly, if a locative argument is relativised, the verb in the relative clause must be derived as a locative-effect verb, and if a benefactive argument is relativised, the verb in the relative clause must be derived as a beneficiary-effect verb, as in:

Iyon	*ang*	*sakong*	*aalisan*	*ko*	*ng*	*bigas.*
that	spcf.	sack = lig.	will.take.out.from	gen.1.sg.	obl.	rice

'That's the sack that I'll take some rice out of.'

Iyon	*ang*	*batang*	*ipagluluto*	*ko*	*ng*	*pagkain.*
that	spcf.	child = lig.	will.cook.for	gen.1.sg.	obl.	food

'That's the child I'll cook some food for.'

If one attempts to relativise a non-subject argument, the result is ungrammatical, e.g.

*Iyon	ang	babaeng	iluluto	ang	isda.
that	spcf.	woman = lig.	will.cook	spcf.	fish

Although verbs and nouns are clearly distinguished from one another on a *morphological* basis in Tagalog (see Section 4), distributionally or syntactically they are rather similar. We have already seen that they can serve as predicates. In addition, they can serve as (heads of) arguments or as modifiers. A verbal argument may be analysed as a headless relative clause. For example, compare the following with the last grammatical example cited:

Iyon	ang	ipagluluto	ko	ng	pagkain.
that	spcf.	will.cook.for	gen.1.sg.	obl.	food

'That's the one I'll cook some food for.'

Here the phrase headed by the verb *ipagluluto*, which has the form of a relative clause, is functioning as the absolutive argument of the sentence. Some relevant examples involving adjectival verbs are:

Sino	ang	batang	pinakamatalino	sa	klase?
who	spcf.	child = lig.	smartest	loc.	class

'Who is the smartest child in the class?'

Sino	ang	pinakamatalino	sa	klase?
who	spcf.	smartest	loc.	class

'Who is the smartest one in the class?'

We have already seen various types of verbs (in relative clauses) serving as modifiers, in highly similar constructions involving a ligature between the head and the modifier. Nouns too occur as modifiers in this type of construction: e.g. *gulay na repolyo* 'vegetable dish made from cabbage' (cf. *gulay* 'vegetable (dish)', *repolyo* 'cabbage'), *laruang kalan* 'toy stove' (cf. *laruan* 'toy', *kalan* 'stove'). Thus the syntactic similarities among nouns and verbs in Tagalog are quite striking, although, as we shall see, there are clear morphological grounds for distinguishing them.

4 Morphology

Tagalog verb morphology is quite complex. The verb stem may be polymorphemic and there are obligatory subject-marking and aspectual affixes – which may be prefixes, suffixes or infixes – as well as affixes with a wide range of other functions. The following selective summary of Tagalog verb morphology treats, in order: stem formation, subject-marking affixation, other non-aspectual affixation and aspectual affixation.

Many Tagalog verb stems consist of a single morpheme: e.g. *abot* (cf. *umabot* 'reach for', which consists of the intransitive verbal affix *-um-* plus *abot*), *iyak* (cf. *umiyak* 'cry'), *uwi* (cf. *umuwi* 'go home'). However, there are also a great many verb stems that are analysable as consisting of two or more morphemes. Of these, the most common are those involving the stem-forming prefixes *pag-* and *paN-*.

Pag- combines very productively with nouns to form verb stems that denote character-istic activities involving the referents of the nouns. For example, *pagbus* is the stem of the intransitive verb *magbus* 'ride a bus', *pag-Ingles* (cf. *Ingles* 'English') is the stem of *mag-Ingles* 'speak English', *pagtsinelas* (cf. *tsinelas* 'slippers') is the stem of *magtsinelas* 'wear slippers', and *pag-ingat* (cf. *ingat* 'care') is the stem of intransitive *mag-ingat* 'take care', and transitive *pag-ingatan* 'be careful of s.t.'. (In intransitive verbs, the initial /p/ of *pag-* and *paN-* is assimilated to the intransitive prefix *m-*, historically a reflex of Proto-Austronesian **-um-*.) For some purposes – see below – it is convenient to refer to the resultant forms, *mag-* and *maN-*, as if they were single affixes rather than composites.

In addition, *pag-* combines with certain simple verb stems to form the stems of 'inten-sive' verbs, i.e. verbs that designate intense, frequent or prolonged performance of the activity designated by the simple stem. For example, *pag-* combines with *kain* 'eat' to form the stem of *magkain* 'eat (repeatedly, etc.)' and with *lakad* 'walk' to form the stem of *maglakad* 'walk (repeatedly, etc.)'. *Pag-* also forms verb stems with adjectival verbs, which may themselves be morphologically complex – e.g. *pagmabait* (cf. *mabait* 'kind', *bait* 'kindness'), which is the stem of intransitive *magmabait* and transitive *pagmabaitan* 'pretend to be kind to s.o.' – and even with certain compounds – e.g. *pagmagandang-gabi* (cf. *magandang gabi* 'good evening (the greeting)'), which is the stem of *magmagandang-gabi* 'wish good evening'.

Like *pag-*, but less productively, *paN-* combines with nouns to form stems that denote characteristic activities involving the referents of the nouns. For example, *pamangka* (cf. *bangka* 'boat' – see Section 2 for the assimilation of certain morpheme-initial consonants to prefixal /N/) is the stem of the intransitive verb *mamangka* 'go boating', and *panganak* (cf. *anak* 'child, offspring') is the stem of intransitive *manganak* and tran-sitive *ipanganak* 'give birth to s.o.'. *PaN-* also combines with certain nouns and simple verb stems to form stems that denote destructive or harmful activity and with certain other simple verb stems to form stems that denote activity directed towards multiple objects. For example, *paN-* combines with *walis* 'broom' to form the stem of *mangwalis* 'hit with a broom' and with *kain* 'eat' to form the stem of *mangain* 'devour'; it also combines with *kuha* 'get' to form the stem of *manguha* 'gather' and with *tahi* 'sew' to form the stem of *manahi* 'sew (a number of things, or professionally)'.

There is also a *paN-*-stem-forming prefix – distinguishable from the one just dis-cussed on the basis of a different pattern of morphophonemic alternations – that forms the stem of instrumental-effect verbs. This type of stem may occur independently as a noun with instrumental meaning. Examples are *pam(p)unas* 'something to wipe with' (cf. *punas* 'sponge bath'), which is the stem of the instrumental-effect transitive verb *ipam(p)unas* 'wipe with s.t.', and *pan(s)ulat* 'something to write with' (cf. *sulat* 'letter'), which is the stem of the instrumental-effect verb *ipan(s)ulat* 'write with s.t.'.

Among the other stem-forming affixes that deserve mention are two different redu-plicating prefixes, one monosyllabic, the other disyllabic. The monosyllabic redupli-cating prefix is in general a copy of the first consonant and vowel of the following simple verb stem (but see the discussion of aspectual reduplication below). In one of its uses it combines with *pag-* to form certain additional intensive verbs: e.g. *pagtatapak* the stem of the transitive verb *pagtatapakan* 'step (repeatedly, etc.) on s.t.' (cf. *tapakan* 'step on s.t.') and *pagbabagsak*, the stem of transitive *ipagbabagsak* 'drop (repeatedly, etc.) on s.t.' (cf. *ibagsak* 'drop s.t.').

The disyllabic reduplicating prefix generally consists of a copy of the first two (usually the only two) syllables of the following simple stem. One use of the disyllabic reduplicating prefix is to form the stem of 'moderative' verbs, i.e. verbs that designate activities performed in moderation, occasionally, at random, etc. Some examples are *hiya-hiya*, the stem of intransitive *mahiya-hiya* 'be a little ashamed' (cf. *mahiya* 'be ashamed') and *linis-linis*, the stem of transitive *linis-linisin* 'clean s.t. a little' (cf. *linisin* 'clean s.t.').

As indicated above, the subject-marking affixes are said to mark the semantic role of the absolutive phrase. Among the roles that may be affixally marked are: actor, patient, location, beneficiary and instrument. (Others, which will not be discussed here, include location, reason and referent ('about' object).) The affixes that most commonly mark these roles are shown in Table 49.3.

The affixes that signal that the absolutive noun phrase expresses an actor form verbs that are either monadic or dyadic intransitives. The other affixes typically occur in canonical transitive constructions, although they may also occur in a small number of clearly intransitive constructions in which the subject is experiencer of an 'afflicted' or 'adversely affected' state, e.g. *antukin* 'feel sleepy'(cf. *antok* 'drowsiness'), *lamukin* 'be infested with mosquitos' (cf. *lamok* 'mosquito'), *langgamin* 'be infested with ants' (cf. *langgam* 'ant'), *kilabutan* 'feel terrified' (cf. *kilabot* 'goose pimples'), *pawisan* 'sweat', etc. These also include physical conditions derived from the following nouns: *sipon* 'cold', *lagnat* 'fever' and *malat* 'hoarseness', as well as natural phenomena, such as *ulan* 'rain', *bagyo* 'storm', *lindol* 'earthquake', etc. (De Guzman 1978).

The forms of the affixes given in the table are those that occur in infinitives. Some subject-marking affixes assume different forms in certain finite (i.e. aspect marked) verbs. These forms will be presented later, in connection with the discussion of aspectual affixation.

As Table 49.3 shows, there are several different affixes that signal actor, patient and location subjects. The choice among these affixes is lexically determined and to some extent idiosyncratic, although there are certain generalisations that can be made.

The intransitive affixes, all of which mark that the actor is subject and all of which involve the phoneme /m/, are the infix *-um-* and the prefixes *m-*, *ma-* and *maka-*. *-um-* is infixed between the first consonant and first vowel of the stem, e.g. *humingi* 'borrow' (stem: *hingi*), *sumulat* 'write' (stem: *sulat*), *tumakbo* 'run' (stem: *takbo*). (In the written form of verbs whose stem-initial consonant is /ʔ/, *-um-* appears as a prefix, since /ʔ/ is not represented in the standard orthography: e.g. *umabot* /ʔumabot/ 'reach for' (stem: *abot* /ʔabot/)). *-um-* is the most common affix in intransitive verbs with actor-subject verbs having single-morpheme stems and its occurrence in certain subclasses of verbs is predictable, e.g. in verbs of 'becoming' where the stem also occurs as the stem of a *ma-* adjectival verb, cf. *gumanda* 'become beautiful', *maganda* 'be beautiful', *tumaas* 'become tall', *mataas* 'be tall'.

The prefix *m-* replaces the initial *p-* of the stem-forming prefixes *pag-* and *paN-*, resulting in the forms *mag-* and *maN-* respectively, as in *magbigay* 'give', *magluto* 'cook',

Table 49.3 Affixes

Actor	-um-, m-, ma-, maka-
Patient	-in, i-, -an, ma-
Location	-an, -in
Beneficiary, Instrument	i-

mangisda 'fish' (cf. *isda* 'fish (noun)'), *mangailangan* 'need' (cf. *kailangan* 'need (noun)'). As indicated above, *mag-* occurs productively in verbs that express a characteristic activity involving the referent of the noun that underlies them (e.g. *mag-Ingles* 'speak English'). There are also certain regular correspondences between *-um-* and *mag-* verbs formed with the same stem, e.g. cases in which the *-um-* verb takes two arguments and the *mag-* verb three, such as: *pumasok* 'come/go into' and *magpasok* 'bring/take into', *lumabas* 'come/go outside' and *maglabas* 'bring/take outside'. *MaN-* too has certain characteristic uses – for example in verbs indicating destructive activity, such as *mangwalis* 'hit with a broom' (cf. *magwalis* 'sweep') – but it is considerably less common than *mag-*.

Intransitive *ma-* (there is also a transitive *ma-*) occurs productively in verbs of 'becoming' whose stems are unaffixed adjectival verbs – e.g. *mabingi* 'become deaf' (cf. *bingi* 'be deaf'), *mamahal* 'become expensive' (cf. *mahal* 'be expensive') – and idiosyncratically in a relatively small number of other common verbs, e.g. *matulog* 'sleep', *matuto* 'learn'. *Maka-* occurs idiosyncratically in a few common verbs, e.g. *makakita* 'see', *makarinig* 'hear'. (*Maka-* also occurs productively in abilitative verbs – see below.)

The most common affixes marking simple transitive verbs are *-in* and *i-*. *-in* is the most frequent transitive counterpart of intransitive *um-* verbs in corresponding sets formed with the same stem (e.g. intransitive *humuli* 'catch'/ transitive *hulihin* 'catch s.t.') and *i-* is the most frequent counterpart of intransitive *m-* verbs, (though there are also a good many intransitive *m-*/transitive *-in* correspondences, including some cases where *-in* and *i-* are apparently in free variation, e.g. intransitive *magluto* 'cook'/transitive *iluto* ~ *lutuin* 'cook s.t.'). The stem-forming prefix *pag-* that occurs in intransitive *m-* verbs is often obligatorily absent – less often optionally absent – from the corresponding simple transitive verbs. (This is also true of locative-effect verbs formed with *-in*, and of both simple transitive and locative-effect transitive verbs formed with *-an* – see below.) For example, the transitive counterpart of intransitive *magbigay* 'give' is *ibigay* 'give s.t.' and the transitive counterpart of intransitive *magkaila* 'deny' is either *ikaila* or *ipagkaila*. (On the other hand, the transitive counterpart of intransitive *magbili* 'sell' is *ipagbili*, in which *pag-* is obligatorily retained.) Much less commonly, a stem-forming prefix *paN-* that occurs in an intransitive verb is omitted from the transitive counterpart, e.g. the patient-transitive counterpart of intransitive *mangailangan* 'need' is *kailanganin*.

The suffix *-an*, which is the most common locative-effect affix, occurs less frequently as a simple transitive affix, often in verbs that express actions involving surface contact with, or surface effect on, the patient, e.g. *labhan* 'launder s.t.', *pintahan* 'paint s.t.', *walisan* 'sweep s.t.', *hawakan* 'hold s.t.'. *Ma-* is the transitive counterpart of intransitive *maka-* and occurs idiosyncratically in a few verbs: e.g. *makita* 'see s.t.', *marinig* 'hear s.t.'.

Some examples of locative-effect verbs with *-an* are: *puntahan* 'go to some place', *up(u)an* 'sit on s.t.', *masdan* 'look at s.t.', *bilhan* 'buy from some place' (also functioning as a beneficiary-effect verb with the meaning 'buy for someone'). The suffix *-in* occurs idiosyncratically as a locative-effect affix in a few verbs – e.g. *pupuin* 'use *po* (sir/madam) in addressing someone' – and more systematically in certain other cases, among them cases in which locative-effect *-an* is, as it were, pre-empted. These are cases in which *-an* is used as the locative-effect affix of a three argument verb and *-in* as the locative-effect affix of a two-argument verb formed with the same stem: e.g. *pasukan* 'bring/take into some place' vs *pasukin* 'come/go into some place', *labasan* 'bring/take to some place outside' vs *labasin* 'come/go to some place outside'.

Beneficiary-effect verbs are formed with *i-* or *-an*, depending on the verb class. Any stem-forming *pag-* or *paN-* in the corresponding intransitive verb is retained. Examples are: *ipirma* 'sign for s.o.' (cf. intransitive *pumirma* 'sign'), *ipaglaba* 'launder for s.o.' (cf. intransitive *maglaba* 'launder'), *ipanguha* 'gather for s.o.' (cf. *manguha* 'gather').

Instrumental-effect verbs are also formed with *i-*, but in this case the stem must usually be formed with the prefix *paN-*, as in *ipam(p)unas* 'wipe with s.t.', *ipan(s)ulat* 'write with s.t.' However, if the simple stem itself designates an instrument, alternative instrument-effect formations without any stem-forming prefix or with the stem-forming prefix *pag-* also occur. Thus, the stem *suklay* 'comb' occurs in instrumental-effect *isuklay* and *ipagsuklay* as well as *ipan(s)uklay* 'comb with (a certain comb)', and the stem *gunting* 'scissors' occurs in instrumental-effect *igunting* and *ipaggunting* as well as *ipanggunting* 'cut with (a certain pair of scissors)'.

Apart from affixes which signal the semantic role of the grammatical subject (often referred to as the 'voice' affixes), there are a good many other non-aspectual affixes, among them affixes with abilitative and causative meanings. The abilitative affixes are *maka-* and *ma-*. *Maka-* occurs in intransitive verbs, in which it replaces *-um-* or *m-*, e.g. intransitive *makaawit* 'be able to sing' (cf. *umawit* 'sing'), intransitive *makapagluto* 'be able to cook' (cf. *magluto* 'cook'), intransitive *makapangisda* 'be able to fish' (cf. *mangisda* 'fish'). *Ma-* occurs with transitive verbs. It replaces *-in*, but co-occurs with *i-* or *-an*: e.g. transitive *magamit* 'be able to use s.t.' (cf. *gamitin* 'use'), benefactive-effect transitive *maibili* 'be able to buy for s.o.' (cf. *ibili* 'buy for s.o.'), locative-effect transitive *mapuntahan* 'be able to go to some place' (cf. *puntahan* 'go to some place').

Causative verbs are all formed with the causative stem-forming prefix *pa-*, which occurs in addition to the voice affixes. Causative verbs, in a sense, have two actors, one causing the other to act. However, morphologically (as well as syntactically), only the 'causer' is treated as an actor, while the 'causee' is treated as a kind of patient. Thus, when the causer is the grammatical subject, the intransitive voice affix *mag-* (*m-* + *pag-*) is invariably used, but when the causee is the subject, the transitive affix *-in* is invariably used: e.g. causative intransitive *magpapunta* 'cause to go'/causative transitive *papuntahin* 'cause s.o. to go' (cf. non-causative intransitive *pumunta* 'go'), causative intransitive *magpatsinelas* 'cause to wear slippers'/causative transitive *papagtsinelasin* 'cause s.o. to wear slippers' (cf. non-causative intransitive *magtsinelas* 'wear slippers').

There are also causative verbs in which the subject is some argument other than the causer or the causee. Under these circumstances, the same voice affix that occurs in the corresponding non-causative verb is ordinarily used, except that *-in* (which is, as it were, pre-empted, to mark the causee as subject) is replaced by *i-* in basic causative transitive verbs and by *-an* in causative location-effect verbs. Thus causative transitive *ipalinis* 'cause to clean s.t.' (cf. *linisin* 'clean s.t.') has as its grammatical subject the object cleaned, while *palinisin* 'cause s.o. to clean' has as its subject the causee, the one caused to do the cleaning. Similarly, causative location-effect *papasukan* 'cause to enter some place' (cf. transitive *pasukin* 'enter some place') has as its subject the place entered, while *papasukin* 'cause s.o. to enter' has as its subject the one caused to enter. Some other relevant examples are: *papintahan* 'cause to paint s.t.' (cf. *pintahan* 'paint s.t.'), *pasulatan* 'cause to write to s.o.' (cf. *sulatan* 'write to s.o.'), *ipabili* 'cause to buy for s.o.' (cf. *ibili* 'buy for s.o.').

Turning now to aspectual affixation, let us begin with a brief overview of the Tagalog aspect system. Tagalog, then, makes no true tense distinctions like the English past–non-past distinction, but instead makes a distinction between events viewed as actual, or realis and events viewed as hypothetical, or irrealis. Among the actual events, there is a distinction between those viewed as complete and those viewed as incomplete. Events viewed as complete are in the *perfective* aspect, those viewed as incomplete are in the *imperfective* aspect and those viewed as hypothetical are in the *contemplated* aspect. The perfective aspect is often translated into English by the past or the present perfect, the imperfective aspect by the simple present or by the present or past progressive and the contemplated aspect by the future, e.g. perf. *nagwalis* 'swept, has swept', imperf. *nagwawalis* 'sweeps, is/was sweeping', cont. *magwawalis* 'will sweep'. There are, however, other translation equivalents in certain cases. For example, the imperfective rather than the perfective form is used for the equivalent of the English negative perfect. Thus 'hasn't swept yet' is expressed by *hindi pa nagwawalis*, not **hindi pa nagwalis*. (*Hindi* is a negative form, *pa* an enclitic adverb.)

From a morphological point of view, aspect is marked in Tagalog by two patterns of affixation, one of which is common to imperfective and contemplative verbs, the other to imperfective and perfective verbs. The pattern that is common to imperfective and contemplated verbs can be called 'incompleteness' marking (since hypothetical events are necessarily incomplete), while the pattern common to imperfective and perfective verbs can be called 'actuality' marking.

Incompleteness marking involves a monosyllabic reduplicating prefix. This prefix normally consists of a copy of the first consonant and first vowel of the following syllable, except that the vowel of the reduplicating prefix is always long, whatever the length of the vowel in the following syllable. (Vowel length distinguishes this aspectual reduplication from the stem-forming reduplication mentioned above, which always involves a *short* vowel. Compare, for example, the aspectual reduplicating prefix /la:/ in *maglalakbay* /magla:lakbay/ 'will travel' and the stem-forming (intensive) reduplicating prefix /la/ in *maglalakbay* /maglalakbay/ 'travel (repeatedly, etc.)'.)

The rules for the placement of the aspectual reduplicating prefix in relation to other prefixes are rather complex. Some prefixes always precede the reduplicating prefix, but others may either precede or follow it, resulting in the possibility of alternative orderings. For example, in the contemplated and imperfective forms of the verb *maipabili* 'be able to cause to buy', the reduplicating prefix follows the abilitative prefix *ma-* but may either precede or follow the transitive prefix *i-* and the causative prefix *pa-*; thus cont. *maiipabili*, *maipapabili* and *maipabibili* 'will be able to cause to buy' are all well formed.

Actuality marking, which is common to imperfective and perfective verbs, in most cases involves an affix that contains the phoneme /n/. The sole exceptions to this generalisation are verbs whose infinitives are formed with the actor-trigger infix *-um-*, in which actuality marking consists simply in the retention of this infix. The infix, in other words, is present in imperfective and perfective forms, but absent from contemplated forms. For example, the imperfective and perfective forms of the verb *pumunta* 'go' (stem: *punta*) are, respectively, *pumupunta* and *pumunta*, while the contemplated form is *pupunta*. (As these examples illustrate, the perfective forms of *-um-* verbs are identical with the infinitives.)

There are three actuality-marking affixes that contain /n/, the prefix *n-*, the prefix *ni-* and the infix *-in-*. The prefix *n-* occurs as a replacement of *m-* in all prefixes that begin with the latter in the infinitive. For example, *nagwalis* and *nagwawalis* are the perfective and imperfective forms corresponding to the infinitive *magwalis* 'sweep'. Similarly, *nangisda* is the perfective form of *mangisda* 'fish', and intransitive *nakakita*/transitive *nakita* are the perfective forms of intransitive *makakita*/transitive *makita* 'see s.t.'. The prefix *ni-* and the infix *-in-* occur in all other cases as either free or morphophonemically conditioned alternants. For example, the perfective form corresponding to the infinitive *lagyan* 'put on s.t.' may be either *nilagyan* or *linagyan*, but the perfective form corresponding to *iabot* 'hand to someone' must be *iniabot* and that corresponding to *hiraman* 'borrow from someone' must be *hiniraman*.

If the verb marked by *ni-* or *-in-* contains the prefix *i-*, this always precedes the *ni-* or *-in-*, as in *iniyuko ~ iyinuko*, the perfective forms of *iyuko* 'bend s.t.', or *ibinigay*, the perfective form of *ibigay* 'give s.t.'. Otherwise, *ni-* is always word-initial and *-in-* always follows the first consonant of the word. A special property of verbs whose infinitives are formed with the suffix *-in* is the loss of this suffix in the actuality-marked forms. Thus, corresponding to the infinitive *yayain* 'invite someone', we find perfective *niyaya ~ yinaya* and imperfective *niyayaya ~ yinayaya* (cf. the contemplated form *yayayain*, in which the suffix *-in* is retained).

The morphology of adjectival verbs in Tagalog is also rather complex. Probably the most common formations are those involving the prefix *ma-*, e.g. *mabuti* 'be good' (cf. *buti* 'goodness'), *masama* 'be bad' (cf. *sama* 'badness'), *malaki* 'be big' (cf. *laki* 'bigness'), *maliit* 'be small' (cf. *liit* 'smallness'). There are also many unaffixed adjectival verbs – e.g. *mahal* 'be expensive', *mura* 'be cheap', *hinog* 'be ripe', *hilaw* 'be raw' – as well as many that are formed with various other affixes, e.g. *-an*, as in *putikan* 'be virtually covered with mud' (cf. *putik* 'mud'), *-in*, as in *lagnatin* 'be susceptible to fever' (cf. *lagnat* 'fever') (and other 'adversely affected' forms), and *maka-*, as in *makabayan* 'be patriotic' (cf. *bayan* 'country').

In certain cases adjectival verbs may be morphologically marked for number or gender. Many *ma-* adjectival verbs are marked as plural by a monosyllabic reduplicating prefix occurring between *ma-* and the stem: e.g. *mabubuti* 'be good (pl.)', *masasama* 'be bad (pl.)'. Such plural marking is, however, optional, and the non-pluralised forms may in general be used with plural as well as with singular referents. Gender marking is restricted to certain borrowed forms from Spanish, which occur in two gender-marked forms, a feminine form ending in *-a* and a masculine form ending in *-o*, e.g. *komika* (f.)/*komiko* (m.) 'be funny', *simpatika* (f.)/*simpatiko* (m.) 'be pleasing', *tonta* (f.)/*tonto* (m.) 'be stupid'.

Adjectival verbs may also be morphologically marked as intensive or moderative. Intensive formations involve the prefix *napaka-* (which replaces the *ma-* of a *ma-* adjectival form), while moderative formations involve disyllabic reduplication. Examples are: *napakabuti* 'be very good', *napakamahal* 'be very expensive', *mabuti-buti* 'be rather good', *mahal-mahal* 'be rather expensive'.

The comparative of equality is marked by *(ka)sing-*, e.g. *(ka)singbuti* 'be as good as', *(ka)singmahal* 'be as expensive as', and the superlative is marked by *pinaka-*, e.g. *pinakamabuti* 'be best', *pinakamahal* 'be most expensive'. (Note that the *ma-* of a *ma-* adjectival verb such as *mabuti* 'be good' is dropped after *(ka)sing-* but retained after *pinaka-*.) The comparative of inequality is, however, expressed syntactically (by a preceding *mas*, *lalong* or *higit na* 'more' and a following *kaysa* or *(kaysa) sa* 'than').

Tagalog noun morphology is relatively simple. Nouns are not inflected for case or number (there is, however, obligatory *syntactic* role marking involving case-marking forms like *ng* and *sa* – see above – as well as optional syntactic pluralisation, involving the plural form *mga*), and only certain nouns borrowed from Spanish are marked for gender: e.g. *amiga* (f.)/*amigo* (m.) 'friend', *sekretarya* (f.)/*sekretaryo* (m.) 'secretary'. Nonetheless, a good many morphologically complex nouns occur and some of these reflect quite productive patterns of affixation. Among the latter are: affixation with *-an* to express a place associated with what the stem designates, as in *aklatan* 'library' (cf. *aklat* 'book'), *halamanan* 'garden' (cf. *halaman* 'plant'); affixation with *-in* to express the object of the action expressed by a verb formed with the same stem, as in *awitin* 'song' (cf. *umawit* 'sing'), *bilihin* 'something to buy' (cf. *bumili* 'buy'); and affixation with *taga-* to express the performer of the action of a verb formed with the same stem, as in *tagasulat* 'writer' (cf. *sumulat* 'write'), *tagapagbili* 'seller' (cf. *magbili* 'sell'), *tagapangisda* 'fisherman' (cf. *mangisda* 'fish').

The Tagalog personal pronoun system is summarised in Table 49.4. The person–number categories that are distinguished are first, second and third person, singular and plural. There are, however, two distinct types of first person plural. When the addressee is not included in the group being referred to (i.e. when the meaning is 'he/she/they and I'), the *exclusive* forms are used. When, on the other hand, the addressee *is* included in the group being referred to (i.e. when the meaning is 'you (and he/she/they) and I'), the *inclusive* forms are used. Some dialects of Tagalog also make a distinction between first person inclusive and first person dual forms, although the distinction is lost in the dialect commonly used in Manila. Note that no gender distinctions are made: the same third person singular forms are used to refer to males and females. While, in general, Tagalog personal pronouns are, strictly *personal*, in the sense that they are used to refer only to human beings (and to humanised animals, such as pets or animals in folktales), the third person singular *siya* can also be used for a non-human referent. However, where English would use *it* (or *they* with a non-human referent), Tagalog commonly uses either no pronoun at all or a demonstrative.

Table 49.4 Personal Pronouns

	Genitive	*Locative*	Unmarked
Singular			
1st person	ko	akin	ako
2nd person	mo	iyo	ka/ikaw
3rd person	niya	kaniya	siya
Plural			
1st person-exclusive	namin	amin	kami
1st person-inclusive	natin	atin	tayo
2nd person	ninyo	inyo	kayo
3rd person	nila	kanila	sila

Each personal pronoun category is associated with three distinct forms, except for the second person singular, which is associated with four. The genitive is the form that occurs in the same contexts as personal noun phrases marked by *ni*, that is personal actors of transitive sentences and possessors of nouns. The locative is the form that occurs after the preposition *sa* or as a prenominal possessive pronoun. This set of pronouns is labelled by some analysts as dative. The unmarked form is that which occurs in most other contexts, e.g. in isolation, as a nominal predicate, as a fronted topic or when the pronoun functions as the grammatical subject of the clause. In the case of the second person singular pronoun, there are two forms: *ka*, an enclitic pronoun which functions exclusively as a subject and is unambiguously absolutive, and *ikaw*, which is a free form that occurs in unmarked contexts such as in isolation, as a nominal predicate or a fronted topic.

A similar three-way distinction is made in the demonstrative pronouns, as shown in Table 49.5.

Table 49.5 Demonstrative Pronouns

	Genitive	Locative	Unmarked
'this'	nito	dito	ito
'that (near addressee)'	niyan	diyan	iyan
'that (not near addressee)'	niyon, noon	doon	iyon

Three demonstrative categories are distinguished, one equivalent to English 'this' and two that divide the range of English 'that', one of them used when the referent is near the addressee, the other when it is not. Again the genitive forms are those that occur in the same contexts as common nouns marked by *ng* (*niyon* and *noon* are free variants), and function as actors of transitive sentences or as demonstrative possessors of nouns. The locative forms of the demonstratives occur in the same contexts as *sa* phrases (including directional and locative *sa* phrases, in which case the demonstratives have the meanings 'here' and 'there'). And the unmarked forms occur in most other contexts.

Finally, it may be mentioned that there are also three contextually distinguished forms of the personal-name marker, i.e. the marker that is used when the head noun is a personal name: the *ng* form *ni*, the *sa* form *kay* and the unmarked form *si*. Such formal distinctions within the nominal system serve to identify the semantic and/or syntactic roles of arguments more or less unambiguously, thus allowing for the freedom of word order which, together with the voice-marking system and the complex verbal morphology, constitute perhaps the most striking typological features of Tagalog.

Bibliography

Tagalog grammar was first studied by Spanish missionaries in the sixteenth century, but it was only in the twentieth century that the language was analysed on its own terms, rather than on the basis of often inappropriate European models. Bloomfield's (1917) influential grammar, written from a classic structuralist perspective, served as the basis for the first grammar by a native speaker of the language, Lopez (1940). The most comprehensive grammar of the language written to date is Schachter and Otanes (1972). Various descriptions of the morphology and syntax of Tagalog have appeared since then, including De Guzman (1978), Kroeger (1993) and Maclachlan (1996). Ramos and Bautista (1986) is a handbook of Tagalog verbs with permissable affixation. Himmelmann (2004) provides an excellent description of Tagalog morphology. Recent chapters giving overviews of Tagalog include De Guzman (2001) and Himmelmann (2005).

References

Bloomfield, Leonard. 1917. *Tagalog Texts with Grammatical Analysis*. University of Illinois Studies in Language and Literature, vol. III (University of Illinois, Urbana)

De Guzman, Videa P. 1978. *Syntactic Derivation of Tagalog Verbs*. Oceanic Linguistics Special Publication, vol. 16 (University of Hawai'i Press, Honolulu)

—— 2001. 'Tagalog', in Jane Garry and Carl Rubino (eds) *Facts about the World's Major Languages: An Encyclopedia of the World's Major Languages, Past and Present* (D.H. Wilson, New York and Dublin), pp. 703–7

French, Koleen Matsuda. 1988. *Insights into Tagalog: Reduplication, Infixation, and Stress from Nonlinear Phonology* (The Summer Institute of Linguistics and the University of Texas at Arlington, Arlington, TX)

Himmelmann, Nikolaus P. 2004. 'Tagalog', in Geert Booij, Christian Lehmann and Joachim Mugdan (eds), in collaboration with Wolfgang Kesselheim and Stavros Skopeteas, *Morphology: An International Handbook on Inflection and Word-formation, Vol. 2, 1473–90* (de Gruyter, Berlin)

—— 2005. 'Tagalog', in Alexander Adelaar and Nikolaus P. Himmelmann (eds) *The Austronesian Languages of Asia and Madagascar* (Routledge, New York), pp. 350–76

Kroeger, Paul. 1993. *Phrase Structure and Grammatical Relations in Tagalog.* Dissertations in Linguistics (Center for the Study of Language and Information, Stanford)

Lopez, Cecilio. 1940. *The Tagalog Language (An Outline of its Psycho-morphological Analysis)* (Bureau of Printing, Manila)

Maclachlan, Anna E. 1996. 'Aspects of Ergativity in Tagalog' (PhD dissertation, McGill University)

Ramos, Teresita V. and Bautista, Maria Lourdes S. 1986. *Handbook of Tagalog Verbs, Inflections, Modes, and Aspects* (University of Hawai'i Press, Honolulu)

Schachter, Paul and Otanes, Fe T. 1972. *Tagalog Reference Grammar* (University of California Press, Berkeley)

Zorc, David Paul. 1993. 'The Prehistory and Origin of the Tagalog People', in Øyvind Dahl (ed.) *Language – A Doorway between Human Cultures: Tributes to Dr Otto Chr. Dahl on his Ninetieth Birthday* (Novus, Oslo), pp. 201–11

50

Niger-Kordofanian (Niger-Congo) languages

Douglas Pulleyblank

Niger-Kordofanian is the family to which the vast majority of the languages of sub-Saharan Africa belong. Hundreds of languages fall into this group and about 350,000,000 people speak Niger-Kordofanian languages. Geographically, this group ranges from Senegal in the west to Kenya in the east and extends as far south as South Africa.

The proposal for the group 'Niger-Kordofanian' dates from Greenberg's (1963) classification of the languages of Africa into four families: Niger-Kordofanian, Nilo-Saharan, Afroasiatic and Khoisan. Greenberg's creation of Niger-Kordofanian differed from earlier work on the classification of the relevant languages with respect to both larger and smaller groupings, as well as in its assignment of certain languages to particular subgroups. For example, at the level of large groupings, he included 'Kordofanian' and 'Niger-Congo' within a single family; at the level of smaller groupings, he argued that Bantu was actually a sub-sub-subgroup of Niger-Congo – not an independent family of its own; with respect to particular languages, he argued (for example) that Fula properly belongs to the West Atlantic subgroup of Niger-Congo. The basic subdivisions for Niger-Kordofanian proposed by Greenberg are as follows: NIGER-CONGO: (1) West Atlantic, (2) Mande, (3) Gur (Voltaic), (4) Kwa, (5) Benue-Congo, (6) Adamawa-Eastern; KORDOFANIAN: (1) Koalib, (2) Tegali, (3) Talodi, (4) Tumtum, (5) Katla. (Note that in more recent work, the language family as a whole is usually called 'Niger-Congo', with Kordofanian as one of its branches, rather than 'Niger-Kordofanian'; to avoid confusion, we retain Greenberg's original terminology here.)

There are several problems encountered in the classification of the languages of this group. Apart from general problems involved in the classification of any group of languages, one finds a number of specific problems. There are very few historical records of these languages that go back more than a couple of hundred years and yet we are dealing with a very large, very diverse group of languages which has been splitting apart for thousands of years. Obviously the details of larger genetic groupings will ultimately depend on the reconstruction of smaller groups – a task that is a large one given the number of languages involved and the limited amount of knowledge about many of them. To illustrate this point, work by Elugbe and Williamson (1976) on the reconstruction of Proto-Ẹdo and Proto-Ịjọ (two subgroups of Kwa) calls into question the legitimacy of the distinction between Kwa and Benue-Congo. They show that properties considered to be identifying characteristics of Benue-Congo must also be reconstructed for 'Proto-Ẹdo-Ịjọ'. Their conclusion is that there is no evidence for separating Kwa from Benue-Congo, and that the two groups really constitute a single 'Benue-Kwa' subfamily of Niger-Congo. It is not within the scope of this short survey to review the work that has been done on the classification of African languages since Greenberg's influential work (although it is worth noting that studies such as that of Elugbe and Williamson serve to refine – not refute – Greenberg's work). Consequently, I will refer to languages and language groups according to their positions within Greenberg's (1963) classification. I stress that this is not intended as a rejection of refinements to the 1963 classification, but simply because that classification is the most familiar.

Because of the large number of languages in the Niger-Kordofanian family, it is probably impossible to make any general statements that hold true of all member languages. And even if one were to have access to a comprehensive reconstruction of Proto-Niger-Kordofanian, this would tell us relatively little about the presently attested characteristics of many (most) of the descendants of that language. For example, while most Niger-Kordofanian languages are tonal (and the proto-language surely was), there are important exceptions in languages like Fula (West Atlantic) and Swahili (Bantu; Benue-Congo). Moreover, even in the 'tonal' languages, the actual properties of the tonal systems vary considerably; languages may employ a fairly restricted system – for example, two tones and a fairly predictable distribution of the tones – or languages may employ highly articulated systems involving several distinct tones, essentially unpredictable lexical placements of the tones, complex realisation rules, etc. Languages also differ, for example, as to whether tones are used for lexical and/or grammatical (e.g. tense) contrasts. In the following discussion, I will survey languages and language characteristics of Niger-Congo. Niger-Congo languages will be concentrated on since the Kordofanian group is more limited both in terms of number of speakers and in terms of geographical distribution (all the Kordofanian languages are spoken in the relatively small Kordofan area of Sudan). The languages that will be mentioned were chosen by virtue of being spoken by large numbers of people (although numbers vary from hundreds of thousands to tens of millions); topics to be discussed, however, have been chosen more in terms of anticipated interest than necessarily because they involve pan-Niger-Congo features. For example, perhaps all Niger-Congo languages have dental or alveolar stops while only an important subset of the family has doubly-articulated stops. But in such a case, the doubly-articulated stops will be discussed.

The westernmost branch of Niger-Congo is 'West Atlantic'. The languages of this group are concentrated in the extreme western portion of West Africa, ranging basically from Senegal to Liberia. This said, the list of languages included in this group will begin with an exception. Fula (Fulani, Fulfulde, Peul, Fulbe, etc.), which is perhaps the most well-known language of this group, is spoken essentially throughout West Africa in a sub-Saharan belt that extends from Senegal in the west to as far east as Chad. Closely related to Fula is Serer, a language spoken predominantly in Senegal and also in Gambia. Still closely related is Wolof, centred in Senegal but also spoken in Gambia, Mali, Mauritania and Guinea. Other important languages in the West Atlantic group include Dyola (Senegal; also Gambia and Guinea), Balante (Guinea-Bissau; also Senegal), Temne (Sierra Leone), Kissi (Sierra Leone, Guinea; also Liberia), Gola (Liberia; also Sierra Leone) and Limba (Sierra Leone and Guinea).

Despite its not being a very unified group, it is typical for a West Atlantic language to have noun classes and a system of consonant mutations (Sapir 1971). Class systems of the type generally associated with Bantu languages (see, for example, Chapter 52 in this volume) are found in languages of the West Atlantic group. Classes may have phonological, morphological, syntactic and semantic correlates. The morphological indicators of noun class membership generally involve prefixation and/or suffixation (for example, Temne has class prefixes while Fula has suffixes); in a language like Wolof, however, class membership is not morphologically marked and can only be deduced from the effect a noun has on governed elements. The important syntactic effect of noun classes is in determining properties of agreement. The various elements that can occur within a noun phrase will typically be marked to agree in class with the head of the noun phrase. Agreement can extend beyond the noun phrase to include elements such as the verb. The number of noun classes found in a particular language varies considerably within the West Atlantic group. For example, a language like Nalu has only three classes while certain dialects of Fula have up to twenty-five. While classes are generally not definable in terms of their semantics, certain generalisations can often be made. Classes are typically associated with either singular or plural nouns; classes may indicate notions such as 'augmentative' or 'diminutive'. A particularly interesting phonological property that is related to the noun class system is consonant mutation. In Fula, for example, changes in the phonological nature of the initial consonant of a stem accompany the assignment of a particular class suffix. Hence in addition to the suffix marking the appropriate singular or plural class, examples like the following involve changes in the initial stem consonant: *pul-lo* 'a Fula'; *ful-ɓe* 'Fulas'. In the singular class, the initial stem consonant must appear in its 'stop grade'; in the plural class, the initial stem consonant appears in its 'fricative' grade; other classes could require either of the above grades or a third 'nasal grade' (which for the *p/f* series would also be *p*, but which for many other series would be a prenasalised consonant). Although such consonant alternations correlate with noun classes in Fula, this is not always the case. In Serer, for example, the appropriate consonant grade is determined by an interaction between noun class membership and other lexical stem properties. As a final point, consonant mutation is not restricted to nouns; consonants of adjectives, verbs and even (in Fula) certain suffixes may alternate. For example, the following verbs from Fula illustrate the appearance of the fricative grade in the singular and of the nasal grade in the plural: *laamɗo warii* 'the chief came'; *laamɓe ngarii* 'the chiefs came' *(w/ng)*.

Mande languages, the second group to be considered here, are spoken as far west as Senegal and as far east as Bourkina Fasso (Upper Volta) and Ivory Coast. The largest languages in this group are Maninka-Bambara-Dyula and Mende. Maninka-Bambara-Dyula refers to a group of very closely related dialects/languages spoken in several countries including Senegal, Gambia, Guinea, Mali, Sierra Leone, Ivory Coast and Bourkina Fasso; Mende is spoken in Sierra Leone. Other languages in the Mande group include Soninke (Mali), Vai (Sierra Leone), Susu-Yalunka (Guinea, Sierre Leone), Loma (Liberia, Guinea), Kpelle (Liberia, Guinea), Mano (Liberia, Guinea), Dan-Kweni (Ivory Coast, Liberia), Samo (Bourkina Fasso, Mali) and Busa (Benin, Nigeria). Note that Busa is exceptional geographically for Mande, occurring as far east as Nigeria.

In contrast with the West Atlantic languages, Mande languages do not have noun classes. Interestingly, however, certain Mande languages do have systems of consonant mutation. Changes in the initial consonant of a word can correlate with properties of definiteness, can occur with particular pronominal elements, can occur in particular syntactic contexts, etc. (Welmers 1971: 132). Moreover, there are cases where segmental properties of consonants interact in very interesting ways with tonal properties. While it is not uncommon in general to observe that voiced consonants have a lowering effect on the pitch of an adjacent vowel while voiceless consonants have a raising effect, it is interesting that in a Mande language like Kpelle the presence or absence of a low tone actually correlates with the presence or absence of voicing. Hence a voiceless stop like *p* has a counterpart in Kpelle that is heavily voiced and bears a low tone (Welmers 1962: 71–2).

In general, the tonal properties of Mande languages are of considerable interest and importance. The observation that tone must be assigned in certain cases to morphemes rather than to some smaller phonological unit such as the syllable was first made by Welmers with respect to Kpelle (Welmers 1962: 85–6). Using examples from Mende (Leben 1978) as illustration, it can be shown that words such as the following all involve a single high–low pattern: *mbû* 'owl', *ngílà* 'dog', *félàmà* 'junction'. The high and low tones are realised on a single vowel (the only vowel) in the first example, on the first and second vowels in the second example, and in the third example, the high appears on the first vowel while the low appears on the second and third vowels. Consideration of such cases has been instrumental in determining that phonetic contour tones are best represented as involving sequences of phonologically level tones and that certain vowels that phonetically bear tones are best viewed as receiving their tones by the interaction of general principles with tonal sequences that are assigned underlyingly to morphemes rather than to specific vowels or syllables.

The Gur, or Voltaic, languages are primarily spoken in southeastern Mali, Bourkina Fasso and northern Ghana, although they extend through Togo and Benin as far east as Nigeria. The largest language of this group is Moore (also known as More, Mossi, etc.), spoken in Bourkina Fasso, Ghana and Togo. Other languages include Dagari (Ghana, Bourkina Fasso), Dagomba (Ghana, Togo), Dogon (Mali, Bourkina Fasso), Gurma (Bourkina Fasso, Ghana, Togo), Lobiri (Bourkina Fasso, Ivory Coast), Bwamu (Bourkina Fasso), Senari (Ivory Coast) and Suppire-Mianka (Mali) – these last two largest 'Senufo' languages –, Tem (Togo, Benin, Ghana) and Bariba (Benin, Togo, Nigeria).

Like the West Atlantic languages (and indeed typical of Niger-Kordofanian in general), Gur languages commonly manifest systems of noun classes (Bendor-Samuel 1971: 164–71). Unlike the most common Niger-Kordofanian pattern of prefixes, however, Gur languages generally have class suffixes. It should be noted, moreover, that the presence of class systems in widely diverse languages is more than simply a typological similarity. For example, it is typical of Gur that there be singular and plural person classes marked by the affixes *a* or *u* (singular) and *ba* or *bi* (plural); there is typically a class not involved in a singular/plural pairing that is used for mass/liquid nouns and generally marked by a nasal affix. Such characteristics, while typical of Gur, are widely attested throughout Niger-Kordofanian.

The morphology of Gur languages presents numerous properties of considerable phonological interest. Consider, for example, the following imperfective forms in Dagara (*ré* 'imperfective'): *dì* + *ré* → *dìré* (*dɪ* 'eat'); *tú* + *ré* → *túúr* (*tú* 'insult'); *cè* + *ré* →*cìér* (*cè* 'construct'). In the first example, the imperfective suffix surfaces basically without modification. In the second example, however, the vowel of the suffix is lost while the stem vowel is lengthened. And in the third example, there is not only loss of the suffix vowel and lengthening of the stem vowel, but, in addition, the stem vowel is diphthongised. Determining the precise conditions under which these types of changes take place involves rather intricate interactions between properties of vowel quality, syllable structure and tone.

Another point concerning the morphology of Gur languages is the high frequency of compounding. For example, it is common for adjective–noun sequences to appear as a compound rather than as a syntactic sequence. In such a case, the noun stem will appear followed by the adjective followed by a single class suffix. When adjectives do appear as a syntactic constituent, there are three basic possibilities: they may be invariant; they may be marked for noun class membership just as nouns – but not participate in agreement; or they may take class affixes that agree with the head noun (Bendor-Samuel 1971: 171–2). It should be noted before leaving the topic of adjectives that this category is a very restricted one throughout Niger-Congo. Typically, the types of meanings that might be expressed by adjectives in a language like English are expressed in Niger-Congo languages by constructions involving either verbs or nouns.

Gur languages manifest some variation with respect to basic word order. For example, although the general order for subject, object and verb in Gur is SVO, certain Gur languages (e.g. Senari) have the basic order SOV. It is worth noting that Gur reflects the overall Niger-Congo patterning in this regard – in general, the Niger-Congo basic order is SVO, although in a group such as Mande it is SOV.

The Kwa languages are found in an area extending basically from Liberia in the west to Nigeria in the east. The four largest languages in the Kwa group are Akan (Ghana), Ewe (Ghana, Togo, Benin), Yoruba (Nigeria, Benin, Togo) (see Chapter 51 in this volume) and Igbo (Nigeria). Other languages in this group include Bassa (Liberia), Kru (Liberia), Baule (Ivory Coast), Bete (Ivory Coast), Gã-Adangme (Ghana), Nupe (Nigeria), Gwari (Nigeria), Ebira (Nigeria), Bini (Nigeria), Igala (Nigeria), Idoma (Nigeria) and Ijo (Nigeria). It might be noted that there is some disagreement as to whether Ijo really belongs to the Kwa group or to the Benue-Congo group. Of course, such a question ceases to be an issue if it turns out that Kwa and Benue-Congo actually form a single branch of Niger-Congo (as mentioned above as a possibility).

A striking phonetic property of a typical Kwa language is the presence of doubly-articulated 'labial-velar' stops. While such segments appear in numerous non-Kwa languages, in Kwa they are commonplace. Ladefoged (1968: 9) notes that there are at least three ways for a doubly-articulated stop like [k͡p] to be produced: the labial and velar closures may be released on an air-stream that is (1) pulmonic egressive only (e.g. Guang (Ghana)); (2) pulmonic egressive and velaric ingressive (e.g. Yoruba); (3) pulmonic egressive, velaric ingressive and glottalic ingressive (e.g. Idoma).

Another typical phonetic property found in Kwa (although in no way restricted to Kwa) is tonal downstep. Although a language may contrast only two phonological tone levels, it may have a number of phonetic pitch levels that is in principle unlimited. In Igbo, for example, two adjacent high-toned syllables will normally be produced on the same pitch. If, however, a low-toned syllable intervenes between the two high tones, then the second high tone will be produced on a lower pitch than the first one. In an appropriate sequence of alternating tones (e.g. HLHLH ...), a series of gradually lowered high tones will be produced. Such completely transparent examples of phonetic downstepping are often complicated by the presence of 'floating' tones in a language's phonological representations. That is, tones may be phonologically present in certain cases even though there is no vowel available for the tone to be pronounced on. Consider again the type of HLH sequence in a downstepping language where the second high tone will be produced on a slightly lower pitch than the first. If the vowel bearing the low tone were to be deleted for some reason, then in many cases the low tone itself would remain and continue to play a role in the tonal phonology of the sequence in question – for example, by triggering the phonetic lowering of the second high tone. Hence the phonetic sequence of a high tone followed by a slightly lower tone (but not low) is in many cases the phonetic realisation of a H–L'–H sequence (where L' indicates a floating tone). In many other cases, such a slightly lower tone may of course be correctly analysed as a mid tone – phonologically distinct from either high or low. Determining the correct analysis of such non-high tones is often a major problem of tonal phonology.

With respect to syntax, one interesting construction found in a number of Kwa languages is that of the 'predicate cleft'. In this construction a predicate is focused by placing a copy of the verb in a fronted position. The following example is from Yoruba:

rírà	ni	bàbá	ra	bàtà
buying	foc.	father	buy	shoe

'Father *bought* shoes.'

In this example, the verb *rà* is focused by placing a nominalised form of the verb in the initial focus position. This construction therefore makes it possible to focus syntactically virtually any constituent of a basic Yoruba sentence – noun phrase subjects, objects, etc., being typical focused constituents.

The Benue-Congo languages are distributed throughout east, central and southern Africa, extending as far west as Nigeria. Four sub-branches of Benue-Congo can be distinguished, of which the most important is Bantoid – the branch including the Bantu languages. Since a separate chapter in this volume is devoted to Bantu, the discussion here will concentrate on Benue-Congo languages other than Bantu. With respect to the number of speakers, the Bantu languages stand in marked contrast to the other languages of Benue-Congo. Whereas a large proportion of the speakers of Niger-Kordofanian languages speak Bantu languages, only relatively small groups tend to speak other Benue-Congo languages. Two exceptions to this generalisation are Efik-Ibibio (Nigeria) and Tiv (Nigeria), both spoken by large populations.

When the Bantu group is compared with the rest of the Benue-Congo group, it is striking that there is much more variation within the group not including Bantu than there is within the Bantu group itself. For example, the features that characterise the Bantu group are its systems of noun classes and agglutinative verb morphology and it is generally fairly straightforward to establish correspondences between the particular forms of one language and those of another – or between the forms of one language and the reconstructed forms of Proto-Bantu. Of course, a major reason for including Bantu in the Benue-Congo group is that the typical 'Bantu' properties can be demonstrated to occur in other languages of the Benue-Congo group. But typically, the Benue-Congo languages other than Bantu show considerable diversity in their manifestations of such properties.

Consider, for example, Benue-Congo noun class systems. While noun class systems demonstrably corresponding to Bantu are typical of Benue-Congo, there are Benue-Congo languages that have lost their class systems (e.g. Jukun). And while noun classes are morphologically marked by prefixes in Bantu, in a very closely related language like Tiv, noun classes are marked by both prefixes and suffixes.

The morphology of the Tiv noun class system is quite complex. For example, the singular person class is marked either by the absence of class marking or by a low tone prefix in conjunction with labialisation of the initial stem consonant. An example of the latter possibility is *ꞌkwásé* 'wife', where *ꞌ* indicates an initial downstep triggered by the low tone prefix, and labialisation of the stem *kásé* has taken place because of the singular prefix. The plural person class is marked either by a suffix *v* (e.g. *kásév* 'wives') or by one of the prefixes *ù* or *mbà*. Apart from the phonological properties of the singular affix, an interesting property of the class morphology concerns the appearance of class suffixes on nouns within prepositional phrases (Abraham 1940). One observes that class suffixes cannot occur with a preposition like *shá* 'on': *shá ꞌkwásé* 'on the wife'; *shá ùkásé* 'on the wives'. In this example, the suffix *v* that normally appears in the plural of *kásé* has been replaced by the prefix *ù* within a prepositional phrase. However, class suffixes can occur within a prepositional phrase if the relevant noun is followed by a demonstrative, possessive pronoun, etc. Compare the following examples involving the stem *gèrè* 'water': *ḿgérĕm* 'water' (prefix *ḿ*; suffix *ḿ*) *shím m̀gèr* 'in the water' (prefix *ḿ* only; final stem vowel is deleted by a regular phonological rule); *shím m̀gérĕm mèrá* 'in that water' (prefix *ḿ*; suffix *ḿ*). Not only is the suffix not present in the form *shím m̀gèr*, but the class prefix has lost its normal high tone.

The final branch of Niger-Congo to be considered is Adamawa-Eastern or Adamawa-Ubangian. Geographically, the languages of this group are found as far west as Nigeria (although concentrated groups of Adamawa languages do not begin until Cameroon) and extend as far east as Sudan; the northern and southern extents of Adamawa-Eastern are Chad and the Congo. The largest language of this branch is Gbaya, spoken in the Central African Republic, Cameroon and the Congo. Two other Adamawa-Eastern languages are Banda (Central African Republic, Congo) and Zande (Sudan, Central African Republic, Congo).

Just as most other branches of Niger-Congo, Adamawa-Eastern shows reflexes of a Niger-Congo noun class system. Typically, the class markers in this branch are suffixes, although in some cases they can only be reconstructed through the comparison of 'stem'-final consonants in languages which have ceased to operate a synchronic class system (Boyd 1974: 56–7). Reduplication, in addition to forms of affixation, is a common morphological process in this group (and also common in other groups of Niger-Congo). As a final point concerning morphology in a broad sense (and again actually a more general point than simply relating to Adamawa-Eastern), one should take note of the class of words referred to as 'ideophones'. Although notoriously difficult to define, ideophones form an identifiable class of words in many languages (see pages 873–874 for a discussion of Yoruba ideophones). Typically, they exhibit certain morphological properties such as reduplication; phonological properties such as specific tonal patterns and the occurrence of special phonemes; syntactically, they are often used in adverbial configurations and are often idiomatically restricted to appearing with particular predicates.

With respect to phonology, this branch has a number of interesting properties (where it should be stressed that while such properties may be typical of Adamawa-Eastern, they are not restricted to it). Prenasalised segments are common; in a language like Duru (Cameroon; Boyd 1974: 24), a prenasalised stop series is attested, while in a language like Mbum (Cameroon; Hagège 1970: 54), there are both prenasalised stops and prenasalised fricatives. Evidence that such prenasalised segments belong to a single syllable – even intervocalically in a sequence such as [... aŋga ...] – can be found in the language games of a language like Gbaya (Monino and Roulon 1972: 110–11). Also with respect to nasalisation, one observes in a language like Mbum (Hagège 1970: 62) that if there are two vowels in a word, then either both will be nasal or neither will be nasal – different values for the two vowels are not attested. Also with respect to Mbum, Hagège notes (Hagège 1970: 48, 54) that glides ([y, w]) are in complementary distribution with their corresponding vowels: glides appear initially before a vowel as well as intervocalically, while the vowels appear elsewhere (e.g. *mbòì* 'follow'; *mbóyà* 'to follow'). A final general point can be made about the distribution of consonant phonemes. One typically observes that the full range of contrasts is possible only in initial position; only a restricted inventory may appear in intervocalic positions and an even more limited set is all that is possible in final position.

To close this discussion, a few brief comments will be made about the syntactic possibilities of this group, starting with a construction that is not attested: in the Adamawa-Eastern group, as in certain other groups, there is typically no morphologically marked passive construction. On the other hand, a construction that typically is found is one involving a proximate/obviative distinction between pronouns. That is, a pronoun in an embedded sentence that is coreferential to the matrix subject is distinguished morphologically from a pronoun that is disjoint in reference from the matrix subject (for Yoruba examples, see pages 878–879). Finally, one observes interesting word order properties in a language such as Duru. Boyd (1974: 52) notes that in a morphologically unmarked tense such as the past (perfective), predicates exemplify the more common pattern of this group in placing the object after the verb. But in the present (imperfective) tense, an object in Duru precedes the verb – appearing immediately after a particle that occurs in post-subject position. Hence the basic word order of a sentence depends on its tense.

Bibliography

For the establishment of the Niger-Kordofanian family, reference should be made to Greenberg (1963). For current views on the family and its internal composition, see Bendor-Samuel and Hartell (1989) and Williamson and Blench (2000). Welmers (1973) is an account of a number of recurrent structural properties of sub-Saharan African languages, with emphasis inevitably on Niger-Congo languages. Ladefoged (1968) is a detailed phonetic study of some of the less usual phonetic segments occurring in West African languages.

References

Abraham, R.C. 1940. *A Dictionary of the Tiv Language* (Stephen Austin, Hertford)

Bendor-Samuel, J.T. 1971. 'Niger-Congo, Gur', in T.A. Sebeok (ed.) *Current Trends in Linguistics, Vol. 7, Linguistics in Sub-Saharan Africa* (Mouton, The Hague), pp. 141–78

Bendor-Samuel, J.T. and Hartell, R.L. (eds) 1989. *The Niger-Congo Languages: A Classification and Description of Africa's Largest Language Family* (University Press of America, Lanham MD)

Boyd, R. 1974. *Étude comparative dans le groupe Adamawa* (SELAF, Paris)

Elugbe, B. and Williamson, K. 1976. 'Reconstructing Nasals in Proto-Benue-Kwa', in A. Juilland (ed.) *Linguistic Studies Offered to Joseph Greenberg*, vol. 2 (Anma Libri, Saratoga, CA)

Greenberg, J.H. 1963. *The Languages of Africa* (Indiana University, Bloomington; Mouton, The Hague)

Hagège, C. 1970. *La Langue mbum de Nganha* (SELAF, Paris)

Ladefoged, P. 1968. *A Phonetic Study of West African Languages* (Cambridge University Press, Cambridge)

Leben, W.R. 1978. 'The Representation of Tone', in V.A. Fromkin (ed.) *Tone: A Linguistic Survey* (Academic Press, New York), pp. 177–219

Monino, Y. and Roulon, P. 1972. *Phonologie du Gbaya Kara 'Bodoe* (SELAF, Paris)

Sapir, J.D. 1971. 'West Atlantic: An Inventory of the Languages, Their Noun Class Systems, and Consonant Alternation', in T.A. Sebeok (ed.) *Current Trends in Linguistics, Vol. 7, Linguistics in Sub-Saharan Africa* (Mouton, The Hague), pp. 45–112

Welmers, W.E. 1962. 'The Phonology of Kpelle', *Journal of African Languages*, vol. 1, pp. 69–93

—— 1971. 'Niger-Congo, Mande', in T.A. Sebeok (ed.) *Current Trends in Linguistics, Vol. 7, Linguistics in Sub-Saharan Africa* (Mouton, The Hague), pp. 113–40

—— 1973. *African Language Structures* (University of California Press, Berkeley)

Williamson, K. and Blench, R. 2000. 'Niger-Congo', in B. Heine and D. Nurse (eds) *African Languages: An Introduction*. Cambridge: Cambridge University Press, pp. 11–42

51

Yoruba

Douglas Pulleyblank

Revised by Ọlanikẹ Ọla Orie

1 Historical Background

Yoruba belongs to the Yoruboid group of languages, a group belonging to the Benue-Congo branch of the Niger-Congo language family. Other Yoruboid languages include the group of dialects referred to collectively as the Akoko cluster and Igala. Yoruba has about twenty distinct dialects (for example, Ọyọ, Ekiti, Ẹgba, Ijẹbu, Ijẹṣa, Ifẹ, Igbomina, Ondo, Ọwọ, Yagba). The vast majority of the speakers of Yoruba are found in Nigeria (upwards of 20 million), located particularly in Lagos, Ọyọ Ogun, Ondo, Ekiti, Ọsun, Kogi and Kwara states – states that essentially make up the southwestern corner of the country. Speakers are also found in southeastern sections of the Republic of Benin, as well as central and northern Togo.

It is interesting, however, that the study of Yoruba did not begin in any of the places just mentioned. In the early nineteenth century, Yorubas began to form a large percentage of the slaves being exported from West Africa. As this period also marked the beginning of the British suppression of the slave trade, it turned out that many of the freed slaves being resettled in Freetown, Sierra Leone, were speakers of Yoruba. When linguistic work undertaken in Freetown was extended to include languages not indigenous to Sierra Leone, Yoruba (or 'Aku' as it was commonly called) was a natural choice for study because of the large number of speakers residing in Freetown. In fact, as early as 1831, Yoruba was selected as one of two African languages to be used as the medium of instruction in a Sierra Leone girls' school. In the 1840s, however, the study of Yoruba began to shift to Yorubaland itself. The sending of the Niger expedition by the British government signalled the beginning of CMS (Church Missionary Society) missionary activity in Yorubaland. One of the central figures in the early study of Yoruba was Samuel Crowther. Crowther was a Yoruba slave who was liberated and settled in Freetown. There he received an education and began his study of Yoruba. After accompanying the Niger expedition to Yorubaland, he both became a priest and published his first work on Yoruba (a grammar and vocabulary). The CMS established itself in Abẹokuta; translation of the Bible was undertaken, primers were prepared and a Yoruba periodical was produced (from 1859 to 1867 – perhaps the earliest such vernacular periodical to be published in West Africa).

One of the particularly important things that happened at this time was a concerted group effort aimed at establishing an efficient orthography for Yoruba. The result, which included digraphs for certain phonemes and diacritically modified letters for others, involved contributions from scholars and missionaries in Europe, Freetown and Abẹokuta. Crowther's adoption of the revised orthography in conjunction with his considerable success as a translator did much to establish and promote standard Yoruba. The orthography adopted by Crowther and others in the 1850s was revised in the 1960s and 1970s by the Yoruba Orthography Committee. This committee was charged with the responsibility of resolving issues pertaining to inconsistencies in the orthography.

Before entering into a discussion of issues of Yoruba orthography and grammar, it is appropriate to note the influence that Yoruba language and culture have had in a variety of areas outside Yorubaland. Yoruba slaves were extremely influential in certain areas of Brazil and Cuba. For example, the Nagos (Yorubas) of Bahia in Brazil preserved Yoruba as a ceremonial language at least until very recently. And there are reportedly still small numbers of Yorubas in Sierra Leone. Yoruba has also undergone revivals such as that exhibited in Ọyọtunji village of the United States. Even where Yoruba has ceased to be spoken, it has often exerted a considerable impact on the languages that have replaced it – such as Krio in Sierra Leone.

In Yorubaland itself, Yoruba has an established and thriving literature, including books, newspapers, picture magazines, etc. Today, Yoruba is acquired as a first language in Yoruba-speaking homes and as a second or third language by high school students who are compelled by the National Policy on Education to learn a major Nigerian language in addition to their mother tongue. At the tertiary level, Yoruba programmes are quite vibrant. Currently, Yoruba serves as the medium of instruction for courses in Yoruba linguistics and literature in several Nigerian universities. In the 1950s and 1960s, when the Yoruba curriculum consisted mainly of reading classical novels composed of themes illustrating Yoruba customs and traditions, there was no difficulty in teaching Yoruba through Yoruba. However, much difficulty was encountered as higher level technical linguistic concepts were taught in the 1970s. To address this issue, the National Educational Research Council sponsored a Yoruba Metalanguage Project, which the Yoruba Studies Association (YSA) executed. The association has produced two volumes of the Yoruba metalanguage edited by A. Bamgboṣe (1984) and O. Awobuluyi (1988). One remarkable success of this project is that language and literature theses up to the doctoral level can now be written completely in Yoruba.

In the media, Yoruba is well established as a broadcasting language for both radio and television. It is used in government circles in the Yoruba-speaking states for political campaigns and public enlightenment. Furthermore, there is a thriving Yoruba movie industry, which is an offshoot of the traditional travelling theatre. These Yoruba movies use Yoruba language and drama to illustrate the Yoruba cultural cosmos (for example, *Ayé* 'Life!' by H. Ogunde), and are thus popular among Yorubas in Africa and Diaspora.

2 Phonology

The segmental phonemes of standard Yoruba are laid out in Table 51.1. The oral vowels form a straightforward seven-vowel system. Orthographically, [ɛ] and [ɔ] are represented as *ẹ* and *ọ* respectively, while the other vowels are represented as they appear in the table (that is, *i*, *e*, *a*, *o* and *u*). Although the nasalised vowels appear to represent a fairly symmetrical subset of the oral vowels, the symmetry would perhaps better be represented as deriving from a three-way contrast between high front, high back and low nasalised vowels. This is because the vowel [ɛ̃] has an extremely limited distribution (appearing in standard Yoruba in only a few lexical items, such as [ìyɛ̃] 'that'), and [ɔ̃] and [ã] are variants of a single phoneme. Orthographically, the nasalised vowels are represented as a vowel + *n* sequence when immediately following an oral consonant, and as a simple vowel when immediately following a nasal consonant: *sìn* [sĩ̀] 'accompany', *fún* [fṹ] 'give', *pọn* [kpɔ̃] 'draw (water)', *tán* [tɔ̃́] 'finish', [mɔ̃́] 'know'.

With respect to the consonant inventory, several comments are in order. Four basic places of articulation are distinguished for Yoruba stops, namely bilabial, alveolar, palatal and velar. While alveolar and velar places of articulation include both voiced and voiceless phonemes, the bilabial and palatal positions allow only voiced ones. In addition to the four places of articulation just referred to, Yoruba has two stops that are doubly articulated – with simultaneous labial and velar closures. These labial-velar stops are orthographically represented as *p* [kp] and *gb* [gb]; the simple letter *p* suffices for the voiceless labial-velar stop since there is no voiceless bilabial stop in the language.

There are four fricatives in Yoruba, all of which are voiceless. Orthographically, the labial, alveolar and glottal fricatives are represented as *f*, *s* and *h*; the palato-alveolar fricative is represented by the dotted *ṣ* consonants [ʃ].

The remaining consonants in Table 51.1 are the sonorants, *m*, *l*, *r*, *y* and *w*. Orthographically, these segments are written as just listed and therefore require no special comment. Phonologically, on the other hand, these segments exhibit certain interesting properties that will be discussed shortly. First, however, it is necessary to discuss two types of phonemes not included in Table 51.1. The first is the syllabic nasal. Such nasals are orthographically represented as *n* or *m* but their pronunciation depends on the nature of the following segment. If the following segment is a vowel (which occurs in a fairly limited set of circumstances) then the syllabic nasal is pronounced as a velar,

Table 51.1 Segmental Phonemes of Yoruba

Oral vowels	i		u				
	e		o				
	ɛ		ɔ				
		a					
Nasalised vowels	ĩ		ũ				
	ɛ̃		ɔ̃				

	Stop		*Fricative*	*Nasal*	*Lateral*	*Tap*	*Glide*
Bilabial		b		m			
Labio-dental			f				
Alveolar	t	d	s		l	r	
Palato-alveolar			ʃ				
Palatal		j					y
Velar	k	g					w
Labial-velar	kp	gb					
Glottal			h				

as in *ŋ ò lọ* 'I didn't go'. When the syllabic nasal is followed by a consonant, the nasal is homorganic to the following segment: *ḿbọ̀* [m̩bɔ̀] 'is coming', *ńfọ̀* [ɱfɔ̀] 'is washing', *ńsùn* [n̩sũ̀] 'is sleeping', *ńjó* [ɲjó] 'is dancing', *ńkà* [ŋkà] 'is reading'. Note that the syllabic nasal is generally only written as 'm' before 'b'. In medial position, there is potential confusion over whether an orthographic *vowel–'n'–consonant* sequence represents a phonetic *nasalised vowel–consonant* sequence or a *vowel–syllabic nasal–consonant* sequence. For example, the phonetic sequence [… ɔŋk …] and [… ɔ̃k …] would both be represented orthographically as '… ọnk …'. Where such cases arise, they can be disambiguated by tone-marking the syllabic nasal – which, of course, bears a tone by virtue of being syllabic. This brings us to the second phoneme type not represented in Table 51.1, namely tone.

Tone is of major importance in Yoruba. Three tones must be distinguished underlyingly: high, mid and low. High is orthographically represented by an acute ' '' accent, Low is represented by a grave accent ' '' and Mid is generally left unmarked (although if it is necessary to mark it – such as with a syllabic nasal – then a macron '¯' is used). The functional load of tone is considerable in Yoruba. For example, numerous sets of lexical items are distinguished solely by tone: *igbá* 'calabash', *igba* 'two hundred', *ìgbá* 'garden egg (aubergine, eggplant)', *igbà* 'time', *ìgbà* 'climbing-rope'; *ọbẹ̀* 'soup', *ọ̀bẹ* 'knife'; *ọkọ̀* 'vehicle', *ọkọ́* 'hoe', *ọko* 'husband', *ọ̀kọ̀* 'spear'. Tone may also serve a grammatical function. For instance, declarative sentences have a high tone between the subject and the verb: *Ayọ̀* (a name); *Ayọ̀ ọ́ ra ọkọ́* 'Ayọ bought (a) hoe.'

Tones are modified in a number of ways before reaching their actual phonetic manifestations. For example, although the contrastive tones are all level, phonetic contours occur in certain environments. A high tone immediately following a low tone is realised as a rising tone: *ìwé* [ìwě] 'book', *ọ̀ré* [ɔ̀rě] 'friend', *ìgbá* [ìgbǎ] 'garden egg'. A low tone immediately following a high tone is realised as a falling tone: *owó wà* [ōwó wâ] 'there is money', *ó dùn* [ó dû] 'it is tasty', *ó kéré jù* [ó kéré jû] 'it is too small'. Note that there is an asymmetry with respect to a tone's potential to create a contour tone between high and low tones on one hand and mid tones on the other. This asymmetry is also seen in other areas of Yoruba tonal phonology. For example, when a mid-toned vowel is deleted, both vowel and tone disappear. But when a high-toned vowel or a low-toned vowel is deleted, the high or low tone will generally continue to have an effect on adjacent tones (Bamgboṣe 1966: 9–10). For example, in connected speech, the i of *ìgbá* 'garden egg' is deleted in a phrase such as the following: *fẹ́ ìgbá* [fɛ́ ìgbǎ] *fẹ́ gbá* 'want a garden egg'. In the phrase that has not undergone vowel deletion, the final high of *ìgbá* is realised as a rising tone because of the immediately preceding low tone; in the phrase where vowel deletion has taken place, one also observes a rising tone in spite of the apparent deletion of the low-toned vowel. Deletion of a low-toned vowel before a mid-toned vowel can actually derive a level tone that is phonetically distinct from the three basic-level tones – namely, a lowered-mid tone (indicated by a vertical accent in the following example): *fẹ́ ìwo fẹ́ wọ̇* 'want a horn'. Orthographically, the deletion of a low-toned vowel is often indicated by including a dot where the low-toned vowel had been. A tonal rise, a lowered-mid tone, etc., can then be straightforwardly inferred. For example, the two cases just discussed could be represented: *fẹ.gbá* and *fẹ.wo*. In cases such as these where it is a high-toned vowel that undergoes deletion, one observes that a vowel adjacent to the deleted vowel acquires a high tone: *rí aṣọ → r áṣọ* 'see cloth'.

Tone is used in other contexts, for example, whistled Yoruba and the Yoruba talking drum. Whistled Yoruba is a language used to communicate over long distances on farms.

Typically, short phrases are whistled. The whistled language is composed of [h], the vowel [u] and the tones of the intended utterance. For example a non-whistled greeting such as *ẹ kú iṣẹ́ o* 'greetings at work' becomes *u hú uhú u* in whistled speech.

Tone is a key feature of *Dùndún*, the Yoruba talking drum, a pressure drum, which accompanies singing during festivals and important ceremonies. This drum 'speaks' by reproducing the tones of vowels. For example, a king is hailed with the tones of these words using drums: *èrù ọba ni mo bà, ọba tóo* 'it is the fear of the king that I have; all hail the king!' The tonal nature of the talking drum makes its language potentially ambiguous. Speakers actually thrive on generating multiple interpretations from a given drum language. For example, the signature tune of Radio Nigeria Ibadan, which has the following tonal sequence High High Low Low High High Mid High High Mid Low, is often assigned different interpretations – *rédíó nàìjíríá la tí ń fọhùn* 'we are broadcasting from Radio Nigeria'; *tólúbàdòn bá kú ta ní ó joyè* 'if the king of Ibadan dies, who will succeed him?'; *súlé gàgàgúgú onímú orù* 'Big Sule with humongous nose'; *nínú kòkò dúdú la ti ń sèbẹ̀* 'we cook soup in a black pot'.

Turning to matters of phonological organisation, consider first possible syllables in Yoruba. Essentially, a syllable may consist of a vowel nucleus with or without a consonant onset: V-syllable: *a* 'we', *iwé* 'book'; CV-syllable: *rí* 'see', *gbà* 'take'. Consonant clusters are not permitted (recall that orthographic 'gb' in an example like *gbà* represents not a sequence of phonemes but a single multiply-articulated phoneme). On the other hand, long vowels are attested. Compare, for example, *oògùn* 'medicine' vs *ògùn* '(name of a river)'; *aago* 'bell' vs *ago* 'cup'. In many cases, long vowels can be seen to derive from disyllabic sequences that have undergone consonant deletion (for example, *agogo* ~ *aago* 'bell') or to derive from morphological juxtaposition of vowels that does not result in vowel deletion (for example, in the reduplicated form *ọsọ̀ọsẹ̀* 'every week' derived from *ọsẹ̀* 'week').

The syllable plays a crucial role in regulating two common vowel processes, deletion and assimilation. These processes affect sequences of adjacent vowels in connected speech. Deletion applies when a monosyllabic verb or noun precedes nouns: *rí aṣọ* → *ráṣọ* 'see cloth', *ra epo* → *repo* 'buy oil'. On the other hand, if a disyllabic noun or verb precedes a noun, assimilation applies: *tọrọ aṣọ* → *tọra aṣọ* 'beg for cloth', *tọrọ epo* → *tọre repo* 'beg for oil'. This asymmetry is viewed as resulting from prosodic requirements (Orie and Pulleyblank 2002). A vowel is deleted when a preceding verb or noun is not a two-syllable foot but retained when a word has at least two syllables.

There are a number of restrictions on the occurrence of vowels in Yoruba. For example, in the standard language, vowel-initial nouns cannot begin with [u]; they cannot begin with a nasalised vowel or a high tone vowel. However, when these vowels are preceded by a consonant, the forbidden forms do occur in word-initial position: *dúdú* 'black', *tuntun* 'new', *wúrà* 'gold'. These restrictions are also seen as syllable-based. Although the features high-back, nasal and high tone are banned when a syllable without an onset occurs at the beginning of nouns, they freely occur in the same position if the syllable has an onset (Ọla 1995).

Apart from restrictions involving word-initial placement of vowels, certain vowels cannot co-occur. In three papers in volume 6 of the *Journal of African Languages*, O.Awobuluyi and A. Bamgboṣe show that two basic patterns of vowel harmony hold. On the one hand, the mid vowels *e* and *o* do not co-occur with the mid vowels *ẹ* and *ọ* (*esè* 'foot', *èfọ́* 'vegetable', *ọsẹ̀* 'week', *ọkọ* 'husband'; *ètè* 'lips', *epo* 'oil', *òwe* 'proverb', *owó* 'money'; but **oCọ, *oCẹ, *eCọ, *Cọo, *eCẹ*, etc.); on the other hand, front and back vowels do not co-occur in monomorphemic ... CVCV ... sequences (*ìrókò* '(kind of tree)', *àbúrò* 'younger sibling', *ìràwọ̀* 'star', *ahéré* 'hut', *òkìkí* 'fame', *àtíkè* 'make-up powder', etc.). In longer VCVCV words with medial high vowels, initial and final mid vowels do not always harmonise in the standard dialect: in examples such as *èbúté* 'harbour', *ewúro* 'bitter leaf', mid vowels flanking high vowels harmonise; on the other hand, disharmonic mid vowels flank high vowels in forms such as *orúkọ* 'name', *ewúrẹ́* 'goat' (Archangeli and Pulleyblank 1989). On the whole, these harmonic restrictions operate to define possible morpheme shapes in synchronic Yoruba.

3 Morphology

In this section, two morphological properties will be presented. The first is the minimal word phenomenon. The second is word formation strategies.

Consider first the minimal word. In many languages, free morphemes such as roots and stems are required to have a minimal phonological size (McCarthy and Prince 1986). In standard Yoruba, a root must minimally contain a CV syllable (for further discussion, see Ọla 1995). For instance, verbs are canonically monosyllabic as follows: *lọ* 'go', *wá* 'come', *fò* 'jump'; English loan verbs truncate to the initial CV, and the resulting form signifies action carried out secretly: *pá* 'pass', *fé* 'fail', *pọ́* 'pump'; consonant deletion is possible in a noun if and only if there is at least one CV remaining in it. Intervocalic *r*-deletion illustrates this constraint. In the example *oríkì* 'praise name/ poem', intervocalic *r*-deletion produces *óiki*, then progressive vowel assimilation applies, causing the output form to have a long vowel, *oókì*. However, if a word has two intervocalic [r]s they can be eliminated if there are other consonants in the word which will enable the word to obey the CV constraint. For example, *ìrágberí* 'city name' becomes *àágbeé*, but in *orórì* 'mausoleum', the only possible output is *oórì*; **oóì* which involves deletion of the two [r]s is unattested. Furthermore, deletion is blocked if there is only one [r] in a word: *orí* 'head' **oí*. Consonant deletion blockage can be viewed as resulting from the CV minimal requirement. If *r*-deletion were to apply, the resulting form would have a sequence of V syllables, violating the obligatory CV minimal requirement.

Consider next attested word formation processes. Yoruba word formation processes are for the most part derivational and not inflectional. Although certain pronominal forms do vary as a function of tense/aspect (to be discussed below), both nouns and verbs are essentially invariant – for example, nouns are neither declined for case nor inflected for number and verbs are not conjugated for person, number or gender. Yoruba has two morphological properties of high significance. Word formation in Yoruba involves three basic processes: affixation, compounding and reduplication. I will begin by looking at these processes and then go on to examine certain morphological properties of pronominal forms and ideophones.

There are several ways of deriving nominal forms from verbs (for some discussion, see Rowlands 1969: 182–93). These processes fall basically into two classes: an 'abstract' class and an 'agentive' class. Prefixes of the 'agentive' class include *a* and *ò-*. The prefix *a-* productively attaches to verb phrases – that is, a verb plus complements. Consider the following examples: *apẹja* 'fisherman' (*pa* 'kill', *ẹja* 'fish'), *akòwé* 'clerk' (*kọ* 'write', *ìwé* 'paper, book'), *akọrin* 'one who sings songs' (*kọ* 'sing', *orin* 'song'), *asẹ́gità* 'firewood seller' (*sẹ́* 'snap off ', *igi* 'wood', *tà* 'sell'), *abẹnilórí* 'executioner' (*bẹ* 'cut off', *ẹni* 'person', *ní* ('syntactic marker' – see discussion in Section 4), *orí* 'head'), *abáolóńjẹkú* 'glutton' (*bá* 'accompany', *olóńjẹ* 'eater', *kú* 'die'). In all the above examples, one observes a verb with one or two objects, in certain cases with an additional verbal complement. Although the above cases all illustrate derived nouns that denote a *person* who performs the relevant action, nouns derived with *a*- can also indicate the *object* that performs the action: *abẹ* 'razor, penknife', *bẹ* 'cut, slit', *ata* 'that which stings' (*ta* 'sting'), *asẹ* 'strainer', *sẹ* 'strain'.

The prefix *ò*- is comparable to *a*- except that it is less productive. Phonologically, *ò*-harmonises with the base to which it attaches producing the two variants *ò/ọ* (although this harmony does not appear to be fully productive); in addition, this prefix induces certain tonal changes in the verb. Consider the following examples: *ọmọ̀wé* 'educated person', *mọ̀* 'know', *ìwé* 'book', *ojíṣẹ́* 'messenger', (*jẹ́* 'answer', *iṣẹ́* 'message'), *ọmùtí* 'drunkard' (*mu* 'drink', *ọtí* 'spirits'). This prefix appears to be involved in the very large class of nouns derived from a verb phrase headed by the verb *ní* 'have, possess': *oníbàtà* 'shoe-maker' (*bàtà* 'shoes'), *onímọ́tò* 'car-owner' (*mọ́tò* 'car'), *oníbọtí* 'maltseller, owner of malt' (*bọtí* 'malt'). These derived nouns have the meanings 'owner of X' or 'person who deals with X' (such as a seller of X or a person who makes X); they can also mean 'thing that has X' (for example, *aṣọ ọlọ́nà* 'cloth which has decorations on it' (*aṣọ* 'cloth', *ọnà* 'decoration'), *ọbẹ̀ ẹléran* 'stew with meat in it' (*ọbẹ̀* 'stew', *ẹran* 'meat')). The last two examples illustrate the application of some completely regular phonological processes that affect these words. In Yoruba, [n] is an allophone of /l/: /n/ precedes nasal vowels while /l/ occurs before oral vowels. Therefore, when the noun following /lí/ ([ní]) begins with an oral vowel, the vowel of lí deletes: /o+lí-ẹrã/→ o+l+ẹ́rã. Since there is no longer a nasalised vowel to trigger nasalisation of /l/, /l/ surfaces in its oral form. In addition, these forms show evidence of a morphophonemic rule of vowel assimilation: the [o] of the agentive prefix completely assimilates to the following vowel when the nasality of *ní* is lost: o+l+ẹ́rã → ẹ+l+ẹ́rã. The following are some additional examples of these processes: o+ní+aṣọ → aláṣọ 'cloth-seller' (*aṣọ* 'cloth'), o+ní+epo → elépo 'oil-seller' (*epo* 'oil'). Note that if the object of *ní* begins with *i*, there is no loss of nasality and no assimilation: o+ní+igi → onígi 'wood-seller' (*igi* 'wood').

With respect to the prefixes that form abstract nouns from verb phrases, there are basically two: *ì*- and *à*-. Both prefixes may attach to a simple verbal base: *ìmọ̀* 'knowledge' (*mọ̀* 'know'), *àlọ* 'going' (*lọ* 'go'). In such cases, however, the *à*- derivative will tend to be used in wishes and prayers (Rowlands 1969: 185), while the *ì*- derivative has a more neutral usage. When the base involves serial verb sequences (see Section 4), the tendency is to use *à*-: *àṣejù* 'doing to excess' (*ṣe* 'do', *jù* 'exceed'), *àṣetán* 'doing to completion' (*ṣe* 'do', *tán* 'finish'), *àṣetì* 'attempting to do and failing' (*ṣe* 'do', *tì* 'fail'). Words derived with the prefix *à*- can also have a locative interpretation (for example, *àká* 'granary' (*ká* 'reap')) or a resultative interpretation (for example, *àfimọ́* 'appendix to a book' (*fimọ́* 'add thing to another thing')). Although the first example with the prefix *ì*- was with a simple verb stem, it is much more common to find *ì*- with a verb plus complements: *ìbínú* 'anger' (*bí* 'annoy', *inú* 'stomach'), *ìnáwó* 'expenditure of money' (*ná* 'spend', *owó* 'money'), *ìlọsíwájú* 'progress' (*lọ* 'go', *sí* 'to', *iwájú* 'front'). In many cases, *ì*- and *à*- can be freely substituted for each other (for example, *ìsọyé*, *àsọyé* 'explanation'). Finally, *ì*- (like *à*-) can have non-abstract interpretations in certain cases: *ìdì* 'bundle' (*dì* 'tie'), *ìránṣẹ* 'messenger, servant' (*rán* 'send', *iṣẹ́* 'message'). One morphological difference between *ì*- and *à*- lies in their ability to appear in combination with certain other affixes. This question will be returned to below.

The two prefixes *àti-* and *àì-* are used in 'infinitival' or 'gerundive' forms; *àti-* is used in affirmative forms while *àì-* is used in negative forms: *àtilọ* 'act of going, departure' (*lọ* 'go'), *àti pa á* 'to kill him' (*pa á* 'kill him'), *àti raṣọ yẹn* 'to buy that dress' (*rà* 'buy', *aṣọ* 'dress', *yẹn* 'that'), *àtisùn* 'sleeping' (*sùn* 'sleep'); *àìdára* 'not being good' (*dára* 'be good'), *àìlówótó* 'not having enough money' (*ní* 'have', *owó* 'money', *tó* 'be enough'), *àìnínkan púpọ̀* 'not having many things' (*ní* 'have', *ńkan* 'thing', *púpọ̀* 'many'), *àìmọ̀* 'ignorance' (*mọ̀* 'know').

Another type of affixation attested is infixation. For example, the infix *kí*, a well-known nominaliser, is inserted between two identical nouns: *[X]+kí+[X]*. The resulting nouns mean 'any kind of X' and often have a derogatory connotation. Examples are: *ilékílé* 'any house, bad house' (*ilé* 'house', *ki* 'infix' *ilé*), *ọmọkọ́mọ* 'any child, bad child' (*ọmọ* 'child', *kí* 'infix', *ọmọ* 'child').

Compounding is also used for forming words. Compounds are derived by deleting the initial vowel of two nouns in juxtaposition, for example, *ẹranko* 'animal' (*ẹran* 'meat', *oko* 'farm'), *ọmọjá* 'delinquent child' (*ọmọ* 'child', *ajá* 'dog'), *ewébẹ̀* 'vegetable' (*ewé* 'leaf', *ọbẹ̀* 'soup'), *ojúde* 'front yard' (*ojú* 'face', *òde* 'outside').

Among the more interesting word formation processes of Yoruba are a variety of types of reduplication – both partial reduplication and complete reduplication. In some cases, the process involves the addition of affixal material while in other cases reduplication is all that is involved. Complete reduplication can be used to express intensification: *púpọ̀* 'much', *púpọ̀púpọ̀* 'very much'; *díẹ̀* 'little', *díẹ̀díẹ̀* 'very little'. Complete reduplication can also be used with numerals to mean 'a group of X' (where X is a number) or 'all X'. Cardinal numerals in Yoruba have two forms, a morphologically simple form used for counting and a prefixed form used as a noun or adjective. To obtain the 'group' interpretation, the prefix (*mú*) is added prior to reduplication: *méjìméjì* 'two by two' (*èjì* 'two'), *mẹ́tàẹ́tà* 'three by three' (*ẹ́tà* 'three'), *mẹ́rìndínlógúnmẹ́rìndínlógún* 'sixteen by sixteen' (*ẹ́ẹ́rìndínlógún* 'sixteen'). To obtain the universally quantified form, reduplication takes place prior to prefixation of *mú*: *méjèèjì* 'both' (*mú+èjì+èjì*: *èjì* 'two').

It is also possible in Yoruba to derive agentive nominals by reduplicating a sequence of a verb and its object: *jagunjagun* 'warrior' (*jà* 'fight', *ogun* 'war'), *kólékólé* 'burglar' (*kó* 'steal', *ilé* 'house'), *bẹ́ríbẹ́rí* 'executioner' (*bẹ́* 'cut off', *orí* 'head'), *jẹdíjẹdí* 'haemorrhoids' (*jẹ* 'consume', *ìdí* 'bottom').

Apart from such examples of complete reduplication, Yoruba has a productive process of partial reduplication that is used to derive a nominal form from a verb. For this process, the initial consonant of a verb is copied and this copied consonant is followed by a high-toned [í]: *lílọ* 'going' (*lọ* 'go'), *rírí* 'seeing' (*rí* 'see').

Before leaving the topic of reduplication, it is appropriate to discuss at least briefly the phenomenon of ideophones. Ideophones are notoriously difficult to define – both in general and with respect to a single language. What is clear, however, is that there is a class of words in Yoruba which have rather distinctive and interesting properties. Reduplication is one of these properties – although as has already been seen above, reduplication is not restricted to ideophones. Consider the following examples: *kẹ́sẹ̀kẹ́sẹ̀* 'of surrounding being dead quiet', *rokírokí* 'of being red', *ròdòrodo* 'of being bright', *rùbùtùrubutu* 'of round object', *kọ̀rọ̀bọ̀tọ̀kọrọbọto* 'of being fat', *pọ̀tọ̀pọ́tọ̀* 'soft mud', *dòdoòdò* 'of coming up brightly', *ramúramù* 'of a loud noise (e.g. lion's)', *gbàlágbàlá* 'of wobbling movement (e.g. of a fish)', *jálajàlajàlàjala* 'of shabby appearance', *gógórogògòrogògòrògogoro* 'of several things being tall', *súúsùùsúú* 'of perching or assembling in an area'. The above ideophones involve two, three or four repetitions of a sequence. The tonal possibilities for ideophones correlate in many instances with semantic information – for example, the LHLH pattern of *gbàlágbàlá* seen above occurs in forms indicating lack of smoothness of activity. Changes in the tonal pattern of an ideophone can have marked semantic consequences. For example, in the following set of ideophones, a low tone correlates with largeness or heaviness, a high tone correlates with smallness or lightness and a mid tone indicates an average value: *rò2gòdò* 'of a big round object', *rogodo* 'of an average round object', *rógódó* 'of a small round object'. Moreover, the quality of the vowel in such words turns out to be semantically significant in such ideophones as well. While *o* indicates roundness, replacement of *o* by *u* serves to indicate weight (with the same degree distinction possibilities correlated with tone): *rùgùdù* 'large (heavier) object', *rugudu* 'medium (heavy) object', *rúgúdú* 'small (slightly heavy) object'. In some cases, there is no obvious source for an ideophone (or at least, no semantically related source). In other cases, an ideophone can be related both semantically and phonologically to a source morpheme. For example, *kéékèèkéé* 'in small bits' can be seen to derive from *kéré* 'small' with the application of reduplication, *r*-deletion and certain tonal changes. In this respect, it should be noted that rules applying to ideophones can typically be observed to apply elsewhere in the language – to non-ideophones. For example, *r*-deletion applies in the derivation of many ideophones but also applies in many other cases – such as, in deriving the variant *oókì* for *oríkì* (as mentioned above, vowel assimilation in this example is triggered by *r*-deletion).

Although it was noted at the beginning of this section that Yoruba word formation processes tend to be derivational, this section will conclude with a short discussion of certain inflectional processes observed in the pronominal system. Yoruba has two classes of pronouns (weak and strong pronouns – to be discussed further in Section 4). While one class of pronouns is invariant (just like regular nouns), the second class of pronouns varies as a function of grammatical relation and tense/aspect/polarity. For illustration, examples will be given of first and third person singular pronominal forms: subject (for appropriate tense/aspect/polarity): *mo bínú* 'I was angry' (*mo* 'I'), *ó mọ Èkó* 'he/she knows Lagos' (*ó* 'he/she'); subject (before the negative marker *kò*): *n kò mò* 'I don't know' [ŋ (k)ò m ̀ɔ̃] (*n* 'I') or *mi kò mò* [mi (k)ò m ̀ɔ̃] (*mi* 'I'), *kò mọ̀* 'he/she doesn't know' (∅ 'he/she'); subject (before the future marker *á*): *mà á lọ* 'I will go' (*mà* 'I'), *á á lọ* 'he/she will go' (*á* 'he/she'); object: *ó rí mi* 'he/she saw me' (*mi* 'me'), *mo rí i* 'I saw her/him/it' (*i* 'her/him/it'), *jẹ ẹ́* 'eat it' (*ẹ́* 'it') *fà á* 'pull it' (*á* 'it'). The last three examples illustrate the fact that the form of the third person singular pronoun object is dependent on the verb that it follows: whatever the quality of the vowel of the verb, the pronoun will have the same quality. Moreover, the tone of object pronouns depends on the tone of the verb: if the verb is mid or low, then the pronoun is high; if the verb is high, then the pronoun is mid. The above examples are not exhaustive – for example, additional forms are required in possessive noun phrases. But they are representative of the morphological changes in both segmental make-up and tone that characterise the various syntactically determined pronominal forms.

4 Syntax

In this section, three basic areas of Yoruba syntax will be discussed: word order properties, clitic pronominals and serial verbs. Consider first properties of word order. Given the paucity of inflectional morphology – in particular, the absence of morphological case marking – it is relatively unsurprising that Yoruba is highly configurational. In the following discussion, word order properties of major constituents will be described and illustrated.

With respect to basic word order, Yoruba is SVO (subject–verb–object):

bàbá   ra   bàtà
father   buy   shoes
'Father bought shoes.'

If a verb takes more than one object, then both objects follow the verb. The second object in such a case is preceded by a semantically empty preposition *ní*:

Adé fún   Tolú ní   owó
Ade give   Tolu prep.   money
'Ade gave Tolu money.'

In a comparable fashion, when a verb takes a verbal complement, such a complement follows the verb:

Táíwò   rò   pé   ó   sanra
Taiwo   think   that   he/she   fat
'Taiwo thought that he/she was fat.'

Adverbials generally follow the verb (as in the first example below), but there is a small class of adverbials that precede the verb (as in the second example):

kò   sanra   rárá
neg.   fat   at all
'He/she is not fat at all.'

ó   sèsè   lo
he/she   just   go
'He/she has just gone.'

Tense and aspect in Yoruba are expressed by particles that appear between the subject and the verb. For example, the following sentences illustrate the placement of the perfective aspect marker *ti* and the future tense marker *á*:

ó   ti   kú
he/she   perf.   die
'He/she is/was dead.'

òré   mi   a   lo
friend   my   fut.   go
'My friend will go.'

To form a yes–no question, a particle can be added at the beginning of the sentence (*sé*, *ǹjé*) or at the end of the sentence (*bí*):

șé	Òjó	lọ?
ǹjẹ́	Òjó	lọ?
Òjó	lọ	bí?

'Did Ojo go?' (lọ 'go')

Turning our attention to the noun phrase, it can be seen that the head of the phrase appears in initial position. Hence, adjectives occur postnominally:

ajá	funfun
dog	white

'white dog'

Possessive noun phrases appear after the noun possessed:

filà	Àkàndé
cap	Akande

'Akande's cap'

Determiners and demonstratives appear after the head noun:

ọmọ	náà
child	the

'that child' (definite determiner)

Similarly, a relative clause is placed post-nominally:

ẹni	tí	ó	wá
person	rel.	he/she	come

'the person who came'

As far as numerals are concerned, the appropriate word order depends on the individual case. For examples below one hundred and ninety, numerals that are *not* multiples of ten are placed after the noun:

ajá	méjì
dog	two

'two dogs'

Numerals that are multiples of ten are placed *before* the noun (starting from 'twenty'):

ogún	ajá
twenty	dog

'twenty dogs'

But in spite of the prenominal appearance of a numeral like 'twenty', derivatives of such a numeral appear post-nominally:

ajá	méjìlélógún
dog	twenty-two

'twenty-two dogs' (two over twenty)

876

As can be seen from the above examples, noun phrases and verb phrases are head-initial. Prepositional phrases are also head-initial (as is obvious from the terminology):

ní   ọjà
at   market
'at the market'

Hence in general, the head of a phrase in Yoruba comes at the beginning. While a short discussion such as this cannot even attempt to cover all important properties of word order in Yoruba, it would nevertheless be remiss to wind up without at least mentioning the extremely common 'focus' construction. This construction is derived by fronting a constituent which is marked by the morpheme *ni*. The fronted constituent can be an argument of the verb (for example, subject or object); it can be an adjunct (for example, a locative or temporal adjunct); the fronted constituent can even be the verb itself ('predicate cleft'):

èmi ni   Tolú rí
me foc.   Tolu see
'It's me that Tolu saw.' (object)

ní   ilé   ni   ó   ti   bèrè
at   house   foc.   it   perf.   start
'It was in the house that it started' (adjunct)

rírà   ni   bàbá ra bàtà
buying   foc.   father buy shoes
'Father BOUGHT shoes.'

As can be seen in the last example, when the emphasised element is the verb, a nominalised form of the verb appears in focus position and the verb itself continues to appear in its appropriate place inside the clause. In a similar way, if the subject is focused, a pronominal form must replace the fronted noun phrase in subject position:

èmi   ni   ó   lọ
me   foc.   3sg.   go
'It's I that went'

Note that in such constructions, the 'third person singular' pronoun can be used without actually implying any qualities of person or number; in such a sentence, the pronoun serves simply to mark the subject position that the fronted constituent came from. It is possible to focus the possessor of a noun phrase. In such a case (as with subjects), a pronominal form will replace the fronted noun phrase; and as with subjects, the 'third person singular' morphological form may be used with a semantically neutral interpretation in such cases:

bàbá   ni   ilé   rè   wó
father   foc.   house   his   collapse
'It was Father whose house collapsed.'

As a final point about the focus construction, content questions are formed by placing the appropriate question word in focus position. The properties of such sentences are comparable to those of the non-interrogative focus sentences seen above. Two examples are given below:

ta	ni	Tolú	rí	ọ̀rẹ́	rẹ̀
who	foc.	Tolu	see	friend	his/her

'Whose friend did Tolu see?'

ní	ibo	ni	ó	lọ
at	where	foc.	he/she	go

'Where has he/she gone?'

At several points in the above discussion, reference has been made to pronominal forms. For example, in the discussion of morphology, it was seen that pronominal forms vary as a function of their syntactic environment and it was noted above that pronominal forms fill in certain positions in focus constructions. As mentioned in the morphology section, however, there are two classes of pronouns in Yoruba – and both properties just mentioned hold of the 'weak' class. In fact, the 'weak' and 'strong' classes turn out to be distinguished on phonological, morphological and syntactic grounds. The strong pronouns behave simply like a true noun phrase. Phonologically, they fit the canonical pattern for Yoruba nouns; morphologically, they are invariant. Syntactically, their distribution parallels that of non-pronominal noun phrases. The weak pronouns, on the other hand, are systematically distinguished from non-pronominal noun phrases. Phonologically, weak pronouns are the only nominal forms that can be of a single syllable. They are also the only forms whose tonal specifications can vary depending on the context – as seen above with weak object pronouns. It has already been shown that the morphological form of weak pronouns varies, unlike regular nominals. Syntactically, the distribution of weak pronouns is quite restricted. For example, weak pronouns cannot be conjoined or modified (although strong pronouns and regular nouns can be). Weak pronouns occur only in a restricted set of syntactic positions; for example, they cannot appear in focus position and they cannot appear with interrogative particles such as *dà* 'where?' and *ńkọ́* 'what about?' (while both strong pronouns and non-pronominal noun phrases can). Such properties suggest that the strong pronouns are indeed pronominal *nouns* – and therefore show the distribution of nouns. Weak pronouns, on the other hand, can be analysed as clitics – with their morphological and phonological shape dependent on the constituent to which they are attached. By analysing them as clitics, their restricted syntactic distribution can be explained.

Apart from the properties just mentioned, there is a particularly interesting set of differences between the two pronominal sets. Consider the following sentences:

Dàda	rò	pé	ó	sanra
Dada	think	that	he	fat

'Dada thought that he (someone else) was fat.' (weak pronoun)

Dàda	rò	pé	òun	sanra
Dada	think	that	he	fat

'Dada thought that he himself was fat.' (strong pronoun)

In the sentence with the weak pronoun, the pronoun must refer to someone other than Dada; in the sentence with the strong pronoun, the pronoun must refer to Dada. This difference in interpretation involves reference to the syntactic configuration; it is not due simply to lexical properties of the strong and weak pronouns. Compare, for example, the following sentence including a strong pronoun with the sentence above that also had a strong pronoun:

Tolú	sọ	pé	òun	ni	ó	wá
Tolu	say	that	he/she	foc.	he/she	come

'Tolu said that it was he/she who came.'

In this sentence, the pronoun *òun* (a strong pronoun) may either refer to Tolu or to someone else. That is, the pronoun *òun* in the sentence with an embedded focus construction may or may not refer to the preceding subject. But the pronoun *òun* in the sentence with a simple (non-focus) embedded clause must refer to the preceding subject. Comparable syntactic considerations also determine whether a weak pronoun is interpreted as coreferential to a preceding subject. Compare the above example with a weak pronoun to the following sentence:

Dúpé	ń	ta	aṣọ	bí	ó	ṣe	ń	ta	ọsàn
Dupe	prog.	sell	cloth	as	she	do	prog.	sell	orange

'Dupe sells cloth the way she sells oranges.'

In this sentence, unlike the previous one, the weak pronoun not only can be interpreted as referring to the preceding subject, but it is normally interpreted in that way. The difference in interpretation is again due to syntactic differences: the weak pronoun in the earlier sentence is contained in a clausal complement to the verb in the main clause; the weak pronoun in the later sentence is contained in a manner adjunct. The correct interpretation of a pronoun in Yoruba therefore depends on two basic factors: (1) whether the pronoun belongs to the strong class or the weak class; and (2) the nature of the syntactic configuration within which the pronoun appears.

Serial verb constructions are the final topic to be discussed in this section. In Yoruba, as in many Kwa languages, one finds sentences in which strings of verb phrases appear consecutively without any intervening conjunction or subordinator. Such sentences are extremely common and exhibit a number of interesting properties. Consider the following examples:

ó	gbé	e	wá
he/she	carry	it	come

'He/she brought it.'

wọ́n	gbé	e	lọ
they	carry	it	go

'They took it away.'

In this type of example, the second verb indicates the direction in which the first action took place. In such a case, the subject of the second verb is also the subject of the first

879

verb. It is also possible, however, for the subject of the second verb to be the object of the first verb:

ó tì mí ṣubú
he/she push me fall
'He/she pushed me and I fell.'

In such a sentence, it is the object of *tì* 'push' who falls – and not the subject. Two transitive verbs can be combined in a serial verb construction. In some such examples, the serial verb sequence will have two object noun phrases:

ó pọn omi kún kete
he/she draw water fill pot
'He/she drew water and filled the pot.'

In many examples, however, a single object appears in between the two transitive verbs – and is interpreted as the object of both verbs:

ó ra ẹran jẹ
he/she buy meat eat
'He/she bought meat and ate it.'

ó ra màlúù tà
he/she buy cow sell
'He/she bought a cow in order to sell.'

In many examples syntactically comparable to the last two, the meaning of the pair of verbs ranges from being idiomatic but related to the individual verbs' meanings to being completely opaque:

ó gba òrò náà gbọ́
he/she accept matter the hear
'He/she believed the matter.' (gbà … gbọ́ 'believe')

ó ba kèké mi jẹ́
he/she   bicycle my
'He/she spoiled my bicycle.' (bà … jẹ́ 'spoil')

Many constructions that might be thought to involve categories other than verbs can be shown to involve serial verb sequences. For example, consider the word *fún* in the following sentence:

ó tà a fún mi
he/she sell it 'to' me
'He/she sold it to me.'

One might think that *fún* in such a sentence is a preposition. In fact, however, the properties of this word are verbal and not prepositional. For example, it can take object clitics such as *mi*; prepositions do not take pronominal clitics. The word *fún* can be nominalised by the process of partial reduplication: *fífún* (just like a verb). In addition, *fún* appears as a main verb meaning 'give':

ó	fún	mi	ní	owó
he/she	give	me	prep.	money

'He/she gave me some money.'

Recall that the *ní* that appears in such a sentence is a semantically empty preposition marking a second object to a verb.

The above discussion of serial verbs does not even vaguely attempt to be exhaustive. Serial verb constructions are used in many ways other than those described here – and in many cases the syntactic properties are somewhat different. Without a doubt, what are being called 'serial verb constructions' actually refer to several distinguishable syntactic types. What is probably of most interest is that various syntactic constructions use morphologically indistinguishable verbs and use them in syntactic phrases that themselves do not involve overt markers to distinguish construction types.

5 Politeness

Politeness is an essential aspect of Yoruba culture and language is used to convey respect, especially for older people and those in authority. Politeness can be expressed by the choice of pronouns in reference and address. For instance, the plural forms of the second and third person pronouns (*èyin* 'you pl.', *àwọn* 'they') are considered honorific and appropriate whereas singular forms are considered impolite (*ìwọ* 'you sg.', *òun* 'he/she').

The choice of names and nicknames is another way of expressing politeness. For example, it is impolite to refer to uncles and aunts by name; they are considered 'small or younger' fathers (*bàbá kékeré*) and mothers (*ìyá kékeré* or *màmá kékeré*). Consequently, a child typically has multiple fathers and mothers.

Women who have children show respect to their husbands by addressing them as Father of X (where X is the name of the first child). Furthermore, nicknames are used by women in addressing children who were born before they were married into the family (Oyelaran 1976). Although a woman may refer to a child after her marriage by name, she cannot address those born before by name because they deserve respect on account of existential precedence. Therefore, women invent a nickname for each senior child. Examples are *Ẹléyinjúẹgẹ́* 'delicate eyes', *Ayílukọ* 'plump girl/woman', *Péléyejú* 'facial marks befit face'.

Bibliography

Bamgboṣe (1966) is the standard reference grammar. The grammatical notes in Rowlands (1969) are very useful; the volume includes translation exercises. Two pedagogical grammars are Bamgboṣe (1967) and Awobuluyi (1978). For the development of Yoruba orthography, see Ajayi (1960). Hair (1967) is an interesting discussion of early work on Yoruba, including a bibliography up to 1890.

References

Ajayi, J.F.A. 1960. 'How Yoruba was Reduced to Writing', *Odu: A Journal of Yoruba, Edo and Related Studies* (Ministry of Education, Ibadan) pp. 49–58

Akinlabi, A. 1984. 'Tonal Underspecification and Yoruba Tones' (PhD dissertation, University of Ibadan)

Archangeli, D. and Pulleyblank, D. 1989. 'Yoruba Vowel Harmony', *Linguistic Inquiry*, vol. 20, pp. 173–217

Awobuluyi, O. 1978. *Essentials of Yoruba Grammar* (Oxford University Press (Nigeria), Ibadan)

Bamgboṣe, A. 1966. *A Grammar of Yoruba* (Cambridge University Press, Cambridge)

—— 1967. *A Short Yoruba Grammar* (Heinemann Educational Books (Nigeria), Ibadan)

Hair, P.E.H. 1967. *The Early Study of Nigerian Languages: Essays and Bibliographies* (Cambridge University Press, Cambridge)

McCarthy, J. and Prince, A. 1986. 'Prosodic Morphology' (unpublished manuscript, University of Massachusetts and Rutgers University)

Ọla, Ọ. 1995. *Optimality in Benue-Congo Prosodic Phonology and Morphology* (PhD dissertation, University of British Columbia; published by LINCOM EUROPA, Munich)

Orie, Ọ.Ọ. and Pulleyblank, D. 2002. 'Yoruba Vowel Elison: Minimality Effects', *Natural Language and Linguistic Theory*, vol. 20, pp. 101–56

Oyelaran, O. 1976. 'Oriki,' a paper presented at the Yoruba Studies Association Meeting, University of Ibadan, 30 January

Pulleyblank, D. 1986. *Tone in Lexical Phonology* (Dordrecht, Reidel)

Rowlands, E.C. 1969. *Teach Yourself Yoruba* (English Universities Press, London)

52

Swahili and the Bantu languages

Benji Wald

1 Historical and Social Background

The Bantu languages dominate the southern half of the African land mass and are spoken as first languages by an estimated 220 million speakers, nearly a third of Africa's total population. In their geographical extent, they come into contact with representatives of all the other major African language families: Cushitic (of Afroasiatic superstock) and Nilo-Saharan languages in the north-east, Khoisan in the south (and minimally in the north-east due to the retention of the Khoisan language Sandawe in north-eastern Tanzania, surrounded by Bantu languages) and its closest relatives among the Niger-Congo languages in the north-west.

The Bantu languages are thought to have originally spread from the West African transitional area of eastern Nigeria and Cameroon, which now marks the westernmost expansion of Bantu in Africa. From this area Bantu languages were carried eastward and southward in several waves of migration, responsible for the oldest dialect divisions among the languages, and starting no later than the early centuries of the first millennium AD. It was early recognised, for example, that a major dialect division is into West and East Bantu, symptomatised by the distinction between reflexes of the lexical item 'two': Proto-West *bàdé* and Proto-East *bèdé*. West Bantu shows more syntactic diversity than East Bantu, particularly in the north-west, where the morphological richness of the majority of Bantu languages begins to give way to the more isolating syntactic tendencies of the neighbouring Benue-Congo and Kwa languages of Nigeria, e.g. the passive verbal suffix *-o- is totally replaced by the impersonal construction, i.e. 'they saw me' replaces 'I was seen'.

The vast majority of the speakers of Bantu languages are directly involved in agricultural production. In this they contrast traditionally with the hunters and herders they came into contact with from other language families in much of their present areas, frequently effecting language shift on earlier populations, whether or not the latter maintained their modes of production. More recently, the agricultural majority also contrasts with the growing number of city dwellers involved in distribution and services, as the rapid urbanisation of Bantu Africa continues.

The distinctive typological nature of the Bantu languages and their close genetic relationship were recognised early by scholars. The label Bantu was established by Bleek

Map 52.1 The Bantu-speaking Area.

in 1862 as the reconstructed word for 'people'; the modern Proto-Bantu reconstruction is *ba-ntò*, plural of *mo-ntò* 'person'. Bantu speakers themselves tend to recognise the essential unity of their own and neighbouring Bantu languages with which they are familiar.

Consequent to the high degree of structural unity among most Bantu languages, together with the wide area of contact among them, a great deal of mutual influence among Bantu languages in contact renders detailed subclassification according to the tree theory of genetic relations problematic. Usually, broad areas reflecting isogloss bundles clearly circumscribe certain dialect groups despite internal diversity. Between such clear groups transitional areas are often apparent, giving the appearance of a dialect continuum.

Swahili is the most widely spoken of the Bantu languages, and is the only one to have international status, as one of the official languages of both Tanzania and Kenya and an important regional language in the urban centres of southern and eastern DR Congo.

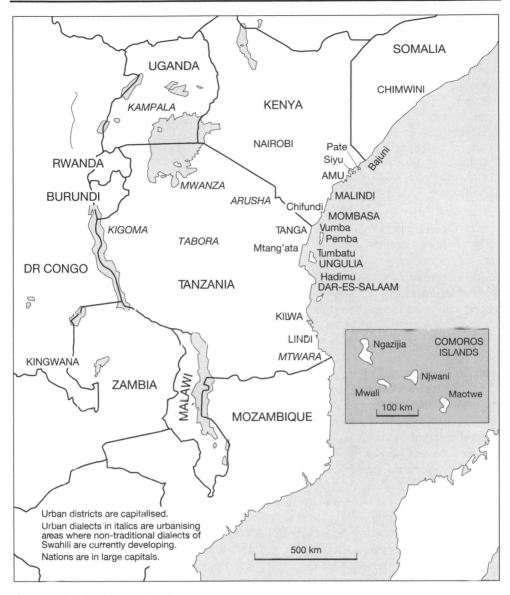

Map 52.2 The Swahili-speaking Area.

Swahili is a North-East coastal Bantu language, extending northward into southern Somalia, where ChiMwini and the northern Bajuni dialects are spoken, southward to northern Mozambique, where the southern coastal dialects are more widely understood than spoken, eastward to the major Indian Ocean islands of Pemba, Zanzibar, the Comoros and the northern tip of the Madagascar subcontinent, where the urban dialect of Zanzibar City has spread amid numerous distinctive and non-mutually intelligible rural dialects of earlier provenience, and, finally westward into Uganda, Rwanda, Burundi and eastern and southern DR Congo, primarily as an auxiliary language, except in the

Lubumbashi area of southern DR Congo, where an urban dialect of Swahili usually called KiNgwana has arisen since the late nineteenth century.

The distinctive social status of Swahili as an international language reflects the strategic location of the traditional Swahili dialect area on the coast of East Africa, whence it spread, through the role of urban Swahili communities as intermediaries in commerce between the interior peoples, mostly Bantu-speaking, and the South Asian communities from Arabia to China. Swahili is thought to have first arisen through contact between southern Arabian entrepreneurs and speakers of closely related coastal Bantu languages in the latter centuries of the first millennium. The origin of the label *Swahili* is the Arabic word *sawa:ḥil* 'coasts'.

Urban Swahili communities grew on the coast of southern Somalia, Kenya, Tanzania and the off-shore islands such as Zanzibar, as Indian Ocean commerce increased. Particularly in its southern forms, Swahili spread as a lingua franca among other Bantu speakers in the interior. During the European colonial period of the late nineteenth and early twentieth century, Swahili became even more widely used, as communications and transportation networks developed on an increased scale. British control over the major Swahili areas of Kenya and Tanzania in the twentieth century allowed the development of an international standard Swahili language, propagated through the educational system and mass media, based on the cultivated southern urban dialect of Zanzibar City, a variety close to the basic form of Swahili already used as a lingua franca in precolonial times.

By the mid-1980s the estimated number of speakers of Swahili was nearly 50 million, the majority residing in Tanzania and Kenya. Most speakers use Swahili as an auxiliary language and have a different first language, also Bantu. First-language speakers traditionally tracing their ancestors back to other Swahili speakers number about two million. However, with the rapid urbanisation of East Africa and the prominence of Swahili as a lingua franca among working-class East Africans, possibly another four million have come to adopt Swahili as either an only first language or simultaneously with their ethnic language, e.g. in Dar es Salaam, Mombasa, Nairobi, Lubumbashi and smaller urban centres.

Swahili, particularly the standard variety, is currently written in the Roman alphabet, using Latin vowel conventions and simplified English conventions for consonants. A modern Swahili literature has been developing since standardisation in the 1920s. Traditionally Swahili was written in a modified Arabic script, used to commit to paper verse meant to be recited. Manuscripts going back to the early eighteenth century reveal a written poetic tradition originating in the northern area and spreading southward. The literate poetic tradition is strong enough to occasion the reservation of space in standard Swahili newspapers for readers to submit poems.

Among speakers from traditional Swahili communities, Swahili is perceived as a cover term for a series of dialects among people who share a historic cultural as well as linguistic heritage. The dialects themselves are associated with local names reflecting local territoriality and ethnicity. There are three fairly distinct dialect groups:

(1) Northern: includes the sharply distinct urban dialect of ChiMwini in Brava, Somalia (not considered Swahili by its own community or other Swahili speakers); the Bajuni dialects of more southern Somalia and northern coastal Kenya; the urban island dialects of Lamu, Siyu, Pate and the transitional to Central dialect of urban Mombasa, Kenya.

(2) Central: most of these dialects are rural and spoken by relatively small communities on and off the coast of southern Kenya, northern Tanzania and the Comoros. Among these dialects are ChiFundi and Vumba of the Kenyan coast; Mtang'ata of the northern Tanzanian coast; Pemba, Tumbatu and Hadimu of the off-shore Tanzanian islands of Pemba and Zanzibar; Ngazija, Nzwani and Mwali of the Comoro Islands. These dialects are the most distinct and internally varied of the Swahili dialects.

(3) Southern: includes Zanzibar City and the urban districts of coastal Tanzania, e.g. Tanga, Dar es Salaam, Kilwa.

In some respects, the Northern and Southern dialects show more affinity to each other than they do to the Central dialects, particularly in their verbal systems, leading to the impression of a basic distinction between urban and rural dialects overlying the tripartite dialect division.

Among Bantu languages, all Swahili dialects are most striking in the adstratum of Arabic vocabulary in their lexicons while retaining the distinctive Bantu grammatical type, somewhat more extensive than the proportion of Anglo-French loanwords used in English in everyday conversation, e.g. the numerals 'six', 'seven, 'nine' and all higher multiples of 'ten' have replaced Bantu roots with Arabic loans. However, even more extreme than Swahili in its lexical borrowing is the northern Tanzanian language of Mbugu, retaining a Bantu grammar and inventory of grammatical morphemes, but almost totally non-Bantu in its lexicon (mostly of Cushitic origin). The lexical and grammatical effect of non-Bantu languages on Swahili will be discussed separately from its essential Bantu nature.

2 Phonology

The syllabic structure of the reconstructed Common Bantu word is relatively simple, consisting of CV(V) syllables only. However, the transparency of this structure is modified somewhat in various Bantu languages, where nonprominent syllables have been subject to altered glottalic and timing mechanisms which reduce their nuclei to short unvoiced vowels, or completely omit them in some cases. Apocope is most characteristic of certain North-West Bantu languages, where final consonants are found, e.g. in the Cameroonian language Fang.

Most recent reconstructions of the Common Bantu consonantal system display three manners and four points of articulation.

```
p     t     č     k
b     d     j     g
m     n     ny    ng'
(and        y in some reconstructions)
```

Typologically the system is unusual in the absence of a distinctive phoneme /s/, but /s/ is not necessary for reconstructive purposes. This and many other phonemic fricatives exist in most Bantu languages, at least in part due to assimilatory changes caused by adjacent vowels or, through a large part of the area, the shift of the non-nasal palatals to sibilants. Southern Swahili is unusual in its area in retaining the original palatals. The Northern dialects are distinctive in the shift of the original voiceless palatal to a dental

887

stop. Dentalisation of palatals and/or fricatives is characteristic of the Thagicu languages of interior Kenya and adjacent northern Tanzanian languages, e.g. Northern Pare, but not resulting in dental stops, cf. Thagicu [ðeka], Northern Pare [θeka], Northern Swahili [teka] and Southern Swahili [čeka] for Common Bantu *čèka 'laugh'. Alveolar affricates are the reflexes of the palatal stops among the Miji Kenda languages of the north-east coast of Kenya, relatively closely related to the adjacent forms of Swahili, e.g. [tseka] 'laugh', but in Swahili these reflexes of the palatals are only found in the isolated Comoros dialects, possibly a relic of this stage of development among the Northern dialects.

In view of their historical evolution in various Bantu languages, the prenasalised series of Common Bantu should probably be treated phonologically as an independent series rather than as a cluster of nasal + stop.

| mp | nt | nč | nk |
| mb | nd | nj | ng |

The voiceless prenasalised series shows considerable instability across many Bantu languages, e.g. with loss of nasalisation among some languages, voicing assimilation to a voiced prenasalised series in others and loss of the stop in still others, cf. *ba-ntò* 'people' > [wa-t'u] in Swahili, [a-ndū] in the Thagicu languages of interior Kenya, [wa-nu] in Luguru (among other Central coastal Tanzanian languages). The widespread areal feature of aspiration of the voiceless prenasalised consonants gave rise to a distinct opposition between an aspirated and unaspirated voiceless series upon the denasalisation of the prenasalised voiceless stops in Swahili, e.g. *kaa* 'charcoal' vs *k'aa* 'crab' < *n-kádá. This contrast is more typical of traditional Kenyan Swahili communities than of Southern Swahili, where the two series have merged fairly recently through the unconditioned aspiration of the original voiceless stop series.

The prenasalised voiced series is more stable and often shows behaviour parallel to or rotational with the original voiceless stops. Thus, the Common Bantu prenasalised palatal *nj* shifts parallel to *č* to dental in Northern Swahili, e.g. [ndaa], cf. Southern Swahili [njaa] 'hunger'. Most interesting among the Sotho group of Southern Bantu is the rotational shift of consonants, so that the Common Bantu prenasalised voiced series becomes a voiceless aspirated stop series concomitant with a shift of the Common Bantu voiceless stops to fricatives (the Common Bantu apical series is postalveolar, resulting in a flap-like liquid *r* or *l* in the lenition processes which have affected the voiced apicals), e.g. Sotho *xo-rutha* from Common Bantu *ko-túnda* 'teach', cf. Swahili *ku-fund-isha*, with a verbal suffix added.

There is a great deal of variety in the glottalic mechanisms by which the Common Bantu stop series is realised across the current Bantu languages. In Swahili, the set of voiced stops is 'implosive' (preglottalised), rather than truly voiced. This set of voiced stops is largely of secondary origin, sometimes due to back-formations based on prenasalised forms, where the stops are truly voiced and not preglottalised. Thus, *ki-ɓovu* 'rotten' (class 7 concord) is a back-formation from *m-bovu* 'rotten' (class 9 concord), cf. *mwovu* 'rotten' (class 1 concord) and *-oza* 'rot (v.)' with lenition and loss of initial *b*. Lenition of the voiced non-prenasalised series to corresponding fricatives or sonorants is common in most of the Bantu area, resulting in a series:

[β/w l/r z/ž ɣ/y/∅]

Swahili shares with a number of North-East Bantu languages a tendency towards further lenition of glides so that Common Bantu *d is lost, primarily in the vicinity of back vowels. However, Swahili is more conservative than many of its North-East relatives in having lost w and y only before high vowels of like fronting, though also variably before a in vernacular speech. The Northern dialects have gone slightly further in loss of y (< *g) before an unlike high vowel as well, e.g. Northern *hu-u* 'this one (anim.)' < *hu-yu*, still the Southern and standard form. Glide deletion is most advanced in the Thagicu language Kamba, e.g. -o- 'buy' < *-gòd-, -a- 'divide' < *-gàb-.

In some areas, e.g. in the north-east, lenition also commonly affects some or all of the members of the voiceless series, cf. Giriama *henza* for earlier North-East Bantu *pɛnja 'love (v.)', cf. Swahili *penda*; Giriama *moho* for Common Bantu *mo-yɔ́tɔ̀ 'fire', cf. Swahili *moto*. Lenition of *p is particularly widespread, while the velar *k is most resistant to lenition.

A widespread tendency towards word-level manner of articulation prosody is shown in some of the more striking consonantal changes affecting large areas in the north-east and extending towards the south-west, e.g. the following dissimilatory changes: Dahl's Law, originally noted in Nyamwezi of interior Tanzania, but of a much wider area, dissimilates the voicing of the first of two consecutive voiceless stops, e.g. -bita ⋍ -pita 'pass (v.)'; the Ganda Law, originally noted for LuGanda, dissimilates the first of two consecutive voiced prenasalised stops to the corresponding nasal, e.g. *ng'ombe* 'cow' (where *ng'* is the orthographic representation of [ŋ]) < ngòmbè. Finally, in much of West Bantu a morphophonemic process of nasal harmony is found, changing /d/ to /n/ in verbal suffixes following a root-final nasal, e.g. Luba (southern Zaire) -kwac-ile 'having caught' < *kóát-edɛ, but -dim-ine 'having sown' < *dèm-edɛ.

In contrast to the consonantal system, the vowel system of Common Bantu has remained relatively stable in the various languages. The reconstructed system is a symmetrical seven-vowel system with four degrees of height:

i   e   ɛ

       a

u   o   ɔ

Prosodically, one vowel per word could be distinctively long or short and each vowel of a stem could have a high or low tone. The tonal distinctions are preserved in most of the area, with reduction of the full domain of the original tonal distinctions in large areas of the north-east and south-west. Total loss of lexical tone is unusual and confined to a few languages in the north-east, including all dialects of Swahili. The loss of distinctive vowel length is characteristic of most of the western Bantu area and a large area of the east, including Swahili along with most of the coast. Reduction of the original seven-vowel system to five vowels is characteristic of most Bantu languages, with the exception of an extreme northern band extending from the west coast almost to the east coast and the Sotho group of South-East Bantu. For the most part this five-vowel system is derived from the mergers of the highest two tiers of vowels. Unusual is the merger of Common Bantu *u into *e in part of the southwestern area, e.g. Umbundu *o-mbela* < *mbúdà 'rain', cf. Swahili *mvua*.

In most of the five-vowel area, the merger of the highest two tiers of vowels did not occur before influencing the manner of articulation of the preceding consonant, generally through fricativisation of the preceding consonant before the highest original vowels *i* and *u*. In the largest area of this shift, reduction of point of articulation contrasts accompanied the fricativisation process. In Swahili, all fricatives became labial before *u*, e.g. *-chofu* 'tired' < *-čɔk-u*, cf. *-choka* 'tire', *fua* 'forge (v.)' < *túda*, *-ongofu* 'deceitful' < *-ɔngɔp-u*, cf. *-ongopa* 'lie (v.)'. However, the situation is much more complicated before *i*. Generally, the point of articulation of the resulting fricative is preserved, producing regular morphophonemic alternations such as the following:

-pi*k*a 'cook (v.)'	-pi*sh*-i 'cook (anim. n.)'
-fua*t*a 'follow (v.)'	-fua*s*-i 'follower'
-li*p*a 'pay'	-li*f*-i 'payer'

In the most northern dialects of Amu and Bajuni, the merger of the labials into the apicals is general, e.g. majority Swahili *fimbo* > *simbo* 'walking stick' and *vita* > *zita* 'war, battles'. A few lexical items, e.g. *mwizi* 'thief' where *mwivi* is expected (and attested, but not common), have become usual in Southern Swahili. The same merger is also characteristic of the Comoros dialects, e.g. Ngazija *-zimba* 'swell', cf. Southern Swahili *-vimba*. Otherwise, this merger is general to all urban Swahili dialects only within lexical items where *i* is immediately followed by another vowel, reflecting a Common Bantu double vowel, e.g. *zaa* 'bear children' < *bíáda* or *soma* 'read' < *píɔma*. Many rural dialects show resistance to merger even under these conditions, as is typical of the North-East coastal Bantu languages outside of Swahili and Giriama, e.g. Vumba *vyaa*, *fyoma*.

Bantu vowel harmony consists of lowering *e* and *o* to *ɛ* and *ɔ* following a syllable whose nucleus is already at that degree of height. In all the Bantu languages, this is reflected in the use of this type of vowel harmony in the vowel of many verbal extensions, a morphophonemic process, e.g. Swahili *pit-i-a* 'pass by', *pand-i-a* 'climb onto', *shuk-i-a* 'come down to', but *tok-e-a* 'come from' and *end-e-a* 'go towards', where the prepositional extension *-i/e-* < *-e/ɛd-* in Common Bantu is determined by the vowel of the preceding syllable. Bantu polysyllabic roots and stems also tend to adhere to this vowel harmony, so that *Cɛ/ɔCe/ɔ* is much more common than *Cɛ/ɔCe/o*.

Generally, the variety of tonal changes that have affected various Bantu languages can be traced back to a two-tone system, e.g. *-bàd-* 'count': *-bád-* 'shine' (Swahili *-waa*). The total loss of lexical tone distinctions is confined to a few languages of the north-east. Geographically intermediate are languages like LuGanda which appear to be pitch-stress languages with only one distinctive tone per word. Even among fully tonal languages, especially in the southern Bantu area, there is a tendency for one syllable per word, usually the penultimate, to have special prominence through lengthening. Swahili conforms to the penultimate stress pattern, with regular high pitch and lengthening of the penultimate vowel. Exceptions to this pattern are secondary through borrowing or clipping of reduplicated forms, e.g. *kátika* 'in' < *kàté-kàté*, reduplication of *kàté* > Swahili *káti* 'among'. While traditional Swahili communities maintain the antepenultimate stress of the clipping, second-language speakers tend to regularise stress to penultimate.

3 Morphology

Bantu languages have long been appreciated by scholars for their distinctive morphology, highly agglutinative and allowing great structural complexity to nominal and even more so to verbal forms.

Basic to Bantu nominal morphology is the division of nouns into numerous noun classes, the precise number of which varies from language to language due to syncretism and secondary developments. Traditionally, each reconstructed noun class has been assigned a number. The reconstructed Common Bantu noun classes number nineteen. Each is associated with a different class prefix preceding the noun stem. It is thought that the Bantu noun classes arose in pre-Bantu times from a system of classifiers, probably from nouns even earlier, adding content to the nouns they introduced. The semantic content of many of the classifiers is transparent because of their role in nominal derivation. Some of the noun classes specialise in marking collective or plural nouns and many of the pairings of classes into singular and plural found in the current Bantu languages are traceable to Common Bantu. The list given here presents the reconstructed Bantu noun classes with a rough indication of their semantics. Their semantics is most evident when they are used derivationally. Lexically, there is greater unpredictability for whether a noun of a particular meaning belongs to a certain class, both within and across the various languages.

Class (singular)		*Class (plural)*	
1	* mo- 'human singular'	2	* ba- 'human plural'
3	* mo- 'thin or extended objects, trees, singular'	4	* me- 'plural of class 3'
5	* di/e- 'singular of objects that tend to come in pairs or larger groups, fruits'	6	* ma- 'collective or plural of class 5'
7	* ke- 'instrument, manner'	8	* bi- 'plural of class 7'
9	* ne- 'miscellaneous, animals'	10	* di-ne- 'plural of class 9'
11	* do- 'extended body parts'		'Use class 6/10 plural'
12	* ka- 'diminutive'	13	* to- 'plural of class 12'
14	* bo- 'abstract nouns, qualities'		
15	* ko- 'body parts'		'Use class 6 plural'
16	* pa- 'place where'		
17	* ko- 'place around which, infinitive'		
18	* mo- 'place in which'		
19	* pi- 'diminutive'		'Use class 6/8/10/13 plural'

Exemplifying from Swahili when possible: (1) *m-tu* 'person', pl. (2) *wa-tu*; (3) *m-ti* 'tree', pl. (4) *mi-ti*; (5) *ji-cho* 'eye', pl. (6) *ma-cho* (Swahili also uses this class pair for augmentatives, e.g. (5) *ji-tu* 'giant', pl. (6–5) *ma-ji-tu*); (7) *ki-tu* 'thing', pl. (8) *vi-tu* (Swahili also uses this class for diminutives, e.g. (7–5) *ki-ji-ji* 'village', pl. (8–5) *vi-ji-ji*, cf. (3) *m-ji* 'town', pl. (4) *mi-ji*); (9) *ng'ombe* 'cow', pl. (10) *ng'ombe* (**di-* is not prefixed to plural nouns in most North-East Bantu languages, cf. Zulu (9) *i-n(-)komo* 'cow', pl. (10) *i-zi-n(-)komo*); (11) *u-limi* 'tongue', pl. (10) *n-dimi*; (12) Gikuyu *ka-ana* 'small child', pl. (13) *tw-ana* (the urban Swahili dialects have lost this pair and switched their functions to (7)/(8), as shown above; *ka-* remains lexicalised in *ka-mwe* 'never' < '(not even a) little one'); (14) *u-baya* 'evil' < *-baya* 'bad'; (15) Gikuyu *kũ-gũrũ* 'leg', pl. (6) *ma-gũrũ* (Swahili has shifted this class of nouns to (3) *m-guu*, Southern pl. (4) *mi-guu*, Northern pl. (6) *ma-guu*); the locative classes (16) to (18) can be directly prefixed to nouns in most Bantu languages, cf. coastal southern Tanzanian Mwera (16) *pa-ndu* 'at a place', (17) *ku-ndu* 'around a place', (18) *mu-ndu* 'inside a place', but Swahili uses an associative construction, (16) *p-a nyumba-ni* 'at-of house-loc.', i.e. 'at home', *kw-a nyumba-ni* 'around-of house-loc.' i.e. 'at/around home', *mw-a nyumba-ni* 'in-of home', i.e. 'inside the house'; (19) Kongo (north-west DR Congo) *fi-koko-koko* 'little hand', pl. (8) *vi-koko-koko* (this class is largely restricted to West Bantu and does not occur in Swahili).

Regardless of various rearrangements of the noun classes, class concord is a pervasive feature of many grammatical categories in all Bantu languages. All categories modifying a noun have concordial prefixes determined by the noun. In addition, coreferential markers in the verb phrase, such as the subject, object and relative markers, also show class concord. The form taken by the class prefix is determined by the category to which it is prefixed. A secondary set of class prefixes is general for the nasal prefixes, formed by replacing the nasal with *g (> *y* in Swahili). Which categories take the primary vs the secondary prefixes varies across the Bantu area. Swahili restricts the nasal class prefixes to adjectives and numerals, except for the retention of nasal class 1 for the object marker, i.e. *m(u)-* rather than *yu-*. The following examples are illustrative of the syntactic extent of class concord in Bantu languages (cp = class prefix, cc = concord):

yu-le	*m*-tu	*m*-moja	*m*-refu	*a*-li-	*y*-e-	*ki*-soma	*ki*-le	*ki*-tabu	*ki*-refu
cc-	cp-	cc-	cc-	cc-	cc-	cc-	cc-	cp-	cc-
that	person	one	tall	he past	rel.	it read	that	book	long

'That one tall (1) person who read that long (7) book.'

wa-le	*wa*-tu	*wa*-wili	*wa*-refu	*wa*-li	*(w)-o-*	*vi*-soma	*vi*-le	*vi*-tabu	*vi*-refu
cc-	cp-	cc-	cc-	cc-	(cc-)	cc-	cc-	cp-	cc-

'Those two tall (2) people who read those long (8) books.'

An interesting further development of concord has occurred among Swahili and some adjacent North-East coastal Bantu languages: animate concord. This device extends class 1/2 concord to animates, regardless of their lexical noun class. For example, most animals are class 9/10 nouns, e.g. *simba* 'lion', *njovu* 'elephant', *ndege* 'bird'. One result of animate concord is the distinction between *ndege yu-le* 'that bird' with a class 1 animate concord marking the demonstrative and *ndege i-le* 'that aeroplane' with a strictly syntactic class 9 concord on the demonstrative. It must be noted that animate concord is atypical of Bantu languages on the whole. Even in Swahili, when the class of the noun is determined by a semantic rather than a lexical process, class concord overrides animate concord. Thus, *ki-jana yu-le* 'that youth (e.g. teenager)' shows animate concord on the demonstrative, illustrating the perceived lexical arbitrariness of the class 7 prefix on the noun, but *ki-jana ki-le* 'that little-old youth' with class 7, where the class prefix to the noun functions as a diminutive. As a local innovation in North-East coastal Bantu, animate concord serves to illustrate that even though the original semantic motivation for noun class is often obscure for individual lexical items, the syntactic resources of class concord continue to be exploited for semantic purposes.

In addition to the class prefix, it is probable that Common Bantu had a preprefix marking definite and generic nouns and their modifiers. This preprefix survives in various forms and functions in the interior and south-west, usually anticipating at least the vowel of the class prefix, e.g. Zulu *u-mu-ntu* 'the person', *a-ba-ntu* 'the people'. The preprefix has been lost in much of the eastern coastal area. A relic remains in the Northern Bajuni dialects of Swahili in *i-ṯ'i* 'land(s)' < *e-n(e)-čé*, Southern Swahili *nchi*. In most dialects of Swahili, the preprefix was lost earlier than voiceless nasals. With the loss of the preprefix penultimate stress was transferred to the nasal, which prevented the loss of the nasal despite its voicelessness. The opposite chronological sequence is evident for Bajuni. When removed from stress, the voiceless nasal and preprefix are lost in all dialects, cf. Bajuni *ṯ'i-ni*, Southern Swahili *chi-ni* 'below' (i.e. 'on the ground').

The personal pronouns have a variety of specific forms in Bantu, according to the grammatical category to which they are attached. The chart shows the Swahili pattern, indicative of the formal variation, though not the precise shapes, of the personal pronouns in Bantu.

	Independent	Possessive	Subject marker	Object marker
'I'	mimi	-ngu	ni-	ni-
'you'	wewe	-ko	u-	ku-
's/he'	yeye	-ke	a-/yu-	m-
'we'	sisi	-itu	tu-	tu-
'you (pl.)'	ninyi	-inu	m(w)-	wa-
'they'	wao	-(w)o	wa-	wa-

The *k*-forms of the second and third singular are usual in Bantu and also appear as the subject markers *ku-* and *ka-* respectively in a few languages (including the central dialects of Swahili). Some Bantu languages have independent pronouns for the other classes, but Swahili uses demonstratives instead, e.g. for class 7 *hi-ki* 'this thing', *hi-ch-o* (< *hi-ky-o*) 'that thing (proximate)', *ki-le* 'that thing (distal)'.

Nominal derivational processes have already been alluded to above in the discussion of noun classes and class concord. In some Bantu languages these provide sufficient resources to nominalise verb–object predicates, e.g. Swahili *m-fanya-kazi* 'worker' with class 1 animate prefix, < *-fanya kazi* 'do work'. However, all Bantu languages also show extensive use of nominal suffixes, converting verbs to nouns, e.g. *-ɔ: Swahili *nen-o* 'word' < *-nen-a* 'say', *-i: Swahili *u-zaz-i* 'parenthood' < *-zaa* 'bear children' via *bo-biád-ı, *-u: Swahili *-bov-u* 'rotten' < *-oza* 'rot' via *-bɔd-u. Note that the suffix *-u* derives stative qualities from process verbs and forms the basis for derived adjectives as well as nouns. Morphologically nouns and adjectives are not distinct in the Bantu languages. Among the noun derivational suffixes is the locative *-ni*, corresponding in function to the locative prefixes. Suffixed to a noun, *-ni* marks the noun as head of a locative phrase, e.g. Swahili *kazi-ni* 'at work', *mto-ni* 'at the river'. Historically, these derivational suffixes are indicative of a syntactic system quite different from the current Bantu systems and well advanced in the process of morphologising by Common Bantu times. This will be further discussed on pages 899–901.

Bantu verb morphology shows the fullest extent of Bantu agglutinative word structure. Central to the verb is the root, which may be extended to a more complex stem by the addition of derivational suffixes. Final modal suffixes *-a and *-ɛ distinguish the indicative and subjunctive respectively. In the indicative mode this is sufficient complexity for the imperative, e.g. Swahili *fany-a* 'do (it)'. Obligatory elsewhere is a subject marker, referring to and concording with the subject of the clause. Since lexical subjects which are inferrable in the context of discourse need not be expressed, the subject marker is often the only reference to the understood subject in a clause and thus functions as a pronoun. The independent pronouns are not obligatory in the clause. The subject marker is sufficient to form a subjunctive clause in most Bantu languages, e.g. Swahili *a-fany-e* 'he should do (it)'. In the indicative mode, at least one more element is necessary for non-imperatives: the tense/aspect marker. The tense/aspect marker may immediately follow the subject marker, preceding the verb, in which case it is called a tense prefix, or it may be suffixed to the verb stem and its extensions, depending on the particular tense/aspect marker and the language, in which case it is called a tense suffix, e.g. Gikuyu *a-gwat-ire* 'he held (today)' suffixes *-ire* 'an action which has taken place on the day of speaking' to the verb *-gwata* 'catch/hold', but *a á-gwata* 'he just held' prefixes *-á-* 'an action taking place immediately before the time of speaking'. Most Bantu languages show a richer paradigm of tense prefixes than of tense suffixes, but all show traces of the Common Bantu tense suffix system. Thus, most Swahili dialects and the standard language retain a tense suffix only for the 'present negative' *h-a-fany-i* (neg.-he-do-pres.) 's/he doesn't do/isn't doing (it)'. The Bantu 'tense' suffix *-(n)ga*, marking 'habituality', is found among interior North-East Bantu languages, e.g. Gikuyu *a-ra-gwata-ga* 's/he kept holding' combining the tense prefix *-ra-* 'action took place no earlier than the day before the day of speaking' with the tense suffix *-ga* 'habitual'. It survives in Swahili only as a common suffix for verb nominalisation, e.g. *m-sema-ji* 'speaker' < *sema* 'speak' via *mo-sema-ga-i* (note that the root *sema* is largely restricted to Swahili and is probably not of Bantu origin).

While all of the tense suffixes are traceable to Common Bantu, some tense prefixes are traceable to other grammatical categories. For example, the urban Swahili perfect *-me-*, as in *a-me-fanya* 's/he has done it', is traceable to Bantu *-màda* 'finish' (surviving also in Swahili *mal-iza* 'bring to an end, complete') via *-màd-idɛ* > *-mez-ie* (surviving in Bajuni) with the perfect suffix *-idɛ*. Nevertheless, many of the tense/aspect prefixes are traceable to Common Bantu, showing that at that stage Bantu had already set a precedent for further development of the tense prefix system in the individual languages.

Bantu languages vary in how negation interacts morphologically with particular tenses. In the subjunctive mode the negative marker immediately follows the subject marker, e.g. Swahili *a-si-fany-e* 's/he shouldn't do (it)', where *-si-* < *-ti-* is the negative marker. In the indicative mode, both suffixation and prefixation of the negative to the subject marker are commonly found, e.g. Swahili *h-a-ta-fanya* 's/he won't do (it)' with the negative marker *h(a)-* prefixed to the complex *a-ta-fanya* 's/he will do (it)'. This absolute first position in the verb complex for the negative marker is obligatory with most tenses. With a very few tenses there is dialect division between prefixing and suffixing of a negative, e.g. with the hypothetical marker *-nge-*, Southern *h-a-nge-fanya* and Northern *a-si-nge-fanya* 's/he should/wouldn't do (it)', cf. *a-nge-fanya* 's/he would do (it)'. In a few areas, the negative is an independent particle following the entire verbal word, e.g. among the Chagga dialects (northern Tanzania) *a-le-ca fo* 's/he didn't come' beside *a-le-ca* 'he came', where *-le-* is the tense prefix for 'action took place yesterday or earlier'.

As some of the glosses above suggest, the tense/aspect systems of many Bantu languages are quite extensive, marking a variety of tenses, aspects and moods. The fine distinction between degrees of pastness is particularly striking as unusual among world languages, e.g. Gikuyu *a-gwat-ire* 's/he held' (current (today) past), *a-ra-gwat-ire* 's/he held' (recent (yesterday) past), *a-à-gwat-ire* 's/he held' (remoter past). Among Bantu languages with such distinctions, some show tense concord between the initial tense and consecutive tense markers, e.g. Giriama *a-dza-fika a-ka-injira* 's/he arrived and entered (today)' vs *w-a-fika a-ki-injira* 's/he arrived … (yesterday or earlier)'. The consecutive marker, common in east coast Bantu and extending into the interior, functions as a perfective, necessarily giving a consecutive interpretation to verbs so marked with respect to the preceding verb.

A great many Bantu languages allow concatenation of particular tense/aspect markers, e. g. Gikuyu *ĩ-ngĩ-ka-na-endia* 'if I should ever sell (it)' where *-ngĩ-* is 'hypothetical', *-ka-* is 'future' and *-na-* is 'indeterminate time'. Along the east coast this degree of morphological complexity is largely reduced to a single tense prefix per verb. Thus, in Swahili 'compound tenses' allow two tenses to mark a clause through the device of an auxiliary verb *-ku-wa* 'be(come)' supporting the first tense, e.g. *a-li-ku-wa a-ki-fanya* 's/he used to do it' where *-li-* is the 'past' marker and *-ki-* is 'habitual/progressive'. The construction *a-li-ki-fanya* survives in Northern Swahili with the same meaning.

Both the reduction of some of the paradigmatic complexity and the introduction of new tense-aspect markers in specific contexts have led to extensive asymmetry between affirmative and negative tense/aspect markers among the east coast languages. Swahili provides many examples. Many scholars caution against direct comparison of the semantics of the affirmative and negative tenses. Thus, the chart given here is approximative, in order to indicate differences in the affirmative and negative tenses.

Affirmative		*Negative*
-na/a-	'progressive/general'	-∅-...-i
-me-	'perfect'	-ja-'not yet'
-li-	'past/anterior'	-ku-
-ta-	'future'	-ta/to-
-nge/ngali-	'hypothetical'	-nge/ngali-
-ki-	'participial, progressive'	-si-po-'unless'
-ka-	'perfective/consecutive'	(use neg. subjunctive) 'without then V-ing'

This standard Swahili paradigm is general to most urban Swahili dialects. The rural dialects show various differences, e.g. *-na-* is 'today past/perfect' in the rural coastal dialects, *-∅-...-ie-* < **-idɛ* serves a similar function in the Bajuni dialects and ChiMwini (*-ire*), Comoros dialects use *nga-...-o* rather than a tense prefix for the 'progressive/general', e.g. *ng-u-som-o* 's/he's reading', cf. standard *a-na-soma*. In addition to the above markers standard Swahili uses *hu-*, usually considered a tense/aspect marker but not admitting a subject marker (< *ni+ku-* = copula + infinitive marker), to mark 'occasional recurrent action' (i.e. 'sometimes'). In the Northern dialects, *hu-* is generally used as the 'progressive/habitual', and *-na-* only occurs in speech to speakers of other varieties of Swahili.

An optional element of the Bantu verb is the object marker, placed immediately before the verb stem. Common to all Bantu languages is the use of an object marker anaphorically to refer to an understood second argument of the clause, not expressed in the clause itself, e.g. Swahili *a-me-vi-ona* 's/he has seen them', where *-vi-* refers to some class 8 object such as *vi-su* 'knives' (pl. of *ki-su*). The invariant reflexive object marker, *-ji-* < **gi* (many Bantu languages use a reflex of **ke-*) marks subject–object coreference, e.g. *a-me-ji-kata* 'he cut himself', *tu-me-ji-kata* 'we cut ourselves', etc.

Many Bantu languages allow multiple object markers, e.g. Umbundu *w-a-u-n-dekisa* 's/he showed him/her to me', where *-u-* is the class 1 object marker 'him/her' and *-n-* is the first person singular object marker 'me'. On the east coast and spreading inland towards the south is the restriction of the object marker to one per verb. In some languages, either of two object arguments may be represented by the object marker, the other being expressed anaphorically by an independent pronoun or demonstrative. Most investigated languages indicate that there are further restrictions on which object may be so represented. Swahili is highly developed in this respect. Animates are selected over inanimates and there is a hierarchy of roles from agent down to direct object. These roles are determined either lexically or by verbal extensions. The verbal extensions will be discussed immediately below. First, however, it is worth mentioning that Swahili is unique in gravitating towards the object marker as an obligatory verbal category, though only for reference to human objects. The use of the object marker with expressed indefinite human objects in the same clause is generally tolerated in Bantu only by those North-East coastal languages which have been in contact with Swahili for several generations (e.g. the Kenyan coastal languages Pokomo and Miji Kenda), but is obligatory in urban dialects of Swahili and the standard language, e.g. *a-li-mw-ona mtu* 's/he saw somebody', where *-m(w)-* class 1 refers to *mtu* 'person' and the referent is not yet known to the addressee. Elsewhere in Bantu the object marker must have an anaphoric reference.

The verbal extensions are verbal suffixes which define the role of one argument of the verb. They are directly suffixed to the verb root or to each other when grammatically possible. All the verbal suffixes are inherited from Common Bantu. The system has undergone little semantic change and a moderate amount of formal change in the current languages. Swahili will serve to illustrate the basic system common to all Bantu languages.

In Swahili the regular causative is *-i/esha* (the vowel determined by the vowel harmony rule discussed on page 890), e.g. *pik-isha* 'cause to cook', *chek-esha* 'make laugh'. Its origin appears to be a sequence of stative + causative. The *-ya* causative survives in a few transparent lexical items, e.g. *on-ya* 'warn', cf. *ona* 'see', *on-esha* 'show'. The causative focuses on the agent of the root verb if a specific agent referent is understood. If not, it may focus on the object of the root verb, e.g. *a-li-zi-jeng-esha* 's/he had them built', where 'them' refers to a class 10 noun such as *nyumba* 'houses'.

Causative	-ya, i/esha	< *-ia, *-e/ɛk-ia, respectively
Stative	-(i/e)ka	< *-(e/ɛ)ka
Prepositional	-i/ea	< *-e/ɛda
Reversive	-u/oa	< *-o/ɔda
Reciprocal	-ana	< *-a-na
Passive	-(i/e)wa	< *-(e/ɛd-)oa

The stative suffix focuses on the state or potential of the subject. With the perfect *-me-* it focuses on state, e.g. *i-me-vunj-ika* 'it is broken' < *vunja* 'break', *i-me-poto-ka* 'it is twisted' < *potoa* 'twist'. With the general 'present' *-na-*, *-a-* or *hu-* it may focus on a potential, e.g. *i-na-vunj-ika* 'it is breakable' (i.e. 'it can get broken'). With some verbs the stative form is *-i/ekana* as if from stative + reciprocal, e.g. *i-na-pat-ikana* 'it is obtainable' < *pata* 'get'. Sometimes the stative interpretation remains with this tense, e.g. *i-na-jul-ikana* 'it is known' < *jua* 'know'. A number of stative verbs show lexicalisation of the stative marker, e.g. *amka* 'awaken (intr.)', *choka* 'be tired', where no simpler forms of the verb exist.

The prepositional suffix (also called applicative) covers the semantic range of the most common prepositions in English. It may be benefactive, e.g. *ni-li-m-pik-ia* 'I cooked *for* her', directive, e.g. *ni-li-lil-ia kijiko* 'I cried *over* a spoon', directional, e.g. *ni-li-m-j-ia* 'I came *to* him', instrumental, e.g. *ni-li-l-ia kijiko* 'I ate *with* a spoon', affected participant, e.g. *wa-li-m-f-ia* 'they died *on* him'. That is, the prepositional suffix focuses on the role of some argument other than the direct object. The particular role focused on in context is a matter of the lexical meaning of the verb and inference, e.g. *ni-li-mw-ib-ia* may mean either 'I stole *for* him' or 'I stole *from* him'. As with other extensions, in some cases they have lexicalised, e.g. *-ambia* 'say to' < *amb-i-a*, where the verb *-amba* 'say' survives in Swahili elsewhere only as a complementiser, e.g. *nimesikia kwamba a-me-fika* 'I heard *that* he has arrived'. Double prepositional verbs have a 'persistive' meaning, e.g. *tup-il-ia* 'throw (far) away', *end-el-ea* 'continue' < *end-e-a* 'go in a certain direction' < *enda* 'go'.

The reversive suffix functions to undo the action of the root verb, e.g. *fung-u-a* 'open, untie' < *fung-a* 'close, tie', *chom-o-a* 'pull out' < *chom-a* 'stick in, skewer'.

The reciprocal suffix indicates reciprocal roles for two subjects or a subject and the object of a *na* 'and/with' phrase, e.g. *wa-li-pig-ana* 'they fought (with each other)' < *piga* 'hit', *a-li-pig-ana na-ye* 's/he fought with him/her', where *na-ye* consists of *na* 'with/and' and a cliticised form of the independent pronoun *yeye* 'him/her'.

The passive focuses on the non-agentive status of the subject, e.g. *a-li-shind-wa* 's/he was defeated' < *shinda* 'defeat', *a-li-on-esh-wa* 's/he was shown' (… 'see' + causative + passive). Only an object which can be referred to by an object marker with the active verb can be the subject of the passivised verb in Swahili. Thus, the only passive corresponding to the active sentence, *ni-sha-ku-on-esha watu* 'I already showed the people to *you*', is *u-li-on-esh wa watu* 'you were shown the people'. The direct object *watu* 'people' cannot be passivised over the indirect object, just as it cannot be represented by an object marker while there is an indirect object in the clause. The passive is always the last verbal extension in the Swahili verb. This appears to be quite general to Eastern Bantu. However, in the south-west the passive may precede the prepositional if the subject has the role of direct object of the active verb, e.g. Umbundu *onjo y-a-tung-iw ila ina-hé* 'the house was built for his/her mother' < *tunga* 'build', where the subject of *tung-iw-* 'build-passive' is *onjo* 'house' and *ina-hé* 'mother-his/her' is the object of *-ila*, the prepositional suffix. A number of other verbal extensions are extant in Bantu, but are no longer productive, cf. Swahili *kama-ta* 'seize' < *kama* 'squeeze', *nene-pa* 'get fat' < *nene* 'fat (adj.)', *ganda-ma* 'get stuck' < *ganda* 'stick to'. Still further verbal extensions are recognisable through Niger-Congo reconstruction, e.g. **bí-áda* (Swahili *zaa* 'bear children') contains **bi*, a Niger-Congo root for 'child' not common in Bantu.

To complete discussion of the morphological complexity of the verb structure, the relative marker must be mentioned. In most of the Bantu area relativisation is a syntactic process which does not interfere with the verbal complex. However, among the North-East coastal languages, including Swahili, a relative marker may be infixed in the verbal complex by suffixation to the tense prefix. The relative marker in such cases is itself complex, consisting of a secondary class concord marker + the referential morpheme *-o*, e.g. *ni-li-p +o-fika* 'when I arrived'. Here the relative marker *-p +o-* consists of the concord for class 16, a locative used here as a temporal, and the referential *-o*. The form functioning as a relative marker here occurs throughout Bantu in a demonstrative series, e.g. the Swahili proximate 'that' *hu-y +o* (cl. 1), *hi-l +o* (cl. 5), etc. In the languages which have the infixed relative marker it only appears with a few tense prefixes. In all cases these tense prefixes are innovations developing later than the Common Bantu period. The origin of this infixation is postposing of the relative marker to the entire verbal complex. This process survives on the north-east coast and in the south-east, when there is no tense prefix on the verb, e.g. Swahili *mwezi u-∅-ja-(w+)o* 'the month which is coming', i.e. 'next month', where the *-∅-* marks the absence of a tense prefix and the relative marker is suffixed to the verb *ja* 'come', or Pokomo *want'u wa-∅-j-ie-(w+)o* 'the people who came', with the addition of a tense suffix *-ie* to the verb *-ja* 'come'. The tense prefixes which allow the infixed relatives originate in aux-iliaries where the relative marker was postposed, e.g. Swahili *-li-* 'past/anterior' < (*-a-* 'remote past') + *li* 'copula'. The tense prefix *-na-* 'general, progressive' regularly takes infixation in the standard and Southern dialects, but is largely resisted by the Central dialects, e.g. standard Swahili *watu wa-na-(w+)o-sema* 'the people who are speaking', while Central Swahili prefers *watu amba-(w+)o wa-na-sema* 'the people who have spoken', where the relative marker cliticises to a complementiser *amba* introducing the relative clause. This device is used for relativisation in all dialects and is the only option with tense prefixes which do not allow relative infixation.

4 Syntax

Bantu languages have a basic verb-medial word order with a strong tendency towards subject first. Auxiliaries precede the verb (itself usually in infinitive form with **ko-* prefixed). All noun modifiers follow the noun in most of the Bantu area: adjectives, numerals, demonstratives, relative clauses. However, most languages optionally allow demonstratives to precede the noun to mark definiteness. The basic possessive (or 'associative') pattern is *Possessed cc-a Possessor*, where *-a* is the associative marker 'of', and the class concord prefix concords with the possessed noun. As discussed on page 893, the pronominalised possessor takes a special form, which is suffixed to *-a-*; thus, Swahili *ngoma z-a-mtu* '(the) drums of/for (the) man' with the class concord *z-* (class 10) concording with *ngoma* 'drums' and *ngoma z-a-ke* 'his/her drums' with the special possessive form of the pronoun suffixed to *-a-*. Most Bantu languages show concord for the class of the pronominalised possessor, but Swahili uses *-ke* for all classes except the animate plural (class 2).

With the exception of **nà* 'and/with', Common Bantu does not appear to have pre-positions. Beside the prepositional extension, Swahili uses both verbs and nouns to function like English prepositions, e.g. *a-me-fika toka Dar* 'he has arrived *from* Dar', where *toka* is the verb 'come from'; *a-li-tembea mpaka Dar* 'he walked *to* Dar', where the noun *mpaka* 'boundary' is used as a vector to mean 'up to, until'. Commonly, the possessive construction is used prepositionally, e.g. *chini y-a nyumba* 'under (of) the house', where *chini* 'down, under' etymologically displays *nchi* 'ground' + *-ni*, the locative suffix. The possessed concord ignores the locative and concords directly with the root noun. The possessive construction is also used with the locative concords prefixed, especially *ku-* (class 17), to express locative, instrumental and manner relations, e.g. *kw-a Fatuma* '*at* Fatuma's (place)', *kw-a nyundo* '*with* (a) hammer', *kw-a nguvu* '*by* force'. In all cases, these preposition-like uses of constructions are noun-second. In all respects, then, Swahili and the other Bantu languages are very much like the proto-typical SVO language.

However, word order is not invariant. Topicalisation is possible, e.g. *kitabu ni-li-ki-kuta* 'the book, I found it'; note the usual use of the object marker (*-ki-* (class 7) in this case) in the topicalised construction. In Swahili a topicalised possessive construction is optional with animate possessors: *mtu ngoma zake* 'the man, his drums'. Some Bantu languages require a cleft construction for interrogatives, equivalent to Swahili *ni nani uliyemwona?* 'who did you see?' lit. '(it) is who that you saw?', where the interrogative pronoun *nani* 'who' is introduced as the predicate of the copula *ni*, a marker used to focus on noun phrases or entire clauses in the Bantu languages. In Swahili, topicalisation is never obligatory. The usual form of the question leaves an object interrogative in object, i.e. post-verbal, position, e.g. *ulimwona nani*? 'you saw who?' The widespread use of Bantu interrogative pronouns ending in *-ni*, e.g. Swahili *na-ni* 'who?', *ni-ni* 'what?', *li-ni* 'when?', *ga-ni* 'what kind?' indicates the earlier prevalence of topicalisation in *wh*-questions in Bantu, still found in Bantu's Benue-Congo and Kwa relatives, where cognates of *ni* (< **ne*) are suffixed to topics, whether interrogative or otherwise, e.g. in Yoruba (see pages 877–878).

Beside its predicate-marking function, the particle *ni* (usually called a copula because of its equative function in Bantu languages, e.g. *Fatuma ni m-Swahili* 'Fatuma is a Swahili speaker') functions in some North-East interior languages to mark a main clause, e.g. Gikuyu *nĩ-a-gwat-ire* 'he held (it)' as main clause, but *mũndũ ũ-ria a-gwat-ire*, 'the man who held (it)', where *a-gwat-ire* is relativised by means of the demonstrative *ũ-ria* (Swahili *yu-le*) introducing the relative clause. Another Bantu 'copula' reflected in Swahili *-li* acts like a verb in taking tense prefixes and is used for both equative and locative purposes in most Bantu languages (replacing *ni* as equative with non-third persons). In Swahili, equative and locative predicates are strictly distinguished, so that *skuli ni hapa* means 'this place is a school' but *skuli i-ko hapa (iko < i-li-ko)* means 'the/a school is in/around here'.

Despite its typically verb-second syntax, much of the morphology of the Bantu languages indicates a verb-last origin, only sporadically found among the Niger-Congo languages. Signs of verb-last syntax are found in the preposing of the object marker to the verb stem (as if of OV origin), the postposing of the verbal extensions and mode markers (as if of verb-auxiliary origin), the suffixing of the locative marker *-ni* to the affected noun (as if of noun-postposition origin), the class prefix on nouns (as if of modifier-noun origin) and probably the postposing of the relative marker to the non-tense-prefixed verbal complex surviving on the north-east coast and in the south-east (as if of clause-relativiser origin). Otherwise, with its obligatory subject marker and tense prefixes in that order, and its noun-genitive possessive construction, the Bantu languages resemble the majority of their Benue-Congo and Kwa neighbours in the north-west.

The variation in position of some Bantu categories, most characteristic of the north-west, suggests an intermediate stage of evolution between an analytical verb-final syntax and the strict verbal morphology of Swahili and the east coast, with maximally a single tense prefix and object marker per verb. In particular, the morphologisation of auxiliary-like categories, both pre- and post-verbal, does not appear to have occurred uniformly over the Bantu area as the languages assumed their current verb-medial syntax. The slight ordering freedom of verbal extensions, e.g. in the Umbundu example on page 897, suggests the relatively late survival of pre-Bantu verbal extensions as a separate word class in part of the southwestern area. The prepositional verbal extension *-e/ɛda*, as well as the use of verbs for prepositional direction, e.g. Swahili *(ku)toka* 'come (from)' and *kw-enda* '(go) towards', suggest the serial verb constructions general to Niger-Congo languages, including Bantu's north-west relatives (see pages 879–881). In the process of evolution towards complex verb morphology, the attraction of these auxiliaries to the preceding verb precluded a preverbal position for the object of the 'prepositional' verb and may have precipitated verb-medial syntax. The Bantu languages which still allow multiple object-markers, the interior east and most of the west (in the north-west object markers have been partially lost in favour of post-verbal independent pronouns), indicate the retention of verb-final syntax, allowing two or more preposed objects, but only for a pronominal form of the object. That is, where O is a lexical object and o is a pronominal object, O–V O–aux. appears to have evolved into O–V+aux. O and finally V+aux. O O, but o–V o–aux. evolved into o–o–V+aux. In most contexts, languages like Swahili have gone further in reanalysing the object of the extension as the only object of the main verb. Syntactically, focusing options have been maintained in Swahili through the development of a new prepositional device, using the possessive construction for instrument discussed above, e.g. *a-li-pig-i-a nyundo msumari* 'he hit the nail with a hammer' (i.e. he used a hammer to hit the nail), with the extension focusing on the instrument, and *a-li-piga msumari kwa nyundo*, with the same meaning but use of the possessive construction, reversing the order of lexical objects. Interestingly enough, the instrumental use of the prepositional extension in Swahili still allows an object marker for the direct object despite the presence of the instrument in the clause, e.g. *a-li-u-pig-i-a nyundo msumari* (where *-u-* refers to *msumari* 'nail'). All other uses of all verbal extensions allow the object marker only to refer to the object of the extension when that object is mentioned in the clause. Amid variation in the position of the negative marker across Bantu languages and according to tense/aspect within the languages, the widespread use of a post-verbal negative marker in the northwest (and in Chagga, as discussed above) suggests an auxiliary origin in verb-final syntax for negation: verb negative (= auxiliary). The preverbal position of the negative marker **ti* (Swahili *si*) appears to be a manifestation of the shift to verb-medial syntax. This **ti* is also the negative copula, e.g. Swahili *mnyama si mtu* 'an animal is not a person'. In the same way that there are traces of a post-predicate position for the currently prepredicate copula **ne* (Swahili *ni*) among the interrogative pronouns, as discussed earlier, the negative 'copula' appears to have shifted to a preverbal auxiliary: negative (= auxiliary) verb. The other forms of negation, which place the negative before the subject marker, appear to be even later developments within the Bantu area, evolving from verbs with inherent negation, e.g. Swahili *ha-* < *nk'a-* (still common in the Central dialects) perhaps developing from *ni* 'copula' + *kana* 'deny'.

Bantu subordination patterns are relatively consistent across languages. Relativisation is generally introduced by a demonstrative or, among languages with preprefixes, a preprefix when the subject is relativised, e.g. Zulu *a-bantu a-ba-funa-yo* 'people who want' (note the final relative marker *-yo* used with no tense prefix). The preprefix itself may derive from an earlier demonstrative in concord with the head noun and subject of the relative clause. Complement clauses and even adverbial clauses are generally introduced by verbs etymologically meaning 'say' (as generally in Niger-Congo), e.g. Swahili *kw-amba*, Southern and Central Bantu *ku-ti*, and/or 'be(come)', e.g. Swahili *ku-wa*. Thus, *-amba-* in Swahili may introduce reported speech, a relative clause and earlier introduced the protasis of conditional sentences, e.g. *na **kwamba** moyo ni chuo ningekupa ukasome* 'and **if** the heart were a book, I would give it to you for you to read' (a verse from the early nineteenth-century Mombasan poet, Muyaka). This last use of *kwamba* has been replaced by *kama*, of Arabic origin, also used as the preposition 'like'. In the rural dialect of Chifundi *ku-wa* 'be(come)' retains this function, cf. Zulu *u-ku-ba* and *u-ku-ti* which also may function like this. In Swahili *ku-wa* may also introduce reported speech and other complements of verbs of communication or mental action, e.g. 'think'.

In sum, the syntax of the Bantu languages reflects an SVO language which has evolved out of a language with both SOV characteristics and interclausal relations common to Niger-Congo languages of either basic word order. It is most distinctive among Niger-Congo languages in its noun-class system and its verb morphology. Among Niger-Congo class languages it is specifically distinctive in the complexity of its verb morphology. For example, the distantly related West Atlantic language Fula is also a class language, but the class markers follow rather than precede the noun and there are no tense prefixes or object markers preceding the verb root. Like Bantu, Fula is currently verb-medial showing the prevalence of this type of syntax throughout Niger-Congo.

5 Non-Bantu Influence on Swahili

In view of its general, even extreme, adherence to the Bantu type (extreme, for example, in the extent of its obligatory verb morphology), Swahili is usually viewed as minimally affected in its syntax by non-Bantu influence. In contrast, the Swahili lexicon shows massive borrowing from Arabic and more recently from English. In addition, as the traditional medium of communication between the Indian Ocean commercial network and the Bantu interior, it has accepted words and concepts from numerous other languages, both Bantu and foreign, e.g. Portuguese (in the sixteenth century), Persian and Hindi. Among traditional Swahili communities, words originating in Arabic often maintain some features of their Arabic pronunciation, e.g. *baxt(i)* 'luck' with a consonant cluster and the foreign phoneme /x/. However, as Swahili has spread to non-Arabicised Bantu peoples and everyday usage in traditional Swahili communities, certain Bantu processes of nativisation have taken place, e.g. *bahati* with typical Bantu syllable structure and nativisation of /x/ > /h/. In both the standard language and the traditional dialects the Arabic interdental fricatives have been adopted, e.g. *dhani* 'think', *thelathini* 'thirty'. Among the new urban Swahili communities such as Dar es Salaam in Tanzania, these interdentals are non-standardly replaced by post-alveolars, e.g. *zani*, *selasini*. The phonological nativisation process for loanwords from languages allowing word-final consonants consists of using the vocalic quality of the final consonant as the nucleus of a final syllable, e.g. *-jibu* 'answer' < Arabic *jib*; *-skwizi* 'hug romantically' < English *squeeze*, *starehe* 'relax' < Arabic *-stariħ*. An interesting detail concerning loan verbs is that they do not take the modal suffixes. Thus, the subjunctive and indicative are distinguished only by the presence or absence of a tense prefix, i.e. *a-∅-jibu* 'he should answer' must be subjunctive because there is no tense prefix on the verb.

Bantuisation of loan nouns occurs where the loan is analysable into a class prefix + stem, thus *ki-tabu*, pl. *vi-tabu* 'book' < Arabic *kita:b*. This tendency to metanalyse also occurs within Bantu words when possible, e.g. *chupa* 'bottle' < *ne-čópà* is metanalysed in the newer urban Swahili communities as *ch-upa*, pl. *vy-upa*, by analogy with class 7/8 nouns, e.g. *ch-uma* 'iron' < *ke-ómà*, pl. *vy-uma*. This tendency is not seen in Northern Swahili communities where the reflex *t'upa* is unmistakably class 9, pl. *t'upa* (class 10).

A fuller understanding of the impact of other languages, particularly Arabic through continual contact for a millennium, awaits further examination of the semantics and rhetorical patterns of Swahili and other Bantu languages. Beside the cultural influence of Arabic reflected in Swahili's vocabulary, the use of Arabic adverbials and conjunctions is striking, e.g. *lakini* 'but, however', *au/ama* 'or', *halafu* 'then', *baada* 'after'. As rhetorical style is expressed in art, Swahili poetry has adopted numerous Arabic metres and the use of vocalic rhyme. Vocalic rhyme is unknown in traditional Bantu verse (in contradistinction to tonal rhyme), but Swahili has used the identity of word-final syllables to create a tradition of rhyme schemes far more intricate than in the Arabic source, e.g. the regular form of the Swahili quatrain (four-line stanza) has the rhyme scheme ab/ab/ab/bc, which repeats as de/de/de/ec. Note that only the final rhymes of each stanza are related. This typical pattern of stanza rhyme suggests the refrain pattern of a repeated coda line, marking the end of each stanza, commonly used in Bantu and West African song and often in Swahili song as well. This blending of Bantu and non-Bantu traditions is suggestive of more prosaic adaptations of non-Bantu rhetorical patterns which remain to be described in Swahili.

Bibliography

For Bantu as a whole, Guthrie (1967–70) is the most extensive classification and reconstruction. Nurse and Philippson (2003) is the most recent overview of the Bantu languages, including outline descriptions of several individual languages. Nurse and Philippson (1975) and Nurse and Hinnebusch (1993) present a classification of Swahili's nearest geographical relatives.

For Swahili, Polomé (1967) is a conveniently arranged introduction to the dialects and the basic structure of the language. Ashton (1944), a pedagogical grammar, is still the most complete introduction to the standard language, while Hinnebusch (1979) presents a descriptive synopsis. Vitale (1981) is a highly comprehensive generative treatment of Swahili syntax; although it offers little in the way of new data, it relates Swahili grammar to issues in generative grammar and organises topics accordingly. Stigand (1915) is still the most extensive English-language discussion of Swahili dialects, excluding most of the Central rural dialects. Whiteley (1969) presents a sociohistorical discussion of the development of standard Swahili.

References

Ashton, E.O. 1944. *Swahili Grammar (Including Intonation)* (Longman, London)
Guthrie, M. 1967–70. *Comparative Bantu*, 4 vols (Gregg International Publishers, Farnborough)
Hinnebusch, T.J. 1979. 'Swahili', in T. Shopen (ed.) *Languages and Their Status* (Winthrop, Cambridge, MA), pp. 204–93
Nurse, D. and Hinnebusch, T.J. 1993. *Swahili and Sabaki: A Linguistic History* (University of California Press, Berkeley)
Nurse, D. and Philippson, G. 1975. 'The North-Eastern Bantu Languages of Tanzania and Kenya: A Classification', *Kiswahili*, vol. 45, pp. 1–28
—— (eds) 2003. *The Bantu Languages* (Routledge, London)
Polomé, E.C. 1967. *Swahili Language Handbook* (Center for Applied Linguistics, Washington DC)
Stigand, C.H. 1915. *A Grammar of Dialectic Changes in the Kiswahili Language* (Cambridge University Press, Cambridge)
Vitale, A.J. 1981. *Swahili Syntax* (Foris, Dordrecht)
Whiteley, W.H. 1969. *Swahili: The Rise of a National Language* (Methuen, London)

Language Index